James Beard's

AMERICAN COOKERY

Books by James Beard

James Beard's Hors d'Oeuvre and Canapés

Cook It Outdoors

Fowl and Game Cookery

The Fireside Cookbook

Paris Cuisine *(with Alexander Watt)*

James Beard's Barbecue Cookbook

James Beard's New Fish Cookery

The Complete Book of Outdoor Cookery
(with Helen Evans Brown)

How to Eat Better for Less Money
(with Sam Aaron)

The James Beard Cookbook

James Beard's Treasury of Outdoor Cooking

Delights and Prejudices

James Beard's Menus for Entertaining

How to Eat (and Drink) Your Way Through a French (or Italian) Menu

James Beard's American Cookery

Beard on Bread

Beard on Food

James Beard's Theory and Practice of Good Cooking

The New James Beard

Beard on Pasta

Love and Kisses and a Halo of Truffles
(John Ferrone, editor)

James Beard's

AMERICAN COOKERY

Little, Brown and Company
New York Boston London

Little, Brown and Company
Hachette Book Group
237 Park Avenue, New York, NY 10017
www.hachettebookgroup.com

First Edition: May 1972
First paperback edition: September 1980
Republished hardcover edition: October 2010

Illustrations by Earl Thollander

Library of Congress Cataloging-in-Publication Data

Beard, James.
James Beard's American cookery / by James Beard ; with illustrations by Earl Thollander ; new foreword by Tom Colicchio.—Republished hardcover ed.
p. cm.
Includes index.
ISBN 978-0-316-09868-7
1. Cookery, American. I. Title.
TX715.B3715 2010
641.5973—dc22 2010020003

10 9 8 7 6 5 4 3 2 1

RRD-VA

Printed in the United States of America

This book is dedicated to my favorite great ladies of the American kitchen:

Eliza Leslie
Mrs. T. J. Crowen
Sarah Tyson Rorer
Fannie Merritt Farmer
Irma Rombauer
Helen Evans Brown
June Platt

Contents

Foreword

I never met James Beard, but I feel like I know him. In 1984 I was a wet-behind-the-ears young chef in Millburn, New Jersey, working at a restaurant where each day's menu was dictated by the greenmarket. To a kid raised on macaroni and Sunday gravy, this was a novel departure, the stepping-off point for a lifetime obsession with seasonal ingredients. And yet I knew enough to realize the concept wasn't new, even if it was only gaining cachet at the time; James Beard had been cooking with high-quality, locally sourced ingredients since the 1950s. On the day he died, we dedicated a menu at 40 Main Street to him. I felt as though a personal mentor had passed away.

As my career has evolved from cook to chef to restaurateur to guy on TV, I'm reminded that here James Beard was a pioneer too. Along with Julia Child, he used television as a way of bringing food and cooking into American homes, setting the stage for today's revolution in food programming. One of the things I'm proudest of is that hundreds of people write me letters saying that, thanks to *Top Chef,* their kids have an interest in eating a variety of foods, and the family now cooks together, trying new things and bonding along the way. The show has helped to usher in the very thing that James Beard cared about most—food as a means of connecting people to loved ones and friends. Would there be a *Top Chef* today without James Beard's first-ever cooking show in 1946? Maybe, maybe not. But he certainly set the stage.

I consider myself an American chef because I was born here, but also because I borrow from all the traditions that have made their way over to our shores—including the Italian cooking of my parents and the French of my early training—which is a uniquely American pattern. In this, too, James Beard led the way; just as all politics is local, he felt that all cuisine was regional, because at its core, great cooking is about bringing something personal to the task. James Beard celebrated the regional cuisines of Cajun New Orleans, the Pacific Northwest, and just about everywhere in between. His influence persists in the modern revival of locavore eating—it might feel new to many, but James Beard was preaching that gospel before most of us geniuses were born.

The beauty of this book is that it allows you—the enthusiastic home chef (or armchair cook)—to experience firsthand what made James Beard special and unique. His voice can be heard through his no-nonsense recipes and the choices he made that celebrated even simple, humble dishes for what they were: good food.

We hear a lot today about what makes someone a "real" chef—is it the guy at the stove? The one teaching future chefs? The one on TV? The one championing important causes? Or the one traveling with his craft and running a successful business? James Beard showed us a great chef could be all of those things, gracefully and without compromising his ideals, and for that I am truly grateful.

Tom Colicchio
New York City, April 2010

James Beard's

AMERICAN COOKERY

Introduction

Food and eating habits have fascinated me throughout my life, and after sixty-five years I have come to the conclusion that perhaps American cookery is one of the most fascinating culinary subjects of all. When I was very young I knew ranch food and other Western-style cooking. I knew elegant hotel food as well as American plan hotel food, with all its faults and its few merits. I have known home cooking all the way from the very simplest to the most luxurious. I have eaten, cooked, observed, and taught in many sections of this country. And I have lived long enough to have experienced the glories of native cookery in the early years of this century, the decline in good cooking that followed the disappearance of hired help from American households, and, since the mid-1940's, a renaissance of interest in food.

Today American cookery is at a crossroads somewhere between technology and tradition. On the one hand we have a tremendous boon of items on the market called convenience foods — prepared dishes, mixes, freeze-dried dishes, frozen foods of all kinds, and complete frozen dinners. While these have seldom improved the American palate they have helped the less enterprising cook, whose approach to food is a matter more of necessity than of creativity, and have permitted some cooks to serve better food than they could ever have produced themselves.

On the other hand we have a widespread vogue for fine traditional cookery. French cuisine is the goal of every amateur in the kitchen. One must do all of the famous provincial dishes, and the bourgeois dishes, and now and again attempt to reconstruct some of the monuments of grande cuisine, an aspiration that often leads the novice into techniques far beyond his depth. Without question it is a delight to follow the meticulously planned trail of Julia Child or read the sublime evocations of Elizabeth David, but we should also look into the annals of our own cuisine. We have so much to complain about in the quality of food served in many restaurants and in not a few homes that we forget what distinguished food Americans have produced in several periods of our history.

The beginnings of a native cuisine must have been modest enough. Quite likely until the end of the eighteenth century and the start of the next, the only food of consequence was to be found in a few great houses in parts of the South and in New York, Boston, and Philadelphia. Elsewhere the food served at many tables was undoubtedly overcooked and underseasoned. As Americans began to travel more and sophistication grew, there was greater daring in making dishes that were not purely functional, and with the arrival of immigrants in number the cultural mix mingled cuisines as well.

Eventually in many small communities excellent natural cooks began to blossom, whom all the local ladies tried to emulate. These gastronomic voices of the hinterland are evident when one peruses collections of recipes compiled by the Ladies Aid societies, missionary societies, hospital volunteer groups, neighborhood houses, and women's exchanges all through the country. It is fascinating to see, for example, how successful recipes inspired envious cooks to compete. Thus we find Mrs. Doctor Joseph Niemyer's Chicken with a Savory Sauce turning up in other cookbooks as Chicken with a Savory Sauce or Savory Sauced Chicken. Occasionally a recipe such as Mrs. Niemyer's is improved upon, perhaps by a housewife with a different ethnic background. So runs the pattern through all these remarkable paperbound cookbooks for almost two centuries. They, as much as anything, record the history of our cuisine. Through them it is possible to trace the march of recipes westward and to see which of the great recipes survived through generations of change.

As cooking became more easily regulated with the availability of better stoves, we find an increasing number of recipes for baking appearing in cookbooks. The rather heavy cakes of Colonial days become more and more refined until we achieve the light and delicate cakes of the last fifty years. Some earlier cakes — sponge cakes, pound cakes, fruit cakes, and the famous One-Two-Three-Four Cake — have weathered the years. Other longtime favorites, like Pork Cake and Election Cake, are seldom to be found. The baking powder layer cake, with its varied fillings and icings, has become a standby. But so have cake mixes, unfortunately, and artificial flavorings. Mixes do produce cakes, I confess, with decent texture which for the most part are better than cakes available in the average bakery these days. The younger generation is developing a pleasure in baking that often begins with mixes, and leads through curiosity to preparing a recipe from scratch. I have watched children of nine to fifteen baking cakes and pies partly to satisfy their appetites and partly to find out what happens when one performs a chemical experiment with flour, eggs, and other ingredients. People are also trying to achieve good honest bread in their own kitchens once again, and that is perhaps the healthiest sign of all — a return not only to home baking but also to the most fundamental traditions of American cookery.

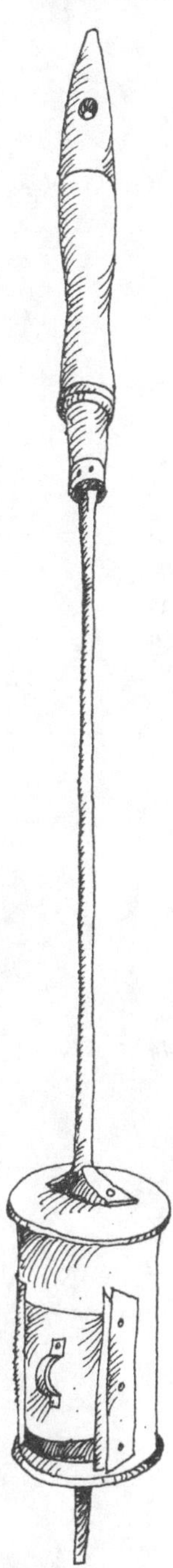

It goes without saying that when we talk about American cookery we are not referring to regional food alone. The inspiration for incalculable numbers of our dishes came with immigrants from Europe and the Orient. I think, for example, of the mother of a Chinese friend of mine, a restaurateur of high rank in this country. Her husband was a Christian preacher in the wilds of eastern Oregon during the early part of the century, and for years they trekked to small towns and villages — wherever there might be a colony of Chinese workmen. She cooked Chinese food with almost none of the necessary ingredients, substituting what she found at hand, creating new dishes within a traditional style of cooking. Some of her inventions, served in her son's restaurant, have also taken a place in the standard cuisine of this country. Even professional chefs from abroad had to improvise when reproducing their native dishes here, and frequently they brought forth entirely new dishes that became world-famous. Then there were pioneers of French cookery, like M. Pierre Blot, who taught the principles of grande cuisine throughout the hinterland, and many other unsung gastronomic stalwarts who showed our grandparents American bounty through foreign variations.

In fact, very few foreign dishes survive in their pure form when they become nationally popular; they take on the stamp of the

American kitchen — so quickly that in many cases they cease to be exotic and are accepted as casually as a plate of ham and eggs. Often ethnic restaurants, observing what appeals to American taste, begin to pass off adaptations (and occasionally travesties) of their cuisine as the real thing. Many Italian restaurants fashion food to suit Americans' ideas of Italian cookery, and this is why our countrymen traveling to Italy for the first time will astonish us by considering the food in Rome less good than Italian food in Chicago or San Francisco. The first thing an amateur chef will tackle is a spaghetti sauce, which, he may boast, took two or three days to prepare. We can be sure it bears little resemblance to the sauce found in Bologna. The same can be said of Oriental food — an American sitting down to a genuine Chinese or Japanese dinner would be apt to find it unpalatable. One of the reasons so-called Polynesian food is so popular here is that it is an idealized version of Oriental food. It is frequently tasty, though hardly authentic — except, perhaps, authentic Trader Vic's.

For these reasons I have sometimes during the course of this book offered an original foreign recipe along with its American version. It is not my intention to pronounce the adaptations inferior — they may in some cases be improvements; it is a matter of taste — but only to show how they have acquired American accents.

It should be apparent that this is not a book of regional cookery, it is not a collection of family recipes, it is not primarily a critique of American cuisine. It is simply a record of good eating in this country with some of its lore. To compile it I have used a large number of published books and manuscript cookbooks in my possession or at my disposal. What interests me is how the quality of cooking in this country can be followed from a period of simplicity and function to one of goodness and bounty, then to an age of elaboration and excess, back again to functional (and for the most part, mediocre) eating. Finally, we hope, we are now in another epoch of gastronomic excellence.

The written record of our cuisine is in many ways more complete than that of any other country. Beginning with Amelia Simmons we have the wisdom of such notables as Eliza Leslie, Catharine Beecher, Mrs. T. J. Crowen, Marion Harland, Maria Parloa, Mrs. Sarah Tyson Rorer, Mrs. Mary Lincoln, and Fannie Merritt Farmer. And since the turn of the century there has been an unceasing flow of cookbooks, which can only grow larger. The present one is added to their numbers.

Not all of our food history is set down in cookbooks. I think of the influence of itinerant cooks, many of them foreign, like the wife of the Chinese missionary who traveled between logging camps or ranches. And anyone fortunate enough to have eaten in the old days in these camps and on some of the larger ranches will remember that the meals were an amazing and rather splendid demonstration of gargantuan feeding with the simplest and best of ingredients.

While I do not overlook the grotesqueries of American cooking, I believe we have a rich and fascinating food heritage that occasionally reaches greatness in its own melting pot way. After all, France created French cuisine over centuries, and I daresay some of it was purely experimental cookery. Italian, Austrian, and Scandinavian cookery, as well, has had generations of change and tradition. We are barely beginning to sift down into a cuisine of our own. This book is a sampling of that cuisine, and inevitably it reflects my own American palate.

Cocktail Food

The cocktail party grew out of the Prohibition era and out of the decline in entertaining with pomp and servants. At the same time new standards of living and a new tempo of living inspired informal, friendly gatherings of anywhere from ten to five hundred people for the purpose of sipping drinks and munching on small snacks. As we well know, these gatherings continue to this very day and have become so much a part of our lives that we take them for granted. Ironically enough, they can sometimes be as deadly as the most formal of gatherings. It takes imagination to throw a successful cocktail party, and part of the success depends on the quality of the food you offer.

With the advent of the cocktail party a new style of food was created — what is known in the trade as "finger food": quite simply, food that can be eaten with the fingers without dribbling over clothing, rugs, and furniture. Many of the snacks created for such occasions are excellent, and many of them are garbage. One owes it to his guests to know the difference. Some of the more evil items are commercial dips dreamed up by those who have a product to sell, and others are concoctions fabricated with pastry bag and tube on small bits of soggy bread or toast. These are to be avoided at all cost. Nevertheless, there are many good edibles in the realm of cocktail hors d'oeuvre. Experiment until you find items that are easy to prepare and are never left behind on the plate. Do not attempt a great variety. Content yourself with a few things well done and in sufficient quantity. Sometimes nowadays hosts offer fare more substantial than the usual snacks so that guests will feel reasonably fed. This has its advantage in preventing oversaturation, and guests can go home or on to other engagements without bothering about dinner.

A few simple rules: Provide small plates and plenty of paper napkins of convenient size. Serve food that looks delightful and tastes even better. Remember that highly seasoned food stimulates drinking, and substantial food moderates it.

For appetizer recipes in other chapters, see the index.

Raw Vegetables

Cocktail food falls into a number of categories. One of the most indispensable is raw vegetables. Americans are greater consumers of raw vegetables than any other people. It is natural, then, that vegetables have become an important part of the cocktail hour. At their best they are crisp and accompanied by a dressing or dip that is well seasoned and interesting (see Dips, Sauces, and Spreads, below). They have the appeal of being not too filling, and for the most part are not highly caloric.

The choice of items available for use in a raw vegetable bowl is bountiful. Naturally one should choose the most perfect the market affords, and they should be nicely cut, thoroughly cleaned, and beautifully arranged. It is best to set them in crushed ice in a container to keep them crisp and cold. They should not, however, swim in melting ice and water — if this occurs, the ice should be replenished. Here is a list of candidates for the raw vegetable bowl, to be served with a dressing or dip.

Artichokes. Tiny artichokes, quartered, with their chokes removed.

Asparagus. Tiny tips of raw asparagus have delightful flavor and texture and are good with a pungent sauce, or just with salt, plain or seasoned.

Avocadoes. Small finger avocadoes are excellent when thoroughly ripe. A receptacle has to be provided for the skins.

Fava beans. Select young beans and either remove them from the pods or leave them for guests to pod themselves. Serve with coarse salt.

Green beans. Tiny ones are quite delicious raw.

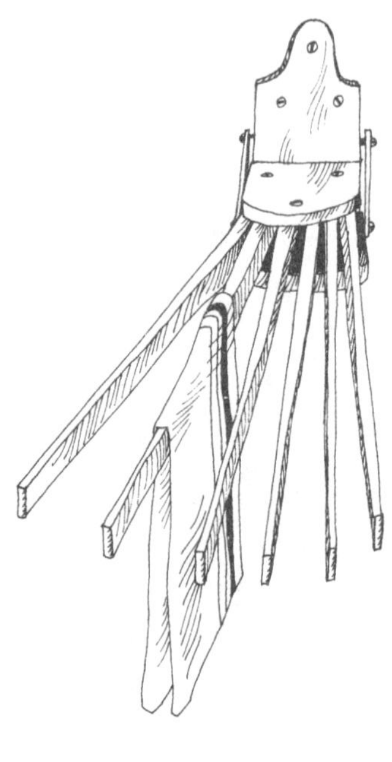

Broccoli buds. Chill and serve with a dressing.

Brussels sprouts. Tiny ones, nicely trimmed and crisped in cold water, are delicate in flavor and pleasant in texture.

Carrots. These are naturally a standby, for they seem to have been one of the first vegetables eaten raw by children. Who of my generation cannot remember pulling young carrots in a garden patch, wiping them clean, and eating them right there on the spot. Carrots should be cut in long julienne strips or in smallish wedges. Serve crisp and cold.

Cauliflower. Break into small flowerets. They must be fresh, white, and crisp.

Celery. Another staple, whether served alone or with other vegetables. Cut into strips or trimmed pieces.

Cucumber. Strips or slices of peeled cucumber are perfect for the vegetable bowl — best when seeds are removed and the flesh is cut in strips.

Endive. Quartered or broken into leaves, it is refreshing and pungent.

Mushrooms. A must in any collection of raw vegetables. Choose smallish ones, as fresh as possible.

Onions. Green onions, peeled and chilled, are essential for most vegetable platters.

Peas. Tiny sweet new peas, served in the pod or shelled.

Peppers. Seeded, stripped green or red peppers or tiny whole ones, both sweet and very hot.

Radishes. All the different forms of radishes — the little red ones with their plumage, if it is fresh; the long icicle radish; and the great black-skinned white radish, sometimes sliced and at other times shredded and blended with chicken fat. These are exceptionally good with other vegetables and served with a sauce.

Tomatoes. Cherry tomatoes, currant tomatoes, plum tomatoes, both the yellow and the red, are absolute necessities for a vegetable arrangement.

Turnips. Young turnips sliced thinly or cut in thin strips have great flavor and texture.

Watercress. Available in markets nearly everywhere in the States, and a decorative and peppery addition to a vegetable group.

Dips, Sauces, and Spreads

As I noted above, the dips and sauces conceived for vegetables are legion and frequently indigestible. However, there are several standard ones which can be depended upon and which lend themselves to variations. Most useful of all, perhaps, are the mayonnaises and other dressings (see page 75). See also the chapter on Sauces for such recipes as Elena Zelayeta's salsa fria, a superb cocktail dip.

Sour Cream Dips

There are several extremely good sour cream dips which may be used with vegetables. I'll eschew the obvious ones like the dried onion soup dip, clam dip, and others which have run the gamut of television and radio commercials.

Sour Cream Herb Dip I. To each cup of sour cream add ¼ cup each of chopped parsley and chives. Add salt and freshly ground pepper to taste.

Sour Cream Herb Dip II. To each cup of sour cream add ¼ cup finely chopped parsley, 2 finely chopped garlic cloves, and chopped fresh dill or dillweed to taste.

Sour Cream Roquefort Cheese Blend. This is ideal to make if you have dry ends of Roquefort cheese on hand. Merely shave them until you have a cupful or more, or crumble ½ pound fresh Roquefort cheese. Add ¼ teaspoon Tabasco or to taste, enough softened butter to make a smooth paste when creamed in the electric mixer or with a heavy fork, and about 3 or 4 tablespoons Cognac or bourbon. Blend this with 1 to 1½ cups sour cream, and add salt if necessary after allowing the mixture to rest for 2 hours.

Sour Cream Curry Sauce. Sauté 3 finely chopped shallots or 6 scallions, cut very fine, in 4 tablespoons butter until just limp. Add 1 tablespoon curry powder, or to taste, and blend well over low heat for 4 minutes. Stir occasionally. Add to 1½ cups sour cream along with 2 tablespoons chutney, and toss well. Correct the seasoning.

Note. Never add raw curry powder to such a dip. It will be far more subtle to the taste if first cooked.

Sour Cream Chili Dip. Sauté 1 cup very finely chopped onions in 4 tablespoons butter till just wilted and soft. Add 1½ tablespoons chili powder, 1 teaspoon ground cumin, ¼ teaspoon Tabasco, 3 tablespoons sesame seeds, and, if you like, ½ teaspoon oregano. Cook over low heat 3 or 4 minutes. Correct the seasoning and cool slightly before folding into 2 cups sour cream.

Liptauer (Cream Cheese Spread)

Mix the cream cheese, butter, and cream until fluffy. An electric mixer is good for this (use small bowl). Shape into a mound on a

2 8-ounce packages cream cheese
¼ cup butter (½ stick)
2 tablespoons heavy cream
Chopped onion, chopped anchovy fillets, capers, chopped chives, radish roses

decorative dish and surround with the chopped onion, anchovy fillets, capers, and chopped chives. Decorate with radish roses. Serve with small pieces of rye bread (not sweet), thinly sliced.

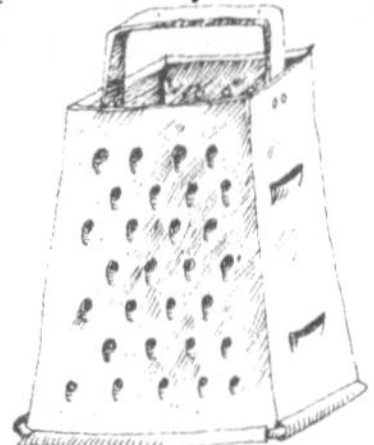

Cheese and Ham Spread

1½ pounds grated Swiss Emmenthaler cheese
1 pound ground baked ham with some of the fat
2 teaspoons prepared mustard (Dijon preferred)
Mayonnaise to bind
Chopped parsley

Mix the cheese and ham well with the mustard, and blend in just enough mayonnaise to moisten and bind. Press into a bowl from which you can serve it, and chill for an hour or two. Sprinkle with chopped parsley just before serving. Serve with small slices of rye bread or pumpernickel, and provide knives.

Note. For other cheese spreads, see Cheese for Cocktails, page 13.

Shrimp Butter

2 pounds shrimp
1 teaspoon mace
1 teaspoon finely chopped onion
¼ cup finely chopped parsley
½ to 1 cup softened butter

Clean and devein the shrimp, and cook in boiling salted water for 3 or 4 minutes after they come to a boil. Cool and chop coarsely, and blend with seasonings and enough softened butter to make a thick paste. Chill, but remove from refrigerator an hour to an hour and a half before serving to soften the butter. Serve with small rounds of bread, Melba toast, and lemon halves or quarters.

Baked Liver Pâté

2½ pounds pork liver
3½ pounds fresh pork with fat
2 medium onions, finely chopped
3 cloves garlic, finely chopped
1 teaspoon thyme
1½ tablespoons salt
2 teaspoons freshly ground pepper
½ cup Cognac
4 eggs
½ cup flour
Thin slices fresh pork siding

Pâtés have become exceedingly popular as cocktail food. This one is fairly simple and keeps well. Serve with toast or rounds of French or rye bread.

Grind the pork liver and meat with a good deal of the fat, using medium to fine blade of meat grinder. Mix in the next six ingredients well. Beat in the eggs one at a time, and stir in the flour. (All this can be done with an electric mixer.) Line 5 or 6 small 2-cup casseroles with thin slices of pork siding. (This is the same cut as bacon, but has not been salted and smoked.) Almost fill the casseroles, leaving room for expansion during baking. Top with more thin slices of pork siding. Cover the casseroles with several layers of aluminum foil that can be tied on tightly. Place them in a baking pan or dish deep enough to accommodate boiling water reaching slightly more than halfway up the sides. Bake in 350-degree oven for 2 hours. Remove from the oven and cool for 15 minutes. Remove the coverings, fit new foil inside the tops, and weight down until cooled thoroughly.

Quick Liver Pâté

½ pound braunschweiger (smoked liverwurst) at room temperature
½ cup butter at room temperature
2 teaspoons scraped onion
2 tablespoons finely chopped chives
2 tablespoons finely chopped parsley
2 tablespoons Cognac or bourbon

Put all ingredients into small bowl of electric mixer and mix well, or mash and mix with fork. Spread on bread for sandwich filling or on buttered cocktail rye, French bread, or Melba toast for appetizer. Decorate with tiny sprigs of parsley, small pickled onions, strips of green pepper, or strips of pimiento.

Or form into one large ball or two smaller balls or a log, then roll in chopped chives, parsley, or toasted chopped nuts. Wrap and chill until firm. Serve on a platter or cheese tray with crackers or cocktail breads.

To use as a dip, thin with sour cream or cream, and serve with crackers or potato chips. This can be frozen, wrapped in moisture-proof, vaporproof material. Stir after thawing.

Chili con Queso

2 cloves garlic, finely chopped
1 28-ounce can Italian plum tomatoes
Salt and freshly ground pepper
2 cans peeled green chilies, finely chopped and seeded
1½ cups rich cream sauce
1 pound shredded jack or medium sharp Cheddar cheese

A Mexican dish that is excellent as a dip for breadsticks, corn chips, small pieces of crisp tortilla, or celery or cucumber sticks.

Combine the garlic, tomatoes, and salt and pepper to taste. Cook down 20 minutes over medium heat, stirring occasionally. Add the chopped green chilies. Cook and stir until the mixture is thick and pasty. Add the cream sauce and cheese. Serve warm from a chafing dish or electric skillet kept at low heat. Do not let it boil or the cheese will become stringy.

Cheese for Cocktails

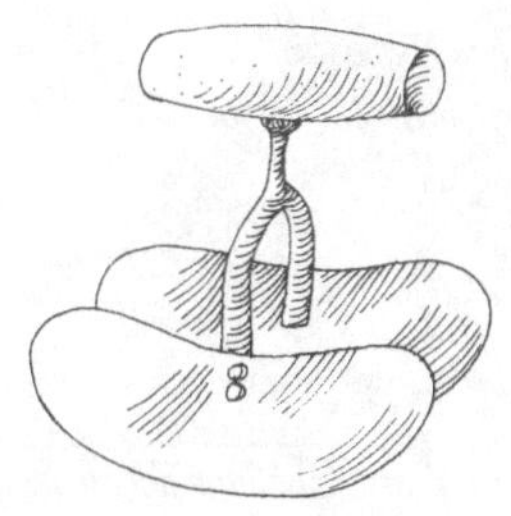

We have always been good cheese eaters, although cheese has never figured as a separate course in our meals as it does in France. Cheese, for us, has been a snack, a luncheon food, an accompaniment to pies, and, of course, cocktail food. With the enormous variety of cheese to be found throughout the country now, it is a simple matter to assemble a staggering cheese board.

One thing most of us have not learned is the proper temperature for serving cheese. It should be at room temperature and not at refrigerator temperature. If you are serving it with cocktails, let the cheese stand out of the refrigerator most of the day. It develops full flavor and bouquet that way, which makes a great deal of difference in the pleasure of eating it.

If you are serving a cheese board or tray, be sure to have either one magnificent cheese — and that in sufficient quantity — or several cheeses which are varied in flavor, texture, and shape. For example, choose one cheese of high and rich flavor, a milder one of firmer texture and another which has a markedly different quality from either, and finally one which is mild, for those who think they like cheese but really only like the idea of cheese. Always serve butter with cheese, and it is a good idea to serve thinly sliced breads as well as good crackers.

Cheese logs or balls are completely American and have become important fixtures at cocktail parties. I know of several cheese purveyors and supermarkets in the countryside who have these already prepared for sale. However, they are rather amusing to make and are delightful to see when made correctly. Any of the mixtures may also be made into small balls and rolled in chopped nuts or in chopped parsley and chives.

Blue Cheese Spread, Dip, or Ball

¼ pound blue cheese at room temperature
½ cup butter at room temperature
1 small clove garlic, minced
1 tablespoon finely chopped parsley
2 tablespoons finely chopped chives
Few drops Tabasco
3 tablespoons Cognac or Armagnac

Blend all ingredients in small bowl of electric mixer or mix with a fork. This can be spread on buttered bread for sandwiches or on tiny pieces of toast or cocktail white or rye bread.

Or form into a ball, log, or small balls, then roll in chopped parsley or chopped, toasted nutmeats. Wrap and chill. Serve on a cheese tray or plate surrounded by small cocktail bread or crackers.

For a dip, add cream or milk, a very little at a time, and stir until of a good consistency for dipping crackers, fresh vegetables, or potato chips.

This spread can be frozen — see note under next recipe.

Cheddar Cheese Spread, Dip, or Ball

½ pound sharp Cheddar cheese, grated (2 cups)
2 canned peeled green chilies, chopped

Have all ingredients at room temperature. Mix in small or large bowl of electric mixer or mash with a fork by hand. If this seems too stiff to spread, add cream or milk, a very little at a time, until of a good consistency. Serve as a spread, or form into one large or two small balls or logs and roll in chopped toasted nuts or chopped parsley or chives. Serve on a cheese board or tray surrounded with crackers, cocktail rye bread, French bread, or Melba toast.

½ canned pimiento, chopped
1 small clove garlic, grated
Few drops Tabasco
½ cup butter, softened
3 to 4 tablespoons Cognac, sherry, or bourbon
Salt to taste

This can be made into a dip by adding more milk or cream, and is especially good with raw vegetables such as celery, carrot sticks, cucumber sticks, radishes, endive, cherry tomatoes, or sweet pod or snow peas.

Note. The cheese balls or spread can be frozen after wrapping in polyethylene freezer bags and sealing. Be sure to thaw several hours before using. The dip can be frozen in moistureproof or vaporproof freezer containers. It will appear to separate when thawed but can be stirred again to original consistency.

A Cheddar Cheese Log

3 pounds soft Cheddar cheese, grated
1 4-ounce can peeled green chilies, finely chopped
½ teaspoon Tabasco
Coarsely chopped walnuts

This is for a fairly large party, although leftovers can be saved for a couple of weeks by wrapping in plastic wrap and refrigerating.

Blend the cheese well with the chilies and Tabasco, and form into a large sausage-like roll. Chop the nuts and spread on a piece of waxed paper or foil about 13 to 14 inches long. Place the cheese on the paper or foil and roll tightly so that the cheese collects the nuts. Pat extra nuts on with your hands to distribute evenly. Serve the roll with breads and crackers.

Cheddar Cheese Roll

2 pounds grated soft Cheddar cheese
1 tablespoon Dijon mustard or to taste
½ teaspoon Tabasco
½ cup finely chopped parsley
¼ cup finely chopped pimientos
Chopped pecans or pecan halves

Work the various seasonings into the cheese with your hands until it is a smooth mixture. Correct the seasoning. Form a long roll or ball of the cheese. Sprinkle a long piece of waxed paper or foil with the chopped or halved pecans and roll the cheese in the nuts.

Roquefort Cheese Log

2 pounds Roquefort cheese
1 pound cream cheese
½ pound butter
2 teaspoons dry mustard
¼ cup Cognac
Chopped parsley and chives

Crumble the Roquefort and blend well with the cream cheese, butter, and seasonings. Correct the seasoning to taste. I sometimes find it will take more mustard and more Cognac. Mold into a ball or roll and chill for a few minutes. Sprinkle parsley and chives on a piece of waxed paper or foil, and roll the cheese in the herbs until completely covered. Serve with breads and crackers.

Note. For storing, it is better to roll this in chopped nuts. Fresh herbs do not keep as well.

Vegetable Appetizers

See Raw Vegetables, page 9.

Baked Potato Hors d'Oeuvre

Scoop out the meat from baked potatoes, scraping the inside of the skins thoroughly, and cut the skins carefully into long strips about 1 to 1½ inches wide. Brush them lavishly with softened butter and sprinkle with salt and freshly ground pepper. Broil about 6 to 7 inches from the broiling unit until browned and crisp. Watch carefully. Serve hot.

Katherine Smith's Small Potatoes

One of the most satisfying snacks I have ever had with drinks was served in Washington at a party several years ago. It should become a classic.

Choose very small new potatoes and scrub them well. Boil them in their jackets until just pierceable. Remove. Hold each one with tongs or with a soft cloth and scoop out a little well in the top. The potatoes must be able to stand without rolling, so you may have to trim off a thin slice to form a base. Fill the hollows with sour cream blended with freshly chopped chives and crumbled crisp bacon, and serve. Or do not scoop them out, but serve as they are with a bowl of coarse salt and freshly ground pepper mixed. Either way they are excellent and filling.

Eggplant Caviar

2 rather good-sized eggplant
3 cloves garlic, crushed
1 medium onion, finely chopped
1½ teaspoons salt
1 teaspoon freshly ground pepper
¼ teaspoon cinnamon
½ cup chopped parsley
2 tablespoons vinegar
6 tablespoons olive oil
1 tablespoon grated lemon rind
1 tablespoon lemon juice
1 teaspoon chopped mint or basil

This is a Near Eastern dish which has become inordinately popular, perhaps because of the magic of the word caviar — for it is related to the real thing in name only. It is, however, a pleasant hors d'oeuvre.

Bake the eggplant whole in a 350-degree oven 1 hour, or until they are soft and cooked through. Slit them so the steam will escape. Peel, and chop them very fine. Add the seasonings and mix well. Let stand several hours or overnight in the refrigerator before using. Serve as hors d'oeuvre or with drinks, spooned on small bits of toast.

Eggs for Cocktails

Stuffed Eggs

From the beginning of good eating in this country stuffed eggs and pungent eggs have been part of the picture. Stuffed or deviled eggs were picnic fare and fare for the supper baskets prepared by cooks for basket socials. The attractively packaged baskets were auctioned off to raise funds for a new carpet for the church or a stove for the minister's house, and many a romance was started between an unattached lady and a man bidding for her pretty supper basket.

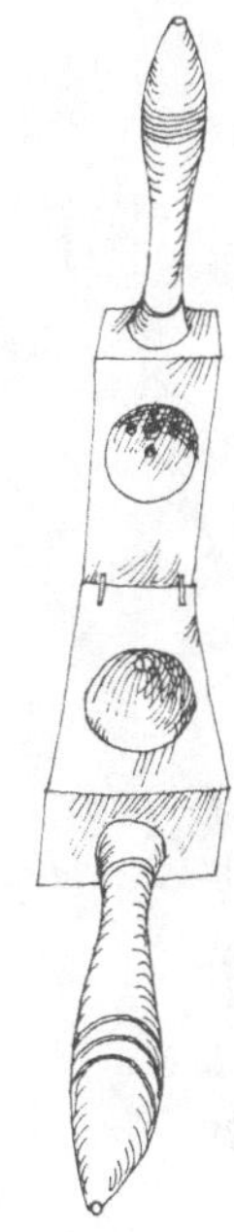

Deviled eggs were then a much enjoyed delicacy, and even today, if you have taken care to observe at a cocktail party, nothing disappears as quickly as the eggs.

To prepare, hard-boil the eggs (see Eggs chapter), stirring them gently at the beginning so the yolks will be better centered. Transfer the eggs to cold water at once. Cut them into halves vertically, horizontally, or diagonally. Carefully transfer the yolks to a bowl. Combine with seasonings. Stuff the whites with the aid of a pastry tube fitted with a large rosette tube, or spoon in the filling, smooth it off, and garnish. Estimate 4 stuffed halves per person for a large party and 3 per person for a smaller party.

Deviled Eggs. Mash the yolks of 12 eggs and combine with 2 teaspoons Dijon mustard, 1/4 teaspoon Tabasco, 1/2 teaspoon salt, 1/2 teaspoon freshly ground black pepper, 1 tablespoon grated onion, and enough mayonnaise to bind the mixture into a smooth paste. Fill the whites as directed above. Garnish with parsley sprigs or chopped parsley.

Caviar Eggs. Combine the mashed yolks of 12 eggs with 2 tablespoons grated onion, 2 to 3 ounces caviar (adjust caviar content to suit your taste and your purse), 2 tablespoons chopped parsley, and enough sour cream to bind the mixture. Fill egg whites as directed above. Garnish with chopped parsley.

Mexican Eggs. Combine 12 mashed egg yolks with 3 tablespoons finely chopped green chilies (the canned roasted variety), 2 teaspoons chili powder, 2 tablespoons chopped fresh coriander or parsley, and enough sour cream to bind. Stuff egg whites and decorate with fresh coriander or finely chopped pimiento.

Olive-Stuffed Eggs. Combine the mashed yolks of 12 eggs with 1/4 cup each of chopped stuffed or ripe olives, 1/2 teaspoon freshly ground black pepper, and enough mayonnaise to bind. Stuff the eggs as directed above. Decorate with toasted almonds or pecans.

Herbed Stuffed Eggs. Combine the mashed yolks of 12 eggs with 2 tablespoons each of chopped chives, chopped dill, and chopped parsley. Add 1/2 teaspoon salt and enough mayonnaise to bind. Stuff the eggs as directed above. Decorate with finely chopped herbs.

Salmon-Stuffed Eggs. Combine the mashed yolks of 12 eggs with 1/2 cup finely chopped smoked salmon, 2 tablespoons fresh dill, and 2 tablespoons chopped capers. Bind with mayonnaise. Stuff the eggs as directed above. Decorate with strips of smoked salmon or sprigs of dill.

Ham-Stuffed Eggs. Combine the mashed yolks of 12 eggs with ½ cup finely ground cold baked ham, ¼ cup finely chopped sweet gherkins, 1 teaspoon Dijon mustard, and enough mayonnaise to bind. Stuff the eggs as directed above.

Roquefort-Stuffed Eggs. Combine the mashed yolks of 12 eggs with ¼ cup finely crumbled Roquefort cheese and 2 tablespoons Cognac. Bind with enough sour cream to make it firm and smooth. Stuff the whites as directed above. Garnish with watercress sprigs.

Scotch Eggs

6 hard-boiled eggs
1 pound well-seasoned sausage meat
Flour
2 eggs, lightly beaten
Bread crumbs

Peel the eggs and flour them lightly. Divide the sausage meat into six portions and flatten each section a bit. Flour your hands and wrap the sausage meat around the eggs to form a firm egg-shaped covering. Flour the eggs, dip in beaten eggs and roll in crumbs. Fry in deep fat at 375 degrees until nicely browned and cooked through. Drain on absorbent towels. Serve either whole or carefully cut in halves. Best served cold.

Meat and Fish Appetizers

Chili con Carne

6 tablespoons butter, margarine, or salad oil
6 medium onions, sliced
3 pounds ground beef
3 cans (20 ounces each) tomatoes
1 can (6 ounces) tomato paste
1 cup beer or ale
1 tablespoon salt
½ teaspoon Tabasco
2 to 4 tablespoons chili powder
2 cans (12 ounces each) whole-kernel corn

A sound, all-around chili, made distinctive by the addition of corn. Serve in tiny cups with small spoons or in little croustades for cocktails. Or serve with hamburgers or frankfurters on buns for a more substantial cocktail snack.

Melt the butter, margarine, or oil in a large saucepan. Add the onions and cook until tender but not brown. Add the ground beef and cook until lightly browned, breaking up with a fork. Add the tomatoes, tomato paste, beer, salt, Tabasco, and chili powder. Cover and simmer 45 minutes. Add the corn and simmer 15 minutes longer.

Tortilla Snacks

36 small tortillas, about 3 inches in diameter

Heat the tortillas on a lightly greased griddle until crisp and keep warm by placing on a hot plate and covering with a cloth, or put in slightly warm oven, covered with a cloth. Heat refried beans until bubbling. Heat shredded chicken or pork just until hot. Top each tortilla with refried beans, then a little of the meat, and finally a spoonful of sauce. Put into hot oven for few minutes to heat through.

1 #2 can Mexican refried beans (frijoles refritos)
1 to 1½ cups shredded roast chicken or pork
Mexican barbecue sauce or salsa fria

Sausages with Cocktails

Sausages with drinks is hardly a new idea. It has been known here among the German, French, and Italian groups for generations. However, the greater variety of sausages on the market and new ideas for serving them, such as metal trees designed for hanging sausages, have made them more sophisticated fare in the past fifteen years or so. Because most people love to carve for themselves (even though most of them are poor carvers), it is best to have a large board of sausages, or one of the now fashionable trees, with various sausages hanging from its iron limbs. Provide one or two good boards, sharp knives, and a selection of breads — rye, pumpernickel, perhaps Near East bread, if available, and certainly various kinds of crackers and rye hardbreads. Also lay out butter, horseradish, mustards, perhaps a sauce or two, relishes, dill pickles (if you can find good ones) and small sour pickles.

Here are some of the better-known sausages suitable for service with cocktails.

Salami. Italian, Jewish, or German, to say nothing of Hungarian-style salami. All are pretty much available throughout the country. Buy a whole one. It will keep for a long time and doesn't even need refrigeration. Serve it sliced paper-thin.

Summer sausage. A dry, fine-grained sausage without too much high seasoning. Excellent with rye bread or with certain crackers. Must be thinly sliced.

Bologna. Our old standby. Very good bologna can be found if you shop for it. If not, buy mortadella.

Mortadella. This Italian sausage is like bologna except that it has small pieces of larding pork in it that make a mosaic when sliced. Best to have the mortadella sliced by machine when you buy it, for it must be sliced very, very thin.

Liverwurst or braunschweiger. These two standard sausages may be successfully used for cocktails, either sliced or as a spread, depending on consistency. More or less a poor man's pâté.

Pepperoni. The rather hot, dry Italian sausage which can be thinly sliced by hand.

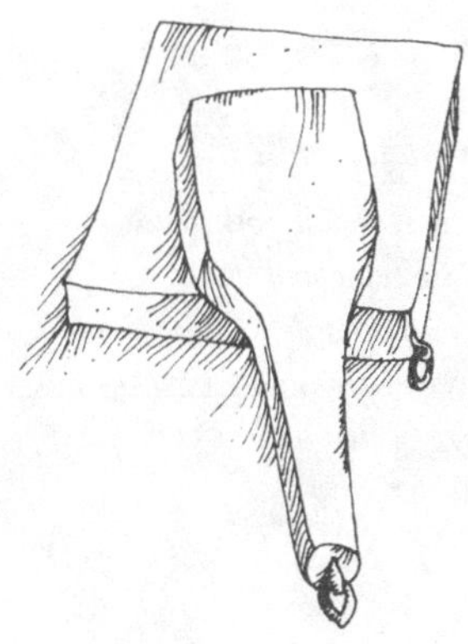

Capocollo. Cured pork rather than a sausage, but it resembles sausage. Pungent and well-flavored.

Yachtwurst. Spicy German-style sausage with pistachio nuts strewn through it. Excellent when sliced not too thin.

Teewurst. A rather soft, nicely spiced sausage which may be used as a spread with crackers, toast, or bread.

Lebanon bologna. The typical Pennsylvania dry sausage, nicely flavored and related somewhat to summer sausage.

Sausages to Be Served Hot with Drinks

You should have a chafing dish or an electrically heated tray, and don't let the sausages linger too long on the table once they have been heated lest they cool, shrivel, and become unappetizing.

Frankfurters. Small and large frankfurters have been standard cocktail fare for ages. The tiny ones are easy to serve with toothpicks. The larger ones may be served with hot dog rolls, relishes, and chili — rather hearty fare for cocktails but much appreciated by guests who would rather have one large snack than ten little ones.

Knockwurst. Large juicy ones may be cut in slices and served with mustards and relishes for dipping. Extremely good and simple to do.

Pork sausages. Tiny pork sausages grilled or sautéed have been favorites with drinks for years. Serve them with good mustards and with chutneys.

Kielbasy. The Polish sausages are ideal with drinks. Serve cold, or heat them in white or red wine flavored with chopped onion and serve hot in inch-long pieces with mustard or a barbecue sauce.

Bratwurst. Grill, sauté, or roast bratwurst and serve with rolls and perhaps a relish or mustard. Excellent flavor and a texture different from most of the other sausages.

There are other local sausages which are worth trying and adding to the list given here.

Sausage Rolls

12 to 18 small pork sausages
White wine and water
Dijon mustard
1 recipe cream cheese pastry
1 egg beaten with 1 tablespoon water

These rolls have a Scottish background but have been served in this country for generations. Superb when hot from the oven and even good when reheated.

Poach the sausages in a frying pan in half white wine and half water for about 10 minutes. Drain on absorbent paper and cool. Using half the pastry at a time, roll out on a lightly floured board into a square or rectangle about ¼ inch thick. Cut into smaller rectangles with a knife or pastry wheel, making each rectangle slightly longer than the sausage. Spread each rectangle with mustard to your taste, place a sausage on it, and roll it up. Place seam side down on a baking sheet. Brush with beaten egg. Bake in a 450-degree oven 10 minutes. Reduce heat to 350 degrees and continue baking 10 more minutes or until the pastry is nicely browned. These rolls are good hot or cold. They can be made in advance, wrapped in moistureproof, vaporproof freezer bags, and baked on the day you plan to use them.

Ginger Sausage Balls

1½ pounds pure pork sausage meat
1 clove garlic, finely minced
1 tablespoon grated fresh (green) ginger or slightly more candied ginger
3 eggs, separated

Slightly Oriental in feeling, these sausage balls have character and flavor.

Mix the sausage with the garlic, ginger, and egg yolks. Beat egg whites and fold into the mixture.

To deep-fry, drop by small teaspoons into deep fat heated to 370 degrees. Do not fry too many at once or the fat will cool and they will become grease-soaked. The balls should be quite small, about the size of a filbert or hazel nut. When browned, remove from fat and drain on paper towels.

To bake, chill the mixture, then form into small balls. Place on a baking pan about 1 inch apart. Bake in 425-degree oven about 10 minutes or until lightly browned.

These sausage balls can be made ahead, wrapped, and frozen, either baked or unbaked, until ready to use. They should be served hot.

Sauerkraut Balls

1 large onion, finely chopped
5 tablespoons butter
1 garlic clove, finely chopped
1½ cups finely ground cold corned beef
½ cup finely ground cold ham
½ teaspoon freshly ground pepper
½ teaspoon Tabasco
6 tablespoons flour
2 eggs, lightly beaten
2 cups well drained sauerkraut, coarsely chopped
2 tablespoons chopped parsley

COATING

Flour
2 eggs, well beaten
2 to 2½ cups dry breadcrumbs
Fat for frying

Sauté the onion in butter until wilted. Add the garlic, meat, and seasonings and mix thoroughly. Cook over medium heat. Add the flour and blend thoroughly. Mix the eggs with the sauerkraut and parsley, add to the meat mixture and stir until thickened. Chill. Form into small balls. Roll the balls in flour, dip in well-beaten egg, and roll in crumbs. Fry in hot fat at 375 degrees until nicely browned and crisp. Drain on absorbent paper and serve hot. It is best to cook only a few of the sauerkraut balls at a time. Overloading tends to make the balls greasy.

Tartar Steak

2 pounds freshly ground lean beef put through the grinder twice — top or bottom round, or chuck with little fat, or top sirloin
12 anchovy fillets
1 medium onion, very finely chopped
2 teaspoons or more Dijon mustard
3 raw egg yolks
2 teaspoons salt or to taste
1 teaspoon freshly ground pepper
4 tablespoons Cognac

This way of serving it has convinced many people that raw meat can be thoroughly delicious.

Spread the chopped meat on a chopping board in a rectangle. Chop the anchovies very fine. Blend them into the meat with two heavy-bladed knives, using a spreading stroke with one hand and a chopping stroke with the other. Fold the meat in from the edges to the center and then spread it out as before. Add the onion, mustard, and egg yolks and spread and chop. Fold in again from the edges to the center. Spread and chop until it is a rectangle once more. Add the salt and freshly ground pepper. You may add Tabasco and Worcestershire, if you like, but I feel it is not necessary. Spread and chop, this time very well, and again bring in the edges to form a large patty. Turn over, spread and chop again, and re-form a large patty. Place in a bowl and cover with chopped parsley and chives, or form a nice patty and arrange on a board or platter. Garnish with chopped parsley. Serve with rye or pumpernickel breads. Tartar steak may also be shaped into small balls and rolled in chopped parsley or chopped nuts. Serve with toothpicks.

Grilled Flank Steak Sandwiches

2 flank steaks
1 cup dry red wine
½ cup salad oil
1 clove garlic, chopped
1 onion, sliced
½ cup chopped parsley
Salt and freshly ground pepper
2 medium-size loaves French bread
Butter
1 clove garlic, crushed
¼ teaspoon thyme

Remove the tough outer membrane from the meat. Put the wine, oil, chopped garlic, sliced onion, and parsley in a shallow bowl. Let the meat marinate at least 2 or 3 hours, or better, overnight, in the refrigerator. Turn the meat several times while marinating. Flank steak should be at refrigerator temperature when grilled, so store it until the last minute. Grill it quickly over charcoal. The coals should be hot enough and the grill close enough to the coals to cook the steak to a crusty brown on the outside and red rare in the center in 4 minutes on each side. This is a cut that must not be well done. Brush with the marinade as it cooks and season to taste with salt and pepper.

In the meantime, prepare the bread: Split the loaves the long way. Mix the butter — a lot or little, as you prefer — with the garlic and thyme and spread on each half loaf. Put the loaves together again, wrap in foil, and heat on the back of the grill before you start the steak.

When the steak is ready, remove it to a cutting board and with a very sharp knife cut it in thin diagonal slices. Place on the lengths of French bread. Make open-faced sandwiches or cover with another length of bread, as you choose. Cut crosswise in a convenient size. Serve as an accompaniment to drinks, and provide mustard, barbecue sauce, pickles, chowchow, and the like. For a large party, one person should be assigned to grill the steaks and serve them as fast as they are demanded. This is one of the best and easiest of hors d'oeuvre I know.

Cocktail Reuben Sandwiches

These can be prepared well ahead, toasted in the broiler oven as needed, and served piping hot.

Spread slices of cocktail rye bread with butter. On half of the slices place a thin slice of corned beef topped with a thin slice of Swiss cheese. Add a few shreds of sauerkraut that has been well washed and drained. Top with another slice of bread. Press together. Toast when ready to serve.

Tiny Pizzas

1 yeastcake or package of dry yeast
2 teaspoons sugar
1¼ cups warm water (105 to 110 degrees)
3 to 3½ cups all-purpose flour
1 tablespoon olive oil
1 tablespoon salt

The pizza epidemic broke out after the Second World War, and since then they have become one of the three or four most popular snacks in the country. Inevitably they have come to the cocktail table in smaller versions, which can be extremely attractive.

To make the dough, dissolve the yeast with the sugar in ¼ cup warm water, and stir and let stand till it proofs. Combine the rest of the water with 1 cup flour, the oil, and salt. Mix well, add the yeast mixture, and stir in enough flour to form a fairly stiff dough. Knead lightly for 5 minutes, place in an oiled bowl, and set in a warm spot to rise until double in bulk — about 1½ hours.

Punch the dough down and divide it in three pieces. Roll out, cut with a 3 or 4 inch cutter and form small pizzas, or form the individual pizzas with your hands. The center of the dough should be thinner than the edges. Place the pizzas on an oiled baking pan. Pat oil on surface with the fingers. Add any of the fillings (or a combination) presented below. Then let the pizzas rise for about 12 minutes. Bake them in a 375-degree oven for 12 to 15 minutes or until they are throughly cooked through and the filling is perfectly done.

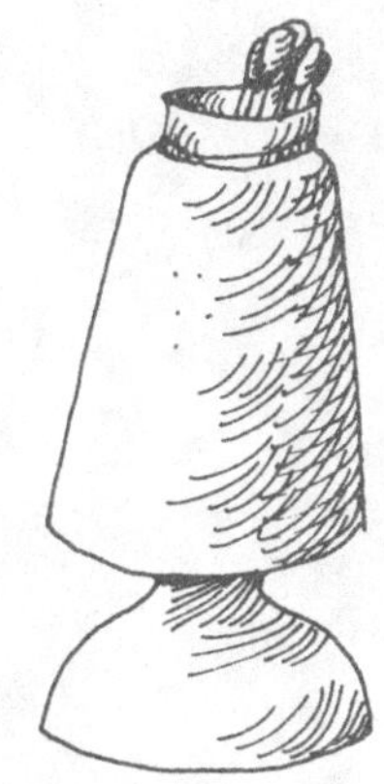

Suggested Fillings

Onions. Slice onions very thin or chop them, and steam in butter (for 1½ cups onions use about 3 tablespoons butter) in a heavy covered saucepan for 15 minutes over fairly low heat.

Tomato sauce. Use tomato purée, well seasoned, or follow recipe for tomato sauce, pages 461-463.

Sausage. Use thinly sliced pepperoni or salami, or any other sausage you prefer.

Anchovies. Boneless are the best. Traditional with onion, tomato, and cheese; or with soft black olives, onions, and grated Parmesan (without tomato sauce).

Garlic. Add minced garlic to taste to any combination of seasonings.

Herbs. The best herbs for pizzas are basil, which combines beautifully with tomato, or oregano, a pungent and sometimes too pungent herb if used with a heavy hand. Chopped parsley is always good, especially the flat-leafed Italian variety.

Sauerkraut. May be combined with sausage, Emmenthaler cheese, and onion to make a most delicious and unusual pizza.

Cheeses. Mozzarella, Monterey jack, Gruyère, or Emmenthaler for melting cheeses; and freshly grated Parmesan, Asiago, or Romano for grating cheeses.

Bacon-Wrapped Hors d'Oeuvre

Sometime about the middle of the 1920's I seem to remember my first bacon-wrapped snack, served to accompany bathtub gin martinis. Good bathtub gin was not without its merits, but it needed food to keep one in shape for the second and third drink, so snacks became more hearty. I'm certain the first snack of this type I had was one I find often these days in trekking around the country — a bacon-wrapped crisp cracker or saltine. It still makes one of the more successful items in this genre, although practically everything you can think of has been wrapped in bacon these last years. However, one must use excellent bacon — sometimes a chore to find these days, but nevertheless possible. Also, there is an important point overlooked by many cooks. The bacon should be partially cooked before wrapping and broiling or baking so that a good deal of the excess fat and moisture (prevalent nowadays in bacon) is cooked out.

Crackers in Bacon. Use saltines or the long crackers called Waverly, among other names. (Each biscuit company has a different appellation, but they come four to a section and are short and crisp.) Wrap pieces of partially cooked bacon around the crackers and secure with toothpicks. Arrange on a rack in a broiling pan or shallow roasting pan and broil 5 inches from the heating unit, or bake in a 450-degree oven until bacon is crisped. Do not burn the crackers, however. Turn once if necessary. Serve hot.

Olives in Bacon. These are superb even though served rather frequently. Wrap partially cooked bacon around large stuffed olives and secure with toothpicks. Place on rack in broiling pan. Broil 5 inches from broiling unit or bake in 450-degree oven till bacon is crisp.

Sausages in Bacon. Blanch tiny pork sausages, tiny frankfurters, or chipolata sausages 4 minutes in boiling water. Wrap in partially cooked bacon strips and secure with toothpicks. Place on rack in broiling pan or shallow roasting pan and broil 5 inches from broiling unit or bake in oven at 450 degrees. Turn once if necessary.

Crabmeat Chunks or Legs in Bacon. Chunks of backfin crabmeat from blue crabs or legs of Dungeness crabs are excellent wrapped with partially cooked bacon strips and broiled or baked. Broil about 5 inches from the heat unit, and turn the pieces once, or bake at 450 degrees, in which case turning is probably not necessary. Be careful not to overcook the crabmeat; merely heat through.

Shrimp in Bacon. Marinate 24 large shrimp 1 hour in ½ cup soy sauce, ¼ cup oil, 2 finely chopped garlic cloves, and ¼ cup chopped parsley. Wrap each shrimp in a strip of partially cooked bacon, place on rack in broiling pan, and broil until bacon is cooked, turning once.

Chicken or Duck Livers in Bacon. Cut chicken or duck livers into sections large enough to be rolled in bacon. Season with salt and Tabasco and wrap in partially cooked bacon strips. Broil on rack about 4 inches from heat until liver is delicately brown and bacon is crisp. Turn once during cooking.

Rumaki. This comes from the Polynesian school of cookery, which is a combination of American, Hawaiian, and Oriental, popularized by Trader Vic and his imitators. Very good some of it is, too. Buy 1 pound chicken livers and cut each liver in half. Marinate 1 hour in ½ cup soy sauce, ¼ cup oil, 2 finely chopped garlic cloves, and 1 teaspoon curry powder. Slice 3 or 4 water chestnuts fairly thin. Wrap a piece of liver and a slice of water chestnut in partially cooked bacon strips, and secure well with a toothpick. Place on a rack in a broiling pan and broil till bacon is crisp, turning once.

Tiny Sandwiches in Bacon. Very tiny sandwiches filled with cheese and/or peanut butter may be wrapped in partially cooked bacon and broiled on a rack about 5 inches from the heat. Turn once during the broiling. Do not let the sandwiches get too brown.

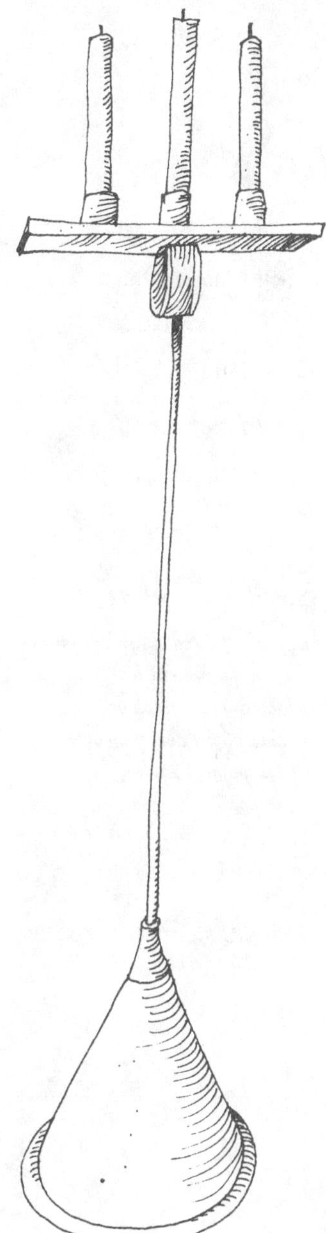

Small Skewers as Hors d'Oeuvre

Small metal or bamboo skewers of food are excellent drink accompaniments, especially for outdoor cooking in summer. Merely string cubes of marinated meat — beef, lamb, pork, or chicken — on small skewers, leaving no space between the pieces. Marinate the meat for several hours in ½ cup each of soy sauce, oil, and sherry or red wine, 2 or 3 finely chopped garlic cloves, 1 teaspoon dry mustard, ¼ teaspoon Tabasco, 1 teaspoon rosemary, and ¼ cup chopped parsley. Turn the meat in the marinade several times. Bamboo skewers should soak in water for an hour. Invite guests to broil skewers to their own taste. Serve bowls of mustard, chili sauce, and soy sauce for dipping.

Tiny Chicken Legs

Follow any of the recipes for fried chicken, using only very small chicken legs or legs of Rock Cornish game hens. Put a paper frill on the legs, and serve them hot as finger food.

Tiny Lamb Chops

Small lamb chops — rib chops trimmed of their fat and the bone scraped to make a good handle — may be broiled and served very hot with a curry mustard sauce or a chutney sauce. Put a paper frill on the bone, and serve from a hot platter or from the grill.

Small Hamburgers

1 pound ground chuck or round with 25 percent fat
3 tablespoons grated onion
3 tablespoons heavy cream
¼ teaspoon Tabasco
1 teaspoon salt
¼ teaspoon freshly ground pepper

Here is an idea that came from one of the finest catering services in the country, Yours Truly, in Portland, Oregon. Prepare small hamburgers and season well. Cook to taste and pop into buttered hot buns, along with a thin slice of onion and a brush of mustard. Small hamburger buns can be ordered from good bakeries throughout the country. This hors d'oeuvre is invariably a hit.

Blend the ingredients well and form into small patties. Grill or sauté in butter. You should get 8 or even 9 patties to a pound, depending upon the size buns you choose.

Individual Oyster or Clam Cocktails

Sake cups have flooded the market during these last years, and they make efficient containers for individual oyster or clam cocktails, to be passed on a tray. To eat, one simply tips the cup to the lips, consumes the tiny oyster or clam and sauce, and returns the cup to the tray. In effect, one drinks the clam or oyster. Use petite points or Olympias from the Pacific coast, or very small Eastern oysters, or any small clam of your choice. Top the oyster or clam with a small amount of cocktail sauce or a sauce of your own creation, and serve at once.

Codfish Balls

1 pound salt codfish
2 cups freshly mashed potatoes (instant may be used)
¾ teaspoon freshly ground pepper
½ teaspoon powdered ginger
4 eggs, beaten

These were in style in the East during speakeasy days and continued in style after Prohibition was ended. They are simple but extremely good when well made. Today, unfortunately, most people know only commercial codfish balls, which are frequently reduced in flavor to the point where they are without character.

Soak the codfish in cold water for several hours, changing the water after 2 hours. Place in fresh water and bring to a rolling boil. Drain and flake the fish and combine with the mashed potatoes and seasonings. Add the beaten eggs and beat well. One or 2 finely chopped garlic cloves may also be added to the mixture if you like (it gives a magnificent flavor although it is not traditional). Drop by teaspoonfuls into fat heated to 375 degrees, and cook until nicely browned and crisp. Serve with drinks.

Smoked Fish for Appetizers

Quantities of smoked and cured fish are available throughout the country, particularly in the Northwest, the Middle West, and the Northeastern States, as well as in Canada. In Florida, California, and other coastal states where sport fishing is popular, an interesting variety of smoked and hot-smoked fish is marketed locally and is smoked to order for fishermen. And in the large cities one usually finds an excellent selection of fish, some of the finest on sale in Jewish delicatessens.

It is nearly impossible to list all the small smoked fish on the market, so we must settle for the choices found most frequently. If available, assemble several different kinds of smoked fish, either sliced or whole, for your cocktail board or platter. Serve along with thin rye bread, pumpernickel, bagels, if you like, capers, olive oil, chopped onion, butter, and lemon or lime. (See also Smoked Fish in the Fish chapter.)

Smoked Fish

Salmon. If you are throwing a large party and you have someone to carve, purchase a side of smoked salmon. It should be sliced with a very sharp slicing knife in long, thin diagonal slices, not in thick chunks as is so often the case.

Sturgeon. Cut the same way as salmon, but it is impossible to cut it quite as thin. Often it is wiser to have it sliced in the shop where you purchase it.

Eel. Should be skinned, filleted, and removed from the bone. The larger eel are usually the juiciest and the best.

Whitefish. Should be skinned and filleted with a knife and fork. The meat is very tender, so treat it gently.

Trout. Should be skinned and filleted. It is good served with horseradish mixed with sour cream or whipped cream.

Winnipeg goldeye. Serve like smoked trout, skinned and filleted, or heat and serve warm.

Butterfish. Should be served whole, skinned if possible.

Tuna. Smoked tuna has a tendency to be quite dry, so slice cautiously.

Smoked shrimp. Usually smoked in the shell and served that way.

Kippered Fish

The terms "smoked fish" and "kippered fish" are frequently used interchangeably. However, kippered fish is really hot-smoked, a process that cooks it at the same time. It is quite delicious. These are the kippered fish found most commonly:

Salmon. Comes in small pieces, which should be carefully sliced.

Cod. Best when heated, but may be sliced and served cold.

Sablefish. Wonderfully flavored. Slice fairly thin and carefully. May also be served heated.

Cold Shrimp

From the very beginnings of cocktail snacks, shrimp have taken first place. One seldom goes to a cocktail party where they are not served in one form or another. However, they are frequently not as good as they ought to be. The failing of shrimp served both in restaurants and in most homes is that they are cooked with little or no salt and, in addition, are overcooked. For rules on cooking shrimp, refer to the section on fish.

To serve cold shrimp, use the largest or next to largest shrimp you can get — under 12 to a pound or larger. If the larger ones do not appeal to you, use those under 15 to a pound. Arrange the shrimp in bowls set within larger bowls of cracked or shaved ice. They will look especially handsome if first arranged on a bed of parsley heads. Provide bowls of mayonnaise, herbed mayonnaise, mustard mayonnaise, or Thousand Island dressing to be used as a dip. Napkins and small plates are helpful for this type of service.

Marinated Shrimp

4 to 5 pounds shrimp, poached, peeled, and chilled
1 large or 2 medium onions, sliced paper-thin
2 or 3 lemons peeled and sliced paper-thin
1 bunch fresh dill, broken into small clusters of leaves
Chopped parsley
Freshly ground pepper
3 garlic cloves, crushed and wrapped in cheesecloth
1½ to 2 cups olive or half olive and half peanut oil
3 bay leaves

You will need a large tureen or casserole for this, from which the shrimp can be served.

Alternate layers of shrimp, onion, lemon, dill clusters, and chopped parsley. Grind fresh pepper over each layer of shrimp. Place the bag containing the garlic in the center of the dish, where it can be removed before serving. Add the oil, which should come almost to the top of the shrimp. Cover the tureen or casserole, and let it rest in the refrigerator for 18 to 24 hours. Just before serving, remove the garlic bag. Sprinkle with chopped parsley, and add the bay leaves. Serve from the tureen, and provide small plates and picks or small forks.

Small Pacific or Maine Shrimp

The tiny sweet shrimp of the Pacific Coast and those from the waters of Maine are reminiscent of the Icelandic and English shrimp prevalent in Europe. Some are offered already cooked and shelled. The best way to serve them for cocktails is merely to have a bowl of them on a table and let guests eat them up as they do peanuts or popcorn.

Shrimp in Shells

3 to 4 pounds smallish shrimps (15 to 30 to a pound)
COURT BOUILLON
2 full heads of garlic (not cloves), crushed (you need not peel; merely crush well)
1 bottle (fifth) of white wine
1 cup white wine vinegar
3 cups water
2 tablespoons Tabasco, or to taste
1 tablespoon freshly ground pepper
3 or 4 sprigs of fresh dill or 1 tablespoon dillweed
1 tablespoon salt or more to taste

Serve the cooked shrimp in shells. Don't worry about the black vein, it is not necessary to remove it. Place empty containers nearby to collect discarded shells.

Bring the court bouillon mixture to a boil and simmer 10 minutes. Taste and correct the seasoning. Add the shrimp and let return to a boil. Boil 3 minutes. Remove the shrimp and reserve the bouillon. Cool both shrimp and bouillon, then return the shrimp to marinate in the bouillon 2 to 3 hours. Chill thoroughly and serve in a bowl set over crushed ice.

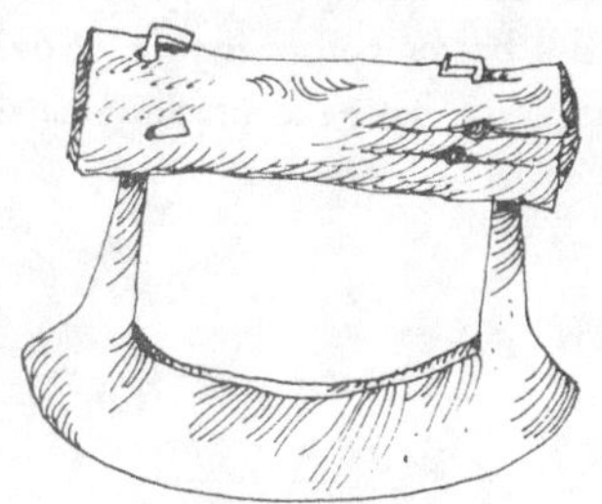

Fried Shrimp

3 to 4 pounds shrimp, cleaned but with the tails left on

BATTER

2 eggs
1¾ cups beer or water
1 cup flour
2 tablespoons cornstarch
¼ cup cornmeal
½ teaspoon salt
½ teaspoon baking powder

These must be served piping hot and never allowed to cool, else they will become soggy. Nothing except perhaps a cold fried clam can be as horrible as a cold fried shrimp.

To prepare the batter, beat the eggs and add 1 cup beer or water. Sift the flour, cornstarch, cornmeal, salt, and baking powder together, and combine with the egg mixture. Stir in additional beer or water to make a thick batter. You may not need all the liquid.

Heat oil or shortening in a deep fryer to 375 degrees. Dip the shrimp in the batter and fry them until delicately brown and crisp. Serve very hot with any of the sauces recommended for cold shrimp, above, or set out hot mustard and chili sauce in separate bowls. If you use mustard mayonnaise, make it very pungent.

Helen Evans Brown's Shrimp on a Stick

2 to 3 pounds large shrimp

COURT BOUILLON

2 cups white wine
6 cups water
¼ cup vinegar
1 onion, sliced
1 carrot, sliced
1 tablespoon salt
2 whole cloves
1 rib celery, sliced
3 or 4 sprigs parsley
1 teaspoon dillweed or 2 tablespoons chopped fresh dill

DILL BUTTER

½ pound butter
2 tablespoons chopped fresh dill or 1½ teaspoons dillweed
1½ teaspoons lemon juice
¼ teaspoon Tabasco

Clean the shrimp and impale each one firmly on a bamboo skewer, inserted at the tail of the shrimp and running through to the other end. Arrange on a platter or plate, cover with plastic wrap. and refrigerate until serving time.

Put the ingredients for the court bouillon in an electric skillet or similar appliance that can be used efficiently on a serving table in the living room or on the terrace.

To prepare the dill butter, cream the butter well, and beat in the dill and other seasonings. Do not refrigerate too long before serving; the butter should be creamy and not firm. Divide it among several small bowls, and set around the table.

Cook the court bouillon 10 minutes. To serve, add several skewers of shrimp to the bouillon, and when it returns to a boil, let the shrimp cook about 3 or 4 minutes. Each person helps himself to a skewer and dips it into the dill butter before eating. Provide guests with napkins and small plates, and have receptacles available for used skewers.

Shrimp-Cucumber Cups

2 to 3 long cucumbers
1 pound shrimp, cooked and chopped fine
1 cup butter (2 sticks)
1 teaspoon salt
½ teaspoon mace
Dash of Tabasco
Chopped parsley

These we invented years ago when I had an hors d'oeuvre business in New York. They make a wonderful snack, delightful to look at and good to taste. You may use a crabmeat, chicken, or lobster combination instead of the shrimp.

Wash the cucumbers but do not peel. Combine the chopped shrimp, butter, salt, mace, and Tabasco. Cut the cucumbers in ¾-inch slices. Use a small, fluted pastry cutter to make the edges more decorative. Form into little cups by scooping out some of the seeds with a melon ball cutter. Stuff with the shrimp mixture and decorate with a wreath of parsley, or put a tiny sprig of parsley in the top. Place these on a platter or in a baking pan, cover lightly with foil, and chill thoroughly. These can be made ahead very nicely and left to chill for up to 4 or 5 hours. Makes about 20 small cups.

Fruit for Cocktails

Piquant Tangerine Sections

2 cups tangerine sections
½ cup honey
½ cup water
⅓ cup cider vinegar
2 to 3 tablespoons Jamaica rum
½ tablespoon finely chopped onion
1 tablespoon rosemary
1 teaspoon soy sauce

Boil the honey and water for 1 minute. Add the remaining ingredients except the tangerine sections. Stir well. Pour the mixture over tangerine sections and let them marinate 3 to 4 hours or overnight. Serve with small picks and provide small plates or paper napkins.

Ham with Fruit

Italian prosciutto with halved fresh figs or with slices of melon, papaya, or pineapple makes a delicious and now quite standard appetizer. But very thin slices of cooked Virginia ham are even better. Either drape the ham over the fruit and serve on a plate as a first course, to be eaten with knife and fork, or cut the larger fruit into small sections, wrap securely with the ham, and secure with a toothpick. Serve as a cocktail snack and provide small plates or napkins.

Bacon with Fruit. Secure crisp bacon slices to fruit with a toothpick, if you like.

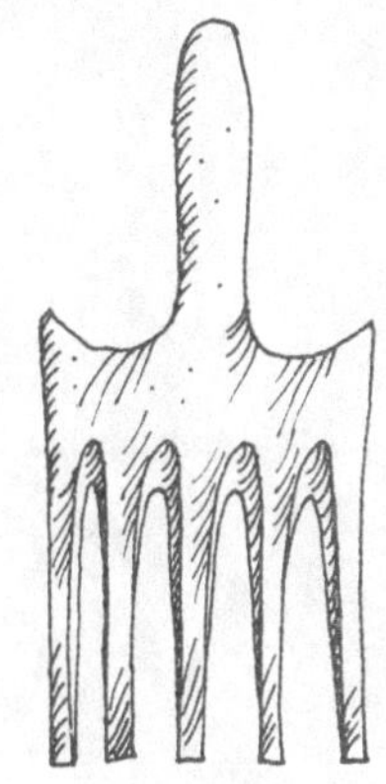

Fruit with Curry Dunk

3 to 3½ cups rich chicken broth
2 tablespoons curry powder
2 tablespoons arrowroot
⅔ cup seeded raisins, puffed in warm water
2 cups toasted Brazil nuts or almonds, finely chopped
2 cups coconut, fresh grated or dried
Fresh fruits

Originally a California idea, this cocktail delight has become known in other parts of the country and is especially good for summer parties in the garden or on the terrace.

Heat the broth and blend in the curry powder. Stir a little water into the arrowroot and stir slowly into the broth. Cook and stir until thickened. In the meantime put the raisins in hot water to puff them. Drain, add to the sauce, and heat through. Keep the sauce hot in a chafing dish over hot water or in an electric skillet on very low heat (the mixture will thin out if too hot).

Arrange two bowls, one containing the chopped nuts and the other the coconut. On a bed of ice, place fingers of chilled fresh fruit, such as pineapple, melon, banana, papaya, mango, or halved plums or apricots, whole figs, sliced peaches, or pear quarters. Brush with lemon juice to keep them from discoloring. Invite the guests to dunk a piece of fruit into the curry sauce and then into the chopped nuts and coconut.

Raw Vegetables with Curry Dunk. Substitute fresh, crisp vegetables, such as celery stalks, radishes, green pepper strips, cucumber fingers, fresh raw asparagus, raw baby carrots, and scallions. This is also a delicious luncheon dish served with rice, chutney, crisp toast, and cool white wine.

Avocado Balls Piquant

1 cup avocado balls
⅓ cup olive oil
¼ cup cider vinegar
1 small clove garlic, crushed
2 tablespoons Jamaica rum

Mix the olive oil, vinegar, garlic, and rum, and pour over the avocado balls. Marinate for 3 to 4 hours, or overnight if possible. To serve, drain from the marinade. Serve as an appetizer in a small bowl sprinkled with a bit of chopped parsley. Provide toothpicks. Or serve as a beginning course in cocktail glasses on a bed of shredded lettuce with perhaps a bit of lettuce leaf at the sides, or serve on a small plate in a cupped lettuce leaf.

Salads

American salads, unlike good, simple French salads, have traditionally tended to be "composed salads" or the elaborate sweet-sour combinations that have been especially popular in the hinterland. Even plain greens are tossed with a sweetened French dressing, and many commercial mayonnaises have a high sugar content. Often those who like a tart salad ignore lettuce in favor of green leafy vegetables or raw vegetables, dressed with vinegar, salt, and pepper. As a matter of fact, the earliest salad recipes treated cucumbers or sliced onions in this way — these dishes still persist in certain regions — and pickled beets have never lost their appeal, though sometimes they taste as strongly of vinegar as any edible food can.

An even earlier form of salad is coleslaw, which came to the American Colonies with the Dutch and has gone through many stages before arriving at the more or less standard recipe.

The dish we normally associate with the word salad — greens, with or without other ingredients, mixed with a dressing — did not come into use till the late nineteenth century, and not until the early twentieth century, about 1912, did the balance in flavor of sour to bland begin to achieve sophistication.

Following this came a period of fancy salads made with fruits and cheese and nuts. Some of the more outlandish were called Butterfly Salad, Candlelight Salad, and Santa Claus Salad. They prevailed at luncheons and dinner parties and were served up covered with appalling sweet dressings and decorated with maraschino cherries.

When a Pennsylvania housewife won a national prize for a jellied salad in 1905, she unleashed a demand for congealed salads that has grown alarmingly, particularly in the suburbs. The jellied salad does have its delights, though, and it is without question an American innovation.

As of this writing, the tossed salad, green salad, or whatever you wish to call it, has taken over. And though it seems a simple thing to prepare, a fine salad is an art. The greens must be fresh, crisp, and cool. They should not sport a drop of moisture when they are placed in a bowl. They should be broken into bite-size pieces or left in large pieces to be cut at table. The salad should not be tossed till just before eating. The perfect dressing should be neither oily nor acid. Sugar has no place in the dressing. Each leaf should be coated with sauce and remain crisp and fresh to the palate.

Selecting Salad Greens

There are many members of the lettuce family, varying widely in texture and taste. These can be supplemented with vegetables which double as salad greens, such as spinach and cabbage, and also with certain fresh herbs, which may be added to salads in substantial quantities, thus acting as an extra green.

Iceberg lettuce. This widely available lettuce is the most generally maligned and mistreated of them all. The hearts, well crisped and broken into manageable chunks — not huge wedges — have good flavor and interesting texture.

Bibb or limestone lettuce. Bibb comes in small heads, is exceptionally green and crisp, and maintains its crispness extremely well in a salad. However, it is difficult to clean and requires thorough rinsing and soaking, for dirt lurks in the most inaccessible spots. Tear off the leaves, or break the heads into quarters or halves, according to size (they vary from small to medium).

Boston or butter lettuce. A pale green, loosely packed, tender round lettuce found in the market throughout most of the year that has a pleasing flavor and takes dressing well. Boston is very fragile and must be washed and dried with care.

Romaine or Cos lettuce. One of the most satisfactory and sought-after members of the lettuce group. Romaine has crisp long bright green leaves and good flavor. Discard the coarse outer leaves, but retain the core of the lettuce, which has a pleasantly bitter taste; trim it and slice it into the salad.

Leaf lettuce. This category includes several varieties of loose-leafed lettuce that do not form heads. The curly green and curly red-tipped are the most common, the latter adding a contrasting color to a largely green salad. There are also a number of flat-leaf lettuces with such names as "salad bowl" and "ivy leaf." Leaf lettuces have delicious tender leaves, rather soft in texture compared to romaine or Bibb. They should be washed, dried and used quickly, and not overtossed, as they wilt easily.

Chicory or curly endive. A slightly bitter curly green lettuce usually partially blanched before marketing, which makes its heart white and the outer leaves a bright green. Because of its bitter taste, it is best when combined with other greens.

Dandelion greens. Both commercially grown and wild dandelion greens are excellent in salad. They have a refreshingly bitter taste, good alone or with other greens.

Escarole. Although it somewhat resembles chicory, escarole is heavier and tougher in texture and the leaves are not so feathery. It, too, is slightly bitter in taste and has its center leaves blanched to a creamy white.

Endive. This small, elongated, tightly packed lettuce is always bleached before being sent to market. Formerly all of it came from Belgium (hence the general term Belgian endive), but some is now being raised in this country. It is fairly expensive, particularly in the West and Middle West, although better distribution is helping to lower prices. Endive is one of the cleanest of all lettuces, requiring very little washing. It has a crisp texture and a delicately bitter flavor.

Spinach. An increasingly popular salad green, either alone or mixed with other types. The leaves should be fresh, young, and thoroughly washed.

Watercress. The quality of this peppery-tasting green varies greatly across the country, but it is generally fresh, crisp, and deep green in color. Although it is frequently mixed with other greens in salads, in my opinion it is best when served alone, without dressing, or as a garnish for composed salads, as it wilts rapidly when dressed.

Arugula or Rocket. A small flat-leaved green shaped somewhat like radish tops, with a well-defined bitter flavor that makes it a delicious addition to other greens. It is sold in Italian markets.

Field salad or corn salad. These small darkish green leaves, which are sold with roots attached, are tedious to clean but worth it.

Their flavor is tangy and stimulating, especially when combined with a small quantity of cooked beets. Difficult to find in this country except in Eastern markets in the late fall and winter.

Cabbage. Green, red, or Savoy cabbages are often used in salads with a combination of greens. The cabbage should be shredded very fine and either crisped or wilted, depending on the salad recipe.

Chinese cabbage. A pale green and white cabbage that forms long heads. It is usually added to other greens. Before shredding it should be crisped and the tough outer leaves removed.

Basil. Especially good in salads with tomatoes, beans, or tuna fish.

Burnet. A mildly peppery herb, not widely known. The roots and flowers are excellent in a spring salad.

Chervil. Good in any delicately flavored salad.

Coriander. If you like its rather strange flavor, a wonderful addition to a salad.

Dill. A very agreeable herb, especially good with salads containing cucumbers and tomatoes.

Italian or flat parsley. An easily available herb that imparts a lively taste to salads.

Sorrel. A few leaves, shredded, give a delicious tartness and unusual flavor to salads.

Tarragon. Tarragon leaves combined with greens give almost any salad distinction.

Preparing Green Salads

A common fault of many salads is that the greens are not thoroughly dried after washing, and the accumulated moisture dilutes the dressing, rendering the salad tasteless and soggy. It is best to wash greens carefully well ahead of time. In the case of Boston lettuce, romaine, or chicory the heads should be left intact during the washing and crisping process. Shake excess water off the greens, roll in several thicknesses of paper toweling or in a dish towel, and place in a plastic bag. Crisp in the refrigerator — as much as 12 to 24 hours ahead. Take care that the refrigerator temperature is not unusually low, for greens freeze easily and become translucent, wilted, and quite unusable. Also, be careful when breaking greens. Certain varieties, such as Boston lettuce, are extremely tender and bruise easily.

When you are combining several greens in a salad, consider which need emphasis. Such delicate greens as field salad or Boston lettuce should not be overpowered by heavier, tougher greens like escarole or chicory.

How much salad per person should you allow? This question is seldom confronted by cookbook writers or is evaded with "It all depends on how hungry your guests are." According to my experience, you should plan on a minimum of 2 cups of loosely packed greens per person, or slightly less if other ingredients are to be added to the salad.

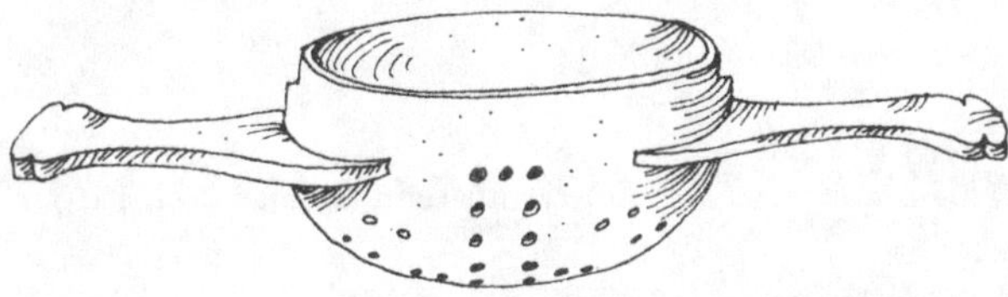

Simple Composed Salads

The ingredients listed below can be added to a basic mixture of greens to create a simple but substantial salad, appropriate for serving as a light luncheon, as an hors d'oeuvre at dinner, as part of a buffet, or at supper. Although a salad of this type fits into almost every menu, it has no place in a formal dinner or a dinner that is especially heavy. For each serving you will need 1 cup of greens and 1 cup of additives.

(1) Add orange sections, rosemary, and onion rings. Toss with a vinaigrette made with lemon juice instead of vinegar and strongly flavored orange juice.

(2) Add grapefruit sections, onion rings, and avocado slices or cubes. Toss with a vinaigrette heavily flavored with garlic.

(3) Add grapefruit and orange sections, onion rings, avocado slices, and thin cubes of fresh pineapple. Toss with a vinaigrette briskly flavored with garlic and rosemary.

(4) Add sliced radishes, sliced scallions, cubed and seeded cucumber, tiny cherry tomatoes (peeled, if you like) and chopped fresh basil. Toss with a vinaigrette.

(5) Add chopped fresh basil, cubed cucumber, cherry tomatoes, and sliced raw mushrooms. Toss with a vinaigrette.

Chiffonade Salad

1 head romaine, shredded
1 grapefruit, peeled and sectioned
2 green peppers, shredded
3 or 4 small tomatoes, peeled and quartered
Rosemary-flavored vinaigrette sauce

This used to be considered a most stylish salad to serve with dinner. Actually, it's quite a pleasant salad, though one hears of it much less often nowadays.

Make a bed of romaine on a platter or in a shallow bowl. On it arrange the grapefruit sections, peppers, and tomatoes. Dress with the vinaigrette sauce.

Bibb and Mushroom Salad

4 to 6 heads Bibb lettuce, cut in quarters
½ pound white mushrooms, stemmed and thinly sliced
2 tablespoons chopped parsley
Vinaigrette sauce flavored with basil

Since the Bibb lettuce is being used in quarters, it will require extra care in washing. Place the Bibb and mushrooms in a bowl, sprinkle with the parsley, and toss with the vinaigrette.

To Dress Lettuce as a Salad

This is a rather early nineteenth-century salad recipe from Miss Leslie.

"Strip off the outer leaves, wash the lettuce, split it in half, and lay it in cold water till dinnertime. Then drain it and lay it in a salad dish. Have ready two eggs boiled hard (which they will be in twelve minutes), and laid in a basin of cold water for five minutes to prevent the white from turning blue. Cut them in half and lay them on the lettuce.

"Put the yolks of the eggs on a large plate; with a wooden spoon mash them smooth, mixing them with a tablespoon of water, and two tablespoonfuls of sweet olive oil. Then add, by degrees, a saltspoonful of salt, a teaspoonful of mustard, and a teaspoonful of powdered loaf sugar. When these are all smoothly united, add, very gradually, three tablespoonfuls of vinegar. The lettuce having been cut up fine on another plate, put it to the dressing, and mix it well. If you have the dressing for the salad made before dinner, put it into the bottom of the salad dish. Then (having cut it up) lay the salad upon it, and let it rest till it is to be eaten, as stirring it will injure it.

"You may decorate the top of the salad with slices of red beet, and with the hard white eggs cut into rings."

Wilted Lettuce

2 heads lettuce or the equivalent in other greens
4 to 6 slices bacon or salt pork, cut into small dice
⅓ cup sugar
⅓ cup vinegar
1 teaspoon mustard
Salt (optional)
2 tablespoons or more chopped onion (optional)

This is one of the oldest and probably the most functional of salads. It can be made with nearly any type of greens and needs so few ingredients that it could be prepared en route in the covered wagon, in camp, or in the most primitive house. Its earthy quality makes it an interesting salad still, with certain dishes. I can remember wilted lettuce prepared in a large iron skillet at the beach and served from a warmed bowl. It is one salad where warm ingredients and warm utensils are in order.

Clean and dry the lettuce or other greens and arrange in a warmish salad bowl. Try out the bacon or salt pork in a heavy skillet, and when it is crisp, transfer to the salad bowl. Add sugar, vinegar, mustard, and salt, if needed, to the skillet. Swirl ingredients to blend well and simmer till the sugar is dissolved. Pour over the lettuce and toss lightly. Add chopped onion and egg if you like, and serve at once. This is excellent with chops, steak, or pot roast.

1 hard-boiled egg, chopped (optional)

Wilted Dandelion Salad

Approximately 1 pound dandelion greens, trimmed, washed, and dried
6 slices bacon, cut in rather small dice
2 garlic cloves, finely chopped
1/3 cup red wine vinegar
2 teaspoons sugar
1/2 teaspoon salt (optional)
2 tablespoons chopped parsley
3 tablespoons coarsely chopped fresh mint
1/2 teaspoon freshly ground pepper

Italians make a dish similar to the one above, using fresh dandelion greens, which can be gathered in the spring.

Sauté the bacon and garlic together. Add the vinegar, sugar, salt if necessary, and finally the parsley and mint. Pour over the dandelion greens, grind pepper over the top, and toss gently.

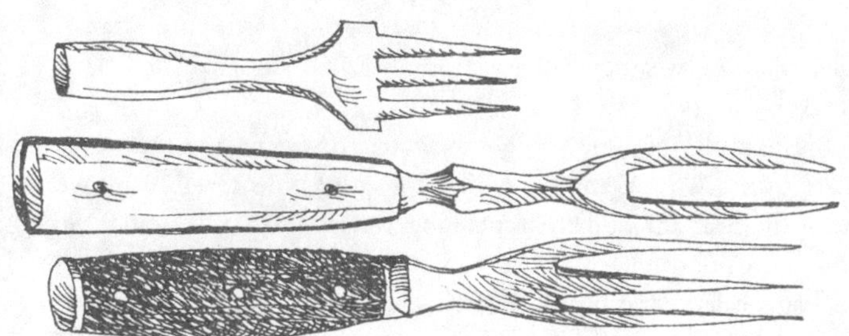

Caesar Salad

2 heads romaine or the equivalent in Bibb or iceberg lettuce
2 cups diced white bread of good quality — homemade type preferred
4 tablespoons plus 8 tablespoons olive oil
3 garlic cloves, crushed
1 teaspoon salt, or to taste
12 to 15 anchovy fillets, finely cut
2 tablespoons lemon juice
1 egg, raw or coddled 1 minute
1 teaspoon freshly ground pepper, or to taste
1/2 to 3/4 cup freshly grated Parmesan cheese

This salad, which has become an American classic, was created by a restaurateur in Tijuana, Mexico, in the 1920's, and its vogue has never ceased. There are many recipes for this salad. This one I find works exceedingly well.

Wash the romaine or lettuce thoroughly and dry well. Wrap in a tea towel or paper towels and refrigerate until ready to serve. Sauté the diced bread in 4 tablespoons olive oil with the garlic cloves. Shake the pan well and cook over medium heat until the croutons are delicately browned and crisp. Add additional oil if necessary. Remove the garlic and drain the croutons on absorbent paper. In a chilled salad bowl, break the greens in bite-size pieces. Add the 8 tablespoons olive oil and toss well so that each leaf is coated. Add the croutons, salt, anchovies, pepper, and lemon juice. Break the egg into the bowl (there has been great discussion as to whether it should be a raw or a 1-minute coddled egg). Toss again and add the grated Parmesan cheese.

Cabbage Salads

Cabbage salad and coleslaws have been standard dishes in this country since the early eighteenth century — ever since it was discovered that winter cabbage kept very well and afforded a crisp green vegetable long after most other greens had succumbed to the frost. For coleslaws and sauerkraut salads, see the cabbage section in the Vegetables chapter.

Perfection Salad

1 envelope unflavored gelatine
1¾ cups water
½ cup sugar
¼ cup vinegar
1 tablespoon lemon juice
½ teaspoon salt
¾ cup finely shredded cabbage
1 cup diced celery
1 pimiento, chopped
Greens
Mayonnaise

This historic salad, which has become a standard in American cuisine, won the third prize in a contest sponsored by Charles Knox in 1905. Fannie Farmer was one of the judges. The winner, Mrs. John E. Cooke of New Castle, Pennsylvania, was rewarded with a hundred-dollar sewing machine and enduring gastronomic fame. The salad has weathered the years and seems as popular now as it was early in the century.

Sprinkle the gelatine in ½ cup water to soften. Add the sugar, place over low heat, and stir until the gelatine is dissolved. Remove from the heat and add the remaining water, vinegar, lemon juice, and salt. Chill to the consistency of unbeaten egg white. Fold in the cabbage, celery, and pimiento. Pour into a 4 or 5 cup mold or into individual molds, and chill till firm. Serve on a bed of greens with a well-seasoned mayonnaise.

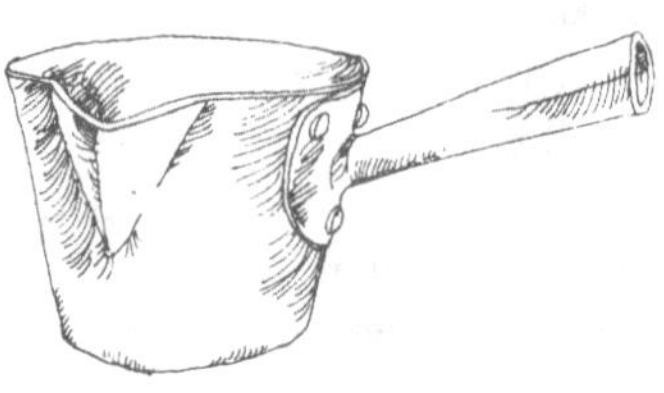

Potato Salads

Potato salads are not as old as lettuce salads, tomato or cabbage salads. But then, the potato didn't come into common use as early as most people think it did. Once potato salad was invented, however, it became an all-time favorite. There are many recipes for it, nearly all of them good.

One of the first potato salads I remember was prepared for a picnic by Polly Hamblet. It is different from the accepted version of today and extremely good.

Polly Hamblet's Potato Salad

6 to 8 medium-size cold boiled potatoes in their jackets
1 medium onion, finely chopped
3 ribs celery, finely chopped
Salt and freshly ground pepper
4 hard-boiled eggs
2 tablespoons chopped parsley
Mayonnaise
Ripe olives

Peel and dice the potatoes and combine with the onion and celery. Toss gently. Salt and pepper to taste. Chop two of the eggs rather fine and add to the mixture, along with the parsley. Bind to your taste with mayonnaise. Garnish with the two remaining eggs, quartered, and ripe olives.

Note. The same salad may be mixed with a boiled dressing, which changes its character completely.

Picnic Potato Salad

6 medium-size potatoes, boiled in their jackets
1 clove garlic
2 small cucumbers, peeled and seeded
1 teaspoon or more salt
½ teaspoon freshly ground pepper
2 tablespoons hot bacon drippings
1 medium onion, finely chopped
4 tablespoons olive oil
1½ tablespoons vinegar
Greens
Paprika

Peel the potatoes while they are hot. Place in a bowl which has been well rubbed with garlic. Let them stand till cool. Slice the cucumbers, and add salt and pepper. Slice the cooled potatoes and pour heated bacon fat over them. Combine with the cucumbers and onion and toss lightly. Add the oil and vinegar, and again toss lightly. Let stand 2 hours before serving. Add more oil and vinegar, if needed. Arrange on a bed of greens and sprinkle with a touch of paprika.

Peggy Martin's Potato Salad

8 or 9 medium-size potatoes, waxy ones if possible
1½ cups dry white wine
½ cup finely chopped onion
½ cup shredded carrot
¾ cup olive oil
3 tablespoons wine vinegar
Salt and freshly ground pepper
½ cup slivered blanched toasted almonds
4 tablespoons mayonnaise
3 hard-boiled eggs
2 tablespoons chopped parsley

This delicious salad is a relative of Alexander Dumas's recipe for potato salad, which appears in his great dictionary of gastronomy. Peggy Martin used it successfully for a picnic salad years ago.

Boil the potatoes till just pierceable. Peel as soon as possible and break apart with two forks. Pour the white wine over them. Cool. Add the onion, carrot, oil, vinegar, and salt and pepper to taste. Chill several hours. When ready to serve, toss with the mayonnaise and garnish with the almonds and hard-boiled eggs. Sprinkle with chopped parsley.

Oil and Vinegar Potato Salad

6 to 9 medium-size potatoes or 12 small new potatoes
6 tablespoons olive oil
1 teaspoon salt
1 teaspoon freshly ground pepper
2 or 3 tablespoons wine vinegar
⅔ cup finely cut green onions, including green tops
4 tablespoons chopped parsley

This was a French potato salad originally, but various additives have given it new definition.

Boil the potatoes till just pierceable. Peel as quickly as possible and slice fairly thin. Add the olive oil, salt, pepper, and vinegar, and allow the potatoes to cool. When ready to serve add the green onions, parsley, and additional oil and vinegar if needed. Serve cool, but not chilled, with cold or hot meats.

Note. You may substitute chopped chives for the onions, and instead of additional oil and vinegar, add ½ cup mayonnaise blended with an equal amount of sour cream. Garnish with chopped fresh tarragon and parsley.

Bacon Potato Salad

8 medium-size potatoes
6 rather thick slices bacon
1 cup thinly sliced onion
3 tablespoons wine vinegar
1 teaspoon (or more) salt
1 teaspoon freshly ground pepper
2 tablespoons chopped parsley

Boil the potatoes, and when nearly done, sauté the bacon so it will be ready at the same time. Peel the potatoes at once and slice into a warm bowl. When the bacon is crisp, break it into small pieces. Add to the potatoes, along with the onion. Add the vinegar, salt, and pepper to the bacon fat, and heat thoroughly. Add to the salad and toss well. Correct the seasoning, sprinkle with parsley, and serve hot.

Hot New Potato Salad

12 to 16 tiny new potatoes
6 tablespoons olive oil
2 or 3 tablespoons wine vinegar
1 teaspoon salt
1 teaspoon freshly ground pepper
Chopped chives
Chopped parsley

This is an Americanized version of the French pommes à l'huile, which is excellent with hot sausages, ham, sausage in a crust, corned beef, or tongue.

Cook the potatoes until tender, then peel and halve or quarter them. Return them to the pan and add the oil, vinegar, seasonings, and herbs. Toss lightly and reheat. Serve at once.

Russian Salad I (Vegetable Macédoine)

1 cup finely diced cooked potatoes
1 cup finely diced cooked carrot
1 cup very small cooked peas, fresh or canned
1 cup finely cut cooked green beans
2 tablespoons (or to taste) finely chopped onion
Mayonnaise

Closely related to potato salad, this dish is an import from Europe and is often used with other dishes as a garnish. Rather dull actually.

Combine the vegetables and bind with mayonnaise. Use the salad to stuff tomatoes or cucumbers, or use as a garnish for cold lobster or other cold seafood, cold chicken, or cold meats of any kind.

Combine all the ingredients except the greens and sliced eggs and toss well. Arrange in a large salad bowl lined with greens and garnish with the hard-boiled eggs and a dollop of mayonnaise.

Russian Salad II

6 medium-size cold potatoes cooked in their jackets
1 cup finely diced onion
2 tablespoons chopped chives
½ cup diced cold ham
1 cup diced unpeeled apple
1 cup diced cooked cold beet
2 tablespoons capers
1 chopped gherkin
2 tablespoons chopped parsley
Mayonnaise to bind
Greens
2 or 3 sliced hard-boiled eggs

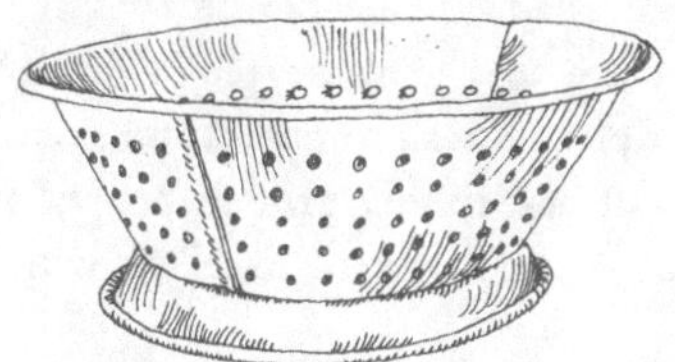

Herring Salad

1½ cups diced cooked cold potatoes
1½ cups diced cooked cold veal
1½ cups diced peeled apple
1½ cups diced cooked cold beet
1½ cups diced marinated herring
2 tablespoons capers
¾ cup finely chopped onion
Mayonnaise
Sour cream
Greens
Hard-boiled eggs
Sliced cooked cold beets

This is a version of the Russian salads above. Hearty and exceptionally flavorful, it serves as a main course for a luncheon or a principal item for a cold buffet. It is even better the second day.

Combine the diced ingredients, capers, and chopped onion, and toss well with equal parts of mayonnaise and sour cream to bind. Arrange on greens in a bowl or a platter. Decorate with hard-boiled eggs and sliced beets and add a dollop of mayonnaise.

Tomato Salads

A good ripe tomato usually needs no peeling. But if the skin appears to be coarse, it is better peeled. To peel, either drop the tomatoes in scalding water for a moment — the water should be at the boil — and remove them at once, or hold them over the gas flame for a moment or two, turning them until the skin pops.

Combination Salad

For years this salad appeared on menus throughout the country, but it has now apparently dropped out of fashion. Yet it was a good, honest salad. To make it, merely arrange lettuce, sliced tomatoes, and sliced cucumbers in a bowl or on a large plate. Serve with cruets of vinegar and olive oil. Each person dresses his own salad to taste.

Beefsteak Tomatoes and Onions

A pleasant, simple salad or first course typical of steakhouses throughout the East and to a lesser degree in the West. It consists of thickish slices of ripe beefsteak tomatoes and good sweet onions, usually eaten with salt and freshly ground pepper and sometimes with oil and vinegar, served in cruets. Excellent with broiled foods.

Tomato and Onion Salad. For an exquisite salad in summer, combine slices of freshly gathered ripe tomatoes — red and sweet to the taste — and either young onions from the garden or sweet Italian onions. Toss together with fine olive oil and a touch of lemon, vinegar, or lime juice.

Sliced Tomatoes

The most prevalent salad in this country outside of potato salad is probably the sliced tomato. This is especially true in season, for many people who eschew salad as salad will sit down happily to a plate of ripe tomatoes sliced or cut into wedges.

I feel that tomatoes should not be chilled before serving; they are so much better served with some of the natural warmth left in them. Arrange on an attractive plate or in a salad bowl, glass, or earthenware, and dress in any of the following ways:

(1) At the moment of eating, sprinkle with coarse salt and freshly ground pepper.

(2) Add fine olive oil, vinegar, salt, and freshly ground pepper. Use 3 parts oil to 1 part vinegar.

(3) Add finely chopped green onions (scallions) to #2.

(4) Add chopped parsley and chives to #2.

(5) Add chopped fresh basil and parsley, preferably the Italian flat-leaf variety, to #2.

(6) For an old-fashioned touch, sprinkle with sugar and add vinegar or sour cream.

(7) Add a light sprinkling of lime juice and salt and freshly ground pepper.

(8) Add finely chopped garlic and chopped fresh basil to #2.

(9) Spoon mayonnaise over the tomatoes just before serving.

(10) Place strips of crisp bacon across the tomatoes and add oil and vinegar dressing (#2). This is sometimes called a Greased Pig Salad if served on greens.

(11) Add finely chopped hard-boiled eggs, green onions, oil, vinegar, salt, and freshly ground pepper.

Stuffed Tomatoes

There is a famous stuffed tomato dish in Provençal cookery that provided the original inspiration for our many variations on the idea.

Tomatoes for stuffing should be either small round ones or beefsteaks. If they are particularly beautiful and ripe they will not need peeling. If they do, see page 43. Then remove the tops and very carefully scoop out the seeds and some of the meat. Do not pierce the shell of the tomato. Some good fillings are:

(1) Any chicken salad (pages 73–74). Garnish with ripe olives and pimientos or with parsley.

(2) Russian salad. Use as a garnish with cold meat or fish dishes.

(3) Shrimp (see shrimp-stuffed tomato, page 54).

(4) Crabmeat and mayonnaise or crabmeat and a Louis dressing. If using canned or frozen crabmeat, marinate it in a little vinaigrette sauce before filling the tomatoes and adding the dressing.

(5) Tiny raw bay scallops, marinated in vinaigrette for an hour, mixed with a small amount of finely chopped olives or green onion, and then tossed with mayonnaise.

(6) Lobster chunks, sliced hard-boiled eggs, and homemade mayonnaise. Garnish with a piece of lobster claw or with a thin slice of lemon.

(7) Fine white-meat tuna fish and a garlic-flavored mayonnaise. Garnish with an anchovy fillet.

(8) Tuna fish salad made with celery and onion and tossed with mayonnaise. Garnish with ripe olives and a ring of green pepper.

(9) Cold salmon and mayonnaise. Top with sliced crisp cucumbers.

(10) Rice salad. Garnish with chopped parsley and a slice of hard-boiled egg.

(11) Smothered cucumbers. Garnish with chopped dill and parsley.

(12) Beet and egg salad. Garnish with sliced eggs and olives.

(13) Herring salad. Garnish with diced pickled beets and onion rings.

(14) Sliced raw mushrooms marinated in vinaigrette sauce. Garnish with finely chopped tarragon, parsley, and chives.

Other Vegetable Salads

Asparagus Salad

Fresh asparagus cooked until tender but still firm makes an ideal salad when served with either a well-seasoned vinaigrette sauce or a mayonnaise. In many parts of the country it was commonly served with a mayonnaise rich in mustard. Decorate the asparagus with strips of pimiento if you like. When served cold in this manner the asparagus is better if peeled.

Canned Asparagus Salad. I have always felt this is quite a different vegetable from the fresh, and often serve the giant white stalks with mayonnaise or with a vinaigrette. The texture of the white variety is smooth and the flavor superb.

Asparagus and Egg Salad

2 bunches asparagus
Greens
4 hard-boiled eggs, quartered
½ cup finely cut chives
½ cup chopped parsley
Vinaigrette sauce
½ cup grated Parmesan cheese

Cook the asparagus until tender but firm, and cut off the tips with about 2 inches of stalk (the rest of the stalks may be used for soup). Arrange on a bed of greens like the spokes of a wheel with egg quarters in between. Sprinkle with the chives and parsley and pour vinaigrette sauce over the top. Sprinkle with the cheese.

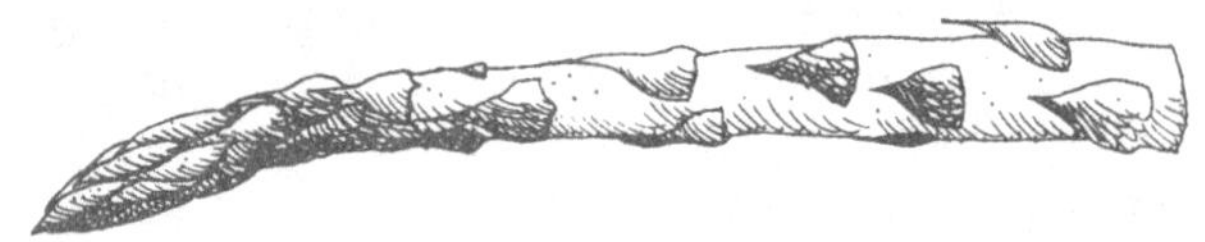

Green Bean Salad

For this purpose the beans should be picked when they are quite small. Trim the ends but leave whole. Cook in boiling salted water till they are tender but a touch crisp; or cook to your taste. Drain them well and marinate in a good vinaigrette sauce for two hours in the refrigerator. Drain them, and serve in a shallow ravier or salad dish. Garnish with finely chopped chives and parsley or with onion rings. One pound of beans serves 4 sparingly.

Variations

(1) Do not drain the beans after marinating, but serve as they are.

(2) After marinating, drain well and serve with a masking of mayonnaise. Garnish with chopped chives and parsley.

(3) The beans are delicious served with tiny wedges of tomato, onion rings, shaved almonds, and additional vinaigrette sauce flavored with tarragon and parsley.

Beet and Egg Salad

2 to 3 cups coarsely chopped cooked beets
½ cup finely chopped onion
3 or 4 hard-boiled eggs, peeled and coarsely chopped
Mayonnaise
Additional hard-boiled eggs for garnish
Greens

For many years, a standard salad for luncheons and buffets.

Combine the chopped beets and onions with the eggs and enough mayonnaise to bind. Taste for seasoning, and if necessary add more salt, pepper, or vinegar. Spoon the salad into an oiled mold and chill for an hour. Unmold on greens and decorate with slices of hard-boiled eggs.

Variations

(1) Arrange good-quality boneless and skinless sardines around the salad. Serve with wedges of lemon.

(2) Add 1 cup each of cold coarsely chopped boiled potatoes and carrots to the mixture and season well. Serve with thinly sliced onion rings and anchovy fillets.

Broccoli Salad

Cook broccoli spears till they are just tender but still crisp. Do not under any circumstances cook till they are very tender or you will have mush. Arrange them on a serving dish, dress with a well-garlicked vinaigrette, and garnish with chopped hard-boiled egg.

Cauliflower Salad

Cold cooked cauliflower — either the whole head or flowerets — makes a most attractive salad when presented with a good dressing and nicely arranged on greens.

Cook the cauliflower till just tender. Undercooking leaves it rather tough and hard at the core; overcooking will make it very mushy. Drain it well and cool. Arrange on a bed of greens on a platter or chop plate or in a rather shallow bowl. Cover with mayonnaise, Thousand Island dressing, or a vinaigrette sauce. Sprinkle with finely chopped radish and parsley, and serve with cold meats, cold chicken, or a platter of cold fish.

Celery Salad

This was one of the first salads made in America and seems to have been a great favorite. Celery was originally cultivated throughout the Atlantic seaboard, and in the westward trek it was established in Colorado and eventually in the coastal states, where it still flourishes. Here is an early celery salad from Mrs. Crowen — really two recipes incorporated into one.

"Put a bunch of celery into cold water, cut it loose from the stalk end. Cut off the green part and any imperfections, and serve in a celery glass [a tall vaselike glass that held a whole bunch], with vinegar, oil, and made mustard in the caster.

"Or, cut the white part in thin slices across, and put it into a salad bowl or deep dish, put a wreath of the most delicate leaves around the edge, put a sprig in the middle, and pour a salad dressing over the whole."

The latter version remains a delicious salad if properly dressed.

To ½ cup good vinaigrette sauce add 2 tablespoons Dijon mustard. Toss with the celery, let it mellow 2 hours and toss again. Makes a crisp yet slightly wilted salad, excellent in flavor. Good with game or poultry.

Smothered Cucumbers

2 fairly good-sized cucumbers
1 tablespoon vinegar
1 teaspoon salt
1 tablespoon fresh dill, finely chopped, or 1 teaspoon dillweed
¾ cup mayonnaise
½ cup sour cream
Parsley, chopped (optional)

Peel the cucumbers, split them in half, and remove all seeds. Slice them rather thin, sprinkle with the vinegar and salt, cover, and let stand a half hour. Drain them well, pressing them to extract as much liquid as possible. Add the dill, mayonnaise, and sour cream. (The measurements are approximate; you may need more or less, depending upon flavor or moistness.) Place in a bowl, cover, and shake well. Allow the cucumbers to ripen in the refrigerator several hours before serving. Top with additional chopped dill and with chopped parsley, if you like.

Cucumber and Onions

2 cucumbers, peeled and sliced thin
1 medium onion, sliced thin
1 teaspoon salt
1 teaspoon freshly ground pepper
Vinegar
Water
Sugar (optional)

This was once a staple salad relish, and it seems to have lingered on.

Combine the cucumber and onion slices. Dress with salt and pepper and a mixture of vinegar and water — the proportions depend on your taste and the strength of the vinegar. Some people like to add sugar to the mixture. Let the cucumbers and onions marinate several hours. Before serving, pour off the marinade and reserve it for storing any leftover cucumber. Extremely good with fish or cold meats.

With Dill. Fresh dill or dillweed is often added to this salad and gives it a brilliant flavor. In this case, I feel that some sugar should be added.

Bohemian Cucumber Salad. Omit the onion and water. Dress with salt, pepper, vinegar to taste, and heavy cream or sour cream. Let it ripen a half hour in the refrigerator before serving.

Lentil Salad

3 cups cooked lentils
1 cup chopped red onion or green onion, including some tops
¾ cup garlic-flavored vinaigrette
2 tablespoons chili sauce
1 cup crisp bacon bits
½ cup finely cut chives
½ cup chopped parsley

Mix the lentils, onion, vinaigrette, and chili sauce. Refrigerate 12 hours or more. Arrange on greens and garnish with bacon, chives, and parsley.

Spinach Salad

1 pound spinach, washed, dried, and crisped
⅓ cup toasted sliced almonds
⅓ cup crisp bacon bits
1 medium onion, thinly sliced and separated into rings
Vinaigrette sauce

Combine all ingredients and toss. This salad is especially good with grilled meats or with fish.

Wilted Spinach Salad

4 tablespoons olive oil
1 large or 2 small cloves garlic, crushed and chopped
2 tablespoons soy sauce
½ cup thinly sliced water chestnuts
Freshly ground pepper
2 tablespoons lemon juice
1 pound spinach, washed, dried, and crisped
Salt to taste
2 hard-boiled eggs, coarsely chopped

Cook olive oil and garlic over medium heat for 2 minutes. Add the soy sauce, water chestnuts, and pepper. Cook 1 minute, tossing the water chestnuts. Add the lemon juice and blend. Then add the spinach and toss as you would a salad until the spinach is just wilted. Taste for salt and correct the seasoning, if necessary. Transfer to a salad bowl and garnish with the chopped egg. Serve warm.

Health Salad

Chicory, Bibb, or lettuce of your choice
1 cup freshly shredded raw carrots
1 cup freshly shredded young raw beets
½ cup or more freshly shredded Japanese radish or black radish
¾ cup freshly shredded raw young turnips
1 small cucumber, seeded and shredded
Cherry tomatoes
Celery sticks

This delicious and attractive salad isn't really a health salad, but it is often served in health food shops and restaurants.

Arrange the lettuce on a platter or in a shallow bowl. Heap the vegetables on the greens in individual mounds to make an appealing assortment of color. Serve with vinaigrette sauce.

Note. This salad can be enlarged with ½ cup raw young peas, shredded snow peas, or sliced raw mushrooms.

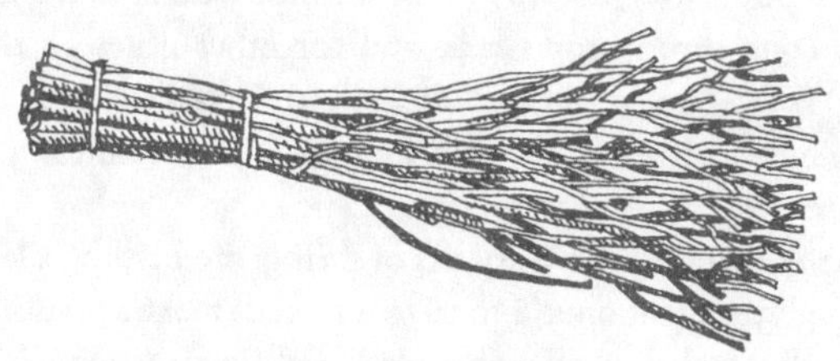

Buffet Vegetable Salad

Line a large platter or chop plate with fresh greens — chicory, romaine leaves, Bibb lettuce quarters, or curly leaf lettuce. On the greens arrange nests of the following vegetables to make a handsome display. Serve with a well-herbed vinaigrette or with yoghurt dressing.

Cauliflowerets, cooked just until tender and marinated in 2 parts oil to 1 part vinegar.

Tiny fresh raw peas.

Fresh asparagus tips, cooked until tender but still crisp.

New potatoes, cooked, sliced thin, and dressed with oil, wine vinegar, salt, and pepper.

Tiny whole green beans, cooked until tender but still crisp.

Cherry tomatoes or sliced ripe tomatoes.

Rice Salad with Vegetables

4 cups cooked rice
½ cup vinaigrette sauce (more if necessary)
Salt and freshly ground pepper to taste
⅔ cup finely chopped green onion
½ cup finely chopped green pepper
½ cup finely chopped, peeled, and seeded tomatoes
½ cup finely chopped celery
⅓ cup chopped parsley
½ cup thinly sliced red radishes

Toss the hot rice with the vinaigrette sauce and allow to cool. When it is cold, correct the seasoning, add the chopped vegetables, and toss well. Add additional vinaigrette sauce if necessary. Sprinkle with chopped parsley and arrange in a salad bowl with or without greens.

Shrimp Salads

For some reason shrimp has always far exceeded any other seafood in popularity, and the list of shrimp salads is long and inviting.

To cook shrimp for salads, and for other notes on shrimp, see page 153. Canned shrimp are already cooked and should be well chilled before being used in a salad. The result is a far better texture.

The medium or tiny varieties of shrimp are best for salad making, although the giant ones (8 to 10 to a pound) make a beautiful garnish. They also make an effective salad with just mayonnaise or Louis dressing, but a fork and knife to eat them are required.

Perfect Shrimp Salad

This salad is simple, elegant, and the most satisfying of all the shrimp platters.

Arrange a bed of crisp watercress, Bibb lettuce, or shredded lettuce on a 12 or 14 inch chop plate, serving dish, or platter. On the greens arrange 3 pounds cooked shrimp (15 to 20 per pound), peeled and deveined. Garnish the plate with tomato quarters. Cover the shrimp with homemade mayonnaise just before serving. Add a few capers and a tablespoon or two of chopped parsley. Pass additional mayonnaise, and serve with hot rolls or crusty bread, preferably homemade, and butter.

This can be served as a luncheon dish, an hors d'oeuvre, or a supper dish. Particularly pleasant as a luncheon specialty for outdoor eating.

Note. You may substitute Thousand Island dressing, an herbed mayonnaise, or a Louis dressing if you like. However, to my mind, a plain well-seasoned mayonnaise cannot be improved upon.

Old-Fashioned Shrimp Salad

1½ cups cooked or canned shrimp broken into small pieces
1 cup finely chopped celery
2 tablespoons grated onion
Mayonnaise
Greens
A few whole shrimp
1 tablespoon capers

A typical shrimp salad from the turn of the century.

Combine the shrimp, celery, and onion, and toss well with enough homemade mayonnaise to bind. Arrange on individual dishes or in one large bowl lined with greens. Top with mayonnaise and garnish with a few whole shrimp and capers.

Shrimp and Cabbage Salad

2 cups cooked shrimp broken into smallish pieces, and a few whole shrimp for garnish
½ cup chopped celery
½ cup chopped shredded cabbage
Mayonnaise
1 tablespoon prepared mustard
Salt and freshly ground pepper to taste
Watercress or sliced tomatoes
Hard-boiled eggs, sliced

Combine the shrimp, celery, and cabbage, and toss well with mayonnaise and mustard. Correct the seasoning and let the mixture ripen in the refrigerator 2 or 3 hours. Arrange on a bed of watercress or surround with a ring of sliced tomatoes. Garnish with additional mayonnaise, sliced hard-boiled eggs, and whole shrimp. Serve as a main course for lunch or supper.

Mrs. G. W. Sanborn's Shrimp Salad

1 pint large shrimp, canned or fresh
Same quantity celery, chopped fine
4 hard-boiled eggs, chopped fine
4 cold boiled potatoes of medium size, cut into small pieces
Mayonnaise
Lettuce

This recipe was created by a delightful hostess who came from one of the great fish-packing families on the West Coast.

Break the shrimp into several pieces. Add the celery, eggs, and potatoes. Mix well with a well-seasoned mayonnaise dressing. Serve on lettuce leaves.

Note. To decorate Mrs. Sanborn's salad, I like to use chopped parsley, black olives, and additional hard-boiled eggs.

Shrimp and Orange Salad I

2 cups cooked shrimp
1 cup coarsely broken walnut meats
2 cups orange sections, or mixed grapefruit and orange sections
Mayonnaise
3 tablespoons dry sherry
Greens
Whole shrimp and orange sections for garnish

The combination of orange (grapefruit may be used if preferred) and shrimp is a piquant one. Here are three widely different versions — each good in its way. All three come from the West Coast, where the idea of composed salads seems to have had a head start, just as the molded or "congealed" salad had great popularity, and still has, in the South.

Toss the shrimp, nuts, and fruit sections with mayonnaise and sherry. Arrange on greens — watercress or chicory are particularly nice with the mixture. Garnish with orange sections and whole shrimp.

Shrimp and Orange Salad II

1 large or 2 medium heads romaine
2 or 3 large oranges, peeled and sectioned
1 large red Italian onion, peeled and cut in paper-thin slices
2 cups large cooked shrimp
½ teaspoon rosemary, well crushed
6 tablespoons olive oil
1 tablespoon lemon juice
1 tablespoon vinegar
1 teaspoon salt
1 teaspoon freshly ground pepper
2 tablespoons chopped parsley

Break up the romaine and place in a large salad bowl with the orange sections, onion rings, and shrimp. Blend in the rosemary with the oil, lemon juice, vinegar, and seasonings. Pour over the salad just before serving and toss well. Garnish with the parsley, Serve with toast, hot rolls, or herbed bread.

Shrimp and Orange Salad III

1 ½ cups large cooked shrimp
1 bunch watercress, washed, dried, and crisped
2 oranges, peeled and sectioned
1 medium red onion, peeled and sliced very thin
1 avocado, peeled and cubed
1 cup cherry tomatoes

DRESSING

1 tablespoon chopped fresh tarragon or 1 ½ teaspoons crumbled dried tarragon
6 tablespoons olive oil
2 teaspoons fresh lemon juice
1 tablespoon vinegar (optional)
1 teaspoon salt
½ teaspoon freshly ground pepper

Combine shrimp, watercress, orange sections, onion, avocado, and tomatoes. Blend the dressing, pour it over the salad just before serving, and toss.

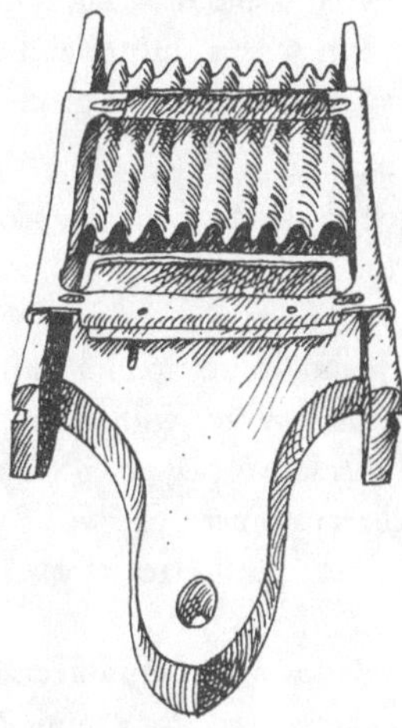

Cucumber and Shrimp Salad, Mrs. Dewitt

6 medium-size fresh cucumbers
2 cups or more finely chopped cooked fresh shrimp or canned shrimp
2 tablespoons finely chopped onion
1 tablespoon prepared mustard (Dijon type preferred)
Mayonnaise
Salt to taste
Greens

Striking in color and good in flavor, this is from an early Los Angeles cookbook.

Peel the cucumbers and cut off one end. Scoop out all the seeds. Salt lightly and chill 3 hours. Blend the shrimp with the onion, mustard, and mayonnaise to bind. Taste for salt and add more if needed. Remove the cucumbers from the refrigerator and dry the interiors with paper toweling. Stuff with the shrimp mixture. Cut into rings about 1 inch thick and arrange on six plates lined with greens. Garnish with additional mayonnaise.

Shrimp-Stuffed Cucumber

For each serving, peel a ripe cucumber, cut in half lengthwise, and scrape clean of its seeds. Cut a thin slice from the outer side of each half so that it will rest flat when served. Salt the cucumbers and let them stand in ice water for an hour. Remove, and dry on absorbent paper towels. Arrange on greens or watercress on a serving plate or individual plates. Fill the cavities with shrimp, preferably small ones — larger shrimp require especially careful arranging to look attractive. Garnish with capers and ripe olives; cherry tomatoes also add a nice touch of color to the greens and the shrimp. Dress with mustard mayonnaise or green mayonnaise.

Shrimp-Stuffed Tomato

For each serving, remove the top of a fairly good-sized ripe tomato and scoop out the flesh. Stuff with shrimp — the very small Pacific shrimp are by far the best for this purpose. Dress the shrimp with cocktail sauce, Thousand Island dressing, mustard mayonnaise, or rémoulade sauce. Garnish with a shrimp and a black olive or a round of cucumber. Serve on watercress or greens.

Shrimp-Stuffed Tomato with Egg. Place a hard-boiled egg, or a cold poached egg cooked fairly hard, in the scooped-out tomato before filling with shrimp.

Shrimp-Stuffed Avocado

Split avocadoes, which should be ripe but not too mushy. Use a half per serving. Heap the cavities with shrimp and arrange the halves on greens or on attractive plates with a simple garnish of parsley and perhaps a cherry tomato or two. Serve with a Louis dressing, and sprinkle with chopped black olives.

Shrimp-Stuffed Artichokes

This is not as spectacular as a whole stuffed artichoke, but it is delicious. (The leaves may be reserved for a soup. Put the tender ones through a food mill together with the edible ends of the tougher ones.)

With a heavy kitchen knife cut through the artichoke, leaving only the bottom and about ½ inch of the leaves. Trim the bottom, removing the stem. Cook the bottoms in boiling salted water till tender. Cool, remove the choke with a spoon, and trim again around the edge till you have a well-tailored artichoke bottom. Wrap in plastic and chill. When ready to serve, arrange the bottoms on a serving dish, fill with shrimp, and garnish with chopped green and black olives. Pass a rémoulade sauce or a Thousand Island dressing.

Shrimp and Pimiento Mold

3 envelopes unflavored gelatine
½ cup cold water
2 cans (10 to 12 ounces each) consommé
3 tablespoons lemon juice
1 teaspoon salt
⅛ teaspoon white pepper
1 pound fresh or frozen shrimp, cleaned, cooked, shelled, and chilled

Soften the gelatine by sprinkling over the cold water. Bring the consommé to boiling point, add the gelatine, and cook until clear. Remove from the heat, stir in the lemon juice, salt, and pepper, and chill until syrupy. Chill well a 7-cup mold. Meanwhile, prepare garnishes for your mold, using shrimp split lengthwise, pimiento, and hard-boiled eggs. (If you like, make pimiento fans: cut a pimiento pod in half, then cut from the open end toward the base at ¼-inch intervals, leaving 1 inch at the base uncut. Spread to make a fan.) When the garnishes are made, chop the remaining shrimp, eggs, and pimiento, and combine with the chopped chestnuts. Place a little syrupy gelatine in the mold and rotate to distribute evenly over bottom and sides. Garnish the mold and chill briefly to set. Combine the remaining gelatine with the chopped shrimp mixture. Gently pour into the mold and chill 2 to 3 hours until set. Unmold; decorate with salad greens. Serve with lemon mayonnaise (blend the lemon juice thoroughly with the mayonnaise; keep it cold until ready to serve).

1 can (4 ounces) pimiento
2 hard-boiled eggs
½ cup (5-ounce can) chopped water chestnuts
Salad greens for garnish

LEMON MAYONNAISE

1 cup mayonnaise
2 tablespoons lemon juice

Tomato Ring with Shrimp

2 pounds shrimp, cooked, shelled, deveined, and chilled
1½ cups tomato juice
1 onion, cut in thin slices
1 clove garlic, crushed
1 bay leaf
1 clove
1 teaspoon dried or 2 tablespoons fresh basil
¼ teaspoon Tabasco
Salt and freshly ground pepper
2 tablespoons tomato paste
2 envelopes unflavored gelatine
½ cup cold water
2 tablespoons cut chives
2 tablespoons chopped parsley
2 tablespoons lemon juice
Mayonnaise
Cherry tomatoes

Combine the tomato juice, seasonings, and tomato paste. Bring to a boil and simmer 10 minutes. Soften the gelatine in the cold water, combine with the tomato mixture, bring to a boil again, and stir until the gelatine is melted. Strain into a 2-quart ring mold which has been washed out with cold water. Cool, then chill until firm. When ready to serve, unmold the ring on a serving plate. Toss the shrimp with the chives, parsley, and lemon juice. Fill the ring with the shrimp, top with mayonnaise, and surround with cherry tomatoes. Pass additional mayonnaise.

Shrimp and Tomato Mold. Use a 3-quart mold. Incorporate the shrimp with the tomato mixture and chill. Unmold, garnish with additional shrimp, and serve with an herbed mayonnaise.

Shrimp and Tomato Ring. Omit the chives. Incorporate the shrimp into the mixture and add 1 cup shredded cucumber. Fill the ring with cherry tomatoes, and dress with equal quantities of sour cream and basil-flavored mayonnaise, combined. Garnish with chopped parsley.

Shrimp Aspic, Helen Evans Brown

2½ pounds fairly large shrimp, sliced in half lengthwise
2 egg whites
2 envelopes unflavored gelatine
½ cup cold water
Stuffed olives

A delicious aspic, which requires a lot of work, created by the late Helen Evans Brown.

Combine the ingredients for the court bouillon, and cook a half hour over medium heat. Peel and devein the shrimp. Cook them in the bouillon for 3 or 4 minutes after they return to the boil. Drain, and return the bouillon to the saucepan. Reduce to about 4 cups, over medium high heat. Whisk the egg whites lightly, add to the bouillon and continue to whisk till the bouillon boils. Remove

Watercress or chicory
Sliced hard-boiled eggs
Cherry tomatoes
1 1/2 cups mayonnaise
1/4 cup cut chives
1 small cucumber, peeled and grated

COURT BOUILLON

3 tablespoons soy sauce
6 cups chicken or fish stock
1 cup cut green onions
1 tablespoon grated fresh ginger
1 1/2 teaspoons salt

from heat, and let it stand for several minutes. Strain through a linen cloth.

Soften the gelatine in the cold water and add to 3 3/4 cups of the hot bouillon. Stir until dissolved. Ladle a small amount of it into a fish mold and let it set very quickly. Arrange the shrimp halves on the gelatine so that they resemble fish scales. Use a slice of stuffed olive to serve as an eye. When the rest of the gelatine is thickish and cooled, ladle over the shrimp very carefully so as not to disturb the pattern. Chill thoroughly. Unmold on a bed of watercress or chicory. Garnish with stuffed olives, sliced eggs, and tiny cherry tomatoes. Serve with a mayonnaise to which you have added the grated cucumber and cut chives.

Marinated Shrimp Salad

2 pounds cooked shrimp, peeled and deveined
6 tablespoons olive oil
1 teaspoon salt
1 tablespoon Dijon mustard
1 tablespoon chopped fresh dill or 1 1/2 teaspoons dillweed
1 garlic clove, crushed and finely chopped or put through a press
1 to 2 tablespoons finely chopped onion
1 tablespoon chopped parsley
1/4 teaspoon Tabasco
2 to 3 tablespoons vinegar or to taste
Greens

Combine all ingredients for the dressing and pour over shrimp. Cover and chill several hours. Mix with romaine, quartered Bibb lettuce, or a combination of chicory and Belgian endive.

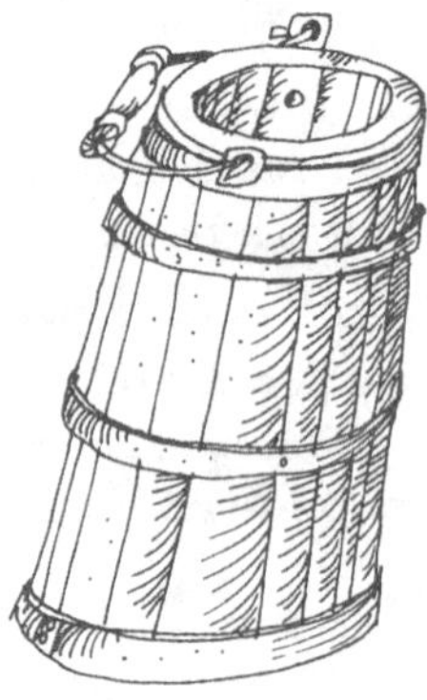

Crabmeat Salads

There are many different crabmeats available throughout the country, and they are all suitable for salads, except that Dungeness crab should be used in recipes which call for crab legs of large size. Having been brought up on Dungeness, I prefer it above other crabmeat, although I confess that Maryland and Florida lump crabmeat can be superb when used in a salad. Alaska king crab can also be used in salads, but it is not as delicate in texture or flavor as others.

Crab Salad, Miss Boelling

4 yolks of raw eggs
2 yolks of hard-boiled eggs
4 tablespoons or more olive oil
1 tablespoon good vinegar
1 teaspoon hot mustard
A dash of cayenne
1 teaspoon salt
½ teaspoon freshly ground pepper
Leg and body meat from 2 Dungeness crabs
Lettuce leaves

This is an old recipe from a woman who lived near Puget Sound, one of the major sources of crab.

Blend the raw and cooked yolks thoroughly with a fork, and gradually stir in the oil till the mixture thickens. Add the vinegar, mustard, cayenne, and salt and pepper. Arrange the crabmeat on the lettuce leaves, and spoon the sauce over the salad.

Crab Salad

For each person:
About 2 cups greens
½ to ⅔ cup crabmeat
2 tablespoons capers
½ cup finely cut celery
¼ cup finely cut onion
Mustard mayonnaise diluted with a little heavy cream

A simply prepared crab salad is best — see the classic crab salad below. Here, however, is another salad that has distinction, which Leon Lianides serves at the Coach House in New York.

Toss all the ingredients. Serve on a chilled plate with a few slices of cucumber as a garnish.

Classic Crab Salad

Watercress or Boston lettuce
1½ pounds crabmeat
Homemade mayonnaise, well flavored
Hard-boiled eggs
Ripe olives
Cherry tomatoes

Arrange the greens on a large serving dish and heap the crabmeat on them. (It must be the choicest crabmeat available.) Top with mayonnaise and garnish with quartered hard-boiled eggs, ripe olives, and cherry tomatoes. Pass additional mayonnaise with the salad.

With Dungeness Crab. Arrange 1 pound crabmeat on the greens and top with mayonnaise. Arrange giant crab legs around the crabmeat, and garnish as above. Serve additional mayonnaise.

Crab Louis

This delicious dish originated in San Francisco and Portland at about the same time and has become tremendously popular everywhere. It consists of a bed of shredded lettuce topped with a good serving of crabmeat and Thousand Island or Louis dressing and garnished with hard-boiled eggs and ripe olives. It makes a full-size luncheon dish or, served in smaller portions, a first course for dinner. It is best made with Dungeness crab, but lump crabmeat is almost as good.

Lobster Louis. This is prepared exactly like crab Louis. Meat from frozen lobster tails works quite successfully for this salad.

Louis Dressing

I don't think anyone is certain of the recipe for the dressing in the original crab Louis, of which there have been many different and many horrible versions. However, this one comes from a great restaurant where crab Louis was served during its heyday — the Bohemian in Portland.

Combine 1 cup mayonnaise with 1/3 cup whipped cream, 1/3 cup chili sauce, 1 tablespoon grated onion, and a touch of cayenne.

Solari's Crab Louis Dressing

In her *West Coast Cookbook*, Helen Brown writes that the former San Francisco restaurant, Solari's, claimed to have served the first crab Louis. Others say it was originated at the St. Francis. Here is Solari's dressing. Combine 1 cup mayonnaise, 1/2 cup heavy cream, 1/4 cup chili sauce, 1/4 cup chopped green pepper, 1/4 cup chopped green onion, 2 tablespoons chopped green olives, salt to taste, and lemon juice.

Crab Legs Palace Court

Another crabmeat dish that originated in San Francisco. The first one I remember consisted of a slice of tomato arranged with lettuce leaves, on which was placed a large artichoke bottom. This was topped with a mound of Russian salad and crab legs were set in a design around and over the salad. It was served with a masking of Russian dressing. Helen Brown, who got the recipe directly from Lucien, chef at the old Palace Court, states that although the dish was originally made with crabmeat it was subsequently made with shrimp or lobster and sometimes with a mixture of all three. Nowadays the Palace Court serves the crab salad on an artichoke bottom decorated with Russian dressing and garnished with chopped hard-boiled eggs and pimiento strips.

A Baltimore Crab Salad

1 1/2 cups backfin lump crabmeat
1 cup finely cut celery
2 tablespoons grated onion
Mayonnaise
Greens
Cherry tomatoes or sliced hard-boiled eggs

Toss the crabmeat, celery, and onion together thoroughly but carefully, to avoid shredding the crabmeat. Blend lightly with a mayonnaise, heap onto greens, and decorate with cherry tomatoes or sliced hard-boiled eggs.

Crabmeat Salad

1 pound crabmeat
1 head romaine
¾ cup sliced green onions, including some of the green tops
2 hard-boiled eggs, coarsely chopped
6 tablespoons oil
2 tablespoons vinegar
1 teaspoon salt
½ teaspoon freshly ground pepper
2 tablespoons chopped parsley

Combine the crabmeat, romaine, onions, and eggs in a salad bowl. Make a dressing of the oil, vinegar, and seasonings, and pour over the salad. Toss lightly and serve on chilled plates.

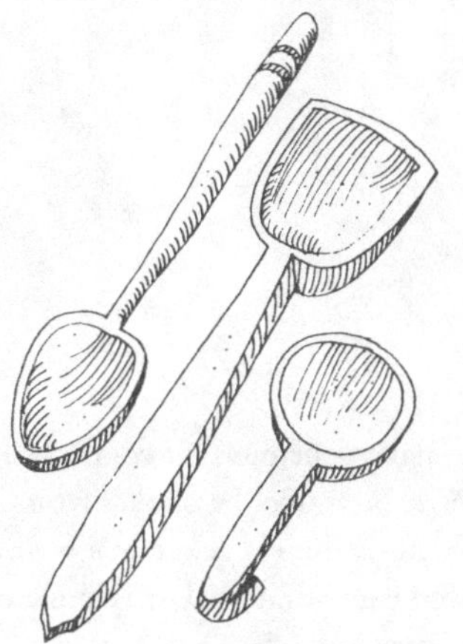

A Piquant Crab Salad with Cabbage

1 pound crabmeat
1½ cups finely chopped cabbage
½ cup finely chopped onion
½ cup finely chopped green chilies
½ cup finely chopped green pepper
Greens

DRESSING

6 tablespoons salad oil
1 tablespoon sugar
3 tablespoons vinegar
1 teaspoon salt
1 teaspoon mustard seed
½ teaspoon freshly ground pepper

I have eaten this in several parts of the country. I have no idea of its origin, but it is extremely good.

Combine the crabmeat and vegetables. Mix the ingredients for the dressing and taste very carefully. Some vinegars are excessively sharp. This dressing should have a sweet-sour flavor, so balance the vinegar and sugar accordingly. Pour over the salad and toss. Let stand in the refrigerator an hour or so before tossing again and serving on a bed of greens.

Crabmeat Coleslaw. Crabmeat mixed with shredded cabbage and dressed with a boiled dressing makes a superb salad for a picnic or a large buffet gathering.

Cucumber and Carrot Ring with Crabmeat

2 envelopes unflavored gelatine
½ cup cold water
1½ cups boiling water
2 tablespoons lemon juice

Another of the jellied salads so popular for looks as well as flavor for buffets and luncheons. This recipe is rather simple and extremely good.

Soak the gelatine in the cold water. Combine the boiling water and soaked gelatine and stir until thoroughly dissolved. Add the seasonings and cool till the gelatine is thick and syrupy. Add the

1 cup white vinegar or white wine
1 teaspoon salt
¼ teaspoon Tabasco
1½ cups grated cucumber, well drained
½ cup grated carrot
2 tablespoons chopped parsley
Greens
Crabmeat
Mayonnaise
Sliced hard-boiled eggs

cucumber, carrot, and parsley, and ladle into a 6-cup ring mold. Chill until set. Unmold on a bed of salad greens, and fill the center with crabmeat. Dress with mayonnaise, and garnish with sliced hard-boiled eggs.

Crab-Stuffed Vegetables

These make delicious first course or luncheon dishes.

Artichoke. Remove the chokes from boiled artichokes and fill the cavities with crabmeat mayonnaise or a crab Louis mixture. Serve on greens. Pass additional mayonnaise, Thousand Island dressing, or Louis dressing.

Avocado. Avocado halves are excellent filled with crabmeat and dressed with a tarragon-flavored vinaigrette, a Thousand Island dressing, or a dill-flavored or mustard-flavored mayonnaise. Serve on watercress.

Tomato. Scoop out ripe beefsteak tomatoes and fill with crab mayonnaise, crab Louis, or crab rémoulade. Arrange on greens and top with a fine crabmeat lump or leg of crabmeat and a sprig of watercress. Sometimes called "Tomato surprise"!

Crabmeat Rémoulade

2 cups crabmeat
Salad greens
1 hard-boiled egg, finely chopped
Capers

RÉMOULADE SAUCE

1 cup mayonnaise
¼ cup chopped parsley
1 teaspoon tarragon
¼ cup onion, chopped
1 clove garlic, finely chopped
1 teaspoon Dijon mustard

For rémoulade sauce, combine the mayonnaise with the parsley, tarragon, onion, garlic, and mustard, and allow to stand an hour or so. Arrange the crabmeat on the greens, dress with the sauce, and garnish with the chopped egg and capers.

Crabmeat Orientale

3 cups cold cooked rice
½ pound raw mushrooms, sliced
1 cup thinly sliced water chestnuts
1 cup finely chopped green pepper
3 pimientos, finely cut
2 cups crabmeat
¼ cup chopped parsley
¼ cup chopped chives

DRESSING

1 cup olive oil
3 tablespoons soy sauce
3 tablespoons vinegar
½ teaspoon Tabasco
2 teaspoons Dijon mustard
Greens

Combine the rice, mushrooms, water chestnuts, green pepper, pimientos, crabmeat, and herbs. Blend together the oil, soy sauce, vinegar, Tabasco, and mustard. Pour over the salad mixture and toss well. Arrange on a bed of greens.

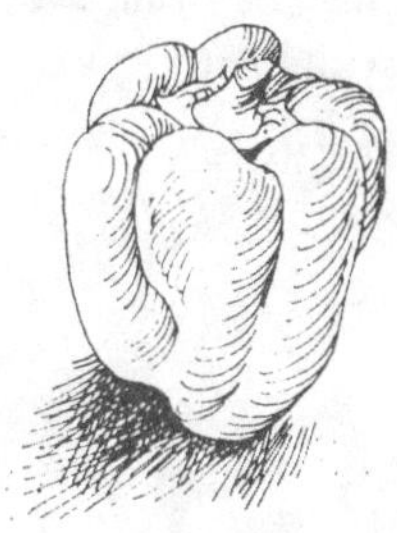

Lobster Salads

Traditionally, lobster salad is one of the great luxury dishes, and it is the ultimate among elegant salads. It should only be served lavishly and is therefore no dish with which to economize. While one can make very good salad from frozen lobster tails, true lobster salad is made from freshly cooked lobsters that have been cooled but not refrigerated.

Lobster Salad

An all-time favorite, as elegant as any dish can be.

Cut cooled cooked lobster meat into medium-size pieces, arrange on a bed of lettuce or other greens, and top with the finest possible mayonnaise. If you have the tomalley and coral, combine with the mayonnaise. Garnish, if you will, with a wedge or two of tomato, slices of hard-boiled egg, or perhaps a few capers, but nothing more. The salad may be served with the claws as a decoration, in which case you will have to provide lobster crackers and some extra mayonnaise. Crisp toast or tiny hot biscuits go well with this.

Variations

(1) Add 1 cup very finely diced celery.
(2) Add 1 cup shredded raw celery root.
(3) Use equal portions of lobster and cooked shrimp, combined.
(4) Combine the lobster with one seeded and finely diced cucumber and ½ cup sliced raw mushrooms.

Lobster Rice Salad

3 cups cooked rice
½ cup finely chopped celery
½ cup finely chopped onion
½ cup finely chopped seeded and peeled tomato
2 tablespoons chopped parsley
1 tablespoon chopped fresh tarragon or 1½ teaspoons dried tarragon
1½ to 2 cups lobster meat, cut in bite-size pieces
A well-seasoned vinaigrette sauce
Tomato wedges, hard-boiled eggs, lobster claws

This gracious salad holds well for taking to a picnic and makes an excellent buffet dish that can easily be stretched.

Combine the cooked rice with the vegetables, herbs, and lobster. Toss well with vinaigrette sauce, and arrange in a salad bowl of earthenware or porcelain. Garnish with tomato wedges and halved hard-boiled eggs. Lobster claws make an elegant garnish as well.

Note. This salad also may be made with crabmeat or shrimp or a combination of both with lobster.

Lobster and Cauliflower Salad

1 large head raw cauliflower, washed and cut into paper-thin slices
Vinaigrette sauce
1½ to 2 cups cooked lobster chunks
Mustard mayonnaise or Thousand Island dressing
Watercress
2 hard-boiled eggs
Black olives

Marinate the cauliflower in vinaigrette sauce 2 hours. Drain. Combine with the lobster and toss with the dressing. Serve on watercress and garnish with eggs and black olives.

Note. This recipe may also be made with shrimp.

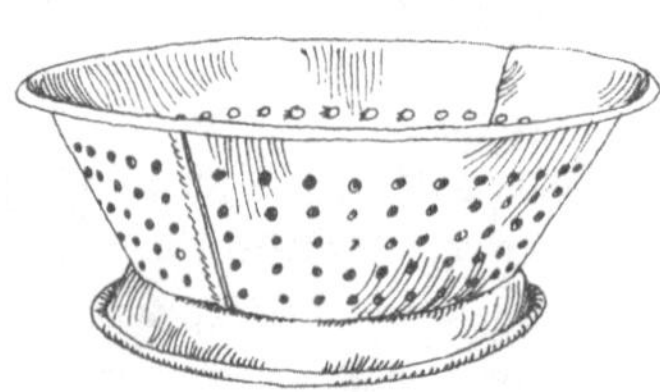

Lobster, Avocado, and Tomato Buffet Salad

About 6 to 8 ounces cooked lobster meat per person
Vinaigrette sauce
½ avocado per person
2 small tomatoes or 1 medium tomato per person
2 stuffed egg halves per person

One of the stretchable salads that hostesses in this country have enjoyed using for years.

Marinate the lobster in vinaigrette sauce. Peel and section the avocados and also marinate in vinaigrette sauce. Peel the tomatoes and cut into sixths or eighths. Cook and stuff the eggs according to your favorite recipe. When ready to assemble, make a bed of shredded lettuce on a large platter or chop plate. Arrange romaine or butter lettuce leaves around the edge. Heap the lobster meat in the center. Make a wreath of avocado slices and then one of tomato wedges alternated with stuffed eggs. Garnish with chopped herbs or chopped parsley. Serve with a choice of vinaigrette and mayonnaise.

Note. This salad may be combined with shrimp or crabmeat; or both may be combined with lobster to make a stupendous buffet dish.

Shredded lettuce and crisp butter lettuce or romaine
Chopped herbs or chopped parsley
Mayonnaise

Lobster and Chicken Salad

For each serving:
1½ cups greens
½ cup cooked lobster chunks
½ cup cooked chicken breast, diced
4 cherry tomatoes
¼ cup finely chopped celery
Vinaigrette sauce flavored with tarragon

Arrange the greens in a salad bowl. Add the lobster, chicken, tomatoes, and celery. Dress with vinaigrette. Toss.

Variations

(1) Add cherry tomatoes and chopped hard-boiled egg. Serve with a basil-flavored vinaigrette.

(2) Add diced cucumber and chopped hard-boiled egg. Serve with a tarragon-flavored vinaigrette.

(3) Add diced avocado and finely chopped onion. Serve with a vinaigrette with lobster coral and tomalley beaten into it.

(4) Add chopped peeled and seeded tomatoes, thinly sliced green onions, and chopped parsley. Serve with a basil-flavored vinaigrette.

Other Seafood Salads

Scallop Salad

1 pint or more bay scallops
2 cups water
1 cup white wine
1 teaspoon salt
1 very small onion
1 sprig parsley
4 or 5 smallish cold boiled potatoes, sliced very thin
2 tablespoons finely chopped onion or chives
2 tablespoons finely chopped parsley
1 tablespoon finely cut dill or 1 teaspoon dillweed
Vinaigrette sauce
Greens

Tiny bay scallops make a delicious salad, as many Long Islanders will tell you. They must be very lightly cooked, which is true for all scallops, and then combined with savory ingredients. This is a typical Long Island recipe.

Poach the scallops about 2 minutes in the water combined with the wine, salt, onion, and parsley — just long enough for them to lose their translucence. Drain and cool. Combine with the potatoes, chopped onion, and herbs. Toss well with a nicely flavored vinaigrette sauce. Serve on greens.

Note. You may also prepare the bay scallops as for seviche (page 169): Cover with lime juice or lemon juice for 2 to 3 hours, then drain. In this case, use no vinegar in the dressing, but simply mix oil, salt, pepper, an herb, and perhaps a couple of spoonfuls of chopped green chilies.

Mussel Salad

2 cups mussels steamed in white wine or broth (see page 164)
1 tablespoon chopped parsley
1 tablespoon chopped fresh tarragon or 1 teaspoon dried tarragon
Mayonnaise to bind
Greens
Tomato wedges
Hard-boiled eggs

Toss the mussels, herbs, and mayonnaise together and place in a bowl lined with greens. Decorate with tomato wedges and hard-boiled eggs.

Variations

(1) Add thinly sliced boiled potatoes and 1 tablespoon chopped onion to the mussels before tossing with mayonnaise. This salad is excellent when 1 tablespoon Dijon mustard is added to the mayonnaise.

(2) Omit the parsley and add 6 finely cut green onions and ½ cup finely cut celery. Bind with Thousand Island dressing instead of mayonnaise.

(3) Follow #2, but instead of Thousand Island dressing use a dressing prepared as follows. Combine ½ cup peeled, seeded, and coarsely chopped fresh tomato, ½ teaspoon salt, ½ teaspoon freshly ground pepper, and enough homemade olive oil mayonnaise to bind.

Mixed Seafood Salad

For each serving:
1½ cups greens
1 cup mixed seafood
¼ cup orange sections
¼ cup onion rings
4 to 6 black olives
Vinaigrette sauce flavored with basil

This can be a mixture of shrimp, crabmeat, lobster, and scallops, in proportions of your own choosing.

Arrange the greens in a salad bowl. Add the seafood, orange sections, onion rings, and black olives. Dress with vinaigrette sauce. Toss.

Variations

(1) Add onion rings and green pepper rings. Serve with a plain vinaigrette.

(2) Add avocado cubes, onion rings, cherry tomatoes, and fresh dill. Serve with a dill-flavored vinaigrette.

Seafood Rice Salad

2 cups cooked rice
Tomato-flavored vinaigrette sauce
2 5½-ounce cans or jars tiny Icelandic shrimp, drained
2 8-ounce cans crabmeat, flaked
½ cup diced cucumber
½ cup diced red onion
Chopped dill

Marinate rice in tomato-flavored vinaigrette sauce. Mix in seafood, cucumber, and onion, and sprinkle with dill.

Oyster Salad

1 pint well-drained oysters
2 cups finely chopped celery
6 hard-boiled eggs, chopped
Greens
Mayonnaise

This was a great favorite in the neighborhood of oyster beds in New England, Maryland, and the Northwest. It was commonly served for lunch as a main course and sometimes as a first course.

Toss the oysters, celery, and eggs together. Heap into a bowl lined with salad greens. Top with mayonnaise and serve. Pass additional mayonnaise.

Note. One old recipe calls for a few French peas for color.

Seafood Salads as a Stuffing for Vegetables

Vegetables stuffed with seafood salads have been most popular among those who feel that pretty salads are a mark of distinction in entertaining. Any of the following vegetables are suitable for stuffing: ripe tomatoes (see page 45), cooked celery root, cucumber halves, grilled and peeled green peppers or pimientos, cooked zucchini, and cooked eggplant. It is best to lightly marinate the vegetables in vinaigrette sauce before stuffing. Then arrange with greens on plates. Top the stuffed vegetables with a bit of mayonnaise and garnish with morsels of seafood, chopped hard-boiled eggs, sliced olives, or tiny cherry tomatoes.

Fish Salads

Halibut, red snapper, salmon trout, sea trout, striped bass, and many other fish may be used in salads in the same way as salmon or tuna in the following salads.

Codfish Salad

2 cups cold poached codfish, broken into large flakes
2 cups sliced boiled potatoes, preferably waxy new potatoes
1 cup finely chopped or thinly sliced onions
¼ cup chopped parsley

DRESSING

½ cup olive oil
3 tablespoons vinegar
½ teaspoon freshly ground pepper
1 garlic clove, crushed
½ teaspoon dry mustard

This salad undoubtedly came from the Portuguese on Cape Cod or Nantucket.

Combine the fish, potatoes, onions, and parsley in a salad bowl. Blend the dressing thoroughly, pour over the salad, and let it mellow an hour or so before serving.

Note. The same salad may be prepared with salt cod.

Fresh Salmon Salad

2 cups flaked cold poached salmon
1 cup sliced peeled and seeded cucumbers
½ cup finely cut celery
½ cup finely cut green onions
1 tablespoon capers
Greens
Mayonnaise
Hard-boiled eggs and ripe olives for garnish

Combine the flaked salmon with the cucumbers, celery, green onions, and capers. Toss well with mayonnaise, and arrange in a salad bowl lined with greens. Top with additional mayonnaise and garnish with sliced eggs and ripe olives.

Variations

(1) Mix 2 tablespoons chopped fresh dill into 1 cup mayonnaise. Toss the salad with the mayonnaise and ½ cup sour cream. Decorate with dill sprigs.

(2) Toss the salad with Green Goddess dressing.

(3) Marinate 2 cups sliced cucumbers in a good French dressing. Arrange them on a plate with the celery and onions, and top with the salmon. Cover with Green Goddess dressing and decorate with anchovy fillets, sliced hard-boiled eggs, and ripe olives. Serve with watercress.

Salmon and Spinach Salad

2 medium cucumbers
Spinach leaves, thoroughly rinsed and drained
2 cups fresh cooked salmon
⅓ cup each of chopped parsley and chives
Mayonnaise flavored with chopped fresh tarragon or dried tarragon

A pleasant and unusual version of salmon salad.

Peel and seed the cucumbers. Slice thin and wilt by sprinkling with salt and pressing between two plates until limp. Drain. Arrange the spinach leaves in a bowl. Top with the salmon and cucumber and sprinkle with chives and parsley. Serve with tarragon-flavored mayonnaise.

Canned Salmon Salad I

Greens
2 7-ounce cans salmon or 2 of the salmon steaks in cans
1½ cups finely cut celery
1½ cups finely cut green onion
1 cup shredded raw carrot
1 medium cucumber, peeled, seeded, and thinly sliced
Vinaigrette sauce
4 hard-boiled eggs
1½ cups mayonnaise
2 tablespoons chopped fresh dill
1 tablespoon chopped parsley

All too often canned salmon salad is turned into a stretcher salad with several additives and very little salmon — the result, a salmon-*flavored* salad. This one is more generous with the salmon content and allows the people at table to assemble their own dish.

Arrange a bed of greens on a chop plate or platter. On this carefully unmold the salmon so that each portion remains in one piece. Toss each of the vegetables with a little vinaigrette sauce and arrange in mounds around the salmon. Garnish with quartered hard-boiled eggs. Mix mayonnaise with dill and parsley and allow to stand about an hour before serving. Top the salmon with some mayonnaise and reserve the rest to serve with the salad. Each guest chooses his own accompaniments to the salmon.

Canned Salmon Salad II

1½ cups canned salmon
1 cup finely cut celery
1 cup finely cut cabbage
2 tablespoons chopped onion
2 tablespoons chopped pimiento
Mayonnaise
Greens

A plain old-fashioned salmon salad, as simple as can be.

Flake the salmon, mix with the vegetables, and bind with mayonnaise. Arrange on a bed of greens.

Smoked Salmon Salad

1 cup thinly sliced smoked salmon cut into small strips
1 large red or Spanish onion cut in rings
2 tablespoons capers
⅓ cup dill sprigs cut rather fine
¾ cup mayonnaise
½ cup sour cream
Greens
Cucumber slices
Cherry tomatoes

This highly unusual blend of flavors may be served as a salad or as an hors d'oeuvre.

Toss the ingredients together. Chill in the refrigerator 24 hours. Serve on greens with a garnish of cucumber slices and cherry tomatoes, or serve on greens as an hors d'oeuvre.

Jellied Salmon Mold

Yolks of 2 eggs
1 teaspoon salt
1 teaspoon dry mustard
1 teaspoon paprika
1½ tablespoons melted butter
¾ cup milk
2 tablespoons wine vinegar or lemon juice
1 envelope unflavored gelatine dissolved in ¼ cup cold water
2 cups flaked canned or cold poached fresh salmon

This is typical of dishes served at the turn of the century, when molds were in vogue for luncheons and for buffet parties. In fact, what are known in the South as "congealed salads" are still considered a necessary item for any entertainment.

Beat the egg yolks lightly and add the salt, mustard, and paprika. Combine with the butter, milk, and vinegar. Cook in a double boiler or in a heavy enameled pan, stirring constantly, till the mixture thickens. Add the softened gelatine and stir till dissolved. Add the flaked salmon and mix. Turn into a 6-cup mold which has been rinsed in cold water. Chill, and when firm unmold on a platter decorated with greens. Serve with mayonnaise.

Note. This mold can be prepared with tuna fish or with crabmeat.

Jellied Salmon Ring with Cucumber Sauce. Use a 6-cup ring mold, and serve with the center filled with a cucumber sauce, made as follows. Peel, seed, and chop 1 medium cucumber. Combine with 1 cup heavy cream, whipped. Season with ½ teaspoon salt, ½ teaspoon freshly ground pepper, and 1 tablespoon fresh dill, finely chopped, or 1 teaspoon dillweed.

Tuna Fish Salad I

2 7-ounce tins white-meat tuna or chunk-style tuna
1 cup or more finely cut celery
¼ cup finely chopped onion
½ teaspoon salt
½ teaspoon freshly ground pepper
Mayonnaise
Greens

Since tuna fish in oil first became a staple item on grocery shelves, it has been one of the great American standards for salads. Here is the basic tuna fish salad, which is also very often used as a sandwich filling.

Flake the tuna, combine with celery, onion, and seasonings, and bind with mayonnaise. Serve on greens.

Cheryl Crawford's Tuna Fish Salad. Add 1 finely diced ripe apple and ¾ cup white grapes. Makes a delightful change from the usual blend.

Tuna Fish Salad II

For each serving:
1½ cups greens
¾ cup tuna
1 sliced hard-boiled egg
2 tablespoons capers
¼ cup onion rings
¼ cup diced avocado
Vinaigrette sauce

Imported or domestic tuna preserved in olive oil is preferable for this type of salad. Imported white tuna has a firmer flesh and breaks into nicer pieces than most other tuna products. A 7-ounce can of tuna mixed with greens will serve two persons very well; it can be stretched to serve three or four by adding a quantity of other ingredients, but a tuna salad, after all, should be heavy on tuna. If the preserving oil is olive, also use it in preparing the vinaigrette sauce.

Put the greens in a salad bowl. Add the tuna, egg, capers, onion rings, and avocado. Dress with a plain vinaigrette sauce, and toss lightly.

Variations

(1) Add thinly sliced fennel and chopped onion. Serve with a plain vinaigrette.

(2) Add 2 or 3 chopped anchovies, black olives, and cherry tomatoes. Serve with a vinaigrette flavored with fresh basil.

Tuna Fish Dandelion Salad

1 quart shredded dandelion greens
1 7-ounce tin tuna in olive or vegetable oil
8 to 10 anchovy fillets, chopped
½ cup chopped pitted ripe or green olives
1 hard-boiled egg, chopped
½ cup shredded salami
½ cup shredded green pepper
Garlic vinaigrette

Combine all ingredients and toss well. Serve as a first course or as a luncheon dish or salad.

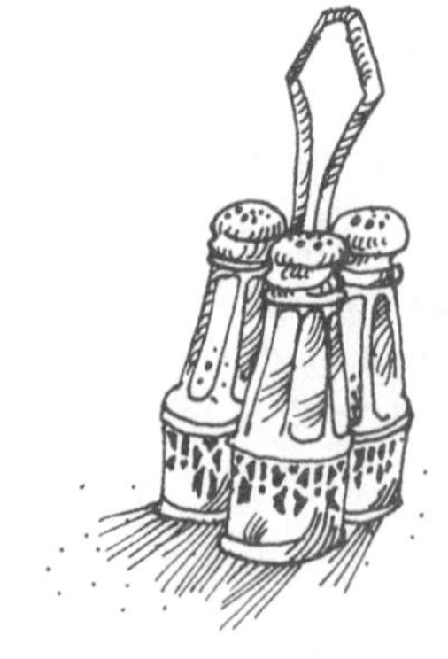

Shad Roe Salad

1 head romaine
1 bunch watercress, nicely trimmed
2 pair shad roe, poached and cooled
1 medium potato cooked, and sliced
1 small onion, thinly sliced
1 teaspoon dried basil or 2 tablespoons fresh basil
2 tablespoons chopped parsley
6 tablespoons olive oil
2 tablespoons wine vinegar or to taste
1 teaspoon salt
¾ teaspoon freshly ground pepper

Shad was exclusively an Eastern fish till about the last quarter of the nineteenth century, when it was planted in the Sacramento and Columbia rivers. It thrived in both of them, and shad roe became one of the great spring delicacies. A few imaginative cooks used it for salad.

To prepare roe for salad, first poach it 8 or 9 minutes in a well-seasoned court bouillon or in salted water flavored with parsley, onion, and tarragon. Drain and cool.

I. For each person arrange a bed of greens — watercress, romaine, or Belgian endive are all nice for this. On the greens arrange a good slice of cooked celery root and top it with a roe which has been poached and cooled. Mask with mayonnaise and decorate with tomato wedges.

II. Break the romaine leaves and roe into pieces. Combine with the watercress, potatoes, onion, basil, and parsley in a large salad bowl. Mix the oil, vinegar, and seasonings. Pour over salad at the last moment, and toss lightly.

Scandinavian Herring Salad

12-ounce jar herring tidbits, cut julienne
1 cup diced ox tongue
1 cup diced cooked veal
1 diced crisp unpeeled apple
1 cup diced cooked potatoes
Mayonnaise
2 hard-boiled eggs, quartered
Chopped parsley and chopped green onion tops
12 canned baby beets

Combine the herring, tongue, veal, apple, and potatoes. Toss with mayonnaise. Garnish with the eggs, chopped parsley, and onion. Surround with a ring of baby beets.

Meat Salads

Many of the meat salads served in this country originated as a way of using up leftover meats, usually boiled, and sometimes vegetables as well. A salad of cold corned beef is not uncommon, and neither is one of cold boiled beef, which is made in sundry combinations and lends itself to improvisation. Pork had its vogue in salad during the reign of the food titans in the early part of the century, when it was often suggested as a substitute for chicken salad. And it is true that if the pork is delicately white and tender it makes as good a salad as chicken. Veal, too, was frequently used as a substitute for chicken in the days when veal was cheap and chicken expensive. Sweetbread salads and salads made with ham and tongue also used to be quite common, and the Germans and Dutch added cervelat salad and other sausage salads to our repertory.

Pork Salad

2 cups cold cooked loin of pork or pork tenderloin cut in ½-inch dice
1 cup finely cut celery
2 tablespoons chopped onion
1 teaspoon salt
½ teaspoon freshly ground pepper
Mayonnaise to bind
Greens
Hard-boiled eggs for garnish
Cherry tomatoes for garnish
Capers

Mix the pork, celery, onion, and seasonings, and toss well with mayonnaise. Let the salad stand an hour in the refrigerator before dressing on a bed of greens. Garnish with sliced eggs, cherry tomatoes, a dollop of mayonnaise, and capers.

Variations

(1) Sometimes a brisk mustard mayonnaise is used, made by adding 2 tablespoons prepared mustard (Dijon type) to 1½ cups mayonnaise and mixing well.

(2) Half an apple, diced, is sometimes added to the salad.

Ham Salad

2½ cups diced cold ham
½ cup finely chopped celery
½ cup finely cut green onions
¼ cup finely chopped pickles — sweet or mustard pickles
Mayonnaise
Salad greens
Hard-boiled eggs
Olives
Sliced tomatoes

Combine the ham, celery, green onions, and chopped pickles, and bind with mayonnaise to taste. If you like, add some mustard to the mayonnaise. Arrange on a bed of greens and garnish with eggs, olives, and sliced tomatoes. Serve with buttered toast. For picnics and other events this ham salad was sometimes mixed with cold macaroni and additional mayonnaise. It is still often prepared in that fashion.

Miss Parloa's Beef Salad

I like the final line of this recipe; Miss Parloa was practical!

"One quart of cold roasted or stewed beef — it must be very tender, double the rule for French dressing, one tablespoonful of chopped parsley, and one of onion juice, to be mixed with the dressing. Cut the meat in *thin* slices, and then into little squares. Place a layer in the salad bowl, sprinkle with parsley and dressing, and continue this until all the meat is used. Garnish with parsley, and keep in a cold place for one or two hours. Any kind of meat can be used instead of beef."

Beef Salad

1 head romaine or 4 heads Bibb lettuce
4 1-inch slices lean cold boiled beef or corned beef, cut into ¾ to 1-inch squares
6 to 8 small new potatoes cooked in their jackets, peeled and sliced
4 tomatoes peeled and cut into wedges, or 18 to 20 cherry tomatoes
6 hard-boiled eggs, halved
2 medium onions, cut into rings
1 tablespoon capers
2 tablespoons chopped parsley
¾ cup vinaigrette sauce flavored with thyme and garlic

One of the best beef salads ever eaten used to be served in the historic old Astor Hotel on Broadway at 44th Street. In its heyday the Astor harbored the greats of the theater and music as well as the fashionable set. The food for many years was exemplary. The beef salad was long a favorite of mine before a matinee. It was similar to this salad.

Wash, dry, and crisp the greens. When ready to prepare the salad, tear the greens into manageable pieces and arrange in a bowl. Add the meat, potatoes, tomatoes, eggs, onions, and capers, and sprinkle all with parsley. Just before serving, add the vinaigrette sauce and toss.

Special Beef Salad. A good salad for outdoor eating or for a buffet. Add 1½ cups thinly sliced celery, ¾ cup shredded green peppers, and ¾ cup thinly sliced raw mushrooms to the ingredients. Toss with mustard-flavored vinaigrette sauce and pile in the center of romaine or chicory leaves arranged around a serving ravier or a bowl. Reserve the hard-boiled eggs for garnish, and add a few parsley sprigs and olives.

Veal Salad

2 cups cold roast veal cut in small dice
4 hard-boiled eggs, coarsely chopped
1 cup finely cut celery
1 tablespoon fresh tarragon or 1 teaspoon dry tarragon
Mayonnaise to bind
Greens
Tomato wedges
Ripe olives

Many of the earlier cookbook writers swore one could never tell the difference between veal and chicken if the salad was well made. I am one to doubt it, although I agree that a veal salad is attractive eating. It is best if served on greens on a large platter or chop plate with green beans marinated in a vinaigrette sauce as an accompaniment. Top the bean salad with a few onion rings.

Toss the veal, eggs, celery, and tarragon lightly but thoroughly with mayonnaise. Arrange on salad greens and garnish with tomato wedges and ripe olives.

Note. Occasionally anchovy fillets were served as a garnish. A few capers along with the anchovies is also a good idea.

Beef or Lamb Vinaigrette

This should be made with very rare slices of beef or lamb. Alternate the meat slices with paper-thin slices of sweet onion and a few capers. Cover with a well-seasoned vinaigrette sauce, preferably flavored with Dijon mustard. Add chopped parsley, cover, and put in the refrigerator to mellow several hours before serving.

Variations

(1) For a rather hearty luncheon dish, dice the meat, add to a green salad and toss.

(2) Add to the first variation 1 cup finely diced celery marinated in vinaigrette sauce, tomato wedges, and sliced hard-boiled eggs. Toss and serve as a luncheon salad or an hors d'oeuvre.

Tongue and Spinach Salad

1½ cups julienne of tongue
2½ cups spinach leaves
½ cup crisp bacon bits
⅓ cup shredded fresh horseradish or 2 tablespoons prepared horseradish
Vinaigrette sauce

A somewhat different approach to the traditional combination of tongue and spinach.

Toss the tongue, spinach, bacon, and fresh horseradish with vinaigrette sauce (if prepared horseradish is used, mix it into the sauce).

German Salad

4 large knockwurst
1 cup julienne of Gruyère or Emmenthaler cheese
½ cup diced celery
1½ cups cooked sliced potato
6 green onions, chopped
Mustard mayonnaise

This knockwurst version of a cervelat salad is thoroughly hearty and brilliant in flavor — a perfect salad for a picnic.

Simmer the knockwurst in water 8 to 10 minutes. Drain, cool, peel, and slice. Combine with the cheese, celery, potato, and onions, and dress with mustard mayonnaise.

Sweetbread and Cucumber Salad

1 pair sweetbreads
Ice water
Chicken broth to cover
Salt and freshly ground pepper to taste
1 small onion stuck with 2 cloves
2 cucumbers, peeled, seeded, and thinly sliced
Vinaigrette sauce
Chicory, watercress, or lettuce

This was a favorite with Miss Farmer in early editions of her cookbook. She offered several versions, of which this is by far the most interesting. I take the liberty of poaching the sweetbreads in chicken broth and find the difference in flavor extraordinary.

Plunge the sweetbreads into ice water and let them soak 20 minutes, then drain, and poach them in seasoned chicken broth 15 to 20 minutes. Remove from the broth and cut away all membrane. Chill several hours. (The broth may be saved for a soup or for poaching vegetables.) Cut the sweetbreads into dice and combine with the cucumbers. Toss well with vinaigrette. Arrange on a bed of greens and garnish with additional cucumber slices.

With Celery. Use only one cucumber and substitute an equal quantity of thinly sliced celery.

Chicken Salads

The finest of chicken salads — and recipes for it are found all through the recent literature of American cuisine — is the basic chicken salad below. However, there are many other ideas of what chicken salad should be. Naturally for the most part they include mayonnaise, but there are some dissenters.

Chicken Salad

Combine well-cooked chicken cut in pieces, not too small, with homemade mayonnaise prepared with the best olive oil. Garnish with capers, ripe olives, and hard-boiled eggs, and serve with greens. It is, like lobster salad, simple, elegant, and delicious.

Traditional Chicken Salad

2 cups diced cold chicken
1 cup finely chopped celery
Mayonnaise (homemade)
Greens
Hard-boiled eggs, ripe olives, and capers

The chicken must be tender and not overcooked, and the celery must be cold and very crisp. Combine the two and toss with mayonnaise — olive oil mayonnaise is best, or failing that, peanut oil mayonnaise is next best. Arrange the salad on greens, and garnish with hard-boiled eggs, ripe olives, and capers.

Variations

(1) Serve on a plate surrounded by cooked whole green beans which have been marinated in a well-seasoned vinaigrette.

(2) Use only ½ cup celery and add 1 cup broken cooked chestnuts.

(3) Add 1 cup toasted English walnuts.

(4) Add 1 cup white grapes and ½ cup blanched toasted almonds.

(5) Add 1 cup soy bean sprouts, and add 1 tablespoon Japanese soy sauce to the mayonnaise.

(6) Add ½ cup shaved toasted almonds or Brazil nuts. Use nuts and black olives for garnish.

(7) Add 1 cup cold marinated cooked green peas. Garnish with chopped egg and raw peas.

Club Salad

Chicory, Bibb lettuce, Boston lettuce, or escarole
12 thin slices white meat of chicken
24 slices ripe tomato
12 rashers crisp bacon
Olives and gherkins
Mayonnaise

A favorite salad served by the women's committee of the Baltimore Museum, this is really a club sandwich without the bread.

Place the lettuce leaves on a large chop plate or platter, and on them arrange layers of chicken, tomato, and bacon. Garnish with olives and gherkins. Serve mayonnaise separately. Also serve crisp toast, if you like.

Mrs. Rorer's Philadelphia Chicken Cream Salad

1 4-pound chicken
1 pair sweetbreads
Tarragon vinegar
2 cloves garlic
Piece of stale French bread
1 Bermuda onion
¼ teaspoon Tabasco
1 tablespoon soy sauce
1 teaspoon salt
½ pound Jordan almonds, sliced and toasted
1 tablespoon lemon juice
1 cup heavy cream
1 cup mayonnaise
2 heads lettuce, washed, dried, and crisped
Black olives and pine nuts

Mrs. Rorer flourished in the time when composed salads were extremely fashionable for luncheons and ball suppers. This example is elaborate but most rewarding.

Poach the chicken as directed on page 197, and cool. Wash the sweetbreads, cover them with boiling water, and simmer 20 minutes. Plunge into ice water, and when cool enough to handle, break them up into smallish pieces. Sprinkle with tarragon vinegar. Make a chapon by rubbing the bread with the garlic cloves, and place the sweetbreads on top. Cover, and let stand several hours. When the chicken is cold, cut the meat into cubes. When ready to assemble the salad, remove the sweetbreads from the chapon and blend with the chicken. Grate the onion into the mixture, and add the Tabasco, soy, and salt. Add the almonds and lemon juice. Toss well. Whip the cream, and combine with the mayonnaise. Blend about half the dressing with the chicken. Arrange the salad on greens. Top with the remaining mayonnaise and garnish with black olives and pine nuts.

Reception Salad

1 envelope unflavored gelatine
¼ cup cold water
1 cup mayonnaise or boiled dressing
1 cup cream, whipped
¼ teaspoon salt
1½ cups diced chicken
¼ cup chopped blanched almonds
¾ cup white grapes, peeled and seeded
Greens

This is an old recipe from Knox's Gelatine which has been in use for over fifty years and is still found in many places on buffet tables.

Soften the gelatine in the cold water. Place the dish over boiling water and stir until the gelatine is dissolved. Cool, and combine with the mayonnaise, whipped cream, and salt. Fold in the chicken, almonds, and grapes. Turn into 6 individual molds which have been rinsed in cold water. Chill. Serve on a bed of greens with additional mayonnaise mixed with whipped cream.

Flowers for Salads

Many flowers are quite edible and provide a change of texture and flavor for the salad bowl. On the other hand, like mushrooms, some are not only inedible but poisonous. One should consult a good book on the subject before eating from the garden. Here are a few of the flowers most commonly used in salads.

Chrysanthemums. The petals of both yellow and white blossoms can be used, either straight from the flower or slightly blanched. The flavor is somewhat bitter, but pleasing.

Marigolds. The petals of this flower make a pungent and novel addition to composed salads of almost any type.

Nasturtiums. Both the blossoms and leaves can contribute to a summer salad.

Roses. Added to some salads, notably those with fruit in them, the petals give a surprising flavor with a bit of bite to it, not to mention the visual effect of bright petals among the greens.

Violets. The flowers make a beautiful and exciting ingredient when used suitably. They are especially good in a mixture of Bibb lettuce and sliced raw mushrooms dressed with a well-seasoned vinaigrette made with lemon juice instead of vinegar. Sometimes baby beets are added to this salad for flavor and color.

Salad Dressings

Many other dressings are scattered through the book, in this chapter and others. For those, see the index.

Mayonnaise

1 egg yolk
1 teaspoon salt
½ teaspoon dry mustard
¼ teaspoon freshly ground pepper
Lemon juice or vinegar
1 cup olive oil, or peanut or other oil

Mayonnaise has been made in American households since early in the nineteenth century. Today most people use a commercial mayonnaise (I often do myself), which, though accepted in nearly all quarters, does not satisfy the taste buds of those who hanker for old-fashioned mayonnaise made with fresh eggs, good olive oil, and muscle. This basic recipe makes approximately 1 cup.

Mayonnaise, being an emulsion, should be carefully handled. Drop the yolk in a bowl, add the seasonings and lemon juice, and whisk or beat vigorously with a fork, whisk, or rotary beater until the mixture is well blended. Now add oil, practically drop by drop, whisking or beating vigorously until the mixture begins to thicken and become emulsified. The remaining oil can be added more rapidly — by tablespoons — or in a steady stream if you are using a rotary or portable electric beater. If the dressing seems to be too thick, thin it with additional lemon juice or vinegar. Also, it will thicken slightly after it is made. Keep it in a cool place.

If your mayonnaise should curdle, it is because you have added oil too fast and not beaten or whisked enough. Put another egg yolk in a fresh bowl, and after beating in a small amount of oil, start adding the curdled mayonnaise gradually, beating vigorously after each addition. The mayonnaise will thicken and become smooth.

To make mayonnaise in an electric blender, place the egg yolk and seasonings in the blender jar, turn on and immediately off at "blend" or "low," then turn on at "blend" again, and pour the oil in a steady stream. The mixture will thicken within a half minute and give you a cup of excellent mayonnaise. Use a rubber spatula to remove the dressing.

Horseradish Mayonnaise. Blend 1 tablespoon horseradish (or to taste) into 1 cup mayonnaise.

Mustard Mayonnaise. Add dry mustard or Dijon mustard to taste to the finished mayonnaise. About 2 tablespoons dry mustard or 1 tablespoon Dijon to 1 cup mayonnaise is right for my taste.

Sour Cream Mayonnaise. Blend equal parts sour cream and mayonnaise. Used as a dressing, this gives a richer, creamier taste to certain salads. For an easy coleslaw dressing (I), add 1 tablespoon Dijon mustard per cup of the mixture, or to taste. Blend with shredded cabbage and let stand several hours before serving. For another easy coleslaw dressing (II), blend 1 cup sour cream, ½ cup mayonnaise, and ¼ cup sugar. This is unusual and quite good.

Yoghurt Mayonnaise. Yoghurt may be substituted for sour cream in the recipe above — a combination which seems to have gained favor in the last two or three years.

Thousand Island Dressing. This is similar to Louis dressing, and there is a good deal of doubt in my mind whether or not the original recipe was ever recorded. However, if you blend ½ cup chili sauce, 1 finely chopped pimiento, 1 tablespoon grated onion, and 2 tablespoons finely chopped green pepper with 1 cup mayonnaise, you will approximate the first Thousand Island dressing. In fact, it is a very good dressing.

Garlic Mayonnaise. Add 2 finely chopped garlic cloves to 1½ cups mayonnaise, or use 3 garlic cloves and ¼ cup olive or peanut oil and whirl in the blender. The garlic content will depend on your taste and how daring you can be with your guests.

For a large party it is perhaps best to make a garlic mayonnaise from scratch. Blend 2 garlic cloves for each cup of oil you expect to use. Proceed to make the mayonnaise, and fold in the garlic flavoring last. Allow it to rest for several hours before serving.

Garlic Herb Mayonnaise. To 4 cups garlic mayonnaise add ½ cup finely chopped parsley, ½ cup finely chopped fresh spinach, ½ cup chopped fresh dill, or any other fresh herb you like — chervil, tarragon, thyme, oregano. Salt and pepper to taste.

Dill Mayonnaise. Simply add fresh dill, chopped rather fine, to taste' to mayonnaise. Also add chopped onion or chives, if you like.

Anchovy Mayonnaise I. Add 12 to 18 finely chopped anchovy fillets to 2 cups mayonnaise. A finely chopped or crushed garlic clove may be added as well.

Anchovy Mayonnaise II. Combine 18 anchovies, 15 soft black olives (the Greek or Italian ones), 2 garlic cloves, and 1 tablespoon chopped fresh basil or 1 teaspoon dried basil. Chop all ingredients or whirl them in the blender. Combine with 2 cups mayonnaise.

Anchovy Mayonnaise III. To 4 cups mayonnaise add 1 or 2 garlic cloves, chopped or blended, 12 anchovy fillets, chopped, a 4-ounce can of tuna fish, finely shredded, 2 tablespoons chopped fresh basil, or 1½ teaspoons dry basil, 2 tablespoons tomato paste or chili sauce, and a dash of lemon juice. Blend thoroughly and dust with chopped parsley just before serving.

Curry Mayonnaise

1 tablespoon butter
2 teaspoons curry powder
Dash of Tabasco
1 cup mayonnaise

One of the greatest gastronomic mistakes made by many cooks is to add raw curry powder to dressings. Curry powder straight from the jar or tin is not as flavorful as that which has been cooked a few minutes.

Heat the butter in a small saucepan or pipkin. When it is bubbling, add the curry powder and a dash of Tabasco and let it simmer in the butter over low heat 3 or 4 minutes, stirring it rather well. Cool, and add it to the mayonnaise.

Note. You may use curry powder to your own taste, using just a hint or as little as ¼ teaspoon up to 1 tablespoon.

Green (Herbed) Mayonnaise

2 cups mayonnaise
¼ cup finely chopped raw spinach
1 tablespoon chopped parsley
1 tablespoon chopped chives or green onion tops

Blend well and let stand for an hour or two before serving. Use other herbs to your taste as follows: tarragon, fresh or dry; chervil, fresh or dry; fresh dill or dillweed; fresh mint if the flavor is enjoyed.

Note. If a deeper color is desired, add additional chopped spinach.

Russian Dressing

2 cups mayonnaise
1 teaspoon dry mustard
2 tablespoons finely chopped onion
1 tablespoon Worcestershire sauce
2 tablespoons caviar (certainly not the best beluga)

This is an excitingly good Russian dressing which I had served to me many times in a small New York restaurant in the 1920's. It is classically different from the usual Russian dressing served today, which resembles Thousand Island dressing.

Fold the dry mustard and other ingredients into the mayonnaise, and blend well. Chill.

Vinaigrette Sauce

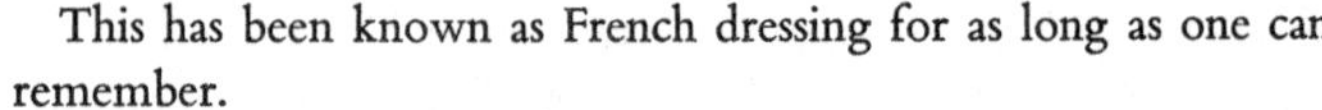

This has been known as French dressing for as long as one can remember.

The French dressings that have been dreamed up the country over, especially in the last forty years, are a far cry from the simple classic oil and vinegar dressing, even though good olive oil was imported on the Pacific Coast a hundred years ago (probably before then, in small quantities) and must have been available on the Atlantic and Gulf coasts since the eighteenth century. One recipe I found calls for 2 tablespoons vinegar or lemon juice to 1/3 cup olive oil, plus 1 tablespoon sugar, salt, pepper, 2 tablespoons catsup or 3 tablespoons pickle relish, and garlic powder. It also recommends adding cream to this mixture. No wonder salads were unpopular with many people.

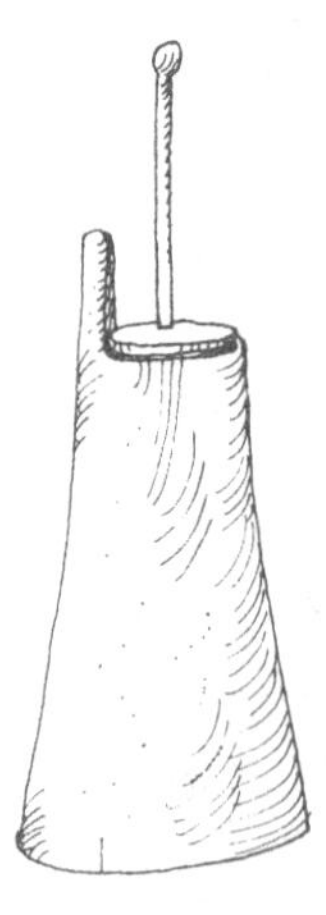

To make a basic vinaigrette sauce, use about a fifth or a quarter as much vinegar as oil. (If you like the flavor of olive oil, it should shine through.) For best results start with 8 tablespoons oil, 1 teaspoon salt, 1/2 teaspoon freshly ground pepper or 1 teaspoon Dijon or English mustard, and 1 tablespoon vinegar or lemon juice. Mix, and then add vinegar to your taste. It is easier to add vinegar than to try to counteract it.

This basic salad dressing is appropriate for all salads save those which are better with a mayonnaise or a boiled dressing.

Herbed Vinaigrette. Fresh or dehydrated herbs may be added to the dressing according to taste. The herbs I most prefer for salad are three, in addition to the standard parsley and chives. They are tarragon, basil, and dill. But do not combine them. One fine herb flavor is enough — with the addition of parsley if you like. Chervil, a difficult herb to cultivate, is also a good friend of salads. However, dehydrated chervil is not very expressive of the true flavor of fresh chervil.

Garlic Vinaigrette. A garlic-flavored vinaigrette is excellent with most salads. Garlic powder and garlic salt I find completely unacceptable. There are several ways to introduce garlic into a salad:

(1) Rub the heel or a piece of dry bread with a peeled garlic clove till most of its juice is absorbed in the bread. Toss this with the salad and leave it in the bowl. It is a delicious bite after the salad is eaten.

(2) Rub a peeled garlic clove into coarse salt to be used in the dressing.

(3) Chop garlic exceedingly fine or put through a press, and add directly to the dressing.

Roquefort Cheese Dressing. Add to the basic vinaigrette sauce recipe 2 tablespoons crumbled Roquefort cheese — or more, to taste — and blend well.

Helen Corbitt's Poppy Seed Dressing

1½ cups sugar
2 teaspoons dry mustard
2 teaspoons salt
⅔ cup vinegar
3 tablespoons onion juice
2 cups vegetable oil — not olive oil
3 tablespoons poppy seeds

Helen Corbitt, who has furthered the cause of good food in Texas over a great period of years, understands American food as few people do, and she is a genius in preparing things that will enchant the eye and the palate at the same time. This unusual dressing created by her is excellent with fruit salads.

It is best to make this in an electric mixer or a blender at low speed. Combine the sugar, seasonings, vinegar, and onion juice, and beat for a few minutes. Then gradually beat in the oil as if you were making a mayonnaise. When it has thickened, gradually beat in the poppy seeds and continue beating until the seeds and dressing are well blended.

Sour Cream Fruit Salad Dressing

To 1 pint sour cream add about 1 cup crushed or frozen fruit, folded in. Crushed or frozen strawberries or raspberries, apricot preserves, or preserved cherries may be used very successfully. I usually add a few drops of lime or lemon juice and a little salt to the mixture.

Chiffonade Salad Dressing

1 hard-boiled egg, finely chopped
1 teaspoon finely cut chives
1 tablespoon chopped green pepper
1 tablespoon chopped red pepper
1 teaspoon each of salt, freshly ground pepper, and paprika
1 teaspoon tarragon vinegar
½ cup olive oil
3 tablespoons cider vinegar

Here is a recipe from the old Elite in Los Angeles — one of the most delightful restaurants in the earlier days of that city. Though the Elite is gone, some of its dishes still linger with Californians.

Combine the ingredients in a pint jar and shake well.

Original Recipe for Green Goddess Dressing

10 fillets of anchovy, finely cut
1 green onion, finely sliced
½ cup chopped parsley
2 tablespoons finely cut tarragon
¼ cup finely cut chives
3 cups mayonnaise flavored with 2 tablespoons tarragon vinegar

Created by the Palace Hotel in San Francisco and named for a play starring George Arliss, the great English actor.

Combine all ingredients. Let stand to mellow at least an hour before using. This is a thoroughly rewarding dressing for all seafood and fish salads.

Soups

Soup was one of the stalwarts of early American diets — not soups such as we know today but those based on game animals, game birds, and often on vegetables, flavored with cured meats or fats from cured meats. Seafood and fish were available for chowders and stews.

Very few directions of any consequence on soup making come from earlier cookbooks. In fact, some cookbooks all but ignored soup. Miss Leslie, in the 1837 edition of her book, offers this bit of sage advice: "Always use soft water for making soup, and be careful to proportion the amount of water to the amount of meat. Somewhat less than a quart to a pound of meat is a good rule for common soups. Rich soups, intended for company, may have a still smaller allowance for water." Fifty years later Mrs. Rorer in her first book makes very much the same statement about soft water and goes on to say that salt should never be added till the soup is done and that the soup should never boil. Both Mrs. Rorer and Miss Leslie felt that soup made from leftover meats could not equal that made from raw meat. Miss Farmer, however, states in the 1904 edition of her book: "Large families need seldom buy fresh meat, provided all leftovers are properly cared for."

Soups in early America were functional. In Pennsylvania, Maryland, and other nearby states turtle and snapper soups flourished and still do. Terrapin became a stew — really a very substantial soup in Maryland; in the South the Huguenot influence in Charleston produced the famous she-crab soup; and elsewhere in the South gumbos flourished — chicken, crab, shrimp, and crawfish gumbos — and reached into Kansas and Missouri; chowders and stews, which varied greatly throughout the country, were often served as a main dish. Dried beans and peas formed rich and satisfying pottage with a bit of salt pork or a ham bone added to give strength and flavor. Some of these soups, notably the black bean, have survived as representatives of our finest cuisine. Cream soups were created as cream and milk became more plentiful, and when canning became part of the daily routine the vegetable soups extended into winter. Winter vegetables also had their place in the soup pot and were well thought of, although many of these vegetables are now almost forgotten. Here, for instance, is an old recipe for parsnip soup, from a manuscript cookbook.

Parsnip Soup

"The meat for this soup may either be fresh beef, mutton or fresh venison. Remove the fat, cut the meat into pieces, add a little salt, and put it into a soup pot with an allowance of rather less than a quart of water to each pound. Prepare some fine, large parsnips by first scraping and splitting them, and cutting them into pieces; then putting them in a frying pan and frying them brown in fresh butter or nice drippings. When the meat has been boiled till the meat is all in rags and well skimmed — put into it the fried parsnips and let them boil about ten minutes, but not until they break or go to pieces. Just before you put in the parsnips stir in a tablespoon of thickening made with butter and flour, and mixed to a smooth paste. When you put it into the tureen to go to table be sure to leave in the pot all the shreds of meat and bits of bone."

This is a superb soup if you like parsnips as I do. The same manuscript cookbook whence this came gives practically the same recipe for turnip soup and carrot soup and then recommends that you combine all three, with the addition of an onion.

Perhaps my favorite recipe is one in Miss Eliza Leslie's 1857 edition. It is called "portable soup" and is worth repeating for its intelligence and for the amusement it now provides. Imagine doing this in a small apartment kitchen.

Portable Soup

"This is a very good and nutritious soup, made first into jelly and then congealed into hard cakes, resembling glue. If well made, it will keep for many months in a cool dry place and when dissolved in hot water or gravy [in reality it is much like glace de viande – JB] will afford a fine liquid soup, very convenient to carry on a journey or sea voyage, or to use in a remote place where meat for soup is not to be had. A piece of this glue the size of a large walnut will, when melted in water, become a pint bowl of soup; or by using less water you may have it much richer. If there is time and opportunity, boil with the piece of soup a seasoning of sliced onion, sweet marjoram, sweet basil, or any herbs you choose. Also, a bit of butter rolled in flour.

"To make portable soup, take two shins or legs of beef, two knuckles of veal, and four unskinned calf's feet. Have the bones broken or cracked. Have the whole put in a large clean pot that will hold four gallons of water. Pour in, at the beginning, only as much water as will cover the meat well and set it over the fire so that it will heat gradually till it almost boils. Watch and skim carefully while any scum rises. Then throw in a quart of cold water to make it throw up all the remaining scum, and then let come to a complete boil, continuing to skim as long as any scum appears. In this be particular. When the liquid appears clear and completely free from grease, pour in the remainder of the water and let it boil very gently for eight hours. Strain it through a very clean hair sieve into a large stoneware pan and let it cool quickly. Next day remove all the grease and pour the liquid as quickly as possible into a three-gallon stew pan, taking care not to disturb the settlings at the bottom. Keep the pan uncovered and let boil as quickly as possible over a quick fire. Next transfer it to a three-quart stew pan and skim it again if necessary. Watch it well and see that it does not burn, for that would spoil the whole. Take out a little in a spoon and hold it in the air to see if it will jelly. If it will not, boil it a little longer. Till it jellies it is not done. Have ready some small white-ware preserve pots clean and quite dry. Fill them with the soup and let them stand, undisturbed, till the next day. Set over a slow fire a large flat-bottomed stew pan, one third filled with boiling water. Place in it the pots of soup, seeing it does not reach within two inches of their rims. Let the pots stand uncovered in this water, hot, but without boiling, for six or seven hours. This will bring the soup to a proper thickness, which should be that of a stiff jelly when hot, and when cold it should be like hard glue. When finished turn out the

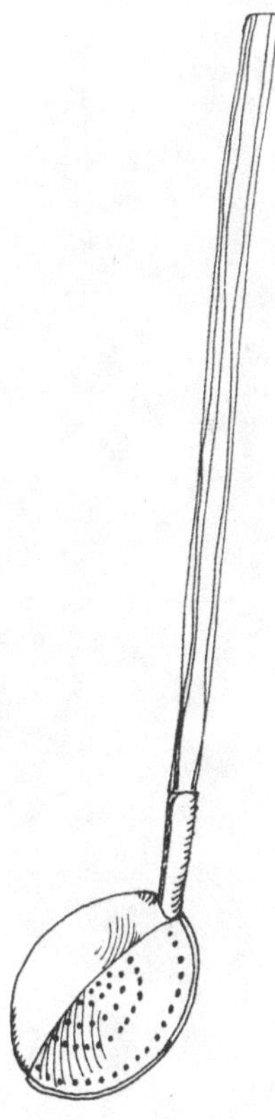

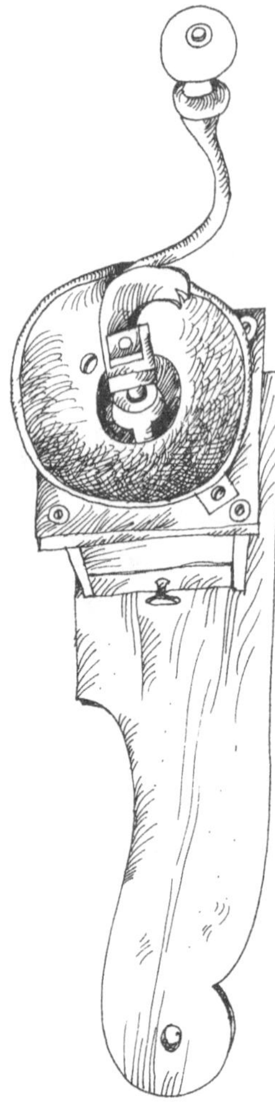

molds of soup, and wrap them up in clean brownish paper, and put them up in boxes, breaking off a piece when wanted to dissolve the soup.

"Portable soup may be improved by the additions of three pounds of nice lean beef, to the shins, knuckles and calf's feet, etc. The beef must be cut into bits.

"If you have any friends going the overland journey to the Pacific, a box of portable soup may be a most useful present to them."

In the late nineteenth and first part of the present century soups played a much more important part in diet than they now do. Many families had a soup every night at dinner, and soup and salad luncheons or dinners were common. Nearly every kitchen boasted a stockpot, and soup bones were given away by the family butcher for the asking.

Now that convenience food is upon us, canned and dehydrated soups are available in abundance, to say nothing of frozen soups. The idea of the stockpot is quite remote, even if there were room for one in the average kitchen. Instead, one buys canned beef broth, chicken broth, and consommé.

There is, of course, an endless variety of other canned soups on the market which may be used plain or with additives to make them more distinctive. Sometimes several different canned soups are combined in the same kettle, and the resulting bisque or purée is remarkable for its inventiveness if for nothing else. One recipe I found recently calls for canned mushrooms, canned tomatoes, canned potatoes, canned chicken broth, canned chicken gumbo, canned beef bouillon, frozen mixed vegetables, and chicken breasts! This, with herbs and onions and about eight different steps for preparation — obviously more trouble than starting from scratch.

Stock, Broth, and Consommé

Stock — both beef and veal — is a wonderful additive to have in the kitchen. It may be frozen successfully and kept for soups, for cooking vegetables and meats, and for sauces. Chicken broth, which is virtually indispensable in the well-run kitchen, is easy to make at the last minute, but it may also be frozen and kept for various uses. As a substitute, canned chicken broth is generally an excellent product. But although canned beef bouillon is good for many kitchen uses, it does have a fairly strong flavor and is not always a reliable substitute for meat stock, since it can overpower delicate flavors. Be certain you do not confuse it with canned consommé, which is very highly seasoned and often has gelatine added for serving cold and jelled.

Brown Soup Stock

3 to 4 pounds shin of beef with bone
2 pounds marrowbones cut in 2 to 3 inch lengths
1 calf's foot, pig's foot, or veal knuckle
3 quarts cold water
10 peppercorns
1½ teaspoons thyme
A few celery leaves or 1 rib celery
2 sprigs parsley
1 onion stuck with 2 cloves
1 large or 2 small carrots
1 leek, if available
1 turnip — a very small one; the flavor of turnip is aggressive
Salt

There are different ways of preparing basic brown stock. Here are two methods which have merit and may be used with ease and success. It is important to have an 8 to 10 quart pot for making large amounts of stock.

Cut the meat into 1½-inch cubes. Place the bones, meat, and foot in a large roasting pan and either brown in a 450-degree oven or set under the broiler about 6 inches from the heat. Turn the meat once or twice and allow it to brown well. If the broiler is used, let the meat get quite brown and the bones color a bit.

Transfer the meat, bones, foot, and pan juices to an 8-quart kettle. Add the peppercorns, thyme, celery, parsley, and water. Bring to a fairly slow boil, and skim off all the scum which forms on top of the liquid. Cover the kettle and simmer very slowly for 2 hours. Add the vegetables, and continue simmering for another 2 to 2½ hours. Salt the broth during the last half hour of cooking. If any additional scum forms on top, be certain to skim it off. Taste for salt after it has been in the broth about 10 minutes, adding more if necessary. Strain the broth into a large bowl, and cool. Chill it in the refrigerator, and remove the coating of fat that rises to the top.

To clarify stock. Return the broth to a 4-quart saucepan. Use one egg white and shell for each quart of stock. Beat the egg slightly with a whisk, combine with the crushed shell, and stir into the broth. Bring to a boil, stirring constantly with a whisk or a wooden spoon. When it reaches a boil, continue to boil for 2 minutes. Then place it on a cold burner of the range, turn to simmer, and let it simmer over very low heat for 10 to 15 minutes. Skim off any scum that forms, and strain the stock through muslin or several thicknesses of cheesecloth.

Note. Freshly ground beef (½ pound per quart) is often used to clear stock as well. Add to stock with the egg whites, bring to a boil, and allow to simmer for 10 to 15 minutes. Then strain.

Ordinary Beef Stock

3 to 4 pounds shin of beef with bone
2 pounds marrowbones cut in 2 to 3 inch pieces
1 calf's foot, pig's foot, or veal knuckle
2 or 3 leeks, if available
2 garlic cloves
1 onion stuck with 2 cloves
1 teaspoon thyme
Several sprigs parsley
1 rib celery or a handful of celery leaves
1 bay leaf
10 to 12 peppercorns
1 carrot
4 quarts cold water
Salt

Put all ingredients except the salt in an 8 to 10 quart pot. Bring slowly to a boil and skim off all scum as it rises to the surface. Let the broth boil for 20 minutes or so, reduce the heat to a faint simmer, and cover and simmer for 2 hours. Add salt, and skim off any scum that may linger. If you plan to use the meat, remove it if it is tender. Simmer for another hour or two and let the broth cool. When it is thoroughly cold, remove the fat and the vegetables and bones. Clarify the broth if you like.

Venison Broth. This was commonly made in the earlier part of our history. To make, use the ordinary beef stock recipe, substituting venison for beef.

Oxtail Consommé or Bouillon

2 oxtails cut in sections
1 onion stuck with 2 cloves
1 bay leaf
10 peppercorns
1 teaspoon thyme
Few celery leaves
1 sprig parsley
3 quarts water
Salt

Combine all the ingredients except salt. Bring to a boil over medium heat. Skim off all scum very carefully. Cover, reduce the heat, and simmer for 2½ to 3 hours. Add salt to taste after 2 hours' cooking, and a half hour later taste for seasoning. Remove cover and allow the soup to cook down over high heat till it is reduced by one third. Strain, and when it is cold remove the fat. Clarify and serve as a clear soup with the addition of a tablespoon of Madeira per cup of broth. Or use as a base for a vegetable soup.

Veal Broth

4 pounds neck of veal
1 veal knuckle
1 calf's foot, if available
1 onion stuck with 2 cloves
1 teaspoon or more tarragon
1 bay leaf

Delicate, gelatinous, and a delightful base for sauces and aspics.

Put all ingredients except the salt in an 8-quart soup kettle. Bring slowly to a boil over medium heat and skim off all scum which forms atop the liquid. When it is free from scum, cover, reduce the heat to simmer, and simmer for 2½ hours. Add salt to taste, and skim off any additional scum which may have appeared. Continue cooking another hour or hour and a half. Remove the broth from the heat and strain. Allow it to cool thoroughly, and then remove the fat. Clarify if you wish. Store and use as needed.

A few celery leaves
1 sprig parsley
3 quarts cold water
Salt

Veal Aspic. This will probably make a strong jelly when chilled in the refrigerator. If additional stiffening is necessary, use up to 1 tablespoon gelatine per pint of hot broth.

Basic Chicken Broth

2 to 3 pounds necks and backs
2 pounds gizzards
1 onion stuck with 2 cloves
1 teaspoon thyme
6 peppercorns
1 or 2 leeks
3 to 4 quarts cold water
Salt

Now that chicken in parts is commonly available, I find that the backbones and necks, combined with gizzards, yield a rich and thoroughly flavorful broth. The gelatinous quality of the gizzards gives body to the broth not achieved otherwise.

Place chicken parts in an 8-quart pot, add seasonings, and cover with cold water. Bring slowly to a boil over medium high heat, and skim off any scum which forms on the surface. Add salt to taste. Cover, reduce heat to simmer, and simmer for an hour. Taste for seasoning. Simmer another hour to an hour and a half. Strain through muslin or several thicknesses of cheesecloth and allow to cool thoroughly. Remove the fat. Clarify the broth, if you like, according to the instructions under beef stock.

Double Chicken Broth. To a batch of well-made, strained chicken broth add a whole fowl or chicken and bring to a boil. Skim off any scum that forms and simmer till the chicken is thoroughly tender, about an hour for a young chicken and 2 to 2½ hours for a fowl. This yields a doubly rich, delicious broth, with a lovely texture almost unique among soups. Served clear or with a small amount of rice or tiny pasta it makes one of the most elegant of clear soups for a company dinner. And it is invaluable in making rich cold soups for summer. The chicken may be used for made dishes.

Pheasant or Wild Turkey Broth. These were often made when game birds were plentiful. They are made in the same way as chicken broth except that once the broth is prepared it is often supplemented with another bird, as in double chicken broth.

Chicken and Tomato Bouillon

1 quart rich chicken broth
1 number 303 can Italian plum tomatoes, or 6 ripe tomatoes peeled and quartered
1 teaspoon basil
Salt and freshly ground pepper

Combine chicken broth, tomatoes, and basil, bring to a boil, and simmer for 45 minutes. Correct the seasoning, and strain through several thicknesses of cheesecloth. The tomatoes should be quite ripe and should color and flavor the chicken broth. Serve the bouillon as is or with a dollop of salted whipped cream and a sprinkling of chopped parsley.

Clam and Tomato Bouillon. This recipe can be done very successfully substituting clam broth for chicken broth. It can be served hot but is also excellent served icy cold with a dollop of sour cream and chopped parsley and chives.

Vegetable and Meat Soups

A Hearty Main-Dish Soup

1½ to 2 quarts beef broth
½ cup each diced onion, celery, carrot, turnip, green beans, potato, and cabbage
1 teaspoon thyme or sage
1 cup diced cooked meat
¾ cup shell beans or lima beans
2 cloves garlic, finely chopped
1 cup elbow macaroni

This is typical of the soups served in the farm country when stockpots were kept going on the back of the stove and when one's own garden provided vegetables in late summer and fall. Some of the soup meat was removed before it had cooked to rags and strings, and it was freed of all fat and cut into fairly hearty dice.

Combine all ingredients but macaroni and bring to a boil. Reduce heat to simmer and cook until vegetables are tender and just slightly overcooked. Add macaroni and cook till it is tender. Serve in warm soup bowls with chopped fresh herbs and, if you like, with grated cheese. With the addition of buttered toast or hot rolls and butter, perhaps sliced tomatoes dressed with oil and vinegar, and beer, you have a good hearty supper. This type of supper calls for a good dessert — a hot apple pie or simple lemon pudding.

Hot Beef Borsht

3 quarts beef broth
Some of the meat from the broth cut into dice
4 young beets or 5 small ones, shredded
4 potatoes, peeled and thinly sliced
2 medium onions, coarsely chopped
2 cups finely shredded raw cabbage
½ cup lemon juice
2 or 3 tablespoons sugar
2 cups sieved tomatoes (optional)

Borsht comes in endless variety. This recipe I have known since I was young, and I continue to make it from time to time.

Bring broth to a boil. Add the beets and cook for 15 minutes. Add the potatoes, onions, and cabbage, and cook till the cabbage and potatoes are somewhat overcooked. Add lemon juice and adjust the seasoning, adding sugar if it is needed. There should be a sweet-sour balance in the dish. If you like, add the tomatoes and heat the soup thoroughly. Serve in large heated bowls or soup plates. This makes an excellent supper dish when made with plenty of meat in it and served with good black bread and sweet butter, followed by a cheese platter and fresh fruit.

Variations

(1) Serve with whole boiled potatoes, added at the last minute.
(2) Serve with macaroni instead of potatoes.
(3) Serve with sour cream.

Chicken and Noodle Soup with Vegetables

A 5 to 6 pound fowl or 2 pounds chicken backs, 1 pound gizzards, and 1 pound legs and thighs

Place the whole chicken or the backs and gizzards in a heavy 6-quart kettle with the water, onion stuck with cloves, leek, carrot, 1 tablespoon salt, and peppercorns. Bring to a boil and skim off any scum that forms on top. Reduce the heat and simmer for 2 hours. Correct the seasoning. If you are using chicken parts, add the legs and thighs, and cook until they are tender — 45 minutes to an hour. Remove the chicken, skim excess fat from the broth, and then

3 quarts water
1 onion stuck with 2 cloves
1 leek
1 carrot
Salt
10 peppercorns
½ cup finely chopped onion
½ cup finely diced carrot
½ cup finely cut green beans
4 ounces egg noodles
1 cup frozen or fresh peas
Chopped parsley

remove the vegetables. (If you are not serving the soup till the next day, it will be easier to remove the fat if the broth is cooled and then chilled.) Pour the broth into a container, wash out the kettle, and then return the broth to it. Add the cut vegetables, the meat from the legs and thighs cut into small dice, and the gizzards thinly sliced. Bring to a boil again and cook just until the vegetables begin to tenderize and are pleasantly firm. Add the noodles (increase the amount if you like a very thick soup) and peas, and boil for 5 to 9 minutes or until they are cooked. Serve in heated soup plates or bowls and sprinkle with some chopped parsley.

This deliciously filling soup is ideal for a Sunday supper, accompanied by buttered toast or hot rolls, perhaps followed by a salad or some excellent cheese and a bottle of red wine.

Note. Other vegetables, such as spinach, cabbage, and zucchini, as well as mushrooms, may be added to the soup during the final cooking.

Scotch Broth

2½ pounds shoulder and neck of lamb
1 onion, thinly sliced
1 medium turnip, diced
2 carrots, peeled and diced
1 rib celery, cut into thin slices
1 tablespoon chopped parsley
1 teaspoon thyme
½ cup pearl barley
1½ quarts water
1 tablespoon salt or to taste
1 tablespoon softened butter
1 tablespoon flour
¾ teaspoon Tabasco
2 tablespoons chopped parsley

The Scot is anonymous who introduced this dish to American cookery, but it has remained a favorite for more than a century. As is true of many soups, its contents vary a good deal. The following recipe, if not the original, is a very sound one.

Remove the meat from the bones. Combine with the vegetables, herbs, barley, water, and salt. Bring to a boil and skim off the scum carefully. Reduce the heat and simmer for 2 hours. At the same time boil the bones for 2 hours in a pint of water, adding more if it cooks away. Strain the resulting broth, and add to the meat and vegetable mixture. Taste for seasoning. Blend the butter with the flour, and stir into the soup. Add the Tabasco and continue stirring until the soup is thickened slightly. Serve in heated soup plates with a garnish of chopped parsley.

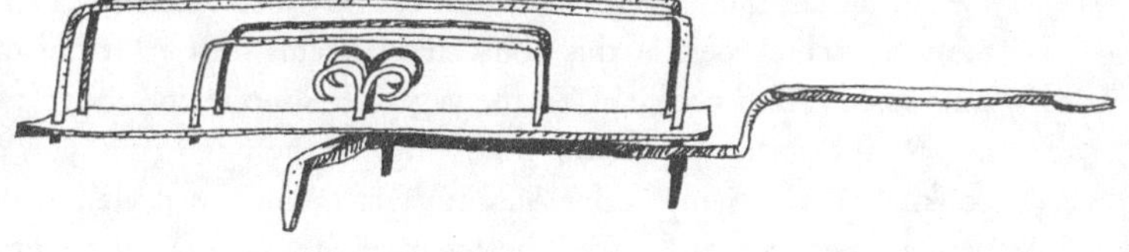

Pepper Pot

1 veal joint (knuckle of veal)
1 bunch herbs (I use a leek, sprig of parsley, thyme, and bay leaf)
3 quarts water
4 pounds tripe (honeycomb and cooked tripe is best)
2 onions, chopped
1 tablespoon salt
1½ teaspoons freshly ground pepper
1 teaspoon Tabasco, or to taste (original called for red pepper pods) or 1 or 2 hot red peppers
4 to 5 potatoes, peeled and diced
2 tablespoons chopped parsley
½ pound beef suet, finely chopped
2 cups flour

Typically Philadelphian, this soup used to be hawked in the streets by women cooks, and was usually dispensed from pushcarts. I have always had a hunch that pepper pot is not a Dutch soup. And since Philadelphia was such a cosmopolitan city in its early days, there is a very good chance that the soup is of French or English origin. Both cuisines are partial to tripe.

This is an old recipe to which I have added a few notes to make it sounder.

Place the veal knuckle and herb bouquet in the water, bring to a boil, and skim off any scum that forms. Cover and simmer for 2½ hours. Strain the broth, strip the meat from the bone, and cube it. Cut the tripe into small squares. Combine with the veal meat, strained broth, chopped onions, salt, freshly ground pepper, and the Tabasco or a red pepper or two. Simmer for an hour and a half. With your fingers blend the beef suet and flour, and work them together very well. Blend with water to a paste and make into tiny balls. Drop into the soup. Add the potatoes and chopped parsley and cook for another hour. Correct the seasoning. Serve in heated soup bowls with toast.

Vegetable Soups

Old-Fashioned Family-Style Vegetable Soup

2 quarts beef stock
2 small carrots or 1 large one, finely cut
2 medium onions, coarsely chopped
1 turnip, finely diced
⅔ cup finely cut green beans
½ cup finely cut celery
2 leeks, thinly sliced
1 cup fine pasta — pastina or finely cut macaroni or alphabets
1 cup fresh peas or frozen peas

Combine beef stock and vegetables, except for the peas. Bring to a boil over medium high heat and simmer till the vegetables are just beginning to tenderize. Add the pasta and the peas, and continue cooking till vegetables and pasta are very tender. Correct the seasoning — it may need additional salt. Serve in hot soup plates or bowls. Also serve grated cheese and buttered toast if you like.

Note. Any seasonal vegetables may be used for this soup and the soups that follow — green beans and shell beans, zucchini, squash, peppers, green onions, shredded cabbage, kohlrabi, asparagus — anything, that is, except beets, which color the soup too much.

Vegetable Soup with Beans and Lentils. It was formerly the custom to add dried beans to vegetable soups, soaking the beans overnight, cooking them slowly with seasonings, and then adding them to the soup at the last minute. However, one can buy such excellent canned beans and chick peas at this point that it seems folly to spend the time soaking and cooking. To the vegetable soup recipe above add a 1-pound can of any of the following for the last 10 minutes of cooking: red or white kidney beans drained and rinsed well, chick peas drained and rinsed well, butter beans (or use a jar of flavored butter beans), fava beans or lima beans, or a combination of beans. Chopped fresh parsley, chives, and fresh basil are pleasant additives to such soups, as well as grated Parmesan cheese. Oven-toasted slices of bread (melba toast) — toasted till crisp and dry — are an ideal accompaniment.

Onion Soup

5 tablespoons butter
2 tablespoons oil
5 medium onions, peeled and very thinly sliced
1 teaspoon or more sugar (optional)
1½ teaspoons salt
6 cups beef broth
1 cup red wine or port
8 slices crisp toast, preferably crusty French bread
Grated Parmesan or Asiago cheese

Onion soup is believed to be typically French, but it was brought to this country a century and a half ago and has remained a popular soup. It turns up in the South around New Orleans, in New York State, and in the Far West around San Francisco. It has certainly become Americanized in these last years with the appearance of dehydrated and canned versions. You can greatly improve dehydrated onion soups, incidentally, by using good stock with them and a touch of wine.

Sauté the onions in butter and oil in a heavy skillet over medium heat until they are soft and take on color. You may sprinkle them with a small amount of sugar and toss them so that the sugar caramelizes and colors them. Salt them. Add boiling broth and wine — I happen to prefer port, for it was the onion soup I grew up on. Blend over medium heat. Serve in heated bowls with Parmesan cheese and crisp slices of hot toasted French bread.

Variations

(1) Ladle soup into ovenproof dishes and add slices of toast heaped with grated Switzerland cheese and some Parmesan. Place in a 350-degree oven for 10 minutes or so till the cheese melts and bubbles. Serve at once with additional toast and bowls of grated Switzerland cheese and Parmesan.

(2) Instead of the port or red wine add ⅔ cup applejack to the soup.

Onion Soup Made with Chicken Broth. Substitute rich chicken broth for the beef broth and white wine for the red. This is a very delicate and delicious version of onion soup which I first discovered in upper New York State.

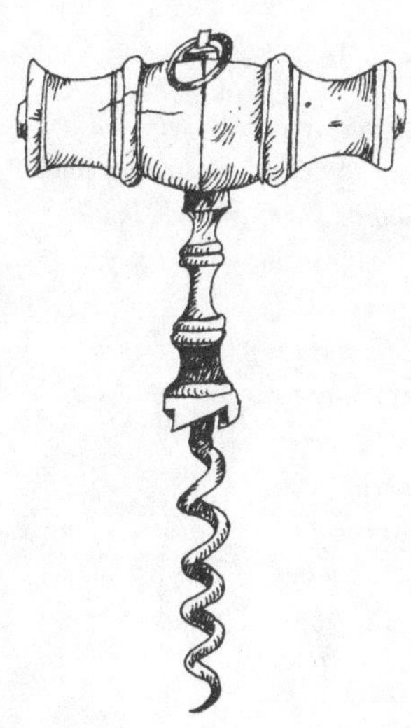

An Old Leek and Potato Soup

5 or 6 leeks
3 tablespoons butter
3 cups diced potatoes
1 quart chicken broth
2 teaspoons salt or to taste
¼ teaspoon cayenne
½ teaspoon nutmeg
2 tablespoons butter
2 tablespoons flour

Although there are many different recipes for potato soup, the one most appreciated is a potato and leek soup. In a different guise it is the basis for the cold soup which Louis Diat made famous under the name of Vichyssoise, served first at the Ritz Carlton in New York when Diat was chef. Its popularity has grown immeasurably since then.

Wash the leeks, split them lengthwise, and cut into thin slices after removing all sand. Sauté in 3 tablespoons butter in a large skillet for 4 minutes. Add the potatoes and the broth, and bring to a boil. Boil for 2 minutes. Reduce heat, and simmer till potatoes are tender. Season to taste with salt, cayenne, and nutmeg. Strain out the vegetables and put through a food mill or ricer. Return to the broth. Melt 2 tablespoons butter in a saucepan over low heat and stir in the flour. Add 1½ cups of the broth and blend well till the mixture thickens. Return to the kettle, and stir till soup comes to a boil. Serve in hot soup plates with a dash of cayenne or nutmeg.

Vichyssoise. Prepare soup as above and allow it to cool. Add 1½ cups heavy cream and blend well. Chill in refrigerator. Serve in chilled cups with a garniture of chopped chives.

Or chill the soup without the heavy cream. Serve in chilled cups with a large spoonful of sour cream and chopped chives.

Still another variation: Do not put the vegetables through a food mill, but serve pieces of leek and diced potatoes in the thickened soup.

Split Pea Soup

1 pound split peas, well washed
A meaty ham bone or ham hock
2 quarts water (include liquid from cooking a ham if you have it)
1 onion stuck with 2 cloves
1 rib celery
1 or 2 carrots
2 garlic cloves
1 bay leaf
Salt to taste

The dried pea — both the green and the yellow — has been with us for centuries, and nearly every Western country has one or more ways of preparing it for soup, purées, and various other dishes. In this country dried peas have traditionally been combined with a meaty ham bone or the liquor in which a ham was cooked to make a rich, thick soup. However, in recent years there have been a number of soups based on chicken broth and dried peas, notably a delicious summer soup, which I think is one of the greatest of all cold soups (see recipe following this).

The finest peas and lentils now come from Idaho and Oregon. The legumes no longer require long soaking before cooking. One can start a split pea soup in the morning or early afternoon and have it for dinner.

Combine the well-washed peas (either green or yellow) with the ham bone or hock, water, and other ingredients except the salt. Bring to a boil. Cover the pot tightly, reduce the heat, and cook for 2 hours, stirring occasionally. Taste for salt — the ham will provide salt — and add more to taste. Remove the ham bone. Cut off any bits of meat that linger and cut them into small dice. Put the soup through a food mill, removing the vegetables and the cloves as you do so. Return the soup to the pot along with the ham bits, and if necessary, dilute the soup with heavy cream, broth, or even water. Serve it very hot with thinly sliced sausages, crisp croutons, or crisp bits of bacon.

Split pea soup, in any of its variations, makes a delicious supper dish for entertaining. It is simple to reheat and has great appeal when served with good bread and butter, followed by a salad or some cheese.

Variations

(1) Dilute the soup with tomato purée and serve with finely chopped fresh tomatoes and croutons.

(2) Add sherry or Madeira to the soup just before serving and garnish with chopped ham.

Lentil Soup. Follow the recipe for split pea soup, puréeing the lentils or leaving them whole, as you like. It is excellent served in any of the fashions described for split pea soup.

Cold Pea Soup with Mint

1½ cups green split peas, well washed and picked over
4 cups salted water
4 cups chicken broth
1 small onion, sliced
2 garlic cloves, crushed
1 sprig fresh mint
Salt to taste
2 cups heavy cream
Fresh mint leaves, finely chopped

I used to serve this soup many years ago as standard summer fare. It is one of the most refreshing of cold soups.

Wash the peas, bring them to a boil in salted water, and boil for 5 minutes. Remove from the heat and let stand for 1 hour. Drain. Add the chicken broth to the peas and bring to a boil. Add the onion, garlic, mint sprig, and salt to taste. Reduce the heat, cover, and simmer the peas in the broth till tender. Put the peas through a food mill, discarding the onion, garlic, and mint.

Chill the soup overnight or for 24 hours. When ready to serve, stir in chilled heavy cream. Serve the soup cold in small iced bowls or cups with finely chopped mint leaves as a garnish. Makes about 8 to 10 cups.

Note. You may add 1 cup cream to the pea purée, or adjust the amount of cream to your taste. You may also add a dollop of sour cream to each serving in lieu of the sweet cream.

Boula Boula

I don't know if this name is derived from the famous Yale song, but I do know that in the last fifty years the soup has become a top-drawer soup for company. Although it is very simple, it is delicious

4 tablespoons butter
3 tablespoons finely chopped onion
2 8-ounce packages frozen peas or 2½ cups cooked fresh peas
½ cup water or broth
1½ teaspoons salt or to taste
¼ teaspoon Tabasco
3 cups canned turtle soup, strained
Turtle meat (from the soup), diced
1 cup heavy cream
¼ cup dry sherry
Whipped cream, slightly salted

and just different enough to be distinguished. It is an American invention.

Melt the butter in a heavy saucepan, add the onion and cook till it is just soft. Add the peas, water, salt, and Tabasco. If frozen peas are used, let them cook in the water over medium heat till just tender; then add the turtle broth. If cooked fresh peas are used, add the turtle broth along with the salt and Tabasco. Cook for 5 to 8 minutes. Remove from heat and run through a food mill to purée the peas and onion. Return to heat, and stir in the cream, diced turtle meat, and sherry. Reheat. Pour the soup into heatproof bowls or crocks and top with slightly salted whipped cream. Run under the broiler for a few minutes to color the cream. Serve with crisp buttered crackers or souffléed crackers.

Navy Bean Soup

3 cups cold baked beans
6 cups water or stock
4 tablespoons chopped onion
½ cup chopped celery
1½ cups cooked or canned tomatoes, strained
Salt and pepper
2 tablespoons butter
2 tablespoons flour
Crisp bacon

This was a soup made in New England from the remains of Saturday's baked beans. The recipe spread gradually to other parts of the country and now has many different variations. The original one was made without tomatoes and was not as interesting a soup as the later versions.

Combine the beans, water or stock, and vegetables. Bring to a boil in a heavy saucepan and simmer for 20 minutes. Put through a food mill, season to taste, and return to heat. Stir in the butter and flour, kneaded together, and stir until thickened. Serve topped with crisp crumbled bacon.

Black Bean Soup

2 cups black beans
4 tablespoons butter
2 large onions, coarsely cut
2 crushed garlic cloves
3 leeks, coarsely cut
1 celery stalk, coarsely cut
2 bay leaves
2 or 3 cloves
Split ham shank with bone and rind
3 pounds beef or veal bones
8 peppercorns

This great soup is a specialty of Leon Lianides at the Coach House in New York.

Soak the beans overnight in water to cover. Next day melt the butter in a stockpot, add the vegetables, bay leaves, and cloves, and sauté 3 minutes. Add the ham shank and beef or veal bones and cook 3 to 4 minutes, then add the peppercorns and flour and blend well. Cook 2 to 3 minutes more, then add the water and bring to a boil. Reduce the heat, skim, and simmer about 8 hours, covered (leave a small air space). Strain the soaked beans, add to the pot, and simmer 2½ hours more, stirring occasionally. Add more water if the mixture gets too thick or the beans are not completely covered. Remove from the heat, discard the bones, and put the soup through a food mill or coarse strainer — you must really purée the beans. Taste, correct the seasoning, add the Madeira, and bring to a boil. Turn off the heat and serve immediately, garnished with the parsley, chopped eggs, and lemon slices.

2 tablespoons flour
4 to 5 quarts water
½ cup Madeira
Chopped parsley
2 or 3 finely chopped hard-boiled eggs
Very thin lemon slices

Cream of Tomato Soup

2 cups canned tomatoes (solid pack or Italian plum tomatoes are probably best for today's needs, unless you have home-canned ones)
1 tablespoon butter
1 tablespoon flour
½ teaspoon bicarbonate of soda
1½ cups heavy cream (evaporated milk may be substituted quite successfully)
Salt and freshly ground pepper
Chopped parsley

There are many versions of this, for it was decidedly one of the more fashionable soups for a company dinner. In winter it was especially simple to prepare, for the larder was filled with canned tomatoes which could be turned into very acceptable, fresh-tasting dishes. This recipe and my mother's (below) are two good ones suitable for present-day entertaining.

Cook the tomatoes down over medium low heat for a half hour or until they are fairly thick. Break them up with a wooden spatula or spoon. Stir in the butter and flour, kneaded together, and continue to stir until slightly thickened. (If you like, strain the soup before adding the thickening.) Add the soda, and let it cook with the tomatoes for a few minutes. Remove the saucepan from the heat. Add some of the tomato mixture to the heavy cream, which should be heated in advance. Slowly stir this back into the rest of the tomato mixture. Add salt and freshly ground pepper to taste. Serve with a dash of chopped parsley.

My Mother's Standard Cream of Tomato Soup

3 cups canned tomatoes or Italian plum tomatoes
1 cup beef broth or veal broth
1 small onion stuck with 2 cloves
1 teaspoon salt
1 teaspoon basil
½ teaspoon freshly ground pepper
¼ teaspoon bicarbonate of soda
1½ tablespoons flour
1½ tablespoons butter
1½ teaspoons sugar (if needed)
2 cups heavy cream, heated to almost the boiling point
Chopped parsley

Cook the tomatoes, broth, and seasonings in a covered saucepan 30 minutes over low heat. Strain through a fine sieve. Add the soda and correct the seasoning. Blend the butter and flour together with a fork until it is a smooth paste. Stir it along with the sugar into the tomato mixture and cook over medium heat until slightly thickened. Add the heated cream to the tomato mixture very slowly off the fire to prevent curdling, return to the heat and bring the soup very slowly almost to the boil. Serve with a garnish of chopped parsley.

Cream of Mushroom Soup

1 pound mushrooms
1 quart chicken broth
2 tablespoons butter
3 tablespoons flour
2 tablespoons sherry or Cognac (optional)
2 cups heavy cream
1½ teaspoons salt, or to taste
¼ teaspoon Tabasco

Although canned mushroom soup has dominated the country for years, there really was a fresh cream of mushroom soup before that time. I remember a delicious one from a restaurant on the West Coast. This is the recipe. Unlike the canned variety, it does not double as a sauce.

Remove the stems from the mushrooms, combine with the chicken broth, and simmer for 35 to 40 minutes or until the mushroom flavor has thoroughly permeated the broth. Strain the broth through cheesecloth, and return to a saucepan. Bring to a boil again, stir in the butter and flour, kneaded together with a fork to a very smooth paste. Stir well until slightly thickened. Add the mushroom caps, which have been thinly sliced, and simmer for 8 to 10 minutes. Heat the cream, and stir into the broth (add sherry or Cognac before the cream, if you like). Add the salt and Tabasco. Heat through thoroughly. Taste for seasoning. Serve in heated soup plates or cups.

Lentil Soup with Chard and Lemon (Adas bi Haamud)

1½ cups lentils
2½ pounds fresh Swiss chard
½ cup olive oil
¾ cup chopped onion
3 to 4 garlic cloves
Salt
1 stalk celery, chopped
¾ cup lemon juice
1 teaspoon flour
Chopped chives (for garnish)

A Syrian version of lentil soup, found in Virginia, where there is a Middle Eastern community.

Wash and pick over the lentils. Cover them with fresh cold water, and cook, covered, until tender. Wash the Swiss chard leaves and chop them. Add these and a cup of water to the lentils. Continue cooking until the Swiss chard is done, adding more water if necessary. Heat the olive oil in a skillet and add the chopped onion. Crush the garlic cloves with salt, and add these and the chopped celery to the onion. Continue cooking until the vegetables are tender and blended. Add to the lentil mixture. Mix the lemon juice with the flour and stir it into the soup. Cook gently, stirring occasionally, until the soup is rather thick. Taste for seasoning.

Serve chilled with chopped chives in soup bowls, and pass crusty French or Italian bread to sop up the juices.

Quick Iced Tomato Soup

1 can tomato soup
1½ cups sour cream
1 teaspoon basil
1 tablespoon grated onion
½ teaspoon salt
½ teaspoon freshly ground pepper
Ice cubes
Chopped parsley or chopped hard-boiled eggs (for garnish)

Use a large cocktail shaker, and prepare the soup just as you are ready to serve it. Combine all ingredients (except the last) with ice cubes in the shaker and shake vigorously till well blended and chilled. Pour into chilled cups and garnish with chopped parsley or chopped hard-boiled eggs.

Chilled Cucumber Soup

2 cups chicken broth
2 cucumbers, peeled, seeded, and cut into strips
1 tablespoon finely chopped onion
Salt and freshly ground pepper
1 teaspoon fresh dill or dillweed
2 cups yoghurt
Finely chopped cucumber or chopped fresh dill or dillweed (for garnish)

Combine the broth, cucumbers, and onion, and cook over low heat till cucumbers are just cooked tender. Whirl in a blender with salt and pepper to taste and the fresh dill or dillweed. Cool. Combine with the yoghurt and correct the seasoning. Chill and serve in chilled cups with the chopped cucumber, dill, or dillweed.

Chilled Avocado Soup

1½ cups avocado, puréed
1½ cups hot chicken broth
1 teaspoon or more dried tarragon or 1 tablespoon fresh, chopped
¼ teaspoon Tabasco
1 tablespoon lemon juice
½ cup heavy cream
½ cup sour cream
Chopped fresh tarragon or chives (for garnish)

Sieve the avocado into the chicken broth and add the seasonings. Blend and chill well. Combine with the cream and sour cream and chill again. Serve in chilled cups with chopped tarragon or chives.

Gazpacho

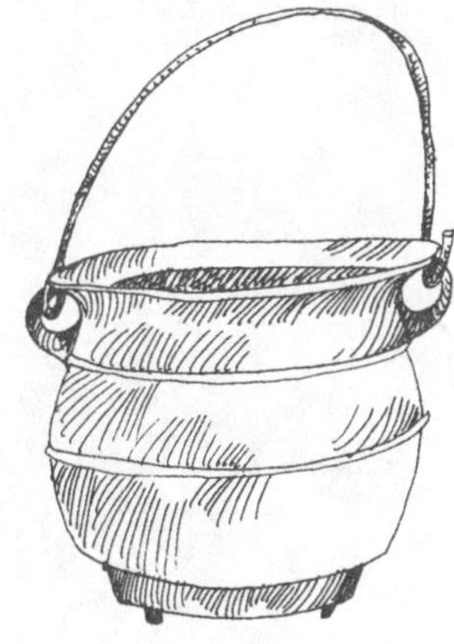

Oddly enough, Mrs. Mary Randolph, in her classic *The Virginia Housewife* (1836), classified her recipe for "gaspacho" under salads. This is an interesting way of considering it, but perhaps even more interesting is the question of how this old Spanish summer soup reached the South early in the nineteenth century — by way of a Virginian who had traveled abroad or by way of the Spanish embassy in Washington? In any event, it is now only one of many versions that have become standard hot-weather fare for many Americans north and south.

"GASPACHO — SPANISH. Put some soft biscuit or toasted bread in the bottom of a salad bowl, put in a layer of sliced tomatoes with the skin taken off, and one of cucumbers sprinkled with salt, pepper and chopped onion; do this until the bowl is full; stew some tomatoes quite soft, stir in the juice, mix in some mustard oil and water, and pour over it; make it two hours before it is eaten."

California Gazpacho

1 clove garlic
3 pounds tomatoes
2 cucumbers
½ cup minced green pepper
½ cup minced onion
2 cups iced tomato juice
⅓ cup olive oil
3 tablespoons vinegar
Salt and freshly ground pepper
¼ teaspoon Tabasco

A much later recipe.

Chop the garlic very fine and add to a large bowl with the tomatoes peeled, seeded, and chopped. Try to save as much of the tomato juice as you can. Peel and seed the cucumbers and add to the bowl with the pepper, onion, and tomato juice. Add the olive oil and seasonings, cover and chill thoroughly. Taste for seasoning — for my taste this will take much more garlic — and serve in chilled bowls with an ice cube of frozen tomato juice in each bowl. Serve small croutons with it.

Cherry Soup

2 pounds tart red cherries, pitted
2 cups water
2-inch piece of cinnamon bark or 1 teaspoon cinnamon
2 cloves
¼ teaspoon salt
2 cups red wine (port or medium sherry may be used if a sweeter soup is desired)
Sugar to taste
2 egg yolks, well beaten

The Scandinavians who migrated to this country and pushed on to the Northwest found many of the fruits they knew at home. This inspired them to reproduce their wonderful fruit soups, especially cherry soups, which they served cold in summer.

This particular soup is best made with red cherries — May Dukes, Kentish, or Montmorency — the tart cherries used a great deal for cookery and pastry making.

Cook the cherries in the water, with the cinnamon, salt, and cloves, until they are quite soft. Rub them through a fine sieve, or remove the cinnamon bark and cloves and whirl in a blender together with some of the cooking liquid. Return to the saucepan, and add the wine and sugar to taste. (If you use port or sweetish sherry you will need no sugar.) Mix a little of the soup with the egg yolks, stir into the mixture, and reheat, stirring, till slightly thickened. Cool and chill well in the refrigerator. Serve cold with a garnish of fresh cherries.

Wheat Bread Soup

This was a popular dish of the Plains States that came to us with the Bavarians, the Bohemians, and other Central Europeans. It's as homely as any dish can be, but there are those who are fond enough of it to want it often.

Boil 4 or 5 thick slices homemade wheat bread in 1 quart salted water or broth for 15 minutes. Beat three eggs with a cup of cream. Remove the pot from the heat and stir the egg-cream mixture in vigorously so it will not curdle. Add 2 tablespoons butter and a touch of mace. Serve at once in heated bowls.

Cheddar Soup

1 small onion, finely chopped
3 tablespoons butter
1 clove garlic, finely chopped
1 cup mashed potatoes (instant may be used)
1 cup chicken broth
2 cups milk
1 cup shredded sharp Cheddar cheese
¼ teaspoon Tabasco, or to taste

With Cheddar, "store," or "rat" cheese being as much a staple as it was across the country — it used to be made in every state where there was a dairy industry — it is natural that many dishes were built around it. This was long before the days of processed cheese and controlled flavors. For my taste, the sharper and more aged the cheese, the better the flavor of the soup. Do not try this with processed cheese, or you'll have a pretty sticky mess.

Wilt the chopped onion in butter in a 2-quart saucepan. Do not allow it to color. Add the garlic and cook 2 minutes. Then add the mashed potatoes, stock, and milk. Stir over medium heat till it is smooth. Simmer 4 to 5 minutes, after which add the shredded cheese and Tabasco. Stir gently till the cheese is melted. Add salt if needed. Serve very hot with toast.

Helen Evans Brown had a recipe from Oregon which included a half-cup of sliced ripe olives, added at the last moment. This gives the soup completely another quality.

Fish and Shellfish Soups, Stews, and Chowders

For these, see pages 172–183 in the Fish and Shellfish chapter of this book.

Eggs

Eggs as a main course, except at breakfast, have never become as established in the United States as they have in other countries. One or two dishes such as Eggs Benedict and Eggs Florentine have become standard luncheon fare, and omelets are becoming more and more popular, but we do not begin to approach the number of attractive egg dishes found daily on menus throughout France, Spain, or Italy. However, I'm sure we lead the world, as we always have, on the subject of breakfast eggs. Our variety of egg and meat combinations for this meal is unequaled when we begin to tally ham and eggs, bacon and eggs, Canadian bacon and eggs, jowl slices and eggs, and sausage, meat or link, and eggs. And we are the only country I can think of where potatoes are important as a breakfast food — hashed brown or country-fried or cottage-fried potatoes — combined with eggs or meat and eggs.

The stereotype of eggs for breakfast has made our egg cookery less varied, but it has nevertheless given us some good dishes and in some cases has developed excellent techniques for cooking eggs.

Fried Eggs

Probably the most common of all ways to serve eggs is not really fried but panned. They are served with the yolks brilliantly glazed, known as "sunny side up," or turned briefly, known as "over easy." In the past, eggs were cooked in bacon or sausage fat after the meat was removed. This makes delicious eggs, but it is hazardous today, considering the modern techniques of curing bacon and ham. The excessive sugar content in much of the present-day bacon causes the eggs to stick to the pan and the whites to break up. The best way to fry eggs, I find, is in Teflon, using a minimum of butter. Drop the eggs into the pan when it is well heated and the butter is warm. Let the whites solidify, and if you want your eggs over easy, turn with the aid of a spatula. If you want them sunny side up, add a few drops of hot water to the pan and cover for a minute or two with the heat off. A delicate film of cooked egg white will form on the yolks. Shake the pan gently before removing the eggs.

In diners and small restaurants fried eggs are typically prepared in a small 6 or 7 inch pan that will just hold two eggs easily. The butter is ample — at least a good tablespoon for each pan of eggs — and when it foams the eggs are dropped in and cooked to the required state. Eggs prepared in this manner will slide from the pan with the greatest of ease. One can keep one or more such pans ready for fried eggs, using them exclusively for that purpose.

Poached Eggs

Poaching is extremely easy, and is even easier if you take a few steps not generally mentioned in the rules. But first we'll begin with the most generally recommended method. Pour enough water into a small, shallow pan to cover the eggs. Bring to a gentle boil, not a rolling boil. Add a little vinegar, and start swirling the water to create a miniature whirlpool. Break the egg into the center of this, and then gather the white together with a spoon or other tool. If you are deft, this produces a beautiful rounded egg. Cook it — do not boil it — until the white is firm. Remove it from the water with a slotted spoon or slotted lifter (there are excellent ones to be found in Japanese shops). Dry on paper towels or a dish towel. If you are going to use the eggs later, either cold or reheated, for a dish, store in a bowl of cold water. When ready to use, remove carefully and dry on a towel.

It is probably much easier for most people to follow one of these two methods of poaching eggs:

(1) Prepare water for poaching and let it heat to the feeble ebullition stage. Gently break each egg to be poached into a small cup — measuring cups with handles are ideal for this purpose. Carefully turn the cup over into the water, holding the cup inverted over

the egg for a few seconds. This holds the white intact until it sets. Continue poaching as above, basting the eggs with a little hot water, if you like. Transfer them carefully to a paper towel or dish towel.

(2) There are rings equipped with folding handles available on the market for frying eggs in perfect circles. If you place these in a pan of water and invert the eggs (in cups) into the rings, they will poach perfectly.

Boiled Eggs

There are three ways to boil eggs:

(1) Place the eggs in cold water, and let them come to a boil. Remove from the heat and allow to stand for 30 seconds for very soft eggs and 1 minute for firmer eggs. For hard eggs, let them boil for 3 minutes. Remove from heat and allow to stand for 20 minutes. Plunge into cold water at once. If you stir the eggs about during cooking it sometimes helps to keep the yolks centered.

(2) Put the eggs in cold water and bring to a real rolling boil. Reduce to a simmer and let them cook 3 minutes for very soft eggs and 4 for a firmer egg. For hard-boiled eggs let them cook for 10 to 12 minutes. Plunge into cold water at once.

(3) Use an electric egg cooker, which is the latest development in the field. It works with a minimum of trouble and gives extremely good results.

Coddled Eggs

Lower the eggs gently into boiling water, and immediately remove the pan from the heat. Cover, and let stand 4 minutes for very soft eggs, 6 minutes for firmer.

Scrambled Eggs

For years the best restaurant-scrambled eggs were to be found in diners and at small counters, where short-order cooks had the knack of making creamy, large-curd scrambled eggs that were soft and flavorful. It is now a lost art in restaurants, but one can do it at home with ease.

There are two methods that work very well and a third that I consider to be a bit tedious. Also, the advent of Teflon pans has made the process a great deal easier, although I do not believe in using Teflon without some butter.

Estimate 2 eggs per person. To 4 eggs add 1½ tablespoons water, ½ teaspoon salt, and a dash or two of Tabasco. Beat lightly with a fork. Melt 1 to 2 tablespoons butter in the pan you will use.

(1) Use a 10-inch skillet — preferably Teflon-lined. Place the pan over low heat, and when the butter is just melted, add the eggs. Let them heat through, and as they do, increase the heat slightly. Using a wooden spatula or spoon, push the eggs from the bottom

of the pan in long strokes to form rather long curds. Continue this with increasing speed as the pan grows hotter. Remove from heat if it grows too hot. The eggs should be loose, creamy, and not the least bit overcooked. Scrape them onto warm plates, and serve at once.

(2) Do not use a Teflon pan for this method. Simply heat the butter in a skillet, add the eggs, and mix with a fork as the eggs form a solid mass at the bottom of the pan. Gauge the size of the curds you want as you manipulate the fork.

(3) Heat the eggs in melted butter in the top of a double boiler over boiling water. Stir with a wooden spoon or spatula till the eggs are creamy and curded.

Eggs may be scrambled with any of the following additives. For 4 or 5 eggs:

½ cup crisp bacon bits
2 tablespoons chopped fresh herbs
½ cup finely diced ham
½ cup grated Cheddar or Swiss cheese
Thinly sliced cooked sausages
1 cup whole kernel corn and 3 tablespoons melted butter in addition to butter in pan
1 cup flaked cooked finnan haddie or codfish
Strips of chipped beef blanched 3 minutes in boiling water

Tomato Scrambled Eggs. For 6 eggs, peel, seed, and chop 3 ripe tomatoes. Sauté them in 3 tablespoons butter, and add salt, pepper, and basil to taste. Combine with the 6 eggs slightly beaten. Scramble in the usual way. A bit of raw onion may also be added to the eggs.

Omelets

Omelets have figured in our pattern of eating for over a hundred years. Some of the recipes are startling, and others are for a true French omelet, made as we do it today. The soufflé (puffy) omelet — one in which the yolks and whites are beaten separately and then combined — used to be the most popular type of omelet; they were often started on top of the stove and finished off in the oven. Other omelets had the yolk and milk mixture thickened with cornstarch before the whites were folded in, as in a soufflé. Then the double omelet pan arrived and is still with us for those who cannot fold an omelet in an ordinary pan. This horrible invention has been the ruination of omelet making for a long period of years.

"Egg Omelet — A Nice Breakfast Dish"

Here's an 1884 omelet recipe which is like no other we have today.

"Let 1 teacup of milk come to a boil; pour over it one teacup of breadcrumbs and let stand a few minutes. Break six eggs into a bowl. Stir till well mixed. Then add the milk and bread; mix, season with salt and pepper and pour into a hot spider in which you have melted a large piece of butter. Fry slowly. Cut into squares; turn, fry to a delicate brown and serve at once."

The Puffy Omelet

6 eggs, separated
1 teaspoon salt
½ teaspoon freshly ground pepper
½ cup milk or cream
5 tablespoons butter

Separate the eggs, and beat the yolks fairly well, till they are light and lemon-colored. Add salt and pepper. Beat in the milk or cream. Then beat the whites till they are stiff but not dry, just beyond the soft-peak stage. Fold the yolk mixture into the whites very lightly. Heat a heavy 12-inch skillet until very hot. Add the butter and melt quickly but do not brown. Add the omelet mixture and cook over medium heat till it is just set on the bottom. Carefully place the pan in the oven preheated to 375 degrees. Cook till the omelet is puffed and just delicately browned and set. Serve at once with creamed crab or shrimp, with a cheese sauce, or merely with sausages.

A True Omelet

The pan is the most important thing in making an omelet. I like to use either a rather heavy French iron pan with rounded sides or a 10-inch Teflon-lined heavy aluminum pan. However, you can use just about any pan that has a shallow bowl shape.

The second most important thing is to have the pan hot enough. It should make a drop of water race across the surface when it is ready. Also, it is important to reheat the pan between omelets. Those who make omelets in quantity nearly always have several pans ready and change from one to the other so that the pans not in use reheat.

If the omelet sticks to a perfectly seasoned pan, the answer is probably that the pan was not hot enough. If there is residue in the pan, use coarse salt and a paper towel to remove it. Then rub it well with a little oil and dry with paper towels. Except for Teflon pans, it is better to wipe pans with a damp cloth than to wash them. Never put through a dishwasher. With Teflon-lined pans, however, this rule does not hold. The pan may be put to other uses as well for as long as the Teflon lining lasts.

Certainly I have seen omelet pans which suffered by not being washed and on which the outside became so dirty and unappetizing that one would question the advisability of eating an omelet issuing therefrom. So even though you protect the patina of the inside of the omelet pan from soaps and detergents, there is no reason why the exterior need collect the dirt and bits of egg. Wash it!

Count on about 2½ eggs per omelet if you are making them in quantity. Beat the eggs lightly, and for every two eggs I like to add 1 tablespoon water. Also add salt to taste and a healthy dash of Tabasco. If you are making five to ten omelets, mix the eggs, water, and seasonings, beat lightly with a fork or whisk, and then strain through a coarse sieve into another bowl.

Have the pan hot, as described above. Add a good piece of butter — about 1 tablespoon per omelet — and swirl the pan around by the handle to distribute the butter. It should bubble and foam. If it should brown or burn, the pan is too hot. Pour off the butter, wipe out the pan, and start again.

When the butter is properly heated, add the egg mixture (when making in quantity, ½ to ¾ cup of the mixture is about right). When the eggs hit the pan shake it well in a circular motion and, if you like, stir the eggs lightly with a fork, being careful not to disturb the bottom of the omelet. If there is a great deal of liquid in the pan, carefully pull the sides of the omelet up from the edge a bit and allow the liquid to run underneath. Continue to shake the pan well, and when the omelet is set, give the pan a forceful shake with a firm grip on the handle and the pan inclined away from you, so the omelet will roll toward the opposite side of the pan from the handle. (Some cooks shake and also give the handle of the pan a forceful bang with a clenched fist, and sometimes one needs the aid of a fork or spatula.) Then change your grip so you can tip the pan and roll the omelet out onto a hot plate. Serve at once. If the omelet should stick, shake the pan well and loosen the sticking point with a spatula or fork. Before reusing, wipe out the pan with a little coarse salt and a paper towel. Reheat and proceed with your omelet making.

If you are filling the omelets, start rolling them, add two or three spoonfuls of the filling and then continue to roll out as directed above. If you are using fines herbes or grated cheese, sprinkle on the omelet as you begin to roll it.

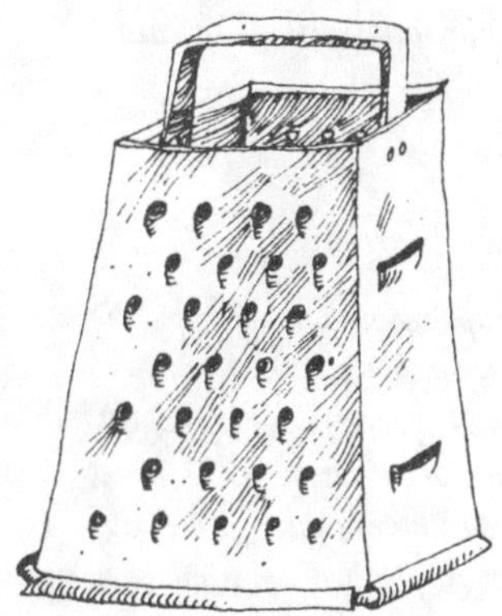

Use any of these fillings for omelets:

Cheese — grated Cheddar, Swiss, Parmesan, Munster, Roquefort, feta, or practically any melting cheese
Chopped fines herbes or merely chopped chives
Sautéed onions
Bacon
Sautéed mushrooms
Cooked, drained, chopped, and buttered spinach
Smoked salmon
Red caviar and sour cream
Jelly or jam
Curried chicken or seafood
Chili
Tomatoes
Finnan haddie
Clams in sauce

Egg Dishes

Eggs Benedict

For each person:
1 slice bread or a muffin, toasted and buttered
1 medium thick slice of ham, sautéed in butter
1 poached egg
Hollandaise sauce and a slice of truffle

Often mistakenly called Eggs Benedictine, which is the name of a French dish made with codfish and topped with eggs, this delectable luncheon dish is really named Eggs Benedict.

The oldest recipe I have found for Eggs Benedict does not use English muffins but rather toast or toasted rolls. Another later recipe calls for very thin toast and still another for toasted buns — similar to those used nowadays for hamburgers, only firmer. Otherwise the dish in each case is quite the same.

The ham goes on the toast, and the egg atop the ham. Even the Midwestern and Western books call for truffle as a garnish — not the slice of ripe olive some restaurants cheat with.

Asparagus with Egg and Bacon

An old and established West Coast favorite. Merely top 5 or 6 perfectly cooked stalks of peeled asparagus with a poached or fried egg and 2 strips well-cooked bacon. A perfect luncheon dish.

Eggs Florentine

2 cups chopped, cooked, and drained spinach
2 tablespoons butter (optional)
1 teaspoon salt
A dusting of nutmeg
4 eggs, poached and trimmed neatly
½ cup grated Parmesan cheese

These have been a standard in American cookery for years. Now they seem to be having a renaissance with those who are watching their calories.

Blend the chopped spinach with the butter, salt, and nutmeg, and heat through. Arrange in 4 baking dishes or ramekins. Top each with a poached egg. Sprinkle with a little grated Parmesan, and pop into a 375-degree oven for 5 minutes. Serve at once.

Note. You may want to double this recipe and serve each person 2 eggs.

Poached Egg in Tomato

Another delight which used to grace luncheon and breakfast tables. This version is from *Lowney's Cook Book*, 1907. For each person, cut the stem end from a smallish tomato. Remove the seeds and some of the pulp. Place the tomato in a ramekin or a small baking dish. Drop an egg into this, and add salt and freshly ground pepper. Cover with buttered paper and bake in a pan of water in a 350-degree oven till the egg is set. Serve at once with buttered toast fingers.

Baked Eggs with Tomatoes

Butter
2 cups cooked or canned tomatoes
½ cup finely chopped onion
1 teaspoon salt
½ teaspoon freshly ground pepper
3 tablespoons butter
2 tablespoons flour
1 teaspoon sugar
6 or 12 eggs
¾ cup grated cheese — Cheddar or Swiss

Tomatoes and eggs have always been paired since the "love apple" became common food in the United States. This is a rather delicious combination and a good Sunday breakfast dish when served with sausage patties and crisp toasted muffins and jam.

Butter 6 ramekins or small baking dishes well. Combine the tomatoes, onion, salt, and pepper, and simmer 15 to 20 minutes. Add the butter and flour, which have been kneaded together, and stir until the mixture is thickened. Add the sugar and taste the mixture for seasoning. Spoon the sauce into the ramekins or baking dishes. Break an egg (or 2) into each dish. Sprinkle lightly with cheese and bake at 350 degrees 15 minutes or until the white is set.

Deviled Poached Eggs

Butter
1 cup catsup
½ cup water
1 teaspoon Worcestershire sauce
½ teaspoon Tabasco
2 teaspoons dry mustard
4 tablespoons butter
6 eggs

This old recipe is quite similar to the one above.

Butter 6 ramekins or baking dishes well. Heat the catsup, water, and seasonings together. Add the butter bit by bit, and blend thoroughly. Spoon the mixture into the baking dishes and break an egg into each dish. Bake in a 350-degree oven till the eggs are set. Serve with crisp bacon and toast for a Sunday breakfast. Buttered asparagus is also a good accompaniment.

Puffed Eggs

4 eggs
4 slices toast
Butter
¾ cup finely chopped ham
2 tablespoons well-seasoned mayonnaise
1 teaspoon hot mustard
Salt and freshly ground pepper
Chopped parsley

Incredibly fashionable as a luncheon or breakfast dish at the turn of the century, puffed eggs are seldom encountered any longer. They are delicious — except when they are overcooked.

Separate the eggs, placing the whites in a bowl and each of the yolks in a separate cup, being very careful not to break them. Butter the toast, mix the ham and seasonings, and spread a layer on each piece of toast. Beat the whites till they are firm but not dry, adding a little salt to them. Spoon the whites on the toast. Make a hollow in each portion large enough to hold one yolk. Carefully drop the yolks into the whites and sprinkle with a bit of freshly ground pepper. Place on a baking sheet and bake in a 350-degree oven till the eggs are set and the whites are delicately colored. Garnish with parsley, and serve at once.

Eggs Suzette

6 baked potatoes
6 tablespoons butter
3 tablespoons sour cream
1 tablespoon chopped chives
1 tablespoon crumbled bacon
2 teaspoons salt
1 teaspoon freshly ground pepper
6 eggs
Grated Cheddar cheese

Split the potatoes. Scoop out the meat and blend well with the butter, sour cream, chives, bacon, and salt and pepper. Beat lightly and spoon back into the shells. Make a hollow in the top of each potato and into this drop a raw egg. Sprinkle lavishly with grated Cheddar cheese, and place in a 350-degree oven long enough to cook the eggs and melt the cheese. Makes a delicious breakfast or supper dish.

Gypsy Eggs

4 tablespoons chopped green pepper
4 tablespoons chopped onion
2 tablespoons oil
2 tablespoons tomato catsup
2 tablespoons grated cheese
Salt and freshly ground pepper
6 eggs beaten with ½ cup milk or cream
Toast

This is so reminiscent of the piperade from the Basque country that it must have originated there and been brought over by the Basques who settled in great numbers in Oregon, Nevada, and California and who still maintain colonies in those states, working mostly as shepherds and sheep ranchers.

Sauté the green pepper and onion in oil till wilted. Add the catsup and cheese and season to taste. Add the egg-milk mixture, and stir until the eggs are set and fluffy like scrambled eggs. Spoon on toast, and serve with slices of frizzled ham.

Note. I find the dish is much better if 2 tablespoons water are added to the eggs instead of the milk or cream, or the eggs are cooked as they are. Also, ½ teaspoon each of salt and pepper, and a dash of Tabasco, improve the dish for me.

Spanish Omelet

½ cup finely chopped green pepper
¾ cup finely chopped onion
2 tablespoons butter
4 tablespoons oil (preferably olive)
1 cup sliced mushrooms
2 cups cooked or canned tomatoes
1 clove garlic, finely chopped
1 teaspoon salt
1 teaspoon freshly ground pepper
¼ teaspoon Tabasco
4 to 6 individual omelets

Hardly Spanish, this dish has had a long career and has weathered the poor preparation it frequently gets. Done properly, it can be excellent. The combination seems to have originated in Colorado, California, or Texas.

Sauté the green pepper and onion in butter and oil till they are limp. Add the mushrooms, tomatoes, and garlic, and cook 5 minutes. Add the seasonings, and simmer till the mixture is well blended and slightly thickened. Prepare the omelets the usual way, and add a healthy filling of the sauce as you roll them. You may add sliced ripe olives and a little chopped parsley, which are later variations on this dish.

Note. If you add several chopped green chilies to the above mixture, you will have a Mexican omelet.

Eggs à la Livingston

Spread 4 well-buttered pieces of toast with caviar. Scramble 6 eggs with 1 cup cooked shrimp, either small or chopped large ones. Spoon over the caviar toasts, and serve very hot.

Bombay Toast

A once popular dish similar in style to the one above. Spread buttered toast with anchovy paste and top with scrambled eggs. I find that anchovy fillets make this dish even better.

Oyster Omelet, Palace Hotel

This was a great favorite in the days of the old Palace Hotel in San Francisco, and was made at one time with California native oysters, a small type, similar to Olympias, which were superb. If you make it now, use any of the oysters available in the East, and in the West use the petite points or Olympias.

Merely make your best omelets, and roll freshly creamed oysters into each omelet. Sprinkle with a little chopped parsley. For 4 omelets, use 1 cup cream sauce, and 1 cup oysters.

Oyster Omelet (for small oysters only)

1 pint small oysters
Flour
2 eggs beaten lightly with ½ cup heavy cream
2 to 3 cups freshly made bread-crumbs
6 to 8 tablespoons butter
1 teaspoon salt
½ teaspoon Tabasco
8 eggs, slightly beaten with 1 tablespoon water
Toast
Chopped parsley

Drain the oysters well, dip in flour, then in the egg-cream mixture, and finally in crumbs. Heat the butter in a 10 or 12 inch skillet and add the oysters. Brown well on both sides. Add the salt and Tabasco. Then add the eggs beaten with water and stir until the eggs are set. Spoon over hot toast, and garnish with chopped parsley.

Western (Denver) Omelet or Sandwich

There is no true recipe for this. Sometimes a cook who is fond of what he's doing will give you a memorable version, and other times it is bland and horrible. Correctly made in one of the iron skillets that used to abound in diners and greasy spoons, a western took a deft hand.

Basically it is a combination of chopped onion, green pepper, and ham or bacon, seasoned well and sautéed in a little butter a few minutes till the onion and pepper are limp. Then 2 or 3 eggs, lightly beaten, are added, and the whole is cooked brown on one side and then turned to brown on the other. Season well with salt, freshly ground pepper, and Tabasco. Serve on hot well-buttered toast or a toasted bun, and you have a good dish. Here again liberties may be taken with the basic recipe. I've had chopped tomato and crisp bacon in it, among other variations.

Eggs St. Denis

6 tablespoons butter
¾ cup sliced green onions
¾ cup chicken livers, finely chopped
¾ cup mushrooms, finely chopped
1 garlic clove, finely chopped
⅓ cup white wine
2 tablespoons lemon juice
1 teaspoon salt
½ teaspoon freshly ground pepper
6 pieces ham, cut to fit toast
6 eggs
6 rounds or squares of toast
Chopped parsley

This Creole recipe was once very popular in New Orleans.

Heat the butter in a rather heavy 9 or 10 inch skillet, and sauté the onions, livers, mushrooms, and garlic 4 to 5 minutes over medium heat. Turn often. Add the wine, lemon juice, and seasonings. Grill the ham slices. Fry the eggs in butter in small pans to keep them in rounds and more trim. Arrange the ham on toast, top with an egg, spoon the sauce over all, and serve with a garnish of chopped parsley. Or make a layer of toast on a platter, top with ham, arrange eggs over all, and serve the sauce separately.

Eggs Foo Yung

2 tablespoons peanut oil
½ cup cut green onions
½ cup bean sprouts
¼ cup chopped celery
¼ cup chopped water chestnuts
½ cup finely cut shrimp or crabmeat
2 tablespoons soy sauce
2 tablespoons flour
6 eggs lightly beaten
½ to ¾ cup peanut oil

SAUCE

1½ cups chicken broth
½ cup soy sauce
4 teaspoons cornstarch blended with 2 tablespoons water
Fresh coriander if available, or chopped parsley

A Chinese dish which has been pretty thoroughly Americanized and which inspired one of our standard sandwiches — the western or Denver. Both of these must have originated with the many Chinese chefs who cooked for logging camps and railroad gangs in the nineteenth and early twentieth centuries.

There are so many different versions of Eggs Foo Yung that it is impossible to select an authentic one. However, most recipes begin with the same ingredients.

Heat the peanut oil and sauté the chopped vegetables and shrimp or crabmeat lightly. Season with the soy, add the flour, and stir well. Cool slightly and blend with the beaten eggs. Drop by spoonfuls into hot oil in a heavy skillet, and cook till brown. Turn as you would hotcakes. Transfer to hot plates, and serve with the sauce.

To make the sauce, combine the broth and soy, and thicken with the cornstarch blended with water. Cook until transparent, and add fresh coriander or parsley.

Note. The crab or shrimp may be replaced by ham, tongue, chicken, duck, or mushrooms, among many choices. You may vary the seasonings as well.

Creole Eggs

3 tablespoons butter
3 tablespoons flour
2 cups cooked tomatoes or tomato purée
½ teaspoon freshly ground pepper
1 teaspoon salt
2 tablespoons chopped onion
2 tablespoons chopped green pepper
8 hard-boiled eggs, peeled and quartered
¾ cup grated American cheese or Monterey jack
6 strips bacon

Combine the butter and flour in a heavy saucepan, blend, and cook 2 to 3 minutes. Gradually stir in the tomatoes and seasonings and cook until thickened. Add the onion and green pepper and cook 4 minutes. Arrange the eggs in a 6-cup baking dish and pour the sauce over them. Add the cheese and bacon strips and bake at 375 degrees 20 to 25 minutes, or until the cheese is melted and the bacon cooked.

Scalloped Eggs with Cheese

6 hard-boiled eggs cut into quarters
2 cups white sauce
1 cup grated American cheese
Tabasco
½ cup breadcrumbs

Arrange half the eggs in a well-buttered 1-quart baking dish. Add half the sauce, a few dashes of Tabasco, and a heavy sprinkling of the cheese. Add another layer of eggs and sauce, a few more dashes of Tabasco, and the rest of the cheese. Sprinkle with breadcrumbs, and bake at 350 degrees 15 to 20 minutes, or until the cheese is melted and the sauce is bubbly. Serve with sausages.

Goldenrod Eggs

6 hard-boiled eggs
2 cups white sauce
¼ teaspoon salt
Few grains cayenne
¼ teaspoon freshly ground pepper
2 teaspoons chopped parsley
6 slices buttered toast

A rather dreary recipe which once had great standing. It was taught in domestic science classes and in cookery schools and was probably the dish brides felt comfortable in preparing for their husbands, who sooner or later might well have found the dish grounds for divorce. This is Maria Willett Howard's recipe in *Lowney's Cook Book,* published in 1907.

Shell the eggs, chop the whites fine, and add to the white sauce. Press the yolks through a fine sieve and season with the salt, pepper, cayenne, and parsley. Arrange the toast on a platter and spoon the creamed whites over it. Sprinkle the chopped yolk mixture over the toasts in any pattern you wish. Serve at once. A border of chopped ham makes this dish a little pleasanter.

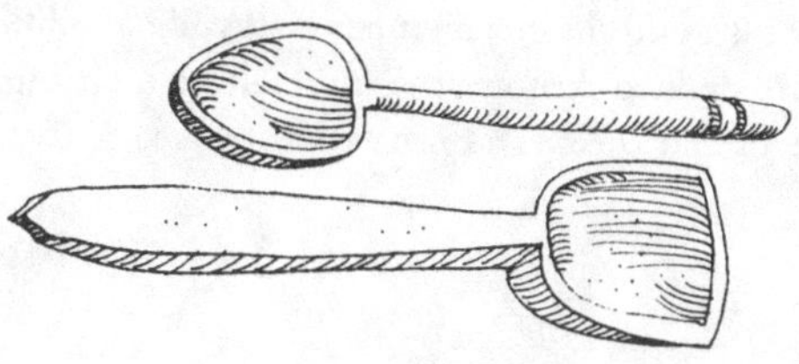

Frittata

1 or 2 cloves garlic, finely chopped
1 onion, thinly sliced
4 tablespoons olive oil
2 cups cooked, drained, and chopped spinach
1 teaspoon salt
½ teaspoon freshly ground pepper
¼ teaspoon nutmeg
8 eggs
½ cup grated Parmesan cheese

The Italian version of a pancake omelet has long been a dish served in American restaurants and diners under a variety of names. In San Francisco frittatas have been served for a hundred years, made with a great variety of vegetables. One of the most successful frittatas uses spinach flavored with garlic and a bit of onion. Others are made with potatoes and onions and sometimes ham or bacon; or zucchini and prosciutto; or onions, chicken, almonds, olives, chilies, and grated Parmesan cheese. And frittatas are good cold if made properly. Here is one example — a spinach frittata.

Sauté the garlic and onion in the olive oil until just wilted. Add the spinach, which has been cooked until just limp in a small amount of water (you will need about 2 pounds raw spinach, or you may use 3 packages frozen spinach, in which event thaw but do not cook it, drain well, and press to remove all water). Heat the spinach through, blending with the garlic and onion. Add the seasonings. Beat the eggs lightly and pour over the vegetables. Cook over medium heat. When the eggs are set, invert the pan onto a hot plate, slide the omelet back into the pan, sprinkle with the cheese, and cook till set on the reverse side; or sprinkle with the cheese and run under the broiler until nicely browned, being very careful not to scorch the eggs. Slide onto a hot platter, and serve cut in wedges.

Variations

Many other vegetables, combinations of vegetables, or vegetables and meat may be used in place of the spinach.

(1) A bit of shredded prosciutto or other type of ham is particularly good with zucchini.

(2) Tomatoes, peeled, seeded, and chopped, are a delicious filling when complemented with garlic, onion, and some basil.

(3) Peas, potatoes, and onions are a good combination. The potatoes should be sliced cooked potatoes, preferably new potatoes, which are somewhat waxy.

(4) Potatoes, onions, and bacon make a delicious combination. The bacon should be precooked and on the crisp side.

(5) For an unusual frittata, combine 1½ cups bean sprouts (available fresh in Chinese shops or canned in many supermarkets) with 1 cup cut green onions, and sauté in oil till limp. Add to this 1 can drained shrimp or 1 cup small fresh shrimp, and blend. Add the eggs and cheese and proceed as above.

(6) Combine garlic-flavored croutons of bread, 3/4 cup crisp bacon bits, and the eggs and cheese.

(7) Combine 1/2 cup peeled and diced canned green chilies, a thinly sliced onion, 1 1/2 cups diced chicken, and 1 cup sliced ripe olives. This delicious recipe is, as are most of these variations, a California adaptation of the original frittatas.

Curried Eggs

1 medium onion, finely chopped
4 tablespoons butter
1 tablespoon curry powder
3 tablespoons flour
1 cup chicken broth
1 teaspoon salt
1/4 teaspoon Tabasco
Dash nutmeg
1/2 cup or more heavy cream
6 hard-boiled eggs, shelled and sliced

A great chafing dish favorite when the chafing dish was in vogue.

Sauté the onion in the butter until it is just limp. Add the curry powder and blend well. Then blend in the flour and cook over low heat 3 minutes. Stir in the chicken broth, and continue stirring till thickened. Add the seasonings, and stir in enough cream to thicken to your taste. Correct the seasoning — you may want additional curry powder, in which case allow the sauce to simmer a few minutes longer. Add the eggs and blend well. Serve with rice or toast and chutney, chopped cucumber, peanuts, and raisins soaked in sherry.

Mushroom Curried Eggs. Curried eggs are often made with sautéed mushrooms — about 1/4 pound sliced and sautéed in butter to which a little curry powder and 1/4 cup heavy cream are added. Combine with the eggs just before serving.

Mrs. Mary Randolph's Fricasseed Eggs

"Boil six eggs for five minutes, lay them in cold water, peel them carefully, dredge them lightly with flour, beat one egg light, dip the hard eggs in, roll them in breadcrumbs, seasoned with pepper, salt and grated nutmeg; cover them well with this and let them stand some time to dry — fry them in boiling lard, and serve them up with any kind of rich, well-seasoned gravy, and garnish with crisped parsley."

Cheese

Our tradition of cheese came from the English, of course, which accounts for the fact that most of the cheese made in this country up until the early twentieth century was a version of Cheddar. In the last sixty or seventy years Swiss and French cheeses have gained a greater foothold and are now made in many states. Cheddar is produced in New York state, Vermont, Wisconsin, Illinois, California, Oregon, and Washington. Swiss-type Emmenthaler cheese is produced all through the country from the Atlantic to the Pacific, some of the best being made in Wyoming, Montana, Utah, Wisconsin, and a little in Oregon and Washington. We also have various of the soft cheeses made in fine fashion — an excellent Brie in Ohio and Illinois and a fine Brie in northern California. Blue cheeses flourish in the country too, and among them one finds blue cheese which can compete among the world's greatest. Blues are made in Iowa, Wisconsin, Oregon, and various other parts of the country.

Cheese has never been as vital a part of our diet in the United States as it has been in Europe. Here, cheese has been used as a snack, as a filling for sandwiches, and for cooking. Even so, there are no great original American cheese dishes, which seems rather strange. The closest thing to it, I suppose, would be the American toasted cheese sandwich, which is hardly original except for the type of cheese used. It resembles the croque monsieur of the French and the melted cheese dishes that the English very often present to you. Our macaroni and cheese is a version of an Italian dish. We have, however, contributed one or two interesting uses of cheese — for example, Roquefort cheese dressing, which can be a delicious item or utterly pedestrian. And Roquefort cheese has come to play an important role in meat cookery. Another meat and cheese combination, the cheeseburger, by no means originated in this country, but it has become one of the most common dishes.

In the last twenty-five years the popularity of cheese has grown by leaps and bounds. Americans now spend a great deal of time picking good cheeses and learning to distinguish between the mediocre and the fine. It's heartwarming to think that in the next twenty-five years we may develop a new cheese of our own and several great cheese dishes. However, never believe that we have not produced some extraordinarily fine cheeses already. Some of the New York Cheddars and the Bries that I spoke of and many individual cheeses are of high quality. And one Liederkranz, if not a complete invention, is fairly American in its adaptation and presentation. Fortunately for all of us, its producers have maintained a great quality, and it has remained one of the best natural cheeses made and sold in the United States.

The best way to sample the full range of American cheeses is to travel about the country to hunt down the places where cheese is produced. Oftentimes you will find unusual varieties that you would never believe existed here.

Mrs. Burgess's Cheese Soufflé

6 thin slices white bread
Butter
¾ cup shredded sharp cheese
1½ cups milk
1 teaspoon salt
⅛ teaspoon cayenne pepper or ¼ teaspoon Tabasco
3 eggs, slightly beaten

Though soufflés are really part of Continental cuisine, they have figured for a great many years in American cookery. Here are several versions of the cheese soufflé.

This first is not a soufflé at all, according to our standards, but was called such for many years. The recipe is from Mrs. Burgess of Webster City, Iowa.

Butter the bread slices and cut in fingers. Arrange them in a buttered 1½-quart baking dish in layers, alternating with the shredded cheese. Add the seasonings to the milk, and mix together with the beaten egg. Pour over the bread and cheese, and let stand 30 minutes. Bake at 350 degrees 25 to 30 minutes, or until brown and puffy.

Note. This same dish was often done with soda crackers instead of bread.

A Kansas "Soufflé Omelet." This so-called omelet is simply another version of the recipe above. Butter a 1-quart pudding dish, and cover the bottom with thin slices of cheese. Cover the cheese with thin slices of buttered bread, spread with prepared mustard. Add a few sprinkles of cayenne and of salt. Add enough layers to fill the dish. Pour over it 2 eggs beaten with 1¼ cups milk. Bake 30 minutes in a moderate oven (350 degrees).

Fannie Farmer's Cheese Soufflé

2 tablespoons butter
3 tablespoons flour
½ cup scalded milk
½ teaspoon salt
Few grains cayenne
½ cup grated Cheddar cheese
3 eggs, separated

Miss Farmer was one of the first to offer a real soufflé. Here is one of her early recipes.

Melt the butter, add the flour, and when well mixed gradually add the scalded milk. Then add the salt, cayenne, and cheese. Remove from the fire; add the egg yolks beaten until lemon-colored. Cool the mixture, and fold in the egg whites beaten stiff but not dry. Pour into a buttered 1½-quart mold, and bake 30 to 35 minutes at 375 degrees.

Swiss Cheese Soufflé

3 tablespoons butter
3 tablespoons flour
¾ cup scalded milk
4 egg yolks, slightly beaten
¾ teaspoon salt
1 teaspoon dry mustard
1 cup grated Swiss cheese
5 egg whites

This is a much later version of the cheese soufflé.

Melt the butter in a heavy saucepan and blend with the flour over medium high heat. Simmer 3 minutes. Gradually stir in the scalded milk, and stir till thickened. Remove from the heat and beat in the egg yolks. Return to heat for just a minute to set the egg yolks. Add the seasonings and cheese, and remove from the heat. Let stand while you beat the egg whites stiff but not dry. Fold into the cheese mixture, folding in about a quarter of the beaten whites quite well and the rest more lightly. Pour into a buttered 1½-quart soufflé mold and smooth lightly. Bake at 375 degrees 30 to 35 minutes, or until the mixture is well risen and delicately brown and puffy. Serve with a cheese or tomato sauce, if you like, and a salad.

To achieve a puffier soufflé, you may put a collar on the baking dish. Use a piece of brown paper, wax paper, cooking parchment, or foil. Butter well and wrap it around the soufflé mold so that it rises about 4 to 5 inches above the rim of the dish. Tie it with twine, and then add the soufflé mixture to the mold. Bake as above, and remove the collar before serving.

Cheese Fondue (Cheese Custard)

½ cup dried breadcrumbs
¼ teaspoon paprika
¾ cup boiling water
1 teaspoon dry mustard
1 tablespoon butter
½ cup milk
1 cup sharp cheese, finely diced or shredded
2 egg yolks, lightly beaten
½ teaspoon salt
2 egg whites, beaten stiff but not dry

The term "fondue" in American cookery originally had nothing whatever to do with the typical fondue of the last ten years, which has been adapted from the Swiss. This fondue was essentially an American innovation that might be called a pudding as well.

Combine the breadcrumbs, boiling water, and paprika, and gradually add the other ingredients. Fold in the egg whites, and pour into a buttered 1-quart baking dish. Bake at 350 degrees 25 to 30 minutes, or until brown and puffy, and serve at once.

Cheese Dreams

6 slices white bread or 3 English muffins, split
Butter
6 slices or pieces sharp Cheddar or Munster (American type)
6 slices tomato
Salt and freshly ground pepper
12 slices bacon, partially cooked to remove most of the fat

Still very much fancied, these were musts on tea room menus and were a staple dish to serve evenings when guests dropped in for cards or talk.

Toast the bread, or heat the English muffins, and butter well. Place a slice of cheese on the buttered toast, then add a slice of tomato, seasoned with salt and pepper. Top with two rashers of bacon, crossed. Run under the broiler till the cheese is melted and the bacon crisped. Or, if you prefer, broil without bacon, and add crisp bacon before serving. Serve at once with pickles and radishes, etc. One or two of these makes a portion, depending upon the appetite.

Cheese Croquettes

4 tablespoons butter
5 tablespoons flour
1 cup milk
4 tablespoons cream
1 teaspoon salt
¼ teaspoon cayenne
½ pound sharp cheese, shredded
2 egg yolks, well beaten
Flour
2 eggs, well beaten, mixed with ½ cup milk
Freshly made breadcrumbs

These were very fashionable as an entrée in the early part of this century. Sometimes they were served with a tomato sauce or sometimes with a very piquant sauce — almost a barbecue sauce.

Make a heavy cream sauce: Melt the butter, work in the flour, and cook 3 to 4 minutes to blend well. Stir in the milk and cream, and continue stirring until the mixture is well thickened. Add the salt and cayenne. Then add the cheese, and when it is melted, add the beaten egg yolks. Pour into a 9×9-inch pan to cool.

When ready to make the croquettes, form the mixture with your hands into rolls, pyramids, or cubes. Dip them into flour, then into beaten eggs and milk, and finally roll them in crumbs. Fry in deep fat at 375 degrees, turning once, till nicely browned and crisp. Serve at once with tomato or devil sauce.

Welsh Rabbit

1 tablespoon butter
1 pound sharp Cheddar cheese, shredded
1 cup ale or beer
1 egg, slightly beaten (optional)
½ teaspoon salt
¼ teaspoon Tabasco
1 teaspoon dry mustard

Although it was an English dish when imported to this country, this has become an American chafing dish specialty and a favorite late night snack.

Melt the butter in a chafing dish or upper part of a double boiler, and add the cheese. When the cheese begins to melt, add the beer, stirring in well until nicely thickened. Carefully stir in the egg, if you like, and seasonings. Serve on toast, on English muffins, or over a hamburger on a bun.

Blushing Bunny

1 tablespoon butter
½ pound shredded cheese
1 can tomato soup
1 tablespoon Worcestershire sauce
½ teaspoon mustard
Toast or crackers

This oddly named dish originated in the early part of the century. It is also known as Dinah de Ditty and tomato rarebit. It is not as bad as it may sound and has weathered well through the years.

Melt the butter in a chafing dish or double boiler. Add the cheese, and when it begins to melt, add the tomato soup and Worcestershire sauce. Stir in the mustard, and when properly blended and thick, serve on toast or crackers.

For a cheese pudding to serve as a savory or light entrée, see page 727.

Fish and Shellfish

In earlier centuries this country was blessed as few countries have been with a wealth of fish, in staggering quantity and variety. Unfortunately progress and pollution, which seem to be fellow travelers, have taken their toll. And so have foreign fishing fleets, operating just outside our territorial limits. Certain of our greatest catches, now scarce in our own waters, have to be bought from other countries.

It is hard to believe that lobster of startling size once so abounded around Cape Cod that people apologized for serving it to guests. Nowadays our supply seems to grow shorter each year, and we depend on Canada for a good percentage of it — a deplorable lack of a shellfish unique in the world and, for many tastes, by far the finest of all lobsters. Salmon once flourished around New England waters and was traditionally, for the Fourth of July, served boiled, with egg sauce, new green peas, and the very first new potatoes. It is now completel gone. West Coast salmon is fast disappearing, and the end of that wonderful fish is now predicted. I can remember when Astoria at the mouth of the Columbia was the center of the salmon industry, a city on piers, with canneries and nets and fishing boats strung along the waterfront as far as the eye could see. We could go to a cannery, ask one of the Chinese foremen for fifty cents' worth of salmon cheeks, and return in an hour to collect a huge measure of this delicacy. Alas, all this has changed.

Shad, native to the East and transplanted to Western rivers, is also on the critical list because of pollution — the taste of Hudson shad at this point is a mixture of crude oil and filth. Our superb varieties of fish in the Great Lakes region seem to have all but vanished — the perch, lake trout, and whitefish — and to think that the lakes once harbored sturgeon from which caviar was procured, not as fine as the Persian or Russian, but nonetheless caviar.

It must be said that there have been some conservation efforts to protect and increase the supply of fish. Trout farms flourish in many states, and trout are planted in streams and lakes. Catfish are planted also. Striped bass are protected on the West Coast, and many other fish are under strict surveillance. As a result, we still have a heritage of fish to be thankful for. Some are not equaled anywhere in the world. Certainly the great West Coast Chinook salmon, while it lasts, is peer of all. The pompano of the Gulf is found only in those waters, and is unlike any other fish. Our striped bass is the equal of the bar in France, and our lake trout compares more than favorably with the Omble Chevalier of Europe. Our catfish and whitefish and wall-eyed pike are all superb, though they have gone unappreciated over the centuries.

Oddly enough, a few of our most prized shellfish also went unappreciated in earlier times. Of crab, Miss Leslie writes in the 1857 edition of her cookery book that they "are seldom eaten except at the seashore, where there is a certainty of their being fresh from the water. They are very abundant, but so little is in them that when better things are to be had, they are scarcely worth the trouble of boiling and picking out the shell." Today we pay five dollars a pound for the finest lump crabmeat.

So it was with shrimp. The same valuable source, Miss Leslie, says: "At good tables they are only used as sauce for large fish, squeezed out of the shell, and stirred into melted butter." On the other hand, some items have declined in favor. Turtle used to be extremely popular on the East Coast not only for soup but for pies and stews. And, of course, the classic terrapin was America's answer to caviar. Up to World War II I knew of families who kept a constant supply of terrapin in the refrigerator, ready to be reheated at the command of the head of the household.

Another practice no longer seen, which flourished during the nineteenth century in the Middle West, was the storing of barrels of oysters, sent inland during the winter months. The mollusc was enjoyed in quantity both raw and cooked, the reason for so many oyster recipes throughout that section of the country. Salt fish used to be consumed more widely in the East and Northwest than it is today. Salt mackerel was a standard breakfast dish, and in the West salmon tips, salmon bellies, and salt salmon were once common dishes. At present, cod and herring are the only fish that are readily available salted.

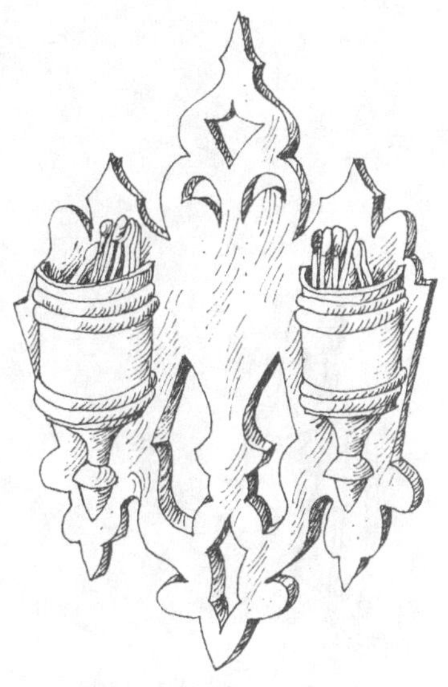

Fish has always played an important part in our celebrations — clambakes in New England; the cioppino in California, originally a communal dish cooked on the beaches; fish fries in the South. And in the Acadian country splendid crawfish feasts are often sponsored by the volunteer fire departments. Many other regional events center around fish runs. Herring runs in New England, when the fish tear upstream and practically overrun the banks, provide a chance to fish and gossip. Grunion runs on the West Coast, when the grunions come ashore to dig holes in the sand for their eggs, attract thousands of people. The smelt runs in the Sandy River match the herring runs of the New England coast for sheer excitement, as people line the shores with orange crates, baskets, billowing skirts — anything to scoop up the millions of fish.

Considering our bounty of fish, it is surprising we did not learn how to prepare it properly until the twentieth century. Until then it was generally overcooked, and whitefish was cooked with a good deal of fat. Many fish were fried in crumbs or cornmeal till crisp, which entirely ruined the texture and flavor. It remained for Evelene Spencer, who worked for the Federal Bureau of Fisheries and afterward taught at the University of Washington, to revolutionize, in the 1920's, fish cookery in this country. It was she who discovered the quick high heat methods that have become part of our fish cookery. One still finds Spencer methods set forth in various publications. More recently, the Japanese have added their touch, too. Many Americans have become fans of sushi, the service of finely cut raw fish.

It is a pity that enlightenment on preparing fish should come when our supply is diminishing. More than ever we should enjoy its delights.

Fish

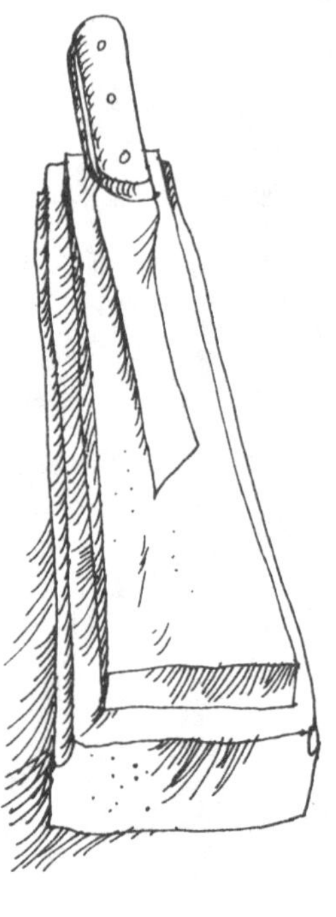

Shopping for Fish

Whole fish. The fish should be mild in odor (one must learn to distinguish a healthy fish smell from the strong smell of stale fish); the eyes clear and bright; the gills free of slime and usually bright red; the scales lustrous; the flesh firm but elastic to the touch.

Fillets and steaks. Again, the fish should smell fresh. It should also look freshly cut, with no sign of dryness or discoloring, and be firm but elastic to the touch.

Frozen fish. Look for packages that are solidly frozen and tightly wrapped, with little or no air space between fish and packaging. The flesh should be firm, glossy, and free of dryness, discoloration, or freezer burns.

Quantities to buy. Naturally one cannot establish a standard serving, but these quantities will provide fairly generous portions. *Whole or roundfish*: not dressed, a pound per serving; dressed and drawn, 3/4 pound per serving. *Pan-dressed fish,* with head and tail removed, cleaned: a pound will serve two. *Steaks*: 1/2 to 3/4 pound per serving. *Fillets*: a pound will serve 2 or 3, depending upon appetites.

Storing Fish

Fresh fish should be used as soon as possible. Wash it, wrap it in wax paper, and keep in the refrigerator until ready to use.

It is best to keep frozen fish solidly frozen in an unopened package at a −10 degree temperature. Do not store more than 2 or 3 months. Frozen fish is best cooked in its frozen state to retain its juices, unless it is to be stuffed. If it must be thawed, do so at refrigerator temperature. Cook as soon as it has thawed. Do not refreeze it, or it will lose its flavor and texture.

Cleaning and Dressing Fish

Most fish we find in the markets is already cleaned and dressed. Your fish dealer will fillet a fish, cut it into steaks and bone it for you. However, if you are an angler, you will be faced with scaling and cleaning your own catch, unless you have a friendly fish man who will do it. Here is the method:

(1) *Scaling.* Place the fish on a table, holding it firmly by the head with one hand. In the other hand hold a sharp knife or fish scaler, and starting from the tail, scrape toward the head, taking off the scales. Be sure to remove all scales around the fins and the base of

the head. Wet fish can be scaled more easily than dry, so you can simplify this job by soaking the fish in cold water a few minutes before you begin work.

(2) *Cleaning.* With a sharp knife, slit the belly of the fish the full length from the vent (anal opening) to the head. Remove the intestines. Next, cut around the pelvic fins (on the underside toward the head) and pull them off, being careful not to tear the fish. Take off the head by cutting above the collarbone, and also remove the pectoral fins (on either side just back of the gills). If the backbone is too large to cut through, cut to it on each side of the fish; then place the fish so the head hangs over the edge of the table and snap the backbone by bending the head down. Cut any remaining flesh that holds the head to the body.

Cut off the tail. Next remove the dorsal fin (on the back of the fish). Cut along each side of it and give a quick pull forward toward the head to remove the fin and its root bones. Take out the ventral fins (at the back on the underside) in the same way. Do not take fins off with shears, for simply trimming them will not remove the little bones at the base.

Wash the fish in cold running water to free it of any membranes and viscera. It is now dressed and ready for cooking. Large fish may, of course, be cut crosswise into steaks.

(3) *Filleting.* With a sharp knife, cut along the back of the fish from the tail to the head. Next, cut down to the backbone just back of the head on one side of the fish. Then, laying the knife flat, cut the flesh down one whole side, slicing it away from the ribs and backbone. Lift the whole side off in one piece. Turn the fish over and repeat on the other side.

Cooking Time for Fish

The Canadian Department of Fisheries has worked out what I believe is the most dependable and most revolutionary rule for fish cookery. It is an evolution of Evelene Spencer's method, and several years of experience with it have made me fully confident that it is foolproof. It is as simple as this: measure the thickness of the fish at its thickest point, and estimate 10 minutes cooking time per inch, whatever the cooking method. Thus, if you are poaching a whole salmon that measures 4 inches at its thickest point, you will poach it 40 minutes. If a fillet is half an inch thick you will sauté or poach it 5 minutes. To broil a steak of salmon or halibut 1½ inches thick, allow 7½ minutes a side.

For frozen fish, double the cooking time.

Broiled Fish Steaks

Fish steaks take wonderfully to broiling.

Place the fish on the rack of the broiling pan, brushing both the fish and rack with olive oil or melted butter. Broil fresh fish about 4 inches from the heat unit, frozen fish 5 to 6 inches. Estimate 10 minutes cooking time per inch of maximum thickness (see page 123), and for frozen fish twice the time.

Most whole fish and steaks should be turned after half the cooking time has elapsed. Brush the other side with oil or melted butter, and season with salt and freshly ground pepper. Continue broiling for the allotted time. When done, transfer to hot plates or a platter, garnish with sprigs of parsley or watercress, and serve with wedges of lemon or lime.

Broiled Salmon Steaks

2 salmon steaks 1 inch thick
6 tablespoons melted butter
2 teaspoons lemon juice
Salt and freshly ground pepper
Watercress or parsley

This and the following fish steak recipes may be used for preparing and broiling any fish steak, as well as the one specified in each recipe.

When I was living in Oregon, I recall, fresh Chinook salmon was brought to the house the afternoon it was caught, sliced into rather thick steaks, and broiled for dinner. Sometimes it was served with a dill butter and sometimes a Béarnaise sauce. It is surely one of the great fish dishes of the world, and it is eaten in this fashion wherever salmon occurs. New potatoes, dressed with parsley butter, and peas are excellent accompaniments; and for drinking, serve a beer or a rather robust white wine, such as a Meursault, or a vigorous Muscadet.

Rub the grill or broiling rack well with oil. Brush the salmon steaks well with melted butter and lemon juice. Place them on the rack of a broiling pan or on a hinged grill and broil about 4 inches from the broiling unit, allowing a total of 10 minutes. Turn after 5 minutes and brush with the butter-lemon mixture. Sprinkle with salt and pepper to taste. Continue broiling for the second 5 minutes. Transfer to hot plates or a platter, and serve with dill butter or Béarnaise sauce. Garnish with watercress or parsley.

Peppered Swordfish Steaks

2 swordfish steaks 1½ to 2 inches thick
1½ tablespoons coarsely crushed pepper
1 to 2 teaspoons salt
Olive oil
Freshly chopped parsley

With the heel of the hand, press the crushed pepper into the flesh of the steaks. Salt to taste. Brush well with oil and broil about 4 inches from the broiling unit for a total of 15 to 20 minutes (10 minutes per inch of thickness). Turn the steaks once during cooking and brush lightly with oil. When done, place on a hot platter and garnish with chopped parsley. Serve with tiny new potatoes and a crisp romaine salad.

Grilled Garlic-Flavored Halibut Steaks

2 halibut steaks about 1 inch thick

MARINADE

1 large or 2 small cloves garlic, finely chopped
6 tablespoons olive oil
1 teaspoon dried basil
1½ teaspoons salt
1 teaspoon freshly ground pepper
1 tablespoon lemon or lime juice
Chopped parsley

Combine the ingredients for the marinade and marinate the steaks 2 hours. Place on a well-oiled rack in a broiling pan or on a hinged grill. Broil 5 minutes on each side about 4 inches from the broiling unit, brushing with the remaining marinade. Serve at once on hot plates with crisp fried zucchini and boiled potatoes. Garnish with chopped parsley.

Broiled Swordfish Steaks

1 or 2 swordfish steaks 1½ inches thick

MARINADE

¼ cup soy sauce
2 garlic cloves, finely chopped
¼ cup olive oil
1 tablespoon finely chopped fresh ginger
1 tablespoon grated orange peel
¼ cup sherry or Madeira

Combine the marinade ingredients and marinate the fish 1 hour, turning several times. Place the steaks on an oiled rack in a broiling pan and broil about 4 inches from the heat unit for a total of about 15 minutes. Turn once during the cooking and brush well with the marinade. Serve on a hot platter with mounds of rice. Pour the remaining marinade over the steaks.

Broiled Cod Steaks

4 cod steaks about 1 inch thick
Salt

BASTING MIXTURE

½ cup melted butter
2 tablespoons grated onion
2 tablespoons lemon or lime juice
¼ cup chili sauce
1 teaspoon dried tarragon
1 teaspoon paprika
2 tablespoons chopped parsley

Rub the steaks well with salt. Combine the remaining ingredients and brush the mixture on one side of each steak. Place the steaks on a well-oiled broiler rack and broil about 4 inches from the broiler unit 5 minutes. Turn, brush well with the butter mixture, and broil another 5 minutes, basting once more during the cooking period. Transfer to a hot platter. Serve with tiny boiled new potatoes and chopped buttered spinach, and if you like, drink a pleasant Pinot Blanc.

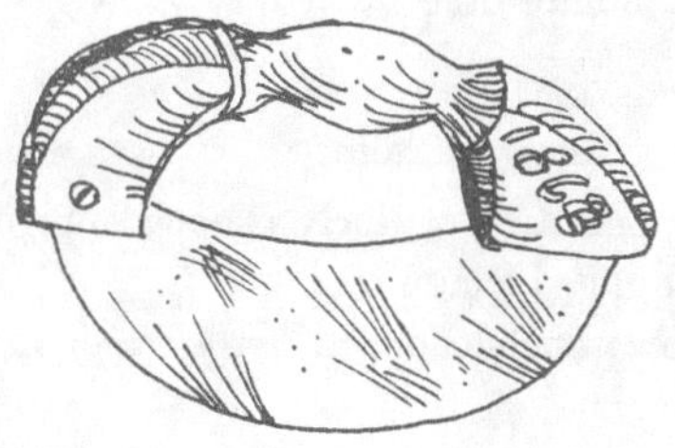

Broiled Fillets of Fish

2 pounds fish fillets
BASIC BASTING MIXTURE
½ cup melted butter or oil or a mixture of both
1 teaspoon salt
¼ teaspoon freshly ground pepper
2 tablespoons lemon juice

Filleting was one of the arts of the kitchen in the eighteenth and nineteenth centuries, and even later, I remember, many women kept filleting knives — usually a good knife worn down to filleting size by continued sharpening. They could fillet a whole fish or a piece of cod or salmon deftly and quickly. Sometimes skin was left on one side, and sometimes it was removed entirely.

Fillets are now universally available, either frozen or fresh, and the technique of filleting is largely a lost art, except behind the fish counter. (However, if you are faced with filleting a fish, see page 123.) One can buy fillets of such fish as cod, haddock, flounder, rex sole, dabs, salmon (usually the tail piece), rockfish, whiting, plaice, striped bass, sea bass, and shad. One can also buy just "fillets" — which means any of a variety of fish. Often it is wise to cut fillets into serving-size pieces and to trim the edges before cooking.

Even as far back as Mrs. Lincoln and the early Miss Farmer, various cooks have recommended the use of a hinged grill for cooking fish. Several different ones are available for this purpose, but the smaller the mesh, the more easily the delicate fish can be handled. Fillets are quite tender when broiled, and great care should be taken to avoid breaking them when removing from the grill. Firm sharp-edged spatulas or long-bladed professional turners are ideal for the purpose. If fillets are quite thin it is often more desirable to broil them on one side only, and if they are put on buttered or oiled foil for broiling, they can be easily transferred to plates or a platter.

Place the fillets on a well-buttered or oiled rack (or foil) and brush with the basting mixture. Broil anywhere from 2 to 4 inches from the broiler unit. For cooking time, estimate 10 minutes per inch of maximum thickness, although it is best to undercook a bit if the fillets are thin at one end and thicker at the other. If they are thick enough, turn after half the cooking time and brush again. If too thin to turn, baste. When done, transfer the fillets carefully to hot plates or a platter, pour over them any of the basting mixture left in the pan, and garnish with chopped parsley or watercress. Serve with wedges of lemon or lime.

Variations

Add to the basic basting mixture:

(1) One tablespoon each of finely chopped onion and parsley, and a teaspoon of grated lemon rind.

(2) A garlic clove, finely chopped, and 1 teaspoon crushed dried tarragon.

(3) A tablespoon each of tomato paste or chili sauce, chopped onion, chopped parsley, and Worcestershire, and ¼ teaspoon Tabasco.

(4) Three tablespoons dry white wine, 1 teaspoon crushed dried tarragon, 1 tablespoon chopped parsley, and 2 tablespoons chopped chives.

(5) Two tablespoons soy sauce, ¼ teaspoon dry ginger, and 1 tablespoon grated orange rind.

(6) Use the basic mixture, and after broiling several minutes, sprinkle the fillets with sliced buttered and toasted almonds.

Broiled Whole Fish

Broiling whole fish, either tiny ones or those of fairly good size, produces as satisfactory a fish dish as one can imagine, excelled, perhaps, only by a poached whole fish. The skin is crisp, sometimes enhanced by the subtleties of herbs, and the meat is tender and juicy.

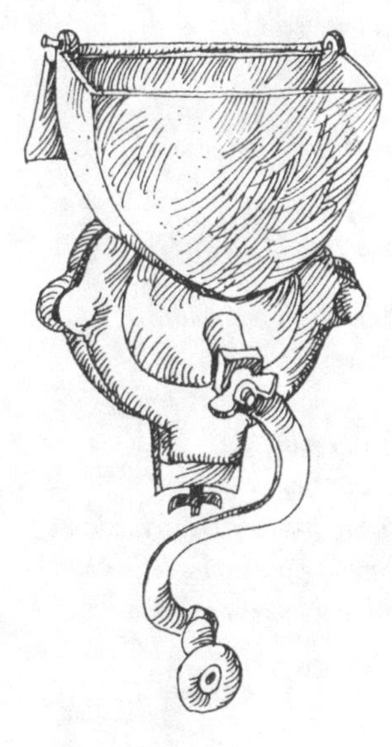

Naturally the size of your grill or broiling oven will guide you in choosing a fish of appropriate dimensions. The fish should be scaled and gutted, and although the head and tail are usually left intact, of course remove them if the fish proves too large for your cooking facilities.

Oil the fish well on both sides and rub with salt and freshly ground pepper. Slash the skin in two or three places with a sharp knife. Stuff with herbs if you like, or rub crushed or chopped herbs on the skin. Fennel, thyme, rosemary, and summer savory are suitable.

Oil the broiler rack or grill well, or a hinged grill, which is considerably easier for handling a whole fish. Measure the fish at the thickest part. Place on the rack and broil, turning once, allowing exactly 10 minutes per inch of maximum thickness. Broil large fish 4 to 6 inches from the heat unit, and smaller fish 2 to 4 inches away. Be very careful not to overcook. When done, transfer to a hot platter and serve at once with any of various fish sauces, such as mustard sauce, Béarnaise sauce, barbecue sauce, Hollandaise sauce, caper sauce, or sweet and sour sauce.

Flambéed Fish

This elegant way of treating fish was introduced into this country by French settlers. Our striped bass closely resembles the Mediterranean loup de mer of the original dish and is frequently used as a substitute.

Broil the fish whole, as above, and place on a hot platter on a bed of dried wild fennel. (This grows along the roads in many parts of the country.) Pour warmed Cognac around the fish and ignite. Traditionally, the flames are beaten out with a bunch of parsley. The burning fennel sends a heavenly smell through the air and flavors the skin, which is crisp and delicious, as well as the flesh. If you don't have fennel, you may use fennel seeds or thyme branches, rosemary, sage, or oregano.

Other fish which may be broiled whole and flavored in the same manner are sea trout, mountain trout, lake trout, crappies, whitefish, sablefish, red snapper, sea bass, flounder, rex sole, smelts, redfish, mackerel, butterfish, and bluefish.

Sturgeon Kebabs

3 pounds sturgeon in one piece
Oil
Salt and freshly ground pepper
Sesame seeds (optional)

Remove the skin from the sturgeon and cut the fish into 1½ to 2 inch cubes. Skewer the cubes, keeping them about ½ inch apart. Three or four cubes is an ample serving. When ready to broil, brush the cubes well with oil and salt and pepper them to taste. Broil about 4 inches from the heat unit (or coals) about 5 minutes. Turn, brushing again with oil, and broil another 5 to 6 minutes. If you like, dip the fish into sesame seeds and return to the broiler 2 to 3 minutes to brown the seeds. Excellent with sautéed potatoes and asparagus or crisp snow peas.

Pan-Fried Fish

Fish, about 2 pounds
1½ teaspoons salt
½ teaspoon Tabasco
½ cup milk
½ cup flour
¾ cup fine dry breadcrumbs or freshly made blender crumbs
Oil and butter or clarified butter

Pan-frying used to be one of the more popular methods of preparing small fish, fillets, or steaks, and has a long history in American cookery. However, when fish is cooked in this manner special care must be taken to keep it from drying out. Unfortunately, the mania for having fish "golden brown" has frequently resulted in disregard for texture. There are times, therefore, when you will have to choose between toothsomeness and what many consider eye appeal.

In former days fish was customarily fried in bacon fat or rendered salt pork or lard. Often it was rolled in cornmeal beforehand, especially trout — a favorite way for fishermen to cook their catch, accompanied by a few rashers of bacon. Despite what some snobbish critics may say, this makes a tasty dish. Bacon fat is still excellent for pan-frying fish, but the use of oil, butter, or vegetable fat is more common today. Clarified butter is ideal for this purpose, since it doesn't burn and gives a delicious flavor to the fish. Butter and oil in equal proportions is next best, providing the flavor of butter while the oil prevents burning. Olive oil or any other vegetable oil may be used successfully as well.

Combine the salt, Tabasco, and milk in a soup plate or shallow pan. Dip the fish in the milk, roll in flour, dip in milk again, and roll in breadcrumbs. You may also roll the fish in cornmeal after it has been dipped in milk the second time, which will give a nice crunchy finish. Heat oil and butter or clarified butter in a heavy skillet to a depth of about ¼ inch. When the fat is hot but not smoking, cook the fish quickly till nicely browned on both sides, turning once, allowing 10 minutes per inch of thickness measured at the thickest point. Serve piping hot on hot plates. Lemon wedges and tartar sauce go well with this.

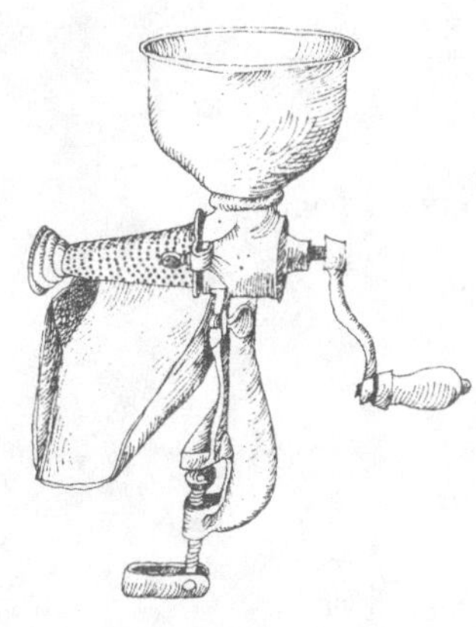

Pan-Fried Fillets. Cut the fish into serving-size pieces, and handle them carefully. Time as above. The cooked fish should be a delicate brown on both sides. Drain lightly on absorbent paper and serve at once on hot plates with tartar sauce or a very spicy tomato sauce. A good coleslaw is a welcome addition.

Variations

(1) Add 1 teaspoon tarragon to the milk.

(2) Use cornmeal instead of crumbs.

(3) Instead of milk, use tomato juice seasoned with Tabasco, Worcestershire sauce, and lemon juice.

(4) Add finely grated garlic to the milk.

(5) Mix grated Parmesan cheese with crumbs in equal parts.

(6) Substitute finely chopped nuts for the crumbs. Almonds or peanuts are the best choices for this.

Pan-Fried Smelts

2 pounds smelts
1 large or 2 medium eggs
3 tablespoons cream or milk
1½ teaspoons salt
½ teaspoon Tabasco
1½ cups breadcrumbs
6 tablespoons clarified butter or 3 tablespoons each butter and oil

Clean the smelts, removing the heads and tails if you prefer. However, they look better on a dish if they are left intact. Beat the eggs and combine with the cream or milk, salt, and Tabasco. Dip the smelts into this blend and then into breadcrumbs. Heat the fat in a large heavy skillet. If the skillet is not large enough, you may have to cook the smelts in two batches. If so, wipe out the pan and add additional fat before cooking the second batch. Cook the fish till lightly brown on both sides, taking care you do not overcook them. Smelts are delicately meated fish, and it is better to sacrifice color than to cook them dry. Serve with a dill sauce or tartar sauce.

Other fish that can be cooked in this way are trout, butterfish, perch, pickerel, crappies, porgies, sea squab or blowfish, and catfish.

Sautéed Fillets of Pompano

People rave about the elaborate dishes of pompano en papillote served in New Orleans, in Florida, and in many fancy restaurants elsewhere. However, this excellent fish, declared by many to be the finest in American waters, is at its best when sautéed simply as it has been done at the Four Seasons in New York.

Either fillet the fish yourself or have the fishmonger do it, allowing 1 pompano per person — thus 2 fillets of rather small size. Dip the fillets in milk and then in flour, and proceed as for Sauté Meunière, below. Serve very hot with lemon wedges and tiny boiled potatoes.

Forget all the fancier treatments, which smother the delicacy of the fish.

Sauté Meunière

This French term began to turn up in manuscript cookbooks during the last century after M. Pierre Blot toured around the country giving demonstration cooking classes. Mrs. Rorer used it and so did Miss Farmer (it's lacking in Mrs. Lincoln's cookbook), and it has found steady usage in cookery books and on menus ever since.

There is no simpler way of preparing fish — especially small whole fish such as trout, butterfish, sand dabs, sole, and flounder. Clarified butter is ideal for the fat; otherwise use a mixture of equal parts of butter and oil.

Use a weighty skillet. Heavy-duty aluminum Teflon-lined pans are excellent, and so are old-fashioned iron pans, including the oval French iron pans designed for fish cookery. A 10-inch skillet will take 3 trout or 2 sole or flounder of medium size; a 12-inch skillet will take 4 to 5 trout or 3 to 4 flatfish, such as sole, flounder, or plaice.

For a 10-inch skillet you will need 6 tablespoons butter or 3 each of butter and oil; for a 12-inch skillet, 8 tablespoons butter or 4 each oil and butter. Allow an additional 2 tablespoons butter, 1 tablespoon lemon juice, and 2 to 3 tablespoons chopped parsley for the finishing process. Naturally salt and pepper to taste are in order, but I think the lemon juice suffices for this delicately cooked fish.

Heat the butter or butter and oil in the skillet. Dip the fish in milk and then in flour, or merely flour them. Sauté in the hot — but not burning — fat till delicately browned, turning once. Time according to the rule of 10 minutes cooking time per inch of maximum thickness — the average small fish (sole, trout, butterfish) will take about 3 to 5 minutes on each side. Be certain not to overcook. Transfer to a hot platter. Add a little more butter to the pan along with some lemon juice and chopped parsley. Swirl around in the pan for a minute, then pour over the fish. Garnish with parsley and lemon wedges. This is best accompanied by boiled potatoes, with perhaps asparagus or a salad to follow. Also serve a rather brisk white wine.

Walnut-Breaded Sole

6 fillets of lemon sole or flounder
Flour
2 eggs, slightly beaten, mixed with 2 tablespoons cream
1 cup breadcrumbs
1½ cups coarsely chopped black walnuts or English walnuts
Butter and oil — about 3 tablespoons of each
Salt and pepper
Lemon wedges

Flour the fillets. Dip into the beaten eggs and cream, then into the crumbs and nuts. Sauté quickly in the oil and butter until delicately browned on both sides. Salt and pepper to taste. Serve with lemon wedges. Boiled potatoes, a cucumber salad, and a good Alsatian Riesling are delicious with this unusual dish.

Mackerel in Escabeche

6 to 8 mackerel
Flour
4 tablespoons butter
4 tablespoons oil
Salt and pepper
½ cup lime juice
½ cup orange juice
½ cup olive oil
1 onion, finely chopped
2 peeled green chilies, finely chopped
2 cloves garlic, crushed
Fresh chopped coriander (cilantro or Chinese parsley) if available, or chopped parsley

In the Southwest, and particularly in California, where there is such a wealth of fish, many old Mexican and Spanish dishes have remained in vogue. This delicious escabeche is typical of some of them, and a thoroughly good dish for summer or for the hors d'oeuvre table at any time.

Flour the fish lightly and sauté in the butter and oil until golden brown on both sides. The average mackerel will take about 3 to 4 minutes on each side, according to the thickness of the fish. When done, salt and pepper to taste and transfer to absorbent paper to drain. In the meantime combine the fruit juices, oil, onion, chilies, and garlic. Arrange the mackerel in a serving dish and add the sauce. Cool, then chill for 24 hours. Sprinkle with chopped coriander or parsley before serving.

Deep-Fried Fish

In America, this is the most typical way of preparing fish, which also partly accounts for its lack of popularity for many years. One was often — and still is — served fish so heavily breaded, and fried so long in deep fat, that it resembled a board dipped in sawdust. Restaurant cooks outside the main cities — and some in the cities — are prone to overcook fish anyway. However, modern equipment and thermometers to gauge the heat of the fat have helped the deep-frying process enormously, and those who must have deep-fried

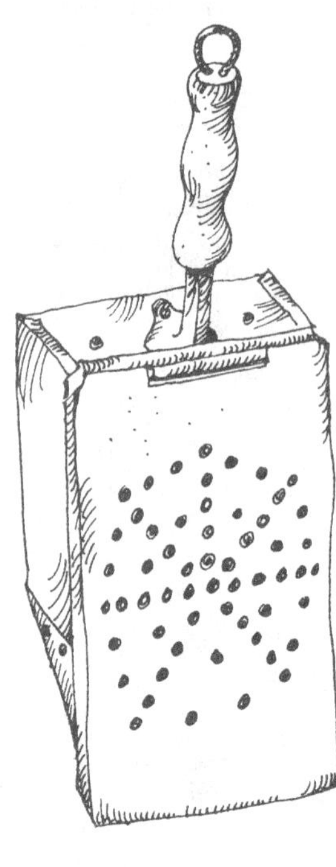

fish can now have it scientifically produced to the point where it is more attractive and more palatable.

Boiling lard was used most often for frying fish in the early days of the country. One cook warns that the lard must be "deep enough to float the fish lest the fish be soggy and soft." Modern methods have proved vegetable oil or a solidified vegetable fat to be best for frying fish. Peanut oil and corn oil are both very satisfactory.

If you are using fillets, cut them to uniform size. If they are very thick, make tiny slits in the sides to enable the fish to cook more evenly. Sprinkle the fish with salt, then prepare for frying in any of the following ways:

(1) Dip in flour, then milk, then crumbs.
(2) Dip in milk, then flour.
(3) Dip in milk, then flour, then beaten egg, and finally crumbs.
(4) Dip in flour, then a batter (see below).
(5) Dip in flour, then beaten egg, then finely chopped nuts — almonds, peanuts, and walnuts are best for this.

Place a single layer of fish in a frying basket. (The greatest fault of deep-frying is overcrowding.) Fry the fish at 375 degrees about 3 to 4 minutes till nicely brown. Transfer to absorbent paper and keep warm while you cook the next batch. Be certain to reheat the fat to 375 degrees before adding more fish. This is very important. If the fat is not hot enough, the fish will absorb it.

When the fish is done, transfer from the absorbent paper to hot plates or a platter. Garnish, if you like, with parsley or watercress. Serve with a sauce — tartar sauce, mustard sauce, rémoulade sauce, lemon butter, parsley butter, and dill butter all are excellent with deep-fried fish.

Note. Shellfish, fish cakes, and croquettes can be cooked in the same way.

Batters for Deep-Frying

Each of these will make enough batter to coat 2 pounds of fish for frying.

Lemon Batter

1 egg
3/4 cup water
1 1/2 tablespoons lemon juice
1 cup flour
1 teaspoon baking powder

Beat the egg well till it is light, add the water and lemon juice, and blend well. Stir in the dry ingredients and mix lightly.

A Tender Batter

1½ cups flour
1 tablespoon baking powder
1 teaspoon salt
2 eggs
¼ teaspoon Tabasco
1 cup milk

Sift the dry ingredients together. Beat the eggs well, and mix with the Tabasco and milk. Combine with the dry ingredients and stir until smooth.

Crisp Batter

1 cup flour
1 teaspoon baking powder
1½ teaspoons salt
1 tablespoon salad oil
1 cup stale beer
½ teaspoon Tabasco

Blend and sift the dry ingredients. Make a well in the center and pour in the liquids, stirring the while until smooth.

Tempura Batter

2 eggs
1 tablespoon peanut oil or other oil
1 tablespoon soy sauce
¾ cup beer, preferably stale
1 cup cornstarch, sifted
1 teaspoon dry mustard or ginger

In the last twenty years the American palate has taken to Japanese food, and one of the specialties of that cuisine, tempura, has become a national favorite. Shrimp and other fish take to this treatment delightfully.

Separate the eggs. Beat the yolks with the oil, soy sauce, and beer. Combine the cornstarch and mustard or ginger. Blend well with beaten yolk mixture. Beat the whites till they are stiff but not dry. Fold into the yolk mixture.

Fried Catfish

A traditional fish dish in the Middle West, catfish is hardly known in the coastal regions of the country. It is tremendously good if properly done and is superb at fish fries. Frying is the usual method of preparation. For all methods of preparation, the fish must be skinned before it is cooked. To skin it, draw a very sharp knife around the fish just in back of the gills. Strip off the skin by hand or with tweezers. It can, of course, be bought already skinned and dressed. Choose cleaned and skinned catfish of similar size, or use pieces of fish.

To fry, dip in milk and then roll in crumbs or cornmeal. Fry in about an inch of fat till nicely brown on both sides.

To deep-fry, heat the fat in your deep fryer to 375 degrees. Beat 2 eggs lightly. Roll out cracker crumbs or breadcrumbs or use cornmeal. Dip the fish in flour, then in beaten egg, and roll in the crumbs. Fry 3 to 5 minutes, depending on the size of the fish. Drain and season to taste. Serve with tartar sauce.

Poached Fish

Poaching in water or a court bouillon is one of the prized fashions of cooking fish. In old cookery books this process was always referred to as "boiling," but poaching or keeping the liquid just under the boil at a faint bubbling is really what was meant. Mrs. Mary Henderson in her *Practical Cooking and Dinner Giving* has this to say about it:

"Among professional cooks, a favorite way of boiling a fish is in water saturated with vegetables, called *court bouillon*; consequently, a fish cooked in this manner would be called, for instance, 'Pike, *au court bouillon*.' It is rather a pity this way of cooking has a French name; however, if one is not unduly scared at that, one can see how simple it is.

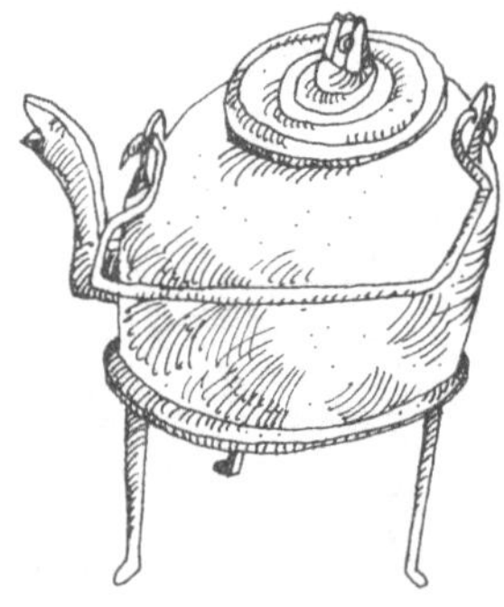

"Mince a carrot, an onion, and a small piece of celery; fry them in a little butter, in a stewpan; add some parsley, some peppercorns, and three or four cloves. Now pour on two quarts of hot water and a pint of vinegar. Let it boil a quarter of an hour; skim it, salt it, and use it for boiling the fish.

"It is improved by using white or red wine instead of vinegar; only use then three parts of wine to one of water. These stocks are easily preserved, and may be used several times.

"To boil the fish: Rub the fish with lemon juice and salt, put it in a kettle, and cover it with *court bouillon*. Let it only simmer, not boil hard, until thoroughly done. Serve the fish on a napkin, surrounded with parsley. Serve a caper, pickle, or any kind of fish sauce, in a sauceboat."

Fish boilers are available for cooking whole fish or parts of fish. They are equipped with a rack, are extremely simple to use, and if you do a good deal of fish cookery they will be a godsend. In lieu of a rack, one can wrap the fish in cheesecloth, leaving loose lengths at each end or at each side to serve as handles. If the fish is placed on a wide band of aluminum foil, this too will enable one to turn the fish and to lift it more easily. If lacking a fish boiler, a baking pan, oval skillet, or even an oval dishpan will do handsomely. It is important for the fish to be covered by the bouillon. If not, you must turn the fish and baste it with a large bulb baster.

The court bouillon should be simmered a half hour before adding the fish. Allow the bouillon to return to the simmering point and poach 10 minutes per inch of thickness, measured at the thickest part of the fish.

Remove the cooked fish from the bouillon as soon as it is done. If it is to be served hot, keep it in a warm place on a hot platter while you make the sauce. If it is to be served cold, allow it to cool to room temperature. Serve with a béchamel or velouté made with fish stock, a parsley or egg sauce, or Hollandaise.

Note. Fish can also be poached delicately in milk, a treatment which especially suits smoked fish.

A Simple Court Bouillon

½ cup white or red wine
½ cup vinegar
1 tablespoon salt
1 rib celery
1 onion stuck with 2 cloves
1 carrot, thinly sliced
1 teaspoon thyme
8 or 9 peppercorns
1 bay leaf
2 or 3 sprigs parsley
6 cups boiling water

This quantity may be doubled or tripled as needed. It is not the richest of court bouillons, but it is quite adequate for most cookery.

Combine all ingredients in fish boiler or pan. Cover and simmer 15 minutes.

Fish Stock. A court bouillon in which fish has been cooked is the fish stock called for in some recipes; the bouillon must be reduced, strained, and clarified. If you don't have it, canned or bottled clam juice will serve as a substitute.

A Fine Court Bouillon for Fish Aspics

1 pound fish heads and tails or a small bony fish
6 cups water
2 cups white wine
1 teaspoon thyme
1 leek
1 onion stuck with 2 cloves
1 carrot, diced
2 cloves garlic
1 bay leaf
Salt
Peppercorns or freshly ground pepper

This will accommodate a striped bass, a small salmon, or lake trout. For larger fish double the recipe.

Cook the fish heads and tails in water 30 minutes or more. Strain through cheesecloth and add to the remaining ingredients. Bring to a boil and simmer 20 minutes. Add whatever fish is to be poached. When done, remove the fish, cook the bouillon down for a few minutes, till it is reduced enough for your recipe, and strain.

Fish Aspic. Reduce the strained stock to about 3 cups; then clarify: Add 3 slightly beaten egg whites. Stir vigorously with a wire whisk over high heat till the mixture comes to a boil. Let it rest off the heat several minutes, then strain through a linen napkin or towel. Measure the clarified stock and use 1 tablespoon gelatine for each pint of liquid. Soften the gelatine in a little cooled stock, stir into the hot stock, and chill until it has thickened enough for you to use in molding or coating.

Mrs. Simeon Reed's Spiced Salmon

"Boil three pounds of fresh salmon in water. Then put to boil one pint of vinegar, two tablespoons melted butter, two tablespoonfuls whole allspice, two tablespoons mixed mustard, one teaspoonful salt, one quarter teaspoon cayenne pepper. Let the above mixture boil for ten minutes, then pour hot over the fish. Set away to cool for twelve hours before using. Serve cold."

Cold Trout with Dill Sauce

6 to 8 trout
Court bouillon
Dill, parsley, and chives, finely chopped
Cucumber and hard-boiled egg, sliced

DILL SAUCE

1 ½ cups sour cream
1 tablespoon fresh dill
1 teaspoon grated onion
1 teaspoon dry mustard
½ cup finely chopped hard-boiled egg
Salt and freshly ground pepper to taste

Poach the trout in court bouillon 5 minutes, or until they are just cooked through. Chill thoroughly. Remove part of the skin from the top of the trout, leaving the heads and tails intact. Sprinkle with the chopped herbs. Arrange alternate slices of the cucumber and egg on each fish. Serve with the sauce.

Cold Poached Salmon Steaks

Court bouillon
6 small or 3 large salmon steaks (halve the large ones for cooking and serving) about 1 inch thick
Watercress or lettuce leaves
Lemon slices
Mayonnaise

Prepare a court bouillon in a fish cooker, deep skillet, or kettle large enough to accommodate all the steaks at one time. If you must use a smaller pan, cook three at a time, using the same court bouillon.

Arrange the salmon on a rack that can be lowered into the bouillon. Failing that, arrange on a piece of cheesecloth or foil with ends protruding from the pot so they can be used to lift the fish out with the aid of a spatula. Lower the fish into the hot court bouillon, allow it to come to the boiling point, and immediately turn the heat to simmer or slightly below. Poach the fish for a bit less than the standard rule of 10 minutes per inch of maximum thickness. Remove from the bouillon and allow to cool. Arrange attractively on a serving dish and chill till serving time. Garnish with greens and lemon slices, and serve with a good mayonnaise. Cucumber salad and hot rolls would be excellent accompaniments, and a dry white wine would make the meal really festive.

Smoked Fish Fillets Poached in Milk

2 pounds smoked fish fillets
Milk
4 tablespoons butter
Chopped parsley
½ teaspoon freshly ground pepper

This is a delicious Sunday breakfast or lunch dish for four persons.

Place the fillets in a heavy skillet and add milk to barely cover. Put a lid on the skillet, and poach the fish until it is just cooked through, allowing about 10 minutes per inch of maximum thickness. Remove to a hot platter, dot with butter, and sprinkle with chopped parsley and pepper. Serve with tiny boiled potatoes and scrambled eggs.

Sweet and Sour Salmon

4 to 6 salmon steaks, 1 inch thick
2 cups water
1 cup vinegar
1 cup brown sugar
3 or 4 cloves
1 onion, thinly sliced
Salt and freshly ground pepper
1 cup sultana raisins
6 to 8 lemon slices
12 to 14 gingersnaps, crumbled

A superb traditional Jewish recipe which has been used for many kinds of fish but is at its best with salmon. This was Mrs. Leon Hirsch's recipe and has been handed down for three generations.

Cut the salmon steaks in half lengthwise. Combine the water, vinegar, sugar, cloves, and onion. Bring to a boil in a deep skillet or oval fish dish and add the fish. Poach about 10 minutes. Transfer to a serving platter. Add the raisins to the bouillon and cook down 4 or 5 minutes or until reduced by one-third. Add gingersnaps and stir till thickened. Pour over the salmon. Serve either warm or cold.

Note. Sherry (½ cup) may be added along with the raisins.

Blue Trout

Travelers to Switzerland and France, fishermen among them, have brought back with them a love for this extremely simple dish. Those who fish in trout streams find it is no more difficult to prepare on the scene than pan-fried trout, and besides, it is a much more delicate dish. It can be done at home if you have a trout tank. Few of us do.

Take live trout, gut them quickly, and plunge into a boiling bath composed of 3 parts water to 1 part vinegar and seasoned with a little salt and a few peppercorns. Simmer the trout just long enough to cook them through — about 4 or 5 minutes. Remove from the liquid and eat with butter and salt and pepper. Boiled potatoes are an excellent companion to this classic dish.

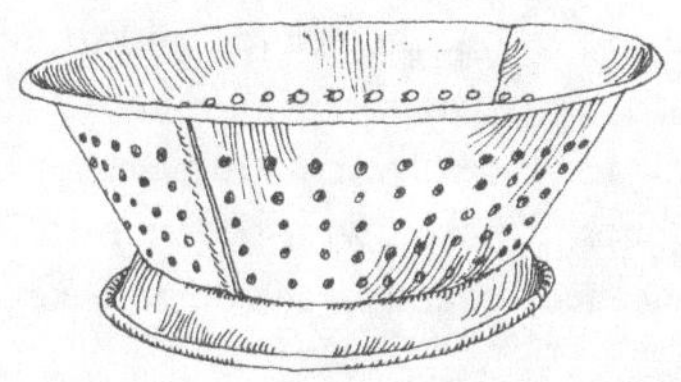

Steamed Fish

Whole fish or fillets may be delicately steamed in a basket or colander over boiling water. This is an excellent way to prepare fish for salads when the flavor of a court bouillon is not suitable. It is also superb cookery for an invalid's diet or for other special diets.

Salt the fish and wrap in cheesecloth, leaving long enough ends to hang outside the pot to use for handles. Place in a colander or on a rack over rapidly boiling water. The water must not touch the fish. Cover tightly and steam, allowing 10 minutes cooking time per inch of maximum thickness. Remove, and either serve hot with parsley butter or cool and use in a fish salad.

Sweet and Sour Carp

1 carp, 4 to 5 pounds, cleaned and scaled
¾ cup pineapple juice
½ cup wine vinegar
½ cup sugar
½ cup water
3 tablespoons cornstarch
1 tablespoon soy sauce
½ cup each of green onion, green pepper, and pineapple, cut in thin slivers

A recipe with a Chinese background that I remember being prepared by Let, our Chinese cook.

Place the fish, wrapped in cheesecloth, on a rack over hot water so that the fish does not touch the water. Cover, and steam until it is firm — about 25 minutes or so. Arrange on a serving dish. Cook together the pineapple juice, vinegar, sugar, and water. Thicken with cornstarch, and season with soy sauce. Add the slivered green onion, green pepper, and pineapple, and cook these in the sauce just long enough for the onions and pepper to turn bright green. Serve over the fish.

Braised Fish

This is an especially good way to prepare delicately flavored and textured fish. You will need a fairly large, thick piece for best results, either a whole fish of about 3 to 4 pounds or a thick steak cut of 4 to 5 inches.

On the bottom of a saucepan, fish cooker, braising pan, or Dutch oven, put a layer of chopped or sliced carrot, celery, and onion. If you like, melt butter in the pan first, and sauté the vegetables a few minutes. Also, if you like, add chopped garlic, herbs, or other seasonings. Place the fish on the bed of vegetables, sprinkle with salt and a few grinds of pepper, and lay on it a strip or two of bacon or salt pork, or dot it generously with butter. Pour into the pan enough liquid — wine, fish stock, water, or a combination — to half cover the fish. Bring it just to a boil, then cover, and simmer very gently (or bake in a 350-degree oven) about 25 minutes, or until the fish is done. Remove the fish carefully to a hot platter. Strain the liquid, and reduce to 1½ cups. Thicken with beurre manié (small balls of butter and flour kneaded together), season to taste, and serve as a sauce with the fish.

Braised Halibut with White Wine

4 to 5 pound halibut steak
2 medium onions, thinly sliced
2 stalks celery cut in thin strips
1 carrot cut in thin strips
3 sprigs parsley
1 leek, well cleaned and cut in strips

Place the sliced onions, celery, carrot, parsley sprigs, and leek in the bottom of a fish cooker or a braising pan with the butter, and let simmer over a medium flame until the onions are wilted. Rub the halibut with about 2 teaspoons salt and with pepper, and place it on the bed of vegetables. Add wine to half the depth of the fish, then add the thyme and bay leaf and let it just come to a boil. Cover the fish with a piece of well-buttered parchment or brown paper and place in a 425-degree oven. Cook about 20 to 25 minutes, or until the fish is just barely cooked through. While the fish is cooking, brown the onions in half the additional butter and let them cook through in a covered pan with the addition of a little white wine. Sprinkle them lightly with granulated sugar and shake the pan well while they caramelize a bit. Sauté the mushrooms lightly in the remaining butter and season to taste. They and the onions should be ready when the fish is done. Remove the fish from the pan and arrange on a hot platter, surrounded by the mushrooms and the onions. Strain the sauce and thicken it with beurre manié. Taste for seasoning and correct it. Serve the sauce separately, and garnish the fish with chopped parsley. Plain boiled potatoes and white wine go extremely well with this.

5 tablespoons butter
Salt and freshly ground pepper
Red or white wine, preferably white
1 teaspoon thyme
1 bay leaf
18 small white onions
6 tablespoons additional butter
Granulated sugar
1 pound mushrooms
Beurre manié
Chopped parsley

Braised Sturgeon, Sweet and Sour

Sturgeon (a 4-pound piece)
2 pieces barding pork
3 carrots, finely chopped or sliced
3 medium onions, finely chopped
2 ribs celery cut in thin strips
1 leek
1 bay leaf
1 teaspoon thyme
1 tablespoon salt
2 cups white wine

SAUCE

¼ cup vinegar
½ cup brown sugar
2 tablespoons soy sauce
2 tablespoons cornstarch mixed with a little water
⅔ cup preserved pineapple chunks
½ cup shredded green pepper
⅓ cup sliced preserved ginger
(OR use 1½ to 2 cups Chinese mixed pickle — available in many Chinese groceries — instead of pineapple, green pepper, and ginger)

This has Chinese overtones, and is one of the finest sturgeon dishes I have ever had. It is a West Coast recipe from Astoria.

Bard the sturgeon and tie it firmly. Place the cut vegetables on the bottom of a heavy braising pan or Dutch oven. Arrange a rack in the pan, and on this place the sturgeon. Add the leek, herbs, salt, and wine. Bake in a 375-degree oven, allowing 10 minutes per inch of thickness, measured at the thickest point. Transfer the fish to a hot platter, remove the barding pork, and carefully remove the skin. Keep the fish warm while you prepare the sauce.

Strain off the juice from the pan, pressing the vegetables well. Pour into a saucepan and reduce by about one-third over a brisk flame. Stir in the vinegar, sugar, and soy, and continue to stir until well blended. Taste for seasoning and for sweet-sour balance. Stir in the cornstarch, and continue stirring until the mixture thickens and becomes rather translucent. Add the pineapple, pepper, and ginger, and just heat through. Spoon over the fish and serve with rice. Follow with a good salad.

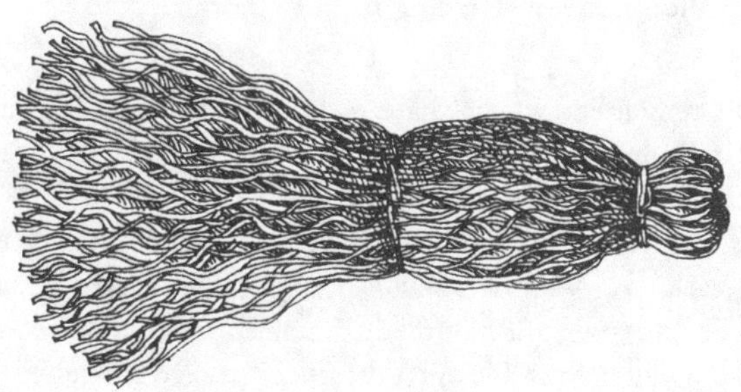

Baked Fish

If you are baking a whole fish, remove the scales, fins, and viscera, or have the fish dealer prepare it for you. The fish is more attractive when served with the head and tail intact. If the fish is to be stuffed, remove the backbone. Use any of various types of stuffing — forcemeat, nuts and crumbs, or vegetable stuffing. Clip the sides together, tie firmly with twine, or sew up the sides. Oil the fish well, and place in an ovenproof serving dish or on buttered foil in a baking pan. Bake at 450 degrees, allowing 10 minutes per inch measured at its thickest part. Garnish with parsley or watercress and serve with wedges of lemon or lime.

Baked Fish Fillets. Cut into serving-size pieces, if you like. Brush with the basic basting mixture under broiled fillets (see page 126) and baste once or twice during cooking.

Baked Crumbed Fillets. Dip the fillets in milk seasoned with Tabasco and salt (1/4 teaspoon Tabasco and 1 teaspoon salt to 1/2 cup milk) and then roll in crumbs. Arrange in a buttered baking dish and dot generously with butter. Bake approximately 10 minutes. Serve with lemon slices, sautéed potatoes, and perhaps tiny new peas.

Stuffed Baked Striped Bass

A striped bass about 5 pounds, with backbone removed
1 cup finely cut green onions
6 tablespoons butter
1 teaspoon salt
1/2 teaspoon Tabasco
1 tablespoon dried tarragon
3 cups soft breadcrumbs (blender-made crumbs are ideal)
Butter
Salt and freshly ground pepper
Lemon slices
Watercress or parsley

Sauté the onions in the butter till just limp. Do not let them brown. Add the salt, Tabasco, and tarragon, and blend well. If the mixture seems to have absorbed all the butter, add a spoonful or two more. Blend with the crumbs. Stuff the fish lightly — do not press into the fish. Either close the opening with small skewers and tie with twine, or sew up the opening. Butter the fish well and place on a piece of buttered foil in a baking pan or on a buttered rack in a baking dish or pan. Salt and pepper the fish and bake at 450 degrees, allowing 10 minutes per inch of thickness measured at the thickest point. When cooked, transfer to a hot platter, remove the skewers and twine, and decorate the fish with lemon slices. Garnish with watercress or parsley and serve at once. Steamed cucumbers dressed with butter make a perfect accompaniment. For wine, serve Muscadet or a Johannisberg Riesling from California.

My Favorite Baked Striped Bass

1 striped bass or other fish, about 5 pounds, with backbone removed
1 large or 2 medium onions, thinly sliced
1 green pepper, seeded and sliced

I can't remember when I haven't known this dish. It is utterly simple, refreshing, and delicate. The recipe can also be used for other kinds of fish.

Stuff the fish with alternating layers of the sliced vegetables, dotting each layer with butter and sprinkling with chopped parsley. Salt and pepper well. Secure the fish with skewers or leave as it is; the stuffing will not tumble out if the fish is handled carefully. Butter the fish well, salt and pepper it, and place on a piece of buttered foil in a baking pan. Bake in a 450-degree oven, allowing 10 minutes per inch measured at the thickest part of the fish. It will take 30 to 35 minutes. Transfer to a hot platter and remove the skewers. Decorate with lemon wedges and watercress, and surround with tiny boiled potatoes.

4 or 5 ripe tomatoes, thinly sliced
½ cup chopped parsley
Butter
1½ teaspoons salt
½ teaspoon or more freshly ground pepper
Thinly sliced lemons

Baked Stuffed Whitefish

1 whitefish, 4 to 5 pounds
6 rather thick onion slices
3 tablespoons butter
6 rather thick slices ripe tomato
6 good-size mushrooms, sliced
1 tablespoon fresh dill, finely chopped, or 1 teaspoon dillweed
4 or 5 sprigs parsley
Salt and freshly ground pepper
Additional butter or oil
Tomato sauce

Sauté the onion slices lightly in the butter till delicately brown. Turn them carefully with a spatula so that they remain whole. Prepare the fish for stuffing. You may choose to remove the backbone completely. Stuff with the onion slices, tomato slices, mushrooms, fresh dill or dillweed, and parsley. Salt and pepper it well. Secure with skewers and twine or sew up the opening. Place the fish on a piece of buttered foil in a baking dish or pan and dot with butter or rub well with oil. Salt it lightly. Bake at 450 degrees 30 minutes. Transfer to a hot platter and remove the skewers and twine. Serve with a tomato sauce.

Savory Baked Smelts

4 dozen smelts, cleaned
2 medium onions, thinly sliced
3 garlic cloves, finely chopped
2 small carrots, grated
2 bay leaves
10 peppercorns
1 lemon, thinly sliced
1 tablespoon salt
1 teaspoon paprika
½ teaspoon Tabasco
3 cloves
Small piece cinnamon bark
¾ cup olive oil
¾ cup white wine or vinegar
1 cup water or to cover

A most delicious dish, with a Mediterranean background, which I have enjoyed since I was a child. The smelts make a superb light meal served cold with a simple salad, or they might be served as a first course for dinner.

Smelts differ from region to region of the country. In the West, for example, they are much fatter than in the East. And while they are really a saltwater fish, they have survived their transplanting into the lakes exceedingly well.

In a baking dish from which the smelts can be served, arrange a layer of smelts, a layer of onions, garlic, and carrots, and finally another layer of smelts. Combine all the remaining ingredients. Bring to a boil and simmer 5 minutes. Pour over the smelts and bake at 375 degrees 20 minutes, or until the fish are just cooked. Allow to cool in the bouillon, and chill.

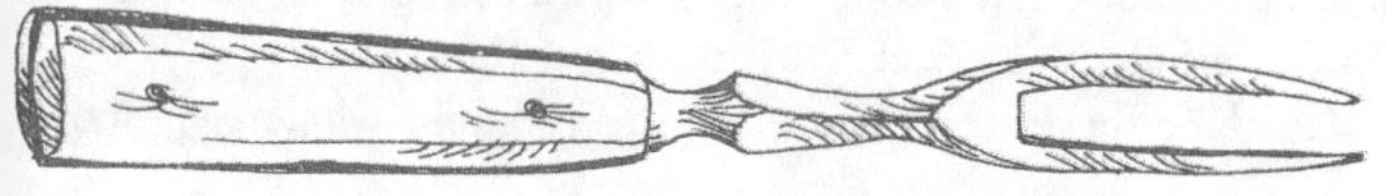

Spanish Mackerel in Papillote

6 pieces aluminum foil
6 Spanish mackerel
Butter
Lemon slices
¼ cup chopped parsley
Salt
Made mustard or Dijon mustard

A famous American ichthyologist named Mitchell, in describing this fish, wrote "A fine and beautiful fish, comes in July." It *is* fine and beautiful, and delicious as well. This is a recipe I remember from the twenties. They didn't use foil then, but to a great extent it has succeeded cooking parchment for this purpose.

Measure the length of the fish. Cut six pieces of foil the same length plus 3 inches. Fold each piece over once and cut so it will form a heart shape when opened. Butter the foil well and on each half place a slice of lemon and a bit of chopped parsley. Salt the mackerel and brush heavily with made mustard (dry mustard mixed with water) or Dijon mustard. Place atop the lemon slices and dot with butter. Fold the other half of the foil over the fish and crimp the edges to seal. Place on a baking sheet. Bake at 450 degrees 18 minutes. Serve in the papillotes.

Miss Leslie's Baked Shad

"Keep the head on and fins. Make a forcemeat of grated bread-crumbs, cold boiled ham or bacon minced fine, sweet marjoram, pepper, salt, and a little powdered mace or cloves. Moisten it well with beaten yolk of egg. Stuff the inside of the fish with it, saving a little to rub over the outside, having first rubbed the fish all over with yolk of egg. Lay in a deep pan, putting the tail in its mouth. Pour into the pan a little water, and add a gill of port wine, and a piece of butter rolled in flour. Bake it well, and when it is done, send it to the table with the gravy poured round it. Garnish with slices of lemon. Any fish may be baked in the same manner."

Salmon Loaf

2 cups flaked salmon, either cold poached fresh salmon or canned
2 cups cooked rice
½ cup milk
3 eggs, beaten
1½ tablespoons minced parsley
1 tablespoon melted butter
1½ teaspoons salt
1 tablespoon lemon juice

Although this dish has been especially well known in the West, it still ranks as a universal favorite. It is an excellent change from standard fish dishes.

Combine all the ingredients, mold into a loaf, and spoon into a well-buttered baking dish. Bake at 375 degrees approximately 40 minutes. Unmold on a hot platter. Serve with a tomato sauce or Hollandaise. A cucumber salad is delightful as an accompaniment — or asparagus, which has a special affinity for salmon.

Note. This recipe is delicious with the addition of 1 teaspoon dillweed or 1½ tablespoons chopped fresh dill.

Codfish Cakes

1½ cups flaked cooked codfish
2 cups hot mashed potatoes, beaten with 3 tablespoons butter

My mother made superb codfish cakes, which she learned how to make from our Chinese cook. They were delicate, thoroughly crusty on the outside, and soft and appealing in texture inside.

Combine the fish, potatoes, and the yolk and whole egg, and

blend thoroughly. Taste for salt, and add to taste, along with the ginger. Form the mixture into round flat cakes. Heat butter in a heavy skillet, and brown the fish cakes on both sides, turning once.

1 yolk and 1 whole egg
1 teaspoon salt, if needed
½ teaspoon ground ginger or more to your taste; or ¼ teaspoon grated fresh ginger
Butter for sautéing

Smoked Fish

Smoked fish is only now gaining substantially in favor throughout the country, although the processes of smoking and kippering fish were known to the American Indians before the white man arrived, and they no doubt taught him this technique of preservation as well as salting and drying.

There are numerous ways of smoking fish. One of the typical ways is cold-smoking over a long period of time, a very mild cure that produces fish which is delicately flavored and moist, with practically no hint of salt. Raw salmon is treated in this way, for example, and makes the very choicest smoked fish. Kippering or hot-smoking is another method, and it results in fish of firmer texture and smokier flavor. Here are the fish in these categories most commonly found (see also Smoked Fish for Appetizers in the chapter on appetizers).

Smoked salmon. The finest in North America are the Chinook and the Nova Scotia because they contain a generous amount of natural oil. They should be cut in paper-thin slices and served as an hors d'oeuvre or as a main course for luncheon, in which case they are generally dressed with oil, lemon juice, freshly ground pepper, and sometimes capers or chopped onions.

Lox. This is smoked salmon also, but is somewhat saltier than the top grades. It can be used in the same way, however. It is often eaten with bagels and cream cheese and is sometimes scrambled with eggs or steamed over potatoes to make a delicious breakfast dish.

Kippered salmon. This is firmer, more cooked, and smokier in flavor than smoked salmon. It is served cold in slices or in salads.

Smoked sturgeon. One of the most delicate of fish unless it is oversmoked, when it becomes dry and dull. Creamy in color, it is a splendid fish to serve thinly sliced for an hors d'oeuvre; or in a sandwich with onion, perhaps, and with thinly sliced cucumber.

Kippered sturgeon. The texture is apt to be quite dry. The flavor, however, is delicate and appealing.

Smoked tuna. Most of the "smoked" tuna one finds is really

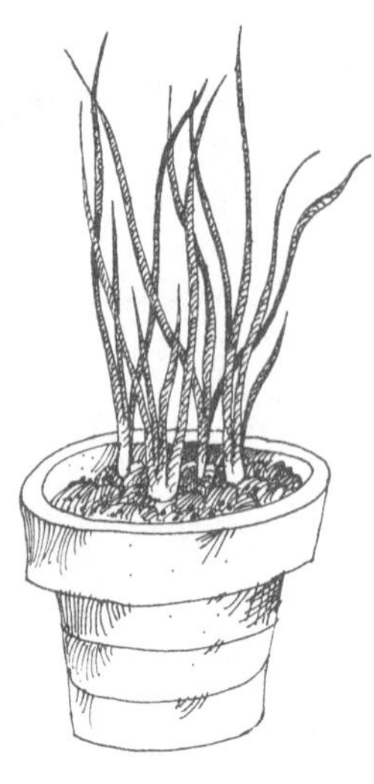

kippered tuna, and as with kippered sturgeon it must be smoked properly to prevent a dry texture. It can have excellent flavor. Serve it cold in a salad or with scrambled eggs.

Smoked whitefish. This is delicate in flavor, light in texture, and one of the more desirable of all the smoked fish. It comes in various sizes and is usually bought whole, except for large fish, which are sold in sections. It is often served on rye bread with onion and capers. It is also served for breakfast as an accompaniment to scrambled eggs and lox.

Kippered sablefish. Called on the West Coast "black cod." Delightful when steamed and served with drawn butter or lemon butter for a breakfast dish. It was one of the specialties of the Palace Hotel in San Francisco until only recently.

Other fish occasionally found smoked are shad, which is quite oily and rich; trout, which is excellent served with a horseradish cream; butterfish, which is small and delicate; and barracuda, which is coarse and rather poor in texture.

Salt Fish

Salt salmon, salmon bellies, salmon tips, mackerel, and other fish — apart from cod — used to be much more generally available than now. Almost all salt fish has to be freshened in water before being cooked. It is usually broiled or poached, and served with butter sauce, herbed butter, or béchamel sauce. It is often flaked and combined with a cream sauce after poaching. At this writing, the only salt fish available in the markets are cod, stockfish, and occasionally mackerel.

Shellfish

Lobster

Boiled Lobster

Bring salted water (about 1 tablespoon salt per quart of water) to a rolling boil in a deep kettle. Use water enough to immerse the lobster thoroughly. When the water is at a rolling boil, plunge the lobster in head first. Cover, return to the boil, then reduce the heat and simmer 5 minutes for the first pound and 3 minutes more for each additional pound. Remove the lobster from the water, place it on its back, and use a heavy knife (with a mallet if necessary) to split it from end to end, starting at the head. Retain the green liver (tomalley) and (in female lobsters) the roe (coral). They are both delicious whether eaten with the lobster or used in a sauce. Crack the large claws so the meat can be taken out at the table. Serve hot with melted butter and lemon wedges, or cold with good homemade mayonnaise, either plain or in one of its variations such as rémoulade sauce or green mayonnaise.

Note. You will need to cook one 1½-pound lobster for each person. Put no more lobsters in the kettle at once than will fit easily on the bottom, and have enough water so the rolling boil is scarcely interrupted, if at all, and the lobsters are well covered with water.

Broiled Lobster

For whatever reason, this has a great reputation in the United States. Have plenty of butter on hand before you start; otherwise the lobster will be dry. A 1½ to 2 pound lobster makes one serving.

If you plan to have the fish dealer split and clean lobsters for you, don't buy them until shortly before cooking time. To split and clean a lobster yourself, first kill it by inserting a sharp knife between the body and tail shells, which cuts the spinal cord. Then, with the lobster on its back, split it as described under boiled lobster, cutting right through the back shell. The stomach and intestinal tract, which runs down the tail section near the back, should come out, but leave the liver (grayish before cooking) and the coral.

Butter each lobster half very well, place on the broiler rack with the cut side up, and broil in a thoroughly preheated broiler 12 to 15 minutes, basting frequently with melted butter. When done, salt and pepper to taste, remove to very hot plates, and serve with more melted butter and lemon wedges.

Lobster Franco-American

For 2 people:
2 lobsters, 1½ to 2 pounds each
⅓ cup olive oil
2 medium onions, finely chopped
2 cloves garlic, finely chopped
1 cup tomato sauce or tomato soup
Salt and freshly ground pepper
¼ cup Cognac
2 tablespoons meat glaze
⅓ cup sherry or Madeira
2 tablespoons additional Cognac
2 tablespoons chopped pimiento

A version of a classic dish, lobster à l'Américaine, and long popular in this country.

Plunge the lobsters into rapidly boiling water for 1 minute, to kill them. Cut in half, and save the liquid inside and the liver and intestines (also the coral, if there is any). Heat the olive oil in an ovenproof pan, then add the onions, garlic, lobster halves, and tomato sauce, and season to taste. Cook gently 4 minutes, then pour in the ¼ cup Cognac and bake, covered, about 18 minutes in a 400-degree oven. Remove the lobster halves to hot plates or a platter, and keep them warm while you make the sauce. Strain the contents of the pan through a fine sieve, then reheat it, adding the rest of the ingredients and the liver, coral if any, intestines, and liquid from the lobsters. Pour the sauce over the lobster. This is traditionally served with rice.

Lobster Fra Diavolo

2 lobsters, 1 to 1½ pounds each
6 tablespoons olive oil
4 tablespoons chopped parsley
1 teaspoon thyme or oregano
1 small onion, chopped fine
1 clove garlic, chopped fine
Pinch of cloves
Pinch of mace
Salt and freshly ground pepper to taste
2 cups cooked tomatoes
¼ cup Cognac, warmed

An Italian version of lobster à l'Américaine.

Kill, split, and clean the lobsters as for broiled lobster above. Heat the olive oil, and cook the lobster halves until the shells are red. Continue cooking gently about 10 minutes, then add the other ingredients except the Cognac. Cover, and continue to cook gently about 15 minutes, stirring frequently. Arrange a ring of rice around a heated serving dish, and put the lobster halves in the center. Pour the sauce over them. Just before serving, pour the warmed Cognac over, and blaze.

Lobster Thermidor

2 lobsters, 2 pounds each
Salt and freshly ground pepper
Olive oil
1 cup dry white wine
1 cup bouillon (fish or meat stock)
2 tablespoons chopped green onion
2 tablespoons chopped fresh tarragon or 2 teaspoons dried
1½ cups béchamel
1½ cups heavy cream, mixed with 4 egg yolks
1 teaspoon dry mustard
Grated Parmesan cheese
Melted butter

Kill, split, and clean the live lobsters as for broiled lobster, above. Sprinkle with salt and pepper, then brush with olive oil and bake at 425 degrees about 18 minutes, basting frequently with additional olive oil. Let the lobster cool enough to handle, and remove the meat from the body and claws, keeping the body shell intact. Dice the meat. Cook the wine, bouillon, green onion, and tarragon together until the mixture is reduced to practically a glaze. Combine this with the béchamel, stir in the cream-yolk mixture, and heat through, but be sure not to boil. Stir in the mustard and taste for seasoning. When the sauce is well thickened, add the lobster meat, heat through, and fill the shells with the mixture. Sprinkle with grated Parmesan cheese, brush with melted butter, and run under the broiler a moment or two to brown.

Lobster Sauté with Curry

1 stick (½ cup) butter
½ cup shredded blanched almonds
2 tablespoons grated onion or shallot
1 pound cooked lobster meat cut into scallops
1 tablespoon chopped parsley
2 teaspoons curry powder
½ cup heavy cream
Salt and freshly ground pepper
Fried toast rounds

Melt the butter in a large skillet, add the almonds and grated onion, and cook and stir 3 to 4 minutes. Add the lobster meat, and toss lightly. Stir in gently the parsley, curry, and cream. Let the mixture come just to a boil, and simmer 3 minutes. Taste for seasoning. Serve on the toast rounds.

Lobster au Gratin

3 cups cooked lobster meat cut into scallops
6 tablespoons butter
¼ cup Cognac
¼ cup white wine
½ cup heavy cream
Hollandaise sauce

Melt the butter. Sauté the lobster meat just long enough to heat it, then pour the Cognac over it and ignite. Add the white wine and cream, and simmer gently 5 minutes. Pour into a buttered heated casserole and top with Hollandaise sauce. Run under the broiler long enough to glaze, and serve with rice.

Lobster Newburg I

1½ cups heavy cream
3 well-beaten egg yolks
Salt, freshly ground pepper, cayenne
3 cups cooked lobster meat
1 tablespoon butter
1 tablespoon sherry

Although this appears in a number of French books, including Montagne and Salles' *Grand Livre de la Cuisine*, it is definitely an American dish. It was originally made for a man named Wenburg, not Newburg, so the story goes. However, no one has, to my knowledge, ever turned up the very first recipe for the dish. One thing that remains consistent in all versions is the use of cream and egg yolks. Beyond that, some recipes call for sherry, others for Madeira, and still others for brandy or Cognac. Whatever the version, it is a delicious dish. This one is from the State of Maine.

Heat the cream over hot water. Remove from the heat and stir in the egg yolks and seasoning to taste. Return to cook over hot water (simmering gently — do not allow it to boil), and stir until the mixture is thick enough to coat the spoon. Add the lobster and continue to cook over hot water 5 minutes or till it is heated through. Add the butter and sherry and cook 1 minute longer. Spoon over toast, into patty shells or into the center of a rice ring.

Lobster Newburg II

2 cups raw lobster meat
5 tablespoons butter
1 teaspoon salt
¼ teaspoon Tabasco
⅓ cup Cognac
1½ cups heavy cream
3 egg yolks

This version seems more authentic to me, since it uses raw lobster meat, as do most French recipes.

Heat the butter in a medium skillet and sauté the lobster with the salt and Tabasco about 4 minutes. Heat the Cognac, ignite, and pour over the lobster. Heat the cream and egg yolks over hot water, stirring constantly till the mixture coats the spoon. Add the sautéed lobster and heat through, being certain the hot water under the mixture does not boil. Correct the seasoning and serve as above.

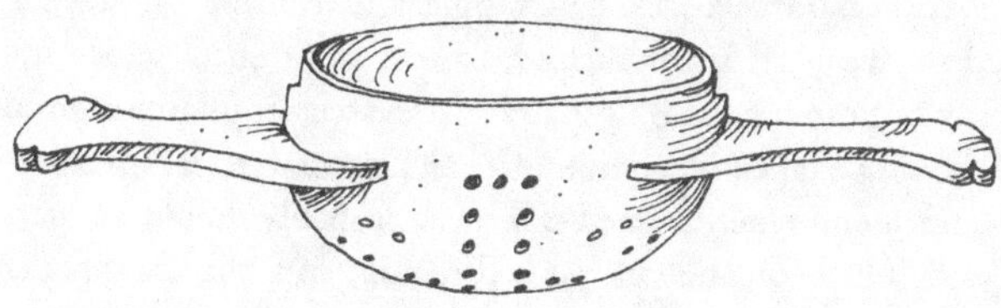

Crab

Crab is probably the most American of all shellfish. It is eaten to some extent in England, where it is properly considered a great delicacy, but in France it is seldom served, and in other countries it is never found in the abundance that we enjoy. Each region of the United States has its own tempting type of crab, and people are quite partisan about which they prefer.

In the West there is the superb Dungeness, with its meaty and delicious claws and the lump crabmeat in the back. Blue crab is found in the Atlantic and in the Gulf, and in addition the Gulf yields buster crabs. Stone crabs, found in Florida, are unique, since only the large claws are used, broken off live crabs, which are returned to the sea to grow new ones. Finally there is the huge Alaskan king crab, sometimes measuring as much as nine feet across. The claws alone are giant in size and can be bought frozen for broiling. The meat is also available in frozen blocks. Meat from this type of crab is not as delicate as that of other varieties, but it is well flavored and lends itself to many crab dishes. Dungeness crabs are flash-frozen and shipped East. Maryland and Florida crabmeat — the backfin lump being the best — is sent to the market refrigerated and is tremendously expensive at this point. Stone crabs are largely served locally in Florida and occasionally reach New York. Blue crabs are found live in the market from time to time along the Atlantic and Gulf Coasts.

Softshell crabs. Softshell crabs are unique to the Southern section of the United States. They are not a distinct species but simply blue crabs that have moulted and not yet grown new shells. The smaller they are, the better. Two or three softshell crabs are sufficient for a serving, although a colossal appetite may require 6 to 8.

One usually buys softshell crabs in the market cleaned and ready for cooking. If not, you are obliged to do it yourself, thus: With a small sharp knife make incisions at the points in the back and remove all the spongy bits you find there. Turn the crab and remove the tiny apron at the front.

Certainly the best possible way to prepare them is by sautéing (see below and pages 150–151).

Canned and frozen crabmeat. Crabmeat is available in the shell, chilled and very often pasteurized, frozen, and tinned, which quite honestly one can use for almost any of these recipes interchangeably. Care should be taken when using frozen king crab to remove bits of bone and membrane. Canned crabmeat probably should be marinated with a little oil and vinegar before using in a salad, and perhaps a little dash of white wine or French vermouth before using in a cooked dish. A tablespoon or two of wine will give a pleasant flavor to the canned fish.

Quantity of crabmeat to buy. One pound of crabmeat will make 3 ample servings or 4 lesser ones.

To sauté crabmeat. Crabmeat is easily ruined by overcooking. People seldom realize that it is ready for eating when bought. It is a delicately fibered shellfish, and excess cooking makes it stringy and tough. To sauté, cook gently in butter until heated through.

Sauces for crabmeat. All too often crabmeat, with its delicate flavor, is served with what Helen Brown long ago labeled in a remarkable article in the *Territorial Enterprise* "the Red Menace" — that standard tomato cocktail sauce which is poured in quantities over all kinds of shellfish. It has the effect of smothering the natural flavors of the crabmeat, which you are left to imagine. A pox on the inventor.

Crabmeat should not be swimming in "the Red Menace." It should be served with a good homemade mayonnaise, a tarragon-flavored vinaigrette, or a good rémoulade. It can also be served with a Thousand Island or Louis dressing, which seems to have a particular affinity for crab.

Cracked Crab with Mayonnaise

Dungeness crab is the only variety served in this manner, usually a half crab per portion. The legs are cracked and the back section cut in slices so the meat can be extracted easily. A good homemade mayonnaise should be served with it. Some people eat the meat as they extract it; others do all the work first.

Crab Soufflé

3 tablespoons butter
1 small onion, finely chopped
3 tablespoons flour
3 tablespoons tomato paste
½ cup cream
1 teaspoon salt
½ teaspoon freshly ground pepper
Dash Tabasco
1 teaspoon tarragon
2 tablespoons Cognac
4 egg yolks
6 egg whites
1 pound crabmeat (leg meat or lump)

Sauté the onion in the butter till soft. Add the flour, stir, and cook a minute or so. Add the tomato paste and cream and stir till smooth. Add the seasonings and cool slightly. Stir in the egg yolks and beat well. Beat the egg whites till firm but not dry, and fold into the mixture. Butter a 1½-quart soufflé dish. Place a layer of crab leg or lump meat on the bottom. Add one-third of the soufflé mixture, then another layer of crab, and finally the remaining soufflé mixture. Bake at 375 degrees approximately 30 to 40 minutes, or until puffy and browned. Serve with a Hollandaise if you like.

Sautéed Crabmeat with Pine Nuts

4 tablespoons butter
1 tablespoon finely chopped onion
1 tablespoon finely chopped parsley
¼ cup sherry
Salt and freshly ground pepper
1 pound crabmeat
⅓ cup pine nuts
Rounds of fried toast
Additional chopped parsley

Heat the butter and sauté the onion 1 minute over medium heat. Add the parsley, sherry, and salt and pepper to taste. Immediately add the crabmeat and pine nuts and just heat through, shaking the pan well. Spoon over rounds of fried toast and serve with additional chopped parsley.

Crabmeat Casanova

6 tablespoons butter
4 small slices French bread cut quite thin
2 tablespoons chopped shallots
1 pound crabmeat
⅓ cup Cognac
1 tablespoon or more grated carrot
½ cup white wine
Salt and freshly ground pepper
¼ cup chopped parsley

This dish was named not for the great lover but for a maître d'hôtel who is a spectacular tableside cook. It was designed for a chafing dish or table stove and is most impressive prepared that way.

Heat the butter over fairly high heat and delicately brown the pieces of bread in the butter, turning once. Transfer to a hot dish. Add the shallots and let them cook just a minute or two to melt them into the butter. Add the crabmeat and toss well. Reduce the heat. Add the warmed Cognac and ignite. Add the carrot, wine, salt and pepper to taste, and parsley. Let the crabmeat just heat through, tossing the mixture lightly to blend well. Correct the seasoning, and spoon the crabmeat over the toast. Serve at once.

Sautéed Crabmeat with Curry and Almonds

¾ cup sliced toasted almonds
2 tablespoons oil
5 tablespoons butter
¼ cup finely chopped onion or green onion
¼ cup finely chopped green pepper
1 tablespoon curry powder
1 teaspoon chili powder
1 pound crabmeat
1 cup heavy cream
1 teaspoon salt
Rice ring
¼ cup chopped parsley

A venerable Western specialty.

Place the almonds on an oiled baking pan or cookie sheet and toast briefly in a 350-degree oven, stirring frequently, till they are lightly browned and crisp. Set aside to cool. Heat the oil and butter in a 9-inch skillet, and when fairly hot add the onion and green pepper. Let them cook several minutes over medium heat. Add the curry powder and chili powder and mix well. When the pepper and onion are somewhat tenderized but not browned, add the crabmeat and toss until merely heated through. Add the cream and salt and let the mixture blend well and cook through. If the crab absorbs too much cream and the mixture looks dry, add more cream. Meanwhile, cook the rice, put into a buttered ring mold, and unmold on a hot platter. Spoon the crab mixture into the center, and top with the chopped parsley and toasted almonds. Serve with chutney and, if you like, bananas baked in their skins.

Herbed Sauté of Crabmeat

5 tablespoons butter
3 tablespoons oil
1 pound crabmeat
½ cup chopped chives
½ cup chopped parsley
½ cup chopped fresh basil or 2 teaspoons dry basil
⅔ cup white wine
1½ teaspoons salt

Heat the butter and oil in a skillet, add the crabmeat and the herbs, and toss well. Add the white wine and salt. Cook till heated through, shaking the pan and tossing the crabmeat lightly. Spoon over rice or fried toasts. Serve with an orange and onion salad.

Note. Tarragon may be substituted for basil and a few thinly sliced toasted almonds added.

A Very Old Southern Recipe for Deviled Crab (Miss Boelling's)

4 tablespoons butter
1 medium onion, finely chopped
4 tablespoons flour
1½ cups fish stock, chicken broth, or clam broth
2 teaspoons salt
½ teaspoon freshly ground pepper
½ teaspoon cayenne
1½ teaspoons mustard
1 tablespoon chopped parsley
1 tablespoon Worcestershire sauce
4 egg yolks
1 pound crabmeat
1 cup breadcrumbs
Butter

Sauté the onion in butter very lightly, and blend in the flour. Cook 3 or 4 minutes, stir in the stock and the seasonings, and continue stirring till the mixture thickens. Simmer several minutes. Beat the egg yolks lightly. Blend a little of the sauce into the eggs and then stir the mixture thoroughly into the rest of the sauce. Fold in the crabmeat and heat till warmed through. Do not let it boil after the egg yolks have been added. Spoon into baking shells or a serving dish, top with crumbs, and dot with butter. Place in a 375-degree oven to glaze and brown the crumbs.

Broiled Softshell Crabs

8 to 12 softshell crabs, depending on size
Flour
1½ teaspoons salt
1 teaspoon paprika
About ½ teaspoon Tabasco
Butter

Dredge the crabs lightly with flour and sprinkle with salt and paprika. Add a few drops of Tabasco to each one and dot well with butter. Place on a broiling rack and broil about 4 inches from the heat unit. They will take about 4 minutes on each side. When you turn them, dot well with butter again and sprinkle lightly with salt and Tabasco. Place on a hot platter and pour the pan juices over them. Serve with a tartar sauce.

Softshell Crabs Sauté

8 to 12 softshell crabs, depending on size
Flour
8 tablespoons (1 stick) butter, and another 2 or 3 tablespoons
3 tablespoons oil
1 ½ teaspoons salt
1 teaspoon freshly ground pepper
2 tablespoons chopped parsley
Lemon slices

You will need a 12 to 14 inch skillet. Dredge the crabs lightly with flour. Heat the butter and oil in the skillet till quite hot. Add the crabs and sauté over moderate heat till they are delicately browned on one side. Turn, and brown on the other side. Salt and pepper to taste. Sprinkle with chopped parsley and transfer to a hot platter. Melt additional butter in the pan — 2 or 3 tablespoons — and pour over the crabs. Garnish with lemon slices. Serve with a mustard or tartar sauce. Also serve crisp shoestring potatoes or chip potatoes and a good Chablis or Muscadet.

Softshell Crabs with Toasted Almonds. Add 1 cup toasted blanched whole or sliced almonds to the skillet to cook in the butter for a moment or two. Spoon over the crabs.

Fried Softshell Crabs

8 to 12 softshell crabs, depending on size
1 cup flour
1 ½ teaspoons salt
1 teaspoon freshly ground pepper
2 eggs beaten lightly and seasoned with 1 teaspoon Tabasco
Breadcrumbs or cracker crumbs

This is probably the way softshell crabs were cooked originally, and no doubt overcooked. They needn't be.

Dredge the crabs well with flour mixed with the salt and pepper. Dip them into the egg mixture and then roll well in crumbs. Fry in deep fat (heated to 375 degrees) just long enough for the crabs to brown nicely. Cook only a few at a time and transfer to absorbent paper on a hot dish to keep warm. Serve with tartar sauce and hash-brown potatoes.

Shrimp

More shrimp are consumed in this country than any other shellfish. Their popularity has never waned, even when much of the country had only canned shrimp. Fortunately, fresh shrimp are available today in profusion, and frozen as well, and there is little need for the canned.

Shrimp have always been plentiful along our coasts, and in many varieties. These include the tiny Pacific shrimp, which are pink and tender and may be eaten by the handful; the sweet tiny shrimp from Maine; the very large, rather gray-green Gulf shrimp; and the Florida shrimp, which are of medium size and quite pink. Shrimp also come to our markets from Spain, Panama, Guatemala, and India, some weighing two and three to a pound and others over a hundred to a pound.

A note is in order here concerning scampi. Despite what most cookbooks and restaurateurs tell you, scampi are not shrimp. They are more closely related to the Dublin Bay prawn or the langoustine. Furthermore, they are not native to our waters, and you are unlikely to have them served to you in any restaurant, unless they have been flown in from Italy, Iceland, or Ireland.

Cooked Shrimp

Shrimp are all too often overcooked and undersalted. Their flavor and appearance are improved if they have been shelled and deveined before cooking, or at least split and deveined, despite the fact that the Shrimp Association says there is no danger in eating shrimp which have not been deveined.

To cook, bring well-salted water to a boil, and add the shrimp. Return to a boil and cook 3 to 4 minutes (ocasionally, very large shrimp may take up to 4 minutes). Remove from the water at once.

Be sure the liquid is well seasoned, for one of the faults of shrimp cooking the country over is the lack of salt or flavor in the finished product. If you are making an aspic or a dish with a sauce, you will probably want to cook the shrimp in a court bouillon (see page 135).

Shrimp Cocktail

In all the country there is no first course as popular as a cocktail of shrimp with a large serving of cocktail sauce. Some restaurants are learning that other sauces for this dish are as good, and gradually some of the restaurant patrons are learning the same thing. For example, one can serve vinaigrette sauce with chopped fresh herbs, herbed mayonnaise, curried mayonnaise, mustard sauce, or dill sauce — all most effective as a complement to the shrimp in a cocktail server or on greens on a plate. If you are entertaining, serve two or three sauces and allow guests to choose for themselves.

For the average shrimp cocktail serve 6 shrimp. If the shrimp are small, serve 8. If you are serving the very tiny Alaska, Maine, or Pacific shrimp, you will want ½ to ⅔ cup of shrimp for each serving. Toast, crackers, or thin rye bread and butter sandwiches are nice to serve with the shrimp cocktails.

Spiced Shrimp

2 to 3 pounds shrimp, medium size, cooked, shelled, and deveined
3 red Italian onions, thinly sliced
2 lemons, thinly sliced
3 bay leaves
¼ cup chopped parsley
1 teaspoon tarragon
Salt and freshly ground pepper to taste
Olive oil

A favorite dish of Liz Lucas in Rochester.

Alternate layers of shrimp, onions, and lemons, together with the various seasonings, in a deep casserole that can be covered. Add enough olive oil to just cover the shrimp, and allow them to marinate 12 to 24 hours. Arrange in a serving dish.

Southern Shrimp Paste

1½ pounds shrimp, cooked, shelled, and deveined
½ cup soft butter
Salt to taste (about 1½ teaspoons)
½ teaspoon freshly ground pepper
1 tablespoon Worcestershire sauce
¼ teaspoon Tabasco
½ teaspoon nutmeg
Breadcrumbs
Additional butter

This dish from the Carolinas resembles the potted shrimp of England, which is where it probably originated. For another version, see shrimp butter (page 12).

Chop the shrimp exceedingly fine or put through a grinder, using a fine blade. Blend with the softened butter and beat thoroughly. Add the seasonings, pack into a 9-inch loaf pan, and press down firmly. Sprinkle with breadcrumbs and dot with additional butter. Bake 12 minutes at 450 degrees. Remove, cool, then chill thoroughly. Cut in thin slices and serve with cocktails, as a first course, or as a buffet dish. Pass green mayonnaise with it, and garnish with chopped parsley.

Barbecued Shrimp

2 pounds shrimp (about 15 to the pound)
1 cup olive oil
1 teaspoon salt
2 cloves garlic, chopped
¼ cup chili sauce
3 tablespoons Worcestershire sauce
½ teaspoon Tabasco
1 teaspoon salt
1 teaspoon basil

Shell and devein the shrimp, leaving the tail shells on. Arrange in a shallow oblong dish approximately 6 × 9 inches. Mix the seasonings well and pour over the shrimp. Toss thoroughly and allow to stand several hours, turning occasionally. To broil over charcoal, string the shrimp on metal or bamboo skewers and invite each person to grill his own over medium coals, or place all the shrimp in a wire grill and broil them over the coals. To broil in a gas or electric broiler, arrange the shrimp on a flat pan and run under the broiler about 4 inches from the heat unit for about 3 to 5 minutes or until the shrimp have turned color and the flesh is tender.

Polynesian Broiled Shrimp

2 pounds large shrimp, shelled and deveined, with tails left on
MARINADE
½ cup peanut oil
1 large garlic clove or 2 small ones, finely chopped
½ cup soy sauce
¼ cup sherry
1 tablespoon grated orange rind
¼ cup finely chopped or grated fresh ginger (or use candied ginger, washing off most of the sugar)
1 teaspoon salt

Always a delight for hors d'oeuvre or for a main course, served with rice, this dish is part of the soy sauce and teriyaki school of cookery, an outgrowth of Japanese cuisine, with a heavy West Coast accent.

Put the shrimp in a deep dish approximately 11 × 14 inches. Combine the rest of the ingredients and pour over the shrimp. Marinate 1½ to 2 hours, turning the shrimp several times. Broil the shrimp in any of three ways: (1) Skewer, allowing space between them, and broil 5 to 6 minutes over coals or in the broiling oven about 4 inches from the heat unit, turning once. For an hors d'oeuvre 3 shrimp to a skewer are enough; for a main course, 6 to 8. (2) Place the shrimp in a wire grill basket and broil 5 to 6 minutes over charcoal or in the broiling oven about 4 inches from the heat unit, turning once and brushing with the marinade. (3) Arrange the shrimp in a broiling pan, pour the marinade over them, and broil

6 to 7 minutes about 6 inches from the heat unit. These need not be turned.

Serve the broiled shrimp with steamed rice and an orange and onion salad.

Butterfly Shrimp

3 pounds large shrimp
Flour
3 eggs, lightly beaten
Cracker crumbs or breadcrumbs
Oil for frying
Salt and freshly ground pepper

These were adopted from the Orientals with added flourishes.

Shell and devein the shrimp, leaving the tails on. With a sharp knife cut each shrimp almost in half lengthwise. Flatten them out on a piece of foil. Heat the oil to 370 degrees. Dip each shrimp in flour, then into beaten egg, and finally press into crumbs. Cook a few at a time in a frying basket. Be certain to let the temperature of the oil return to 370 degrees after each frying. Salt and pepper them and drain on absorbent paper. Serve with a tartar sauce, rémoulade sauce, or tomato sauce.

Shrimp Creole

2 to 2½ pounds shrimp, shelled and deveined
4 tablespoons butter
1 large onion, finely chopped
1 green pepper, finely chopped (optional and not absolutely traditional)
1 cup finely cut celery
1 #2½ can Italian plum tomatoes or 2½ cups stewed fresh tomatoes
1 teaspoon sugar
2 teaspoons salt
2 bay leaves
1 teaspoon thyme
½ teaspoon Tabasco

Although this is an American classic, I feel it does an injustice to shrimp, which in most versions is generally overcooked.

Heat the butter and sauté the onion gently until just wilted and lightly colored. Add the pepper and cook gently several minutes. Add the celery and tomatoes and bring to a boil. Reduce the heat, add the seasonings, and simmer 12 minutes. Correct the seasoning, add the raw shrimp, and simmer 8 minutes longer or until the shrimp are cooked and blended with the sauce. It is obligatory to serve rice with this dish.

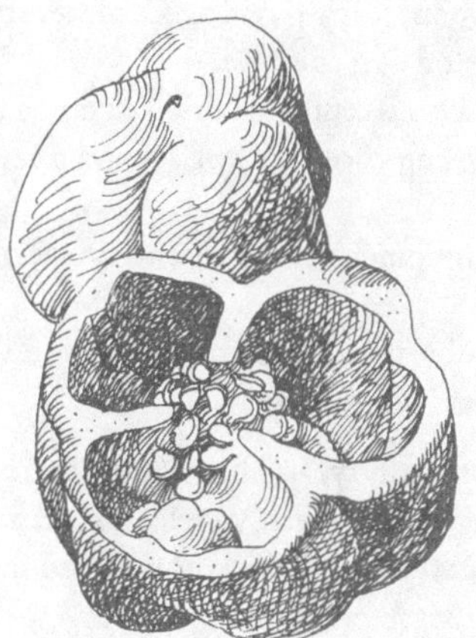

Creamed Shrimp

3 pounds shrimp
Boiling salted water or court bouillon
3 tablespoons butter
3 tablespoons flour
1½ cups shrimp stock
1 teaspoon salt
¼ teaspoon nutmeg
2 egg yolks
½ cup cream
Patty shells, toast points, or rice
Toasted almonds or chopped parsley

This dish has been a perennial favorite through the years for luncheon and late supper parties, even when canned shrimp were the only ones available. And of course it has been a standard item for chafing dish enthusiasts.

Shell and devein the shrimp. Bring salted water or court bouillon to a boil. Plunge the shrimp into the liquid and cook 3 minutes after it returns to the boil. Remove the shrimp as quickly as possible. Add the shells to the liquid and boil it down to use in the sauce. Strain and reserve. When you are nearly ready to serve, melt the butter in a heavy saucepan or in a chafing dish over hot water. Add the flour, blend thoroughly, and simmer a few moments to cook out the raw flour taste. Stir in 1½ cups of the cooking liquid and continue to stir until thickened. Season with the salt and nutmeg. Beat the egg yolks lightly, and combine with the cream. Stir 2 spoonfuls of the sauce into the cream mixture to temper it, then gradually stir back into the hot sauce. Add the shrimp. Stir over low heat till the shrimp have heated through and the sauce is blended. Do not let the sauce boil after adding the egg yolks. Serve with heated patty shells, toast, or rice. Garnish with toasted almonds or chopped parsley.

Variations

(1) Add 1 teaspoon paprika and ¼ cup Madeira or sherry to the sauce, and let it blend well for the alcohol to cook out before adding the shrimp.

(2) Add 1 tablespoon tomato paste and ¼ cup dry white wine to the sauce.

(3) Add 2 tablespoons grated onion to the butter–flour mixture, then add 1 tablespoon curry powder. Cook several minutes before adding the cream and egg mixture.

(4) Add 1½ teaspoons crumbled dried tarragon to the sauce. Then add the shrimp, ¼ cup chopped parsley, and a few drops of lemon juice.

(5) Add a healthy pinch of saffron and 2 tablespoons Cognac to the sauce.

(6) Add 1 teaspoon mustard and 1 teaspoon dillweed or 1 tablespoon chopped fresh dill to the sauce.

Shrimp Wiggle. For many years this was in the repertoire of every coed with a chafing dish and every girl who had a beau to cook for. Add tiny French peas (petits pois) to the creamed shrimp in whatever quantity you like. Serve on toast.

Curried Shrimp with Pilaff

1 cup clam or other fish broth
3 tablespoons cream
2 pounds shrimp, shelled and deveined
1 teaspoon curry powder
2 green cooking apples, grated
2 tablespoons butter
1 tablespoon flour
Salt and freshly ground pepper
½ cup heavy cream
3 egg yolks
Dash Tabasco

Combine ½ cup broth and the cream in a large kettle. Add the shrimp, curry powder, and grated apple. Cover, and steam over medium heat till shrimp are cooked — about 8 minutes. Shake the pan vigorously from time to time. Melt the butter in a small saucepan, add the flour, and blend. Cook for a few minutes. Stir in the rest of the broth and continue to stir until thickened. Season to taste. Remove from the heat. Mix the heavy cream and egg yolks together. Add a couple of spoonfuls of sauce to temper the mixture, then stir back into the sauce. Continue to stir over medium heat till just thickened. Do not boil. Stir sauce into the shrimp. Serve with rice pilaff and chutney.

Baked Shrimp

2 pounds (approximately 30) shrimp
3 shallots, finely chopped
4 to 5 sprigs parsley, finely chopped
1 clove garlic, finely chopped
1½ sticks (¾ cup) butter
1 teaspoon Worcestershire sauce
½ teaspoon Tabasco
½ teaspoon salt
2 tablespoons sherry
Croutons ⅛ to ¼ inch square

Blend the shallots, parsley, and garlic with the butter. Add the Worcestershire sauce, Tabasco, salt, and sherry, and cream very briskly. Shell the shrimp, leaving the tails on. Plunge in boiling salted water and cook for 3 minutes after it returns to the boil. Arrange the shrimp (tails up) in buttered ramekins or small soufflé cups, 5 or 6 to a serving. Add a spoonful or two of the seasoning mixture, another dash of sherry, and the tiny croutons, which have been browned in the oven very lightly or sautéed in butter until crisp and delicately brown. Dot with a tiny bit more of the seasoned butter and bake at 400 degrees until the butter is melted and the shrimp are heated through. Garnish with a small amount of chopped parsley, and serve very hot.

Oysters

As late as thirty years ago there was as great a selection of oysters in our waters as one could find anywhere in the world. Some came very close to being as magnificent as the Galway Bays, the Belons, and other oysters from France and England. Alas, pollution has smothered much of our oyster crop, and the starfish and other sea pests have been even more destructive. It is criminal that our sea resources have been allowed to dwindle in this manner.

Despite the hazards, there are still fine oysters to be had, and some of the larger cities are lucky enough to get many varieties flown in. The Quilcenes and the fabulous Olympias from the Pacific Coast, the Malpecques from Canadian waters, the Chincoteagues, the

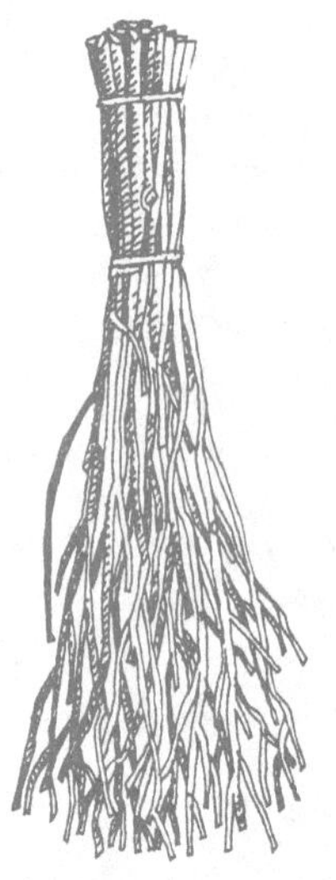

Bluepoints, and the Cotuits from the Eastern seaboard, and the Gulf oysters are all available.

Oysters vary in size, flavor, saltiness, and texture. Even oysters from the same small bay can be entirely different if they come from different beds. If you are not familiar with the oysters in your area, ask the advice of your fish dealer, or try the various kinds available and decide which you like best. Like clams, they are sold shucked by the pint or quart or in the shell or on the half shell.

The American Indians ate quantities of oysters, as mounds of shells at various sites along our coasts testify. They also probably roasted them in the coals, as people are still wont to do. As they heat through, the shells begin to open. This is the moment to force the top shell off with an oyster knife and treat the oysters with melted butter, a sauce of your own choosing, or merely lemon and a little Tabasco. With plenty of bread and butter and an assortment of relishes one can devour untold numbers in this way. As a matter of fact, we have become pretty dainty in our appetites. Our forefathers thought nothing of eating several dozen oysters just as an appetizer. To most people nowadays, six seem a great deal.

In the nineteenth century, when railroads pushed through the hinterland, oysters went along with progress. It is amazing to read in cookery books and memoirs of the period about the quantities of oysters which were shipped to homes in the Middle West and central states. Many people had them sent every two weeks, and others stocked them for holidays and special occasions. There were many instances of barrels of oysters being kept in the coolth of the springhouse or barn and meted out for various and sundry occasions. Some memoirs boast of oyster stew every Sunday night and others of proper oyster feasts during the season. It is reasonable to believe that oysters have been one of the greatest of delicacies throughout the country for over a hundred years.

Some uses for oysters which are delicious and unusual:

(1) When you make a beefsteak and kidney pie, add 12 oysters that have been poached in their own liquor or in a little beef or chicken stock.

(2) Oysters added to your favorite chicken pie recipe will give it an exciting new flavor and texture.

(3) Crisp fried oysters or poached oysters are delicious combined with a broiled steak. Time was when a "pocketbook" or "carpet-bag" steak meant a thick fillet of beef cut with a pocket to be filled, just before serving, with fried oysters.

(4) Of course you know that oysters can enhance your favorite stuffing. Try them with a stuffing of bread crumbs, butter, onions, and loads of tarragon.

(5) For a sensational soup, serve double chicken consommé boiling hot with one or two oysters placed in each cup. The same can be done with beef consommé.

(6) Combine a few oysters with a blanquette of veal or veal fricassee.

Oysters on the Half Shell

At their best, oysters are eaten on the half shell with nothing to enhance them except lemon, a bit of grated fresh horseradish, or a mignonette pepper sauce. If you do not like the natural flavor of oysters, and find that you must cover them with quantities of red cocktail sauce, then perhaps you shouldn't be eating them.

Use 6 or 12 or 18 oysters for a serving, depending on appetites. Serve on a plate with crushed ice, and with some sort of dark bread — rye, whole wheat, or pumpernickel — and butter. Beer, ale or stout, or a dry white wine would be an excellent accompaniment.

Miniature Oysters

6 lemons
3 dozen small Eastern oysters, or 10 dozen Kissling or Olympia West Coast oysters
2 tablespoons finely chopped fresh herbs (chives, tarragon, green onions, shallots)
2 tablespoons lemon juice
Salt and freshly ground pepper (coarse grind)
¾ cup heavy cream sauce
Sauce mousseline (Hollandaise folded with whipped cream)

Cut the tops from the lemons and scoop out the interiors, carefully removing all pulp. Balance the lemon shells in muffin cups or custard cups. Poach the oysters in their own liquor just until the edges curl. Set them aside and strain the juice. To the juice add the herbs, lemon juice, salt and coarse pepper to taste, and the heavy cream sauce. Bring to a boil and mix with the oysters. Spoon the mixture into the lemon shells and mask each with the sauce mousseline. Glaze under broiler.

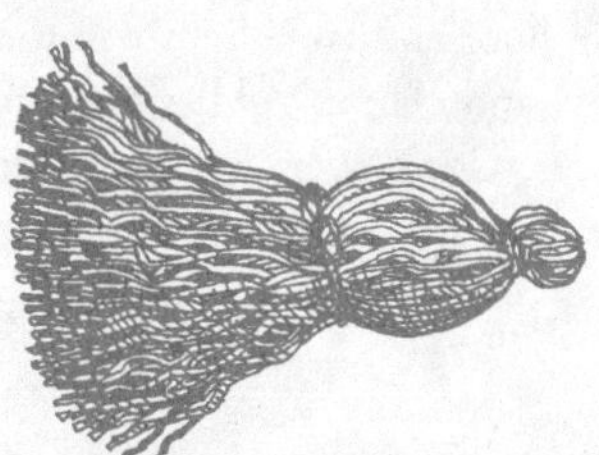

Harry Hamblet's Fried Oysters

I was brought up on these. Harry Hamblet was one of the first men to transplant the Eastern oysters to the Northwest beds in Shoalwaterbay, Washington. He loved oysters (and living, generally) and was a superb cook. His fried oysters are impossible to beat.

Heat butter and oil, to a depth of a half-inch, in a heavy 12-inch skillet. Beat the eggs lightly, and beat in the cream. Have plenty

Butter — or butter and oil mixed
3 eggs
3 tablespoons heavy cream
1 quart oysters, medium size
Freshly rolled cracker crumbs (not crackermeal)
Salt and freshly ground pepper

of rolled crackers on a piece of foil or wax paper. Dip the oysters in the egg mixture and then in the cracker crumbs. Let them stand several minutes on a piece of foil or wax paper. Fry them (do not crowd them in the skillet) just long enough to brown nicely and heat through. Salt and pepper them as they cook. Serve on hot plates with lemon wedges or tartar sauce. Six to twelve oysters is a portion, depending upon the appetite. Coleslaw and either boiled or hash-brown potatoes are fixtures with this.

French-Fried Oysters. Fry the oysters in deep fat, having not more than 4 or 5 at a time in the frying basket to keep them from touching. Fry for 2 minutes or until they are golden brown. Serve piping hot.

Hangtown Fry I

6 to 8 oysters
Beaten egg and cracker crumbs
Butter
6 eggs, well beaten
2 tablespoons water
Salt and pepper
Crisp bacon

Legend has it that this recipe came from the "last breakfast" in a frontier town for a man who was about to be hanged. He was trying to combine all his favorite foods for the last meal before paradise or eternal burning. This is a recipe for which there seem to be dozens of different versions. I like to think that one of these is authentic because they are all so delicious.

Dip the oysters in beaten egg, then in cracker crumbs, and fry in plenty of butter. When they are golden brown pour the well-beaten eggs, which have been mixed with water and seasonings, over them and cook as you would an omelet. Pull the egg from the sides of the pan with a spatula, and when the omelet is cooked but not dry roll it onto a hot platter. Garnish with strips of crisp bacon. A perfect Sunday breakfast dish or dinner entrée.

Hangtown Fry II

8 large oysters
Flour
6 tablespoons butter
6 eggs
3 tablespoons cream
¼ cup chopped parsley
¼ cup grated Parmesan cheese
Salt and freshly ground pepper

Dip the oysters in flour and sauté lightly in the butter. Blend the eggs, cream, parsley, and cheese. Add salt and pepper to taste and pour over the oysters. Cook over low heat until the eggs are set. Place under broiler to brown lightly. Serve from the skillet or slice onto a hot platter.

Hangtown Fry III

Merely add fried oysters to scrambled eggs, allowing 2 oysters to each egg. Sprinkle with parsley and serve with crisp bacon. This is probably as close to the original as you'll find.

Oyster Patties

1 pint of sauce velouté made partially with oyster liquor
¼ cup sherry or Madeira
1½ pints oysters
Warmed patty shells
Chopped parsley

Oyster patties are little more than creamed oysters served in patty shells. When properly made, they are quite delicious, and they look impressive as well. They can be made very nicely in a chafing dish or on a table stove. No collation in the 1890's or early 1900's was complete without this delicacy if oysters were in season. They were served at luncheons and at receptions of all sorts, and my mother used to serve them for late evening supper parties, which I was too young to stay up for. Sometimes I was lucky enough to get them for supper. I can still recall her giving instructions for cooking the oysters till the edges barely curled.

Prepare a velouté, using about ½ cup of the oyster liquor. Add the sherry or Madeira and simmer several minutes. Add the oysters and heat just until the edges curl. Spoon into heated patty shells, sprinkle with chopped parsley, and serve at once. This will make 6 to 8 servings, depending upon the size of the shells.

Oyster Pie. Double the recipe, cool slightly, and place in a deep 9-inch baking dish with a pie stand or egg cup in the center. Top with a rich crust. Brush with an egg and cream mixture (beat 1 egg with 2 tablespoons cream). Bake at 425 degrees 18 to 25 minutes, or until the crust is brown and cooked through.

An Illinois Recipe for Oyster Balls

3 cups mashed potatoes, mashed until light and creamy with 4 tablespoons butter, 3 tablespoons oyster liquor, and 1 tablespoon lemon juice
1½ cups chopped oysters
1½ teaspoons mustard
½ teaspoon Tabasco
1½ teaspoons salt
½ cup chopped parsley
Flour
2 eggs, lightly beaten
1 cup (or more) thinly sliced almonds or chopped almonds
Oil for frying

Combine warm mashed potatoes with the chopped oysters, seasonings, and chopped parsley. The mixture should be fairly stiff. Form into balls and cool. When thoroughly cool, roll in flour, dip in beaten egg, and roll in sliced or chopped almonds. Fry until nicely browned in oil heated to 370 degrees. Serve with tartar sauce and a cucumber salad.

Oysters Casino

24 oysters on the half shell, arranged on beds of rock salt
1 cup butter
½ cup each of chopped shallots, parsley, and green pepper
2 tablespoons lemon juice
1 teaspoon salt
½ teaspoon freshly ground pepper
6 strips bacon, partially broiled

It is certain that green pepper and bacon are two of the original ingredients for this dish. The others remain a mystery, so many different versions of the dish have there been.

Blend the butter, shallots, parsley, and green pepper together well, and add the lemon juice, salt, and pepper. Dab each oyster with some of the herbed butter and top with a small piece of bacon. Run under the broiler just long enough to heat the oysters and brown the bacon.

Variations

(1) Bake in a 425-degree oven instead of broiling, just long enough to cook the bacon.

(2) Some of the "original" recipes call for a spoonful of catsup under each oyster before adding the herbed butter. Works very well, too.

Clams Casino. Clams may be treated the same way.

Oysters Rockefeller

2 dozen oysters on the half shell
¼ cup chopped shallots, or green onions if shallots are not available (as a matter of fact in New Orleans they call green onions shallots)
¼ cup chopped celery
1 teaspoon chopped chervil
⅓ cup chopped fennel
⅓ cup chopped parsley
½ pound butter
2 cups watercress
⅓ cup breadcrumbs
⅓ cup Pernod
Salt and freshly ground pepper
Cayenne

This great dish, which was originally made in New Orleans, has become a much misquoted classic. There seem to be as many recipes as there are cookbooks. This one comes from a good source, which is important.

Sauté the green onions, celery, and herbs in 3 tablespoons of the butter for 3 minutes. Add the watercress and let it wilt. Scrape out into a blender, add the Pernod, and blend 1 minute. Blend with the crumbs and remaining butter. Season well. Arrange the oysters on beds of rock salt in metal containers which may be carried to table. Dampen the salt lightly. Spoon about 1 good teaspoonful of the mixture on each oyster. Bake at 450 degrees about 4 minutes, or just long enough for the oysters and sauce to heat through.

Scalloped Oysters

1 stick (½ cup) butter
1 to 1½ cups freshly rolled cracker crumbs
1½ pints oysters
Salt and freshly ground pepper

This dish, with the addition of more cream or milk, is what was originally called chowder.

Butter a 1½-quart baking dish and cover with a layer of cracker crumbs. Add a layer of half the oysters and another of cracker crumbs. Dot with butter and add seasonings. Make another layer of oysters and another layer of cracker crumbs. Dot again with butter and add seasonings. Pour the liquids over the top. Finally sprinkle with buttered breadcrumbs. Bake 25 minutes at 400 degrees. Serve with beef, as an entrée for luncheon, or as the hot item with a cold supper. It can also be served with chicken, hot or cold turkey, or cold ham.

Tabasco
½ cup oyster liquor
½ cup heavy cream
Buttered breadcrumbs

Oyster Pan Roast I

½ cup (1 stick) butter
1 pint oysters
2 tablespoons chili sauce
1 teaspoon salt
½ teaspoon Tabasco
1 teaspoon Worcestershire sauce
Lemon juice
Crisp buttered toast

There are many versions of this dish, of which this is my favorite.

Melt the butter, add the oysters, and let them just heat through till the edges curl. Add the seasonings and a dash of lemon juice, and boil up for 1 second. Spoon over crisp toast.

Oyster Pan Roast II

6 tablespoons butter
1 tablespoon chili sauce
1 tablespoon Worcestershire sauce
1 teaspoon salt
½ teaspoon Tabasco
1½ cups cream
½ cup oyster liquor
1 pint oysters
Crisp toast

Melt the butter, add the seasonings, and blend well. Add the cream and oyster liquor and bring to the boiling point. Add the oysters and heat till the edges curl. Serve in bowls or cream soup cups with crisp buttered toast.

Oyster Loaf

This was what gentlemen who lingered too long in their favorite bar took home to the little woman as a peace offering. There were two different types of oyster loaf, both delicious. Both used a loaf of French bread, either round or long, with the top third sliced off and the inside scooped out. This shell was then toasted and buttered. In one version, the shell was filled with golden fried oysters and the top replaced to keep them warm. In the other, the shell was filled with either a pan roast without too much liquid or with creamed oysters and the top replaced.

I have seen individual oyster loaves made with largish French rolls, and I have also seen one made with a regular pan loaf of bread, prepared as above, and filled with fried oysters.

Spaghetti with Oyster Sauce

4 tablespoons olive oil
3 cloves garlic, finely chopped
½ cup oyster liquor
½ cup white wine
½ pound spaghettini
1 pint chopped oysters
½ cup chopped parsley

This recipe comes from Lester Gruber, owner of the well-known London Chop House in Detroit.

Heat the garlic in the olive oil and cook till barely browned. Add the oyster liquor and white wine and simmer several minutes. Cook the spaghetti to taste in well-salted water. Drain well, Add the oysters and parsley to the sauce and just heat through. Arrange the spaghetti on two or three plates and top with the sauce. Serve at once.

Spaghetti with Clam Sauce. This same sauce can be made with minced clams.

Mussels

Although our coastal waters abound with wonderful mussels, they remain the most neglected of all our shellfish. Granted, on the Pacific Coast there are periods when they are inedible, but this does not account for their lack of popularity when in season. Furthermore, our indifference to mussels seems to go back into our history, since few of the older cookbooks mention their existence. Possibly they are too tedious for most people to prepare. Because of the "beard" and vegetation that linger on the shell, each mussel must be scrubbed thoroughly with a wire brush.

It is difficult to gauge how many mussels a person will eat. When they are good one can go on eating them forever. To make the consumption of them easier, use an empty mussel shell as you would a pair of tongs to remove the other mussels from their shells.

Steamed Mussels

2 to 3 quarts mussels
1 onion, thinly sliced
3 or 4 sprigs parsley
1 rib celery, sliced
2 tablespoons lemon juice
4 tablespoons butter
1 teaspoon salt
¼ teaspoon Tabasco

Scrub and beard the mussels. Place them in a kettle that can be tightly covered and will hold 6 to 8 quarts. Add the onion, parsley, and celery and shake together well. Cover, and simmer over low heat just till the mussels open. Add the lemon juice, butter, salt, and Tabasco, and heat through for 3 minutes or so. Serve the mussels in soup bowls along with some of the mussel broth. Also serve plenty of crisp rolls or bread.

Mussels Steamed in White Wine. Use 2 crushed garlic cloves instead of celery, 1 cup white wine instead of lemon juice, and 1 teaspoon freshly ground pepper instead of Tabasco.

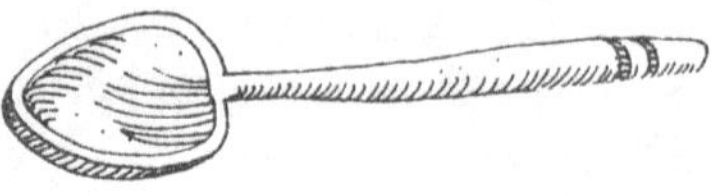

Mariner's Mussels (Moules Marinière)

2 to 3 quarts mussels, scrubbed and bearded
1 garlic clove, crushed
1 large onion, thinly sliced
2 to 3 sprigs parsley
4 tablespoons butter
1 teaspoon salt
1 teaspoon freshly ground pepper
½ cup white wine
4 tablespoons additional butter
½ cup chopped parsley
¼ teaspoon Tabasco

Place the garlic, onion, parsley sprigs, butter, and seasonings in the bottom of a large kettle. Add the cleaned mussels and pour the wine over them. Cover tightly and cook over low heat till the shells open. Transfer the mussels to a large tureen. Add the additional butter, parsley, and Tabasco to the liquid in the kettle. Correct the seasoning. Present the mussels in soup plates along with some of the broth. Serve plenty of crisp bread or rolls.

Variations

(1) After removing the mussels, add 1 cup scalded heavy cream to the broth. Blend well, and if you prefer it thickened add small balls of flour and butter kneaded together and stir over medium heat until you achieve the consistency you wish. Add 1 tablespoonful lemon juice and serve.

(2) Add 1 tablespoon curry powder to the cream in the variation above and thicken. Omit the lemon juice.

(3) Add a little saffron to the cream in the first variation.

Maine Baked Mussels

2 quarts mussels, scrubbed and bearded
1 small onion, finely chopped
½ cup chopped parsley
1 teaspoon salt
½ teaspoon freshly ground pepper
6 rashers lean bacon, partially cooked
½ cup grated Cheddar cheese (optional)

Probably the finest mussels we have come from the state of Maine, where they have long been known and appreciated.

Steam the mussels in salted water (1 teaspoon salt and a pint of water). When they have opened, remove them and extract the mussels from the shells. Put into a 1-quart baking dish and toss with the onion, parsley, and seasonings. Top with the bacon rashers, and bake at 375 degrees until the bacon is cooked through, about 15 minutes. If you like, sprinkle with grated cheese 5 minutes before removing from the oven.

Fried Mussels. Dip the cooked mussels in flour, then in beaten eggs, and roll them in cracker crumbs. Fry in butter and oil about 1 inch deep. Cook quickly, turning once, till lightly browned.

Clams

Steamed Clams

You will need 20 or so clams per person — more or less according to the diners' appetites and the quantity of other food you are serving.

Scrub the clams thoroughly with a brush and rinse several times. Be sure they are tightly closed. Place them in a large kettle with a half inch of salted water at the bottom, and cover the kettle tightly. Steam just until the shells open, which will take about 6 to 10 minutes. Serve immediately, and do not use any clams that do not open. Taste the broth for seasoning, and serve in cups to accompany the clams. Provide plenty of melted butter in bowls for dipping the clams as they are removed from the shells.

Clams on the Half Shell

Use littleneck or cherrystone clams, and ask the fish dealer to remove half the shell. Serve 6 to 8 per person, on a bed of crushed ice on a plate. If you must, provide "cocktail sauce," but they are best eaten with lemon juice, a little pepper, and if you like, a little grated fresh horseradish.

Stuffed Clams

24 steamed clams (keep one half-shell for each)
1 tablespoon each of chopped onion, parsley, and tarragon
½ cup buttered breadcrumbs, and more for topping
½ cup thick béchamel, made partly with the clam broth or other fish stock
Salt and freshly ground pepper
Cayenne, a few grains
1 tablespoon sherry
Butter

Chop the steamed clams very fine and mix with the rest of the ingredients except butter, using just enough béchamel to bind them. Fill the clam shells, dot with butter and more crumbs, and brown very quickly under the broiler.

Note. These are best if set on hot rock salt to cook. Use foil or other inexpensive pie plates, and put a layer of rock salt in each. Heat in a 425-degree oven, then put the clams on the bed of salt and cook. Serve them right in the pan, as they come out of the broiler.

Sautéed Clams

Use littlenecks or cherrystones, and buy them shucked. A quart should be enough for 4 people. Drain, and trim off any tough part. Sauté gently in butter until the edges curl and the clams are heated through and plumped up. Season with salt, freshly ground pepper, and a little paprika. Serve on crisp hot buttered toast, with chopped parsley sprinkled on top, and lemon wedges nearby.

Note. If you like, dip the clams in flour, or in beaten egg and then crumbs, before cooking.

Clam Hash I

6 tablespoons butter
1 tablespoon finely minced onion
1½ cups finely diced cooked potatoes
1½ to 2 cups minced clams
Salt and freshly ground pepper

Melt the butter in a heavy skillet and sauté the onion until just transparent. Stir in the finely diced potatoes and minced clams. Press them down with a spatula, salt and pepper lightly, and add a few flecks of nutmeg. Let cook about 10 minutes, then stir with a fork or spatula, mixing in some of the crust which has formed on the bottom, and press down again. Beat the egg yolks well and combine with the grated cheese and heavy cream. Pour this very gently over the hash, and cover tightly. Cook just until the egg is set — a few minutes.

Nutmeg, a few grains
4 egg yolks
4 tablespoons grated Parmesan cheese
6 tablespoons heavy cream

Clam Hash II. Use 2 medium onions, finely chopped. Omit the nutmeg, eggs, and cream. After the hash is cooked, stirred, and pressed down again, cook a few minutes more, then top with the grated cheese and 6 slices bacon which have been crisply fried and crumbled. Cover briefly to let the cheese melt.

Scalloped Clams

½ cup butter
½ cup toasted breadcrumbs
1 cup cracker crumbs
Salt and freshly ground pepper
Paprika
2 cups minced clams
2 tablespoons finely minced onion
2 tablespoons finely minced parsle
Additional butter
½ cup cream

Melt the butter and mix it with the breadcrumbs and cracker crumbs. Add salt and pepper to taste and a dash of paprika. Set aside ⅓ cup of this mixture for the top of the casserole. Mix the rest with the clams, onion, and parsley. Pour into a well-buttered baking dish and top with the remaining crumb mixture. Dot with additional butter and pour the cream over all. Bake in a 375-degree oven 20 to 25 minutes.

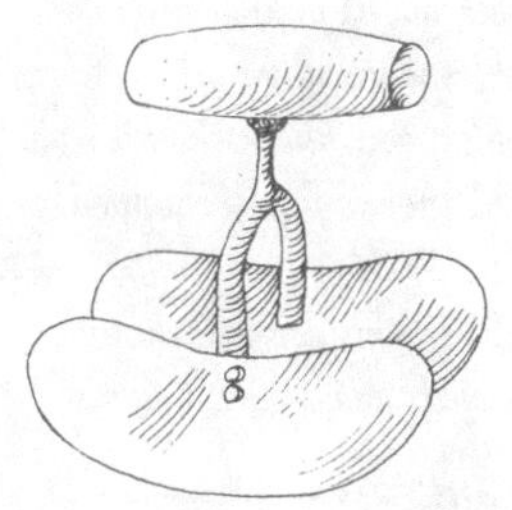

Abalone

This extraordinarily delicious shellfish is difficult to come by, and its supply is limited pretty much to California. Even there the laws governing the fishing of it are very rigid at this time. If you find yourself lucky enough to acquire it, here is how you treat it.

Cut the foot of the fish from the shell, and slice into steaks. Pound with a mallet to tenderize. Dip in flour and, if you like, in beaten egg and then crumbs. Cook very quickly in hot oil in a heavy skillet. Usually ½ minute per side is sufficient. Serve with a Béarnaise sauce or merely with lemon butter.

Scallops

Broiled Scallops

Wash 1½ pounds bay scallops carefully and drain very dry on absorbent paper. Dip the scallops in milk or beer and roll them lightly in freshly made crumbs. Arrange in a shallow metal or foil pan which will fit on the broiling rack. Add salt and freshly ground pepper to taste. Spoon melted or clarified butter over the scallops. Broil 4 to 5 inches from the broiling unit just until the crumbs are lightly colored. Do not overcook. Remove from the broiling oven, arrange on a serving dish, and garnish with additional melted butter and chopped parsley.

Deep-Fried Scallops

Wash, drain, and dry the scallops. Heat fat or oil for deep frying to 370 degrees. Dip the scallops into beer batter, and drop by spoonfuls into the hot fat. Cook 3 to 5 minutes, or just long enough for them to brown nicely. Drain on absorbent paper. Serve with tartar sauce.

Scallops en Brochette

Partially cook 6 rashers of bacon until a good deal of the fat is rendered but the bacon remains fairly soft. Wash 1 pound bay or sea scallops and dry on absorbent paper. Attach one end of the bacon to each of 6 metal or bamboo skewers. Add a scallop, skewer a loop of bacon around it, add another scallop, another loop of bacon, and continue until you have used up the bacon and scallops. Arrange on a broiling rack and broil about 4 to 5 inches from the heat unit, turning several times, until the bacon is crisp and the scallops are just cooked through. Sprinkle them with salt and freshly ground pepper to taste. Add a little chopped parsley.

Sautéed Scallops

1½ pounds bay or sea scallops
Milk or beer
Flour
4 tablespoons butter
4 tablespoons olive oil
1 tablespoon finely chopped garlic
2 tablespoons finely chopped parsley
2 tablespoons cooked, chopped, peeled, and seeded tomato

Wash the scallops and dry on absorbent paper. Dip them in milk or beer and roll lightly in flour. Combine the butter and olive oil in a heavy skillet. When the fat is quite hot, add the scallops and shake the pan well so they do not stick. Sauté very quickly, adding the garlic and parsley, and just before removing to a hot dish add the tomato. It is important to keep the scallops in motion most of the time they are cooking, else they will stick and break apart. Speed is essential. A Teflon-coated skillet is ideal for this operation.

Coquilles St. Jacques, Monteil

1½ pounds bay scallops
2 tablespoons butter
6 shallots or green onions, finely chopped
Bouquet garni (parsley, onion, celery leaves, thyme, bay leaf, tied in a twist of cheesecloth)
1½ cups white wine
2 tablespoons additional butter
12 mushrooms, chopped fine

Wash the scallops and put in a saucepan with the butter, chopped shallots, bouquet garni, and wine. Simmer about 4 to 6 minutes, or until the scallops are just cooked. Drain, and save the liquid. When the scallops are cool enough to handle, cut in small pieces. Melt the additional butter, and stir in the mushrooms, water, lemon juice, and salt and pepper. Drain the mushrooms, saving the liquid. Combine the mushroom liquid and the scallop liquid, drop in the beurre manié, and stir over a medium flame until thickened. Taste, and correct the seasoning. Add the scallops, let them heat in the sauce, and cool slightly. Combine the egg yolks and heavy cream and stir into the mixture. Continue stirring over a low flame until the mixture is well thickened, being very careful not to let it boil. Add the

1/3 cup water
Juice of 1 lemon
1/2 teaspoon salt
1/4 teaspoon freshly ground pepper
Beurre manié made with 3 tablespoons butter and 2 to 3 tablespoons flour
4 egg yolks
1 cup heavy cream
Grated Parmesan cheese
Breadcrumbs

mushrooms, stir in gently, and heap the mixture into scallop shells or individual casseroles. Sprinkle with the cheese and breadcrumbs, and run under the broiler to glaze.

Poached Scallops. Scallops poached in white wine are delicious served with chopped parsley and lemon juice, or a sauce made with the wine, or cold in salads. To prepare, cook as at the start of this recipe, omitting the butter.

Miss Farmer's Deviled Scallops

1 quart scallops
1/3 cup butter
1/3 teaspoon mustard
1 teaspoon salt
A few grains cayenne
2/3 cup buttered cracker crumbs

Clean the scallops and heat to the boiling point in their liquor; drain and reserve the liquor. Chop the scallops. Cream the butter with the salt, mustard, and cayenne. Blend in 2/3 cup reserved liquor, and the scallops. Let stand a half-hour. Put in a baking dish, cover with crumbs, and bake at 425 degrees 15 to 20 minutes.

Scallops Seviche

2 pounds scallops, preferably small bay scallops
Juice of 8 to 10 limes or lemons
1/2 cup olive oil
2 garlic cloves, finely chopped
1/4 cup finely chopped green onions
1/4 cup finely chopped green chili peppers
1/4 cup chopped parsley
Fresh cilantro, if available
1 1/2 teaspoons salt
Dash or two of Tabasco

This has become an extremely popular recipe in the United States. It is based on a Mexican recipe which came into favor in Texas and California for various kinds of fish; but with scallops, it's rather special.

Pour the lime or lemon juice over the scallops so that they are completely covered, and let stand in the refrigerator several hours. You will notice that their color will turn from a rather translucent quality to a much more opaque or cooked quality. The texture will also change. Drain well. Toss well with the oil and other ingredients. Arrange in a glass dish and garnish with fresh cilantro or fresh coriander or chopped chives or chopped parsley. This may be served as a first course or for a summer luncheon dish.

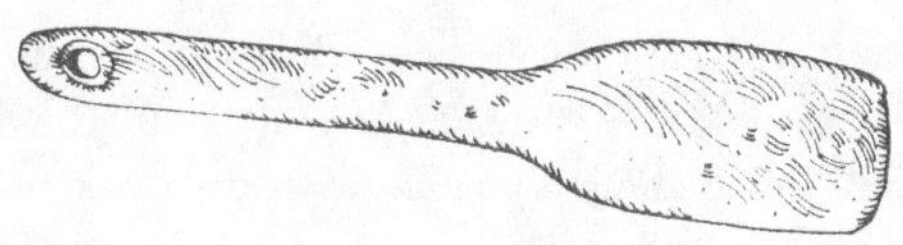

Fish and Shellfish Pies

Any type of firm-fleshed cooked fish or shellfish makes a tasty base for a pie. In very early cookbooks one reads of such fish pie specialties as "Star Gazy," in which small whole fish were baked, with tails hanging over the edge and heads popping through holes in the top crust. In the late nineteenth century, chefs created such delicacies as small trout, boned, stuffed with a mushroom or crab and mushroom filling, encased in puff paste shaped to the fish, and served individually as the fish course of a dinner. In this book we are offering much simpler recipes.

Fish Pie

4 tablespoons butter
2 teaspoons minced onion
1 tablespoon minced celery
4 tablespoons flour
¼ teaspoon dry mustard
Salt and freshly ground pepper
½ teaspoon Worcestershire sauce
2 cups milk or light cream
½ tablespoon lemon juice or 1 tablespoon dry sherry
2 cups flaked cooked fish or shellfish
Pastry for double or single crust

Sauté the onion and celery in the butter over low heat until translucent. Blend in the flour, mustard, salt and pepper to taste, and Worcestershire sauce. (The amount of salt will depend upon type of fish used. Such fish as crab and shrimp are often rather salty. Finnan haddie, smoked salmon, smoked cod, or such fish as salt salmon, even though soaked in several changes of cold water, will also probably require no salt in the sauce.) Add the milk or cream, stir, bring to a boil, and simmer several minutes. Cool. Add the lemon juice or sherry. Fold the fish into the sauce and turn into a pastry-lined 9 or 10 inch pie pan or, if using only the top crust, a shallow 1½ to 2 quart casserole. Adjust the top crust as for any meat pie (see page 633), and bake at 450 degrees 15 minutes. Reduce the heat to 350 degrees and bake 20 to 25 minutes longer.

Fish Pie with Biscuit Crust. Use 3 cups milk, light cream, court bouillon, chicken broth, or consommé in the sauce. Put the hot filling in a 2 to 3 quart casserole or deep baking pan. Top with biscuits, using 1½ cups flour in the recipe. Bake at 400 to 425 degrees 20 to 25 minutes.

Fish Pie with Mushrooms. Use less fish, about 1½ cups, and add ½ to ¾ cups sliced fresh mushrooms, sautéed.

Crab and Chicken Pie. Use 1 cup flaked cooked crab and 1 cup cubed cooked chicken. Also add ½ cup sliced fresh mushrooms, if you like. For the sauce use 1 cup chicken broth and 1 cup light cream.

Crab and Sweetbread Pie (Usually made in larger quantity than the basic recipe). Double the sauce recipe and combine with 2 cups cooked crabmeat and about a pound of sweetbreads that have been simmered (page 355), trimmed, and cut into small pieces. You may sauté the cooked crab and sweetbreads lightly in 3 tablespoons butter before adding to the sauce.

Oyster and Sweetbread Pie. Follow directions for crab and sweetbread pie (above), using (instead of crabmeat) 1 pint whole small oysters or large oysters cut into halves or quarters. Heat in the sauce just until the edges begin to curl. Add the sweetbreads and cool. Put into a 2 to 3 quart casserole or baking pan and cover with pastry made with 2 cups of flour.

Oyster Pie

1 pint oysters, picked over, with their liquor
4 tablespoons butter
1 to 2 tablespoons minced onion (optional)
5 to 6 tablespoons flour
2 cups milk or thin cream
Salt and freshly ground pepper
¼ teaspoon Tabasco
Rich pastry for double or single crust pie

Melt the butter in a saucepan and sauté the onion lightly. Blend in the flour, then the milk or cream. Stir while bringing to a boil. Simmer several minutes. Add the oysters (large ones are usually cut in halves or quarters) and simmer until the edges curl. If using a bottom crust, cool the filling, then pour it in a pie pan 9 or 10 inches in diameter lined with pastry. Moisten the edge, top with pastry, cut steam vents, and crimp the edge all around, pressing down to seal it. If you are using only a top crust, turn the filling into a 1½ to 2 quart casserole and top with pastry (see page 633). Either way, bake at 450 degrees 15 minutes, then reduce the heat to 350 degrees and bake about 25 minutes longer.

Oyster Pie with Biscuit Crust. Use only 3 tablespoons flour to thicken the milk or cream. Turn the hot filling into a 2-quart casserole. Top with biscuits made with 1 to 1½ cups flour and cut about ½ inch thick. Bake at 400 to 425 degrees 20 to 30 minutes, or until the biscuits are a light brown.

Simple Oyster Pie. Line a pie plate with rich pastry, fill with oysters that have been picked over to remove the shells, dot plentifully with butter, season with salt, freshly ground pepper, and (if you like) a little finely cut celery, sprinkle with a bit of flour, top with pastry, and bake at 450 degrees 15 minutes, then at 350 degrees 20 minutes longer. If the oysters are very large, it is customary to cut them in pieces. This is a favorite recipe along the Eastern seaboard.

Clam Pie

Found in many early cookbooks, this is still served in restaurants along the Eastern seaboard. The only change in the recipe over the years is that now canned clams can be used.

Trim the clams, if necessary. The black tip of the neck of most clams is cut away, as well as the stomach and intestinal tract of larger clams. With some types of clams, the neck is cut away entirely

3 cups drained (reserve the juice), trimmed and cleaned fresh steamed clams or canned clams (4 cans 7 to 7½ ounces each)
4 tablespoons butter
1 tablespoon minced onion
1 tablespoon minced celery (optional)
4 tablespoons flour
2 cups combined clam juice and rich milk or light cream
Salt and freshly ground pepper
Dash of Tabasco or ½ teaspoon dry mustard
¼ teaspoon dried basil (optional)
Pastry, using 2 cups flour

and ground, for it is apt to be tough. Use the liquid in which the clams were steamed as part or all of the liquid called for in the recipe. If using no milk or cream, increase the amount of butter. If using whole or minced canned clams, drain off the juice and use it. Cut whole clams in halves or quarters, if you wish.

Melt the butter in a saucepan or skillet and sauté the onion and celery just until translucent. Blend in the flour, then the clam juice and milk or cream. Remove from the heat and add the clams. Return, stir until thickened, and simmer several minutes. Season to taste with salt, pepper, and Tabasco or dry mustard; or use dry basil instead of the pepper sauce and mustard or in addition to them. Line a 9-inch pie pan with pastry, trim the edge, and moisten it. Turn the clam filling into the pan and top with pastry. Cut vents in the center, crimp and seal the edge. Bake 15 minutes at 450 degrees, then reduce the heat to 350 degrees and bake 20 minutes longer. Serve very hot.

Clam and Egg Pie. Use only 1½ cups drained clams and add 4 sliced hard-boiled eggs. Season with dry mustard and about ½ teaspoon Worcestershire sauce.

Clam Quiche. Line the pie pan with butter pastry for a one-crust pie. Sauté the onion and celery in only 1 tablespoon butter and add the clams, using no flour. Add the clam juice and milk or (preferably with this) cream to 3 eggs beaten slightly, and combine with the clam mixture. Use mustard for the extra seasoning, and also, if you like, add up to ¼ cup minced onion before pouring the filling into the pan. Sometimes a mild cheese such as jack or Emmenthaler is sprinkled over the top. Bake 10 minutes at 450 degrees, then reduce to 325 degrees and bake just until the center is firm.

Note. If you wish to partially bake the quiche crust before filling, cover the pastry shell with aluminum foil, fill with dried beans to hold the crust in place, and bake 10 minutes at 450 degrees. Lift out the beans and cool the crust slightly before pouring in the filling.

Fish and Shellfish Soups, Stews, Chowders

Every country in the Western world has its distinctive fish stews. The famous bouillabaisse and the bourride of France and the zuppa di pesce of Italy are but a few. We have created some of our own. Most notable, I suppose, are the shellfish soup-stews of the Northeast. Of these, clam chowder must stand as the earliest as well as one of the greatest. Fish chowder and eel stifle are two other delights that came from New England and took hold throughout the country. There is oyster stew, also, and scallop and lobster stew. In New Orleans the ethnic mix of French, Spanish, and African groups brought forth some Gallic-named but entirely original stews, such as the Court Bouillon (not to be confused with the bouillon used for poaching fish). Also the gumbos and gumbo filés are part of the repertoire. The West contributed cioppino, which is said to have been made originally over bonfires on the beach by Portuguese fishermen. In Washington and Oregon, where so many New Englanders settled, one finds clam chowder and fish chowder again. Occasionally, too, because of the Russian influence in that part of the country after World War I, one finds the wonderful Russian stew solianka, which is not surprising considering the availability of one of its chief ingredients, salmon.

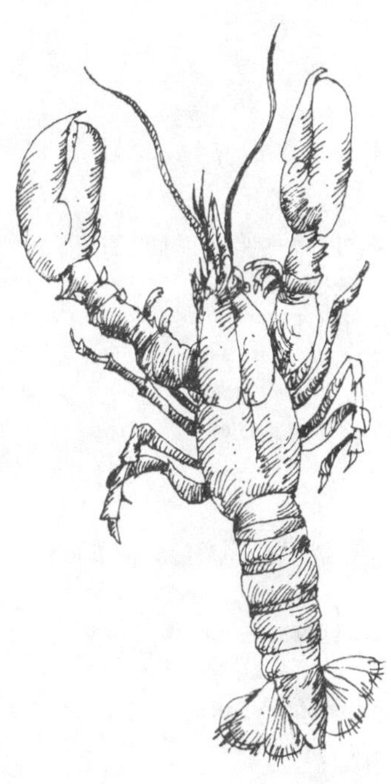

I am sure that clam chowder as it is known today did not originate before the nineteenth century. Before that time clam soups or chowders were done, perhaps, with salt pork, milk, onion, and common crackers. Since potatoes were not in general use till the eighteenth century, it is unlikely that our standard chowder developed until much later. *The Webfoot Cook Book*, published in Portland, Oregon, in 1885 and a scarce book on the market, gives a recipe layering clams, potatoes, onions, and crackers, covering with boiling water and simmering 2 hours. Something of a clue is also provided by Mrs. Crowen's recipe for clam chowder, given below, published in the 1847 edition of her *American System of Cookery*.

Mrs. Crowen's Clam Chowder

"Butter a deep tin basin, strew it thickly with grated breadcrumbs or soaked crackers; sprinkle some pepper over and bits of butter the size of a hickory nut and, if liked, some finely chopped parsley; then put a double layer of clams, season with pepper, put bits of butter over and then another layer of soaked cracker; after that clams and bits of butter; sprinkle pepper over. Add a cup of milk or water, and lastly a layer of soaked crackers. Turn a plate over the basin and bake in a hot oven for three quarters of an hour."

I have made this recipe in a copper braising pan and in a copper saucepan, as well as in an aluminum heavy-duty pan with a tight-fitting cover. It is a delicious dish, but not so much a chowder as a first-class stew. I used cracker crumbs rather than soaked crackers —

about a cup for 1 quart clams — and used 1 cup clam juice (or, in another case, cream) for the liquid. It is helped by shaking vigorously several times while baking (about 35 minutes in a 350-degree oven), and a dusting of chopped parsley after it is ladled into soup plates.

Clam Soup I

3 cups milk
2 cups minced clams (preferably razor clams)
3 tablespoons butter
1 ½ teaspoons salt
½ teaspoon freshly ground pepper
Chopped parsley

In the West we often served clam soup for a luncheon dish, and it was always a dish fed to those with upset stomachs or patients recuperating from an illness. It is not only simple but extraordinarily good.

Heat the milk to the boiling point. Add the minced clams, butter, salt and pepper. Heat till the clams are just hot and the butter melted. Ladle into warm bowls, garnish with parsley, and serve with crisp soda crackers.

Clam Soup II

2½ cups minced clams with broth
2 cups heavy cream
2 tablespoons butter
1 teaspoon salt
¼ teaspoon Tabasco
Chopped parsley

This version of clam soup may be served at formal meals.

Whirl the clams in a blender and combine with the cream, butter, and seasonings in the top of a double boiler. Heat through thoroughly over hot water. Serve in heated cups with a dusting of chopped parsley.

Oyster Soup. Oysters may be treated in exactly the same fashion. Serve with a garnish of one small oyster in each cup.

Old Western Clam Chowder

5 or 6 rashers smoked bacon, cut thick, or salt pork (they give entirely different flavors, both excellent)
1 small onion, finely chopped
3 to 4 smallish potatoes, peeled and diced
1 teaspoon salt
1½ cups clam broth
Water
1 teaspoon freshly ground pepper
½ teaspoon thyme
1 quart milk or half and half
2 to 3 cups minced razor clams or other clams
Butter
Chopped parsley

This is made with razor clams, and a most delicious chowder it is. Our family recipe — given here, and the recipe of most of our friends — was different from the run-of-the-mill chowder and considerably better.

Cut the bacon or salt pork into small squares and try out in a large, heavy skillet till crisp. Remove, add the onion, and sauté in the fat until just wilted. Transfer to absorbent paper, and pour off the fat from the skillet. Add the potatoes to the pan with the salt. Combine clam broth with enough water — or use additional clam broth — to just cover the potatoes. Cook until the potatoes are quite tender. Transfer to a 3 to 4 quart saucepan and add the onion mixture, pepper, thyme, and milk or half and half. Bring to the boiling point, add the clams, and cook just long enough to heat them through. Correct the seasoning. Serve in chowder bowls or large cups with a small piece of butter and a sprinkling of chopped parsley.

Standard New England Clam Chowder

1 quart clams
1 cup water
4 slices salt pork cut into small pieces
1 medium to large onion, thinly sliced
3 cups potatoes, peeled and diced
1 tablespoon salt
½ teaspoon freshly ground pepper
2 cups boiling water
1 quart scalded milk
8 soda crackers soaked in milk
1 tablespoon flour
1 tablespoon butter

This is more or less the standard clam chowder. My objection to it is that the clams are cooked too much. But it has had a long history.

Scrub the clams. Place them in a large kettle with 1 cup water, cover, and cook over medium high heat till they open. Remove the clams, strain the liquid, and chop the clams. Try out the salt pork in a skillet, and when crisp, transfer to absorbent paper. Pour off all but 2 tablespoons fat from the skillet and sauté the onion slices lightly for 4 to 5 minutes, turning them with a wooden spatula several times. Parboil the potatoes 5 minutes in salted water to cover. Arrange the onions in the bottom of a heavy saucepan and top with a layer of half the potatoes. Add the salt pork pieces, then the chopped clams, then another layer of potatoes and salt and pepper. Add the boiling water and cook 10 minutes. Add the scalded milk and bring to a boil. Add the soaked crackers and liquid the clams cooked in. Finally add the flour and butter kneaded together. Bring to the boiling point and correct the seasoning. Serve in hot chowder bowls.

Note. If you are using canned minced clams, add the broth to the chowder as above, but do not add the clams till the very last minute. If you are using tiny, tender clams, add some minced tougher clams earlier, and reserve 1½ to 2 cups of the tender clams to add at the very last minute.

A touch of thyme and a dusting of parsley help the chowder enormously.

Miss Farmer's Recipe for Rhode Island Clam

"*1 quart clams*
3-inch cube salt pork
1 sliced onion
½ cup cold water
4 cups potatoes cut in ¾-inch cubes
2 cups boiling water
1 cup stewed and strained tomatoes
¼ teaspoon soda
1 cup scalded milk
1 cup scalded cream
2 tablespoons butter
Salt and pepper
8 common crackers"

This is the closest bridge I have found to that rather horrendous soup called Manhattan clam chowder. It is a sensible recipe and takes away the curse of the other, which resembles a vegetable soup that accidentally had some clams dumped into it.

"Wash clams and reserve liquor. [Miss Farmer means scrub the unopened clams, steam open in water (1 cup), then strain and reserve the liquid.] Cook pork with onion and cold water for 10 minutes. Parboil potatoes for 5 minutes and drain. To potatoes add reserved liquors, hard part of clams, finely chopped, and boiling water. When potatoes are nearly done add tomatoes, soda, soft part of clams, milk, cream and butter. Season to taste with salt and pepper. Split crackers, soak in cold milk to moisten, and heat in chowder."

Mrs. Lincoln's Clam Chowder

"*½ peck clams in the shells*
1 quart of potatoes, sliced thin
A 2-inch cube of salt pork
1 or 2 onions
1 teaspoonful salt
½ teaspoon white pepper
1 tablespoon butter
1 quart milk
6 butter crackers"

Here is Mrs. Lincoln's rule for clam chowder (from the 1903 edition of her cookbook), one of the few that does not stew the clams to death.

"Clam chowder is made in the same manner as fish chowder, substituting half a peck of clams for the fish. Clams in their shells are better, as you then have more clam liquor. Wash with a small brush, and put them into a large kettle with half a cupful of water, or just enough to keep the under ones from burning; set them over the fire. When the clams at the top have opened, take them out with a skimmer. And when they are cool enough to handle, take the clams from the shell; remove the thin skin; then with the scissors cut off all the black end, cut the leather straps into thin pieces leaving the soft part whole. Let the clam liquor settle, and pour it off carefully. Use half water and half clam liquor. Fry the pork and onion the same as for Fish Chowder; add the potatoes, which have been soaked and scalded, and boiling water to cover. When the potatoes are soft add the clam liquor, the seasoning and the clams. When warmed through add the hot milk and turn into the tureen. Do not put the clams into the chowder until the potatoes are nearly done, as prolonged boiling hardens them."

My Favorite Clam Chowder

1½ cups chopped razor clams or other clams, and their liquor
3 slices salt pork, or thickly sliced bacon cut in small shreds
1 medium onion, finely chopped
2 medium potatoes, thinly sliced
2 cups water, salted
Salt and freshly ground pepper
3 cups light cream
Butter
Thyme
Chopped parsley

This is my own version of clam chowder, with no bows to tradition whatsoever save those my mother created. The recipe is made with razor clams, although it will be quite — well, not quite — as good if done with cherrystones or quahogs or littlenecks.

Drain the clams of their liquor and set both aside. (If you are grinding the clams be sure to catch the liquor.) Cook the salt pork or bacon in a skillet over medium heat until crisp. Transfer to absorbent paper. Add the onion to the fat in the skillet and brown lightly. Cook the potatoes in the boiling salted water until just tender, then add the bacon, onion, salt and pepper to taste, and clam juice, and simmer 5 minutes. Add the cream, and bring to a boil. Correct the seasoning, add the clams, and just heat through. Serve with a dollop of butter, the merest pinch of thyme, and a bit of chopped parsley.

Oyster Stew

5 tablespoons butter
1 cup milk
2 cups cream
1½ pints oysters and liquor

If there is a traditional Christmas Eve dish in the United States, it is oyster stew.

This may be made with cream only or with milk. Heat soup bowls. Add a good pat of butter to each bowl. Keep piping hot. Drain the oysters, then heat the milk, cream, and oyster liquor to the boiling point. Add the oysters and bring again to the boiling point. Season to taste with salt, pepper, and cayenne. Ladle into the hot bowls and add a sprinkling of chopped parsley or of paprika.

Salt and freshly ground pepper
Cayenne
Chopped parsley or paprika

Sautéed Oyster Stew. Combine the oysters and butter in a skillet and cook until the edges curl. Add the hot cream and milk, and bring to the boiling point. Season, ladle into hot bowls, and serve with crisp biscuits or buttered toast.

Lobster Chowder

1 cooked lobster, 1½ pounds
3 soda crackers
¼ cup butter
1 teaspoon salt
Dash cayenne
1 quart milk

Lobster chowder was almost as well known as clam chowder in certain parts of New England.

Remove the meat from the cooked lobster and cut into fine dice. Remove the tomalley and reserve. If there is any coral, add it to the tomalley. Roll the crackers fine and combine with the butter, tomalley, salt, and cayenne. Blend into a smooth paste. Bring the milk to a boil in a heavy saucepan, stir in the paste, and add the diced lobster. Bring to a boil again and serve at once.

Lobster Stew

1 2-pound lobster or 2 1½-pound lobsters
1 stick (½ cup) butter
1 quart milk

The success of this is largely dependent upon the stirring and aging. Some old Maine authorities claim a stew should age as long as 4 or 5 days after making, but these are the extremists. It is best if aged for 5 to 6 hours before reheating gently and serving.

Boil the lobster. Immediately remove the meat, tomalley, and (if there is any) coral. Scrape the thickish white substance from inside the shell as well. Cut the lobster meat in generous pieces. Sauté the tomalley, coral, and the white substance in butter several minutes over rather low heat. Add the lobster meat. Cook about 5 minutes over low heat. Cool 5 to 8 minutes. Then very slowly add the milk, stirring constantly. Allow this to stand 5 to 6 hours before reheating and serving. It usually needs no salt. A little freshly ground black pepper is good added at the last to each serving.

She-Crab Soup

12 she crabs (female crabs)
Butter (about 2½ tablespoons)
1 small onion, finely chopped
Dash of Worcestershire sauce
1 cup milk
1½ cups cream
1 tablespoon flour
2 tablespoons dry sherry
Salt
½ teaspoon freshly ground pepper
Chopped parsley

Long a delight of Charleston and other Southern cities, this soup is cookery of the old South at its very best.

Cook the crabs in boiling salted water for approximately 18 to 20 minutes. Cool, crack, and remove the meat. Place the crabmeat in the upper part of a double boiler, adding roes of the crabs as well, 1½ tablespoons butter, the finely chopped onion, and the Worcestershire sauce. Heat over boiling water. Heat the milk and cream separately, add the flour kneaded with 1 tablespoon butter, and stir until slightly thickened. Combine with the crabmeat mixture, and add the sherry, salt to taste, and pepper. Simmer, covered, about 10 to 15 minutes or until the soup is well blended and smooth. Serve with buttered toast. Garnish with chopped parsley.

Crab Soup Elizabeth Alward

1 pound crabmeat
4 tablespoons dry sherry
4 tablespoons butter
1 medium onion, finely chopped
½ medium green pepper, finely chopped
2 teaspoons chili powder
½ teaspoon sugar
2 tablespoons flour
Salt to taste
1 pint coffee cream or thin cream

Using Dungeness crab of the West Coast and the spicings of the Southwest, this is quite unlike she-crab soup, but is just as good and as completely original.

Combine the crabmeat and sherry in the top of a double boiler and heat over hot water. Melt the butter in a heavy skillet, and sauté the onion and pepper until tender. Add the chili powder, sugar, and flour and season to taste with salt. Blend well and stir in the cream. Continue to stir until smooth and just slightly thickened. Pour over the crabmeat mixture in the double boiler and heat through. Serve at once in heated cups or plates.

This is a very substantial soup for four persons. It makes a good luncheon meal served with buttered toast, a salad, and cheese.

James Beard's Fish Chowder

2 cups minced onions
4 tablespoons olive oil
4 large ripe tomatoes, or two #2 cans (19 ounces each) tomatoes, preferably Italian plum
½ cup chopped kosher fresh dill pickles packed in brine, not vinegar
½ tablespoon each of chopped capers, green olives, and black olives
3 to 3½ pounds skinless and boneless fillets of cod, hake, haddock, or other lean fish, either fresh or frozen
1½ quarts fish stock, or 4 cups bottled clam juice and 2 cups water
1 bay leaf
Salt and freshly ground pepper to taste
Chopped parsley
3 tablespoons chopped fresh dill or ½ teaspoon dried dillweed
6 to 8 slices of lemon

Tomatoes, pickles, olives, and capers give this fish chowder, first brought to the Northwest by the White Russians, a most original and special flavor. It somewhat resembles a San Francisco cioppino but is more subtle.

Cook the onions in the olive oil in a 3 to 4 quart stainless steel or enameled saucepan until they are limp and translucent. If using fresh tomatoes, peel, seed, juice, and chop them; add to the onions and cook several minutes until the tomato pulp is soft. If using canned tomatoes, drain through a sieve, gently press out excess liquid, then force the pulp through the sieve into the onions, leaving the seeds behind. Add to the pan all the chopped pickles and half the chopped capers, green olives, and black olives. If using frozen fish, thaw it in cold water until just soft enough to be cut with a heavy knife. Cut fresh or frozen fish into strips about 1 inch wide and 3 inches long. Place in the saucepan, cover with the fish stock or clam juice and water, and add the bay leaf. Bring to the boiling point, season lightly. Cook fresh fish gently for 10 to 12 minutes. Frozen fish will take 15 to 18 minutes. Correct the seasoning. For serving, pour into a tureen and stir in the parsley, dill, and remaining chopped capers and olives. Garnish with lemon slices.

Superb Fish Chowder

3 pounds boneless and skinless cod, hake, haddock, or other lean fish, either fresh or frozen (with bones, heads, and trimmings, if available)
About 1 pound peeled and sliced potatoes
2 quarts milk
½ pound salt pork, cut into ½-inch dice
2 cups sliced onions
¼ pound pilot or common crackers or 1¼ cups stale French or Italian breadcrumbs
Salt and freshly ground pepper to taste

This recipe, from Julia Child's sister-in-law, is a version of Alice Lee Myer's Camden Fish Chowder. It is typical of various fish chowders and delicious in its blend of flavors.

The secret of such a chowder as this is to have all ingredients of the same temperature when blended. The fish simmers in water or broth; the potatoes cook in milk; and the onions, salt pork, and crackers are sautéed. If necessary, reheat the ingredients just before blending. Also, do not add salt until the end of the process, inasmuch as the salt pork will contribute a certain amount of seasoning.

If you have the fish trimmings, place them in a 3-quart saucepan with 2 quarts water, and simmer 30 minutes. Strain, and return the cooking liquid to the pan. Add the fresh or still frozen fish fillets to the liquid, bring to a simmer, and cook 10 to 15 minutes, until the fish is just tender. Be careful not to overcook.

Simmer the sliced potatoes in the milk in a soup kettle 10 to 15 minutes or until just tender.

Cook the salt pork in a large frying pan over moderate heat until the fat is rendered out and the pork begins to brown lightly. Stir in the onions and cook over low heat until they are translucent but not browned. Crumble the crackers, and gradually stir in enough of them to absorb the pork fat.

For the final combination, stir the warm cooked fish gradually into the warm potatoes and milk, and gradually stir both in the warm salt pork mixture. Heat to just below simmer for 4 or 5 minutes to blend flavors. If the chowder seems too thick, stir in some of the fish-cooking liquid. Serve with additional pilot biscuits and butter.

Old-Fashioned New England Fish Chowder

¼ cup diced salt pork
¼ cup sliced onions
2 cups diced potatoes
2 cups hot water
1½ pounds fillet of haddock, cod, or ocean perch
Salt and freshly ground pepper
2 cups cream
Butter

This is one of many, many fish chowders.

Try out the salt pork in a skillet until it is nicely browned. Add the onions and sauté gently. Add the potatoes and hot water and cook a few minutes, or until the potatoes are partly done. Then add the fish fillets and cook until they are easily flaked with a fork. Season to taste with salt and pepper and add the cream. Let it all heat through. Serve in bowls, topping each with a generous pat of butter.

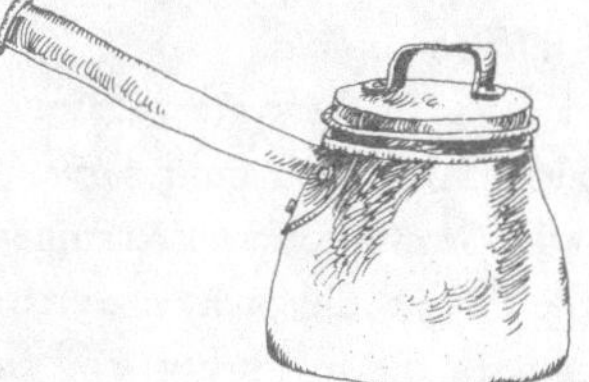

Fish Chowder from The Webfoot Cookbook

This layered dish is a type of simple fish stew that has been a standard item in New England cuisine for many generations. Any type of firm-fleshed fish can be used: cod, halibut, whitefish, lake trout are all good choices.

"Take four or five slices of salt pork; fry them brown in a spider. Cut in bits and turn into your chowder kettle. Pare half a dozen medium-sized potatoes and cut them into four or five pieces. Put into your kettle a layer of any kind of firm hard fish cut into small pieces. Next put in a layer of potatoes and onion if liked. Season each layer and continue till you have the desired quantity. Pour over all hot water enough to cover and boil one hour. Crackers broken into pieces may be used instead of potato."

Nowadays, one is apt to use butter — a good deal — rather than salt pork, and separate layers are made of fish fillets, sliced potatoes, sliced onions — each seasoned lightly — and cracker crumbs. Cook it gently until the fish and vegetables are just done, and if you like pour in a cup of rich cream before serving in large bowls.

Eel Stifle (Eel Chowder)

6 eels
6 large potatoes
4 onions
Butter
Flour
Freshly ground pepper
Salt pork
Water

This dish with the amusing name is an old New England specialty. It is simple but exceedingly tasty.

First you must skin the eels. Cut the skin around the head and then peel it back, stripping it off as you would a glove. You may need to use a pair of pliers to start it peeling. Cut off the heads and then cut the eels into 3-inch pieces. Using a knife or fork, force the intestines out of each segment. Wash the pieces thoroughly. Peel and slice the potatoes and onions. Butter a good-sized casserole or baking dish and place a layer of half the potato slices in the bottom; add a layer of half the onions and then a layer of half the eel. Sprinkle each layer with a bit of flour and pepper. Top with small pieces of salt pork and repeat the layers. Add water to barely cover. Cover the casserole and bake in a 375-degree oven (or cook slowly on top of the stove) just until the eel and vegetables are done.

Solianka

2 pounds fish bones and heads or a 2-pound bony fish with head
1½ quarts water
Salt and freshly ground pepper
3 large ripe tomatoes, peeled, seeded, and chopped
3 tablespoons butter
1½ pounds salmon cut in strips
2 onions, finely chopped

This rather interesting stew is found often in the Northwest, where it was introduced by the White Russians, who arrived via China after the Russian revolution. It is particularly suited to that part of the country, where salmon abound.

Cook the fish bones and heads in the water, seasoned with salt and pepper, 1½ hours. Drain off the broth and reserve. Simmer the tomatoes in butter 15 minutes. Season to taste. Arrange the salmon strips in a deep pot with the onions, dill pickles, tomatoes, capers, and chopped olives. Cover with the fish broth, add the bay leaf, and simmer 12 to 15 minutes. Add the 4 tablespoons butter. Serve in bowls garnished with chopped olives, chopped parsley, and lemon slices.

Note. A tablespoon or more of chopped fresh dill or 2 teaspoons dillweed makes this a most appetizing soup with another accent.

4 dill pickles, finely chopped
2 teaspoons capers
1 tablespoon each of chopped black olives and chopped green olives
1 bay leaf
4 tablespoons additional butter
Chopped parsley, additional chopped olives, and lemon slices for garnish

Cioppino

3 pounds sea bass, barracuda, halibut, or a variety of firm fish
1 large cooked Dungeness (hard-shell) crab or a cooked lobster
1 pound (or more) jumbo shrimp
1 pint clams, mussels, or oysters, or all three

SAUCE

3/4 cup olive oil
1 1/2 cups chopped onion
1 cup chopped green pepper
3 cloves garlic thoroughly mashed with 1 teaspoon salt
1 #2 1/2 can of tomatoes
The broth of the molluscs
2 cups red table wine
2 cups tomato juice
2 cups fish stock made from the crab shell or lobster body and fish trimmings
Herb bouquet (bay leaf, parsley, basil)
1/2 cup minced parsley
Salt and freshly ground pepper to taste

Cioppino is a complicated stew, and there are many versions of it. Seasonings vary from area to area, and the fish used varies with the day's catch. In addition, individual cooks often change the ingredients to suit their own tastes. Some prefer white wine to red; others use sherry. Many like to make it with the addition of exotic tidbits such as octopus, squid, or eel. Or the fish may be omitted and only shellfish used. Often dried mushrooms that have been soaked are included. Here is the basic recipe; master it and then try your own versions.

Cut the fish into good-sized serving pieces. Crack the crab and remove the top shell but keep it for making stock. If you use lobster, cut the tail in pieces and reserve the body to make stock; if you use Eastern lobster, cut the tail in sections and crack the claws. Split the shrimp shells down the back and remove the black vein. Steam the molluscs in a small amount of water just until they open. Remove the top shells and save the broth.

To prepare the sauce, sauté the onion and green pepper in olive oil until just soft, add all the other ingredients except parsley, and cook 10 minutes. Remove the herb bouquet and taste for seasoning.

Select a large casserole or kettle with a cover and arrange the fish and shrimp in it in layers. Pour the sauce over them and cover the pan. Simmer over a low flame or in the oven 20 to 30 minutes or until they are just done. Five minutes before removing from the heat, add the crab or lobster, and in another two minutes add the molluscs. Taste for seasoning. Serve in deep bowls, shells and all, and sprinkle liberally with minced parsley. Have plenty of napkins on hand, because this will require some eating with the fingers. Also serve hot crusty French or Italian bread and a robust red wine.

Louisiana Court Bouillon

1 1/2 pounds red snapper fillets
1/2 cup flour
1/4 cup olive oil
1/4 cup butter

This classic dish of Creole origin should not be confused with the seasoned broth, also called court bouillon, used for poaching fish. The Louisiana Court Bouillon is a rich and elegant stew, one of America's great contributions to the fine art of cooking.

Blend the oil and flour in a large skillet, stirring constantly until

1 pound onions, peeled and chopped
2 stalks celery, chopped
2 cloves garlic, chopped
1 sweet pepper, seeded and chopped
6 ounces tomato paste
3 cups boiling water
1 cup red wine
2 teaspoons Worcestershire sauce
½ lemon, sliced
6 to 8 sprigs parsley
1 bay leaf
Salt and freshly ground pepper
Fried croutons

it forms a thick roux. Then add the butter and chopped vegetables, and blend in the tomato paste. Slowly add the boiling water, stirring to be sure the mixture does not lump. When it is smooth and blended, add the wine, Worcestershire sauce, lemon slices, parsley, bay leaf, and salt and pepper to taste. Simmer gently 30 minutes, then add the fish. Cook just until the fish flakes easily. Taste for seasoning, and serve in large bowls with fried croutons.

Gumbos

There is such a quantity of gumbo recipes — and such a deep feeling in my heart that they are not the culinary achievement they have been made out to be. If you follow the first recipe below, which is an old one from New Orleans, you too will ponder if it could possibly be good. Some of the modern adaptations seem to be better but are still not really great dishes. They are typical of Creole cuisine and became fashionable, I wager, because this is what the cooks of the day, who at times were pretty dictatorial, chose to serve up.

Old New Orleans Gumbo

2 tablespoons lard
2 medium onions, finely chopped
2 pounds fresh okra, cut in thin slices
3 pounds shrimp, peeled
2 or 3 cloves minced garlic
3 quarts water
Salt
Gumbo filé
Boiled rice

Melt the lard in a large skillet, add the onions, and cook over medium heat until they are delicately colored. Add the sliced okra, shrimp, and garlic, and cook slowly over low heat for 1 hour, stirring occasionally. Add the water cupful by cupful. Salt to taste. Cover and cook another hour. Correct the seasoning, and sprinkle with gumbo filé. Serve in soup plates with a spoonful of cooked rice.

A Modern Gumbo

1 tablespoon bacon fat
5 or 6 rashers of bacon, cut in small pieces
16 to 18 okra pods, cut in thin slices

This adaptation shows some regard for cooking shrimp and for proportions of the ingredients.

Sauté the bacon in the bacon fat 3 minutes, then add the okra, onion, and pepper, and sauté 5 minutes more. Add the garlic, sprinkle with flour, and stir well. Stir in the broth, celery, tomatoes, thyme, bay leaf, Worcestershire, and salt and pepper to taste. Cover and simmer 1 hour, then add the shrimp and crab. Cook about 10 minutes. If the mixture seems too thick, add a little more hot broth. Serve in bowls or soup plates with a sprinkling of gumbo filé and a spoonful of rice.

1 large onion, thinly sliced
1 small green pepper, finely chopped
2 garlic cloves, crushed and chopped
Flour
3 cups stock or broth
1½ cups diced celery
1 cup tomatoes — canned or fresh, peeled, seeded, and chopped
1 teaspoon thyme
1 bay leaf
1 tablespoon Worcestershire sauce
Salt and freshly ground pepper
2 cups shrimp
1 cup crabmeat
Gumbo filé
Boiled rice

Another New Orleans Gumbo

2½-pound chicken cut as for frying
Flour
4 tablespoons butter and 4 tablespoons oil
Salt and freshly ground pepper
2 pounds okra, cut in ¼-inch sections
2 medium onions, sliced
8 tablespoons butter
¼ pound boiled ham, diced
2 cups cooked or canned tomatoes
Oyster liquor (from oysters below)
2 quarts stock (chicken or beef broth will do) or water
1 bay leaf
1 tablespoon chopped parsley
16 large oysters
1 pound shrimp
1 pound crabmeat
Gumbo filé
Boiled rice

This is a variation on the old theme, but in flavor and texture it is a far more interesting soup.

Flour the chicken, and sauté in the butter and oil till nicely browned on both sides. Salt and pepper. Sauté the okra in 4 tablespoons butter. In a separate pan sauté the onions in another 4 tablespoons butter till brown. Combine the chicken, okra, onions, ham, tomatoes, oyster liquor, stock, and herbs. Cover and simmer 1½ to 2 hours. Add the oysters, shrimp, and crabmeat, and cook just 5 minutes. Correct the seasoning, sprinkle with gumbo filé, and serve in soup plates with rice. This serves ten and can be used as a main course for lunch or brunch. It's a history-making item but not one to repeat often.

Frog's Legs

As Mrs. Lincoln states: "Frogs are considered a delicacy by those who have cultivated a taste for them." That number is legion, and frog's legs have been a dish in great favor in the West, the Middle West, and along the Atlantic seaboard.

These amphibians are delicately fleshed and lend themselves to a variety of preparations. In this country the most famous is fried frog's legs, a simple but exceedingly good treatment and traditionally one of the specialty dishes in rather fancy restaurants and roadhouses in the hinterland.

Frog's legs found nowadays in markets range in size from the very tiny ones, which require 6 to 8 pairs per serving, to the giant ones, which need only 3 or 4 pairs for a good serving. The large ones are best for frying and the smaller ones for sautéing.

Fried Frog's Legs

Heat oil or fat for deep-frying to 370 degrees. Wash the legs. Dip them in flour, then in beaten egg, and then in crumbs. Fry 2 or 3 at a time in deep fat about 2 to 3 minutes or just till they brown nicely. Drain on absorbent paper, keep warm, and serve with tartar sauce or a tomato sauce.

Note. You may dip the frog's legs in flour and then in a beer batter rather than in the egg and crumbs.

Sautéed Frog's Legs

One must be careful in sautéing frog's legs to keep them from sticking to the pan. The flesh will tear easily unless they are kept in almost constant motion while cooking. Teflon skillets are ideal for the operation. Unfortunately, our ancestors had no such help. I have watched many a cook sautéing legs, in a heavy iron skillet usually, shaking the pan and using a spatula to turn them very carefully and often. Also, do not overcrowd the skillet. It is best to sauté a few legs at a time, keeping them warm on a hot platter, till all are cooked. Some people soak the legs in milk for an hour or so before sautéing, but I feel this takes away some of the flavor.

Terrapin

Mrs. Craig D. Ritchie's Recipe for Terrapin

This is a Philadelphia recipe from 1897.

"To begin, the terrapin must be plunged into boiling water and allowed to boil a few minutes; then it is put on a platter and allowed to cool. With the assistance of a knife, the shell must be removed and this must be done with great care that the gall may not be broken. Remove this and draw what is necessary. Next, pick the flesh from the bones and take off the skin. The terrapin is then ready for the chafing dish. When the dish is well heated by the lamp, put into it a lump of butter, an ounce or two, according to the quantity of the meat. When the butter is hot, pour in the terrapin and several spoonfuls of boiling water. Let the compound boil well a few minutes, stirring to keep from burning. When ready to serve add salt and pepper. This is a non-spirituous dish to which the artist can add a few cloves if he likes. If wine is added it must be poured in at the last moment and Madeira is the best for the purpose. The terrapin is not consulted as to what he would rather be drowned in and in default of Madeira sherry may be used. As some prefer none and others more or less wine, a decanter should be on the table and the terrapin can be served with its own flavor. Any other to be added by the person to his share on his plate."

Poultry

Chicken raising now constitutes a major industry in this country, and millions of the birds are conducted through a scientifically controlled cycle of nine to twelve weeks before being sacrificed to the American menu. Few have the delicate, delicious flavor of the old barnyard chicken, which may not have been raised so pristinely and plucked so cleanly but tasted of chicken and had excellent texture. Only the "natural" capon still has these qualities.

Next to chicken, our native turkey has been the most popular of our birds, and a food source of great importance. Initially the wild turkey afforded a fine addition to the rather limited fare of the early settler. Then, as the bird was domesticated, it became a household luxury, reserved for celebrations and especially for the Thanksgiving and Christmas tables. It was also carried to other countries and has become a part of French and English cuisines. Eventually, as more poultry farmers turned to turkey as a paying business, it has become a year-round staple on the market, available in all its butterball, white-meated glory. In its modern transformation it is an item for daily consumption, reasonably priced, useful in many different dishes, and sold whole and in parts, fresh and frozen. It has come a long way from the native wild bird known to our forebears.

Chicken

In former days, the farmer's wife made the rounds of the neighborhood, selling sweet butter, eggs, and chickens, which had to be ordered a day or two in advance. These chickens were well fed with bits of bread and such from the house, and they got around and scratched the yard for other morsels and became nicely fatted. They were hand-plucked, deftly drawn, and singed of all pinfeathers and hairs, and when cooked, they were delicious in flavor. Rhode Island Reds were considered best for frying, White Leghorns good layers, and Buff Orpingtons great for poaching.

Today's chickens are "design bred." They are taken from hatcheries to growing farms, where for nine weeks they are fed scientifically and watched carefully so they all develop in exactly the same way. They come to the market uniform in size, uniform in color, and uniform in lack of real flavor. They require a good deal of seasoning to give them any character, and they fail to produce a rich broth.

However, these nine-weeks wonders are beautiful to look at, perfectly drawn and cleaned, and come so pure they do not even have to be washed before cooking. Certainly chicken has never been so popular as it is today. Drive-ins line the highways boasting Kentucky or Tennessee fried chicken. Quick-frozen chicken pies and TV chicken dinners are sold by the millions. And chicken parts are dispensed throughout the country in supermarkets as well as in shops specializing in chicken. In addition, chicken can be bought whole, cut up for frying, and split for broiling. Among the many byproducts of chicken available are such items as chicken frankfurters, chicken bologna, chicken sticks, and chicken loaf.

There was a time when chicken was a Sunday dinner dish and could be found in most homes stuffed and roasted, stewed with dumplings, or fried and served with cream gravy. Now it is daily food, propagandized for its low calorie count.

The tight polyethylene packaging used for chickens in most markets is not intended for long storage in the refrigerator. To store for 3 days or less, remove the plastic covering and wrap loosely. For longer storage, wrap and freeze.

Here are the various types of chicken found in markets — some only in specialty markets and some in every supermarket in the country. When buying chicken, estimate at least 3/4 pound for a serving. A 3-pound chicken will serve 4 comfortably but not lavishly. A 2-pounder will just serve 2.

Squab chicken. Tiny broilers that weigh about 1 pound. Broiled split or whole, they can be excellent. Only available in specialty markets. Very expensive.

Broiler fryer. A rather new term that covers chickens from 1½ to 3½ pounds — those nine weeks old. They are advertised as all-purpose chickens for broiling, frying, roasting, or poaching. The meat is moist and has very little flavor.

Roaster. A 12-week-old bird weighing from 3½ to 5 pounds — a little larger than the broiler fryer and firmer fleshed. Probably the best buy.

Bro-hen. I don't know who dreamed up this ridiculous label, but it is a somewhat evasive way of designating a fowl or hen weighing 4½ to 6 pounds. These birds are for poaching and braising. They are also the best source, apart from backs, necks, and gizzards, of broth.

Capon. Genuine capons are usually superb to eat. Artificial capons, created with hormones, are not. A true capon, surely everyone knows, is an unsexed male bird whose sedentary habits endow it with a greater amount of flesh, which is tender and high in fat content. Always considered tops in poultry service.

Broiled Chicken

Next to roasting, broiling has been the most prevalent way of preparing chicken in all regions of the country except the South. Miss Leslie gives a broiling recipe as early as 1837 (but none for frying), prescribing 45 minutes over the coals for a large chicken, broiling only on one side. It was also standard in her day to place a split chicken, bone side down, on the gridiron and cover the skin side with a plate.

Today's Broiler Council calls for broiling a chicken 20 to 25 minutes per side, always starting with the bone side to the heat — 3 to 6 inches away under a gas broiler and 6 to 9 inches under an electric broiler. Since I do not like overcooked chicken, falling from the bones, I disagree with that timing. Here are my ideas about how chicken should be broiled.

Basic Broiled Chicken

Brush chicken halves with butter (or use any of the seasoned butters below) or oil before, during, and after cooking. Broil 4 to 6 inches from the heat unit, whether using gas or electricity. Rather large broilers or those dressed with a sauce should be placed about 6 inches from the heat. Allow 13 to 16 minutes per side, according to the size of the bird. Turn once, brush well with butter or oil, and season to taste. Watch carefully and brush again. Move the chicken up to the top rack of the broiler for the last 2 to 3 minutes of cooking to get a little char, but make certain it doesn't scorch. When done it should be firm in flesh with a bit of pink at the leg joint.

Chicken can be broiled without basting if you prefer to avoid fats. Merely season and proceed, but watch extra carefully to prevent burning.

Lemon Broiled Chicken. A chicken dish that is refreshing as it can be in the summer and thoroughly delightful at any time. Brush and baste the chickens with lemon butter (see below). Salt and pepper to taste and continue basting with the lemon butter until done. Garnish the plate with watercress and serve with lemon wedges, crisp potato chips, and cherry tomatoes.

Seasoned Butters

Instead of plain butter, use any of these for brushing and basting broiled chicken. Quantities are for 2 good-sized broilers. Spread a good layer over the rib cage side of each broiler and stuff a little under the breast skin. Brush the breast with additional butter, and salt and pepper well. Broil as in the recipe above, brushing with more butter if needed.

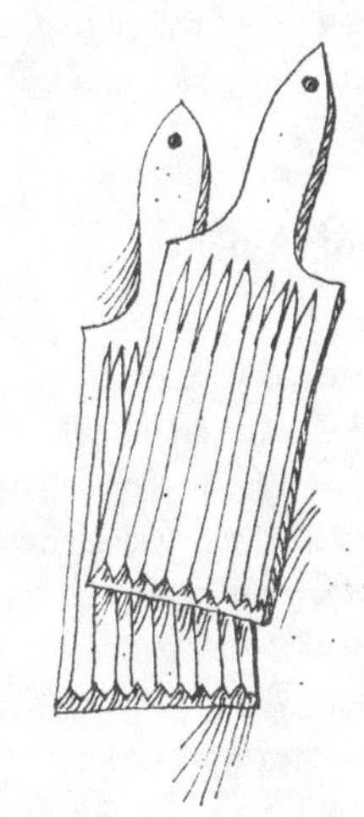

Garlic Butter. Chop 4 large cloves of garlic very fine. Blend with 6 tablespoons butter, 1 teaspoon salt, and 1 teaspoon freshly ground pepper.

Lemon Butter. Combine ½ cup softened or melted butter with ¼ cup lemon juice — or more or less, depending on your taste.

Parsley Butter. Combine ⅓ cup finely chopped parsley with 6 tablespoons butter, and blend well. Add 1 teaspoon salt and ½ teaspoon freshly ground pepper.

Rosemary Butter. Combine 6 tablespoons butter with 1 teaspoon well-crushed dry rosemary or 2 teaspoons finely chopped fresh rosemary. Add 1 teaspoon salt and ½ teaspoon freshly ground pepper.

Tarragon Butter. Combine 1½ teaspoons crushed dried tarragon or 2 tablespoons chopped fresh tarragon with 6 tablespoons butter, 1 teaspoon salt, and ½ teaspoon freshly ground pepper.

Tabasco Butter. Cream 1 stick (½ cup) butter with 1 teaspoon Tabasco. Before broiling, rub each broiler well with salt and Tabasco. Baste with Tabasco butter during broiling.

Chive Butter. Combine ⅓ cup each finely cut chives and chopped parsley with 8 tablespoons butter. Add 1 teaspoon salt and ½ teaspoon freshly ground pepper.

Curry Butter. Combine 1 tablespoon curry powder, 1 teaspoon salt, and 2 finely chopped garlic cloves with 1 stick (8 tablespoons) butter.

Teriyaki Broiled Chicken

Broiler halves

TERIYAKI MARINADE AND BASTE

½ cup olive or peanut oil
⅔ cup Japanese soy sauce
2 tablespoons grated fresh ginger or 1 chopped candied ginger washed free of all sugar
2 garlic cloves, finely chopped
1 tablespoon grated orange rind or (preferably) tangerine rind
¼ cup sherry

Travelers to Honolulu brought this dish back to the Pacific Coast, and at present it is probably the most popular method of broiling chicken throughout the country.

Blend all the marinade ingredients well and pour over the broiler halves in a shallow dish or pan. Press the broiler halves into the marinade and turn several times while they marinate, which may be anywhere from an hour to 24 hours. Place the broilers a little farther from the heating unit than usual to prevent the soy sauce from caramelizing. Brush them with a little oil, and broil according to the basic rule for broiling. Brush several times with the marinade. Spoon the pan juices over the chicken.

Barbecued Broilers

Broiler halves

CHICKEN BARBECUE SAUCE

½ cup olive oil or peanut oil
2 garlic cloves, finely chopped, or 1 large onion, finely chopped
½ cup red wine or sweet vermouth
3 tablespoons tomato paste
¼ cup lemon juice
1 teaspoon dried basil or 2 tablespoons fresh basil, finely chopped
½ teaspoon Tabasco
1 teaspoon salt

Blend the ingredients together well and pour over the broiler halves to marinate, turning frequently. Broil according to directions above and brush with marinade. Be careful not to place the broilers too close to the heat lest they burn.

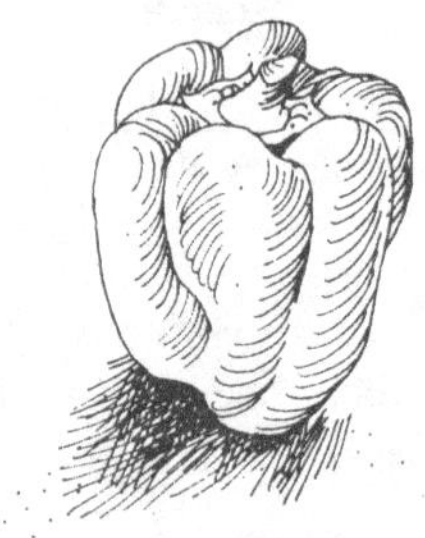

Broiled Deviled Chickens

4 broiler halves, 1½ to 2 pound birds, preferably
Crushed garlic, soy sauce, olive oil

Rub the broilers well with the crushed garlic, soy sauce, and oil. Broil and turn according to directions above. After they have broiled 10 minutes on the skin side, remove, brush well with oil, and press each one into the breadcrumbs to coat the skin side. Sprinkle with a few drops of oil, and season with salt and pepper. Move the broiler rack to a lower position and brown the broilers slowly, watching carefully that the crumbs do not burn. This will take about 3 to 4 minutes. Serve with a Hollandaise blended with tarragon or serve with a good tartar sauce.

Note. Instead of brushing the broilers with oil before crumbing, you may brush heavily with Dijon mustard or dry mustard and water mixed to a paste.

½ cup oil
¾ cup breadcrumbs
Salt and freshly ground pepper
Hollandaise, tarragon-flavored, or tartar sauce

Fried Chicken

Although everyone thinks fried chicken is as American as blueberry pie, it did not originate here. We have made it our own dish, however, and it stands or falls on a great tradition. Some of it served to people along the road and in many restaurants is best forgotten — batter-soaked as it is, dropped in stale deep fat and cooked until rather slimy, fatty, and indigestible. When correctly prepared, few dishes can be so good. At its best it resembles a Viennese dish called Wiener Backhendl, a favorite in Austria for generations. The only significant difference is that there is a larger amount of lemon juice in the Viennese recipe, which gives it a more attractive flavor.

Whether it is cooked in lard, in butter, in oil — olive or otherwise — or in bacon fat; or whether it is dipped in flour only or in flour, beaten eggs, and crushed cracker crumbs, fried chicken can come through with honors. Cold, it is delicate, satisfying, and as good as hot chicken if not better. And for a picnic menu it is incomparable (especially if it has been cooled to room temperature, not chilled in the refrigerator) when offered along with potato salad, onion sandwiches, whole ripe tomatoes, and perhaps a good chocolate cake and watermelon or ice cream.

White meat of chicken cooks faster than the dark. Consequently, when frying chicken, add the white meat after the dark meat is on its way to browning. Or, if you are frying two or more chickens, have a separate skillet for white and dark meat and time them accordingly. The white meat will take about two-thirds as long as the dark. And I beg of you do not overcook either the white or dark sections. Chickens are much better undercooked than overcooked.

Southern Fried Chicken I (Mrs. Henderson)

Despite its countrywide popularity today, Southern fried chicken did not find much acceptance in the North till the last quarter of the nineteenth century. Miss Leslie does not even mention it in the 1837 edition of her book, but in 1877 Mrs. Henderson had this to say: "The Southern Negro cooks have certainly the best way of cooking spring chicken, and the manner is very simple. Cut them into pieces, dip each piece hastily in water, then sprinkle it with pepper and salt and roll it in plenty of flour. Have some lard in a sauté pan very hot, in which fry, or rather sauté, the chickens, covering them well and watching that they may not burn. When done arrange them on a hot dish; pour out the lard from the spider, if there is more than a teaspoonful; throw in a cup of flour, more of milk, or better, cream thickened with a little flour; stir it constantly, seasoning with pepper and salt; pour over the chickens. It makes a pleasant change to add chopped parsley to the gravy."

Southern Fried Chicken II

2 frying chickens cut into serving pieces
Seasoned flour (salt, pepper, paprika, cayenne)
Fat for frying — lard, oil, or vegetable shortening
2 tablespoons flour
1 to 1½ cups milk or light cream
Salt and freshly ground pepper

This is a recipe from the Southern coastal states and is only one of many ways of deep-frying chicken.

Heat the fat in a deep skillet (a heavy iron one is best for this purpose) to a temperature of about 370 degrees. Roll the chicken pieces in seasoned flour or shake them in a bag. Drop in hot fat deep enough to cover and fry 6 to 8 minutes. Turn and continue cooking. Turn once more and cook until the chicken is well browned and tender to the fork. Transfer the pieces to absorbent paper and then to a hot platter to keep warm while you make the gravy. Pour off all the fat from the skillet except 2 tablespoons. Do not pour off the small crisp bits in the bottom of the pan. Add the 2 tablespoons flour and blend well. Gradually stir in the milk or cream and continue to stir until thickened. Salt and pepper to taste. Serve with the chicken and mashed potatoes.

A Modern Way to Fry Chicken

1 large frying chicken cut into serving pieces
Seasoned flour (salt, pepper, cayenne)
4 tablespoons butter
6 tablespoons oil (or use 8 tablespoons oil and omit butter)
3 tablespoons flour
1 to 1½ cups milk or light cream
Salt and freshly ground pepper

Place the chicken pieces in a bag with the seasoned flour, shake vigorously, and remove the chicken. Heat the fat in a heavy skillet over high heat. Brown the chicken pieces well, skin side first. Do not crowd the pieces in the skillet or you will not achieve evenness of color. Turn the chicken, reduce the heat, and brown well on the other side. Turn again, and continue cooking till the chicken is tender. You may, if you like, cover the chicken after browning on both sides and let it simmer very gently till tender. Transfer to absorbent paper and then to a hot platter. Pour off all but 2 tablespoons of fat, add 3 tablespoons flour, and stir well. Gradually stir in the milk or cream, and continue stirring until the gravy is thickened. Season highly with salt and pepper. Mashed potatoes, peas, and hot biscuits and honey are traditional with this.

Tabasco Fried Chicken

1 frying chicken cut into serving pieces
Milk
2 tablespoons Tabasco
6 tablespoons flour
6 tablespoons butter and 6 tablespoons oil
3 tablespoons butter (for gravy)
Salt, freshly ground pepper, and Tabasco

I first ate this on a picnic on a yacht at Avery Island. The recipe is from the McIlhenny archives.

Cover the chicken with milk. Add the Tabasco and salt and allow to soak several hours. Remove the chicken (reserve the milk) and roll the pieces in the flour. Heat the butter and oil in a heavy skillet till hot and fry the chicken, skin side down, 10 minutes or until well browned. Turn and brown the other side. Cover, and simmer about 10 minutes. Remove the cover, turn the chicken again, and test for tenderness. Transfer to a hot platter to keep warm while you make the gravy. Pour off all fat from the skillet except 2 tablespoons. Add the butter. Blend well over medium heat until it is bubbly and has browned with the fat in the skillet. Pour in 1½ cups of the milk used to marinate, and stir until thickened. Season with salt, pepper and Tabasco.

Bacon-Fried Chicken

8 rashers of bacon
1 3-pound frying chicken, cut into serving pieces
Salt and freshly ground pepper
3 tablespoons flour
1½ cups light cream
Tabasco
2 tablespoons brandy

This is a recipe my father often made.

Cook the bacon till it is done to your taste. Transfer to absorbent paper and keep it warm. Flour the chicken pieces and brown them well in the bacon fat over brisk heat, adding the white meat last. Season to taste and reduce the heat to simmer. Continue cooking, turning occasionally, till the chicken is tender. Transfer to a hot platter. Pour off all but 3 tablespoons of the fat and add the flour. Blend well and cook about 3 minutes. Gradually stir in the cream and continue stirring till it is nicely thickened. Season well with pepper and a dash of Tabasco and add the brandy. Let it cook up for a moment and serve with the chicken. Also serve little new potatoes and salad.

Chicken à la Maryland or Chicken Maryland or Maryland Fried Chicken

There are so many recipes for fried chicken, but none is as famous as Chicken Maryland. Strange as it may seem, no two recipes have any similarity when you compare them. Furthermore, there is no other American chicken recipe quite so internationally famous as Chicken à la Maryland. Even Escoffier has it in his book *Ma Cuisine*, and his recipe calls for a chicken to be floured, coated with egg and breadcrumbs, and cooked in clarified butter until golden brown. This was put on a serving plate with sweet corn fritters, potato croquettes, bacon and banana, and served with a béchamel sauce to which M. Escoffier had added a little horseradish. Also, he suggested serving it with a tomato sauce.

Well, that is one version. Then a very old Maryland and Virginia cookbook says that it must be breaded with flour and cooked in boiling lard about 2½ inches deep in a skillet and served with a milk gravy made with some of the drippings from the chicken, flour and milk, and seasoned with salt and pepper. This was to be served with rice. Another interesting Maryland recipe calls for the chicken to be merely floured, cooked in a very small amount of lard and butter mixed, and served with a milk gravy again. Still another recipe calls for it to be served with potato pancakes, another with mashed potatoes, and another with corn oysters. So I am not quite sure whom to believe on the subject of Chicken Maryland.

Creole Fried Chicken

1 3-pound frying chicken cut into serving pieces
Flour
5 tablespoons oil
5 tablespoons butter
1 clove garlic
1 tablespoon chopped onion
1 teaspoon thyme
½ cup diced ham
3 medium tomatoes, peeled and cut into wedges
1½ teaspoons salt
1 teaspoon freshly ground pepper
½ cup white wine
2 tablespoons chopped parsley

This rather pleasant recipe, mindful of Provence in its way, is significant for a particular reason. It is one of the first of the early recipes which mention adding the white meat after half the cooking is over.

Flour the chicken pieces very lightly. Heat the oil and butter in a skillet till hot. Brown all the chicken pieces except the breast meat. Turn the pieces and push to one side of the skillet. Add the breast meat and brown skin side first. Add the garlic, onion, and thyme. Turn the breast meat, add the ham, and cook 5 minutes. Then add the tomato wedges, blend well with the chicken, and cook till the tomatoes are just heated through and the chicken is tender but not overcooked. Season with salt and pepper. Transfer the chicken and other ingredients to a hot platter. Rinse the pan with the white wine, scraping up the delicious browned bits. Pour over the chicken, and sprinkle with the chopped parsley. Serve with rice or crisp fried potatoes and a salad.

Morton Clark's Shenandoah Fried Chicken

2 3-pound frying chickens cut into serving pieces
3 eggs
½ cup milk
Flour (about 1 cup)
Cracker crumbs
Butter and oil, oil only, or lard
Salt and freshly ground pepper

FOR THE GRAVY

3 tablespoons fat from the frying
3 tablespoons flour
2 cups light cream, heated
Salt and freshly ground pepper

Combine the eggs and milk and beat lightly. Spread the flour on wax paper. Roll crackers rather coarsely for the crumbs. Preheat the oven to 350 degrees. Place a large serving dish or casserole in the oven. Heat enough butter and oil, oil, or lard in a large skillet to reach a depth of 1 inch. Dip the pieces of chicken into the flour, then into the egg-milk mixture, and finally press into the crushed crackers. Brown the dark meat pieces and wings in the hot fat first, turning once and seasoning well with salt and a good deal of pepper. When the pieces are beautifully browned, place in the heated casserole in the oven, handling carefully with tongs. Now prepare the white meat pieces in the same way, using additional fat if necessary. Transfer this to the casserole also, cover loosely with a piece of foil, and heat in the oven 15 minutes. Pour off the fat from the pan, leaving 3 tablespoons plus all the crisp little bits which linger there. Stir in the flour and let it brown with the fat. Gradually stir in the hot cream and continue to stir until thickened. Season well with salt and pepper. Serve this deliciously crisp chicken with mashed potatoes, plenty of the cream gravy, and watermelon pickles.

Country Captain (Miss Leslie's)

Aside from Southern fried chicken, probably this is the most important chicken dish we have inherited. It was not an American dish originally, but is an American adaptation. The first published recipe I know of appeared in *Miss Leslie's New Cookery Book* in 1857.

"This is an East India dish and a very easy preparation of curry. The term 'Country Captain' signifies a captain of the native troops (or Sepoys) in the pay of England; their own country being India, they are there called generally the country troops. Probably this dish was first introduced at English tables by a Sepoy officer.

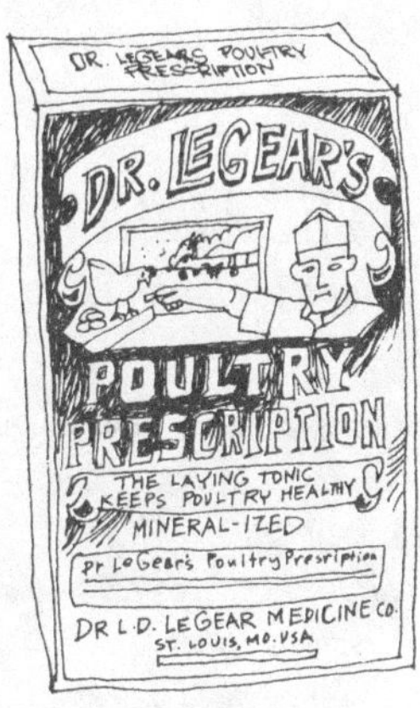

"Having well boiled a fine full brown fowl, cut it up as for carving. Have ready two large onions, boiled and sliced. Season the pieces of chicken with curry powder or tumeric, rubbed well into them all over. Fry them with the onion in plenty of lard or fresh butter, and when well browned they are done enough. Take them up with a perforated skimmer and drain through its holes. It will be a great improvement to put in, at the beginning, 3 or 4 tablespoonsful of finely grated coconut. This will be found an advantage to any curry.

"Serve up, in another dish, a pint of rice, well picked, and washed in two or three cold waters. Boil the rice in plenty of water (leaving the skillet or saucepan uncovered); when it is done drain it very dry, and set it in a dish before the fire, tossing it up with two forks, one in each hand, so as to separate all the grains, leaving each one to stand for itself. All rice for the dinner table should be prepared in this manner. People accustomed to rice never eat it watery or clammy or lying in a moist mass. Rice should never be covered, either when boiling or when dished.

"We recommend this 'country captain.'"

Country Captain (Alexander Filippini)

Next the great Filippini gave his version of the dish and served it in Delmonico's. It is a definite advance over Miss Leslie's because by this time tender frying chickens were available and it was not necessary to first boil a fowl.

"Cut the head and feet off a tender 3-pound chicken. Singe, draw, and cut it in 12 even pieces. Heat 2 tablespoons melted butter in a saucepan, add the chicken, and gently fry 10 minutes, occasionally turning the pieces. Add one finely sliced onion, one ditto green pepper, and a bean [clove] of sound garlic finely chopped; then brown 10 minutes, stirring meanwhile, and moisten with 2 gills water. Season with a good teaspoon salt, ½ teaspoon pepper, and 1½ teaspoons curry powder, freshly chopped parsley, and a saltspoon powdered thyme. Stir well, cover pan, then set in oven 45 minutes, remove, and keep hot. Scald, peel, and roast to a nice golden color a quarter of a pound almonds, add to the chicken with 3 tablespoons picked dried currants, lightly mix, cook 5 minutes, dress on a hot dish. Arrange a rice for curry around the chicken. Place six thin slices crisp, freshly broiled bacon over and serve with Indian chutney, separately, and Bombay duck if at hand."

Cecily Brownstone's Country Captain

1 frying chicken (about 2½ pounds ready-to-cook weight)
¼ cup flour
1 teaspoon salt
¼ teaspoon freshly ground pepper
4 tablespoons butter
⅓ cup finely diced onion
⅓ cup finely diced green pepper
1 clove garlic (crushed)
1½ teaspoons curry powder
½ teaspoon dried crushed thyme
1 can (1 pound) stewed tomatoes
3 tablespoons dried currants (washed and drained)
Blanched toasted almonds

Cecily Brownstone, Associated Press's adroit columnist on things gastronomical, has made a thorough study of this dish, which has fascinated her over a period of time. She has constructed a version of it which was published in *Specialty of the House*, a cookbook compiled for the benefit of the Florence Crittenton League. It's a delicious dish and one which bears repetition.

Have the chicken cut so there are 2 pieces of breast, 2 wings, 2 legs, and 2 second joints; reserve the back, wing tips, neck, and giblets for another use. Wash and drain the chicken; coat with a mixture of the flour, salt, and pepper. Heat the butter in a large skillet; brown the chicken. Remove the chicken, and add the onion, green pepper, garlic, curry powder, and thyme to the skillet. Stir over low heat to loosen the browned particles. Add the stewed tomatoes, including the liquid. Return the chicken to the skillet, skin side up. Cover, and cook slowly until tender — 20 to 30 minutes. Stir the currants into the sauce. Serve accompanied by almonds.

Note. After the chicken is browned and the sauce is made, the dish may be baked, covered, in a slow (325 degrees) oven until tender — about 45 minutes.

Baked or Oven-Fried Chicken

This is an old recipe from Miss Farmer which I have used for years and liked. It far predates any of the oven-fried chicken recipes that we have had since, and it is extremely good and easy.

Dress, clean, and cut up two chickens. Place in a dripping pan, sprinkle with salt and pepper, dredge with flour, and dot with ¼ cup butter. Bake 30 minutes in a hot oven, basting every five minutes with ¼ cup butter, melted, and ¼ cup boiling water. Serve with gravy made by using fat in pan, ¼ cup flour, 1 cup each chicken stock and cream, salt and pepper.

Corn Crisped Chicken

1 cup cornflake crumbs
1 teaspoon salt
1 teaspoon freshly ground pepper
½ teaspoon crushed rosemary
½ cup evaporated milk
6 chicken legs and thighs

A rather recent addition to American food classics, this dish became popular in record time after it was introduced. It is unbelievably simple, but results in chicken that is well flavored and crisp. I use only thighs and legs here because I prefer dark to white meat. You may substitute breasts if you like, but reduce the cooking time by about one-fourth.

Line a shallow baking pan with aluminum foil. Combine the seasonings with the cornflake crumbs. Dip the chicken pieces in evaporated milk and roll in the seasoned crumbs. Arrange in the baking pan and bake in a 375-degree oven 35 to 45 minutes, or until the chicken is nicely browned and tender but not overcooked.

Florence Bingham's Easy Chicken

2 frying chickens cut into serving pieces, or use 8 thighs and legs or 8 breasts
¼ cup honey
¼ cup soy sauce
½ cup catsup
¼ cup lemon juice
Salt and freshly ground pepper

Line a shallow baking dish with foil and place the chicken pieces in it loosely. Mix the flavoring ingredients and pour over the chicken. Allow to marinate several hours, turning once or twice. Place a piece of foil over the chicken and bake 1 hour at 325 degrees. Remove the foil and baste the chicken. Return to the oven without the foil for an additional 20 to 30 minutes. Serve with rice.

Boiled (Poached) Chicken

A so-called boiled chicken should be cooked in broth or water so that it steams and poaches at the same time. If the chicken is a good one — a rarity sometimes — this is surely as flavorful and as satisfying a way to prepare it as any. A mature bird, called a fowl, or a young bird of some fat and taste both make excellent fare when properly poached. The secret lies, as Miss Leslie mentioned in the earlier editions of her cookbook, in cooking the bird slowly enough to allow it to absorb the juices in the pot rather than give them out. One must be as wary of overcooking as when broiling or roasting. A few minutes may mean the difference between good juicy breast meat and powdery, grainy meat. A perfectly poached bird should be as moist when it is cold and sliced, to be eaten with mayonnaise or mustard dressing, as it is the minute it is taken from the pot. I'm not sure that such art has always been observed in poaching chickens, for many of the older recipes advise cooking till the meat literally falls from the bones — quite as undesirable as cooking till tough.

Any chicken may be poached, from a young broiler fryer to a fowl. I remember when laying chickens were sold for poaching with unformed eggs inside, which were delicious tidbits in themselves.

For the poaching liquid use water, broth, or a combination of water and white wine. White wine was used a good deal in the nineteenth century for chicken dishes, according to some of the more reliable cookbooks, probably the result of a wine industry that once flourished in twenty states. The wines were often of types different from those accepted today, but they were nonetheless used for the table, and some found their way into the kitchens of the more imaginative cooks. Often, also, the chicken was cooked in a broth made from chicken carcasses or other bits of the bird. If you choose to do this, make a broth with backs, wings, and gizzards. Gizzards, especially, make fine rich broth with a gelatinous quality — a broth that increases the flavor of a bird when used for poaching.

However, water is quite satisfactory, and most American recipes, apart from those that come from certain Latin or Scandinavian sections of the United States, call for nothing but this, often seasoned with vegetables and herbs. Leeks, onions, carrots, turnips, and garlic are possible choices among the vegetables, and rosemary, thyme, and tarragon are appropriate herbs to use. When using an herb in the poaching liquid, add it to the accompanying sauce as well. Also, vegetables may be added to the broth 45 minutes before the chicken is done, to be served along with the bird.

To estimate quantity for chicken salads or other dishes using cooked chicken, use the following gauge:

A poached 3-pound chicken will yield about 2½ cups meat and at least 2 cups stock; a 5-pound chicken about 4½ cups meat and 3½ to 4 cups stock; and a 6-pound (or more) fowl at least 5 cups meat and 5 cups stock.

Basic Boiled (Poached) Young Chicken

1 chicken, 2 to 3½ pounds
1 onion stuck with a clove
1 bay leaf
1 sprig parsley
Herbs to taste (use any you prefer, or reserve the herbs for the sauce)

In a deep pot arrange the chicken, trussed or not, depending on how it is to be served. Add the seasonings and water or broth. Bring to a boil. Reduce the heat and cover the pan tightly. Simmer 45 minutes to 1 hour, or until the breast seems firm and the legs give slightly when you move them. Do not overcook, as is so often done. Transfer the chicken to a hot platter and keep it warm. Strain the broth.

To serve with cream sauce: Melt the butter in a heavy saucepan or skillet and add the flour. Blend thoroughly and add the salt. Gradually stir in the strained chicken stock (or stock and white wine) and continue to stir until thickened. Correct the seasoning. Blend the egg yolks with the heavy cream. Temper the mixture by adding a little of the hot sauce, then gradually stir back into the sauce, and stir till well blended and thickened. Chopped fresh herbs may be added at this point — tarragon, basil, thyme, or parsley are commonly used; sometimes tarragon is blended with chervil; and occasionally other herbs, such as dill or sage, are used. A bit of fresh lemon peel, or a tablespoon or more of lemon juice, adds a delicious flavor. Simmer the herbs or peel in the sauce 2 to 3 minutes. Serve the chicken with the sauce, rice (see chicken and rice recipes below), and buttered peas or peas and tiny onions, fresh salad, homemade rolls, and perhaps for dessert a peach pie or apple pie.

To serve without cream sauce: Serve in any of the following ways. The same accompaniments would be good.

(1) With boiled potatoes or noodles and the broth.

(2) With a cup of broth and buttered noodles. Coarse salt and freshly ground pepper are in order here.

(3) Add thinly sliced carrots and tiny onions to the pot during the cooking. Serve the vegetables with the chicken, broth, and some good pickles.

(4) With a sauce made simply of chicken broth thickened with a roux and seasoned to taste.

1 tablespoon salt
½ teaspoon freshly ground pepper
2 to 3 cups broth or water

CREAM SAUCE (optional)

2 tablespoons butter
3 tablespoons flour
½ teaspoon salt
1½ cups strained chicken stock (or use part white wine)
2 egg yolks
½ cup heavy cream
Chopped herbs to taste
Lemon peel
Salt and freshly ground pepper to taste

Chicken Tarragon. Use tarragon in the water when poaching the chicken, and add 2 tablespoons chopped fresh tarragon to the sauce when it is thickened. Blend well. Chicken prepared in this way has been a favorite in this country since people began herb gathering over a hundred years ago. Serve with rice (see Chicken and Rice I, below).

Boiled (Poached) Fowl. If you are stuffing the fowl, sew it up securely and truss it well. Or merely insert herbs in the cavity and sew it up; truss or leave untrussed, as you like. Use 3 to 4 cups water, broth, wine and water, or wine and broth. Skim off any scum that forms as you bring it to a boil. Allow about 25 to 30 minutes of simmering per pound, and cook very slowly till the fowl is tender but not overcooked. There should be no break in the skin, and the breast meat should be moist.

Chicken with Rice I. Strain the broth from a poached fowl — you should have about 4 cups — and skim off excess fat. Remove the skin from the chicken and cut the meat into serving pieces. Remove the breast from the bones in two pieces and cut them in half. Separate the thighs from the legs and remove the bones. Use the wings as they are, and cut the back and the rib section into two pieces. While you are carving, cook 1 cup rice in 2 cups chicken broth. Make a rich cream sauce as in the basic recipe. Arrange the cooked rice in a mound on a platter or serving plate, and arrange the chicken pieces around the rice. Spoon sauce over the chicken, and serve the remaining sauce in a sauceboat. Garnish the plate with parsley or tarragon sprigs.

Chicken with Rice II. Do not skin and carve the fowl. Serve whole surrounded by mounds of rice and decorated with chopped parsley. Pass the sauce in a sauceboat. Carve the chicken at table.

Stuffed Poached Chicken

1 fowl, about 6 pounds
Juice from half a lemon
4 tablespoons butter
4 tablespoons oil
1 cup finely chopped onions
½ pound lean ground pork or sausage meat
¼ cup chopped parsley
1 teaspoon thyme or sage
½ teaspoon freshly ground pepper
4 cups breadcrumbs
4 eggs (if to be served cold, 2 more eggs)
2 teaspoons salt

Wash the chicken or fowl and rub the interior with lemon juice. Heat the butter and oil in a 12-inch skillet, add the onions, and sauté lightly. Add the ground pork or sausage meat, break it up with a fork, mix with the onions, and cook 2 to 3 minutes. Add the parsley, seasonings, and breadcrumbs and blend well. Transfer to a bowl, add the eggs, and mix thoroughly with the hands or with a large spoon. Correct the seasoning and stuff the chicken, not too firmly. Place a triple-thick square of foil over the stuffing, close the vent, and sew so that the liquid in the pan will not seep into the stuffing. You may want to stuff the neck cavity as well. If so, secure the neck skin firmly to the chicken's back with a needle and twine. Truss and tie the bird. Place in a large saucepan or braising pan and add water or broth to cover the chicken halfway. Poach as in the basic recipe, allowing about 30 minutes of simmering per pound. When the fowl is tender, transfer to a hot platter. Prepare a cream or velouté sauce, using the poaching broth. Serve the stuffed chicken with noodles or creamy mashed potatoes. A spinach soufflé or spinach ring filled with tiny buttered carrots would be a pleasant accompaniment. For an excellent contrast, also serve a sharp pickle or pickled peaches.

Cold Stuffed Poached Chicken. The fowl and stuffing are extremely good served cold for a picnic or a cold supper. Carve the fowl into serving pieces, then cut the carcass with shears or a sharp knife. The stuffing should come out in one piece so that you can slice it. It makes a delightfully different stuffing cold. Serve the fowl and stuffing with a good mayonnaise or rémoulade sauce and watermelon pickle.

Poached Young Chicken with Hollandaise

2 chickens, 2½ pounds each
1 lemon
1 sprig rosemary or 1 teaspoon dry rosemary
1 onion stuck with clove
1 rib celery or a few celery leaves
1 sprig parsley
1 tablespoon salt

Stuff each chicken with one or two slices of lemon and a few leaves of rosemary. Truss and tie the birds. Place in a heavy kettle with the onion, celery, parsley, and salt. Add 2 cups water and bring to a boil. Reduce the heat, and when the broth is barely simmering, cover the pan tightly. Let them simmer gently 40 minutes, then test for tenderness. When they are done the breast will feel firm and the legs will move fairly freely at the joint and will also feel quite firm. It is safe to assume they will not take more than an hour, but younger birds are often ready at 35 to 40 minutes. Consequently be very certain not to overcook. Transfer the chickens to a hot platter. Strain and skim the broth. Serve with a Hollandaise sauce, and rice cooked in some of the strained and skimmed broth. Save the rest of the broth for future use.

Creamed Chicken Dishes

Of all chicken dishes, this has the most unpleasant associations for most people. A rather recent addition to the country's cuisine, it is all too often badly prepared and carelessly served. When I was young it always seemed to appear at children's parties, and when I was a teen-ager it turned up at every dance supper party. It continues to be a dish universally produced for large luncheons where economy is a factor, and in one guise or another it is apt to be served up anywhere at a moment's notice. Nevertheless, it can still be a first-rate dish if carefully done.

Creamed Chicken

2 cups diced cold or freshly cooked chicken
1½ cups béchamel sauce
¼ cup heavy cream
Salt and freshly ground pepper
Dash of Tabasco
Dash of nutmeg

Heat the chicken, sauce, cream, and seasonings in the upper part of a double boiler till well blended and hot. For a softer, more runny dish, add ½ cup more sauce. Correct the seasoning and serve on toast, toasted English muffins, or thin waffles (crisp, well-made waffles are typical for chicken); or in crisp patty shells or toast croustades, or rolled in thin pancakes; or over rice, noodles, or mashed potatoes; or in éclair or cream puff shells or popovers.

Creamed Chicken and Mushrooms. Make the béchamel with chicken broth and add ½ pound mushrooms sliced and sautéed in 5 tablespoons butter. Omit the Tabasco and nutmeg.

Creamed Chicken and Clams. Add a 7-ounce can of minced clams, drained; the liquid may be used in the sauce. Correct the seasoning.

Creamed Chicken with Oysters. Add 1 dozen oysters and cook just long enough to heat through until their edges curl slightly. It is interesting to use 1 cup oyster liquor for making the sauce.

A Richer Creamed Chicken. Use velouté or supreme sauce rather than béchamel, and omit therefore the ½ cup heavy cream in the recipe. Use chopped parsley instead of nutmeg and Tabasco. To enhance the flavor, you may add during the last few minutes of cooking 2 tablespoons sherry, Madeira, or Cognac. Allow the alcohol to cook out of the mixture.

Creamed Chicken à la King

¼ pound mushrooms
3 to 4 tablespoons butter
2 tablespoons chopped green pepper
1 tablespoon grated onion
3 tablespoons chopped pimiento
3 cups diced cooked chicken breast
3 to 4 cups sauce velouté
¼ cup dry sherry
Salt and freshly ground pepper
2 tablespoons chopped parsley
6 patty shells, croustades, or potato or rice nests

Chicken à la king was an American invention at about the turn of the century, and found a great and ready public for many years. It still has a limited public. Usually prepared in mediocre fashion, it is found in many tea rooms and restaurants. Their version has little to do with the original, which is really quite good if done with care and fine ingredients. It should be served at once and not kept hot over water for hours — this can kill even the best of food.

Slice the mushrooms rather thin and sauté in butter 3 minutes. Add the green pepper, onion, and pimiento and sauté 2 minutes. Combine with the chicken in the velouté sauce and heat over hot water. Add the sherry and cook a few minutes longer. Correct the seasoning. Sprinkle with chopped parsley. Serve in the shells, croustades, or nests.

Chicken Tetrazzini

3 cups diced chicken — breast preferred
2½ cups sauce velouté
¾ pound spaghetti
1½ tablespoons salt
Water
Butter
⅓ cup sherry
½ cup buttered crumbs
½ cup grated Parmesan cheese

This was named after the fabulous coloratura who reigned almost supreme in opera during the early years of this century. She had an astounding girth as well as a thrilling voice and was famous as a gourmande. As is true of most Italians, she was devoted to pasta, which forms the base of this dish. It was probably created in San Francisco, where she loved to sing and eat. Chicken Tetrazzini is not a dish to keep standing. Eat it freshly made.

Combine the chicken and sauce in the top of a double boiler, and heat over hot water. Meanwhile, boil the spaghetti in salted water till it is just al dente. Drain well. Arrange in a buttered baking dish which can be used for serving. Add the sherry to the chicken and sauce and spoon over the spaghetti. Dust with the crumbs and sprinkle with the cheese. Either run the dish under the broiling unit or place in a 475-degree oven for a few minutes to glaze the topping. Serve at once. This is, if correctly made, a rather pleasant buffet dish, especially when served with a purée of broccoli and a good salad, followed by perhaps cheese and fruit.

Chicken in Noodle Ring

Creamed chicken with oysters or chicken à la king
Freshly grated Parmesan cheese

NOODLE RING

2 cups cooked noodles
2 cups milk
6 eggs, separated
1 teaspoon salt
½ teaspoon Tabasco
¼ teaspoon nutmeg
Butter

A noodle ring was for many years considered a most sophisticated base for various made dishes. While it is still occasionally found here and there, it is more of a novelty now than a regular. Nevertheless, I feel it is worth recording. It may be used not only for chicken, but for chicken livers, sweetbreads, turkey supreme, and fish dishes.

Drain the noodles. Beat the milk lightly with the egg yolks and combine with the noodles. Season with the salt, Tabasco, and nutmeg. Beat the egg whites till they hold peaks but are not dry. Fold into the noodle mixture and pour into an 8-cup ring mold generously buttered. Put the ring into a pan of hot water. Bake at 350 degrees 45 to 50 minutes, or until set. Remove from the water. Loosen the ring around the edge with a knife and invert on a large hot plate. Fill with the chicken mixture and sprinkle with freshly grated Parmesan cheese.

Blanquette of Chicken (Mrs. Lincoln)

1 cup rich cream sauce
2 cups diced cooked chicken
1 tablespoon chopped parsley
Salt and freshly ground pepper
2 egg yolks
2 tablespoons cream

There are many recipes to be found for blanquette, which is French in name only. Evidently it sounded attractive to ladies of the 1890's, when it was at the height of fashion, but it subsequently disappeared from cookbooks.

Combine the sauce and chicken in the top of a double boiler over hot water. Cover, and heat through. Add the chopped parsley, and when the mixture is heated through correct the seasoning. Blend the egg yolks and cream, temper with 2 tablespoons of the hot sauce, and then stir back into the chicken mixture. Blend well, and spoon into a rice ring or a ring of mashed potatoes.

Chicken Fricassees and Stews

A Country-Style White Chicken Fricassee

1 fowl cut up for fricassee
Boiling water
1½ teaspoons salt
1 rib celery
1 onion

SAUCE

3 tablespoons flour
3 tablespoons butter
2 cups chicken stock
3 egg yolks
1 cup heavy cream
¼ teaspoon nutmeg

Often nowadays fowl found in the market are very fat. Remove excess fat, wash the fowl, and place in a heavy braising pan or saucepan. Barely cover with boiling water. Add the salt, celery, and onion, bring to a boil, and boil 5 minutes. Remove any scum that rises to the top of the pan. Reduce the heat to simmer, and poach the chicken gently till it is quite tender — about 1½ to 2 hours. Do not let it get to the falling-off-the-bones stage. Transfer to a hot platter and keep warm. Strain the broth through cheesecloth or filter paper, skim off the excess fat, and reduce the broth to 2 cups. Blend the flour and butter in a heavy enamel or stainless saucepan. When cooked and bubbly, stir in the chicken stock and continue stirring till it is thickened. Combine the egg yolks and cream and temper them by stirring in some of the sauce. Stir back into the rest of the sauce until nicely blended and thickened. Add the nutmeg. Spoon some of the sauce over the chicken and serve the rest separately. Rice is perfect with this good country dish.

Note. (1) The juice of half a lemon added to the sauce during the last few minutes of cooking greatly improves the flavor. (2) Add 1 tablespoon Hungarian paprika to the butter and flour when making the sauce.

A Brown Fricassee

1 chicken, 2½ to 3½ pounds, cut for fricassee
3 tablespoons olive oil
Salt and freshly ground pepper
1 tablespoon chopped parsley
1 small onion, sliced
1 bay leaf
1½ cups water or chicken broth (approximately)
Chopped parsley

MUSHROOM SAUCE

1½ cups chopped mushrooms
3 tablespoons butter
3 tablespoons flour
1 cup cream
Salt and freshly ground pepper
Nutmeg

Heat the olive oil in a heavy skillet and brown the pieces of chicken on both sides over fairly high heat, turning them twice. Salt and pepper the chicken and add the parsley, onion, and bay leaf. Cover, and cook 5 minutes. Add the broth or water to just cover the chicken. Simmer till tender — about 30 minutes. Watch carefully. Transfer the pieces to a hot platter when done — the white meat will probably be cooked first. Strain the broth and skim off any excess fat. While the chicken is cooking, sauté the mushrooms in the butter, add the flour, and stir well. Then stir in the cream and season highly with salt, pepper, and a touch of nutmeg. Stir this into the broth in the pan, bring to a boil, and cook 2 minutes. Pour over the chicken and garnish with chopped parsley. Serve with mashed potatoes and a salad.

A Mature Hen, Pot-Roasted

1 large fowl, about 7 pounds
2 tablespoons butter
2 ribs celery cut rather fine
1 teaspoon tarragon or to taste
1 bay leaf
1 tablespoon salt
1 teaspoon freshly ground pepper
½ cup chicken stock or water
2 medium onions sliced paper-thin
1 clove garlic
1 carrot, shredded

One used to put old chickens in a pig's bladder and cook them long and carefully in water to achieve a deliciously flavored bird. This is a more modern version of the dish.

Rub the chicken well with butter. Place it on its side on a piece of foil on a rack in a baking or roasting pan. Roast a half hour in a 375-degree oven, then turn it over and roast another half hour. Remove from the oven. Have ready three large pieces of foil that will completely envelop the fowl. Place the celery, a bit of the tarragon, bay leaf, and some of the salt and pepper in the cavity. Set the chicken on the foil and pour stock or water into it. Bring the foil up around the sides. Top the chicken with the sliced onions, garlic, carrot and some tarragon, salt, and pepper. Close the foil tightly and return the chicken to rack and roasting pan. Reduce the heat to 200 degrees and roast 6 to 7 hours in the foil, being certain it is airtight more or less. Test for tenderness. Fowl vary a great deal in quality and some take longer to cook than others. Serve the chicken with the pan juices, saffron rice, and sliced tomatoes and small sour pickles. If you choose to make a sauce, prepare a roux of 3 tablespoons flour and 3 of butter. Stir in the pan juices and ½ cup heavy cream, and continue to stir until the mixture thickens.

Chicken Hash

4 tablespoons butter
2 medium onions peeled and thinly sliced
2 cups diced cold chicken
1¾ cups cold saffron rice
2 hard-boiled eggs, coarsely chopped
1¾ teaspoons salt
½ teaspoon Tabasco
1 teaspoon freshly ground pepper
3 tablespoons shredded carrot — about half a carrot
¾ cup heavy cream
2 eggs, lightly beaten
3 tablespoons chopped parsley
¾ cup grated Parmesan cheese

A wonderful use of the chicken left over from the recipe above.

Cook the onions in butter, covered, over low heat about 10 minutes till quite limp and delicately colored. Add the chicken, rice, hard-boiled eggs, seasonings, and shredded carrot. Press down well and let the mixture cook uncovered over medium heat about 5 minutes. Cover, and cook over low heat 10 minutes. Add the cream, beaten eggs, parsley, and cheese, and simmer about 4 minutes or until the eggs are set and the cheese is well blended with the parsley. If you like, increase the number of eggs to 4 and instead of the final simmering brown under the broiling unit a few minutes.

Old-Fashioned Chicken and Dumplings

1 fowl, 4 to 6 pounds, cut as for fricassee
2 teaspoons salt
½ teaspoon freshly ground pepper
1 rib celery with tops cut up fine
1 or 2 carrots, thinly sliced
2 medium onions, thinly sliced
½ teaspoon mace
Boiling water

DUMPLINGS

2 cups sifted all-purpose flour
3 teaspoons baking powder
1 teaspoon salt
2 eggs
⅔ cup milk

A favorite Sunday dinner in the nineteenth century. I feel this is a dish to enjoy once or twice a year — never more than that. It has a homely appeal and can be a surprisingly good dish to serve for Sunday lunch with really good light dumplings, watermelon pickle, perhaps salad, and a bottle of pleasant white wine well chilled.

Arrange the pieces of chicken and the giblets in a heavy skillet or braising pan and add the seasonings and boiling water to barely cover. Cover, and bring to a boil. Reduce the heat and simmer approximately 1½ hours, or until tender. If the breast pieces are tender first, which is likely, transfer them to a hot dish to keep warm. When all the meat is cooked and keeping warm in the dish, make the dumplings. Sift the dry ingredients, beat the eggs and milk together lightly, and blend with the flour mixture to a fairly stiff dough. Drop by spoonfuls into the boiling broth, cover tightly, and cook 15 minutes without removing the cover.

Note. For a lighter dumpling, separate the eggs, beat the yolks with the milk, and fold in the whites beaten to soft peaks. Sometimes tiny bits of chicken fat, well chopped, were added to the dumpling mixture, which left golden streaks in the cooked dumplings.

To serve, arrange the dumplings and chicken on a hot platter and pour broth over all. Serve with corn on the cob, creamed corn, or succotash.

A Chicken Stew with White Wine

1 roasting chicken, 4 pounds, cut as for fricassee
1 lemon cut in half
3 tablespoons butter
3 tablespoons oil
Salt and freshly ground pepper to taste
1 large onion, sliced thinly
¼ pound mushrooms, sliced
White wine, approximately 2½ cups
1 teaspoon tarragon or more to taste
1 cup béchamel sauce
Chopped parsley

This recipe must have a French background, but is pretty thoroughly Americanized. It is extremely good when properly made.

Rub the pieces of chicken with the lemon and let stand 15 minutes. Heat the butter in a heavy skillet with the oil until hot but not smoking. Add the chicken and cook on both sides till the skin is a light ivory color. Do not brown. Salt and pepper to taste. Add the onion and mushrooms and mix with the chicken pieces. Barely cover with white wine, add tarragon, and bring to the boiling point. Reduce the heat and simmer, covered, till the chicken is tender, removing the breast pieces first. Do not overcook. When all the chicken is done, skim off any excess fat from the pan juices. Reduce to ½ cup over brisk heat. Combine the juices and béchamel sauce thoroughly, and cook down several minutes. Correct the seasoning. Serve the chicken with the sauce and with noodles. Garnish with chopped parsley.

Chicken Terrapin

Chicken Terrapin was a great favorite in the nineteenth century and was probably so called because it was prepared somewhat like genuine terrapin. However, it was far easier to make and more within reach of the average cook. This old recipe came from one of the ex-pupils of Mrs. Goodfellow's cooking school in Philadelphia.

"Boil a tender chicken weighing about 4 pounds. When cold remove the skin and cut the meat both light and dark into small pieces as for a chicken salad. Put the meat into a porcelain-lined stewpan with a pint of cream. Mix together until creamy ⅛ pound of butter and 4 tablespoons of flour. Add this to the chicken and cream. Put over a moderate fire and stir carefully until the mixture is quite thick. Season highly with red pepper and salt. Just before serving add sherry wine to taste and 2 hard-boiled eggs chopped fine. Serve very hot."

Another old Philadelphia recipe (this one from Grandmother Hannah Wadsworth) adds 1 sweetbread to the mixture and omits the hard-boiled eggs.

Pickled Chicken

1 fowl, 5 to 6 pounds, cut up as for fricassee
1 tablespoon salt
3 medium onions, sliced
2 bay leaves
12 allspice berries
1 sprig parsley
1 teaspoon freshly ground pepper
Water
1 to 1½ cups vinegar or to taste

This recipe, from the *Twentieth Century Cookbook*, used to be a rather popular way in the West to present chicken in summer. It was probably appealing for its keeping quality and for its refreshingly tart fiavor on a hot day. Strangely enough, I recently stumbled upon a restaurant serving pickled giblets for a first course, garnished with chopped parsley and chives, and they turned out to be quite good. No doubt the treatment was the same used here.

Arrange the chicken pieces in a heavy saucepan or braising pan. Add the seasonings and water to cover, and bring to a boil. Reduce the heat to simmer, cover the pan, and cook slowly 2 to 3 hours, or until the chicken pieces are quite tender. About 15 minutes before finishing, add the vinegar. Arrange the chicken in a mold or bowl. Cook the broth down a bit, pour over the chicken, and chill. This dish is always eaten cold and may be served with mayonnaise or a mustard sauce.

Chicken California

½ cup olive oil
1 large chicken, 4 to 5 pounds, cut for fricassee
½ cup cornmeal, ground on a metate if possible
Salt
1 cup finely chopped onion
3 garlic cloves, finely chopped
½ teaspoon nutmeg
1 teaspoon cumin seed
1 teaspoon ground coriander
1 cup red wine
1 cup water
4 tablespoons chili powder
1 cup blanched almonds
1 cup green olives
Cornmeal for thickening
Fresh coriander (cilantro) if available
1 teaspoon sesame seeds

A remarkable old San Joaquin Valley recipe which has some authentic Mexican touches but is more interesting as an excellent example of California ranch cookery at the beginning of the century.

Heat the olive oil in a deep braising pan or heavy iron or cast aluminum skillet. Roll the chicken in the cornmeal and brown quickly on both sides. Salt while it is browning. When nicely colored, add the onion, garlic, nutmeg, cumin, and ground coriander. Turn the chicken so that the flavors blend. Add the water and wine and reduce the heat. Cover and simmer till the chicken is just tender, about 45 minutes to 1 hour. Do not let it overcook. Add the chili powder, turn the chicken pieces, and simmer a few minutes more. Transfer the chicken to a hot platter. Add the almonds and olives to the sauce. Blend a little cornmeal with water and stir into the sauce. Continue to stir until it thickens slightly. Correct the seasoning and pour over the chicken. Sprinkle with chopped coriander if available. Serve with rice or cornmeal and a good salad of oranges and onions flavored with a little rosemary. Beer goes well with this menu.

Mrs. Roberts' Chickens for Supper

2 chickens
6 to 8 hard-boiled eggs
⅓ cup chopped parsley
Broth
1 envelope unflavored gelatine
¼ cup cold water

A recipe from Utica, New York, 1868. Poach the chickens, and when they are done remove from the liquid and cool enough to handle. Skin them and cut the meat from the bones in rather small pieces. Cool in the refrigerator. Add the bones to the broth and simmer another half hour or so, then reduce rather rapidly till you have about 2 cups liquid. Strain through a cheesecloth or a linen towel. Soften the gelatine in the cold water and blend with the broth to dissolve. Correct the seasoning. Arrange layers of chicken, hard-boiled eggs, and chopped parsley in a 1-quart mold. Pour broth over to just cover the mixture, and chill. Unmold on a serving dish and garnish with seasonal greens and tomatoes or radishes. Serve with mayonnaise.

Tomato Chicken

1 large roasting chicken cut in quarters
1 lemon cut in half
2 medium slices ham cut in dice
8 to 10 large tomatoes, peeled and seeded
1 onion, sliced
1 clove garlic, crushed
2 tablespoons chopped fresh basil or 1 teaspoon dried basil
1 fairly good-sized green pepper seeded and cut into strips
2 tablespoons butter rolled in flour
½ teaspoon or more mace
1 tablespoon salt
1 teaspoon freshly ground pepper
½ teaspoon Tabasco
1 cup water
Cooked rice
Chopped parsley

This excellent recipe, which was known in Philadelphia circa 1865, resembles in some ways a chicken dish I have had prepared for me in Provence a number of times. It is especially delicious if made with perfect ripe tomatoes.

Rub the chicken well with lemon. Combine all the other ingredients except parsley and place over low heat in a saucepan or braising pan. Cover, and simmer 20 to 25 minutes to blend the flavors. Remove the cover, add the quartered chicken, and continue simmering till the chicken is tender but not overcooked. Correct the seasoning. Serve on a bed of rice with the sauce spooned over it. Garnish with chopped parsley.

Chicken and Tongue Ring

2 chickens, 3½ to 4 pounds
1 onion stuck with a clove
1 bay leaf
1 tablespoon salt
1 teaspoon freshly ground pepper

Rather a splashy entrée for luncheon or a buffet supper. It is traditional in the Middle West and the West, where the tendency to be "fancy" with dishes is prevalent.

Poach the whole chickens with the onion, bay leaf, salt, pepper, and parsley in enough boiling water to half cover them. When just tender — not overcooked — remove them and cook the broth down for 20 minutes. Cool the broth and skim off the fat. Remove the meat from the legs and thighs and grind it rather fine with the tongue, pecans, and water chestnuts. Add the beaten egg yolks and light cream, and blend well. Fold in the whites, beaten until stiff but not dry. They should hold firm peaks. Butter a 6 to 8 cup ring mold well and pour the mixture into the mold. Set in a pan of hot water and bake at 350 degrees approximately 45 minutes, or until puffy and rather firm to the touch.

While the ring is baking, sauté the mushrooms in butter and oil, and cut the white meat of the chicken into cubes. Prepare the sauce: Melt the butter over medium heat, blend in the flour, and cook a minute or two. Add the broth, stir until nicely thickened, then add the cream. Combine with the chicken white meat and the mushrooms, correct the seasoning, add the Madeira, and cook several minutes.

Invert the ring on a hot platter or chop plate. Fill the center with the chicken-mushroom mixture and garnish with chopped parsley. Serve with saffron rice and watermelon pickle.

2 or 3 sprigs parsley
Boiling water
3 thick slices smoked tongue
½ cup pecans
4 or 5 water chestnuts
4 egg yolks, beaten
1 cup light cream
4 egg whites
1 pound mushrooms sautéed in 3 tablespoons each of butter and oil
Chopped parsley

SAUCE

3 tablespoons butter
3 tablespoons flour
1 cup broth from the chicken
½ cup cream
Salt and freshly ground pepper
⅓ cup Madeira

Variations

(1) Add 1 cup finely cut celery, 1 pint oysters, and additional sauce to the filling.

(2) Fill the center with braised sweetbreads and mushrooms instead of creamed chicken.

(3) Double the amount of sauce and flavor it with 1 tablespoon curry powder and ½ teaspoon finely chopped garlic. Combine with chicken and mushrooms as above, and fill the ring. Serve with chutney and rice.

Chicken in Casserole

Both whole and cut up chickens are suitable for casserole dishes. The following is simple and most attractive when served in a nice cocotte or casserole. Since the chicken is really braised in this type of dish, special care must be taken to prevent overcooking. This is particularly true with many of the chickens we have nowadays, which are exceptionally tender to begin with.

Truss the bird well. Heat the butter and oil in a skillet and brown the chicken well on all sides over fairly brisk heat. Salt and pepper to taste and sprinkle with rosemary. Melt the additional butter in the casserole and arrange the chicken in it breast side up. Cover, and bake in a 375-degree oven 45 minutes. While the chicken is cooking, brown the onions, potatoes, and ham in the butter and oil

1 broiler roaster, 3½ to 4 pounds
4 tablespoons butter
3 tablespoons oil
Salt and freshly ground pepper
¼ teaspoon rosemary
4 tablespoons additional butter
12 small white onions, peeled
3 potatoes cut into 1-inch dice
1 thick slice ham cut in small dice
1 crushed garlic clove
2 tablespoons chopped parsley

remaining in the skillet. Add the garlic. Season with salt and pepper. Remove the casserole from the oven and add the contents of the skillet. Return to the oven and continue cooking until the chicken is tender and the vegetables are done. Do not overcook. Remove the cover and add the parsley. Serve at table in the cocotte. Also serve a good salad. Dress the chicken with the juices in the casserole.

Verna Ross's Chicken Casserole

1 6-pound fowl
1 onion stuck with cloves
2 carrots
1 tablespoon salt
1 large onion, finely chopped
1 pound mushrooms, chopped
4 tablespoons oil
4 tablespoons butter
Salt and freshly ground pepper
2 12-ounce cans whole-kernel corn
2 packages frozen peas, the tiny ones preferred
1 2½-pound can Italian plum tomatoes
1 teaspoon basil
1 teaspoon oregano
1½ pounds seashell macaroni
1 cup breadcrumbs
½ pound sharp Cheddar cheese, diced

A typically American chicken dish from the turn of the century, brought up to date.

Poach the chicken in water to cover with the onion, carrots, and salt. When tender, remove from the broth; when cool enough to handle, strip the meat from the bones and cut into serving-size cubes. Reserve the broth. Sauté the chopped onion and mushrooms in the butter and oil until limp, adding more oil if needed. Salt and pepper to taste. Add the corn, peas, tomatoes, and herbs, and cook together 5 minutes, breaking up the tomatoes with a wooden spatula. Cook the macaroni in the broth till just tender, and drain. Mix well with the chicken and the vegetables. Place in a 6-quart casserole or baking dish. Correct the seasoning. Sprinkle with the breadcrumbs and dot with the cheese. Bake at 375 degrees 20 to 25 minutes, or until nicely browned on top. Serve with a good salad, crusty rolls, and a light California red wine. This is a nice dish for outdoor dining in summer.

Roast Chicken

A perfectly roasted chicken is as fine a dish as one can have. However, it is all too seldom perfect, because the average person fears a few drops of pink juice when the chicken is tested at the joint. If roasted till the juice runs clear the white meat is ruined and the bird is as desiccated as one picked off a spit in a delicatessen. Therefore, either resign yourself to a bit of pink or roast the dark and white meat separately.

This is by no means a new battle. The French, bless them, have always known how to roast a chicken properly, and occasionally in this country one finds a cook who follows in their tradition. I was surprised and delighted recently when a charming woman roasted a chicken for me and said she liked her chicken a little pink always, and she hoped I found it to my taste. I did indeed.

Basic Roast Chicken

Wipe a 3½ to 4 pound chicken well with a damp cloth and rub the interior with a half lemon. Place a large piece of butter inside the bird with a sprinkling of salt. Rub the bird lavishly with butter on all sides. Place on its side on a rack in a shallow roasting pan — I often use the rack of the broiling pan. Roast 25 minutes at 375 degrees, baste with melted butter, turn onto the other side, and roast another 25 minutes. Baste well with the fat in the pan. Turn the chicken on its back and baste again. Roast 15 minutes, baste well with pan juices, sprinkle with salt, and continue roasting another 10 to 20 minutes, or until the juice at the joint runs pink. Transfer from the oven to a hot platter and keep warm for about 10 minutes before carving. Serve with the pan juices.

Chicken Roasted with Bacon. Drape the chicken with rashers of bacon instead of buttering it, and move them to the uppermost side of the bird as you turn it. Baste with butter and bacon drippings. This gives a rather delightful and different flavor.

Miss Leslie's Roast Fowls

"Stuff two fowls with a nice forcemeat, made in the best manner, or with good sausage meat, if in haste. Another nice stuffing for roast fowl is boiled chestnuts, stewed in butter or in nice drippings. Mushrooms cut up and stewed in very little butter make a fine stuffing for roasted fowls. Secure the stuffing from falling out by winding a tape or twine around the body of the fowl or sewing it. Roast the fowls before a very clear fire, basting them with butter. When the fowls are done, set them away to be kept warm, while you finish the gravy, having saved the heart, gizzard, and liver to enrich it. Skim it well from the fat and thicken it with very little browned flour. Send it to table with a sauceboat. Serve up with roast fowls dried peach sauce or cranberry. Make all fruit sauces very thick and sweet. If watery and sour they seem very poor and mean.

"Full-grown fowls require at least an hour for roasting; if very large from an hour and a quarter to an hour and a half. Capons are cooked in the same manner as other fowls. They are well worth their cost."

Roast Capon

Capon — when it is really a caponized chicken rather than a hormone-fed bird — is one of the more delicious fowls one can consume. It has become scarce these last few years, but can be found in most cities if one deals with a good butcher or poulterer. Capon makes a superb feast whether roasted stuffed or merely roasted with a sprig of tarragon or a bit of rosemary and plenty of butter.

Roast at 375 degrees as you would a chicken, allowing about 20 to 25 minutes a pound. Place on its side on a rack in a shallow pan, basting well with butter or bacon fat, and turning it after 30 to 35 minutes to the other side. After another 30 to 35 minutes turn it on its back and continue to baste. When the juice at the joint runs rather pink, it is done to my taste. If you must, cook till the juice runs clear, and overcook the lovely white meat. A fine capon is excellent served with sautéed potatoes or tiny new potatoes and a very good crisp salad. Use the degreased pan juices for a sauce.

Cold Capon. A wonderful dish for cold suppers in summer or for a picnic lunch. It is best to roast it with no stuffing and allow it to cool without chilling in the refrigerator. Really, it is at its peak when tepid. A good homemade mayonnaise and perhaps a string bean salad dressed with vinaigrette sauce or a well-seasoned cucumber salad are delightful with it.

Chicken Pie

There are innumerable versions of chicken pie to be found over the countryside. Some use chicken especially prepared for the pie, others use leftover chicken, and still others use a combination of chicken and other ingredients.

Originally a suet crust was used for chicken pie. Nowadays rich pastry is used as well as biscuit dough, puff paste, or rough puff paste. (Tart pastry and a flaky pie pastry are not suitable.) The crust is best if rolled about 3/8 to 1/2 inch thick. Thin crusts, while crisp and delicious at first, have a tendency to become soggy because of the steaming sauce underneath. Most of the old chicken pie recipes called for a bottom as well as a top crust. This resulted in a fairly sauce-soaked base, which is not to my taste, nor is it to the taste of most modern cooks, who prefer to use a top crust only.

For best results prepare the chicken and sauce and let them cool thoroughly in the refrigerator. Prepare the crust and roll it out. Fill the pie dish with chicken and sauce, and place an egg cup or something of that shape and size in the center of the dish to support the crust — specially designed porcelain birds are also available for this purpose. Arrange the crust over the cooled filling — sometimes it is pressed down on a moistened strip of pastry set around the circumference of the dish. Crimp the edge well, make slits for steam, and bake. By using a cooled filling you will get a better crust and a more unified dish.

Chicken pies are best eaten as soon as possible after baking. However, some pies — those with a minimum of creamy sauce — can be delicious eaten cold. For another chicken pie, see the variations on Brunswick stew in the Game section.

Old-Fashioned Rich Chicken Pie

1 chicken, 3 to 4 pounds
12 small white onions
2 carrots cut in thin slices
1 clove garlic, crushed
¼ cup chopped parsley
3 tablespoons butter
2 tablespoons flour
1 cup heavy cream
Salt and freshly ground pepper
½ teaspoon Tabasco
Rich pie crust
1 egg yolk blended with 1 tablespoon cream

Poach the chicken and allow to cool. Reserve the broth. Cook the vegetables until just tender in some of the chicken broth, seasoned with garlic and parsley. Melt the butter in a saucepan or skillet, blend with the flour, and cook several minutes. Gradually stir in 1 cup of the broth and continue stirring till the mixture thickens. Cool slightly, stir in the cream, and season with salt, pepper, and Tabasco. Cut the meat from the breast, legs, and thighs into substantial pieces. Add smaller bits of chicken to the sauce. Place the large pieces in a 1½-quart baking dish. Set a cup in the middle to hold up the crust. Arrange the onions and carrots over the chicken and pour the sauce over all. Allow the mixture to cool thoroughly. Prepare the pastry and roll out to fit the baking dish with about 1½ inches overlap. Roll up the edges and crimp with the tines of a fork to make it adhere to the top of the baking dish. If there is any pastry left over, cut decorations in the shape of small leaves or flowers and attach to the top crust with a little water. Make a vent in the center of the pastry to allow steam to escape. Brush the pastry well with the cream and egg yolk mixture. Bake 15 minutes in a 450-degree oven. Reduce the heat to 350 degrees and continue baking till the crust is nicely browned and cooked through, about 35 minutes. Serve with either a green vegetable, such as peas or snap beans, or a salad.

Chicken and Oyster Pie. Considered an elegant dish for supper, especially during the holidays in the late nineteenth century. To make, prepare chicken and thickened broth as above but omit the onions and carrots. Bring the broth to a boil. Add 1 quart of picked-over, medium-size oysters. Bring just to the scalding point, and remove from the heat. Add the chicken, 2 tablespoons chopped parsley, and ¼ cup dry white wine. Stir gently to combine. Arrange in a 3-quart casserole. Top the hot mixture with biscuit dough cut in rounds or squares and brushed with melted butter, and bake at 400 degrees for 25 to 35 minutes. Or cool the filling and top with a thick pastry as for chicken pie.

A Very Old-Fashioned Country Chicken Pie

1 large fowl, about 6 to 7 pounds, cut as for fricassee
Flour, salt, freshly ground pepper, paprika
4 tablespoons butter
3 tablespoons lard or oil
1 large onion, thinly sliced
2 carrots cut in quarters
Boiling water
2 ribs celery cut in thin slices
12 small white onions
¼ cup chopped parsley
3 tablespoons butter
2 tablespoons flour
1 cup light cream
Liver of the chicken, chopped
Rich pastry
1 egg yolk blended with 1 tablespoon cream

This is the chicken pie I used to have when we went to a farm in Hood River, Oregon, where they took paying guests in the summer. One ate great quantities of berries and fresh fruits and rich, delicious farm fare. This dish was a favorite.

In a heavy paper sack, combine about 3 tablespoons flour with salt, pepper, and paprika to taste. Add the chicken pieces and shake well. Heat the butter and other fat in a heavy deep skillet or braising pan and brown the pieces of chicken well over rather brisk heat. When nicely browned and crusty add the onion, carrots, and enough boiling water to just barely cover the chicken. Bring to a boil, then reduce to a faint simmer. Cook the chicken till just tender — do not overcook. Transfer the chicken pieces to a large baking dish that will hold the chicken and sauce. Add the celery and small white onions to the broth and cook gently till just tender. Transfer the vegetables to the baking dish.

Combine the butter and flour in a small saucepan, and when bubbling and cooked slightly, stir in the cream and continue to stir till thickened. Skim excess fat from the chicken broth and stir the cream sauce into the broth. Pour enough over the chicken pieces to cover well. Cool thoroughly.

Roll out pastry to fit the top of the baking dish and allow for overlap — about 1½ inches. Place the pastry over the dish, secure the edges, and crimp with the tines of a silver fork. Brush the pastry with the egg-cream mixture. Cut a vent in the center for steam to escape. Bake at 450 degrees 10 minutes, reduce the heat to 350 degrees, and continue baking another 20 to 25 minutes, or until the crust is golden and crisp.

Betty Groff's Pennsylvania Dutch Pot Pie

2 roasting chickens, 4 to 4½ pounds
1 tablespoon salt
1 teaspoon freshly ground pepper
½ teaspoon saffron
3 or 4 ribs celery, chopped medium fine
2 large potatoes, peeled and cut into ½-inch slices

In many sections of America, especially in the South, "chicken and dumplings" means fresh noodles (sometimes called "slick dumplings") 1 to 2 inches wide and 2 to 3 inches long, dropped into simmering chicken broth. The Pennsylvania Dutch refer to this as bot boi or pot pie, and are justly famous for it. Betty Groff is remarkable for her ability to make recipes of the seventeenth and eighteenth centuries taste as if they were being made for the first time. This is her version of the old, old Dutch pot pie recipe.

Poach the chickens in a deep pot, in water to almost cover, seasoned with salt, pepper, and saffron. Simmer 1 to 1½ hours, or until just tender but not overcooked. Remove, and cool enough to handle. Strip the meat from the bones and reserve for the finished dish. Return the bones to the broth and cook 30 minutes. Strain, and return the broth to the pot. Skim off excess fat. Make the dough:

Beat the eggs slightly, add the shortening in small pieces, then the water, and season with salt. Add 2 cups flour and blend thoroughly with the hands, incorporating the fat into the mixture. Transfer to a floured board. Knead, adding enough additional flour to make a soft dough that can be rolled very thin. When the dough has reached the required consistency, cover with foil or plastic wrap and let rest on the kneading board 30 minutes. Roll very thin and cut into 3-inch squares. Bring the broth to a boil and add the potatoes and celery. Cook till they are soft. Correct the seasoning. Add to the boiling broth the pieces of pot pie dough, one by one, and let them cook till just tender. Then add the chicken and heat through. Serve from a large heated bowl. Hot rolls and perhaps buttered green beans or peas would be an excellent accompaniment, and some good pickles will help to make the meal more authentic.

DOUGH
4 eggs
2 tablespoons butter or shortening
⅓ cup water
½ teaspoon salt
All-purpose flour to make a softish dough

Chicken Breasts

Dishes made with chicken breasts have not had a long tradition in this country but have increased in popularity in the last forty years. Possibly the original stimulus was the "supreme" or "filet," called for in so many French dishes, that became fashionable in the cities and spread to the hinterlands. One reason chicken breasts are so prevalent today is that chicken in parts is available everywhere. Another is that they make an ideal dish for the modern cook — easy and quick to prepare, versatile, and good-looking on the plate.

Many dishes call for boned breasts. Of course the butcher will bone them for you, but it is no great task to do them yourself.

Breaded Chicken Breasts

6 chicken breasts (3 whole chicken breasts boned and cut in half)
Flour
2 eggs, beaten well with 4 tablespoons cream
Fresh breadcrumbs
6 tablespoons butter
3 tablespoons cooking oil
Salt and freshly ground pepper
Tabasco
Lemon slices

Among the simplest forms of chicken cookery, these breaded breasts are versatile enough to work for many different occasions. They may be served hot with just lemon or with a sauce; or they can be served cold with a mayonnaise; or they can be prepared as an elegant dish for a company dinner.

Place each boned breast between two sheets of wax paper. Pound with a meat pounder or the flat side of a cleaver till the fillet (for that is really what it is) is flat and about ⅜ inch thick. Dredge each fillet in flour, then dip in the beaten egg and cream, and press thoroughly into the crumbs. Place on individual pieces of wax paper and stack in the refrigerator to set the coating. Heat the oil and butter — more may be necessary — in a heavy skillet. When bubbly and hot, place the fillets in the pan, two or three at a time, and brown quickly on both sides. If the fat is hot and the heat steady and medium high, the pieces should take about 2 minutes each side. Season well with salt, pepper, and Tabasco. Transfer to a hot platter and garnish with lemon. Serve at once with tiny buttered new potatoes and a purée of broccoli.

Variations

(1) Flame the sautéed fillets with ½ cup Cognac or whiskey. Add 2 tablespoons flour to the fat in the pan. Blend well over medium heat, and when the flour has cooked 2 to 3 minutes, add 1 cup heavy cream. Stir until thickened and bubbly. Add salt and freshly ground pepper, if needed, and spoon some of the sauce over each fillet.

(2) Serve the sautéed fillets with a well herbed tomato sauce.

Basic Cutlet Kiev

6 flattened chicken breasts (3 whole, boned and cut in half)
6 fingers frozen butter
Flour
2 eggs, beaten lightly
Freshly made breadcrumbs seasoned with salt and freshly ground black pepper
Oil for deep frying
Watercress

In the past twenty years, chicken cutlets of various kinds have come into prominence. People who have eaten them in restaurants become curious about how they are prepared. So it is not unusual to find a housewife in any part of the country serving Côtelettes Kiev with the greatest ease. They are even available frozen and ready for cooking. Naturally, with popularity came experimentation, and now there are many different versions of chicken cutlets, all of which are excellent.

In boning the breasts, instead of cutting off the shoulder or wing bone, remove the meat about halfway up the bone and cut it there, so that the fillet has a handle. Flatten the fillet between two sheets of wax paper, as in breaded chicken breasts, being careful you do not hit the bone or sever it from the flesh.

Flatten the boned breast, leaving the skin on if you like. Trim any rough edges. Place a finger of frozen butter in the center of each one. Roll the fillet around the butter, first tucking in the ends. The butter should be completely sealed in, so that it does not run out during cooking. Dip it at once into flour, then into beaten egg, and then roll well in breadcrumbs. Arrange the breasts on a plate and chill thoroughly in the refrigerator, at least for several hours. Then heat the oil in a deep-fry kettle to 360 degrees. Cook the cutlets one or two at a time till they are golden brown. Drain on absorbent paper. Attach a paper frill to each bone, arrange the cutlets on a hot platter, and garnish lavishly with watercress.

Note. A word of warning, if you have never made chicken cutlets. When they are served they are very hot, and the butter sometimes spurts when they are first cut into. Caution your guests!

Variations

There are many other ways to prepare these cutlets, as noted above. The following are merely a few.

(1) Give the finger of frozen butter a healthy sprinkling of chopped garlic, salt, and freshly ground pepper before rolling it in the cutlet.

(2) Add chopped garlic and chopped fresh or pulverized dried basil to each cutlet before rolling with the butter. Serve with tomato sauce.

(3) Sprinkle the butter with either chopped fresh tarragon or dried tarragon before rolling. Serve with a tarragon-scented cream sauce.

(4) Before rolling, brush each cutlet with mustard, place the frozen butter on it, and sprinkle with pepper. Serve with a mustard sauce.

(5) Dust the cutlet with ground ginger before adding the frozen butter. Serve with a ginger-flavored velouté sauce.

(6) Roll finely chopped mushrooms with the frozen butter in each cutlet. Serve with a rich mushroom sauce.

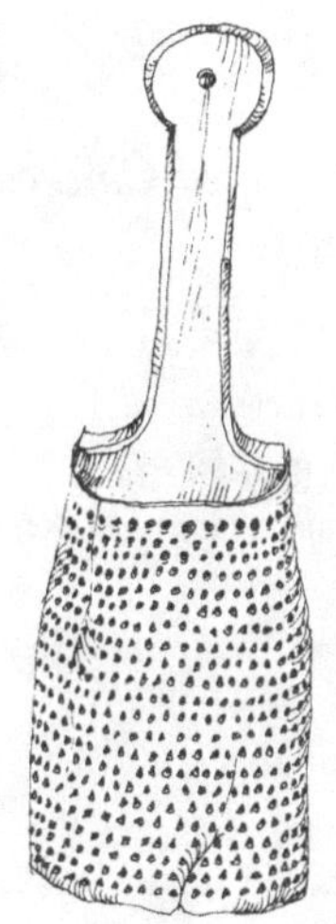

Chicken Strips

3 chicken breasts, if large; otherwise 4
Flour
1 tablespoon salt
1 teaspoon freshly ground pepper
1 teaspoon crushed thyme
1 teaspoon paprika
6 tablespoons butter
6 tablespoons oil

This is another rather modern invention that has developed from the availability of chicken in parts in most supermarkets and shops.

Bone out the chicken breasts, remove the skin, then cut the meat in strips ½ to ¾ inch wide. Combine flour, salt, pepper, thyme, and paprika, and shake the strips a few at a time in the mixture. Heat the butter and oil to a fairly high temperature. Sauté the strips a few at a time, turning them once. They will take only about 3 minutes a side to cook. Drain on absorbent paper, then arrange on a hot platter. Garnish with slices of crisp fried cornmeal mush or with green rice. Serve with a lemon-flavored velouté sauce made with chicken broth and cream, or with a very well seasoned tomato sauce.

Variations

(1) Cut the strips in halves or thirds and add 1 teaspoon dry mustard to the flour mixture. Fry very quickly in oil ½ inch deep and drain on absorbent paper. Sprinkle with Tabasco, and serve with picks for a cocktail hors d'oeuvre or on buttered noodles with a tomato sauce for a main dish.

(2) Before cooking, soak the chicken in highly seasoned milk — to 2 cups add 2 teaspoons salt, 2 teaspoons mustard, and 1 teaspoon

Tabasco. Blend well. When ready to cook, drain the chicken and shake in a bag with the seasoned flour and then with grated Parmesan cheese.

Poached Stuffed Chicken Breasts

6 small chicken breasts (3 whole, boned and cut in half)
1 stick (½ cup) butter
3 tablespoons chopped shallots or onions
4 tablespoons chopped parsley
1 teaspoon thyme or 1½ teaspoons tarragon
1½ teaspoons salt
Chicken broth

SAUCE

3 tablespoons butter
3 tablespoons flour
2 egg yolks, slightly beaten
1 cup cream
1 teaspoon or more lemon juice
Chopped parsley

This is a recipe of my mother's. She would disjoint 3 small chickens, use the breasts for this dish, and roast the legs and thighs another day.

Remove the skin from the chicken breasts. Cream the butter and blend in the shallots, herbs, and salt. Spread a generous amount of butter on one side of each breast and fold over the other half. Secure with small skewers or toothpicks. Place in a large skillet or braising pan and just cover with well-seasoned chicken broth. Bring the broth to a boil over medium high heat and reduce to simmer. Simmer about 12 minutes, or until the breasts are just tender. Turn them once during the cooking process. Transfer to a hot platter. Reduce the broth over high heat for a few moments, and make the sauce. Melt the butter in a heavy saucepan, blend with the flour, and cook 2 to 3 minutes. Stir in 1½ cups strained chicken broth and continue stirring till the mixture thickens. Combine the egg yolks and cream. Spoon a little of the sauce into the egg mixture to temper, and then stir back into the sauce. Stir in the lemon juice and taste for seasoning. Heat till thickened, but do not let it boil. Spoon over the stuffed chicken breasts in an ovenproof serving dish. Place under the broiler or in a 450-degree oven for just a moment to glaze it. Sprinkle with chopped parsley and serve at once with buttered noodles or whipped potatoes.

Sautéed Stuffed Chicken Breasts with White Wine

6 small chicken breasts (3 whole, boned and cut in half)
½ pound mushrooms
6 tablespoons butter
1 teaspoon salt
1 teaspoon freshly ground pepper
Flour
4 tablespoons additional butter
4 tablespoons peanut oil or other oil
Additional salt and freshly ground pepper
¾ cup white wine
2 tablespoons chopped parsley

Chop the mushrooms very fine, and sauté them in the butter until they are very dark — about 12 to 15 minutes over medium to low heat. Salt and pepper to taste; they must be well seasoned, and a teaspoon of pepper is not too much. Spoon some of the mushroom mixture on each breast, fold in half, and secure with small skewers or toothpicks. Roll in flour. Sauté the breasts in the oil and additional butter about 4 minutes on each side over fairly high heat to brown them lightly. Season with additional salt and pepper. Add ½ cup white wine and let it cook up for 1 minute. Reduce the heat to simmer. Cover the pan, and let simmer 3 to 4 minutes. Turn the breasts, cover the pan again, and simmer about 3 minutes longer. Test the chicken for doneness. If not yet ready, cover, and cook 2 minutes more. Transfer the breasts to a platter. Add the remaining wine to the pan, cook it down for a moment, and add the parsley. Rinse the pan well with the wine and pour over the chicken breasts. Serve with crisp fried potatoes and salad.

Club Sandwich or Club-house Sandwich

This must be included in the chicken chapter, for it is one of the great sandwiches of all time and has swept its way around the world after an American beginning. Nowadays the sandwich is bastardized because it is usually made as a three-decker, which is not authentic (whoever started that horror should be forced to eat three-deckers three times a day the rest of his life), and nowadays practically everyone uses turkey and there's a vast difference between turkey and chicken where sandwiches are concerned.

The perfect club sandwich starts with a piece of freshly made crisp buttered toast. On this goes a leaf of lettuce and a bit of mayonnaise, slices of chicken breast, slices of peeled ripe tomatoes, a sprinkle of salt, crisp bacon rashers, more mayonnaise, and a second piece of toast. Some people toss in an additional piece of lettuce, but it isn't necessary. Green olives and sweet pickles are standard garnish.

For a large party, serve a hot platter of bacon, a platter of cold sliced chicken, and a platter of tomatoes. Also have ready a plate of lettuce and olives and a bowl of mayonnaise. Make toast for guests and let them build their own sandwiches.

You may also follow the pattern of the Baltimore Museum's restaurant and serve a Club Salad (see page 73), which is an unassembled array of lettuce, sliced chicken, sliced tomatoes, crisp bacon, toast, and a small pot of mayonnaise. It may be eaten as a salad or made into several open-face sandwiches.

Chicken Legs and Thighs

Stuffed Chicken Legs

6 chicken legs and thighs (preferably large ones)
1 stick (1/2 cup) butter
1/2 cup finely chopped onions
1 clove garlic, finely chopped
1 cup soft breadcrumbs
1/4 cup finely chopped parsley
1 teaspoon thyme
1/2 teaspoon freshly ground pepper
1 teaspoon salt
1/2 cup finely chopped pecans
1/4 cup sherry
Flour for coating
6 tablespoons or more melted butter

I have always preferred the dark meat of chicken and turkey, which has a juiciness and flavor never found in the white meat; therefore it is not surprising that I should remember a dish similar to this from my childhood, when I was taken to lunch one day in Marshall Field's. At that time they had great dining rooms and exciting menus. I have never forgotten something called "stuffed chicken legs," which turned out to be the thigh and leg boned, stuffed, sautéed, and served with a delicious sauce. I was not going around asking for recipes in those days, so that particular dish was never recorded. However, since then I have found a pleasant substitute which is quite like the original but more modern in treatment.

Lay the chicken legs and thighs skin side down on a board. With a sharp knife — a small pointed boning knife, if possible — split the flesh along the bone of the thigh. Using the point of the knife and your fingers, work the flesh away from the bone. Cut around the joint and push the flesh of the leg back about halfway. Sever the

3 tablespoons flour
1 cup cream
Additional salt and freshly ground pepper

bone with shears, leaving just the end. The thigh and part of the leg are thus completely boned.

Melt the butter in a skillet over medium heat, add the chopped onion and garlic, and sauté gently till the onions are just transparent. Add the crumbs, herbs, and seasonings, and toss well. Then add the nuts and sherry and blend. Stuff the legs and thighs and secure with small skewers. Roll well in flour, and place in a well-buttered baking dish which will accommodate them without crowding. Brush with melted butter, and then pour a little more over each leg and thigh. Bake in a 400-degree oven about 40 minutes, or until they are just tender. Baste occasionally with butter. Transfer to a hot platter. Combine the degreased pan juices with 3 tablespoons flour in a heavy skillet or saucepan and blend well. Scrape all the residue from the baking dish into the pan. Gradually stir in the cream and continue to stir till thickened. Season with additional salt and pepper. Spoon the sauce around the legs and thighs. Serve with crisp sautéed or baked potatoes and tiny sautéed young beets.

Baked Legs and Thighs

Few dishes are simpler to prepare or more beneficial for the dieter. Merely rub salt, freshly ground pepper, and a little soy into the skin of the legs and thighs. Place them in an ungreased baking dish, skin side up. Bake at 375 degrees 35 to 40 minutes. Excellent hot or cold.

If you can afford butter in your diet, melt several tablespoons of it in the baking dish before adding the chicken, and baste every ten minutes with melted butter which has been blended with 2 finely chopped garlic cloves. Salt and pepper to taste. Serve with crisply fried potatoes and braised celery.

Chicken Thighs and Legs in Teriyaki Marinade

Marinate legs and thighs in a teriyaki marinade (see page 190) for 2 hours or more according to taste. Remove from the marinade, arrange in a baking dish, and brush with oil. Bake at 375 degrees 35 to 40 minutes, basting with the marinade every 10 minutes. Serve with rice blended with crisp onions, raisins, and nuts.

Hungarian Chicken

6 chicken legs and thighs
1 cup flour or more
1 tablespoon paprika
2 teaspoons salt
½ teaspoon freshly ground pepper
4 tablespoons butter

This is from *The Neighborhood Cook Book* of 1914, and is undoubtedly an adaptation of a classic chicken paprika. Nevertheless, it has a quality all its own and is worth trying.

Put the chicken pieces in a bag with the flour and seasonings and shake well. Heat the butter and oil in a heavy skillet till quite hot, and brown the chicken pieces well on both sides. Transfer to a piece of foil or absorbent paper. Add the onions to the skillet and brown very well, using additional butter and oil if needed. Return the chicken pieces to the pan with the broth and the additional paprika and simmer, covered, till the chicken is just tender — about 20 minutes. If the broth is absorbed, add more. Transfer the chicken to a hot serving dish. Add the sour cream to the pan off the heat, and stir into the pan juices. Heat for 1 minute. Pour over the chicken pieces. Sprinkle the lemon rind on top. Serve with grilled tomatoes and with noodles tossed with butter and crisp croutons.

4 tablespoons oil
1½ cups chopped onions
Additional butter and oil if needed
1 cup broth, and more if needed
1 tablespoon additional paprika
1 cup sour cream
1 tablespoon finely cut lemon rind

Chicken Giblets

Giblets, except for the livers, have been neglected in certain parts of the country. I have always found them delicious, and years ago our poultry man made a point of saving them for me. It was nothing to come away with a pint of hearts and a good number of gizzards when we went to buy chickens. I much preferred these to the livers, which seemed to appeal to most people.

Chicken Hearts

Chicken hearts floured and tossed in the pan with a frying chicken prove to be delicate morsels, and they are delicious cooked along with a broiler. They may also be strung — 2 to 5 — on small bamboo skewers, marinated in a teriyaki marinade (see page 190) and then broiled, in which form they are elegant fare for cocktails.

Chicken Gizzards

Floured gizzards may be cooked along with a fried chicken. Or they may be sautéed until brown on both sides, then covered, cooked till tender, and highly seasoned with salt and freshly ground pepper. Add a little heavy cream for the last 5 minutes of cooking. They may also be broiled or poached, along with a chicken or alone. They are excellent for making broth.

Chicken Livers en Brochette

For each person:
4 to 6 chicken livers
2 slices lean bacon
Melted butter
Salt and freshly ground pepper
Parsley

Break the livers in two pieces and discard the little bits of tendon. Partially cook the bacon and cut into squares. Place in a 325-degree oven on a rack 5 minutes or so, until some of the fat is tried out. Alternate pieces of liver and squares of bacon on skewers. Do not press them too close together. Brush well with melted butter and sprinkle with salt and pepper. Broil about 4 inches from the heat unit, turning two or three times. Brush with melted butter. They will cook rare in about 4 to 5 minutes. Serve with rice.

Rumaki. If the livers are marinated in teriyaki marinade and then each is wrapped in partially cooked bacon and skewered with a piece of water chestnut, they become rumaki, highly favored for cocktail hors d'oeuvre and also a pleasant main course when served with rice and fresh ginger. (See page 25.)

Sautéed Chicken Livers

1 ½ pounds chicken livers
4 tablespoons butter
4 tablespoons oil
1 small onion, finely chopped
Salt and freshly ground pepper
Buttered toast
2 tablespoons chopped parsley

Clean the livers and remove any trace of connective tissue. Heat the butter and oil and sauté the onions till just transparent. Add the livers and shake the pan well. Sauté just 4 to 5 minutes, shaking the pan from time to time to cook the livers on all sides. Add salt and pepper to taste, and when the livers are nicely browned transfer to a hot platter arranged with triangles of crisp buttered toast. Sprinkle with the chopped parsley and serve at once.

Variations

(1) Add a good dash of Tabasco and ¼ cup sherry. Serve either on toast or on well-buttered noodles, or see below.

(2) Prepare as in above paragraph and serve on spaghetti that has been cooked al dente and mixed with a small amount of good tomato sauce. Pass additional tomato sauce. Grated cheese is sometimes added as well. The resulting dish was originally named for Caruso by one of the better New York Italian restaurants.

Chicken Liver Omelet. Fold sautéed chicken livers into omelets. Sprinkle with chopped parsley.

Chicken Liver Timbales

6 chicken livers
2 slices bread soaked in milk and squeezed dry
1 tablespoon grated onion
1 tablespoon chopped parsley
½ cup heavy cream
3 or 4 mushrooms, sliced
3 egg yolks
1 teaspoon salt
½ teaspoon Tabasco
3 egg whites
Chopped parsley for garnish

In the days when large menus were offered for lunch and dinner, timbales were at the height of their popularity. Something between a mousse and a soufflé, they graced many a table and were much admired for their delicacy and often for their originality. The present recipe was a favorite thirty years ago and was sometimes served with a chicken velouté sauce and with — as one cookbook put it — "chopped truffles if they lie within your budget." I have modernized the recipe to use the blender, which makes a better timbale anyway.

Combine all the ingredients except the last two in a blender jar and blend 1 minute, or until finely ground. Pour into a bowl and taste for seasoning. Beat the egg whites till they are stiff but not dry and will just hold peaks. Fold into the liver mixture and pour into buttered timbale molds. Place in hot water and bake at 375 degrees 20 to 25 minutes. Unmold on a hot platter and cover with a velouté made with chicken stock. Garnish with chopped parsley.

Sautéed Giblets

½ pound each of gizzards and livers, and a few hearts if available
3 tablespoons butter

Wash and cut the gizzards into thin slices. Remove any tissue on the livers. Melt the butter in a skillet and add the oil. When hot, add the giblets and shake the pan well. Add the onion, chives, and parsley, and cook rapidly over fairly high heat till nicely browned. Add salt and pepper to taste. Add the wine and reduce the heat, then add the additional pat of butter and simmer 4 to 5 minutes. Serve on saffron rice or buttered noodles.

3 tablespoons oil
2 tablespoons chopped onion
1 tablespoon chives
1 tablespoon chopped parsley
Salt and freshly ground pepper
¼ cup sherry or Madeira
1 tablespoon additional butter

Chopped Giblet Sandwich. A delicious luncheon dish. Chop sautéed giblets fairly coarsely and season with additional salt, freshly ground pepper, and a dash of Tabasco. Mix with a few spoonfuls of mayonnaise and spread on slices of toast. Top with toast and reheat 5 minutes in a hot oven. Serve at once. Tiny sandwiches filled with this mixture are good served with cocktails.

Turkey, Duck, Goose

Called the Great American Bird, the turkey is a native of the Western Hemisphere and as early as the sixteenth century was domesticated in Mexico, where it was to that country what beef is to the United States. The wild turkey, which used to be found in profusion in this country, provided food for the colonists, although it is unlikely that the Pilgrims feasted on the bird for the first Thanksgiving. Turkey has, of course, become the hallowed dish for that holiday, as well as for Christmas and other celebrations. With increased methods of raising and processing turkeys and wider marketing of them, they are now available around the calendar and are one of the cheapest and most satisfactory food buys for families.

Unhappily, the domesticated turkey has never equaled the flavor of the wild birds, and it continues to be transformed in shape and size to meet the demands of modern taste. The craze for white-meated birds has resulted in the production of turkeys with abnormally large breasts and less and less of the delicious dark meat. Some birds, cultivated especially for small ovens, are compact and meaty and weigh only 5 to 8 pounds. There are also on the market now turkeys that have been shot with fat after they have been killed and cleaned, which makes them self-basting.

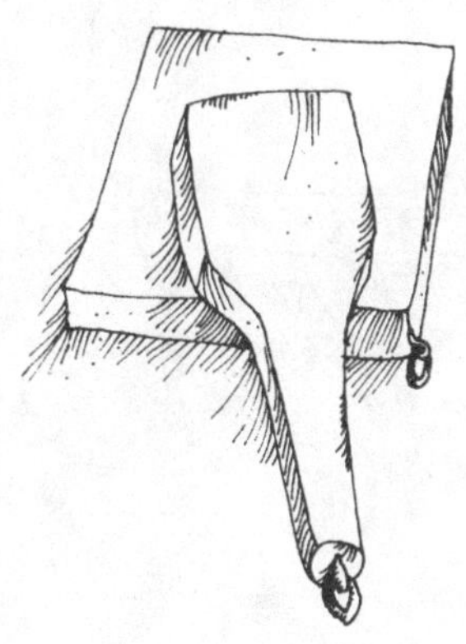

Most people overcook turkey, since they time it to achieve well-done dark meat. While the legs might still be juicy, the breast meat is inevitably dry. There is no solution to this unless you are prepared to accept a bit of pink around the joint of the leg and thigh. If the pink juices are not to your taste, you can always carve off the leg and thigh and cook it under the broiler for a few minutes or in a hot oven. But who ever started the nonsense that you can't have a bit of pink in the dark meat, anyway?

If you are using a frozen turkey, carefully read the directions provided on the label (most packagers give explicit ones), since turkeys vary a great deal in type and in processing.

Mrs. Harland's Roast Turkey

Some of the old-time writers gave turkey a big play, notably Mrs. Harland, who has a rather unusual recipe for roasting and stuffing a bird.

"Clean and wash out the crop and body of the turkey with soda and water, rinsing it out afterwards. Stuff with a forcemeat made of crumbs, a little cooked sausage, pepper, salt, and a little butter. Truss the turkey neatly. (Salt the giblets and set aside for tomorrow's soup.) Lay it in the dripping pan, pour boiling water over it, and roast about ten minutes to a pound after cooking actually commences. Cook slowly at first or it will be dry without and raw within. Baste often and freely. Ten minutes before taking it up sprinkle with flour and baste with butter. Pour off the fat from the top of the gravy, thicken with browned flour, and season. Boil once and serve in a boat."

To Roast a Turkey

Still earlier, Mrs. Randolph, in one of her nicer moments, gave us this delightful turkey.

"Make the forcemeat thus: take the crumb of a loaf of bread, a quarter of a pound of beef suet shredded fine, a little sausage meat or veal scraped and pounded very fine, nutmeg, pepper and salt to your taste; mix it lightly with three eggs, stuff the craw with it, spit it, and lay it down a good distance from the fire, which should be clear and brisk; dust and baste it several times with cold lard; it makes the froth stronger than basting it with hot out of the dripping pan, and makes the turkey rise better; when it is enough, froth it up as before and swish it, and pour on the same gravy as for boiled turkey, or bread sauce; garnish with lemon and pickles and serve up. If it be of a middle size it will require of an hour and a quarter to roast.

"To make sauce for a turkey [bread sauce], cut the crumb of a loaf in thin slices, and put it in cold water with a few peppercorns, a little salt and onion; then boil it till the bread is quite soft, beat it well, put in a quarter of a pound of butter, two spoonsful of thick cream, and put it in the dish with the turkey."

Boiled Turkey

15 oysters
A little milk
Breadcrumbs from a loaf
Butter
Seasonings
Wheat flour

In the early nineteenth century and on through to the earlier years of the twentieth century, boiled turkey and turkey fricassee both served in many a cook's repertoire. These dishes are worth reviving. Here is Mrs. Harland's recipe for boiled turkey.

"Chop about fifteen oysters and work up with them breadcrumbs, a spoonful of butter, with pepper and salt. Stuff the turkey as for roasting; sew it up neatly in a cloth fitted to every part, having dredged the cloth inside with flour; boil slowly, especially at first, allowing fifteen minutes to a pound. The water should be lukewarm when the turkey goes in. Salt and save the liquor in which the fowl was boiled. Serve with oyster sauce."

Roast Wild Turkey

1 turkey, 10 to 12 pounds
Half a lemon
6 to 8 cups stuffing
Butter
Salt
Freshly ground pepper

SAUCE

3 tablespoons flour
1½ cups stock or milk
Salt and freshly ground pepper
¼ cup sherry or Cognac (optional)
½ cup heavy cream (optional)

Wild turkeys may be ordered from certain butchers and are worth experimenting with if you can get them. They have delicious flavor and remind me of the turkeys one ate before production became so scientific.

A wild turkey should be stuffed with a simple well-seasoned bread stuffing or a cornbread stuffing seasoned with thyme, sage, or summer savory. Sometimes oysters or sausage are introduced into the stuffing and at other times black walnuts, pecans, or brazil nuts are added.

Wash the turkey well and rub the interior with the lemon. Dry the exterior and then stuff both the neck and body cavities with your favorite stuffing. Truss with a trussing needle and string. Close the vent of the body cavity with a needle and twine. Rub the turkey vigorously with a generous amount of soft butter, then season. Place on a rack in a rather shallow baking pan. Roast at 350 degrees, allowing about 20 minutes per pound or less. Baste well with butter from time to time. When done, transfer to a hot platter and allow to rest 10 minutes. Remove the trussing twine. Garnish to your taste.

To make the sauce: Leave about 4 tablespoons fat in the roasting pan and add the flour to it. Blend over low heat, scraping the pan to loosen all the bits of caramelized drippings. Gradually add the stock or milk, and stir until the sauce begins to thicken. Add seasonings to taste, and, if you like, the sherry or Cognac and cream. Correct the seasoning and serve in a sauceboat.

Traditionally, mashed potatoes, sweet potatoes, creamed onions, and mashed turnips are the vegetables to accompany the turkey, together with cranberry sauce of one type or another.

My Own Favorite Roast Turkey

1 turkey, 18 to 20 pounds
1 onion stuck with 2 cloves
1 sprig parsley
Additional salt and pepper
½ teaspoon thyme
1 quart water
Half a lemon
1 stick (½ cup) or more softened butter
Strips of fresh or salt pork, or bacon rind
4 tablespoons flour
¼ cup Cognac or Madeira (optional)

STUFFING

½ cup butter
1 cup finely chopped shallots or finely cut green onions
1½ tablespoons dried tarragon or 3 tablespoons fresh tarragon, finely cut
1 tablespoon salt or to taste
1½ teaspoons freshly ground pepper
½ cup pine nuts
Additional melted butter, if needed
10 to 12 cups fine fresh bread-crumbs

Much of this fashion of roasting a turkey came from my family. I have changed and embellished it a bit, and the final recipe is the one I use for Thanksgiving or other traditional holidays.

Make the stuffing first. Melt the butter in a heavy skillet — a 12-inch one if possible. Add the shallots or green onions and the tarragon and allow to cook until the shallots are just wilted. Add the salt, pepper, pine nuts, and then additional butter as needed — I should say another ½ to 1 cup butter, depending on the amount the onion has absorbed. Finally add the crumbs and toss well. Taste the mixture and add more of any of the ingredients if required. A clove or two of garlic may also be added to the mixture.

Remove the neck from the bird if not already done, and put it in a 2-quart saucepan with the liver, gizzard, heart, and the onion, parsley, 2 teaspoons salt, and the thyme. Add the water, bring to a boil, and boil 5 minutes, after which reduce the heat and simmer, covered, 1 hour. Drain and reserve for the sauce. If you like, chop the gizzard, heart, and liver to add to the sauce.

Rub the inside of the turkey with the lemon, and dry with paper towels. Fill the body cavity and neck cavity with stuffing, but not too tightly — the crumbs should remain somewhat loose. Truss the turkey with a trussing needle, by hand-tying the piece of neck skin to the back of the turkey, or by sewing with a needle and twine. Close the vent of the bird, and either secure with skewers and twine or sew it up. Tie the legs together firmly, and then tie them to the tail of the bird. Massage the turkey well with softened butter, and then salt and pepper it. Line a rack with strips of fresh or salt pork or with the rind of bacon, which you can sometimes buy from your butcher when he cuts down a whole slab. Set the rack in a fairly shallow roasting pan, and place the turkey breast side down on the rack. Roast 1 hour at 350 degrees. Remove the pan from the oven, turn the turkey on one side, and rub with softened butter. Return the turkey to the oven and roast another hour. Remove the pan, turn the turkey on its other side, and rub with butter. Roast for another hour, turn the turkey on its back, and rub the breast with butter. Return to the oven and continue roasting till the turkey tests done. Remove from the oven and place on a hot platter. Allow it to rest 15 minutes if being served hot. If being served tepid, let it cool gently at room temperature. Remove all the twine and skewers.

For the sauce, remove all the fat from the roasting pan save 4 tablespoons. Over medium heat add the flour to the pan and blend thoroughly, scraping to loosen bits of caramelized dripping. If there are any juices, add those (skimmed of fat) as well. Gradually stir in 2 cups or more of the turkey broth and cook, stirring constantly, till the mixture thickens. Correct the seasonings. Add the chopped giblets, if you like, and Cognac or Madeira, and simmer about 4 to 5 minutes. Serve with the turkey and stuffing.

Note. If you prefer variety in the stuffing, stuff the neck cavity with a mixture of 1 pound ground pork, 1 pound ground veal, 1 teaspoon salt, ½ cup finely chopped shallot, 1 egg, 1 cup breadcrumbs, and ¼ cup Cognac.

Turkey Hash

5 tablespoons butter
½ cup finely chopped onion
2 garlic cloves, finely chopped
½ green pepper, finely chopped
3 cups diced cold turkey
1 cup cold stuffing
Salt and freshly ground pepper
⅔ cup pitted black olives
½ cup toasted almonds
⅔ cup heavy cream
Chopped parsley

When the turkey is cold, remove about 1½ cups of stuffing and store in the refrigerator.

Melt the butter and sauté the onion, garlic, and pepper until they are limp and just delicately brown. Add the turkey and stuffing and toss well with the onion and green pepper. Salt and pepper to taste Allow the mixture to cook over medium heat till thoroughly warmed through. Turn and blend the mixture well, and add the almonds and olives. Dribble the cream over all, and let the hash cook down thoroughly till nicely blended and piping hot. Add chopped parsley and turn the hash out onto a heated platter or serve from the skillet in which it was made.

Variations

(1) Blend 4 well-beaten eggs with the cream and allow the hash to cook slowly till the eggs are just set. Sprinkle with ½ cup grated Switzerland cheese and run under the broiler for a minute or two to melt the cheese and solidify the egg mixture.

(2) Combine 3 well-beaten eggs with ½ cup freshly grated Parmesan cheese and 2 tablespoons chopped parsley. Pour gently over the hash. Place under the broiler to brown and cook the egg-cheese mixture.

(3) Blend into the hash 1 teaspoon ground cumin seed and 1 tablespoon chili powder, and use ½ cup sherry instead of cream. Sprinkle with freshly grated Parmesan cheese and run under the broiler for a few minutes to brown the cheese.

Turkey Pie

Make turkey pie like chicken pie, with or without vegetables. Usually a small turkey or a piece of turkey breast is used. However, the leftover roast turkey can end nobly in a pie. Cube the meat and make a broth with the turkey carcass, cold water, and seasonings. Simmer about 3 hours. Remove the bones and strain the broth. Simmer uncovered to reduce.

Cooled Turkey

Follow any of the recipes for roasting turkey and let the bird cool slightly, but under no circumstances allow it to be refrigerated. Serve with a potato salad or coleslaw and hot rolls.

Turkey Casserole (Fricassee)

1 small turkey, 6 to 8 pounds, cut up as for fricassee
Flour
½ to ¾ cup (1 to 1½ sticks) butter
1 cup white wine
1½ cups finely cut bacon, blanched 5 minutes in boiling water and drained
1½ cups finely chopped onions, sautéed in 4 tablespoons butter
Chopped giblets of the turkey
1 tablespoon salt
1½ teaspoons thyme
1 bay leaf
1½ cups turkey stock or chicken broth
1 cup heavy cream
Beurre manié
½ cup bourbon (optional)
Chopped parsley

An old-fashioned turkey dish that an old friend of mine, Mabelle Jeffcott, used to prepare in a large black casserole which held untold quantities. It was a most satisfying dish for a large party.

Dredge the turkey pieces lightly in flour. Melt the butter in a large skillet, and when it is foaming brown the pieces of turkey in the fat, adding more butter if needed. Transfer the turkey to a large (6 to 8 quarts) casserole or baking dish. Rinse the skillet with the white wine, and add to the turkey along with the bacon, onion, giblets, seasonings, and broth. Cover the casserole and bake in a 325-degree oven 1½ to 2 hours, or until the turkey is just tender. Remove from the oven and drain off the liquid, leaving the turkey in the casserole.

Skim off any excess fat from the liquid. Pour the liquid into a saucepan, add the heavy cream, and bring to a boil. Drop small balls of kneaded butter and flour (beurre manié) into the sauce, stirring constantly till the mixture has thickened. Correct the seasoning and add the bourbon, if you like. Return the thickened sauce to the casserole and bake another 15 minutes. Sprinkle with chopped parsley, and serve with mashed potatoes, fresh carrots or turnips, and crisp fresh rolls.

Duck

Most ducks sold in the United States are a strain known as Long Island Duckling, which has been developed from the White Canton strain. They have a fairly thick layer of fat beneath the skin and are not too heavily endowed with meat. Therefore it is best to estimate half a bird per serving unless they are extremely large. Ducks should be free of feathers, including pinfeathers, which are rarely found in a dressed bird. They should be washed, and the inside of the cavity rubbed with a half lemon. Because of the fat content it is best in most cases to cook duck at a fairly low temperature, and on a rack in a roasting pan so that the fat can drip. If the duck is roasted on the bottom of the pan it will stew in its own fat and never brown and become crisp.

A Simple Roast Duck

1 duck, 4 to 5 pounds
Salt and freshly ground pepper
½ teaspoon thyme
1 sliced lemon
1 small onion, peeled

Wash the duck, rub it with lemon, and rub salt and pepper into the skin along with the thyme. Put additional thyme, slices of lemon, and the onion into the cavity. Tie the legs together and twist the wings under the back. Place the duck on a rack in a shallow roasting pan and roast 2½ hours in a preheated oven at 350 degrees. Remove from the oven, prick the skin thoroughly with a fork, increase the heat to 500 degrees, and return the duck to the oven for another 15 minutes to brown until the fat oozes out. Turn the duck once or twice during this period. Remove to a hot platter and garnish with parsley or with candied orange slices or tiny green peas. Serve the duck with saffron rice, puréed parsnips, glazed carrots, or braised celery.

Note. You may do the final crisping of the skin under the broiler unit if you wish, but you must watch very carefully to see that it does not burn.

Roast Duck with Sage and Onion Stuffing

2 ducks, 4 to 5 pounds each

STUFFING

6 tablespoons butter (more if needed)
1 cup finely chopped onion
4 cups breadcrumbs
1 teaspoon sage
2 teaspoons salt
½ teaspoon freshly ground pepper
2 tablespoons chopped parsley
½ cup applejack

Melt the butter in a heavy skillet, and when it is foaming and bubbling sauté the onions until just translucent. Add the breadcrumbs and toss well with the onion, salt, sage, and pepper. If additional melted butter is needed you may add it at this time. Add the applejack and parsley and taste for seasoning. Stuff the birds lightly and sew up the cavity or slip several thicknesses of foil over the stuffing. Tie the legs together and slip the wings under the back. Place the ducks on a rack in a roasting pan and rub them with salt. Roast 30 minutes at 425 degrees. Remove from the oven, prick the skin with a fork, and continue roasting at 325 degrees for 1½ to 2 hours, or until the skin is nicely browned and crisp. Serve with baked apples and baked sweet potatoes.

Broiled Peppered Duckling

2 ducks, 4 to 5 pounds, each split, neck and wings removed
Half a lemon
1 tablespoon salt
2 tablespoons crushed black peppercorns

Wash the ducks, rub the bone side with lemon and the skin side with salt. Arrange the ducks bone side up on a broiling pan. Place under the broiler about 6 inches from the heat and broil very carefully approximately 20 minutes. Remove from the oven, turn the duck pieces, prick the skin well with a fork, and return to the broiling oven for 10 minutes. Remove, and holding each half with several thicknesses of absorbent paper or with towels, place the pieces into the crushed pepper so that each half is very well coated. Return to the broiling pan skin side up and continue broiling for another 10 to 15 minutes, or until the ducks are crisp on the skin side and well browned. Remove the browned duck halves from the oven and arrange on a serving dish with tiny new potatoes boiled and buttered, and a big bouquet of watercress. Serve at once on very hot plates.

Duck Casserole with Pinto Beans

2 cups brown pinto beans
1 duck, 5 to 6 pounds, cut in serving pieces
Seasoned flour
3 strips salt pork, cut into small dice
1 medium onion, finely chopped
Pinch of sweet basil
Freshly ground pepper
½ teaspoon dry mustard

Soak the beans in cold water overnight. Drain, and simmer them in lightly salted water until just tender. Drain again, reserving the liquid, and place them in a casserole. Dredge the pieces of duck with seasoned flour. Try out the salt pork in a skillet till crisp. Place the bits of pork in the casserole with the beans and brown the duck quickly in the pork fat. Transfer the duck to the casserole. Add the onion, basil, pepper, and mustard. Work the pieces of duck down into the casserole so that the beans cover them; do not crush the beans. Add boiling water or bean liquid just to cover, cover the casserole, and place in a 350-degree oven. Cook until the duck and beans are well done — 1½ to 2 hours. Add more water if necessary, but when done, the casserole should not have too much liquid. This would be excellent with some buttered turnips and an endive and beet salad.

Goose

Strangely enough, although goose has been traditional in many of the countries from which people came to the United States, the number of recipes for this bird are very few. Even more astonishing — goose is a very difficult bird to find except occasionally at holiday time. At one point, small geese called junior geese were raised in the West. They had less fat on them, and more compact body frame, but even these are now practically unknown. A Mennonite group in Ontario, Canada, has developed a remarkably good strain — not as fat as a French goose but tender and deliciously meaty. The average goose one finds in a market is frozen.

Charcoal-Roasted Goose

1 goose, 12 to 14 pounds
Salt and freshly ground pepper
Half a lemon

Probably the most delicious way to roast a goose is on a spit. Since we are a country of outdoor cooks and spit-roasters, this is not too difficult a procedure.

Rub the goose well with salt and pepper. Rub the inside with lemon. Truss and spit the goose, and balance it on the spit. Roast over medium coals, having placed a dripping pan beneath the goose to catch the fat, with the coals around it. Prick the skin with a fork as it turns on the spit and cook until the leg moves rather easily in its joint, about 2¼ to 2¾ hours. Remove from the spit, and serve with sauerkraut cooked in red wine with juniper berries and fried potatoes cooked in some of the goose fat.

Garlicked Goose

This is an old Hungarian recipe found in the manuscript cookbook of a Midwestern housewife. It calls for 2 pounds of garlic cloves to be crushed and stuffed into the cavity of the goose before roasting. It proves to be a most exciting flavor additive. The garlic need not be peeled and the goose should be sewn up before it is spitted or roasted in the oven.

Oven-Roasted Goose

Oven-roasted goose is prepared for the roasting as it is for the spitting. Place the goose on a rack in a roasting pan and cover it with foil. Roast in a 375-degree oven about 2 hours. Remove the foil, prick the skin of the goose very well, pour off the fat from the pan and reserve, and continue roasting ½ to ¾ of an hour longer until the skin is brown and crisp. Serve the roast goose with mashed potatoes with a little of the goose fat added to them, and braised red cabbage.

Roast Goose with Chestnut and Fruit Stuffing

1 goose, 9 to 12 pounds
24 to 30 prunes which have been brought to the boil and marinated 1 week in sherry or port to cover
6 cooking apples, peeled, cut into sixths, and rolled in sugar and lemon juice
2 to 3 cups whole shelled and skinned chestnuts (canned chestnuts in brine are excellent for this)
2 tablespoons grated lemon rind
2 tablespoons grated orange rind
Salt and freshly ground pepper

Prepare the goose for roasting. Roll the marinated prunes in the grated lemon rind, the apples in sugar and lemon juice, and the chestnuts in the grated orange rind. Stuff the bird with alternate layers of these three ingredients. Close the cavity with several thicknesses of foil or sew it up. Rub the goose with salt and pepper and prick the skin. Place on a rack in a roasting pan, cover with foil, and roast at 375 degrees about 2¼ hours. Remove the foil, prick the skin of the goose very well, and return to the oven for 15 to 25 minutes or until the skin is crisped. Remove to a hot platter and serve surrounded by baked or candied sweet potatoes. This is good with an endive salad made with sliced oranges and onions and tossed with a vinaigrette sauce.

Stuffings

Bread stuffings have always been the most popular of stuffings in this country. The early ones called for a great deal of sage, cubes of bread, and sometimes broth or water, and were often very soggy. I find this rather disagreeable in a stuffing and also find a lot of sage more than the palate can bear. So here are two or three stuffings I have found hither and yon over the years that I think are extremely good. This basic stuffing can be varied in many ways.

Basic Bread Stuffing (Forcemeat)

½ pound butter (approximately)
1 cup finely chopped shallots, green onions, or onions
8 cups (approximately) fresh breadcrumbs, crust and all
1 tablespoon fresh tarragon or more to taste, or 2 teaspoons dried tarragon moistened in a little white wine for 1 hour
1 cup finely chopped parsley
1 tablespoon salt or to taste
1½ teaspoons freshly ground pepper

The breadcrumbs can be made in the blender or grated on a coarse grater; or the bread can be lightly toasted and the crumbs made from that. Estimate 1 cup stuffing per pound of bird. Thus, this recipe will stuff a 10-pound turkey. You will have to adjust the ingredients for larger turkeys. Place the butter in a heavy skillet, and when it is bubbling add the shallots or onions and let them soften in the butter very slowly over medium heat. Add the crumbs, and if all the butter is absorbed, you may add more. Combine with the rest of the ingredients and toss well. Taste for seasoning. This simple basic stuffing makes a very pleasant dressing, but it can be varied in the following ways.

Variations

(1) With homemade sausage. Work into the basic mixture about 1 pound ground pork which you have blended well with 1 teaspoon salt, 1 teaspoon freshly ground pepper, ½ teaspoon ginger, a large dash of Tabasco, ½ teaspoon thyme, and one finely chopped garlic clove.

(2) With commercial sausage. To the basic stuffing add 1½ pounds commercial sausage meat, but reduce the butter content by one-fourth, as there is usually a good deal of fat in commercial sausage.

(3) With nuts. For a very delicate and distinctive texture, add 1 cup toasted almonds, toasted brazil nuts, toasted pecans, or pine nuts.

(4) With chestnuts. Wash and drain canned chestnuts and add to the stuffing according to taste. About 1 cup should be ample for a 10 to 15 pound turkey. Add ½ teaspoon thyme or a little rosemary if you wish.

(5) With oysters. You may add a pint of oysters to any of these stuffing mixtures if you wish, along with their liquor.

(6) With liquor for seasoning. Cognac, whiskey, bourbon, or any of the standard liquors make an extremely pleasant flavoring for a stuffing. For the amount of stuffing in these recipes use 1/3 to 1/2 cup.

Potato Filling

1 large onion, finely chopped
1 small clove garlic, finely chopped
1/3 cup bacon or chicken fat
6 to 8 ounces (about 3/4 to 1 cup) chopped turkey, pork, or chicken liver
1/3 cup chopped celery
2 1/2 cups mashed potatoes blended with 1/2 teaspoon baking powder
4 cups of 1/2-inch croutons of bread which have been dried out in the oven
1/4 cup chopped parsley
1 tablespoon salt
1 teaspoon thyme
1/2 teaspoon freshly ground pepper
1/2 teaspoon Tabasco

The Pennsylvania Dutch are very fond of what they call potato filling for turkeys and other birds. It is not as delicate as some stuffings, but it's unusual, delicious, and typical of the region.

Sauté the onion and garlic in a large skillet in the fat, and when they are nicely browned add the chopped liver. Cook, shaking the pan well, until the liver just changes color. Add the celery and cook about 3 minutes more. Blend this in with the mashed potato, which has been blended with the baking powder. Scrape the sauté pan well or rinse it with a tiny bit of sherry or white wine. Add to the stuffing along with the croutons and the seasonings and blend thoroughly. This is enough for a 12-pound turkey or, with a few more croutons added, for a 15-pounder.

Corn Bread Stuffing

10 tablespoons butter
1 1/2 cups finely chopped onions
1 pound well-seasoned sausage meat
The liver of the turkey, finely chopped
About 8 cups coarsely crumbled corn bread
1/2 to 2 teaspoons salt to taste
2 teaspoons freshly ground pepper
1 teaspoon thyme
1/2 teaspoon sage
1/4 cup finely chopped parsley
1/2 cup Madeira

Throughout the country, and in the South especially, corn bread stuffings have always been highly popular for any bird. This is a particularly good one.

Sauté the onions in the butter in a large skillet until they are just pale gold. Remove to a mixing bowl. Add the sausage to the skillet, break it up with a fork, and let it cook several minutes over medium heat. When it is lightly browned, add the chopped liver. Brown it for 2 to 3 minutes with the sausage meat, and add it to the onions in the bowl. Add the corn bread crumbs, salt, pepper, and the rest of the seasonings. Mix well with the hands and add the Madeira. Taste for seasoning and stuff the bird.

Variations

(1) Add 1 cup pecans to the stuffing.

(2) Instead of using sausage, add additional livers — 5 or 6 chicken livers finely chopped — and an additional 1/4 cup Madeira.

(3) Add 3/4 cup pine nuts to the stuffing at the very last minute.

Game

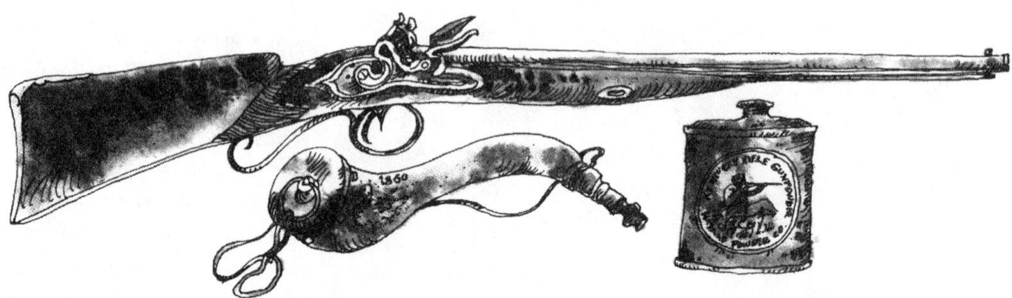

In the late nineteenth century, game was so abundant in markets and restaurants that hunting quotas had to be introduced before the choicest animals disappeared from our wilds entirely. Today game is eaten largely as a delicacy. Despite strict controls, there is still enough available to allow people to stock their freezers in season, and a certain supply comes from game farms. But it is not plentiful, except for smaller animals such as squirrels and rabbits.

Then, too, some game is imported from countries where controls are not as conscientious. For example, many American and Canadian birds are protected by law in North America, but when they migrate south of the border they are all too frequently slaughtered in great number. I have seen teal served in Yucatán that carried tags from game preserves in British Columbia.

Venison

In earlier times, so common was venison in the average diet that cookbooks listed it along with other meats rather than under the separate heading of "game." Evidently it used to be the custom to hang it for long periods, and frequently it was brought into city markets in a rather putrefied condition. Some food writers took up the banner for fresher venison, including Miss Leslie, who has something to say on the subject during the course of this delicious recipe below.

A Fine Venison Pie

"Cut steaks from a loin or haunch of venison, which should be as fresh as you can get it. The strange and absurd prejudice in favor of the hard black-looking venison (that has been kept till the juices are all dried up) is fast subsiding; and no one now eats any sort of food in which decomposition has commenced. Those who have eaten venison fresh from the forest, when the deer have fattened on wild grapes, huckleberries, blackberries, cranberries, etc., will never again be able to relish such as is brought in wagonloads to the Atlantic cities, and which has been kept till full of those fine threads that are in reality long thin whitish worms, and which are often seen in very old hams. Having removed the bones and cut the meat into steaks and seasoned it with salt and pepper, put the venison into a pot with merely as much water as will cover it well. Let it stew till perfectly tender, skimming it occasionally. Then take it out and set it to cool, saving the gravy in a bowl. Make a nice puff paste; divide the paste into two equal portions and roll it out rather thick. Butter a deep dish and line it with one of the sheets of puff paste rolled rather thin at the bottom. Then put in the stewed venison. Season the gravy with a glass of *very good* wine (either Madeira or sherry), a few blades of mace, and a powdered nutmeg. Stir into it the crumbled yolks of some hard-boiled eggs. Pour the gravy over the meat and put on the other sheet of paste, as the lid of the pie. Bring the two edges close together so as to unite evenly and notch them handsomely. Set it immediately into the oven and bake it well. If a steady heat is kept up it will be ready in an hour. Send it to the table hot. Instead of wine you may put into the gravy a half a pint of black currant jelly, which for venison is thought preferable to red. Either will do."

Note. The pastry is best if brushed with an egg wash before placing in the oven. Bake at 375 degrees 1 hour, or until beautifully browned. Also the addition of a bit of thyme and a little chopped parsley improves the flavor of the dish, and you may wish to thicken the sauce with beurre manié.

Broiled Venison Steaks

Steaks from young or properly hung tender animals are thoroughly delicious. Have them cut 1 to 1½ inches thick. Press coarsely ground pepper and coarse salt into the flesh and broil at high heat close to the broiling unit, turning them once. They will take approximately 4 to 5 minutes per side unless you like them really "blue," when they will take 3 minutes a side. While the steaks are broiling, heat a platter with 2 tablespoons finely chopped onion or shallot and about 6 tablespoons butter on it. Add a dash of salt and a few dashes of Tabasco. Place the broiled steaks on the buttered platter and top each with another pat of butter. Turn the steaks on the platter several times. Carve in strips and serve with generous spoonings of the platter juices. Fried hominy or crisp fried potatoes are a perfect accompaniment.

Venison Hamburgers

Before the word "hamburger" came into common usage, tougher cuts of venison ground together were used often for main courses. The meats should be ground as for any other ground meat dish. Form into oval cakes of 4 to 8 ounces each and about 1½ to 2 inches thick. Season with salt and freshly ground pepper, adding a bit of crumbled rosemary if you like. For best results sauté the hamburgers in 3 tablespoons each of butter and oil in a heavy skillet, turning them once or twice during the cooking. The 8-ounce patties will take about 4 minutes a side, and smaller patties 2 to 3 minutes a side. Excellent with sautéed mushrooms and fried onions.

Spitted Boned Leg or Haunch of Venison

Naturally most venison was spit-roasted in the earlier days, and this method works quite as well today with our larger grills equipped with revolving spits. It is probably the most delicious way to prepare the meat.

Nowadays most people take their kill to an accommodating butcher to skin, hang, and cut. If you do this, have him bone out the haunches and roll and tie them, trying to achieve a fairly even circumference the length of the meat.

Prepare small pieces of fat salt pork to lard the haunch. Either use a larding needle and draw several pieces of pork through the roast or make deep incisions with a small sharp knife and force in pieces of the salt pork. Venison is not a well-marbled meat by nature, and larding lubricates and helps to tenderize the meats.

Balance the meat on a spit and roast over a bed of live coals until the interior temperature reaches 125 or 130 degrees. Baste or brush with the liquid (below) from time to time, and salt well about 15 minutes before removing from the spit. If it is possible, arrange the coals around a pan which can serve to catch the drippings. Some large grills on the market are already equipped with a dripping pan.

Remove the roast from the spit and let it rest 10 minutes before carving. Serve with fried hominy squares or with puréed chestnuts mixed with butter and cream. The pan juices, with fat removed, are delicious served on the meat.

Basting Liquid for Spitted Boned Haunch of Venison

½ cup olive or corn oil
1 cup red wine
1 teaspoon rosemary
3 crushed garlic cloves
½ teaspoon Tabasco

Everything from combinations of currant jelly and consommé to good wine and soy mixtures has been used for basting venison. This is one of my favorite preparations.

Combine the oil and wine. Crush the rosemary leaves and garlic with a small mortar and pestle or chop very fine, and add, with the Tabasco, to the mixture. Let stand a couple of hours.

Roast Haunch of Venison

1 haunch of venison
3 cloves garlic, finely chopped
1½ teaspoons freshly ground pepper
1 teaspoon rosemary, thyme, or savory, finely crushed
6 tablespoons softened butter
Salt
¾ cup melted butter or olive oil
1 cup venison or beef broth
½ cup Madeira or sherry
½ teaspoon additional freshly ground pepper
¼ teaspoon Tabasco
Beurre manié or 1½ teaspoons arrowroot mixed with 1 tablespoon or more water

If you have the haunch of a young animal, it should hang about 10 to 12 days before roasting.

Rub the meat well with the garlic, pepper, and herb, and let it stand 2 hours. Rub in the softened butter and salt to taste. Set the oven at 450 degrees. Arrange the haunch on a rack in a rather shallow roasting pan and have the melted butter or olive oil ready for basting, beginning when the haunch has cooked 15 minutes. Place the haunch in the oven, roast at 450 degrees 30 minutes, then reduce the heat to 325 degrees and continue roasting till the temperature of the meat is 125 degrees, for rare, when tested in the thickest part with a meat thermometer.

Transfer the roast to a hot platter and let it rest in a warm place 10 to 12 minutes before carving. Skim most of the fat from the pan juices. Place the pan over medium heat and add to it the broth, wine, additional pepper, and Tabasco. Bring to a boil and scrape all the caramelized bits into the sauce. Thicken with the beurre manié or arrowroot. Stir until thickened and correct the seasoning.

Serve the venison haunch with a purée of parsnips, perhaps some currant jelly, and a salad. Venison calls for a good red wine — a Pinot Noir from California or a good French Burgundy, such as a Fixin or a Gevrey-Chambertin.

Roast Saddle of Venison

Saddle of venison
Oil
Salt and freshly ground pepper
1 cup strong broth
Beurre manié
1 to 2 tablespoons chopped parsley

MARINADE

½ cup olive or vegetable oil
2 carrots cut in rounds
1 large onion, thinly sliced

A roasted saddle has become one of the luxury dishes for a great dinner — a revival of a custom from the mid-nineteenth and late eighteenth century, when it was also considered a pièce de résistance for a formal gathering. The saddle should be roasted rare — very rare, by preference — and should be marinated several days before it is roasted.

Rub the saddle well with oil, place it in the marinade, and let it remain several days, turning it once or so a day.

Remove the meat from the marinade and wipe it dry. Place on a rack in a rather shallow roasting pan. Roast at 450 degrees 30 minutes. Reduce the heat to 400 degrees and continue roasting till the internal temperature, when tested with a meat thermometer,

1 rib celery cut in chunks
2 crushed garlic cloves
2 or 3 sprigs of parsley
1 teaspoon rosemary
½ teaspoon savory
1 bay leaf
1 teaspoon freshly ground pepper
1 bottle (⅕ gallon) red wine

reaches 125 degrees. Salt about 15 minutes before removing from the oven. Transfer to a hot platter.

While the roast is cooking, strain the marinade and reduce it to 2 cups over high heat. Reserve half of it for future use — for a marinade or a sauce. Combine 1 cup with the broth, and correct the seasoning. Stir in the beurre manié and continue stirring until thickened. Reduce the heat and let the sauce simmer 20 to 25 minutes, stirring occasionally and taking care it does not burn. Add the chopped parsley and serve with the roasted venison. Also serve puréed chestnuts mixed with butter and cream, and buttered brussels sprouts.

Roast Young Saddle of Venison

1 saddle of young venison
1 teaspoon freshly ground pepper
1 teaspoon thyme
¼ teaspoon Tabasco
1½ teaspoons salt
6 tablespoons softened butter
Melted butter
Red wine
1½ cups chicken, beef, or venison broth
Beurre manié
½ cup Madeira or sherry
2 tablespoons chopped parsley

If the venison was quite fresh and young it was very often roasted without the marinade.

Rub the saddle well with the pepper, thyme, Tabasco, salt, and softened butter. Roast on a rack in a shallow pan at 450 degrees 30 minutes, and then at 400 degrees till it registers 125 degrees on the meat thermometer, for rare. It will average about 10 to 12 minutes per pound. Baste occasionally with a mixture of melted butter and red wine in equal quantities. Transfer the saddle to a hot platter and let stand in a warm place at least 10 minutes before carving.

If there are any juices left in the roasting pan rinse them out with the broth. Bring to a boil, stir in the beurre manié, and continue stirring until thickened. Add the Madeira or sherry and let the sauce simmer 5 minutes. Correct the seasoning and add the chopped parsley. Serve with a purée of sweet potatoes dressed with butter — eschew the traditional marshmallows, please — and buttered kale.

Note. It was the custom when making the sauce for venison roasts to incorporate a half glass or more of currant jelly. This nineteenth-century nicety may be followed if desired.

Broiled Venison Tenderloin

One of our older cookbooks states that nothing could be more unappetizing than rare venison. How wrong its author was.

Recently I had a windfall of six magnificent tenderloins, a gift from a friend who doesn't like venison. They were tender, fresh, and as beautiful a collection of meats as I had seen for a long time. I rubbed them well with pepper, a little ginger, garlic, and a touch of thyme. Then I rolled them in oil and broiled them quickly under the highest heat, brushing from time to time with butter and sprinkling with salt and pepper. Served with Béarnaise sauce, crisp sautéed potatoes, and grilled tomatoes, they were a dinner of extraordinary magnificence.

Pot-Roasted Venison

Cut of venison for pot-roasting
Oil
Thyme or sage
Cut clove of garlic
Salt and freshly ground pepper
Beef suet
1 onion stuck with 2 cloves
3 cloves garlic
1 bay leaf
2 or 3 small carrots
1 leek
1 teaspoon savory
2 cups red wine
Beurre manié or 1 can beef gravy

Quantities of older venison as well as elk and moose were shot in the pioneering and homesteading days. It was easier to long-cook such meat than to marinate and attempt to tenderize it.

When dealing with a less tender piece of venison it is always best to lard it well with salt pork — and if you like you can soak the larding pork in brandy, bourbon, or gin beforehand. Using a larding needle, plunge the pieces of salt pork deep into the meat. You may add slivers of garlic and bits of carrot to your larding as well.

Rub the meat well with the oil, herb, and cut garlic. Sprinkle with pepper and salt. Brown quickly on all sides in a Dutch oven or braising pan in melted beef suet or oil. Reduce the heat. Add the onion, garlic, bay leaf, carrots, leek, savory, and wine. Bring to a boil. Reduce the heat again, cover, and simmer 2½ to 3 hours, or until the meat is quite tender. Transfer it to a hot platter. Remove the vegetables and skim the fat from the pan juices. Place the braising pan over high heat and reduce the pan juices by one-third. Thicken the sauce with beurre manié or canned beef gravy. Stir over medium heat until thickened to your taste. Serve the venison pot roast with macaroni. Pour the sauce over both. Watermelon pickle and a good salad will complete this hearty and delicious meal.

Other Venison Uses

Venison hams. When deer were part of the daily routine, venison hams figured greatly in the list of keepables for the winter. The hams were cured with salt, sugar, and saltpeter, and stored in pickle 2 weeks, after which they were rolled in sawdust and smoked. The resulting meat was more like dried beef than ham, and it was used like dried beef. Only occasionally was it cut in a great chunk and stewed in water or broth as a ham might be.

Venison chili. Venison is often made into chili. For a well-flavored, delicious dish use the recipe on page 18, substituting ground venison for the beef.

Venison sausage. Venison sausage is famous throughout parts of the country. It is made with 3 parts venison to 2 parts pork, seasoned with garlic, salt, red pepper flakes and black pepper, and stuffed into casings and smoked. It was a great favorite of former President Lyndon Johnson and often served at his ranch.

Dried venison. Jerky, or air-dried venison, is used like dried beef and has a particularly good flavor. I can remember it from childhood, when I felt it was a novelty and grew quite fond of its rather gamy flavor.

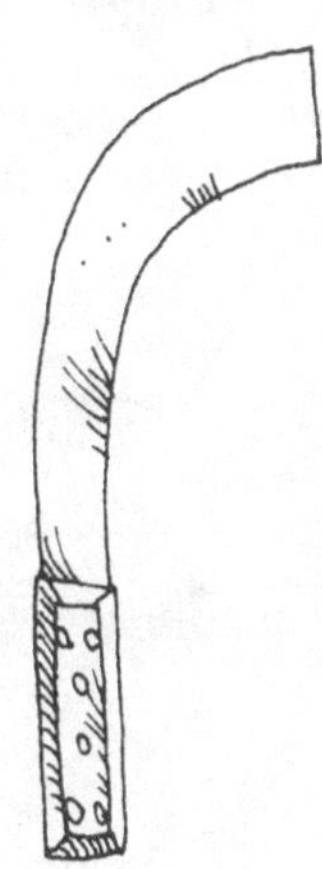

Mock Venison

It is interesting to note the number of mock game dishes which appeared in early cookery books. There was a mock recipe for almost every game bird and animal. Here is Mrs. Hale's recipe for mock venison:

"Hang up, for several days, a large fat loin of mutton; then bone it, and take off all the kidney fat and the skin from the upper fat. Mix together one ounce of ground allspice, two ounces of brown sugar and one ounce of ground black pepper. Rub it well into the mutton; keep it covered with the skin; rub and turn it daily for five days. When to be roasted cover it with the skin and paper it [parchment] the way venison is done. Serve it with made gravy and currant jelly. It must be washed from the spices before it is roasted."

Note. Not too unlike some of the spiced beef recipes in England, and the resulting roast is quite good.

Pheasant

Fried Pheasant

1 young pheasant
½ cup flour seasoned with 1 teaspoon salt, ¾ teaspoon freshly ground pepper, and a touch of thyme
4 tablespoons butter
4 tablespoons oil
½ cup stock, wine, or water
3 tablespoons flour
1½ cups cream
Salt and freshly ground pepper

This was one of the standard recipes for pheasant in the West and to a lesser extent in the East and South after the bird became plentiful.

Cut the pheasant in serving pieces as you would a chicken. Shake the pieces in a plastic bag with the seasoned flour, to coat them. Heat the butter and oil in a heavy skillet. Brown the pieces of pheasant well on both sides over rather high heat. Reduce the heat and add the liquid. Cover the skillet, let cook a few minutes, then remove the cover and allow the bird to cook till tender. The breast will cook much faster than the legs and thighs, and since pheasant meat is drier than that of most birds, the pieces of white meat should be removed the moment they are tender and kept warm on a hot platter. Continue cooking the legs and thighs till tender, and transfer to the platter. Remove all but 3 tablespoons fat from the pan and add the flour. Blend and cook a few minutes to color the flour and scrape up all the bits of residue in the pan. Add the cream and cook over fairly brisk heat, stirring constantly till the mixture thickens. Season with salt and pepper, and serve with the pheasant. Mashed potatoes, made with butter and cream, and braised cabbage are excellent with this dish.

Sautéed Pheasant with Cabbage

2 young pheasant
1 cup flour seasoned with 1½ teaspoons salt, 1 teaspoon freshly ground pepper, 1 teaspoon well-rubbed sage
10 tablespoons butter
8 tablespoons oil
½ cup water, white wine, or chicken broth
1 small head cabbage, finely shredded
6 tablespoons additional butter
½ cup heavy cream
1 teaspoon salt
½ teaspoon freshly ground pepper
Fresh dill sprigs or 1 teaspoon dillweed

Cut the pheasant into serving pieces. Shake the pieces in a plastic bag with the seasoned flour, to coat them. In each of two skillets heat half the butter and half the oil. When quite hot, add the dark meat sections to one skillet and the breasts to another. Cook over high heat till nicely browned on both sides. Reduce the heat to low, and add the water, wine, or broth to the pan containing the dark meat. Cover, and simmer 10 minutes. Allow the white meat to cook gently, basting with the pan juices and additional butter if necessary till just cooked through. Do not overcook. While the pheasant is cooking, steam the cabbage in the additional butter in a heavy copper, aluminum, or stainless steel skillet. Cover tightly, and cook over low heat till the cabbage is just wilted. Add the cream, salt, pepper, and fresh dill or dillweed. Cover, and cook 3 minutes. Transfer the pheasant pieces to a hot platter and arrange the cabbage at the end of the platter. Serve with boiled new potatoes and pickled peaches or watermelon rind.

Note. Prairie chickens can be prepared in the same way.

Braised Pheasant with Sauerkraut

2 pounds sauerkraut
2 cups broth
8 crushed juniper berries
4 tablespoons butter
1 or 2 pheasant, singed and cleaned
3 tablespoons oil or 6 tablespoons clarified butter
1 teaspoon salt
1 teaspoon freshly ground pepper

Sauerkraut became a common food to serve with game throughout the countryside because it was available in winter, had a pleasant taste, and provided a change of diet when other vegetables were scarce.

If you are especially fond of sauerkraut you may add more to the recipe. Wash it, combine with the broth and juniper berries, and simmer 1 hour, covered, in a large braising pan or Dutch oven. Heat the fat in a heavy skillet and brown the pheasant on all sides over fairly high heat. If you are cooking two birds it is wiser to brown one at a time. When they are nicely browned, salt and pepper them and place in the braising pan on the sauerkraut. Cover, and bake in a 375-degree oven 45 minutes, or until the pheasant is tender. Arrange on a platter with the sauerkraut and serve with fried hominy squares.

Roast Pheasant

To roast a pheasant properly it is important to bard the breast well with salt pork. You may stuff the pheasant or not, as you like. If you do not, it is nice to put a good chunk of butter in the cavity along with some tarragon or crushed juniper berries. (Tarragon and pheasant are a particularly delightful combination of flavors.)

Place the bird or birds on a rack in a shallow roasting pan. Roast from 45 to 60 minutes at 375 degrees, breast side down for half the time, then turn for the remaining time. Baste frequently with melted butter. For the last few minutes remove the barding pork and baste thoroughly.

If you use juniper berries in the bird you may want to blaze it with gin before serving. Serve with the pan juices, fried breadcrumbs, and bread sauce. A purée of parsnips or chestnuts is also a good accompaniment.

Bread Sauce

Cook 1 small onion stuck with 2 cloves in 2 cups milk for 5 minutes. Remove the onion and add enough freshly grated white breadcrumbs to form a mixture about the texture of heavy cream. Add 2 tablespoons butter and simmer, stirring constantly, till the mixture is quite thick. Correct the seasoning.

Casserole of Pheasant

1 pheasant cut as for sautéing
Flour
Salt, pepper, paprika
4 tablespoons butter
3 tablespoons oil
1½ cups heavy cream
2 tablespoons finely cut fresh tarragon or 1½ teaspoons dried tarragon
¼ cup brandy

Dredge the pheasant in flour seasoned with salt, pepper, and paprika. Brown well in the oil and butter, turning several times to give an even color. Transfer to a 2-quart casserole. Pour off all but 2 tablespoons of the fat in the pan, add the cream, and bring to the simmering point. Stir well and pour over the pheasant. Add the tarragon and brandy, cover the casserole, and bake at 325 degrees 1 to 1¼ hours, or until tender. Serve with mashed potatoes or with noodles dressed with butter.

Variation. Use thyme instead of tarragon. Add 12 small parboiled onions, 4 parboiled carrots, ½ pound mushroom caps, 1 cup cream, and ¼ cup sherry. Bake 1 hour. Serve with crisp fried cornmeal mush.

Quail

Quail has always been plentiful and has invariably been overcooked by those priding themselves as fine quail cooks. The birds, if they are young and tender, are so delicate that it is folly to cook them an hour or more as some of the old Southern recipes recommend. Mrs. Faber Jones, in a cookbook from Webster City, Iowa, dating from the early part of this century, has a recipe I admire:

"Cut bird up back, keeping breast whole. Put a piece of bread under each bird (breast up) to catch the drippings. Season with salt and pepper. Dredge with flour and baste with butter. Roast 20 to 25 minutes with a sharp fire. When done cut the bread in diamond shape. Serve with gravy, garnish with slices of lemon."

Roast Quail

To roast whole quail, place a large lump of butter inside the cavity along with some salt and freshly ground pepper and a leaf or two of tarragon. Arrange the quail on a rack, butter them well, and sprinkle with salt and pepper. Roast at 450 degrees about 20 minutes, basting well once during that time. Remove from the oven and let stand in a warm place 5 or 6 minutes before serving.

Variations

(1) Wrap the quail in barding pork and roast as above, giving them 25 minutes instead of 20.

(2) Rub the quail well with butter, then bard with pork, wrap in grape leaves, and tie. Roast at 375 degrees 40 to 45 minutes. Serve them on squares of cornmeal mush fried crisp in butter, and with a giblet gravy, if you like. These delicious birds are also excellent for eating cold and taking along for a picnic.

(3) Stuff the quail with oysters and a large lump of butter, and add some pepper and salt. Roast about 35 minutes at 375 degrees, and baste well with melted butter.

Fried Quail for Breakfast

6 quail
½ cup flour seasoned with 1 teaspoon each of salt and freshly ground pepper
6 to 9 thick rashers bacon
Parsley sprigs

GRAVY (optional)

2 tablespoons flour
1 cup milk
Salt, freshly ground pepper, and Tabasco

Split the quail and shake them in a plastic bag with the seasoned flour. Cook the bacon in a heavy skillet till just crisp. Transfer to absorbent paper and keep hot in the oven or warming oven. Sauté the quail in the bacon fat over medium high heat till nicely browned on both sides. Reduce the heat and let them cook, turning once or twice, till just tender. Transfer to a hot platter, top with the bacon slices, and garnish with parsley sprigs.

If you choose to serve a gravy, remove all but 3 tablespoons fat from the skillet and add the flour. Mix well with the fat and pan juices over medium heat and stir till well blended and smooth. Gradually stir in the milk and continue to stir until the mixture is thickened. Season to taste with salt, pepper, and Tabasco. Serve with small new potatoes and hot biscuits and honey.

Partridge

In addition to wild partridge, domestically raised birds can be obtained during most of the year from game farms. Except for those brought in during the first days of the partridge season in France, I have seldom tasted a fine tender bird. Roast partridge, it seems, has a habit of being tough and resistant to the knife and needs very careful cooking.

Roast Partridge

To roast, you need a fine young bird. Clean it well and singe. Bard the breast with a thin piece of fresh or salt barding pork and tie securely. Place the bird on one side on a rack in a rather shallow roasting pan. Roast in a 450-degree oven 5 minutes, then turn onto the other side and roast another 5 minutes. Repeat the process once more so that each side has 10 minutes roasting in all. Reduce the heat to 375 degrees and place the bird on its back. Roast breast up 20 to 25 minutes, according to size. Season with salt and freshly ground pepper and serve, with the barding pork on, on slices of fried bread. If you like, spread the bread first with the giblets, which have been chopped, quickly sautéed in butter, and seasoned with salt, pepper, and Madeira. Serve crisp shoestring potatoes and fresh watercress. Drink a good light Burgundy.

Small Game Birds

In former times small birds such as robins, thrush, snipe, and woodcock were roasted and greatly savored. (Today people who grow fruit would often like to declare open season on robins — but this never happens.) And it used to be the custom — it still is to some extent in England — to roast a small bird with the "trail" or intestines left in the bird and with toast placed under the bird to catch the drippings from the trail. This early recipe of "A Rule for Woodcocks or Snipe" describes the practice.

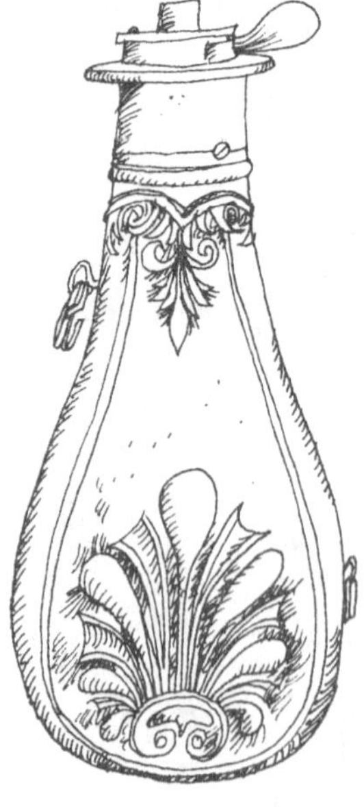

"Be very careful in plucking these to pull out the feathers as carefully and handle them as lightly as possible; for the skin is very easily torn or broken. Do not draw them, for epicures have decided that the trail (as they call the intestines) is the most delicious part of the bird, and by all means should be saved for eating. Having wiped the outside carefully with a soft cloth, truss them with the head under the wing and the bill laid along upon the breast. Keep the legs bent from the knees, retaining that posture by means of a splinter skewer. Suspend the birds to a bird-spit, with their feet downward. Melt some fresh butter in the dripping pan and baste them with it, having first dredged the birds with flour. Before the trail begins to drop (which it will as soon as they are well heated) lay a thick round of very nice toast (with the crust pared off) buttered on both sides and placed in the dripping pan beneath, so as to catch the trail as it falls; allowing a slice of toast to each bird with the trail spread equally over it. Continue the basting, letting the butter fall back into the basting spoon. When the birds are done — which will be in less than half an hour at a brisk fire — carefully transfer the toasts to a very hot dish; place the birds upon them and pour some gravy round the toasts."

Reedbirds or Ricebirds

These are seldom to be had nowadays and are a great loss. I can remember eating them when I was a child. They were so tiny one had merely a bite from each fat little body — something like an ortolan's, if you have ever eaten them. They used to be brought to market strung on a twig or sometimes wrapped in vine leaves. These morsels were roasted quickly, basted with butter and their own fat, and were consumed by the fours or sixes.

Birds in a Grove

This is a rather quaint old recipe, which can be made easier to prepare by using a pastry bag fitted with a large star tube for the potatoes.

"Having roasted some reedbirds, larks, plovers or any other small birds such as are usually eaten, mash some potatoes with butter and cream. Spread the mashed potato thickly over the bottom, sides, and edges of a deep dish. Nick or crimp the border of potatoes that goes round the edges, or scallop it with a tin cutter. You may, if you choose, brown it by holding over it a salamander or a red hot shovel. Then lay the birds in the middle of the dish and stick among them, very thickly, a sufficient number of sprigs of curled or double leaf parsley."

Broiled Doves

6 doves
Half a lemon
1 cup finely chopped tart apple
¾ cup finely chopped onion
1 teaspoon salt
¼ teaspoon nutmeg
4 tablespoons butter, melted
6 thick slices bacon
Salt and freshly ground pepper
½ cup medium sherry or Madeira

Superb when properly cooked, doves are often ruined by overcooking, which makes them dry as dust. They are very plentiful in the South, and the usual way of preparing them is "smothering" in one form or another. One of the best doves I ever ate was simply prepared with bacon.

Clean the doves and wipe them out with the half lemon, pressing the fruit pulp against the flesh of the interior so that the juice runs a bit in each bird. Combine the apple, onion, salt, nutmeg, pepper, and butter, and spoon some of the mixture into each dove. Wrap with bacon (if the bacon is small, use 2 slices for each bird). Place the birds on a broiling rack and broil over medium coals or about 6 inches from the broiling unit. Turn them often till nicely colored and tender. Transfer to a rack in a roasting pan or heated casserole. Add the sherry or Madeira, cover the pan or casserole, and roast in a 250-degree oven 10 minutes. Serve the birds with the wine poured over them. Corn pudding or spoon bread and salad are excellent accompaniments.

Note. The birds may be stuffed with small green olives and a clove of garlic in each.

Bear

Bear is one of the most delicious of game animals. It is best when it is young and tender if the steaks, saddle, or leg are to be served rare. However, because of the danger of trichinosis, bear must either be frozen at 5 to 10 degrees below zero for several weeks or be cooked to a temperature of over 160 degrees. Therefore, if you can freeze the bear meat and then cook it rare, it is worth the trouble. Bear steaks are cooked like venison steaks.

Saddle of bear is roasted like a saddle of lamb or venison. Bear pot roasts are prepared like venison. Also the same marinades used for venison are appropriate for bear.

Rabbit

Wild rabbit or young hare used to be extremely plentiful and still is in some parts of the country. It has never been as popular a game food here as it has been in Europe or even in Mexico or Canada, and no one can explain why. Maybe it's due to our worship of the Easter Bunny, or possibly to our making pets of rabbits. At any rate, it is as delicious as squirrel, if you like squirrel, and if you are in a region where it is in good supply, avail yourself of the opportunity and eat a great deal of it.

Sautéed Rabbit with Bacon and Sour Cream

1 young rabbit or hare
½ cup flour seasoned with 1 teaspoon salt, 1½ teaspoons dry mustard, 1 teaspoon thyme, ½ teaspoon freshly ground pepper
5 or 6 rather thick slices bacon
½ cup chicken or beef stock
1 cup sour cream
2 tablespoons chopped parsley
1 teaspoon salt

Cut the rabbit in serving pieces. Shake the pieces well in a plastic bag with the seasoned flour. Sauté the bacon until just crisp. Remove and keep it warm wrapped in absorbent paper. Heat the bacon fat and brown the rabbit pieces in the fat on both sides. Reduce the heat and add the stock. Cover the pan and simmer 10 to 15 minutes, or until the rabbit is tender. Transfer to a hot platter and skim off all but 2 tablespoons of fat from the pan. Add the sour cream, chopped parsley, and salt. Stir over medium heat till well mixed and heated through, but do not let it boil. Spoon the sauce around the rabbit and serve with mashed potatoes and corn oysters.

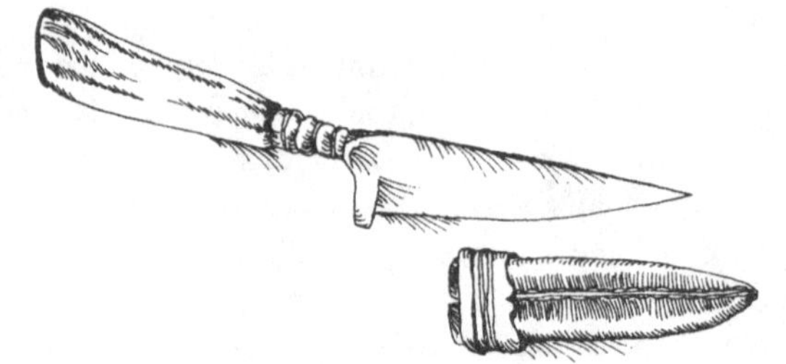

Saddle of Hare

4 saddles of hare
Dijon mustard
1 cup white wine
6 tablespoons butter
3 tablespoons oil
Salt and freshly ground pepper
1½ cups heavy cream

The saddle is probably the most rewarding section of the hare, and if it is a large one the meat thereon will serve one or two persons amply. Here is one of the most delicious ways to prepare it.

Brush the saddles with a generous amount of Dijon mustard, then add the wine. Cover, and let the saddles rest for 2 days. When ready to cook the saddles, heat the butter and oil in a large, heavy skillet. Add the saddles and let them cook slowly 25 minutes, turning them once. Salt and pepper them, add the cream, and let them simmer till just tender — about 10 minutes. Transfer to a hot platter and cook the sauce down for a moment or so. Pour over the saddles and serve them with crisp fried squares of hominy grits.

Squirrel

Squirrel has been written about rapturously for years, and it has long been associated with elegant dining as well as with the simple food of the trapper and the nomad. Fortunately it is plentiful.

Novels and books on the old South and on the trek westward abound with references to squirrel pies, squirrel stews, Brunswick stews, and other dishes using this ever-present little animal. Squirrel is as typical of America as grouse is of Scotland.

Note. The squirrel recipes below are applicable to wild rabbit as well.

Broiled Squirrel

Surely the simplest way of cooking squirrel, if it is young and tender, is to broil it. Skin the animal, draw, and split it. Rub well with salt, freshly ground pepper, and a bit of dried sage or thyme. Butter well, place on a broiling rack, and broil about 4 inches from the heat unit, allowing about 12 to 14 minutes per side. Brush with butter during the broiling process, and turn once or twice before finishing off. Serve with home-fried potatoes, hot biscuits and currant jelly. A beet and endive salad will balance the meal nicely.

Fricasseed Squirrel

2 squirrels cut in serving pieces
¼ cup flour
1 teaspoon salt
1 teaspoon freshly ground pepper
1 teaspoon sage
6 tablespoons bacon fat or butter
1½ cups chicken broth

Cut up the squirrel and rub the pieces well with the flour and seasonings, or put all in a plastic bag and shake the pieces in it. Heat the bacon fat or butter in a skillet and brown the pieces of squirrel on both sides over rather high heat. When they are nicely colored, add the chicken broth and reduce the heat. Cover, and simmer until tender — 45 minutes to an hour. Correct the seasoning and add the bourbon.

While the stew is cooking, brown the onions in butter, glaze

¼ cup bourbon
Chopped parsley
12 small white onions
5 tablespoons butter
Sugar

with sugar, and cook, covered, over low heat until just tender. Arrange the squirrel on a serving dish with the onions and the sauce, and garnish with chopped parsley. Serve with hot biscuits or dumplings, and pear preserve or currant jelly.

Roast Squirrel

Roast young squirrel is indeed good eating. Clean and skin the squirrel and stuff it with your favorite stuffing. I find that either a very highly seasoned sausage meat or ground veal and pork mixture, well seasoned and with a little garlic, is extremely good. Butter the squirrels well, place on a bed of sliced carrots, onions, and parsley, and dot with butter or bacon fat. Roast in a 450-degree oven, basting often with melted butter and white wine in equal quantities. It will take 45 minutes to an hour to be tender. Serve with baked sweet potatoes and pickled peaches or pears.

Brunswick Stew

Bacon fat (about 4 tablespoons)
2 to 3 onions, sliced very thin
1 garlic clove, finely chopped
2 or 3 squirrels
Flour
1½ teaspoons salt
1 teaspoon freshly ground pepper
1 teaspoon rosemary or thyme
2 cups chicken or veal stock
1 bay leaf
½ cup Madeira
1 tablespoon Worcestershire sauce
¾ cup peeled, seeded, and chopped tomatoes
1 cup freshly shelled lima beans or frozen limas
1 cup whole-kernel corn or corn cut from the ear
1 cup cut okra
Buttered crumbs
Chopped parsley

This is one of the most famous of American dishes, and I doubt if there are two recipes alike for it. One simply has to guess whether or not he is making the right choice. This is a Kentucky recipe.

Heat the bacon fat in a heavy skillet. Add the onions and garlic, and cook till soft but not browned. Transfer to a braising pan. In a plastic bag, combine the flour, salt and pepper, and rosemary or thyme, and shake the squirrel pieces in this mixture. Brown the squirrel in the skillet, and when it is nicely colored, transfer to the braising pan. Add the broth, bay leaf, Madeira, and Worcestershire sauce to the skillet, rinse it well, and pour into the braising pan. Cover, and simmer the mixture 35 minutes. Remove the cover, add the tomatoes and other vegetables, and simmer until the squirrel is tender and the vegetables are cooked. Correct the seasoning, adding more Madeira if it seems necessary. Add the buttered crumbs and parsley and cook another 15 minutes. Serve the stew with baked potatoes or sweet potatoes, relishes, and a good salad.

Variations

(1) This is sometimes made with chicken or with a combination of chicken and squirrel.

(2) The stew is sometimes prepared, cooled thoroughly, topped with a rich pastry crust, which is brushed with beaten egg yolk and cream, and baked at 375 degrees till the crust is lusciously browned and the stew thoroughly reheated. In this case the stew would be baked in an earthenware baking dish. The crust should be very rich and rolled about ⅜ inch thick. A vent should be cut in the center

and a small cone of paper inserted to take care of juice that may boil over.

Wild Duck

Wild duck are now in short supply, but I can remember the days when they were still plentiful. We might have as many as twenty at a time hanging in the basement — teal, canvasbacks, mallards — all ready to be plucked, drawn, and roasted. We were a family of individuals when it came to cooking them. My father liked them stuffed and roasted for 45 minutes to an hour. My mother liked them roasted about 40 minutes with no stuffing, and I liked them rare as rare could be, stuffed with an onion and a bit of thyme and basted with butter and red wine. We all agreed on teal for some reason, which were cooked at high temperature, basted with red wine and butter, and served with a glaze of currant jelly.

The traditional seasonings for duck were usually sage and thyme, though juniper berries have since come into style, as well as the related flavor of gin, which is used for flaming and saucing. Game, and especially wild duck, flamed with gin is so agreeable that it is astonishing it is not done more generally.

Duck are a tedious job to pluck, since their down is stubborn and difficult to remove. However, one must persevere if the local butcher, who used to be obliging, is no longer interested in plucking your duck. Some people plunge the birds into scalding water to make the process easier. Others use a coating of paraffin. I prefer to do the task with no help, apart from singeing off some of the downy feathers and using tweezers for pinfeathers.

One duck per person is not too large a serving, although a half is usual; if you are serving teal, 2 per person is the usual portion. Be certain to have a good supply on hand before you invite friends in for a feast.

Rare Roast Wild Duck

Place a piece of onion and a bit of orange rind inside each duck. Wrap the breast with a piece of salt pork and tie it securely. Roast at 400 to 425 degrees, 20 minutes for a smallish duck and 25 for a large one. Baste every 5 to 7 minutes with equal parts of red wine and melted butter. Sprinkle with salt and freshly ground pepper after they are removed from the oven, although the salt pork will provide a certain amount of salting.

Serve on a hot platter and pass the degreased pan juices. Fried parsley and either brown rice with chestnuts or wild rice (to me a gross extravagance) go well with it. Currant jelly is a traditional condiment. For wine, serve a fine Bordeaux or Burgundy or a California Cabernet.

Variations

(1) Use crushed juniper berries and a bit of orange rind to stuff each duck, and baste with melted butter only. When the duck are removed from the oven, flame them with warmed gin.

(2) Use sage, thyme, and an onion in the duck, and baste with orange juice. You may add a bit of Cointreau at the end of the cooking period if you like. In this case, an orange and onion salad is ideal with the bird, as well as mashed chestnuts or fried sweet potatoes.

Mary Hamblet's Famous Roast Duck

4 wild duck
Salt barding pork
1 cup chopped onion
1 cup finely chopped parsley
1 teaspoon thyme
½ teaspoon sage
2 cups dry breadcrumbs or prepared stuffing
1 teaspoon salt
1 teaspoon freshly ground pepper
½ to ¾ cup melted butter, or more

My old friend has a reputation for wild duck in Portland, and invitations to feast on this dish — which was originally her mother's — are much sought after.

Combine the onion and all the following ingredients in a mixing bowl, adding enough melted butter to make a moist mixture. Stuff the duck and tie a piece of salt barding pork over the breasts. Place on a rack and roast in a 350-degree oven 45 minutes to an hour. Baste with melted butter several times during the roasting period.

Teal would take about 30 minutes to roast this way. These are superb, and should please those who have not accustomed their palates to bloody duck.

An Old West Coast Recipe for Wild Duck

This recipe, from Mr. Charles S. Houston (1893), is not the clearest one to follow, but is different from most others for wild duck, and is delicious in flavor.

"Mallards 45 minutes. Teal 30. Salt, pepper, a little garlic and onion rubbed well into the bird. Brown quickly. After the bird is thoroughly browned add a little water and baste well for 45 minutes. This is so there will be no blood when the bird is cooked providing the oven has been the right temperature.

"When duck has cooked 45 minutes put a fork into the thickest part of the breast and pull out quickly. If done clear water will run immediately out. Remove at once. Fine gravy can be made of the juice in the pan by putting in ½ can tomatoes (1½ cups) 2 tablespoons Worcestershire sauce, a little Tabasco. Always keep about 1 cup (small) of the juice and pour it over the duck. When carving dip the breast in juice. It greatly improves the flavor."

General Frost's St. Louis Wild Duck

This came from a bonviveur in the post–Civil War days. It is one of the most amusing duck recipes I know.

"These ducks are cooked on top of the stove in a thin pan which will hold two ducks. Over high heat melt enough fat to half cover the ducks. (This should be about 2½ to 3 cups). You may use all lard or half lard and half butter. The fat should boil in the pan. This means the butter should be clarified. When the fat boils put in the ducks, breast down, and partially cover the pan. Leave it for seven minutes, then remove the lid and turn the birds over. After they are turned put two tablespoons Italian vermouth over the breasts, then put the lid on and allow to cook for another seven minutes. Take the lid off again, turn the ducks over on their breasts again, and pour a little of the vermouth over their backs and let them stay another two minutes.

"Now turn the birds again and test with a fork. If blood comes out they must be turned again for two minutes. If a clear liquid comes out they are done. Remove the ducks to a warm pan. Place the pan in which you cooked the ducks into a large pan of ice water and allow it to cool rapidly. As soon as practical pour off the fat so that merely the juices are left in the pan. [It may be siphoned off with the aid of a baster.] To the juice left add 3 tablespoons thinly sliced orange peel, ½ cup Italian vermouth and about ¾ cup currant jelly. Heat to boiling and pour over the ducks on a hot platter and serve,"

Rice with herbs or rice with mushrooms is a fine accompaniment. The dish is delicious as well as having an interesting background.

Harriet Coe's Special Wild Duck

4 wild duck
4 apples
3 large onions
4 ribs celery with tops
Butter
Salt
Freshly ground pepper
¾ cup currant jelly
⅓ cup brandy

Pick and clean the duck and dry them inside and out. Stuff each one with a piece or two of apple and a piece of onion and celery, all brushed with some softened butter. Rub the outside well with butter, and sprinkle with salt and pepper. Place the birds on a rack and roast at 400 degrees for 10 minutes. Combine the melted jelly and brandy and baste them well with mixture. Continue basting every 10 minutes till the duck have been in the oven 35 minutes for rare, or 45 minutes for medium rare. Transfer to a hot platter and pour the pan juices over them. Serve with crisp fried grits and sautéed apples.

Broiled Wild Duck

Nothing could be simpler. Split the duck — good carving shears are indispensable to the person who carves game a good deal, for they cut through raw or cooked duck with efficiency. Rub the duck well with lemon juice and then with softened butter and salt and freshly ground pepper. Broil, bone side down, about 1[illegible] or 12 minutes. Turn, and broil till done to your taste. About 18 minutes is the usual time for a normal-size duck. Brush with butter if needed. Serve with turnips and mushrooms, or perhaps baked yellow squash or kale.

Spitted Wild Duck

Perhaps the finest duck I have ever eaten in all these years were prepared by General Harold Barton in California. They had been rubbed with olive oil and thyme the day before and oiled again the next day. He spitted them through the middle in a row, head to tail, put two steel knitting needles through them at either end, and finally put the spit clamps on so they would stand firm. They were revolved over good coals for exactly 23 minutes, and the fire was brought up for the last few minutes. He then flambéed them with warmed Cognac, which produced quite a flame. They were allowed to rest a few minutes before being served.

Salmi of Wild Duck

1 or 2 cold duck and bones from those served the night before
1 small onion stuck with 2 cloves
1 teaspoon thyme
1 teaspoon salt
½ teaspoon freshly ground pepper
1 tablespoon Worcestershire sauce
2 tablespoons soy sauce
4 cups stock or beef bouillon
4 tablespoons butter
5 tablespoons flour
2 cups duck broth
½ cup port wine
1 tablespoon grated orange rind

This has always been a good leftover dish. My mother, in the days when wild duck were bountiful, would have a couple of extra on hand to use for a salmi for luncheon during the week. Such luxury nowadays would be an occasion for a special dinner.

Remove the meat from the bones and cut into large serving pieces. Combine the bones, onion, thyme, and other seasonings with the stock or bouillon, bring to a boil, and simmer 2 hours. Strain the broth and correct the seasoning. Combine the butter and flour in a heavy pan or skillet, and let it cook 5 to 6 minutes to color slightly. Stir in the broth, and cook until nicely thickened. Correct the seasoning, add the pieces of duck, and simmer approximately 25 to 30 minutes, or until the duck is tender and the sauce richly flavored. Add the port and orange rind and heat again. Serve on a bed of rice, with noodles, or on squares of fried cornmeal mush. Garnish with green olives which have been heated slightly in broth.

Beef

Beef has been a mainstay in American life for over two centuries. In limited supply during Colonial times, it was usually eaten in minced form or in a ragout because of the lack of forks until well into the seventeenth century. (Governor Winthrop is supposed to have been the first fork owner.) In the post-Revolutionary period we find some reference to spit-roasting of beef, one recipe going as far as to recommend 15 minutes per pound for tender beef and longer for older and tougher beef.

As the West opened up and cattle raising developed into a profitable industry, beef became more plentiful. Great herds of cattle were tended until ready to be driven to the nearest railroad, where they were loaded on cars and shipped to the big meat centers — Chicago, Omaha, and Kansas City. Here they were fattened up, slaughtered, and then sent throughout the country in refrigerated cars. In earlier days butchers bought whole carcasses or halves and disposed of them in their own way. Choice bits were hung to tenderize them and enrich their flavor, and less choice cuts were sold without further processing. Nowadays beef is inoculated with hormones before slaughtering to increase fat and tenderness. In fact, tenderness has become such an end in itself that texture and flavor are hardly considered. Many people feel that most prime and choice grades of beef are simply pap. I must confess that I also prefer my beef properly aged, as it is no longer, and with a slight chewiness to it. Otherwise it can be quite boring, which I think is true of the celebrated Japanese beef, which has been developed to a high degree of tenderness. Another result of this trend is that cuts of meat formerly used in long-cooking dishes are now unsuitable for that treatment, and one must beware of overcooking.

It is alarming to think that government inspection and grading of meats did not go into effect until 1927. And already grading has lost much of its original force, because of changes in processing and pressures from the meat industry. Beef that seems to be much too fatty because of the hormone treatment gets into our markets as "choice" or "prime." It is difficult to escape this commercially established pattern. With much meat prepackaged and with individual butchers buying not whole carcasses but smaller pieces, one must settle for what he is given. In rare instances it is still possible to win the cooperation of a butcher who will hang a particular cut of beef to your specifications.

Another problem for the consumer has been created by the confusion of names used by supermarkets in their competitive merchandising. Names that have never appeared on official meat charts are seen with increasing frequency in advertisements — some names positively misleading and some simply fanciful. Uniformity of cutting and nomenclature would do much to improve the situation.

However, nothing has dimmed the ever increasing popularity of beef, beef, beef. It is the leader in food markets and a favorite with promoters of recipes. Certainly its availability and the ease with which it can be prepared partly account for its vogue. Despite the complaints one can level at the beef industry, American beef is by and large the finest to be had.

Grading of beef

U.S. Prime is the top grade most consumers see, although there is a still better grade, a more heavily fatted beef, that does not flow through the average supermarket. This beef, which used to be known as U.S. Prime, is specially raised and fattened for the luxury market — particularly for the restaurant trade — and brings a premium price. If the housewife were to find this grade of meat at her butcher's, most likely she would complain of the fat content, but it is this additional fat or "marbling" in the lean that yields greater tenderness.

What is now called Prime was formerly an intermediate grade that never appeared on Department of Agriculture charts, but was usually known as *Prime Choice* or *Top Choice*, the cream of *U.S. Choice* grade.

Nowadays, most of the large food chains offer *U.S. Choice* as their top grade of beef, and ordinarily it is extremely good beef — good enough, in fact, for certain of the chains to have built reputations on their beef alone.

U.S. Good is just that — good but no better — and requires no further definition here.

The other grades, *U.S. Commercial* and *U.S. Utility*, never reach normal retail outlets and are solely for commercial uses.

Steak

Buying steak

In buying steak the grade of beef must be considered in conjunction with the cut. Naturally, the better the grade, the tenderer the cut. But the best cuts are sometimes quite acceptable in a lesser grade. For example, a tenderloin of *Good* grade can be well-flavored and tender and cost far less than the same cut of a better grade. On the other hand, inferior cuts must be of top grade if they are to be cooked quickly. Rump, flank, and skirt steaks are delicious for broiling, grilling, or sautéing, provided they are of *Prime* or *Choice* grades — otherwise they are only suitable for braising.

Shop for well-marbled (fatted) meat, cherry-red in color and velvety in texture. The fat should be rather creamy in color and, in some cuts, especially around the kidneys, it should be flaky. With so much meat ready-packaged nowadays, it is sometimes difficult to find steaks of uniform thickness. Uniformity is essential to achieve evenly cooked meat, and it is usually wise to have steaks specially cut for you. This is possible in most supermarkets and certainly in those that belong to the three or four major chains.

I well remember the days when meat was allowed to hang a far longer time — 6 to 8 weeks — than the 3 weeks that is now customary. Good steaks were considered by many (including the author) to be those that came from short loins, heavily fuzzed with green mold and, when broiled, distinctly gamy in flavor. However, it is rare that one finds such beef today and only possible if the butcher who supplies you and other discriminating customers can afford the shrinkage and loss in weight such hanging entails.

Tenderizers

One of the standard items in American kitchens throughout the nineteenth century was a steak beater, a wooden paddle used to pound tough meat and break its fibers, thus tenderizing it. After this came the mallets called "cubers." Neither of these was truly a tenderizer. Each made the meat easier to cut and chew, but in so doing also gave it a somewhat masticated texture.

A genuine tenderizer did not appear until the late 1940's, after two young men discovered a restaurateur in California who served good steaks for very little money. They learned he had a secret process for tenderizing his steaks and paid him a rather indifferent sum for the formula. This was more or less the start of a commercial meat tenderizer based on use of the papaya enzyme. It was not exactly a new idea, for the Central and South Americans had been using papaya leaves to tenderize for generations. However, it was entirely new and magical to North America, and soon the market was flooded with tenderizers of different brands and qualities. Through continued research the effectiveness of the original tenderizer has been improved far more than most of the others.

It is true that if you follow directions faithfully a tenderizer can give remarkably satisfactory results. Tenderizers are available in liquid and powdered form, seasoned and unseasoned. I myself prefer the unseasoned variety. There is even a minute marinade available for meats that accomplishes in a short time the tenderizing and seasoning that normally would require several days. Many restaurants have made fortunes by serving inferior grades of beef, tenderized and attractively cooked, to a public who could not afford the prices of steaks in fine restaurants.

There is even some beef available that is tenderized before slaughtering by being fed the papaya enzyme. This meat is handled by two of the big supermarket chains.

Porterhouse Steak

This was named after the porterhouses or coach stops during the eighteenth and early nineteenth centuries, when this cut was often served to travelers. It is the part of the short loin comprised of the sirloin and the tenderloin with a T-shaped bone between (usually a piece of the backbone and the finger bone). It is apt to have a bit of kidney fat as well, and often, though less so than formerly, a tailpiece of the flank is attached. In France the sirloin and tenderloin sections are called the *filet* and the *contre-filet.*

A porterhouse steak for broiling should be cut not less than 2 inches thick and is better when cut 2½ to 3 inches thick. For pan-broiling or sautéing, 1½ inches is ideal.

The three methods of preparing a porterhouse are:

(1) *Broiling.* Broil 3 to 5 inches from the source of heat. The steak should cook somewhat slowly, rather than charring at once, so heat can penetrate the meat evenly. Turn midway in the cooking.

(2) *Pan-broiling.* If cooked in an ordinary flat pan, the meat should be cooked relatively slowly without fat or liquid, and the fat poured off as it accumulates. Some people prefer to first sprinkle the pan with a layer of salt, but it seems to me that the salt does nothing but absorb the fat, which then smokes a good deal. There are pans on the market designed for stove-top broiling that have ridged bottoms. If cooked in one of these, steak can be done at a rather high temperature, since the fat collects between the ridges and can be readily poured off. Whichever pan is used, turn the steak often during cooking.

(3) *Pan-frying or sautéing.* Brown the steak in a small amount of beef fat over quite high heat. Turn several times. Reduce the heat and let the steak finish cooking over moderate heat.

In Mrs. Crowen's *The American System of Cookery*, published in 1847, the author states, "Sirloin and what is known in the New York markets as porterhouse steaks are the choicest cuts. . . . Broiling is by far the best manner of cooking steaks." Here are Mrs. Crowen's instructions:

"Have a bright clear fire of coals, rub the gridiron bars with a bit of suet, lay on the steak, and let it broil gently until one side is done, then take the steak over the steak dish to catch the blood before turning it, then lay the upper side to the fire. For a fine steak (weighing about two pounds and a half) take a quarter of a pound of sweet butter on the dish, work a small teaspoonful of fine pepper and a large one of salt into it. When the steak is done, put it on the butter; when it melts a little turn the steak; repeat the turning once or twice, then put a tin cover over and serve quickly; the dish must be hot.

"Beefsteaks are generally preferred broiled so the middle will be slightly red; tomato catsup to be served with the beefsteak."

To serve a porterhouse. Using a sharp knife, cut out the bone. Then cut in medium-thin slices across the filet and the contre-filet, so that each slice contains some of both sections. Serve with any of the following:

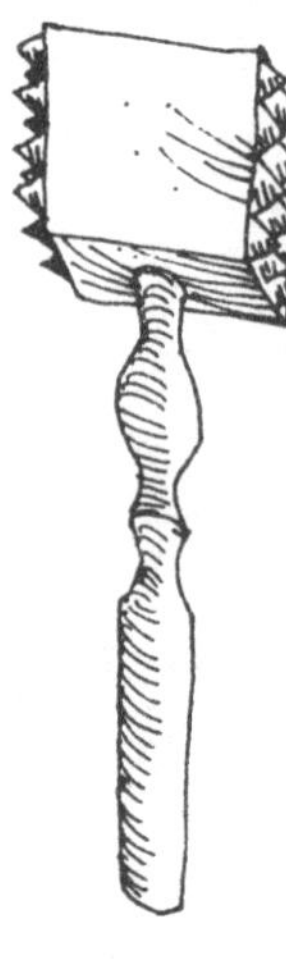

(1) The pan juices and a lump of butter mixed with pepper and salt.

(2) A rich Béarnaise sauce.

(3) Bordelaise sauce.

(4) A large bowl of sautéed onions, brown and almost crisp, or a covering of sautéed mushrooms — this is the old-fashioned way.

(5) Garlic butter or anchovy butter.

(6) Pizzaiola sauce. (Many people eat their steak with catsup, a similar idea.)

(7) Barbecue sauce, if it is an outdoor meal.

However, considering the excellent quality of beef available, and the price one pays for it, it seems a pity to dress a good steak with more than butter, salt, and pepper. Its own character can be savored so much better that way.

The following accompaniments are traditional with porterhouse.

Potatoes. Crisp sautéed or fried potatoes, or hash-brown potatoes, which are more traditional. Baked potatoes have become a standard with steak in many homes and restaurants.

Onions. These have been mentioned in connection with steak since the earliest American cookbooks. Raw thick slices alternated with thickish slices of beefsteak tomato have been much favored in steak houses through the years. Other good versions are fried onion rings, dipped in a buttermilk batter and cooked until brown and crisp; or sautéed sliced onions cooked until soft with a bit of crispness here and there — these smothering the steak.

Salads. Plain watercress; a tossed green salad dressed with oil and vinegar; a tomato salad; romaine or endive and raw mushrooms dressed with oil and vinegar; or the old favorite, lettuce hearts with Roquefort dressing.

Mushrooms. Sautéed mushrooms, broiled mushroom caps, or mushrooms and turnips — all are traditional and appropriate.

Tomatoes. Grilled or baked tomatoes have been a popular accompaniment for steak since the 1840's.

Drinks. Americans began by drinking beer, ale, or porter with steak meals. As we became more expansive in our living habits, we turned to red wines — fine Burgundies and Bordeaux, and later the fine wines of California. Today most people are apt to choose a Burgundy or a California Pinot Noir, although there are still many who prefer to drink a pint or so of good beer.

T-Bone Steak

This is practically the same as a porterhouse, save that the amount of tenderloin in a T-bone is smaller, and should not be considered an inferior cut. It can be treated in exactly the same way as a porterhouse and served with the same accompaniments.

Boneless Loin

Also called *shell steak, strip steak, boneless sirloin, New York steak,* and sometimes *club steak.* Don't let the variety of names for this cut confuse you. Look for its location on a meat chart, fix it in your mind once and for all, and if you find yourself in another part of the country, check a meat chart with the butcher for the local nomenclature. This cut may be the porterhouse or T-bone steak without fillet. It is usually cut without bone and its eye is fairly small, but contains the very choicest meat. It is expensive. A single steak should be cut 1½ to 2 inches thick, a double steak up to 3½ inches, and a steak for three or four persons is sometimes cut as much as 4½ inches thick and broiled on all four sides. Treat this cut as you would a porterhouse. The same accompaniments are appropriate.

Sirloin

The sirloin is a short piece of meat that extends along the short loin to the round. It varies considerably in bone and muscle structure and is usually offered in several cuts:

Pinbone sirloin contains a good deal of bone, but also a nice section of the tenderloin and some of the sirloin. If it is cut thick — 2½ to 4 inches — it makes an excellent steak for a large number of people.

Wedgebone sirloin has a small amount of bone and a rather good expanse of muscle. It is an extraordinarily well-flavored piece of meat, and it carves nicely once the bone has been extracted. It should be cut 2 to 4 inches thick.

Boneless sirloin, as its name clearly indicates, is boned sirloin, without the tenderloin. It is a successful steak if cut about 3 inches thick for two persons, or 4 inches thick for three or more persons.

Top sirloin remains after all bone, the sirloin, and extra fat have been removed from the whole loin. It is a good choice for broiling, has no waste, and is usually less expensive than porterhouse or T-bone. Especially good for steak sandwiches and for thin-cut sliced steak, it is sometimes called *Delmonico steak.*

To cook sirloin steak, follow the directions for preparation and serving of porterhouse steak.

Rump Steak

This steak, cut from the rump, is highly prized among some nationalities, notably the English and the French. Although in the nineteenth century it was one of the most popular cuts of meat, its popularity has since diminished, and for no apparent reason. It can be cooked like other choicer cuts and is particularly good pan-fried or sautéed.

Rib Steak

Cut from the ribs — the rack that constitutes a standing rib roast — this steak is highly favored by the French and seems to grow in esteem generally with people who are beef fanciers. It is sometimes called by its French name, *entrecôte* or *côte de boeuf.* A double rib steak of fine quality, cut with the bone in, is excellent broiled and served with a good sauce. To carve, remove the bone and slice the steak diagonally.

Spencer Steak

This is a trimmed eye of the rib steak and is to be classed with the finest of steaks. Comparatively new to the list of beef cuts, it is found mostly in the West.

Tenderloin

A prized piece of meat in all countries, the tenderloin is also known as the *filet* or fillet. It is expensive, but has no bone and precious little fat. In the United States, until the end of the nineteenth century, it was used mainly as a roast, elaborately larded. But as French cookery became better known throughout the country, through the cooking classes of M. Blot, the spreading fame of New Orleans cuisine, and the appearance of French and continental restaurants in cities on both coasts, we began to find more varied uses for the tenderloin. Today we divide it as the French do into a number of cuts. However, the whole tenderloin is still used for broiling, especially over charcoal, and is often marinated beforehand. (See tenderloin roast, page 280.)

Chateaubriand

Cut from the thickest part of the tenderloin, this usually serves two. Originally this steak was cooked in a wrapping of less tender pieces of meat, which were later put in a press to extract juices for the sauce. Today the Chateaubriand is broiled without wrapping until it is crusty brown outside and red rare inside. It is traditionally served with either a Chateaubriand sauce or a Béarnaise.

Fillet Steak, Tournedos, Tenderloin Steak

These steaks, cut from the tenderloin, are usually about 1 inch thick. The tournedos are customarily wrapped with fat and tied into rounds. Though all of these steaks can be broiled, they are much better when sautéed in butter, butter and oil, or beef fat, and then served with a sauce, such as Bordelaise or Béarnaise. These delicate and elegant morsels were exceedingly popular in the grand era of cookery and are still much in use for dinner parties and in first-rate restaurants.

Filet Mignon

This term, which is often applied to all tenderloin steaks cut from the fillet, really means the "little fillet," the end piece. It is thinner than the rest of the fillet and is more or less triangular in shape. It can be sliced and sautéed for Beef Stroganoff or cut into cubes and cooked on skewers. Though quite as tender and choice as the rest of the fillet, it is limited in use because of its size and shape.

Flank Steak

In recent years flank, which was formerly used almost entirely for braising and stewing, has become a choice cut for grilling. It is also known as London Broil, a standard luncheon dish in restaurants throughout the country. Although other cuts are sometimes substituted for London Broil, including hip and tenderized chuck, the use of flank steak continues to grow. Since there are only two flanks to each steer, these steaks have become hard to find and increasingly expensive.

Flank steak is broiled either plain or after being marinated in a teriyaki or barbecue marinade. It cooks quickly, taking 5 to 7 minutes to reach the rare state, and then must be carved on a sharp diagonal in very thin slices. If treated with teriyaki marinade, flank steak goes well with rice and stir-fried vegetables. It is equally at home with any of the crisper forms of fried potatoes, with good fresh salads, and with fried onions or sautéed mushrooms. Flank is an ideal cut of beef to use for outdoor parties. Several steaks can be marinated at a time and cooked so quickly that no one has to wait for food. Uncooked leftover steaks can be kept in the marinade and refrigerated for as much as 4 to 5 days for later use.

Skirt Steak

A thin, narrow piece from the plate, skirt steak is similar to a flank steak in texture and quality. Rich in flavor and quick-cooking, it is a pleasant change from some of the more familiar steak cuts. It is sometimes rolled and skewered for broiling, but normally it is broiled flat and carved as one does a flank steak. It lends itself nicely to marinating and seasoning.

Minute Steak

As it is cut now, minute steak is neither minute nor capable of being cooked in a minute. It is, however, a small steak, usually about 6 ounces in weight, and a favorite with dieters and those with modest appetites. It is cut from the strip or from the sirloin and has no fixed shape. It can be treated like the more impressive steaks and served with the same sauces and accompaniments, but is really best served quite plain, with little to enhance it other than salt and pepper.

Paillard

This is more nearly a minute steak in terms of cooking time. It is a piece cut from the sirloin, usually, and pounded thin enough to cook in a trice — merely browned quickly on each side. A paillard can be delicious and is especially suitable for those with dietary problems. Like the minute steak, it is best served plain.

Chuck Steak

This cut is less tender than any of the preceding steaks and is used for broiling, pan-broiling, or sautéing only when it comes from top-grade meat. A cheaper grade can be broiled, however, if tenderized (see page 256). See also roasted chuck steak (page 293).

Cold Steak

One of the most enjoyable forms of beef is cooked steak cut in thin slices and served cold. It is elegant enough to appear on the summer menus of a restaurant like the Four Seasons in New York. I myself often broil a thick steak in summer, allow it to cool without refrigeration, and serve it in very thin slices with a salad or a hot vegetable for dinner or for Sunday lunch. It is also excellent for breakfast served with hot toast. And steaks that have been marinated in a teriyaki mixture invariably seem to taste even better cold than hot.

Steak Sandwich

Steak sandwiches are usually made with a loaf of split and toasted French bread that has been spread with a seasoned butter, such as mustard, garlic, or anchovy butter. The steak should be broiled rare, sliced thin, and arranged on one half of the bread, then topped with the other half and cut in slices. Condiments are generally offered with the sandwiches, and if the steak is cooked outdoors a barbecue sauce is used to baste the meat as well as flavor the sandwiches.

Steak au Poivre

This French dish has always been popular in this country and may have come into usage as a means of serving well-aged steak — a taste that used to be more prevalent in the United States than it is today. The crust of pepper disguised the high flavor of the meat and at the same time transformed it into a dish worth remembering. Today one finds steak au poivre in one version or another in steak houses — and naturally in French restaurants — across the country. It has also become a favorite steak variation for the outdoor chef.

Although it can be grilled with success, traditionally steak au poivre is pan-broiled or sautéed. For one person, use a minute steak; for two persons, a thickish sirloin of about 2 pounds; and so on. If the steaks are to be cooked in a skillet, they should not be more than two inches thick. The pepper for steak au poivre must be crushed in a mortar, cracked with a rolling pin, or whirled in a blender to make rather coarse pieces. Ordinary ground pepper — even that produced by the average pepper grinder — is not suitable. Do not be afraid to use a generous amount. Freshly crushed pepper is not hot.

About 30 minutes before cooking, press the crushed peppercorns into both sides of the steak, using the heel of your hand. Gauge about 1 tablespoon for a 2-pound steak. After a first try, your own taste should be your guide. Heat a heavy skillet, and rub the surface with beef fat trimmed from the steak. Sear the steak on both sides very quickly over high heat. Reduce the heat and cook to the state you prefer. Salt the steak, transfer to a hot platter, and serve with a large dollop of butter.

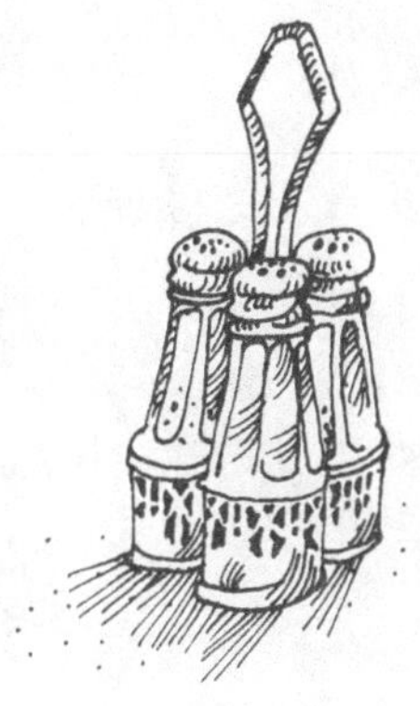

Steak au Poivre Flambé. When the steak is done, quickly flame it with ¼ cup (or more, to your taste) of heated Armagnac, Cognac, or bourbon. Remove the steak to a hot platter, rinse the pan with a touch of the same liquor, and pour over the steak. Or, after flaming, you may add (for 4 persons) ¼ cup of additional liquor and 1 cup of brown sauce. Blend well, bring to a boil, and correct the seasoning. Serve over the steaks or pass separately.

Salt-Broiled Steak

This has been an accepted method of cooking meat for generations. I cannot endorse it with any enthusiasm, although I recognize its appeal for many people.

Pepper a 2 to 3 pound sirloin or T-bone steak. Spread a thin layer of prepared mustard over the meat, and then add a paste made with salt and a little water. Coarse salt, such as kosher or an even heavier variety, is best for this procedure. Broil as you would a plain steak of the same size. The salt will color during cooking and form a hard cake. This is chipped off before carving, and oddly enough the steak will not be oversalted. After removing the salt, give the steak a generous covering of butter.

Roquefort Broiled Steak

Roquefort, which has been called by many a gastronome the king of cheeses, has been in demand in this country since the turn of the century, and probably before that. When I was a child my family and our friends always delighted in a good wedge of Roquefort. It has found a steady use in our cooking habits, indoor and out, and is a standard item in restaurants.

Prepare a paste with ½ pound mashed Roquefort, ¼ pound softened butter, a garlic clove put through a press or finely minced, and 2 tablespoons brandy or bourbon. Blend until creamy. Spread it on the steak after it has been broiled or just before taking it from the broiler. In the latter case, the steak should be 4 to 5 inches from the broiling unit and should remain just long enough to bring the cheese to a bubbling golden brown.

If cooking steak on a charcoal grill, cover the top of the steak with the cheese mixture just before the steak is done, allowing enough time for the cheese to heat through and melt. Serve with a sprinkling of chopped parsley.

Herbed Steak

Rosemary is the preferred herb to use in steak cookery, largely because of the tradition established by French and Belgian immigrants who grew the herb in their own gardens. The recipe I've known all my life, made by a Belgian-Flemish family, calls for a crust of fresh rosemary pressed into the steak with the heel of the hand. During grilling or broiling, the leaves become charred and flavor the steak. Although, again, this method may have originated as a means for disguising gamy meat, it happens to produce an excellent and unusual steak. After cooking, the charred covering should be discarded and the rosemary needles thoroughly brushed away. The steak may be flamed with brandy or bourbon.

Cooking steak over herbed fires. In the West and the North, where such wild herbs as rosemary, fennel, and thyme are found growing in profusion, as in Provence, Spain, and other Mediterranean lands, it is often the custom to grill food over coals heaped with herbs. The food thus acquires a delicious smoky, herby flavor.

Jessie Duncan's Steak Three Inches Thick

A very thick (3 to 4 inches) sirloin or shell steak trimmed of excess fat
2 large onions, thinly sliced
3 green peppers, seeded and thinly sliced
1 lemon, peeled and thinly sliced
Salt and freshly ground pepper
1½ cups tomato catsup
1 cup bouillon or stock

This is a turn-of-the-century dish that borrows something from the Italians and something from the Westerners, of whom Jessie was one.

Set the steak on a rack in a shallow roasting pan and top with the onions, peppers, and lemon slices. Salt and pepper to taste, and add the catsup. Roast in a 450-degree oven 20 to 30 minutes for rare to medium rare. After five minutes add the bouillon or stock and baste the meat often until done.

A New Version. This is improved if the steak is first seared and then covered with the onions, peppers, lemon slices, and a ripe tomato, peeled and sliced. Season and roast on foil in a shallow pan, basting with ½ cup tomato paste blended with 1 cup broth.

Another Version. Sear the steak and place in a hot casserole with the onions, peppers, lemon slices, tomato slices, salt and pepper, and 1 cup catsup. Cover, and bake 30 minutes at 375 degrees.

"Sons of Rest" Beefsteak

Here is another old steak recipe, of anonymous origin, although the Sons of Rest evidently relished good food.

Broil a thick porterhouse steak very rare. Leave it on the broiling rack and quickly cut rather deep diagonal gashes in it about 1½ inches apart. Spread lavishly with softened butter, pressing it into the incisions. Then spread with mustard of your choice — English, Dijon, or other prepared mustard. Salt and pepper to taste. Pour ½ cup sherry over the steak. Place in a 450-degree oven for 10 to 12 minutes. Transfer to a hot platter and pour the pan juices over it. Garnish with chopped parsley.

A New Version. Although the sherry gives a nice flavor, this recipe is better, I believe, if the steak is flamed with brandy or bourbon after it is removed from its final cooking in the oven.

An Old Recipe for Mignon Fillets

An American regional cookbook of the last century credits a Mrs. C.C.B. with this delicious recipe.

Cut slices about 5/8 inch thick from the end of a fillet of beef. Press and trim them into circles. Dredge with salt and pepper, and sauté in butter. Spread Béarnaise sauce on a hot dish and lay the fillets on it, each fillet on a crouton of the same size, and top each with a spoonful of peas or a macédoine of vegetables.

Mignon Fillets, Boston Cooking School

In an early edition of her cookbook, Miss Farmer proposes two ways of treating "mignon fillets." One shows a definite English influence, and the other has a French touch.

In both cases, the fillets are first sautéed in butter in standard fashion. The English version calls for a garnish of poached marrow for each fillet and a Madeira sauce. The other calls for a mound of chestnut purée on each fillet, a delightful idea.

Beefsteak Stanley

This dish was a favorite in New York — especially at the Algonquin Hotel — as late as the 1940's. Broil or sauté a fillet steak to your taste. Top with a broiled banana, and serve with potatoes and a salad.

Planked Steak

One of the more spectacular dishes produced in this country until World War II, planked steak is still occasionally found on a restaurant menu here and there, or in homes where the great traditions of food are maintained. The steak was generally a thick porterhouse, nicely trimmed, or on occasion a sirloin. The plank was a well-aged one of the furrowed well-and-tree style. After the plank was rubbed with salad oil, a wreath of duchesse potatoes was piped around its edge and often around the eventual resting place of the steak and around the vegetables. The vegetables were arranged in beautiful bouquets — tiny green beans, French peas, stuffed or broiled tomatoes, baby carrots, broiled mushroom caps, and in later years, as the dish became more popular, fried or sautéed zucchini. The steak was broiled separately to the rare state and positioned on the plank. Then the entire affair was transferred to a very hot oven to brown the potatoes lightly or to cook the steak a little longer. The steak was topped with a dollop of butter, sprinkled with chopped parsley, and perhaps garnished with watercress before it was borne to the table to be carved and served. Surely this was a *pièce montée américaine* if there ever was one.

Carpetbag or Pocketbook Steak

This combination of steak with oysters used to be in fashion especially in New Orleans and on the West Coast. There were several different versions of the dish, of which this is probably the most common.

Cut a pocket in a very thick shell steak or a thick cut of the tenderloin. Broil the steak. Crumb and fry 8 to 10 oysters. Fill the pocket of the steak to overflowing with the golden-fried oysters. Serve with a Hollandaise or Béarnaise sauce.

Beefsteak with Oyster Blanket. In this other popular version, the steak should be a large sirloin or porterhouse. Broil until nearly done. Spread a pint of fine oysters over the steak, salt and pepper, and dot with butter. Run the steak under the broiler or place in a very hot oven for a few minutes, just long enough to plump the oysters. Sprinkle with chopped parsley and chopped chives.

Beefsteak à la Mirabeau

Porterhouse or rump steak
½ cup butter
2 garlic cloves, finely chopped
Salt and freshly ground pepper
6 anchovy fillets
½ cup pitted green olives
2 tablespoons chopped parsley

SAUCE

2 tablespoons butter
2 tablespoons flour
½ teaspoon freshly ground pepper

This once commonplace Western specialty is still seen occasionally on menus in some of the older restaurants in Oregon and California. It called for a fine broiled porterhouse or rump steak with a garnish of anchovy fillets, pitted green olives, butter, and chopped parsley. Fried potato balls and stuffed baked tomatoes were set around the steak, and it was served with a sauce made with butter, flour, chicken broth, catsup, salt, and pepper. If the recipe had included a little rosemary or basil, it would have been a close cousin of a Provençal steak, which it may have been originally.

Let us remake the recipe in this fashion. Spread the broiled steak with the butter blended with the garlic cloves, salt and pepper. Top with anchovy fillets, green olives, and chopped parsley. Serve with the sauce made as follows:

Melt the butter in a saucepan over low heat. Add the flour, blend well, and cook for a few minutes. Add the seasonings and then stir in the bouillon or broth. Taste for salt — this will depend on the salt content of the bouillon — and correct the seasoning. Continue stirring until thickened. Add some of the degreased pan juices from the steak, if you like.

2 tablespoons tomato paste or catsup
1 teaspoon basil
1 cup bouillon or broth

Steak with Wine Sauce

This very old recipe with English overtones is more a curiosity than a dish suitable for today's repertory.

"Broil your steak as usual, but when you lay it on the hot water dish, have ready this sauce: 1 glass of brown sherry, 1 large spoonful of walnut or mushroom catsup, a tablespoonful of butter rolled in a mere dust of flour, pepper and salt to taste. Bring quickly to a boil in a saucepan, and when it has been poured upon the steak, cover and let stand a few minutes before you serve."

An Early Polish-American Recipe for Steak

Rub well with olive oil a choice porterhouse, T-bone, or sirloin steak about 2½ inches thick. Top with a layer of thinly sliced onions. Let it stand for 3 hours. Remove the onions and sauté them in 4 tablespoons butter. Sauté ¼ pound sliced mushrooms in 4 tablespoons butter. Heat together ½ cup each of Madeira and bouillon. Broil the steak according to your taste. Salt and pepper it, garnish with the onions and mushrooms, and pour the sauce over it.

Old-Fashioned Steak with Gravy

This recipe was much in style when meat was not as tender as it is nowadays. There were a number of versions, but this was the one most used in the North and in the West.

For each person:
A slice of top round steak about ½ inch thick
Seasoned flour
Oil and butter (or lard or shortening)
Salt and freshly ground pepper
Stock or hot water

Pound the flour into the steaks until they are saturated and quite thin. (The flour may be seasoned beforehand with salt, pepper, and paprika and a dash of cayenne, Tabasco, or herbs.) Heat the fat to a depth of 1 inch in a large skillet. Cook the steaks very quickly, turning once, until a beautiful brown, and then remove to a hot platter. Pour off all but 2 or 3 tablespoons of the fat. Add an equal amount of flour, brown well over brisk heat, and then add 1 to 1½ cups stock or water. Stir until thickened, season to taste, and pour the gravy over the steaks or serve separately.

Chicken-Fried Steak

Similar to old-fashioned steak with gravy, this is also less in evidence than it used to be.

Pound flour into slices of top round steak, as for old-fashioned steak with gravy, and fry quickly in fairly hot fat deep enough to immerse. When nicely browned, cover, and simmer for a few moments, as with fried chicken. Transfer to a hot platter. Pour off all but 2 or 3 tablespoons of fat from the pan, add an equal amount of flour, and then add 1 to 2 cups milk or water. Scrape up any brown particles left on the bottom of the pan and incorporate them in the sauce. Season with salt and freshly ground pepper, or with catsup, or add very finely chopped fresh tomato and green pepper and salt and pepper to taste.

Mashed potatoes or rice were always considered *de rigeur* with this dish.

Swiss Steak

2 pounds boneless round steak, 1½ inches thick
Seasoned flour
4 tablespoons butter
2 tablespoons oil
1 garlic clove
1 onion sliced very thin
Bouillon or water

This is a braised or smothered steak — the English call it "stewed steak" — not to be confused with either chicken-fried steak or old-fashioned steak. It is similar to the extent that it is cut from the round, but even then it is cut 1 to 2 inches thick. The basic dish can be varied endlessly, and it is, in its way, a minor classic in American food.

Using the side of a plate, pound the seasoned flour thoroughly into both sides of the steak. Let the steak stand ½ hour. Heat the butter and oil in a skillet, and brown the steak very well on both sides. Add the garlic and onion. When the meat is nicely browned and crusty, add bouillon or water to half cover the meat. Place a tight lid on the pan. Simmer 45 minutes to 1 hour, until the meat is tender and the sauce is rich and thickened. Correct the seasoning. Serve with tiny new potatoes and fresh peas.

Variations

(1) Season with thyme, sage, basil, rosemary, and other herbs.
(2) Season with chili powder and tomato sauce.
(3) In place of the bouillon or water, use broth, beer, wine, tomato sauce, or milk.

Note. Swiss steak can be finished off in the oven. After the meat is thoroughly browned, transfer to a shallow covered baking dish. Add all other ingredients, cover tightly, and bake in a 325 or 350 degree oven 1 to 1½ hours or until the steak is tender, which will depend upon the thickness of the meat and its quality.

Swiss Steak with Wine

2½ pounds round steak 1½ to 2 inches thick
Flour seasoned with thyme, salt, pepper, and cayenne

Pound the seasoned flour thoroughly into both sides of the steak. Let it stand for ½ hour. Sprinkle with chopped garlic. Heat the butter and oil in a heavy skillet. When bubbling hot, add the steaks and brown very well on both sides, turning often. Reduce the heat, and add the onions and the rosemary. Then add the wine and enough

2 garlic cloves, finely chopped
6 tablespoons butter
3 tablespoons oil
2 medium onions, finely chopped
½ teaspoon rosemary
1 cup red wine
Broth or water
½ cup chopped parsley

broth or water to half immerse the meat. Cover the skillet and simmer ½ hour. Uncover, turn the meat, and cover again. Simmer until the meat is thoroughly tender — another 45 minutes to 1 hour. Remove to a hot platter and allow the sauce to cook down slightly. Correct the seasoning, add the chopped parsley, and spoon over the meat. Garnish with whole boiled potatoes and sautéed mushroom caps.

Swiss Steak with Tomatoes

3 pounds round steak 2 inches thick
Flour seasoned with salt, freshly ground pepper, 1 teaspoon basil, and ½ teaspoon mixed spices (nutmeg, ginger, clove, and cinnamon)
2 garlic cloves, finely chopped
6 tablespoons olive oil
3 small onions, thinly sliced
1 green pepper, seeded and sliced into rings
1 #2½ can Italian plum tomatoes
4 tablespoons tomato paste
1 teaspoon basil
3 tablespoons chopped parsley

Pound the seasoned flour into both sides of the steak. Let it stand ½ hour. Sprinkle with the garlic. Heat the oil in a heavy skillet and brown the steak very well on both sides. Add the onions and green pepper, and cook 5 minutes. Add the tomatoes and reduce the heat. Cover and simmer 1 hour. Add the tomato paste and continue simmering until the meat is tender. Correct the seasoning, add the basil and parsley, and cook another 3 minutes. Transfer to a hot platter. Cover with the sauce, and serve with rice or noodles.

Steak Pizzaiola

PIZZAIOLA SAUCE
⅓ cup olive oil
3 garlic cloves, finely slivered
2 cups peeled and seeded ripe tomatoes or canned Italian plum tomatoes (the latter are usually better in most parts of the United States)
1 teaspoon basil or oregano
1 teaspoon salt
1 teaspoon freshly ground pepper
2 tablespoons coarsely chopped parsley

The enormous population of Neapolitans in the United States have promoted their cookery, through restaurants and pizzerias, to the point where it has become standard American fare. This dish is therefore a legitimate part of our steak repertoire.

Broil or pan-broil very rare — it will get additional cooking — any of the following steak cuts: top sirloin, tenderized chuck, minute steaks cut from the rump, or flank steak. Beforehand prepare the sauce.

Heat the oil over moderate heat in a skillet, add the garlic and cook for a minute or so, but do not brown. Add the tomatoes and seasonings and cook down, uncovered, over low heat for about 15 minutes. Correct the seasoning.

Place the cooked steak in the sauce. Cover and simmer for 5 minutes. Serve on very hot plates.

Beefsteak with Onions

Although Mrs. Harland, the author of *Common Sense in the Household*, warned her readers not to serve onions to anyone without asking their permission, onions have been the natural ally of steak for generations. Even Mrs. Harland relented enough to offer a recipe for steak served with butter in which onions had been fried; she did not indicate what was to be done with the onions.

For years steak smothered with onions was traditional from coast to coast. Sometimes it was served on a giant ironstone platter, sometimes right in the skillet. The latter style is found even today in a few of our more posh restaurants, notably the Four Seasons in New York and the Brown Derby in California.

To make, sauté sliced onions in butter over moderate heat until nicely browned. Season to taste. For a more delicate flavor, add a touch of Madeira to the pan just before they are done. Meanwhile, broil or pan-broil a steak to your taste. Season, and top with the onions.

Beefsteak with Mushrooms

Although we still serve a broiled mushroom cap or a small helping of sautéed mushrooms with steak, the old-fashioned way of serving a steak smothered with mushrooms seems to have lost its appeal. It is well worth reviving, however. As formerly done, the steaks — seldom the choicest cuts — were broiled or pan-broiled rare. They were then heaped with button mushrooms or sliced mushrooms sautéed to a deep brown in plenty of butter, seasoned with salt and pepper, and often flavored with a touch of Worcestershire.

Butterfly Steak, Albert Stockli

4 shell steaks or boneless strip steaks 3/4 inch thick, split almost through and spread open ("butterflied")
1 1/2 to 2 pounds chopped beef
1 cup chopped parsley
1 cup chopped shallots or green onions
2 teaspoons salt
Butter and oil
Parsley butter

This imaginative recipe, invented by the former executive chef of Restaurant Associates in New York, has gained favor in many parts of the country in a relatively short time.

Blend the chopped meat and the seasonings. Place a quarter of the mixture on one-half of each steak. Fold the other half over and press it down rather firmly. You will now have a stuffed steak. Heat about 4 tablespoons each of butter and oil in a large heavy skillet. Brown the steaks very quickly on both sides over high heat. Reduce the heat and cook until they are done to your taste. Ideally, the outside of the steak should be nicely browned, and the chopped meat should be no more than warmed through. Serve on a hot platter, giving each steak a generous dollop of parsley butter (chopped parsley blended with softened butter).

Teriyaki Marinated Steak

By far the most prevalent marinade in the United States is what is known as a teriyaki marinade. This is one of the many recipes to come out of the craze for Polynesian food, which is essentially a Hawaiian adaptation of Chinese and Japanese cookery.

The base of a teriyaki marinade is made with equal parts of soy sauce (and it must be a good Japanese or Hong Kong version of soy), sherry, and oil. To this is added crushed or chopped garlic, grated orange or tangerine rind, and grated or sliced fresh ginger to taste. Fresh ginger is available in Chinese markets, in many general produce markets, and sometimes in supermarkets, where it is found in the vegetable and fruit section. If you cannot buy fresh ginger, use candied or preserved ginger, washing off the sugar and cutting it very fine. This will not produce exactly the same flavor, but it is a good substitute. I also like to add a dash of Tabasco and freshly ground pepper to my teriyaki marinade, which makes it less Oriental but improves its quality.

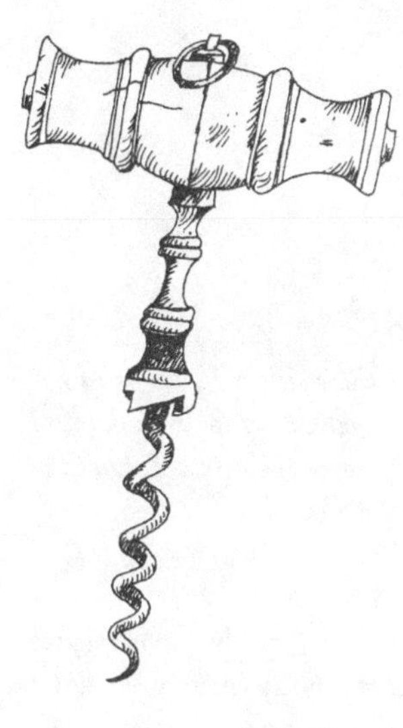

Allow the steak to marinate at least 2 or 3 hours. Some people marinate flank or skirt steak a week or more. And if it is kept refrigerated, the marinade can be reused.

To cook marinated flank or skirt steaks, broil 5 or 6 minutes, turning once. They will develop a rich brown color and great flavor and juiciness. Broil larger steaks according to general instructions, and carve in thin diagonal slices. It would seem a pity to marinate a fine sirloin or porterhouse in this way, but a whole fillet, yes!

Fondue Bourguignonne

This Swiss dish, which is table cookery at its most functional, has become increasingly suited to the present age. It enables the host or hostess to assemble an entire meal ahead of time while the guests do much of the actual cooking. A fondue, with its attendant sauces, potatoes, bread, salad, and fruit and cheese or a simple dessert, makes an ample meal — also an attractive one, when an array of sauces and relishes are arranged around platters of red beef cut into cubes. Admittedly, it is not the most interesting of dishes, and the prolonged smell of hot fat can be unappetizing, but for many people the novelty of communal cooking and the absence of last-minute kitchen work are reward enough.

Use metal fondue pots, or chafing dishes, or electric skillets. Also use proper fondue forks, which are thin and elongated and have insulated handles. Provide two forks per person — a fondue fork for cooking and an ordinary fork for eating. Obviously, it is hazardous to eat directly from a fork that has been sitting in bubbling fat.

Gauge ½ to 1 pound meat per person, according to appetites. By rights the meat should come from the fillet, with all fat trimmed, cut into ½ to 1 inch cubes. I have found, however, that sirloin of good quality works quite as well. Arrange the meat into individual portions in small bowls or dishes.

Place equal quantities of butter and oil in the pots, chafing dishes, or skillets, to a depth of 2 to 3 inches or enough to immerse the cubes of meat, and heat to 360 to 375 degrees. Each person cooks the meat to his own taste and dips it into the sauces gathered on his plate. Crisp fried potatoes, tiny new potatoes cooked in butter, or good potato chips are nice accompaniments. Salad and crusty bread are almost indispensable. This meal calls for beer or a light red wine, such as a Beaujolais or Valpolicella.

Steak Diane I

4 slices sirloin ¼ to ⅜ inch thick, pounded as for a paillard, to approximately the size of a dinner plate
½ pound butter
½ cup oil
Salt and freshly ground pepper
1 cup finely chopped shallots or green onions
Dijon mustard
Worcestershire sauce
½ cup brown sauce or 3 tablespoons meat glaze
Madeira
Lemon juice
Chopped parsley

This table-cooked steak is a restaurant showpiece, and many enterprising amateur cooks as well enjoy producing it for friends. One should be equipped with a table stove or chafing dish and a large pan, similar to those used for crêpes Suzette, or a handsome copper skillet. An electric skillet can be used with equal flair. In addition to stove and pan, a heated platter is needed to hold the steaks while the sauce is made, and it is best to assemble the ingredients for the sauce on a tray. To produce this dish for more than four people requires the participation of two cooks, each with his own set of equipment.

Heat the pan or skillet. (If manageable, use two pans simultaneously.) Place 2 tablespoons butter and 1 of oil in the pan, and heat until bubbling. Sear a steak quickly on each side, and sprinkle with salt and freshly ground pepper. Then, using two forks, roll the steak and transfer it to a hot platter. Repeat this procedure with the other three steaks.

Add 2 tablespoons butter to the pan together with the shallots or green onions. Cook briefly — 2 minutes or so — shaking the pan. Salt and pepper the shallots. Add 1 or 2 teaspoons Dijon mustard and about 2 tablespoons Worcestershire sauce. Blend well. Then add either the brown sauce or meat glaze. Blend well again, and add Madeira to taste. Stir, add a few drops of lemon juice, and taste for seasoning. Sprinkle with more freshly ground pepper if needed. Finally add another tablespoon or two of butter, and stir in the chopped parsley. Spoon over the steaks or bathe the steaks in the sauce before serving.

Steak Diane II

4 slices sirloin, as above
½ cup butter and ¼ cup oil

Cook the steaks in butter and oil as directed above; season with salt and pepper. Flambé in the pan with Cognac or Armagnac, using about 2 tablespoons for each steak. Roll and transfer to a hot platter. Add to the pan the butter, garlic, onions, brown sauce, chives, pepper, mustard, and Madeira. Bring to a boil and cook rapidly about 3 minutes. Stir in the additional butter and the chopped parsley. Unroll the steaks and spoon sauce over each, or dip the rolled steaks into the sauce and spoon remaining sauce over them. Serve with small triangles of fried toast.

½ cup Cognac or Armagnac
Salt and freshly ground pepper
6 tablespoons butter
4 cloves garlic and 4 small onions, finely chopped
½ cup brown sauce
1 teaspoon freshly chopped chives
½ teaspoon freshly ground pepper
1 teaspoon Dijon mustard
2 tablespoons Madeira
1 tablespoon additional butter
2 tablespoons chopped parsley

Fillet of Beef Stroganoff

1½ pounds fillet of beef cut in thin strips 3 inches long, 1 inch wide
3 tablespoons oil
3 tablespoons butter
Salt and freshly ground pepper
3 tablespoons finely chopped shallots or scallions
¼ teaspoon Tabasco
½ teaspoon dried tarragon or 1 tablespoon fresh tarragon
1 tablespoon Worcestershire
1 tablespoon tomato paste (if you like)
1 to 1½ cups sour cream

To most people this well-known dish is a variety of stew, and little wonder. When made with lesser cuts of meat and braised, as it frequently is, about the only resemblance it bears to the original recipe is its use of sour cream. Properly done, this is a dish that is cooked quickly, often at table, and served at once. It calls for tenderloin, which can be sautéed rapidly and gives delicacy to the finished dish.

If cooking in your kitchen, use a heavy skillet; if at table, use an electric skillet or a skillet over an alcohol burner. Heat the butter and oil in the skillet and brown the fillet strips very quickly on both sides. Salt and pepper and transfer to a hot platter. Add the shallots or scallions to the skillet, more freshly ground pepper, Tabasco, tarragon, Worcestershire, and tomato paste. Blend thoroughly. Remove the skillet from the heat and carefully stir in the sour cream. It should just heat through. Under no circumstances should it boil, which causes it to curdle. Spoon the sauce over the beef. Serve with rounds of fried toast and sautéed mushrooms. Garnish with chopped parsley.

Note. In recent years there has been a vogue for serving two 1-inch-thick slices of tenderloin for each person. This involves fewer pieces of meat in the cooking, looks better on the plate, and makes a more agreeable dish.

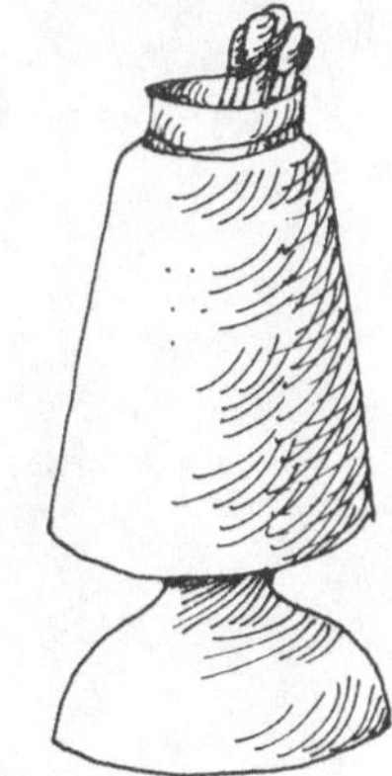

Roast Beef

Beef was largely spit-roasted in this country until the early nineteenth century when the reflector oven was introduced. This was a small metal piece, rounded in shape, which could be set before the coals of a fireplace. The roast, salted and peppered, was placed upon a trivet or muffin rings, with a dripping pan underneath, filled with boiling water. It was then positioned between the reflector and the coals. The roast thus had both direct and reflected heat. It roasted rather quickly in this fashion, for Mrs. Crowen gives directions for roasting 15 minutes per pound. The secret of its success was frequent basting with the drippings. When the meat was half done, it was often pushed nearer the coals, the thickest part foremost. The pan was kept replenished with boiling water, so that at least a pint of dripping would remain at the end of the roasting period. Fifteen minutes before the roast was done, its fatty covering was dredged with flour. This in turn was basted with drippings to make a crusty finish. The roast was then removed to a hot platter and covered while the drippings were mixed with a bit of flour and strained into a small sauceboat. Mrs. Crowen adds that the correct accompaniments were plain boiled or mashed potatoes, boiled spinach, beets or dressed celery, mashed turnips or squash. Pickles or horseradish were also allowed.

In the eighteenth and nineteenth centuries it was necessary to baste a good deal when roasting a major cut of beef, largely because the heat of most wood or coal fires was so uneven and beef was not as well marbled with fat as it is today. It was not unusual to find a recipe that called for a cup of boiling water to be thrown over the roast, after which it was to be basted copiously with the water and pan juices. Nowadays this procedure is unnecessary.

By the mid-nineteenth century ovens were becoming more common, but they were primarily used for baking. When they were put into use for meat, the results were called "baked meats." Mrs. Crowen states that with proper handling a good piece of meat could be baked in a stove oven so nearly to resemble a roast as to be mistaken for it! Here, too, the meat was placed on a trivet or muffin rings to bake. There was little means for controlling heat, but cooks were warned that if the oven became too hot, the oven door should be opened to cool it a bit.

In both the 1886 and 1902 editions of her book, Mrs. Rorer of Philadelphia still refers to the "tin kitchen," which was a more modern form of the reflector oven. It had more space and a deeper well for the dripping pan. Also it is interesting to note that Mrs. Rorer suggests maintaining a temperature of 300 degrees for beef after searing it. And for baking in the oven, this same culinary genius suggests 400 degrees to start and 240 degrees after the meat is well browned. This was quite advanced thinking for her day, and unfortunately most cooks went on testing the oven with the hand, and thus roasting was largely a hit or miss affair. Even Miss Farmer, up to the 1914 edition of her book, had no thoughts on meat temperature at all and simply recommended an hour and five minutes for a 5-pound roast and one hour and thirty minutes for a 10-pound roast in a hot oven. Only since the development of good ranges and accurate oven thermometers has the subject of meat temperatures become essential.

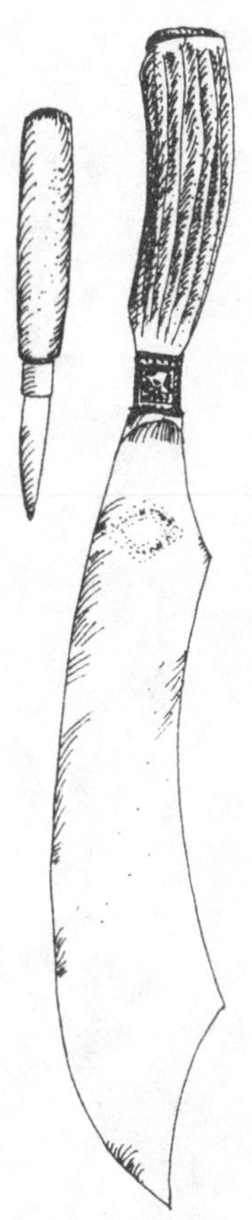

Today there are four or five favorite attacks on the roasting of beef. Each is successful in its way, and it remains for the cook to compare results.

To buy beef for roasting

Look for cherry red, well-trimmed beef with good marbling in it and with creamy fat. It should be U.S. *Choice* or *Prime*. If you have a butcher who indulges you, order your roast well ahead and ask him to hang it a little longer than is customary nowadays.

Estimate ¾ to 1 pound of meat per person, especially if there is much bone. Have no fear of leftover roast. To many palates it is even better cold than hot and can be used in a variety of ways.

Boned roasts. It is still common practice for the French and Italians to bone out roasts, and bard and tie them. The idea went with them to the New World, and thus in earlier days butcher shops offered boned and barded rump roasts or boned and rolled ribs of beef. Rolled roasts are less common today (although at this writing I have a piece of contre-filet, thinly barded and beautifully tied, roasting in the oven), except in food shops and delicatessens where beef is machine-sliced. If you are serving a large roast, it is always handsomer to see it carved from the bones, and the bones themselves can be saved for delectable leftovers, deviled beef bones.

Prime (Standing) Rib Roast

The first three ribs are considered the best, although in my opinion a larger roast is preferable — the first five ribs, well trimmed, so that carving will be easy. This means a "7-inch cut," with the short rib section cut off and the chine bone, back cord, and feather bone removed. It is wise to have the roast barded with an extra piece of suet.

(1) *Low-heat method.* This requires a well-insulated, well-regulated oven. It is much in favor and works successfully with beef that is well fatted. Place the roast on a rack in a shallow pan and rub it with freshly ground pepper and, if you choose, with a little rosemary or thyme or garlic. However, fine beef should be roasted as simply as possible — peppered before roasting, salted later — with additional flavorings reserved for the sauce. Preheat the oven to 180 or 200 degrees, and place the roast in the oven bone side down. Allow it to roast without basting approximately 23 to 24 minutes per pound, until it achieves an internal temperature of 120 to 125 degrees for rare meat; or, for medium, approximately 28 minutes per pound until it achieves an internal temperature of 140 degrees. Salt the roast, remove it from the oven, and allow it to settle about 10 minutes before carving.

(2) *Medium-heat method.* This is more or less the standard method. Preheat the oven to 300 or 325 degrees. Prepare the roast as above. Roast, allowing 15 to 17 minutes per pound for rare (meat thermometer, 120 to 125 degrees) or 17 to 20 minutes per pound for medium rare (meat thermometer, 140 degrees). Allow the roast to stand 10 minutes before carving.

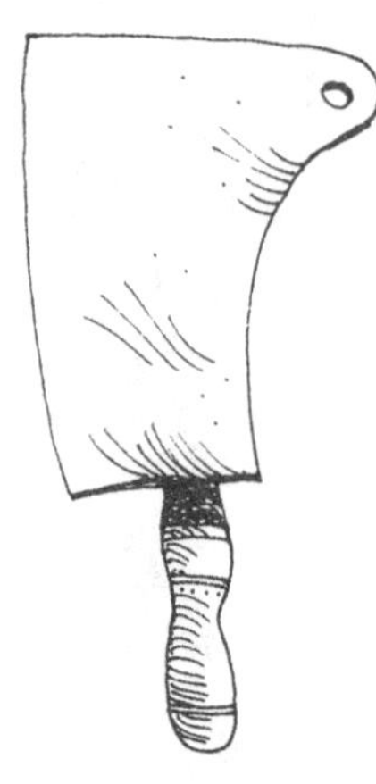

(3) *Searing method.* Preheat the oven to 425 to 450 degrees. Prepare the meat as above. Roast 30 minutes. Reduce the heat to 325 degrees and continue to roast, allowing about 12 minutes per pound for rare (meat thermometer, 120 to 125 degrees) or 14 to 15 minutes per pound for medium (meat thermometer, 140 degrees). Allow it to stand 10 minutes before carving.

(4) *Western method.* This is much used by Western housewives who lead active lives and entertain a great deal. The roast is started before midday for serving at dinner in the evening. For a 7:30 dinner, set the oven at 375 degrees at 11 A.M. (for an 8:30 dinner, advance it an hour to noon, and so on). Put the roast on a rack and place in the oven. Roast 1 hour. At the end of that time, turn off the heat, but do not open the door of the oven. Leave the roast in the oven until evening. Approximately 1 hour before you are ready to serve, turn on the oven to 375 degrees and roast the meat another 45 minutes to an hour. Remove to a hot platter and let it stand 15 minutes before carving. Roasts of varying weight, up to 11 or 12 pounds, will cook in the same time by this method — the outside nicely

browned and the inside rare. For roasts of more than 12 pounds, the final roasting should be started an extra hour in advance.

(5) *Spit-roasting.* To assure even turning, whether it is over charcoal, in front of the fire, or in a rotisserie oven, it is essential to have the roast perfectly balanced on the spit. If one end of the roast seems much heavier than the other, run the spit through so that the heaviest part of the beef is held by the center of the spit.

For charcoal roasting use a medium heat, to achieve a grill temperature of 300 to 325 degrees. A five-rib roast or a large sirloin roast will take from 1¾ to 2½ hours to reach the rare state, or an internal temperature of 120 to 125 degrees. At this point douse the fire and allow the roast to settle about 10 minutes longer.

What to serve with roast beef

See recipes below for roast beef gravy and Yorkshire pudding.

Potatoes. One of the more traditional accompaniments is oven-browned potatoes, cooked in drippings with the roast. These are difficult to achieve in a slow oven unless they are parboiled. Uncooked potatoes cooked with a roast that is seared at high temperature and finished off at a slower heat will be done in about an hour. However, they are best when boiled 15 minutes, peeled, cut in long strips about an inch wide, and transferred while still hot to the pan drippings. Mashed potatoes are also excellent with beef and are especially popular with those who revel in mounds of potatoes and rivers of gravy.

Other vegetables. Green beans are a favorite with roasts, as are mashed turnips — either the swedes or yellow turnips — cabbage, brussels sprouts, and peas.

Condiments and sauces. Some people demand grated fresh horseradish; others, horseradish cream sauce. Still others use mustard, and there are those who insist upon catsup. (And see roast beef gravy, below.)

Wines. A noble roast of beef deserves a good Burgundy. The choice can begin with a modest Beaujolais, Juliénas, or Fleurie and progress to the fine Échézeaux, the Grands Échézeaux, and the Chambertins. Among the American wines, one might choose a Pinot Noir or a Cabernet Sauvignon.

Roast Beef Gravy

However you roast beef, you most likely will want to serve it with a sauce. The sauce most used throughout our history is known as roast beef gravy. It was advocated by all of the early food experts as a necessary accompaniment to beef, and thus it became a classic. Traditionally it was made by combining four tablespoons of fat from the roasting pan with an equal amount of flour and stirring over medium heat till the flour browned slightly. Then 1½ to 2 cups of boiling water were added, followed by seasoning — salt and pepper and occasionally some sweet herbs. This was stirred over low heat till thickened, and it was sometimes strained. Mrs. Harland alone offered a variation by suggesting the use of stock from yesterday's soup to make a richer gravy. In the days when starchy diets were more acceptable, roast beef gravy was made in quantity to be used for a second or third meal over bread or potatoes.

Yorkshire Pudding

2 eggs
1 cup milk
1 cup sifted all-purpose flour
½ teaspoon salt
½ teaspoon freshly ground pepper
Beef drippings

This gift from England did not appear in the United States as early as one might suppose, but begins to turn up on menus as late as the middle of the nineteenth century. Mrs. Crowen fails to mention it as an accompaniment to roast beef, and so does Mrs. Rorer, who is supposed to have originated the popover, a close relative of Yorkshire pudding. It is not to be found in *The Yankee Cook Book* either. So it may well be that the English in Maryland or the Carolinas brought it into fashion. Mrs. Harland is the first writer of note to include it in a cookbook. She broke with tradition in suggesting that the pudding be made with separated eggs, the beaten whites folded into the yolk and flour mixture. Since then practically every standard cookbook carries a recipe for Yorkshire pudding. Miss Farmer, in early editions of her book, gave credit to Miss C. J. Wills for her recipe. At any rate, this famous pudding is now served with roast beef throughout the country. Needless to say, some of it is inedible, to say nothing of being indigestible. One must remember that formerly it was made by pouring the batter into the dripping pan under the roast. As it baked it was flavored by drippings from the roast, and when served with juicy rare meat it was a most delectable dish.

The standard recipe used today resembles the popover recipe. Usually it is baked in a flat pan (11 × 14 × 2½) swathed with plenty of hot beef drippings. It is also baked in muffin pans or in a 2-quart ring mold.

If you are making pudding for a large group or for large appetites, it would be wise to double the quantities given here.

Beat the eggs until quite light and gradually beat in the milk and sifted flour. Or put all at once into an electric mixer or blender and beat or whirl for a few seconds just until the batter is smooth. Flavor with salt and pepper and add, if you like, 2 tablespoons drippings. Heat the pan, muffin tins, or mold, and pour in a heavy layer of hot drippings. Then pour in the batter and bake at 450 degrees about 10 minutes. Reduce the heat to 375 degrees and continue baking 15 to 20 minutes or until beautifully brown and puffy. Do not open the oven door during the first 20 minutes of baking.

Note. Some people like to add a clove of garlic to the beaten batter, which is removed before the batter is poured into the pan, or they rub the pan with garlic before adding the drippings.

Mrs. Harland's Yorkshire Pudding

2 cups milk
4 eggs, whites and yolks beaten separately
1 teaspoon salt
2 cups sifted all-purpose flour

Beat the yolks with the milk and salt, and gradually beat in the flour. Fold in the whites and pour into a hot pan with drippings. Bake at 425 degrees 20 minutes and then turn to 375 degrees and continue baking till light and puffy. This was originally baked beneath the roast.

Rolled Rib Roast

The same cut as prime rib roast above, but boned, tied, and secured with skewers. This makes a very handsome roast if prepared by a good butcher. However, such a roast loses some of the grandeur of the standing roast.

Rolled rib roast can be cooked by any of the methods under prime rib roast, and served with the same accompaniments. The timing is apt to differ from a bone-in-roast.

Eye of the Rib Roast

The center portion of the rib roast, with all the bone and less tender meat removed. It should be barded with suet. It cooks much faster than the ordinary rib roast and is delicious and tender, comparable to a tenderloin in its appeal. (See also tenderloin roast, below.)

Shell (Boneless Sirloin) Roast

This is the boned cut used for shell steaks. It will cook in a shorter time than prime rib roast (above) and is easy to carve, since it is boneless. It makes a tender and delicious as well as luxuriously expensive roast. A shell roast must be cooked on a rack.

Because this roast cooks quickly, it requires extra attention. It would be depressing to have such an expensive cut of meat overcook. I usually gauge about 10 to 12 minutes per pound at 350 degrees in order to achieve 120 degrees on the meat thermometer. The thickness of the cut may vary. Watch carefully.

If the roast is quite thin with a good layer of fat at the top, it can be broiled. Begin fat side up, turn to the meaty side, and turn again to finish off on the fat side. A meat thermometer can be used during broiling provided it is of the type with a long, thin shaft that is plunged into the roast for a reading and then withdrawn.

Porterhouse Roast

This used to be known as a sirloin roast, once considered elegant fare in this country and still considered so in England. It is comprised of the fillet and the contre-filet with the T-bone left in. Actually, the shell roast is a much better choice, not only because of the ease in carving it, but because it roasts evenly. In a porterhouse roast, the fillet generally becomes overcooked if the contre-filet is done just right. Furthermore, few American butchers are familiar with this cut any longer. Follow the recipe for prime rib roast (above).

Pinbone Roast

Another roast formerly popular and almost forgotten today is the pinbone section of the sirloin, either boned or with the bone left in. An extraordinarily tender roast, it is, unfortunately, difficult to come by in butcher shops. If you find it, follow the directions for prime rib roast, above. Timing may differ, but the internal temperature is the same.

Rump Roast

A delicious and all too little known roast, although it is much used in restaurants and in delicatessens. It should be of good quality beef, boned and tied, usually with extra barding fat added. Follow directions for prime rib roast, above, being careful about timing.

Roast Fillet of Beef (Tenderloin Roast)

The whole tenderloin is frequently used as a roast. It is either barded with fat and roasted or trimmed carefully of fat, brushed well with oil and butter, and basted frequently during roasting. While it is considered an elegant roast for important occasions, an eye of the rib roast or a shell roast has more flavor and makes just as handsome a presentation.

Fillets weigh from 4 to 10 pounds and have a coating of kidney fat on one side and a membrane that often runs the entire length of the cut. These should be removed before cooking. It is a fairly simple operation that anyone can do, even though his butcher may turn out a more finished product.

It is my belief that this roast and the eye of the rib, which are usually thin, without bone, and with little fat, cook better at high temperatures, such as 400 to 450 degrees. An average fillet takes about 35 minutes to reach the very rare state, which is what it should be. An eye of the rib may take slightly longer because of its greater thickness, but surely not more than 50 minutes. Test with a meat thermometer for an inner temperature of 120 to 125 degrees for rare and 140 degrees for medium rare. Salt the roast about 10 minutes before removing from the oven. Allow to stand 10 to 15 minutes before carving.

Fillet of Beef Flambé

Fillet of beef, 5 to 6 pounds trimmed weight
4 tablespoons olive oil
1 teaspoon freshly ground pepper
Salt
⅓ cup Cognac or Armagnac
Butter
Chopped parsley

Rub the fillet well with oil and freshly ground pepper. Place on a well-oiled rack in a rather shallow roasting pan. Roast at 400 to 450 degrees about 35 minutes or until it has achieved an internal temperature of 125 degrees. Brush with oil occasionally if necessary. When done, salt the roast and let it rest 10 minutes. Just before carving, blaze the roast with warmed Cognac. Add a little butter, sprinkle with chopped parsley, and serve with the pan juices. Broiled tomatoes and watercress make nice accompaniments.

Marinated Fillet of Beef

Fillet of beef, about 5 to 6 pounds

MARINADE

Oil
1 cup Japanese soy sauce
3 finely chopped garlic cloves
2 tablespoons grated fresh ginger or the equivalent in washed candied ginger
½ cup sherry
¼ cup peanut oil

This is a result of the vogue for seasoning Oriental-style. It is a delicious and unusual dinner dish.

Trim the fillet and rub it well with oil. Place in a container with the other ingredients and turn it to bathe all sides. Let it stand several hours, and turn occasionally. Transfer to a rack in a rather shallow baking or roasting pan. Roast in a preheated 400 to 450 degree oven 30 to 35 minutes, basting occasionally with the marinade. It is done (rare) when a meat thermometer registers 125 degrees internal temperature. Remove to a hot platter and pour pan juices over it. Let it stand 10 minutes. Garnish with sautéed mushroom caps, and serve with mounds of rice topped with buttered toasted almonds.

Stuffed Fillet of Beef

Fillet of beef, about 5 pounds, trimmed well and with mignon removed
½ pound foie gras, or more
Several truffles
Cognac
½ cup butter
Freshly ground pepper
Salt

This recipe came from a small French restaurant in California called Fleur de Lys, where I ate many years ago. It is thoroughly delicious and shows what the French influence did, even in the remote West, where these restaurant folk cooked with great care and enjoyment.

With the aid of a larding needle or an apple corer, run a hole straight through the fillet. Soak the truffles in Cognac for a half hour. Cut the foie gras into small medallions. Stuff the fillet alternately with cubes of truffle and medallions of foie gras. Rub the fillet with softened butter and pepper. Place on a rack and roast at 375 degrees 35 to 40 minutes, or until the internal temperature registers 125 degrees. Baste with melted butter, if needed. Remove to a hot platter, salt well, and pour the pan juices over it. Garnish with parsley sprigs and chopped parsley, and serve with a truffled brown sauce.

Fillet of Beef Bouquetière

This was considered a very stylish way to serve a roast fillet throughout the country. After one look I always found it rather a bore, largely because I do not care for so many vegetables with any dish of meat, and especially with such a prize cut.

Roast the fillet to your taste. Arrange on a magnificent hot platter — preferably a large oval one. Surround with a bouquet of perfectly cooked buttered or glazed vegetables: tiny whole carrots, tiny whole onions, tiny peas, tiny beans, tiny zucchini, tiny grilled tomatoes, artichoke hearts, tiny potatoes, etc., etc., etc. Impressive, but such a display for one lonely little fillet!

Fillet of Beef Wellington

Pastry — rough puff paste or brioche dough
Fillet of beef, about 5 pounds, well trimmed
Butter
Freshly ground pepper
⅓ cup Cognac
Salt
2 cups (about) duxelles (see recipe below)
Foie gras, mousse of foie gras, or homemade pâté
1 egg white
1 egg yolk lightly beaten with ¼ cup heavy cream

DUXELLES

1 or 2 shallots, finely chopped, or 1 small onion, finely chopped
½ cup butter
1 pound mushrooms, finely chopped
Salt

Since the Second World War this has blossomed from a dish found in a few restaurants to one that everyone prepares for dinner parties and special events. It is in my opinion less than superb, but it makes an effect and thus is tremendously popular.

Prepare the pastry. If it is rough puff paste, make two pounds; if brioche, make 1 recipe. Chill the dough till needed.

Rub the fillet well with butter and pepper. Roast on a rack in a 400 to 450 degree oven till it registers 120 degrees — it must be very, very rare. Flame with the Cognac. Remove to a rack and salt to taste. Allow it to cool completely before making the roll. If you do not, the pastry will melt in spots, causing it to be flabby and break when you cut into it. If both pastry and meat are cool, the final baking will brown the pastry and heat the meat without overcooking it, which so often happens.

While the fillet is cooking, prepare the duxelles. Cook the shallots or onion in 6 tablespoons butter over low heat until translucent. Add the finely chopped mushrooms and the additional 2 tablespoons butter. Cook *very* slowly to dehydrate the mushrooms completely. They should turn quite dark. Stir occasionally. They will take about 1 hour or slightly longer to cook down. Cool after cooking.

To assemble the dish: Measure the circumference of the fillet, and roll out the pastry to a size that will envelop it completely, with overlap at the ends and at the bottom. Reserve the trimmed-off pastry for decorations. Spread the fillet with a thin coating of foie gras or mousse of foie gras (these can be purchased in small oval tins in most good food shops and many of the better supermarkets). Then spread the pastry with cold duxelles. Place the fillet in the center of the pastry. Bring the edges of the pastry together, moisten with white of egg, and secure. When sealed, the roll should look rather smart and well tailored. Roll onto a piece of sulfurized paper or foil, and transfer to a baking sheet or shallow pan. Cut small leaves and rosettes from pastry trimmings and fasten them to the roll with egg white. Brush the pastry with the egg yolk and cream mixture. Bake in a preheated 425-degree oven 10 minutes. Reduce the heat to 375 degrees and bake another 20 minutes or until the crust looks cooked through and golden brown. Remove from the oven and allow to stand 10 to 15 minutes before sliding onto a platter. Garnish with watercress or parsley, and send to the table with a bowl of brown sauce or Bordelaise sauce.

To carve through both pastry and meat it is best to use a serrated slicing knife. Each slice should be 3/4 of an inch thick. Tiny Parisienne potatoes and a purée of green beans are pleasant accompaniments. And with this, one should drink a great Burgundy — an Échézeaux, perhaps.

Post-Roast Beef

In addition to the classic cold roast beef, there are two post-roast beef dishes that are delicious and a definite part of our American tradition, roast beef hash and deviled bones.

Cold Roast Beef

Cold beef, sliced exceedingly thin, is a dish with perhaps more distinction than hot beef. If it has not been touched by the chill of the refrigerator and is allowed to cool at room temperature, there are few meats to equal it in flavor. If refrigeration is necessary, by all means remove the beef long enough before serving to restore some warmth.

Cold beef calls for salad, possibly hot vegetables, and good home-made pickles. In the days when people did a great deal of pickling, the standard items were mustard pickles, onion pickles, and chow-chow. In any family with an English background the chowchow was sure to be Crosse and Blackwell's, which had a very sharp turmeric-mustard flavor and quite crisp vegetables.

Cold beef is also often served with thin slices of cold tongue for a contrast of flavor. The accompaniments given above are suitable. And it goes without saying that thin pink slices of beef make a wonderful filling for sandwiches.

Roast Beef Hash

2 small onions or 1 medium onion, finely chopped
5 tablespoons beef drippings or 3 tablespoons butter and 2 tablespoons oil

I think the best roast beef hash I ever had was in a small country hotel in Minnesota. I had a hunch that this was the time and the place for it and I was not disappointed. The beef was beautifully cubed and the seasoning was just right. In fact, it was a minor triumph.

Sauté the onion in the beef drippings till just transparent. Add the

1½ cups finely diced boiled potatoes
2½ cups cold roast beef, diced, with some fat
Salt and freshly ground pepper
Thyme
Chopped parsley
½ cup heavy cream (optional)

potatoes and brown them well over medium heat, until crisp at the edges. Add the beef. Season to taste, blend well, and cook down till the beef is brown and the mixture is crisp. If you wish, add heavy cream and press the hash down in the skillet. Raise the heat a bit and let the cream cook out, so that it helps to form a crust on the bottom. Serve the hash with poached or fried eggs, if you like, and a generous sprinkling of chopped parsley. It is also traditional to serve chili sauce with the hash. To my taste the chili should be slightly warmed before serving.

An Old Recipe for Baked Hash

1 large onion, finely chopped
5 tablespoons beef drippings or butter and drippings
1 large ripe tomato, peeled, seeded, and chopped
2 cups finely chopped cold roast beef with some fat
1 teaspoon salt
½ teaspoon freshly ground pepper
2 tablespoons Worcestershire sauce
3 cups mashed potatoes
Butter

Sauté the onion in the drippings, and when it has begun to color, add the tomato and the meat and brown well. Add the seasonings and cook for a minute or so. Line a casserole or baking dish with the mashed potatoes, rather like a bottom crust. Fill the center with hash and dot with butter. Bake at 350 degrees for 20 to 25 minutes or until crusty and brown. Serve with homemade pickles and chili sauce.

Deviled Beef Bones

4 or 5 ribs
1 cup or more melted butter
2 cups or more breadcrumbs
1 teaspoon Tabasco
1 teaspoon salt, or to taste
1 teaspoon freshly ground pepper
1 teaspoon dry mustard

When carving a standing rib roast, cut the meat so that some meat is left on the flat side of the bones. When ready to cook, cut the ribs apart, leaving meat between the bones as well. Allow them to stand at room temperature.

Mix the crumbs with the seasonings. Dip the ribs in melted butter and press into the crumbs. Brush with melted butter. Broil 5 to 6 inches from the heat until nicely brown and crisp on both sides. Serve with a sauce diable.

In an early edition of her book, Mrs. Rorer offers another version of deviled ribs, one of the few recipes for this dish I have found published. She sawed the ribs in half and dipped them in melted butter, but instead of coating them with crumbs, she rolled them in chopped green peppers. Salt and pepper were the only seasonings. There is no mention of a sauce.

To assemble enough beef bones to serve a group of people, freeze the beef bones each time you have a rib roast until you have acquired the proper amount.

Pot Roasts

Although the term Yankee Pot Roast appears on restaurant menus everywhere, it is difficult to track down its origin. There are no recipes at all for pot roast in early cookbooks, although in *The Yankee Cook Book* Imogene Wolcott comes through with a recipe from New Hampshire. This calls for raisins, along with the usual vegetables, and the author counsels that sometime during the cooking process the meat should be allowed to stick to the bottom of the pot just to gain color.

In *The Yankee Cook Book* one will find recipes for "à la mode" beef, which is practically the same as pot roast. From this evidence one might conclude that the dish derives from the French immigrants, who cooked their meats "à l'étouffée" or in an étouffade. There was sufficient French influence in New England, especially in New Hampshire and Maine, to have inspired this delicious way of tenderizing meat. Later, the German immigrants, who settled in Pennsylvania and moved on to the Middle West, produced the sauerbratens, the vinegar-marinated roasts, which were larded and cooked a long time to make them spicy and tender. In the South, daubes became popular, and the daube glacé of New Orleans cuisine is as much a daube Provençale as those of Aix, Avignon, and Carpentras. Also, Jewish cooks brought with them their adaptations of Hungarian, Austrian, or Russian beef dishes that were braised and long-cooked.

It is no longer necessary, as in earlier days, to lard beef for a pot roast. Through new methods of feeding livestock and processing meat, beef comes to us tenderer than our forebears knew it, and few of us buy meat that is not U.S. *Choice* or *Prime*. In a way, it is a pity that larding is outmoded, for it produced checkerboard slices when carved that looked as decorative as could be on the plate.

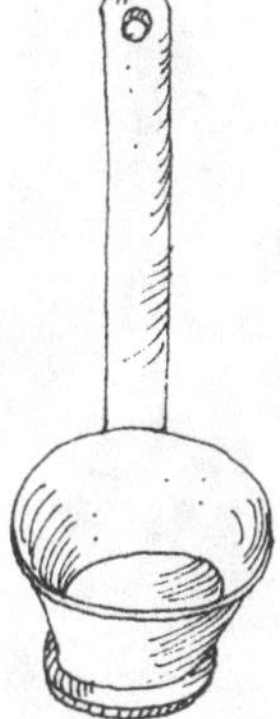

Any one of a number of different pots may be used for pot roasts, étouffades, and à la mode dishes. Traditionally, New Englanders used a heavy iron pot that became known as a Dutch oven. Nowadays one can choose among enameled iron, heavy aluminum, and copper lined with stainless steel.

Normally braising of this sort is done on top of the stove, but the oven can be used with equal satisfaction. The best cuts of beef for a pot roast are rump, round, and chuck. Whatever the cut, it should be boned and tied or rolled and tied. Tying not only gives a better-looking roast; it also produces more compact slices of meat. We have learned from the French that a calf's foot, pig's foot, or a little necklace made of pieces of pork skin added to the pot will give the sauce a wonderful gelatinous quality as well as flavor.

Pot roasts and any braised or smothered dish of this type are much better if cooked one day, left to cool, and reheated the next. For one thing it is easier to remove excess fat if the sauce is cool, and more important, the meat seems to gain in flavor if it rests in the sauce for 24 hours.

Basic Pot Roast of Beef

4 to 5 pounds rump, chuck or round
Flour
Several pieces of beef suet, or 4 tablespoons each of butter and oil
1 onion stuck with 2 cloves
1 bay leaf
1 teaspoon freshly ground pepper
2 tablespoons salt
1½ teaspoons thyme
1 cup broth or water
6 carrots
12 small white onions
2 turnips
Beurre manié

Rub the roast with flour. Try out the beef fat or heat the butter and oil. Brown the meat slowly on all sides in the hot fat, turning with the aid of wooden spoons or spatulas. When it is well colored, add the onion, seasonings, and liquid and reduce the heat. Cover the pot and simmer atop the stove or in a 300-degree oven. Continue cooking for about 2 hours. Test the meat, and if it is on the way to being tender, add the vegetables. Cover again and continue cooking until the meat is tender and the vegetables are cooked. If they cook too quickly, transfer them to a hot dish and keep them warm.

When the roast is finished, remove and keep it warm on a hot platter. Skim the excess fat from the sauce in the pan and, if you wish, thicken it with beurre manié (small balls of butter and flour kneaded together). Taste for seasoning. Serve with plain boiled potatoes with or without jackets. A good salad of endive and beets will round off the meal.

Boeuf à la Mode

This French dish in various versions has long been a great favorite with cookbook writers and with ladies who put together the bits of culinary Americana. Here is Mrs. Crowen's recipe, which is found copied in a number of other small recipe books, including a benefit book published in Detroit some thirty years after Mrs. Crowen. One is astonished at the number of cloves recommended in this recipe, but otherwise it seems to be pretty sound. It does taste rather good and is interesting for its time.

"Take a piece of the round or any lean piece of beef; take out the bone and fill it with a stuffing made of bread, made moist with hot water, and seasoned with pepper and salt and a bit of butter or chopped suet; make a mixture of a tablespoon of pepper, same of salt and of sweet herbs nicely powdered; rub the seasoning well into the meat. Stick cloves over the whole surface. Tie a tape around it to keep it in shape, then put it in a bake pan or a dinner pot with water nearly to cover it, over a gentle fire; cover the pot as closely as possible. Let it simmer or boil gently, according to its weight, allowing fifteen minutes for each pound of meat. When the meat is tender, and the water nearly out, dredge flour over until it is nearly white, then turn it over, add a teacup of butter and a minced onion or leek; cover the pot and set it nearer the fire, to brown the meat; scrape a carrot and cut it in slices a quarter of an inch thick; notch the edges of the slices neatly and put them in a stew pan with boiling water, and set it over the fire; when it is tender take up with a skimmer; dip a bunch of parsley into boiling water and cut it into small pieces and add it and the carrot to the meat; after having turned them again let them stew for a few minutes; then take the meat on a dish, take off the tape, dredge a little flour to the gravy, add a small teacup of boiling water, stir till smooth; then pour over the meat and serve. A glass of wine or vinegar may be put into the gravy instead of the water, or a large tablespoon of tomato catsup."

This became something of a standard recipe for years to come and was only relieved about the time of Mrs. Rorer and Mrs. Lincoln. Mrs. Rorer, in 1886, published a recipe almost identical save that she adds cinnamon and ground pork to the stuffing and uses some stock. She comments that "in winter it will keep for two weeks and may be served cold with its amber jelly."

Chilied Pot Roast

5-pound eye of round roast, tied
3 cloves garlic cut in slices
Flour
Beef suet or drippings
4 medium onions, sliced
1 teaspoon oregano
½ teaspoon cumin seed
½ teaspoon coriander
2 tablespoons chili powder, or more, to taste
Salt
¼ teaspoon Tabasco
1 cup broth
½ cup tomato sauce
Chopped fresh coriander or parsley

This adds the favorite seasoning of California, Texas, and New Mexico. It is a delicious dish with polenta or with tortillas and hominy.

Cut several incisions in the meat and insert thin strips of garlic. Sprinkle with flour. Melt the suet or heat the drippings in a braising pan and brown the meat well on all sides. Take care not to use a fork, but turn with the aid of two wooden spoons or a pair of spatulas. When the meat is nicely colored, add the onions and cook until they are brown. Add the seasonings, sprinkling the chili evenly about the pot, and cook in the fat. Add the broth and the tomato sauce and bring to a boil. Reduce the heat, cover the pot, and simmer very slowly about 2 hours, turning the roast every half hour. Should the sauce become too thick, add more broth to it.

When tender, remove the roast to a hot platter. Skim excess fat from the sauce. Correct the seasoning. Spoon over the roast. Garnish with fresh coriander (cilantro) or parsley. Serve with hominy and tortillas.

Pot Roast with Tomatoes

5-pound chuck or round roast, rolled and tied
Beef fat
1 veal knuckle
4 cloves garlic
1 onion stuck with 2 cloves
1 teaspoon thyme
1 teaspoon or more dried basil or 2 tablespoons chopped fresh basil
¼ teaspoon Tabasco
2 teaspoons salt
1 teaspoon freshly ground pepper
2 cups fresh tomatoes, peeled and seeded, or canned Italian tomatoes
½ cup red wine
2 tablespoons tomato paste

This recipe resembles in some ways certain Southern French daube recipes.

Sear the beef well in a small amount of beef fat till it is well browned. Add the veal knuckle. Siphon off excess fat and add the onion, seasonings, tomatoes, and wine. Bring to a boil, uncovered. Place a sheet of buttered paper over the meat. Reduce the heat and cover. Simmer gently on top of the stove or in the oven at 300 degrees approximately two hours. Test for tenderness and correct the seasoning. Stir in the tomato paste and continue cooking till the meat is tender. The cooking time will, of course, vary with the cut of meat and the grade. Remove from heat, let stand for 10 to 12 minutes, then remove excess fat from the sauce. This dish is excellent served with macaroni or noodles and a crisp salad.

Marinated Pot Roast with Italian Overtones

5 pounds beef rump, rolled and tied with a little barding fat
2 cups red wine
1 onion, sliced
4 cloves garlic
1½ teaspoons dried basil or ⅓ cup chopped fresh basil
2 or 3 sprigs of parsley
6 tablespoons olive oil
Salt and freshly ground pepper
1½ cups Italian plum tomatoes
1 cup soft black olives, pitted — the soft Italian type
Chopped parsley

The tremendous Italian influence in our cooking is certainly evident in this recipe. It's a rather strange combination but very good.

Place the meat in a deep bowl with the wine, onion, garlic, basil, and parsley. Turn several times. Marinate for two days, turning several times each day. When you are ready to cook, remove the meat and dry it well; also remove the onions, garlic, and other seasonings, and reserve. Cook the wine down to half its volume. Sear the meat in olive oil on all sides in a braising pan and add the onion and other seasonings from the marinade. Salt to taste, and add about ten grinds of the pepper mill. Pour the hot wine over the roast and cover. Simmer for about 2 hours. Test the meat for tenderness, and add the tomatoes. Continue simmering till the meat is quite tender. Just before serving, add the olives and allow them to cook for 5 minutes. Remove the roast to a hot platter. Skim off the excess fat and strain the sauce over the meat. Sprinkle with chopped parsley. Serve with rice or with green noodles and grated Parmesan cheese.

A Simple Braised Brisket Pot Roast

4-pound piece of brisket
4 tablespoons beef suet, finely chopped
1 onion, thinly sliced
2 bay leaves
2 teaspoons salt
2 cups boiling water

SAUCE

2 tablespoons butter
2 tablespoons flour
1 cup stock
2 teaspoons onion juice
½ teaspoon salt
¼ teaspoon freshly ground pepper

Brisket is one of the more successful pieces of beef for braising or pot-roasting because of its fat, usually on either side, and the fact that it is boneless and makes beautiful slices. Further, I find it much juicier than many of the other cuts.

This is a turn-of-the-century recipe, included here because its sauce is typical of the cookery in the average good kitchen of that period.

Melt the suet in a braising pan, and when hot, brown the meat on all sides. Add the onion to cook in the hot fat for a few minutes; then add the bay leaves, salt, and finally the boiling water. Cover the pan and cook 15 minutes per pound over medium heat. Test for tenderness and continue cooking. Remove the cover toward the end of the cooking so that the liquid cooks down. Transfer the brisket to a hot platter. Skim off any fat in the pan and use any remaining liquid for the sauce.

For the sauce, brown the flour in the butter, stirring the while. Add the stock, the pan juices and onion juice, and continue stirring till the sauce browns well and thickens. Salt and pepper to taste. Serve with the roast. Also serve baked potatoes, braised turnips, and braised carrots.

Edith Hirsch's Pot Roast

4 tablespoons butter
2 tablespoons oil
1 large onion, sliced
4 pounds brisket, lightly floured
2 cups canned tomatoes, preferably the little Italian plum variety
1 small green pepper, cut into strips
1 bay leaf
6 whole allspice
1 teaspoon paprika
Salt and freshly ground pepper to taste
Small piece of stale lebkuchen or a crust of rye bread
Butter and flour for thickening, if desired

This recipe, which must have had a Western European beginning, is from the manuscript cookbook of a Portland, Oregon, hostess.

Brown the onion in the oil and butter, and when nicely colored add the meat and brown well on all sides. Add the tomatoes and seasonings. Cover and simmer approximately 2½ hours. Test for tenderness. Add liquid if necessary, cover, and continue simmering until the meat is tender. Remove the meat to a hot platter and skim the excess fat from the sauce in the braising pan. Add the lebkuchen or crumbled rye bread to the sauce and stir to dissolve. This will often thicken the sauce sufficiently. Or thicken with butter mixed with flour. Spoon over the roast, and serve with baked potatoes or potato pancakes.

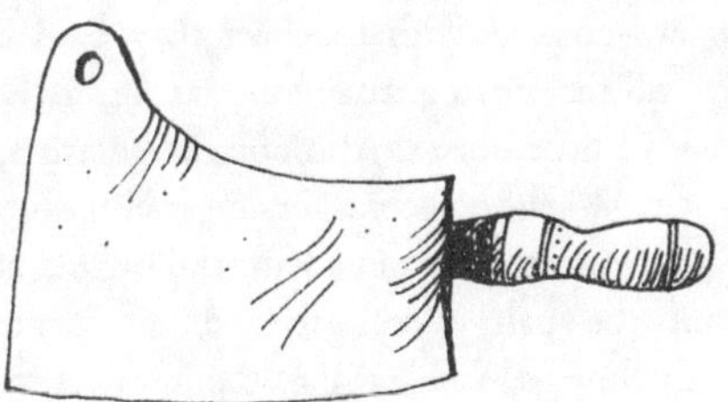

Sauerbraten

4-pound rump roast, rolled and tied
1 cup wine vinegar
½ cup white wine
½ cup cider vinegar, if you like this dish very sharp
2 onions, peeled and sliced
2 carrots, peeled and sliced
1 rib celery, chopped
2 bay leaves
6 whole allspice, crushed
2 cloves
1 tablespoon crushed peppercorns
1 tablespoon salt
4 tablespoons butter and 4 tablespoons oil, or 8 tablespoons beef drippings
3 tablespoons butter and 3 tablespoons flour
1 tablespoon sugar
1 cup crushed gingersnaps

A distinctly German version of braised beef, this pungent dish uses a sour marinade which is cooked and thickened with sweet ingredients. It never ceases to be popular.

Wipe the meat well with a damp towel. Place in a deep bowl. Combine all the liquids, vegetables, and seasonings in a heavy saucepan. Bring just to the boiling point and pour over the meat. Turn the meat in the mixture several times. Cover and refrigerate for three days, turning the meat several times each day. Remove the meat from the marinade and dry it thoroughly with a towel. Heat the oil and butter or the drippings in a braising pan and sear the meat on all sides. When it is nicely browned, remove to absorbent paper. Pour off the fat from the pan. Return the meat to the pan, heat the marinade, and pour it over the meat. Simmer about 3 hours or until the meat is tender. Pour off the liquid, strain, and remove the excess fat. Leave the meat in the braising pan to keep hot.

Melt 3 tablespoons butter in a saucepan, add the flour, and blend well. Add the sugar and blend again. Gradually pour in the strained and degreased marinade, and stir till the sauce is well blended. Add the gingersnaps and allow the sauce to simmer for several more minutes. Correct the seasoning and serve with meat and potato dumplings or potato pancakes.

Bordelaise Brisket of Beef with Carrots

5-pound piece of brisket, well trimmed
Flour
6 tablespoons beef drippings or rendered suet
1 tablespoon salt
Freshly ground pepper
1 bay leaf
1 teaspoon thyme
1 teaspoon marjoram
1 onion stuck with 4 cloves
14 carrots
1½ cups beef broth
6 large or 12 small potatoes
Chopped parsley

This has found its way to the West Coast, where many French have congregated. Some are sheepherders, some work in the vineyards, and others work in the olive groves. This must have come from vineyard workers, for it resembles a Bordeaux dish often served at the time of the grape harvest.

Flour the meat lightly. Melt the fat in a braising pan. When the fat is hot, sear the meat on all sides. Season it with salt and pepper. Add the herbs, the onion, and one carrot. Then add the broth, heated, cover the pan, and simmer the meat until tender.

Meanwhile, cook the carrots. (I prefer to do them separately, for when they are cooked with the beef they tend to dominate the flavor.) Boil till tender in a small amount of salted water or broth, and glaze with a little butter. Also boil the potatoes, in their jackets, in salted water. When the beef is tender, transfer to a hot platter and carve into even slices. Surround with the carrots and the potatoes, peeled. Pour the pan juices, strained and degreased, over all. Sprinkle with chopped parsley. Pass the mustard with this dish, and with it drink a pleasant young red wine, such as a Pinot Noir or a Juliénas, even though it is basically a Bordeaux dish.

Étouffée of Beef

8 tablespoons pork drippings or goose fat
5-pound piece of rump or top sirloin, rolled and tied
2 carrots
2 onions stuck with 4 cloves
4 crushed garlic cloves
½ cup Cognac
2 cups red wine
1 pound streaked salt pork freshened in water
2 pig's feet
1 bay leaf
1½ teaspoons thyme
Salt and freshly ground pepper
Chopped parsley

This is also a dish with French background that settled in with a California family.

Place the drippings or goose fat in a deep braising pan. Sear the roast slowly on all sides to give it a fine color. Add the salt pork, pig's feet, carrots, onions, and garlic, and place in a 450-degree oven for 15 minutes. Add the Cognac, wine, and seasonings. Cover and cook over low heat or in a 250-degree oven, preferably, for 3 to 3½ hours.

It is delicious served hot with small new potatoes or served cold with a good salad and some pickles.

Daube Provençale

3 to 5 pounds brisket, rump or round, in cubes or in one piece
1 calf's foot, split, or a pig's foot, split
2 carrots cut in quarters
6 cloves garlic, peeled and lightly crushed
2 leeks cut in 1-inch pieces
1 bay leaf
1 teaspoon thyme
1 teaspoon summer savory
1 tablespoon salt
1 teaspoon freshly ground pepper
Red wine to cover
2 tablespoons tomato paste
16 to 18 black soft olives, pitted
Macaroni

There are many different forms of this famous dish. This one resembles the New Orleans version that follows this recipe. One also finds daubes in Canada and in some of the New England states, where the influence of French Canadian cookery is noticeable. Traditionally, the daube, prepared in a pottery "daubière," was put to cook overnight on a metal plate under a removable tile in the fireplace and was ready for lunch the next day. A daube can be eaten either hot or cold. If hot, the sauce is usually poured over macaroni, as in this recipe — a dish called macaronade, as authentic as the daube itself. Sometimes the daube is made with meat cut into cubes and sometimes with the meat in one piece, as for a pot roast. In either form the same recipe applies.

Use a pottery casserole for this or an enameled iron, aluminum, or copper braising pan. Place the meat and all the other ingredients, save the tomato paste, olives, and macaroni, in the pan and cover with wine. It is better if left overnight to marinate and then cooked the next day. Bring the liquid to a boil, cover, and let the meat simmer gently atop the stove or in a 275-degree oven for several hours until it is tender. A half hour before serving add the tomato paste and the olives.

Cook the macaroni in boiling salted water. When done, drain and mix with the sauce. Serve with the meat. This dish is almost better cold, when the sauce will be jellied.

Boeuf en Daube Glacé

1 large slice larding pork
¼ cup sherry
1 teaspoon each of thyme and chopped parsley
3 to 4 pounds boneless rump or top round, rolled and tied
4 tablespoons butter or beef fat
2 tablespoons oil
2 large onions stuck with cloves
4 small carrots, scraped and sliced
1 very small turnip
2 pig's feet
2 pounds veal neck
1 bay leaf
Salt, pepper, and cayenne
Water or stock

This was a famous old New Orleans recipe and is still served at one or two of the traditional New Orleans restaurants. It is very like the previous recipe from Provence, where the daube used to be a weekly dish. This version is meant to be served cold.

Cut the larding pork into long strips, soak in sherry 15 minutes, then roll in thyme and parsley. Push through the center of the meat with a larding needle — nowadays this is more for looks than for tenderizing. Rub the herbs and sherry into the surface of the meat and let it stand for an hour. Brown the meat in hot oil and fat in a braising pan, turning to get a rich color on all sides. Add the onions, carrots, turnip, pig's feet, veal neck, and bay leaf, and simmer uncovered 20 minutes. Salt to taste, and add a generous grinding of fresh pepper and a dash or two of cayenne. Barely cover with boiling water or stock, cover, and simmer 3 to 3½ hours. When the beef is tender, remove it and allow the broth to cook down 20 minutes. Remove the veal neck and pig's feet from the broth, tear the meat from the bones and add to the beef in a large bowl or mold. Pour the strained broth over the meat and let it cool 24 hours. Remove the fat from the top. Serve cold with a good salad.

Note. When the meat is cold enough to handle, I prefer to slice it and arrange it in a mold with the bits of veal and pig's feet and then pour the reduced broth over it. This is easier to serve and makes a handsome appearance when unmolded. I also like to serve horse-radish cream or mustard and some pickles with the cold daube, as well as a salad.

A New Daube Glacé

4 pounds brisket of beef
¾ cup chopped beef suet
⅓ cup Cognac
Salt and freshly ground pepper
2 cups white wine
1 leek cut in 1-inch pieces
1 bay leaf
1 teaspoon thyme
1 teaspoon rosemary
1 pig's foot, split
1 cup stock or bouillon
6 young carrots, scraped and sliced
12 small white onions, peeled
Butter, sugar, and wine or water

And now a modern recipe for the same dish, also to be served cold — excellent for luncheon or dinner with a potato salad or a rice salad and perhaps a hot vegetable.

Brown the beef very well in rendered beef suet. Pour off some of the fat and blaze the meat with Cognac. Salt and pepper to taste and add the white wine, leek, herbs, pig's foot, and stock. Bring to a boil, cover, and simmer 2½ hours. While the meat is cooking, cook the carrots and drain. Sauté the onions in butter, and sprinkle with a little sugar to brown. Add a touch of wine or water, cover, and steam till still crisp but tender.

Test the meat for tenderness. If done, remove, and reduce the liquid a bit over high heat. Remove the pig's foot and strip the meat from the bones. Strain the liquid and skim off excess fat. Slice the meat and arrange in a mold or dish. Surround with the small onions, carrot slices, and bits of pig's foot, and pour the broth over all. Chill overnight. Remove any fat that has risen to the top. Invert the mold on a serving dish and serve garnished with pickles, sliced tomatoes, and sliced onion.

Marinated Chuck Steak

1 cup salad oil — peanut or corn
2 cups beer or ale
¼ cup lemon juice
2 cloves garlic, crushed
1½ teaspoons salt
1 teaspoon freshly ground pepper
1 teaspoon dry mustard
2 bay leaves
1 teaspoon basil
1 teaspoon oregano
1 teaspoon thyme
1 8 to 10 pound chuck steak of top quality, cut thick and tied

This delicious, unorthodox dish demands top-quality chuck, and the roast must be thick and tied securely.

Combine all ingredients in a deep bowl; put the meat in last and turn it several times. Marinate for two days, turning several times each day. Place the meat on a rack in a roasting pan, baste with the marinade, and roast at 425 degrees for 3½ hours, for rare meat. For better done, medium steak, roast at 425 degrees for 1 hour, then cover and reduce the heat to 300 degrees. Continue cooking for 4 hours, basting periodically with the marinade. When done, transfer to a platter or board and carve.

This is wonderful with slices of cornmeal mush crisply fried in butter and with braised cabbage.

Short Ribs, Stews, Boiled Beef, Corned Beef

Braised Short Ribs of Beef

5 to 6 pounds short ribs of good quality
1 onion, sliced
1 teaspoon rosemary
1 teaspoon thyme
3 garlic cloves, finely chopped
Salt
Freshly ground pepper
2 tablespoons butter
2 tablespoons oil
½ cup finely chopped onion
4 carrots, peeled and halved
12 small white onions, peeled
1 cup stock or bouillon

Short ribs have become increasingly popular in the last sixty or seventy years, and even more so in the last thirty years because of the shorter cutting of ribs and the higher quality of beef offered in the markets. Although short ribs are sometimes quite fat, the flavor when cooked is delicious. It is wise, therefore, to buy a greater quantity than you might ordinarily buy for braised beef.

This is my favorite preparation of short ribs. It is not traditional, but I prefer the flavor and texture of this version.

Spread the sliced onion over the bottom of a broiler pan, from which the rack has been removed. Place the short ribs on their sides atop the onions. Sprinkle with the herbs and the chopped garlic and broil about 6 inches from the heat till beautifully brown. Turn the ribs and broil on the other side till well browned and crisp. Salt and pepper. Stand the ribs on the bone side, and return to the broiler for a few moments.

While the ribs are broiling, heat the butter and oil in a braising pan and sauté the chopped onion and carrots. Add the small white onions, cover, and cook over low heat until the onions are just tender. Remove the ribs to absorbent paper and pour off the fat from the broiling pan. Place the ribs in the braising pan and spoon about 3 tablespoons of the fat from the broiling pan over them. Add the stock or bouillon. Bring to a boil and cover tightly. Simmer either atop the stove or in a 300-degree oven till the ribs are perfectly tender. This will take from 45 minutes to 1½ hours, depending upon the quality of the meat. Correct the seasoning. Serve with the vegetables and with the pan juices, which can be thickened with beurre manié, if you like. Potatoes, either baked or boiled in their jackets, coleslaw, and beer are excellent with this dish.

Another Braised Short Rib Recipe

5 pounds short ribs
Flour
4 tablespoons beef or bacon fat
Salt
Freshly ground pepper
2 garlic cloves, finely chopped
8 small onions
6 carrots, scraped and halved
1 bay leaf, crumbled
½ teaspoon rosemary
1 cup stock or bouillon or boiling water
Chopped parsley
Butter and flour kneaded together (optional)

This is a much more traditional recipe, and extremely good it is.

Dredge the ribs lightly with flour and brown them well on all sides in the fat — adding more fat if necessary. This may be done in a large heavy skillet or in the braising pan you will use for the simmering. Season the ribs with salt and pepper, and when they are deeply colored, add them to the braising pan. Add the garlic, vegetables, and herbs. Heat the stock to the boiling point. If you browned the ribs in a separate skillet, rinse it out with the liquid and pour over the ribs. If not, pour the liquid over the ribs in the braising pan. Cover and simmer over low heat or in a 300-degree oven until the ribs are tender — from 1½ to 2 hours.

Taste the sauce for seasoning. Remove the ribs and the vegetables to a hot platter. Thicken the sauce, if you wish, with tiny balls of butter and flour kneaded well together. Or just serve the sauce as it is with some of the fat skimmed off. Noodles or boiled potatoes, perhaps sliced tomatoes, and a bottle of a light red wine — a California Mountain Red or a Beaujolais — will complete this meal.

Mrs. Rorer's Short Ribs

"For this use the ends from the rib roast. Cut through between each rib. Put two tablespoons of butter in a saucepan; when hot add an onion sliced, 1 carrot and 1 turnip cut into dice, shake until brown, add the ribs and one quart of good stock. Cover and simmer one hour, then add a teaspoon of kitchen bouquet, one of salt, a saltspoon of pepper, and two bay leaves. Simmer one hour longer. Lift the vegetables with a skimmer, put them in the center of a chop plate, dish the ribs around; outside of this put a border of mashed sweet or white potatoes. Thicken the sauce with 2 tablespoonfuls of flour moistened, and strain it over the center; cover with chopped parsley."

Beef Stews

Brown Beef Stew

3 pounds lean beef from the round or the chuck
1 onion, minced

The first stews produced in America were hardly recognizable as the dish we now call beef stew. They were quite simple, prepared with a bouquet of vegetables and a delicate sauce. In many of them the meat was put on to boil, and then seasonings and flour were added. The beef was cooked down to a rather grayish brown. Later in history browned stews came along, with only onion for an additive. During the last 15 minutes of cooking light dumplings were dropped on the stew, and the pot was covered tightly. This made a meal in a pot, as it were. Finally Mrs. Harland came forth with a more intricate brown beef stew.

Cut the beef into strips two inches long. Add the minced onion, cover with water, and simmer 2 hours, or until just tender. Add the remaining ingredients except fried bread and parsley, stir in well, and simmer till thickened. Correct the seasoning, adding salt as needed, and cook up for a few more minutes. Pour over the fried bread, garnish with chopped parsley, and serve.

Water
2 teaspoons marjoram
1 teaspoon thyme
Chopped parsley
1 tablespoon browned flour
1 teaspoon Worcestershire sauce
1 tablespoon tomato catsup
1 glass wine
Juice of half a lemon
A bit of the peel
1 cup chopped mushrooms
Diced fried bread
Salt and freshly ground pepper to taste
Chopped parsley

American Beef Stew

2 pounds beef — chuck, bottom round, rump brisket
Flour
About 5 tablespoons fat — butter, oil, beef fat, etc.
2 large onions, sliced
1 bay leaf
1 teaspoon thyme or rosemary
2 teaspoons salt
Freshly ground pepper to taste
Water
Flour and butter kneaded together

Our traditional stew seems to have been handed down from one generation to another. It was the basic stew made on the prairies, sometimes with buffalo meat, sometimes with beef, sometimes, I suppose, with horsemeat. All other versions have grown out of it.

Flour the beef thoroughly. Melt the fat in a heavy skillet, stew pan, or braising pan. Use beef fat or drippings or half oil, half butter. Sear the floured beef well on all sides till it has a pleasant brown color. Add the onions, and cook them till lightly brown. Add the seasonings and water to barely cover, and bring to a boil. Cover tightly and simmer 1½ to 2 hours. Test the beef for tenderness and for seasoning, and cook till tender. To thicken the sauce, add pea-sized balls of flour and butter kneaded together, and stir over low heat until the desired thickness has been reached. Serve with boiled potatoes in their jackets.

Southwestern Beef Stew

2 pounds round steak
Water
3 tablespoons lard or beef fat
6 tablespoons chili powder
1 teaspoon or more salt
1 teaspoon oregano
1 clove garlic, chopped
1 cup tomatoes

Barely cover the round steak with water and bring to a boil. Cover and simmer till barely tender. Remove and cut into 1½-inch cubes. Reserve the stock. Brown the meat in the lard or beef fat, add the chili powder, salt, oregano, and garlic, and cook a few minutes. Add the tomatoes and 1 cup of the meat stock reserved from cooking the steak. Simmer ½ hour. Correct the seasoning.

Stew with Green Chilies. Substitute 1 cup chopped canned green chilies (roasted and peeled) for the chili powder. Increase the salt to 2 teaspoons and omit the oregano and garlic.

Cicely's Beef Stew

4 pounds brisket of beef cut in 2-inch cubes
Flour
6 tablespoons rendered beef fat or 3 tablespoons each of butter and oil
1 onion stuck with 2 cloves
1 leek
1 carrot
1 small turnip
1 bay leaf
1 teaspoon thyme
Water or beef stock
6 carrots, scraped and cut in thin strips
12 small white onions
3 ribs celery cut in thin strips
3 cloves garlic, finely chopped
2 medium potatoes, either finely diced or grated
1 tablespoon salt
1 teaspoon freshly ground pepper
½ pound snap beans, previously cooked in salted water
½ pound peas, previously cooked in salted water
Chopped parsley and chives

This is an old Pennsylvania dish that I enjoyed in a lovely restored farmhouse, whence came many wonderful American meals.

Brown the floured beef cubes very well in beef fat or the oil and butter mixture. Add the onion stuck with cloves, the leek, carrot, turnip, herbs, and water or stock to cover. Bring to a boil and reduce the heat. Cover and simmer 1½ hours or until the meat begins to become tender. Add the carrots, onions, celery, garlic, potatoes, and salt and pepper. Cook until the meat is thoroughly tender. Correct the seasoning. The potatoes should thicken the sauce and make it thoroughly smooth. Arrange in a tureen and add the beans, peas, parsley, and chives. Serve with boiled or baked potatoes, a hot bread and a salad.

Note. This stew may also be done very successfully with half broth or water and half red or white wine.

An Old New Mexican Stew

2½ pounds chuck in one piece
2 quarts water
½ pound snap beans, cut in pieces
3 ears corn, cut in 2-inch pieces
4 small squash — zucchini or tiny yellow squash
6 squash blossoms
½ cup each of green onion tops, fresh garlic tops (or 2 cloves garlic) and coriander leaves
1 tablespoon salt

Simmer the chuck in the water approximately 2 hours or until tender. Remove and cut into 1½-inch cubes. If the water has cooked down, add enough more to make 1 quart. Cook the beans, corn, and squash in the water until the beans are tender. Add the meat and the rest of the ingredients, and simmer 25 minutes. Save some of the greens to sprinkle on top.

Boeuf à la Bourguignonne

3 pounds beef (chuck, rump, or brisket), cut in 2 × 1½-inch pieces, with fat removed
Red wine to nearly cover beef—a Pinot Noir or Barbera
1 bay leaf
1 onion stuck with 2 cloves
1 clove garlic
6 ounces streaky salt pork, cut in 1 × ½-inch pieces, blanched 10 minutes in boiling water (or thick bacon may be used)
5 tablespoons butter
3 tablespoons flour
1 teaspoon thyme
1 leek
1 sprig parsley
1½ cups stock or bouillon
Salt and freshly ground pepper

18 small white onions
3 tablespoons butter
1 teaspoon sugar

18 mushroom caps
4 tablespoons butter

Beurre manié (optional)
Chopped parsley

This dish, under various names, has become a great favorite in our country. In the middle of the nineteenth century it was highly popular around San Francisco, in New York and in New Orleans. Gradually, through the lessons of M. Blot and his venturesome students who traveled and collected recipes, it became part of our repertoire. It is often poorly prepared, but it remains the great joy of hostesses when entertaining a large number of people. Boeuf à la Bourguignonne is not just a beef stew with wine. It is a rather special dish that takes time to do well. Whether or not you marinate the beef is up to you, but the final dish is a much better one if you do. It can be made a day or two in advance and reheated.

Let the beef marinate several hours with the red wine, bay leaf, onion, and garlic. The wine should be one with flavor. The Pinot Noir may not be heavy enough, but I usually find it so; the Barbera certainly is.

Blanch the pieces of salt pork or bacon in boiling water 10 minutes. Remove and dry on absorbent paper. Melt 2 tablespoons butter in a heavy braising pan of enameled iron, cast aluminum, or copper lined with stainless steel. Sauté the salt pork or bacon quickly in the butter until nicely browned but not crisp. Remove to absorbent paper. Remove the beef from the marinade, drain it, and dry it well. Add 3 tablespoons butter to the braising pan. Dust the beef with the flour and brown it in the butter and pork fat, turning it often with wooden spoons or spatulas. When well browned, add the thyme, leek, parsley, stock, salt and pepper, and just enough of the marinade, together with the onion and garlic, to cover the meat. Bring to a boil. Reduce the heat, cover, and simmer gently about 2½ hours, or until the meat is tender but not dry and stringy.

Meanwhile cook the white onions in butter in a skillet, and sprinkle with sugar to give them a nice glaze. Shake the pan to give the onions even color. Cover the pan and let them steam till tender but still crisp. Sauté the mushroom caps in butter till just nicely colored. Salt and pepper them to taste. Add the pieces of salt pork to either the onions or the mushrooms. When the meat is quite tender, correct the seasoning and remove with a slotted spoon or skimmer to a hot container. Reduce the sauce slightly, and if necessary thicken a little with beurre manié. Return the meat to the sauce and bring to a boil. Spoon onto a deep platter and garnish with the mushrooms, onions, salt pork, and chopped parsley. Boiled potatoes are good with this, as is rice, but I prefer the former.

Goulash (Gulyas)

6 medium onions, peeled and thinly sliced
4 tablespoons butter
2 tablespoons oil
¼ cup Hungarian paprika
¼ cup wine vinegar
3 pounds rump or chuck, cut into 2-inch cubes
Salt and freshly ground pepper
1 teaspoon thyme
2 tablespoons tomato paste
2 cloves garlic, chopped
3 to 4 tablespoons flour
Beef broth, about 2 cups
Zest of 1 lemon
1 tablespoon caraway seeds

Every Middle European country has its own version of this dish, using veal, beef, or pork, and every version is good. This is one I myself have found immensely satisfactory over a long period of time.

Brown the onions well in the oil and butter till they are almost golden brown. Add the paprika, then the vinegar. Cook 4 minutes, add the meat, and cook it with the onions and seasonings, turning it with wooden spoons or spatulas till it is brown. Add salt and pepper to taste, the thyme, tomato paste, and garlic. Stir and cook until it is practically a glaze. Sprinkle with flour and mix well till the flour is colored. Add the broth, cover, and simmer till the mixture is blended well and the meat is tender. Whirl the lemon zest and caraway in a blender, sprinkle over the top of the goulash, and serve with spaetzle or noodles.

Another Goulash

4 large onions, finely chopped
4 tablespoons butter and 2 tablespoons oil, or 5 tablespoons beef fat
2 pounds chuck or rump beef cut in 1½-inch cubes
2 teaspoons salt
1 teaspoon freshly ground pepper
2 tablespoons paprika
1½ cups boiling water or broth
1 green pepper, seeded and finely chopped

This one is of Yugoslavian origin and came to the Middle West with many of the Middle European groups. It varies from most others, is very simple, and is pleasant served with dumplings or noodles.

Brown the onions in the fat and add the meat. Brown lightly. Add salt and pepper, cover the pan, and simmer gently about 1 hour. Add the paprika, let cook a few minutes, then add boiling water or broth. Cover and simmer until the meat is tender and the liquid is blended with the other ingredients. Add the finely chopped green pepper and cook 10 minutes more.

Note. Sometimes spoonfuls of sour cream are heaped on the goulash when served, which enhances its flavor and appearance.

Burgoo

7 pounds shin of beef or 4 pounds chuck
1 stewing hen, 5 to 6 pounds
Salt
6 medium potatoes cut into large cubes
8 carrots cut into thick slices
6 medium turnips cut into large cubes

An old friend, Zula Ferguson, sent me this recipe for burgoo with the following letter about it. "This inspired combination of soup and stew had its origin around campfires. So while I have adapted this recipe to use in any kitchen, the burgoo of our childhood, which we still remember nostalgically, was made of wild duck and squirrel in a huge black kettle at the edge of a Kentucky lake where our parents and their friends 'went camping' every fall. With the wild game, beef was simmered in water till very tender. Then vegetables in abundance and variety were added and cooked till done. The burgoo was ladled into tin cups. Corn bread squares, hush puppies, or corn dodgers were served with this one-dish meal, which was eaten with a spoon." Her modern adaptation is for twelve to fifteen.

Put the beef and fowl into enough cold water to more than cover them, and add 1 tablespoon salt for each quart of water. You will need a pot for all this that holds 12 to 15 quarts, or two 8-quart ones. Bring to a boil and cook 5 minutes, skimming off any scum that forms at the top. Cover and simmer till the beef and fowl are extremely tender. Remove them from the broth, and when cool enough to handle cut into bite-size pieces. Return to the broth, bring to a boil, and add the vegetables in the order given. When the mixture comes to a full rolling boil, add the thyme and pepper, and simmer until the vegetables are cooked — about 45 minutes. Add salt if needed after tasting. Serve in bowls. Hush puppies are an agreeable accompaniment.

1 large head celery cut into 1-inch pieces
4 medium onions, sliced
1½ quarts canned tomatoes
2 pounds green beans cut into 1-inch pieces
3 pounds peas, shelled
2 pounds butter beans, shelled
12 ears corn cut from the cob
1 head cabbage, shredded
1 pound okra cut into 1-inch pieces
1 cup chopped parsley
10 small red peppers
1 bell pepper cut into strips
1 tablespoon thyme
Freshly ground pepper

Beef Birds

In France, where this dish originated, these are called alouettes sans têtes. They are made with beef or veal, stuffed in various ways, and braised. This is one of the more pleasing versions.

Make the stuffing first. Sauté the onion in the butter till just soft, and add the seasonings, ham, and crumbs. Bind with the egg and add the parsley. Pound the squares of meat to make them a little thinner. Place a small amount of stuffing on each one, roll, and tie securely with twine. Dredge the rolls well with flour and brown quickly in the butter and oil in a large braising pan or two heavy skillets with lids. When nicely browned salt and pepper to taste, and add broth to cover the bottom of the pan or pans. Add the garlic and thyme, cover, and simmer 1 hour, or until the rolls are tender. Turn several times during cooking. Serve the beef birds on a bed of noodles with the pan juices spooned over them. Sprinkle with chopped parsley.

18 4 × 5 × ½-inch squares of round steak
Flour
5 tablespoons butter
3 tablespoons oil
Salt and freshly ground pepper
2½ cups broth, or half broth and half white wine
1 garlic clove, crushed
1 teaspoon thyme
Chopped parsley for garnish

STUFFING

½ cup finely chopped onion
4 tablespoons butter
1 teaspoon summer savory
1 teaspoon freshly ground pepper
½ teaspoon salt
½ pound cold ham, ground
1 cup fresh breadcrumbs
1 egg
¼ cup chopped parsley

Beef Rolls with Anchovies and Red Wine

1 large onion, coarsely chopped
10 tablespoons olive oil
1 teaspoon basil
12 olives, pitted and coarsely chopped
16 to 18 anchovy fillets, coarsely chopped
18 4 × 5 × ½-inch slices beef round, pounded thin
Flour
2 cloves garlic, crushed
Salt and freshly ground pepper
1 cup or more broth or red wine
1 cup tomato sauce
1 teaspoon basil
2 tablespoons tomato paste
Chopped parsley

Anchovies have been popular in this country over a long period of years due to the French, the Italians, and the English.

Sauté the onion in 4 tablespoons of olive oil. Add the basil, olives, and anchovies, and toss well. Spread the mixture on the squares of beef, and roll. Tie the rolls securely and flour lightly. Brown in the remaining olive oil in a large pan that can be tightly covered. Toss the rolls so that they color on all sides. Season with garlic, freshly ground pepper, and some salt, although there will be a goodly salt content in the anchovies. When nicely browned, add broth or wine, tomato sauce, and basil. Cover and simmer 1½ hours or until very tender. Add the tomato paste to the sauce and stir well. When ready to serve, place the beef rolls on a bed of rice or green noodles and sprinkle with chopped parsley. Spoon most of the sauce over the beef. Serve the rest separately. Serve with crisp bread and a salad.

Tongue-Stuffed Birds

18 4 × 5 × ½-inch squares round steak
½ cup horseradish blended with ½ cup softened butter
18 slices smoked tongue, cut paper-thin
Flour
4 tablespoons butter
4 tablespoons oil
2 cloves garlic, finely chopped
1 teaspoon thyme
1½ cups broth
Salt and freshly ground pepper
¼ cup Madeira or sherry
Chopped parsley

Beat the slices of round steak with a meat pounder, spread each one with the horseradish butter, and top with a slice of tongue. Roll and tie securely. Flour the rolls lightly. Brown them quickly in the oil and butter, turning on all sides and shaking the pan repeatedly. Add the garlic, thyme, and broth. Cover the pan and simmer very gently for 1½ hours, or until the rolls are quite tender. Salt and pepper to taste, and add the Madeira or sherry. Let the juices cook down over brisk heat. Serve the rolls around a mound of mashed potatoes, and spoon the sauce over them. Garnish with chopped parsley.

Boiled Beef

Aside from steaks, boiled beef has little competition for popularity among beef dishes. Every European country has its own version. The boiled beef of England is well known. France has its pot au feu,

Italy its bollito, Poland its beef with horseradish, and Austria its various boiled dishes. Early American families adopted the dish, too, combining their soup and meat as their ancestors had done for generations, even centuries, before. Unlike their ancestors, they added vegetables. Some people also served dumplings or steamed suet puddings with their boiled beef, and some added toasted bread to the broth to soak up the goodness.

By far the best cuts for boiling are the cross ribs, the deckle, and the brisket. Our ancestors liked the rump or the round, but this cooks too dry. The French use a great deal of shin, which has a delicious juiciness but often much tendon and gristle as well. I happen to like it very much, but there are many who do not agree with me.

Basic Boiled Beef Dinner

4 to 5 pounds beef brisket, cross ribs, or short ribs
1 onion stuck with 2 cloves
1 bay leaf
1 clove garlic
1 rib celery
1 leek
Cold water
1½ tablespoons salt
1 teaspoon freshly ground pepper
1 teaspoon rosemary
6 carrots
6 turnips
6 additional leeks
12 medium potatoes in their jackets
1 head cabbage, cut in sections

Place the brisket in a deep kettle with the onion, bay leaf, garlic, celery, and leek. Cover with cold water and bring to a boil. Boil 5 minutes, removing scum that may form on top. Add the salt, pepper, and rosemary. Cover and reduce the heat to simmer. Cook approximately 2 hours. Add the carrots, turnips, and leeks. Cover and simmer 25 minutes. Add the potatoes and correct the seasoning. Cook the cabbage separately in boiling salted water until done to the crisp stage.

To serve, arrange the meat on a platter and carve in medium slices. Surround with the vegetables, and pour a little of the broth on the meat. Give each person a cup of broth, some toast, grated horseradish, sour pickles, and coarse salt. Also have mustard on hand. Let each person help himself to meat and vegetables.

Cold Pressed Beef

This is made the same way as pot au feu, save that a calf's foot or 2 pig's feet are included with the meats, and the broth is cooked down when the beef is done. Place the beef into a deep bowl or mold and pour the broth over it. Press the meat by covering it with a plate and placing 8 to 10 pounds of weight on it (scale weights, large cans of vegetables and fruits, or bricks will do the trick). Chill at least 12 hours, unmold, and serve cold, cut in thin slices, with a hot vegetable or a salad. This also makes excellent sandwiches.

Pot au Feu

3 to 4 pounds brisket of beef
2 to 3 pounds shin of beef
Salt pork in one piece, about 1 pound
1 onion stuck with 2 cloves
1 garlic clove
6 leeks
1 carrot
1½ teaspoons rosemary
Cold water
1 tablespoon salt
6 medium onions
6 additional small carrots
6 turnips
6 to 8 pieces marrow bone
1 tablespoon freshly ground pepper
Croutons of crusty French bread
Grated cheese
Boiled potatoes
Boiled cabbage
Coarse salt
Sour gherkins
Mustard

This has come to be a standby in such restaurants as "21," the Four Seasons in New York, and Chasen's in Los Angeles, as well as in "continental" restaurants all across the country. It differs little from boiled beef, but it does have some flourishes not found in the ordinary recipe.

Put the brisket, shin, and salt pork into a large kettle with the onion, garlic, leeks, carrot, and rosemary. Add cold water to cover and bring to a boil. Boil rapidly 5 minutes, removing any scum that forms on the surface. Add salt, cover, and simmer 2 hours. Then add the onions, carrots, turnips, and marrow bones. Simmer another hour or until the meat and vegetables are tender. Meanwhile cook the potatoes and cabbage, each separately. Finally add pepper to the pot au feu, and correct the seasoning.

Serve the broth in bowls with croutons and cheese. Follow with the beef, marrow bones, and vegetables. Pass the coarse salt, gherkins, and mustard.

Corned Beef

For generations of Americans the drying, smoking, and corning of meat was essential to having meat on hand through the winter. The favorites for corning were pork and beef, as well as tongue, and corned beef became one of the most popular of all meat dishes. We haven't lost our taste for corned beef, but the quality of the product that we find in the markets today is frequently inferior to the one that used to be prepared. When done at home it was a task of some magnitude, as this recipe for putting down beef will show.

"Cut up a quarter of beef. For every hundredweight take half a peck of coarse salt, quarter of a pound of saltpeter, the same weight of saleratus, a quart of molasses, or two pounds of coarse brown sugar. Mace cloves and allspice may be added for spiced beef.

"Strew some of the salt in the bottom of a pickle tub or barrel; then put in a layer of meat and salt and meat alternately until all is used. Let it remain one night. Dissolve the saleratus and saltpeter in a little warm water, and put it to the molasses or sugar, then put it over the meat, add enough water to cover the meat, lay a board on it to keep it under the brine. The meat will be fit for use after ten days."

All less tender cuts of beef, beef tongues, and beef livers were treated this way. Sometimes the tongues, liver, and brisket were smoked after the corning period.

Home-Corned Beef

You can, in these days of small kitchens and, for the most part, no barns and cellars, corn your own beef in the refrigerator. You must have space for a large container of enameled metal, glass, porcelain, or earthenware (never unlined metal), and you must, of course, choose a container that will accommodate meat and liquid to cover. For every gallon of water you will need:

2 cups rock salt or curing salt
2 cups dark brown sugar
1½ teaspoons bicarbonate of soda
4 teaspoons saltpeter (available in most drugstores as sodium nitrate)

You may add spice — whole allspice, pepper, and mace blades — or a clove or two of garlic if you like. Mix the ingredients with 1 quart lukewarm water, and when blended and dissolved, add the remaining water.

I think that the best cuts for this treatment are brisket, flanken, or rump, and I prefer brisket or flanken because of the better texture and the marbling of fat. Wipe the meat with a damp cloth and pierce it deeply with a heavy fork or pick so that the brine will penetrate it. Place it in the container specified above and add brine till the meat is immersed. Then cover it with a board weighted in place. Add brine, if necessary, to reach a level of 1½ inches over the meat. Store the beef in the refrigerator at least 8 days. I myself would leave it 12 days. The beef will become saltier the longer it is soaked.

When ready to cook the beef, discard the brine. It is simple to make again, and you may wish to change the proportions of the ingredients next time. Other meats suitable for corning in this manner include fresh tongue, pieces of pork, spareribs, and pig's feet.

To cook corned beef, rinse in cold water, place in a kettle of cold water, and bring to a boil. Simmer 1 hour. Pour off the water and add boiling water to cover. Simmer until tender, 4 to 4½ hours altogether.

New England Boiled Dinner

Piece of corned beef, preferably brisket, 4 to 5 pounds
6 white onions
4 to 5 small to medium turnips
6 to 8 potatoes
6 carrots
1 head cabbage
6 to 8 beets, cooked separately

This has been in continuous favor not only in New England but across the country. To my taste, the boiled dinner is better with most of the vegetables cooked individually — cabbage cooked by itself has a much fresher taste, and potatoes cooked separately in their jackets are far more delicious than those cooked with the beef — but this is a break with tradition. (*Note.* Potatoes were a late additive — about 1725 or even later.) Here is the standard way.

Wash the corned beef, place in a kettle of cold water, and bring to a boil. Reduce heat and simmer 2½ to 3 hours. Add the onions and turnips and cook 30 minutes more. Add the carrots and potatoes and simmer 15 minutes. Add the cabbage, cut in quarters or sixths. When the meat and vegetables are tender, transfer the meat to a hot platter and surround with the vegetables. Serve with horseradish or mustard. This is also sometimes served with a sauce made of the broth and melted butter. Beets were traditionally served with the boiled dinner, cooked separately.

Corned Beef and Turnips. Another popular and flavorful version of corned beef. Add turnips for the last 35 or 40 minutes of cooking time and serve with the beef along with boiled potatoes. Omit the other vegetables.

Vermont-Style Glazed Corned Beef

This is prepared by simply studding a piece of corned brisket with cloves, usually after it has been boiled. Then maple syrup is poured over it and it is placed in a 375-degree oven to glaze. This same process is often accomplished with cloves, brown sugar, and mustard. And sometimes the beef is deviled by having brown sugar, mustard, Tabasco, and crumbs rubbed into its surface. Then cloves are inserted, and it is finished off in the oven and basted with a little wine or broth as it crisps.

Corned Beef Hash

2 pounds cold corned beef
4 to 6 cold boiled potatoes of medium size, coarsely chopped
1 medium size onion, finely chopped
Freshly ground pepper
¼ teaspoon nutmeg
Butter or beef drippings
Heavy cream or boiling water (optional)

For many people this is the best part of the corned beef. It has been a breakfast dish for generations, and it is one of the more popular luncheon dishes to be found anywhere — with a bit of chili sauce, usually, and a poached egg for garniture. This is a standard hash, rich in flavor, but the proportions may be altered to suit your taste.

Chop the meat fairly fine with a knife rather than put it through the grinder. Combine the potatoes and onion with the meat and add a few good grinds of black pepper and the nutmeg. Blend well and allow to rest in the refrigerator several hours or overnight. When ready to cook, melt just enough butter or beef drippings in a heavy skillet to cover the bottom — 4 to 6 tablespoons. Add the hash and press down somewhat firmly. When the hash begins to develop a crust on the bottom, turn with a spatula so that some of the crust is brought to the top. At this point many people add about ½ cup of heavy cream or some boiling water, which enables the bottom crust to form more quickly. I prefer to cook the hash slowly to develop the crust, turning it several times. When it has crusted nicely, loosen it with a spatula, fold it once, and turn it out on a platter, crusty side up. Serve with poached eggs, toast, and chili sauce.

Note. Some recipes include finely chopped green pepper, to be added to the corned beef along with the onion.

Red Flannel Hash. Beloved of New Englanders, this is a corned beef hash to which one adds coarsely chopped cooked beets to taste before crisping in the skillet — not pickled beets, but preferably leftover beets from the boiled dinner.

Quick Corned Beef Hash

1 can corned beef
1 can corned beef hash
1 small onion, finely chopped
½ teaspoon freshly ground pepper
¼ teaspoon nutmeg
5 tablespoons butter or beef drippings
Poached eggs
Chopped parsley

A reasonably good corned beef hash can be achieved with canned beef.

Chop the canned corned beef rather coarsely and combine with the corned beef hash and chopped onion. Heat the butter or beef drippings in a heavy skillet, and cook the hash, pressing it down well to start a crust. Scrape the bottom with a spatula and bring some of the crisp bits to the top. Continue doing this till the crusty and the soft parts are equally mixed. Then let the bottom crust uniformly. Using a spatula, fold over the hash as you would an omelet and turn out on a hot platter. Serve with poached eggs and chili sauce, and garnish with chopped parsley. If you want more potato in your hash, combine the can of corned beef with 2 cans corned beef hash.

Baked Corned Beef Hash

4 to 5 cups corned beef hash
Butter
⅔ cup heavy cream
Freshly ground pepper
Poached eggs
Chopped parsley

Butter a 1½-quart baking dish or casserole, fill with corned beef hash, and press it down firmly. Dot with butter, add the cream and about 5 grinds of the pepper grinder. Bake at 375 degrees 20 to 25 minutes or until nicely crusted. Serve with poached eggs and garnish with chopped parsley.

Cold Corned Beef

Cold corned beef can be a great delicacy if it is of good quality and is sliced thin. It should be served with a potato or rice salad and various types of pickles and relishes. Of course, it also makes excellent sandwiches. The flavor of rye breads and pumpernickel are somehow particularly complementary to it.

Pastrami

This close relative of corned beef originated in Rumania, became very popular in Jewish delicatessens in Europe, and with the growth of the Jewish population in this country has become equally popular here. It is now a definite part of the American food pattern, served warm, usually, rather than hot or cold, as a filling for sandwiches. It is also delicious sliced and served with salad. As with corned beef, one must search out pastrami of good quality, for frequently it is quite inferior.

Homemade Pastrami

4 or 5 pieces of brisket (about 20 pounds)
2 cups salt
½ cup sugar
4 teaspoons saltpeter (sodium nitrate)
½ cup ground ginger
½ cup crushed pepper
4 or 5 cloves garlic, crushed

It is easy to make homemade pastrami if you have facilities for smoking meat. There are many small smokers available on the market these days. I have found them efficient for smoking a piece of meat of moderate size, such as pastrami, as well as a tongue or salt fish.

Pastrami is best cut from the brisket with the deckle removed.

Rub the meat well with the other ingredients, and place it in an enamel pan or porcelain or glass dish. Cover with foil and on this place a board that can be weighted down. Store in the refrigerator 20 days. At the end of that time dry under a fan or in a warm dry room. Then smoke 3 to 4 hours at 150 to 175 degrees.

To cook, cover with water and simmer 3 to 4 hours. The less fat left on the pastrami after cooking, the better. If you do not wish to cook all of the meat after smoking, it can be frozen. Do not store in the freezer for more than 5 or 6 months.

Note. Beef tongue can be treated in exactly the same fashion as pastrami and results in a tongue superior to most.

Dried (Chipped) Beef

For Americans of an earlier era, what salt pork was to the hog so dried beef was to the steer. It is evident that either the Germans from Bavaria or the Swiss brought the idea of curing and air-drying beef as a means of preservation, for it is very similar to the viande de grisons or Bundnerfleisch found in Switzerland and some parts of Germany. The Swiss use it as they would ham, for an hors d'oeuvre or served paper-thin with fresh asparagus, a most agreeable union of flavors and textures. In this country, although dried beef is occasionally used for cocktail snacks, it is mainly served creamed or with eggs.

Chipped beef is sometimes quite salty and must be covered with boiling water for a few minutes and then drained before use. It is available on the market in jars or packages and is always sliced exceedingly thin. In some markets it can be had sliced to order. Six ounces, or even less, is an ample quantity for a dish that serves four.

Chipped Beef with Scrambled Eggs

4 ounces chipped beef
Boiling water
8 eggs
2 tablespoons water
1 teaspoon salt
Dash of Tabasco
5 tablespoons butter
Freshly ground pepper
Chopped parsley

Pour boiling water over the beef and let it stand 5 minutes. Drain, and shred the beef into fine pieces. Combine the eggs, water, salt, and Tabasco. Beat lightly with a whisk or fork. Melt the butter in a heavy skillet and add the chipped beef. Let it frizzle just a bit in the butter —"frizzling" is sautéing lightly until the beef curls at the edges — then add the eggs. With a wooden spatula scrape the eggs from the bottom of the pan as the curds begin to form. Keep the heat at medium low and be patient. Eggs that are scrambled this way are much more delicious and tender, and the curds will be larger and filled with bits of the pungent beef. Do not overcook, for eggs continue cooking when you dish them on a hot platter or plate. When done, give them a few grinds of black pepper and a dash of chopped parsley. This makes a delicious breakfast dish for four or a good hot hors d'oeuvre for luncheon.

Creamed Chipped Beef with Baked Potatoes

6 ounces dried chipped beef
Boiling water
4 freshly baked floury potatoes
Butter
Chopped parsley

CREAM SAUCE

4 tablespoons butter
4 tablespoons flour
1 cup milk, heated
1 teaspoon freshly ground pepper
½ teaspoon mustard
¼ teaspoon ground ginger
½ cup heavy cream

This is an old favorite, and though a bit corny it is still a cozy dish for supper, or lunch, or after the theatre — if you have someone to watch the potatoes.

Cover the chipped beef with boiling water and let it stand 5 minutes. Drain, and cut into strips. Prepare the cream sauce — melt the butter in a saucepan over medium heat, add the flour, and cook till well blended and just pale gold. Stir in the hot milk, and when the sauce has begun to thicken add the seasonings and cream. Stir till thickened and smooth, and simmer 5 minutes. Add the chipped beef and keep hot over hot water. To serve, split the freshly baked potatoes and add a cube of butter to each. Transfer to serving plates. Spoon the chipped beef over the potatoes. Add another dot of butter and a little chopped parsley.

Creamed Chipped Beef with Mushrooms

6 ounces chipped beef
Boiling water
½ pound mushrooms, thinly sliced

Pour boiling water over the chipped beef and let it stand 5 minutes. Drain, and cut into strips. Sauté the mushrooms in the butter and oil over medium heat. Add the pepper and Worcestershire sauce. When the mushrooms are just tender, add the chipped beef and remove from the heat. Taste for salt. To make the sauce, melt the butter in a heavy pan, add the flour, blend, and cook several

4 tablespoons butter
3 tablespoons oil
Freshly ground pepper
1 teaspoon Worcestershire sauce
Crisp toast slices or rice

CREAM SAUCE

5 tablespoons butter
5 tablespoons flour
1 cup chicken broth
¾ cup heavy cream

minutes till just pale gold. Stir in the chicken broth and continue stirring till the mixture is thickened. Mix a little of the sauce with the cream, and then stir this back into the sauce. Stir again till thickened. Combine with the mushrooms and chipped beef and taste for seasoning. Heat through thoroughly and spoon over crisp toast or over rice. Serve with a good salad.

Ground Beef

Ground, chopped, minced, or hashed beef grew up with the United States. We have a legacy of early recipes for meat balls from the Dutch in New Amsterdam and Pennsylvania, from the Swedes in Delaware, and the French and English in the Carolinas. But it was not until the twentieth century, when the hamburger achieved fame and the meat loaf became prevalent, that ground beef became a mainstay of American cooking.

Choosing ground beef. Beef for grinding should be of good grade and contain not more than 25 per cent fat. Chuck and rump are suitable for the purpose, and top round is excellent. The tails from the short loin are often used by restaurants.

Meat Loaves

Meat loaf is a modern development. To be sure, Europeans long ago made pâtés of various kinds to be eaten cold as special treats. But the meat loaf we use so constantly nowadays is a product of the present century.

The best loaves are those made with a combination of meats, honestly flavored, and still moist when cooked. The average loaf served today is apt to be overcooked and dry because of the filler put into it; one finds recipes calling for oatmeal, corn flakes, and other cereals, as well as for condensed soups and canned vegetables. A good meat loaf is similar to a country pâté. It should be highly seasoned and firm but not dry. It is much better eaten cold, when it slices nicely and holds its shape. It should have a pleasant texture and never be grainy. It may be served hot with a good tomato sauce, a brown sauce with mushrooms, or an onion sauce. When served cold, all it needs is a horseradish sauce or a Cumberland sauce, or merely pickles, relishes, and a good salad. Cold meat loaf also makes a perfect filler for sandwiches, flavored with a touch of mustard or chili sauce. And for picnics it is an ideal dish that packs easily and travels well.

Individual Meat Loaves. I am told that many younger people like to make meat loaf into individual servings. These bake in about 25 or 30 minutes at 350 degrees and are served unmolded on a plate. The leftovers also may be served individually or used for lunch boxes or picnic baskets. Merely grease or butter individual pans (such as small bread pans, muffin tins, glass baking cups, or other small utensils), pack with the meat loaf, and arrange on a baking sheet. Top each one with a bit of fat or butter and bake till done.

Meat Loaf with Icing. Any meat loaf may be iced with mashed potatoes. Bake the loaf as directed. When it is done, cover with rich mashed potatoes or instant mashed potatoes beaten with milk, butter, salt, and pepper. Dot with butter, or brush with some of the fat in the pan, and return to the oven 15 minutes to lightly brown the potatoes.

Note. Chopped sweet herbs — dill, parsley, chives, etc. — may be added to the potatoes to give flavor and color.

Beef Loaf

4 pounds of the round
1 pint breadcrumbs
2 tablespoons chopped parsley
1 level teaspoon pepper
4 eggs
1 good-sized onion
2 teaspoons salt

One of the very first published recipes for a meat loaf appeared circa 1900 in Mrs. Rorer's cookbook. Her contemporaries, oddly enough, fail to mention it. But then, ground beef wasn't as highly regarded or as well promoted as it is nowadays. For its time this is a fairly good recipe, and the way in which it is cooked appeals to me.

"Chop the meat very fine; add all the ingredients and mix well; add the eggs unbeaten. Pack this down into a square bread pan until it takes the shape of the pan. Turn it out carefully into a greased baking or roasting pan and bake it in a moderately quick oven for 2 hours, basting every 15 minutes with a little hot stock. When done, stand away until perfectly cold. Serve, cut in thin slices, with horseradish cream or cold tomato sauce."

Favorite Meat Loaf

2 pounds ground beef
1 pound ground pork (sausage meat will do)

Thoroughly blend the meats, garlic, onion, seasonings, and crumbs. Add the eggs and blend again. Arrange the bacon or salt pork slices on the bottom of a shallow baking pan or dish 1 to 1½ inches deep. Form the meat into a loaf of rather even proportions

2 garlic cloves, finely chopped
1 fairly large onion, finely chopped
1½ teaspoons salt
1 teaspoon freshly ground pepper
1 teaspoon thyme
1 teaspoon summer savory
½ cup dry breadcrumbs
2 eggs, lightly beaten
Bacon or salt pork cut in strips

and lay it upon the strips. Lay a few additional strips of bacon or pork across the top of the loaf. Bake at 350 degrees 1 to 1½ hours. Test with a meat thermometer, and when its center has reached 150 degrees it is done. Baste several times during the baking. Serve hot with a tomato sauce and scalloped potatoes, or cold with mustard or Cumberland sauce and a salad.

Note. Although done less frequently these days, there was a great vogue a few decades ago for putting a series of hard-boiled eggs in the center of the loaf. To do this, arrange half the meat in a pan and then top with peeled hard-boiled eggs. Cover with the remaining meat. Bake as above.

Beef Loaf with Tomato

2 pounds ground beef
¾ teaspoon salt
1 finely chopped garlic clove
¼ cup finely chopped celery
½ cup chopped onion
1 cup fine bread or cracker crumbs
1 cup tomato juice
2 tablespoons catsup
2 slightly beaten eggs

Mix the ingredients well with the hands. Pack the mixture into a very well greased or buttered loaf pan or casserole. Bake at 350 degrees 1 to 1¼ hours or until the top is nicely browned. Unmold and serve either hot or cold.

Three-Meat Meat Loaf

2 pounds ground beef
1 pound ground pork or sausage meat
1 pound ground veal
1 cup finely cut green onions or shallots
1 small carrot, coarsely grated
2 teaspoons salt
1½ teaspoons freshly ground pepper
1 teaspoon rosemary
¼ teaspoon nutmeg
½ teaspoon Tabasco
3 eggs, slightly beaten
¾ cup fresh breadcrumbs soaked in ½ cup milk or cream
Bacon strips or salt pork strips

This makes a much more juicy meat loaf because of the gelatinous quality of the veal and fattiness of the pork. Furthermore, it keeps juicy much longer than the usual loaf.

Combine the meats and seasonings. Blend thoroughly with the eggs and soaked crumbs. Form into a large loaf and place on a bed of bacon or salt pork strips. Arrange additional strips across the top. Bake at 350 degrees 1½ to 2 hours. The result is much better if the loaf is basted several times in the process. If wrapped tightly in foil and weighted as it cools, this makes a perfectly textured loaf.

Another Version of Three-Meat Meat Loaf

2 pounds ground beef
1 pound ground pork
1 pound ground veal
4 garlic cloves, ground with 1 large onion
1 cup whole stuffed olives
½ cup tomato paste
2 teaspoons basil
1 cup breadcrumbs soaked in red wine
3 eggs
2 teaspoons salt
1½ teaspoons freshly ground pepper
½ cup chopped parsley
Bacon strips or salt pork strips

Combine all ingredients and form into a loaf as above. Place on a bed of bacon or salt pork slices and lay strips of bacon or salt pork across the top. Roast at 350 degrees 1½ to 2 hours, basting with red wine.

Warning. It is true that good bacon makes flavor for a meat loaf. It is also true that much of the bacon one gets nowadays is highly artificial in flavor and texture. Consequently, you may wish to substitute some good streaky salt pork or even streaky fresh pork.

Meat Loaf with Cream

3 pounds ground beef
1 pound ground pork
¼ pound beef kidney fat, finely chopped
1 cup dry breadcrumbs
1 medium onion, finely chopped
2 egg yolks
¼ pound finely chopped salt pork
2 teaspoons salt
1 teaspoon freshly ground pepper
1 teaspoon summer savory
Butter
1 tablespoon flour
¾ cup heavy cream

This is a loaf much favored by Polish groups in the United States and one which has distinction for its flavor and juiciness.

Combine meat and all other ingredients except the butter, flour, and cream. Mix well with the hands. Make several slight indentations across the top. Bake at 350 degrees about 1¼ hours or until brown. Baste several times with butter. Just before the loaf is done, sprinkle with the flour and gently spoon the heavy cream over the loaf.

Hamburgers

The origin of the hamburger is undoubtedly European. *Larousse Gastronomique* lists a Bifteck à l'Hambourgeoise, which is also called a German steak — this, mixed with crumbs, sautéed until pink in the center, and served with a topping of fried onions. Indeed, the first hamburgers I remember were nearly always served with fried onions.

Early in this century the idea of a hamburger on a bun caught on after two world fairs had introduced it. Circa 1911–1912 hamburgers were already in use as picnic or beach food, I recall, and hamburger stands were springing up at resorts. By the 1920's, hamburger stands, especially in California, were fabled for their inventive variations on the hamburger and often for the quality of their product. One of the best known, the White Spot, began on Wilshire Boulevard in Los Angeles and soon had branches over the entire city. The owner of this chain shared his knowhow with a man named Yaw in Portland, Oregon, who went on to create his own empire of Yaw's Hamburger Shops.

The original White Spot hamburger was cooked to order and served on a toasted bun with butter, onion, relish, tomato, sliced dill pickle, lettuce, mayonnaise, and, if you wanted it, catsup as well. It cost fifteen cents and made a full meal.

From the 1920's on, the hamburger began its reign as America's most popular form of meat. It was considered *au fait* for children's and many grown-ups' parties. It became a "steak" in size, and even such fleshpots as "21," the Colony, and Chasen's began to offer plump patties of prime meat on their menus, serving them with flair, as they still do today.

The hamburger is the universal entrée for those on diets, and it is the delight of outdoor cooks, who, as often as not, maltreat it. Some people, I am convinced, eat it three times a day. The version one usually finds at stands and lunch counters is a mercilessly flattened patty of indefinable flavor, cooked to a state of petrifaction and placed on a cold bun, then to be doused with catsup. If its quality varies, so does its price, which can range anywhere from 19 cents for a quick-order sandwich to $4.50 for an elegantly planked hamburger steak.

At its best — juicy, filled with flavor — it is an excellent dish, not to be regarded with condescension. Certainly it has stimulated a great deal of innovation, both good and bad, in American cookery.

Broiled Hamburgers

Unless the hamburgers are thick and juicy and to be served very rare, they are best pan-broiled or sautéed in a little fat. The average serving for a sandwich is 4 ounces, and for a main dish 8 ounces. A 4-ounce hamburger should be seared quickly on both sides in a little butter, oil, or beef fat, and then cooked over moderate heat until done to your taste. Fair warning — after the rare stage has been reached, the texture of the meat decreases progressively in appeal until, when well done, it becomes dry and crumbly, no matter how good the beef may be. Add salt and freshly ground pepper to taste.

For a juicier and more flavorful hamburger, place a little cream or butter and a chip of ice inside each patty. The cream or butter keeps the interior moist, and the ice prevents it from overcooking. Some people achieve moistness by adding finely chopped onion to the meat, and the addition of finely chopped celery is said to be the secret of a renowned hamburger served by one of the great restaurants in New York.

Any of the recipes given in this section can be broiled.

Oven-broiled. Place the hamburgers on a broiling rack about 4 inches from the heating unit. Brush with butter or oil, or a mixture of the two. Broil at high heat till nicely browned on both sides, turning once. A hamburger 1 inch thick will take about 3 minutes a side. A thinner patty will take about 2 minutes a side if the broiler is very hot.

Broiled over charcoal. A 1-inch hamburger will take about 4 minutes a side for very rare, 5 minutes a side for rare to medium rare, and 6 minutes a side for medium.

Peppered Hamburgers. Press coarsely ground or cracked pepper into hamburger patties, as for steak au poivre. Sauté in beef fat or butter and oil until done to your taste.

Giant Broiled Hamburgers. Restaurant hamburgers are usually formed into oval cakes about 1½ inches thick or more and containing as much as ¾ pound of beef. If you are broiling such giants at home, it is best to place a little heavy cream or melted butter inside the meat before broiling. Then brush well with butter and broil 4 to 5 inches from the heating unit. Cook quickly to get a good crust while the interior remains pink or rare. Salt and pepper to taste.

Stuffed Hamburgers. Place a slice of onion between two thin patties of ground beef and press firmly together. Pan-broil to your taste and serve in a sandwich. The same idea can be executed with a thin slice of cheese as a filling, or a slice of ripe tomato salted and peppered.

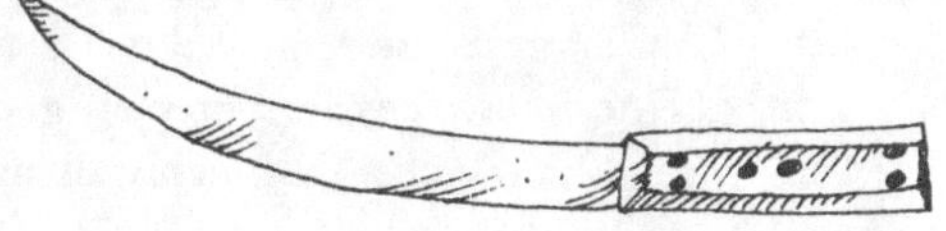

Cheeseburgers

2 pounds chopped chuck or top round
1 cup grated sharp Cheddar cheese, or grated Switzerland Gruyère, or crumbled Roquefort, or crumbled blue cheese
2 tablespoons Worcestershire sauce
½ teaspoon Tabasco
1 teaspoon salt
2 finely chopped garlic cloves

Ordinarily this means a piece of processed cheese placed atop a cooked hamburger patty and broiled just long enough to melt. It is not very good. This, on the other hand, is.

Mix all ingredients together thoroughly and form into cakes — 8 portions for sandwiches, 4 for "steaks" — and broil or pan-broil to your taste.

Garlicked Hamburgers

Hamburgers such as these used to be served in a delightful spot — a joint, really — in the North Beach section of San Francisco. They averaged 6 to 8 ounces apiece and were about 1½ inches thick and rather wide.

For four patties, use 1½ to 2 pounds ground beef. Heat 6 tablespoons olive oil in a large heavy skillet. Add 5 finely chopped garlic cloves. When the garlic begins to color, add the patties and cook quickly, turning once. Add additional garlic, if you like, at this point. When done to your taste, salt and sprinkle with freshly ground pepper. Serve, as these were originally, with sautéed green peppers and crisp Italian bread.

Norman Foster's Hamburger Steak

This man — a rare character and a good sculptor — was as much admired for his hamburger steak as anything else.

For 4 people, use 3 pounds of very lean top sirloin ground coarsely. Form into a thick cake. (For more than 4 people, do not increase the size of the cake, but make a second one and use two skillets.) Heat a heavy iron skillet till very hot and sprinkle heavily with salt. Place the cake in the skillet and cook over high heat, turning once — you will need two spatulas — till charred on both sides but still almost raw in the center. Sprinkle generously with freshly ground pepper during cooking. When done, top with a large piece of butter. Serve cut in wedges. Any leftovers are quite delicious cold and sliced.

Chuletas

2 pounds ground beef
2 cups minced parsley
2 cups chopped onion
2 large eggs

These nicely flavored patties are a specialty of the well-known authority on Mexican food Elena Zelayeta. A favorite dish in California, they arrived via the early Spanish settlers and the Mexicans. They are extremely good broiled and even better sautéed.

Mix together thoroughly all ingredients except the breadcrumbs

1 tablespoon salt
½ cup grated Parmesan cheese
½ teaspoon Tabasco
1 teaspoon freshly ground pepper
3 cups sifted breadcrumbs

and form into about 30 small balls. Sprinkle breadcrumbs over a pastry board, and pat each ball in the crumbs to make a thin patty 3 to 4 inches in diameter. Turn to crumb the other side. Chill well. Then sauté in olive oil, or grill on an oiled fine-meshed grill, 2½ to 3 minutes on each side. Serve with frijoles refritos and salsa fria.

Hamburger Pizza

1½ pounds ground beef
⅓ cup dry breadcrumbs
¼ cup tomato sauce
1 egg
2 garlic cloves, finely chopped
⅓ cup finely minced onion
1 teaspoon salt
½ teaspoon basil or oregano
Butter
½ cup tomato sauce
3 slices mozzarella cheese
4 anchovy fillets (optional)
12 soft black olives
¼ cup grated Parmesan cheese
Additional basil or oregano

With the success of pizza as one of the country's most ubiquitous short-order dishes, it was only a matter of time before it was combined with another short-order favorite to make hamburger pizza.

Combine the meat, crumbs, tomato sauce (¼ cup), egg, garlic, onion, and seasonings. Blend lightly but thoroughly. Butter a square of aluminum foil, place the mixture on it, and mold into a flat, round cake the size of a medium-size pizza. Shape a rim on it to keep the sauce from spilling over. Spread with ½ cup tomato sauce, slices of cheese, anchovy fillets, and olives. Sprinkle with grated Parmesan cheese and with more basil or oregano to your taste. Slide the pizza onto a cookie sheet, foil and all. Bake at 450 degrees approximately 15 minutes, or slightly less if you prefer it rare.

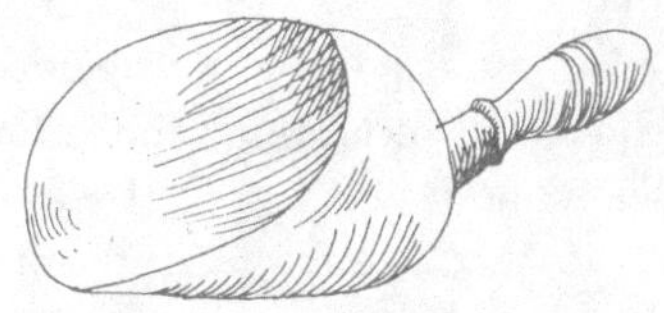

Mrs. Rorer's Hamburg Steak

2 pounds lean beef
1 teaspoon salt
1 tablespoon grated onion
1 saltspoon pepper

This is how ground beef was treated at the beginning of the century.

"Purchase the upper portion of the round or rump steak. Trim off the fat and skin and put the meat twice through a meat chopper; add onion and pepper and form at once into small steaks, being careful to have them of even thickness. Place these on the broiler, broil over a slow fire for ten minutes. It takes longer to broil a Hamburg steak one inch thick than it does an ordinary steak of the same thickness. Dish on a heated plate, dust with salt, put a little butter on top of each, and send at once to the table; or they may have poured over them tomato sauce, or you may serve them with brown or sweet pepper sauce. Where broiling is out of the question, these may be pan-broiled."

An Old Recipe for Almond Steak

2 pounds lean beef
¼ pound blanched almonds
1 teaspoon salt
Freshly ground pepper
Butter

Grind the beef and the almonds and mix in the seasonings. Form into a large steak and place in a hot buttered skillet with an ovenproof handle. Dot with butter and place in a 400-degree oven for 15 to 20 minutes, or until steak is beautifully browned on top. Eat with a good Béarnaise sauce.

Sloppy Joes

1½ pounds ground beef
2 tablespoons butter
1 cup finely chopped onion
½ cup finely diced celery
½ cup finely chopped green pepper
¼ cup Worcestershire sauce
½ cup catsup
½ teaspoon Tabasco
1 teaspoon salt or to taste
1 cup water
4 to 6 toasted hamburger rolls, buttered

This is a product of the modern age, and though it is not a palate-tingling delight it has a large public.

Brown the beef in the butter and break it up well with a fork. Add the onions, celery, pepper, seasonings, and water. Cover and simmer, adding more liquid if it gets too dry. Correct the seasoning. Spoon onto toasted buns, and if you want, add a bit of chopped green parsley or chopped green onion.

My Favorite Hamburger

2 pounds ground chuck or round with a minimum of fat
3 tablespoons grated onion
1 teaspoon salt
½ teaspoon freshly ground pepper
2 tablespoons heavy cream
3 tablespoons oil
3 tablespoons butter

I learned this recipe years ago from a magnificent cook named Jeanne Owen, who wrote deliciously about food and cooked even better than she wrote.

Pat the meat into a rather flat cake. Grate the onion directly into the center. Add the salt and pepper and carefully spoon the heavy cream into it. Blend well with the hands and form into one large cake or 4 smaller ones. If you want the meat rare, have the cakes about 1½ inches thick. Heat the oil and butter in a heavy skillet. When quite hot, add the meat and cook to your favorite state of doneness. Turn once or twice during the cooking process. Add salt and pepper to taste. If you make one large cake, use two very wide spatulas to handle the difficult job of turning it. Serve at once, along with sautéed potatoes and a tomato and onion salad.

Beef Offal

Beef Liver

Surprisingly little is written in cookbooks about beef liver. Americans tend to look down on it, as the great Escoffier did, when he termed all liver merely bourgeois food. In some parts of our country we have something known as baby beef liver. This is the liver from rather mature veal that cannot be sold as calf's liver. It is extremely good, and so is beef liver, if properly handled.

Beef Liver Steak

Have the liver cut 1 to 1½ inches thick. For rare, broil about 4 inches from the heat approximately 5 minutes on each side. For medium, broil 7 minutes on each side. Brush well with butter and serve with Béarnaise sauce or, if you are broiling over charcoal, a barbecue sauce.

Beef Liver en Brochette

Skewer 1½-inch cubes of beef liver alternated with rather thick slices of small rolls of bacon. Broil about 4 inches from the heat or over charcoal until the liver is nicely done on all sides and the bacon is fairly crisp. Allow enough space between the pieces of liver so they will cook on all sides. Serve with mustard and crisp fried potatoes or sautéed potatoes.

Roast Beef Liver

For 6 persons you will want a piece of liver 4½ to 5 pounds, well tied, and rolled. Bard it with bacon or salt pork and roast on a rack in a rather shallow baking pan at 325 degrees for about 15 minutes per pound. The liver should register about 150 degrees on the meat thermometer to be done with a pinkish center. Transfer to a hot platter and let rest 10 minutes before carving it in medium-thin slices. Serve with a bowl of crisp crumbled bacon, sautéed onions, and tiny boiled new potatoes.

Note. For a more elegant dish, soak 8 pieces of larding pork, 4 inches long and about ½ inch square, in 3 tablespoons Cognac for several hours. Then lard the liver with a larding needle. Roast as above.

Beef Liver à la Bourguignonne

4 slices beef liver
Flour
4 tablespoons butter
3 tablespoons oil
6 slices salt pork, diced
3 additional tablespoons butter
4 medium onions, thinly sliced
1 cup red wine
Salt
Freshly ground pepper
Chopped parsley
8 small croutons sautéed in butter with 2 garlic cloves, finely chopped

I discovered this recipe on the West Coast and have served it over a period of years. Its name, evidently, refers to the garniture of red wine, onions, and salt pork.

Flour the liver and sear quickly in the butter and oil. Transfer to a warm plate and cover. Add the salt pork to the pan and cook till nicely brown and well tried out. Transfer to absorbent paper, and pour excess fat from the pan. Add the additional butter to the pan and sauté the onions till delicately colored and just tender. Cover them for 5 minutes and let them steam over medium heat. Add the red wine and let it come to the boiling point. Then add the salt pork, liver, and salt and pepper to taste. Cook 5 minutes over medium heat. Transfer the liver slices to a hot platter, spoon the onion and salt pork mixture over them. Garnish with chopped parsley and the croutons. Serve with crisp sautéed potatoes.

Beef Kidneys

Beef kidneys were often used in a beefsteak and kidney pie or pudding. Although they have been largely displaced by veal kidneys, whose flavor many people prefer, they are still popular for kidney stew, served for Sunday breakfast to kidney fanciers or for a good winter dinner.

Beef Kidney Stew

1 beef kidney
Flour
1 teaspoon thyme
1½ teaspoons salt
1 teaspoon freshly ground pepper
3 tablespoons oil
3 tablespoons butter
2 medium onions, thinly sliced
½ teaspoon Tabasco
1 cup red wine
Chopped parsley
Boiled potatoes

After removing the tubes and membranes, soak the kidney 2 hours in water to cover and 2 tablespoons vinegar, or in milk to cover. Combine the flour and seasonings. Remove the kidney from the liquid and dry on a towel. Slice rather thin and dredge well with seasoned flour. Heat the butter and oil in a sauté pan, and when bubbling hot add the kidney and brown very quickly. Add the onions and cook with the kidney till both are blended and the onions are lightly colored. Add the Tabasco and red wine, cover the pan, and simmer approximately 15 minutes or until the kidney is tender. Correct the seasoning. Arrange the boiled potatoes around the edge of a rather deep platter or serving dish and spoon the kidney mixture into the center. Sprinkle with chopped parsley. The addition of a light red wine and a salad makes this into a rather pleasing dinner or supper.

Beef Heart

Strangely enough, while beef kidney and liver were more or less avoided by early Americans, save the Pennsylvania settlers, heart was given a rather prominent place in cookery.

Beef heart should be thoroughly cleaned by cutting out the tough top cords, and in some cases soaked in milk or acidulated water, but it is not generally necessary nowadays, since it is marketed in a much trimmer state than it used to be.

Broiled Beef Heart

Cut the heart in 1-inch slices and broil as you would liver or kidneys — rather quickly — and season with salt and freshly ground pepper. Serve with rosemary butter.

Beef Heart Hamburgers

Grind a beef heart rather coarsely. Season with salt, freshly ground pepper, a bit of finely chopped onion, and a dash of Tabasco. Form into patties and wrap each one in foil. Broil on the grill as you would an ordinary hamburger, about 4 minutes on each side for a package 1¼ inches thick. Serve with parsley butter, seasoned with garlic, and baked potatoes. Eat the hamburger from the foil.

Stuffed Beef Heart

1 beef heart
Bread or forcemeat stuffing
2 cups dry breadcrumbs
Butter
½ cup chopped parsley

Clean the heart well and stuff it with a forcemeat stuffing or a well-herbed bread stuffing. Sew the heart together with a large needle and heavy cord till it resembles its original shape. Either wrap the heart in foil and secure it tightly or wrap in muslin and tie. Place in a deep kettle and cover with cold water. Bring to a boil. Boil 5 minutes and remove any scum which forms on the top. Cover and simmer 2 hours. Remove the heart from the water. Remove the covering and roll the heart in the crumbs. Dot with butter, place in a shallow roasting pan, and roast 30 minutes at 375 degrees, basting well with melted butter three times. Do not let the crumbs burn. If they get too brown place a piece of foil on top for a few moments. Serve the heart with horseradish cream.

Beefcheek

This is known to the French as museau de boeuf and to the Germans as Ochsenmaul and is greatly used for an hors d'oeuvre as a salad. The French one is far better than the German because the French have far greater respect for the flavor and the Germans for the texture. As a result the French vinaigrette has oil and vinegar and the German vinegar and oil.

Unless one has access to heads it is rather difficult to make it. However, it may be found in many shops where charcuterie is found.

Head Cheese

This was a favorite dish in earlier America when people cooked in large kitchens. It was rather easy to cook a whole head and then pick the meat and sections to pieces and make a well-seasoned head cheese.

Tripe

Despite the number of people who tell you they won't eat tripe, it has a history of popularity in the country which is incredible. This seems to continue through the modern age, for many restaurants offer tripe dishes and many markets offer it frequently for general distribution. Tripe has had its champions for generations and there are some extremely interesting recipes for it.

As everyone knows, tripe is the muscular lining of the ox stomach. The process of readying it was long and tedious. It had to be scraped and soaked in cold water. Then it was soaked in a lime solution and scraped again, then in a salt and water solution and scraped again, and finally in buttermilk for a day. It was then boiled in clear water and stored in vinegar or vinegar and water to preserve it till ready to use. For the last hundred years, however, in New York and since then in most cities, tripe may be bought all prepared and nearly completely cooked. Otherwise, I'm afraid few people would ever bother to buy it and prepare it.

Beef Tongue

Beef tongue is found in a variety of forms. To many people fresh tongue is the most delicious of all, although sometimes difficult to come by. It is very versatile, lending itself to braising and serving with a number of sauces. Smoked tongue, especially good served cold, is much more easily available, and corned tongue is also found in certain markets.

Tongue is an international favorite. The English definitely fancy it, the French have many ways of saucing it, and the Polish, Swiss, and Italians all have brought their recipes for it to these shores. Tongue is one of the few meats that cans very well, and whole tongues, nicely trimmed, have been a choice item in food shops for many years.

Cold Smoked Tongue

Cold smoked tongue is excellent sliced thin and neatly and served with perhaps cold chicken, cold ham, or cold turkey. It is a pungent, moist meat and makes an attractive item for buffet service. It can be served with a mustard mayonnaise, a horseradish and whipped cream sauce, or a gribiche sauce, which complements it especially well.

Boiled Smoked Beef Tongue

1 smoked tongue, 3 to 4½ pounds
1 onion stuck with 2 cloves
2 or 3 garlic cloves
1 slice lemon
1 sprig parsley
1 bay leaf
Water

Place the tongue in a large kettle or braising pan and cover with water. Bring to a boil, and let it bcil 5 minutes. Remove any scum that forms on the surface. Add the onion, garlic, and seasonings and reduce the heat to simmer. Continue cooking till tender, allowing about 50 minutes per pound. When the tongue is cooked remove it from the broth. As soon as it has "set," after about 5 minutes, remove the skin. For this you will need a sharp knife with a narrow, supple blade. Run the knife edge under the skin and when it loosens you can pull off large sections of the skin at a time. Trim some of the root end of the tongue as well, so that it will look more attractive. Oftentimes the entire root end is trimmed and the tongue is sent to table propped up, with a curled end. To achieve this, the tongue must be stood on a piece of bread (called a socle) and its base masked with a sauce such as chaudfroid, for cold tongue, or a hot garniture. Tongue should be served in very thin, even slices. Traditionally, a purée of spinach and boiled potatoes go with it. As for sauces, a horseradish sauce, a mustard sauce with finely chopped pickle and capers in it, or a raisin sauce are all acceptable.

Tongue Hash

2 cups cold tongue, finely chopped
1 cup finely chopped potatoes (cold boiled or baked potatoes)
1 small onion, finely chopped
Salt and freshly ground pepper
5 tablespoons butter

Cold tongue, especially the root end and the tip, make an unusual version of hash.

Combine the tongue, potatoes, and onion and blend well. Season to taste. Melt the butter in a heavy skillet and add the tongue mixture, press flat and cook slowly, pressing the hash down lightly until it begins to crust on the bottom. Run a spatula under it and bring some of the well-done bits to the top. Continue turning till it has nicely browned. Fold over with the aid of a spatula and roll on hot plate. Garnish with fried eggs and chopped parsley. Serve with mustard or mustard sauce.

Tongue and Eggs in Aspic I

1 quart veal aspic
12 to 14 neat slices of tongue
6 cold poached eggs, well trimmed
Tarragon leaves or dill sprigs
Mustard mayonnaise

This was a dish often served for lunch during our summers at the Oregon beach. It was accompanied by summer vegetables prepared with French dressing and very often by tiny hot rolls. So pleasing was it in flavor and appearance that I have never forgotten it.

Prepare a veal aspic (page 87) and have it just at the syrup stage when ready to assemble the dish. Cut the tongue slices with a razor-sharp knife to approximately the same size and thickness. Poach the eggs rather firmly so that there is just a slight running in the yolk. Trim the whites as needed for a regular appearance (or use molds for poaching, if you like).

To assemble, rinse out a mold with cold water. Cover the bottom of the mold with a thin layer of the aspic. Carefully arrange a sunburst of tarragon leaves or dill sprigs in the center. Lift it very carefully and transfer to the freezer compartment for a few minutes to set. Once it is set, arrange the tongue slices, overlapping, around the tarragon or dill. Then arrange the eggs in a circle on the slices of tongue. Carefully spoon the aspic over all. Chill in the refrigerator overnight and unmold carefully on a serving plate. Garnish with a few sprigs of watercress. Serve with mustard mayonnaise.

Tongue and Eggs in Aspic II

1 quart veal aspic at the syrupy stage
Dill, tarragon, or parsley
16 slices cold smoked tongue cut in thin uniform slices
6 to 8 hard-boiled eggs, sliced
6 finely minced gherkins

Pour a layer of aspic in the bottom of a 2-quart oval or round dish. Arrange a center piece of fresh dill, tarragon leaves, or parsley sprigs, or a combination of them. Chill in the freezer a few minutes till set. Arrange alternating layers of tongue and hard-boiled eggs and sprinkle with the chopped gherkins. Spoon aspic on very carefully so as not to float the ingredients and disturb your pattern. Chill overnight in the refrigerator. To serve, unmold on a platter decorated with greens, and serve with mustard mayonnaise and a rice salad.

Simmered Fresh Tongue with Vegetables

1 fresh tongue, 4 to 5 pounds
1 onion stuck with 2 cloves
2 leeks
2 cloves garlic
1 carrot
1 rib celery
1 bay leaf
1 teaspoon thyme
1½ tablespoons salt
1½ teaspoons freshly ground pepper
6 medium onions
6 turnips
6 additional leeks
6 additional carrots

The tongue is treated similarly to boiled beef in a pot au feu and is thoroughly exciting in flavor.

Place the tongue, onion stuck with cloves, leeks, garlic, carrots, celery, and herbs in a large kettle. Fill with water to reach about 2 inches above the tongue. Bring to a boil and boil 5 minutes. Remove any scum that forms at the top. Cover and simmer, gauging about 45 minutes per pound of meat. One hour before it is ready, add the salt, pepper, and onions. After 20 minutes add the turnips and the additional leeks and carrots. When the tongue is tender, transfer to a platter and carefully remove the skin. Loosen it at the ends and pull off with the fingers or with a fork. Trim the root. Return to the broth to reheat. Serve on a hot platter surrounded with the vegetables. Grated fresh horseradish, mustard, and potatoes in their jackets complete the meal.

Braised Tongue with Tomato Sauce

1 tongue, 4 to 5 pounds
1 onion stuck with 2 cloves
1½ teaspoons basil

Cover the tongue with cold water and add the onion stuck with cloves, basil, garlic, and salt and pepper. Bring to a boil and boil 5 minutes. Remove any scum that rises to the top. Cover, reduce the heat, and simmer approximately 45 minutes per pound. While the tongue is cooking, sauté the chopped onion and chopped garlic in the oil and butter in a large skillet or braising pan, and when just colored, add the tomatoes, salt, pepper, and basil. Cook to a smooth sauce, stirring occasionally. Add the tomato paste and the olives, and simmer 20 minutes.

When the tongue is cooked, remove from the broth. When cool enough to handle, peel off the skin. Loosen it with a very sharp knife and pull it off with your fingers or a fork. Trim the root. Place the tongue in the tomato sauce and turn it several times. Add 1 cup of the broth from the tongue. Cover and simmer 20 minutes, turning the tongue once during that time. Arrange on a platter with the sauce poured around it and garnish with chopped parsley. Serve with steamed rice and a purée of spinach.

2 cloves garlic
1 tablespoon salt
Freshly ground pepper
Chopped parsley

TOMATO SAUCE

1 cup finely chopped onion
2 garlic cloves, finely chopped
4 tablespoons butter
2 tablespoons olive oil
2½ cups fresh tomatoes, peeled, seeded, and chopped, or 2 cups Italian plum tomatoes
1 teaspoon salt
1 teaspoon freshly ground pepper
1½ teaspoons basil
3 tablespoons tomato paste
24 soft black olives, pitted

Oxtails

The gelatinous texture of a fine ragout of oxtails is rich, flavorful, and most satisfying. Seasoning must be subtle, and the sauce to be really fine must not be thick but should have a wonderful lip-sealing quality.

Oxtail Ragout

5 or 6 pounds oxtails, disjointed
Flour
¼ cup chopped suet, melted
5 tablespoons butter, melted
3 large onions, thinly sliced
2 cloves garlic
4 carrots, thinly sliced
1 turnip, thinly sliced
Stock
Red wine
1 bay leaf, crushed
1 teaspoon summer savory
1 teaspoon thyme
1 tablespoon or more salt
1½ teaspoons freshly ground pepper
½ teaspoon ground ginger
Beurre manié, if desired

Here is a favorite ragout. It is a perfect supper dish for a large group — but is utterly rewarding at any time.

Flour the joints and brown them well in a skillet in the melted suet and butter. It is wise to brown only part of them at a time, transferring the finished pieces to a braising pan. When they are all browned, add more butter to the skillet if necessary, and brown the onions and garlic lightly. Add to the braising pan along with the carrots and turnip. Just barely cover with two-thirds stock and one-third red wine. Bring to a boil and cook 5 minutes, removing any scum that forms on the surface. Reduce the heat, and when the liquid begins to simmer add the seasonings and cover. Simmer approximately 3 hours or until the joints are quite tender. Remove the joints to a hot platter. Skim off the fat from the broth and reduce the stock over high heat for about 3 minutes. If you wish to thicken your sauce, add beurre manié and stir into the hot stock until it is sufficiently thick. Return the oxtails to the sauce and reheat for just a minute. Serve with a garnish of plain boiled potatoes and sprinkle with chopped parsley.

Beef Pies

Early English settlers in America brought a heritage of enclosing practically everything edible in a pie crust, and meat pies were a common way of using up leftover roasts combined with vegetables. Frequently the pies were baked in large outdoor ovens or in ovens built alongside the fireplace. Sometimes, too, they were made in pottery bowls that were put into a large kettle, which in turn was buried in hot coals. Old cookbooks sometimes explained how to listen for signs that the pie was done.

There were also "pot pies." The big iron kettle was lined with not very rich pastry and then filled with meat, generally cooked or partly cooked, parboiled potatoes, and perhaps onions and other vegetables. A top crust was added with a hole in the center so that water or broth could be poured in from time to time. Then the lid was put on the kettle and it was set to cook slowly in hot ashes. To brown the crust before serving, a hot shovel or shovel full of hot coals was held over it.

The Pennsylvania Dutch idea of pot pie was a well-greased kettle lined with strips of freshly rolled-out noodle dough and filled with meat, gravy, and vegetables.

Pot pie to many Americans today is a stew topped with dumplings, or with the freshly made, thinly rolled noodle strips dropped into the broth.

Beef Pie

3 pounds beef — chuck, rump, or round — cut into strips 1½ by 2 inches
3 to 4 tablespoons flour
1 tablespoon salt
1 teaspoon freshly ground pepper
6 tablespoons finely chopped beef suet
1 onion stuck with 2 cloves
1 clove garlic
1 carrot

This pie can be made almost entirely in advance. Customarily, the meat and sauce are prepared the day before cooking and cooled or chilled, and the crust is fitted on the dish just before it is placed in the oven. Puff pastry or rough puff pastry work extremely well for this purpose, and a suet pastry or cream cheese pastry are quite successful also.

Combine the flour with the salt and pepper, and dredge the meat in it. This is most easily done by putting the flour mixture and meat in a paper or plastic bag and shaking it. Melt the suet in a large skillet or braising pan, and when it is quite hot, sear the meat quickly on all sides. When it is nicely browned, add the onion, garlic, carrot, summer savory, and thyme. Pour in water or bouillon to just cover the meat, bring to a boil, then reduce the heat. Simmer about 1½ hours. The meat should be tender, but not completely cooked.

1 teaspoon summer savory
1 teaspoon thyme
Water or bouillon to cover
3 or 4 veal kidneys
4 tablespoons butter
2 large onions, sliced
¼ cup chopped parsley
Pastry
1 egg
2 tablespoons heavy cream

While the meat is simmering, remove the core from the kidneys and slice them rather thin. Melt the butter in a hot skillet, and toss the kidney slices in the butter for a minute or two to brown them. Salt and pepper them lightly. Remove the kidneys, and add the sliced onions to the pan. Cook over moderate heat until the onions become translucent.

Allow the cooked beef to stand about 15 minutes, then remove the onion, garlic, and carrot. Skim off any excess fat that rises to the surface. In a 2½-quart baking dish arrange alternate layers of beef, kidneys, and onions; pour the sauce over all, and add the parsley. Allow to cool an hour or so. If it is to be cooked the next day, cover and refrigerate. At least an hour and a half before cooking, prepare the pastry and chill it. Roll it out, and cut off a thin strip to fit around the edges of the dish. Moisten it slightly. Cover the dish with the remaining pastry, trim, and press to seal against the moistened strip. Crimp the edges, and cut a vent in the center. If you like, place a paper cornucopia in the vent as a funnel for steam. You may also decorate the top with leftover pastry cut into flower and leaf shapes, moistening the sides to be attached. Brush the entire pastry with the egg beaten together lightly with the cream.

Bake 10 minutes at 425 degrees. Reduce the heat to 375 degrees and continue cooking until the crust is nicely brown and steam is rising through the vent, about 45 minutes to 1 hour. Serve at once. A purée of carrots or turnips is a pleasant accompaniment.

Beef Pie with Potatoes. Spread the bottom of the baking dish with well-seasoned mashed potatoes, and sprinkle with flour. Then add the meat, kidneys, and onions, and proceed as directed above.

Variations

(1) You may substitute mushrooms for the kidneys or use both — 2 kidneys and 12 mushroom caps.

(2) Beef kidney may be used instead of veal, but since it is rather strong in flavor, it is apt to overwhelm the savory quality of the pie. Before using, clean it and allow it to soak in a covering of milk about 2 hours.

Leftover Beef Pie

1½ cups cubed cooked beef
5 tablespoons fat, drippings, butter, or margarine
4 tablespoons flour
1 or 2 tablespoons minced onion
1 or 2 tablespoons minced celery
3 cups beef bouillon or consommé
1 to 1½ cups cooked vegetables (tender but still crisp), such as carrots, peas, green beans, green lima beans, whole-kernel corn, cubed zucchini, or a combination of any of these
Salt and freshly ground pepper to taste
¼ cup red wine (optional)
1 teaspoon Worcestershire sauce
Dash of Tabasco
Pastry or biscuit recipe using 1½ cups flour

A perennial favorite for stretching the leftover Sunday oven roast or pot roast.

Cut any excess fat away from the meat before cutting into cubes. Melt the fat in a saucepan or frying pan. Blend in the flour and stir until lightly browned, adding the onion and celery towards the last of the browning. Add the beef bouillon or consommé. Stir until the mixture is thickened, and simmer several minutes. Add the lightly cooked vegetables and seasonings. Add the meat and cool. Line the sides of a deep 2-quart casserole with thin pastry and let it overhang about ½ inch. Invert a small custard cup or short egg cup in the center of the casserole (this will gather gravy and prevent the filling from boiling over). Pour the filling into the pastry-lined casserole. Roll out the top pastry to allow a margin of about 1 inch around the casserole. Moisten the edge of the bottom crust, lay the top crust over it, and seal and crimp the edges. Cut steam slits in the top. Bake 10 to 15 minutes at 450 degrees, then reduce the heat to 350 degrees and bake about 20 minutes longer. When you start to serve the pie, tip the inverted cup inside to let the gravy run into the filling.

Beef Pie with Biscuit Crust. Pour the hot filling into an unlined casserole. Place ½-inch thick biscuits on top, and bake 25 minutes in a 400-degree oven.

Veal Pie. Use chicken broth to make the gravy, or half chicken broth and half rich milk. Season with tarragon or basil. Green beans or broad beans are especially good in this.

Pork Pie. Use chicken broth or chicken broth and rich milk for the gravy, as in veal pie. The Pennsylvania Dutch season the gravy with about 1 teaspoon brown sugar and ⅛ teaspoon ground cloves, in addition to salt and pepper. Pork pie is generally topped with biscuits.

Lamb Pie. Follow the beef recipe.

Beefsteak and Kidney Pie

1 to 1½ pounds round steak
1 veal kidney or small beef kidney
½ cup chopped onions
5 tablespoons tried-out beef fat, butter, or margarine
4 tablespoons flour

Although this is famed as a British dish, many American homes serve it regularly, especially along the Canadian border. The recipe appears in various forms in a goodly number of old sectional cookbooks of the Northern states.

Trim the fat from the steak and put it in a frying pan over medium heat to melt. Cut the steak into cubes, ¾ inch to 1 inch. Cut the kidney meat away from the white fibers and remove the fat. Cut the kidney into small chunks. When the beef fat is tried out, remove the solid parts left in the pan. Add butter or margarine to the pan (if needed) to make 5 tablespoons. Sauté the onions very lightly in the fat. Stir in the flour and blend well. Add the bouillon or consommé and stir until thickened. Season with the salt, pepper, and Worcestershire sauce. Add the meat and cool.

3½ cups beef bouillon or consommé
1 to 1½ teaspoons salt
¼ teaspoon freshly ground pepper
1 teaspoon Worcestershire sauce
Pastry of your choice, using 2 to 4 cups flour

Have ready a 2-quart casserole or baking pan of comparable capacity. If using a bottom crust as well as top, the pastry will require 3 or 4 cups of flour. Follow the recipe for suet, or regular, or lard and butter pie crust. If using a top crust only, prepare any of these or a meat puff paste. Like many meat pies, this will be better if a custard cup or egg cup is inverted in the center of the pie to hold up the crust and to gather the gravy during baking. Put the filling into the casserole or pan, top with pastry, and bake 20 minutes at 450 degrees. Reduce the heat to 325 degrees and bake 35 to 45 minutes longer.

Beefsteak and Kidney Pasties. The mixture of finely cubed steak and kidneys is very good used in place of the steak or chuck steak cubes as the filling for Cornish pasties (see page 329).

Beefsteak, Kidney, and Oyster Pie

2 pounds chuck or rump cut into strips 1½ × 2 inches
Flour
4 tablespoons butter
3 tablespoons oil
2 to 3 veal kidneys, according to size, trimmed and thinly sliced
12 mushroom caps
1 cup chopped onions
2 tablespoons chopped parsley
½ bay leaf crumbled
1 teaspoon thyme
1½ teaspoons salt, or to taste
1 teaspoon freshly ground pepper
12 oysters
2 cups brown sauce
Pastry enough for a two-crust pie

This pie is quite good in flavor and comparatively easy to prepare. Time was in this country when it used to be made with puff paste, as it still is in England and wherever the cook happens to be a fine patissier. Today homemakers use their favorite pastry, and I can recommend a cream cheese pastry, which seems to lend itself to the prolonged cooking period.

Flour the beef lightly, and brown in a mixture of the butter and oil in a heavy skillet. Arrange the meat around the sides of a baking dish approximately 9 × 12 inches and 3 inches deep. Add the sliced kidneys, mushroom caps, and onions, and sprinkle with the seasonings. Finally add the oysters. Pour the sauce over all.

Roll out the pastry more than large enough to make a top crust for the baking dish. From this, cut off a strip about 1 inch wide and long enough to fit the circumference of the dish and slightly overlap its edges. Dampen it slightly. Now set the remaining pastry in place to make a top crust, fitting it to overlap the moistened strip. Press to seal the two edges together. Make a vent in the center of the crust and place a small paper cornucopia in it to provide a funnel for the steam. Shape leftover pastry into simple flowers and leaves, moisten, and use to decorate the crust. Bake at 350 degrees about 2 hours or until the meat is thoroughly tender. If the crust begins to brown too quickly, cover it lightly with foil.

Leftover Beefsteak Pie

2 pounds leftover beef steak
24 small white onions
6 tablespoons butter
½ pound good bacon, cut in small pieces
24 oysters (optional)
Pastry enough for a 2-crust pie
2 cups brown sauce or beef gravy
1 egg
2 tablespoons cream

This dish is from Pierre Caron, a French chef in New York who eventually became chef at Delmonico's. He left many recipes behind him, which were translated and published in 1886.

Cut the meat into small cubes. Brown the onions in butter, cover, and let them steam until tender but crisp. Try out the bacon pieces and transfer to absorbent paper. Roll out the pastry and put a strip 2 inches wide around a 2-quart baking dish, slightly overlapping the top edge. In the dish place alternate layers of beef, onions, bacon, oysters if wished, and sauce. Dampen the pastry strip, then cover the dish with a top crust, pressing it against the strip to seal it and turning it under. Crimp the edges and make a vent in the center of the crust. Brush the pastry well with the egg and cream beaten lightly together. Bake at 425 degrees for 10 minutes. Reduce the heat to 375 degrees and cook until the crust is done and the meat is thoroughly cooked — another 35 to 40 minutes.

Beefsteak Pudding

Suet crust, using 2 cups flour
2½ to 3 pounds round steak 1 inch thick, cut into strips 1 by 2 inches
3 or 4 veal kidneys, cut in thin slices
2 onions, finely chopped
1 teaspoon thyme
¼ cup chopped parsley
Salt and freshly ground pepper
Stock or water to cover

Mrs. Crowen offers a curious version of this dish. It is made with a steak beaten almost to a paste, seasoned with salt and pepper, dotted with butter, then rolled into a pastry prepared with beef dripping, and wrapped in a pudding cloth. It is boiled for two hours, cut in slices, and served with melted butter and catsup.

However, the traditional version, which was established in this country by the English settlers, is surely the favorite. It was occasionally made with game — bear, venison, and smaller game — instead of beef.

Line a 2 to 2½-quart pudding bowl or mixing bowl with suet crust, allowing enough to overlap the edge. Flour the steak. Place in the bowl in a layer, and alternate with layers of kidney slices and onions, sprinkling each layer with seasonings, until the layers almost reach the top of the bowl. Pour in stock or water to fill ¾ of the bowl. Dampen the edge of the bottom crust. Put a top crust on and secure it to the bottom crust. It is best to allow enough pastry, top and bottom, so that the two crusts can be pressed together and turned under, making a firmer seal. Next take a heavy cloth, wring it out in hot water, and sprinkle liberally with flour. Tie this carefully over the pudding so that no water can penetrate during the steaming process. Place the bowl in a large kettle. Pour in water to cover ⅔ of the bowl. Place a lid on the kettle, and boil for about 4 hours. Remove the pudding cloth.

Serve from the bowl placed on a platter and surrounded with boiled potatoes and, perhaps, Brussels sprouts.

Note. Some recipes add mushrooms to the pudding; or finely grated potato; or mushroom catsup, tomato catsup, or Worcestershire sauce; or pickled onions and catsup. However, none of these additives is true to the original dish.

Tamale Pie

4 cups boiling water
1½ cups yellow cornmeal
2 cups cold water
1½ teaspoons salt
¼ to ½ cup lard, butter, or margarine
½ pound bulk sausage
2 tablespoons chili powder
¾ teaspoon ground cumin or comino
1 clove garlic, minced
1 to 1½ cups finely chopped onion (2 large onions)
1 small green pepper, seeded and chopped
1 cup finely cut celery
1½ teaspoons additional salt
1½ pounds ground beef
3 cups Italian canned tomatoes or 3½ to 4 cups peeled and seeded fresh tomatoes
2½ cups canned whole-kernel corn with juice or 2½ cups fresh corn cut from cob with ½ cup water or tomato juice
1 cup pitted ripe olives
1½ to 2 cups grated medium or sharp Cheddar-type cheese

Mexican tamales, wrapped in corn husks and steamed, are standard fare along the southern border of the United States. Homemakers of early "border" living also developed this pan version, which omits the corn husk procedure. It has been a favorite throughout the United States for serving large numbers.

Bring 4 cups water to boil in a 3-quart kettle. Stir the cornmeal into the cold water and then stir this into the boiling water. Continue to stir while returning to boil. Turn the heat low to keep the mixture simmering. Stir in the salt and lard, butter, or margarine (lard is preferred by Mexican cooks). Cover, and simmer 30 to 40 minutes.

In a kettle or large frying pan, mash the sausage and cook over medium heat until it begins to lose color. Add the chili powder and cumin or comino, and stir and cook several minutes. Add the garlic, onions, green pepper, celery, and additional salt. Stir and cook until the vegetables are limp. Crumble the beef into the pan and mash and cook until the raw color disappears. Add the tomatoes and corn and let the mixture simmer 15 to 20 minutes. Grease or oil a baking pan about 10 × 14 × 2 inches. Spread about two-thirds of the cornmeal mixture on the bottom and up the sides of the pan. Spoon in the filling and distribute the olives evenly around. Spoon the remaining cornmeal over the top and sprinkle with the cheese. Bake in a 350-degree oven about 1 hour.

Cornish Pasties

Pastry, using 5 to 6 cups of flour
2 pounds round steak or boneless chuck roast
2 or 3 medium-size potatoes, peeled and cut into ½-inch cubes

Wherever there were mines in America the miners of Cornwall and Wales could be found. They introduced their famous "lunch," Cornish pasties (pronounced past-ees), made of large rounds of pastry filled with cooked or uncooked cubed or chopped meat, onion, potatoes, and sometimes carrots, turnips, and other root vegetables. Usually the pastry was made with a "tough" or not very fat pastry so that the miners could wrap the pasties in cloth or

1 turnip (optional), peeled and cut into ½-inch cubes
1 carrot (optional), peeled or scraped and cut into ½-inch pieces
½ to ¾ cup finely chopped onion (½ to 1 onion)
1½ teaspoons salt
¼ teaspoon freshly ground pepper
1 teaspoon Worcestershire sauce

newspaper, tuck them into a pocket, and go down into the mines to work.

Pasties are still made by bakers in many of the American mining communities and are on the menus of restaurants and lunch counters. They vary a bit from state to state. Since they are now made to be carried in the hand, like a hamburger sandwich or hot dog, or to be eaten with a fork, the pastry is richer and the pasties vary in thickness.

Prepare the pastry. Use standard pastry (page 634), rough puff paste (page 640), or suet pastry (page 640). Use 5 cups of flour if you are rolling the pastry less than ¼ inch thick; use 6 cups for a thicker crust. This amount of pastry will yield 8 or 9 turnovers.

Trim the fat off the meat and mince enough of the fat to make about 1 teaspoon per pasty. Put it into a bowl. Cut the meat into small cubes about ½ inch square. Add to the bowl, along with the vegetables and seasonings. Roll out the pastry and cut into 8 or 9 8-inch rounds. (A plate makes a good pattern.) Moisten the edges of the pastry with water or egg white. Put filling on one half of each pastry round, fold the other half over the filling, and crimp the edges. Prick the top two or three times.

Place the pasties on a shallow baking pan and bake at 450 degrees 10 to 12 minutes. Reduce the heat to 350 degrees and bake about 25 to 30 minutes longer. Serve hot. If you like, serve with hot beef consommé to pour into the center of each pasty.

Pasties with Gravy. Mix about 1½ cups thickened beef consommé with the meat and vegetables before filling the pasties.

Fish Pasties. Combine cooked firm-fleshed fish, such as salmon, halibut, cod, red snapper, or even canned tuna, with potatoes and a small amount of chopped onion. Sometimes cooked or slightly cooked peas or green beans are added as well. The filling is best if moistened with a thickened court bouillon or fish broth or a well-seasoned cream sauce. Otherwise the pasties are apt to be a bit dry.

Appetizer Pasties. Fine eating for the cocktail hour. Combine ground steak with a bit of fat in it with finely chopped potato and onion. Increase the seasonings or Worcestershire sauce, if you like, and add a few drops of hot pepper sauce. Cut the pastry rounds about 2½ to 3 inches in diameter and fill with about a rounded teaspoon of the beef mixture. Bake about 5 minutes at 450 degrees and about 20 minutes at 350 degrees.

Veal

Veal, like lamb, has suffered from overcooking in this country and has been treated with little regard for the delicacy of its texture and flavor, or for its wonderful capacity to absorb other flavors. One of the first to realize its qualities was Mrs. Rorer when she gave directions for a certain veal dish, "never forgetting," added the sage of Philadelphia, "that veal cooked slowly in butter absorbs the flavor of the fine butter because the flesh is more absorbent."

Until the 1930's most American cooks parboiled veal steaks or chops, thus robbing them of much of their flavor before they were given a final cooking. No wonder veal has never had the popularity here it has maintained in France, Italy, Austria, and Hungary. It was probably the advent of immigrants from those countries, especially the French and Italians, that eventually changed our culinary approach to veal.

Good veal has always been difficult to find. But recently a Dutch process has come to our shores and is giving us a limited quantity of much finer veal than was generally available before. Several years ago my New York butcher, one of the first to carry this grade of veal, used to send it via air to customers as far away as California and Florida. Now there are several farmers using the Dutch process, and the veal is a little more plentiful. The process consists simply of taking calves from their mothers' milk to small stalls, where they are fed with vitamins and powdered milk that contains no iron to darken the flesh. Also, the calves are kept comparatively quiet during their milk regime. Thus, they have a delicate whitish-pink flesh and clear fat and are deliciously tender. Such veal is called plume de veau and is available at this writing in a few cities but will certainly be produced in greater quantity across the country. For the time being it is an expensive process, and thus the veal is far more costly than that commonly sold.

Veal Roasts, Pot Roasts, Fricassees

Roast Veal

Our early cooking authorities felt that veal should be slow-roasted, although Mrs. Rorer does suggest putting the loin into a hot oven and cooking for 15 minutes, after which the oven was to be cooled by closing the drafts and if necessary taking a lid off the stove. Miss Farmer barded her veal, placed it on a rack, and dredged it with flour. She roasted it slowly for several hours and basted every fifteen minutes, which would be quite a chore for today's busy cook.

You may become confused when you shop for veal because of the discrepancy between the names of cuts used in butcher shops and the terminology used in cookbooks. These are the official cuts for roasting listed by the American National Livestock and Meat Board, although even this isn't the final word, since the board changes terminology sometimes to suit itself. (1) Standing rump roast, with bone, from the leg. (2) Shank half of the leg with bone. (3) Rolled leg (a desirable buy). (4) The loin — divided nowadays into a sirloin and a loin. Either one of them boned and tied makes an excellent roast. (5) Double loin, with the bone, is a saddle roast. Excellent and spectacular for a party. (6) Crown, prepared by some butchers as they do a crown of pork. (7) Rack.

It is best to roast veal with some moisture and to keep it covered for most of the cooking. Here are some rules which apply for practically all veal roasting:

(1) Have the butcher bone, bard, and tie the roast. To bard it yourself, wrap (then tie) the roast with thin slices of fat pork or salt

pork which has been freshened in water to remove some of the salt. Bacon may be used, but it is sometimes very flavorful and is apt to dominate the flavor of the veal.

(2) Seasonings such as a carrot, an onion, a leek, or garlic, may be added to the pan with the veal. They not only give flavor but also add moisture to the cooking and contribute to a juicier veal.

(3) Season the veal well with whatever herb you choose, forcing some into the flesh and rubbing the outside thoroughly. Certain herbs go well with veal, but not many. Dill with veal is very popular with Scandinavian people of the Middle West and Far West. The French generally prefer tarragon or chervil. Central Europeans like paprika, usually the sweet; and the Italians, thyme or oregano or sage. Sage must be used cautiously, however, lest it smother rather than enhance the flavor of the veal.

There are two methods for roasting veal.

I. Use a deep braising pan of copper, stainless steel, or enameled iron, with a lid. Heat fat in the braising pan, and when it is bubbling hot sear the meat well on all sides over a fairly brisk heat. Butter and oil, mixed, are excellent for this purpose, or if you are planning to season Italian or Provençal style, use pure olive oil. When the veal is seared, add a sliced carrot or two and an onion stuck with 2 cloves, and cover the pan. Roast in a 325-degree oven, allowing about 25 minutes per pound. It is wise to baste the roast occasionally with pan juices, with butter and white wine, or with broth. Veal should be cooked to an internal temperature of about 160 to 165 degrees. It should be well cooked but not to the point where it is dry and tasteless. It doesn't matter if there is the faintest tinge of pink in the meat as you slice it. Transfer the veal to a hot platter and allow it to rest for 10 minutes before carving. Serve with the pan juices, or if you like, prepare a sauce.

II. Place the roast on a rack in a shallow roasting pan. Rub well with butter or butter and oil and seasoning to taste. Roast uncovered at 425 degrees for 20 to 30 minutes. Reduce the heat to 350 degrees, cover the roast with a piece of foil or some buttered parchment, and continue roasting, basting occasionally with pan juices or with butter and white wine in equal parts. Gauge approximately 15 minutes per pound, and roast till the meat reaches an internal temperature of 165 degrees when tested with a meat thermometer. Transfer the meat to a hot platter and garnish. Allow it to rest 10 minutes in a warm place before carving. Serve with pan juices or a brown sauce.

Basic Sauce for Roast Veal

To make a sauce of some distinction for your roast of veal, buy a veal knuckle and save some of the bones from the boning of your roast. Arrange them in a roasting pan, add a garlic clove and an onion or two, and place under the broiler to brown thoroughly. The bones should be about 5 inches from the broiling unit and must be carefully watched so that they achieve good color but do not char. Sprinkle with 3 tablespoons flour and let that also brown slightly with the bones.

Transfer all to a deep saucepan, and add 1 carrot, 1 onion, 1 teaspoon thyme, a bay leaf, 2 or 3 sprigs of parsley, 1½ quarts water, and 1 cup red wine. Bring to a boil; then add 1 tablespoon salt and ½ teaspoon freshly ground pepper. Cover, and simmer for 2½ to 3 hours. Allow it to cool for 1 hour, then skim off excess fat. Strain through a linen or muslin cloth, and correct the seasoning. Reduce the sauce by ⅓ by boiling rapidly over a high heat. This will give you the basic broth for several sauces. It may be thickened with browned flour and butter. Pan juices may also be added to it and the seasoning adjusted to your taste.

A Double Loin of Veal Larded with Ham

1 double loin of veal, boned and barded
8 strips of Maryland or Virginia ham about 6 to 8 inches long (any good country ham will be satisfactory)
1¼ cups Madeira
Butter and oil
1 carrot
1 onion stuck with 2 cloves
Salt and freshly ground pepper
1 cup brown sauce

This had its origin in Maryland or Virginia, where ham was an important part of the diet and where, because of a certain amount of cattle raising, veal was not an unusual dish. The use of Madeira makes it even more typical of that section.

Soak the ham in 1 cup Madeira 1 hour. Then lard the veal with the ham, using a larding needle or cutting deep incisions in the veal with a sharp knife and forcing the ham in. Sear the veal in butter and oil in a deep braising pan or Dutch oven (preferably not a black iron one, since wine is being used). When it is nicely seared on all sides, add the carrot, onion, salt and pepper, the Madeira from the ham, and an extra ¼ cup. Cover and roast at 325 degrees, allowing about 15 minutes a pound. Baste occasionally with the pan juices. When it has reached an inner temperature of 165 degrees, transfer the veal to a hot platter. Let it rest for 10 minutes before carving. Serve it with the pan juices, or add pan juices to the basic sauce and thicken it with browned flour and butter. Au gratin potatoes and a purée of spinach would be admirable accompaniments.

Vitello Tonnato (Veal with Tuna Fish Sauce)

3-pound roast of veal from the loin or the leg, boned and tied
14 to 16 anchovy fillets
2 7-ounce cans tuna fish in oil, preferably olive oil

A delicious dish that has become very popular in this country as a summer specialty. There are several different ways of preparing it. This is a particularly good one.

Make a few incisions in the veal and insert a few of the anchovies. Reserve 2 anchovies for a garnish. Place the veal in a deep casserole and place on top of it the rest of the anchovies, together with half the tuna. Add the knuckle, onion, and seasonings, and the wine and water heated together. Cover, and roast in a 350-degree oven for

1½ hours or until the veal is just tender. Let it cool in the casserole. When ready to serve, skim off any excess fat from the jellied liquid and transfer the jelly to a bowl. Remove the strings, carve the meat into thinnish slices, and arrange on a serving plate. Melt the jellied liquid just enough to spoon over the veal slices. Return to the refrigerator to harden the jelly.

Crush the contents of the second can of tuna fish, fold into the mayonnaise, and add a tiny bit of the oil from the anchovies. Spoon the tuna mayonnaise over the jellied veal slices and decorate with anchovy fillets, capers, and chopped parsley. Serve with a rice salad.

Note. Some people prefer to combine the mayonnaise with an equal quantity of sour cream, blended with tuna fish to taste.

Veal knuckle
1 large onion stuck with cloves
1 bay leaf
1 sprig parsley
1 cup white wine
½ cup water
1½ cups homemade mayonnaise
Capers
Chopped parsley

Another Vitello Tonnato

Merely slice cold roast veal and dress it with a tuna-flavored mayonnaise as above. Serve with anchovy fillets and capers, and decorate the platter with sliced hard-boiled eggs and watercress. Serve with a rice salad.

Kidney-Stuffed Loin of Veal

1 double loin of veal, boned, stuffed with veal kidney, tied
Thyme
Garlic
6 tablespoons butter
3 tablespoons oil
Madeira
Salt and freshly ground pepper
Veal broth

This was brought to America by the English, the French, and the Germans, who had prepared veal in this fashion for generations.

Season the meat well with thyme and a little garlic. Sear thoroughly in hot butter and oil in a deep roasting pan or an enameled iron, aluminum, or copper braising pan. When nicely browned, cover, place in a 350-degree oven, and roast approximately 15 minutes per pound or until the roast registers 165 degrees on a meat thermometer. Baste two or three times during roasting with the pan juices and a little Madeira. Salt and pepper to taste. Transfer to a hot platter to rest 10 minutes before carving. Add a cup of broth to the pan and a little additional Madeira, and reduce slightly over high heat. Correct the seasoning and serve with the roast.

Carve the meat in fairly thin slices so that everyone gets veal and kidney. Crisp sautéed potatoes and puréed string beans go very well with the roast. Drink a fine Meursault, a Chassagne Montrachet, or a fine California Sauvignon Blanc.

Stuffed Shoulder of Veal

1 shoulder of veal, boned and cut with a pocket
Stuffing
6 tablespoons butter
3 tablespoons oil

The shoulder, boned and cut with a pocket, is perfect for stuffing. Use any of the stuffings given on pages 232–233.

Stuff the shoulder, sew it up with a large needle and twine, and shape it into a sausage-shaped roll or oblong "cushion." Sear in the hot butter and oil in a deep roasting pan or enameled braising pan. When nicely browned, add about 1 cup of broth, cover, and place the pan in a 325-degree oven. Roast about 18 minutes per pound,

Veal broth (about 4 cups)
3 tablespoons additional butter
3 tablespoons browned flour
Salt and freshly ground pepper
Chopped parsley

basting from time to time with additional broth. When the shoulder is done (the internal temperature should be 165 to 168 degrees), transfer to a hot platter to rest 10 minutes before carving. Skim off any excess fat from the pan juices. Measure, and add enough broth to make 2 cups. Thicken the sauce with brown roux made with browned flour and additional butter. Let the sauce simmer 5 minutes, stirring the while. Season with salt and pepper and add a generous amount of chopped parsley. Slice the veal so that everyone has both meat and stuffing. With it serve the sauce and a purée of carrots. If you would like additional starch, also serve steamed rice.

Stuffed Shoulder in Jelly

1 shoulder of veal, boned and cut with a pocket
Stuffing
Garnishes

BROTH

2 veal knuckles
Bones from the shoulder
1 onion stuck with 2 cloves
1 leek, if available
1 carrot
1 rib celery
2 sprigs of parsley
1 bay leaf
Large sprig of tarragon or 1½ teaspoons dried
Salt and freshly ground pepper
2 tablespoons lemon juice

Prepare a very rich broth, as follows: Combine the bones and other ingredients with water to cover. Bring to a boil and boil 5 minutes. Remove any scum that forms on top, and reduce the heat to simmer. Cover, and simmer 2½ hours. Strain, and remove 1½ to 2 cups for the roast. Let the remaining strained broth cool. Prepare the stuffed shoulder as in preceding recipe. When it is roasted, allow it to cool. Pour off the pan juices and combine with broth to make 2 cups. Bring to a boil and cool. Skim off the excess fat. Place the cooled roast in a bowl or other container, weight slightly, and cover. Store in the refrigerator overnight.

Before serving, slice the roast and arrange the slices on a platter. The broth, which will have jellied, should be heated just enough to be spooned over the slices. Return to the refrigerator to set. Garnish the platter with watercress, tiny gherkins, capers, and sliced hard-boiled egg. Serve with a well-seasoned mayonnaise or a rémoulade sauce.

Braised Stuffed Breast of Veal

1 breast of veal with pocket
Stuffing (a forcemeat or a true bread stuffing)
1 clove garlic, chopped
1 teaspoon thyme
1 teaspoon salt
6 tablespoons butter
3 tablespoons oil
1 cup white wine or broth
Salt and freshly ground pepper

The breast lends itself to a rather spectacular stuffing. One old recipe calls for a pork, breadcrumb, and herb stuffing placed in long gashes cut between the ribs. However, doing it in that fashion would rob the dish of its rather magnificent appearance. A savory potato stuffing was often used, as was an excellent crumb and nut stuffing. Occasionally one finds a stuffing with dried prunes as a principal ingredient.

A stuffed breast in the modern manner — and it is comparatively recently that it has come into general use — means an entire breast with a deep pocket cut in it. A rather thin piece of lean meat which is not especially tender covers the breast bones. When a pocket is cut, this covering layer provides an attractive band of meat over the stuffing in the finished dish. When you order a breast with pocket, ask your butcher to remove as many of the rib bones as he can without breaking the flesh.

Stuff the pocket. Cover the open end with a piece of aluminum foil folded four times, molding it around the stuffing to seal it completely. Secure it with skewers, or sew up the opening. Rub the breast well with the garlic and thyme blended with salt. Sear on both sides in the butter and oil until nicely brown. Add the wine or broth and salt and pepper to taste. Place in a roaster and cover, or cover with foil. Roast in a 325-degree oven, allowing about 18 to 19 minutes per pound. It must be thoroughly cooked through the stuffing. Baste occasionally with the pan juices. Add a little more liquid if needed. When the veal is tender, uncover to let the top brown a little more. Remove from the pan and extract any remaining bones. Place on a hot platter to rest 10 minutes before carving, while you make the sauce.

Melt the butter and sauté the onion lightly. Add the flour and blend well, stirring with a wooden spatula. Gradually stir in the pan juices skimmed of excess fat. Add enough broth to make a cup. Stir until thickened. Correct the seasoning and stir in the cream. Let it simmer a few moments. Add the chopped parsley, and serve the sauce with the stuffed breast. The stuffed breast may also be served cold with a well-seasoned mayonnaise.

SAUCE
3 tablespoons butter
1 onion, finely chopped
3 tablespoons flour
Pan juices
Broth
½ cup heavy cream
2 tablespoons chopped parsley

Veal en Daube

A boned loin roast of veal, barded and tied
2 cloves garlic
6 slices thickly cut bacon
1 tablespoon or more paprika
1 red chili
Bacon fat or butter and bacon fat
2 carrots, finely chopped
2 ribs celery, finely chopped
1 green pepper, finely chopped
12 to 14 small onions
1 teaspoon thyme
2 cups red wine
Salt and freshly ground pepper
Chopped parsley

Creole cooks created many dishes that became famous during the French era of New Orleans. The popularity of some reached as far as Virginia and Kentucky. This one is reminiscent of a dish as it is prepared in the southern part of the Rhône Valley.

With a very sharp knife make about 12 incisions in the veal. Cut the bacon into small slices and roll in the paprika. Insert the pieces of bacon, slivers of garlic, and bits of chili in the meat. In a deep braising pan or roasting pan of enameled iron or aluminum, melt 4 tablespoons each of bacon fat and butter. Add the carrots, celery, green pepper, small onions, and thyme, and sear the meat lightly on all sides over medium heat. When nicely colored, add the red wine. Place in a 325-degree oven and roast, allowing about 18 minutes per pound of meat. Salt and pepper to taste and add chopped parsley. When cooked, transfer the veal to a deep bowl or oval dish and strain the broth. Arrange the small onions around the meat. If you want, purée the other vegetables and blend with the broth, or use the broth as it is. Pour over the daube and allow it to cool for 24 hours. This is excellent served cold with a good salad and perhaps a hot vegetable. This may be served from the mold or, if jellied sufficiently, unmolded and served.

White Fricassee of Veal

2½ pounds breast of veal cut in serving-size pieces
1 onion stuck with a clove
1 rib of celery
1 carrot
1 bay leaf
Sprig of parsley
8 peppercorns
Water
Salt and freshly ground pepper
Butter and flour blended together (about 3 tablespoons each) to make small pea-size pieces
Chopped parsley

This derived, as you will see, from the French dish blanquette de veau. A white fricassee used to be considered a great delicacy and was sometimes served as a ladies' luncheon dish. Oftentimes dumplings were cooked in the fricassee at the last, or it was served with rice or mashed potatoes.

The breast meat should not be cut in great chunks but in rather neat pieces. Combine with the vegetables and seasonings and just cover with water. Bring to a boil in a good-sized saucepan, preferably a quite heavy one. Let boil for 5 minutes. Remove any scum that forms at the surface. Add 1 tablespoon salt, reduce heat to simmer, and cover the pan. Simmer till the veal is tender. Test after about 1½ hours. Transfer the pieces of meat to a hot container and keep warm. Strain the broth through linen or muslin and taste for seasoning. Skim off any excess fat, then let it boil up quickly to reduce it a bit. Lower the heat and thicken the broth slightly with the butter and flour mixture. Place the meat in a deep platter or a bowl, spoon the sauce over it, sprinkle with chopped parsley, and surround with garnitures. Suggested garniture: 12 small onions, peeled and cooked in a small amount of water; 3 carrots cut in strips and boiled in salted water till just tender.

Fricassee with Cream. Reduce the broth by ½ and thicken as above. Add 1 cup heavy cream blended with 2 egg yolks and stir in gently but do not allow to boil. Correct the seasoning and garnish as above. This even more closely resembles the classic blanquette of France.

Ossi Buchi (Braised Veal Knuckle)

4 pieces of veal knuckle cut about 2 inches thick
6 tablespoons butter
2 tablespoons oil
1 cup white wine
Salt and freshly ground pepper
6 ripe tomatoes, peeled, seeded, and chopped
½ cup stock or broth
1 tablespoon chopped garlic
2 tablespoons chopped parsley
1 tablespoon coarsely grated lemon rind

Under its Italian name, braised veal knuckle is tremendously popular in all parts of the country. It is a rich, deliciously sauced dish that is especially satisfying with saffron rice, which invariably goes with it.

Sauté the knuckles in the butter and oil until lightly colored. Add the white wine and salt and pepper to taste, and let the wine boil up for about 5 minutes. Add the tomatoes, and let them soften in the wine and butter. Add the stock. Cover, and simmer the bones 1 to 1½ hours or until tender. Do not overcook or the meat becomes stringy and falls from the bones. Transfer the knuckles and sauce to a hot platter. Combine the garlic, parsley, and lemon rind. Sprinkle it on top of the meat. Serve with saffron rice.

Stewed Knuckle of Veal

4 good-size pieces of veal knuckle 3 to 4 inches thick
½ pound raw ham, cut in dice
1 onion, sliced
3 carrots "cut in fancy shapes"
1 bay leaf
Salt and freshly ground pepper
2 quarts water
1 cup rice

This is a mid-nineteenth-century, pre-Italian version of veal knuckle.

Combine the knuckles, ham, onion, carrots, bay leaf, and salt and pepper to taste. Add the water. Bring to a boil, cover, and simmer 1¾ hours. Add the rice and simmer till the rice is soft. Serve the meat surrounded by rice. Garnish with chopped parsley.

Blanquette de Veau

2½ to 3 pounds shoulder or breast of veal or a combination of the two
2 onions stuck with cloves
1 carrot
Bouquet garni (leek, parsley, bay leaf, sprig of thyme, all tied together)
8 to 10 peppercorns
Salt
Water
1 cup white wine
Melted butter
½ cup cream
3 egg yolks
2 tablespoons lemon juice
12 small white onions poached in broth
12 mushroom caps, blanched and poached in acidulated water
Chopped parsley
1 garlic clove, finely chopped

Combine the meat, vegetables, and seasonings, and barely cover with water. Add the white wine. Bring to a boil and continue to boil 5 minutes. Skim off any scum that collects. Cover, and simmer approximately 1½ hours or until the veal is tender but not overcooked. Transfer to a hot dish with a bit of melted butter in it, and keep warm. Strain the broth through a linen or muslin cloth and remove all fat. Reduce by ⅓ over brisk heat. Lower the heat to just below boiling and stir in the cream blended with the egg yolks. Continue to stir until it thickens slightly, making certain the mixture does not boil. Stir in the lemon juice. Add the meat. Serve in a deep dish surrounded by the onions and mushrooms and sprinkled with the blended chopped parsley and garlic. Serve with rice.

Note. An early twentieth-century recipe for blanquette of veal combined 2 cups cold roast veal cut in strips with 1½ cups rich cream sauce heated over hot water. This was served in a potato border with chopped parsley for garnish.

Brown Fricassee of Veal

2 pounds loin or shoulder of veal cut in 2-inch dice
Flour
Salt and freshly ground pepper
4 tablespoons butter

Brown fricassee of veal also used to be very popular, and it too resembles a famous French dish, Veal Marengo, which follows this recipe.

Dredge the veal well with flour, adding salt and pepper to taste. Brown well in the hot butter and oil in a heavy skillet which can be covered. When nicely brown add the onion, carrot, garlic,

3 tablespoons oil
1 onion, finely chopped
1 carrot cut in thin slices
1 clove garlic
1 cup stewed tomatoes (or use 2 tablespoons tomato paste instead)
Water or stock
1 tablespoon lemon juice
1 tablespoon Worcestershire sauce (or substitute basil or tarragon to taste)
Chopped parsley
Chopped tomato

tomatoes or tomato paste, and boiling water to barely cover the meat. Bring to a boil. Reduce the heat, cover, and simmer about 1½ hours or until the meat is tender. Add the lemon juice and Worcestershire sauce and correct the seasoning. Garnish with chopped parsley and finely chopped tomato. Serve with boiled potatoes dressed with parsley butter.

Note. Worcestershire sauce was a commonplace seasoning at the turn of the century. Nowadays many prefer to flavor the dish with some basil or tarragon instead.

Veal Marengo

3 pounds veal riblets
Flour
1 large onion, finely sliced
2 garlic cloves, finely chopped
⅓ cup olive oil
Salt and freshly ground pepper
8 ripe tomatoes, peeled, seeded, and finely chopped
1½ cups stock
4 tablespoons tomato paste
1 cup white wine
12 small onions
Butter
12 mushroom caps
Butter and oil
Lemon juice
Chopped parsley

For Marengo, use cuts from the breast that include the rather gristly sections; one buys them in the shops now as "riblets."

Dredge the riblets with flour. Sauté the onion and garlic in oil in a heavy skillet. Add the meat and brown well, adding additional oil if needed and sprinkling with salt and pepper. When the meat is browned, transfer it to a deep braising pan or heavy saucepan with a cover, and pour over it whatever remains in the skillet. Rinse out the skillet with the stock, and add the stock and scrapings to the meat pan with the tomatoes, tomato paste, and white wine. Bring to a boil. Reduce the heat, cover, and simmer for about 1½ hours or until tender.

While the meat cooks, brown the small onions in butter, cover, reduce the heat, and let them steam till just tender. Sauté the mushroom caps in butter and oil. When the meat is tender transfer it to a hot dish or skillet containing a little oil. Correct the seasoning of the sauce. Skim off any excess fat, and let the sauce cook down for a few minutes till smooth and well blended. Add a touch of lemon juice and, if desired, another freshly chopped garlic clove. Arrange the meat on a serving dish, cover with the sauce, and garnish with chopped parsley. Surround with the small onions and the mushroom caps, and serve with rice.

Veal Cutlets, Scallops, Chops

Breaded Veal Cutlets

2 good-size veal cutlets cut about ¾ inch thick
Flour
1½ to 2 cups dry breadcrumbs or rolled fresh cracker crumbs
Salt and freshly ground pepper
5 tablespoons butter
2 tablespoons oil
2 eggs, lightly beaten
Lemon slices
Chopped parsley

If any dish is thoroughly American, it is a breaded cutlet, although it resembles the Italian veal Milanese and the Viennese Wiener Schnitzel. In our terminology the cutlet is cut from the leg, preferably with the round bone in it, anywhere from ½ to an inch thick. A breaded veal cutlet can be tender and delicious. It can also be something one wouldn't believe possible as it is served in many restaurants. It has been a favorite for probably a century and no doubt will remain one.

One cutlet will serve one or two, depending on the size of the veal. This recipe should serve four people.

Put the flour on one large plate and breadcrumbs on another, or put on separate pieces of aluminum foil. Season the crumbs with salt and freshly ground pepper. Heat the butter and oil in a large heavy skillet. When the fat is bubbling hot, dip the cutlets in the flour, then into the beaten egg, and last into the seasoned crumbs. Place in the skillet, being sure the fat is hot but not boiling. Sauté the cutlets on both sides till they are nicely browned and cooked through. This will take about 10 minutes. Turn them carefully so that the breading does not tear away from the meat. Transfer to a hot platter. Garnish each cutlet with two thin lemon slices and a bit of chopped parsley. Traditionally, mashed, creamy potatoes are served with cutlets.

Veal Cutlets with Cream Sauce. Keep the cutlets hot on the platter. Pour off all but 2 tablespoons fat from the pan and add 2 tablespoons flour. Blend well with the fat and allow it to brown slightly. Stir in 1 cup heavy cream and continue stirring till thickened. Simmer for a minute or two and add freshly ground pepper and salt to taste. Serve with the cutlets.

Veal Cutlets Milanese. Before cooking the cutlets, flatten them with a heavy cleaver or meat pounder and soak in milk for an hour. After they are dipped into the flour, egg, and crumbs, cook them in clarified butter till beautifully brown on both sides. Traditionally they are served with thin lemon slices and chopped parsley.

Wiener Schnitzel. Another ancestor of our veal cutlets, this Austrian specialty has a great history and is undoubtedly the national meat dish of many Austrians. The veal is pounded to a thickness of ¼ inch or even thinner. It is then prepared as the other cutlets above, but cooked in deeper fat — either oil or a blend of oil and lard — about an inch deep. The schnitzel is cooked very quickly and served piping hot, always with salad — a cucumber salad or a tossed salad.

Veal Cordon Bleu

4 veal cutlets (one to a person) pounded about 1/4 inch thick
4 slices ham — raw ham of the prosciutto variety or boiled ham — cut to fit the veal slices
4 slices Switzerland Emmenthaler or Gruyère, about half the size of the cutlet and 1/4 inch thick
Salt and freshly ground pepper
Flour
2 eggs, beaten lightly
1 1/2 to 2 cups breadcrumbs or freshly rolled cracker crumbs
Peanut oil or corn oil
Lemon slices
Parsley

This variation on the cutlet is becoming so much a part of American cuisine that it must also be included. Originally it probably came from Vienna, but the Swiss have more or less claimed it, and it has become almost the national dish of Switzerland.

Place a slice of ham on each of the cutlets, then fold the veal and ham in half with a slice of cheese sandwiched between. Secure with small skewers or toothpicks. Salt and pepper to taste. Dredge with flour, dip in beaten egg, then in crumbs, and cook very quickly in hot oil, turning carefully. Transfer to absorbent paper to drain and serve very hot with a garnish of thin lemon slices and parsley.

Veal Cutlets Parmigiana

6 veal cutlets or scallops cut from the leg, of even size and about 3/4 inch thick
2 eggs
3/4 cup milk or light cream
1 1/2 to 2 cups freshly made crumbs
Salt and freshly ground pepper to taste
1/2 teaspoon dried basil
3 tablespoons grated Parmesan cheese
Flour
1/2 cup olive oil (approximately)
Grated Parmesan cheese
6 slices mozzarella or Monterey jack cheese

This Italian dish was created here in this country for the American public and is served now not only in Italian restaurants but everywhere. More often than not it is badly prepared, but it is delicious when carefully executed.

Beat the eggs and milk or cream together lightly. Mix the breadcrumbs with salt and pepper, and the basil and cheese. Dip the cutlets in flour, then in the beaten egg and milk, and finally in the crumb mixture. Place them between sheets of wax paper and refrigerate while you prepare the tomato sauce. Blanch and peel the garlic and combine with the tomato purée, tomato paste, and seasonings. Bring to a boil and simmer 10 minutes. Correct the seasoning and add a small amount of sugar if the sauce is too acid. Remove the cutlets from the refrigerator. Heat enough oil in a heavy 12 or 14 inch skillet to cover the bottom to a depth of 1/4 inch. Cook the cutlets quickly, being careful not to burn the breading. When nicely browned on one side, turn carefully with the aid of a spatula and brown the other side. Salt and pepper the cutlets during cooking. Spread a layer of tomato sauce in an ovenproof serving dish and arrange the cutlets on the sauce. Spoon additional sauce over the cutlets. Place a large thin slice of mozzarella or jack cheese atop each cutlet and sprinkle well with Parmesan. Place in a 400-degree oven to melt the cheese and heat the cutlets and sauce. Serve at once along with buttered green noodles, sprinkled with grated cheese, and a crisp green salad.

SAUCE

6 to 8 cloves garlic, blanched in boiling water 5 minutes
2 cups tomato purée or sauce
6-ounce can tomato paste
1½ teaspoons basil
1 teaspoon salt
½ teaspoon freshly ground pepper
Sugar, if needed

Minced Veal with Cream

1 pound boneless veal cutlets, cut in thin strips about 1 inch wide and 2 inches long
Flour
6 tablespoons butter, melted
Salt and freshly ground pepper
½ cup dry white wine
½ bay leaf
1 cup sour cream

This treatment of veal probably derives from Swiss cookery.

Roll the veal strips in flour and sauté in a skillet in the butter over rather high heat. This will only take a minute or so. Salt and pepper the meat and transfer to a hot platter. Add the wine, bay leaf, and sour cream to the pan and stir over low heat to blend thoroughly with the pan juices. Do not let the cream boil or it will curdle. Return the veal to the sauce and reheat for a minute. Serve with rice and a baked casserole of tomatoes and eggplant.

Veal Birds (Alouettes sans Têtes, Rollatine, Rouladen)

Every country seems to have a version of the bird. The French call theirs alouettes sans têtes; the Italians, rollatine or rola; the Middle Europeans, rouladen; and we have birds, mock birds, veal birds, and so on. Most all of them are cutlets pounded rather thin, rolled with a stuffing, browned, and braised.

Use veal cutlets about 3 × 5 inches and approximately ¼ inch thick. Pound with meat pounder if necessary. Spread each bird with a filling (see recipes below or make up your own). Roll and tie with twine or secure with skewers or toothpicks. Brown in oil and butter, add liquid — wine, stock, or water — and braise. Make a sauce or serve with the pan juices.

Miss Jessie Duncan's Mock Birds

8 slices veal cutlet pounded thin
4 tablespoons butter
3 tablespoons oil
Flour
1 cup stock or hot water
Chopped parsley
1 cup sour cream

This recipe comes from a benefit cookbook published in the West circa 1910. It makes approximately 4 servings.

Blend all the ingredients for the stuffing. Spread a little on each piece of veal. Roll and secure with toothpicks or with string. Heat the butter and oil in a heavy skillet. Flour the birds, and brown them in the hot fat, turning to color evenly on all sides. Add the stock or hot water and simmer, covered, for about 25 minutes or until the birds are just tender. Transfer them to a hot platter and remove the skewers or strings. Sprinkle with the parsley. Bring the sauce to a

STUFFING
1/4 cup finely chopped ham
2 tablespoons chopped onion
1 tablespoon or more softened butter
3 tablespoons chopped parsley
Salt and pepper

boil, correct the seasoning, and cook down a few minutes. Stir in the sour cream and just heat through. Do not let it boil. Pour over the veal and serve at once with new potatoes.

Boston Cooking School Veal Birds

8 pieces of veal 4×6 inches
Trimmings from the veal
2 or 3 thick slices bacon
1 cup crumbs
1 tablespoon finely chopped onion
1/4 teaspoon Tabasco
1 teaspoon salt
1 teaspoon freshly ground pepper
1 tablespoon lemon juice
1 egg, lightly beaten
Flour
6 tablespoons butter
1 cup cream
Pieces of trimmed toast

Grind the bacon and veal trimmings. Combine with the crumbs, onion, and seasonings, and moisten with beaten egg. Spoon a small amount of the stuffing on each piece of veal. Roll and tie or secure with skewers. Flour the veal birds. Heat the butter in a skillet and brown the birds on all sides. Add the cream and turn each bird to coat it. Cover the skillet and simmer for 20 minutes. Correct the seasoning. Serve the birds on small sections of crisp toast with the sauce spooned over.

California Veal Birds

6 veal slices 4×6 inches, cut from the leg and pounded
1 onion, finely chopped
1 garlic clove, finely chopped
11 tablespoons olive oil
1/2 cup finely chopped ripe olives
12 anchovy fillets, finely chopped
3/4 cup breadcrumbs
Salt and freshly ground pepper
1 teaspoon basil
1/2 cup red wine
Chopped parsley

Sauté the onion and garlic in 5 tablespoons olive oil. Add the olives, anchovies, crumbs, and seasonings, and blend thoroughly. Correct the seasoning. Place a small amount of the filling on each piece of veal. Roll and tie or secure with skewers. Heat the rest of the oil and brown the birds, turning often to give an evenness of color. Reduce the heat. Add the red wine, cover, and simmer the birds for about 30 to 35 minutes or until just tender. Transfer to a platter of buttered noodles. If the sauce has cooked down too much you may need to add another 1/2 cup wine to the pan. Allow the sauce to cook for several minutes, then pour over the birds and sprinkle with chopped parsley.

Thoroughly Western Veal Birds

8 pieces of veal cutlet 4×6 inches
1 onion, finely chopped
3 tablespoons butter
½ cup finely ground ham
1 garlic clove, finely chopped
1 teaspoon dillweed or 8 thin slices dill pickle
1 cup breadcrumbs, freshly made
1 egg
Salt and freshly ground pepper
5 tablespoons butter
3 tablespoons oil
1 cup broth
½ cup cream
Additional dillweed
Flour and butter for thickening
Chopped parsley

Pound the pieces of veal to make them very thin and supple. Sauté the onion in butter and stir in the ham, garlic, dillweed, crumbs, and egg. Season well with salt and pepper. Stuff the birds and roll (if you use the dill pickle, place one slice under the stuffing in each bird before you roll it). Secure with string or with skewers. Brown the birds on all sides in the butter and oil. When nicely browned add the broth and cover. Simmer 30 to 35 minutes or until the birds are thoroughly tender — do not overcook them. Transfer them to a hot platter. Add the cream and a little more dill to the pan juices. Thicken, if needed, with butter and flour kneaded together and stirred into the sauce over low heat. Spoon the sauce over the birds and add the chopped parsley. Serve with rice and a purée of spinach mixed with butter, a little onion, and nutmeg.

Veal Rolls

Here are two interesting variations of the veal roll — one Italian and the other Lithuanian — which have come into being in this country, more or less faithful adaptations of the original recipes.

Veal Roulade Lithuanian

3 veal cutlets or steaks cut across the leg about ¾ inch thick, with bone removed, and pounded to approximately 14–16 inches long and 6–8 inches wide
½ pound ground veal
¼ pound bacon, diced
2 hard-boiled eggs, chopped
1 large onion, finely chopped
1 stalk celery, finely chopped
1 cup breadcrumbs
2 teaspoons salt
½ teaspoon freshly ground pepper
¼ teaspoon nutmeg
5 or 6 large knockwurst

Arrange the veal cutlets on a board so they overlap slightly. Pound overlapping edges lightly to join the pieces. Do not mind if there are occasional holes in the veal. Blend together the ground veal, bacon, chopped hard-boiled eggs, onion, celery, breadcrumbs, salt, pepper, and nutmeg. Spread this filling on the cutlets. Arrange the knockwurst and hard-boiled eggs on the filling. Roll the veal carefully, and secure with skewers or tie with string. Place on a rack in a baking pan and cover with bacon strips. Add the white wine to the pan. Place in a preheated 350-degree oven and bake, covered with a sheet of foil for the first 30 minutes, for 1 hour and 15 minutes. Baste with the white wine pan juices from time to time. Transfer the veal to a hot platter. Cook the pan juices until reduced by half, correct the seasoning, add chopped parsley, and serve with the veal. Garnish the veal with chopped parsley.

Note. This roulade may also be sewn into a cloth, tied securely, and poached in veal broth seasoned with 2 bay leaves, 1 onion

About 6 more hard-boiled eggs
8 or 9 slices of bacon
2 cups white wine
Additional salt and pepper if needed
Chopped parsley

stuck with 2 cloves, 1 garlic clove, and salt and pepper. Poach 20 minutes per pound, or about 2 hours. Transfer to a cool place, weight on all sides, and let cool. Serve with a mayonnaise or an herbed dressing.

Veal Roll Sicilian

3 veal cutlets or steaks cut across the leg ¾ inch thick, with bone removed, and pounded to approximately 14–16 inches long and 6–8 inches wide
½ pound prosciutto, sliced very thin
¼ pound mortadella or large bologna, sliced
¼ pound salami
Freshly ground pepper
Chopped parsley
3 garlic cloves, finely chopped
1 teaspoon basil or 2 tablespoons fresh basil
Omelet made with 3 or 4 eggs, chopped parsley and chives, and rolled
8 strips bacon
2 cups tomato purée
1 teaspoon basil

This has found great popularity in the Eastern United States during the last twenty years. It can be served either hot or cold.

Spread out the veal cutlets to overlap slightly and pound them if they are too thick in places. Lay the prosciutto across one end of the cutlets and follow with the mortadella and the salami. Add freshly ground pepper. (The salt content of the cured meats is generally sufficient to season the dish.) Sprinkle with chopped parsley, garlic, and basil.

Make the omelet — do not overcook — and roll it right onto the middle of the veal. Roll the veal and filling and secure with skewers or tie. Place in a baking dish and strip with the bacon. Surround with the tomato purée seasoned with basil, and bake at 350 degrees for 1 hour and 10 minutes. Transfer to a hot platter if serving hot, or allow it to cool in the dish if serving cold. Serve with polenta.

Veal Scallops

Scallops are cut from the leg and are specially sliced from a certain section of the muscle. They should be pounded to almost filmy thinness. When they are cooked with plenty of butter and with the proper additives, they are as delicate and as unique a meat dish as one could want. They should be eaten hot; holding makes them dry and unpalatable. Scallops were, of course, made popular by the Italian immigrants who started restaurants all across the country in the early part of the century. Today, wherever you find good veal, you are sure to find scallops.

Scallops are best when they are dipped lightly into seasoned flour and cooked quickly in butter. Since our butter has more milk left in it than most European butter, it is best to add a little oil to the pan as well or to use clarified butter. Estimate 3 scallops, properly cut and pounded, per person.

Veal Scallops with Lemon

12 veal scallops
1/3 cup flour seasoned with 1 teaspoon freshly ground pepper and 1 teaspoon salt
6 tablespoons butter
2 or 3 tablespoons oil
2 or 3 tablespoons broth
Lemon juice
Sliced lemon
Chopped parsley

Dip the scallops in the seasoned flour — add 1/2 teaspoon basil or oregano, if you like, but I prefer merely salt and pepper for this particular dish. Melt the butter in a heavy skillet and add the oil. When the fat is hot and bubbling, brown the floured scallops quickly on both sides. Add the broth to the pan, and give each scallop a good squeeze of lemon juice. Reduce the heat and let them cook about 5 or 6 minutes in all, turning once more on each side. Transfer to hot plates. Place a slice of lemon on each plate, and sprinkle the scallops with chopped parsley.

Veal Scallops with Marsala

This is by all odds the most common way of serving scallops. Dip them in seasoned flour and brown them in the fat as above. Then add about 1/3 cup Marsala and let it bubble up. Turn the scallops and reduce the heat. Add about 3 tablespoons veal or chicken broth and let the dish cook slowly for about 3 minutes or until the alcohol has cooked away and the sauce is well cooked down. Transfer to hot plates, and serve with sautéed mushrooms.

Saltimbocca

12 thin veal scallops
12 thin pieces of ham the same size as the veal
12 sage leaves
6 to 8 tablespoons butter
Salt and pepper
1/4 cup Marsala
2 or 3 tablespoons broth

This delicious Roman treatment of veal scallops has also developed a great public here.

Place a slice of ham on each slice of veal and top this with a sage leaf. (Sometimes a leaf with a bit of stem is used and stuck through the two pieces of meat.) Secure the meats with a toothpick or tiny skewer. Melt the butter in a heavy skillet, and when bubbling add the veal and cook slowly, turning carefully till nicely colored on each side. Add the Marsala and broth and cook gently over low heat till the meat is tender.

An Early American Way of Doing Scallops

Evidently this was inspired by a trip to Europe. It combines two dishes. Veal scallops were prepared with seasoned flour and browned in butter as above. They were served on a platter surrounded by a ring of macaroni. Breadcrumbs and grated Parmesan cheese — 4 tablespoons of each — were blended in the pan in which the scallops were cooked and spooned over the macaroni and scallops. Melted butter was poured over the macaroni, and it was sprinkled with more cheese and sent to the table at once.

Paillard of Veal

Paillard of veal has become a very fashionable luncheon dish in New York and is spreading through the country. It is excellent in flavor and is filling and attractive as well, but its chief appeal lies in the fact that it is low in calories. If you are not counting calories, it is more delicious served with a little butter.

A paillard is a very thin slice from the leg, pounded even thinner to about 6 inches square. Brush with oil or butter, and broil very quickly under high heat, turning once. It is brown only where it touches the gridiron. Serve at once with lemon and watercress.

Veal Chops

Veal chops, loin or rib, are not commonly used in this country. For one thing they are rather uninteresting when broiled, and in the United States chops mean broiling. They require long cooking, and even then are not usually particularly tender or distinctive. Sautéed, they need plenty of added flavor to make them as good as they should be. Only the French have been successful with veal chops, although the Italians, too, have proved that when the chops are pounded thin and served well cooked, they can be quite delicious.

Broiled Veal Chops with Herbs

Have loin chops cut about ¾ to 1 inch thick. Oil them well and rub with tarragon and a little chopped onion. Broil slowly about 6 inches from the source of heat and brush frequently with tarragon-flavored butter. The chops should take about 20 minutes. Add salt and freshly ground pepper. Serve with crisp sautéed potatoes and a good salad.

Italian Veal Chops

4 to 6 rib veal chops cut ½ inch thick
2 eggs
1 cup breadcrumbs
1 cup flour
6 tablespoons butter
4 tablespoons oil
Salt and freshly ground pepper
Lemon slices

Pound the chops very thin, leaving the bone in. Beat the eggs quite lightly. Put the breadcrumbs on a plate or square of foil, the flour on a second one. Heat the butter and oil in a heavy skillet. Dip the chops in the flour, then in the beaten egg, and finally in the crumbs. Cook in the hot fat very quickly, browning well on each side. Season with the salt and pepper. Serve at once on hot plates with a thin slice of lemon on each one.

Note. A variation of this has come into favor. The chops are cooked as above and presented with lemon, about 3 anchovy fillets per serving, and a few capers. This version looks appetizing and tastes extremely good.

Russian or Polish Veal Chops (Ciliece)

Prepare 6 chops as above: Pound, and dip in flour, beaten egg, and breadcrumbs. Cook in a heavy skillet in 6 tablespoons butter and 4 tablespoons oil. When they are beautifully browned, add 1 cup heavy cream to the pan, cover, and simmer them about 15 minutes. Season to taste with salt, freshly ground pepper, and sweet paprika (about 1 teaspoon). These are delicious served over rice or noodles.

Russian Veal Chops (Pojarsky)

6 veal chops with meat removed from bone and chopped very fine or ground
1 teaspoon salt
¼ cup melted butter
1 tablespoon chopped parsley
1 tablespoon flour
¼ cup heavy cream or more, depending upon how much the meat will absorb
5 tablespoons butter
3 tablespoons oil
Salt and freshly ground pepper
Chopped parsley

Combine the chopped meat with the salt, melted butter, parsley, and flour. Add enough cream to make a workable mixture and form into round flat cakes, or shape into cutlets. Flour them lightly. Melt the butter and heat with the oil in a heavy skillet. When bubbling hot, add the meat patties and sauté rather slowly, turning once during the cooking process. They should be just cooked through and rather crusty on the outside but still juicy inside. Season to taste. Serve on a hot platter with a garnish of chopped parsley. Delicious served with creamed fresh mushrooms.

Sautéed Veal Chops in the French Manner

6 thickish veal loin chops
Flour
6 tablespoons butter
3 tablespoons oil
1 large onion, finely chopped
2 cloves garlic, finely chopped
2 ripe tomatoes, peeled, seeded, and chopped
½ cup white wine
1 teaspoon rosemary, crushed
¼ cup chopped parsley
½ cup soft black olives
12 mushroom caps sautéed in butter
Freshly ground pepper
Salt, if needed

You will find chops done this way in many of the small French restaurants in New York, New Orleans, and San Francisco. It is a delicious and a different approach to the dish.

Dredge the chops with flour. Heat the butter and oil until bubbling, then brown the chops quickly on both sides. Transfer them to a hot plate. Add the onion and garlic, and sauté till nicely colored. Add the tomatoes and cook down 5 minutes. Add the chops, wine, and rosemary. Cover and simmer 25 to 30 minutes or until the chops are tender. Do not overcook; they must be still slightly firm, not mushy. Add the parsley and black olives and correct the seasoning, adding pepper, and salt if needed. Transfer to a hot platter and surround with saffron rice. Spoon the sauce over all and garnish with the mushrooms and additional chopped parsley.

Veal Loaves

When I was young, the ladies loved to show off with a veal loaf when entertaining at a whist luncheon or a bridge drive, either serving it hot in delicate slices with vegetables or cold with dainty salads. Today, alas, the standard meat loaf has so displaced the veal loaf that one seldom encounters it. But a number of pleasant recipes for it still survive in old cookbooks.

Miss von Destinon's Veal Loaf

2 pounds cold veal, chopped fine
1 pound cold ham, chopped fine
1 teaspoon grated lemon peel
½ teaspoon powdered mace
1 tablespoon chopped parsley, and more for garnish
1 cup grated breadcrumbs, dry and fine
1 cup brown gravy
Cayenne
Lemon juice
Salt and pepper
Yolks of 3 eggs
1 egg for glazing

This recipe comes from a benefit cookbook issued in Portland, Oregon, in 1913. Miss von Destinon, who was a fine cook, called it by its generic name, "pain de veau."

Mix all the ingredients, except half of the gravy and the egg for glazing, adding the yolks of eggs last. The mixture should be just firm enough to hold shape when molded into a loaf. If it is too soft, add more breadcrumbs. Flour your hands and mold the mixture into a loaf rather more than twice its breadth in length. (If longer it will crack in serving.) Flour the outside well and place it in a greased pan large enough to permit you to remove the loaf after cooking without danger of disfiguring it. Cover the loaf and place it in a 375-degree oven for about 25 minutes. Remove the cover and allow it to brown quickly. Remove from the oven and brush with beaten egg. Reduce the heat to 325 degrees. Return the loaf to the oven, and cook till it is firm and deliciously brown, 45 to 60 minutes. Transfer the loaf to a hot serving dish. Handle it very carefully. Serve with the pan gravy or with a mushroom sauce or tomato sauce. Miss von Destinon adds that it is delicious served with a salad.

Mrs. Rorer's Veal Loaf

3½ pounds ground veal
½ pound ground ham
1 cup dry breadcrumbs
1 teaspoon salt (it will take 2 teaspoons)
1 teaspoon onion juice (I find 3 teaspoons better)
½ teaspoon sage
⅛ teaspoon cloves
⅛ teaspoon allspice
2 eggs, beaten
Melted butter

Mrs. Rorer's loaf of the '80's resembles a mild pâté, for it is made with a good deal of seasoning.

Mix all the ingredients except the butter well; add the beaten eggs last and reserve a little for the outside. Press the mixture into a mold, and then unmold on a baking pan which has been well buttered. Brush the loaf with beaten egg and bake at 300 degrees 1½ to 2 hours. Baste occasionally with a mixture of melted butter and water. Serve cold cut in slices. I would suggest serving it with a sauce rémoulade or a chili sauce and a good salad.

Jellied Veal Loaf

1 knuckle of veal
2 pounds neck of veal
1 onion stuck with 2 cloves
1 rib celery
1 small carrot
1 clove garlic
1 teaspoon thyme or tarragon
1 sprig parsley
1 tablespoon Worcestershire sauce
Dash of Tabasco
Water
Salt and freshly ground pepper
8 hard-boiled eggs, halved or sliced
Fresh tarragon, watercress, or parsley for garnish

Here is another form of loaf that was exceedingly popular in summer fifty or sixty years ago. It was ideal picnic food, if one could keep it cool, and was also superb for cold luncheons on the terrace. Many a cook made lovely patterns in the jelly.

Combine the veal, vegetables, and seasonings, and cover with water. Bring to a boil and skim off any scum that rises. Cover, reduce the heat, and simmer about 3 hours. Remove the meat and cool. When cool, remove the fat and gristle and chop the veal coarsely. Strain the liquid, and if you want it very clear, strain it through several layers of cheesecloth or through a linen napkin. Return the broth to a clean pan and cook without a cover until it is reduced about one-third. Cut the meat from the bones and remove all fat. When the broth is reduced, pour a thin layer in the bottom of a square, round, or oblong dish or a loaf pan. Chill this layer in the refrigerator until almost firm. Arrange half the sliced eggs in the bottom of the dish or pan, garnish with leaves of tarragon or tiny sprigs of parsley, and gently spoon enough of the partially jellied broth over the eggs to more than cover. Chill until firm. Add the chopped veal and more sliced eggs, and cover well with the broth. (Heat a little if it has chilled until firm; it should be slightly thinner than egg white.) Chill the mold or pan overnight until very firm. Scrape off any excess fat. Unmold on a platter and garnish with tarragon, watercress, parsley, or other small salad greens. Serve in thin slices.

Lemon Veal Loaf

3 pounds veal, ground fairly fine
1/2 pound fat pork, finely ground
2/3 cup chopped onion
1 teaspoon grated lemon peel
3 eggs, lightly beaten
1 cup well-seasoned tomato sauce
Salt and freshly ground pepper
Tabasco
1 cup (approximately) dry breadcrumbs
6 slices bacon
2 lemons, peeled and thinly sliced
Additional breadcrumbs
Melted butter

An unusual form of veal loaf, this old Southern recipe is interesting enough and delicious enough to repeat here.

Combine the meat, onion, lemon peel, eggs, tomato sauce, seasonings, and enough breadcrumbs to make a firm mixture. Form into a loaf and place on the strips of bacon in a shallow baking dish or pan. Sprinkle with additional breadcrumbs. Cover with thin slices of lemon and bake at 350 degrees 1 hour. Remove the lemon slices. Baste with melted butter and return to the oven for about 15 minutes to brown lightly. Serve either hot or cold.

Veal Loaf with Boiled Eggs

2 pounds chopped veal
1 medium onion, finely chopped
½ teaspoon freshly ground pepper
1 teaspoon salt
½ cup breadcrumbs
1 teaspoon tarragon
½ cup stock or bouillon
1 egg
⅓ cup melted butter
2 or 3 hard-boiled eggs
Butter for top of loaf

Mild, pleasantly different, and typical of cooking during the early years of this century.

Mix all the ingredients together except the last two. Butter a loaf pan and put in a layer of the veal mixture. Press the eggs into the meat and cover with the remaining veal. Dot the top with butter and bake in a 350-degree oven approximately 1 hour. Weight it down slightly while it cools. Remove from the pan when cooled and serve cold with a good salad.

Dijon Pâté

3 cups or more cooked rice
2 raw eggs
⅓ cup heavy cream
4 hard-boiled eggs
2½ cups minced cooked veal
½ cup gravy or melted butter
1 small onion, finely chopped
2 tablespoons chopped parsley
1 teaspoon freshly ground pepper
Salt

This unorthodox version of a veal loaf, circa 1878, is from Mrs. Harland.

Mix 1 cup of the rice with the 2 uncooked eggs and the cream. Press into the bottom and sides of a 2-quart pudding mold. Add the sliced hard-boiled eggs. Mix the veal with the gravy or butter, onion, parsley, pepper, and salt if needed. Add to the mold and cover with the remaining rice. Place the lid on the mold and steam in boiling water 1 hour. Remove and unmold on a hot platter. Decorate with watercress, and serve with a tomato sauce.

Veal Offal

Calf's Liver

In the United States and in a number of European countries, this is the most expensive of all meats. It is considered to be a delicacy by many, and is equally shunned. In the last few years it has become a sought-after food in certain diets and thus is always in great demand. In many large cities kosher liver is considered the finest, for it is consistently the freshest.

To be at its best, liver should be cut either very thin or quite thick, in which case it is known as liver steak. It should be served on the pink side or, in the case of the steaks, quite rare. Once it is overcooked it loses its delightful texture and becomes grainy and disagreeable.

Sautéed Calf's Liver with Bacon

Have the liver cut about 1/4 inch thick. Flour lightly and brown quickly on both sides in butter and oil. Salt and pepper, and serve on a hot platter with strips of bacon and boiled new potatoes.

Sautéed Calf's Liver with Onion. Sauté thin slices of calf's liver as above, and serve on a hot platter with a covering of sautéed onions.

Sautéed Calf's Liver with Herbs and Madeira

4 slices calf's liver
Flour
2 tablespoons butter
2 tablespoons oil
4 or 5 shallots, finely chopped
Salt and freshly ground pepper
1/4 cup Madeira
1/4 cup chopped parsley

Dredge the liver in flour. Heat the butter and oil in a heavy skillet. Add the shallots and sauté gently for 2 minutes. Increase the heat, add the liver, and cook quickly on both sides. Salt and pepper, and add the Madeira and parsley. Shake the pan and turn the liver once. Transfer to a hot platter and pour the pan mixture over.

Broiled Liver Steak, Sauce Béarnaise

Have the liver steaks cut about 1 to 1 1/2 inches thick (although a 2-inch steak is also delicious). Brush with butter or oil and broil about 4 inches from the heat unit, brushing with butter from time to time. A 1 to 1 1/2-inch steak will take about 7 to 8 minutes for rare and a 2-inch steak about 8 to 10 minutes. Salt and pepper the steaks and serve on a hot platter with Béarnaise sauce and boiled potatoes.

Larded and Braised Whole Calf's Liver

1 whole calf's liver
Salt pork or larding pork
4 tablespoons butter
3 tablespoons oil
1 medium onion, thinly sliced
Approximately 1/3 cup sherry or Madeira
Salt and freshly ground pepper
Chopped parsley

Buy an entire liver. Cut about 6 to 8 lardoons of the pork. Lard the liver with the lardoons, using a larding needle. Sear the larded liver quickly in butter and oil in a heavy skillet. Add the onion and place in a 325-degree oven for about 35 minutes. After 5 minutes add the sherry or Madeira. After 10 minutes turn the liver and add a bit more butter if needed; after another 10 minutes turn again, and add more wine if needed. Continue roasting for another 10 minutes or until done to your taste. When the liver is done, transfer to a hot platter and pour the pan juice over all. Garnish with chopped parsley and watercress, and serve with potatoes Anna.

Baked Whole Liver

1 or 2 calf's livers, about 4 to 5 pounds, rolled and tied (if using 2, roll together)
1½ pounds bacon
Freshly ground pepper
Chopped parsley and garlic

An expensive but spectacular dish for 6 to 8 persons.

Arrange the liver on a rack in a roasting pan and cover completely with strips of bacon. Roast at 375 degrees, allowing about 15 minutes per pound of liver. The bacon will take care of basting. Transfer the liver to a hot platter. You may remove the bacon strips, or if you want to serve them, arrange on the platter around the liver. Pepper the liver and sprinkle with the chopped parsley and garlic mixture before sending to table. Serve in medium thick slices with a Béarnaise sauce, boiled parsley potatoes, and a purée of peas. This also deserves a fine red Burgundy — a Chambertin or a Corton.

Liver on Skewers

Strips of calf's liver about 2×3×1 inches are best for this dish. Thread the liver on skewers with strips of bacon. Start with the bacon and wrap it under a piece of liver, then over a piece of liver, and so on, so that bacon separates each piece of liver from the next. Brush the skewers well with olive oil and broil over charcoal or in a broiling unit about 4 inches from the heat. Turn often, brush with oil, and season with salt and freshly ground pepper. Serve with wedges of lemon and sautéed onions.

Liver and Veal Loaf, to Be Eaten Cold

1 pound bacon
1 pound veal scallops cut thin and pounded
½ cup finely chopped onion
½ cup chopped parsley
1½ teaspoons thyme
1 pound thinly cut calf's liver
Salt and freshly ground pepper
¼ teaspoon Tabasco
1 bay leaf
1 cup white wine

Line a 9-inch loaf pan with the bacon strips so that they extend over the edge. Make a layer of veal scallops and sprinkle with chopped onion and parsley and a dusting of thyme. Add a layer of liver, salt and pepper it, and continue alternating meats and seasoning till all is used. It is best to finish with a layer of veal. Add the Tabasco. Place a bay leaf on top, and add wine to come almost to the top of the loaf. Cover with bacon and then with foil. Bake at 350 degrees 1½ hours. Remove from the oven, and after it has cooled for a half hour, place another piece of foil on top of the loaf and weight down to cool completely. Chill in the refrigerator 12 hours or more before slicing down thinly and serving. Serve as an hors d'oeuvre or as cold meat with salad.

Sweetbreads

Sweetbreads, which are part of the thymus gland of the calf or sheep, are delicate morsels and deserve kind and tender treatment to be at their best. They come in pairs and are surrounded with bits of tissue and tubes that have to be removed before cooking. Nowadays there is discussion as to whether sweetbreads are made more delicate by being blanched before cooking. I have tried cooking them blanched and unblanched, and although there is no great difference, I tend to agree blanching does make a more delicate finished dish.

Soak the sweetbreads in cold water about 1 hour. Then simmer them 15 minutes in 1 quart water to which ½ teaspoon salt and the juice of half a lemon have been added. This is ample blanching time for a pair of sweetbreads. Plunge into ice water. Let them stand till cooled, adding more ice if necessary. Trim them of all tubes, heavy bits of membrane, and any discolored portions. Some people then weight them down under a plate for an hour so that they yield more uniform slices when cut. One pair serves two to four persons.

Since sweetbreads are among the more delicate of foods, they require subtle treatment. Many old recipes called for piquing or larding them, a process which in the days of haute cuisine made an enchanting-looking dish but is quite unnecessary today. Probably the oldest way of doing sweetbreads was creaming them. This version is a typical one from around the turn of the century, when cream sauces were much used in our cookery.

Sweetbreads à la Crème

1 pair sweetbreads
½ pound mushrooms, finely chopped
5 tablespoons butter
Salt and freshly ground pepper
1½ cups rich cream sauce
Patty shells or toast cases

Blanch and trim the sweetbreads and cut into small dice. Sauté the mushrooms and sweetbreads in butter for 4 to 5 minutes and combine with the rich cream sauce. Heat through and correct the seasoning. Spoon into hot patty shells or bread cases and garnish with a tiny sprig of parsley.

Mrs. Rorer's Sweetbreads à la Béchamel

3 tablespoons butter
2 tablespoons flour
⅔ cup chicken broth or veal broth
Salt and freshly ground pepper
1 pair sweetbreads blanched and cut in ¾-inch dice
8 mushroom caps, finely chopped
2 tablespoons sherry
⅔ cup cream
2 egg yolks

Blend the butter and flour in a heavy saucepan. Stir in the broth and continue to stir until it thickens. Correct the seasoning and add the sweetbreads, mushrooms, and sherry. Heat through over low heat. Blend the cream and egg yolks. Into this stir a spoonful of the sauce. Then carefully stir back into the mushroom-sweetbread mixture. Stir till it thickens, but do not allow it to boil.

Sweetbreads Country Style

3 pairs sweetbreads, blanched, trimmed, and weighted
Salt and freshly ground pepper
¼ pound (½ cup) butter
6 slices bacon

A very popular dish, rather delicious in its way. Some will think the bacon is too strong an additive, but it does give an agreeable flavor.

Butter a baking dish well and arrange the sweetbreads in it. Salt and pepper to taste. Pour two or three spoonfuls of melted butter over each pair of sweetbreads and top each one with a slice of well-cured bacon. Bake at 375 degrees for approximately 20 minutes, basting twice.

Sweetbreads sous Cloche

6 rounds of bread 3½ to 4 inches in diameter, toasted and buttered
6 rounds of ham (Smithfield by preference)
6 pieces of sweetbread cut to fit the toast rounds as well as possible
6 tablespoons butter
Salt and freshly ground pepper
Paprika
6 tablespoons heavy cream
6 mushroom caps sautéed in butter
Chopped parsley

For many years, during the 1880's and up to the early 1900's, serving *sous cloche* was extremely fancy and fashionable.

You will need 6 ramekins or baking dishes with glass bells to fit. Butter the dishes and place a piece of the buttered toast on each one. Top with a piece of ham. Sauté the sweetbreads in butter in a heavy skillet and season with salt, pepper, and paprika. Add the cream and let it cook down with the butter. Place the sweetbread on the ham and spoon the sauce over. Top with a large beautiful mushroom cap sautéed in butter, and sprinkle some chopped parsley. Cover with the glass bells and place in a 350-degree oven for about 10 minutes.

Note. This was sometimes enhanced with ¼ cup sherry or Madeira, added before the cream.

Broiled Sweetbreads I

Parboil and trim sweetbreads. Dip each one into heavy cream, then into beaten egg and finally roll in crumbs. Broil slowly about 5 inches from the broiling unit until the crumbs brown, then turn to brown on the other side. Serve with lemon wedges or Hollandaise sauce.

Broiled Sweetbreads II

Combine equal parts grated Parmesan cheese and fresh crumbs. Dip parboiled and trimmed sweetbreads in melted butter then into the cheese-crumb mixture. Broil as above. Season with salt and freshly ground pepper.

Broiled Sweetbreads III

Combine about 1½ cups freshly made crumbs with 1 tablespoon freshly chopped parsley, 1 tablespoon chives, and 1 tablespoon chopped fresh tarragon or 2 teaspoons dried tarragon. Dip parboiled and trimmed sweetbreads in butter and then into herbed crumbs. Broil carefully about 5 inches from the broiling unit. Turn once, and season with salt and freshly ground pepper.

Smothered Sweetbreads

2 pair sweetbreads, parboiled and trimmed
½ pound butter (1 cup)
Salt and freshly ground pepper
Toast
Lemon wedges
Chopped parsley

This is the simplest form I know of preparing sweetbreads, and I'm not sure it is not the best.

Melt the butter in a rather heavy skillet or a large saucepan with a cover. Dip each parboiled sweetbread in the butter and turn to coat both sides. Cover and simmer about 15 to 20 minutes. Add salt and pepper to taste. Serve on crisp pieces of toast with lemon wedges. Garnish with chopped parsley.

Kidneys, Sweetbreads, and Sausages

1 pair sweetbreads
3 veal kidneys
1 pound small pork sausages
6 shallots (green onions), finely chopped
6 tablespoons butter
4 tablespoons oil
Salt and freshly ground pepper
½ teaspoon tarragon
¼ cup Cognac
¼ cup Madeira
1½ cups broth
Beurre manié (mixed flour and butter)
Chopped parsley
Patty shells, warmed
Mushroom caps, fresh

This is often served as a brunch dish.

Blanch the sweetbreads, trim well, and cut into small pieces. Trim the kidneys and cut in thin slices. Cut the sausages in small sections and blanch 3 minutes in boiling water. Pour off the water and brown the sausages just until cooked through. Sauté the shallots in half the butter and oil until translucent — about 3 minutes. Add the sweetbreads and sauté 4 to 5 minutes, shaking the pan from time to time to cook the pieces evenly. Season to taste with salt, pepper, and tarragon. Sauté the kidneys very lightly in the rest of the butter and oil. Season well with salt and pepper, flame with the Cognac. Combine the Madeira and broth in a medium-size saucepan. Simmer until reduced to one-third. Thicken with beurre manié made by working flour into butter with fingertips. Combine with sweetbreads, kidneys, and sausages. Correct the seasoning, heat to boiling point, and sprinkle with chopped parsley. Serve in heated patty shells. Garnish with sautéed mushroom caps. Serve immediately.

Sweetbreads, Oysters, and Veal in Pastry

Rich pastry for a 9-inch pie
1 pair sweetbreads, blanched and cut in 1-inch dice
1½ cups diced cooked veal or ham
18 oysters
¾ cup finely chopped mushrooms sautéed in 4 tablespoons butter
1½ cups rich cream sauce
¼ cup Madeira or sherry

This early nineteenth-century recipe still has merit today as a thoroughly delicious "made dish" for luncheon or supper.

Combine the meats, oysters, and mushrooms, and stir in the cream sauce. Add the Madeira or sherry and the chopped parsley. Correct the seasoning. Place the mixture in a 2-quart baking dish or casserole and allow it to cool thoroughly. Roll out the pastry about ⅜ inch thick. Cut a strip about 1½ inches wide and fit it around the outer edge of the casserole so that it will overlap the top edge slightly. Brush with water, arrange the pastry top over the casserole, and pinch the two edges of pastry together to seal and to make a pleasant pattern. Cut a hole in the top and fit with a small cornucopia of

3 tablespoons chopped parsley
Salt and freshly ground pepper
1 egg beaten with 3 tablespoons cream

pastry to allow the steam to escape. If you have pastry left over, cut out small leaves or flowers, moisten with water, and attach to the top crust. Brush the pastry with the cream and egg mixture and bake at 375 degrees about 25 to 30 minutes or until the pastry is beautifully browned. Serve hot.

Sautéed Sweetbreads

2 pairs sweetbreads, blanched and trimmed
Flour
2 eggs, lightly beaten
1½ cups freshly made dry breadcrumbs
6 tablespoons butter
3 tablespoons oil
Salt and freshly ground pepper
Lemon
Chopped parsley
Optional: 2 tablespoons flour and 1 cup heavy cream

Cut the sweetbreads into serving-size pieces. Dip first in the flour, then the beaten eggs, and lastly the crumbs, and sauté gently in the butter and oil till nicely browned on both sides. Season with salt and pepper. Transfer to a hot platter, sprinkle with chopped parsley, and serve with lemon wedges. To serve with a cream sauce: Remove all but two tablespoons fat from the pan, add two tablespoons flour, and brown well with the remaining fat. Gradually stir in 1 cup heavy cream, and cook until nicely thickened. Season well with freshly ground pepper.

Calf's Brains

Brains were a common food in the eighteenth and nineteenth centuries and only recently seem to have declined in use, perhaps because they require a little more preparation than today's housewife has time for. Nevertheless, brains are one of the most delicate of all offal. They are quite perishable and should be stored in the refrigerator until ready for use.

To prepare, wash the brains well, and soak them in ice water 20 to 25 minutes. Remove the membrane and any remaining blood. Simmer about 15 minutes in salted water or a light court bouillon made with approximately 1 quart water, an onion stuck with a clove, salt, two tablespoons vinegar or white wine, a few peppercorns, and a sprig of parsley. One pair will serve two persons.

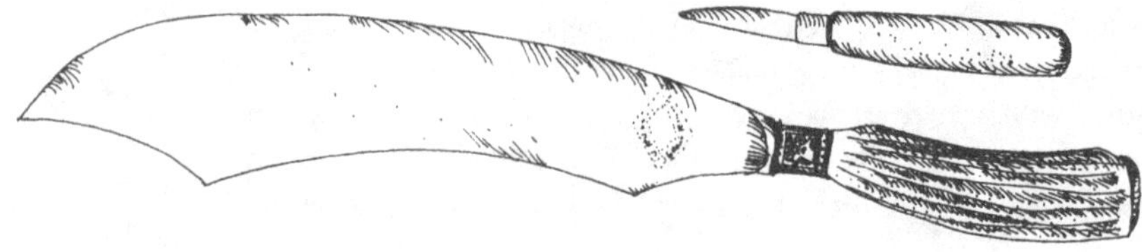

Scrambled Eggs and Brains

1 pair parboiled brains
6 eggs
1 tablespoon water
1 teaspoon salt
¼ teaspoon Tabasco
5 tablespoons butter
Freshly ground pepper

I have served this on many occasions as a luncheon dish, and many a club has featured it on certain days of the week. It makes a delicious first course dish served in small pastry shells or tiny patty shells and looks handsome when served in a large patty shell, garnished with parsley and chives.

Parboil the brains according to directions above. Cool and cut into small dice or very thin slices. Beat the eggs slightly and add water, salt, and Tabasco. Melt the butter in a heavy skillet, add the brains, and heat through thoroughly. Add the eggs and scramble with a spatula, pushing the mixture into thin curls as it firms on the bottom of the skillet. When the eggs and brains have formed large curds, turn out onto a hot platter. Add some freshly ground pepper and garnish with watercress or chopped parsley.

Sautéed Brains

For 2 persons, parboil a pair of brains as directed above. Dip the brains in flour, then into beaten egg, and last into freshly made breadcrumbs. Sauté in butter very quickly till just golden brown and cooked through. Season with salt and freshly ground pepper, and serve with lemon wedges.

Fried Brains

Parboil brains as above. Cool and cut in slices. Dip in flour and beer batter and fry until well browned in deep fat heated to 375 degrees. Drain on absorbent paper and serve with fried parsley and lemon wedges.

Crumbed and Sautéed Brains

1 pair brains
Court bouillon (page 358)
Flour
Beaten egg
Crumbs
6 tablespoons olive oil

MARINADE

½ cup olive oil
3 tablespoons lemon juice
1 teaspoon salt
¼ teaspoon Tabasco
1 tablespoon chopped parsley
1 tablespoon chopped chives

Parboil the brains as above. Allow to cool, then slice. Mix the marinade and marinate the slices several hours. To cook, dip first in flour, then beaten egg, then crumbs, and sauté in the olive oil until nicely browned. Drain on absorbent paper and serve with lemon wedges.

Brains in Black Butter

1 pair brains
Court bouillon (page 358)
BLACK BUTTER
6 tablespoons butter
3 tablespoons vinegar or lemon juice
2 tablespoons chopped parsley
½ teaspoon freshly ground pepper
3 tablespoons capers

Clean a pair of brains and let them soak in ice water 2 hours. Poach about 20 minutes in the court bouillon as given above. To make the black butter, melt the butter over medium heat and let it brown. Tilt the pan back and forth so the butter does not burn. Add the vinegar or lemon juice, parsley, pepper, and capers, and cook 2 minutes. Spoon over the poached brains.

Mrs. Wight's Entrée of Brains

2 pairs brains, cleaned and soaked in ice water
4 tablespoons butter
1 cup stock or bouillon
1 cup white wine
1 tablespoon vinegar
1 tablespoon chopped tarragon
1 small clove garlic, finely chopped
1 tablespoon parsley, finely chopped
1 bay leaf
Salt and freshly ground pepper

This interesting recipe comes from the Portland, Oregon, *Woman's Exchange Cookbook* (1913).

While the brains are soaking, brown the butter lightly in a saucepan. When it is well colored, add the liquids and seasonings, bring to a boil, and simmer 10 minutes. Add the brains and poach about 20 minutes. Transfer the brains to a hot dish. Reduce the sauce and serve over the brains. Garnish with capers and chopped parsley. Serve with rice and a well-flavored but not too tart tossed salad.

Brain Timbales

1 pair brains
2 medium-thin slices bread, soaked in 1 cup milk
1 teaspoon salt
½ teaspoon ground ginger
Freshly ground pepper
4 eggs, lightly beaten
Butter

Parboil the brains as directed above and while still hot put them through a food mill or sieve to make a purée. Purée the bread slices as well, and season with the salt, ginger, and a few grinds of pepper. Combine with the lightly beaten eggs and fill 6 buttered timbale molds or one 6-cup mold. Cover, and steam in hot water 40 to 45 minutes. Unmold on a hot platter and serve with a Hollandaise or mushroom sauce.

Calf's Head

As we become more civilized in culinary matters, it becomes more and more difficult to find good hearty things like calf's head, calf's feet, and sheep's trotters. However, calf's head is still available in some cities. In New York I have to order it a week ahead. So if you manage to find a source, you would be well advised to experiment and learn its delights. I remember a small restaurant in New York where calf's head appeared on the menu and was so much in demand that it had to be offered several times a week.

Our earlier cookery books were filled with recipes for this delicacy, and that in the days when one had to singe and remove hairs from the snout and go through other less attractive preparations. One delight which I have always threatened to make is a calf's head parboiled, dipped in beaten egg, crumbed, and baked, to be served sitting on a collar of leaves and crowned with leaves as well. But the thought of carving such a dish at table has kept me from following through.

French butchers, bless their hearts, will bone and tie a calf's head. Or rather, they will make a head into two rolls with an ear topping each half. You may be able to find a friendly butcher who will do the same thing for you. If not, have the butcher split the head and bone it (unless you can perform that task yourself. Then you may roll and tie it before cooking or cut into sections as you wish.) Or you may merely split the head, remove the brains, then cut the flesh from the bone after cooking.

To prepare a calf's head, put the tongue and head into a large pot with enough water to cover and bring it to a boil. Cook 10 minutes, remove any scum that rises, and pour off the water. Add fresh water and bring to a boil again. Remove the scum, and add an onion stuck with 2 cloves, a carrot, ½ cup wine vinegar, and about 1 tablespoon salt. Cover and simmer 1½ hours. While this is cooking, prepare and soak the brains as directed on page 358. Remove the skin and let them soak again in the salt water 2 minutes. Poach them in salted water to which has been added an onion and a tablespoon of lemon juice. They will take about 20 minutes of poaching (water below simmer). Remove the head and tongue from the kettle. Save the broth, for it is rich and useful for other dishes. Peel the tongue carefully and cut into slices. Cut the head into nice serving pieces and arrange on a napkin or a hot platter. Slices of head, slices of tongue, and slices of brain should be arranged in separate sections of the platter. Many like to serve hard-boiled egg slices and plain steamed potatoes on the same platter. Serve with a fine vinaigrette sauce that includes chopped capers, chives, onions, hard-boiled eggs, parsley, and so forth. The head may also be served with a sauce poulette, a tomato sauce, or a béchamel.

Veal Kidneys

Veal kidneys, of all the offal, are by far the most delicious and succulent bits, but are too often ruined by overcooking, a fault also true of the treatment accorded kidneys in early American recipes. Alas! it is no longer possible to buy veal kidneys encased in their fat. Because of this, many of the delicious ways of preparing them are lost to us. They were excellent baked in the shell of fat, split, and then either flambéed with brandy and eaten rare or taken from their protective case, sliced thin, and sautéed in butter, with seasonings and wine or spirits. Or they were skewered and broiled till crisp on all sides, split, seasoned with salt and Tabasco, then flamed with brandy or bourbon, and served "on the half shell."

Broiling is one of the simplest and most pleasing methods of preparing the veal kidney. Overcooking or fast cooking toughens it and makes it less attractive to the bite and to the taste.

Some people like to soak kidneys in salted water, wine, or milk before cooking. For fresh veal kidneys this is really unnecessary. Simply split the kidneys before broiling and remove the cores. One kidney is usually an ample serving.

Kidneys make superb summer fare when cooked on the outdoor grill over charcoal and are excellent served with mustard, shoestring potatoes, and a crisp coleslaw or a salad.

Broiled Veal Kidneys

Split the kidneys, remove the core, and brush with butter or oil. Broil 5 to 12 minutes according to size. Brush several more times with melted butter or oil and turn once. If broiling in an oven, place 3 to 4 inches from the source of heat. When cooked properly they should be delicately brown outside and a rich pink inside; or, for more robust persons, fairly rare in the center. Transfer to a hot plate, salt to taste, and add freshly ground pepper. Spoon a bit of melted butter over each one, and sprinkle with chopped parsley or buttered crumbs.

Miss Farmer suggested serving broiled kidneys on pieces of toast and seasoning them with salt, cayenne, and lemon juice.

Deviled Kidneys. Broil the kidneys till almost done. Dip in melted butter seasoned with lemon juice and Tabasco. Roll in crumbs, return to broiler, and brown the crumbs. Serve with a mustard sauce.

Broiled Kidneys and Sweetbreads

Blanch a pair of sweetbreads and weight them under a plate. Cut into 1½-inch cubes. Cut 2 kidneys into pieces of similar size. Thread the sweetbread and kidney pieces alternately on skewers. Brush lavishly with melted butter or oil. Broil, turning on all sides so they will color nicely. Brush with additional butter or oil. If the pieces are not too closely pushed together, they will take only about 6 minutes to broil. Season with salt. Serve with melted butter and lemon.

Miss Farmer suggests alternating pieces of bacon and kidney slices on skewers and broiling them. However, she first requires cooking the kidneys in stock for 10 minutes. (I think that much cooking would toughen the kidneys, but the bacon and kidney combination is a good one.) This is to be served with a Madeira sauce.

Middle Western Kidneys Sauté

2 veal kidneys
Flour, seasoned with salt, freshly ground pepper, paprika, and a bit of sugar
4 tablespoons butter or other fat
2 tablespoons oil
3 tablespoons sherry

Slice the kidneys and parboil in salted water 2 minutes. Remove, dip in the seasoned flour, and sauté in the fat and oil till lightly brown on both sides. They should be cooked quite quickly and removed to a hot platter. Spoon off most of the fat, rinse the pan with sherry, and pour over the kidneys.

Kidney Stew

3 veal kidneys, cored and thinly sliced
Flour
6 tablespoons butter
3 tablespoons oil
2 medium onions, finely chopped
2 green peppers, seeded and finely chopped (these were formerly used in season only)
2 tablespoons lemon juice
2 cups stock or chicken broth
Salt, freshly ground pepper, and cayenne
⅓ cup sherry or Madeira
Chopped parsley

Many Midwesterners and Far Westerners used to entertain handsomely at Sunday breakfast. The groaning board included sausages and kippers and bacon and eggs, and nearly always a kidney stew with rice or, farther south, with grits. Although the kidney dish was overcooked for my palate, it had good flavor and some imagination.

Slice the kidneys and flour them. Sauté lightly in the butter and oil (about 5 minutes). Add the onions and peppers and continue cooking another 5 minutes. Add the lemon juice, stock, and seasonings. Cover, and simmer about 20 minutes. Correct the seasoning, add the sherry or Madeira, and allow to boil up. Serve in a ring of rice or with grits and crisp buttered toast. Sprinkle with chopped parsley.

Mrs. Harland's Veal Kidney Sauté with Wine

"Cut the kidneys into thin slices and cook 10 minutes in a little drippings in a frying pan. Take out and lay upon a hot water dish, covering closely. Add to the dripping in the pan a little gravy — beef will do or a little of your soup; season with a chopped onion, salt, parsley, and pepper and thicken with a little browned flour. Boil up. Add a glass of good wine and the juice of half a lemon. Pour upon the kidneys and set upon boiling water 5 minutes. If kidneys are cooked too long, they will toughen."

Veal Kidneys in Sherry Sauce

4 veal kidneys
2 tablespoons butter
2 tablespoons olive oil
¼ cup diced ham
1 medium onion, finely chopped
⅓ cup sherry
1 clove garlic, crushed
1 tablespoon chopped parsley
Dash of white pepper
½ cup tomato pulp, skin and seeds removed
½ cup veal or chicken broth
Toast triangles

Remove the membrane and cores of the kidneys and cut in small pieces. Heat the butter and oil over fairly high heat and sauté the kidneys quickly. Remove from the pan. Add the ham and chopped onion to the pan, sauté lightly, and remove. Add the sherry to pan and reduce over high heat. Add the seasonings, tomato, and broth. Simmer for a few minutes to reduce slightly. Add the meats and onion and simmer to blend flavors and heat through. Serve garnished with toast triangles or in a ring of white rice. Serve with any light, pleasant red wine — a lesser red Bordeaux or a claret or Zinfandel from California.

Lamb

Though there has always been an abundance of lamb in this country, it has long been the most neglected and most poorly prepared of all the meats. In recent years people have at last begun to realize how delicious it can be when properly cooked, and it is ironical that we are now faced with a diminishing supply.

We are accustomed to what is known as "yearling" lamb, which is somewhat older than the lamb one finds in France and England and other countries where this meat is much appreciated. However, prime grade lamb is tender and well flavored, and occasionally one finds baby lamb in some of our markets, which is indeed small in size, though well meated, and needs different treatment from older lamb. The parts most desired are the leg, chops, rack, saddle, and shoulder, in that order. It is best, with the lamb available here, to bone the shoulder and remove some of the fat before cooking.

Mutton. This delicious meat is nearly impossible to find any more. A few butchers who pride themselves on being great suppliers, such as Milton Kaufman of the Maryland Market in New York, will find good mutton a few times a year and alert their best customers. And infrequently, it will turn up in California, Chicago, or some remote spot. Mutton needs long hanging and should be well ripened before cooking. Also it is usually very fat and requires a good deal of trimming. Any of the recipes for leg of lamb or shoulder of lamb will work as well with good mutton.

Leg of Lamb

It used to be, and is still often true, I'm afraid, that this delicious joint arrived at table, was hacked to chunks, and proved to be rather gray-brown, overdone meat with a strongish flavor. No wonder it was not popular. Today, for the most part, it is treated with greater care with a consequent improvement in flavor.

Legs are now cut two ways primarily. The French cut has the shank bone left in; it is not cracked or broken elsewhere; and it sometimes contains the tail and hip bones as well as the leg and shank. The American cut has some of the sirloin and the shank bone removed. For carving, the French leg is an easier one to work with. Half legs are sometimes sold, and one can choose either the shank half or the sirloin half.

A thin membrane known as the fell covers the meat, and if the butcher has not removed it, it is wise to do so before roasting.

Plain American Roast Leg of Lamb, Modern Style

Rub the lamb slightly with flour, salt, and freshly ground pepper, and place it on a rack in a shallow roasting pan. Roast in a 325-degree oven approximately 11 minutes per pound or until the interior temperature registers 140 degrees (for medium rare) when tested with a meat thermometer. (In the absence of a thermometer you can tell by pressure of the finger if a roast is done; it will be fairly firm.) Salt and pepper it well, and transfer to a very hot platter. Allow it to rest 10 minutes in a warm place before carving it.

The average American likes gravy or mint jelly with his lamb. The latter is a newcomer which has taken the place of the famous English and earlier American mint sauce. Oven-browned potatoes have always been popular with roast lamb. Other typical companions are new potatoes dressed with butter and mint or parsley, and buttered green peas.

It is interesting to note that the first American cookery book to discuss this dish — Mrs. Crowen's — suggested putting the lamb leg on muffin rings or a trivet if the roast was going into the oven. Also she favored high heat and much basting. And it probably turned out very well.

Lamb Gravy

Siphon off all but 3 tablespoons of the fat from the pan juices. Combine the juices with 3 tablespoons flour, and cook over medium heat till thickened and smooth. Gradually pour in 1½ cups water, milk, or broth, and stir again until the mixture thickens. Season to taste with salt and freshly ground pepper, and serve with the roast.

Garlic Roast Leg of Lamb

The French influence, which was particularly strong in New York, parts of the Middle West, and California, introduced the use of garlic and herbs with lamb. Thus we find these next two favorites, dating from the mid-nineteenth century.

Use a French cut leg for this version. Remove the fell and excess fat. Make slits with a sharp knife and insert small slivers of garlic, using 4 to 6 cloves for the average-size leg. Rub it well with oil and rosemary leaves, either fresh or dehydrated, and roast on a rack as above. Add salt and freshly ground pepper about midway in the roasting process. When the roast has achieved the internal temperature of 140 degrees (for medium rare) transfer it to a hot platter and pour the pan juices over it. Let it rest 5 to 8 minutes before carving. Serve with white beans flavored with a touch of garlic, chopped parsley, and a bit of oil. Spoon the pan juices over the slices of meat and the beans.

Roast Leg of Lamb, Searing Method

There are at least two schools of thought on roasting lamb. Some people prefer to use a low temperature throughout, as in the "modern style" recipe given above. Others feel that searing the meat briefly and then reducing the temperature yields a better-flavored meat and prevents juices from running. I do not agree with the latter method. I have tried out both ways simultaneously, with twin legs, and have found the lower temperature gives a more even coloring throughout. However, for the benefit of those who believe in the searing, I am offering a recipe for it.

Make slits and insert tiny shreds of garlic into the lamb, using 4 to 6 cloves for a leg of 6 to 7 pounds. Rub the meat well with freshly ground pepper and butter. Arrange the leg on a rack in a baking pan and place in an oven preheated to 450 degrees. Roast 20 minutes, turning and brushing with butter several times. Reduce the heat to 325 degrees and continue cooking, allowing 10 to 11 minutes per pound from that point. Salt and pepper the lamb well. It should reach an internal temperature of 140 degrees (for medium rare) when tested with an efficient thermometer. Transfer the roast to a hot platter and let it rest 10 minutes before carving. Serve with the pan juices. Also serve sautéed potatoes and perhaps a purée of peas prepared with butter and chopped parsley.

To Make Lamb or Mutton Taste Like Venison

1 leg of lamb
Oil

MARINADE

1 fifth red wine
1 tablespoon salt
1 tablespoon crushed peppercorns
1 rib of celery cut in julienne strips
1 teaspoon thyme
1 onion stuck with two cloves
1 bay leaf, crushed

The origin of this dish is rather dim. The French, Italians, and English have all done it for centuries, and early cooking authorities in the United States differ a good deal about the preparation. Mrs. Crowen feels the leg should be rubbed with 1/4 pound brown sugar and then put to marinate with 1 pint port wine and 1 pint vinegar. The meat is turned in this for several days, then washed, wiped dry, and roasted, using some of the marinade for a baste. Mrs. Crowen also suggests using it for a pie.

Mrs. Rorer in an early edition of her book recommended washing the leg with vinegar and then letting it hang for a week, after which, for two days in succession, it was to be rubbed with allspice and pepper and then hung for another week. When ready to roast, the pieces were washed off with vinegar — wine, we hope — and the leg was roasted in the usual way. Just before removing it from the roasting rack one poured a tablespoonful of mushroom catsup over the lamb along with a tablespoon of Worcestershire sauce, and, adds Mrs. Rorer, "if you use wine, four tablespoons of sherry." It was served with blackcurrant jelly.

Here is a modern version of this dish that is similar to the old recipes.

Rub the leg well with oil and marinate 3 to 6 days. Turn the leg each day. The longer you leave it the gamier the flavor will be. Roast the meat on a rack at 375 degrees, basting from time to time with the strained marinade, till it achieves an internal temperature of 135 to 140 degrees (for medium rare). Transfer to a hot platter. Add the remaining marinade to the roasting pan and bring to a boil. Serve separately with the roast, along with a purée of chestnuts or slices of cornmeal mush sautéed in butter till crisp. A robust red wine, such as a fairly good Médoc or a California Cabernet, would go extremely well with this meal.

Grilled Leg of Lamb

With the advent of charcoal cookery, this has become more and more popular. It is also an extremely interesting dish when done in an electric or gas broiler. In fact, there are some people who insist that the flavor of the grilled leg is superior to a roast.

The leg should be boned (leaving the shank bone) and split so that it is open and flat, although some spots will be thicker than others. The fell should be removed. Rub the meat lightly with olive oil flavored with a little tarragon or rosemary. Broil cut side down, at least 5 or 6 inches from source of heat, about 20 minutes. Do not allow it to char. Turn it and broil another 15 to 20 minutes, depending upon the thickness of the meat. Gauge it almost as you would a thick steak. Salt and pepper well, using freshly ground pepper. Transfer to a hot platter. Allow to stand 5 minutes. Carve in diagonal slices across the leg.

Garlic Leg of Lamb. Stud the leg with garlic cloves cut in slivers, and rub with rosemary or tarragon before grilling.

Marinated Leg of Lamb. Marinate the boned leg as in the directions for making lamb or mutton taste like venison. Remove from the marinade and dry thoroughly. Rub well with oil and broil according to directions above. Baste two or three times with the marinade. Serve with the marinade, added to the pan juices and cooked down for 3 minutes. Garnish with chopped parsley.

Swedish Leg of Lamb

One finds this from time to time in the Middle West among people of Swedish descent, and it was popularized a number of years ago through an article by the actor and director Alfred Lunt.

Prepare a leg of lamb for roasting. Roast at 325 degrees for a half hour, then baste with a cup of hot coffee made with cream and sugar. Continue roasting and basting, adding more coffee if necessary, until the lamb is done. Sprinkle with salt and freshly ground pepper just before removing from the oven. Skim off excess fat from the coffee-flavored pan juices, correct the seasoning, and serve as a sauce.

Boned and Stuffed Leg of Lamb

Leg of lamb, boned, with shank bone left in
6 cloves garlic, finely chopped
½ cup each of chopped mint leaves and chopped parsley
1 teaspoon salt
2 teaspoons freshly ground pepper
2 teaspoons brown sugar
1 tablespoon lemon juice
½ cup each of red wine and melted butter

This recipe I ran across at a house party on Long Island where each person contributed a course for the Saturday night dinner. One guest, whose name is long since forgotten, made quite a production of this lamb dish, which was interesting enough to record here.

Have the butcher bone the leg, leaving the shank bone in. Combine the garlic, mint, parsley, salt, pepper, brown sugar, and lemon juice. Spread this mixture over the inner surface of the meat, then roll and tie it. Place on a rack in a roasting pan and roast at 325 degrees, basting with the wine and melted butter added to the pan juices. When the lamb is done, salt and pepper it and transfer to a hot platter. Serve with the pan juices, tiny new potatoes, and a purée of green peas.

Weeping Leg of Lamb

Leg of lamb 5 to 5½ pounds
6 to 8 potatoes, thinly sliced
Butter
Salt and freshly ground pepper
Garlic
1½ teaspoons dried tarragon or 2 or 3 sprigs fresh
1½ to 2 cups beef bouillon or stock
½ cup grated Parmesan cheese
Chopped parsley

This was originally a Southern French recipe from the region around Avignon, but it has gained a public in the United States and seems to be one of the more interesting fashions of preparing a leg of lamb. No doubt it was first done on a spit before an open fire, but this modern method produces good results. It requires the use of an oblong or oval baking dish large enough to catch the drippings from the leg placed on a rack above it — thus, the leg "weeps."

Butter the baking dish well and arrange the sliced potatoes in it in layers. Butter each layer, and salt and pepper to taste. The quantity of potatoes required will depend on their size, but I find 8 potatoes of good size are usually ample for 2 to 3 layers. Add 1 to 1½ cups broth — enough to barely cover the potatoes. Preheat the oven to 325 degrees. Remove the excess fat and fell from the lamb and pique it on both sides with 5 or 6 cloves of garlic, slivered. Rub the leg well with tarragon and sprinkle additional tarragon on the leg. If fresh tarragon is available attach the sprigs to the leg. Place the baking dish, containing the potatoes, on the lower rack of the oven. Oil the rack above and place the leg on it, centered directly over the baking dish, making certain that no drippings will fall on the surface of the oven. Roast until the leg achieves an interior temperature of 140 degrees (for medium rare), about 12 minutes per pound. Salt and pepper the leg just before it is done. Remove the leg and the rack. Sprinkle the potatoes with grated Parmesan cheese and some chopped parsley, and return to the oven for just a minute. Transfer the lamb to a hot platter and allow to rest for 5 minutes. Serve with the lamb-flavored potatoes. Follow this with a good green salad lightly tossed with olive oil and wine vinegar. A good Bordeaux wine or a Cabernet would be a welcome addition.

Note. Another version of weeping leg of lamb adds 12 to 14 anchovy fillets to the potatoes and omits salt. It also piques the lamb with anchovies and garlic and omits salting. Otherwise it is the same. The potatoes make a dish which the Swedish call Jansen's Temptation.

Leg of Baby Lamb

Baby lamb is becoming more and more common in this country, due probably to the influence of the Italians, the French, and the Middle Eastern people, who have always prepared it so well. The small legs will cook very fast, and they are best, to my thinking, baked at a brisk temperature — between 375 degrees and 400 degrees. The total cooking time is 45 minutes to an hour, depending upon the size of the leg. If the number to be served is rather large, it is wise to buy two legs, still attached, which is a cut known as the baron. This looks superb on a platter surrounded by young spring vegetables, and it provides ample food for 6 to 8 people, depending upon appetite.

Roast Leg of Baby Lamb I

Some restaurants, notably the Forum of the Twelve Caesars in New York, have made a specialty of tiny legs of lamb roasted to order for two persons.

Rub the leg well with butter or olive oil — remember, there is very little fat on young lamb. Place on a rack and roast quickly at 375 degrees, allowing about 45 to 60 minutes for it to achieve an internal temperature of 150 to 160 degrees (it should not be served quite as pink as older lamb). About 10 minutes before it is done, sprinkle with salt and freshly ground pepper and add a sprig of fresh thyme, if you have it, or a teaspoon of dried thyme. Transfer to a hot platter to settle 5 minutes. Serve with steamed rice, tiny asparagus tips, and the pan juices.

Roast Leg of Baby Lamb II

Prepare leg as above, and begin roasting. Meanwhile, pare off a strip of skin around 24 to 30 small new potatoes, and boil them till tender. Also peel 24 to 30 small white onions and parboil them till tender but still crisp. Butter the potatoes and add to the roasting pan for the last 10 minutes of cooking. Drain the onions, sprinkle lightly with sugar, and also add to the pan for the last 10 minutes. About 5 minutes before removing the pan from the oven, sprinkle the meat and vegetables with salt and freshly ground pepper. Transfer the leg to a hot platter to rest for 5 or 6 minutes. Allow the vegetables to stay in the pan till ready to serve. Serve around the roast, sprinkled heavily with chopped parsley.

Roast Leg of Baby Lamb III

Prepare the leg for roasting by rubbing well with olive oil or peanut oil. Place on a rack in a shallow pan and roast in a 375-degree oven approximately an hour, or slightly less. After 40 minutes salt and pepper the leg well, and place on it three peeled and sliced garlic cloves and a sprig of fresh rosemary or 1 teaspoon dried rosemary. Continue cooking till it reaches an internal temperature of 150 degrees. Transfer to a hot platter to rest 5 to 8 minutes before carving. Add the pan juices to the platter. Serve the lamb with crisp sautéed potatoes.

Boiled Leg of Lamb

An early Middle Western recipe for "boiled leg of mutton," as it was called, reads: "Plunge the leg of mutton into boiling water and let it scald fifteen minutes for every pound; in extremely cold weather allow half an hour extra boiling. Serve with drawn butter and Nasturtium [sic] or capers." The English brought with them their version of boiled lamb, which is, I'm afraid, rather dull fare unless perfectly prepared. It is perpetually served with a rather pasty caper sauce, which could be much more deftly prepared.

Boiled Leg of Lamb with Caper Sauce

Rub a leg of lamb with salt and freshly ground pepper and put it into a kettle of boiling water to which you have added 1 tablespoon salt, 1 teaspoon freshly ground pepper, 1 teaspoon thyme, and an onion stuck with two cloves. Bring back to a boil, reduce the heat, and poach till the lamb is tender and still pink. It is best to allow 12 to 14 minutes per pound after the liquid has returned to a boil. Transfer the lamb to a hot platter and allow it to rest for 5 to 8 minutes before carving. In the meantime, prepare the caper sauce (below). Serve the lamb and caper sauce with buttered spinach and steamed rice, sprinkled with chopped parsley.

Caper Sauce

3 tablespoons butter
3 tablespoons flour
1½ cups lamb broth
Salt and freshly ground pepper
1 tablespoon lemon juice
½ cup capers

Melt the butter, blend in the flour, and cook 3 to 4 minutes over low heat. Add the broth, and stir well until thickened. Taste for seasoning and add salt and pepper if needed, remembering that the capers will add a certain amount of salt. Add the lemon juice and capers, and simmer for a minute or two.

A More Elegant Boiled Leg of Lamb

1 leg of lamb, boned and tied
Bones from the lamb leg and an additional lamb shank
1 tablespoon salt
2 onions stuck with cloves
1 teaspoon freshly ground pepper
1 teaspoon thyme
2 garlic cloves
3 quarts water

Put the bones, shank, seasonings, and cold water in a large kettle, and bring to a boil. Boil about 10 minutes and remove any scum that forms. Cover, and simmer 1½ hours. Again, skim off any excess fat or scum. Rub the lamb with salt and place in the kettle. Bring to a boil again and simmer, allowing 12 minutes per pound. Transfer the lamb to a hot platter. Prepare a caper sauce (above) made with the lamb broth, or simply serve the lamb broth as the sauce, along with boiled potatoes and peas. Sprinkle the lamb with chopped parsley before serving and garnish with fresh watercress.

June Platt's Rare Leg of Lamb, Boiled

1 leg of lamb
2 to 3 quarts water
1 onion stuck with 2 cloves
3 cloves garlic
1 bay leaf
1 teaspoon thyme
½ cup pepper

SAUCE

12 anchovy fillets, finely chopped
2 crushed garlic cloves
2 teaspoons Dijon mustard
2 tablespoons chopped capers
½ teaspoon Tabasco
½ cup hot broth from lamb

Mrs. Platt, one of the more distinguished writers on food in our gastronomic history, offers this superb version of boiled leg of lamb.

Bring the water and seasonings to a boil in a 10 to 12 quart kettle and simmer 30 minutes. Place a rack in the bottom of the kettle, or improvise one using a plate turned upside down. Wrap the leg of lamb in a heavy linen napkin and tie it securely. Place in the bouillon and let it come to the boil again. Count exactly 12 minutes per pound from that point. Remove from the broth and from the napkin and place on a hot platter. Surround with boiled new potatoes. Serve this deliciously spicy lamb with the sauce, which is made with a small amount of the broth blended together with the other ingredients. It is rather a thickish sauce, and a small amount is sufficient for each serving. A casserole of eggplant goes extremely well with this dish. For an appropriate wine choose a Beaujolais; the peppery quality of the lamb does not lend itself well to a more important wine.

Sauce for Boiled Leg of Lamb

1 pint oysters and their liquor (should be about 1 cup)
3 tablespoons butter kneaded with the same amount of flour (beurre manié)
Salt to taste
Cayenne or Tabasco and nutmeg
⅔ cup heavy cream, scalded
Half a lemon

Mrs. Harland offered this sauce for boiled leg of lamb one hundred years ago in a cookbook of dinners. It is deliciously different from the usual caper sauce.

Drain the oysters and bring the liquor to a boil. Thicken with beurre manié. You may not need as much as called for. Season with salt and spices, and add the oysters. Cook just long enough for them to heat through. Add the hot cream and blend thoroughly. Remove from heat and add juice of lemon. Serve at once with the boiled lamb.

Note. Should there not be enough oyster liquor for the sauce and the oysters, you may add milk or fish broth to compensate.

Shoulder of Lamb

To be really practical, this cut must be boned and rolled. In the eastern part of the United States it is usually sold this way, but there are some parts of the country where butchers are not so accommodating. Therefore, either learn to bone this cut yourself or avoid it, since the carving problem is almost insurmountable. Also there is a certain amount of fat in the shoulder, which a knowing butcher will remove. The meat is thoroughly delicious and has a sweetness which is sometimes more interesting than the leg.

Roast Shoulder of Lamb

A boned and rolled shoulder may be roasted in almost any way prescribed for a roast leg of lamb.

Roast Shoulder of Baby Lamb

A boned and rolled shoulder of baby lamb is excellent eating. A small boned shoulder weighs about 2 pounds and will roast in about 45 minutes at 375 degrees or in about an hour at 325 degrees. Small amounts of rosemary or fresh mint and a clove or two of garlic, crushed and placed in the lamb, will help define the flavor. Try adding ½ to ¾ cup heavy cream to the pan juices after you transfer the roast to a hot platter. This will make a most interesting sauce for the meat and whatever vegetables are served with it. Let the cream and the pan juices cook down about 3 minutes and correct the seasoning. Pour off into a sauceboat.

Braised Shoulder of Lamb with Lentils

1 pound lentils
1 onion
1 bay leaf
Salt
1 shoulder of lamb about 4 to 4½ pounds, boned and tied after most of the fat is removed
2 garlic cloves
Freshly ground pepper
3 medium onions, peeled and thinly sliced
½ cup water
¼ cup chopped parsley

Lentils appear to have lost favor in this country, probably because they have not had the benefit of intensive advertising. They were standard fare for generations, prepared in a variety of styles by the German, French, Italian, and Indian immigrants. They are grown in Colorado and in the Far West with great success. This is but one of the many good dishes made with lentils.

Soak the lentils overnight, unless they are the quick-cooking variety, in which case follow the directions on the package. Add the onion, bay leaf, and salt, and bring to a boil. Simmer till tender but still on the firm side — they will be recooked later. Pique the lamb shoulder with slivers of garlic, and rub it well with pepper. Melt some of the lamb fat in a heavy skillet, Dutch oven, or braising pan made of iron, enameled iron, copper, or stainless steel. Brown the lamb on all sides until it has a nice golden color. Pour off practically all the fat from the pan, add the onions, and let them cook 4 to 5 minutes over rather brisk heat. Reduce the heat, cover the pan, and cook about 4 minutes. Add the water, cover, and simmer 1 hour or bake in a 300-degree oven. Add the lentils and a little of their liquid and continue slow cooking till the lamb is tender — ½ to 1 hour. Salt to taste. The meat should not be brown and stringy but should still have a faint touch of pink in it.

Transfer the lamb to a hot platter. Drain the lentils, reserving the pan juices. Arrange the lentils around the lamb and sprinkle generously with chopped parsley. Serve the pan juices apart. A salad and a bottle of California Mountain Red wine would go well with this dish.

Shoulder of Lamb Braised with Vegetables

1 lamb shoulder, boned and rolled after some of the fat is removed
Lamb fat or 4 tablespoons oil (peanut or olive oil)
1 teaspoon thyme
1 teaspoon freshly ground pepper
½ cup water, broth, or vegetable juice
6 to 8 medium potatoes, peeled
6 to 8 medium onions, peeled
6 to 8 medium carrots, scraped
6 small turnips, peeled
2 or 3 leeks
2 pounds fresh peas, shelled, or 1 package frozen peas
Salt and freshly ground pepper
Water or broth, if needed

This may be prepared on top of the stove, but it is best done in the oven at 300 degrees, in which case it should be started atop the stove. Heat the lamb fat or oil in a Dutch oven, covered casserole, or braising pan. Rub the meat well with the thyme and pepper. Brown it evenly on all sides over rather high heat, turning it often. Pour off most of the fat. Add ½ cup of liquid, cover the pan, and simmer atop the stove or bake in the oven. After 20 minutes, add all vegetables except the peas, arranging them around the meat or putting the meat on a rack over the vegetables. Add about 2 teaspoons of salt and ½ teaspoon of freshly ground pepper to the vegetables. Cover, and continue cooking 1 hour. Test for tenderness. The vegetables and lamb should be almost ready to serve. Do not allow the vegetables to become mushy. Cook the peas separately in boiling salted water. Drain and butter.

When done, transfer the lamb to a hot platter and remove the strings. Arrange the vegetables around the lamb, and garnish with the peas. Serve the pan juices apart. This is a complete meal for 6 persons. A good choice of wine to go with it would be a Beaujolais or perhaps a California Zinfandel.

Shoulder of Lamb with Okra and Tomatoes

About 3 to 4 pounds shoulder of lamb, boned and rolled after some fat is removed
4 to 5 tablespoons olive oil
Salt and freshly ground pepper
3 onions, thinly sliced
3 cloves garlic, finely chopped
1 green pepper cut into julienne strips
1½ cups tomato juice
1 can tomato paste
1 pound okra washed and split in halves
1 tablespoon lemon juice

The Creoles and Southerners used a great deal of okra in their cookery. In this dish it is more important for texture than flavor, which is principally supplied by the tomato, onion, and garlic.

In a heavy skillet, Dutch oven, or braising pan, sear the lamb in olive oil, turning on all sides to acquire an evenness of color. Salt and pepper to taste. Reduce the heat slightly, add the onions and garlic, and cook 4 to 5 minutes. Add the pepper and tomato juice. Cover, and simmer atop the stove or bake in a 300-degree oven 45 minutes. Stir in the tomato paste and okra. Taste for salt and pepper. Cook, covered, another 30 minutes or until the lamb is tender but not overcooked. Transfer to a hot platter. Add the lemon juice to the pan juices. Garnish the platter with steamed rice and parsley, and serve the sauce apart. Also serve a salad.

Broiled Shoulder of Lamb

One finds recipes for this dating from the early part of the nineteenth century. It was greatly favored as a breakfast dish, served with boiled hominy or potatoes. The shoulder was boned, with most of the fat removed, and then broiled like the leg. Plenty of butter, pepper, and salt were the only condiments. While you may not want to have it for breakfast, it is a dish which would double successfully for the broiled leg in outdoor cooking. You might serve it with a barbecue sauce or an anchovy-flavored Hollandaise.

Rack, Crown, and Saddle of Lamb

Next to the leg of lamb, the rack or rib end of the saddle is the most popular lamb roast. It is a fairly modern dish, and until restaurants and the French and English influences in cookery created such a demand for it, it was generally cut into chops or incorporated with the shoulder for a roast. Few things are better if roasted quickly and sliced properly. A rack is just enough for two servings as trimmed and served in most restaurants. The butcher should French the ribs for you — remove the fell and flesh and scrape them so that they project. Cover the ends with foil during roasting, and replace with paper frills for presentation at table.

Rack of Lamb Parslied and Crumbed

1 rack of lamb (about 6 chops)
2 cloves garlic, very finely chopped
¾ cup dry toasted breadcrumbs
½ cup chopped parsley
Salt and freshly ground pepper
Butter

Trim most of the fat from the lamb. Mix the chopped garlic, crumbs, and parsley, and season with salt and pepper. Wrap the ends of the rib bones with a little foil. Rub the rack with butter and pepper. Place fat side down in a shallow pan and roast 20 minutes at 500 degrees. After 20 minutes, reduce the heat to 400 degrees, invert the lamb, and roast 10 minutes. Spread the crumb mixture on the roast, pressing it in firmly. Dot with butter and return to the oven to brown, or if your stove can accommodate it, run it under the broiler, about 8 inches from the heat, to brown. It will take 5 minutes. Watch carefully. Transfer to a hot platter. Let rest 3 minutes. Carve into chops and serve with sautéed potatoes, a salad, and a pleasant claret. It may also be carved parallel to the bones in medium slices.

One rack will serve two. You may do 2 or 3 racks at a time if you plan to serve more people. It will be a major carving job, however, and one should not attempt it alone.

Simple Rack of Lamb

Small rack of lamb (about 6 small chops), well trimmed, with bones Frenched (page 379)

This rack is served frequently in restaurants, carved parallel to the rib bones in long, thin slices. The pink slices look magnificent on a plate, and the tiny rib bones, served separately, make delicious picking.

Rub the lamb with garlic, butter, salt, and pepper, and put it to roast on a rack in a shallow pan at 400 degrees. Give it just about 20 minutes to reach 135 to 140 degrees (for medium rare). Transfer to a hot platter, sprinkle with chopped parsley, and allow it to rest 5 minutes. Carve parallel to the bones in long, thin slices. Cut the bones into separate ribs, and serve later or on the same plate. Spoon the pan juices over the meat. Serve with sautéed potatoes and watercress, and drink a red Bordeaux or a Cabernet Sauvignon.

Garlic
Butter
Salt and freshly ground pepper
Finely chopped parsley

Crown Roast of Lamb

Since the nineteenth century, this has achieved a social status for elegant entertaining that no other roast has done save a fillet of beef. I don't ever remember having had one presented to me at table that was not overcooked. However, the presentation is handsome, and if you try, you can avoid overcooking.

First of all, find a butcher who knows how to prepare a crown. He should French the ribs (page 379). One crown will usually yield twelve small chops, thus allowing two each to six persons, which is not a lot of meat. If you serve a second crown, it should be timed to come out of the oven about 15 minutes after the first one.

Usually the center of a crown is stuffed. One of the more repulsive fillings, served all too often, is the butcher's contribution — ground lamb, completely unseasoned, which overcooks during the roasting. Some pleasanter fillings, added after the roast is cooked, might be:

Rice pilaff blended with chopped toasted almonds and saffron.
Bulgur or wheat pilaff.
Wild rice with toasted filberts.
Grilled lamb kidneys.
Purée of chestnuts with whole chestnuts as a garnish.
Tiny, crisp, well-buttered Brussels sprouts, and braised chestnuts.
Tiny new peas or new peas with tiny onions.
Sautéed mushrooms tossed with fresh parsley, dill, and chives, and perhaps a bit of cream.

Season the roast with freshly ground pepper and perhaps dried or fresh tarragon, and, if you like, rub it with garlic. Place the crown on a rack in a shallow roasting pan. Crumple a piece of foil into a ball large enough to fill the middle of the crown so it will hold its shape while roasting. Rub the meat well with butter or olive oil, and roast in the oven at 350 to 375 degrees approximately 30 to 35 minutes, for pink lamb. Baste it with melted butter twice during that time.

It is difficult to take a temperature reading on a crown roast, although you can try it. It is best to gauge cooking time by the size of the chops. About 9 to 10 minutes per pound is generally right, but the eye of the meat differs so much in size that this can only be approximate.

Salt the meat well before removing from the oven. Transfer the crown to a hot platter and remove the foil. Fill the crown with one of the fillings given above. Garnish the platter with watercress or with cooked artichoke bottoms, nicely trimmed and filled with Béarnaise sauce for the lamb. To serve, carve into chops, allowing two per person. Potato puffs and a Bibb lettuce salad made with a French dressing, or perhaps fresh asparagus, in season, would make splendid accompaniments. Since this is a luxury dinner, drink a good St. Emilion, such as a Cheval Blanc or an Ausone.

Saddle of Lamb

The saddle is the double loin of lamb with the tiny fillets left in, which may be removed and cooked separately. This cut is usually folded and tied, and it makes as elegant an appearance as the crown.

Season the meat well with freshly ground pepper, and rub with rosemary or tarragon, if you like. Place on a rack in a shallow roasting pan and roast at 325 degrees, allowing 14 to 15 minutes per pound, or until it reaches an internal temperature of 135 to 140 degrees (for pink lamb). Transfer to a hot platter, and remove the twine used in tying it.

Carve in long slices parallel to the spinal column. Then turn the saddle, remove the fillets or tenderloins from underneath, and serve in small rounds. Or you may cook them separately and use them for a garnish. Sometimes the saddle is garnished with broiled fillets and broiled or sautéed kidneys. Thus each person has a long thin slice of the saddle, a kidney, and a round of the fillet.

Serve the meat with the pan juices, a Béarnaise sauce, or a mustard Hollandaise. Tiny potatoes browned in butter or potatoes Anna are a delightful accompaniment. Grilled or baked tomatoes sprinkled with crumbs and a hint of garlic are excellent also. Drink a fine Burgundy with this — a Chambertin or a Clos de Vougeot.

Lamb Chops

There are five different chops from five different sections of the animal, plus two or three variations in cuts:

(1) *Sirloin chop.* From the end of the leg, this is rather a large chop, containing some of the backbone and a little of the hip bone. Each chop seems to vary in shape. Not the most elegant chops, but they are flavorful and pleasant to the palate.

(2) *Loin chop.* Considered by many people to be the choicest, this corresponds to the porterhouse cut in beef, for there is the fillet, a little of the kidney fat on one side of the backbone, and the loin on the other side, lined with fat and the fell removed. May be cut as thick as desired.

(3) *English chop.* Usually the saddle chop or a double chop cut across the saddle, it is often boned and tied, sometimes with a kidney inserted and secured with a small skewer. Usually cut 1½ to 2½ inches thick. Sometimes an English chop means a triple loin chop or a quadruple rib chop.

(4) *Rib chop.* This has the rib bone and some of the backbone. It is cut thick or thin, and French chops have the bone scraped clean from the end of the chop almost to the eye of the meat. Often served with paper frills.

(5) *Arm chop.* From the arm side of the shoulder, this has some of the round bone and cross rib bones. Not as choice as the other chops and is best for braising or for outdoor grilling.

(6) *Blade chop.* This contains some of the blade bone and some of the backbone. Not too choice in appearance and taste but excellent for braising or for made dishes.

Broiled Lamb Chops

Lamb chops usually bear a good portion of fat, which creates a problem, since most people like lamb chops on the rare or pink side but don't want underdone fat. In the average broiling oven it is best to begin the chops about 4 inches from the source of heat, moving the rack closer to the heat later. If you are broiling over charcoal, you should have coals at medium heat at first, increasing the heat later if you want to char the chops. Salt and pepper them as they are turned.

APPROXIMATE BROILING TIME FOR CHOPS

Thickness	*Rare*	*Medium rare*
1 inch	6–8 minutes	12–14 minutes
1½ inches	7–9 minutes	12–14 minutes
2 inches	9–12 minutes	16–20 minutes

For medium chops add 2 to 3 minutes to the longest broiling time.

Naturally, timing depends on the character of the broiling unit. No two stoves are guaranteed to deliver the same intensity of heat. Often, for example, I find that a gas broiler will take longer than a good electric one. Therefore, the table given above is truly approximate. The only test you can be sure of is to slit the flesh next the bone with a fine pointed knife to see if the meat is done enough for your taste.

Serve broiled chops on hot plates, for lamb fat congeals quickly and makes an unappetizing garnish. For accompaniments serve crisp fried potatoes and watercress or grilled tomatoes and watercress.

To Broil Extra Thick Chops (English Chops) I. If your broiling unit is a good one, there should be no difficulty in broiling a thick chop. Merely start with the rack about 6 inches from the source of heat and broil on each side for 4 minutes. Then bring the chops closer to the heat and broil about 3 minutes longer on each side. Slit one of the chops near the bone to test for doneness, or test with a meat thermometer. Salt and pepper the chops when you turn them for the first time, and for a finer flavor and finish, brush the chops with butter.

To Broil Extra Thick Chops II. This method has been employed by many restaurants where very thick chops are a specialty. Start the chops under the broiler almost 6 inches from the heat and sear them quickly on each side. Then place them in a very hot oven — 450 to 500 degrees — for 10 minutes, and finally finish them with high heat under the broiler, turning on all sides. Test after about 15 or 18 minutes. Serve with crisply fried potatoes or a stuffed baked potato and a fine dish of coleslaw, which seems to accompany the thick chop nicely. Also, it is sometimes a good idea to serve the chops with a devil sauce or other hot sauce.

Pan-Broiled or Sautéed Lamb Chops

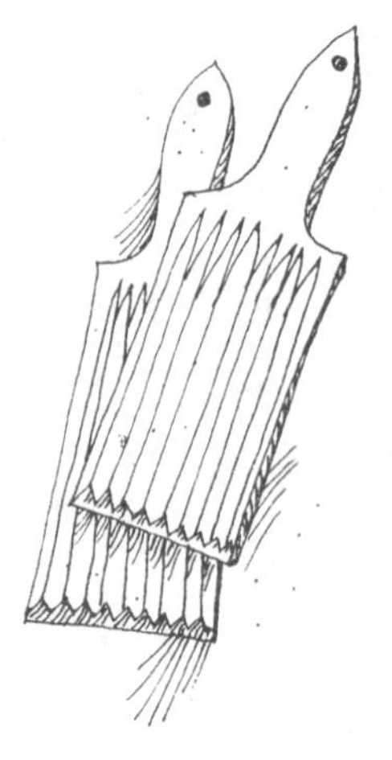

This has always been a favorite way of preparing chops, especially when a good broiler isn't available. It requires the use of a heavy skillet of cast aluminum, iron, or stainless steel.

Heat the skillet until it is quite hot, and melt a little of the lamb fat in the pan — just enough to make a thin film of fat. Sear the chops very quickly in the pan, and when they have taken on a nice color reduce the heat and cook, turning quite often, till they are done to your taste. Salt and pepper the chops midway in the cooking. This method is not recommended for extra thick chops.

Broiling chops in stove-top broiler pans. Heavy iron pans with deep ridges in the bottom, for broiling small steaks or two or three chops, are very efficient and may be used successfully for lamb chops. Heat the pan till quite hot, and rub with a little of the lamb fat. Proceed to broil the chops — which should not be extra thick ones — turning them several times, till done to your taste.

Herb-Stuffed Lamb Chops

6 lamb chops, 2 to 2½ inches thick, with pockets cut in them
1 stick (¼ pound) butter
3 finely chopped garlic cloves
1 tablespoon finely chopped tarragon or 1½ teaspoons dried tarragon
3 tablespoons chopped parsley
1 teaspoon salt
½ teaspoon freshly ground pepper

Stuffed broiled lamb chops are extraordinarily good and can be prepared for broiling an hour or two in advance of dinner or lunch. Have a small pocket made in thick rib or loin chops.

Cream the butter and combine with the herbs and seasonings. Stuff each chop with some of the herbed butter, retaining a small amount for the finished chops. Secure the pockets with skewers or toothpicks. Broil slowly about 6 inches from the source of heat, turning once or twice, till the chops are almost done. Salt and pepper each side. Then move them closer to the heat and finish off. Transfer to a hot platter and dot with the reserved herbed butter. Serve with grilled tomatoes, watercress, and crisp bread.

Mushroom-Stuffed Lamb Chops

6 thick lamb chops with pockets cut in them
1 pound mushrooms, finely chopped
1 stick (¼ pound) butter
3 to 4 green onions or scallions, finely chopped
Salt and freshly ground pepper

Sauté the mushrooms slowly in butter in a skillet until they are dark brown. Add the green onions and salt and pepper to taste. Continue cooking, over very low heat, till the mushrooms are well done — they should be almost black — turning them from time to time. This filling may be made a day or two in advance and refrigerated. Stuff the mushroom filling into the pockets of the chops and secure with small skewers or toothpicks. Broil about 6 inches from the source of heat, turning several times, until the chops are done to your taste. Salt and pepper the chops as you turn them. Serve with rice mixed with butter, chopped parsley, and anchovies. Also serve a tossed green salad.

Lamb Chops Stuffed with Chicken Livers

6 lamb chops, 2 inches thick or more, with pockets cut in them
6 chicken livers, trimmed
4 tablespoons butter
Mushroom filling (see recipe above)
1 tablespoon chopped parsley
¼ cup sherry
Salt and freshly ground pepper

Sauté the chicken livers very lightly in butter, and when they are still rather pink inside, remove from the pan and chop coarsely. Combine with the mushroom filling, parsley, and sherry, and cook about 3 minutes. Stuff the chops with this mixture, and secure with skewers or toothpicks. Start broiling about 6 inches from the source of heat and gradually move closer to the heat as they become cooked. If any of the stuffing is left, put a spoonful on each chop and run them under the broiler a minute before transferring to a hot platter or hot plates. Salt and pepper the chops. Serve with crisply sautéed zucchini prepared with a touch of garlic, and a Bibb lettuce salad.

Mrs. Leon Hirsch's Recipe for Planked Lamb Chops

This recipe comes from a manuscript cookbook dating from the early years of this century. It calls for English kidney chops cut 1½ inches thick. Broil the chops in the usual manner just until nicely browned on both sides, but do not cook through. Then place in the center of a well-seasoned oak plank. Pipe duchess potatoes around the plank with a pastry tube. (Duchess potatoes differ from mashed potatoes in that they have the yolks of eggs beaten into them.) Garnish the plank with mounds of boiled cauliflower flowerets that have been dipped in butter and sprinkled liberally with paprika. Between the mounds, place tomatoes that have been cut in half, dotted with butter, sprinkled with grated cheese, and grilled. Also add medium-size parboiled onions, and fill up the remaining space with cooked green string beans or carrots, which may be sliced or cut in fancy shapes with a vegetable cutter. Place the plank in a moderate 350-degree oven for 25 minutes until the chops are done and the vegetables browned.

Ragout of Lamb Chops with Chestnuts

10 to 12 lamb chops (2 per person) cut from the shoulder, with fat removed
Salt and freshly ground pepper
Thyme
2 onions cut in thin slices
6 tablespoons butter
2 cups peeled chestnuts (canned whole chestnuts may be used)
1½ to 2 cups liquid (broth or half broth and half wine or water)
Chopped parsley

Butter a rather deep baking dish or casserole equipped with a cover. In it arrange half of the chops. Salt and pepper them, and add a touch of thyme. Add a layer of half of the onion rings and dot with butter. Add a layer of half of the chestnuts, a layer of chops, a layer of onions, and finally a layer of chestnuts. Add broth to barely cover the dish. Dot with butter, and season with salt, pepper, and thyme. Cover, and bake at 350 degrees for an hour. Test the chops for doneness by cutting a slit near the bone. If not done, return to the oven for 15 to 20 minutes. Serve with braised brussels sprouts. Garnish with chopped parsley.

Note. The addition of a couple of cloves of garlic to the recipe enhances it considerably.

Shoulder Lamb Chops Braised with Onions and Peppers

6 shoulder chops, arm or blade, cut about 1 inch thick
4 medium onions, thinly sliced
3 green peppers, seeded and thinly sliced
Salt and freshly ground pepper
¾ cup tomato sauce
1 teaspoon basil

Sear the chops quickly in lamb fat rubbed onto the surface of a heavy skillet. Add the onions, green peppers (the peppers will be more delicious if they are held over a flame to burn off most of the skin), and salt and pepper to taste. Add the tomato sauce, and bring to a boil. Cover, and simmer 25 to 30 minutes. Add the basil, correct the seasoning, and cook, covered, another 5 to 10 minutes. Serve with rice or noodles.

Braised Shoulder Lamb Chops with Mushrooms and Onions

6 shoulder chops, arm or blade, cut about 1 inch thick
2 cloves garlic, finely chopped
2 onions, finely chopped
½ pound mushrooms, finely chopped
Butter, if needed
Salt and freshly ground pepper
2 tablespoons chopped parsley

Rub a heavy skillet well with lamb fat. Heat and sear the chops on both sides until they are a pleasant brown. Add the chopped garlic, onions, and mushrooms. Cook 4 to 5 minutes over rather brisk heat. Cover, reduce the heat to simmer, and continue cooking 20 minutes. If the mixture seems dry, add 2 or 3 tablespoons butter. After 20 minutes, add salt and pepper to taste and chopped parsley. Continue cooking 5 to 6 minutes. Transfer to a hot platter, and serve with buttered boiled potatoes and a purée of spinach.

Breaded Lamb Chops I

These have been popular from the 1870's and '80's up to the present day — one still finds them on menus. They should properly be served with an onion sauce. Any cut of chop may be used for the dish, but it seems rather a waste of good and expensive meat to use loin or rib chops when the arm or blade chops will do just as well. You will need a heavy skillet for this and enough fat — peanut oil, butter and peanut oil, or any other oil you choose — to reach a depth of ¾ to 1 inch. The fat should be heated to 360 degrees.

For 6 thickish shoulder chops, prepare dried breadcrumbs seasoned with salt and freshly ground pepper. Beat up two eggs with 2 tablespoons milk. Have a plate of flour ready. Dust the chops with flour, dip both sides in the egg mixture, then press into the crumbs. Fry them quickly in fat, turning once, and drain on absorbent paper. Transfer to a hot platter. Serve with lemon wedges and onion sauce. Buttered peas are a natural complement.

Breaded Lamb Chops II

Prepare the crumb mixture as above, but add finely chopped parsley and a little nutmeg. For 6 thick chops, beat eggs and milk as above. Melt 6 tablespoons butter in a heavy baking dish or pan, and heat well in a 350-degree oven. Dust the chops with flour, dip into the egg mixture, then press into the crumbs. Arrange the chops in the baking dish and place in the oven. When they have just begun to cook baste with a mixture of boiling water and butter, and continue basting every fifteen minutes for an hour. Remove the chops, dot with butter, and serve either from the baking dish or on a hot platter. Serve with an onion sauce and broiled or grilled tomatoes. Garnish with chopped parsley.

Note. For a more sophisticated dish, add finely chopped garlic and some tarragon to the crumb mixture.

Teriyakied Lamb Chops

Teriyaki has become an almost universal method of preparing meats of all kinds. It is amazing to see how this primarily Pacific Coast version of Oriental cookery has swept the country and is now as popular in South Carolina as it is in Washington or California. Any of the chops mentioned above are good for teriyaki broiling, either over charcoal or in your broiler. For outdoor cooking, arm and blade chops are superb fare when cut good and thick.

For teriyakied lamb chops, marinate the chops overnight or a few hours in a teriyaki marinade (page 190). Broil to your taste, and serve with broiled eggplant slices, well seasoned with salt and freshly ground pepper.

Lamb Steaks

Although I find the lamb steak less toothsome than other cuts of lamb for broiling, there is a great demand for this particular cut. You may prepare it in any of the prescribed fashions for chops. However, I find it is best marinated in teriyaki sauce (page 190) and then broiled. It is also very good brushed with oil, rubbed with garlic and a generous dose of tarragon, and then broiled or pan-broiled.

Lamb on a Skewer

Americans have been broiling meat on skewers and sticks for over three hundred years — not only lamb but all kinds of meats and game and even fish, cooked over open fires and in fireplaces. In the nineteenth and early twentieth centuries, immigrants from the Near East and Mediterranean countries began to spread the cult of the shish kebab, and after the First World War the Russians arrived in force in the Northwest and brought their version of skewered meat, shashlik. Today there is no lamb dish more varied in preparation or more in evidence. It is a favorite item for outdoor cookery, and it has found its way onto the menus of every steak and chop house across the country, a sure token of cultural acceptance.

Basic Shish Kebab

For 4 persons, you need 3 pounds of meat or more. The best meat for shish kebab is certainly the leg of lamb, and the second choice is the shoulder with some of the fat removed. The meat should be cut into cubes 1 to 2½ inches square, depending upon individual taste and the size of the skewers, and marinated 2 to 48 hours (see Basic Marinade, below).

Use skewers of steel, iron, or even hard wood, if well soaked. If you want rare and juicy pieces, string them close together. For crisp and medium rare pieces, space them some distance apart. For very juicy and flavorful kebabs, place pieces of lamb fat between the pieces of lean. For vegetables to alternate on the skewer with the lamb, see basic marinade recipe below. When you have strung the skewers, brush them with oil or butter and broil over charcoal or in the broiler oven, about 3 inches from the source of heat. Turn the skewers often, and brush with oil. Broiling time will be 9 to 12 minutes, for medium rare to medium. Salt and pepper the meat as you turn it. This simple seasoning is all that is needed. Serve the kebabs very hot with rice, bulgur, or kasha.

Basic Marinade for Shish Kebab

1 cup olive oil
1/3 cup lemon juice
2 garlic cloves, crushed
Salt and freshly ground pepper to taste

Add any of the seasonings given below, and marinate the cubes of meat in this mixture for 2 to 48 hours. String on skewers and broil.

Greek fashion. Add either oregano or sage to the marinade, and alternate the lamb with quarters of onion and squares of green pepper.

Iranian. In Iranian restaurants and homes in the United States, the lamb is cut about two and a half inches long, an inch wide, and an inch thick. These pieces are strung on smallish skewers, marinated with yoghurt and thyme for 12 to 24 hours, and then grilled with the yoghurt covering. The kebabs are served with rice, fresh radishes, and onions and are completely delicious.

Lebanese. Add mint or thyme to the marinade. Usually the lamb is alternated with green pepper squares and onions, and sometimes tomatoes are added.

Rumanian. Usually oregano is added to the marinade and the lamb is alternated with eggplant cut in cubes and sometimes with tomato and green pepper as well.

Turkish. Season the marinade with crushed bay leaves and see that some is spread on the kebabs when broiled. Sometimes the meat is alternated with pieces of sweetbread, onion, and quartered tomatoes or whole cherry tomatoes.

Shashlik

2 pounds cubed leg of lamb (see Basic Shish Kebab)

MARINADE

1 cup oil (it can be corn oil or peanut oil)
1 cup red wine

The Russian influence in cookery first made itself felt in the Northwest states, and it has gradually spread throughout the country. This Russian version of shish kebab has been extremely popular. The first one I recall eating was made with mutton and contained a great deal of fat, which when broiled down was redolent with the flavors of the marinade.

Sometimes pomegranate juice is substituted for the wine and

3 bay leaves, crushed
Fresh dill or parsley
2 tablespoons wine vinegar
3 garlic cloves, crushed
1 teaspoon freshly ground pepper
½ teaspoon ground allspice

wine vinegar, a very interesting change. Marinate the lamb as for shish kebab and broil. Pieces of onion and tomato may be combined with the lamb.

Ground Lamb Kebabs

2 pounds ground lamb
2 garlic cloves, finely chopped
½ cup pine nuts
½ cup chopped parsley
1 teaspoon salt
1 teaspoon freshly ground pepper
¼ cup dry breadcrumbs
2 eggs

Mix ingredients well and taste for seasoning (raw lamb is quite palatable). Mold around skewers, brush with olive oil, and broil over coals or in a broiling oven. These should be eaten on the rare side. Serve with broiled eggplant and tomatoes.

Broiled Breast of Lamb

Choose young breast of lamb, which is not too fat, allowing 1 breast for 2 persons. Rub well with garlic and a little Tabasco and rosemary. Place on a rack and broil about 8 inches from the source of heat, or weave on a spit and broil over charcoal. The breast should broil slowly in order to cook out most of the fat and become crisp. Salt and pepper well, and serve cut in strips as you do spareribs. A salad of sliced onions and tomatoes and some crisp rolls or bread make a very good accompaniment to this dish.

Note. Breast of lamb may be placed on a rack and roasted in a rather hot oven (400 degrees). Turn two or three times while roasting and allow to get crisp and thoroughly well done. This will take about an hour to an hour and a quarter.

Marinated Breast of Lamb

5 pounds breast of lamb
½ cup oil
1 cup red wine
2 cloves garlic, crushed
1 teaspoon rosemary or sweet basil
1 large onion, finely chopped
1 teaspoon freshly ground pepper

This originated as a specialty for outdoor cookery. However, if you have a rotisserie oven in your kitchen, you can do these breasts quite as well indoors as out.

Place the lamb in a shallow dish. Combine the other ingredients, and pour over the lamb. Let it stand for several hours. Weave the breasts on a spit, and roast slowly, basting from time to time with the marinade until they are quite well done and beautifully browned — about 1 to 1½ hours. Serve with a rice pilaff and a watercress salad.

Stuffed Breast of Lamb

2 breasts of lamb
1 large onion, chopped
2 garlic cloves, chopped
4 tablespoons butter
2 cups soft breadcrumbs
1 teaspoon thyme
¼ cup chopped parsley
Salt and freshly ground pepper
1 egg, lightly beaten
Additional melted butter, if needed
3 tablespoons flour
Stock or water

You must try to find very young lamb for this dish, for you want as little fat as possible. It is a dish which has come to us from various sources — France, North Africa, the Middle East. In this country it first caught on in the West, but it has gradually become known in the East as well.

Sauté the onion and garlic lightly in the butter, and combine with the crumbs and seasonings, using 1 teaspoon salt and ½ teaspoon pepper. Blend in the egg. If the stuffing is too dry, add melted butter. Place the stuffing between the two breasts of lamb and tie them together securely. Arrange on a rack in a roasting pan. Roast in a preheated 350-degree oven, allowing 15 to 18 minutes per pound of meat, until brown and rather crisp. Salt and pepper the meat before transferring to a hot platter. Pour off the pan juices and skim off excess fat. Combine 3 tablespoons of the fat with the flour, and blend over medium heat to make a brown roux. If there are pan juices, add them. If not, add 1½ cups stock or water, blend well, and stir until it thickens slightly. Season to taste and add a few dashes of Tabasco. Serve the brown gravy with the lamb and buttered peas. Or you might prefer to serve a well-seasoned tomato sauce, as many people do. Also, if you want, add 3 to 4 tablespoons dried currants or sultana raisins to the stuffing, which gives it a rather different quality.

Breast of Lamb, Poached and Breaded

2 breasts of lamb
1 or 2 onions stuck with cloves
Sprig of parsley
Water
1 tablespoon salt
Flour
2 eggs slightly beaten
Dry breadcrumbs mixed with 1 teaspoon salt and 1 teaspoon freshly ground pepper
6 tablespoons oil
4 tablespoons butter

This recipe is similar to a dish made in France and in England, served with a different sauce in each country. It was much in vogue for luncheons in this country around the turn of the century and is worth perpetuating.

Trim excess fat from the breasts. Place the meat in a deep saucepan with the onions, parsley, and water to cover. Bring to a boil and add the salt. Cover, and simmer until the lamb is very tender. Let it cook 1 hour and pull out as many rib bones as possible. Place the lamb in a flat dish and weight down. Refrigerate till ready to use. Then cut the breast meat in a size convenient for serving. Flour well, dip in beaten egg, and roll in crumbs till completely coated. Sauté or fry in hot fat until nicely browned on both sides. Drain on absorbent paper, arrange on a hot platter with a garnish of watercress, and have hot onion sauce ready to pour. Serve with a crisp salad.

Stews, Fricassees, Casseroles

A Browned Lamb Stew with Vegetables

3 to 3½ pounds of lamb shoulder or leg cut in 1½-inch cubes
Flour
3 tablespoons oil
4 tablespoons butter
Boiling water
1 tablespoon salt
6 medium small onions
3 large carrots, halved, or 6 small carrots
3 to 4 young turnips, cut in quarters
1 garlic clove, crushed
1 teaspoon thyme
12 small new potatoes, boiled till just tender
2 pounds fresh cooked peas or 1 package frozen peas, cooked
¼ cup chopped parsley
1 teaspoon freshly ground pepper

Here are two versions of the browned lamb stew. The first is the accepted one, and the second was a recipe made by the cook of some neighbors of ours, named Julie. Her French parents had emigrated to San Francisco in the early days. They taught her how to cook, and she maintained some of their culinary secrets for the delectation of others long after.

Remove excess fat from the lamb. Dredge well with the flour and brown small amounts at a time in the hot oil and butter. Add more oil and butter if needed. Transfer the meat to a heavy pot or kettle or Dutch oven. Rinse the pan with enough boiling water to barely cover the lamb and add to the pot. Stir in the salt and bring to a boil. Reduce the heat to simmer and cook for an hour. Add the onions, carrots, turnips, garlic, and thyme. Continue cooking till the meat is tender and the vegetables are cooked through. Remove from the heat and let stand 10 minutes. Skim off the excess fat. Taste for seasoning. Add the potatoes and bring to the boiling point again. Stir in the cooked peas. Arrange the stew on a platter and sprinkle with the chopped parsley and pepper. Serve in rather deep plates with plenty of warmed crisp bread or toast. Along with a good salad, this makes an excellent meal for 4 to 6 persons, depending upon appetites.

Note. This stew is even better if it is allowed to cool overnight before skimming and reheating with potatoes and peas.

Julie's Exceptional Lamb Stew with Vegetables

FOR THE BROTH

2 pounds or more lamb bones and 1-pound piece of neck
2 leeks
2 large onions
2 large carrots
1 turnip
1 teaspoon thyme
2 to 3 sprigs parsley
3 garlic cloves, crushed

This is a long process, but worth it. It is best to start the dish a day in advance. Make the broth first. Brown the bones and neck in a hot oven, 425 to 450 degrees. Combine them with the vegetables, seasonings, and water. Simmer 4 to 5 hours. Cool overnight. Then skim off the fat, strain off the broth, and set aside.

Dredge the shoulder meat with flour and brown in the hot oil and butter. Transfer to a large Dutch oven or braising pot. Add enough boiling lamb broth to just cover the meat, and return to a boil. (Or you may use ⅔ broth and ⅓ white wine.) Rinse the pan used for browning with a little more of the broth and add to the meat. Simmer covered for 1 hour or until the meat is just tender. Drain, and reserve the broth. Keep the meat warm. In the meantime cook the vegetables in boiling salted water — the carrots and turnips in one pan, the onions and leeks in another, and the snap beans in a third.

Add some of the vegetable juices to the meat broth, and reduce over a rather brisk heat. If you like, thicken the sauce slightly with butter and flour kneaded together, and stir until smooth. Taste the sauce for seasoning. Combine with the meat, carrots, turnips, onions, and leeks, and just heat through. Add the green beans and heat another moment. Serve on a hot platter surrounded with mounds of steamed rice, and garnish with chopped parsley. Drink a bottle of Fleurie or a California Cabernet with this.

1½ teaspoons salt
2 to 3 quarts water

FOR THE STEW

4 pounds lamb shoulder, cut in 1½-inch cubes
Flour for dredging
5 tablespoons butter
3 tablespoons oil
12 small carrots or 6 carrots cut in halves
3 small turnips, peeled and quartered
12 small onions
3 leeks cut in 2-inch pieces
1 pound snap beans
3 to 4 tablespoons butter kneaded with the same amount of flour
Chopped parsley

Irish Stew

One of the first Irish stews to be found in an American cookbook was offered by Miss Marion Harland, who made it with beef and served it with a brown sauce, which I'm sure would surprise the Irish. Mrs. Rorer, who gave a recipe for Irish stew in 1886, eschewing the carrots, omits it in her later editions but gives us a Scotch stew with tomatoes which is rather unusual.

3 to 3½ pounds lamb shoulder
1 pound neck of lamb
2 quarts water
1 medium onion stuck with 2 cloves
1 large bay leaf
2 large garlic cloves
1 tablespoon salt
½ teaspoon freshly ground pepper
½ teaspoon thyme
Parsley sprig
3 thinly sliced medium onions
3 leeks split in half and cut in small dice
Additional bay leaf
½ teaspoon additional thyme
¼ teaspoon nutmeg
4 medium potatoes, finely diced
2 tablespoons finely chopped parsley

Have the butcher bone the shoulder and give you the bones. Put the bones and neck in a deep saucepan with 2 quarts water. Bring to a boil and boil 5 to 6 minutes, skimming off the scum from the surface. Add the onion stuck with cloves, and the bay leaf, garlic, salt, pepper, thyme, and parsley. Bring to a boil again, reduce the heat to simmer, and simmer 2½ hours to a strong broth. Strain, and put in the refrigerator overnight. Next day, skim off the fat.

Remove all fat from the lamb shoulder and cut the meat into pieces 1 inch wide and 2 inches long. Put the meat in a heavy pan with the sliced onions, leeks, additional bay leaf and thyme, nutmeg, and enough lamb broth to come 1 inch above the meat. Bring to a boil, skim off the scum, reduce the heat, and simmer, covered, 1 hour, then test the meat for tenderness. If it still seems a bit tough, give it another 15 minutes, then add the diced potatoes. Cook 30 minutes, until the stew is slightly thickened by the potatoes, then taste for seasoning. You will probably find it needs salt — 1 to 2 teaspoons should be sufficient — a few grinds of pepper, and a touch of nutmeg. Let this cook a little to blend with the stew, then add the chopped parsley and cook just 1 minute more.

With dumplings. Make dumplings (see page 205). Drop into the stew, cover, and cook 16 to 17 minutes without removing the cover. Serve the dumplings sprinkled with chopped parsley.

An Early Version of Lamb Curry (Miss Farmer's)

2 pounds lamb shoulder cut in 1-inch pieces
Boiling water (about 1 quart)
3 onions cut in slices
½ teaspoon peppercorns
½ teaspoon thyme
Sprig parsley
3 tablespoons butter
3 tablespoons flour
2 teaspoons curry powder
½ teaspoon salt
½ teaspoon pepper

This is as mild as May but it gives a good idea of how cautiously spice was introduced into our cuisine. New Englanders were the first to use much curry because it was brought back from the Orient by ship.

Cover the meat with boiling water. Add the onions, peppercorns, thyme, and parsley. Bring to a boil and simmer until tender — about an hour. Remove the meat, strain the liquid, and skim off the excess fat. Make a roux with the flour and butter, add the curry powder, and cook a few minutes. Add a bit of the broth and stir into the remaining broth; salt and pepper, and bring to a boil. Heat the lamb in this and serve with steamed rice.

Kapama

3 pounds shoulder lamb cut in 2-inch dice
Flour
4 tablespoons butter
3 tablespoons oil
Salt and freshly ground pepper
3 large onions, finely chopped
3 garlic cloves, finely chopped
1 tablespoon paprika
1 cup water or stock
14 to 16 green onions cut in small pieces
Sour cream

Balkans have brought us many of their native lamb dishes. This particular one comes from the Dalmatian country, where sheep abound and the variety of lamb dishes is astounding. It is easy to make, full of flavor, and a change from the usual.

Dredge the lamb with flour and brown well in the hot butter and oil, salting and peppering it to taste. Transfer the meat to a saucepan or braising pan. Add the onions and garlic to the browning pan, along with more butter if needed, and cook till the onions are translucent. Add the paprika and blend well. Transfer to the pan containing the meat. Rinse the browning pan with water or stock, and add to the meat pan. Cover, and simmer 1 hour, adding more liquid if necessary. At the end of the hour, add the finely cut green onions, and simmer 30 minutes. Serve with rice and sour cream.

Kibbeh Naye

2 pounds ground lamb from the leg, free of any sinew or fat
1½ cups bulgur or cracked wheat

The Kashouty family live in Virginia, where they have maintained some of the great traditions of Mrs. Kashouty's national cuisine and adapted it to American eating. In Lebanese and Syrian restaurants dotted throughout the country and in homes like the

Kashoutys' you are apt to find this typical dish. Kibbeh is done in two ways. One is served raw, as an appetizer, and the other is a baked dish to be served as a main course for lunch or dinner. Both this and the baked kibbeh below are Mrs. Kashouty's.

3 medium onions
Salt and freshly ground pepper to taste (the Syrians use allspice with pepper)
3 ice cubes
Green onions

The dish is best when made just before serving. Place the meat in a good-sized mixing bowl. Grate the onions over it, and add the seasonings and ice cubes (the latter add the necessary liquid and prevent the lamb from turning dark). When the mixture is well blended, remove any excess ice and correct the seasoning. Spread on a cold serving plate. Decorate with shredded green onions. Serve as an hors d'oeuvre with thinly sliced bread or Syrian bread, radishes, and green onions. It is often served with crisp lettuce leaves, also.

Sautéed Kibbeh Naye. The kibbeh may also be formed into balls and sautéed in butter over a rather brisk heat. Serve with a large platter of radishes, scallions, romaine, and endive, accompanied by vinegar and oil cruets.

Baked Kibbeh

1 recipe for kibbeh naye
2 cups chopped lamb from the shoulder with some fat
2 medium onions, coarsely chopped
4 tablespoons butter
½ cup pine nuts
Freshly ground pepper or allspice (or both)
Salt
1 cup melted butter

Sauté the onions and shoulder lamb in the butter, blending well. Add the pine nuts and seasonings, and cook lightly. In an 11 × 14 × 2 inch pan make a layer of half of the kibbeh naye. Then add the filling, and top with another layer of the kibbeh naye. With a sharp knife cut into diamond shapes. Pour the melted butter over the meat, and bake 25 minutes at 350 degrees. Run under the broiler for a few moments to brown more, if you like.

Lamb with String Beans

1 pound young lamb cut in 1-inch cubes
½ cup butter
2 large or 3 medium onions, finely chopped
Salt and freshly ground pepper or allspice (or both)
2 to 3 pounds snap beans cut in 1-inch pieces, tips removed

Cook the lamb in ¼ cup butter till crisp and brown. Add the remaining butter and the onions, and sauté till the onions are just golden. Season well. Put the snap beans in a saucepan and add the lamb, onions, and pan juices. No extra liquid is needed. Cover the pan, and cook over medium heat for about 1 hour, shaking several times to rotate the mixture. Serve with kibbeh.

Lamb with Rice and Pine Nuts (Lebanese)

1 pound lamb, chopped
1 stick (½ cup) butter
1 large onion, finely chopped
Dash of allspice, cinnamon and nutmeg
Salt and freshly ground pepper
1 cup rice
4 tablespoons butter
Broth
½ cup pine nuts

Sauté the lamb in the butter with the onion, shaking the pan and stirring occasionally till the onion is just golden. Add a dash of the spices and salt and pepper to taste. Sauté the rice in butter until golden, and add to lamb and onion. Add broth to more than cover by an inch. Cover the pan and simmer until the meat is tender and the rice has absorbed all the liquid. Add the pine nuts just before serving. This is delicious served with poultry, or just as it is, with a salad or tray of raw vegetables, such as radishes and onions, and various greens.

Haricot of Mutton

Originally this recipe was called *halicot* of mutton, from the French verb *halicoter*, meaning to cut up. It was, in other words, a stew or ragout. But eventually it was corrupted to *haricot* of mutton, misleading anyone who doesn't know better into thinking it is a dish made with beans. It is no wonder then that it is frequently confused with *ragout de mouton aux haricots blancs*, which really *is* a dish prepared with beans. Both dishes are presented here in Anglo-Americanized form — first, two lamb versions of haricot of mutton in its original sense, and then a lamb or mutton dish made with white beans.

Haricot of Mutton (or Lamb)

3 pounds lean lamb cut into strips 3 inches long and about 1½ inches wide and 1 inch thick
Flour
3 to 4 tablespoons butter
2 tablespoons oil
1 onion, thinly sliced
1 cup stock or bouillon
1 cup parboiled sliced carrots
1 cup peas (either fresh or frozen)
Salt and freshly ground pepper
Butter and flour, kneaded together, for thickening
1 tablespoon tomato catsup (I'd settle for 2 tablespoons tomato paste)
¼ cup sherry

This first one, dating from about 1865, is the more typical of the two.

Dredge the meat with the flour and brown quickly in the butter and oil mixture. Add the onion, and brown with the meat. When nicely browned, add the broth, and cover. Simmer 1 hour, or until the meat is beginning to be tender. Add the carrots and peas. Cook 20 minutes, covered. Salt and pepper to taste, and add the beurre manié to thicken (if you like), the catsup or the tomato paste, and the sherry. Bring to a boil, and cook briskly about 3 minutes. Serve with molded potatoes — rich mashed potatoes pressed into a well-buttered mold and then unmolded on the platter.

Mrs. Rorer's Haricot of Mutton (or Lamb)

2 pounds loin chops cut around 1 inch thick
3 tablespoons butter
2 tablespoons oil
2 tablespoons flour
1 cup broth or stock
2 onions cut in thin slices
1 rib celery cut in 1-inch pieces
1 tablespoon mushroom catsup
1 carrot, cut in fancy shapes and parboiled 10 minutes
1 turnip, cut in fancy shapes and parboiled 10 minutes
Salt and freshly ground pepper
1 bay leaf
2 tablespoons sherry

A later version, from the 1880's.

Brown the chops on both sides in the butter and oil. Remove, add the flour to the pan, and make a roux. Stir in the stock, and blend over low heat till it thickens. Add the onions, celery, mushroom catsup, parboiled carrots and turnips, salt and pepper, the bay leaf and the chops. Simmer covered for 30 to 45 minutes, till the vegetables and chops are tender. Do not overcook. Finally add the sherry ("If you use it," Mrs. Rorer adds). Let it boil up thoroughly, and serve with rice or with baked potatoes.

Haricot Mutton (or Lamb) with Beans

½ pound dried white beans, pea beans, or Great Northern
1½ pounds lamb cut in 1-inch cubes
Flour
4 tablespoons butter
2 tablespoons oil
1 medium onion, sliced
1 carrot cut in 1-inch pieces
1 small turnip cut in dice
2½ cups stock or water
Salt and freshly ground pepper
Chopped parsley
Chopped mint, if available

An English version of haricot lamb that found its way to the States and that resembles the French ragout au haricots blancs.

Put the beans in water, bring them to a boil, and boil 5 minutes. Let them cool in the water. Dredge the lamb with flour, and sear in the hot butter and oil till nicely browned on all sides. Add the onion, carrot, and turnip to the pan, and toss well with the meat. Drain the beans and add, with the stock. Cover, and simmer about 2 hours, adding more liquid if needed. Salt and pepper to taste. Serve the mixture in a large bowl, with chopped parsley and mint for garnish. A salad would be the proper accompaniment for this rather heavy dish.

Hot Pot

This dish, which is certainly a relative of the famous Lancashire hot pot, has been known for generations in England, where it is made with fresh lamb. In this country it became a favorite way of using leftover lamb.

American Hot Pot

Butter
3½ cups diced leftover lamb
4 potatoes, diced
2 large onions, diced
1 tablespoon chopped parsley
Salt and freshly ground pepper
2 additional small potatoes, thickly sliced
Broth or stock

Butter a baking dish and in it arrange alternating layers of the meat, diced potatoes, and onions, till all the ingredients are used. Add the chopped parsley and salt and pepper to taste. Arrange the sliced potatoes over the top of the dish. Add broth or stock to come within 1 inch of the top layer, and bake, covered, 1½ hours. Brush the potatoes with butter, and bake uncovered for another half hour to brown them. Serve with a salad or a purée of spinach.

Traditional Lancashire Hot Pot

1½ pounds lean leg lamb cut in thin slices
3 large potatoes, sliced
2 large onions, sliced
Salt and freshly ground pepper
Water or broth
Butter

Arrange alternating layers of the meat, onions, and potatoes in a baking dish equipped with a cover. Salt and pepper each layer and finish with a layer of potatoes. Add boiling water or broth to cover. Place a piece of buttered wax paper, parchment, or foil on top, and cover the dish. Bake at 350 degrees 1¾ to 2 hours. Remove the cover and paper, and dot the top with butter. Return to the oven uncovered for 15 minutes or so to brown the potatoes. Serve with well-buttered fresh peas.

Dishes Made with Cold Lamb

Probably because lamb was never as popular as other meats in earlier years, cookbooks seldom recommended serving it cold. A lamb salad is one of the few instances found. However, nicely sliced cold lamb, served with a good salad or with homemade pickles such as the chowchow or the oiled pickles given in this book, makes a most agreeable meal. Cold lamb also makes delectable sandwiches for lunches and picnics if the lamb is cut without fat in delicate slices and good bread is used, spread with perhaps a garlic butter or a well-flavored mayonnaise.

Shepherd's Pie

3 cups cold lamb ground coarsely (other meats may be mixed with it)

This rather homely dish has long been a common way to use up an old joint or roast, so it is natural that it should have come to America with the English. I doubt if many people recognize it as an old English recipe when they see it on menus across the United States. The American version is basically the same, except that one well-known food writer mixes flour with the mashed potatoes, which makes a much heavier crust.

1 onion ground with the lamb
Salt and freshly ground pepper
7 tablespoons butter
2 tablespoons flour
½ cup stock or milk
4 to 5 good-sized potatoes — mealy potatoes preferred
Milk — ¼ to ½ cup

Grind the lamb and onion, and season to taste with salt and pepper. Melt 3 tablespoons butter over low heat and add the flour to make a roux. Stir in the liquid and continue stirring till thickened. Season to taste. Combine with the meat. Spread into a 2-quart baking dish. Cool thoroughly. Peel the potatoes and cook in boiling water till tender. Drain, mash, and add 4 tablespoons butter, the milk, and seasonings. Let it cool slightly.

When the meat is quite cold, spread the mashed potato over it to make a crust, or force it through a pastry bag, using a large rosette tube. Dot the crust with butter. Add crumbs or grated Parmesan cheese, if you like. Bake at 375 degrees for 35 to 40 minutes or until the crust is nicely brown and the dish is bubbling hot. A coleslaw would make a pleasant accompaniment to this dish.

Although this is a delicious dish as it is, you may want to add some thyme or tarragon or a touch of garlic and tomato to the lamb. Or you may add chopped fresh herbs, such as chives, tarragon, and parsley, to the mashed potatoes.

Lamb Salad

1½ cups diced cold lamb
1½ cups diced cooked potatoes
½ cup finely chopped green onion
¼ cup finely chopped parsley
1 tablespoon capers
2 or 3 gherkins, thinly sliced
Mayonnaise

Toss the first six ingredients together and bind with a good homemade mustard-flavored mayonnaise. Serve on lettuce leaves.

Mrs. Rorer's Chinese Lamb

2 cups cold lamb, finely chopped
1 onion, coarsely chopped
3 tablespoons butter
1 cup fresh peas
1 cup stock, broth, or boiling water in which you have dissolved a bouillon cube
1 small head of lettuce, shredded
Salt and freshly ground pepper

Mrs. Rorer probably calls this Chinese lamb because someone's Chinese cook prepared it for her once and she liked it. Otherwise it has little relation to Chinese cookery.

Sauté the onion in the butter, and add the lamb, peas, and broth. Bring to a boil and reduce to simmer. Add the lettuce and cover. Simmer just till the meat is cooked through and the peas are tender. Correct the seasoning. Serve in a rice ring with a curry sauce or a tomato sauce.

Lamb Rice Casserole

1 large onion, finely chopped
1 clove garlic, finely chopped
Butter
2 cups cold roast lamb cut in 1-inch cubes
Lamb gravy or brown sauce
¼ cup finely chopped parsley
Salt and freshly ground pepper
3 cups cooked rice
Crumbs

This simple dish was a staple for generations of Americans, and it is so good in its way that it should not be forgotten. It probably has no national background but was put together by a creative cook and has been going on ever since.

Sauté the onion and garlic in a little butter. Combine them with the lamb, gravy, and parsley. Season to taste with salt and pepper. Make a bed of rice in the bottom of a 1½-quart casserole or baking dish, and make alternate layers of the lamb mixture and rice, ending with a layer of rice. Top with crumbs, and cover with a piece of well-buttered paper. Bake at 350 degrees for 35 to 40 minutes or until thoroughly heated. Remove the cover for the last 10 minutes to color the top. Serve with sautéed zucchini flavored with garlic and parsley.

Note. You may add condiments to your taste to this dish, such as Worcestershire, tomato sauce, or Tabasco.

Lamb Offal

Lamb's Liver

The liver of the lamb is a rather neglected delicacy. It can be prepared as you do calf's liver. It is thoroughly delicious whether cut in thin slices and sautéed in butter till pink within and brown without or cut into a thick steak (an American innovation, for the most part) and broiled rare.

Cut liver into rather thick slices and brush well with oil. (Olive oil gives more flavor.) Broil over charcoal or in the broiling oven of your range, allowing about 3 to 4 minutes on each side, until the liver is just seared and still quite rare within. Salt and pepper well, and serve with a Béarnaise sauce, plain boiled potatoes, and perhaps sautéed onion rings.

Lamb Kidneys

Lamb kidney has been an international favorite among the French and Italians and also among some of the English.

There are important steps in preparing lamb kidneys for cooking. Anyone who appreciates the texture and flavor of the kidney knows that the less it is cooked the more tender it is. First, remove the tubes and the rather tough white section in the middle of the kidney, which is easily done with a sharp knife or scissors. Second, soak the kidneys in milk or white wine about an hour before they are cooked, which makes them more delicate.

Serve any of the recipes below with crisply fried eggplant or potatoes, watercress, and perhaps sliced tomatoes with oil and vinegar. Serve 3 or 4 lamb kidneys per person. Wine is almost a must with kidneys. Serve a nice Beaune or a light Bordeaux wine.

Plain Broiled Lamb Kidneys

Split the kidneys, remove the cores, and soak in milk or white wine for an hour. Dry with a towel and rub with oil or butter. If you are broiling on a broiling pan, oil the rack and arrange the kidneys on it. Broil in a hot oven about 3 inches from the heat, turning once until nicely browned. This will take 4 to 5 minutes if you like them quite rare. Serve the kidneys on hot plates and salt and pepper them at table. Mustard is favored by many people as a seasoning.

Lamb Kidneys en Brochette I

Mrs. Rorer in 1888 offered "a nice breakfast relish" of kidneys en brochette, alternated with bacon squares, brushed with melted butter, and broiled 5 minutes, basted with butter the while.

Lamb Kidneys en Brochette II

Soak kidneys in milk, dry on a towel, and rub well with olive oil or melted butter. Arrange on skewers. Broil 5 or 6 minutes, basting with oil or butter. Serve with a Béarnaise sauce. This became a favorite in the latter part of the nineteenth century and makes a superb dinner or luncheon dish.

Lamb's Tongues

There was never a time, it seems to me, when there were not some pickled lamb's tongues on the shelf of our family larder. They were used for a quick snack, for a cold supper, for sandwiches, or for picnics. And how tender and delicious they were.

Often when they were being prepared, we would dine on some of the tongues before pickling, served with a version of what might be called a sauce poulette or with a tomato sauce. They were delicate and extraordinarily good. I fear that lamb's tongues are lost to most people today, who won't take the trouble to prepare them and don't know what eating pleasure they are missing.

The tongues are quite small, and several are usually served to a person.

Boiled Lamb's Tongues

Lamb's tongues
SEASONED WATER
3 quarts water
1 tablespoon salt
1 teaspoon freshly ground pepper
1 onion
1 rib celery
1 sprig parsley
1 or 2 slices lemon

Wash and clean the tongues, and simmer ½ to ¾ hour in seasoned water. When they are tender, transfer to a dish. When cool enough to handle, peel and core them. Split and serve hot with tomato sauce or Creole sauce. Or serve cold with horseradish or a mustard vinaigrette.

Pickled Lamb's Tongues. Place the cooked tongues in a large jar. For 12 tongues, cut 1 large onion into thin slices. Add 6 to 8 peppercorns, a clove of garlic, and a sprig of fresh tarragon or a teaspoon of dried tarragon. Add a mild wine vinegar to cover, or use half white wine and half mild cider vinegar. Cover the jar tightly. These will keep 2 to 3 weeks. Serve with a salad — a tossed green salad, a pungent potato or rice salad, or a sauerkraut salad. For sandwiches, slice thin and combine with thin slices of cheese, preferably a Swiss Emmenthaler, and, if you like, a layer of raw sauerkraut.

Mrs. Harland's Fricassee of Lamb's Tongues

12 lamb's tongues
Flour
4 tablespoons butter
3 tablespoons oil
½ cup finely chopped onion
3 tablespoons chopped parsley
½ teaspoon thyme
2 cups broth in which tongues were cooked
Beurre manié
5 or 6 slices lemon
1 tablespoon lemon juice or more

Simmer and peel the tongues according to directions above. Cut them into thickish slices, dip in flour, and sauté in the butter and oil about 5 minutes. Transfer to a hot platter. Add to the pan the onion, parsley, and thyme. Sauté 3 to 4 minutes. Add the broth, and let it reduce to 1½ cups over brisk heat. Add small balls of flour and butter kneaded together (beurre manié), and stir till the sauce has thickened slightly. Add the lemon slices and juice. Cook 1 minute. Pour over the tongues.

Such a fricassee was usually served with mounds of rice and surely needs a green as well, like puréed spinach, to make it agreeable to eye and palate. What Mrs. Harland has given us is in a way a version of sauce poulette.

Sheep's Trotters

16 trotters, prepared by the butcher
3 quarts water
1 onion stuck with 2 cloves
1 or 2 cloves garlic
6 to 8 peppercorns
1 heaping teaspoon thyme
Few grains allspice
2 tablespoons salt

Tender little sheep trotters are now forbidden fare in most of the United States due to the danger of their passing on various maladies. However, since they used to be an important part of diet among some Americans, it is necessary to include them here.

They were sometimes served, either hot or cold, with a vinaigrette sauce. And occasionally, in sections of the country where the French had settled, they could be found served with a rémoulade sauce or a ravigote. At any rate, they are completely delicious. It is still possible to find trotters in France and England, prepared in various ways, so if your curiosity is piqued by the idea, try them the next time you travel.

It takes quite a few trotters to make a meal. The ordinary person can eat at least four.

1 cup white wine or ½ cup vinegar (optional)

SAUCE

1 onion, thinly sliced
4 tablespoons butter
2 tablespoons flour
Salt and freshly ground pepper
1½ cups of the poaching broth
2 egg yolks
¾ cup heavy cream
2 tablespoons lemon juice

Wrap the trotters in muslin or several folds of cheesecloth, and tie securely. To the water, in a large kettle, add the onion, garlic, peppercorns, thyme, allspice, and salt. If you like, add white wine or vinegar. Bring this to a boil and simmer a half hour. Add the wrapped and tied feet, cover, and simmer 1½ hours. Leave the feet in the broth 20 minutes longer, while you make the sauce. Sauté the onion in the butter until it is just translucent. Add the flour, blend well, and simmer 3 minutes. Season to taste. Stir in the broth and continue stirring till the mixture is thickened. Simmer 5 minutes. Beat the egg yolks and cream together. Add a little sauce to the egg-cream mixture, and stir well. Gradually stir into the sauce. Continue cooking and stirring until it begins to thicken. Do not let it boil after you have added the egg-cream mixture. Finally, stir in the lemon juice and correct the seasoning. Transfer the feet to a hot platter, and when cool enough to handle remove the string and the wrappings. Pour the sauce over the feet and garnish with chopped parsley. Serve with steamed rice or boiled potatoes.

Lamb Fries

These are the testicles of young male lambs. In the sheep-raising sections of this country, such as Montana, where many Basque people have settled, they are referred to as "fries" or "mountain oysters." The French refer to them as *frivolités*.

To prepare, clean and remove the outer skin or sac, rinse, and drain well. Cut into slices. Heat butter or butter and olive oil in a skillet, and fry lightly over medium heat. Season with salt and pepper.

Basque-Style Lamb Fries. Clean the lamb fries as above and slice. Heat olive or salad oil in a skillet, and add a clove of minced garlic. Add the sliced fries, and brown lightly over medium heat. Season with salt and freshly ground pepper. The Basques like to fold these cooked fries into an omelet. In sheep country, lamb fries are also often served as a breakfast dish, along with scrambled eggs, bacon, and fried potatoes.

Pork

Few people realize what an astonishing variety of meat comes from the pig. Our earliest settlers made use of every bit of the animal — they had plenty of hogs long before beef was available — and in addition to bacon, ham, roasts, chops, spareribs, and sausage, they ate head cheese, smoked jowl, pig's feet and hocks, tails, livers, and kidneys. The fat was rendered into lard, a pure fat second only to butter in delicacy, and used in pastries, breads, and cakes, as well as in general cooking. And the mouth-watering recipes for dishes made with salt pork make us realize that perhaps we are neglecting some of the more delicious parts of the pig. Today we are eating a much leaner pork then our ancestors knew, though with forfeit of some flavor and texture. Nevertheless, pork continues to be among the most popular of meats consumed by Americans.

The Roasts

There has been much discussion over the years about roasting pork. The earliest books warn you to cook pork until it is well done — as it would be unpalatable otherwise. Later we went through a period when pork was supposed to be cooked to death because of the danger of trichinosis. Then we discovered that the trichina parasite is destroyed at a temperature well below 150 degrees. If you remove a roast at 160 to 165 degrees and let it stand 15 minutes before carving, it will be just right in flavor, texture, and tenderness.

Roast Loin of Pork

By far the most popular of pork roasts. The rack is sold whole or in sections — the rib end or the loin end. Sometimes butchers get very elegant and call the loin end the sirloin roast and the other the rack. In England, the skin is often kept intact so that it can be scored and transformed into crisp cracklings. This was also done in early America, but alas, we now get pork loin stripped of its skin.

When you buy a loin roast you should have the backbone and feather bone split to make for easy carving. Some butchers cut the backbone so that it can be removed entirely when the roast is ready for presentation at table. A loin roast of about 4 pounds will serve 4 persons with some left for a cold meal.

Rub the loin with a little thyme, freshly ground pepper, and some salt. Place on a rack in a shallow roasting pan with the backbone down and roast in a 325-degree oven, without basting, allowing approximately 24 minutes per pound. Or cook until the internal temperature reaches 160 to 165 degrees. Place the pork on a hot platter and let it rest 10 to 15 minutes before carving.

Make a gravy in either of two ways: Skim excess fat from the pan, add 1½ cups hot stock, let it boil down for a moment, and correct the seasoning. Or skim away all the fat from the pan but 3 tablespoons, add 2 tablespoons flour, brown over a fairly high heat, stir in 1 cup boiling water or stock and continue to stir till thickened, and season to taste with salt and freshly ground pepper. Sometimes hot milk is used in place of water or stock and makes a delicious gravy.

Serve the roast loin of pork either with potatoes cooked in the pork fat along with the roast or with creamy mashed potatoes. Also it is traditional to serve sautéed apple slices, fried apples, or applesauce.

Another Way to Roast Loin of Pork

5-pound roast of loin end with fillet
Sage, freshly ground pepper, and salt

Rub the pork well with the seasonings. Place on a rack in a roasting pan and roast at 325 degrees, allowing about 25 minutes per pound. After 1½ hours remove from the oven and pour off excess fat. Add the apples to the pan. Dip them in pork fat and sprinkle lightly with sugar. Return the roast to the oven and continue roasting till the meat is done — about 1 hour. Transfer the roast to

5 or 6 tart apples, peeled and quartered
Sugar
1 cup heavy cream
¼ teaspoon nutmeg

a hot platter to rest 10 to 15 minutes before serving. Pour excess fat from the pan and add the heavy cream, a touch of salt, and the nutmeg. Let this boil down for a few minutes with the apples. Serve with the pork. Braised onions go very well with this combination.

Loin of Pork with Prunes

5-pound piece from center of loin, prepared for roasting
6 to 8 dried prunes
Water or sherry
Walnut halves
Thyme or sage
Freshly ground pepper
Salt

This is a great Swedish and Danish favorite (the French also have a version) and is frequently found in the Middle West.

Bring the prunes to a boil in water or sherry to cover, then drain (reserve the liquid) and pit them. They may be stuffed with walnut halves for added texture. Cut a deep slit in the pork extending from the tip through the thickest part of the meat muscle. Insert the prunes. Press the meat back in place, tie securely, and, if you want, also secure with skewers. Rub the roast well with thyme or sage and pepper. Place it on a rack and roast at 325 degrees, allowing about 24 minutes per pound. Baste occasionally with the pan juices. Salt the roast just before removing, when it has reached an internal temperature of 160 degrees. Transfer it to a hot platter and remove all but about 3 tablespoons of the fat in the pan. Add about 1 cup of heated juice from the prunes — either water or sherry. Bring to a boil and cook for several minutes. Correct the seasoning. Serve with the roast. Also serve mashed potatoes and perhaps some sautéed cabbage.

Loin of Pork Teriyaki Fashion

5-pound loin of pork
1 clove garlic
¾ cup Japanese soy sauce
¾ cup sherry
1½ tablespoons grated fresh ginger
Orange or (better) tangerine zest
Salt

This has become a favorite dish, especially in the West, where the rage for Polynesian or Amerasian food had its start. (It is based a good deal on Japanese marinades, though there have been many additions and changes since the first ones were imported.) Rub the pork well with garlic and insert a few slivers into the flesh. Place the roast in a pan with the soy sauce, sherry, ginger, and a scraping of zest. Turn the roast a number of times and let it rest in this bath for several hours, turning again as often as you can think of it. To roast, remove from the sauce and place on a rack in a shallow baking pan. Roast at 350 degrees, allowing 25 minutes per pound. Baste from time to time with the marinade and the pan juices. Salt the roast just before removing from the oven. It is ready when the meat registers 160 degrees when tested with a thermometer. Transfer to a hot platter and let stand 10 minutes. Spoon some of the pan juices over the roast. Serve with hot mustard, preserved kumquats, and rice. A salad is a perfect accompaniment.

Cold Loin of Pork

There was a great deal of old wives' talk in the older days of the nineteenth and early twentieth centuries about not eating pork in summer. On the contrary, it is thoroughly safe. As a summer meat, eaten cold, it is one of the greatest of delicacies. It is best when cut thin and served with a mustard mayonnaise or a homemade chili sauce or with good pickles. And tender pork sandwiches can be equally mouth-watering.

Crown Roast of Pork

Elegances were typical of the nineteenth century, when people had hired girls and competed at entertaining. Sometimes the competition produced horrors of gastronomic art, and sometimes niceties such as this. The crown can be formed with two loins tied together, bone side in, and tied and trimmed to make a circle or "crown." Or just the center cuts of the loins or the rib cuts can be used. Whatever the cuts, they make a rather spectacular roast and will serve 10 to 16 people. Cover the rib ends of the roast with foil so they do not char during the roasting. Fill the center of the crown with a cushion of foil. Rub the roast well with sage, thyme, and garlic or with coarsely ground pepper and a little rosemary. Place the crown on a rack in a large pan — a broiling pan is suitable. Roast in a 325-degree oven and allow about 25 minutes per pound of meat, being certain to use the dressed weight. Although it is not necessary, the roast will achieve a better finish if it is basted with the pan juices and some white wine or with equal parts of melted butter and white wine. The internal temperature of the meat should register 160 to 165 degrees. Test by inserting a thermometer in the flesh at two or three places. Transfer the roast to a hot platter and remove the foil from the center and from the rib bones. Put paper frills on the bones if you like. Fill the center with any of these:

(1) Braised Brussels sprouts, heaped high. Also serve browned potatoes.

(2) A purée of chestnuts buttered well and flavored with a little ginger and nutmeg. Also serve sautéed apples.

(3) Sauerkraut — about 3 to 4 pounds cooked for 1 hour with 3 cups bouillon and 1 tablespoon juniper berries. Garnish with slices of garlic sausage. Also serve puréed potatoes.

(4) Sautéed apples.

(5) Sautéed lentils tossed with parsley, bacon, chopped onion.

All go exceedingly well with the pork, and all look impressive. A Bibb lettuce salad made with a little grated beet and a vinaigrette dressing will also.

Roast Fresh Ham or Leg of Pork

This roast is often served at Thanksgiving or Christmas instead of the traditional bird. How good it is, and how good the cold meat is the next day.

It is only in the last few years that the term "fresh ham" has come into common usage. (I still prefer to call it a roast leg of pork, which has a more honest sound to it.) The ham or leg will weigh from 8 to 16 pounds. If possible have the skin left on and scored, for it makes the most delicious crackling, which is half the joy of eating this dish.

Slow cooking, about 300 degrees, is preferable for a leg of pork to tenderize it and cook it evenly. However, it is a good idea to increase the heat to 425 degrees at the end of the cooking time to crisp the skin.

Rub the leg with sage, freshly ground pepper, and a bit of garlic. Or use thyme or summer savory instead of the sage. Place on a rack in a rather shallow pan. Roast at 300 degrees to an internal temperature of 160 degrees — about 25 minutes per pound. There is no need to baste during most of the cooking. If the skin is scored, bring up the temperature for the last 20 minutes and baste generously with the pan drippings. This makes the skin crisp and crackly. Salt well. Transfer the roast to a hot platter and let it rest 15 minutes before carving. Decorate the platter with sautéed apples or pickled crabapples.

Make a gravy with the pan juices. Skim off the fat and leave 3 to 4 tablespoons. Add 4 tablespoons flour and stir over rather high heat. Add 2 cups broth, water, or milk, and allow it to cook down and thicken. Correct the seasoning and let it boil up. Serve in a sauceboat. Mashed potatoes, sauerkraut, and apples all go exceedingly well with this great roast.

Leg of Pork to Taste Like Wild Boar

1 leg of pork, about 12 pounds, skin removed
3 cloves garlic, crushed
12 peppercorns, crushed
12 allspice berries, crushed
12 juniper berries, crushed
1 teaspoon thyme
½ teaspoon nutmeg
1 bay leaf, crushed
2 strips orange zest

This dish, of Spanish origin, was often used in the West and has become a favorite around the country. It makes a superb roast for a large buffet or a great dinner party. It is also excellent eaten cold.

Rub all the seasonings save the onion and orange zest into the pork. Place it in a deep bowl or crock, cover with warm red wine, and add the onion and zest. Let stand 6 to 7 days in the refrigerator or a very cool place, and turn two or three times a day. When ready to cook, dry the roast well and rub with oil. Place it in a roasting pan — not on a rack. Roast at 300 degrees, allowing 25 minutes per pound of meat. Baste every 30 minutes with the heated marinade. When the roast has reached an internal temperature of 165 degrees, transfer to a hot platter, strain the juices in the pan, and remove excess fat. Also strain any remaining marinade and add to the pan juices. Cook this down very quickly to 2 cups.

Melt the butter in a saucepan, add the flour, and let it cook several minutes to brown. Gradually stir in the heated and reduced marinade, and stir until it boils and thickens. Correct the seasoning. Add the raisins and pine nuts and let it cook up once more. Pass this sauce separately. Serve the roast with rice pilaff, baked eggplant or purēed chestnuts, and braised onions. Drink a light red wine.

1 large onion stuck with 2 cloves
Oil
Red wine
4 tablespoons butter
4 tablespoons flour
½ cup or more pine nuts
1 cup seedless raisins
Grated orange zest
Salt and freshly ground pepper

Roast Pig to Taste Like Lamb

Mrs. Crowen offered this recipe in 1847. "Take a leg or forequarter of a large roasting pig, skin it, rub it well over with salt and pepper and chopped mint, then roast or bake it, dredge a little flour over and baste with a little butter about fifteen minutes before taking it up — serve with mashed potatoes."

To improve upon this, stud the roast with garlic before rubbing it with salt, pepper, and mint. Roast at 300 degrees allowing 25 minutes to the pound or until it registers 165 degrees on the thermometer. Transfer the meat to a hot platter. Take 3 tablespoons of fat from the pan, combine it with ¼ cup chopped mint, 3 finely chopped garlic cloves, 2 tablespoons tarragon vinegar and ½ cup red wine, and cook for 2 or 3 minutes, adding more wine if needed. This makes a most unusual roast.

Italian-Style Leg of Pork

Leg of pork, boned
Herbs for stuffing
White wine
Chopped parsley
Salt and freshly ground pepper
Basil or sage
Chopped chives

There are several good Italian butchers in my neighborhood, where chairs are provided and the local ladies gossip while they choose their meat for the weekend. It is not unlike the marketplace in the earlier days of the country. Two of the butchers deal in pork. The place I frequent is run by a brother and sister, both of whom are good butchers. They make a great array of sausages and other pork products, and they often have most unusual legs of pork ready to cook that they will do to order on two or three days' notice. The skin is left on half the leg — or all of it — and is scored. The leg is boned and then stuffed with Italian parsley, fresh or dried basil, a bit of thyme or sage, garlic and sometimes bay leaf, and coarse pepper. Then it is rolled and tied. This, of course, makes a very easy roast to carve and the herbs give a splendid flavor.

Unless you have a pork butcher who is prepared to duplicate this roast, have the leg boned and then stuff and roll and tie it yourself.

Place the roast on a rack and roast at 300 degrees, allowing 25 minutes per pound, until it has reached an internal temperature of 165 degrees. Baste with warm white wine every half hour. When done, transfer the roast to a hot platter. Skim most of the fat from the pan, leaving 3 to 4 tablespoons. Add a cup of white wine and bring to a boil. Add chopped parsley, salt and pepper, either basil or sage, and some chopped chives. Serve this sauce with the roast of pork. Steamed rice and a good salad of greens and tomatoes make delicious accompaniments.

Leg of Pork with Cider and Cream

Leg of pork, about 10 pounds
Salt and freshly ground pepper
Nutmeg and a little ginger
Cider
⅓ cup applejack
1½ cups heavy cream
Beurre manié
2 egg yolks

All our apple states — New York, Pennsylvania, Oregon, Washington — have traditional dishes using cider, apple juice, and applejack. This is much like the food one finds in Normandy, where cream as well flows into the good cookery. This roast appears to be a combination of both domestic and Norman dishes.

Rub the roast well on all sides with the salt and spices. Place it on a rack in a baking pan and roast at 325 degrees, allowing about 25 minutes per pound, until an inner temperature of 165 degrees has been reached. Baste the roast often with warm sweet cider. About 20 minutes before the roast is to come out of the oven, flame it with the applejack. Remove the roast and keep it warm on a hot platter. Skim off most of the fat from the pan juices and measure 1 cup of juices. Combine with 1 cup heavy cream and heat in the pan. Add beurre manié (butter and flour kneaded together) and thicken to taste. Mix the remaining half cup of cream with the egg yolks, and stir well into the sauce. Do not let it boil after adding the egg yolks. Correct the seasoning and add a touch of powdered ginger. Serve in a sauceboat. Mashed potatoes, green peas, or a purée of carrots and sautéed apples are the traditional accompaniments. This roast is also delicious eaten cold.

Shoulder of Pork or Picnic Shoulder

Either of these may be treated in the same fashion as a leg of pork. They have different bone structure, of course, and will not carve as well, but the meat is excellent in flavor and texture.

Smoked Loin of Pork

In the last ten years this cut has become increasingly popular and is now available in most supermarkets, as well as in smaller markets where curing and smoking are done by a specialist. Some loins are ready to eat and only require reheating. Others require cooking at 325 degrees for 25 minutes per pound. Ask your butcher which type you are buying. Otherwise, treat a smoked loin as you would a fresh one. It is good, for example, basted with white wine or with sherry. Smoked loin calls for sauerkraut and either mashed or fried potatoes. It is also very good served with braised cabbage or braised Brussels sprouts.

Smoked Crown of Pork

This superb roast is a specialty of several smokehouses in the East who also produce smoked hams and bacon. When ordered, it is usually accompanied by rules for cooking. It is excellent served with a filling of sauerkraut and a garnish of sausages, or with braised chestnuts and Brussels sprouts.

Roast Suckling Pig
(Originally referred to as Sucking Pig)

To the modern cook: Not as Mrs. Glasse, the great eighteenth-century English cooking authority, is reported to have said — "First catch your hare" — but first measure your oven. It was much easier in former days to buy a good small suckling pig. Now you have to order one two or three weeks in advance, and even if you're lucky enough to get a pig of proper size for your oven it is apt to be frozen. Even fifteen or twenty years ago I remember what a common sight suckling pigs used to be hanging in butcher shops during the Christmas holiday and at the beginning of the year. There was a much larger demand for them, and people often cooked them on a spit. They still have a great tradition behind them, and they provide one of the most delectable ways of eating pork — crisp skin shiny and golden; soft, delicate flesh; and tiny bones that are a delight for picking.

Mrs. Harland recommended roasting suckling pigs on their knees. (As a matter of fact this is frequently done if the oven is large enough.) And she adds at the end of her recipe, "Put the innocent — still kneeling — upon a large hot dish; surround with parsley and blanched celery tops. Put a wreath of green around his neck and a sprig of celery in his mouth." I like this garnishing far better than the usual apple and cranberry.

Roast Suckling Pig Stuffed with Herbs

If you prefer not to stuff the pig in the usual manner, rub it well with lemon and stuff (for a 12-pound pig) with two bay leaves, a generous slice of orange zest, 5 or 6 slices of lemon, a sprig of rosemary, and a bunch of parsley. Sew up the pig, and either balance "the innocent" on his knees, as Mrs. Harland suggests, on a rack in a large pan, or rub him well with oil or butter and then place him on his side on a rack. Set him to roast in a 350-degree oven and for the first half hour baste three times with melted butter and cream. After 1½ hours brush well with butter and carefully — if he is on his side — turn him without rupturing the skin. Brush the turned side well with butter and cream, and baste with the pan juices. Roast another hour, and baste with pan juices or butter several times during that time. The skin must begin to glaze and be crisp. Salt the pig and give it a grinding of fresh pepper. When it is cooked, transfer to a hot platter and let it stand 10 to 15 minutes. Skim the excess fat from the pan, add 1 cup broth or bouillon to the juices, and bring to a boil. Serve this in a sauceboat.

To carve the pig, remove the head first and cut down the spinal column, then remove the hams. In this way you will be able to reach the stuffing. Cut the hams in slices. Cut the chops in twos or threes.

Serve surrounded with baked apples flamed with applejack and perhaps diced buttered rutabagas.

Southwestern Tostadas with Pig. This is Christmas food in the Southwest and originally came from Mexico. Roast a pig with herbs and lemon as above. Serve meat and skin on hot tostadas or on hot tortillas, and dress with a bit of salsa fria. Garnish with shredded green onions. This is delightful fare for a Christmas cocktail party (you may need two or more pigs), and in its way it is as delicious as Peking duck served with the thousand-leaf buns.

Stuffed Roast Suckling Pig

1 suckling pig
Olive or peanut oil
Butter

STUFFING

½ cup finely chopped onion or shallot
4 tablespoons butter
1 teaspoon salt
½ cup chopped parsley
1 teaspoon thyme or sage
4 to 5 cups cooked rice
2 tablespoons grated orange rind
2 tablespoons lemon juice
⅔ cup pistachio nuts

Pig should have a simple stuffing — no sausage meat, farce, foie gras, or such things — because the stuffing will absorb fat and juices during roasting and acquire flavor and richness enough. One of the best stuffings I have ever found for it is this one.

Quickly sauté the onion or shallot in the butter till translucent. Add the salt, parsley, and thyme or sage, and toss well with the rice, orange rind, lemon juice, and pistachios. Taste for seasoning. It may need additional salt.

Stuff the pig lightly and sew it up neatly. If it is possible to stand it up on a rack, do so. If it is unsteady, then wire the little front legs to the rack in the roasting pan. Rub the pig well with olive oil or peanut oil and roast in a 350-degree oven. Baste with butter or oil every fifteen minutes for the first hour. Then brush well with the pan juices and additional oil or butter as it roasts. It will take 2½ hours, more or less, depending upon its structure. When it is roasted, transfer, still standing, to a hot platter. Remove the wires, if you have wired it to the rack. For decoration, I would settle for a bunch of parsley in its mouth and a garnish of glazed crabapples, apples, or tiny pickled pears. Skim off excess fat from the roasting pan and add 1 cup broth to the juices. Boil up quickly. Correct the seasoning and serve with the pig. Rice in the stuffing makes it unnecessary to serve a farinaceous food. Sautéed corn and peppers or braised onions cooked with a little sherry or Madeira would go well as accompaniments.

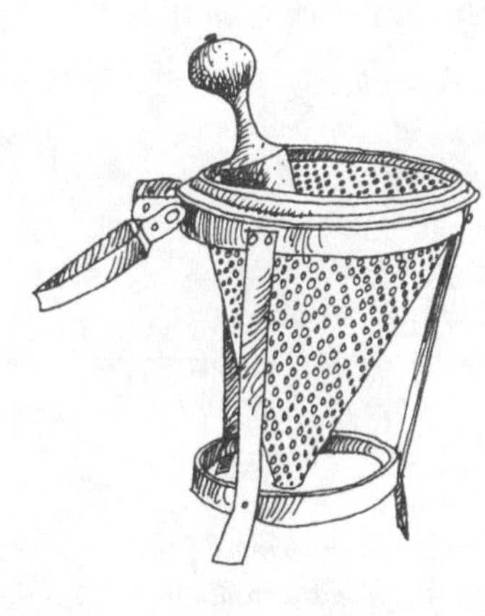

Pork Chops, Tenderloin, Spareribs

The best chops come from the loin and correspond to the porterhouse in beef. These contain some of the tenderloin and some of the loin. They should be cut an inch or more thick. For stuffing, they should be cut two inches and over. The rib chop does not include the tenderloin. Nevertheless, it is a choice cut and is also adaptable for stuffing. A good chop should be cut 1 to 1½ inches thick.

Broiled Pork Chops

This, in my opinion, is the least successful way to cook pork chops. Broiling tends somehow to toughen the meat. To be successful they must be broiled slowly and carefully and then browned at the last in high heat. You may brush them well with a barbecue sauce or with soy sauce while broiling. Or simply salt and pepper. Serve with crisp fried potatoes and green beans.

Plain Pork Chops (sautéed)

These are just simple, flavorful chops. Pork, of course, needs longer cooking than other meats; consequently sautéing is ideal. The chops are seared and then covered and simmered or cooked uncovered over low heat for a long period of time.

Trim the chops well, allowing one good chop or two smaller ones for each person. Trim off some of the fat, melt it in a heavy skillet, and combine with butter. (For 6 chops, add 3 tablespoons butter.) When the fat is bubbling hot but not burning, add the chops and cook over medium heat 6 to 8 minutes. Turn, and let them cook another 6 to 8 minutes, being careful they do not cook too fast. Salt them and give them a few grinds of freshly ground pepper. Transfer to a hot platter and serve.

Pork Chops and Cream Gravy. Keep the chops warm. Remove all but 3 tablespoons fat from the sauté pan. Add 3 tablespoons flour and blend well. Gradually stir in 1 cup milk or light cream and continue stirring until it thickens. Salt and pepper it well and pour into a gravy boat. Serve with the chops, mashed squash, and boiled potatoes.

Breaded Pork Chops

6 thick rib chops
4 tablespoons butter
4 tablespoons oil
Flour
2 eggs, lightly beaten
1½ cups breadcrumbs
Salt and freshly ground pepper
3 tablespoons flour
¼ teaspoon Tabasco
¾ cup milk
2 tablespoons chopped parsley
1 tablespoon chopped dill or 1½ teaspoons dillweed
½ cup sour cream

Heat the butter and oil in a heavy skillet. Dip the chops in flour, then in the beaten egg, and finally roll in the breadcrumbs. Press the crumbs in well. Brown the chops on one side rather slowly over medium heat. Turn carefully and brown on the other side. Season well with salt and pepper. Turn once again. The total cooking will take 15 to 20 minutes. Test with a skewer. When the chops seem quite tender and are nicely browned, transfer them to a hot platter. Remove all but 2 tablespoons fat from the pan. Combine with the flour and brown and blend well over medium to medium high heat. Stir in the Tabasco and milk and stir till thickened. Add the parsley and dill and simmer 2 minutes. Remove from the heat and stir in the sour cream. Heat through but do not let it boil. Serve the sauce with the chops. Also serve potatoes and green beans.

Pork Chops Creole

4 thick pork chops, preferably loin
Flour
5 tablespoons oil
1 large onion, thinly sliced
1 garlic clove, chopped
½ green pepper, finely chopped
1 rib celery, finely cut
2 cups stewed (or canned) tomatoes
1 teaspoon thyme
1 teaspoon salt
1 teaspoon freshly ground pepper
1 teaspoon sugar
¼ teaspoon Tabasco
Chopped parsley

In the nineteenth century nearly every dish made with tomatoes, onions, and peppers used to be called Creole whether it was or not, just as every dish in France made with garlic and tomatoes is called Provençal. This dish was one such "Creole" creation and helped to popularize the flavor of tomato.

Flour the chops lightly. Heat the oil over a rather high heat and brown the chops well on both sides. Add the onion, reduce the heat slightly, and cook just until the onion wilts. Add the garlic, green pepper, and celery, and turn the chops to get the mixture slightly blended. Add the tomatoes and seasonings, and blend with the other ingredients. Reduce the heat, cover, and let the chops simmer in the sauce 15 minutes. Transfer the chops to a hot platter, and let the sauce cook down over a medium high heat for a few moments. Correct the seasoning and pour or spoon over the chops. Sprinkle with chopped parsley. This dish definitely calls for rice.

Chilied Pork Chops

4 thick loin chops
6 tablespoons oil
2 garlic cloves, finely chopped
1 medium onion, finely chopped
1 teaspoon oregano

This Mexican-style dish comes to us by way of California.

Sear the chops very quickly in the hot oil over brisk heat, turning several times until they are nicely colored. Pour off the excess fat. Reduce the heat to medium, add the garlic and onion, and cook till wilted but not brown. Add the oregano, cumin, salt, and tomato sauce. Cover, and simmer 10 minutes. Uncover, add the chili powder and turn the chops. Simmer uncovered 10 minutes. Correct the seasoning. Transfer the chops to a hot platter. Let the sauce boil up for a minute or two and spoon over the chops. Add the chopped chilies and cilantro or parsley. Serve with pinto beans or refried beans.

1 teaspoon cumin
1½ teaspoons salt
1 cup tomato sauce
2 tablespoons chili powder
2 tablespoons chopped peeled green chilies
Fresh cilantro (coriander) or parsley

Pork Chops with Mushrooms

6 rib chops about 1 inch thick
Flour
4 tablespoons butter
2 tablespoons oil
1 teaspoon salt or more to taste
1 teaspoon freshly ground pepper
½ cup white wine or stock

MUSHROOM SAUCE

1 pound mushroom caps — little ones, if possible, or large ones quartered
5 tablespoons butter
1 teaspoon salt
1 teaspoon freshly ground pepper
1 tablespoon Worcestershire sauce
2 tablespoons flour
¾ cup heavy cream

We have always been great lovers of mushrooms, wild and cultivated. This dish was usually made with meadow or button mushrooms, but the cultivated ones will fill in just as easily and be almost as good.

You will need two skillets for this dish — one for the chops and one for the mushrooms. Flour the chops very lightly and brown them well in the butter and oil over brisk heat. Season them, add the white wine, and reduce the heat. Cover, and simmer 10 minutes. Sauté the mushroom caps in the butter and season them. Sprinkle with the flour, and then stir in the heavy cream. Continue to stir until lightly thickened. Transfer the chops to a hot platter. Skim off excess fat from the pan and pour the degreased pan juices into the mushrooms. Stir, and spoon over the chops. This is delicious served with fried hominy and a salad.

Pork Chops with Onions

4 thick loin chops
½ cup (1 stick) butter
3 tablespoons oil
Salt
Freshly ground pepper
3 large onions or 5 medium ones, thinly sliced
⅓ cup sherry or Madeira

Brown the pork chops in 3 tablespoons of the butter and the oil in a large skillet. When they are well browned, season, transfer to a hot platter, and keep warm. Add the remaining butter to the skillet and brown the onions lightly, turning often. When they are nicely colored and beginning to be tender, push them to one side of the skillet. Return the chops to the skillet and heap the onions on top. Reduce the heat, cover, and simmer 10 minutes. Add the sherry or Madeira and simmer another 5 minutes. Serve with hashed brown potatoes and coleslaw.

Piquant Pork Chops

6 rib chops about 1 inch thick
4 tablespoons bacon fat or oil
1 clove garlic, finely chopped
Salt and freshly ground pepper
Chopped parsley

SAUCE

1 cup finely chopped onions
4 tablespoons bacon fat or butter
1 teaspoon sage or thyme
1 teaspoon salt
1 teaspoon freshly ground pepper
½ teaspoon Tabasco
½ cup vinegar (originally 1 cup, but it is too strong)
½ cup white wine
½ cup tomato sauce
1 teaspoon mustard

This is probably a version of the French dish Pork Chops Charcutière, which has been served in this country since the middle of the nineteenth century and no doubt has undergone numbers of changes since the original dish was introduced.

Brown the chops well in the bacon fat or oil and add the garlic and seasonings. Reduce the heat and let the chops simmer while you prepare the sauce. In a separate pan sauté the onions in the bacon fat or butter till they are just wilted. Add the remaining ingredients, blend, and cook down about 5 minutes. Correct the seasoning. Pour over the chops and simmer, covered, 10 minutes or until they are tender and well flavored with the sauce. Transfer the chops to a hot platter, spoon the sauce over them, and sprinkle with chopped parsley.

Stuffed Pork Chops

4 very thick chops cut from the loin or rib, with a pocket
4 tablespoons butter
3 tablespoons oil
Boiling water
1 cup brown sauce or gravy (or 3 tablespoons flour and 1 cup broth)
Chopped parsley

STUFFING

1 medium onion, finely chopped
4 tablespoons butter
1 rib celery, finely cut
1 clove garlic, finely chopped
1 teaspoon thyme or rosemary
3 or 4 mushroom caps, finely chopped
1¼ cups dry breadcrumbs
¼ cup chopped parsley
1 teaspoon salt
1 teaspoon freshly ground pepper

I think this is a purely American invention, for I have never been offered a stuffed pork chop in any other country. It is a hearty, savory dish for a cool night. The chops — either loin or rib — must be very thick, with a pocket cut in the side toward the bone. If you use loin chops, which have a bone dividing the meat, the bit of tenderloin should not be stuffed but will serve as a small garniture.

Make the stuffing first. Sauté the onion in the butter, add the celery, garlic, thyme or rosemary, and mushrooms. Sauté gently 3 or 4 minutes, then add the breadcrumbs, parsley, and seasonings. Blend thoroughly. The mixture should be fairly dry. Fill the cavities in the chops. Secure the opening with small skewers or toothpicks.

Heat the butter and oil in a heavy skillet and brown the chops well on both sides. Add just enough boiling water to cover the bottom of the pan. Cover the skillet tightly. Either simmer atop the stove 35 to 45 minutes or place in a 350-degree oven for the same length of time. The chops should be turned once during the cooking period. They should be tender but not dry. When they are done, transfer to a hot platter and spoon off any excess fat from the juices in the pan. Add brown sauce or gravy to the pan and heat thoroughly. Or add 3 tablespoons of flour, blend well with the pan juices, and let it cook down for several minutes. Then add 1 cup broth or bouillon and stir over medium high heat till the mixture thickens. Correct the seasoning and spoon over the chops. Sautéed apple rings and buttered leaf spinach make good companions.

Pork Chop Sauerkraut Casserole

4 thick slices bacon
4 thickish pork chops
1 garlic clove, chopped
2 pounds sauerkraut
½ teaspoon freshly ground pepper
1 teaspoon juniper berries or caraway seeds
2 cups beer

There are many European and American dishes that combine pork and kraut — a pleasing combination always.

Sauté the bacon in a heavy skillet till just cooked through but not crisp. Transfer to a deep casserole or skillet or an electric skillet. Brown the pork chops quickly in the bacon fat and add the chopped garlic clove. While the chops are browning, add the sauerkraut to the bacon along with the pepper and juniper or caraway. When the chops are nicely browned, season to taste and add to the sauerkraut. Pour the beer over all. Cover the casserole or skillet and simmer on top of the stove for 45 minutes or place in a 350-degree oven for the same length of time. Serve from the casserole or skillet with boiled potatoes and apple slices sautéed in butter.

Pork Chop and Potato Scallop

6 good-sized pork chops well trimmed of their fat
6 fairly large potatoes, peeled and thinly sliced
Salt and freshly ground pepper
1 teaspoon sage
1 tablespoon flour
4 medium onions, thinly sliced
Butter
Milk or broth

This early nineteenth-century Middle Western dish is hearty and flavorful and good for a cold winter's night.

Butter a large, rather flat baking dish about 12 × 16 inches. Arrange a layer of half of the potatoes in it, and season with salt and pepper. Add the chops in a layer, salt and pepper them, and sprinkle with the sage and flour. Add the onions, and finally top with a layer of potatoes. Salt and pepper and dot with butter. Pour over enough milk or broth to come almost to the top of the baking dish. Place in a 350-degree oven and let the dish bake about 1 hour or until the potatoes are cooked, the chops are tender, and the liquid is pretty well absorbed. Serve with glazed beets and a green salad.

Nantucket Fireman's Supper

This robust dish, from a Nantucket cookbook, was the dream dish of firemen once a week.

"Trim pork chops. Put a little fat into an iron spider and fry the chops slowly on both sides. Cover the upper side of the chops thickly with sliced onions. Pare, slice, and add half a dozen potatoes. Season well with salt and pepper. Cover all with cold water. Simmer till potatoes are soft — about half an hour. Keep closely covered. Use the oven or the top of the stove as preferred. Slow simmering is necessary to bring out the juices."

A Pork Goulash

2 large onions, chopped
Butter
3 tablespoons Hungarian paprika
2 pounds lean pork shoulder, diced

Austrian and Hungarian immigrants brought us this dish, which is sometimes known as a Szegediner goulash. It is an exciting blend of flavors.

Sauté the onions lightly in butter until they are just wilted. Add the paprika and mix well. Add the pork and toss with the onions

1½ cups broth
2 pounds sauerkraut
2 tablespoons tomato paste
1 teaspoon freshly ground pepper
Boiled potatoes
Sour cream

and paprika. Add the broth, cover, and simmer gently 45 minutes. Add the sauerkraut, mix with the other ingredients, and simmer another half hour. Add more broth if necessary. Finally, add the tomato paste and pepper and mix thoroughly. Taste for seasoning. Serve on a plate surrounded with potatoes, and top with sour cream.

Pork Tenderloin or Fillet of Pork

The fillet is the tenderloin, which rests at the side of the bone in a loin of pork. Like a tenderloin of beef, it is round and larger at one end than at the other. The fibers run lengthwise. It has a very small amount of fat. When I was a child this cut was one of our standard dishes. Nowadays it is difficult to find in New York and the large metropolitan centers. In Chicago I often see it in certain markets and have taken it with me on the plane to California or New York for dinner the same night. Usually one tenderloin is ample and often more than enough per serving.

Broiled Pork Tenderloins

For each tenderloin take two slices bacon and cross them. Place the tenderloin at the center. Wrap the bacon around the tenderloin, overlapping the ends, and secure with toothpicks. Sprinkle well with freshly ground pepper. Broil about 4 inches from the broiling unit, or over charcoal, for 10 to 12 minutes, depending upon the size of the tenderloin. Serve with a baked potato and sour cream.

Teriyaki Broiled Pork Tenderloins. Marinate the tenderloin in equal parts soy sauce and sherry, 1 garlic clove, finely chopped, and a tablespoon fresh grated ginger. Remove from the marinade and rub well with oil. Broil, as above, brushing from time to time with the marinade. Serve on a bed of rice with snow peas cooked with mushrooms.

Sautéed Pork Tenderloins

4 pork tenderloins
Flour
4 tablespoons butter
3 tablespoons oil
¼ cup brandy
1 cup heavy cream
1 teaspoon salt
¼ teaspoon freshly ground pepper

Dredge the tenderloins well with flour. Heat the butter and the oil in a skillet, and when bubbling hot add the meat. Cook slowly over medium heat till nicely browned on both sides. Be careful not to overcook or the tenderloins will be stringy and dry. When just tender, pour off most of the fat, reserving about 2 tablespoons of it. Flame the meat with brandy. Transfer to a hot platter. Blend 2 tablespoons flour with the fat in the pan. Brown lightly. Add the cream and stir until the mixture has thickened slightly. Add the salt and pepper. Pour over the tenderloins. Serve with tiny parslied potatoes.

Spareribs

These wonderful morsels have been favorites among Americans for generations, and they seem to be peculiarly our own except for the Chinese, who do excellent things with them. Europeans neglect them completely, though they are beginning to achieve a certain popularity in American restaurants in Paris and in larger cities elsewhere.

There are two types of spareribs: the traditional one containing the breastbone, rib bones, and rib cartilages, and the type sometimes referred to as "country spareribs" or "back ribs," which are cut from the back and contain the bones from the ribs and some of the meat from the loin eye. Though the latter are far meatier, the traditional ones are consistently delicious and a delight to nibble with the fingers — for they are definitely finger food. Country ribs may be used in any of the following recipes, though they cannot be woven on a spit in the same manner as the traditional ones.

Boiled Spareribs and Sauerkraut

5 pounds spareribs cut in sections
4 pounds sauerkraut
2 onions, sliced
Juniper berries, if desired
4 cups beef, veal, or pork stock or water

The oldest way I know for preparing spareribs is this one. It was a dish farm folk ate at the time of slaughtering and smoking, and often the back bones were added to the mixture. It smelled wonderful when cooking and had a good, honest blend of flavors in the eating.

Add the onions and juniper berries to the sauerkraut, and place in a deep kettle with enough of the broth to barely cover. Bring to a boil and simmer 1 hour. Add the spareribs, and mix with the kraut. Add more broth if necessary. Cover the kettle and simmer 1½ to 2 hours or until the ribs are tender. Transfer the ribs and kraut to a huge platter, and serve with boiled potatoes, dill pickles, and rye bread and butter. Beer helps this meal enormously.

Another Old Way with Baked Spareribs

2 sides spareribs
3 to 4 pounds sauerkraut
2 potatoes, grated
1 teaspoon freshly ground pepper
2 large onions, thinly sliced
3 apples, thinly sliced
Salt

Mix the sauerkraut with the grated potatoes and pepper. Place in a buttered baking dish. Top with the onions, apples, and spareribs. Sprinkle the ribs with salt and pepper. Bake in a 350-degree oven 1 hour. Turn the ribs and continue cooking another 20 to 25 minutes.

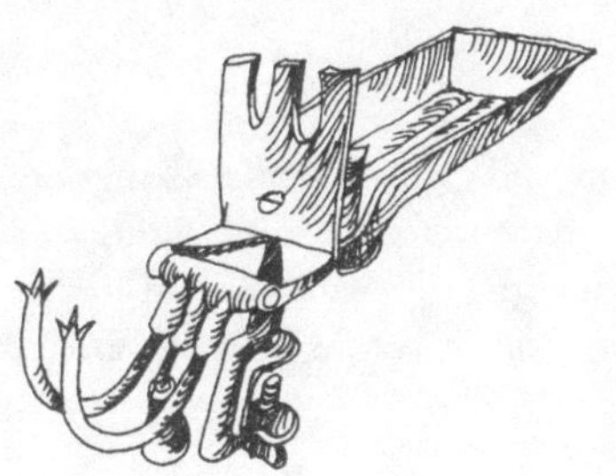

Stuffed Spareribs

3 racks or sides of spareribs, cracked
About 10 cups poultry bread stuffing

This has been a common dish in the Pennsylvania and Ohio countryside for over a century. It is simple, savory, rich, and extraordinarily good.

I break with tradition in the way I do these, but our forebears didn't have aluminum foil. Place a large piece of heavy-duty foil on a rack which will fit in your roasting pan. Place the stuffing on the foil and cover with the three racks of spareribs. Roast at 350 degrees 1 hour and 20 minutes or until the ribs are crisp on top and the stuffing is done. Serve with sautéed apples and good mustard pickles.

To prepare in the traditional way, use only 2 racks of spareribs and 5 to 6 cups of stuffing. Place one rack of ribs on the bottom of the pan, cover with stuffing, and top with the second rack. Roast about 1¾ hours. With this method, however, the bottom spareribs get rather stewed. The dish is immeasurably better if done with foil.

Spitted Barbecued Spareribs

2 sides spareribs
Salt and freshly ground pepper

MARINADE OR BRUSHING LIQUID

½ cup honey
½ cup soy sauce
2 garlic cloves, crushed and chopped
3 tablespoons catsup
½ cup water or white wine

Salt and pepper the spareribs and weave them on the spit. Mix the ingredients for the marinade. Start the ribs revolving and roast slowly, brushing them frequently with the marinade. After 1 to 1½ hours they will be beautifully glazed and will have absorbed the delicious flavors of the marinade. Cut the ribs in sections. Serve as an hors d'oeuvre or as a main course with fried rice and a tomato salad.

Glazed Spareribs

2 sides spareribs
Salt and freshly ground pepper

GLAZING SAUCE

1 cup melted orange marmalade
2 teaspoons Dijon mustard
1 tablespoon lemon juice
1 tablespoon Worcestershire sauce

Season the ribs, weave them on a spit, and roast as above, brushing frequently with the sauce. Keep the sauce warm so that the marmalade does not congeal.

Barbecued Spareribs

2 sides spareribs
Salt and freshly ground pepper

Sauté the onions and garlic in butter till they are just tender. Add the remaining ingredients for the sauce. Bring to a boil and simmer 5 minutes. Sprinkle the ribs with salt and freshly ground pepper. Weave them on a spit or lay them on the grill. Broil very slowly over very low heat. If you spit them, let them roast about 20 minutes and then begin brushing with the sauce. Continue to brush every 15 minutes or so till the ribs are cooked. If you are using the grill, broil the ribs on one side, turn, and brush the finished side with the sauce. When the other side is done, turn and brush also. Repeat the process two or three times till the ribs have a nice glaze but are not burnt.

BARBECUE SAUCE

1 stick butter (½ cup or ¼ pound)
1 cup chopped onion
3 garlic cloves, finely chopped
½ cup catsup
¼ cup brown sugar
1 teaspoon salt
1½ teaspoons freshly ground pepper
¼ teaspoon Tabasco
1 tablespoon lemon juice
1 teaspoon basil or 2 tablespoons fresh basil
1 tablespoon chili powder

Oriental Spareribs

4 pounds spareribs
2 teaspoons sugar

MARINADE

½ cup soy sauce
½ cup sherry
3 finely chopped garlic cloves
2 tablespoons grated fresh ginger or chopped preserved ginger
⅓ cup olive oil
Salt and freshly ground pepper

This dish came to the mainland from Honolulu.

Blend the marinade ingredients and marinate the ribs in the mixture for several hours. Spit the ribs or broil them as you like. Brush well with the marinade several times during the cooking process. Salt and pepper them before removing from spit. When the ribs are done you may sprinkle them with 2 teaspoons or so of sugar and let it caramelize for a few minutes to give a beautiful glaze. Serve with fried rice and a good salad.

Pork Offal

Chitterlings or Chitlins

Chitterlings are the small intestines of the pig and are considered a great delicacy in the South when cooked and served with turnip greens or black-eyed peas. They must first be freed of fatty particles and then thoroughly washed in several changes of water before cooking. Add seasonings to the cooking water — onion, herbs, and garlic — if you like. Cook 3 or 4 hours. Sometimes chitterlings are eaten boiled, along with greens, grits, or other accompaniments. Sometimes they are dipped in batter and deep-fried. However they are done, they are a welcome change and resemble many European dishes made with the same ingredient. They are as old as history and not entirely exclusive to the South, for the intestines of pork make the famous French sausage known as andouillette. Recently I stopped at a huge shop in Los Angeles advertising "Buckets of Chitlins." They were wonderful. You can eat there in the garden or you can literally carry away paper buckets of them.

Pork Liver Polish Style

1 pound liver
Milk
1½ cups vinegar
1 large onion, thinly sliced
6 tablespoons butter
Breadcrumbs
Salt and freshly ground pepper
Broth or water

This part of the pig is much neglected, possibly because it does have a rather strong and distinctive flavor. However, if it is marinated in milk for several hours, it can be sliced and sautéed as any other liver. The Poles, who settled in so many different sections of this country, introduced this liver dish into our cuisine. See also the pork loaves.

Pour boiling vinegar over the liver, let it stand 2 minutes, and drain. Cut the liver into 2-inch strips. Sauté the onion in 3 tablespoons butter until just delicately gold. Add additional butter and push the onions to one side. Crumb the liver strips and sauté very quickly in the same skillet. Toss well till nicely browned. Season with salt and pepper. Transfer the onions to a hot platter and top with the liver pieces. Rinse with a little broth or water. Let it boil up and pour over the liver.

Sautéed Pork Kidneys

4 pork kidneys
Milk
3 slices bacon diced
4 tablespoons butter
½ cup finely chopped onion
Salt and freshly ground pepper

Pork kidneys, like the liver, are little used nowadays. They also need to be soaked in milk or salted acidulated water for some time before cooking, but they can be delicate, tender, and extremely good.

Soak the kidneys in milk 2 to 3 hours. Clean, split, and cut into thin slices. Cook the bacon in butter. Add the onion and then the kidney slices. Sauté gently, adding salt and pepper, till the kidneys are cooked through and tender.

Brawn, Jellied Pork, and Head Cheese

Brawn, jellied pork, and head cheese are all similar in definition and vary little in preparation, although some types are much easier to cook than others.

Jellied Pork

Double recipe for court bouillon (see page 421)
6 pig's hocks
6 pig's feet
2 pounds pork shoulder

This one I find extremely good eating and simple to prepare. Moreover, it will keep for ten days to two weeks if properly refrigerated.

Bring the bouillon to a boil and let it simmer 20 minutes. Add the hocks, feet, and shoulder, and bring to a boil again. Skim off any scum that forms and reduce the heat. Simmer till all the meats are very tender — practically ready to fall from the bones. Remove the meats and set aside. Reduce the broth one-third and correct the seasoning. Strain through a linen cloth or through a paper filter such as used for coffee.

When the meat has cooled enough to handle, bone it and break into fairly small pieces. Taste for seasoning — it may need additional salt. Fill two or three 1-quart earthenware molds with the meat, and ladle some of the broth into the molds. Pierce the meat with a fork, knife, or skewer so that the broth penetrates to the bottom of the mold. Add enough broth to cover the surface of the meat. Cool thoroughly and then chill at least 6 hours. Serve with a mustard mayonnaise, an herbed vinaigrette sauce, or horseradish cream.

Head Cheese or Brawn

Pig's head (boned), tongue, and heart
Court bouillon (page 421)
2 tablespoons salt, or to taste
1 tablespoon freshly ground pepper
1 teaspoon Tabasco
2 teaspoons grated lemon peel
½ teaspoon mace
1 cup white wine
¼ cup wine vinegar

Unless you are deft at boning, better have the butcher bone the pig's head for you. Weigh the meat after it is boned. Make the court bouillon. Place the meats in a large kettle and add the bouillon and enough extra water, if needed, to barely cover the meats. Bring to a boil and remove any scum that forms. Reduce the heat and let simmer feebly till the meats are tender. Gauge roughly 25 minutes per pound. Transfer the meats to a rack in a pan to cool. Peel the tongue and trim the heart. Reduce the broth one-half. Add the rest of the ingredients. Cook down 20 minutes to blend flavors. Taste for seasoning and correct. In the meantime cut the meat into small dice. Add to the liquid and simmer together 10 minutes. Ladle meat and broth into a large mold or several small molds and cool.

Another Way with Head Cheese. Cook the meat as above and dice very fine. Season with sage, salt, freshly ground pepper, and a little allspice. Then ladle meat and broth into a mold, cover with a sheet of foil, and weight it while it cools. About a 6-pound weight will do, as long as it is distributed evenly over the mold.

Souse. In former days, the head meat was sliced, wrapped in muslin, placed in a container, and covered with equal parts broth and vinegar to keep for winter. This was served with a hot slaw or hot potato salad.

Salt Pork

Before the days of any sort of refrigeration, save icehouses and the natural refrigeration of winter weather, people depended upon various pickled and salted meats for their mainstay during the colder months, often eaten in combination with game. There are recipes for many dishes made with salt pork. In all of them the pork should be streaked like good bacon, and if it is very salt it should be put in cold water, brought to a boil, and drained and dried before using. Today we use it as an additive to some braised dishes, notably those of French origin. And it is used for Boston baked beans and for a number of other composed dishes. Salt fat pork is sometimes used for larding and often for barding birds.

Greens and Pot Likker

1 pound salt pork
2 quarts water
3 pounds turnip greens, mustard greens or collards
Salt and pepper

This typically American dish has been in evidence since the late seventeenth century. Strange that in our era, when vegetables are cooked more crisply all the time, it persists. I recall that my father, who had a Kentucky background, believed that green beans should be cooked with jowl for several hours, and also that greens, even spinach, should be cooked with pork or bacon for a long time. These dishes were served with a dash of vinegar.

Boil the salt pork in water about 1 hour. Add the washed and picked greens and boil 1 hour. Remove the greens, cut rather coarsely, and season well with pepper and a dash of Tabasco. Place on a platter with slices of the pork and some of the pot likker. This calls for corn pone, corn bread, or corn dodgers.

Salt Pork Midwestern Style

8 thin slices salt pork freshened in water
4 tablespoons flour
4 tablespoons cornmeal
A little pork fat
1 tablespoon chopped onion or more to taste
2 tablespoons flour
1½ cups milk or thin cream
Freshly ground pepper

Dredge the pork slices with flour and press into the cornmeal. Heat a skillet with a little pork fat and add the pork slices. Cook to a nice brown on both sides and reduce the heat to cook through thoroughly. Transfer to a hot plate. Remove all but 2 tablespoons fat from the pan, add the onion, and cook 3 minutes. Add the flour and blend. Gradually stir in the milk or cream, and stir until thickened. Add some freshly ground pepper to the sauce. Serve with corn bread and perhaps some greens.

Note. The salt pork may be fried without flour and cornmeal. After browning, proceed with the recipe above.

Baked Salt Pork

Salt pork was sometimes baked in milk to cover, after which most of the liquids were poured off and potatoes were added to the pan. To prepare this dish, use a 3-pound piece of salt pork. Bake in milk to cover at 350 degrees for a half hour. Pour off two-thirds of the liquid. Add thickly sliced potatoes. Bake for another hour.

Pig's Feet, Knuckles, Hocks, and Tails

"Pig's trotters" in England, *pieds de porc* in France — I know not what in China — are a favorite food around the world, and they have been standard farmhouse fare in this country from the late eighteenth century through the nineteenth. They have delicious flavor, a tender texture, and a pleasing gelatinous quality. Furthermore, they lend themselves to so many different dishes. Often a pig's foot is included in a dish to give body to the sauce or to provide the jelling ingredient. If you can find feet that are cut long, as they often are in Chinese markets, they will be far more meaty.

Although it is a bother, pig's feet, especially those to be served cold or grilled, are much better if they are wrapped very tightly in a little muslin or cheesecloth and tied securely before cooking. This prevents the skin breaking, which easily happens. If you are serving the pig's feet pickled, have your butcher split them in half, or split them yourself if you're a good enough butcher.

Court Bouillon for Pig's Feet

2 quarts water (or part white wine, part water)
2 carrots
2 onions stuck with 2 cloves
1 teaspoon thyme
1 bay leaf
1 or 2 sprigs parsley
1 tablespoon salt
12 peppercorns, crushed
8 allspice berries, crushed

Combine the ingredients, bring to a boil, and let cook 15 to 20 minutes before using (see recipes below).

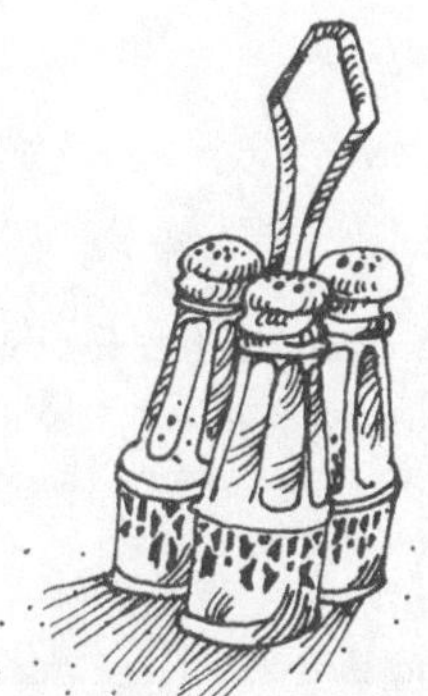

Grilled Pig's Feet

6 pig's feet
Court bouillon (see above)
Oil
Dry breadcrumbs
Sauce diable or barbecue sauce

Wrap the pig's feet well in muslin or cheesecloth and tie firmly. Prepare the bouillon and let it cook 15 to 20 minutes after it comes to a boil. Add the wrapped pig's feet and bring again to a boil. Reduce the heat and simmer 3 to 4 hours. Remove the feet and cool. When ready to broil, unwrap and rub the feet well with oil. Roll in dry breadcrumbs and broil either over charcoal or under the oven broiler. Broil slowly about 5 inches from the heat and brown on all sides, watching carefully so they do not burn. When they are nicely browned and piping hot, transfer to a hot platter. Serve them with a sauce diable, a barbecue sauce, or a good mustard. Garnish with watercress. French-fried potatoes are almost a must.

Pickled Pig's Feet I

6 pig's feet, split
Court bouillon (see above)
2 large onions, sliced
Salt and freshly ground pepper
White wine vinegar or cider vinegar

Wrap and cook the feet in court bouillon as directed above. Remove the feet from the bouillon, and when they are cool enough to handle, discard their wrappings. Place the feet in a bowl or jar with the onions and salt and pepper to taste. Add heated white wine vinegar or cider vinegar to cover. Refrigerate for several days before eating. Eat cold with drinks or with a salad and beer.

Pickled Pig's Feet II. Instead of the flavorings above, pickle the pig's feet in 1 part oil to 2 parts wine vinegar, seasoned with 2 onions cut in thin slices, 1 tablespoon dried tarragon, 2 crushed garlic cloves, and salt and freshly ground pepper.

Cold Pig's Feet with Rémoulade Sauce

6 pig's feet, split, wrapped, and tied
Court bouillon (see above)
2 large onions, thinly sliced
1 green pepper, seeded and thinly sliced
¼ cup chopped parsley
1 cup vinaigrette sauce
Rémoulade sauce

A thoroughly delightful and unusual summer dish with salad, hot bread, and white wine or beer.

Cook the pig's feet in court bouillon as above. When they are cooked, take from their wrappings and place in a large flat dish or a large shallow bowl. Add the onions, green pepper, parsley, and vinaigrette, and allow the feet to cool in the sauce, then chill. Arrange on a platter with some of the onions and pepper and serve with a rémoulade sauce.

Jellied Pig's Feet

8 pig's feet
Court bouillon (see above)

You do not need to wrap the feet for this dish. Simmer them in the court bouillon till tender, about 3 to 4 hours. When they are cooked, transfer them to a rack over a shallow pan. Cook the broth down 20 minutes or so till it is reduced by one-third. As soon as the feet are cool enough to handle, bone them out, discard the bones, and place the meat and skin in a large casserole. Be sure it is quite free from bones. Strain the broth well and ladle enough over the feet to just cover. Cool and then refrigerate to chill. Slice and eat cold with pickles and salad.

Pig's Knuckles and Sauerkraut

3 pounds sauerkraut
6 pig's knuckles
1 onion stuck with 2 cloves
1½ teaspoons freshly ground pepper
1 tablespoon caraway seeds

A prevalent dish everywhere in the country where pork is eaten at all. I remember having it in a restaurant in a little town in Arizona on a blistering hot day! It seemed the most remote dish possible for that climate. But then the entire menu consisted of pork dishes, so it was a question of choosing one's favorite part of the pig.

Place a layer of half of the sauerkraut on the bottom of a large kettle. Add the knuckles and the onion, pepper, and caraway seeds. Then add the rest of the sauerkraut. Pour the broth, beer, or white wine over the kraut and cover. Bring to a boil and simmer gently till the knuckles are thoroughly tender — about 3 to 3½ hours. Add the frankfurters 10 minutes before the dish is done. Serve the knuckles on a bed of sauerkraut with the frankfurters for a garnish. Boiled potatoes are a must, and plenty of good mustard, and perhaps some pickles should be served.

1 pint or more broth, beer, or white wine
12 frankfurters

Jellied Pig's Hocks

6 pig's hocks, brushed and washed
Water to cover
1 large onion stuck with 2 cloves
1 garlic clove, crushed
½ bay leaf
1 tablespoon salt
8 to 12 peppercorns, crushed
Sprig of parsley
1 teaspoon thyme
1 rib celery
¼ cup wine vinegar or 1 cup white wine
Salt and freshly ground pepper

Combine all except the hocks in a large pan, bring to a boil, and simmer 25 minutes. Add the hocks and bring to a boil again. Skim off any scum that forms at the top. Reduce the heat, cover the pan, and cook at the merest simmer about 2 hours till the hocks are tender. Be careful not to cook them too fast or too long, or they will disintegrate.

Remove the hocks from the bouillon and allow them to cool. Reduce the bouillon by one-third over high heat and strain through a linen cloth or the paper filters one uses for making coffee. Allow the bouillon to cool until it forms a thin jelly.

Cut the hocks in half and bone them. They can be arranged in individual molds or one large mold. If using individual ones, place a leaf or two of tarragon or dill at the bottom of the mold and then add a little of the jelly. Cool quickly in the freezer, then top with a piece of pig hock and cover with more jelly. A slice or two of gherkin or other pickle may also be included before the final coating of jelly. If using a large mold, make a design at the bottom of the mold with tarragon leaves or dill sprigs, or a layer of halved hard-boiled eggs and sliced olives. Spoon enough thick broth over the design ingredients to cover. Place in the freezing compartment to set quickly. Then add the hocks and, if you like, additional sliced hard-boiled eggs and slices of stuffed olive or pickle. Cover with jelly. Chill till ready to serve — at least overnight. Serve with a mustard mayonnaise, a vinaigrette sauce flavored with herbs, or a horseradish cream. Nothing but a good potato salad seems right with this dish.

Pig's Hocks Vinaigrette

8 small pig's hocks
Court bouillon (see page 421)
Herbed vinaigrette sauce

This dish is both German and French in origin. The difference in character lies in the acidity of the sauce, the German sauce being much more tart. You should make the vinaigrette sauce to suit your own taste. This makes an interesting summer hors d'oeuvre or a main dish for a summer luncheon, served with a cucumber salad or potato salad.

The pig's hocks should be meaty and appetizing to the eye. Poach them in the bouillon as in the recipe above till they are very tender but still intact. Remove them from the bouillon, and when cool enough to handle, trim them nicely and arrange in a serving dish — a flat ravier, for example, or a handsome shallow dish. Dress them with an herbed vinaigrette sauce and let them marinate at least 2 hours. Add additional chopped herbs just before serving. Serve cold with a potato salad, rye bread, and beer.

Barbecued Pig's Tails

5 pounds pig's tails
Salt
Barbecue sauce used for spareribs (see page 417)
2 cups dry breadcrumbs

Pig's tails are much neglected and can be so thoroughly good. They were often served with pig's feet in the days when people ate more boiled dishes than they do now. If you treat them as you do pig's feet or hocks and cook them with sauerkraut they are excellent. Much eating with the fingers is required and there are many little bones to pick at, but it is rewarding all the same.

This is a great specialty of the section of Canada near Toronto where there is a huge Mennonite colony. It seems to have traveled from there into parts of the northern United States near the Ontario border. For this recipe the tails should be meaty ones — cut rather deeply into the backbone.

Clean the tails — they should merely need washing. Arrange them in a fairly deep pan where they can lie flat. Add about 1½ tablespoons salt. Cover with water. Bring them to a boil very slowly, and when they have boiled 3 to 5 minutes remove any scum that may have formed. Reduce the heat so that they simmer with the barest ripple. Cook about 1½ hours. Let them cool in the water 1 hour, then remove and chill till ready to use.

To barbecue them, brush well with the barbecue sauce and place them on the grill or on the rack of a broiling pan. Broil slowly, turning often and being careful not to break the skin. When they are nicely browned, remove them, brush with sauce again, and roll lightly in crumbs. Broil, basting once or twice, till the crumbs are nicely brown. Serve at once with additional sauce.

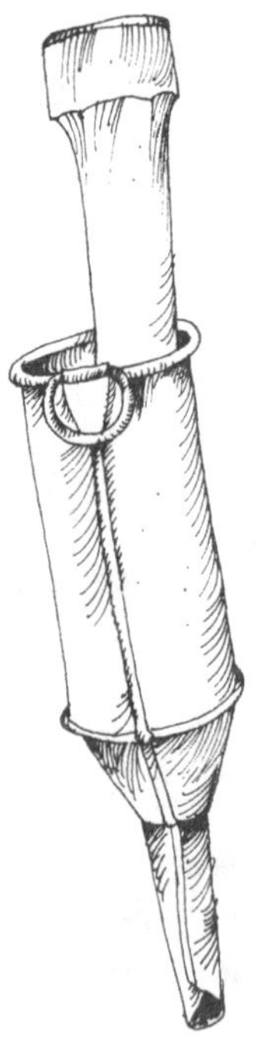

Pork Loaves and Pâtés

While pâtés were not authentically early American, liver and meat loaves were. They came to be eaten cold as well as hot, eventually acquired various seasonings, and developed into a much more specialized dish. Pâtés arrived along with French, Italian, and German immigrant families, who used the products of their new country to create many variations on native dishes. From these experiments have come some remarkably good American loaves and pâtés. (See also the loaves and pâtés in the chapter on appetizers.)

An Old New England Liver Loaf

3 slices salt pork 4 inches long, ¼ inch thick
1 pound pork liver, sliced
1½ cups breadcrumbs or cracker crumbs
1 cup broth or water
2 eggs lightly beaten
¼ cup finely chopped onion
1 teaspoon thyme
1 teaspoon savory
1½ teaspoons salt
1 teaspoon freshly ground pepper
Bacon or salt pork slices to line the pan

Try out the salt pork in a heavy skillet. Add the liver and brown quickly. Grind the liver and the salt pork together. Mix the crumbs with the broth. Combine with the liver and salt pork. Add the beaten eggs, onion, and seasonings. Blend well together with the hands. Form into a loaf. Line a loaf tin or a casserole with strips of salt pork or bacon. Place the loaf on top. Bake at 375 degrees for approximately 45 minutes to 1 hour, or until brown and firm to the touch. Eat the loaf hot or cold. Cold, it makes beautiful slices and has a delicious homely flavor.

A Country Terrine or Pâté

This pâté has no particular nationality. Originally, it might have been French, Italian, or even Scandinavian. It is typical of the type of pâté found in many places in Europe, and it is found here in New York, California, and in certain parts of the Midwest.

2 pounds lean pork, very coarsely chopped
2 pounds finely chopped veal
1 pound ground pork liver
Several slices (about 1 pound) fresh pork siding or rather fat pork, cut in small dice
6 garlic cloves, ground with the liver or the veal
3 eggs
¼ teaspoon nutmeg
¼ teaspoon ginger
⅓ cup whiskey or brandy
1 tablespoon basil
1 tablespoon salt
1½ teaspoons freshly ground pepper
Bacon or salt pork slices to line the terrine

Combine the meats and knead well together. Add the eggs and the seasonings and work the mixture well. Take a bit of it and sauté in a little butter very quickly to check for seasoning. This is important, for it should have good salt content to bring out the flavors. Use either a 2½-quart or a 3-quart dish for the pâté. In the smaller terrine the pâté will round over the top and look quite handsome. Whichever you choose, line the bottom well with salt pork or bacon slices. Fill the bowl or terrine with the pâté and place a slice or two of the salt pork or bacon on top. Place the dish in a 325-degree oven and bake 2½ hours. Cover loosely with a piece of foil the first hour; then remove it so that the pâté browns well but not too much. It will shrink away from the sides when it is done. Cool. Before refrigerating, cover tightly with foil or place in a plastic bag.

Tourtière

Pastry for a two-crust 9-inch pie
1 pound veal chopped
1 pound ground pork
2 slices lean salt pork, cut into small pieces
6 tablespoons butter
1 large onion chopped
1 garlic clove chopped
Salt and freshly ground pepper
¼ cup water

Tourtière is a completely French Canadian invention. It is very often a specialty for Christmas and in its rather rustic way is reminiscent of pâté en croûte, which must have been one of its ancestors. It has crept into New England cooking along with so many of the French Canadian dishes.

Blend the meats. Melt the butter in a heavy skillet and when bubbling add the onion and garlic and sauté lightly. Add the meats and cook 3 or 4 minutes, blending and stirring. Add the water and salt and pepper to taste. Remove from the heat. Roll out half the pastry to make a bottom crust. Arrange it in the pie tin with a little overhang. Fill with the meat mixture and cover with the rolled-out top crust. Press the edges of the crust together and flute them with your fingers. Cut two vents in the top crust. Bake at 375 degrees for 45 minutes. If it is not cooked at that time, reduce the heat to 325 degrees and bake until light brown. This may be eaten hot, but it is much better cold with pickles and beer.

Scrapple (Panhaus)

From New England and Pennsylvania to the Gulf states one can find scrapple or panhaus in one version or another. It is made with bits and pieces of pork cooked down in a rich pork broth and thickened most commonly with corn meal, or sometimes with oatmeal, barley meal, or other meals. The resulting mixture is poured into molds or pans.

To cook scrapple. Slice it thin, flour the slices, and fry in bacon fat or butter till brown. Scrapple is served with eggs or as a base for other dishes. I know, for example, of two or three recipes for quail and partridge served on slices of crisp scrapple, and very good they are.

Scrapple

Pork liver, kidneys, heart (optional), and scraps
Cornmeal or other meal
Salt and freshly ground pepper
Sage or thyme (optional)

Clean the liver and kidneys. Add the heart, if you like, and cook in salted water till just tender. Remove from the pot, chop, and combine with pork scraps. Return to the pot and continue cooking till very, very tender. Then start dribbling meal into the pot, stirring it thoroughly all the time until it takes on the consistency of cornmeal mush and bubbles and pops. (Take care, for sometimes the bubbles burst and spew you with boiling-hot meal.) Season well with salt and pepper and, if you like, some sage or thyme. Pour immediately into pans or molds and allow to cool. To cook, see above.

Philadelphia Scrapple. Use pork shoulder or neck and cook in salted water till it is so tender it can be shredded with two forks. Season with salt and freshly ground pepper; sage or thyme is usual, and sometimes summer savory — I think it best with thyme and a great deal of pepper. Then stir meal into the broth, and continue stirring vigorously till the mixture is well thickened and the meal cooked through. This takes about 15 to 20 minutes. Pour into pans or molds to cool. Then cook, as above.

Sausage and Other Charcuterie

Sausage has been part of our food heritage as long as there has been pork, and before we raised hogs, quite possibly sausage was made from game. Link sausage, sausage meat sewn into bags, smoked sausage — all used to be put down for the winter months in most parts of the country. There are still distinct regional differences in the way sausage is made. Sausages from Maryland and some parts of the Eastern Shore vary in shape, flavor, and texture from most of the other sausages on the Eastern seaboard. In Pennsylvania one is likely to find sausage that is lightly smoked, as well as sausage of beef and pork combined, and each section of the state has its own favorite. In the Midwest one encounters the Bratwurst so dear to the Germans and the Swiss. And in farmers' markets, wherever they still exist throughout the country, one nearly always sees an array of link sausages and, occasionally, the delicacy known by the French as crépinettes — sausage meat rolled in the caul and secured with a small skewer or toothpick. Italian sausages, both sweet and hot, are becoming more commonplace everywhere. The hot ones are seasoned with a dosage of pepper and some anise or fennel. Both hot and sweet are coarsely ground and cook beautifully. Cured sausages are also increasingly in evidence. Polish sausage, or kielbasy, appears to be available in various sizes, shapes, and flavorings from coast to coast. And we have created some native sausages that range from fair to excellent in flavor.

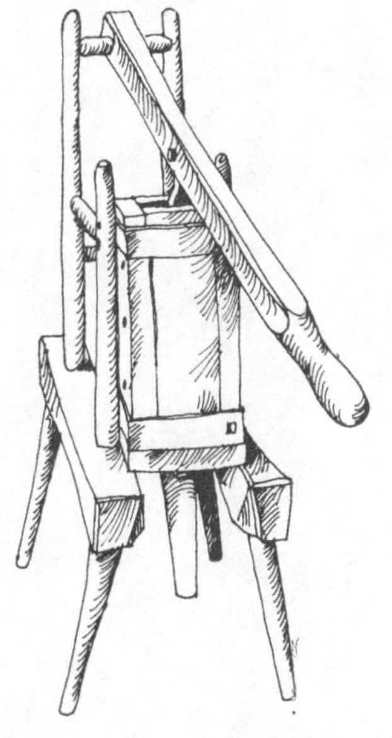

There are at least two types characteristically our own: (1) Summer sausage, a dry smoked sausage with a distinctive pungence. The Swedes, Germans, Hungarians, and other ethnic groups produce their own varieties. The number is endless, and certain types are highly localized. (2) Milwaukee cervelat, which is similar in some ways to the summer sausage and which has a rather haunting flavor unlike any other sausage. It is not to be confused with common cervelat, which is a fine-grained sausage delicious thinly sliced and made into a salad.

These are only the more common varieties one finds. We have been a nation of sausage fanciers for over a hundred and fifty years. This taste grows all the time as our gastronomic curiosity increases. Most of them are good-keeping sausages. One must be a fairly deft carver to do sausage justice, since most types should be cut very thin.

To Make Sausage Meat

It is interesting to make your own sausage and experiment with seasonings and textures. This is a pretty standard recipe for sausage making.

Chop coarsely by hand, or grind, 1½ pounds lean pork and ½ pound pork fat or 2 pounds lean pork and 1 pound pork fat. If you are interested in a particularly fine-grained sausage put it through the grinder twice. For a medium grain put it through the medium grinder. For a very coarse sausage it is best to grind the fat with the medium grinder and then chop or cut the lean with a knife until you achieve the texture you want.

For the basic seasoning add 2 teaspoons salt and 1 teaspoon freshly ground pepper. Here are a few recommendations for further seasonings.

(1) For that old-fashioned country taste add 2 teaspoons sage, well crumbled, and preferably leaf sage that is not too old and dry.

(2) A teaspoon each of thyme and ground coriander, and a touch of basil.

(3) A teaspoon of thyme, ¼ teaspoon nutmeg, and ¾ teaspoon ginger.

(4) A clove of garlic, finely chopped, 1 teaspoon thyme, and ½ teaspoon rosemary.

(5) A half teaspoon crushed aniseeds (use a mortar and pestle), 1 tablespoon paprika, and 1 teaspoon Tabasco.

(6) Two tablespoons each of chopped chives and chopped parsley.

(7) Two finely chopped garlic cloves and a teaspoon of summer savory.

To taste sausage meat for seasoning. Take a small amount of the mixture and sauté it very quickly in a little butter. Let it cool several minutes. In fact, the longer you let it cool, the more honest a taste you will get. Adjust your seasoning after tasting. When you find a combination of seasonings you enjoy, you can make sausage in larger quantities.

To store sausage meat for patties. Sausage meat will keep 2 weeks in the refrigerator if well wrapped and, of course, longer in the freezer. Make muslin bags from oblongs about 12 × 7 inches stitched together on the long side with circular pieces about 3 inches in diameter inserted at each end. Fill the bags with sausage meat and tie securely. You can wrap the bags in foil and freeze them. When ready to use, remove the foil and cut right through the bags to form patties.

To Make Link Sausages

If you wander through some of the great markets — such as the Lancaster market and the Reading market in Pennsylvania or the Farmers Market in Los Angeles — you will see an infinite variety of link sausages. Some are tied, some are twisted, and others just seem to come by the yard and are cut when you say "When." They range from a gray white to deep red in color, and some have the russet brownness of smoke on them. Some are extremely thin and about 3 inches long — a variety of pure pork sausage. Others — German, French, and Italian — are about 2½ inches long and very fat. Then there are the Italian sweet and hot ones which are 4 to 4½ inches long and about 1 inch in diameter. In origin, link sausages are Polish, German, Dutch, French, Czechoslovakian, Chinese, Italian, Spanish, and American, to identify but a few.

To make link sausages you will need casings, which can be bought at a pork butcher's, a butcher supply house, or wholesale markets. While they are clean when you purchase them, they should be cleaned again by running water through them. They should then be soaked in a little acidulated water, dried, and cut into 5-inch lengths. Tie one end securely — sometimes it is secured with a small piece of wood about the size of a toothpick.

Attachments are available for electric grinders and some electric mixers that make the stuffing process quick and easy. However, it can be done by hand, using a stuffer obtainable at butcher supply houses and from mail order houses that supply country districts, such as Sears Roebuck. If you want to experiment before buying all the equipment, you may do so with a pastry bag, using no tube or a very wide plain tube. To stuff the casing, fit the open end of it over the nozzle of the stuffer or the end of the pastry tube and continue to pull the casing over the nozzle or tube until you have reached the tied end. Then force the meat through into the casing. When you have enough for one sausage, either twist the casing around twice (and not too tightly), or tie with string. This will become an easy trick to master, and you'll find it a most rewarding experience to have sausage links of your own making.

Swedish Potato Sausage

1 pound lean ground beef
½ pound lean ground pork
7 cups grated potatoes
1 finely chopped onion
1 tablespoon salt
2 teaspoons ground ginger

Swedish potato sausages seem to be prevalent in all parts of the country especially at Christmastime. This is Helen Evans Brown's recipe.

Mix all the ingredients together and stuff loosely into sausage casings. Each sausage should be about 5 inches long. Cover the sausages with salted water and refrigerate till ready for use. To cook, remove the sausages from the brine and poach in salted water for a half hour. Drain. Melt ⅓ cup butter in a large skillet and brown sausages on all sides.

An Old Maryland Recipe for Sausages

10 pounds fresh pork — 20 percent fat
4 tablespoons salt
2 tablespoons freshly ground pepper
5 tablespoons crumbled sage
¾ teaspoon cayenne
½ teaspoon saltpeter

Combine all the seasonings. Cut the pork into pieces and grind very fine. Mix with the seasonings. Stuff into casings.

Southwestern Sausage Mixture

2¼ pounds lean pork
¾ pound kidney suet
5 cloves garlic, chopped fine
½ cup finely chopped onion
4 to 6 chili peppers, finely chopped
¼ cup brandy
⅓ cup chili powder
½ cup vinegar
1 teaspoon freshly ground pepper
1 teaspoon ground coriander
1½ teaspoons cumin
½ teaspoon Tabasco
Salt to taste

This must have had a Mexican beginning and undoubtedly has undergone a few adjustments. It has great authority and is a pleasing change from the usual sausage.

Chop or grind the pork coarsely and combine with the beef fat. Combine the garlic and onion with chilies, brandy, and seasonings. Blend well. Stuff casings with the mixture, making 4-inch sausages. Hang in a dry place or in front of an electric fan for 24 hours. If necessary, cover with cheesecloth to protect from flies. Store in the refrigerator. These will keep under refrigeration for a fortnight.

To Cook Sausage Meat

(1) Form sausage into cakes of any size you choose — 2, 3, or 4 inches in diameter and about 1 inch thick. Broil slowly about 4 or 5 inches from the heat unit.

(2) Sauté them in a small amount of butter over medium heat so that some of the fat cooks out and they become brown and crisp. Turn often.

(3) Steam them with a small amount of water in a covered skillet until the water is pretty well evaporated. A tablespoon of water for 6 sausage cakes is enough. Then add a small amount of butter and brown the cakes, turning them often.

(4) Make good-sized, rather rounded patties of sausage meat and wrap them securely in aluminum foil. Broil them over coals or under the oven broiler. Split in half and serve them in the foil with a piquant sauce.

To Cook Link Sausages

Much the best way to cook the links is to poach them first. Put them into cold water, bring to a boil, and let them cook 4 to 6 minutes. Drain, and add a bit of butter to the pan. Brown the sausages over low to medium heat, shaking the pan once in a while to turn them. Or pour boiling water over them and let them poach 4 to 6 minutes and then sauté. Or poach them and then broil about 4 inches from the heat till nicely browned, turning from time to time. They will take about 6 minutes.

You may also bake sausages. Place them on a rack in a shallow baking pan and bake for 15 to 20 minutes at 350 degrees till nicely browned and cooked through.

Sausages and Mash

Known in England as "bangers and mash," this dish followed the English to America, where it is frequently served in restaurants as well as in homes.

Cook sausages in any of the ways suggested, allowing about 3 good-sized ones per person. Serve them in a great mound of well-buttered and creamy mashed potatoes. With the addition of a little mustard, you have a delightful entrée.

Sausages in White Wine

18 medium-size sausages
Boiling water
6 tablespoons butter
3/4 cup white wine
1/2 cup brown sauce
Lemon juice

Meaty sausages of generous size are best for this dish, which is French in origin. The tiny, very fat breakfast sausages seem to cook away to nothing.

Poach the sausages in a small amount of boiling water 5 minutes. Drain, and add butter to the pan. Brown the sausages lightly on all sides, shaking the pan to turn them. When they are just delicately brown add the white wine, let it come to a boil, and simmer 5 minutes. Transfer the sausages to a hot platter and let the wine cook down for 1 minute. Add the brown sauce and blend well. Correct the seasoning. Add the lemon juice and boil up for 1 minute. Serve the sausages on a mound of puréed potatoes or puréed peas. Spoon the sauce over. These are also extremely good served on a bed of sautéed lentils. A pleasant luncheon dish.

Smoked Sausages with Hominy

2 pounds smoked pork sausage
Water
10 tablespoons butter (1¼ sticks)
3 cups hominy
½ cup heavy cream
1 teaspoon salt
1 teaspoon freshly ground pepper

The sausage should be the farm-smoked variety — nicely seasoned and hearty in size. It is usually sold in one long link, cut where you want it. When you are ready to cook it, cut into 4 or 5 inch lengths. Place in a skillet and pour boiling water over to cover and poach for 6 or 7 minutes. Drain, add 4 tablespoons butter, and sauté about 6 or 7 minutes until nicely browned and cooked through.

While you are sautéing the sausages, melt 6 tablespoons butter in another skillet and add the washed hominy. (Nowadays it will probably mean canned hominy, because the hominy man is a thing of the past.) Add hominy to the butter, toss thoroughly, and shake the pan often during cooking. If all of the butter is absorbed, add one or two additional tablespoonfuls. Add the cream and the salt and pepper. Shake the pan well, and let the cream cook down with the hominy. Continue to shake the pan several more times. Pepper to taste — it should take a good deal — and it may possibly need more cream. Arrange the hominy in a serving dish and top with the sausages. Serve with a good salad.

Italian Sausage with Peppers

4 or 5 red and green peppers
10 tablespoons olive oil
4 garlic cloves, finely chopped
Salt
1 tablespoon red wine vinegar
18 Italian sausages — either sweet or hot or half and half
Water
2 tablespoons chopped Italian parsley

It may be a bit of work, but the peppers are so much tastier if they are skinned. Put the peppers on a fork and toast them in the gas flame or in the broiler till the skins crack and burn. The flesh of the peppers will blacken a bit, but that will disappear in the cooking. Scrape the skin off. Seed the peppers and cut them in strips. Heat 6 tablespoons olive oil in a heavy skillet and add the garlic cloves. Then add the peppers and let them sauté very slowly, covered, about 20 minutes. Remove the cover and continue cooking till thoroughly tender. Add salt and vinegar at the very last.

Poach the sausages in water 6 minutes. Drain. Add 4 tablespoons olive oil to the pan and sauté gently till the sausages are delicately brown and are cooked through. Place the sausages on a hot platter, top with the sautéed peppers, and sprinkle with chopped Italian parsley. Serve with risotto, polenta, or potatoes.

Sausages with Sauerkraut

2 pounds sauerkraut
1 teaspoon freshly ground pepper
A few juniper berries
2 cups broth or bouillon

Wash the sauerkraut, toss it lightly, and place in a large saucepan. Add the pepper and juniper berries. Bring the broth to a boil, pour over the kraut, and bring to a boil again over rather high heat. Add the potato and mix with the kraut. Reduce the heat and simmer ½ hour. Place the sausages on a rack in a shallow baking pan and bake at 350 degrees till nicely brown. Turn several times. Spoon the sauerkraut onto a deep platter and surround with boiled potatoes. Top with the brown sausages and serve with mustard or horseradish and perhaps a salad of greens and tomato quarters.

1 large potato, grated
18 large pork sausages, Italian or country sausage
Boiled potatoes

Broiled or Sautéed Bratwurst

This coarsely textured sausage is best when it it broiled or charcoaled. Authorities differ about whether it should first be floured. At any rate, it should be broiled slowly and browned well enough to perhaps develop a crack in the skin. Serve with fresh corn, good mustard, and crisp bread.

Another way to prepare bratwurst: Poach 4 minutes, dry thoroughly, and flour lightly. Brown in butter or in pork fat, turning often till nicely colored.

Bratwurst is perfect served along with crisp sautéed onions atop a good helping of Swiss potatoes or hash browns and perhaps a helping of sauerkraut. One bratwurst of normal size is usually ample for one serving. If smaller, as they are in the Middle West, serve two or three bratwurst per person.

Poached Kielbasy in Red Wine

2 large kielbasy
1 cup finely cut green onions or ½ cup chopped shallots
Red wine to cover

HOT POTATO SALAD

24 small new potatoes
½ cup chopped onion or chopped chives
½ cup chopped parsley
½ cup hot olive oil
2 tablespoons wine from the sausage
2 tablespoons wine vinegar, or to taste
1 teaspoon salt

There are at least twenty different kielbasy or Polish sausages on the market and the variety depends upon where you happen to live. The ring-shaped ones are available nearly everywhere. In New York and a few other places we get superb fresh and cured types, which come both in rings and in one straight link. Naturally, the fresh varieties take a little more time to cook than the cured.

Put the sausages in a skillet or sauté pan with the onions and wine. Bring to a boil, and poach about 35 minutes, turning once. The sausages will develop a nice glaze and an excellent flavor. Serve with a little of the sauce spooned over them.

Cook the new potatoes in salted water until just pierceable. Cool with cold water and peel quickly. Cut in halves or quarters and place in a hot ovenproof dish. Add the onion and parsley and toss with the hot oil. Add the wine from the sausage and the vinegar. Add salt if needed.

Bockwurst

This is a predominantly veal sausage seasoned with chives. It is generally on the market in the spring. It should be poached or sautéed and served with eggs or with a purée of peas.

Cotechino or Coteghino

This is another cured sausage available throughout the country wherever you have an Italian population. Since it is dried and requires no refrigeration it is seen hanging in the open in Italian stores along with other cured sausages. Larger in size than most of the others, it is usually 7 to 9 inches long and about 2½ inches in diameter. Cotechino should be poached in water or wine for about an hour. Serve it sliced, with lentils, sauerkraut, beans, or polenta.

Blood Sausage or Boudin

It is difficult to find blood sausage any more, for in some states there is a prohibition on them. However, there are ways and means, and occasionally some extraordinarily good ones are brought forth from under the counter. Boudin should be broiled slowly about 4 inches from the heating unit or charcoal fire. Turn often and cook until well done. Serve with mashed potatoes, applesauce, and sautéed onions. Not a light dish but a rewarding one. It needs beer or a light red wine to help with digestion.

Knockwurst

This larger member of the frankfurter family, sometimes mistakenly called garlic sausage, contains a high percentage of pork, although some kinds have no pork in them at all. At their best they are juicy and of good texture. They require very little cooking and can be prepared in several ways. The most common method is steaming or boiling, which makes an ideal dish for dieters because of the low calorie count. Boiled knockwurst are also excellent as an appetizer with drinks when they are cut in 1-inch slices, impaled on toothpicks, and served with a mustard mayonnaise or horseradish cream. For a more unusual treatment, split knockwurst in half, spread with currant jelly, and sprinkle heavily with cracked pepper. Then broil. Knockwurst are good served with fried potatoes, sauerkraut, puréed split peas, or a green salad.

Breakfast Sausage

Small pork sausages and smoked sausages are preferred for serving with eggs. Salami and other dry sausages are also occasionallv included in the breakfast platter. Salami — especially kosher — is often scrambled with eggs or made into a pancake omelet or frittata. Sometimes a combination of sausage, bacon, mushrooms, and grilled tomato is served for a breakfast mixed grill. A plate of cold sliced sausages and thin slices of cheese is also served as a breakfast dish.

Sausage Rolls

English and Scottish in origin, the sausage roll has been a favorite in this country for over a century. Sausage rolls may be made with small pork sausages previously poached for 5 minutes, rolls of well-seasoned sausage meat, frankfurters, or brown-and-serve sausages. Each sausage is wrapped in puff paste, rich pastry, or cream cheese pastry. You may also use the refrigerated pastry that comes in rolls intended for turnovers, or the refrigerated dough for crescent rolls. This last, which is perforated, will require two sections or 1 complete square of the dough.

You will need a square of pastry just a trace longer than each sausage and wide enough to enfold it and slightly overlap. It is best to try one for size before cutting all of the dough. Roll the sausages in the pastry and arrange on a baking sheet. Brush the pastry well with an egg wash made with 1 egg yolk beaten with 2 tablespoons heavy cream. Bake at 425 degrees for 10 minutes. Reduce the heat to 375 degrees and continue baking till the pastry is nicely brown and cooked through. This should take about 30 minutes. Make plenty of these at a time, because they reheat nicely and freeze well.

Sausage in Crust

Large sausage may be rolled and baked in brioche dough, puff paste — rough puff paste, preferably — or roll or bread dough. Some of the sausages suitable for this dish, notably the French garlic sausage and the Italian coteghino, are best poached for 45 minutes and peeled before baking. They should be cooled completely before rolling in dough. The American knack for adaptation has also led to the use of such ready-to-eat sausages as bologna and kielbasy. This works exceedingly well although these types of sausage lack the proper coarse texture so often found in other sausages.

Roll out brioche, puff paste, or bread dough so that it measures large enough to envelop the sausage completely, with just enough excess to allow tucking in the ends and joining the seam along its length. Seal the seam with a little egg white or water. Place on a buttered baking sheet, seam side down. Brush well with egg wash — 1 egg yolk beaten with 2 tablespoons heavy cream. If using brioche or bread dough, place the roll in a warm place for 15 minutes; then bake in a 375-degree oven for approximately 30 to 40 minutes or until the coating is brown and puffy and gives every sign of being cooked through. If using puff paste or rough puff paste, heat the oven to 425 degrees and bake 10 minutes; then reduce to 350 degrees and continue baking until the pastry is crisp and brown — about 30 minutes. Serve the sausage in slices with a hot potato salad and mustards. A sausage in crust can be reheated and served.

Frankfurters

(1) When you serve frankfurters to a group of people — notably outdoors or at a picnic — have a variety of mustards on hand. The markets are full of various and sundry ones which can enhance a sausage and give it new character. You'll find mustards we have used since long before the First World War, when German mustards were so popular, and now these have been joined by many French and English ones as well.

(2) Try combining 1 part mustard and 3 parts mayonnaise. Add crumbled crisp bacon, chopped onion, and a small amount of tomato sauce or catsup.

(3) For a pleasant change in cooking frankfurters, split them, butter them, and broil quickly.

(4) For frankfurters and beans, see page 599.

Frankfurters in Sour Cream

1 pound frankfurters — the finest quality
½ cup finely chopped shallots or onion
4 tablespoons butter
⅓ cup chili sauce
1¼ cups commercial sour cream
Salt and freshly ground pepper
¼ cup chopped parsley

This dish was made famous by a great fashion designer who offered it at buffet parties as a spécialité of the house. Guests were baffled by it. It is one of those tricky dishes which, when well made, is superb and otherwise completely mediocre.

Carefully cut the frankfurters into halves lengthwise, and then each half into quarters. Sauté the onion or shallots in the butter, add the frankfurters and chili sauce, and heat thoroughly. Stir in the sour cream and heat through without allowing it to boil. Taste for seasoning, and correct. Transfer to a tureen or chafing dish and garnish with the chopped parsley. Serve on fried toast rounds, parslied rice, or toasted English muffins.

Ham and Bacon

Smoking products to preserve them has meant more to people through the ages than almost any other method of preservation. The discovery of how to cure meats was as important as the discovery of bread, of wine, and of cheese. Montagné claims the Gauls discovered the ham process, but this does not explain how the Chinese had ham much like Virginia ham in their cuisine before the Gauls.

In this country, the first smoked meats were certainly done in the fireplace chimney, where they could hang and be what you would certainly call hot-smoked. Later, when spices became plentiful, the hams were rubbed with pepper and spices, sewn into muslin coverings, and hung that way to prevent insects from boring into the meat. In the South, as the planters began building their large estates, a smokehouse was part of the farm buildings, and smoking began to be a major occupation and finally a business.

In Virginia, around the town of Smithfield, a curing process began which was to distinguish itself from others and produce a great ham, comparable in quality to the Parma ham known to us as prosciutto, the York ham from England, the Bayonne ham from the Basque country, and the Ardennes ham from Belgium. So popular did the Virginia ham from Smithfield become that it was necessary to limit the use of the designation to those hams produced in a radius of five counties surrounding Smithfield.

Kentucky started a different cure, and aged Kentucky hams were sold extensively before the war and now are sold at premium prices when you can get them. This is also true of hams from Maryland, Tennessee, the Carolinas, Georgia, and Missouri. The pigs are fed various feed to give the hams a distinctive flavor, a custom that probably originated because certain foods were in more plentiful supply. Thus we have peanut-fed hams, peach-fed hams, artichoke-fed hams (Jerusalem artichokes), corn-fed hams, and so on. As the trek West began and continued, the smoking process became widespread, and eventually country hams and commercial hams were developed in great variety. Nowadays, since the packers have won all the arguments, it is distressing to eat some of the meat served forth as ham. It is filled with water, given a cure consisting of various types of injections and heat treatments (in lieu of smoking), and in general is pretty revolting. The best thing one can say about these hams is that they are labor-saving. But a good ham is worth the trouble.

There are still Smithfield hams available, some aged and some not. Occasionally one gets a Kentucky or Tennessee ham or a Virginia country ham — not a Smithfield. There are country hams from Georgia and North Carolina and Missouri on the market. Also hams are available from Pennsylvania, New York, and other states where there are local smokers who sell from their own ranches. In many instances the hams are available cooked and ready for the table. They are all worth the effort of mailing in for them.

In addition to hams from the hindquarters of the hog, there are picnic shoulders — smoked shoulder ham. They are quite bony and you cannot get fine slices from them, but they have good flavor and for family use are excellent. There are also boneless butts from the shoulder, which are smoked and sold in great quantity, probably because they do not last as long as a ham and are easy to prepare. Sometimes they are mistakenly called smoked tenderloins.

Time was — in the elegant days — when there would be a cooked ham in the household for cold slices, for sandwiches and snacks, and for flavoring, and a raw smoked ham from which to cut slices to cook for breakfast. When the best parts were eaten, the remains would be made into other delicious ham dishes, ending up usually as soup.

To Prepare Hams for Baking

Dried hams. The dried hams from Italy, France, England, and other countries — and the adaptations of those hams made in the United States — require no cooking before eating. They are sliced paper-thin and served for a first course seasoned with freshly ground pepper or accompanied by melon quarters, fresh figs, pineapple fingers, or pears. The Italian Parma ham (prosciutto) is also used in some cookery.

Aged hams. Nowadays one seldom finds a ham aged more than two or three years. Formerly it was not uncommon to find them aged six and seven years, especially from Virginia or Kentucky. They were black, covered with mold, and looked uninviting to the average person, but they gave promise of fine feasting to the ham fancier. Aged hams must be scrubbed with a brush and soapy water, not perfumed detergent but soap such as Ivory, for there is sometimes a patina of spice, dust, and mold that needs to be removed. The ham is then soaked 24 to 48 hours, depending upon its age and dryness, then cooked in water. Finally, the skin is removed and it is baked (see below).

To cook, cover the ham with fresh water, bring it to a boil, and boil 5 minutes or so, removing any scum that forms on the top. From this point on, there are two methods of cooking:

(1) Cover the ham and let it simmer at the barest ripple for 20 minutes per pound. The small bone at the shank end of the ham will be very loose when the ham is thoroughly cooked. Remove the ham from the water at once and allow it to cool.

(2) The other method is to let the ham simmer 2½ hours exactly, then let it cool in the liquid.

To remove the skin from the ham, use a sharp boning knife. When the ham is cool enough to handle, loosen the skin at the butt end, and run your fingers under the skin to loosen it further. Then pull the skin over the shank end, leaving a ham covered with a blanket of creamy fat. If the fat is too heavy, carefully trim some of it off with the boning knife. Do not, of course, cut away all the fat, or the ham will dry out during baking (see page 440).

Country hams. For the most part, producers of the various country hams, such as MacArthur's Smokehouse in Millerton, New York, the Talmadge Farms in Georgia, and the Great Valley Mills in Pennsylvania, are very good about providing printed directions with their hams. However, in the South one occasionally finds hams cured at small farms, and these require your own judgment in preparing them. The smell and feel of the ham should guide you. If it is dry, very hard to the touch, and has a fairly heavy smoky smell, I would treat it as an aged ham.

Ready-to-eat and tenderized hams. The type of ham one ordinarily buys in the store or supermarket is usually marked "ready to eat" or "tenderized." These hams usually need no boiling before you bake them.

Canned hams. These are becoming increasingly standard for many people. They are convenience food at its most unattractive — boned, cooked, defatted, deflavored, and ready to eat! There is absolutely no relationship between an artificially flavored canned pork and a real ham. If you must use them, bake them in a crust or coat with a chaudfroid sauce, a cold sauce made with aspic, or one of the glazes given below.

Baked Aged Cooked Ham

Traditionally the ham fat is covered with brown sugar and crumbs, studded with cloves, and baked in a 350-degree oven to glaze. In my opinion too many cloves overwhelm the flavor, and they are a nuisance to insert, besides. I like to break with tradition and either spread the ham with crumbs, brown sugar, and some dry mustard, or use one of the glazes below.

Aged hams should be served tepid or cold, cut in paper-thin slices with a very sharp ham slicing knife. Spoon bread, hominy in cream, or creamed potatoes are traditional accompaniments. All are excellent. This is also usually the place for watermelon pickles, pickled peaches, or crabapples, perhaps hot biscuit or beaten biscuit, and certainly some preserves. See also the garnishes listed below.

Baked Country Ham

If there are no directions with the ham, cook as above (baked aged cooked ham) — most country hams fare well if they are boiled and baked like aged hams, with or without presoaking. Or they should be prepared as follows. After the skin is removed, place the ham fat side down in a large pan and pour water, wine, cider, or ginger ale into the pan to cover about two-thirds of the ham. Cover tightly with foil. Bake at 325 degrees, allowing approximately 18 minutes per pound. Two-thirds of the way through the cooking, remove the foil and turn the ham. Cover with the foil again and continue cooking. Remove the ham and cool. Cover with crumbs and brown sugar and mustard or with one of the glazes below. Bake at 350 degrees for 1 hour. Serve with spoon bread or corn pudding and a purée of fresh spinach prepared with butter and a touch of nutmeg.

Baked Ready-to-Eat or Tenderized Ham

These hams are quite wet, and if you like a dry texture, be certain to pierce the ham with a fork in several places before baking. The skin can usually be loosened with a knife and pulled off before baking. Glaze the ham (see glazes below), or rub crumbs, brown sugar, and mustard into the surface. Stud with cloves if you like, first scoring the fat in parallel lines with a sharp knife so as to form perfect squares. A clove can be inserted in the center of each square. Bake the ham at 325 degrees approximately 10 to 12 minutes per pound.

Note. You may bake tenderized or ready-to-eat hams fat side down in a pan with a pint of sherry, Madeira, apple cider, or ginger ale. Baste the ham with the liquid from time to time during baking.

Glazes and Garnishes for Baked Ham

Apricot Glaze. An apricot glaze will give a cold ham a beautiful look and a good tart flavor. After baking, cool the ham thoroughly. Bring 1½ pints apricot jam to a boil and let it cook 3 minutes. Add ¼ cup brandy or bourbon, if you like, and put the jam through a strainer. Rub the ham fat with a little dry mustard. Spoon or brush the glaze over the ham to cover it completely. Let it set before serving. Grape, apple, or quince jelly may be used instead of apricot preserves.

Pickled Peach or Watermelon Glaze. During baking, baste the ham often with the syrup from pickled peaches or watermelon pickle, which leaves a pleasant and pungent glaze. Place the ham on a platter. Decorate the platter with pickled peaches or watermelon pickle slices.

Ham with Pineapple. Another ritual — besides inserting cloves in any kind of ham — is to glaze it with pineapple syrup and decorate it with pineapple slices and sometimes maraschino cherries. There is no doubt that the combination of ham and pineapple is very agreeable, and there is no doubt that pineapple slices or "fingers" glazed with butter and a little sugar are decorative. But it is quite another matter to smother an entire ham with pineapple. I recommend a return to the days when ham was discreetly glazed with pineapple syrup (if using unsweetened juice, add sugar in a 1-to-1 proportion) and sautéed pineapple slices, either canned or fresh, were served around the ham as a garnish. This looks and tastes much better. Forget the cherries!

Garnishes and Accompaniments for Baked Hams. If the ham is to be served hot: spinach timbales, artichoke bottoms filled with wild rice, puréed green peas, tomatoes filled with spinach purée, fried apple rings. If the ham is to be served cold it should be sliced very thin and served with a variety of mustards and such relishes for complement and flavor and for garnish as spiced pears, spiced peaches, pickled watermelon rind, or any favorite relish, such as red pepper relish or India relish or the Italian mustard fruits or Chinese mixed pickles. Appropriate dishes to accompany cold sliced ham would be a vegetable salad, potato salad of any kind, coleslaw, a hot dish such as macaroni and cheese, a bean dish, or tiny new potatoes with butter or asparagus, either hot or cold with a vinaigrette sauce.

Country Ham Baked in a Crust

Puff pastry or rich pastry — double recipe for a 2-crust pie
A country ham about 10 to 12 pounds
3/4 cup brown sugar
1 1/2 teaspoons freshly ground pepper
Pinch of ground clove
Dry mustard
Fine breadcrumbs
1 egg yolk
3 tablespoons cream

Prepare the pastry and chill in the refrigerator. Prepare the ham according to the directions provided by the packers, or use the directions for country hams given above. Let the ham cool thoroughly. Mix the brown sugar and spices. Rub the ham well with them and press them into the fat, with the crumbs. Place the ham on a baking pan.

Roll out enough pastry to cover the top and the sides of the ham. No pastry goes on the bottom. To transfer the pastry to the ham, roll it around a floured rolling pin and then roll over the ham. Mold the pastry to the shape of the ham. Mix the egg yolk and cream well and brush the pastry. Cut leftover pastry into rounds and strips, and use your fingers to shape into flower petals, oval leaves, and stems. Or create other decorations of your own. Attach to the pastry with some of the egg wash, brush again with the egg wash, and bake the ham in a 350-degree oven 1 1/4 to 1 1/2 hours. Before serving, cut the crust loose around its perimeter and set aside. Carve the ham lengthwise toward the shank in thin slices. Leave the slices in place and restore the crust. Serve a bit of crust along with each portion of ham.

Ready-to-Eat Ham in Crust

Double 2-crust recipe for plain pastry, rough puff paste, or cream cheese pastry
Ready-to-eat ham
1 1/2 cups breadcrumbs
1 cup brown sugar
1 1/2 teaspoons dry mustard
1 teaspoon freshly ground pepper
2 egg yolks
3 tablespoons heavy cream

Skin the ham. Rub well with the crumbs and seasonings and press down into the fat. Roll out the crust as in the preceding recipe and follow the directions for preparing the ham for the oven. Brush the crust with the egg yolks and cream lightly beaten together. Bake at 325 degrees 1 1/2 hours.

Note. Canned hams may be given the same treatment.

Ham Baked in Bread Crust

A Polish-American recipe for a country ham or aged ham. Boil and skin as directed above, and rub the fat with crumbs, brown sugar, and freshly ground pepper. Cover with rye bread dough filled with caraway seeds and rolled out quite thin. Glaze the dough with egg white beaten with water. Bake a half hour at 375 degrees. Reduce the heat to 325 degrees and continue baking 1 hour longer. At this point some people remove the crust completely. I think it nicer to cut around the edge of the ham and lift off the crust when it arrives at table for carving. Serve each person a bit of the crust along with the slices of ham.

Ham Baked in Cola

1 tenderized ham, about 10 pounds
Cola
1 cup brown sugar
2 teaspoons dry mustard
1 teaspoon freshly ground pepper
1½ cups breadcrumbs

This Southern-style dish has come into fashion within the last twenty or twenty-five years. Do not, of course, use this method with fine aged Smithfield hams or country hams. It works well with tenderized hams.

Place the ham, fat side down, in a roasting pan. Add cola to half cover the ham. Bake at 350 degrees, allowing 15 minutes per pound. Baste the ham frequently with the cola. Remove the ham from the pan, skin it, and rub well with dry mustard, pepper, breadcrumbs and brown sugar. Press the coating into the fat. Place the ham on a rack, return to a 350-degree oven for 35 to 40 minutes, and baste with cola.

Ham Baked in Cider

1 10-pound ham (not aged)
Cider
1 cup brown sugar
2 teaspoons mustard
Cloves
2 cups breadcrumbs

SAUCE

2 cups cider from the ham
¼ cup applejack (optional)
½ cup seedless raisins
¼ teaspoon nutmeg
¼ teaspoon cloves
1 tablespoon cornstarch mixed with 1 tablespoon cider

A dish that used to be favored in New England, Pennsylvania, and sometimes in the West — in fact, wherever apples are a major crop and cider is made in the fall.

Soak the ham in cider overnight, skin side down. Remove the ham and place it on a rack in a roasting pan. Bake at 350 degrees, allowing 20 minutes per pound. Baste from time to time with the cider. Remove the ham from the oven, and strip off the skin. Spread with brown sugar, mustard, and crumbs, and stud with cloves. Return to the oven to glaze for about a half hour at 350 degrees. Baste occasionally with the cider.

When the ham is done, prepare the sauce. Cook the cider, applejack, and raisins about 5 minutes and add the spices. Stir in the moistened cornstarch and continue stirring till it thickens slightly. Serve the sauce with the ham. Also serve fried apple rings and cornmeal mush cut in slices, floured, and fried until crisp in butter.

Ham Stuffed with Fruits and Nuts

1 10-pound country ham, boned, with the shank bone left in, and not tied
1½ cups corn bread crumbs
1 cup finely chopped pecans
1 cup chopped mixed candied fruits
1 cup sultana raisins
½ cup currants
½ teaspoon each of mace and cinnamon
¼ teaspoon cloves
½ cup honey or maple syrup
1 cup Cognac or bourbon
Cider or white wine
1 cup breadcrumbs
1½ cups brown sugar
1 cup sherry

Traditional Southern cooking includes many elaborate stuffed ham dishes, some made with greens and butter, others with nuts and dried fruits, and still others with spiced meat combinations. Sometimes the hams were boned and the resulting cavity filled with stuffing, or deep gashes were made in the hams and the stuffing forced in. There is one recipe which calls for poking holes in the ham with a broomstick and then stuffing it. Surely the modern kitchen that would prepare such dishes would do well to have a big larding needle or such a tool on hand.

Blend together the corn breadcrumbs, nuts, fruits, and spices, and moisten with the honey or syrup and Cognac or bourbon. Stuff the bone cavity of the ham, close with skewers, and tie the ham securely. Place it, skin and fat side down, in a roasting pan. Pour in enough white wine or cider to immerse about one-third of the ham. Cover the pan with foil, sealing it well so that the pan is practically airtight. Bake the ham at 350 degrees, allowing 30 minutes per pound. Remove the ham and skin it. Rub the fat with the breadcrumbs and brown sugar and return to a 400-degree oven. Baste from time to time with the sherry till the crumb and sugar mixture forms a crust. Remove from the oven. Serve cooled but not chilled, with scalloped potatoes and Harvard beets. Drink a chilled rosé wine.

Cold Decorated Ham for a Buffet

A cooked (boiled) ham with the skin removed
Approximately 4 cups chaudfroid sauce, made with ham broth
2 cups aspic jelly
Decorations (see below)

This can make a beautiful buffet dish for a very important party. The ham is covered with a chaudfroid sauce, which is made with ham broth in this case, and then the ham is chilled and afterwards decorated. Finally some aspic jelly is spooned over it and it is chilled again.

Lately I have seen decorations far too elaborate for a ham or any other food, and they hark back to the Victorian age, when people felt compelled to decorate hams with renderings of Niagara Falls or other scenic landscapes. The simpler and more tailored the decorations, the better they will look.

The ham should be quite cold. Place it on a rack in a shallow pan. Cool the chaudfroid sauce to the point of setting. Spoon it over the ham very carefully and quickly, turning the ham from side to side so that the sauce will cover the surface evenly.

For decorating use any of the following: fresh tarragon leaves or leek greens, truffles, thin strips of carrot, hard-boiled egg, red or green pepper, pimiento, parsley sprigs, dill sprigs. Plan your decoration beforehand, and cut truffles, carrot, egg, pepper, or pimiento into the required shapes. For instance, make a rosette of truffle slices in the center of the ham and surround with little crescents of truffle; or decorate with tarragon leaves, or leek greens cut into leaf shapes; or arrange a sunburst effect with a slice of hard-cooked egg at the center and strips of carrot, pepper, or pimiento radiating from it. When your decoration is complete, spoon aspic nearly at the setting stage over the entire surface, being careful to distribute it evenly without disturbing the decorative pattern. Place the ham on a platter and surround it with chopped aspic jelly and sprigs of parsley or dill or other small greens. Put a ruffle on the ham bone. Use the ham as a feature part of the buffet. So that everyone gets a chance to observe your handiwork, you can have a platter of sliced ham ready to serve at first.

Schnitz und Knepp

2 cups dried sweet apples (schnitz)
4 pounds ham — hocks, shank end of a ham, or a picnic ham
½ cup brown sugar
DUMPLINGS (KNEPP)
1 beaten egg
1 cup flour
2 teaspoons baking powder
½ teaspoon salt
Milk
2 tablespoons melted butter

As famous as any of the Pennsylvania Dutch dishes, Schnitz und Knepp was in evidence prior to the American Revolution. It has survived many changes from generation to generation and continues to attract people, I think, because of its intriguing name. Here is an old recipe.

Soak the dried apples in water overnight. Simmer the ham, allowing 25 minutes per pound. Add the schnitz and brown sugar and cook 1 hour. Mix the knepp and drop by spoonfuls into the pot. Cover tightly and boil about 15 minutes. Serve the ham on a platter surrounded with the schnitz and then with the knepp.

For a modern version of this recipe, substitute a boneless butt for ham hocks or other cuts. Cook the butt and soaked apples together, and then drop in the dumplings.

Baked Ham Slice

2-inch slice of ham
¼ teaspoon nutmeg
A tiny pinch of clove
1 teaspoon mustard
½ cup cider
¼ cup maple syrup

Thick slices cut from the center of the ham have been part of American cooking since Colonial times. This is an old New England recipe.

Rub the spices well into the ham. Place it in a baking dish and pour the cider and syrup over it. Bake at 350 degrees, approximately 1¼ hours for cured ham and 45 minutes for tenderized ham. Baste occasionally. A slice of this size will serve two or three persons. Creamed hominy makes a pleasant addition.

A California Ham Slice

1 ham slice 1½ to 2 inches thick
Hot mustard or sweet mustard
Freshly ground pepper
1½ cups red wine

Place the ham slice in a shallow baking dish and spread well on both sides with your favorite mustard. Give it several grinds of fresh pepper. Add the red wine and bake at 350 degrees about 45 minutes or until the ham is tender. Serve this with polenta and with leaf spinach prepared with butter and lemon juice. Drink the same wine used in the cooking, possibly a California Pinot Noir.

Ham Slice with a Mustard Crust

1½-pound slice of ham
4 tablespoons prepared mustard (Dijon, German, or Colman's, as you please)
4 tablespoons flour
2 tablespoons molasses
2 cloves
1½ cups milk

SAUCE

2 tablespoons butter
2 teaspoons finely chopped green pepper
1 tablespoon flour
Milk from the pan
Paprika and freshly ground pepper to taste
Salt, if needed
¼ cup seedless raisins

Place the ham slice in a baking dish. Blend the mustard, flour, and molasses to a paste and spread it on the ham. Stick the two cloves into the ham and pour the milk around it. Bake at 350 degrees 45 minutes or until tender. Baste from time to time with the milk. Transfer the ham to a hot platter. Reserve the milk, and prepare the sauce. Melt the butter and add the green pepper and flour. Blend well and cook 2 or 3 minutes. Stir in the milk and continue stirring until the mixture thickens. Correct the seasoning and add the raisins. Serve with the ham.

Ham Slice in Champagne

1 ham slice about 2 inches thick
Champagne
Granulated sugar

This recipe comes from the turn of the century, when champagne was popular and not expensive.

Place the ham in a baking dish and cover with champagne. Let it marinate several hours, turning it once. Bake in the champagne at 375 degrees about 45 minutes. Ten minutes before the ham is done, sprinkle it lightly with granulated sugar. Return to the oven for 10 minutes, then place under the broiler for a moment or two to caramelize the sugar. Watch it very carefully so it does not burn. Serve with tiny new potatoes dressed with butter and finely chopped parsley and perhaps with tiny buttered green beans. Drink a bottle of your favorite champagne.

Ham Slice with Oranges

1 large ham slice, about 2 inches thick
Orange juice
1 cup orange sections
Granulated sugar
½ teaspoon cinnamon

Slash the fat on the ham to prevent the slice from curling.

Place the slice in a baking dish large enough for the ham and enough orange juice to barely cover. Bake at 375 degrees about 45 minutes, basting occasionally with the orange juice. Just before the ham is served, top with the orange sections and sprinkle with sugar and cinnamon. Run it under the broiler about 4 inches from the heat unit for a moment or two to caramelize the sugar. Serve with rice and a crisp salad.

Boiled Ham and Cabbage

1 ham, picnic ham, or smoked butt
1 bay leaf
1 onion stuck with 2 cloves
½ cup wine vinegar
1 head cabbage
Potatoes

This dish works equally well with a whole ham, a picnic ham, or even a smoked butt. Generally, picnic hams are used, and the left-overs go into ham loaf, ham balls, and such things.

Cover the ham with water, add the bay leaf, onion, and vinegar, and bring to a boil. Boil 5 minutes and remove any scum that forms. Reduce the heat and simmer the ham, covered, about 18 minutes per pound. If you prefer to cook the vegetables with the ham, peel the potatoes and add to the ham 25 minutes before it is done. Cut the cabbage into sixths and add 15 minutes before. To my mind, however, it is far better to boil the cabbage and potatoes (in their jackets) separately and to serve them freshly buttered rather than have everything tasting of ham. Pickles and mustards should accompany this boiled dinner. Use the leftover ham for any of the dishes given on pages 449–452. The bone and cooking broth will make a good lentil or split pea soup.

Fried Ham

Choose slices ⅜ to ¾ inch thick. One large slice of ham from the center cuts should serve two or three, according to thickness and appetites. Timing for different types of ham will vary greatly.

An Old Recipe for Frying Ham

This early nineteenth-century way of frying ham is from a manuscript cookbook.

"Cut some fine slices from the large end of the ham, take off the skin, put them in a frying pan and pour hot water over; set it over the fire and let it boil up once, then pour the water off, take the slices up, put a spoonful of lard in the frying pan, and let it become hot. Dip the slices in rolled cracker crumbs or wheat flour and fry them a nice brown; when one side is done turn to the other, then take them on a dish, pour a very little water in the pan, let it boil up once, put it over the meat. Or, if flour gravy is wanted, make a thin batter with a teaspoonful of flour and stir it into the gravy in the pan; let it brown, and if too thick put a little hot water into it. Stir it smooth and serve with the meat."

Fried (Sautéed) Ham

Sauté ham slices very slowly in a little ham fat and butter in a heavy skillet. Turn several times. The ham should be slightly browned and the fat crisp at the edges and lightly colored. Do not overcook or the ham will dry out.

For a slice of ready-to-eat ham ½ inch thick, allow approximately 10 minutes. For country ham, allow 12 to 15 minutes. For aged ham or very salty ham, first parboil or blanch 5 minutes in water, then remove and dry on absorbent paper or a towel. Sauté in butter (approximately 3 tablespoons for a large slice) 8 to 10 minutes.

Ham and Eggs

Time was — and that within easy memory — when travelers could safely order ham and eggs in any unfamiliar little country restaurant. One was served a respectable cut of ham ranging from 1/4 to 1 inch in thickness, well cooked, with a tang of salt about it, and fine crisp fat. The eggs really looked at you, and a little of the pan gravy from the ham was poured over them. Often lovely brown home-fried potatoes or hash-browns were served too. This used to be a great American dish when prepared well, as thoroughly delicious as anything we have produced gastronomically. It must have been the Dutch who introduced it, for all over Holland one encounters a similar dish, called spek en eiern. Today, alas, ham and eggs in most restaurants means thin rashers of canned or boiled ham and eggs poorly cooked. To prepare this dish at home, it is worth the trouble so seek out well-cured country ham or aged ham.

I recommend cooking the ham and eggs separately. Fry the ham according to the directions above, and cook the eggs in butter. If you want ham flavor with your eggs, spoon pan gravy over them after they are cooked.

Country-Style Ham and Eggs. Prepare ham and eggs as in the recipe above. Add 3/4 cup cream to the pan in which the ham was cooked, blend it well, and allow it to cook down 2 minutes. Spoon over the ham and eggs.

Fried Ham with Red-eye Gravy

This famous dish, which has its points, is not as interesting to me as the age-long discussion of how it originated. Red-eye is really nothing more than ham gravy and water cooked down until it turns lightly pinky red. There is one theory that only Tennessee hams yielded good red gravy. Some of the old books prescribe black coffee instead of water, and of course that would cause it to turn a rather unappetizing reddish brown. Serve with home-fried potatoes and hot biscuits.

Broiled Ham

Broiled Ham Slices

Ham slices broil very well. If broiling a salty aged ham, it is best to first soak it in cold water several hours or put it in cold water and bring it to a boil. Score the fat and brush the ham with a bit of melted butter. Broil about 3 inches from the broiling unit and watch carefully to prevent overcooking. Allow about 6 minutes for a piece of ready-to-eat ham, 8 to 10 minutes for a thick slice of country ham, and 12 to 14 minutes for aged ham ½ to ¾ inch thick.

An Old Manuscript Recipe for Broiling Ham

"Lay ham slices on a gridiron over bright coals. When the outside is browned turn the other, then take the slices on a hot dish, butter them freely and sprinkle pepper over and serve." Or "Dip each slice in beaten egg and then into rolled crackers and broil and serve."

Broiled Ham Slice with Fruit

1 ham steak, ready-to-eat or tenderized, 1½ inches thick
8 poached or canned apricot halves or 4 poached or canned peach halves
GLAZE: *4 tablespoons honey blended with 2 tablespoons lemon juice*

This is typical of a great number of recipes using fruit with ham, making a combination of sweet and savory.

Broil the steak on one side in a broiler, about 4 inches from the source of heat until nicely browned and well cooked. Remove from the broiler. Turn and place the fruit on the uncooked side. Brush with a little of the glaze and return to the broiler. Broil very slowly about 5 to 6 inches from the broiler if possible, and brush with the glaze several times. The fruit must not burn while the ham cooks. Transfer to a hot platter and garnish with watercress. Glazed sweet potatoes and a good salad make appropriate accompaniments.

Using Up Leftover Hams

Some of our best recipes for ham were inspired by leftovers. Ham balls and ham loaf have good flavor and texture and are a nice change from other similar meat dishes. And few things excel real deviled ham as a filler for sandwiches.

Deviled Ham

Combine 2 cups chopped or ground cooked ham with any one of the following:

(1) ⅓ cup chopped sweet pickle and mayonnaise to bind.
(2) ½ cup finely chopped chutney.
(3) 2 teaspoons Dijon mustard and mayonnaise to bind.
(4) ½ cup coarsely chopped salted peanuts and a little mayonnaise.
(5) ½ cup finely chopped dill pickle and mayonnaise to bind.
(6) 2 tablespoons catsup and ¼ teaspoon Tabasco.

Ham Balls, Sweet and Sour

2 pounds ham, ground rather fine
1 pound ground veal or pork
1 teaspoon dry mustard
2 tablespoons finely chopped onion
Dry breadcrumbs (about 2 cups)
1½ cups very heavy cream sauce
Fat for deep frying
Flour
2 eggs well beaten

SAUCE

1 cup honey
½ cup wine vinegar
2 tablespoons soy sauce
½ cup cold water
1 cup Chinese mixed pickles (available in Chinese food stores)

Mix together the ground meats, mustard, onion, 1 cup breadcrumbs, and the cream sauce. Taste for seasoning. Form into balls and chill thoroughly. Prepare the sauce. Combine all the ingredients except the Chinese pickles, bring to the boiling point, and simmer 5 minutes. Add the pickles and heat through. Keep warm. Heat the oil to 365 degrees in a skillet. Roll the balls in flour, then in the beaten egg, and finally in crumbs. Fry a few at a time in fat to cover until nicely browned. Drain on absorbent paper. Serve with the sweet and sour sauce, and with a hot potato salad.

Deviled Ham Toast

8 slices bread, thinly cut, crusts removed, and well buttered
Deviled ham
2 eggs
3 tablespoons cream
Salt and freshly ground pepper
4 tablespoons butter

A nineteenth-century recipe from the West Coast.

Spread 4 slices of bread with deviled ham in any of its versions (page 449). Top with bread and press together firmly. Beat the eggs and cream together lightly and season with salt and pepper. Dip each sandwich into the egg mixture, and sauté quickly in butter in a large heavy skillet till delicately browned on both sides. Serve with an assortment of relishes and pickles and a tomato salad.

Eleanor Lynch's Upside Down Ham Loaf

4 cups ground cooked ham
1 small onion, finely chopped or ground with the ham
2 cups herb-seasoned breadcrumbs or croutons
½ cup hot water
2 eggs, slightly beaten
¼ cup brown sugar
¼ teaspoon ground cloves
4 pineapple slices

Combine the ham and onion. Soak the crumbs or croutons in the hot water and mix together with the ham mixture and the eggs. Line an 8 × 3-inch loaf tin with foil. Sprinkle with the brown sugar and cloves. Place the pineapple slices on the sugar. Press the meat mixture into the pan and bake 1 hour at 350 degrees. Turn out on a heated platter and peel off the foil. Surround with glazed sweet potatoes and crisp watermelon pickle.

Ham in Tomato Cream

6 to 8 ham slices on toast
6 shallots or green onions, chopped fine
4 tablespoons butter
4 tablespoons flour
1 cup white wine
2 teaspoons tomato paste
¾ cup cream

Sauté the shallots or green onions in the butter until just wilted. Add the flour, stir in the white wine, and allow the mixture to thicken. Simmer 5 minutes, stirring frequently. Blend in the tomato paste and finally the cream. Stir until the mixture is thickened. Correct the seasoning. Spoon over 6 to 8 reheated ham slices on toast.

Ham Toasts

8 slices medium thick bread toasted on one side
Butter
English mustard
1½ cups chopped cooked ham
1 finely chopped shallot
¼ teaspoon Tabasco
1 cup grated Cheddar or Gruyère cheese

This recipe comes from a small cookbook written for American women by one of the original chefs at Delmonico's.

Spread the bread well with butter and then with mustard. Mix the chopped ham with the shallot, cayenne, and cheese, and spread on the bread. Place under the broiler long enough for the cheese to melt, and serve at once.

Scalloped Potatoes with Ham

Butter
6 to 8 potatoes peeled and thinly sliced
About 1½ cups ham, diced, chopped or ground
Salt and freshly ground pepper
Milk

Generously butter an oblong or oval baking dish about 9×12 inches. Arrange a third of the potatoes in a layer and spread with half the ham. Make a second layer of potatoes, dot with butter, and season well with salt and pepper. Add the remaining ham and finish with a layer of potatoes. Dot well again with butter, and salt and pepper to taste. Heat milk and pour over the potatoes to cover three-quarters of the way. Bake at 350 degrees about 1 hour or until the potatoes are tender and the top is browned. Serve at once.

Note. This is sometimes topped with grated cheese after a half hour's baking, and sometimes the ham is added in thin slices.

Ham Rolls with Asparagus Tips

6 slices cold ham about 4×6 inches
Asparagus tips (either fresh or canned)
2½ cups cheese sauce (page 459)
Grated cheese

Ham rolls made with various fillings used to be considered quite elegant for ladies' luncheons, and so they were. The dish given here has even been prepared with a filling of bananas.

Roll several asparagus tips in each slice of ham. Place the rolls, seam side down, in a baking dish suitable for serving at the table. Spoon some of the cheese sauce around the rolls, and lay a strip of it down the center of the rolls. Sprinkle with grated cheese and bake at 375 degrees for 15 to 20 minutes, or until the dish is bubbling hot.

Creamed Ham

2 cups diced cooked ham
2 cups rich cream sauce
3 tablespoons finely chopped pimiento
2 tablespoons sherry or Madeira
Salt and freshly ground pepper
6 patty shells or croustades
2 tablespoons chopped parsley

A constant favorite with luncheon-goers, this is often served in patty shells or in croustades and sometimes on toast. It is also very good on toasted English muffins.

Prepare a rich cream sauce, using chicken broth for the basic liquid and adding cream. Keep warm over hot water. Add the ham, pimiento and wine. Heat through and correct the seasoning. The dish must be piping hot. Spoon the creamed ham from a tureen or chafing dish into heated shells or croustades. Garnish with chopped parsley.

Variations

(1) Add 4 or 5 sliced hard-boiled eggs to the ham mixture and slice one for the top as a garnish, together with the chopped parsley.

(2) Add 1/4 pound mushroom caps lightly sautéed in butter.

(3) Add 3/4 cup grated Gruyère or sharp Cheddar cheese to the mixture just long enough before serving to allow it to melt.

Ham and Cheese Soufflé

3 tablespoons butter
3 tablespoons flour
3/4 cup hot milk
6 egg yolks
3/4 cup finely ground ham
1/4 cup grated Gruyère or sharp Cheddar cheese
1 teaspoon salt
1 teaspoon dry mustard
8 egg whites

Melt the butter, add the flour, and blend well over a medium heat, stirring continuously. Add the hot milk and continue stirring till the mixture is smoothly thickened. Remove from the heat and let it cool for a few minutes. Beat the egg yolks lightly and stir in a few spoonfuls of the cooled mixture. Then blend the rest of the sauce into the yolks and stir thoroughly. Return the mixture to the heat for just a few moments to set the yolks with the sauce, but do not allow it to boil. Add the ham, cheese, and seasonings, and blend well. Cool slightly. Beat the egg whites until they are stiff but not dry — just past the soft peak stage. Fold one-third of the egg whites into the sauce quite thoroughly, and fold in the remainder lightly but well. Pour into a buttered 2½-quart mold and bake at 375 degrees for 30 to 40 minutes or until the soufflé is nicely risen and puffy and lightly browned.

Italian Ham and Eggs

For each serving:
1 ramekin or round heatproof dish
2 rounds of buttered toast or 2 English muffin halves
2 slices ham
2 poached eggs
Sauce Mornay
Grated Parmesan cheese

A luncheon delight for many, many years — often found on menus in clubs and restaurants.

Arrange the toast and the ham slices in the ramekins or baking dishes. Top with the poached eggs and spoon Mornay sauce over each one. Sprinkle liberally with grated Parmesan cheese and run under the broiler to glaze before serving. A good green salad is a pleasant accompaniment.

Bacon

Bacon was probably the most prevalent meat in the early nineteenth century. Explorers, prospectors, settlers, and homesteaders, if they ate meat at all aside from game, were likely to eat bacon. It was both meat and cooking fat and had infinite culinary uses. Few things smelled more tantalizing than a pan of bacon cooking slowly over the coals, and bacon fat cooked eggs, potatoes, pheasant, trout, and venison, and provided the shortening for biscuits.

I wonder what the prospector and the hardy pioneer would think of the average water-soaked, artificially flavored, indescribable substance called bacon today. It shrinks to nothing in the pan, tastes sweet, and reeks of artificial smoke. The one thing you can say for it is that it looks pretty in the package. Some good bacon is, however, still available.

Cooked Bacon

It is probably at its best sizzling in the pan over a campfire, but here are some rules for homecooking:

To broil. Broil bacon on a rack about 4 inches from the broiling unit, turning once.

To pan-fry. Bacon is best laid in a cold pan and cooked quite slowly and turned often. It will take from 5 to 10 minutes, depending upon the thickness of the slices and how well done you like it.

To bake. Place the rashers on a rack in a broiling or shallow roasting pan and bake at 325 degrees till done to your taste.

Baked Canadian Bacon

Canadian bacon is back bacon from the loin, extremely lean, and in some cases has all fat removed. It used to be cooked in a little fat as bacon was, and was extremely good. Nowadays, unless you get home-cured Canadian bacon, it is best ignored.

If you are lucky enough to get a whole piece of well-cured Canadian bacon, stud it with cloves, sprinkle with some brown sugar and crumbs, and bake it as you would a ham. It is delicious sliced and served with any of the garnishes you might use for ham.

Sauces for Meats, Fish, Vegetables

American cookery is not notable for its native sauces, and we have borrowed heavily from the French, the Italians, and the English. We have, nevertheless, contributed innovations in the realm of barbecue sauces and marinades, and some of these have distinction if for no reason other than their uninhibited and often wildly imaginative seasoning.

The earliest food authorities — Miss Leslie, Mrs. Crowen, and their contemporaries — offer comparatively few sauces in their books, and even a number of these, such as peach sauce and nasturtium sauce, have long since been forgotten. The latter was a substitute for caper sauce, made from the seed pods of nasturtiums, gathered by housewives and pickled like capers for winter use.

As the French influence in food grew throughout the country in the eighteenth and nineteenth centuries, the basic or "mother" sauces came into general use. In New Orleans and elsewhere in the South the "brown roux" and the "white roux" were the principal sauces. They are still made there and called by their original names.

Thickening Agents

Cornstarch and arrowroot are also used.

Flour. Probably the most common of thickening ingredients for sauces. It is important to cook the flour and fat together well before adding liquid; or if adding a flour mixture to a liquid, simmer for several minutes after thickening to blend and mellow the sauce. Nothing is more disagreeable than the taste of raw flour in a sauce.

Beurre manié. Still another form of roux, often used to thicken liquids and stocks. It is made by thoroughly kneading together equal quantities of butter and flour. Add by spoonfuls to the liquid, being careful to stir in well and to simmer the sauce after thickening. Beurre manié may be formed into small pea-size balls and stored in the refrigerator to be used as needed.

Eggs and cream. A blend of egg yolks and cream is used to thicken very delicate, creamy sauces. Use 2 or 3 yolks to a cup of heavy cream. Beat together, then add some of the hot sauce to temper the egg-cream mixture. Stir this back into the sauce, off the fire. Then reheat carefully, but do not allow to boil, or the eggs will produce a scrambled texture.

Miss Leslie's Drawn or Made Gravy

This is one of the oldest of American recipes to be found on the subject of gravy.

"For this purpose you may use the coarse pieces of lean of beef or veal, or the giblets and trimmings of poultry or game. It must be stewed for a long time, skimmed, strained, thickened, and flavoured with whatever condiments are considered most suited to the dish it is to accompany."

Drawn Butter (White Roux)

½ cup butter
3 to 4 tablespoons flour
2 cups hot water or stock
½ teaspoon salt
¼ teaspoon pepper

More than a white roux, this was the customary sauce to serve with vegetables and fish and even with boiled meats.

Put half the butter in a saucepan over low heat. Do not let it become brown. When melted, add flour, mix well, and simmer for several minutes. Add the hot water or stock a little at a time, and stir as it thickens. When perfectly smooth, add remainder of butter in small pieces, and stir until it is absorbed. Add salt and pepper.

From this basic white roux a number of sauces used to be made. A few of the notable ones are given below.

Caper Sauce (or the above-mentioned pickled nasturtium sauce). Add 6 tablespoons capers.

Egg Sauce. Add 2 or 3 hard-boiled eggs, chopped or sliced.

Mustard Sauce. Add 3 tablespoons prepared or Dijon mustard.

Parsley Sauce. Add 2 tablespoons chopped parsley.

Brown Sauce (Brown Roux)

2 pounds shin of beef with bone
1 veal knuckle
1 large onion stuck with 2 cloves
1 carrot
1 or 2 cloves garlic (optional)
1 teaspoon thyme
1 bay leaf
Several sprigs parsley
5 cups water
2 tablespoons tomato paste
Salt and freshly ground pepper
6 tablespoons or more butter
6 tablespoons browned flour

Basic brown sauce is another "mother" sauce which calls for a roux, made primarily with browned flour.

To prepare browned flour. Spread 1 cup flour on a cookie sheet or a jelly roll pan and brown slowly in a 250-degree oven, shaking the pan from time to time.

Brown the beef and bones well under the broiler, turning several times, or brown in a 450-degree oven for 30 to 45 minutes. Transfer the browned meat and bones to a large pot, and add the vegetables, garlic, herbs, and water. Bring to a boil, reduce the heat, and simmer, covered, for 3 hours. Remove the cover and simmer for another ½ hour. Let the broth settle and cool. Strain, chill overnight and remove the fat. Measure off the stock and heat to the boiling point. Add the tomato paste, taste for salt, and correct the seasoning.

Prepare the roux by melting the butter and blending with the browned flour. Stir in approximately 2½ cups brown stock, and when it thickens, add another cup of stock and continue to simmer very gently until reduced and nicely thickened.

This sauce is the base for other sauces (see list following Quick Brown Sauce), or it can be used as is if thinned with additional liquid. It will keep in the refrigerator for several weeks if carefully sealed, or it can be frozen for a longer period.

Quick Brown Sauce

3 tablespoons butter
3 tablespoons flour
1½ cups canned bouillon, soup stock, or vegetable stock
½ teaspoon thyme
Sprig parsley
Salt and freshly ground pepper

Melt the butter in a heavy saucepan over low heat, add the flour, and blend well over medium heat. Reduce the heat and simmer for several minutes. Heat the bouillon or stock, stir into the roux, and continue stirring until the sauce thickens. Add herbs, reduce heat, and simmer for several minutes. Correct the seasoning.

Serve as it is with meats or other dishes, or use as a base for other sauces.

Madeira Sauce. Combine 1½ cups brown sauce with ½ cup Madeira and simmer till reduced by almost a third. Correct the seasoning.

Piquante Sauce. Combine 1 cup brown sauce with ¼ cup red wine, 1 teaspoon Dijon mustard, 1 tablespoon finely chopped sour pickles, 1 tablespoon chopped capers, ¼ teaspoon Tabasco. Heat and simmer for 4 or 5 minutes. Add 2 tablespoons chopped parsley and serve.

Sauce Diable (Devil Sauce). To 1½ cups brown sauce add 1 tablespoon tomato paste, 1 tablespoon Dijon mustard, 1 teaspoon tarragon vinegar, and ½ cup sherry or Madeira. Simmer for 6 minutes. Add 1 tablespoon chopped parsley. Taste for salt and pepper.

Mushroom Sauce. Sauté 1 cup coarsely chopped mushrooms in 5 tablespoons butter until soft and dark. Season with salt and freshly ground pepper. Combine with 1½ cups brown sauce and ¼ cup Madeira or sherry and simmer for 5 minutes.

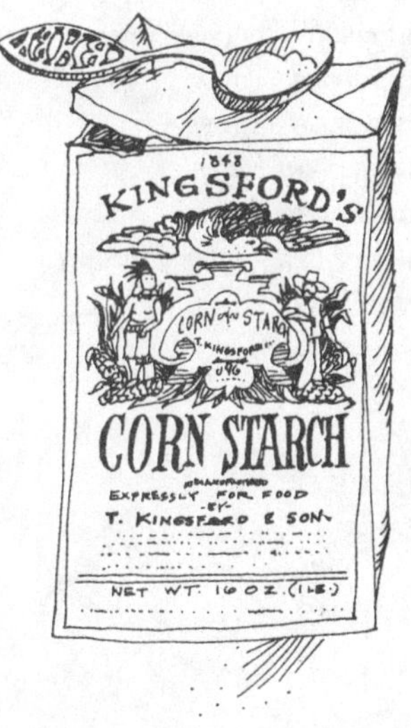

Currant Jelly Sauce for game and turkey. Combine 1 cup brown sauce with ½ cup currant jelly and 1 tablespoon dry mustard. Stir and simmer for 4 or 5 minutes. Add the juice of half a lemon and a few gratings of lemon zest. Correct the seasoning.

Orange Sauce for Duck. Combine 2 cups brown sauce with ½ cup undiluted concentrated orange juice, 3 tablespoons orange zest cut in very thin julienne strips, and 1 tablespoon lemon juice. Simmer 5 minutes and add 2 tablespoons Grand Marnier, Cointreau, or Cognac. Just before serving add ½ cup orange sections. Heat through.

Olive Sauce (for duck or tongue). Combine 1 cup brown sauce, ½ cup red wine, and ¼ cup finely chopped onion or shallot. Cook down for 5 minutes over rather brisk heat. Reduce the heat and simmer for 5 more minutes. Add 1 cup small green olives and simmer again for 5 minutes. Correct the seasoning.

Bordelaise Sauce (for steaks, roast beef, or lamb). Combine 1 cup red wine with ¼ cup shallots and 1 teaspoon thyme. Reduce over a brisk flame to ⅓ cup. Strain into 1 cup brown sauce, and add 1 tablespoon Cognac and 1 tablespoon lemon juice. Simmer for 3 minutes and add 1 tablespoon chopped parsley.

Sauce for Venison. Combine ½ cup port wine, ¼ cup currant jelly, 2 tablespoons orange zest cut into tiny shreds, a dash of Tabasco, and the pan juices from the roast venison. Cook down for 3 minutes, combine with 1 cup brown sauce, and simmer for 5 minutes. Correct the seasoning, and add 2 tablespoons chopped parsley.

White Sauce (Cream Sauce, Sauce Béchamel)

THIN SAUCE

1 tablespoon butter
1 tablespoon flour
Salt and freshly ground pepper
1 cup liquid

One would sometimes think this was the single sauce known to man, so much has it been used to cover everything from fish and shellfish to vegetables of all kinds, meats, and chicken. Creamed food has been more than prevalent — it has been an epidemic in the annals of American cookery, encouraged by the fad for using canned cream soup as a sauce. However, the white sauce base

MEDIUM SAUCE

2 tablespoons butter
2 tablespoons flour
Salt and freshly ground pepper
1 cup liquid

THICKISH SAUCE

3 tablespoons butter
3 tablespoons flour
Salt and freshly ground pepper
1 cup liquid

cannot be ignored, for when treated judiciously it is highly useful and versatile.

Basic white sauce can be made in varying degrees of thickness. The more butter and flour used, the thicker the base. A thick base is made, for example, if the finished sauce calls for additional liquid, which, of course, will thin the base.

Although in the past a white sauce was usually made with milk, we have learned that it can be made with any number of liquids. The resulting base serves as the foundation for an impressive variety of sauces.

Liquids

chicken broth	vegetable broth
veal broth	clam broth
beef broth	fish broth
lamb broth	shellfish broth
pork broth	a mixture of white wine and broth
turkey broth	milk
game broth	cream
mushroom broth	

I have even heard of using Scotch whisky. The choice of liquid, of course, should complement the flavor of the dish being sauced.

The preparation process is the same for all white sauces. Melt the butter in a saucepan, combine with the flour, and cook over low heat a few minutes to cook the starchy taste out of the flour. Stir in the liquid, either hot or cold, and continue stirring until the mixture thickens. Let it simmer for a few minutes, stirring occasionally.

If the sauce should lump, put it through a fine sieve. To keep the sauce until ready to use, place a piece of buttered wax paper over it.

Sauce Velouté. Add ½ cup heavy cream to the finished sauce, and season with a few grains of nutmeg. Simmer a few minutes. Just before serving, beat in 3 to 4 tablespoons butter, 1 spoonful at a time.

Sauce Supreme. Use chicken or veal stock as the liquid, and enrich the finished sauce with 1 cup heavy cream and 3 egg yolks. Beat the yolks slightly, stir in the cream, temper the mixture with a little of the béchamel, then stir it back into the sauce. Reheat, but do not let it boil.

Curry Sauce (similar to some French curries). Cook 2 teaspoons curry powder in the butter for 2 minutes before adding the flour. This is a mild, pleasant curry sauce appropriate for eggs, mushrooms, veal, or chicken. For a more traditional curry sauce, see page 461.

Cheese Sauce. A favorite sauce for vegetables and for some meats. Stir into the finished béchamel ½ cup sharp Cheddar cheese and a dash of Tabasco or dry mustard. Let the grated cheese melt in the hot sauce. Do not stir too much after melting or the cheese may become stringy and rather disagreeable in texture. To vary, use grated Gruyère cheese or Emmenthaler from Switzerland instead of Cheddar.

Sauce Mornay. Used a great deal for dishes to be browned under the broiler, for vegetables, and sometimes for fish and shellfish dishes. Stir ¼ to ½ cup grated Parmesan cheese and 1 or 2 pats of butter into the finished sauce. Simmer 3 to 4 minutes and correct the seasoning. If poured over a dish to be browned in the oven, sprinkle lightly with additional grated Parmesan.

Mustard Sauce. Excellent for fish dishes. Add 2 tablespoons or more Dijon mustard to the finished sauce. Stir in well and simmer 2 to 3 minutes. This makes a fairly hot sauce. For a milder sauce, add less mustard, to taste.

Herb Sauce. Parsley sauce or dill sauce are often used for fish and veal and sometimes for chicken dishes. For *parsley sauce*, stir ¼ cup chopped parsley or more into the finished sauce. For *dill sauce*, stir in chopped fresh dill or dillweed to taste, and add a few drops of lemon juice.

Tarragon Sauce. Use chicken broth for the liquid. Add about 2 tablespoons chopped fresh tarragon and stir. Then stir in 2 egg yolks mixed with ½ cup cream. Heat but do not allow to boil. Serve with roast or poached chicken.

Soubise (Onion Sauce). Add 1 cup puréed cooked onions and ⅓ cup freshly grated Parmesan cheese. Just before serving, beat in about 2 tablespoons butter, a spoonful at a time.

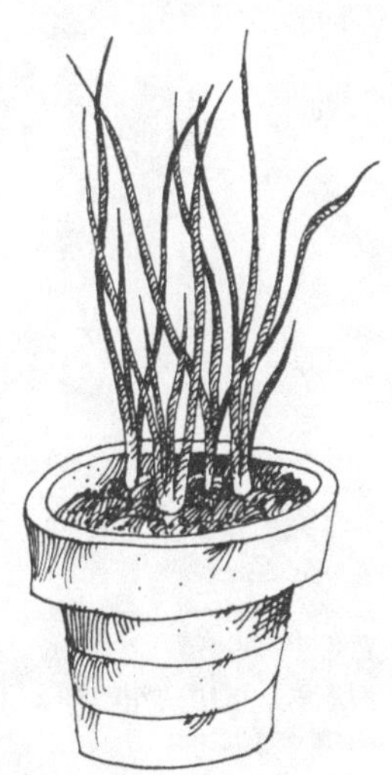

Hollandaise Sauce (Made in a Blender)

4 egg yolks
½ teaspoon salt
Dash of Tabasco
1 tablespoon lemon juice
¼ pound (1 stick) butter, melted

As its name hints, Hollandaise is not a native sauce, but it has been used in this country for well over a hundred years and is one of our two most popular sauces. There are several ways to prepare it, and home cooks make it with varying degrees of success. Certainly the most foolproof Hollandaise is made in the blender.

Combine the egg yolks and seasonings in the beaker of an electric blender. Turn the blender on and off. Melt the butter until it is bubbling but has not yet turned color. Turn on the blender, leaving the inner part of the top off, if your blender is equipped with a two-part top. Gradually pour a thin stream of the hot butter into the egg yolk mixture. It will thicken and become golden in color. Keep over warm water until ready to serve. If this should curdle, pour about a tablespoon of boiling water into the sauce while the blender is turned on. Yield: about 1 cup.

Hollandaise Sauce (Made on the Stove)

3 or 4 egg yolks
½ teaspoon salt
Dash of Tabasco
1 tablespoon lemon juice
½ cup (1 stick) butter

Blend the eggs and seasonings in a heavy saucepan which is barely warm. It should be an enameled or stainless one. Or you may use a double boiler with hot — not boiling — water. In a separate pan heat the butter to the bubbling stage. Place the eggs over medium low heat and pour the hot butter into the egg mixture in a steady stream, stirring or whisking until the sauce thickens. Remove from the heat and stir well till it cools a bit. If this curdles, beat in a little heavy cream.

Mustard Hollandaise. Add 1 or 2 teaspoons Dijon mustard or 1 teaspoon English mustard to the Hollandaise along with the other seasonings.

Tomato Hollandaise (Sauce Choron). Add 1 to 2 tablespoons tomato paste and a touch of lemon juice to the finished sauce.

Maltaise Sauce. Particularly good with asparagus. Add 1 tablespoon grated orange rind to the finished sauce.

Anchovy Hollandaise. Good with certain fish and steaks. Add 4 or 5 anchovy fillets to the finished sauce.

Sauce Mousseline. Add an equal quantity of whipped cream (about 1 cup) to the finished sauce.

Béarnaise Sauce

½ cup white wine
1 tablespoon finely chopped shallots or scallions
1 or 2 teaspoons (or to taste) chopped fresh tarragon

Combine the wine, shallots, and tarragon, and cook till the wine is reduced to a mere glaze. Combine the glaze with the egg yolks and salt in the beaker of an electric blender. Heat the butter till it is bubbling hot. Turn on the blender and turn it off to quickly blend the ingredients. Turn it on again, and gradually pour in the hot melted butter in a steady stream till the sauce thickens. Additional chopped tarragon and parsley may be folded into the sauce.

The sauce may be made on top of the stove according to the directions for making Hollandaise given above.

3 or 4 egg yolks
½ teaspoon salt
½ cup (1 stick) butter

Traditional Curry Sauce

6 tablespoons butter
¾ cup finely chopped onion
¾ cup finely grated apple
¼ cup finely cut celery
Curry powder to taste
¼ teaspoon Tabasco
Salt to taste
1½ cups chicken broth, fish broth or tomato juice
Tomato paste, beurre manié, or potato flour and water
2 tablespoons chutney
Grated orange rind

Melt the butter in a saucepan, add the onion and apple, and allow them to cook down slowly till they are well blended and soft. Add the celery and cook 5 minutes. Blend in the curry powder, and cook 4 minutes more. Add the Tabasco, salt, and liquid, and cook down 5 to 6 minutes. Thicken with tomato paste if you have used tomato juice; otherwise, thicken with beurre manié or with 1 to 2 tablespoons potato flour blended with water. Stir well and simmer 10 minutes, then correct the seasoning. Just before the sauce is ready to take up, add the chutney and a little grated orange rind.

Tomato Sauces

Many old American recipes offer a sauce that is nothing more than a can of tomatoes cooked down. However, the tomato sauces prevalent today are unmistakably influenced by Italian cuisine as practiced by immigrants, especially the Neapolitans. These sauces, like much of the Italian cookery found here, are not particularly authentic but fall into a genre that can only be called Italo-American.

See the index for other tomato sauces.

Fresh Tomato Sauce

3 pounds ripe tomatoes
2 tablespoons oil
6 tablespoons butter
1 cup stock or water
1½ teaspoons salt
½ teaspoon freshly ground pepper
¼ cup finely chopped onion
2 garlic cloves, finely chopped
3 tablespoons tomato paste

A popular sauce, made with fresh tomatoes, this resembles a good sauce found in Italy or the South of France.

Wash the tomatoes and cut in quarters. Heat the oil and butter in a heavy skillet or sauté pan, add the tomatoes, and let them sauté slowly for 10 minutes. Mash down as much as possible. Add the stock or water and the salt and pepper. Bring up the heat and let the tomatoes cook rather briskly for 15 minutes, stirring them from time to time. Remove from the heat and put through a coarse sieve or a foodmill. Return them to the skillet with the onion and garlic and let simmer for 10 minutes. Add the tomato paste and cook down for about 5 minutes. Correct the seasoning, and when the sauce is nicely thickened remove from the heat. Use for pasta or for any recipe calling for a tomato sauce.

You may make exactly the same sauce using a 33-ounce can of solid-pack tomatoes or Italian plum tomatoes. Both make a perfect sauce.

A Favorite Tomato Sauce

6 tablespoons olive oil
1 medium onion, thinly sliced
3 cloves garlic, crushed
3 cups finely cut peeled and seeded ripe tomatoes or 1 33-ounce tin Italian plum tomatoes
2 tablespoons fresh basil or 1½ teaspoons dry basil
1 teaspoon salt or to taste
1 teaspoon freshly ground pepper
1 teaspoon sugar
½ cup tomato paste
¼ cup grated fresh Parmesan cheese

Sauté the onion and garlic in the oil. Add the tomatoes and crush well with a wooden spoon or spatula. Add the basil, salt, pepper, and sugar and simmer for 30 minutes. Add the tomato paste, stir well, and simmer for another 10 minutes. Add the cheese and mix thoroughly. Correct the seasoning. Use for pasta, meats, or fish.

Variations

(1) For a Creole sauce, add ½ cup finely chopped green pepper to this sauce and 1 additional onion.

(2) Substitute thyme or tarragon for the basil.

(3) For a Texas sauce, add 3 tablespoons chopped canned peeled green chilies and 1 tablespoon chili powder.

Elena Zelayeta's Salsa Fria

1 #2 can solid-pack tomatoes or 2 cups chopped very ripe tomatoes
1 onion, finely chopped
1 4-ounce can whole peeled chilies, chopped
1 tablespoon fresh coriander (cilantro) if available
1 teaspoon oregano
2 tablespoons wine vinegar
1 tablespoon olive oil
1-pound can tomatillos (green tomatoes) with hulls removed and chopped
Salt and freshly ground pepper to taste
Chopped coriander (cilantro) to taste, as a garnish

A mixture of Mexican and Spanish, this sauce is delicious on cold or hot meats or fish and superb on hamburgers and hot dogs for cookouts and picnics or as a cocktail dip.

Blend all the ingredients very well, and chill the sauce thoroughly.

Poor Man's Butter

2 very ripe tomatoes, peeled
2 medium quite ripe avocados
3 tablespoons lime juice or wine vinegar
1 tablespoon olive oil
Salt

This is a California version (another of Elena Zelayeta's) of a Mexican sauce, excellent for grilled pork or spareribs or for chicken.

Cut the tomatoes and avocados into small dice and blend with the seasonings. Toss well and let stand for an hour before using.

Note. I like to add 1 or 2 finely chopped cloves of garlic to this sauce and a spoonful of chopped parsley as well.

Barbecue Sauces

Barbecue Sauce

12 to 14 cloves garlic
2 cups boiling water
6 tablespoons olive oil
1 cup finely chopped onions or shallots
2 cups cooked or canned tomatoes (Italian plum are best)
1 tablespoon fresh basil, finely chopped, or 1 teaspoon dried basil
1 green pepper, finely chopped
Salt and freshly ground pepper to taste
3 tablespoons tomato paste
½ cup sherry

Pour boiling water over garlic cloves (they need not be peeled) and simmer for 12 minutes. Drain, and when cool enough to handle remove the skin. Force through a sieve or whirl in a blender with a little water or tomato. Heat the olive oil, add the onions, and sauté until they are just wilted. Add the tomatoes, basil, green pepper, salt, pepper, and garlic. Bring to a boil and simmer for 30 minutes. Add the tomato paste and sherry and cook for 10 minutes. Put the sauce through a food mill or sieve and correct the seasoning. Reheat just before serving.

Variations

(1) You may increase the garlic content to 25 or 30 cloves if you really like the flavor and delicacy of blanched garlic. The short boiling period gives the garlic a quite different and very pleasant quality.

(2) Add to the tomato mixture 1 tablespoon chili powder, or more, to taste.

(3) Add to the onions 1 tablespoon curry powder or more, to taste, and let it cook several minutes before adding the tomatoes.

Soy Barbecue Marinade and Basting Sauce

½ cup peanut oil
½ cup or more soy sauce
½ cup sherry or vermouth
3 garlic cloves, crushed
Several pieces of fresh ginger, sliced, or several slices of candied ginger with sugar washed off
Small piece of orange or tangerine zest
Dash of Tabasco

Sometimes described as Polynesian or Oriental, this sauce is excellent as a marinade for chicken, beef, lamb, and pork. It may also be used for brushing the meat while cooking and for glazing.

Combine all ingredients and taste to decide if you have enough soy sauce in the mixture. Use as a marinade and basting sauce for chicken, duck, squab, guinea hen, steaks, lamb chops and steaks, pork chops, or spareribs.

Note. Honey may be added to this sauce if a heavy glaze is wanted on spareribs, duck, leg of pork, or other roast meats. Add about ½ to ¾ cup.

Cranberry Sauces

Baked Cranberries

2 pounds cranberries
¼ to ½ cup water
2 cups sugar

Wash cranberries well and place in a heavy 2-quart saucepan with the water. Cover and steam over medium heat till cranberries pop. Transfer to a baking sheet, cover with sugar, and bake at 300 degrees till cranberries are thick and clear.

Cranberry-Strawberry Compote

2 pounds cranberries
1 cup sugar
1 pint strawberry preserves

This recipe comes from the cranberry bog region in the West and is a delightful change from the usual cranberry sauce.

Cover cranberries with water in a 2-quart saucepan, and cook, covered, for about 5 minutes after they come to a boil. Add the sugar and the strawberry preserves, and cook for another 5 minutes. Chill.

Cranberry-Orange Compote I

1 pound cranberries
1 large sweet orange, peeled
Sugar to taste

Grind the cranberries with the orange, and stir in sugar to taste. Cover with foil or place in a jar, and refrigerate for a week before serving.

Cranberry-Orange Compote II

2 pounds cranberries
1 peeled orange
1 orange with skin
Sugar
3 tablespoons Cognac or Grand Marnier

Grind the cranberries with the oranges. Add sugar to taste and either the Cognac or Grand Marnier. Blend thoroughly. Correct the flavoring — more sugar or liqueur may be needed. It is best to refrigerate for several hours before serving.

Horseradish Sauces

Horseradish Sauce

Fold freshly grated horseradish to taste into 1½ to 2 cups of sour cream or whipped cream. Add a teaspoon of Dijon or prepared mustard if you like.

Horseradish Applesauce

Add ¾ cup horseradish, freshly grated or prepared, to 2 cups chilled applesauce. Serve with pork, boiled beef or cold meats.

Vegetables

Along with the growth of the organic gardening and the health foods cult, there is a renewed interest in food from the wilds — the same vegetables and greens that sustained our forefathers during the early days of this country and that are still available in profusion if one is willing to search them out. Fiddleheads, wild asparagus, and pokeweed are but a few of the delicacies tracked down by fanciers. Some of our wild greens, such as purslane and sorrel, actually began life here as domesticated plants, imported from Europe. Our first cultivated native crops were corn and beans, sometimes grown together so that the cornstalks served as bean poles. Gradually other native plants, such as pumpkin and various types of squash, were also cultivated, and seeds of vegetables were brought in by immigrants from all parts of the world.

By the nineteenth century domestic gardens supported households with an international round of vegetables. For the winter months, root vegetables were stored in cellars, cabbage was made into kraut, and other vegetables were pickled or salted. The advent of home canning and preserving revolutionized our diet, and commercial canning extended the pattern. The next development, frozen foods, continued the trend toward year-round availability of all vegetables, and the seasonal idea has now all but disappeared, except for the produce one finds in farmers' markets throughout the countryside.

The high point for fresh vegetables was reached in the years immediately following World War I and in the early 1920's, when we received finer produce than we have any time since. The "vegetable dinner" came into fashion then, started in New York by a famous chain of restaurants whose creator had been the produce king. It consisted of simply a huge plate of noble vegetables. By the time the vogue spread through the country, the vegetables presented were considerably inferior in quality, and the idea took a fairly definite exit.

Apart from the great organic gardening kick, the most notable recent development in vegetables has been the interest in "stir-fry" cookery, an outgrowth of the popularity of Chinese food. This quick, efficient method of treating vegetables may help their cause immeasurably. After our experiences with overcooked, greasy vegetables, stale vegetables, over-refrigerated vegetables, and poor frozen vegetables, stir-frying may revive the demand for fine, flavorful, crisp vegetables in their prime.

Artichokes (French or Globe)

There is no printed record of artichokes in America, nor directions for cooking them, before about the third quarter of the nineteenth century. Curiously enough, they were called French artichokes at that time, and no credit was given to the Italians, who must have imported some of the globes as well.

Certainly it was the Italians who planted the artichokes in California and developed them into what is now a major crop. The industry is at present centered around Castroville, but one used to see tremendous fields of artichokes just beyond San Francisco on the drive down the coast. The plants are quite handsome, and the artichokes themselves are as beautiful as they are good to eat. They are, after all, a thistle, and when the vibrant lavender flowers are in bloom they look like something from another planet.

Mrs. Rorer, in her 1886 edition, described them as having a head like a pinecone and advised serving them with Hollandaise. Miss Farmer, in the 1896 and 1904 editions, noted that most artichokes were imported from France, but went on to say that there were those which arrived from California later in the year.

Pierre Caron, who was chef at Delmonico's and published his cookbook, with the aid of Mrs. Sherman, in 1886, was the first, as far as I know, to offer a recipe for raw artichokes with vinaigrette.

He mentions that to be served raw, an artichoke has to be extremely fresh. He must have influenced Miss Farmer, for she has the same recipe.

Although the artichoke is one of the most interesting of vegetables, many people have never attempted to eat one. It is easy to see why. The large globe with a tiny thorn on the end of each pointed leaf must seem formidable indeed to the uninitiated.

To eat an artichoke, tear off a leaf, dip it in sauce, and scrape off the meat between your teeth. Only the bottom portion of the leaf will be edible. Discard the leaves as you proceed. The very center, with its tiny leaves and compact fuzz, is known as the choke, and is not eaten. Remove it with your knife and fork or with a spoon, and you are left with the prize — the bottom or the fond. This is delicious meat and is often served by itself stuffed with a filling.

Because of its rather complicated structure, an artichoke is usually served as a separate course. It may be served hot or cold and is good with a number of sauces — vinaigrette, mayonnaise, Hollandaise, mousseline, rémoulade or merely with herbed vinegar or oil.

Good fresh artichokes are bright green and rather silky, and the leaves are tightly packed. Sometimes one sees brown streaks of frost damage. If it has not penetrated beyond the first leaves, the artichoke is all right — Merely discard the first round of leaves. One should also look for worms in artichokes, but this hazard seems to have been eradicated these last few years. Size makes no great difference in the quality of artichokes, and you should be guided by the way you wish to serve them and by individual appetites. Usually one artichoke per person is ample. In some markets there are very tiny artichokes which may be prepared in several different ways. They are generally used for braising or stuffing, or if very fresh for eating raw.

Artichoke bottoms may be bought canned. Artichoke hearts are small artichokes cut down to tiny hearts, which include the leaves and the fond. They may be purchased frozen (these must be cooked) or canned, which need no additional cooking.

To Cook Artichokes

1 artichoke per person
Salt
1 slice lemon for each two artichokes

Tear off the coarse outside leaves and cut the stem so that the fond (bottom) will rest flat on a plate. Also trim the top, if you like, by slicing off 1½ to 1¾ inches with a sharp, heavy knife. This makes it simple to cook and gives it a neat "crew cut" appearance. Either wash the artichoke under running water or let it soak in acidulated water for a half hour. Some people tie artichokes to hold the leaves together, but I don't think this is at all necessary.

To boil. Place the artichokes in a deep kettle with 1 tablespoon salt for each 3 artichokes and the lemon slices. Add boiling water to cover, and boil 30 to 45 minutes. The artichokes are done when a leaf can be pulled out with complete ease. Remove the artichokes and set upside down to drain. If serving hot, let them drain for only a short time. If serving cold, let them cool this way and then chill, covered, in the refrigerator.

To steam. If you have very heavy-duty cookware — rolled or cast aluminum, heavy stainless steel, or enameled ironware — you may steam the artichokes, tightly covered, with very little water, the lemon, and salt. They take approximately the same length of time as boiled artichokes. Advocates of this method say the vegetables taste better, but I am not convinced of this.

To serve. Serve hot artichokes with melted butter, black butter, Hollandaise, Béarnaise, mousseline, mustard sauce, herbed vinegar (for dieters), bagna cauda, or cheese sauce.

Serve cold artichokes with mayonnaise, rémoulade, vinaigrette, gribiche, mustard mayonnaise, herbed vinegar (for dieters), oil and vinegar with herbs, or Louis dressing.

For an attractive presentation of artichokes, pull the leaves apart and remove the soft center leaves in one piece. Then remove the choke with a spoon. Invert the center leaves in the artichoke and fill with sauce.

Cold Stuffed Artichokes

These make a very pleasant luncheon dish or first course at dinner.

Cook artichokes with the tops cut, and remove the center leaves and choke. Fill the center with any of the following: crabmeat rémoulade, crabmeat salad, lobster salad, shrimp salad, shrimp Louis, crab Louis, avocado cubes with Russian dressing, a macédoine of vegetables with mayonnaise, chicken with mayonnaise, duck with mayonnaise. Serve additional sauce for the leaves and the fond.

Hot Stuffed Artichokes

Cook trimmed artichokes and remove the center leaves and the choke. Then spoon in the filling. If you like, gratiné under the broiler for just a moment or top with buttered crumbs or grated Parmesan cheese. Suitable fillings are crabmeat in cream, lobster Newburg, shrimp in cream, seafood Newburg, clam hash, chicken hash, turkey hash, sweetbreads in cream, braised sweetbreads and mushrooms, mushrooms in cream.

Baked Stuffed Artichokes

6 small or 4 good-sized artichokes
1 clove garlic, finely chopped
6 tablespoons olive oil

This recipe, of French-Italian origin, is thoroughly different and exceedingly good.

Cut the tops from the artichokes, remove the stalks, and cook the artichokes in boiling salted, acidulated water until done. While they are cooking, sauté the garlic in olive oil a few minutes, then add the mushrooms, ham, crumbs, and seasonings. Toss lightly but well. When the artichokes are cooked, remove the chokes and center leaves and spread the surrounding leaves back to provide a well for the filling. Fill with some of the mushroom-ham mixture and also spoon the mixture between the leaves. Tie the artichokes securely around the middle. Sprinkle well with oil, place in a baking dish, and add about 1 inch of broth or white wine. Bake 30 minutes in a 375-degree oven, basting twice with the pan juices. Five minutes before finishing, sprinkle a spoonful of grated Parmesan on each one. Untie, and serve as a main course at luncheon or as a first course at dinner.

½ cup chopped mushrooms
½ cup chopped ham
1 cup dry breadcrumbs
½ teaspoon salt
½ teaspoon freshly ground pepper
¼ teaspoon thyme
¼ teaspoon oregano
Additional olive oil
1 cup broth or white wine, or more
Grated Parmesan cheese

Mrs. Fleischner's Stuffed Artichokes

From *The Neighborhood Cook Book*, published in 1914.

Cut off about 1½ inches from the top of the artichokes and discard. Trim the bottoms so that the artichokes will stand easily. Cook in boiling salted water, to which the half lemon is added, until the artichokes are tender (about 35 to 40 minutes). Remove from the water and drain. When they are cool enough to handle, extract the centers and the chokes. Discard the chokes. The fonds, or bottoms, should now form a cup for the filling. Put the center leaves through a food mill or purée them to retain only the tender meat. Discard the rest. Combine the artichoke pulp with the bread (which has been squeezed dry and broken up into small bits), the cream, and the sherry. Beat together lightly, combine with the sautéed sweetbreads and mushrooms, and heat together over boiling water. Correct the seasoning. When warmed through and well blended, spoon into the artichoke cups. Place in a baking dish with a little bouillon or stock. Cover lightly with buttered foil or paper and bake at 350 degrees for 25 to 30 minutes till piping hot. Top each artichoke with a slice of truffle or a sautéed mushroom cap. Serve as a hot hors d'oeuvre or entrée.

6 artichokes of good size
½ lemon
2 slices of bread soaked in milk
¼ cup heavy cream
¼ cup sherry
1 pair sweetbreads, blanched, diced finely, and sautéed lightly in 5 tablespoons butter
½ pound mushrooms, sliced and sautéed in butter
Salt and freshly ground pepper
1 truffle, sliced, or mushroom caps

Artichoke Bottoms (Fonds)

Artichoke bottoms (fonds) are much used for garnishes and for serving as an appetizer. The artichokes are cooked and the fond trimmed well, sometimes left with just a neat edge line of leaf. Artichoke bottoms may also be bought canned in acidulated water.

To serve artichoke bottoms hot as a garnish, fill with fresh peas, sautéed or broiled small mushrooms, tiny buttered carrots, tiny braised onions, whole-kernel corn, or a mixture of vegetables. To serve cold as an appetizer, fill with pâté or foie gras, Russian salad, chicken salad, fish salad, or tiny tomatoes.

Fried Artichoke Bottoms. Dip canned or fresh artichoke bottoms in beaten egg and crumbs and deep-fry in oil heated to 365 degrees until perfectly browned. Drain on absorbent paper and serve plain or with a tomato sauce.

Stuffed or Dipped Artichoke Leaves

It has become exceedingly stylish at cocktails to dab individual leaves of artichokes with a filling, such as a pâté, ham mousse, or a cheese spread, and arrange them on a large plate. Guests eat the garnish and the end of the artichoke and discard the remainder of the leaf. Also the leaves are sometimes beautifully arranged in plates around a sauce presented in a scooped out artichoke. In either case one must provide plates for the discarded leaves.

Roman Artichokes

This is a recipe I have found in California restaurants and homes. It is a copy of a dish served in Rome, where it is called Jewish Artichokes. It requires extremely fresh artichokes, and so is not apt to be as successful with artichokes that have been shipped cross-country.

You must leave about 2 to 3 inches of stem on the artichokes. Cut off about one-third to one-half of the artichoke tops, and spread the leaves. Cook the artichokes in boiling salted, acidulated water, and as they cook, take them by the stalk and press down so that the leaves spread. When they are tender, transfer to a board and press all the water out of them. Then cook in hot oil, about 360 degrees and about 4 inches deep. With the aid of wooden spoons or forks, turn and press down so the leaves spread even more. Drain on absorbent paper. They come out golden brown and crisp and are extraordinarily good.

Jerusalem or Canadian Artichokes

These peculiar tubers, which have no botanical relationship to the globe artichoke, are natives of the Western Hemisphere. However, one would never guess this if he observed the miles of them which grow wild along the roads in France, where they are called *topinambours*. Strangely enough, many people in the United States have no idea what they are and have never tasted them. They have a delicious crisp quality which does not disappear entirely with cooking.

Jerusalem Artichokes Vinaigrette

8 to 10 Jerusalem artichokes
Greens
Vinaigrette sauce

Peel the artichokes and toss into very cold water or ice water to rest until you are ready to toss the salad. Break up some romaine or Boston lettuce, slice the artichokes very thin, and add to the greens. Toss with vinaigrette sauce.

Jerusalem Artichokes in Cream

12 to 14 Jerusalem artichokes
1½ cups rich cream sauce
Salt and freshly ground pepper

Peel or scrape the artichokes and toss them into very cold water or ice water till ready to cook. Cut in slices about ½ inch thick. Bring water to a boil, add salt to taste, and boil the artichokes about 20 minutes. Drain, and arrange in a heated serving dish. Pour hot cream sauce over all, and garnish with a little chopped parsley.

Note. This may also be served with a Mornay sauce and sprinkled with grated Parmesan cheese.

Asparagus

It is said that the first man to grow asparagus in the American Colonies was Diederick Leertower, who was consul for the royal family of the Netherlands in Massachusetts and New Hampshire and who died in 1798. Undoubtedly wild asparagus was to be found even earlier. Probably green asparagus was the first to be cultivated, particularly in New York, Pennsylvania and the South. (Mrs. Crowen talks of asparagus with tough white ends and instructs one to cut to the green.) Cultivation of white asparagus — in California, the Northwest and the Middle West — most likely did not begin until the latter half of the nineteenth century.

There are now some twenty varieties of asparagus on the world market, and most of them have been grown in the United States at one time or another. We used to produce quantities of white asparagus, both with pink tips and with purple. But the green is most commonly raised nowadays. The Martha Washington and the Washington species grow in profusion in Pennsylvania and New Jersey and throughout New England, and a jumbo asparagus produced in California is much sought after.

Asparagus is available usually from February till fall. It is a joy to eat the first stalks of the season in the early spring, and its fresh, pungent flavor never seems to pall. Do not plan to serve it sparingly. The average appetite can accommodate at least three-quarters of a pound with ease, and dainty appetites probably a half pound. Look for fresh green stalks tightly budded at the end. When asparagus begins to blossom it loses its flavor. Nowadays it is cut shockingly long — obviously to increase the weight — and the waste is tremendous. Try to choose stalks with the least number of tough white ends. Also, choose stalks of even size so they will cook uniformly.

To Cook Asparagus

Although many people differ with me, I feel asparagus is better peeled before cooking — unless it is perfectly fresh from the garden, when you need only break off the white end wherever it breaks easily. Otherwise peel the stalks with a sharp knife or potato peeler. (And don't save the white stalks thinking you are going to make a soup, because you never do. It was different when people always had a soup pot on the stove and could take out a little stock and boil up an asparagus soup.) Then wash thoroughly in several changes of water, for sand can lurk in the tips and under the spurs and be quite gritty and disagreeable.

To boil. Early American cookbooks recommended tying asparagus in bunches and cooking in boiling salted water 25 to 30 minutes. This method has proved workable through the years for many people, and as a result, oblong asparagus cookers with removable trays have been developed. To use this method you must have asparagus of uniform size. The small varieties, about ½ inch in diameter, will cook in 12 to 15 minutes after the water comes to a second boil. Larger ones will take 14 to 18 minutes. Cook covered or uncovered.

To steam. Use a saucepan or asparagus cooker with a tight-fitting lid. Place a small amount of water in the cooker, add salt, cover, and bring to a boil. Add the asparagus, cover tightly, and reduce the heat at once. If using an electric unit, turn to warm for a few minutes, then turn off. If using gas, turn to low for about 5 minutes, then turn off. Allow asparagus to steam 12 to 16 minutes in all, according to its size and how well cooked you like it.

Asparagus can also be steamed standing upright in a deep double boiler with the stalks in water and the heads out. These pots are covered during cooking. Or use an especially designed steamer fitted with a rack. This method keeps the delicate heads out of water during cooking and thus is preferred by many cooks. It will take 12 to 18 minutes.

If you like pressure-cooked vegetables, asparagus can be done by this method in about 2 minutes.

My favorite method: Place asparagus in a skillet. Pour in enough cold water to cover and add salt. Bring to a boil quickly and cook till done to your taste. The advantage of this method is that you can test the asparagus more easily and remove stalks that are done before the others. Furthermore, it is the simplest of all the methods.

Early cookbooks always suggested serving asparagus on buttered toast with some of the cooking broth added. This makes a delicious, soggy mess on your plate which certainly tastes of asparagus. If asparagus is fresh and properly cooked, it needs nothing but freshly ground pepper and salt, and it is best eaten with the fingers. Or you can serve it with melted butter or lemon butter, or with a sauce — Hollandaise, cheese sauce, or mousseline sauce (considered to be the most elegant of sauces with asparagus). The French and Italians like to serve hot asparagus with a vinaigrette sauce.

Cold asparagus may be served with cold vinaigrette sauce and chopped parsley, or with mayonnaise — or a mustard mayonnaise, which is even more complementary, or with sour cream flavored with dill, chives, and parsley.

Dutch-Fashion Asparagus. This is an old way of serving asparagus. Give each person a hard-boiled egg, and pass the mustard and oil. The egg is crushed with a fork, and the mustard and oil — and salt and pepper, if needed — are added to taste. The asparagus is dipped in this sauce as it is eaten.

Asparagus with Parmesan Cheese. Serve hot asparagus with a sprinkling of freshly grated Parmesan cheese. Add melted butter if you like.

Asparagus with Ham. Serve asparagus on a piece of sautéed or broiled ham cut rather thin. Dress with a little melted butter. Add grated cheese as well, if you like.

Asparagus with Egg. For a luncheon plate, top asparagus with either a fried egg or a poached egg, and sprinkle with grated Parmesan cheese.

Asparagus with Dried Beef. Asparagus combines nicely with paper-thin slices of air-dried beef such as the Swiss make and sometimes is made in the United States. Simply arrange the beef over the hot asparagus stalks and serve, or serve cold with the beef and vinaigrette sauce.

Creamed Asparagus

For some reason this used to be considered a rather dressy dish. Actually it is a waste of asparagus. Nevertheless, if it is to your taste, here is how to prepare it. For 6 persons cut 2½ pounds of asparagus into 1-inch sections. Boil in salted water or steam until the asparagus is just tender — about 18 minutes. Drain thoroughly and combine with 1½ cups rich cream sauce. Serve on toast or in croustades.

Asparagus in Ambush

"Green tops of two bunches of asparagus
8 or 9 small light rolls
2 cups milk
4 eggs
1 great spoonful of butter [about 3 tablespoons] rolled in flour"

From the time of Mrs. Harland, who no doubt adapted it from an old English recipe, till Mrs. Rorer came along, it was considered fashionable to serve Asparagus in Ambush. I'm quite sure it was the name and the fun of the dish that made it so popular. It was originally served by Mrs. Harland thus, together with Green Pea Pancakes and Bermuda Potatoes en Robe de Chambre.

"Take out the crumb from the rolls, when you have cut off the tops to serve as covers, and set them open in the oven to crisp, laying the tops by them. Heat the milk, pour upon the beaten eggs; stir over the fire until they begin to thicken, when add the butter and the flour. Lastly put in the asparagus boiled tender and chopped fine. Fill the rolls with this mixture, put on the tops, and serve hot. Good!!!" So well did Mrs. Harland like this recipe that she offered a variation. In this, a hole was made in the top of the roll, and a little piece of asparagus was coyly inserted.

Asparagus in Ambush: A Modern Version

8 French rolls
3 pounds asparagus
Butter
Hollandaise sauce
Strips of pimiento

The dish has now been brought up to date, and is much more attractive and delicious.

Cut the tops from long French rolls and remove the crumb. Toast the rolls and tops lightly under the broiler, then butter and keep them warm. Cut the asparagus to fit the rolls, and then cook it in your favorite way, but do not overcook. Arrange the asparagus in the buttered toasted rolls. Dress with Hollandaise sauce and put a strip of pimiento over each one. Cover with the top of the roll. Dribble sauce over the roll crosswise. Serve as a separate course or as an hors d'oeuvre. Knife and fork are called for with this dish.

Minute Asparagus

2 pounds asparagus
Salt
¼ pound butter
3 tablespoons soy sauce
1 tablespoon lemon juice
Freshly ground pepper

Wash the asparagus and cut into very thin diagonal slices, not over ¼ inch thick and thinner if possible. Place in a colander or cooking basket. Pour enough water in a kettle to accommodate the colander or cooking basket, add salt, and bring to a boil. Heat the butter in a large skillet and have the soy sauce, lemon juice, and pepper at hand. When the water boils, dip the asparagus in, bring to a second boil, and cook for just one full minute. Remove, drain, and toss into the skillet with the butter. Add the other ingredients and toss well over medium heat till the butter has browned and the asparagus is crisp and deliciously flavored.

Wild Asparagus

Tiny stalks of wild asparagus are found in many regions throughout the country in the early spring, pushing through the ground before the feathery green foliage appears. To prepare, wash well and cut in 1-inch pieces. Place in a small colander or cooking basket, as for Minute Asparagus above, and dip in boiling salted water. When the water returns to a boil, cook 2 minutes. Drain, and toss in a skillet with melted butter and freshly ground pepper. Cook quickly over medium heat, shaking the pan, till the butter browns lightly and the smell is nutty and delicious. Do not allow the butter to burn. Spoon into a hot dish and add a few drops of lemon juice. Serve at once.

Green Beans, Snap Beans, String Beans, French Beans, Haricots Verts

Although dried beans were a mainstay of Colonial life and the baked bean of Boston made probably the best-known American dish, green or snap beans figured very little in meals of early America. Until the late nineteenth century they were called French beans. The reason for this is that the green bean, like the potato, traveled from the New World to Europe; its cooking was perfected by the French before it achieved popularity. Our early prescriptions for cooking green beans left them unpalatable. They were to be boiled until they could be mashed between the fingers, or they were cooked for several hours with a piece of fatback or smoked jowl into a gray, greasy mass. The French discovered that when the beans were allowed to become mature, they toughened. They picked the beans while they were young — a lesson we have yet to learn — and cooked them a short period of time, the proper treatment for this delicate vegetable.

When buying, look for beans of uniform size. This used to be fairly easy to do, but the newer varieties produced today make the job increasingly difficult. Of course, look for the smallest and freshest beans. I usually snap one to see how crisp it is and sometimes taste it for freshness. (Nowadays, with all the quick-frozen beans available, many people never bother to buy fresh ones — and little wonder, so difficult is it to find tiny tender beans in the market.) A pound of fresh green beans should supply three good servings.

To prepare green beans for cooking, wash them carefully, and if they are the least bit limp, put them in a plastic bag and freshen them in the vegetable compartment of the refrigerator. When ready to cook, tear off the blossom end and pull down to remove any traces of string. If the beans are tender and young, they can be cooked whole. Otherwise, cut them in long diagonal slices, or split lengthwise. Wash again, and drain.

To Cook Green Beans

To boil. Bring a pan of salted water to a rolling boil — enough to more than cover the beans — and add the prepared beans in several batches in order to keep the water boiling. Cook at a rolling boil a few minutes, then reduce the heat to medium and cook slowly 12 to 15 minutes. Taste from time to time to see if they are done — the raw taste should be cooked away, but the beans should remain fresh-tasting and crisp to the bite.

Drain the beans at once. To serve cold, plunge into cold water and drain again. To serve hot, dry out the pan in which they were cooked by putting it over medium heat for a moment. Add the beans and let them reheat briefly before adding butter and seasonings — shake the pan to prevent scorching.

For buttered green beans, add at least 6 tablespoons butter and ½ teaspoon freshly ground pepper for 2 pounds beans. Shake the pan well. Transfer the beans to a heated serving dish, dot with a little more butter, and serve.

To steam. Use a fairly heavy saucepan with a tight lid. Bring a small quantity of salted water to a boil. Add the prepared beans, cover tightly, and cook over high heat until steam begins to appear around the lid. Reduce the heat at once, and steam slowly 12 to 14 minutes. Drain (if necessary). Melt 6 to 8 tablespoons butter in the pan, and return the beans. Cover, and steam 3 to 4 minutes, shaking the pan well. Season to taste with salt and freshly ground pepper.

Note. The butter can be added to the beans during the initial steaming.

California-Style Green Beans

2 pounds green beans
2 garlic cloves, finely chopped
6 tablespoons olive oil
3 tomatoes, peeled, and cut into sixths
½ teaspoon freshly ground pepper
½ teaspoon oregano
2 tablespoons chopped parsley

Prepare and cook the beans according to instructions above. Drain. Sauté the garlic 2 minutes in the heated olive oil. Add the beans and shake well. Add the tomatoes and seasonings, and shake again till the tomatoes are just heated through. Spoon into a heated serving dish, and sprinkle with chopped parsley.

Note. This may also be served with freshly grated Parmesan cheese. For this amount you will need about ½ cup. Sprinkle on the beans just as they are to be served.

Green Beans with Almonds

2 pounds green beans, cleaned and washed
Salt
1½ cups blanched almonds or sliced blanched almonds
6 tablespoons butter or more

The combination of rather crisp beans and toasted almonds is a most pleasing one. It has become a standard recipe throughout the country within the last twenty years, although it is often ruined by overcooking the almonds. Green beans and almonds go especially well with chicken or veal dishes.

Prepare and cook the beans according to the recipe for boiling or steaming beans. When done to your taste, drain well. While the beans are cooking, sauté the almonds lightly in butter, shaking the pan often. The nuts should brown only slightly and have a cooked, toasted flavor when they are done. Salt them to taste. Return the beans to the saucepan in which they were cooked and shake vigorously over heat to dry them and reheat them. Transfer to a heated serving dish, and spoon the sautéed almonds over them. Serve at once.

Old-Fashioned Hot Green Bean Salad

2 pounds green beans
8 strips bacon or salt pork
3 medium onions, thinly sliced
Salt (if needed)
4 tablespoons mild vinegar (cider or white wine vinegar preferred)
1 tablespoon sugar
1 teaspoon freshly ground pepper
Lemon slices

There are many versions of this dish, which used to be universally popular and was evidently used to start balky children eating vegetables. Some recipes contained much more sugar than this one, and some used salt pork instead of bacon.

Boil or steam the prepared beans according to the basic recipe. Try out the bacon or salt pork in a heavy skillet until crisp. If you use salt pork you may need a little butter in the pan. Transfer the pork or bacon to absorbent paper. Add the onions and sauté in the pork or bacon fat, adding butter if necessary. Taste for salt. Add the vinegar, sugar, and pepper, and shake the pan well. When the beans are drained, reheat them for a few moments, then add the onion mixture and again shake the pan well. Spoon into a heated serving dish and top with the bacon or salt pork. Garnish with lemon slices. Excellent with ham or pork or with such things as spareribs or grilled pig's feet.

Note. This dish is made extremely interesting by the addition of 1 tablespoon or more fresh dill or 1½ teaspoons dillweed. Add with the vinegar, sugar, and pepper.

Green Beans with Cream

2 pounds green beans
Salt and freshly ground pepper
4 tablespoons butter
1 tablespoon fresh dill or 1½ teaspoons dillweed
¾ cup heavy cream
2 tablespoons chopped parsley

Boil or steam the prepared beans according to the basic recipe Drain, and return to the saucepan with the butter. Taste for salt, and add pepper to taste. Shake well over medium heat. Add the dill and cream, and toss with the beans. Spoon into a heated serving dish and top with the chopped parsley. This is pleasant with fish, chicken, or veal.

Joe's Green Beans

2 pounds whole green beans
6 tablespoons olive oil
3 finely chopped garlic cloves
3 tablespoons lemon juice
1 tablespoon finely cut — not grated — lemon rind
1 teaspoon freshly ground pepper
½ cup freshly grated Parmesan cheese

This is from my mother's recipe book. It originally came from our Italian truck gardener, who used to supply us with wonderful vegetables.

Cook the prepared beans according to the basic recipe till tender but still crisp. Drain well. Add the olive oil to the saucepan in which the beans were cooked, and sauté the garlic 1 minute. Add the beans and shake well for several minutes to coat them with the oil and blend in the garlic bits. Add the lemon juice, lemon rind, and pepper. Shake the pan. Spoon the beans into a heated serving dish and sprinkle with the cheese. Serve at once. Excellent with roast chicken or veal scallops, or as a full course after pasta.

Green Beans in Cheese Sauce

1 pound green beans
2 cups cheese sauce, made with sharp Cheddar
½ cup coarsely shredded sharp Cheddar cheese
½ cup buttered breadcrumbs
Salt and freshly ground pepper

Cook the prepared beans according to the basic recipe. Drain, and return briefly to the saucepan to dry out. Season to taste. Arrange in a greased 2-quart baking dish and cover with the cheese sauce. Sprinkle with the shredded cheese and buttered crumbs. Bake at 375 degrees approximately 15 minutes, or until the cheese is melted and the crumbs are browned. Serve with beef or lamb, or whenever the cheese will not overwhelm a delicate flavor.

Note. Both the beans and sauce may be prepared ahead of time. The dish can then be assembled several hours later and baked for a slightly longer time — about 25 minutes at 350 degrees.

Green Beans with Mushrooms I

1 pound green beans
1 pound mushrooms
4 tablespoons butter
2 tablespoons oil
1 teaspoon freshly ground pepper
Salt
¼ cup buttered breadcrumbs

Prepare and cook the beans according to the basic recipe. Drain. Slice the mushrooms rather thickly, reserving the stems for other uses. Sauté the mushrooms in the butter and oil very quickly till they are just cooked through. Salt as needed, and add the pepper. Return the cooked beans to the saucepan over medium heat, shake well, add the sautéed mushrooms, and toss thoroughly. Spoon into a heated serving dish and top with buttered toasted breadcrumbs.

Green Beans with Mushrooms II

1½ pounds green beans, preferably small whole ones
2 cups creamed mushrooms (see page 525)
6 mushroom caps, broiled lightly

This dish has become an American favorite for buffet entertaining, often made with canned mushroom soup and served topped with sautéed blanched almonds.

Prepare and cook the beans according to the basic recipe. Drain well, and reheat till dry in the saucepan. Transfer to a greased 2-quart baking dish and cover with the creamed mushrooms. Top with the broiled mushroom caps and place under the broiler a moment to glaze.

Wax Beans or White Beans

Wax beans have never been quite as popular in the country at large as green beans. Undoubtedly color has something to do with it, for the attractiveness of the green bean versus the yellow in the marketplace or on the table cannot be denied. However, wax beans have a winning quality quite their own. They are available in profusion in our markets.

To Cook Wax Beans

Prepare them as you would green beans. Cut the stem end and pull down to take with it any strings that may be there. Leave the beans whole, cut them in 1½-inch diagonal slices, or shred them.

To boil. Bring an ample amount of salted water to a boil, and add the prepared beans a few at a time. When the water comes to another full boil, reduce the heat and cook uncovered till the beans are just tender — about 12 to 15 minutes, and a little longer for more mature beans. Drain the beans well and return to the saucepan. Shake well and season.

To steam. Pour about ¼ inch of water into a large saucepan, preferably a heavy one, with a tight-fitting lid. Add 2 teaspoons salt, cover, and bring to a boil. Let it boil several minutes. Add the prepared beans and cover tightly. When steam appears around the lid, reduce the heat and steam until the beans are tender.

Wax Beans with Butter. Cook the beans either way, and drain. Add butter (4 tablespoons per pound of beans) and shake well to blend butter and beans. Add salt and freshly ground pepper to taste. Serve at once.

Wax Beans with Onion. Butter and season the drained cooked beans as above, and add finely cut green onions (about 3 tablespoons per pound of beans). Shake the pan well to blend the seasonings. Spoon into a serving dish and sprinkle generously with chopped parsley.

Wax Beans Sweet and Sour

½ cup water
½ cup vinegar
½ cup finely chopped onion
1½ pounds wax beans
4 tablespoons brown sugar
Salt and freshly ground pepper
6 slices bacon cut in small pieces and cooked crisp

Originally this was introduced into lower New York State and Pennsylvania, eventually becoming known through the Middle West. Quite refreshing on a hot day.

Heat the water and vinegar in a heavy saucepan which can be tightly covered. Add the onion, cover, and when the mixture begins to steam, add the beans and cover again tightly. Reduce the heat so the beans will steam very slowly. Add the sugar and stir well. When the beans are tender, shake the pan well to distribute the seasonings. Add salt and pepper as needed. Spoon into a heated serving dish and top with the crisply cooked bacon.

Shell Beans or Cranberry Beans

Much less popular these last twenty-five years than they used to be, shell or cranberry beans have rather speckled pods, and the beans themselves are ivory-colored streaked with red. They are quite mealy in texture, closely resembling some of the dried beans. The pods are rather heavy and you'll need about a pound per person. In some farmers' markets one finds them shelled, though seldom any more — a pity, because the pods are thick and lined with a fuzzy substance, making shelling quite a task.

To Cook Shell Beans

Bring shelled beans to a boil in salted water, then reduce the heat and cook, covered, over low heat until tender. Drain well and return to the pan for a moment to dry out. It used to be customary to add some bacon, smoked jowl, or salt pork to the beans during cooking, and the bits of meat were served with the beans.

Shell Beans with Butter and Onion. Drain and dry the beans well. Add butter (1½ tablespoons per pound of unshelled beans) and chopped raw onion (1 tablespoon per pound), and shake the pan well to blend. Add freshly ground pepper and salt to taste. Serve in a heated serving dish with chopped parsley as a garnish.

Shell Beans with Bacon

4 pounds (before shelling) shell beans
4 thick bacon slices, cut in small squares
2 garlic cloves, finely chopped
¼ cup chopped mint
2 tablespoons vinegar
Salt and freshly ground pepper
Chopped parsley

Cook the beans in salted water as in the basic instructions above. When they are tender, drain and keep them warm. While they are cooking, try out the bacon in a skillet until almost crisp. Add the garlic and just color it slightly. Add the mint, vinegar, salt to taste, and pepper, and let them blend well together. Combine with the hot beans and toss thoroughly. Serve garnished with chopped parsley.

Fava Beans or Broad Beans

Unlike most other beans, which are natives of the Americas, these were imported into the Western Hemisphere by the Italians, or by the English, who know them as "broad beans" — to the rest of Europe they are known as "fave" or "feves." They are now very much ours. Strictly speaking, they are not beans, like haricots or white beans, but belong to another family of plants grown in Europe and Asia for centuries.

When young the beans are quite tender and the skin not too tough. As they grow larger and more mature the skin becomes very coarse and toughens. Then one has to "slip" the beans — that is, remove their outer skins — before eating them. This can be a tedious job, as I know well, having once participated in the slipping of 10 pounds of broad beans for a dinner party. It was worth it. Always try to find the smallest of broad beans. Five pounds of unshelled broad beans will just about serve four.

To Cook Broad Beans

Shell the beans and wash them well. Put them to boil in salted water and cook fairly fast. The tiny ones will cook in 10 to 12 minutes; the larger ones in up to 25 minutes. Drain.

If the skins seem tough, you will have to slip the beans after cooking. Let them cool (this can be hurried by pouring cold water over them); then remove the outer skin of each bean.

Reheat the beans and add seasonings.

Buttered Broad Beans. Return the cooked drained beans to the saucepan and add butter (6 tablespoons per 5 pounds of unshelled beans). Shake the pan over medium heat to coat the beans. Add salt and freshly ground pepper to taste. Serve with chopped parsley.

Frozen Broad Beans. Excellent frozen broad beans are available. They save the time of shelling and are of fairly uniform size. To prepare, blanch them in boiling salted water 4 to 5 minutes. Cool immediately. Slip the outer skin of the beans and reheat with seasonings.

Raw Broad Beans

Broad beans must be very fresh and young to be eaten in this way. Much beloved by the French and Italians, they have begun to be considered good cocktail food here. They are served in the pods, and guests are expected to extract the beans and dip them in coarse salt. Excellent for a tray of crudités. Like nuts, one can't stop eating them.

Garlicked Broad Beans

5 pounds broad beans
6 tablespoons olive oil
3 garlic cloves, finely chopped
½ cup finely chopped onion
1 tablespoon finely cut fresh basil or 1 teaspoon dried basil
Freshly ground pepper (and salt if needed)
¼ cup grated Parmesan cheese
3 tablespoons chopped parsley

Shell the beans and cook as in the basic instructions above. Drain well and, if the skins seem tough, slip them. Heat the olive oil in a heavy skillet. Add the garlic and onion, and sauté 3 to 4 minutes. Add the basil and pepper and combine with the beans. Shake well to blend. Taste for salt. Spoon into a heated serving dish and sprinkle with freshly grated Parmesan cheese and chopped parsley.

Scarlet Runner Beans

These darlings of the English gardener are rarely seen in this country, save for those raised every year for sentimental reasons as much as for enjoyment. Markets rarely feature them. You have to have them as a gift from someone who grows them, or you must grow them yourself.

Not only does this plant provide a good vegetable, but it produces a luxuriant vine and scarlet flowers as well — reminding one of the old saying, "When beans are in flower, fools are in power." The broad pods are sometimes six inches long and are usually filled with large, streaked beans.

To Cook Scarlet Runner Beans

Wash the beans well and shred them diagonally in about ½-inch pieces. Drop by handfuls into boiling salted water and let them cook at a medium boil for about 25 minutes or less according to the tenderness of the bean. Drain them well and return to the saucepan in which they cooked.

With Butter. For 2 pounds scarlet runners, add 6 tablespoons butter and ½ teaspoon freshly ground pepper. Taste for salt. Shake well over medium heat to blend.

Scarlet runners may also be prepared in most of the ways suggested for green beans.

Lima Beans

Fresh lima beans in the markets have greatly improved within the last twenty years. Formerly they were large, full beans, resembling most of the dried limas one buys. But with the advent of several new varieties, notably the Fordhook, and with the harvesting of small beans instead of the large pods formerly offered, this vegetable is far more desirable.

Green lima beans are troublesome to shell, far more so than fava beans, for example, which they resemble. The fava, however, is a delight to the bite and to the taste, and to my palate, the lima is almost without flavor. Neither is it particularly pleasant in texture. It requires the addition of herbed butter or a sauce to give it distinction.

One pound of lima beans in pod will yield about 1 cup of beans. Consequently, for four persons, you will need approximately three pounds. Shelled lima beans are available in many places, but they do not keep especially well and I much prefer frozen lima beans. If you buy beans in the pod, store them in the vegetable compartment of your refrigerator and shell them at the last possible moment. Split the pods at the rounded end, and the beans will come out fairly easily. Watch carefully, and discard any wormy beans.

To Cook Lima Beans

Pour about ¼ inch of water into a heavy saucepan with a tight-fitting lid. Add salt. Cover, and bring to the boiling point. Add the beans, cover tightly, lower the heat, and steam rather gently till the beans are tender, which will take 12 to 20 minutes, depending upon their freshness. Be careful not to overcook. When done, the beans will be tender to the bite with a suggestion of resistance. The interior should never be mushy or starchy. Drain well, and return to the heat for a moment to dry.

For 3 cups cooked beans, treat in any of the following ways.

Buttered Lima Beans. Add 6 tablespoons melted butter and a little freshly ground pepper to taste. Salt if needed. For *Herbed Lima Beans,* use chive butter, dill butter, or herbed butter.

Lima Beans with Sour Cream. Add 4 tablespoons melted butter, freshly ground pepper, salt, and 3 tablespoons sour cream. Do not allow the cream to boil. Add 2 tablespoons finely chopped parsley.

Lima Beans with Mushrooms. Add 2 cups sliced mushrooms which have been sautéed in 6 tablespoons butter. Add freshly ground pepper and salt to taste.

Lima Beans with Bacon. Add ½ cup bacon cracklings (this means 6 to 8 slices bacon cut in small pieces, tried out till crisp, and drained on absorbent paper). Add 4 tablespoons melted butter, salt, and freshly ground pepper.

Lima Beans with Cheese. Transfer the beans to a baking dish. Cover with 1½ cups rich cream sauce. Sprinkle with ½ cup shredded Cheddar cheese (sharp, if possible) and heat in a 350-degree oven about 10 minutes, or until the cheese is melted and bubbling.

Lima Beans with Bacon, Onions and Mushrooms

3 pounds green lima beans
6 slices bacon
1 cup thinly sliced onions
Salt and freshly ground pepper
1 cup sliced mushrooms
4 tablespoons butter
2 tablespoons chopped parsley

I read this recipe in one of the recipe exchange columns in a small-town newspaper some years ago. I tried it, and it's very good.

Shell the lima beans and cook according to the basic recipe. While the beans are cooking, try out the bacon in a heavy skillet. When it is rather crisp, transfer to absorbent paper. Pour off all but 3 tablespoons fat, and sauté the onions lightly. They should be just tender and delicately brown. Salt them to taste. Sauté the mushrooms lightly in butter. Salt and pepper them to taste. Drain the lima beans and return them to the heat to dry for a minute. Add the bacon, broken into small bits. Shake the pan well. Add the onions and mushrooms and shake the pan again to blend the flavors. Spoon into a heated serving dish and garnish with chopped parsley.

Beets

The poor beet has suffered no end of unpopularity. This is quite beyond my understanding, for it is versatile and attractive and has good flavor. It has been in use since the Romans and seems to continue despite its enemies. In the South, beet greens are much favored, as they are in the Middle West. In fact, many people are willing to settle for the greens and not bother about the tubers. In France beets are cooked — usually in the oven — and sold in the marketplace as an additive for salads or as an hors d'oeuvre item. Certainly the English were the first to bring the beet into this country, and the Dutch probably imported it shortly thereafter. In New England cookery there are many dishes which depend on beets — for example, red flannel hash and Harvard beets, and there is a beet dish named for Yale as well.

Small beets, usually sold by the pound or in bunches, are the best buy. The older ones tend to take very long cooking and are sometimes woody to boot. Bunches carry about 5 to 7 beets, and this amount, if they are not too tiny, should serve four persons. If you are lucky enough to find what one used to call "Bitsy Beets," packed in tins or glass, they are quite choice.

To Cook Beets

Beets should not be scrubbed or brushed before cooking. You might puncture the skin, allowing the juice to escape, and you would end up with a colorless, flavorless mess of pulp. Wash the beets gently and leave 1½ to 2 inches of the stems on. Put them in a small amount of boiling water, cover tightly, and simmer slowly till they are tender to the touch of the finger. Don't pierce them with a fork until they are done. They will take from 30 to 45 minutes. Plunge the cooked beets into cold water. As soon as you can handle them, slip the skins off. Then dress them and serve.

Baked Beets. Beets may also be baked in the oven at 325 degrees. They will take about an hour to become tender to the touch.

Buttered Beets. Slice peeled cooked beets or cut into dice. Combine with melted butter in a saucepan (4 tablespoons for 8 medium beets) and shake the pan till the beets are warmed through. Add lemon juice (1 tablespoon for 8 beets), salt, and freshly ground pepper.

Beets with Sour Cream

8 to 10 medium-size beets
4 tablespoons butter
1 teaspoon sugar
Salt
Few grains nutmeg
1 cup sour cream
Chopped parsley

Especially good with a roast of pork or with grilled pork chops.

Cook the beets and slip the skins off, as above. Either dice, slice, or leave whole, and transfer to a saucepan with the butter. Add the sugar, salt, and nutmeg, and heat the beets through. Shake the pan to season evenly. Add the sour cream and just heat through again; do not let the cream come to a boil and "break." Pour into a serving dish and garnish with chopped parsley.

Harvard Beets

12 small beets
½ cup sugar
2 teaspoons cornstarch
½ cup vinegar
2 tablespoons butter

These have been a New England tradition for generations. Whether or not the name is derived from the Harvard "red," I cannot tell. They are a national dish now and are sometimes made in horrendous fashion. This is an old New England rule.

Boil the beets and skin as in the basic recipe. Cut into slices, julienne strips, or dice. Combine the sugar, cornstarch, and vinegar in a small saucepan. Bring to a boil and let it simmer 4 or 5 minutes. Pour over the beets in a larger saucepan and heat through very slowly, shaking the pan several times during the heating. Just as you serve the beets, add the butter and let it melt with the sauce.

Yale Beets. This is exactly the same recipe except that it substitutes ½ cup orange juice and 1 tablespoon lemon juice for the vinegar.

Beets with Onions and Herbs

12 smallish beets
6 tablespoons butter
½ cup finely cut green onions
¼ cup chopped parsley
1 tablespoon freshly cut tarragon or 1 teaspoon dried
1½ tablespoons sugar
¼ cup wine vinegar
Salt and freshly ground pepper

Cook the beets and skin according to the basic recipe. Cut into thin slices. Combine with the butter in a saucepan. Add the green onions and seasonings and heat thoroughly.

Beets with Béchamel

12 to 14 very small beets
1½ cups béchamel sauce
Chopped parsley

Mrs. Rorer thought this made a lovely dish for a pink luncheon.

Cook the beets and skin according to the basic recipe. Arrange in a 1 to 1½ quart flat baking dish. Add the hot béchamel sauce. Reheat in a 350-degree oven 5 minutes. Sprinkle with chopped parsley and serve.

Pickled Beets

12 medium beets
2 medium onions, sliced
Wine vinegar
6 peppercorns
6 whole allspice
3 cloves

Cook the beets and skin according to the basic recipe. Slice, and combine in a bowl with the onion slices. Cover with the vinegar, add the spices, and blend. These will keep for quite a time.

It used to be a common thing for housewives to serve pickled beets and save the juices, in which hard-boiled eggs were then pickled. These were served as snacks with beer. They can still be found at delicatessen counters in Pennsylvania Dutch country.

A Polish Version of Pickled Beets

10 to 12 medium-size beets
1 tablespoon grated horseradish
½ teaspoon caraway seed
1 tablespoon salt
1 tablespoon sugar
2 cups vinegar

This is often found in surprising places in the Middle West and in upper New York State. It is a most pleasant combination of flavors.

Cook the beets and skin as in the basic recipe. Cut in thin slices. In a bowl arrange layers of beets sprinkled with the horseradish and caraway seeds. Heat the salt, sugar, and vinegar together to the boiling point and pour over the beets. Let stand 24 hours before eating.

Beet Greens

2 pounds beet greens
Melted butter
1 tablespoon lemon juice
Salt and freshly ground pepper
Few grains nutmeg

Fresh young greens found on bunches of beets or nowadays sold separately are pungent and pleasing to the palate. A pound will serve two.

Wash the greens well in several waters. Place in a heavy kettle, cover tightly, and let them wilt over medium heat. Toss with a fork several times to mix the top greens with those on the bottom. When they are just wilted and tender, remove them and drain thoroughly, then chop and drain some more. Dress with the melted butter, lemon juice, salt, pepper, and nutmeg.

Beet Greens with Beets. When you are lucky enough to grow your own beets, you may have to thin out the rows. In so doing, you'll gather tops with tiny, tiny beets on them. Cut the beets from the tops and cook them very quickly. Cook the greens separately, as above. Skin the beets and combine with the cooked greens. Add butter, pepper and salt, and a bit of lemon juice.

Broccoli

This member of the cabbage family is known as *chou broccoli* (cabbage broccoli) in France and broccoli-rabe in Central Europe. It was known to the English, and probably also to the early settlers in America, as brockala, and there are occasional recipes for it under that name in manuscript cookbooks.

While broccoli must have been cultivated in this country for generations, it is comparatively recently — in the last forty years — that it has become what we might call a fashionable vegetable. The varieties sold on the markets in the United States today are far better than the vegetable raised in the past century. Modern experimentation has changed its face and figure a good deal. I have a friend in France who grows American broccoli and serves it to astonished Frenchmen, for it is indeed a superior variety.

Broccoli at its peak is tightly budded with bright gray-green leaves and stems of a yellower green. Avoid broccoli with buds bursting into flower, for it is past its prime.

Broccoli is usually sold in 2-pound bunches. Look for bunches with the slenderest stems. Heavy stems are often rather woody, and you will have a great deal of waste. It is in season a good part of the year in most large cities.

To prepare broccoli for cooking, wash it well, wrap it in plastic or foil, and store in the vegetable compartment of your refrigerator. When ready to cook, peel the heavy stems, and remove part of them if they are unusually heavy and seem tough. Break the very thick stems or cut them into smaller bunches for better service. Rinse the broccoli again.

To Cook Broccoli

Since the flowers are much more tender than the stems, they take far less time to cook. That is why one so often sees broken, messy plates of broccoli, which are as unappetizing as any vegetable can be. Therefore be ruthless in your trimming and cook only the choicest portions of the vegetable unless you are doing a purée or a soufflé.

It is best to steam-cook broccoli in a rather deep pot or in a saucepan which can be covered tightly with an inverted pan. The deep round pot with a movable tray the Italians have made for cooking asparagus is ideal.

Tie the broccoli in one large bunch or in several smaller bunches so that it will stand securely. Place it in about 1½ inches of boiling salted water in a saucepan or cooking pot and cover tightly. If your pot will not cover tightly with its own cover or another pot, cover it with foil, and secure it around the edge of the pot. Steam the broccoli about 12 to 14 minutes, or until just tender. Drain well, and serve with melted butter, drawn butter, lemon butter, or a sauce Maltaise or Hollandaise. You will need approximately ¾ to 1 cup of the sauce for four persons.

Cold Broccoli. Arrange cold cooked broccoli on a bed of greens with the stems pointing to the center of the serving dish. Sprinkle the stems with chopped hard-boiled egg and capers and cover with lemon slices. Arrange cherry tomatoes between the stems. Serve with a well-flavored mayonnaise or a vinaigrette sauce. Pass the sauce separately, or arrange the salad on individual plates and dress when it goes to table.

Broccoli Purée

3 pounds broccoli
Salt
6 tablespoons melted butter
1 teaspoon freshly ground pepper
1/4 teaspoon nutmeg
3 tablespoons heavy cream
1/4 cup grated Parmesan cheese

Cut the broccoli in small pieces, separating the flowers and the stems. Boil the stems 10 minutes in boiling salted water, then add the flowers and cook till tender. Drain well. Put the broccoli through a food mill or purée attachment of the electric mixer. Season with the butter, pepper, nutmeg, and cream, and blend well. Taste for salt. Spoon into a 1 1/2-quart baking dish and sprinkle with Parmesan cheese. Heat in a 375-degree oven 10 minutes.

Serve with sautéed chicken, roast duck, or a leg of lamb.

Brussels Sprouts

Brussels sprouts do not figure in early cookery books as broccoli and other members of the cabbage family do. Perhaps they were considered a too difficult crop for many people. Or perhaps they were so badly prepared no one thought them worth writing about. One thing is certain: these miniature members of the family Brassica Olerocea can be as crisp and tender and well-flavored as any vegetable. Therefore it is all the sadder to see how often they are utterly ruined.

The English, on whose tables brussels sprouts appear — often badly cooked — at all times, were most likely responsible for bringing them to the American scene. They are found during a good part of the year in the markets and vary a good deal in size. Time was when they were graded and one could buy small, medium, or large, but nowadays they seem to come in small punnets which contain large and small, and you must gauge the cooking time to cover them all, or cook some longer than others.

Brussels sprouts go well with beef dishes, lamb, fried or roast chicken, duck, pheasant, and roast pork. They should not be served with delicately sauced dishes. One pound of sprouts will serve four persons.

To Cook Brussels Sprouts

Cut off the stem end and remove the outer leaves and any leaves which seem to be yellowed or ravaged with wormholes. Occasionally a sprout will be found still housing a little worm. Discard the sprout. Soak the sprouts in water 15 to 20 minutes before cooking.

To steam-cook. Put a small amount of salted water (about a quarter-inch) in a heavy saucepan and bring to a boil. Add the prepared sprouts, cover tightly, and steam 5 to 10 minutes, or until they are just crisply tender. Test carefully, for there are few things more unpleasant than an overcooked sprout. Drain the sprouts well and return to the saucepan to dry out before seasoning.

To boil. Boil the prepared sprouts in an ample quantity of salted water, uncovered, over brisk heat till they are just tender, which will take 5 to 15 minutes, depending upon the crispness you prefer and the size of the sprouts. Continue as above.

Buttered Brussels Sprouts. Add a large lump of butter to the reheated sprouts and toss well till thoroughly covered — but don't let them cook. Add freshly ground pepper, and salt if needed. For a pound of sprouts you will want about 4 tablespoons butter and ½ teaspoon pepper.

Brussels Sprouts Hollandaise. Spoon cooked, drained, and dried-out sprouts into a warmed serving dish. Spoon Hollandaise over them or pass the sauce at table (1 cup per pound of sprouts).

Brussels Sprouts with Cheese Sauce I. Transfer cooked, drained, and dried-out sprouts to a heated serving dish and spoon cheese sauce over them or pass the sauce at table (1½ cups sauce per pound of sprouts).

Brussels Sprouts with Cheese Sauce II. Dry out the drained cooked sprouts and pour into a well-buttered baking dish. Cover with cheese sauce (1½ cups per pound of sprouts). Sprinkle lavishly with grated Cheddar or Swiss cheese and heat in a 350-degree oven just long enough to melt the cheese.

Brussels Sprouts with Mushrooms. Sauté ½ pound mushrooms (per pound of sprouts) in 3 tablespoons butter. Add to the cooked, drained, and dried-out sprouts with freshly ground pepper, and salt if needed. Toss well. Spoon into a heated serving dish and garnish with chopped parsley.

Brussels Sprouts and Chestnuts

1 pound Brussels sprouts
1 can whole chestnuts in brine (these are imported from France)
6 tablespoons butter
½ teaspoon freshly ground pepper
¼ teaspoon nutmeg

In several states where the chestnut crop was fine, Brussels sprouts and chestnuts became a tradition with turkey or goose for Thanksgiving or Christmas. It's an extraordinarily good combination and one which nowadays is very easy to prepare.

Steam the Brussels sprouts according to the basic recipe, and drain well. Drain the chestnuts well and wash them in a small amount of water. Heat, covered, in a heavy saucepan, and drain again. Combine the chestnuts and Brussels sprouts. Melt the butter, add the pepper and nutmeg, and pour over the vegetables. Shake the pan gently. Transfer to a heated serving dish, and serve. Add a little chopped parsley and additional butter if you like.

Note. If you prefer to use fresh chestnuts, see rule for preparing them, page 511.

Butter-Steamed Brussels Sprouts

6 tablespoons butter or more
1 pound Brussels sprouts
1 teaspoon salt
1 teaspoon freshly ground pepper

Melt the butter in a heavy skillet. Add the sprouts, cover tightly, and steam until they are crisply tender. Shake the pan vigorously from time to time. When they are just tender, add salt and pepper and serve at once. Do not overcook.

Brussels Sprouts with Bacon

1 pound Brussels sprouts
6 slices thickly cut bacon
1 small onion, chopped
1 teaspoon freshly ground pepper
2 tablespoons vinegar

This was one of the earliest American recipes I found for sprouts, and it's rather a nice one.

Steam or boil the sprouts, according to the basic recipe, till tender but still crisp. Sauté the bacon, cut into small pieces. Remove some of the fat, add the onion, and cook just till it wilts. Add the pepper. Drain the sprouts and dry out over the heat for just a minute. Add to the bacon mixture and toss well. Add the vinegar, shake again, and transfer to a heated serving dish.

A California Recipe for Brussels Sprouts

1 pound Brussels sprouts
6 tablespoons olive oil
2 small cloves garlic, chopped
2 tablespoons lemon juice
½ teaspoon freshly ground pepper
3 tablespoons grated Parmesan cheese

Boil or steam the sprouts as in the basic recipe till they are barely cooked through and are still very crisp. Drain, and dry out over the heat for a moment. Meantime, sauté the garlic in the olive oil till just wilted. Add to the sprouts and shake the pan well. Add the lemon juice and pepper and shake again. Spoon into a heated serving dish and sprinkle with grated Parmesan cheese. Serve at once.

Note. For an interesting variation, add about 1 cup shredded boiled ham, baked ham, or prosciutto to this dish.

Cabbage

Cabbage, in one form or another, is probably the most widely used of vegetables next to potatoes. More than likely the Dutch brought cabbage to America, for it is first mentioned in connection with New Netherlands. The Swedish colonies in Delaware grew it too, and it must also have found its way to New England just after the first settlers arrived. Certainly it was soon to be immortalized in the New England boiled dinner.

There are enough different recipes for coleslaw alone to have made cabbage more than a minor crop in this country, and a prodigious amount was also used as sauerkraut. Originally made by the Dutch and Germans, sauerkraut grew quickly in popularity because it proved a good way to preserve cabbage for the winter and gave much-needed acidity to meals. No doubt this is why sauerkraut became traditional with turkey in Maryland and why it came to be served cold with foods as a salad, as well as being prepared hot with other foods and with game such as pheasant and duck.

Cabbage is available in many forms in our markets. The earliest cabbage is generally a rather beautiful green, conical in shape, with large curling outer leaves and a fairly firm head. Later cabbage comes quite heavily headed, with a firm white interior which results from being kept from the sun. The outer leaves are gray-green or a rather bright green. Savoy or curly cabbage is crinkled, delicate in texture, and quite beautiful to the eye. The red or purple cabbage, which has a trim head and a stem that is white inside, is used for special recipes and for pickling.

If cabbage has suffered in reputation for being particularly penetrating in odor, it is largely because of overcooking, an unfortunate heritage from our past. As late as 1837 Eliza Leslie advised: "To prepare a cabbage for boiling, remove the outer leaves and pare and trim the stalk, cutting it close and short. If the cabbage is large, quarter it, if small cut it in half; and let it stand for a while in a deep pan of cold water with the large end downwards. Put it into a pot with plenty of water (having first tied it together to keep it whole while boiling) and taking off the scum, boil it 2 hours, or till the stalk is quite tender. When done, drain it and squeeze it well. Before you send it to the table introduce a little fresh butter between the leaves; or have melted butter in a boat." Two hours! No wonder cabbage had a bad name. It not only smelled up the house but was reduced to a pulp.

Though Mrs. Rorer characterized cabbage as a waste food, it is a delight in many dishes, and since her time has found its champions as far as vitamins are concerned. A cabbage of 2 to 3 pounds will serve 4 persons.

To Cook Cabbage

Remove the outer leaves which are coarse and torn. Trim the stalk. Cut the cabbage in half and cut each half in 2 or 3 sections. Or shred the cabbage very fine with the aid of a sharp knife or a shredder, removing the stem unless you particularly like it cooked with the cabbage. (It is good raw, sprinkled with a little salt and pepper, to munch as you prepare the rest of the cabbage.) Whichever way you cut the cabbage, soak it a half hour in cold water with a touch of salt in it.

Cabbage for stuffed cabbage leaves, etc., may be kept whole for blanching.

Drain the cabbage after soaking in cold water.

To steam. Take a large heavy saucepan or skillet which has a tight lid, and pour in salted water to a depth of about a half-inch. Bring to a boil, covered. When it begins to steam, add the cabbage, cover tightly, reduce the heat, and steam — about 4 minutes for a shredded young cabbage, up to 8 for an older one, and 6 to 8 for a sectioned cabbage. Curly or Savoy cabbage will take about 8 minutes. Shake the pan vigorously several times during the cooking. For shredded cabbage, if you have the strength, grab the pan by the handle, hold the cover on tight, and shake the pan up and down from side to side. When the cabbage is just crisply tender, drain it well.

To boil. Have enough salted water to cover the cabbage, bring to a boil, add the cabbage, and boil over high heat in an uncovered saucepan 8 to 10 minutes, or until just crisply tender. Drain it well.

Buttered Cabbage. Return the drained cabbage to the saucepan or skillet with butter — 6 to 8 tablespoons for a 2 to 3 pound cabbage. If the cabbage is shredded, cover the pan and shake it well to mix. If it is in sections, cover the pan and steam the cabbage for a moment, turning the sections in the butter. Add freshly ground pepper to taste, and taste for salt. Transfer to a heated serving dish, and serve at once.

Braised Cabbage

1 head cabbage, 2 to 3 pounds
4 tablespoons butter, bacon fat, pork dripping, or goose fat
1 teaspoon salt
1 teaspoon freshly ground pepper
2 teaspoons chopped fresh dill or 1 teaspoon dry dillweed (optional)
½ cup stock or white wine

This appears to be a combination of several similar recipes from various parts of the country. The dill was definitely a Pennsylvania additive. The wine came much later in New York State, and the broth was a standard item from the stockpot on the stove. This may be cooked as much as you like, depending upon how strongly flavored you prefer it.

Clean, shred, and soak the cabbage as directed for the basic recipe above. Melt the fat in a heavy skillet which can be tightly covered. Add the drained shredded cabbage and sear it over rather high heat, tossing it with two wooden spoons as you would a salad. When it is lightly browned, reduce the heat and add the seasonings. Add the liquid, cover, and simmer till just tender. Remove the cover and cook down over high heat for 2 minutes. Correct the seasoning. Spoon into a heated serving dish. Especially good with pork dishes, corned beef, or boiled beef.

Smothered Cabbage. Increase the fat to 6 tablespoons, and omit the dill. Brown the cabbage fairly well before you add the salt and pepper. Simmer it with no extra liquid. When it is tender to your taste, add 1 tablespoon vinegar, shake the pan, then add ⅓ cup heavy cream, and toss well with the wooden spoons.

Dilled Cabbage with Ham

2 smallish cabbages, about 2 pounds each
½ pound smoked ham, cooked and cut in julienne pieces
6 tablespoons butter
½ cup finely chopped fresh dill
½ teaspoon freshly ground pepper
Salt

Wash and section the cabbages, and soak as in basic preparations. Cook in boiling salted water till just crisply tender. Drain, chop very fine, and combine with the ham, butter, and dill. Season to taste and reheat a few moments over hot water. Serve in a heated serving dish.

Ladies Cabbage

Ladies cabbage must have been a very fashionable dish, for it appears in recipes by everyone from Mrs. Harland to Mrs. Rorer. Strange how certain dishes have a vogue for years and years and suddenly disappear. No one hears of ladies cabbage nowadays.

Mrs. Harland's Recipe for Ladies Cabbage. Cook a 2 to 3 pound cabbage in sections as directed in the basic recipe. Drain well and cool. Chop it very fine and combine with ¼ cup cream, ¼ cup butter, melted, and 2 lightly beaten eggs. Season to taste with salt and freshly ground pepper. Spoon into a buttered 1½-quart baking dish and bake at 350 degrees 25 minutes. [*Note.* Much better topped with ¼ cup buttered crumbs.]

Mrs. Rorer's Recipe for Ladies Cabbage. Cut the cabbage in eighths and cook as directed in the basic recipe. Remove the sections carefully and arrange in a sunburst on a warmed serving plate. Spoon 1½ cups rich cream sauce over the center of the cabbage. Garnish with chopped parsley.

California Cabbage in White Wine

1 large cabbage, 3 pounds or more
1 teaspoon salt
1 teaspoon freshly ground pepper
½ teaspoon dried basil
California Pinot Chardonnay or Sauvignon Blanc
½ cup melted butter

Cut the cabbage in 1-inch slices and soak in cold water an hour. Place in a large saucepan and add the seasonings. Just barely cover with white wine. Cover, and simmer over very low heat until the cabbage is tender — about 1 to 1½ hours. For those counting calories, it is delicious removed from the wine and served as is. For others, add melted butter and toss well.

Cale-Cannon or Colcannon

Miss Leslie mentions Cale-Cannon, which we have come to know as colcannon and associate with St. Patrick's Day. Hers is an honest recipe and certainly worth knowing. "Boil separately some potatoes and cabbage. When done, drain and squeeze the cabbage, and chop, or mince it very small. Mash the potatoes, and mix them gradually but thoroughly with the chopped cabbage, adding butter, pepper and salt. There should be twice as much potato as cabbage." Cale-Cannon is eaten with corned beef, boiled pork, and bacon.

Cabbage and Zucchini Skillet

6 tablespoons olive oil, bacon fat, or goose fat
1 2-pound cabbage, shredded very fine
1 large onion, thinly sliced
½ cup broth or white wine
1 clove garlic, finely chopped
3 to 4 zucchini, washed and cut in ½-inch slices
Salt and freshly ground pepper

I first ate this dish in Provence many years ago. I was surprised, therefore, when I was offered it again by friends who had emigrated from that part of the world to the Middle West. It had become a common dish among their friends, who liked it very much served with pork sausages. The combination is hearty and good.

Heat the fat in a large, heavy skillet and add the cabbage. Toss it well with two wooden spoons for several minutes to distribute the fat. Add the onion and toss again. Add the liquid to the skillet, reduce the heat, cover, and simmer 40 minutes. Add the garlic and the zucchini, cover again, and simmer another 45 minutes. Season to taste, cover, and cook just 5 minutes more. Transfer to a heated serving platter. Surround with cooked sausages if you like. Or serve in a heated serving dish with braised or boiled meats. It is especially good with corned beef.

Stuffed Savoy Cabbage

1 good-sized Savoy cabbage
1 cup finely chopped smoked ham
1 cup finely chopped cooked veal or pork
½ cup finely chopped onion sautéed in 6 tablespoons butter
½ cup chopped mushrooms sautéed in butter
1 teaspoon thyme
1 finely chopped garlic clove
1 teaspoon salt
¾ teaspoon freshly ground pepper
1½ cups cooked rice
Hollandaise sauce or rich cream sauce
Chopped parsley

This was a most dressy luncheon dish served at the turn of the century and later. It is a dish well worth preserving and is not the trouble it may sound. When properly done, it looks absolutely beautiful on a plate. The ancestry is definitely French.

Soak the Savoy cabbage in cold water 1 hour. Blanch in boiling salted water 10 minutes or so, or until the leaves unfold easily from the head. Drain well and separate (do not detach) all the leaves so that they resemble a huge flower. Combine the meats, onion, mushrooms, seasonings, and rice. Correct the seasoning. Then stuff the cabbage: place a few spoonfuls on each leaf and fold them back into place. Tie the cabbage securely in a triple thickness of cheesecloth. Lower the cabbage into boiling salted water and simmer, covered, 35 to 40 minutes. Remove the cover and carefully lift the cabbage to a rack. Remove the cheesecloth. Place the cabbage on a heated serving plate and top with Hollandaise or cream sauce. Crisp rolls and perhaps a tomato salad would be right with this dish.

Note. For a richer, more flavorful dish, poach the cabbage in chicken broth or veal stock. You may then use the stock afterwards for the basis of a very delicious soup or a borsht.

Creamed Savoy Cabbage I

1 Savoy cabbage, 2 to 3 pounds
1½ cups rich cream sauce
½ cup toasted buttered crumbs
Salt and freshly ground pepper

Shred the cabbage, soak, and cook as directed in the basic instructions. Prepare a rich cream sauce, and taste for seasoning. Toast and butter the breadcrumbs. When the cabbage has cooked till just tender, drain it very well. Taste it for salt. If more is needed, add before baking. Arrange the cabbage in a 2-quart buttered baking dish. Cover with the cream sauce. Top with buttered crumbs and bake 20 minutes in a 350-degree oven. Nice with chicken, turkey, and veal dishes.

Creamed Savoy Cabbage II. Prepare as above, but alternate layers of cabbage and shredded Cheddar or Gruyère cheese. Top with the sauce, sprinkle with more shredded cheese, and add buttered crumbs. Bake at 350 degrees just long enough to melt the cheese without allowing it to become stringy.

Coleslaw, Kohlslau, Coldslaw

One of the more popular ways of using cabbage. Slaw cannot be rightly classed as a salad, but rather it is a way to prepare cabbage as a relish or even as an hors d'oeuvre. It is as old as cabbage and has known many different versions — and strangely enough, practically all of them are good.

There has been, in the last few years, a trend to combine coleslaw with other items. Some of these experiments are quite successful, and others are extraordinarily bad. Finely shredded apple as a second ingredient is extremely good, especially if the slaw is being served with pork. Carrot also goes well with the cabbage, as does a small amount of green pepper. But pineapple and white grapes hold no brief for this palate, and I need hardly comment on one writer who advised using pineapple, white grapes, *and* tiny marshmallows.

Coleslaw in some of its forms makes a superb base for seafood salads, combining equally well with crabmeat, lobster meat, or shrimp.

Mrs. Crowen's Coleslaw

2 to 3 pound cabbage, shredded
6 tablespoons butter
1½ teaspoons salt
1 teaspoon freshly ground pepper
½ cup wine vinegar

I find this 1847 version as good as any slaw I have ever eaten and unusual in its way.

Shred the cabbage very thin. Soak a half hour in cold water. Drain well. Place in a heavy saucepan with a tightly fitting cover and add the other ingredients. Cover tightly and place over rather high heat. Lift the pan, hold the cover on, and shake vigorously several times. The cabbage should steam about 5 to 6 minutes till it is just wilted and the butter and vinegar have permeated it. Turn into a serving dish and serve at once.

The same source of this recipe, Mrs. Crowen, offers a cabbage salad which is considered "very good when celery cannot be had and much less expensive, too." It is merely shredded cabbage dressed with oil and vinegar and tossed.

Hot Slaw

1 cabbage, 2 to 3 pounds, shredded
4 tablespoons butter
1 tablespoon flour
½ cup water
2 eggs
6 tablespoons sugar
1 teaspoon dry mustard
1 teaspoon salt
½ cup vinegar

This is a common dish through the countryside. It probably came originally from Dutch settlers in New York before finding its way over the entire country.

Heat water in the bottom of a double boiler. Melt the butter in the top and stir in the flour until it is bubbling and lightly colored and the raw flour taste has cooked away. Stir in the water and continue stirring till the mixture is smooth and lightly thickened. Beat the eggs with the sugar, mustard, and salt. Spoon a little of the hot sauce into the egg mixture to temper it. Then stir back into the hot base and continue stirring till blended and thickened. Gradually add the vinegar and blend well. Remove from the heat.

Stir, hot or cold, into the shredded cabbage. If you stir in the sauce while it is hot, the cabbage will become very limp and quite pungent with the dressing. If you stir in the sauce when cold, it will keep the cabbage crisp and be entirely different in character.

A Favorite Coleslaw

1 cabbage, 2 to 3 pounds, finely shredded
1 cup mayonnaise, preferably homemade
1 cup sour cream
1 teaspoon salt
½ teaspoon freshly ground pepper

Crisp the cabbage in cold water for an hour. Drain well and combine with the mayonnaise, sour cream, and seasonings. Toss well and let stand 30 minutes, or even longer if you like a rather wilted slaw. Correct the seasoning before serving.

Sweet and Sour Slaw. Add 2 tablespoons sugar, ¼ cup vinegar, 1 teaspoon dry mustard or to taste, and ¼ teaspoon Tabasco.

Chopped Slaw

1 cabbage, 2 to 3 pounds, shredded and finely chopped
½ cup olive oil
2 to 3 tablespoons vinegar, according to taste
1 teaspoon salt
½ teaspoon freshly ground pepper
1 teaspoon celery seed
1 teaspoon mustard seed
1 teaspoon sugar
½ teaspoon dry mustard

This was a favorite in restaurants around the turn of the century and is hard to discover nowadays. However, it is a delicious change from the other slaws.

Combine all the ingredients for the sauce and shake well in a jar or beat well with a spoon. Toss the cabbage with the mixture and let it stand an hour, turning it several times while it mellows.

Miss Farmer's Coleslaw with Boiled Dressing

1 cabbage, 2 to 3 pounds

BOILED DRESSING

1 teaspoon salt
1 teaspoon dry mustard
1½ tablespoons sugar
Dash cayenne
1½ tablespoons flour (1 tablespoon plus 1½ teaspoons)
Yolks of 2 eggs, slightly beaten
1½ tablespoons melted butter
¾ cup milk
¼ cup vinegar

Boiled dressing was much used before mayonnaise was as common as it is now, particularly with potato salad and coleslaw.

Mix the salt, sugar, cayenne, and flour well. Stir in very slowly the beaten yolks, melted butter, milk, and vinegar. Heat over boiling water or over low heat in a heavy enameled saucepan, stirring constantly, till thickened. Strain and cool. Shred the cabbage very fine and soak in very cold water 1 hour. Drain, dry on a towel, and combine with the dressing. Toss, and let stand a half hour before serving.

Harriet Coe's Mustard Ring with Coleslaw

1 medium cabbage

MUSTARD RING

½ cup sugar
3 tablespoons dry mustard (I like to add 1 tablespoon Dijon as well)
1 teaspoon salt
1 envelope unflavored gelatine
¼ cup cold water
¾ cup wine vinegar
4 eggs, lightly beaten
1 cup heavy cream, whipped

BOILED DRESSING

⅓ cup sugar
1 teaspoon flour
⅔ cup vinegar
⅓ cup water
6 tablespoons butter
2 eggs, beaten
½ cup heavy cream, whipped

From *Cooked to Taste: The Junior League of Portland Cookery Book.* A delicious, different way to serve cabbage salad or slaw for a buffet party.

Make the mustard ring first. Mix the sugar, mustard, and salt. Soften the gelatine in the cold water, then melt over hot water. Combine with the vinegar, beaten eggs, and dry ingredients, and stir over hot water until thickened. Cool. Fold in the whipped cream and pour into a 6-cup ring mold rinsed in cold water. Chill.

For the dressing, mix the sugar and flour in the top of a double boiler and add the vinegar, water, and butter. Stir in the beaten eggs and cook, stirring, until thick and smooth. Cool. Fold in the whipped cream.

To assemble, shred the cabbage very fine and blend the dressing with it. Unmold the ring onto a serving dish and fill it with the coleslaw.

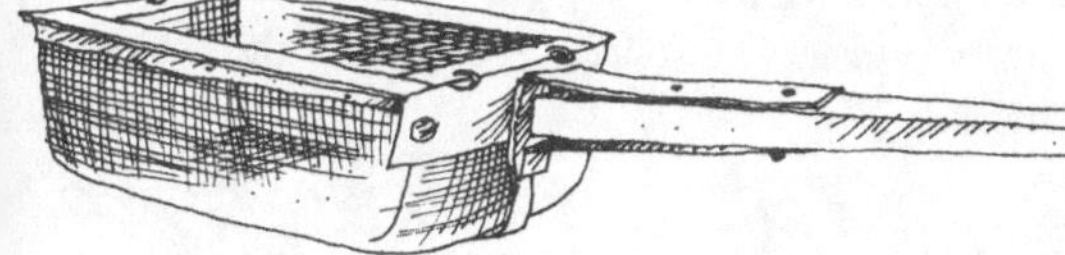

Billy's Coleslaw

½ cup olive oil
2 tablespoons flour
½ teaspoon salt
2 teaspoons dry mustard
Dash Tabasco
6 tablespoons sugar
½ cup wine vinegar
1 cup heavy cream mixed with 2 egg yolks
1 medium cabbage

This is a slaw on which I was brought up. Billy was a Chinese chef, a pal of my mother's chef Let, and his coleslaw was superb. He often mixed it with tiny shrimp, crabmeat, or bits of lobster, which made it entirely different but equally delicious.

Heat the oil in a heavy skillet or sauté pan, add the flour, and blend well. Add the salt, mustard, Tabasco, sugar, and vinegar, and stir until thickened. Combine some of the hot oil mixture with the egg-cream mixture, and then pour into the oil mixture. Stir until it thickens. Shred the cabbage very thin and combine with the hot dressing. Cool and chill several hours. If the dressing is too thick, mix with a little heavy cream or with a touch of mayonnaise.

Pepper Slaw

1 medium head of cabbage, chopped fine
1 medium onion, chopped fine
3 ribs of celery, chopped fine
2 green peppers, chopped fine
1 medium carrot, shredded

DRESSING

½ cup olive oil
1½ teaspoons salt
1 teaspoon freshly ground pepper
2 teaspoons celery seed
2 teaspoons mustard seed
2 tablespoons sugar
3 tablespoons vinegar
1 tablespoon Dijon mustard or 2 teaspoons dry mustard

Combine all the vegetables and blend in the dressing. Toss well and allow to mellow 2 or 3 hours. Toss again just before serving.

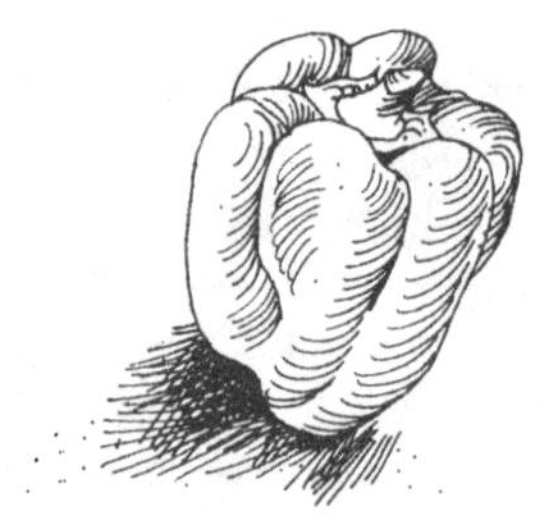

Sour Cream Slaw

3 tablespoons vinegar
1 teaspoon salt
1 teaspoon freshly ground pepper
2 tablespoons sugar
1 tablespoon or more chopped fresh dill
1 teaspoon dry mustard
1 cup sour cream
1 2-pound cabbage, shredded or chopped

This universal favorite has been played with and added to and subtracted from with success everywhere. The version given here I first encountered in Minnesota, but undoubtedly similar recipes can be found in many other states. For example, I have had this dish with 2 teaspoons freshly grated horseradish added to the dressing.

Combine all ingredients except the cabbage and blend thoroughly. Correct the seasoning and let stand in a cool place 1 or 2 hours. Toss with the cabbage and serve at once. Or toss with the cabbage before letting it stand.

Slaw with Egg Dressing

1 cabbage, about 3 pounds, shredded
6 hard-boiled eggs
6 tablespoons olive oil or peanut oil
1 teaspoon dry mustard
1 teaspoon salt
2 tablespoons vinegar
1 tablespoon chopped fresh dill or 1 teaspoon dry dillweed
2 tablespoons finely chopped onion or chives
2 tablespoons chopped parsley
½ cup sour cream
Additional chopped dill and parsley

I was first served this dish in southern California by a friend whose family migrated from Iowa. In all likelihood the recipe was transported along with other family treasures.

Separate the yolks from the egg whites. Chop the whites with some dill and parsley and reserve. Mash the yolks well with a fork and stir in the oil a little at a time until the mixture thickens slightly. Stir in the seasonings and lastly the sour cream. Correct the seasoning and toss with the cabbage. Sprinkle the herbed egg whites over the slaw and serve chilled.

Sauerkraut

Few people make sauerkraut in this age, but it used to be one of the more important domestic processes during the fall for the American household. This was especially true where there was the slightest German, Dutch, French, or Belgian ancestry. Many other nationalities, too, became fond of this dish and prepared it each year. Nowadays we do not have cellars suitable for storing kraut over the winter, and furthermore, such good sauerkraut can be bought — either in bulk or in cans and jars. However, in case you prefer to make your own, this is how it is done.

Homemade Sauerkraut

You will need a stone crock, hardwood keg, or barrel, all very clean, of course. The container also must be free from odors. Line it with clean cabbage leaves.

Sauerkraut requires fall cabbage that is very firm. Take off any ragged or tough leaves. Shred the cabbage quite fine (the old kitchens invariably had a "kraut board" or shredder for this). Weigh the cabbage, and for each 10 pounds cabbage use ½ cup pure pickling salt. Place a layer of salt in the container, then 2 or 3 layers of shredded cabbage, more salt, and so on. Leave several inches between the cabbage and the top of the container. Pound gently with a mallet, wooden potato masher, or the end of a clean two-by-four. Top with a layer of salt. Place a clean hardwood board or a plate over the top of the cabbage and weight down with a rock or perhaps a jar of water. Tie a clean muslin or several layers of cheesecloth over the top of the barrel or crock and store in a cool (45 to 55 degrees) place to ferment.

After several days, the brine will have risen above the board or plate and tiny bubbles will have appeared. There will also be a scum on top of the liquid. Skim this off every day or two; it will ruin the kraut if left. Continue to keep in a cool place until the small bubbles stop rising.

The kraut is now made, and a storage problem will present itself. The usual furnace-filled basement is much too warm for storing kraut, and it cannot be frozen successfully. Therefore it is best to can it. Transfer to regular vacuum-top canning jars, filling them with juice and kraut to within about a half inch of the top. Wipe the sealing edge, dip the little metal disk lids in boiling water, place on the top, and screw the metal bands down tight. Arrange on a rack in a deep kettle, cover with hot tap water, and put the lid on. Bring to a boil and boil very gently 35 minutes. Remove the jars from the water with as little jiggling as possible and set on a rack, board, or several layers of paper. Let cool 12 to 24 hours. They should now be sealed and will keep a long time.

Sauerkraut can also be made right in the canning jars. Tamp shredded cabbage lightly into the jars. Add 1 tablespoon (level) of pure pickling salt per quart jar. Fill with lukewarm tap water to within a half inch of the top of the jar, set the lid on lightly, and put the jar or jars in a moderately warm place to ferment. As soon as the kraut has fermented, wipe the sealing edge and put the rinsed lids on. Tighten the bands, and either process as above or keep for a short time in a cool, dry place before using.

Some people add caraway seeds to their kraut as they make it. Others add juniper berries or dill. Flavor to your taste. Serve with pork, sausages, ham, turkey, boiled dinners, duck, or any meat.

Sauerkraut Slaw

Fresh sauerkraut makes a delicious salad, similar in its way to a slaw.

For a simple sauerkraut slaw, rinse and drain 1½ pounds fresh sauerkraut or a 1-pound 11-ounce can of sauerkraut. Combine with a vinaigrette sauce, mayonnaise, or Thousand Island dressing to taste. Serve as you would coleslaw.

Cooked Sauerkraut Salad

To about 4 cups cooked sauerkraut add ½ cup finely chopped onion and mayonnaise to bind, or a combination of mayonnaise and sour cream. Toss well, and correct the seasoning. Serve with cold meats or poultry. Delicious with cold pork or cold turkey.

Sauerkraut Vinaigrette. Dress the sauerkraut with a good vinaigrette sauce. Garnish with tomato wedges.

4 cups sauerkraut, washed and dried
8 green onions, finely cut
4 tomatoes, peeled and cut into wedges
⅔ cup vinaigrette sauce
2 tablespoons finely chopped fresh dill
Several sprigs fresh dill

Combine the sauerkraut, green onions, and tomatoes and toss well with the vinaigrette and dill. Arrange in a salad dish and decorate with sprigs of fresh dill. Serve with fish or ham.

Red Cabbage

While red cabbage is thoroughly decorative, it does not have the versatility of the white. In fact, braising seems to be the best way to use it except for relishes and pickles.

Braised Red Cabbage with Red Wine

1 3-pound red cabbage
4 to 6 tablespoons bacon fat, goose fat, or butter
Salt and freshly ground pepper
1 cup red wine
2 very tart apples, cored and diced but not peeled
2 tablespoons brown sugar
1 tablespoon vinegar

Definitely German in origin, this has been a favorite dish across the country. It is often served with goose, wild duck, pork, or — when you can get it — wild boar.

Discard the outside leaves of the cabbage and cut it in half. Shred finely and soak in salted water a few minutes. Drain well. Melt the fat in a large skillet — heavy enameled iron or aluminum. Add the drained cabbage and toss well with two wooden spoons or spatulas as you would a salad. When it is beginning to wilt, add salt and pepper to taste and the red wine. Simmer 5 minutes. Add the apples. Sprinkle with the brown sugar and add the vinegar. Cover, and simmer until the apples and cabbage are tender and well blended. This should take about 1 hour at lowest heat.

Baked Red Cabbage

1 red cabbage, about 3 pounds, shredded and soaked
2 smallish onions, sliced
2 cooking apples, cored and diced

This is probably also German in origin, but is somewhat more exotic than the one above.

Prepare the cabbage. Butter a heavy 2½-quart casserole. Make alternate layers of the cabbage, onions, and apples, and season every three layers with salt and spices. Finally pour in the vinegar, orange juice, and wine mixed together. Cover, and bake at 325 degrees 2

1 teaspoon salt
¼ teaspoon cinnamon
¼ teaspoon nutmeg
⅛ teaspoon cloves
1 tablespoon vinegar
½ cup undiluted concentrated orange juice
¼ cup port or sherry
Butter

hours or more until the cabbage is very tender and the flavors have melded. Delicious with pork or duck.

Carrots

No one recorded the first carrot in the United States. But being what it is, almost a staple wherever it goes, it is safe to believe that it came within months of the first settlers. It remains one of our more important vegetable crops, if one takes into account all the raw carrot sticks served in restaurants and at cocktail parties and all the badly cooked carrots served up with peas. Generally unimaginative treatment has given the vegetable a very bad name which it certainly does not deserve.

Carrots are now an all-year crop. In earlier times it was a seasonal vegetable valued because it could be stored in the root cellar for winter use. The carrots so stored were pretty large and not as tender as the small young carrots one finds in the market today.

Carrots come bunched with their delicately feathery green tops — which, by the way, may be combined with other greens for cooking — or they come with the tops removed, packed in plastic bags. They should be firm, well shaped, and bright orange gold in color.

Bunches are supposed to weigh about 1 to 1½ pounds. This quantity will serve 2 or 3 persons. It is a good idea to buy extra, because carrots are always useful for seasoning, for salads, and for appetizer trays.

To Cook Carrots

If the carrots are young and smooth, they will need only a good scrubbing with a firm-bristled brush. If they are older, scrape them or peel them with a very sharp paring knife. They may be cut into dice, sliced across or diagonally, cut into julienne sticks, shredded, or left whole.

To steam-cook. Heat a very small amount of salted water in a heavy saucepan with a tight-fitting cover. Drop in the carrots, cover, and steam gently until tender. Shredded carrots will cook in 3 or 4 minutes; cut pieces in 10 to 12 minutes; and whole carrots in 15 to 18 minutes.

To steam in butter. This requires a heavy-duty pot with a tight-fitting lid. Melt enough butter in the pot to cover the bottom — about 4 to 8 tablespoons. Add the cleaned carrots, cover tightly, and steam over very slow heat till tender. Shake the pan several times to coat the carrots. Whole carrots will take about 20 minutes, and sliced, diced, or julienne carrots about 15 minutes. Be careful not to overcook.

Serve cooked carrots in any of the following ways.

(1) With melted butter and chopped parsley.

(2) With lemon juice, butter, salt, and freshly ground pepper. For 2 pounds carrots you will need 4 tablespoons butter, 2 tablespoons lemon juice, 1 teaspoon salt, and ½ teaspoon pepper.

(3) Carrots take agreeably to marjoram. Add 1 teaspoon to the cooking water. Before serving, add 4 to 6 tablespoons butter, a touch more marjoram, 1 teaspoon salt, and ½ teaspoon freshly ground pepper.

(4) Slice or dice the carrots and add 1½ cups rich cream sauce, to which you may add 1 tablespoon chopped parsley.

Mashed Carrots. For 2 pounds carrots, cooked and drained, add 6 tablespoons butter, 1 teaspoon salt, and ½ teaspoon freshly ground pepper, and mash with a potato masher. Or put them through a food mill and add the butter and seasonings later. Return the carrots to heat for just 2 or 3 minutes before you serve them.

Mashed Carrots and Potatoes. Follow directions above for mashed carrots and combine with an equal quantity of mashed potatoes. Garnish with chopped parsley. This was considered a delicious holiday treat with turkey.

Carrots and Peas

2 cups sliced or diced carrots, cooked according to the basic recipe
2 cups fresh or frozen peas, cooked according to the basic recipe
6 tablespoons butter
Salt
½ teaspoon freshly ground pepper

This is to be feared. It can be delicious only if the carrots are young, well drained, and nicely buttered, and the peas are fresh and perfectly cooked.

Cook the peas and the carrots separately. Drain, and combine with the butter, salt, and pepper. Shake the pan well and correct the seasoning. Both vegetables should taste fresh as the dawn and have no soupy juice about them.

Carrots with Dill

12 medium carrots
1 stick (½ cup) butter
1 teaspoon salt
½ teaspoon freshly ground pepper
1 tablespoon or more finely chopped fresh dill or 1½ teaspoons dry dillweed

This delicately flavored dish one finds in the sections where the Scandinavians or Poles have settled. It has also won favor among other groups.

Steam the carrots and drain well. Melt the butter in a skillet, and add the carrots and the seasonings. Shake the skillet several minutes to coat the carrots with butter and blend the flavors. Extremely good served with veal, chicken, or pork.

Glazed Carrots

12 carrots, left whole, cooked according to basic recipe
6 tablespoons butter
1 tablespoon honey
½ teaspoon freshly ground pepper
½ teaspoon salt

Cook the carrots and drain well. Combine with the butter and honey in a skillet or saucepan. Heat and roll them in the mixture to acquire an even glaze. Cook over medium heat, watching very carefully to prevent scorching, till the carrots are delicately glazed. You may add more honey to the pan if you like. It becomes an oversweet dish if you do, but that satisfies many palates.

Note. Many English and Scottish people add 1 tablespoon chopped mint to this mixture and a touch of lemon juice — about 1 tablespoon.

Variation. Proceed as above, but use 2 tablespoons granulated sugar instead of honey. Add 1 tablespoon lemon juice if you like.

Sautéed Carrots

6 to 8 carrots, scraped and cut in thin strips
6 tablespoons butter or more
Salt
½ teaspoon freshly ground pepper

These are popular in the South and are wonderful served with grilled meats or roasts.

Prepare the carrots and parboil them in salted water for just about 8 minutes — until they are only two-thirds cooked. Drain well. Heat one 12-inch or two 8-inch skillets. Add the butter, and when it is bubbly add the carrots. Sauté quickly over fairly high heat, tossing the pan well till the carrots are lightly browned and cooked through. Add additional salt if needed and freshly ground pepper.

Mrs. Rorer's Carrots in Turnip Cups

"Pare small, well-shaped white turnips. Cut slices from the stem end, and with a potato scoop, scoop out the flesh, leaving a cup. Throw these into salted boiling water and simmer for 20 minutes. Lift each one carefully with the skimmer and turn upside down to drain. While these are cooking, cut young carrots into dice, put them in a kettle of boiling water, and cook below the boiling point for 20 minutes; drain in a colander. Arrange the turnip cups while hot on a heated chop dish; add to the carrots ½ teaspoonful of salt, a saltspoonful of pepper, and ½ cup of good thick cream. Shake over the fire until hot and fill the turnip cups; garnish the dish with parsley and send at once to the table.

"This is an exceedingly sightly dish to serve in the spring at a small dinner or lunch."

Cauliflower

The legend goes that only one family of early Dutch settlers were given cauliflower seeds to take to the New World, which they planted on Long Island near Setauket. And from that original family monopoly presumably our great cauliflower industry sprang. Certainly the cauliflower is a favorite food of the Dutch, and we know that for years the finest cauliflower came from the Long Island acres, so there must be a word of truth in the legend.

However, this vegetable, which had an Oriental beginning, was first made a household delight by the Italians, who grow a purple-headed variety as well as the white. This is available in certain parts of the country, usually in the fall. It can be treated the same as white cauliflower.

Apart from the Italians, we have done more to develop cauliflower than most other people. We have learned the pleasure of the raw vegetable when given a sauce for dipping, and we discovered the secret of undercooking it. It's a long way from Miss Leslie's rule for boiling cauliflower for 2 hours to the latest advice, which recommends a maximum of 30 minutes.

Cauliflower heads should be firm and the flowerets fine and white or creamy white. The surrounding leaves should be fresh-looking and green. Look for heads that are heavy and tightly flowered rather than those with straggly flowerets. A large head will weigh around 3 pounds and will serve 4 persons well.

To Cook Cauliflower

Wash the cauliflower well. Remove the outer leaves and heavy stem, and remove any small bruised sections. Leave the cauliflower whole or break into flowerets.

Cauliflower is best steamed in about 1 inch of boiling salted water in a heavy covered saucepan. The flowerets will take 8 to 15 minuntes and the whole cauliflower from 20 to 30 minutes. The cauliflower should be just crisply tender when you serve it — the mushier it is, the more unpalatable it becomes. Drain it very thoroughly, and serve in any of the following ways.

Buttered Cauliflower. Return the drained cauliflower to the saucepan for a moment or two to dry out over very low heat. Arrange in a warmed serving dish and cover with ½ cup melted butter and freshly ground pepper to taste.

Cheesed Cauliflower. Cook the cauliflower whole, and drain and return to the saucepan as above. Force sticks of Gruyère cheese or Cheddar cheese into the head. Spread with softened butter and sprinkle with 1 teaspoon freshly ground pepper and 1 teaspoon paprika. Cover, and heat 2 minutes. Transfer to a serving dish and sprinkle with grated cheese.

Cauliflower with Black Butter. Drain and dry out as above. Place in a warmed serving dish. Add black butter to taste, and freshly ground pepper.

Cauliflower Mornay. Transfer cooked drained cauliflower flowerets to a shallow baking dish about 8 × 10 inches. Cover with ½ cup grated Cheddar cheese, 1½ cups rich cream sauce, then another ½ cup grated Cheddar. Top with ½ cup buttered crumbs. Heat in a 350-degree oven 15 minutes, or until the cauliflower is brown and bubbly.

Cauliflower Italian. Cook flowerets until just barely tender, drain, and return to the saucepan to dry out as above. Transfer to a heavy skillet in which you have heated ½ cup olive oil and 2 finely chopped garlic cloves. Toss the cauliflower in the mixture over medium heat till it is a delicate brown. Add ½ teaspoon freshly ground pepper and transfer to a heated serving dish. Sprinkle liberally with grated Parmesan cheese.

Herbed Cauliflower. Transfer a cooked, drained, whole cauliflower to a heated serving dish. Dress with ½ cup melted butter and sprinkle with ¼ cup each of chopped chives and parsley.

Cauliflower Parmesan. Transfer a cooked whole cauliflower to a round baking dish about 9 inches in diameter. Cover with ½ cup melted butter, 1 teaspoon freshly ground pepper, 1 cup buttered toasted breadcrumbs, and ¼ cup grated Parmesan cheese. Reheat 5 minutes in a 375-degree oven.

Cauliflower with Almonds or Walnuts. Place a cooked drained whole cauliflower or flowerets in a heated serving dish. Cover with ½ cup melted butter in which you have sautéed ½ cup sliced almonds till just delicately brown. Or instead of almonds use ½ cup finely chopped black walnuts.

Cauliflower Hollandaise. Transfer a cooked, drained, whole cauliflower or flowerets to a heated vegetable dish. Either spoon Hollandaise over the cauliflower and garnish with chopped parsley or sprinkle with chopped parsley and serve Hollandaise sauce separately.

Cauliflower à la Huntington. Miss Farmer recommends this dish in an early edition of her work. Essentially it is cooked drained cauliflower served with a Hollandaise made with olive oil to which a teaspoon of dry mustard and ½ teaspoon curry powder has been added. It is very good and somewhat unusual.

Puréed Cauliflower. Cook cauliflower flowerets somewhat more tender than usual. Drain well and put through a food mill. Mix well with ½ cup melted butter and 1 teaspoon freshly ground pepper and transfer to a heated serving dish. Dot with butter before serving.

Fried Puréed Cauliflower. Purée a cauliflower as in the previous recipe. Heat ½ cup olive oil in a large heavy skillet with 2 finely chopped garlic cloves. Form the cauliflower into a cake as compact as possible on a piece of foil and slide gently into the hot olive oil. Cook slowly to form a crust on the bottom. Turn it out on a large board covered with foil, place fresh oil in the skillet, and slide the cauliflower back to brown the uncooked side slowly. Sprinkle with ½ cup grated Parmesan cheese and serve from the skillet. No mean feat, this, but satisfactory when you achieve it.

Cauliflower with Shrimp

1 cauliflower, steamed as in basic recipe
1½ cups rich cream sauce
¼ teaspoon mace
1 tablespoon tomato paste
1 teaspoon paprika
1 tablespoon lemon juice
2 cups cooked shrimp, whole or coarsely chopped

An old Western recipe which has an unusual quality. The shrimp must be small ones — the tiny bay shrimp preferred.

Drain the cooked cauliflower and place in a heated round serving dish large enough to accommodate the sauce and the shrimp in addition. Prepare the cream sauce and add the seasonings. Add the shrimp and just heat through. Pour over the cauliflower and garnish with a few shrimp and some chopped parsley.

Note. If tiny shrimp are not available, use other shrimp coarsely chopped.

Celery

In earlier generations Americans served raw celery more often than is customary today. It was soaked, some of the tops were removed, some of the outer ribs were split, and it was served in a "celery glass," which closely resembles a flower vase — they are still used in France and in England. In the latter country celery is always served as an accompaniment to cheeses.

In our country celery glasses finally gave way to celery dishes to match the "dinner set," or there were celery dishes in cut glass. These held long stalks of celery or celery hearts and sometimes crushed ice to keep them crisp. Then came the day of the celery curl. Every woman's hidden sculptural talents went into cutting celery so that when dropped into ice water for an hour or two it would curl and bring as fancy a touch to dinner as one could imagine. It was the nineteenth-century and early twentieth-century housewife and hostess who performed the marriage of the olive and celery, and one was practically never seen without the other. One still finds "Celery and Olives" listed on the menu of many old-style restaurants.

Cooked celery has never been quite as popular, possibly because the usual "stewed celery" one is served in restaurants is merely a way to get rid of the outside ribs of the bunch. It is overcooked, strong in celery flavor, and altogether unpleasant. On the other hand, good braised celery, fried celery, and even celery with cheese sauce are quite acceptable dishes.

Incidentally, this is one of the few vegetables you can give great winebibbers, if you are serving remarkably good wines. Celery does not overwhelm the flavor of wine as such things as artichokes, asparagus, and endive are supposed to do.

There are two basic types of celery which we find in the markets nowadays. First and by far the most common is what is sometimes called Pascal celery. It has heavy green ribs, the bunches or stalks are large and full, and the leaves are green. The outer ribs are for dicing and cooking. The inner ribs, or the heart, may be eaten raw or used for braised celery. The second type, golden celery, is bleached; the ribs are white and the leaves yellow. It is very often sold as "hearts" in the market with only the center ribs and the root tied together in bunches of two or three stalks. These are delicious raw and may also be used for braising. For steam-cooking, estimate 1 bunch or stalk (2½ to 3 cups diced or julienne) for 4 persons. For braising, 1 stalk of the heart will make 2 portions.

To Steam-Cook Celery

Strip the leaves from the stalks, and if there are any strings remove them. Dice the celery or cut it in thin julienne strips about 2 to 3 inches long and about ½ inch wide. Pour about ¾ inch of salted water in a heavy saucepan which can be covered tightly. Bring to a steaming boil, and add the celery. Cover, and steam over medium heat 10 to 12 minutes, or until the celery is crisply tender. Celery is also excellent when cooked in chicken or beef broth instead of water.

Serve steamed and thoroughly drained celery in any of the following ways. Quantities are for 4 persons (2½ to 3 cups celery).

(1) Combine with 6 tablespoons melted butter and ½ teaspoon freshly ground pepper. A tablespoon of lemon juice is a welcome addition.

(2) Combine with 1½ cups rich cream sauce and ½ cup buttered toasted crumbs.

(3) Combine with 6 tablespoons melted butter and ½ cup dry roasted peanuts. An old favorite in the South.

(4) Combine with 4 tablespoons oil, 2 tablespoons vinegar, and ½ teaspoon freshly ground pepper. Toss like a salad and serve hot. Add a clove of garlic if you like.

Braised Celery I

3 celery hearts
1½ cups rich chicken or beef broth
1 stick (½ cup) butter
1 teaspoon salt
½ teaspoon freshly ground pepper

Trim the celery hearts, leaving a little of the root on to hold them together. Cut in half. Each half should be about 5 inches long and fairly thick. Poach in the broth in a heavy skillet, covered, till crisply tender. Drain. Reserve the broth for other dishes if you like. Melt the butter in a heavy skillet and braise the celery hearts to brown them lightly. Turn them once or twice. Add the salt and pepper. Arrange on a serving dish and pour butter over them. If you like, sprinkle them with either chopped parsley or grated Parmesan cheese. This is perfectly fine served with chicken, game, or a leg of lamb.

Variation. Use 1 cup white wine instead of broth. Steam the celery, tightly covered, till just tender. Continue as above.

Celery Ring

1 cup dry whole wheat breadcrumbs
1½ cups ground raw celery
¼ bunch parsley, chopped
¾ cup ground roasted peanuts (dry roasted are best)
1 small onion, ground
½ small sweet green pepper, seeded and ground
3 eggs, beaten
3 tablespoons melted butter
1 teaspoon salt
1½ cups milk

The Outing Club in Davenport, Iowa, has been in existence for many years and is a center for the town's social life. This recipe has been a favorite there for luncheons for over fifty years. It's a good dish and is especially pleasant when the ring is filled with sautéed sweetbreads and mushroom sauce, or with creamed fish. It can also be served as a vegetable course filled with a purée of chestnuts or with buttered peas.

Combine the ingredients and let stand about 20 minutes. (The grinding is easier if the celery, pepper, onion, and peanuts are ground all at one time.) Turn into a well-greased 2-quart ring mold and bake in a 350-degree oven 45 to 60 minutes, or until firm when touched lightly in the center. Remove from the oven and let stand a few minutes. Loosen in the pan and invert onto a hot platter.

Sautéed Celery

Cook the celery in julienne strips. Dry thoroughly after draining, and dredge with flour. Fry a few at a time in a heavy skillet in which you have melted 6 tablespoons butter and 4 tablespoons oil. Add salt and freshly ground pepper as you fry them. Drain on absorbent paper. This is another oldish Southern recipe.

Celery Root, Celery Knob, Celery Rave, Celeriac

Celery root, unlike celery, is grown for the root and the root alone. It came into use in this country later than celery and is still not widely known. Yet it is a versatile vegetable, useful in salads both raw and cooked, and it lends itself to combination with various other vegetables, notably potatoes. The bulbs are large and are usually covered with a collection of little roots. Not pretty by any means, it is a delightful change from other vegetables. Estimate 1½ to 2 pounds celery root for 4 persons.

To Cook Celery Root

Cut off the straggling bits of root and the tops and wash well. Unless otherwise directed in a recipe, do not peel. Cover with boiling salted water and cook, covered, from 40 to 60 minutes, or until quite tender. Drain, peel, and either slice or dice as the recipe indicates. Peel just before using, or the vegetable turns dark.

Sautéed Celery Root. Peel and slice the cooked drained celery root and toss into a skillet in which you have melted 6 tablespoons butter. Add salt to taste and ½ teaspoon freshly ground pepper. Sauté gently 4 minutes, turning it often. Transfer to a heated serving dish and sprinkle with chopped chives or chopped parsley.

Celery Root Hollandaise. Peel and dice the cooked drained celery root and transfer to a heated serving dish. Spoon over it a mustard Hollandaise and serve at once.

Mashed Celery Root and Potatoes. Peel and mash cooked drained celery root very well or put through a food mill. Return to the saucepan with 6 tablespoons butter, and combine with an equal quantity of seasoned mashed potatoes (about 1½ cups of each). Blend well and correct the seasoning. Serve in a heated vegetable dish, and top with a piece of butter.

Scalloped Potatoes and Celery Root

2 good-sized celery root, peeled and thinly sliced (raw)
4 or 5 potatoes, peeled and sliced
1 teaspoon salt

This is purely a Pacific Northwest dish, which I remember from my childhood. We never really liked scalloped potatoes in the classic style, and when celery root was at its peak we often had this combination instead.

There is a remarkable dish similar to this in the Savoie in France. It uses slices of a delicious smoked sausage and adds a great deal more cheese. The Gruyère of the Savoie, of course. This makes a pretty remarkable dish.

½ teaspoon freshly ground pepper
Water
1 to 1½ cups beef broth or consommé
1 cup grated Switzerland Emmenthaler cheese

Butter a baking dish — round, oval, or oblong — about 9 × 12 inches. Lay a layer of sliced celery root in the bottom. Dot this with butter and give it a dash of salt and another layer of thinly sliced potatoes. Alternate until you have a top layer of potatoes. Dot with butter and add a cup to 1½ cups broth or bouillon. Cover the pan and place in a 350-degree oven for 45 minutes. Remove the cover and test for doneness. If the potatoes and celery root are tender, add 1 cup grated cheese and return to the oven uncovered and let the mixture cook another 10 to 15 minutes. If they need more cooking before adding the cheese, return them to the oven uncovered and add the grated cheese when the vegetables are tender.

Note. You may add heavy cream to this dish instead of the broth if you wish. That makes something pretty rich but altogether delightful to the palate.

Chestnuts

We used to have quantities of chestnuts in this country, and they were a valuable crop for our forebears, who learned to store them in sand to keep out mold. Over the winter months they were combined with many different ingredients.

However, a great blight hit our chestnut trees, and now we have comparatively few of them. Chestnuts in the market come from Europe and the Orient. We also have, from France, canned chestnuts in syrup or in brine, which saves the labor of peeling and preparing them. In addition, there are skinned dried chestnuts from Italy. These need soaking, like dried beans or peas, and then boiling.

The chestnut has a distinctive flavor not found in any other nut, and it is unique in being used both as a vegetable and in desserts.

To Cook Chestnuts in Their Shells

Split the shell crosswise on the flat side with a very sharp knife. Toss the chestnuts into boiling water and boil 5 minutes after the water returns to a boil. Drain, and remove the shell and the skin. Boil another 20 minutes in salted water. The chestnuts should then be ready for a purée or for other uses.

Chestnuts with Other Vegetables

Whole chestnuts, prepared as in the basic recipe, then heated and buttered well — about 4 tablespoons butter per pound (unshelled) — may be combined with cooked Brussels sprouts, mushrooms, or tiny white onions.

Chestnut Purée

1 pound unshelled chestnuts or 1 can chestnuts in brine
4 tablespoons butter
½ teaspoon salt
¼ teaspoon nutmeg
6 tablespoons heavy cream

As this is very rich, it is served primarily as a garniture.

Prepare raw chestnuts as above, or, if using canned chestnuts, wash and drain them. Force the chestnuts through a food mill or a china cap. Combine with the other ingredients and heat thoroughly. Whip with a wooden spatula or a whisk and correct the seasoning. If you do not feel they are rich enough, add more heavy cream.

Corn

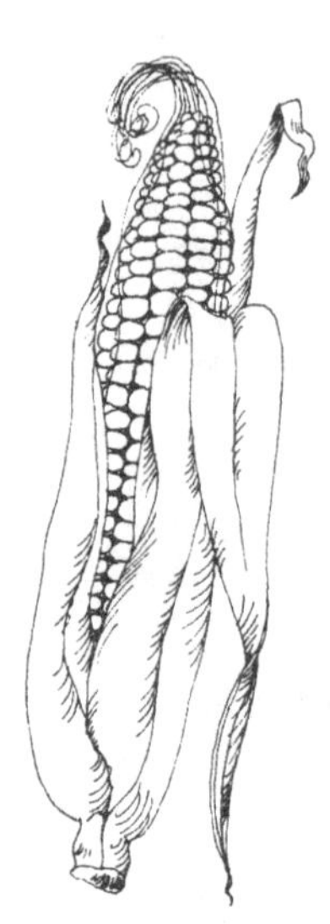

Corn has been an invaluable food throughout the history of this country. It was the crop (along with the bean) that saved the Massachusetts Bay Colony; the South adopted it to the point of almost erasing wheat from their menus; and in the settling of the Southwest it became the mainstay, as it had been in Mexico and Central America.

In early cookbooks corn is mentioned in the making of hominy, samp, breads, and puddings, but apart from clambakes, there is little record of the American custom of eating corn on the cob. We must take it for granted that this was done in season. Occasionally the term "roasting ears" turns up, which indicates that perhaps corn was roasted in front of the fire in its husks after the silk had been removed.

I remember the times when yellow Bantam corn was the first of the season and people looked forward to fall with great appetite for the Shoe Peg and Country Gentleman corn, which were supposed to be so much better. In the case of Shoe Peg, few varieties have outdone it for sheer tenderness and sweetness. Nowadays the season for corn is year-long. Recent experimentation has developed choice strains of sweet corn for the commercial market that are cut and instantly chilled to hold all the starch and sugar. Thus it can be transported with less deterioration. It is a notable improvement over the days when corn had to be cut and rushed to the kitchen pot if it was to be sweet at all.

Here are two early recipes for corn.

Mrs. Harland's Corn on the Cob

"Strip off the outer husks. Turn down the innermost covering, and pull off the silk with great care. Re-cover the ear with the thin inner husk; tie at the top with a bit of thread and cook in salted water from 25 to 30 minutes; cut off the stalks close to the cob, and send the corn to the table wrapped in a napkin."

The Home Messenger's Corn

"Cut the center kernels through lengthwise with a sharp knife; scrape the inside out with the back of a knife; pour over and boil with a very little water. After cooking 10 minutes add milk, salt, a very little sugar and plenty of butter, and let boil gently for 5 to 10 minutes."

Both this and Mrs. Harland's recipe seem so foreign to our method of cooking corn nowadays. Here are two accepted modern rules which seem to be the best at this writing.

To Cook Corn

Naturally the corn should be well filled and plump and the kernels milky when tested with the fingernail. The husks should look fresh and green. Keep it refrigerated till working time, and just before cooking, remove the husks and the silk. Do not cook more than will be eaten at one time. It is best to cook it in two or three batches and have it freshly done. Use either method below.

(1) Cook the corn, covered, in unsalted boiling water to cover for 3 to 5 minutes. Remove and serve at once with butter, freshly ground pepper, and salt.

(2) Put the corn in cold water in a skillet or shallow pan. Bring to a boil over rather high heat and remove when it reaches a rolling boil. Serve at once with butter, freshly ground pepper, and salt.

Sautéed Corn

8 ears of corn
8 tablespoons butter
1 teaspoon freshly ground pepper
1 teaspoon salt

A popular way of serving corn for people who are not prone to eat it from the cob.

Husk the corn and remove the silk. With a very sharp knife, cut the corn from the ears and scrape all the milk and sugar from the cob. Have the butter melted and bubbling when you have cut the last ear. Place the kernels in the pan and sauté gently over medium heat about 4 minutes, or until just cooked through. Shake the pan several times so the corn will not stick. Add the pepper, and at the very last minute, just as you are spooning the corn into a heated serving dish, add the salt.

Variations

(1) Just as the corn is about half done, add ½ cup heavy cream and heat thoroughly.

(2) Sauté 1 medium-size green pepper, cut in fine julienne strips, in 2 tablespoons butter till soft and tender. Combine with the corn just as it is cooked.

Corn Oysters

12 ears of corn
3 tablespoons heavy cream
2 tablespoons sifted flour
1 tablespoon melted butter
1 egg, well beaten

These delicate morsels are simply corn kernels with enough batter to hold them together. If properly made, they are as excellent a dish as there is to serve with chicken or veal. At one time they were served for tea with maple syrup, but the syrup ruins the delicacy of the flavor.

Remove the husks and silk from the corn. Scrape the corn from cob: With a sharp knife cut lengthwise down the center of each row of kernels, then scrape down with the back of a knife to push the meat out of the kernels. Combine the corn, cream, and flour, and add the melted butter and beaten egg. Blend thoroughly. Drop by spoonfuls on a well-buttered griddle or a heavy skillet over medium heat and cook till delicately browned on both sides. Serve at once with chicken, veal or bacon.

Corn Pudding

2 eggs
1 teaspoon salt
½ teaspoon freshly ground pepper
1 tablespoon grated onion
1 teaspoon sugar
2 tablespoons butter
2 cups milk
1 can (1 pound) cream-style corn

This recipe for corn pudding, one of many versions, is from a family who have lived in Florida for generations. It uses canned cream-style corn, which many people favor for the pudding.

Beat the eggs with the seasonings. Heat the butter and milk, and fold into the egg mixture. Add the corn and mix thoroughly. Pour into a shallow 1½-quart baking dish, set in a pan of water, and bake at 325 degrees about 1 hour, or until just set. Serve from the baking dish.

Another Corn Pudding

8 ears of corn
3 eggs
1½ cups milk
2 teaspoons sugar
1 tablespoon melted butter
1 teaspoon salt
1 teaspoon freshly ground pepper
¼ teaspoon Tabasco
6 slices bacon

This one comes from the Middle West — the corn belt — and is made with fresh corn.

Carefully cut the corn from the ears with a sharp knife and scrape all the milk and sugar from the cob. Beat the eggs quite well and add the milk, sugar, butter, and seasonings. Combine with the corn and pour into a 1½-quart greased flat baking dish. Carefully lay the strips of bacon atop the corn pudding. Bake at 350 degrees 45 to 50 minutes, or until the pudding seems just firm to the touch.

Southwestern Baked Corn

1 large onion, finely chopped
4 tablespoons melted butter
2 peeled green chilies, finely chopped
2 cups finely chopped peeled and seeded tomatoes
1 tablespoon chili powder
1 teaspoon salt
6 ears of corn
1 cup grated or shredded jack cheese

Sauté the onion in butter till just limp. Add the chilies and the tomatoes, and simmer 15 minutes. Add the seasonings. Cut the corn from the cobs and scrape off all the milk and starch. Add to the tomato-onion mixture, pour into a 1½-quart greased baking dish, and bake about 45 minutes at 350 degrees. Ten minutes before it is done add the jack cheese and allow it to melt and brown.

Cucumbers

While cucumbers were raised primarily for salads and pickles, there was usually such a plethora that people became interested in cooking them. European immigrants remembered fried ripe cucumber, and the Japanese brought the idea of steaming little lozenges of cucumber to serve with fish. Cooked cucumbers are fresh-tasting and a delightful change from the run of vegetables. Also, in many made dishes they may be substituted for zucchini when necessary.

To Cook Cucumbers

You will want 2 or 3 cucumbers of average size for 4 persons.

To steam. Peel the cucumbers, split them the long way, and remove the seeds. (A teaspoon with a rather rounded bowl is ideal for scraping out the seeds.) Cut the cucumbers into lozenge shapes, using the discard for sandwiches. Cook in a very small amount of boiling salted water for just a few minutes, till they turn a translucent shade of pale jade. Drain them at once and serve with butter and a grind or two of pepper. These are a welcome addition to the vegetable repertoire and are especially good with grilled salmon or other fish.

To sauté. Unless the skin is very thick and heavy or waxed do not peel the cucumbers. Remove the ends, cut in ¼-inch slices, and soak in ice water 2 hours. Dry thoroughly. For 3 cucumbers melt 3 tablespoons butter and 3 tablespoons oil in a heavy skillet. Dip the cucumbers in flour and sauté at medium heat till they are pleasantly brown on both sides. Sprinkle with salt and freshly ground pepper. Transfer to a heated serving dish and serve with Hollandaise sauce or lemon butter.

Dandelions

Among the first harbingers of spring are the tender shoots of dandelions. They appear early enough to tempt one's longing for fresh greens. In early times they satisfied the craving for green food that the winter denied, and they became as welcome in the vegetable world as young rhubarb was on the dessert table. Dandelions should be eaten before they blossom lest they become quite bitter. Use only the tenderest leaves, and if possible gather those that grow in the deepest grass rather than those on well-cared-for lawns. So popular are dandelions that they are also raised as a commercial crop, and like most other greens are available in markets throughout the country for a large part of the year. As a consequence they dc not have quite the same seasonal meaning that they once carried. The roots of the dandelion plant are also edible and resemble salsify in some ways.

Dandelion Greens with Bacon Dressing I

½ pound bacon cut in ¼ inch slices
2 or 3 garlic cloves, finely chopped
½ cup coarsely chopped fresh mint
2 to 3 tablespoons red wine vinegar
1 quart dandelion greens
Salt and freshly ground pepper

This I remember from childhood when our vegetable man, who toured the neighborhood, shared a recipe with my mother. It was a spring staple in the Galuzzo family and startlingly delicious.

Cut the bacon slices into ½-inch bits and sauté with the garlic. Add the mint, wine vinegar, and greens, and toss as you would a salad till they are wilted. Taste for seasoning, and add salt and pepper to taste. Add more wine vinegar if needed.

Dandelion Greens with Bacon Dressing II

4 egg yolks
¼ cup vinegar
¼ cup water
2 tablespoons sugar
1 teaspoon salt
2 teaspoons dry mustard
½ cup sour cream
½ cup crisp bacon bits
½ cup shredded spring onions
1 quart cleaned dandelion greens, broken into pieces

This version is rather typical of early dandelion recipes.

Combine the egg yolks, vinegar, water, sugar, salt, and mustard in the upper part of a double boiler. Cook over hot water, stirring constantly, until the mixture coats the spoon and becomes thick. Cool slightly and beat in the sour cream. Pour over the greens with the bacon and onions and toss well. Garnish with hard-boiled egg.

Eggplant

This magnificent purple vegetable was originally Oriental. Thus it has many, many uses in Oriental and Near Eastern cookery. Some extraordinarily good dishes have sprung from Lebanon, Syria, Greece, and elsewhere on the Mediterranean coast — Italy, Provence, Spain. It is quite probable that the Spanish, Portuguese, or Italians first introduced it into the United States, where it has had what I would call fair acceptance. One reason it is not more popular is that we grow, for the most part, only the large eggplant, which can be rather coarse of seed and flavor. The tiny ones, which one finds only in Italian or Near Eastern markets, seem to have a more delicate flavor and a finer texture.

I grew up in an era when there was an old wives' tale that cautioned one to soak eggplant in salted water and weight it down before cooking. This is unnecessary. Nor is it necessary, unless it is bruised, blemished or waxed, to peel an eggplant before cooking.

Since eggplant is a vegetable used mostly by immigrants in their traditional dishes, most of the recipes we have for it are American adaptations of foreign cookery. We have developed three or four rather interesting ways of preparing it, but it is the combination with olives, oil, tomatoes, anchovies, and other delicious additives that produces our most succulent eggplant dishes.

Miss Leslie warned of the bitter flavor of eggplant and advised people to cook it long and well. She also added that it was sometimes eaten at dinner but as a general rule should be served at breakfast.

One large (1½ to 2 pounds) eggplant will serve 4 persons. Four or five of the smaller ones, or more, depending on size, will serve the same number. Eggplant should be firm, with a shiny, smooth purple skin. As mentioned above, they need not be peeled or soaked before cooking.

Sautéed Eggplant I

Slice the eggplant in ½ to 1 inch slices. Peel it or not according to your taste. Dust the slices with flour. Heat 4 tablespoons butter and 3 tablespoons olive oil — or use all olive oil — in a heavy skillet. Sauté the eggplant slices slowly in the heated fat till nicely browned on one side. Turn, and sauté on the other side. Sauté a few slices at a time, adding more fat when necessary. Crowding the pan will give you poor results. Season with salt and freshly ground pepper. As they are cooked, transfer the slices to a heated serving dish and keep warm in the oven or atop the stove till the rest of the slices are done.

Sautéed Eggplant II

Prepare 2 cups dry breadcrumbs. Beat 2 eggs with 3 tablespoons heavy cream. Have a plate of flour ready. Heat 6 tablespoons olive oil in a heavy skillet. Slice the eggplant as in above recipe, and dip the slices in flour, then in beaten egg, and then in crumbs. Sauté in the olive oil till nicely browned on one side, and continue as above.

Broiled Eggplant

This, I think, is a purely American innovation, for it has become common practice with the outdoor cook. Merely brush thick slices of eggplant well with olive oil, season with salt, freshly ground pepper, and garlic, and place in a hinged broiling rack. Broil over coals or in the broiling oven, brushing with oil from time to time.

This is often used as a base for broiled hamburgers or lamburgers, served with a tomato sauce, which makes an attractive and unusual version of these broiled meats.

Eggplant in Foil

This may be cooked over the grill, in the broiler, or in the oven at 375 degrees. It is an outdoor cook's invention and is simple and very good. Peel eggplant, cut in wedges, and place on squares of foil with a slice of onion, a bit of garlic, and a half tomato. Sprinkle with freshly ground pepper and salt, and add a leaf of fresh basil. Fold the foil like an envelope and cook on the broiler, turning several times, for 20 minutes. Or cook in the broiling oven or in the oven for the same length of time.

Eggplant Parmigiana

2 medium eggplant, sliced
2 chopped garlic cloves
Olive oil
1 pound mozzarella cheese
1½ cups or more tomato sauce
¾ cup grated Parmesan cheese
Salt and freshly ground pepper

By far the most popular of all eggplant dishes in the United States, introduced by the Neapolitans. The version now served in most Italian restaurants is not to be found in Italy, for it is gauged to the American taste.

Sauté the eggplant slices in oil as in the basic recipe, adding the finely chopped garlic cloves. Arrange in layers with alternating layers of sliced mozzarella cheese in a 9 × 12-inch oval baking dish or a round baking dish about 10 inches in diameter. Spread each layer with a little tomato sauce and cover the entire top with tomato sauce. Sprinkle liberally with grated Parmesan. Add salt and pepper to taste, and bake at 350 degrees 20 to 25 minutes. Serve bubbling hot or it becomes a leaden mass.

An Eggplant Casserole

1 large eggplant cut in ½-inch slices
1 large onion or 2 medium, thinly sliced

This also had a Mediterranean origin. It is very good and works nicely as an accompaniment to outdoor foods in summer. It will hold, and seems to become richer as it stands.

Oil a 2½ quart casserole well. Sauté the eggplant slices according to the basic recipe. Salt and pepper them to taste. Sauté the onion and garlic in olive oil till just limp. Arrange layers of eggplant, onion, tomatoes, and chopped pepper in the casserole. Season the layers with salt, pepper, and basil. Cover the casserole and bake at 300 degrees 1 hour. Top with the crumbs and bake uncovered another 30 minutes. Add the Parmesan cheese. Serve with grilled meats or poultry or with roast lamb.

1 clove garlic
¼ cup olive oil
1½ cups cooked tomatoes or canned Italian plum tomatoes
1 green pepper, finely chopped
1 teaspoon salt
Freshly ground pepper
1 tablespoon fresh basil, chopped, or 1 teaspoon dried basil
½ cup toasted breadcrumbs
½ cup grated Parmesan cheese

An Old Southern Version of Eggplant

Butter
8 1-inch slices of eggplant sautéed as above, but not quite cooked through
Salt and freshly ground pepper
¾ cup heavy cream
1½ cups coarsely chopped pecans

Butter a baking dish large enough to hold the eggplant (or two dishes if necessary) and transfer the nearly cooked slices to it. Put 1½ tablespoons heavy cream on each slice. Sprinkle liberally with pecans. Dot with butter. Bake at 375 degrees 10 minutes, or until the butter is melted and the nuts slightly toasted. Serve with fried chicken or with veal. This also makes an interesting luncheon dish served with a salad.

Ratatouille

½ cup olive oil
1 large onion, sliced
2 cloves garlic, chopped
1 or 2 green peppers, seeded and cut in thin strips
1 large eggplant, diced
4 small zucchini cut in ¼-inch slices
8 to 10 very ripe tomatoes, peeled, seeded, and chopped, or 2 cups canned Italian plum tomatoes
1 teaspoon basil
1½ teaspoons salt
1 teaspoon freshly ground pepper

Ratatouille came from Provence in the '40's. Few dishes have gained such popularity in the United States.

Sauté the onion and garlic in the oil in a deep saucepan or kettle. When the onion is just transparent, add the peppers, eggplant, and zucchini, and blend well. Reduce the heat, cover the pan, and let it cook down 7 or 8 minutes or until the eggplant is beginning to soften. Add the tomatoes and seasonings and continue simmering, covered, for 10 minutes. Remove the cover and let the mixture cook down, stirring it often so it will blend. The vegetables should remain somewhat intact while the whole is well mixed and blended. Correct the seasoning. Serve very hot, or serve cold with lemon juice or vinegar and additional oil. The dish may be made the day before and reheated, or served cold with olive oil.

Note. Sometimes mushrooms or fennel are added to ratatouille. The fennel, cut in thin slices like celery, gives it delightful flavor.

Caponata

2 medium onions, sliced
2 ribs celery, thinly sliced
½ cup olive oil
3 or 4 small eggplant, unpeeled and cut in strips, or a 1½-pound eggplant, unpeeled and cut in dice
8 tomatoes, peeled, seeded, and chopped, or 1½ cups Italian plum tomatoes
1½ teaspoons salt
1 teaspoon freshly ground pepper
1½ teaspoons dry basil or 2 tablespoons chopped fresh basil
2 tablespoons tomato paste
½ cup capers
1 cup pitted soft olives — the Italian or Greek variety
1 lemon, thinly sliced

Caponata is served cold as an hors d'oeuvre. However, it has also become a relish to eat with cold meats. It is Italian in origin.

Sauté the onions and celery in the oil till just golden in color. Add the eggplant and toss well. Shake the pan several times to blend the vegetables. Add the tomatoes and cook down, uncovered. Do not overcook, for each vegetable should retain its own personality. Add the seasonings and cook 10 minutes. While it is cooking stir in the tomato paste. Add the capers and olives. Correct the seasonings and chill for a day or two before serving. Serve with lemon slices, and some chopped parsley and quartered tomatoes if you like. It will keep, covered, for a week or so in the refrigerator.

Baked Stuffed Eggplant

2 small eggplant
Olive oil
3 cloves garlic, finely chopped
2 cups croutons or diced bread
20 to 24 anchovy fillets
20 black Italian or Greek olives, pitted and chopped
2 tablespoons capers
1 teaspoon freshly ground pepper
1 tablespoon grated lemon rind
2 tablespoons lemon juice
Salt to taste
1 cup broth or water mixed with a bouillon cube

Another importation from the Mediterranean, which makes a delightful first course or luncheon dish.

Split the eggplant in half. Scoop out the meat, leaving enough on the skin to hold the eggplant together when you bake it. Chop the meat rather fine and sauté it in 4 tablespoons olive oil with 2 of the finely chopped garlic cloves. In another skillet sauté the bread in 4 tablespoons oil with the third garlic clove till the bread is crisp and brown. Chop the anchovies rather fine, combine with the eggplant and the croutons. Add the olives and capers. Season to taste. Add the lemon rind and juice. Stuff the eggplant halves with the mixture and brush with olive oil. Place the halves in a 9 × 12-inch baking dish with 1 cup broth and bake at 350 degrees 40 minutes. Serve at once.

New England Stuffed Eggplant

2 small eggplant
1 pound mushrooms

Split the eggplant and scoop out the meat. Chop the mushrooms quite fine. Peel and chop the onion. Sauté the mushrooms, onion, and chopped eggplant meat in the butter till the onion is melted, the mushrooms are just cooked, and the eggplant is softened.

Season to taste. Mix with the cold meat and stuff the eggplant. Cover with the breadcrumbs. Dot with additional butter. Arrange in a baking dish with the broth or water. Bake at 375 degrees 45 minutes. Serve with a tomato sauce.

1 onion, finely chopped
6 tablespoons butter
1 teaspoon salt
Freshly ground pepper
Pinch of nutmeg
1 cup cold minced veal or pork
1½ cups breadcrumbs, buttered
Additional butter
1 cup broth or water

Greens

All of the greens — mustard greens, turnip greens, kale, collards, chard, escarole, chicory, and so on — have a place in our cuisine. The Chinese and Italians among our population favor the pungent, delicate flavor of mustard greens. Turnip greens are a favorite in the South. Kale is hardy and tough, but a welcome addition to the diet in winter. Chard has tender leaves, and its stalks can be cooked like asparagus. Escarole and chicory are basically salad greens but are delicious when braised with oil and garlic.

In addition to these there are the weeds — dandelion, pigweed, and dock — all of which were in the diet of early settlers and cross-country travelers. Incredibly enough, there are few written recipes for such greens. People apparently knew how to prepare them instinctively. And what they did, according to our standards today, was entirely wrong. On the evidence of what recipes we have, the greens were cooked with ham hocks, salt pork, or bacon for two to three hours. At this point, it can be imagined, they were limp, greasy, and overwhelmed by the smoked pork flavor. We have now discovered that they need far less cooking — more a matter of minutes than of hours.

To Cook Greens

Wash greens with several waters, dry them, and wash again. Discard any brown or faded leaves. What water remains on the greens after the washing is enough for their cooking.

Cook greens in a heavy saucepan with a tight-fitting cover. Place in the pan with salt and cover the pan. Let them wilt over medium heat. This will take approximately:

For escarole, chicory, and lettuce leaves, 15 to 18 minutes.

For mustard greens and Swiss chard without the stems, 15 to 18 minutes.

For collards, 10 to 15 minutes.

For turnip greens and kale, 15 to 25 minutes.

When the greens are cooked, drain them well, and chop them if you like. Dress with melted butter — ¼ cup for each 2 pounds greens — or with crisp bacon cracklings and bacon fat — 4 slices cut in small pieces for 2 pounds greens. Serve with lemon wedges or with a cruet of vinegar.

An Old Southern Recipe for Greens

1 pound each dandelions, collard greens, and mustard greens, washed and left quite damp
1 tablespoon salt
1 cup chopped cooked ham bits with some fat
Pinch of nutmeg
1 tablespoon lemon juice or vinegar
1 cup chopped green onions

Combine the wet greens, salt, and cooked ham in a heavy saucepan. Steam until the greens are wilted, tossing from time to time. Reduce the heat and cook until just tender. Add the nutmeg, lemon juice or vinegar, and green onions. Toss again and serve at once with baked ham or with roast pork.

Braised Mustard Greens or Escarole

2 pounds escarole or mustard greens
6 tablespoons olive oil
1 clove garlic, finely chopped
1 teaspoon salt
Water if needed
1 teaspoon freshly ground pepper

Wash the greens well and pick over. Heat the olive oil in a deep saucepan and add the garlic and greens. Cover, and steam 20 to 25 minutes. Add some water if needed, but none should be needed. Add the salt and pepper. Dish up the greens and serve very hot. Serve with lemon juice or vinegar.

Braised Lettuce. You may braise the outside leaves of lettuce or cook the hearts or, in the case of Bibb, Boston, or romaine (Cos) lettuce, a whole head. Cook and serve in the same way as braised celery or as braised mustard greens above. It makes an excellent accompaniment to chicken or creamed dishes and is a suitably bland vegetable to serve with fine wines.

Kohlrabi

This is rather a bastard vegetable. It is neither turnip nor cabbage and is seldom as tender and crisp as it should be. To me it is a mystery why people really care for it. But they seem to, and it is in the markets all the time and has been for generations, although it was not among the earliest vegetables produced here. Mrs. Rorer felt that kohlrabi was more nutritious than turnips and that it was pleasant served with Hollandaise sauce.

To Cook Kohlrabi

Choose medium-size kohlrabi and gauge one per person. Remove the leaves. Peel, and slice rather thin.

Steam-cook in a very small amount of salted water in a saucepan with a tight-fitting lid. Add the vegetables when the water comes to a steaming boil, and cook gently 25 minutes. Drain, and dress with melted butter — 2 tablespoons for each kohlrabi — and salt and freshly ground pepper to taste. Or serve with a rich cream sauce — 1½ cups for 4 kohlrabi.

Leeks

Called in France the asparagus of the poor, the leek has been more popular here in recent years than it was in the nineteenth century. Mrs. Crowen says it is mainly for soup making. Miss Leslie doesn't even mention it, nor does Mrs. Harland, and most other cookbook writers neglect it as well. This is puzzling, for it is a hardy and quite versatile vegetable.

In the early part of the twentieth century, Louis Diat, at that time chef at the Ritz Carlton in New York, created his cold Vichyssoise soup based on the classic leek and potato soup of his native France. Immediately leeks went up in price, and people began serving them. Nowadays they are expensive and much in demand by more sophisticated cooks.

Leeks come by the bunch or are sometimes sold separately. They hold dirt in between the layers of leaves and are sometimes exceedingly difficult to clean. Cut them to within an inch of the white section. Soak in acidulated water, and run water on them to loosen dirt. Occasionally it is necessary to cut the leeks in half to get all the dirt out of them. Two leeks per person usually make a fair portion.

To Cook Leeks

Steam the leeks in a small amount of boiling salted water until just tender — this will take around 15 minutes. Drain well. Treat cooked and drained leeks in any of the following ways:

(1) Serve hot with melted butter.
(2) Serve hot with Hollandaise sauce or sauce Mousseline.
(3) Chill and serve with vinaigrette sauce.

Braised Leeks

6 to 8 leeks
1 cup or more chicken broth
6 tablespoons butter
Salt and freshly ground pepper

Steam the prepared leeks in the chicken broth with salt to taste in a tightly covered saucepan. When they are tender, drain, and reserve the broth for other dishes. Melt the butter in the saucepan, add the leeks, and let them cook, turning them often, till the butter is lightly colored. Serve on a heated serving dish with the butter poured over them.

Mushrooms

America is rich in mushrooms. Practically every good edible variety has grown here in abundance. To the settler in the seventeenth century it must have been a comfort to have this natural bounty of meadow mushrooms, morels, boletus — everything but truffles, and some say these have been found, but I would have to witness the unearthing to believe it. Even when I was a child a five-pound lard pail of mushrooms gathered before breakfast was no feat in season. Our supply of mushrooms continues to diminish along with our wilderness, but they can still be found in astonishing variety and profusion, especially through Connecticut, New York, and Pennsylvania.

Miss Leslie stated that "Good mushrooms are only found in open fields where the air is pure and unconfined. Those that grow in damp ground and shady places are always poisonous." This is typical of the old wives' tales that have attended mushrooms as food. Any amateur mycologist knows that morels, boletus, and many other excellent mushrooms grow in damp and shady places.

Unlike Miss Leslie, Mrs. Rorer was impressively knowledgeable about mushrooms and was enamored of the many varieties to be found in Pennsylvania. She offers recipes such as Coprinus Micaceus, Steamed; Baked Lepiota Procera; and Deviled Clavaria.

Generations after both ladies, the cultivated mushroom came into being. It began in earnest in Pennsylvania and Delaware, and now it spans the country. The output is tremendous. Nevertheless, many people still prefer to gather wild ones. There is a lively trade in mushroom guides, and the New School in New York had a series of "mushroom walks" for several years to acquaint pupils with various species.

Mushrooms are good whether they are eaten raw in hand or in salads or cooked in the most elaborate fashion. Mrs. Rorer liked to serve them under glass. This enabled each person, as he lifted the glass from his plate, to get the full bouquet of the mushrooms before taking the first delicious bite.

Mushrooms should not be peeled, since most of the flavor is discarded with the peel. Unless they are sandy and mucky, merely wipe them well with a wet cloth. Otherwise wash them well and dry them.

To prepare for broiling, remove the stems and reserve for duxelles (page 282). If slicing for sautéing, remove the stems or leave them, as you like. The slices will look better without them. If cooking small whole mushrooms, trim the stems to meet the cap.

This, too, makes a better appearance. Mushrooms are sometimes quartered, also, for sautéing or other treatment. Simply cut through the stem and cap, or first trim the stem, as for whole mushrooms, and then quarter.

Mushrooms keep rather well. If they turn brown, they are still all right for sauteing, but do not serve them raw. One pound of mushrooms will serve 3 to 4 persons. If they are particularly fond of mushrooms, you had better provide 1½ pounds for 4.

Steamed Mushrooms

1 pound mushrooms
1 tablespoon lemon juice
1 teaspoon salt

Many recipes call for cooked mushrooms as a garnish. These should be steamed rather than sautéed.

Pour about ¼ inch water in a covered heavy saucepan and bring to a gentle boil with the lemon juice and salt. Add the mushrooms, cover, and steam about 5 minutes, shaking the pan from time to time so that the mushrooms will not stick to the bottom. These may be held over hot water — not boiling — if they are to be used later.

Sautéed Mushrooms

4 tablespoons butter
2 tablespoons oil
1 pound mushrooms, quartered, whole or sliced
Salt and freshly ground pepper

Melt the butter in a heavy skillet with the oil. When it is bubbling, add the mushrooms and sauté over medium high heat 6 to 8 minutes. Shake the pan several times, and if necessary reduce the heat slightly. When the mushrooms seem to have absorbed every bit of fat in the pan, shake again vigorously. They will begin to brown delicately and are almost ready for service. Salt and pepper to taste, and place in a heated serving dish or spoon onto pieces of fried toast.

Mushrooms with Herbs and Cream. Just before removing from the heat add ¼ cup chopped parsley, ¼ cup chopped chives, and ¼ cup heavy cream. Shake the pan well to blend.

Mushrooms with Dill. Add ¼ cup chopped parsley and 2 tablespoons chopped fresh dill or 1 teaspoon dillweed. Remove the skillet from the heat and stir in 1 cup sour cream. Heat through, but do not bring to a boil. Serve garnished with additional chopped herbs.

Creamed Mushrooms. Combine the sautéed mushrooms with 1½ cups rich hot cream sauce. Garnish with chopped parsley.

Sautéed Mushrooms and Bacon. This was a favorite dish in restaurants and homes in the nineteenth century and even into this century. The blend of flavors is delightful. Sauté the mushrooms in half bacon fat and half butter, and garnish with curls of fairly crisp bacon. Serve on toast.

Deviled Mushrooms

1 pound mushrooms
4 tablespoons butter
3 tablespoons oil
Salt and freshly ground pepper
¼ teaspoon Tabasco
2 teaspoons Worcestershire sauce
1 tablespoon lemon juice
2 tablespoons dry sherry

This was a great breakfast dish when one could still find fresh meadow mushrooms. They were gathered early in the morning, and served with bacon, toast, and sometimes a broiled tomato. This recipe was also sometimes made in a chafing dish and served for supper.

Sauté the mushrooms in the butter and oil, shaking the pan several times. Season to taste with salt and plenty of pepper. Add the Tabasco, Worcestershire, lemon juice, and sherry, and shake the pan again. Let the mushrooms cook up for a moment or so. Taste the sauce for seasoning — it should have a good bite to it. Spoon over toast.

Broiled Mushrooms

Use large caps for broiling. Brush them well with butter or oil and place them on an oiled broiler rack, cap side up, about 4 inches from the broiling unit. Broil 2 to 2½ minutes, then turn them over. Place a dot of butter, a tiny piece of partially cooked bacon, or a few drops of olive oil into each cap, and add a dash of salt, a dash of Tabasco, and a grind of pepper. Cook under the broiler another 2½ minutes, and they should be done. Transfer them carefully to a serving plate or to slices of toast so they do not lose the bit of seasoning in the cap.

Mushrooms Under Glass

For each serving:
4 to 5 largish mushroom caps
1 round of crisp toast
2 tablespoons herb butter
Salt and freshly ground pepper
2 to 3 tablespoons heavy cream
HERB BUTTER (4 servings)
1 stick (½ cup) butter
1 tablespoon chopped parsley
1 tablespoon chopped shallots or garlic
1 teaspoon dried tarragon or 1 tablespoon fresh
1 tablespoon lemon juice

This was one of the more glamorous dishes in the fine restaurants at the turn of the century. It is a simple feat. Glass bells may be bought in any good kitchen equipment shop and are quite durable. You will need to fit them to small round baking dishes. The enameled iron dishes seem to work exceedingly well. The point of serving under glass is that it retains all the delicious bouquet, which is released when the glass is lifted at table.

Blend the ingredients for the herb butter together with a fork or with the hands till creamy and well mixed. To assemble: Butter the toast on both sides. Place on the bottom of the baking dish. Place the mushroom caps on the toast — and here you may use fluted mushrooms if you've a mind to. Add the herbed butter to the mushrooms, then the heavy cream and a grind of pepper. Cover with the glass bells and bake at 350 degrees about 20 minutes, or until the mushrooms are just cooked through. Do not remove the bells. Set each baking dish on a plate, and remove the bell as you serve it.

Creamed Mushrooms Under Glass

Sauté 1 pound mushroom caps in butter and combine with 1½ cups rich cream sauce (see page 457) flavored with ¼ cup sherry or

Madeira. Arrange rounds of toast, buttered on both sides, in individual baking dishes. Top each with a slice of Virginia ham. Spoon several creamed mushrooms over the ham. Sprinkle with chopped parsley. Cover with a bell, and heat through in a 375-degree oven for about 10 minutes. Serve at once.

Stuffed Mushrooms

16 mushrooms
1/4 pound butter or more
1/2 cup dry breadcrumbs (freshly made, please)
1 tablespoon chopped parsley
1 tablespoon chopped chives or onion
1/4 teaspoon Tabasco
1 teaspoon salt
1 teaspoon freshly ground pepper
2 eggs, lightly beaten
1/2 cup grated Parmesan cheese
Small amount of broth

For stuffing you will need fairly uniform, largish mushrooms. Estimate about 4 mushrooms per person.

Remove the stems of the mushrooms. Peel them and chop very fine. Wipe the mushroom caps with a damp cloth. Melt 4 tablespoons butter in a skillet and lightly sauté the chopped mushroom stems with the crumbs, parsley, chives or onion, and seasonings. Blend with the beaten eggs. Correct the seasoning. Brush the bottom of a shallow baking dish with butter. It should be a 9-inch square or 9 × 12 oval one, just large enough to hold the 16 caps. Brush the caps with melted butter inside and out. Stuff each cap with some of the mixture and place in the baking dish. Brush with melted butter and sprinkle with grated Parmesan cheese. Add a little broth to the pan to keep them from sticking. Bake in a 375-degree oven about 15 minutes or until the mushrooms are nicely browned and tender. You may baste with additional melted butter if you like.

Mushrooms Stuffed with Seafood. Substitute for the chopped mushrooms in the recipe above 1 cup crabmeat or chopped shrimps, and add 1 teaspoon chopped dill or tarragon to the herb mixture.

Mushroom and Potato Pie

2 1/2 cups richly buttered mashed potatoes
Caps from 1 1/2 to 2 pounds mushrooms, sautéed
1 recipe rich pastry
1 egg yolk blended with 3 tablespoons cream

Line a 9 × 12-inch shallow rectangular baking dish with a layer of really rich mashed potatoes, seasoned well with salt and freshly ground pepper. Top with well-seasoned sautéed mushroom caps, heaped rather high, and garnish with chopped parsley. Cool, then cover with a rich pastry crust and flute around the edges. Make a vent in the top and brush with the egg and cream mixture. Bake at 425 degrees 10 minutes. Reduce the heat to 350 degrees and bake until the crust is just brown and cooked through. Serve with beef, chicken, or lamb, or serve as a main course for luncheon with a salad and fruit

Mushroom Spinach Casserole

2 cups chopped cooked spinach, drained and seasoned with salt, freshly ground pepper, and a dash of nutmeg
Caps from 1 pound mushrooms, sautéed in butter
2 tablespoons lemon juice
1 teaspoon dried tarragon or 1 tablespoon fresh chopped tarragon
1 teaspoon salt
½ teaspoon freshly ground pepper
½ pound noodles, lightly cooked
6 tablespoons butter
½ cup freshly grated Parmesan cheese

This standard for buffet parties had its origin as a dish of mushrooms served on spinach. Then someone invented the topping for it, which gives it a pleasant touch.

Line a 2-quart buttered casserole with the chopped spinach. Make a layer of the sautéed mushrooms, and add lemon juice, tarragon, salt, pepper, and the butter from the skillet in which the mushrooms were sautéed. Top with the hot, freshly cooked noodles, tossed with the butter, and sprinkle with the grated cheese. Bake in a 375-degree oven 5 to 6 minutes to reheat and blend. Serve with veal, chicken dishes, or fish.

Mushroom Purée for Seasoning

3 pounds mushrooms, finely chopped
½ pound butter
Salt and freshly ground pepper

This purée is a relative of French duxelles, and delicious it is. Since mushrooms have become relatively cheap in some parts of the country, people can afford to have a jar of this in their refrigerators. A few spoonfuls are superb when swirled into scrambled eggs or used for an omelet. A spoonful added to a cream sauce will give it new perfume. Spread on toast, it is a good snack with cocktails. It is also excellent mixed with cream and used as a filling for crêpes.

You may buy bargain mushrooms that are slightly brown for the purée.

Melt the butter over low heat in a heavy 12-inch skillet. Add the chopped mushrooms and stir for a moment or two. Reduce the heat to warm. Let them cook, stirring occasionally, for 2 to 2½ hours. The liquid will cook out of them and the mixture will turn quite brown — almost black. They must not cook crisp but should remain soft. Add more butter if necessary. Salt and pepper them to taste and spoon into jars. Cover, and store in the refrigerator.

Sometimes this is seasoned with shallots, or garlic and flour are added to it. I find it much more useful in its simpler version.

Okra

Okra is also called gumbo, and is known by that name in most countries outside the United States. It is especially popular in the

South, where it is prepared in many different ways — it is fried; or steamed, rolled in cornmeal, and then fried or sautéed; or made into little fritters and served with various meats. To some people the rather slimy quality of okra is not wholly appetizing. However, it has had a long history. Gumbos would be nothing without it, and most Creole recipes call for it.

Okra should be young and tender, with clean pods which snap easily. Small to medium pods are the best to buy. One pound of okra will serve 4 persons.

To Cook Okra

Wash the okra well and cut off the stems. If the pods are young, leave whole. If older, cut in slices.

Steam-cook in a small amount of boiling salted water about 10 minutes, or till just tender. Overcooking tends to give it a disagreeable texture. Dress cooked okra with any of the following (quantities are for 1 pound):

(1) 6 tablespoons melted butter and ¼ teaspoon freshly ground pepper.
(2) ½ cup vinaigrette sauce.
(3) 6 tablespoons lemon butter.

Okra and Tomatoes with Lemon

1 pound small okra
½ cup olive oil
3 to 4 onions, peeled and coarsely chopped
2 cloves garlic, finely chopped
2 cups canned Italian plum tomatoes
Salt and freshly ground pepper
1 teaspoon ground coriander
Lemon wedges

Trim the tops from the okra, wash it, and dry on a paper towel. Sauté the onions and garlic in the olive oil in a large skillet, and when they are slightly brown, add the okra. Cook 3 minutes. Add the tomatoes and seasonings. Cover the skillet and simmer about 35 minutes. Serve on a bed of steamed rice. Provide lemon wedges for each person.

Note. This is as good a dish served cold as hot. To serve cold, place in a small salad bowl with additional olive oil and garnish with lemon slices and chopped parsley.

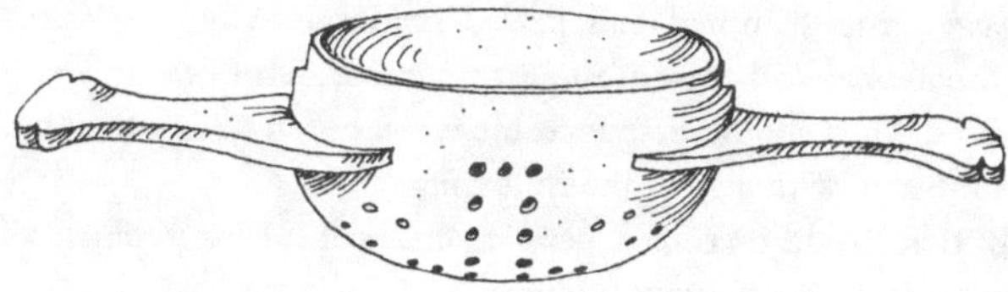

Corn, Okra, and Tomatoes

4 tablespoons butter
½ cup chopped onion
1 small green pepper, seeded and finely chopped
2 cups canned tomatoes, preferably Italian plum tomatoes
1 cup sliced okra
Salt and freshly ground pepper
2 cups fresh corn kernels or drained whole-kernel corn

This is a classic dish from the South, although one finds it prepared differently in different states.

Sauté the onion in butter till limp. Add the green pepper, and when it is just beginning to soften, add the tomatoes and okra. Cook 20 minutes or so, till well blended and smooth. Salt and pepper to taste. Add the corn and cook 5 minutes. Correct the seasoning and serve in a heated serving dish.

Onions

Onions were one of the first crops of our early settlers, who soon were growing shallots and green onions as well. We now have many varieties: small white onions, which are boiled, steamed, or braised, and also used to accompany many different braised dishes; the red Italian onions, which are particularly good for eating raw and for use in salads; and the all-purpose white and brown onions, which can be steamed, boiled, baked, braised, or used for seasoning.

If you pour boiling water over onions, bring them just to a boil again, and let them stand several minutes, they are much easier to peel. First rinse them in cold water so they can be handled. It is claimed that with this method you will not weep either, but this is a fallacy. I once questioned some women who spent eight hours a day peeling and slicing onions, and they said every day for one half hour they wept, and that was it.

To Cook Onions

For boiling or most braising recipes, onions are left whole. If you are careful in cutting the root end and leave a trace of the root, the onions are much less apt to break up during cooking. Some make a cross cut at the root to prevent breaking.

For sautéing and for some braising recipes onions are sliced anywhere from ¼ to ½ inch in thickness.

Estimate 1½ pounds onions for 4 persons — or gauge 1 large, 2 medium, or 3 small onions per person.

To boil. Drop trimmed and peeled onions into boiling salted water. Small ones will cook in about 15 minutes; large ones in about 30 minutes. They should be pierceable when tested with a fork but still firm. Serve with any of the following:

(1) Butter, freshly ground pepper, and salt. A tiny pinch of nutmeg or mace is a pleasant addition.

(2) Rich cream sauce.

(3) Rich cheese sauce. Sprinkle with shredded or grated cheese. Swiss Gruyère is very agreeable with onions, and Cheddar, particularly, goes well with cooked onions.

(4) Tomato sauce, highly seasoned with peppers and garlic.

To steam-cook onion slices. For 4 large, 6 medium, or 8 small onions, which have been trimmed, peeled, and sliced, melt 6 tablespoons butter in a heavy saucepan. Add the sliced onions, 1 teaspoon salt, and a dash of nutmeg or mace, and cover tightly. Steam-cook over low heat approximately 10 minutes. Shake the pan gently a few times during the cooking.

To broil onion slices. Brush thick onion slices with butter, salt them, and arrange on a well-oiled grilling pan. Broil about 4 inches from the heat unit. When they are delicately brown, turn them very carefully with aid of spatulas, and butter and salt the other side. Return to the broiler to brown. Serve these broiled onion slices in the traditional way with hamburgers or with small steaks.

Sour Cream Onion Tart

1 recipe biscuit dough
2 cups sliced sautéed onions
1 teaspoon oregano
1 teaspoon salt
3 eggs, slightly beaten
Additional salt and freshly ground pepper
1½ cups sour cream

This originated in Southern California. It is quick and easy and a good accompaniment to many meat dishes.

Line a buttered 9-inch pie pan with the biscuit dough. Cover with the sautéed onions, salted and seasoned with oregano. Combine the eggs, sour cream, pepper and salt to taste. Pour over the onions. Bake at 400 degrees until the crust is cooked through and the top is nicely browned.

Baked Onions with Cheese

12 medium onions
½ cup beef bouillon or consommé
Salt and freshly ground pepper
Grated Cheddar or Gruyère cheese

In the West and Middle West, this takes the place of creamed onions, in the Thanksgiving feast — which is commendable, since many people, including the author, find that creamed onions have tradition and little else to support them.

Butter a 9 or 10 inch casserole well. Place the onions in it, add the broth, and sprinkle lightly with salt and a few grinds from the pepper mill. Cover, and bake in a 325-degree oven 1 hour, or until the onions are just tender. Replenish the liquid, if need be, during the baking period. Add enough grated cheese to almost cover the onions completely, and run under the broiling unit or return to the oven for a few moments to melt the cheese thoroughly. Serve from the casserole.

Steamed Sliced Onions with Cheese

½ cup beef bouillon or consommé
6 large onions, sliced ½-inch thick
Salt and freshly ground pepper
Grated Cheddar or Gruyère cheese

Bring the bouillon to a boil. Add the onion slices, cover, and steam 10 to 12 minutes, or until they are tender. Correct the seasoning and add the cheese. Shake the pan well in order to mix the cheese with all the onions. Transfer to a heated serving dish.

Braised Onion Slices with Bourbon

2 tablespoons butter
2 tablespoons olive oil
4 large onions cut in 1-inch slices
1 teaspoon salt
½ teaspoon freshly ground pepper
¼ cup bouillon
¼ cup bourbon

Naturally, a Southern recipe.

Heat the butter and oil in a heavy saucepan. Add the onions and sear over high heat for 2 minutes. Add the salt, pepper, and bouillon. Reduce the heat and simmer for 10 to 12 minutes. Add the bourbon and cook down for 3 minutes. Serve with poultry, game, or beef.

Old-Fashioned Fried Onions

6 tablespoons beef drippings or butter
4 medium onions or 3 large ones, thinly sliced
Salt

This is the type of fried onion which was used to smother steaks and hamburgers and other dishes during the earlier years of this century.

Heat the fat in a heavy 12-inch skillet. Add the onions and shake the pan well. Cook over medium heat. Let them color on the bottom for several minutes, then turn with a spatula and continue cooking till the onions are golden brown and wilted. Add fat if needed. The onions should almost be caramelized. Season with salt to taste, and transfer to a heated serving dish. Serve with steaks, hamburgers, pork chops, or other delicious, homely dishes.

Braised Small Onions

18 small white onions, peeled
6 tablespoons butter
2 teaspoons sugar
¼ cup broth or water
Salt to taste

Sear the onions in butter until they are of a golden brown. Sprinkle lightly with sugar and shake well in the pan so they caramelize and brown nicely. Add the liquid, cover, and steam till the onions are just tender. Season with salt. These may be served with braised meats, added to a stew or beef à la mode, or used as a garnish with a roast.

Onions in Onions

6 onions, about 3 inches in diameter

Practically every writer after Mrs. Crowen up to the present day has given one recipe or another for stuffed onions. This one is served in the Four Seasons in New York.

Cook the large onions in boiling salted water, covered, in a heavy saucepan till just barely tender. If they are too tender they will not work for this particular dish.

36 pearl onions (canned, if the fresh are not available)
2 cups rich cream sauce
1 cup buttered breadcrumbs

Cook the pearl onions in a small amount of boiling salted water in a covered saucepan till just tender. If you use the canned onions, merely heat through in their liquid.

Run cold water over the large onions and cut them in half crosswise. Remove the center rings to leave a hole approximately 1 inch in diameter. Fill with 3 or 4 of the tiny onions and place the halves in a buttered and heated baking dish which can be used for serving. Spoon the cream sauce over the onions and sprinkle with the buttered crumbs. Run under the broiling unit about 4 inches from the heat to brown quickly.

This will serve 6 or 12. It is very pretty on a plate with roast beef and a browned potato or with a roast of lamb.

Onions Stuffed with Sausage. Instead of pearl onions, stuff the large onions with enough well-flavored sausage meat so that it makes a mound. Arrange them on strips of bacon in a baking dish and bake at 375 degrees until the sausage is just cooked through — about 20 minutes. Serve with the bacon and baked potatoes.

Green Onions

These are exceedingly delicate in flavor and suffer from overcooking. A most pleasant change as a vegetable. Estimate 3 or 4 green onions per person. Remove the root and any outside loose skin before cooking, and trim the tops neatly.

To Cook Green Onions

Steam-cook the green onions in a small amount of salted boiling water, allowing about 8 minutes. Transfer them carefully with a spatula and fork or spoon to a hot serving plate. Serve with:

(1) Butter, freshly ground pepper, and salt.
(2) Rich cream sauce.
(3) Rich cheese sauce sprinkled with grated cheese.
(4) Hollandaise sauce.

Green Onion Tart

Rich pastry for a 9-inch tart
3 cups chopped onions
4 tablespoons butter
4 eggs, lightly beaten
1½ cups light cream

Line a 9-inch pie pan with rich pastry. Flute the edges. Place a piece of foil in the tart shell and fill with beans or rice. Bake at 425 degrees for 10 to 12 minutes or until the shell is lightly browned. Remove the foil and the beans or rice and keep for another baking. Sauté the onions in the butter very lightly 3 minutes or so, or until they are just limp. Beat the eggs lightly and beat in the cream. Season with salt, pepper, and nutmeg. Spoon the onions into the

1 teaspoon salt
½ teaspoon freshly ground pepper
¼ teaspoon nutmeg

tart shell and pour the custard mixture over them. Place in a 350-degree oven and bake approximately 25 minutes, or until the custard is just set and the top nicely brown.

Parsnips

One of the most neglected and most talked about of the vegetable family. Miss Farmer stated in 1906, "Parsnips are raised mostly as cattle food." And there have been many old wives' tales associated with them — one being that they were poisonous if eaten before the frost bit into them, and another that they were inedible if left in the ground after the first frost. Why parsnips have been thus maligned I fail to understand, for, when properly cooked, they are a most satisfying vegetable. And when puréed, they are my favorite vegetable for a Thanksgiving feast, replacing the traditional, utterly dull sweet potatoes.

Despite all, parsnips are available in the market the year round, and they have been with us for centuries. They were certainly in use as early as the Massachusetts Bay Colony, as this little verse from that date indicates:

For pottage and puddings, and custards and pies
Our pumpkins and parsnips are common supplies.
We have pumpkins at morning and pumpkins at noon.
If it were not for pumpkins we should be undoon.

Especially if you are going to purée them, you will need 2½ to 3 pounds parsnips for 4 persons. There are times when the core is quite woody and the waste is therefore rather large. Select those which have meatiness around the top rather than the long, thin ones, which really are not suitable for puréeing.

To Cook Parsnips

Although most people tell you to scrape parsnips before cooking, when I purée or fry them or use them for fritters, I seldom scrape them but merely brush them well. They are much easier to skin after boiling and take less time for preparation. For buttered parsnips, for example, I find it convenient to boil them unpeeled hours ahead of a meal. Then I let them cool before skinning and cutting them for the final cooking.

Cook the parsnips in sufficient boiling salted water to cover. They will take from 20 to 40 minutes, depending upon the time of the year they are grown and the size of the parsnips. Avoid overcooking. Drain and plunge into cold water to cool so they may be peeled easily.

Buttered Parsnips. After cooking and cooling, peel the parsnips and cut the best parts into attractive serving pieces. To every 3 cups parsnips, add ½ cup butter and reheat over low heat. Add salt and freshly ground pepper to taste.

Parsnip Purée with Madeira

3 pounds parsnips
1 teaspoon salt
1 teaspoon sugar
¼ pound butter, melted
4 tablespoons heavy cream
Madeira — good Madeira — to taste (¼ cup or more)
Buttered breadcrumbs

Cook the parsnips as above. When they are cold, skin and put them through a food mill or a purée attachment on your electric mixer. You should have about 2½ cups purée or more. Combine with the salt, sugar, melted butter, cream, and Madeira. Whip and spoon into a 1-quart baking dish. Dot with butter, sprinkle with buttered breadcrumbs, and bake at 350 degrees 25 to 30 minutes. This is an excellent accompaniment to turkey, chicken or beef.

Parsnip Cakes. Omit the cream. Shape into cakes, dip into flour, and sauté in 6 tablespoons butter, or more as needed, until nicely brown and puffy.

Scalloped Parsnips and Potatoes

4 good-sized parsnips, peeled and cut in rounds
4 large potatoes, peeled and cut in slices about ¼ inch thick
Butter
1 teaspoon salt
1 teaspoon freshly ground pepper
Heavy cream

Butter a 2-quart baking dish. Alternate layers of parsnips and potatoes with dottings of butter in between and a sprinkling of salt and pepper. Barely cover with heavy cream and bake at 350 degrees approximately 1 hour, or until the parsnips and potatoes are done. Definitely not a low-calorie recipe, but truly a fine old farm dish.

Peas

Many people nowadays barely realize that peas come in pods, so prevalent is the custom of eating peas out of cans, boxes, and plastic bags. I feel that children could very well be told of the days when peas were shelled and of the wonderful taste of raw peas straight from the pod. One hostess I knew used to serve bowls of freshly shelled peas from the garden along with cocktails. As I write this, I have been living through a summer with fresher-than-fresh peas picked a short time before being cooked with butter and lettuce leaves. This is another delight we have forgotten.

For the most part, frozen peas are the order of the day — usually cooked too long in too much water. A convenience to the restaurateur but an unexciting event for the guests, such peas are at their worst when combined with canned carrots. Some brands of frozen peas, however, such as the tiny boil-in-bag variety, can be excellent. So can many canned peas if they are treated as carefully as fresh ones.

Peas, being a favorite vegetable of the English, were no doubt among the first vegetables to travel across the Atlantic, and in dried form they were a source of good winter food in soups and purées. It was the Orientals who first domesticated the wild vegetable, which developed into two types — the pea that is shelled and the sugar pea or mangetout, whose edible pod is much used in Chinese cuisine as well as in French, Swiss, and Italian. Petits pois are not a type but simply peas gathered before maturity, and they are considered the best the market affords.

The finest of peas grown in the United States, I maintain, are those produced in the sandy soil of Oregon and Washington. Now that they are increasingly hard to come by, the price is fittingly astronomic. These peas are sweet, tender, and prizewinning, a judgment supported by many people who have sampled them on my recommendation.

Mrs. Harland in her menus for a week in May from her *Dinner Year Book* provides this interesting sidelight on the pea situation during the last century:

"*Green Peas.* I have purposely avoided too early an introduction of green vegetables and other spring dainties, through fear that the high prices demanded for them might make this part of my work useless for housekeepers of moderate means. By the first of May, however, even our Northern markets should be well supplied at reasonable rates with many delightful esculents which are, as yet, brought only from the South.

"Shell the peas and wash well in cold water. Cook in boiling water — for 25 minutes. A lump of sugar will be an addition, and a pleasant one to market peas. Drain well, stir in a great lump of butter and pepper and salt. Serve hot."

This reminds us that peas were once seasonal. They were a tradition for the Fourth of July in New England, along with poached salmon and new potatoes. Presumably the first ones were ready in time for that celebration. Now they are with us always.

Pea pods should be vividly green and rather velvety and fresh-looking. Split one and taste a pea to determine its freshness and sweetness. Shell peas as soon before cooking as possible. Do not wash the peas, and do not salt them till after they are cooked. A teaspoon of sugar will enhance the flavor of most peas.

It will take 3 to 5 pounds of peas in pod, depending on their size, to yield enough for 4 persons.

To Cook Peas

(1) Boil about 8 to 12 minutes in about an inch of water, covered. Add a little sugar, but save the salting for afterwards.

(2) Cover with lettuce leaves, freshly washed, or with a head of lettuce, finely shredded. For 3 pounds peas (before shelling), add 1/4 pound butter, 1 to 2 teaspoons sugar, and about 3 tablespoons cold water. Cook, covered, over very low heat till tender, about 8 to 15 minutes, depending upon the youth of the peas.

(3) Combine with tiny onions and shreds of well-flavored ham and cook, covered, in a heavy saucepan in about 1 inch of boiling water. After the peas are cooked, add salt, if you like, and thicken the sauce with 1 spoonful of beurre manié.

(4) For 3 pounds peas (before shelling), melt 4 tablespoons butter in a heavy saucepan. Add the freshly shelled peas and just cover them with heavy cream. Cook very slowly until the peas are tender. Add 1 teaspoon sugar, and salt and freshly ground pepper to taste. Blend over the lowest heat a few moments before serving.

(5) Serve peas with chopped mushrooms or sliced mushrooms sautéed in butter.

(6) Combine equal quantities of buttered peas and freshly cooked rice. This is an Italian specialty called Risi e Pisi.

Peas in Turnip Cups

For 4 persons choose 4 turnips of equal size — about 2 to 3 inches in diameter. Peel and trim them, and scoop out a bowl in the center with a melon cutter. Boil, covered, in salted water and 3 tablespoons lemon juice until just barely tender. Drain well. Butter the hollows lightly, and set the turnips aside to keep warm until serving time.

Arrange on a heated serving plate. Fill the center with peas prepared in any of the ways given above. Pile additional peas in the center of the dish. Garnish with parsley sprigs.

Peas in Tomato Sauce

3 to 4 pounds (before shelling) peas, cooked as above and lightly buttered
1 large onion, finely chopped
4 tablespoons butter
1 1/2 cups tomato sauce
1 teaspoon salt
1 1/2 teaspoons freshly ground pepper
1 teaspoon basil
3/4 cup prosciutto, cut in fine shreds
1/4 cup chopped parsley

While the peas are cooking, sauté the onion in the butter till just pale golden, soft, and transparent. Add the tomato sauce and seasonings, and cook down for 5 minutes. Drain the peas, add them to the sauce with the prosciutto, and heat through again. Correct the seasoning. Garnish with chopped parsley after transferring to a heated vegetable dish.

Pea Pie

This is a recipe of June Platt's, which she has treasured over a number of years. I find it a most decorative way to serve peas and a thoroughly New England one. We are using it with her permission.

"For this dish make the pastry first. Sift together 1½ cups of pastry flour with ½ teaspoon of salt. Work in with the fingertips ¾ cup of butter. Moisten the flour and butter with a few drops of tepid water, and mix with a large fork until it holds together. Form it into a flat ball, wrap in wax paper, and chill several hours. Shell 8 to 10 pounds of peas, discarding the large tough ones. Wash the peas, put them in a large enamel pan, add a pinch of bicarbonate of soda and 1 teaspoon of salt, and cover with rapidly boiling water. Skim carefully. Cook about 20 to 25 minutes. When done, drain, saving the juice. Put the peas in a deep dish in which has been placed ¼ pound of butter and pour over just enough juice barely to cover the peas. Season to taste with salt and freshly ground black pepper, and allow the peas to cool in their juice.

"When ready to assemble and bake the pie, roll out a small piece of pastry to form a band about an inch wide and long enough to edge the rim of the dish — a 1½ quart deep-dish pie casserole — in which the pie is to be cooked. Paint the rim with beaten egg, then press the strip of pastry securely around the edge. Fill the dish level with peas and their juice. Roll the rest of the pastry to form a circle large enough to cover the dish and overhang about ¾ inch. Paint the strip of pastry around the rim with more egg; then place the top over all, pressing the edges together with floured fingers. Work quickly. Brush the top with egg and make a hole in the center of the crust for the steam to escape.

"Place in the refrigerator for a few minutes; then bake in a preheated, very hot oven (450 degrees) for 15 minutes. Reduce the heat a little and continue cooking about 15 minutes longer, or until the juice in the pie is boiling hot and the crust cooked through. Serve at once."

Pea Purée

This is mostly used for making a border around certain dishes, such as the famous chicken hash of Louis Diat served so long at the Ritz Carlton in New York. A great dish of pea purée is not attractive to serve by itself unless covered with buttered crumbs and either chopped mint or chopped parsley mixed with tarragon.

Shell 4 to 5 pounds fresh peas and cook in water according to the basic recipe. Drain them well and put through the food mill or other purée appliance. Blend with 6 tablespoons butter and salt to taste. Either spoon into a heated serving dish and garnish with chopped mint or chopped parsley and tarragon, as suggested above, or force through a bag with a large rosette tube to make a border around a serving platter. If you must reheat the peas, brush them with lightly beaten egg yolk and place in a hot oven.

Peas with Bacon

3 to 4 pounds (before shelling) peas, cooked in water as in basic recipe
6 thick strips bacon, cut in small pieces
1 clove garlic, finely chopped
1 tablespoon fresh mint
1 tablespoon wine vinegar

A childhood favorite of mine.

The bacon must be very good smoked bacon, thick-cut and cut into pieces ½ inch wide. Try it out in a skillet. Do not let it get crisp, but cook it through. Remove excess fat from the pan and leave perhaps one or two tablespoons. Add the garlic and let it melt in the fat. When the peas are cooked, drain them and add the mint and vinegar to the bacon. Cook for just a minute, add the peas, and toss well. Pour into a warmed serving dish. Salt and pepper to taste, although it may not need salt because of the bacon.

Snow Peas, Mangetout, or Chinese Peas

These are the edible pod peas and may be treated like other peas except that one does not shell them. Break off the stem end, and if there are any strings, remove them. Either cook them whole or shred them. The cooking time is much the same as for shelled peas. They must not be overcooked. Their crispness of pod and unique greenness are the secret of good mangetout. One pound should serve four.

Serve them with butter alone or with sautéed mushrooms, sautéed toasted almonds, or toasted peanuts.

Peppers

Peppers are native to the Americas. Though I doubt that the Pilgrims or the Massachusetts Bay Colonists knew them, they had long been in use through the South and in Mexico. The number and varieties of chilies used by the Mexican and Spanish groups alone is astonishing. It is said that something like twenty-three kinds are required to make a proper mole.

Creole cookery, also, depends heavily on peppers, usually cooked together with tomatoes, a style that seems to derive from Basque, Italian, and Mexican cuisines with a bit of originality thrown in.

Apart from these more exotic examples, cooked peppers were slow to be adopted as part of our common cuisine. It must be that Peter Piper had nothing else *but* pickled peppers to pick, since no recipes for peppers appear in cookbooks until nearly the end of the nineteenth century. Rules for pickling, plain and stuffed, there are aplenty. But even Mrs. Rorer in 1886 neglects peppers completely as a cooked vegetable.

The sweet bell green or red peppers, which are our most common variety, are found in markets everywhere and are in season most of the year. They grow to enormous size at times and are beautiful and shiny and well meated. They are usually darkish green, but in the fall some varieties will turn red or even yellow.

Look for peppers that are firm and well shaped. One pepper is usually considered a serving, but if they are small, count on two.

Although it is a tedious job to skin peppers, it benefits the flavor and the texture of a dish in which they are used. They have to be held over a flame so the skin will burn to a point where it can be scraped with ease. This can be done in an electric broiler, if you watch them carefully, or over open flame, with the pepper impaled on a long fork. Keep turning the peppers. They will be partially cooked by the time the skin is broken and loosened.

If you don't want to take this trouble, they are delicious as they are. In either case, remove the seeds carefully.

For most recipes, cut the peppers in julienne strips or in rounds.

If you are stuffing peppers, they should be left in halves and usually parboiled 10 minutes in a small amount of salted water. If they have been peeled as suggested above, parboiling is unnecessary.

Sautéed Peppers

6 green, red, or yellow peppers, seeded and cut in julienne strips
6 tablespoons olive oil
1 garlic clove, thinly sliced
1 teaspoon salt
1 tablespoon wine vinegar

Clean, seed, and cut the peppers. Heat the olive oil in a rather heavy skillet over low heat and add the garlic. Let it melt in the oil about 4 minutes. Add the peppers and cover. Let them steam in the oil, shaking the pan occasionally, till just soft — about 15 to 20 minutes. Add the salt and wine vinegar and let them cook up for just a moment. Serve with beef, chicken, pork, or a plain roast duck.

Peppers and Corn. Prepare sautéed peppers as above. Omit the vinegar, and add at the last 2 cups corn cut from the cob or 2 12-ounce cans whole-kernel corn, 1 teaspoon freshly ground pepper, 3 tablespoons butter, and 1 teaspoon salt. Shake the pan well and cook 5 minutes over medium heat, uncovered. Shake the pan several more times. Correct the seasoning.

Stuffed Peppers

6 peppers, with the tops removed, seeded
4 tablespoons butter
1 large onion, finely chopped
1 garlic clove, finely chopped

At the turn of the century peppers were used to serve leftovers in a new and different way. It seems that was their sole employment save for pickling. Miss Farmer has two or three recipes for stuffed peppers in her early editions, and Mrs. Rorer, who went one step further, admitted they made a succulent vegetable. She and Miss Farmer both felt that baked peppers, stuffed with equal parts minced leftover chicken, veal, or beef and seasoned breadcrumbs, presented a pretty luncheon or supper dish, or an entrée. And they do.

2 cups finely chopped cooked beef, pork, or chicken (cold roast or boiled meat is perfect)
1 teaspoon salt
2 tablespoons tomato sauce
¼ teaspoon Tabasco
½ teaspoon freshly ground pepper
1½ cups fresh breadcrumbs
Butter
1½ cups stock or bouillon

Parboil the peppers 10 minutes. Sauté the onion and garlic. Add the meat and toss well with the onion and seasonings. Combine with the crumbs and taste for seasoning. Fill the peppers. Dot with butter and cover with the pepper tops. Place them in a deep baking dish, 9×9×3 inches, and add the stock. Bake at 350 degrees 35 to 40 minutes, basting several times. Serve with tomato sauce.

Stuffed Peppers Mediterranean

6 peppers
2 cups finely diced bread
2 garlic cloves, finely chopped
4 tablespoons olive oil
4 tablespoons butter
20 anchovy fillets, coarsely cut
1 large onion, coarsely chopped
¾ cup sultana raisins soaked in a little sherry
½ cup pine nuts
¾ cup chopped parsley
½ cup finely chopped mint
Salt and freshly ground pepper
Additional oil

Cut the peppers in half lengthwise. Sauté the bread and garlic in the oil and butter, shaking the pan and tossing till the bread is crisp. Add additional olive oil if needed. Toss with the anchovies, onion, raisins, nuts, parsley, and mint. Add salt and pepper if needed. Let the mixture stand a few minutes. Meanwhile, steam the peppers 10 minutes. Fill them loosely with the mixture, place in a baking dish with 4 to 5 tablespoons oil, and bake 35 to 40 minutes at 325 degrees. Serve them warm or cold as an hors d'oeuvre or as accompaniment to cold meat or fish.

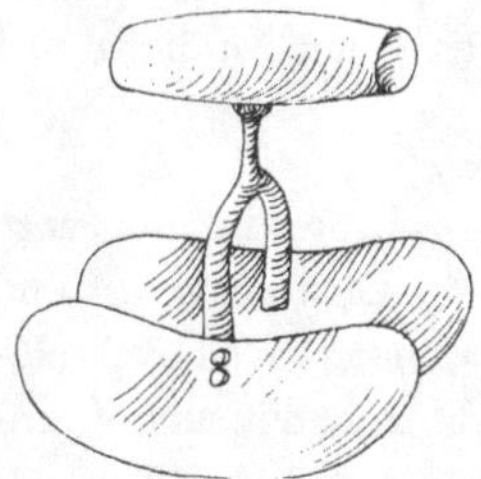

Sausage-Stuffed Peppers

8 peppers, cleaned and seeded
2 pounds sausage meat, not too fat and very well seasoned
1 cup stock, broth or water

This is served as a Sunday breakfast dish at the Tower Suite in New York and is unusual enough to record. It is excellent with fried cornmeal mush slices or fried grits slices.

Use small peppers or large ones cut down so that each serving is not overpowering. Clean and seed, and discard the tops. Prick a few tiny holes at the bottom and sides of each pepper to enable the excess fat to ooze out into the pan while cooking. Steam the peppers 15 minutes. Fill with the sausage meat and place in a 9×9×3-inch pan with a cup of stock or water. Bake at 375 degrees 20 to 25 minutes, or until the sausage is just cooked through.

Peppers Stuffed with Corn

Cut 3 peppers in half lengthwise. Seed them well and steam 20 minutes. Fill with either fresh corn cut from the cob or with whole-kernel canned or frozen corn. Dot each pepper with 1 tablespoon butter, ¼ teaspoon salt, and ¼ teaspoon freshly ground pepper. Place in a 9 × 12 × 3-inch baking dish and add 1 cup water to the dish. Bake at 375 degrees 15 minutes. Serve at once garnished with chopped parsley or finely chopped green pepper.

Pumpkin

Prepare pumpkin in any of the ways mentioned for winter squash.

Salsify or Oyster Plant

Salsify was a popular root vegetable for many generations and then suddenly seemed to drop into disrepute. It was originally called oyster plant because it was said to have the flavor of oysters — so much so, says Mrs. Rorer, that vegetarians made Mock Oyster soups. The claim for its flavor I have never found to be true.

It is in season during the winter months. The roots are long, rather black on the outside, and about 1 inch in diameter at the heart. Usually salsify is sold in bunches.

You will need 2 to 3 pounds for 4 persons. Scrape the roots well and toss into acidulated water, for they turn color if not immediately used.

To Cook Salsify

Either cut the scraped roots in 2 to 3 inch lengths or cook them whole. Boil in salted water to cover in a heavy saucepan until just tender — 12 to 15 minutes. Remove and drain well. Serve in a heated vegetable dish, treated in any of these ways:

(1) Dress with ¼ cup melted butter and freshly ground pepper to taste.

(2) Cut into thin slices. For about 8 salsify, butter a 1½-quart baking dish. Alternate layers of salsify, sprinkled with freshly ground pepper, and rich cream sauce, ending with cream sauce (you will need 1½ cups altogether). Cover the top with freshly made buttered breadcrumbs and heat through in a 350-degree oven 20 minutes, or until bubbling hot.

(3) Drain and purée the salsify, and combine with 3 tablespoons melted butter and 3 lightly beaten eggs. Season with freshly ground pepper and salt. Blend the mixture well. Melt 4 tablespoons butter, combine with 3 tablespoons oil, and heat till bubbly. Drop the mixture by spoonfuls into the hot fat. Cook on one side till brown, then turn and brown on the other. These were called mock oysters.

Spinach

Spinach is available fresh in the market the year round, usually prewashed and packed in bags. It is probably unlike the first spinach introduced to the Western Hemisphere, which more nearly resembled the strongly flavored European spinach.

Like other delicate greens, spinach has been badly treated, which probably accounts for its being in disfavor with many people. It was once thought necessary to cook it for a long time with salt pork or smoked jowl. We know now that it requires only the briefest of cooking.

This versatile vegetable is good whether served alone, used raw in salads, or used as a base for other vegetables, eggs, fish, or meats. It obligingly combines with cheese, eggs, garlic, oil, among other things, and it is also used to color foods green — noodles, cannelloni, mayonnaise for sauce verte. It is even used in sweets. A famous inn on the Ile de Porquerolles near Toulon features a spinach tart made with sugar and flavored with vanilla and glazed with apricot.

As Miss Leslie stated in her cookbook, "Spinach requires close examination and picking, as insects are frequently found among it, and it is often gritty." Gritty it is, and many careful washings are necessary most of the time to make it palatable. It comes to market cleaner than formerly, but one cannot be too careful. Discard the heavier stems. Wash it well again, and it is ready to cook. Lukewarm water removes the dirt more easily.

Usually 2 pounds spinach is considered enough for 4 persons. If the stems are heavy, be safe and buy 3 pounds.

To Cook Spinach

Put the washed spinach in a large heavy saucepan and cover. Add no water. Steam it till it is just wilted thoroughly — about 5 to 8 minutes. Turn it once or twice with wooden spoons. Drain the spinach and serve it *en branche* — as it is — or chop well. Serve it in any of these ways:

(1) For 2 to 3 pounds, add ¼ cup melted butter, 1 teaspoon salt, and ½ teaspoon freshly ground pepper. Add ⅛ teaspoon nutmeg, freshly grated, if you like.

(2) Butter the spinach and arrange in a heated serving dish. Season, and garnish with sliced hard-cooked eggs or with chopped eggs.

(3) Heat 1 garlic clove, finely chopped, with 6 tablespoons olive oil and 1 teaspoon basil. Toss with drained leaf spinach, or mix with spinach before chopping. Add 1 tablespoon freshly squeezed lemon

juice. Season with salt and freshly ground pepper. You may add a sprinkling of grated Parmesan cheese to this dish as well.

(4) *Spinach Purée.* Chop drained spinach very fine, add ½ cup rich cream sauce, 2 tablespoons heavy cream, 1 teaspoon salt, and a few gratings of fresh nutmeg. Reheat, stirring the while. Serve in a heated serving dish with a garnish of buttered crumbs.

(5) Season chopped drained spinach with 1 teaspoon salt, a grating of nutmeg, and about 3 tablespoons heavy cream. Toss well and add a few grinds of the pepper mill. Garnish with finely chopped hard-boiled egg.

(6) Roll seasoned spinach, as in #3, in thin French pancakes or crêpes. Place them in a baking dish 6 × 9 or 9 × 9 × 3 inches and butter them well. Heat in a 375-degree oven 10 minutes. Serve with Hollandaise sauce. Perfect with baked ham or roast chicken.

Tossed Leaf Spinach

2 pounds spinach, washed well
4 tablespoons butter
½ cup chopped filberts
1 tablespoon soy sauce
Salt and freshly ground pepper

Heat the butter, add the spinach, and sauté, stirring or tossing with two wooden spatulas or spoons as you would a salad. Add the filberts, soy sauce, salt, and pepper. Toss until the spinach is just wilted. Serve at once.

Spinach Ring

3 cups chopped cooked spinach, pressed to remove all traces of water
1 cup light cream sauce blended with 2 eggs
Pinch of nutmeg
½ teaspoon freshly ground pepper
1 tablespoon lemon juice

Butter a 1-quart ring mold well. Combine the spinach, sauce, cream and eggs, and seasonings. Mix well. Pour into the mold. Set it in a pan of hot water and bake 45 minutes to 1 at 350 degrees hour, or until the mixture is quite firm. Remove from the oven, unmold at once on a heated serving plate, and fill the center with sautéed mushroom caps, freshly buttered peas, carrot rounds buttered and flavored with dill, or braised onions.

Spinach Roll

3 pounds fresh spinach with stems removed or 3 packages frozen spinach
6 tablespoons butter
Salt and freshly ground pepper
Nutmeg
4 eggs, separated
3 tablespoons butter for the pan

If using fresh spinach, wash it well. Place in a large kettle, cover tight, and steam till it is merely wilted — this is a matter of a very few minutes. Drain well and chop coarsely. If using frozen spinach thaw over low heat and drain very well. Chop if it is leaf spinach. Place the spinach in a bowl. Add 6 tablespoons butter and salt, pepper, and nutmeg to taste. Beat in the egg yolks, one by one. Line an 11 × 15 × ½-inch sponge roll pan with heavy wax paper. Butter it generously with 3 tablespoons butter and sprinkle with the dry breadcrumbs. Beat the egg whites until they hold soft peaks, and fold into the spinach mixture. Immediately turn into the prepared pan and smooth it. Sprinkle the top with grated Parmesan cheese.

Bake immediately in a preheated 350-degree oven 12 to 16 minutes, or until the center feels barely firm when touched lightly with fingertip. Cover with buttered wax paper or foil and invert onto a warm platter or board. Remove the bottom paper and spread the roll with scrambled eggs flavored with Tabasco and tarragon, or with creamed mushrooms. Roll gently by lifting an edge of the paper or foil. Add a dash more grated cheese. Serve with Hollandaise sauce.

½ cup dry breadcrumbs
4 tablespoons or more grated Parmesan cheese
Scrambled eggs or creamed mushrooms

Summer Squash

Three different summer squash are available to us. One is the cymling, sometimes called the patty pan or scalloped squash. These, as late as the 1930's, were allowed to mature till they were 8 or 10 inches across, by which time they were a vegetable much better forgotten. Some enterprising farmer in California decided to sell them small and underdeveloped, and since then they have found a ready public. The same is true of the yellow straight or crookneck squash, which were raised to the point where they looked like the first prize winner for size at the county fair. They were coarse-meated, large in seed, and thoroughly unpalatable. Now one also can buy these in tiny versions, and they are much improved. It is almost impossible, outside of New York and Southern California, to find zucchini, or Italian squash or courgettes, as small as they should be, when they are delicate in texture and flavor. But they are available in certain markets and are worth looking for.

All the old cookbooks provide instructions for cooking mature squash for such a length of time that they could not have any character left in them. Here is Miss Leslie's version:

"Wash them, cut them into pieces and take out the seeds. Boil them about three quarters of an hour, or until quite tender. When done, drain them and squeeze them well till you have pressed out all the water. Mash them with a little butter, pepper and salt. Then put the squash, thus prepared, into a stew pan, set it on hot coals, and stir it very frequently till it becomes dry. Take care not to let it burn."

Thus, it was turned into flavorless pulp, which is what summer squash meant to most people. Fortunately we have now discovered the pleasure of eating young tender squash lightly sautéed in butter or oil, or steamed briefly in a small amount of water.

Depending on additives, 1½ to 2 pounds of summer squash will serve 4.

To Cook Summer Squash

The cymlings may be left whole or cut into quarters. The small yellow crooknecks may be peeled or not according to tenderness. Slice them across or cut them in quarters or sixths lengthwise. Zucchini should be sliced or cut in strips, or, if very small, may be left whole. If by chance you are lucky enough to get them with the blossoms intact at the blossom end, naturally cook the blossoms, too.

To steam-cook. Drop the prepared squash (1½ to 2 pounds) into a small amount of boiling salted water in a heavy saucepan and steam-cook, covered, until they are just crisply tender. Drain and serve at once, as follows:

(1) Add 6 to 8 tablespoons melted butter, 1 teaspoon freshly ground pepper, and 1 tablespoon lemon juice.

(2) Arrange on a heated serving plate or in a heated dish. Add 1 cup Hollandaise sauce well seasoned with lemon juice, or add 1½ cups sauce Mousseline.

To braise or sauté. Cut the squash in rounds or in long fingers and sauté quickly in 6 tablespoons butter or in the same of olive oil, or half butter and half oil. Season with a finely chopped garlic clove, salt, and ½ teaspoon freshly ground pepper. When just tender but still firm, add 2 tablespoons chopped parsley. Serve from a heated serving dish.

Zucchini with Walnuts

6 medium small zucchini
2 tablespoons butter
2 tablespoons olive oil
1 cup walnuts
1 teaspoon salt
½ teaspoon freshly ground pepper

Cut the zucchini in ½-inch slices and sauté in butter and olive oil till tender but still crisp. Shake the pan well and toss the zucchini with a wooden spoon to cook evenly. Reserve ¼ cup walnuts. Chop the remaining ¾ cup and blend with the zucchini along with the salt and pepper. Shake the pan, and when the walnuts are heated and blended with the zucchini, transfer to a heated vegetable dish and garnish with the remaining walnuts.

Sautéed Zucchini with Herbs and Garlic

6 to 8 small zucchini cut in quarters lengthwise
Olive oil
2 finely chopped garlic cloves
1 teaspoon salt
1 tablespoon, or to taste, chopped fresh basil (or another herb)
½ teaspoon freshly ground pepper
2 tablespoons chopped parsley

Cut the zucchini in thin strips. Heat the olive oil in a heavy skillet and add the zucchini strips. Sauté lightly, turning them once or twice, for 5 minutes. Add the garlic, salt, and basil. Cover the pan and simmer about 10 minutes, till the zucchini are just tender to the bite. Add the pepper. Serve in a heated dish with chopped parsley for a garnish.

Zucchini with Tomato Sauce. After adding the garlic and basil, add 1 cup tomato sauce. Cover, and simmer 10 minutes. Serve sprinkled with grated Parmesan cheese.

Winter Squash

Our repertory now includes quite a number of winter squash in addition to the time-honored Hubbard and Golden Hubbard, which were the standbys for generations and which are both extremely good. We have the acorn, banana, butternut, nutmeg, turban, and the Danish squash. Of these the Hubbards are still the best for long-time storage and will be found to be richly meated and moist well into the winter. The acorn should be eaten at its peak and not kept long after harvesting.

The rind of good squash should be very hard. Usually 1 medium squash is ample for 1 or 2 persons. With larger winter squash, you will have to decide according to the size of the pieces how much you should cook.

To Cook Winter Squash

Remove the seeds and clean thoroughly. Some people add bacon or bacon fat to the squash; others butter it well. Acorn squash halves may be filled with well-seasoned sausage meat. Or spread the halves with softened butter and sprinkle well with brown sugar. Bake in a 375-degree oven either in a pan of water or on the rack. An acorn squash cut in half will take about 30 to 45 minutes. The banana squash, and most others of that type will take 30 to 40 minutes. Hubbard will probably take an hour to cook to proper softness without becoming dry.

Save for Hubbard, squash may be served in the shell with salt, pepper, and seasonings such as nutmeg or ginger. Hubbard squash may be served in the shell with plenty of butter, freshly ground pepper, and salt. Or it may be scooped out, put through the food mill, buttered well, whipped, and then reheated in additional butter.

Casserole of Squash

5 pounds squash
½ cup melted butter
1 teaspoon salt
1 teaspoon freshly ground pepper
Pinch of nutmeg
½ cup toasted coarsely chopped pecans, and some whole
3 tablespoons sherry or Madeira

Bake the squash according to directions above. When it is tender, scoop out the meat from the shells and combine with the rest of the ingredients. Put the mixture in a buttered 1½-quart baking dish and sprinkle with additional whole toasted pecans. Dot with butter and bake 15 minutes at 375 degrees. Serve at once.

Tomatoes

The tomato, or love apple, was originally raised as a decorative plant, and because of its relationship to the nightshade family was long suspected of being too poisonous to eat. Whoever ate the first one and lived to tell about it remains unknown to history, but I am convinced that the Portuguese and Italians were the discoverers of its culinary possibilities.

Not until 1820 or slightly earlier was it accepted in American cookery. Most likely it was initially used for preserves and then for salads. After that came its use in sauces and other preparations. The first recorded American recipes I found were in Miss Leslie's books, dating from the 1850's and '60's. Needless to say, once the tomato was introduced, its inimitable delights were soon known throughout the countryside.

Unless you grow your own tomatoes or buy them from a farmer's market there are few delights in today's product. Commercial tomatoes are grown for shelfage rather than for flavor, and one can cook them for hours, it seems, without getting palatable results. Therefore, when fresh garden tomatoes are not available you can successfully substitute canned tomatoes of good quality, especially the Italian plum variety. They work particularly well in such dishes as stewed and escalloped tomatoes.

To peel tomatoes, see page 43.

Stewed Tomatoes

4 pounds tomatoes
4 tablespoons butter
Salt and freshly ground pepper
1 teaspoon or more sugar

If good fresh ones are available this is the way I like to stew tomatoes.

Peel the tomatoes (page 43). Place them with the butter in a heavy skillet and cook slowly, covered, till they break down. Add salt and sugar and continue cooking till the mixture is well blended — about 10 minutes. Correct the seasoning. Serve with additional butter, if desired.

Stewed Tomatoes with Basil. Add 4 tablespoons butter and 2 tablespoons chopped fresh basil.

Stewed Tomatoes with Onion. Cook ½ cup finely chopped onion with the tomatoes.

Stewed Tomatoes with Lemon and Garlic. Cook 1 finely cut garlic clove with the tomatoes. When they are cooked add 1 tablespoon grated lemon zest, 2 tablespoons butter, and 1 tablespoon lemon juice.

Piquant Tomatoes. Ten minutes before serving, add 3 canned peeled green chilies, finely chopped, and 1 garlic clove, finely chopped.

Escalloped Tomatoes

One of the standbys of American cookery. It is found everywhere — in homes, schools, restaurants, and summer camps. It can be horrible and it can also be extraordinarily good. Here is Miss Leslie's recipe, which is a very good one even now.

"Peel some fine large tomatoes, cut them up and take out the seeds. Then put them in a deep dish in alternate layers with grated breadcrumbs and a little butter in small bits. There must be a large proportion of breadcrumbs. Season the whole with a little salt and cayenne pepper. Set in an oven and bake it. In cooking tomatoes care should be taken not to have them too liquid."

If they cook at 350 degrees, they will be about perfect. Six good-sized tomatoes will do the recipe.

Scalloped Plum Tomatoes

2 cups freshly made breadcrumbs
1 can Italian plum tomatoes (32 ounces)
1/4 cup finely minced onion or scraped onion
1 tablespoon sugar
1 teaspoon salt
1/2 teaspoon freshly ground pepper
Butter

Line a 2-quart baking dish with crumbs. Drain off about 1/2 cup liquid from the tomatoes. Combine the tomatoes with the seasonings and add to the casserole. Liberally cover with additional crumbs and dot with butter. Bake at 350 degrees 25 to 30 minutes, or until the topping is beautifully brown and the tomatoes cooked through.

Grilled Tomatoes

6 large ripe tomatoes
Salt and freshly ground pepper
2 slices bread
1 clove garlic
Olive oil
2 tablespoons chopped parsley

Slice the top off the stem end of the tomatoes. Give each tomato a slight squeeze to loosen some of the seeds, sprinkle it with salt, and turn over on absorbent paper to drain.

In the meantime, rub the bread well with garlic and whirl in the blender to make breadcrumbs. Blend with a little olive oil — about 2 tablespoons. When the tomatoes are well drained, spread a little of the crumb mixture over them and add a bit more salt and some pepper. Place the tomatoes on a rack and broil about 5 inches from the broiling unit. As they begin to heat through, raise the rack closer to the heat and continue broiling. Do not let the crumbs burn, but let them brown nicely. Garnish with chopped parsley. Serve with broiled meats.

Broiled Tomatoes Sicilian Style

6 quite firm ripe tomatoes
1/2 cup olive oil
1/2 teaspoon allspice
1 teaspoon cinnamon
3 garlic cloves, finely chopped

These can be found on menus in New York and California. They are unusually good.

Remove the tops of the tomatoes and rub the tomatoes with salt. Squeeze lightly to loosen the pulp, and turn onto absorbent paper. Combine the oil and seasonings, and either whirl in a blender or pound in a mortar. Pour the mixture into a heavy skillet. Place the tomatoes cut side down in the mixture and simmer over medium

¼ cup chopped parsley
1 teaspoon dry basil or 1 tablespoon chopped fresh basil
1 teaspoon salt
½ teaspoon freshly ground pepper

low heat about 30 minutes, till the tomatoes are cooked through. They must not be mushy and overdone. Right them and spoon the pan juices over them.

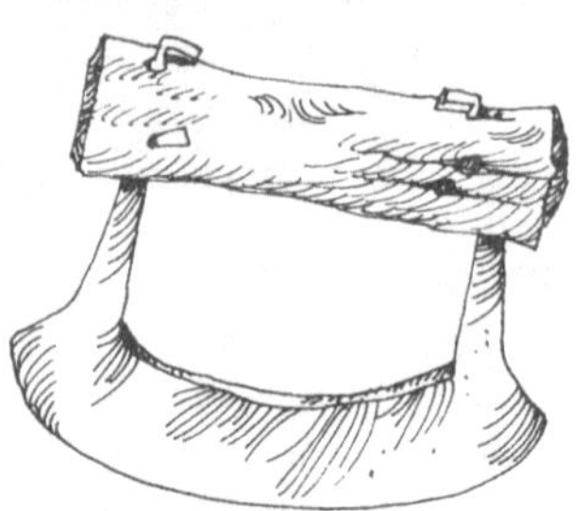

Mrs. Biles's Stuffed Tomatoes

6 largish solid tomatoes, with seeds and most of the pulp removed
2 cups grated corn
1 fairly large green pepper, seeded and finely chopped
½ cup rich cream
½ cup fresh breadcrumbs
1 egg
1 teaspoon salt
½ teaspoon freshly ground pepper
6 slices bacon
1 cup broth
6 toast rounds

This was an old Middle Western recipe and is extremely individual in its flavor.

Prepare the tomatoes. Combine all the ingredients except the bacon, broth, and toast, and blend well. Fill the tomato shells with this mixture. Top each with a slice of bacon. Arrange in a 9×12-inch baking dish. Pour in the broth. Bake 35 minutes at 350 degrees, basting once or twice. Serve on the rounds of toast.

Pennsylvania Dutch Tomatoes

6 tomatoes, ripe but firm
Flour
4 tablespoons butter
4 tablespoons oil
½ cup tightly packed brown sugar
1 cup heavy cream
Salt and freshly ground pepper

Cut the tomatoes in thick slices and press both sides into flour. They must be well floured. Sauté in the hot butter and oil, and while they are browning on one side, sprinkle the other heavily with brown sugar. Turn carefully. As they cook the brown sugar will caramelize and blend with flour. When just browned on both sides, add the cream and let the tomatoes simmer 3 to 4 minutes. Transfer to a hot platter and serve with bacon strips.

Note. Green tomatoes may also be prepared the same way.

Sautéed Crumbed Tomatoes

6 large firm ripe tomatoes
Flour
1 egg lightly beaten with 2 tablespoons cream
2 cups dry breadcrumbs
¼ pound butter
1 teaspoon salt
1 teaspoon freshly ground pepper
½ teaspoon Tabasco
Chopped parsley

Cut the ends off the tomatoes and then cut into ½-inch slices. Press into flour, dip in the egg mixture, and then roll in breadcrumbs. Sauté in bubbling hot (not burning) butter. When browned, turn carefully and add the seasonings. Sauté until the second side is nicely brown. Transfer to a heated plate and sprinkle with chopped parsley. Spoon crumbs and butter from the pan over the tomatoes. Serve with frizzled ham or with bacon for breakfast, or with broiled meats or roasts.

Steamed Cherry Tomatoes

These small tomatoes have crept into popularity within the last twenty years. First they were a novelty for salads and for cocktail hors d'oeuvres. Then people began enjoying their honest tomato flavor and began serving them as a vegetable. If you prefer to peel them, it is a tedious job but rewarding. Choose 1 pint firm tomatoes and pour boiling water over them. Let stand 1 minute and then plunge them into cold water. They will peel easily. Place them in the upper part of a double boiler and add 6 tablespoons butter, 1 teaspoon salt, and 1 teaspoon finely chopped fresh dill. Cover, and steam over hot water till the tomatoes are just heated through. Pour carefully into a heated serving dish and top with additional chopped dill.

If you do not peel these, merely heat them in the upper part of the double boiler with butter and dill, chopped fresh tarragon, or chopped fresh basil. They will be less delicate and less elegant, but they will still be extremely good.

Fried Onions, Tomatoes, and Corn with Olives

3 large onions, peeled and thinly sliced
4 tablespoons butter
4 tablespoons bacon fat or oil
4 large tomatoes, peeled, seeded, and chopped
1½ teaspoons salt
1 teaspoon freshly ground pepper
1½ cups freshly cut corn or whole-kernel corn
1 cup pitted ripe olives

This is definitely in the cooking style of Southern California, New Mexico, and Arizona, and it is a good hearty vegetable combination. Sometimes, in addition to the seasonings suggested here, a tablespoon or two of chili powder is added. It gives excellent flavor.

Sauté the onions in the butter and fat in a heavy skillet till just soft. Add the tomatoes and seasonings, cover, and simmer 25 minutes over low heat till thoroughly blended. Add the corn and olives and heat through for 10 minutes. If using chili powder, add after the corn has cooked 5 minutes. Correct the seasoning and serve with hamburgers, barbecued pork, or barbecued spareribs.

Stuffed Baked Tomatoes

Remove the tops of 6 tomatoes, loosen the flesh with a sharp knife, and scoop out the seeds and flesh in the center, leaving a shell. Stuff in any of the ways given below. Place in a well-buttered baking pan and bake 25 to 30 minutes at 375 degrees, or till the mixture is hot and the tomatoes just cooked through. Some people cover the pan, but I feel it pulls too much of the juice. If the tomatoes appear to be getting dry, you can baste them with a few spoonfuls of butter.

(1) Stuff with freshly cut corn — about 2 cups for 6 tomatoes — blended with a little of the chopped tomato pulp, 2 tablespoons chopped onion, 2 tablespoons chopped parsley, 1 teaspoon salt, ½ teaspoon freshly ground pepper, and 6 tablespoons melted butter. Cover with breadcrumbs and dot with butter.

(2) Blend 2½ cups cooked rice, 2 finely chopped garlic cloves, 1 small onion chopped and sautéed in 6 tablespoons butter, ½ cup finely chopped ham or chicken, ¼ cup pine nuts, 1 teaspoon salt, 1 teaspoon freshly ground pepper, and 1 teaspoon basil or oregano. Fill the tomato cups. Dot well with butter. When done, garnish with chopped parsley.

(3) Stuff with 1 cup mushroom purée or duxelles (see page 528) combined with 2½ cups cooked rice, 3 chopped garlic cloves cooked with 1 chopped onion in 4 tablespoons butter till soft, 1 teaspoon thyme, 1 teaspoon salt, and ½ teaspoon freshly ground pepper.

(4) Combine 2 cups cold cooked rice, 1 cup cold minced lamb, 2 chopped onions, and 2 chopped cloves garlic sautéed in 4 tablepoons butter, 1 teaspoon basil, and a little of the tomato pulp. Stuff the tomatoes and top with fresh breadcrumbs. Dribble olive oil over all and bake at 375 degrees 25 to 30 minutes.

(5) Dice 6 small zucchini and sauté them quickly with 3 finely chopped garlic cloves in 6 tablespoons olive oil. Toss well so that the zucchini browns lightly. Add 1 teaspoon salt, ½ teaspoon freshly ground pepper, and 2 tablespoons chopped parsley. Fill the tomatoes and brush well with olive oil. Bake 25 minutes in a 375-degree oven and serve with additional chopped parsley.

Cheese Tomato Pie

1 recipe biscuit dough
4 to 6 peeled ripe tomatoes, rather thickly sliced
1 teaspoon salt

Really a version of quiche, and an original.

Line a 9-inch pie pan with the biscuit dough. Cover with layers of the sliced tomatoes. Sprinkle with the salt, pepper, and basil. Blend the cheese and tne mayonnaise and spread over the tomatoes. Bake at 400 degrees 15 minutes, then reduce the heat to 350 degrees

1 teaspoon freshly ground pepper
2 tablespoons freshly cut basil or 1 teaspoon dried basil
1 cup shredded cheese — Cheddar, Gruyère, or jack
1½ cups mayonnaise

and bake until the crust is done and the top nicely browned. This will take about 20 additional minutes.

Turnips

Turnips are in our markets most of the year and are used very often for seasoning in stews and soups. In this case, they should be used with great care, as they are strong enough in flavor to overpower almost any other ingredient. Cooked by themselves as a vegetable, they are extremely piquant in flavor and highly individual. Many people find turnips rather unpleasant. I, however, am exceedingly fond of them. About 1½ pounds of turnips should serve four people. Look for the smallest ones, which are more delicate in texture and flavor.

Boiled Turnips

Peel 6 to 8 small to medium turnips and cut them in even dice, rounds, or slices. Cook them in boiling salted water for about 15 to 20 minutes or until just tender. Drain. To serve, add butter, freshly ground pepper, and additional salt if needed.

Turnips with Mushrooms. Combine the buttered and seasoned cooked sliced turnips with an equal quantity of sliced sautéed mushrooms. Add a tablespoon of finely chopped parsley.

Turnips with Cream. Add to the drained cooked turnips 2 tablespoons butter, ½ teaspoon freshly ground pepper, and about 3 tablespoons heavy cream. Toss the turnips well in the mixture and garnish with finely chopped chives and parsley.

Mashed Turnips. Mash the cooked drained turnips and combine with 2 to 3 tablespoons butter, 2 tablespoons heavy cream, salt and freshly ground pepper to taste. Garnish with chopped parsley or paprika.

Braised Turnips

8 to 10 turnips, peeled and trimmed
6 tablespoons butter
1 teaspoon sugar
½ cup beef stock or consommé
Salt
Freshly ground pepper

Peel the turnips. Melt the butter in a heavy skillet, and when it is foaming and bubbly add the turnips and roll them around in the butter over medium heat for several minutes. Sprinkle lightly with granulated sugar and shake the pan so that the turnips begin to caramelize slightly. When they are delicately brown, add the consommé, cover the skillet, and simmer until just crisply tender, shaking the pan from time to time so that they are evenly cooked. Correct the seasoning and serve with the pan juices.

Yellow Turnips or Rutabagas

The English, who have loved this vegetable for years, were the first to bring them to this country under the name which they had used at home — "swedes." They were used for animal feeding and for family feeding. Rutabagas, yellow turnips, or swedes are a traditional part of Thanksgiving dinners in many parts of the country, either mashed or buttered. They have a strong flavor which I find most delightful. One large rutabaga should serve four people and sometimes more.

Buttered Rutabagas

1 large rutabaga
Salt
Freshly ground pepper
Butter

Peel, cut into dice or slices, and cook in boiling salted water to cover over medium heat until they are just tender. (Lately rutabagas have been dipped in wax before being sent to market, so be sure you remove all the wax when you peel the vegetable.) Drain well. If you wish to mash them, mash with a potato masher or electric mixer. Add 4 to 6 tablespoons melted butter for this quantity of diced rutabagas, with plenty of freshly ground pepper and additional salt if needed.

Rutabagas with Mushrooms. Mash the rutabagas, butter and season them, and add 1 cup chopped mushrooms sautéed in butter until they are very dark in color and dehydrated.

Swedes and Potatoes. This was a favorite in England and later throughout the country where the English settled and gardened. Combine an equal quantity of mashed rutabagas and mashed potatoes with butter and a little heavy cream. Pile into a serving dish and top with a good pat of butter before sending to the table. Add plenty of freshly ground pepper.

Deep-Fried Vegetables

Deep-fried foods run the risk of being less than superb — sodden and heavy — unless they are prepared fresh and remain crisp and delicate.

Naturally, first among the deep-fried vegetables in popularity are potatoes, which came to be known in this country alone as "French fries," and probably inspired the designation of "French fried" for any other food fried in deep fat. A runner-up to potatoes is the fried onion ring, without which a steak is not a steak to many people. It can be the saddest of all fried vegetables if it is not crisp, tender, and pungent.

Here are two excellent batters for deep-frying.

Beer Batter

1 12-ounce can light beer
1 cup flour
1 teaspoon salt
¼ teaspoon Tabasco

Beer has long been used as a leavening agent and as an additive to batters for frying and even for crêpes and pancakes.

Sift the flour and salt into the beer and stir until the batter is light and frothy. Add the Tabasco and let stand several hours. Be sure to stir again before using.

Cecily Brownstone's Buttermilk Batter

1 egg
1 cup buttermilk
1 cup flour
½ teaspoon each salt and baking soda

This particular batter is by far the best one I have ever found for deep-frying onion rings. Beat the egg and buttermilk together, and add the dry ingredients.

To Deep-Fry Vegetables

For batter frying, use any of the following:

Artichoke hearts	Eggplant fingers or slices
Artichoke bottoms	Mushrooms
Jerusalem artichokes	Mangetout or snow peas
Asparagus	Pepper strips or rings
Blanched snap beans	Spinach leaves, well crisped
Broccoli flowerets	Fiddleheads (see page 559)
Brussels sprouts	Zucchini

Chill the vegetables and dry them well. Dip in batter and fry at 370 to 375 degrees a few at a time. Drain on absorbent paper and keep hot in a 325-degree oven till all are cooked.

Fried Onion Rings

Cut 3 or 4 large onions into ¼-inch slices and break up into rings. Soak in ice water 2 hours, adding more ice if necessary. Remove, dry thoroughly, dip in batter, and fry in deep fat a few at a time at 375 degrees. Remove from the fat when nicely browned and drain on absorbent paper. Keep warm in the oven till ready to use.

Zucchini Florentine

Slice zucchini paper-thin or in long julienne strips. Chill in ice water. Dry, roll in flour, and fry a few at a time in deep fat at 375 degrees till delicately brown and crisp. Drain, season, and send to table at once.

Vegetable Soufflés

Soufflés have always been a rather festive dish in this country, and people seem to enjoy making them and experimenting with them. Here are a few vegetable soufflés that have been standard for years.

Basic Soufflé Mixture

3 tablespoons butter
3 tablespoons flour
¾ cup milk heated to the boiling point
½ teaspoon salt
Freshly ground pepper to taste or Tabasco
4 egg yolks
Cooked and prepared vegetable (see below)
6 egg whites
½ teaspoon cream of tartar (optional)

Melt the butter and combine with the flour. Cook several minutes to blend thoroughly. Add the hot milk and stir until the mixture is thickened. Add the salt and pepper. Remove from the heat, cool slightly, and add the egg yolks. Return to the heat and stir for just a minute or two. Add the vegetables, blend well, and correct the seasonings. Beat the egg whites until they are stiff but not dry. Classically this is done in a copper bowl with a large whisk. However, it may be done in the mixer, with a rotary beater or with a whisk in any large bowl. If you do not use copper, it is wise to add cream of tartar when the whites begin to foam. Then beat to the soft peak stage. Test the bowl by tipping. If the whites run from the bottom of the bowl they need a little additional beating. You should be able to invert the bowl without having the whites drop out, but they must not be beaten till they are dry and grainy, at which point they are overbeaten.

Take about one-third of the egg whites and blend thoroughly into the egg yolk mixture by folding in with a spatula or with your hand. Then take the remaining two-thirds and fold in carefully but not as thoroughly. Pour the mixture into a 1½-quart buttered soufflé dish, any deep straight-sided dish, or a shallow straight-sided baking dish. Bake at 375 degrees 30 to 35 minutes, or until the soufflé is brown and puffy. It may be left just a bit creamy in the center, which is by far better than having it too firm.

Snap Bean Soufflé. Use 1 cup cooked puréed or finely chopped green beans prepared with butter, salt, freshly ground pepper, and if you like, a touch of fresh tarragon or dill.

Broccoli Soufflé. Use 1 cup cooked puréed or finely chopped seasoned broccoli and ¼ cup grated Parmesan cheese.

Carrot Soufflé. Use 1 cup cooked puréed carrots, well buttered and seasoned with salt.

Corn Soufflé. Use 1 cup grated fresh corn or 1 cup canned whole-kernel or cream-style corn.

Onion Soufflé. Use 1 cup steamed chopped onions, well buttered, and ¼ cup grated Parmesan cheese in the basic soufflé mixture.

Shallot Soufflé. Use 8 finely chopped, sautéed shallots and ¾ cup grated Cheddar cheese in the basic soufflé mixture. Exceptionally good with steak.

Corn and Chili Soufflé

5 egg yolks
3 canned peeled green chilies
1 cup whole-kernel corn, or fresh corn cut from the cob
½ teaspoon salt
1 teaspoon chili powder
6 egg whites

Whirl the egg yolks, chilies, and corn in an electric blender with the seasonings. Beat the egg whites until stiff but not dry. Fold into the corn and chili mixture and pour into a well-buttered 1½-quart soufflé mold or a buttered baking dish. Bake at 400 degrees 25 to 30 minutes.

Spinach Soufflé

Prepare in either of the following ways:

(1) Use 1 cup well-seasoned blanched, chopped, and well-drained spinach in the basic soufflé mixture.

(2) Before pouring the soufflé into the buttered soufflé dish, cover the bottom with a layer of chopped cooked spinach well seasoned with salt, freshly ground pepper, butter, and nutmeg. Use an additional ¾ cup chopped seasoned spinach in the soufflé mixture.

Squash Soufflé

1½ cups puréed winter squash
Butter
Salt and freshly ground pepper
Pinch of cinnamon and nutmeg
5 egg yolks
6 egg whites

Purée the cooked squash, butter it well, and season as usual with salt and pepper, adding a pinch of nutmeg and cinnamon. Beat in the egg yolks thoroughly. Beat the whites until stiff but not dry and fold into the squash mixture. Pour into a well-buttered 1½-quart soufflé dish or baking dish and bake at 350 degrees for 45 minutes, or until nicely puffed and browned.

Canned Vegetables

Canned vegetables were the first of the convenience foods, and they have been with us since the late 1860's and 1870's, when there were both American and European vegetables on the markets. Originally they served to supplement fresh vegetables, but they have now become an important part of our food economy, and improvement in canning methods and flavor control has brought some canned vegetables to the point where they are oftentimes better than the inferior fresh vegetables available — tomatoes, for example. Even with the advent of frozen foods, canned foods remain popular and are, of course, unbeatable for sheer convenience. People sometimes forget that canned foods are ready to eat. They need only some touching up with seasoning and, if they are to be eaten hot, a mere heating through.

Some of the earlier cookbooks had definite ideas about cooking canned vegetables. Mrs Harland warned: "Open a can of peas an hour before cooking them, that there may be no musty, airless taste about them, and turn into a bowl. When ready for them put on in a farina kettle — or one saucepan within another — of hot water. If dry add cold water to cover them and stew about 25 minutes. Drain, stir in a generous lump of butter; pepper and salt."

We know better than that now.

Artichoke bottoms. Useful for baked dishes or for salads and good stuffed. Usually sold in two different sizes in both jars and bottles. Serve in any of the ways suggested for fresh ones.

Asparagus. A vegetable entirely different from the fresh. You either like it or you do not. For lovers of white asparagus, the jumbo spears are excellent hot or cold. We used to have oblong cans of asparagus and occasionally still see them nowadays. This was when there were great fields of white asparagus of superb quality around Sacramento. Never try to fool anyone into thinking that canned asparagus is anything but what it is.

Beans. Cooked dried beans are available in cans and save the time of soaking as well as cooking. If you like the character of canned green or wax beans, excellent ones can be found — whole, cut, or shredded — good for salads or for eating hot. There is a definite flavor change, but the texture and color are quite acceptable.

Carrots. Unfortunately a great many small carrots in cans and jars are being imported, and one or two American packers are offering them. What is more unfortunate, there are many fine restaurants with labor shortages who are serving them to their customers. Canned carrots are of good color, but utterly tasteless and of a disagreeable texture. They are best rejected completely.

Corn. Both the whole-kernel and the cream-style corn have many different uses. The quality varies among packers and brands, but the top grades are excellent for sautés, chowders, soufflés, and puddings.

Mushrooms. They are gummy, flavorless, and of disagreeable color. I find the dried mushrooms much better.

Onions. Some of the small onions in cans are very good and may be used for creamed onions and for combining with other vegetables. Taste the juice to see if it is agreeable, as much of it is, and use some of it for the sauce for creamed onions. They need be only heated, for they are quite well cooked when you get them.

Peas. These were among the very first vegetables to be canned. Some are dreadful, many excellent, and a few superb if treated carefully. They need butter and seasonings and merely heating through. Some of the larger peas are also excellent products, and those combined with tiny onions or with other vegetables are quite successful. On the other hand, avoid the small — not the tiny — peas, which usually have a much starchier texture than the others.

Peppers. Chilies, pimientos, and pepper cups (for stuffing) are all available in cans and are useful and well preserved products.

Potatoes. Well, do what you will with them, they still have the flavor of canned potatoes and will never lose it. They are sometimes a lifesaver but should never become a habit.

Spinach. Too poor for further comment.

Squash and pumpkin. If the dish is to be well seasoned the canned product is very useful. Makes a good hot purée and excellent pies.

Tomatoes. Probably the most valuable of all the canned vegetables. I will go as far as to state that for the most part canned tomatoes are better than fresh for sauces and purées. I tend to use them more all the time. Many of our fresh tomatoes are of a texture that will never melt down and make a rich, thick purée or sauce. One must read the labels carefully, for there are varieties of canned tomatoes which are not good. Buy solid-pack, stewed Italian plum and concentrated tomato paste. Canned tomato sauce is very good when you need a small amount, but it needs seasoning. Most canned tomato purée I find a little thin for general use. It needs cooking down and seasoning.

Edible Weeds

The Indians showed us which weeds and sprouts were edible, and many of these continue to appear on our tables.

Dandelion. The tiny shoots of the dandelion weed are prized by people, though one can buy cultivated dandelions in the market. They are cooked like other greens, or they may be sautéed in oil with garlic, mint, or bacon.

Dock. This is the sour dock, or curly-leafed version of dock, which grows wild through the West and Middle West. The best leaves are the early ones in the spring. They may be cooked and served like spinach or other greens.

Fiddleheads. These shoots of the fern, which are the first pushing through the ground, are considered a great delicacy. They are available canned and frozen in various parts of the country and in Canada. They are cooked in a small amount of boiling salted water and eaten with butter or Hollandaise sauce.

Pokeweed. The young shoots of the pokeweed or pigeon berry weed are often found in farmers' markets in various parts of the country. Usually they are cooked as one would asparagus.

Sorrel. Nowadays we use the domesticated sorrel, but there is a limited quantity of wild sorrel to be found, and it is used in salads or soups or cooked with spinach.

Wild peppergrass. This is sometimes called wild mustard and is cooked like cultivated mustard greens.

Stir-Fry Vegetables

Stir-fry vegetables were inspired by the crisp, fresh-flavored cooking achieved by the Chinese in their round-bottomed cooking pan — the wok — with its conical cover. Characteristically, Americans have adapted this style of cookery to their own use and do not necessarily season their food Chinese style. In fact, those who prefer very little seasoning will find the stir-fry method retains the full flavor of the vegetables and thus requires a minimum of additives.

Root vegetables are not so successful when stir-fried, with the exception of tender, young carrots cut in thin rounds. Most of the others — turnips, rutabagas, parsnips and such — are better if steam-cooked.

To Stir-Fry Vegetables

The method of stir-frying, in case you do not own a wok and a wok-ring for resting the round-bottomed pan over the heat, can be attained with a heavy frying pan with a tight-fitting cover. Since the latter part of the cooking usually requires steam, the lid must fit tightly.

Have the pan hot to begin the cooking. Add as little or as much oil, butter, bacon fat, or other fat as you like to season the vegetables. Turn the prepared vegetables into the pan and toss-stir to heat them quickly. Use a wide spatula or pancake turner. (The Chinese use what looks like a flat soup ladle and a rounded spatula.) When the vegetables show definite wilting, add a small amount of water, broth, or in some cases tomato juice, and seasoning, and turn the heat very low. Cover tightly and let the vegetables steam until just tender. If there is a large amount in the pan, it will, of course, take longer to cook. If the pan contains such things as greens, they should be turned during the steaming. Transfer the vegetables to a hot serving dish when they are just crisp-tender. Even a few seconds can make the difference between being just right or overcooked.

Vegetables must be cut in small sections or pieces so that they will cook quickly. Here are some suggested vegetables and seasonings:

Stir-Fried Asparagus. Asparagus should be cleaned well, broken at the point where it is tender. Cut on a sharp diagonal across the stem in

¼-inch slices or larger, leaving the tip, which is the most tender part. For each 2 or 3 cups, use 1 to 5 tablespoons butter or oil. After about 1 minute of tossing it in the hot fat, add ½ cup chicken or beef broth (preferably chicken), water, or tomato juice, and season with salt and freshly ground pepper or 1 to 2 tablespoons soy sauce. Turn the heat very low and steam about 3 to 6 minutes more — depending upon how thin you cut the asparagus. If using soy sauce for flavoring, salt afterward. The soy may add enough salt.

A Chinese Way of Cooking Asparagus. Soak about 2 tablespoons of the tiny Chinese black beans in the chicken broth an hour or more before adding the broth, with the beans, to the asparagus. Sometimes a thin slice of fresh gingerroot is added with this, and a crushed clove of garlic. The garlic is fished out of the mixture before serving. Oftentimes also the dish includes medium-size tomatoes peeled, cut in sixths, and added at the end of the cooking just long enough to heat through — about 1 to 2 minutes, no longer.

Stir-Fried Broccoli. Broccoli is another good vegetable for stir-frying. Wash very well, and cut the stalk where the knife goes through easily. If the stalk is quite thick, split it in half or even in four pieces from the base to the flower. Cut off the flowers, for they will cook quickly. Cut the stems in diagonal or crosswise slices about ½ inch thick. Sauté the stems quickly, as for asparagus. Add the liquid and flower tops along with the same seasonings used for asparagus. Frozen broccoli pieces can be used for this.

Stir-Fried Green Beans. Green or snap beans should be cut on the diagonal not more than ¼ to ½ inch wide. After the initial tossing, add the seasonings and steam from 5 to 10 minutes, depending upon the type and age of the beans. French-cut frozen beans take kindly to stir-fry cooking. Break them apart quite well before putting into the hot greased pan. Add a bit of onion with the first frying, and use tomato juice instead of broth for the steaming. Or add the broth, and use pieces of fresh tomato, as suggested for asparagus, steamed just long enough to heat them through.

Stir-Fried Cauliflower. Cut into large flowerets, with the tough stem removed, then cut the flowerets into slices not more than ¼ inch thick. Treat as you would asparagus, and it will take about as long to cook. Often strips of seeded sweet red or green pepper are a flavorful addition. Soy also makes a complementary seasoning. And plenty of minced garlic is excellent, especially when the cauliflower is served with lamb or pork.

Stir-Fried Greens. Greens such as kale, Swiss chard, or Chinese cabbage are good stir-fried. Other greens — spinach, mustard, beet — can be stir-fried, but since they require such a short cooking period they do not really benefit by this method. Cut the heavy stems from the greens, then cut the stems into bite-size pieces. Stir-fry these 1 to 2 minutes, then add the leaves with the seasonings and liquid — chicken broth, water, beef broth, or tomato juice — and steam for a very few minutes.

Greens are good with Chinese-style flavorings. Use ½ to 1 teaspoon green ginger peeled and chopped (if you can't obtain the green gingerroot use about ¼ teaspoon ground ginger in the broth) to each pound of greens. Onion and green pepper may also be added to your taste, along with 1 to 2 tablespoons soy sauce. Cook the onion and strips of seeded green or red pepper with the stems of the greens. They should steam until they are crisp-tender.

Stir-Fried Green Peppers. Peppers have better flavor, I think, if peeled first — or remove as much peeling as you can (see page 540). Stir-fried green pepper strips are a favorite with many beef and steak dishes, and they are usually combined with onions cut the Chinese way. The dry onion is peeled and cut in half crosswise, then the onion is turned against a knife, leaving thin strips about 1½ inches long. Or use diagonal sections of young green onion with much of the tops. Add onion to taste. Do not overcook.

Stir-Fried Cabbage. This is delicious, especially when done as the Chinese would do it. For 1½ quarts shredded cabbage add 1 onion and half a green pepper cut in thin strips. Toss for 2 minutes before adding the liquid (½ cup chicken broth or pork broth) and seasonings. Use 1 garlic clove, minced, and if you like, 1 or 2 teaspoons minced green gingerroot; or use ⅛ to ¼ teaspoon powdered ginger in the broth; or wash off candied or preserved ginger and add 1 tablespoon, chopped. Toss well, then steam about 3 to 8 minutes, depending upon how fine the cabbage is cut.

Stir-Fried Squash. Zucchini and other summer squash are delicious stir-fried. Cut small squash into rounds about ½ inch thick. You'll no doubt like onion to your taste with this, and I often add half a young green onion for each small zucchini. Cut the green onion in ¼-inch rounds. Also add green pepper strips, if you like. After tossing the vegetables, add about ¼ cup broth or tomato juice for each 3 cups squash. Add the seasoning — salt and freshly ground pepper, or soy, ginger, and minced garlic — and steam 4 to 6 minutes, or perhaps less if the squash is very young.

Potatoes

The potato was not in general use in America until about 1721, and it did not achieve popularity until the end of that century. It was the French agronomist Antoine-Auguste Parmentier who rescued it from the suspicion of being unfit for food and brought it soundly into fashion. Later, in the United States, Luther Burbank was also to perform a great service for the potato, developing new strains and improving growth.

After Parmentier's experiments the French gave us many of our best potato dishes — puréed potatoes, potatoes baked with cheese in cream or milk, potatoes fried in various fashions, potato soups. Soufflé potatoes originated in France when a train was late in arriving for a formal banquet to christen a railroad line. A hotel chef, who had been keeping the fried potatoes waiting, plunged them into boiling fat for the second time. Much to his amazement, they puffed up, an accident that was to make them the showpiece of potato dishes and the vexation of generations of housewives. The English contributed one great dish — the boiled potato, called by the French even today *pommes à l'Anglaise*. Americans also contributed a number of wonderful dishes, such as hashed-brown potatoes, potatoes hashed in cream, home fries, and fine baked potatoes, along with the potato chips or "Saratoga chips" which were created in Saratoga, New York, when a young chef became provoked over patrons' demands for thinner fried potatoes.

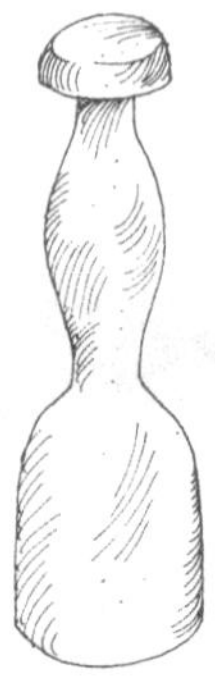

Except for the South, where it is second to rice, corn, and sweet potatoes, the white potato has become the commonest of our vegetables, eaten in some families as often as three times a day. Fried potatoes for breakfast, made from dinner leftovers or from cold boiled potatoes, used to be standard fare and are still much in evidence in the West. But without question deep-fried potatoes — generally called French fries — reign throughout the country. For some people they are a main course, and for others an accompaniment to every dish. Some people eat them with catsup or with mayonnaise and some sprinkle them with vinegar.

To shorten the time needed for preparing potatoes, we now have every possible form of processed potatoes on the market — frozen fried potatoes, frozen mashed potatoes, dehydrated potatoes, freeze-dried potatoes, and there are even some frozen baked potatoes in artificial skins that have been created especially for that dish.

Like most other vegetables, potatoes can be utterly delicious or horrid, depending upon the quality of the raw product and the care in preparation.

Choosing Potatoes

The Idaho potato, used for baking and for dishes requiring a mealy potato, is found throughout the country. But apart from this variety, potatoes differ greatly in every region of the country. In the East, for example, we have Maine potatoes, Long Island potatoes, and new potatoes — both the white and the red (sometimes given an additional coat of dye), found in markets all year. One must simply become familiar with the potatoes in his own section of the country. For use in salads or for frying, waxy potatoes are needed; and for plain boiled or mashed potatoes and for most other uses, a more mealy potato is best.

Buy potatoes that are smooth and have comparatively few eyes to be cut out. Although it is difficult to recommend quantities, 2 pounds will usually serve 4. If using baking potatoes, estimate 1 per person. And for most other purposes one medium-large potato per person is ample. Small new potatoes, however, vary so much in size that you must gauge portions for yourself, using 2 pounds for 4 as a guide.

Preparing Potatoes

Peel potatoes with a vegetable peeler or a sharp knife. The less peel removed, the better, usually, unless you are making olivette or Parisienne potatoes, which require cutting into shapes.

Many people like to boil and serve potatoes in their jackets, especially the thin-skinned new potatoes. The smaller ones are attractive with a strip peeled from their circumference before boiling.

Wash peeled potatoes well before cooking. Some recipes call for soaking sliced potatoes in cold water and then drying them on towels.

If you must slice a great many potatoes you will benefit by using the old fashioned slicer called a mandoline, or you may be fortunate enough to own an electric mixer that is equipped with a vegetable slicer. In either case the thickness of the slices can be made more uniform than by slicing by hand.

Boiled Potatoes

There are two efficient ways to boil potatoes. One is to steam them in a small amount of boiling salted water in a tightly covered heavy saucepan. When they are just tender — in about 20 to 25 minutes — drain and return them to the heat for a few moments to dry out well. The other method is to boil them in salted water to cover in a heavy saucepan. Cook till tender and drain and dry out as recommended above. Serve in any of the following ways.

(1) Serve without butter or seasoning in a heated dish. These might receive a sauce or gravy, or, if served with fish, are good as they are. Butter and salt and freshly ground pepper can always be added at table.

(2) Add approximately 1 tablespoon melted butter per potato; or, in the case of small new potatoes, 6 tablespoons for 2 pounds potatoes. Add a few grinds of pepper.

(3) Add butter and chopped parsley, chives, dill, or mint; or add butter and a combination of parsley and chives.

Creamed Potatoes. These were served at ladies' luncheons and were considered quite elegant. Whether or not they were depended upon the sauce made by the cook or the hostess. They are merely boiled potatoes cut in fancy shapes, cubes, or balls, covered with a rich cream sauce, and usually garnished with chopped parsley.

Baked Potatoes

The best potatoes for baking are the Idahos or the California Whites, or use any local variety which has proved good and mealy. Scrub the skin well. Then bake in any of the following ways:

(1) Rub the potatoes well with butter or oil and make a 1/2-inch slit in each skin with a sharp knife. Bake at 375 degrees an hour or slightly less. Test by squeezing a potato gently with a towel. If it gives and seems soft it is done. Serve the potatoes at once. They

will, if left to keep warm, become soggy and thoroughly unappetizing.

(2) Wash the potatoes well. Do not oil or slit the skins. Bake at 375 degrees approximately one hour, and proceed as above.

(3) If you are cooking outdoors, bury potatoes in the coals and bake 40 to 45 minutes. The skins will burn but the potatoes will be starchy and delicious. Or put potatoes in a heavy iron Dutch oven, cover, and let stand in the coals about 40 minutes.

To eat baked potatoes, split them open and squeeze well to loosen the contents. Then:

(1) Simply eat with salt and freshly ground pepper.

(2) Add butter to taste with the pepper and salt.

(3) Sour cream is often passed, along with accompanying tidbits such as crisp bacon, chopped chives or green onions, parsley, grated Parmesan cheese or shredded Cheddar cheese. However, I feel that this treatment detracts from the elegant flavor of the potato if it is perfectly cooked.

Stuffed Baked Potatoes

4 baked potatoes
4 tablespoons butter
1 teaspoon freshly ground pepper
1 teaspoon salt
4 tablespoons grated Cheddar or Gruyère cheese
2 tablespoons cream
Grated Parmesan cheese

Cut the baked potatoes in half and scoop out the meat into a hot bowl. Blend well with the seasonings, cheese, and cream. Heap into the potato shells, dot with butter, and sprinkle with Parmesan cheese. Return to the oven and bake at 375 degrees until nicely browned — about 15 minutes. Serve with any roast or grilled food. Rich as they are, they also need the company of a sharp salad.

Mashed Potatoes

6 to 8 medium-size potatoes, peeled and quartered
6 tablespoons butter
Salt and freshly ground pepper
½ cup hot cream

Eternally popular with Americans, especially those who are fanciers of potatoes and gravy. This combination was often served as a luncheon dish by itself, with perhaps salad or bread and butter. Basically, mashed potatoes are a purée of potatoes blended with butter and milk or cream and whipped to a creamy consistency with a whisk, wooden spatula, or spoon. Or they are mashed with a potato masher — a wooden or wire one; the butter, seasonings, and milk or cream are added, and all the ingredients are mashed till smooth. There are experts who say that potatoes should only be mashed with an up and down motion and that they should never be whipped. The great Alexandre Dumaine, who ruled over the kitchens in Saulieu at the Hôtel de la Côte d'Or, was one of these. Others feel that whipping aerates the potatoes and gives them perfect texture.

Boil the potatoes as above. Drain and dry. Either put through a food mill or ricer, or mash with a masher. Or prepare in the electric mixer if you have a paddle attachment. Add the butter and mash again well. Add the seasonings and hot cream and beat with a wooden spatula or spoon till light and thoroughly blended. Reheat for a moment over hot water and serve in a heated serving dish topped with a lump of softened butter, unless you are serving gravy.

Variations

(1) Beat chopped parsley or chopped chives into the potatoes.

(2) Combine equal parts of mashed potatoes and mashed celery root.

(3) Combine equal parts of mashed potatoes and mashed yellow turnips. This is often served for holiday dinners.

Mashed Potato Cakes

These are often made with leftover mashed potatoes. You may also beat an egg into the potatoes — they must be cold. Form the potatoes into flat cakes 3 to 4 inches across and 1 to 1½ inches thick. Brush with butter and sauté gently in butter till the cakes are nicely browned on both sides. For 4 potato cakes you will need about 2 cups mashed potatoes and 6 tablespoons butter. Serve very hot. Excellent with chops, steak, or cold meat.

Scalloped Potatoes

4 medium-size potatoes, peeled and sliced about ⅛ inch thick
Butter
1 teaspoon salt
1 teaspoon freshly ground pepper
Milk

This American adaptation resembles in many ways the gratins found in regional French cookery, particularly the Gratin Dauphinois, which comes from the region known as Dauphine. There are two versions of this dish. In one, rather thinly sliced potatoes and rich heavy cream are baked in a garlic-buttered gratin dish. In the other, cheese and egg are added with the cream to the sliced potatoes. Our homely dish is somewhat less rich, but nevertheless no church supper or gathering after the turn of the century was without it. Sometimes the potatoes were scalloped with onion, sometimes with ham, sometimes with parsley.

Soak the sliced potatoes in cold water 30 minutes. Remove and dry on absorbent paper or on towels. Butter a 9×9×3-inch baking dish or an 8 × 10-inch oval baking dish. Arrange a layer of potatoes in it. Dot with butter and season with a little pepper and salt. Continue with layers of potato, butter, and seasoning. Dot the top layer with butter, and add enough milk to just barely cover the potatoes. Bake at 350 degrees 45 minutes to 1 hour, or until the potatoes are tender but not mushy.

Variations

(1) Use beef or chicken broth instead of milk.

(2) Sprinkle each layer of potatoes with grated Cheddar, Gruyère, or Parmesan cheese.

M. Blot's Recipe for Au Gratin Potatoes

6 to 8 cold boiled potatoes
1½ cups rich cream sauce
Cayenne
4 egg yolks, lightly beaten
½ cup shredded Cheddar or Gruyère cheese
Buttered breadcrumbs
Salt and freshly ground pepper

Slice the potatoes rather thick. Make the sauce and season well, adding a bit of cayenne to it. Remove it from the heat, add the egg yolks, and blend well. Add the shredded cheese. Stir well. Spoon a layer of sauce on the bottom of a 9-inch square baking pan or oven-proof dish. Add a layer of potatoes. Alternate layers till material is used, saving sauce for the top. Sprinkle with buttered breadcrumbs and heat in a 400-degree oven 10 minutes. Serve at once.

Home-Fried Potatoes (Made with Boiled Potatoes)

4 or 5 medium-size boiled potatoes, peeled and cut in ⅛-inch slices
4 tablespoons butter or beef dripping
Salt and freshly ground pepper

Melt the butter in a heavy skillet. Add the potatoes and cook slowly to brown on one side. Shake the pan gently two or three times. When they are nicely browned on one side, turn them carefully with a spatula and brown on the other. Season to taste and serve in a heated dish.

Lyonnaise Potatoes

4 to 5 tablespoons butter or beef dripping
1 good-sized onion cut in rings
4 or 5 medium-size boiled potatoes cut in ⅛-inch slices
Salt and freshly ground pepper
Chopped parsley

These are seldom made successfully. The onions are overcooked and the potatoes crumbling, resulting in a not very attractive dish. Use either of these two ways to avoid this.

Method I. Heat the fat in a skillet. Sauté the onion until golden. Transfer to a hot plate while you cook the potatoes. Add more butter or beef fat to the skillet if needed. When the potatoes are nicely browned on both sides, combine with the onions, season to taste, add chopped parsley, and serve in a heated dish.

Method II. Sauté the onions and potatoes simultaneously in separate pans, and combine at the last minute. Add seasonings and chopped parsley, and serve in a heated dish.

O'Brien Potatoes

A turn-of-the-century dish that originated in Jack's, a great restaurant on Sixth Avenue in New York, where every celebrity in the theatre and sporting world ate when after-theatre suppers were still fashionable. To make it, prepare Lyonnaise potatoes, and at the last minute add ¼ cup finely chopped green pepper, ¼ cup chopped pimiento, plenty of chopped parsley, and ¼ cup heavy cream. Let the cream cook down over medium heat. Shake the pan to blend the ingredients, and serve in a hot dish.

Note. Sometimes O'Brien potatoes are diced rather than sliced.

Potatoes Fried with Suet

4 to 5 tablespoons finely chopped beef suet, or substitute beef dripping, chicken fat, goose fat, or pork fat
4 or 5 medium-size raw potatoes, peeled and sliced 1/8 inch thick
Salt and freshly ground pepper

These, in huge quantities, used to be served for breakfast and often for supper in the great ranch dining rooms of earlier days.

Render the beef suet in a skillet till the particles are crisp and the melted fat is hot. Add the potatoes and cook quickly, shaking the pan and turning the potatoes to brown them evenly. When they are tender and crisp, season to taste and serve in a heated serving dish.

An Old Michigan Recipe for Fried Potatoes

Pare and slice the potatoes thin. If sliced in small flakes they look more inviting than when cut in larger pieces. Keep in ice water 2 to 3 hours, then drain them dry, or dry on a towel. Drop them into the boiling lard. When nearly done, take them out with a skimmer and drain them. Let them get cold and drop them again into boiling lard, and fry till well done (this last operation causes them to puff out). Sprinkle with salt and serve hot, but many people like them cold, our recipe says, as a relish for tea or with cold meats.

Hash-Brown Potatoes

As a child I used to be fascinated by short-order cooks at work in a diner or in a thriving railroad café. These cooks were seldom trained chefs, but they were deft and had an innate sense of flavor. Within the limits of their skills, they produced some of our best native dishes. Certainly this was one. They always had a pile of nice waxy boiled potatoes on hand. These were roughly sliced into hot bacon fat, butter, or lard. Sometimes they were also diced on the cutting board beforehand. But the real champions diced them directly in the pan as the potatoes cooked, using a 2-pound baking powder can with holes punched in the bottom. The pan was shaken and tossed, and the potatoes were done to a crusty brown on both sides. Few potatoes ever tasted or looked better to me.

Peel 8 medium or 10 small potatoes and chop them somewhat coarsely. The potatoes should be waxy and not too mealy. Melt 6 tablespoons butter, beef drippings, or bacon fat in a heavy iron or aluminum skillet and add the potatoes, forming them into a flat cake and pressing them down. Let them cook over medium heat about 5 to 6 minutes till they form a crust on the bottom. Run a spatula around the edges to keep them loose, and shake the pan gently from time to time. Add a bit more fat on top and let it trickle through the potatoes. Salt them and give them a few grinds of pepper. Place a large plate or pan over the skillet for a moment or two off the heat and let them steam. Invert quickly onto the plate. Add more fat to the skillet and slide the potatoes back into it to brown the other side. Slide them out onto a hot platter.

Roesti (Swiss) Potatoes

6 to 8 medium potatoes, partially boiled in their skins
¼ pound butter or more
1 teaspoon salt
1 teaspoon or more freshly ground pepper

The potatoes should be about two-thirds cooked. They should not be mealy but should still have a little crispness to them. Cool, and shred them coarsely. Melt the butter in a skillet over medium heat. Add the potatoes and form into a cake, or into several small cakes. Cook rather quickly. Add salt and pepper. Watch carefully until a crust forms on the bottom. Turn with two spatulas or invert on another pan and slide back into the skillet to brown the other side. You will need additional butter. Slide onto a hot platter and serve at once.

The Roesti and hash-browns are really better if they are done in an 8-inch iron skillet with rounded sides. Even if you have to use two skillets at a time, the finished article is easier to handle and looks better.

There are several versions of hashed-in-cream. All of them are rich and good, and your choice may merely depend upon which part of the country you live in. The three recipes given here are Western.

Potatoes Hashed in Cream

6 cold boiled potatoes
6 tablespoons butter, beef drippings, or bacon fat
1 teaspoon salt
1 teaspoon freshly ground pepper
½ cup or more heavy cream

I (*Western Ranch Style*). Peel and chop the potatoes rather coarsely. Sauté quickly in butter or fat, tossing the potatoes so they become crisp on all sides. When they are beginning to be golden brown, add the cream and shake the pan well. Let the cream cook down several minutes, being careful it does not burn but merely helps to make a rich crust. Loosen the potatoes at the bottom of the pan and invert them on a hot platter.

4 cold boiled potatoes
4 tablespoons butter
1 teaspoon salt
½ teaspoon freshly ground pepper
1 teaspoon flour
½ cup heavy cream
2 tablespoons toasted sesame seeds or 2 tablespoons toasted chopped filberts

II. Peel and dice the potatoes. Sauté in the butter till delicately brown. Add the salt, pepper, and flour, and gradually add the cream. Let it cook down until it has formed a crust. Sprinkle with the nuts or sesame seeds and fold over as you would an omelet onto a hot plate. Serve at once.

6 freshly baked potatoes
¼ pound butter
1 teaspoon salt or more to taste
1 teaspoon freshly ground pepper
¾ cup heavy cream
½ cup freshly grated Parmesan cheese

III. This version is especially inventive and is characteristic of the Westerner's more daring approach to food. Slit the potatoes when they come from the oven and squeeze the meat from the skin into a mixing bowl. Hold the potatoes with a towel. You may save the skins for an hors d'oeuvre. Add the butter and toss. Do not mash the potatoes. Cover a flat 11 × 14 × ½-inch jelly roll pan with foil. Butter well. Make a firm ring of foil 10 inches in diameter and 2 inches high. Set this in the center of the pan. Place the potatoes in the ring, and gradually pour the heavy cream over them. Let stand for 15 minutes. Sprinkle with grated Parmesan cheese, and bake in a 375-degree oven 20 minutes, or until nicely browned.

Deep-Fried Potatoes

Early recipes for deep-fried potatoes called them "French" in parentheses, and certainly the French were the first to prepare them in that fashion. They call them *frites.* It is a matter of question whether the French or Americans consume greater quantities of *frites.*

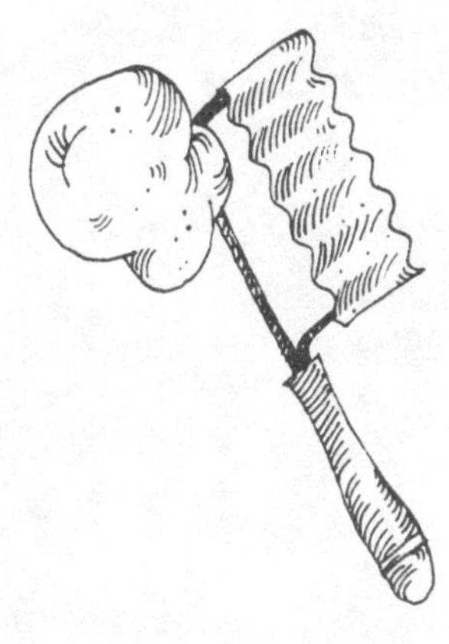

Basic Rules for Deep-Frying

Not all potatoes fry well. The best potatoes for this purpose should be firm, have a certain mealy quality, and hold well after frying. There is only one way to discover the right potato: experiment.

Cut the potatoes in flat rounds or waffle rounds (using a mandoline cutter), in long fingers, in matchsticks, in quarters (if they are small potatoes), or in balls (using a scoop), in which case they are called Parisienne.

Soak in cold water till ready to cook, then dry on toweling.

Pour oil or fat in a deep kettle and heat to 375 degrees. Set the oven at 275 or 300 degrees, and line a large baking sheet with absorbent paper.

Place a few potatoes at a time in the deep-fry basket, and lower into the fat. Cook until they are golden brown and crisp. Shoestring potatoes, waffle potatoes, and potato chips will be done in 1 to 1½ minutes and should be cooked until crisp through. Other forms of potatoes will take about 4 minutes and should be crisp on the outside and soft in the center. For still crisper exterior, fry the potatoes, then cool. Plunge again into deep fat for a minute or two. This is the same principle used in making soufflé potatoes.

When the potatoes are done, drain and transfer to the absorbent paper to drain further. Keep warm in the oven, with the door ajar, till all the potatoes are fried.

Soufflé Potatoes. Prepare and deep-fry as above peeled and sliced large potatoes — the slices should be about 3 to 4 inches long, 1½ to 2 inches wide, and ⅛ inch thick. Heat the fat to 325 degrees, and cook a few at a time just long enough to let them cook through and brown lightly. Drain on absorbent paper and let cool. Just before you are ready to serve, heat the fat to 375 degrees. Plunge the potatoes, a few at a time, into the fat. If the temperature is right and you do not overcrowd the basket, the potatoes will swell. Drain well on absorbent paper and keep warm till ready to serve. Salt before serving.

Almond-Studded Potatoes

1½ cups dry mashed potatoes
Salt and freshly ground pepper
Slivered or sliced almonds
Fat for frying

CREAM PUFF PASTE

1 cup water
5 tablespoons butter
1½ cups flour
3 or 4 eggs

These are a fascinating version of a croquette — puffy, light, and crunchy all at the same time. The base is a cream puff paste.

Bring the water and butter to a boil. Add the flour all at once and stir until it is thick and forms a ball and breaks from the sides of the pan. Remove from the heat and beat in the eggs, one at a time, till the mixture is thickened and waxy-looking. You may need only three eggs if they are large ones. If you need more, at first add only the yolk of the fourth until you see if it forms a firm waxy ball. If not, add the white as well. Add the mashed potatoes and salt and pepper to taste. Blend thoroughly. Form into small balls and roll in sliced or slivered almonds, pressing slightly to make the nuts adhere. Fry a few at a time in deep fat heated to 375 degrees until the potatoes are puffed and browned. Serve hot with meats or as a snack with cocktails.

Potatoes Anna

There has long been a vogue in this country for these delicately browned potatoes cooked in the oven. Originally a French dish, they were often mentioned in the chronicles of food-minded travelers, and not a few recipes have been published for them.

A special utensil has been invented for potatoes Anna which is supposed to steam and brown them all at one time. However, they will cook well without it.

Butter an ovenproof skillet, baking dish, or shallow casserole well on the bottom and sides. Peel several potatoes and slice into thin rounds. Arrange a layer in the bottom, overlapping the potatoes spiral-fashion. Build up three or four layers, dotting each layer with butter and seasoning with salt and freshly ground pepper. Dot the top with butter and cover with a lid or with foil. Bake at 400 degrees for 45 minutes. Remove the cover, test the potatoes for tenderness, and bake uncovered till very tender and browned on top. Invert the baking dish on a hot plate and serve. The potatoes should be crisp and brown on the outside and creamy tender and buttery on the inside.

Galette Potatoes

3 to 4 baking potatoes, peeled and thinly sliced
4 tablespoons butter or beef dripping
Salt and freshly ground pepper
Additional butter

This is a top-of-the-stove version of potatoes Anna.

Melt the butter in a heavy skillet that can be tightly covered. Arrange the potatoes in a spiral, beginning in the center and continuing outward so that the potatoes overlap. Repeat for two or three layers, dotting with butter and adding salt and pepper. Cover the pan and cook slowly over medium heat till the potatoes are tender and the bottom layer is brown and crisp. Either invert the potatoes on a hot platter or invert them on a tray and slip back into the pan with additional butter so that they brown on the other side.

Bouillon Potatoes. Add 1 cup or more bouillon — just enough to cover — and let the potatoes simmer in the bouillon till they are tender.

Browned Potatoes

These used to be more popular than they are now. They are peeled and halved potatoes, cooked with a roast in the roasting pan and basted frequently with the pan drippings.

When we used to roast at high temperatures, the potatoes were sensationally good, but now that most people roast at low temperatures, and on a rack, they are not quite as successful. However, they may be roasted separately in beef dripping or butter in a 350-degree or 375-degree oven and basted frequently. They may also be parboiled 10 minutes and then added to the drippings.

Potato Pancakes

4 medium potatoes
1 medium onion (optional)
1 egg lightly beaten
2 tablespoons fine dry breadcrumbs
1 teaspoon salt
½ teaspoon freshly ground pepper
Butter or bacon fat

A great favorite with the German and Jewish population, these are served with braised meats and very often as a lunch dish with applesauce. Sometimes when they are very crisp they are served as an hors d'oeuvre with caviar and sour cream, which makes a thoroughly wonderful combination.

Wash and peel the potatoes. Grate with a fine grater and drain off all the liquid that collects in the bowl. Grate the onion into the potato and mix in the egg, breadcrumbs, salt, and pepper. Heat the butter (1 teaspoon at a time) in a large skillet or griddle. Put in four large spoonfuls of the mixture to make 4 pancakes. Cook gently until brown on the bottom, turn, and brown on the other side. Add more fat and continue cooking until all are done.

Cecily Brownstone's Savory Potato Pie

2 pounds frozen small whole potatoes
¼ cup frozen chopped onion
1 tablespoon chopped parsley
2 teaspoons salt
⅛ teaspoon freshly ground pepper
2 tablespoons butter
1 cup heavy cream

To make the pastry, sift the flour and salt into a mixing bowl. With a pastry blender, cut in the shortening until particles are fine; cut in the butter until particles are the size of peas. Sprinkle 1 tablespoon of the water over part of the mixture. Lightly mix with a fork until the flour is absorbed, then push aside; in the same way continue adding the remaining water, 1 tablespoon at a time. Gather together the dough with your hands and shape into a ball. Wrap in plastic. Chill.

Let the potatoes thaw at room temperature until they can be sliced easily (1 to 1½ hours, depending on size). Using a knife with a thin serrated edge, cut them into thin slices and place in a bowl (yields 7 cups sliced potatoes). Chop the onion even finer, until

SPECIAL PASTRY
2¼ cups sifted all-purpose flour
1¼ teaspoons salt
½ cup shortening
¼ cup (½ stick) butter
4 tablespoons cold water

finely minced. Add the onion, parsley, salt, and pepper to the potatoes; toss to mix well; set aside.

Roll out half of the special pastry so it is 1½ inches larger all around than the top of a shallow 2-quart oblong glass or similar baking dish — about 11¾ × 7½ × 1¾ inches. Fit the pastry into the dish, fill with the potato mixture, and dot with butter. Trim the pastry even with the dish edge. Roll out the remaining pastry and place it over the potatoes. Trim it 1 inch beyond the dish edge, fold it under the bottom pastry, flute the edge, and cut four 3-inch slits in the top.

Bake in a 375-degree oven 1 to 1¼ hours, or until the potatoes are tender when tested with a fork and the pastry is lightly browned. Remove from the oven. Slowly pour the cream into the slits. Let stand 5 minutes before serving.

Sweet Potatoes and Yams

There are two types of sweet potatoes: the yam, which has an orange-colored flesh, and the plain — sometimes called the Jersey — sweet potato, which is smaller and has a yellowish flesh. The yam is more oily in texture, the Jersey sweet potato is fluffier and drier. They are interchangeable. Sweet potatoes boil extremely well, and they can be recooked, but baking is the simplest and perhaps the best way to cook them. Allow one per person.

Baked Sweet Potatoes

Choose one large or one medium sweet potato per person. Wash and scrub it well. Bake in a 400-degree oven 35 minutes to 1 hour, or until it responds to pressure with a towel wrapped around your fingers. Serve at once with butter, freshly ground pepper, and salt.

Boiled Sweet Potatoes

6 medium-size sweet potatoes
2 teaspoons salt
Freshly ground pepper
6 tablespoons butter

Wash the potatoes well, cut off the tips, but do not peel. Put enough water in a saucepan to cover the potatoes and add 1 teaspoon salt. Bring to a boil, add the potatoes, cover, and cook until tender when pierced with a fork. Drain the potatoes, peel, season with salt and pepper, and serve with butter.

Mashed Sweet Potatoes. Mash the peeled potatoes, and with a heavy whisk beat in about 2 tablespoons butter, 2 teaspoons salt, and freshly ground pepper to taste. If you like, top the mashed sweets with bits of crumbled bacon.

Fried Sweet Potatoes. Slice the peeled potatoes about ½ inch thick. Melt 4 to 6 tablespoons butter in a heavy skillet, add the potatoes, and season to taste with salt and freshly ground pepper. Cook until they have browned lightly and crisply on each side, turning them once or twice during the cooking. If you like, sprinkle them with a little granulated sugar, and toss them well in the pan to caramelize and brown them more definitely.

Candied Sweet Potatoes. Cut the peeled potatoes in ½ to 1 inch slices or in long halves. Arrange them in a 9 × 14 baking dish which has been very well buttered. Sprinkle them with ½ cup brown sugar or about ⅔ cup maple syrup. Dot with butter and add a touch of salt. Place in a 375-degree oven and bake until the potatoes are nicely glazed and lightly browned. Some people in the past have added marshmallows to this dish, which you may do at your own risk.

A Sweet Potato Casserole. Put the boiled potatoes through the food mill or ricer. For 4 cups of purée, blend with 4 tablespoons butter, ¼ teaspoon ground cinnamon, ¼ teaspoon mace, and about ⅓ cup heavy cream. Whip all together and beat in ⅓ to ½ cup Cognac. Season to taste with salt. Heap in a casserole, dot with butter, and sprinkle with finely chopped almonds. Place in a 375 to 400 degree oven until delicately brown.

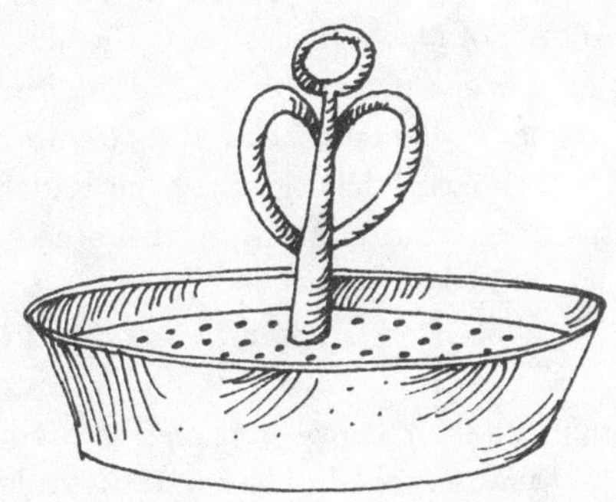

Grains and Pastes

Grains

Rice

Rice has been a staple throughout the country for generations, especially in the South, where it became so popular that potatoes went begging. It was served as a cereal for breakfast; in croquettes or in the famed calas of New Orleans; as a vegetable; as the liaison with meat, poultry, or fish in many casserole dishes; and as a dessert, ranging from simple rice with sugar and cream to the most elaborate rice puddings and molds. Ethnic groups who settled throughout the country extended the uses of rice, and it has been fried, steamed, baked, and made into salads.

Long-grain Carolina rice has become a standard in this country as well as in many parts of the world. Recently Texas, California, and other sections of the country have started producing rice of various types. Brown or unpolished rice is now extremely fashionable among health food fans after many years of eclipse. And in the last ten or twelve years converted rice has become the best-selling variety on the market. Formerly, white rice was processed so that the bran coating was ground off, after which the rice was polished, and much of the food value was polished away as well. The converting process preserves the nutritive values and offers the same benefits, for the most part, as natural brown rice. What is more, converted rice takes much less time to cook, and the results are usually excellent.

Cooking Rice the Old-Fashioned Way

I grew up with a form of rice cookery that is seldom used any more. The rice was washed with several waters (now considered unnecessary by most packagers of the grain), and then at least 2½ quarts of salted water were brought to a rolling boil in a 4-quart saucepan or kettle. The rice was tossed in in small amounts so that the water never stopped boiling. It was cooked until tender, about 15 minutes, and then drained and washed again. Finally it was reheated in a pan and served with butter or a sauce. This produced a well-cooked, flaky rice. When seasoned and tossed with a fork, it was delicious.

Modern Rice Cookery (Boiled Rice)

Long-grain Carolina rice. The packaged Carolina rice no longer requires washing before cooking. The recommended cooking method calls for bringing 2¼ cups of water to a boil and adding 1 teaspoon salt and 1 cup rice. Bring to a boil again, and reduce the heat to simmer. Cover the pan, and cook 15 to 16 minutes, or until all the water is absorbed and the rice is tender to the bite. Some prefer one degree of tenderness and others another. It is best to begin testing it after 14 minutes. Remove the cover if you want the rice to steam slightly drier. Season to taste.

Converted rice. Bring 2½ cups water to a boil with 1 teaspoon salt. Add 1 cup rice, and bring to a boil again. Cover the pan, and reduce the heat to simmer. Cook until the rice has achieved your favorite degree of tenderness. This will be between 13 and 16 minutes. For crisper rice, add only 2 cups water to the pot.

Rice Ring. Press 5 to 5½ cups cooked hot rice into a well-buttered 6-cup ring mold. Press firmly. Invert on a hot serving dish and carefully remove the mold.

Saffron Rice. Add a healthy pinch of saffron to the rice when the water returns to a boil. Toss lightly with a fork. Or you may soak the saffron in a tablespoon of boiling water and add it later with the liquid.

Rice with Stock. Chicken, beef, veal, mushroom, or other vegetable stock or broth may be substituted for the water in cooking rice to produce a dish with more flavor and character.

Rice with Cheese. Toss 4 cups cooked rice with ¼ cup melted butter and ½ cup freshly grated Parmesan cheese. Also add about ¼ cup grated Cheddar or Gruyère if you like. Delicious when served with roasts or with steak.

Crumbed Rice. Combine 4 cups cooked rice with 1 cup buttered dried breadcrumbs and toss well with a fork. Add salt and freshly ground pepper to taste.

Rice with Nuts. Use crisply toasted almonds, filberts, walnuts, pecans, or pine nuts. Chop nuts coarsely, save for pine nuts, which should be whole, and combine with ½ cup melted butter. The quality of the nuts may vary to your own taste, from ½ cup to 1½ cups. Toss into 4 cups cooked rice with a fork. Garnish the top with a few whole nuts.

Green Rice. Combine 4 cups cooked rice with ¼ cup melted butter or heated olive oil and ½ cup each of chopped parsley and chopped chives or green onions, including tops. Or use chopped parsley and finely chopped fresh basil, or ¼ cup fresh tarragon. To serve with certain Oriental and Mexican dishes use chopped fresh coriander, called variously in our markets Chinese parsley or cilantro.

Garlic Rice. Combine ⅓ cup melted butter or olive oil with 2 or 3 finely chopped or crushed garlic cloves and ½ cup chopped parsley. Toss into 4 cups cooked rice with a fork and serve very hot. Extremely good with lamb or with roast chicken.

Brown Rice

Brown rice needs a great deal more cooking than long-grain or converted rice. It is best to follow explicitly the directions on the package. It is also very good when baked in stock. Bring 2½ cups stock to the boiling point, and blend with 1 cup brown rice in a 1-quart casserole. Cover and bake at 350 degrees approximately 1½ hours.

Rice Pilaff

1 cup raw rice (long-grain Carolina or converted rice)
4 tablespoons butter or olive oil
1 small onion, finely chopped
1 teaspoon salt
½ teaspoon freshly ground pepper
1 teaspoon thyme
2½ cups stock or water
Butter
Chopped parsley

Middle and Far Eastern immigrants brought various versions of pilaff with them. These have been more or less combined in one general style of preparing the dish — somewhat changed from the native methods but extremely good, useful, and simple.

Rinse the rice and dry on a towel. Heat the butter or oil in a heavy skillet or a 1½-quart enameled metal casserole, and sauté the onion until it is transparent and soft. Add the rice and sauté 5 minutes over medium flame, then add the seasonings. Pour in boiling stock or water and stir. Cover, and heat in a 350-degree oven 20 minutes, or until all the liquid is absorbed and the rice is tender. Add melted butter to taste and a sprinkling of chopped parsley.

Pilaff with Nuts and Raisins. Add a good pinch of saffron to the rice during baking. When the rice is cooked, transfer to a serving dish and top with ¾ cup toasted sautéed almonds, ½ cup puffed raisins, and, if you like, some crisp French-fried onions (the tinned ones are admirable for this purpose). Excellent with kebabs, lamb, or curried dishes. The amount of nuts and raisins may be increased according to your taste. A few leaves of finely chopped mint added at the last moment give a remarkable quality, as does chopped fresh coriander.

Rice with Peas. This is a variation on a dish brought by the Italians, Greeks and Central Europeans. It is a delight with veal, chicken, or lamb. Furthermore, it serves as two vegetables. A few leaves of fresh mint, finely chopped, also may be added to this recipe. To make it, combine the basic pilaff recipe with 2 cups small green peas — fresh, frozen, or canned — which have been heated, seasoned with salt to taste, and dressed with 3 tablespoons butter. Toss into the rice with a fork.

Mexican or Spanish Rice

4 finely chopped or cut green onions
1 finely chopped green pepper
½ cup olive oil
1 cup raw rice, either long-grain Carolina or converted
1 cup canned tomatoes (preferably Italian plum tomatoes)
1 cup tomato juice
1 cup water
1 teaspoon salt
1 teaspoon oregano or 1 tablespoon chili powder
Grated Parmesan cheese
Chopped parsley

This dish has little relationship to genuine Spanish or Mexican rices. At one time any dish using tomatoes was immediately labeled Spanish, Mexican, or Portuguese. I'm sure this recipe had its start with an experimental American cook trying to think up new ways to dress ordinary food.

Sauté the green onions and pepper in olive oil about 3 minutes, shaking the pan as you do so. Add the rice, shake the pan again, and cook till the rice takes on some color. Add the tomatoes, tomato juice, water, and seasonings. Cover, and cook over low heat till the rice is tender and the liquid is pretty much absorbed. Additional liquid may be needed, so it is wise to test from time to time. Sprinkle with grated Parmesan cheese and a little chopped parsley. Serve as an accompaniment to pork, ham, or stews.

Fried Rice

4 cups cooked rice
2 to 4 tablespoons oil (preferably peanut oil)
3 tablespoons shredded green onions
¼ cup chopped sautéed mushrooms

This is borrowing from the Chinese, long popular in the West and now more popular than ever because of a rise in taste for Oriental dishes and seasonings.

Cook the rice in the oil approximately 5 minutes to heat through, shaking the pan and tossing the rice with a fork from time to time. Add the green onions, mushrooms, and your choice of ham, pork, chicken, or shrimp. Toss in well. Combine the eggs and soy sauce — add additional soy to taste, if you like. Stir into the rice

½ cup or more shredded ham, pork, or chicken, or shrimp cut in pieces
2 tablespoons soy sauce
2 eggs

off the heat and toss with a fork until the eggs are set. Transfer to a heated dish. Garnish with additional shredded green onions or with sliced toasted almonds. For an unusual and delicious flavor, also add chopped fresh coriander.

Rice and Olive Casserole

1½ cups raw rice, either long-grain Carolina or converted
2 finely chopped garlic cloves
3 tablespoons peanut oil
2 tablespoons butter
36 to 40 soft black olives, pitted and cut coarsely
1½ teaspoons salt
1 teaspoon freshly ground pepper
2 teaspoons chili powder
1½ teaspoons basil
5 cups tomato juice
Grated Parmesan cheese
Chopped parsley

Sauté the rice and garlic in the oil and butter till just barely golden in color. Transfer to a 2-quart casserole or baking dish. Add the olives and seasonings, and toss with two forks. Heat the tomato juice to the boiling point, and pour over the rice mixture. Cover, and bake at 350 degrees approximately 1 hour, or until the liquid is entirely absorbed and the rice is tender. Sprinkle with grated Parmesan cheese and chopped parsley.

Note. Instead of Parmesan, shredded Cheddar or Monterey jack cheese may be added for the last 5 to 8 minutes of cooking time.

Hominy and Hominy Grits

Hominy is one of the delights of American food. It is made from white corn and is sometimes called samp. Hominy made from yellow corn is called hulled corn. Both are made by treating the kernels of corn with lye, which dissolves the skin. It is afterwards washed in several waters and then boiled for several hours. One used to find dry hominy in shops, but only a few specialized mail order houses sell it now. Cooked hominy can be bought in cans, ready to wash, heat, season, and serve. It is remarkably good as a change from other starchy vegetables. In Portland, when I was young, the hominy man passed through our neighborhood in his little horse-drawn cart twice a week. Friendly and pleasant, he sold horseradish as well as hominy, and carried all the gossip with him.

Buttered Hominy

2 cans hominy
2 cups milk or water
1 teaspoon salt

Drain the hominy and wash well. Place in a heavy saucepan and just barely cover with the milk or water. Heat till it is at the boiling point and let the hominy simmer several minutes. If you are using milk, be careful it does not scorch. Drain, add the seasonings and butter and shake the pan well. Pour into a serving dish and sprinkle with chopped parsley. Serve with pork, chicken, veal, or game.

1 teaspoon freshly ground pepper
6 tablespoons butter
Chopped parsley

Creamed Hominy. Add ½ cup heavy cream with the butter and seasonings. Let it boil up and cook several minutes, shaking the pan all the while. Serve as above.

Hominy and Cheese Casserole

3 cans hominy, drained and washed
6 tablespoons butter
1½ cups grated or shredded Gruyère or Cheddar cheese
Salt and freshly ground pepper
½ cup buttered breadcrumbs
½ cup cream

Butter a 2½-quart baking dish. In it make a layer of hominy, dot with butter, and sprinkle with cheese. Give a few grinds of the pepper mill and add a touch of salt. Continue this procedure, ending with a layer of hominy. Cover with the buttered crumbs and pour the cream over all. Bake at 350 degrees 20 to 25 minutes or until the crumbs are nicely browned and the cheese is melted. Serve at once. Excellent with broiled dishes or with a roast of lamb.

Hominy with Green Chilies and Sour Cream

3 cans hominy, drained and washed
8 canned peeled green chilies cut in strips
½ pound Monterey jack cheese cut in small cubes
1½ cups sour cream
Buttered crumbs

Arrange a layer of hominy in a 2½-quart casserole. Wrap the cubes of cheese in strips of chili. Place a layer of these on the hominy, and spread with some of the sour cream. Continue making layers in this fashion, ending with hominy. Sprinkle with buttered crumbs and bake at 350 degrees until the top is browned and the casserole piping hot.

Boiled Hominy Grits

2 cups grits
Water
1 teaspoon salt

Hominy grits (which are coarsely ground dry hominy), as they are boiled and served for breakfast in the South, I find a rather revolting food. It is probably fine for those who were brought up on porridge, but I wasn't. As a result it took me a long time to discover that grits are extraordinarily good done in other ways.

If you are using quick-cooking grits, follow directions on the package.

Wash the grits well. Drain. Cover with 1 quart water and soak several hours. Bring to a boil over direct heat in the top of a double boiler, then place over the bottom part of the boiler and cook over simmering water 1 to 1½ hours. Stir occasionally. Serve with butter or cream.

Fried Hominy Grits. Pour boiled grits into a loaf pan or a square or oblong dish and allow to cool. Cut into slices about ½ inch thick. Dip in beaten egg and breadcrumbs, and sauté in butter until nicely browned on each side. Or flour lightly and sauté in butter or oil till nicely browned and crisp at the edges. Delicious with pheasant, wild duck, quail, or any game.

Hominy Grits Casserole. Prepare a double recipe of boiled hominy grits. Combine with 6 tablespoons butter, 3 well-beaten eggs, additional salt if needed, and ¾ teaspoon freshly ground pepper. Pour into a buttered 2-quart baking dish and top with 1 cup grated Cheddar or Gruyère cheese, which should be stirred into the grits. Dot with butter. Bake at 400 degrees just long enough to brown the top — about 15 minutes.

Hominy Grits Spoon Bread

1 tablespoon butter
2 cups cooked hominy grits
3 eggs, separated
½ cup white cornmeal
2 teaspoons baking powder
½ teaspoon salt or to taste
½ teaspoon freshly ground pepper
½ teaspoon Tabasco
Milk (about 1 to 1½ cups)

Combine the butter, hominy grits, egg yolks (which have been well beaten), cornmeal, baking powder, seasonings, and enough milk to make a custard-like consistency. (Grits vary, and it is difficult to say exactly how much milk they will absorb.) Finally, fold in the egg whites, beaten stiff but not dry. If they are beaten in anything but a copper bowl add ½ teaspoon cream of tartar. Pour the mixture into a 2-quart soufflé mold or baking dish and bake at 350 degrees approximately 1 hour.

Cornmeal

Cornmeal Mush

2 cups boiling water
½ teaspoon salt
½ cup cornmeal

If you are using quick-cooking cornmeal, follow directions on the package.

Bring the water and salt to a boil either in the top of a double boiler or in a heavy saucepan. Stirring constantly, pour the meal gradually into the water. When all is added, let it come to a boil and boil 5 minutes. Continue to stir. Then place it over simmering water to cook 1 hour, or if cooking in a saucepan, cook over medium flame 45 to 50 minutes, stirring often. To serve, stir in 6 tablespoons butter and, if you like, ½ cup grated cheese — Parmesan, Cheddar, or Gruyère. Serve with pork, chicken, chili, or other suitable dishes.

Polenta. Polenta is a porridge usually made with cornmeal, but sometimes with barley or chestnut meal.

Fried Cornmeal Mush. Pour the cooked mush into a mold or bread pan and let it chill thoroughly. Remove, cut into slices, and sauté in butter or fat until crisp and brown. Serve as a breakfast dish with syrup or honey and butter, or serve with game or with dishes such as chili, or highly seasoned stews and ragouts.

Cornmeal Mush and Sausages, Italian Style. Pour hot cornmeal mush into a 1½-quart baking dish, preferably a long oval or square one. On it arrange cooked Italian sausages or smoked sausages. Top with a tomato sauce and grated Parmesan cheese, and place in a 350-degree oven to heat thoroughly — a few minutes should be long enough.

Cornmeal Spoon Bread

2 cups milk
½ teaspoon salt
¾ cup cornmeal
4 tablespoons butter
4 eggs, separated

This is really a heavy soufflé. It is a dish that has maintained a remarkable popularity and is excellent eaten with butter, or with sauce from a fricasseed chicken or such things, or as an accompaniment to game.

Bring the milk and salt to a boil and reduce the heat to simmer. Stir in the cornmeal and continue to stir until it thickens. Add the butter. Remove from the heat and beat in the egg yolks, slightly beaten. Cool slightly and fold in the whites, stiffly beaten. Bake in a buttered 1½-quart casserole or soufflé mold at 375 degrees about 40 minutes.

Note. Instead of separating the eggs, you may beat them whole and add to the mush mixture. Place in a buttered baking dish about 9×9×3 inches and bake at 375 degrees 1 hour.

Spider Bread or Spider Corn Bread

4 to 5 tablespoons butter or margarine for the baking pan
⅓ cup all-purpose flour
2 teaspoons baking powder
1 teaspoon salt
1 to 2 tablespoons sugar
1⅔ cups yellow or white corn meal
2 eggs
3 cups milk

The name comes from the frying pans used in fireplace cooking. These were of heavy cast iron and had three legs, usually about three inches long. The batter was poured into the well-greased pan, which was set over coals with a few coals placed on the lid. To bring this up to date, bake in a deep 12-inch skillet in the oven or in a regular baking pan. It has a deliciously soft, custardy texture.

Melt the fat in a skillet that can go in the oven, or a 9×13×2-inch baking pan. Sift the flour with the baking powder, salt, and sugar, and mix with the cornmeal. You can add all the dry ingredients to the flour and then sift, if you wish, but the cornmeal usually just runs through the sieve. Beat the eggs in a mixing bowl. Add 2 cups of the milk and stir. Add the dry ingredients and stir just to wet. Pour immediately into the skillet or baking pan that has had the fat melted in it and been turned so that it is well greased. Some like to have the skillet hot when the batter is poured in. Now pour over the remaining cup of milk, drizzling it evenly over the surface of the batter. Bake immediately in a 400-degree oven until firm, about

25 minutes. If baked in a larger pan, the time required for baking will be slightly less. Serve hot cut into wedges or squares. This will have a slight custard layer and is moist.

Cornmeal and Cheese Casserole

Cooked cornmeal mush (1 recipe)
1½ sticks butter
1 cup or more shredded Monterey jack or Gruyère cheese
1 4-ounce tin peeled green chilies, finely chopped
Salt and freshly ground pepper
½ cup grated Parmesan cheese or additional shredded jack or Gruyère

Pour the cooked mush into a bread pan or mold to cool. Chill overnight. Unmold, and cut into slices approximately ½ inch thick. Arrange a layer of half the slices in a well-buttered oblong or square baking dish (9×9×3) or bread pan, spread lavishly with butter, and sprinkle with half the shredded cheese. Add the peeled green chilies and the rest of the cheese; then arrange another layer of cornmeal. Dot with butter, give it a few grinds of pepper, and top with the Parmesan or additional shredded jack or Gruyère. Bake at 350 degrees approximately 20 minutes, or until the cheese is melted and lightly browned and the casserole is piping hot. Cut into wedges or squares, and serve with beef, pork, lamb, or game.

Barley

Although pearl barley is one of the more delectable grains, it has been badly neglected. Usually Scotch broth and one or two other soups constitute most people's experience with it. An old friend of ours in Seattle originated this rather interesting use for it years ago, and many variations on the theme have resulted.

Barley Casserole (from Mildred Oakes)

3 tablespoons butter
½ pound mushrooms
1 stick (½ cup) butter
2 medium onions, finely chopped
1½ cups pearl barley
About 3 cups chicken broth or beef stock
Salt
Chopped parsley

Melt the butter in a heavy skillet and sauté the mushrooms over medium high heat 4 minutes. Transfer to a small dish. Add the butter to the skillet and heat till the foam has subsided. Add the onions and cook until they are just wilted. Add the barley and stir over medium high heat till it has a rich golden color. Combine with the mushrooms in a 1½-quart casserole or baking dish. Add about 1½ cups hot broth and cover. Bake at 350 degrees 30 minutes, then remove the cover and add another 1½ cups hot broth. Cover again, and bake another 30 minutes. Add salt to the casserole if necessary (the broth should be well seasoned) and additional broth if the barley has absorbed too much liquid before it is tender. Sprinkle with chopped parsley before serving.

Kasha or Buckwheat Groats

Middle Eastern and Jewish cooks use kasha a great deal as a cereal for accompanying meats and fowl. It has a strangely appealing nutty flavor and is a pleasant change from other grain dishes.

To Cook Groats

1 cup brown buckwheat groats
1 egg
2 cups boiling water or stock

Put the groats in a heated skillet over high heat, add the egg, and stir vigorously. When each grain is separated and dry, add the boiling liquid and salt. Cover, reduce the heat to simmer, and steam 30 minutes, or until the liquid is absorbed. Stir in the butter or chicken fat.

1 teaspoon salt
¼ cup butter or rendered chicken fat

Wild Rice

Wild rice is not rice. It is the grain of a wild grass which grows along streams and rivulets in the Northwest and in Canada. It is scarce, therefore astronomically priced, and should be used only when one feels the urge for luxury. Formerly it was used lavishly for stuffings, as a pilaff, and as an accompaniment to game. Recently the producers of one of the finer brands of converted rice have come out with a blend of rice and wild rice which I find exceptionally good. Follow the directions on the package carefully, and the results will be excellent. Sometimes — and this depends upon the source — wild rice is exceptionally dirty. Thus it needs thorough washings before cooking.

Steeped Wild Rice

An interesting method of preparing wild rice, this recipe, which I found in Minnesota, really steeps rather than cooks rice.

Cover 1 cup washed wild rice with boiling water. Cover the pan tightly and let it stand 20 minutes. Drain, and repeat the process three more times. Salt the water for the last steeping. Drain, and let the rice dry a moment or two over low heat. Toss in melted butter or rendered chicken fat. Add salt if needed. Extraordinarily good with wild or domestic duck or with goose.

Boiled Wild Rice

1 cup well-washed wild rice
2 cups boiling water
1 teaspoon salt
⅓ cup melted butter or more, to taste

Stir the rice into the boiling water, add the salt, and allow it to boil 30 minutes. Drain, and shake over the heat a moment or two to dry. Toss with the butter.

Variations

(1) Top with ¾ cup sliced sautéed almonds.

(2) Omit the butter, and top with ½ pound mushrooms sautéed with 1 finely chopped small onion in 6 tablespoons butter.

(3) Omit the butter and top with about ½ cup pine nuts sautéed in ¼ cup butter. Add freshly ground pepper to taste.

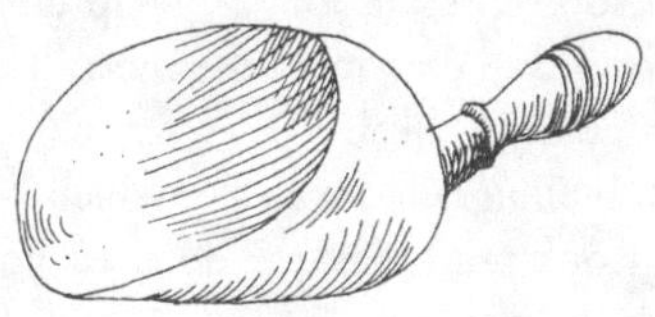

Pastes

Noodles

Of all the pastes which have come into the American cuisine, certainly the egg noodle has been the outstandingly popular one. The Pennsylvania Germans, the French, the Hungarians, and various other middle European groups have always used noodles in great profusion. They are easy to make and are very satisfactory with chicken, veal, and other meats.

To Make Noodles

2 to 2½ cups unsifted flour
½ teaspoon salt
3 eggs
1 tablespoon cold water

The Dutch noodles we offer here originated in Pennsylvania and have been standard throughout the country. They are excellent with many different dishes. When they are rolled, cut in squares, and dripped into a chicken stew, the result is called pot pie (see chicken pot pie, page 214), and they may be bought in that shape and under that name in many of the Pennsylvania Dutch markets. They closely resemble the noodles of the Hungarians and the Poles, the Alsatians and the French.

Combine 2 cups flour and the salt in a deep bowl, and drop the eggs into the center. Work this well with the hands, and continue working till it makes a soft ball. Remove to a floured board and start kneading as you would bread dough. If necessary, add more flour by the tablespoon, kneading it in, until you have a firm dough. Continue kneading another 8 to 10 minutes. Cover the dough with a bowl and let it rest 20 minutes or so. (You can also do all the kneading in an electric mixer fitted with a dough hook; or if you have an Italian pasta machine you can run the dough through that a number times rather than kneading by hand.) After the dough has rested, break it up into four pieces and form them into balls. Place each ball of dough on a floured board and press it down as flat as possible. Then roll out into squares about ⅛ inch thick or less. Cut the dough into strips of any width you choose — from ⅛ inch to 1 inch. Let the strips dry on paper towels or wax paper.

To Cook Noodles

Noodles are best when cooked within an hour or so after they are made. If you wish to keep them longer, wrap them in plastic and refrigerate them for a day or two at the most. They may also be frozen, but rather riskily, I feel.

Cook noodles in boiling salted water to which you add a spoonful or two of oil. Cook until they are done to your taste — they will need about 9 to 12 minutes. Drain the cooked noodles and combine with other ingredients, serve with butter or butter and cheese, or serve plain with a stew or fricassee to be tossed with the sauce or gravy.

Noodles are also excellent when served with a tomato sauce. And they are very often served topped with crisp buttered crumbs, giving them a new dimension, almost as if they had a delicate crust on them.

Poppy seeds, too, are served on buttered noodles, especially with Hungarian dishes, such as a fine goulash, or with certain Polish and Jewish dishes. In this case, the poppy seeds are usually blended with butter and tossed with the noodles just before serving.

Baked Lasagna

1 pound lasagne
Oil
1 recipe tomato sauce with meat (page 589)
2 cups rich béchamel sauce flavored with nutmeg
1½ pounds Italian sausages, sweet or hot, according to taste
1 pound ricotta cheese
1 cup or more freshly grated Parmesan cheese

Delicious wide noodles — lasagne — either spinach noodles or plain, have become a most popular dish in the United States, whether prepared in the Italian fashion or as a simple dish for entertaining that can be prepared ahead. There are dozens of ways to make baked lasagna, but none is really preferred over the other. However, use green noodles if available. One pound will make plenty for a large family or for entertaining.

Cook the lasagne in salted water to which you have added 2 tablespoons oil, or according to package directions. Drain well, stir in a little oil, and keep them warm over hot water. Prepare the tomato meat sauce and the béchamel with nutmeg. Blanch the sausages in boiling water 3 minutes. Drain and broil till cooked through — about 8 minutes. Peel and discard the skins.

Spread a layer of the tomato sauce in the bottom of a large baking dish or pan, preferably one with sharp corners, about 9 × 12 × 3 inches. Then add layers of lasagne, sausage, ricotta cheese, and béchamel. Begin with another layer of lasagne and repeat until the ingredients are used up, reserving some béchamel for the top of the dish. Sprinkle heavily with grated Parmesan cheese and bake in a 350-degree oven 20 to 25 minutes. Remove from the oven and allow to sit in a warm spot 10 minutes before serving. Cut in squares and serve with additional grated Parmesan cheese.

Note. You may use tiny meatballs instead of sausage and use double the amount of tomato meat sauce, omitting the béchamel. You may also add layers of thinly sliced mozzarella or Gruyère cheese, if you wish.

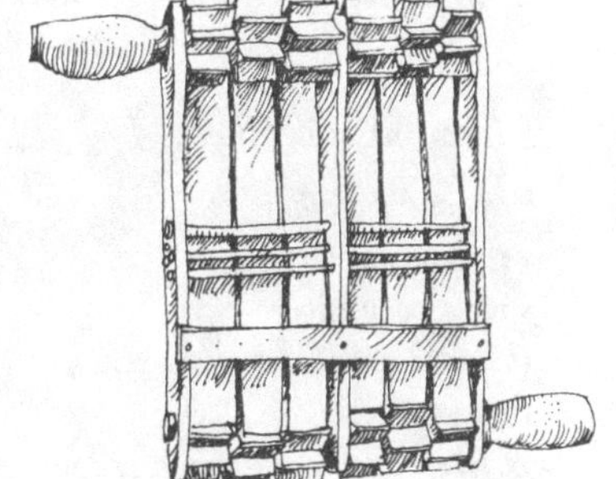

Spaetzle

Spaetzle is used in the country at large, though often people do not know that it originated in central Europe. It consists of rather free-formed bits of pasta that are dropped into boiling water and cook quickly, and it is often used with pot roast, stews, or dishes having a Hungarian or similar middle European background. It has been in the American repertoire for close to two hundred years, but has never been as common as noodles.

Spaetzle is delicious, easy to do, and fun to serve. Although many people merely drizzle these nuggets into boiling water, I strongly suggest that you use a special large-meshed spaetzle sieve, which is generally easy to find and is simple to use. Serve spaetzle either with loads and loads of butter and freshly ground pepper — also a few poppy seeds, if you like — or with the gravy or sauce from a pot roast or braised brisket.

Spaetzle

2 cups flour
1 teaspoon salt
Pinch of nutmeg
Freshly ground pepper
2 lightly beaten eggs
Milk

Mix the flour, seasonings, and eggs together, then add enough milk to make a rather stiff batter. Beat quite well and let the batter stand an hour before cooking. Pour in the spaetzle sieve, let the batter drop into salted boiling water, and cook 10 to 15 minutes, according to your taste. Drain, and run cold or hot water through the spaetzle. To serve, add 1 to 1½ sticks of butter, melted, and ample freshly ground pepper.

Macaroni

Macaroni — also spelled maccaroni in early books — seems to have been the one great pasta dish known in earlier times aside from noodles. Mrs. Randolph in *The Virginia Housewife* gives this rule for macaroni pudding.

"Simmer half a pound of maccaroni in plenty of water, with a tablespoon of salt, till tender, but not broke — strain it, beat five yolks, two whites of eggs, half a pint of cream. Mince white meat (of chicken) and boiled ham very fine, add three spoonfuls of grated cheese, pepper and salt. Mix these with the maccaroni, butter the mold, put in and steam it in a pint of boiling water for an hour — serve with a rich gravy."

Macaroni and Cheese I

½ pound macaroni
3 tablespoons butter
3 tablespoons flour
1½ cups milk
1 teaspoon salt
½ teaspoon dry mustard

Boil the macaroni in salted water till just tender. Drain well. Prepare a white sauce — melt the butter in a heavy saucepan, blend with the flour, and cook several minutes over medium heat. Heat the milk to the boiling point, stir into the flour-butter mixture, and continue stirring till it thickens. Add the seasonings and simmer 4 to 5 minutes. Butter a 2 or 2½ quart baking dish or casserole. In it arrange alternate layers of macaroni, sauce, and cheese, ending with cheese. Cover the top with buttered crumbs. Bake at 350 degrees 25 minutes, or until the top is nicely browned and the sauce is bubbly. Serve at once.

Dash Tabasco
1 to 1½ cups shredded Cheddar cheese
Buttered crumbs

Macaroni and Cheese II

½ pound macaroni
8 to 10 tablespoons butter
Salt and freshly ground pepper
1 to 1½ cups shredded sharp Cheddar cheese

This was another rather popular version, often served with baked ham, for some reason, and crabapple pickle.

Cook the macaroni in boiling salted water until it is just tender. Be careful not to overcook it, lest it become very mushy. Drain. Butter a 2-quart baking dish, and arrange in it alternating layers of macaroni dotted with butter and shredded cheese. Season with salt and pepper, and top with a layer of cheese. Bake at 350 degrees till the cheese is melted and the macaroni is heated through.

Note. Buttered crumbs may be added to this mixture. A few strewn in with the cheese and over the top are sufficient.

Variation. When you have prepared the layers of macaroni and cheese and seasoned the dish, add 1 to 1½ cups hot milk or half milk and half cream. Cover the top with grated or shredded cheese and buttered crumbs, and bake at 350 degrees till the cheese is melted and the mixture has thickened and is bubbly hot.

Spaghetti

Tomato Meat Sauce

2 tablespoons olive oil
4 medium onions, chopped
3 garlic cloves, crushed
2 green peppers, chopped
1½ pounds ground beef
1 pound ground pork or sausage (Italian sausages, skinned)
1 #2½ can Italian tomatoes
2 6-ounce cans tomato paste
½ teaspoon sugar, approximately
2 teaspoons dried or 1½ tablespoons chopped fresh basil
2 small dried red peppers
1½ tablespoons salt, approximately
Freshly ground pepper

Many Americans pride themselves on their sauce for pasta, which is more often than not an elaborate and long-cooking version of a simple, fresh-tasting Sauce Bolognese. This typical sauce comes from a Middle Western cookbook that holds forth on the authenticity of the recipe. It is authentic American, perhaps, but not particularly Italian.

Sauté the onions, garlic, and peppers in the olive oil till just wilted and lightly brown. Add the meats, break up well with a fork, and sauté till delicately brown. Add the tomatoes and other ingredients and bring to a boil. Simmer 3 to 3½ hours, stirring occasionally. Correct the seasoning.

This is often embellished with meatballs, a dish not to be found in Italy, though in this country it is accepted as Neapolitan. I believe it can be considered thoroughly American.

To cook spaghetti. Cook in plenty of boiling salted water to your favorite stage of doneness. Drain well. Toss with a little oil before saucing. Or serve with just butter or butter and cheese.

Meatballs for Spaghetti

2 pounds ground beef
1 pound ground pork
2 teaspoons salt
⅓ cup grated Parmesan cheese
1 teaspoon freshly ground pepper
1 teaspoon dried or chopped fresh basil
½ teaspoon thyme
5 or 6 garlic cloves, chopped
¾ cup crumbs
¼ cup small sultana raisins
¼ cup pine nuts
3 tablespoons chopped parsley
3 eggs
½ teaspoon crushed red peppers

Blend all the ingredients well and roll firmly into tiny balls about 1½ inches in diameter. Heat 4 to 5 tablespoons olive oil in a heavy skillet and add the meatballs. Roll them around well, by shaking the pan, to keep their shape. When they are nicely browned on all sides, drop them into tomato sauce or tomato meat sauce and let them simmer 20 minutes before serving with pasta and sauce and large amounts of freshly grated Parmesan, Romano, or Asiago cheese.

Simple Tomato Sauce

3 tablespoons olive oil or butter
1 garlic clove, finely minced
1 small onion, finely chopped
1 #2½ can Italian plum tomatoes
1½ teaspoons salt
1 teaspoon dried basil
½ teaspoon crushed red peppers
4 tablespoons (or more to taste) tomato paste

Sauté the garlic and onion in the oil 3 to 4 minutes or until they are just wilted. Add the tomatoes and seasonings, bring to a boil, and cook rather briskly 10 minutes, stirring occasionally. Add the tomato paste, simmer 5 minutes longer, and taste for seasoning. Serve on pasta with ample freshly grated Parmesan or Romano cheese.

Spaghetti or Linguine with Clams

1 pound spaghetti or linguine
CLAM SAUCE
4 tablespoons olive oil
3 garlic cloves, chopped
1 cup clam juice or half clam juice and half white wine, or slightly more if necessary
1 teaspoon salt
¼ teaspoon freshly ground pepper
1½ to 2 cups minced or small whole clams

Because of the abundance of clams on both coasts, this relative of the Italian linguine alla vongole has become a first-rate American dish, using various and sundry types of clams. I have made it with minced razor clams on the West Coast, with minced quahogs in New England, and with some delicious canned small whole clams, packed, I believe, in California. The dish is quickly prepared and thoroughly satisfying.

Heat the olive oil and sauté the chopped garlic in it for 2 minutes. Add the liquid, salt, and pepper, and simmer about 8 to 10 minutes. Meanwhile, cook the pasta in boiling salted water. When done, drain at once. Add the clams to the sauce, heat thoroughly, and add the parsley. Serve the pasta in individual dishes, and spoon the clam sauce over it.

¼ cup chopped parsley, preferably the Italian variety

Note. If the clams are fresh they will take slightly longer to cook than tinned clams, and may warrant the addition of more liquid.

Spaghetti Caruso

Named for the great tenor, Spaghetti Caruso is an entirely American invention and enjoyed a rather full popularity for a long time. Lately it seems to have been on the wane, but it is worth preserving.

Prepare a recipe for the tomato meat sauce given above. At the last moment, when the spaghetti is served, add the sauce to each serving and top each portion with 3 or 4 chicken livers sautéed in butter. Sometimes a bit of sautéed mushroom, finely cut, is added to the pan in which the livers are sautéed. Grated Parmesan or Romano cheese always completes the dish.

Dried Beans, Peas, and Lentils

Beans

It is my theory that the word "pease" so often used in early American manuscript cookbooks and letters meant the dried bean as well as the dried pea. Without question beans were known to the American colonists, became a mainstay of their diet, and helped to save the Massachusetts Bay Colony from starvation. Long before the white man arrived, beans had been a standard crop of the North American Indian. The Northeastern tribes grew the pea bean or Great Northern bean, and the Indians of the Southwest developed the darker beans — all of which eventually found their way into our national cuisine.

In the South, where rice and other staples prevailed, beans did not have the acceptance they had in other parts of the colonies. However, a few important bean dishes from that region have survived — black bean soup and Hopping John, for example. And in Florida, especially in the southern part of the state, some delectable bean dishes have been contributed by Spanish and Caribbean people.

Like the potato, another native of the Americas, the edible pod bean achieved general popularity only after it had been introduced into France. Since then it has spread into cuisines all over the world. Puchero, cassoulet, feijoada complela, frijoles refritos, all celebrate the bean, but perhaps none with greater tradition behind it than our own Boston baked beans.

Canned beans. Boston baked beans, bean hole beans, baked beans with tomato sauce and pork, baked beans vegetarian style with tomato sauce — all have found their way into cans. Their quality varies from excellent to mediocre, but they have formed an important addition to the country's food supply. I can remember when no picnic was complete without a large can of either Van Camp or Heinz pork and beans, which were opened and then heated in the can in the coals. They were, with bacon, standard fare for the camper as well.

White Beans

This designation covers several varieties of beans — the small pea bean, sometimes called the "navy bean," dating from the time when beans were a mainstay of the navy and all dried legumes of that type were referred to as "navy beans"; the Great Northern bean, a large plump bean commonly used in the Eastern states; and the white kidney bean, called cannellini by the Italians and much favored by them.

Without doubt the most famous of all our bean dishes is Boston baked beans. It developed as a natural combination of what the New England earth provided and originally was made with maple syrup or maple sugar. This ingredient was replaced by molasses when the shipping industry began to flourish. It is worth noting that beans flavored with rum were not unusual in the South, and the jump from rum to molasses is but a short one.

The worship of Boston baked beans is a mystery to me, since my palate cannot reconcile the sweetness of syrup or molasses and the simple hardy flavor of pork and beans. However, this dish has stood for American cuisine as few other dishes have. The beans used to be a Saturday night ritual, served with brown bread, and they were reheated on the Sabbath when cooking, along with other activities, came to a halt. Many people still like the custom of Saturday night beans.

There have been various departures from the purity of the parent recipe. Occasionally cooks will add onions or an onion stuck with cloves. A bay leaf or touches of sweet herbs have also crept into the

Boston Baked Beans

2 pounds (4 cups) pea beans
½ pound or more salt pork or pickled pork, the skin scored
1 tablespoon salt
½ cup maple sugar or syrup
½ teaspoon dry mustard
Hot water

recipe, and the addition of mustard has become almost a universal practice, but essentially the dish remains the same.

Soak the beans overnight in water twice the depth of the beans. Drain, and renew the water. Add the salt and bring to a boil. Boil several minutes and then simmer till the beans are tender. The old test is to remove two or three beans in a spoon and blow on them. If the skin breaks they are done. But you can simply taste them for tenderness if you want. Transfer the beans to a bean pot and push in the piece of scored salt pork. Add the seasonings and boiling water to cover. Cover the beans and bake 8 to 10 hours in a very slow oven — 250 degrees. Add water if necessary. For the last half hour or so, remove the cover and let the beans form a crust.

Molasses Beans

In Boston baked beans substitute 1/4 cup molasses and 2 tablespoons sugar for the maple sugar or syrup.

Southern Baked Beans

In the early nineteenth century some Southern cooks followed the Boston rule and added either chopped, peeled, and seeded tomatoes or canned tomatoes and ginger. For the proportions given above for Boston baked beans, use 5 or 6 peeled and seeded tomatoes, 1 teaspoon ginger, and an onion, of course.

Pennsylvania Baked Beans

These, an adaptation of Boston baked beans, used pork chops instead of salt pork, and reduced the cooking time to about 3 1/3 or 4 hours.

New York Baked Beans

This greatly advanced method of preparing baked beans was offered by Mrs. Crowen. The beans were soaked overnight and then placed in a kettle with a rib piece of corned pork with bone, a small hot pepper, and hot, not boiling, water. This was cooked about 2 hours, till the beans were tender, then transferred to a buttered baking dish with the beans arranged around the pork in the center. Some liquid was added from the beans and the whole dotted with butter. It was baked for an hour. No sugar was added, but black pepper was often included.

Baked Pork and Beans with Tomato Sauce

These came with the catsup age. Prepare the beans as for Boston baked beans but omit the sugar or syrup. Substitute a cup or more tomato catsup or chili sauce. Reduce the baking time to 4 hours.

Mrs. Rorer's Beans with Tomato Sauce

Mrs. Rorer felt that if one very carefully pulped each bean after they were boiled they would be more wholesome and nutritious. She broke with tradition and suggested adding a mixture of Brazil nuts and pine nuts to the bean and tomato mixture instead of the pork, believing this was a more nutritious addition. She also felt that if you didn't like pork, for which she herself had little use, you might add some chopped beef suet for fat.

Mrs. Harland's Baked Beans

These were boiled without pork, then placed in a baking dish with salt, freshly ground pepper, a good amount of butter, and boiling water. They were covered and baked at 350 degrees about 1½ to 2 hours. The cover was removed, dots of butter were added to the top, and it was browned uncovered. This dish was served with a vegetable and with potatoes.

Bean Hole Beans

These were a favorite of the lumberjacks and should interest outdoor cookery enthusiasts.

A hole about 2 to 3 feet deep and 18 to 24 inches across was dug in ground fairly free from rock (as compared to preparation for the clambake). A fire of hardwood was built in the hole and burned down to fine coals. While this was in progress, the beans, which had been soaked, were set to boil. When they were tender they were transferred to a huge bucket or kettle fitted with a tight cover. More salt pork than usual was added, along with the molasses and sugar or the maple syrup, onion, and mustard. The kettle of beans was covered and then set in the hole. Some coals were heaped on top, then it was covered with soil and left there overnight to cook. The beans were served with the morning meal.

Katie's Pioneer Beans

1 pound (2 cups) pea beans or Great Northern beans
5 cups water
¼ teaspoon soda
½ pound salt pork or bacon cut into cubes
⅓ to ½ cup molasses
1 small onion
½ teaspoon dry mustard
¼ teaspoon ginger
¼ teaspoon allspice

This is the same idea as the Maine bean hole beans but the ingredients are different.

Soak the beans overnight in the water and soda. Put a few of the salt pork or bacon bits in the bottom of a 4-quart kettle equipped with a lid that will fit tightly, or use a bean pot. Make alternate layers of the pork and beans. Add the molasses, onion, spices, and the water in which the beans were soaked. Put the lid on the kettle and cover tightly with foil or seal the top with flour and water mixed together to a thick paste. Place in the bean hole, heap with coals, and cover the hole as above. Cook 6 to 8 hours.

Note. Tomato sauce may be added to this recipe as well.

Boiled Beans

This recipe gives you plain unseasoned boiled beans, useful in other recipes. For serving, you will need to add butter and seasonings, as in the variation below.

Cover 1 pound white beans (about 2 cups) with water and bring to a boil. Cook 2 minutes. Cover, and let stand 1 hour. Simmer until tender. Drain.

Buttered Boiled Beans. Before simmering, add 1 small onion. When the beans are cooked and well drained, add salt and freshly ground pepper to taste, 6 tablespoons butter, and some chopped parsley. Serve with lamb chops or with a leg of mutton.

Bretonne Beans

1 pound beans (Great Northern seem the best)
Salt
2 onions, finely chopped
1 garlic clove, finely chopped
6 tablespoons butter
3 to 4 tomatoes, peeled, seeded, and chopped
½ teaspoon thyme
1 teaspoon freshly ground pepper
Chopped parsley

This has become a classic service with leg of lamb because of the number of small French restaurants, especially on the Atlantic seaboard, which specialize in gigot (leg of lamb) Bretonne style.

Cook the beans as for boiled beans, above. Drain and keep hot, adding salt to taste. Sauté the onions and garlic in the butter, adding more butter if needed. Add the tomatoes and seasonings, and cook till the sauce is nicely blended. Add a tiny bit of water, stock, or tomato paste if more liquid is needed. Pour the drained beans into a heated serving dish. Spoon the sauce over them, and garnish with chopped parsley. Serve with leg of lamb or with meats grilled over charcoal.

Bean Purée

2 cups white beans, boiled as above
4 tablespoons butter
¾ cup heavy cream
Salt to taste
1 teaspoon freshly ground pepper

Prepare the beans, and when they are tender, drain well and put through the food mill to make a purée and to remove the skins. Blend with the melted butter and hot cream to make a light creamy mixture. Season with salt and freshly ground pepper, and serve with almost any meat.

Mrs. Rorer's Polenta

2 cups pea beans, boiled as above
1 tablespoon salt
1 teaspoon dry mustard
2 tablespoons butter
1 tablespoon vinegar
1½ tablespoons molasses (substitute 1 teaspoon sugar)
½ teaspoon freshly ground pepper

I don't know how Mrs. Rorer came to devise this recipe, since it is as far from polenta as it can be. Mrs. Rorer's is made from pea beans. However, it is rather good and unusual, though it is better if 1 teaspoon sugar is substituted for the molasses.

Cook the beans, and when they are tender, drain well and put through a food mill. Add the rest of the ingredients. Cook over medium heat 10 minutes. Pour into a loaf pan or a mold and cool. Cut in slices, dust with flour, and sauté in butter. Or form into cylinders, dip in egg, flour, and crumbs, and deep-fry at 365 degrees.

White Bean Salad

Excellent with cold roast beef, corned beef, ham, or barbecued meats. Use Great Northern beans, pea beans, or any of the varieties of smallish white beans one uses for baked beans or other bean casseroles.

Rub a salad bowl well with the garlic clove, adding a bit of salt to the bowl to get the best result. Add the cooked beans and other ingredients, and toss well. Allow it to stand an hour or two before serving. Use additional chopped parsley or a few red onion rings for garnish.

1 clove garlic
3 cups cooked white beans
½ cup finely chopped onion or green onion
3 tablespoons parsley
6 tablespoons olive oil
2 tablespoons wine vinegar
1 teaspoon salt
Freshly ground pepper

Beans Vinaigrette

2 cups white beans cooked in water, as above
Vinaigrette sauce
1 tablespoon chopped onion
1 garlic clove, finely chopped
2 tablespoons finely chopped green pepper

Cook the beans, and drain well. When cool, blend with vinaigrette and the other ingredients. Serve as an hors d'oeuvre or as an accompaniment to cold meats.

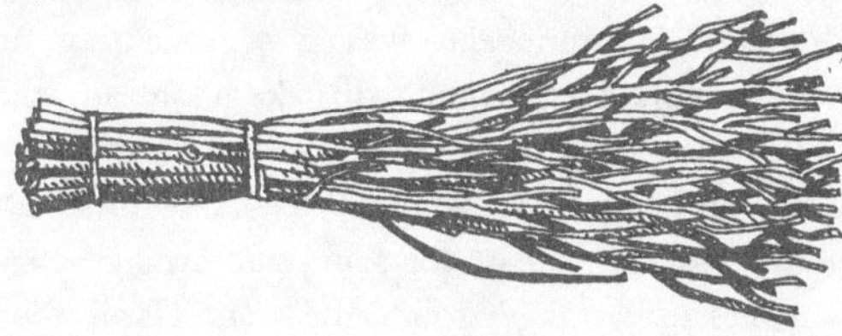

Italian Cold Beans

2 cups cannellini or pea beans, boiled as above
1 7-ounce can tuna fish in olive oil, flaked
1 garlic clove, finely chopped
½ cup finely chopped onion (optional)
1 tablespoon chopped fresh basil or 1 teaspoon dried basil
¾ cup vinaigrette sauce
2 tablespoons chopped parsley

Originally served in Italian restaurants in this country as an antipasto, but now well established in our general cuisine. It is good served as a luncheon dish, as an accompaniment to a cold egg dish or certain kinds of sausage, or as an hors d'oeuvre or a picnic dish.

Cook the beans, drain, and let cool. Arrange in a salad bowl, add the tuna fish, seasonings, and vinaigrette sauce. Toss well and garnish with chopped parsley.

Note. I often toss the salad, then add another can of tuna fillets in olive oil, some black olives, and a few anchovy fillets before garnishing with chopped parsley.

White Beans with Ham

2 cups white beans — navy, Great Northern, or pea beans
1 onion stuck with 2 cloves
1 bay leaf
1 rib celery
A piece of ham shank or ham bone, a small shank half of a ham, or a boneless butt

A treasured old recipe made when a ham was pretty well used and the shank end still had some meat on it. It has a good, homely flavor and makes a very appetizing meal.

Prepare the beans as for boiled beans, above, and after they have rested an hour add the onion, bay leaf, celery, and ham. Cover, and simmer over low heat till the beans are tender and the ham meat is thoroughly done. Drain the beans well. Remove the meat from the ham bone and cut it in small pieces, or if you have used a shank end or a butt, slice the meat. Season the beans to taste and heap on a

Salt, if needed, and freshly ground pepper

hot platter, with the pieces of meat arranged on top. Surround with fried tomatoes or braised Brussels sprouts. Serve with mustard, pickles, and rye bread and butter.

White Beans with Picnic Ham. Simmer a picnic ham in water, add the soaked beans, and continue to simmer until done. This way the flavor of the ham permeates the beans and makes a deliciously satisfying dish. Slice the ham, arrange on a platter with the beans, and serve with sautéed cabbage.

White Beans with Smoked Sausages

2 cups white beans
1 onion stuck with cloves
1 bay leaf
1½ to 2 pounds smoked pork sausages
Salt and freshly ground pepper
Shredded green onions

Cook the beans as for boiled beans, above, and when they are just beginning to be soft to the bite add the smoked sausages — Pennsylvania farm sausage, Italian cotechino, or any smoked sausages of your choice. Simmer the sausages with the beans until both are ready for eating. A cotechino will take about an hour or so; most of the Pennsylvania smoked sausages about 40 minutes; and other country smoked sausages about the same time. Drain the beans (save the liquid as a base for soup) and arrange on a platter. Slice the sausages and arrange around the beans. Garnish with some shredded green onions and serve with pickles, mustard, and a tomato salad.

Cassoulet

3 pounds white beans
Water
3 pounds pork shoulder in one piece
3 pounds lamb shoulder in one piece
Red wine
Salt and freshly ground pepper
1 onion stuck with cloves
2 carrots
Bouquet garni (garlic, celery, bay leaf, thyme, parsley, tied together in a piece of cheese-cloth)
1 pig's foot, split
½ pound lean salt pork
1 large or 2 small garlic sausages (kielbasy, cotechino, or whatever regional sausage is available)

Although it is not an American dish by origin, cassoulet has become a familiar part of our cuisine largely through its frequent appearance on the menus of French restaurants. One of the reasons it appeals so much to Americans is that we have a natural fondness for the bean. Another is that it is highly seasoned and hearty. Then, too, it lends itself to our favorite way of entertaining — the buffet.

Cover the beans well with cold water. Bring to a boil, boil 2 minutes, and then let them rest 1 hour. Put the pork and lamb roasts in a 325-degree oven on a rack and roast 1½ hours, basting occasionally with a little red wine and the pan juices. Salt and pepper well. When done, allow to cool, reserving the pan juices. Add the onion stuck with cloves and the carrots, bouquet garni, and pig's foot to the beans and simmer until the beans are about half cooked. Add the salt pork. Put the sausages to poach in water until they are cooked through. Sauté the onions and garlic in butter till just soft. When the pork and lamb are cool enough to handle, cut them into 1½-inch cubes. Slice the sausages. Drain the beans and reserve the liquid. Taste the beans for seasoning and add salt, pepper, and additional thyme if needed. Remove the meat from the pig's foot and cut into pieces. Dice the salt pork.

4 medium onions, finely chopped
2 cloves garlic, finely chopped
2 tablespoons tomato paste
Breadcrumbs
Lard or goose fat
Chopped parsley

You will need about a 4-quart casserole or baking dish for the cassoulet. Arrange a layer of beans at the bottom, then some of the various meats, and the onions and garlic. Continue with layers of beans, meats, and seasonings, and end with a layer of beans.

Blend the tomato paste with the bean liquid and spoon over the beans until it reaches three-quarters of the way to the top. Cover the top with breadcrumbs and dot with lard or goose fat. Bake at 325 degrees 1½ hours, or until beautifully browned and bubbly and most of the liquid has cooked away. Sprinkle with chopped parsley and serve with a good salad and crusty bread.

Traditionally this dish is served in the middle of the day, since it requires some hours for digestion. So if you are serving it for an evening meal, see that there is to be some activity after dinner. Heavy red wine should accompany the cassoulet.

Frankfurters and Beans

2 cups white beans, Great Northern, cannellini, or pea beans
Water
Salt
1 onion stuck with cloves
4 tablespoons butter
2 garlic cloves, finely chopped
1 large onion, finely chopped
4 tablespoons butter
2 cups canned tomatoes, preferably Italian plum tomatoes
¾ cup catsup
Salt and freshly ground pepper
8 to 10 frankfurters

This is certainly one of the most thoroughly American dishes of all. It can be very poor as served in some of the greasier greasy spoons, but it can also have wonderfully good qualities. I am sure this was a New York invention, although it has become a universal favorite — so much so that they have been canned together, unsuccessfully. Beans can beautifully, but to my taste, frankfurters don't. Interestingly enough, in this age of Americana in Europe, frankfurters and beans are found on a number of menus in American snack bars and such. I had occasion to taste this dish in a restaurant in Brussels, which is part of a chain being created for the European trade. So our modest bean dish is becoming international.

Cover the beans with cold water, bring to a boil, and then let rest 1 hour. Simmer with the salt and onion stuck with cloves until tender. Drain them, reserving about 1 cup of liquid. While the beans are simmering, sauté the garlic and onion in the butter, and when they are just soft add the tomatoes and let them cook down till rather thickish. Add the catsup, pepper, and salt if needed. Combine the sauce with the drained beans, butter, and reserved liquid, and reheat. Heat the frankfurters through in boiling water. Spoon the beans into a hot deep platter. Surround with the frankfurters. Serve with mustard, a hearty salad, and crisp rolls.

Lima Beans

Buttered Lima Beans

1 pound dried lima beans
1 tablespoon flour blended with 2 tablespoons butter

Soak the beans overnight. Drain, cover with boiling water, and cook till the beans are just tender. Drain well, and return to the pan in which they were cooked. Add the flour and butter, well mixed, and the seasonings and cream. Toss well with a fork and taste for

1 tablespoon salt
½ teaspoon freshly ground pepper
1 cup light cream

seasoning. Cook down for a few minutes. Serve with roast meat or fowl.

Note. This recipe is greatly enhanced by adding ½ cup freshly grated Parmesan cheese.

Lima Beans with Mushrooms

1 pound dried lima beans
2 large onions, finely chopped
¼ cup butter
½ pound mushrooms, sliced
2 tablespoons paprika
1 tablespoon salt
1 tablespoon flour
1½ to 2 cups sour cream
Salt
1 cup finely chopped parsley

Soak the beans, cook, and drain well as above. Sauté the onions in the butter in a heavy skillet until almost translucent. Add the mushrooms and cook another 4 minutes, using more butter if necessary. Then add the paprika, salt, and flour. Cook about 3 more minutes before adding the drained beans, sour cream, and parsley. Serve with pork or with chicken.

Casserole of Lima Beans and Pork

1 pound dried lima beans
Water
1 tablespoon salt
1 carrot, grated
1 large onion, finely chopped
½ pound salt pork, finely diced
Salt and freshly ground pepper
1 teaspoon summer savory or thyme
1 cup white wine
1 cup breadcrumbs
¼ cup melted butter
½ cup chopped parsley
2 finely chopped garlic cloves

This is called a "Californian Casserole."

Soak the beans overnight. In the morning simmer in salted water 20 minutes. Drain well, reserving the liquid, and pour into a casserole. While the beans are cooking, sauté the carrot, onion, and salt pork together till the pork is nicely colored and crisp. Add with the seasonings to the beans. Add the white wine and just enough bean liquor to cover. Cover, and bake at 300 degrees until the beans are tender — about 2 to 2½ hours. Combine the breadcrumbs, melted butter, parsley, and garlic. Sprinkle on top of the beans and return to the oven, uncovered, to brown.

Lima Beans with Lemon

3 cups dried lima beans
1 tablespoon salt
6 tablespoons butter
1 teaspoon freshly ground pepper

The recipe of a mid-nineteenth-century French chef who presided at Delmonico's and gave cooking lessons to the ladies of New York.

Cook the beans as for boiled beans, above, adding the salt before simmering. When the beans are tender, drain, and add the butter, pepper, nutmeg, and additional salt if needed. Beat the egg yolks lightly with the water and lemon juice. Toss into the beans and heat briefly, shaking the pan the while. Add the chopped parsley and serve.

¼ teaspoon nutmeg
3 egg yolks
1 tablespoon water
3 tablespoons lemon juice
4 tablespoons chopped parsley

Lima Beans with Tomato Sauce

3 cups dried lima beans
1 tablespoon salt
2 pounds very ripe tomatoes or 1 #2½ can Italian plum tomatoes
1 garlic clove
1 finely chopped medium onion
2 teaspoons dried basil or 2 tablespoons fresh
2 tablespoons concentrated tomato paste (if using canned tomatoes)
4 tablespoons butter
Chopped parsley
Grated Parmesan cheese

Cook the beans as for boiled beans, above, adding the salt before simmering. While they are cooking, simmer the tomatoes with the garlic, onion, and basil. If using fresh tomatoes, add the butter at the very beginning; if using canned tomatoes, add it at the last along with the concentrated tomato paste. Correct the seasoning and cook till thick. If the tomatoes are very sharp, add 2 teaspoons sugar. Drain the beans and place in a deep platter or serving dish. Spoon the tomato sauce over them and sprinkle lavishly with chopped parsley and freshly grated Parmesan cheese.

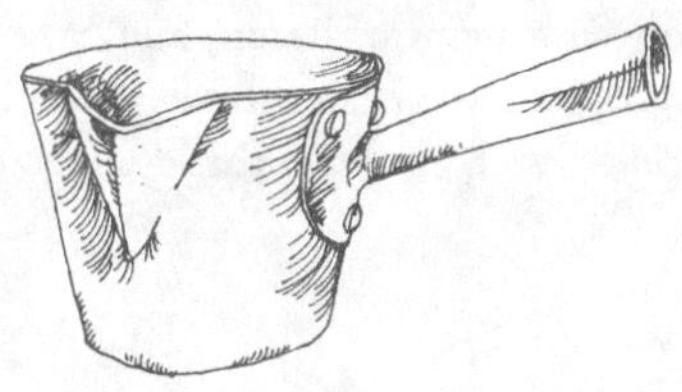

Brown Kidney Beans

The brown kidney bean is rich and creamy. It is not as popular in some sections of the country as the white or pinto bean, but it is widely used in salads. Fresh kidney beans are served mainly with butter or a tomato sauce. The dried ones are prepared like any other dried beans — see boiled kidney beans, below. However, there are quick-cooking processed beans on the market that cut down the cooking time quite noticeably. There are also excellent canned kidney beans available, ready-processed, which need only rinsing before adding to any dish.

Boiled Kidney Beans

Cover the beans with water, bring to a boil, and boil 2 minutes. Allow the beans to rest 1 hour; then simmer till tender, and drain. Serve with plenty of butter, and salt and freshly ground pepper.

Kidney Beans Maître d'Hôtel

2 cups (1 pound) dried kidney beans
¼ pound (1 stick) butter
½ cup minced onion
¼ cup minced parsley
Salt
1 teaspoon freshly ground pepper
3 tablespoons lemon juice

A recipe from the mid-nineteenth century, created by the chef at Delmonico's.

Cook the beans as for boiled kidney beans, above. When ready to serve, reheat the beans and add the other ingredients. Shake the pan well as you reheat. Garnish with additional chopped parsley, if you like. Serve with pork, lamb, or cold meats.

Kidney Beans with Sausage and Red Wine

2 cups (1 pound) dried kidney beans prepared as above or 3 to 4 cans kidney beans, drained and salted
2 kielbasy sausages
1 cup finely chopped onion
2 cups red wine
Salt and freshly ground pepper
6 strips bacon
Chopped parsley

Prepare the beans as for boiled kidney beans, above, or use the canned beans. Combine the sausages, onion, and wine, and poach about 25 to 30 minutes. Add salt and pepper to taste. Remove the sausages and cut in 1½-inch sections. Let the wine and onion reduce over high heat. Place layers of beans and sausages — ending with beans — in a baking dish and pour the reduced wine over them. Cover the top with strips of bacon, and bake at 350 degrees until the bacon is crisp and the bean mixture bubbly. Remove from the oven and sprinkle with chopped parsley.

Kidney Bean and Cheese Cazuela

6 slices bacon cut in small dice
1 cup finely chopped onions
1 garlic clove, finely chopped
1 cup tomato sauce
2 tablespoons chili powder
1 teaspoon salt
3 cans kidney beans, drained and washed
2 cups diced Monterey jack cheese, Cheddar, or Gruyère
Cilantro (fresh coriander) if available

A Southwestern specialty.

Try out the bacon until it is just barely crisp. Pour off all but about 2 tablespoons fat, add the onions and garlic, and let them just wilt with the bacon. Add the tomato sauce, chili powder, and beans, and cook very slowly together. Just before serving, stir in the cheese and let it melt. Sprinkle with coriander leaves, and serve at once.

Ham and Kidney Bean Tureen

3 cups dried kidney beans (1½ pounds) or 6 #1 tall cans
1½ cups finely chopped onions
6 tablespoons butter
1 teaspoon summer savory
1 teaspoon thyme
2½ to 3 cups cooked ham cut in 1½-inch dice
2 cups red wine
2 tablespoons tomato paste
Salt and freshly ground pepper
½ cup finely chopped green onions
¼ cup chopped parsley

Originally from the Napa Valley, where wine is a natural ingredient for recipes, this is excellent for a large party or picnic (pack in a large vacuum container).

If you use dried beans, prepare as for boiled kidney beans, above. If you use canned beans, merely wash them thoroughly. Sauté the onions gently in the butter till wilted. Add the herbs and ham and blend thoroughly. Add the wine and tomato paste, and simmer gently 25 minutes or until all ingredients are well blended. Add salt and pepper to taste. Combine the beans and the ham mixture and heat together until piping hot. Serve from a large tureen or deep bowl and sprinkle with chopped green onions and parsley.

This calls for a crisp salad — a spinach salad with soy dressing or a coleslaw. Also serve corn bread and more red wine, and you have quite a good meal for supper.

Quick Kidney Bean Dish

2 cloves garlic, finely chopped
4 tablespoons olive oil
2 cans kidney beans, drained and washed
½ cup red wine
20 pitted black olives — the soft variety
3 tablespoons chopped parsley

Another recipe from California, where so many bean dishes seem to originate.

Sauté the garlic in oil and add the beans, wine, and olives. Heat thoroughly and serve sprinkled with the chopped parsley.

Kidney Bean Salad

2 1-pound cans kidney beans, drained and washed
1 cup finely cut green onions
1 cup finely chopped parsley
2 tablespoons chopped green pepper
¾ cup garlic-flavored vinaigrette sauce
Greens
Cherry tomatoes for garnish

Excellent with grilled meats, especially for outdoor meals, and pleasant with cold meats or fish. Canned red kidney beans may be used for this — a great saving in time and effort. Wash canned beans well before using them for salads.

Combine the beans, green onions, parsley, pepper, and vinaigrette. Toss, and let stand several hours before serving. Chill in the refrigerator till about a half hour before serving. Arrange on greens and garnish with cherry tomatoes.

Variations

(1) Add ½ cup chopped peeled and seeded tomato and 1 cup chopped peeled and seeded cucumber.

(2) Use equal portions of kidney beans and white beans, and substitute 3 tablespoons chopped pimiento for the green pepper.

Ranch Salad

2 cans kidney beans, drained
2 cans white beans, drained
2 cans garbanzos or chick peas, drained
1 large onion, finely chopped
12 green onions, finely cut
2 green peppers, seeded and diced
1 or 2 hot chilies, finely chopped
4 tomatoes, peeled, seeded, and chopped
Tabasco to taste
Very garlicky vinaigrette sauce
Greens

This salad is basically a cold bean dish. In a few years it has grown from being a California specialty to the point of becoming a national institution. It has many variations. Here are two. Both are suitable for large gatherings.

Wash and drain the beans and garbanzos very well. Combine with the vegetables and seasonings and toss well with the vinaigrette sauce. Heap into a bowl lined with greens, and garnish with sliced tomatoes and hard-boiled eggs, if you like. Perfect with grilled foods, ham, or spareribs.

Ranch Salad with Sauerkraut

2 27-ounce cans sauerkraut
2 cans red kidney beans
2 cans white beans
2 cans garbanzos or chick peas
12 tomatoes, peeled and cut into sixths
2 cucumbers, peeled, seeded, and cut into strips
Garlic vinaigrette sauce or Russian dressing

Drain and wash the sauerkraut and beans. Arrange the sauerkraut in the center of a deep salad bowl and arrange mounds of the various beans around it. Press tomato sixths between the mounds, and surround with strips of cucumber. Add either a fine vinaigrette or a Russian dressing. Serve with roast pork, barbecued pork chops or spareribs, or barbecued beef.

Red Bean Stew

3 cups (1½ pounds) dried red beans — kidney beans, pintos, or bolitas
Water
1 pound pickled pork or salt pork
3 large onions, finely chopped
2 or 3 chilies (tepins)
½ cup chili powder
1 teaspoon Tabasco
2 or 3 green peppers, seeded and chopped
1 pound chaurice or chorizo

One finds this dish all along the Mexican border states and up into the edges of Colorado and Wyoming. It is often made with kidney beans and sometimes with pintos or bolitas.

Cover the beans with cold water and bring to a boil. Boil 2 minutes and let them rest an hour. Bring to a boil again and reduce heat. Simmer with the pork and the remaining ingredients except the sausage. When the beans are beginning to be tender, add the sausage. Cook until the beans are quite soft and the meat is well cooked, about 1½ hours. Cut the pork into small pieces and slice the sausage. Correct the seasoning and continue cooking a half hour. Serve in bowls and top with rice and with additional sausages, if you like.

Pinto Beans and Bolitas

Pintos, a spotted pinkish-brown bean, and bolitas, a roundish brown bean, are the beans most used in the Southwest. They probably came from Mexico originally, but now from Texas to the Oregon line and beyond, the pinto is much in demand. It is a rich-tasting bean and combines beautifully with chilies and other seasonings of a high degree of spiciness.

The pinto bean flourishes in a fairly arid climate and takes longer to cook than some of the other dried legumes. The bolita comes from higher altitudes and cooks in shorter time. Both must be cooked at low temperature for a long time. Traditionally they are cooked in an earthenware pot.

Boiled Pinto Beans or Bolitas (Frijoles)

2 cups (1 pound) dried pintos or bolitas
Water
2 cloves garlic, crushed
1 tablespoon sugar
1 tablespoon salt
½ pound finely diced salt pork

Soak the beans overnight. Drain. Add the garlic and sugar and cover with water. Bring to a boil, reduce the heat, and simmer. Add the salt and salt pork after a half hour. Simmer very slowly until the beans are tender. This will take about 3 hours or more for pintos, 4 to 5 hours for bolitas. These are delicious served with a chili, high seasoned pork, or sausages.

Frijoles con Queso (Beans with Cheese). Add small cubes of Monterey jack or mild Cheddar cheese and give them just enough time to melt. Serve with pork or with any outdoor food. This recipe is also made with frijoles refritos or Southwestern chili beans (below).

Mashed Beans (Frijoles Machacados). Let the beans cook down so that there is little liquid left in the pan. Cook 2 tablespoons lard or olive oil and 2 tablespoons flour for a moment in a large skillet. Mash the beans, add to the skillet, and cook 5 minutes. Add fat if needed.

Frijoles Refritos (Refried Beans)

1 pound pinto beans
½ cup lard or bacon fat (or more)

Refritos are best if cooked at low heat for about 2 hours. Prepare boiled pinto beans as above. When they are almost cooked, melt the lard or bacon fat in a cazuela or a heavy skillet. Mash the beans a few at a time till they are well blended with the fat. Then add more fat to the pan and let them cook slowly, mashing them occasionally so they become rather crisp at the edges. The beans must be very hot, crisp, and creamy.

Southwestern Chili Beans

2 cups (1 pound) pinto beans
¼ pound salt pork
3 tablespoons lard or bacon fat
3 cloves garlic, finely chopped

Many recipes like this have come from Arizona, Nevada, and New Mexico. Although they are similar to one another in some ways, each has character, quality, and originality.

Cook the beans very slowly in water to cover till they are just on the verge of being done. In the meantime try out the salt pork in

2 onions, finely chopped
½ teaspoon oregano
Pinch of ground cumin
3 tablespoons chili powder
Salt and freshly ground pepper
2 cups tomato sauce

a large skillet or earthenware dish, add the lard or bacon fat, and brown the garlic and onions. Add the seasonings, tomato sauce, and the beans. Cook very slowly about an hour. Correct the seasoning. The beans should be soft but not at all mushy, and the flavors should be very well blended.

Chili con Carne con Frijoles (Cowpuncher Beans). Add 1 pound each diced cooked pork and beef to this dish, and perhaps a little more liquid.

California Beans with Cognac

2 cups (1 pound) pinto beans or bolitas
Water
2 cloves garlic, finely chopped
1 onion stuck with 2 cloves
Bay leaf
1 teaspoon thyme
6 tablespoons butter
1 small onion, finely chopped
2 cups tomato sauce or Italian plum tomatoes
¼ cup minced parsley
2 teaspoons salt
⅓ cup Cognac

Soak the beans overnight. The next morning drain and add the garlic, onion, bay leaf, and thyme. Cover with boiling water and cook very slowly until just tender. Drain, and reserve 1 cup of the liquid. Sauté the chopped onion lightly in the butter. Add the remaining ingredients and the reserved bean liquid. Bring to a boil, reduce the heat, and simmer 30 minutes. Mix with the beans and place in an earthenware casserole. Reheat at 325 degrees till just bubbly. Remarkably good with lamb.

Variations

(1) Brown 4 thickish pork chops and place them in the bottom of a large casserole or baking dish. Cover with the beans and sauce, and bake.

(2) Add 1 cup diced cooked ham and 1 pound cooked sausages to the beans and sauce before reheating.

Beans and Rice

2 cups (1 pound) pinto beans
Water
1 tablespoon salt
1 clove garlic, crushed
1 or 2 cloves garlic, finely chopped
Bacon fat, oil, or lard
6 tomatoes, peeled, seeded, and chopped
Freshly cooked rice
Fresh cilantro

Soak the beans overnight. Drain. Add the salt and crushed garlic clove to the beans, cover with boiling water, bring to a boil, then reduce the heat and simmer very slowly till the beans are just tender. Sauté the chopped garlic and tomatoes in fat, oil, or lard. Top the beans with cooked rice, spoon the sauce over all, and sprinkle with chopped cilantro.

Garbanzos or Chick Peas

This firm-textured member of the pea family is in common use throughout the Latin countries, North Africa, and the Middle East. It was introduced into this country by the Spanish in California and by the Middle Eastern people and Italians on the East Coast.

Since garbanzos are tough and require long cooking, I suggest you use canned ones, which are processed and ready to use.

To cook dried garbanzos. Soak overnight in water to more than cover, adding a little baking soda (½ teaspoon for 2 cups dried garbanzos). Next day drain and pick them over, discarding any that seem imperfect. Wash and drain, cover with fresh water, and simmer in a covered kettle until they are tender. Drain well.

Baked Garbanzos

4 cups drained cooked or canned garbanzos
1 teaspoon salt
½ teaspoon freshly ground pepper
3 large tomatoes, peeled, seeded, and chopped
1 large onion, chopped
1 clove garlic, crushed and chopped
1 teaspoon rosemary
½ cup olive oil

Combine all the ingredients in a baking dish and bake at 350 degrees 1 hour or until well blended. Correct the seasoning and serve hot (see note under sautéed garbanzos).

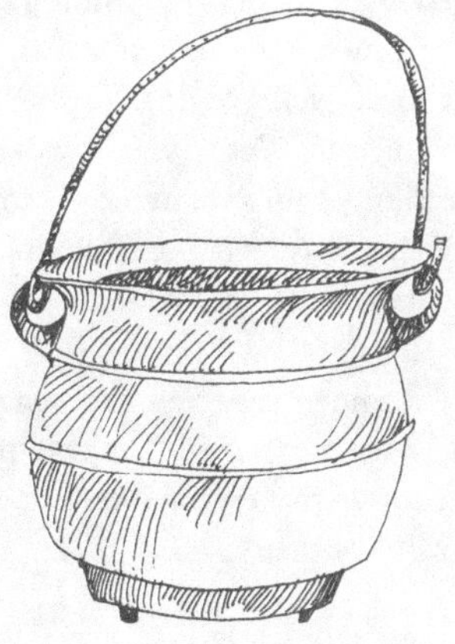

Sautéed Garbanzos

4 crushed garlic cloves
½ cup (1 stick) butter
2 tablespoons olive oil
3 cups drained cooked or canned garbanzos
Salt and freshly ground pepper

Sauté the crushed garlic very slowly in the butter and olive oil. Remove it, unless you like garlic in strength, add the garbanzos, and cook very slowly, shaking the pan well from time to time, until they are colored and quite tender. Salt and pepper them to taste. Serve with lamb.

Note. Baked or sautéed garbanzos are often served with a rice pilaff.

Garbanzos with Sesame Oil Sauce (Hummus bi Tahini)

6 cups drained cooked or canned garbanzos
1 cup sesame or olive oil
1½ cups lemon juice
3 crushed garlic cloves
Salt to taste
Chopped parsley

A Middle East dish usually served tucked into a half round of the puffy, hollow bread called pitta.

Press the well-drained garbanzos through a sieve or food mill to make a purée. Add the oil and lemon juice alternately, a little at a time. Add the crushed garlic and salt to taste. Blend thoroughly. Check for seasoning, adding more lemon juice if necessary. Chill in the refrigerator a few hours before serving.

To serve, heap the mixture in a bowl and top with a liberal sprinkling of chopped parsley. Serve as an appetizer with pieces of the flat Middle East bread, if available, or with very thin slices of your favorite bread.

Lentils

Lentils are supposed to be the "mess of pottage" that figures in the Bible. I have grave doubts that this is so, even though some French cookbooks list lentil soup as *potage Esau*. However, they are indeed an ancient legume, long favored as food in Asia and in Europe and introduced to America by immigrants from those continents. We do not grow the number of varieties that one finds in Europe or Asia, but those we have do exceptionally well. Some of the finest are grown in the West, which provides the market with a large crop. Increasingly lentils are processed for quick cooking and are sold labeled in that way. They enable one to prepare the legume without presoaking and the subsequent long period of cooking.

Lentils have become a much neglected dry vegetable — I think mainly because people have not tasted them at their best. They need complementary flavors to make them interesting, although they have a good earthy quality of their own.

Sautéed Lentils

2 cups quick-cooking lentils
1 tablespoon salt
1 onion stuck with 2 cloves
1 bay leaf
½ pound slab bacon, cut into small dice
1 cup finely chopped onion
2 garlic cloves, finely chopped
Freshly ground pepper
¼ cup chopped parsley

Bring the lentils to a boil in salted water along with the onion and bay leaf. Simmer until they are *just tender*, then drain. You must be very careful not to overcook lentils, lest they become mushy and lose their character. Try out the bacon in a heavy skillet, add the chopped onion and garlic, then add the drained lentils and toss well. Add pepper to taste and the chopped parsley. Serve with spareribs, braised lamb shanks, or braised beef.

Lentil Salad

2 cups quick-cooking lentils
Salt
1 onion stuck with 2 cloves
1 bay leaf
1 teaspoon thyme
1½ cups finely cut green onions
½ cup olive oil
1 garlic clove, finely chopped
3 to 4 tablespoons wine vinegar
1½ teaspoons freshly ground pepper
¼ cup finely chopped pepper (optional)
½ cup chopped parsley

A thoroughly delightful salad which may be used as an hors d'oeuvre for a buffet party or for serving with cold meats. It is of French derivation and has long been a favorite with people in San Francisco.

Bring the lentils to a boil in salted water to which you have added the onion, bay leaf, and thyme. Simmer until the lentils are just tender, then drain, and add the remaining ingredients except for the parsley. Toss well and cool. Add the chopped parsley, correct the seasoning, and serve. This is better made the day before, with the parsley added just before serving. Taste for flavor. You may have to add more oil and vinegar.

Lentils Maître d'Hôtel

4 cups quick-cooking lentils
1 tablespoon salt
1 stick (½ cup) butter
½ teaspoon freshly ground pepper
¼ teaspoon nutmeg
2 egg yolks mixed with 2 tablespoons water
3 tablespoons chopped parsley (and more for garnish)

An old recipe from Delmonico's, dating from about 1885.

Bring the lentils to a boil, add the salt, and simmer till they are just tender. Drain. Add the rest of the ingredients and toss well. Add more parsley for garnish.

Lentil Casserole with Sausage

2 cups quick-cooking lentils
1 tablespoon salt
1 onion stuck with 2 cloves
1 bay leaf
12 Italian sausages, either sweet or hot
½ cup finely chopped onion
4 tablespoons butter
Salt and freshly ground pepper
1 cup red wine

Cover the lentils with water, and add the salt, onion, and bay leaf. Bring to a boil and simmer till the lentils are just tender. Drain. While the lentils are cooking, poach the sausages about 5 minutes in water to cover. Sauté the chopped onion in the butter. Arrange half the sausages in the bottom of a greased 2½-quart baking dish and add half the lentils, a little sautéed onion, and salt and pepper. Make another layer of lentils, and top with the rest of the sausages and onion. Pour in the wine, and bake at 350 degrees about 25 to 35 minutes, or till sausages are nicely brown.

Note. This basic casserole of lentils may also be prepared to great advantage with any of the following substituted for sausage: well-browned pork chops and sliced sauteéd onions; braised lamb shanks; roast duck, cut in quarters just as it is ready to be carved; braised pork tenderloin.

Lentil Purée

3 cups quick-cooking lentils
1 tablespoon salt
1 onion stuck with 2 cloves
1 bay leaf
1 stick (½ cup) butter
¼ teaspoon mace
¼ teaspoon ginger
½ cup heavy cream

Remarkably good with roast duck and superb with game, chicken, guinea hen, or a fine pork roast.

Cover the lentils with water, and add the salt, onion, and bay leaf. Bring to a boil and simmer till the lentils are just tender. Drain, and purée them in a china cap or food mill or with the purée attachment of your electric mixer. Melt the butter, add the spices and cream, and beat into the purée. Taste for salt and the balance of spices, and correct as needed. Serve very hot.

Mrs. Rorer's Egyptian Lentils

2 cups quick-cooking lentils
2 cups rice
2 cups canned or stewed tomatoes (preferably the Italian plum)
1 bay leaf
1 cup finely chopped onion
½ teaspoon mace
1 teaspoon salt
1 teaspoon freshly ground pepper
6 crushed cardamom seeds
3 tablespoons butter

Mrs. Rorer felt that because of their nitrogenous value, lentils should be on every table at least once a week. She also insisted they be served with rice. This recipe combines the two and makes a delicious dish for a buffet or for an accompaniment to grilled foods for outdoor eating.

Cover the lentils with water, bring to a boil, and simmer till just tender. Cook the rice according to your favorite recipe. Combine the tomatoes, bay leaf, onion, mace, salt, and pepper, and cook down until reduced about one-third. When the lentils and rice are done, combine them, dress with the tomato sauce, add the cardamom seeds, and toss well. Drizzle the butter over the top and serve.

Note. The addition of a little tomato paste to the sauce and some chopped parsley to the final service improves the dish.

Dried Peas

Usually split peas are used for soups nowadays, if at all. However, the green ones, especially, make a thoroughly delightful winter vegetable to serve with sausages, browned and sizzling; with thickish pork chops and a natural sauce; with game birds such as wild duck, pheasant, or woodcock; or with roast turkey, in which case it is pleasant to surround the puréed peas with small braised onions.

Purée of Split Peas

2 cups dried peas — green or yellow
Water
Chicken or veal broth
1 onion stuck with 2 cloves

Wash and soak the peas in water several hours. Drain, and add chicken or veal broth to cover by 1½ inches. Add the onion and seasonings and bring to a boil. Simmer gently over very low heat until the peas are soft. Drain, and reserve the broth. Purée the peas, add the butter, and if needed add some of the broth.

1 bay leaf
1 sprig mint
2 teaspoons salt
1 teaspoon freshly ground pepper
3 to 4 tablespoons butter

Black Beans

Sometimes called "turtle beans," black beans have been immortalized in American cuisine by the superb soup (which see). The black bean has smooth texture and rather distinctive flavor. It is often found in the cookery of the Caribbean and Florida and of the Southwest, notably California, where it has been popular as long as I can remember.

Tipsy Black Beans

2 pounds black beans
Water
1 tablespoon salt
1 onion stuck with 2 cloves
1 garlic clove
1 bay leaf
1 teaspoon thyme
1 teaspoon summer savory
1 or 2 sprigs parsley
Ham bone or ham hock
Beurre manié
½ cup Jamaica rum
1 teaspoon Tabasco
Sour cream

Soak the beans overnight. Drain, add the seasonings, herbs, and ham bone or hock, and more than cover with water. Bring to a boil and simmer at the feeblest ebullition until the beans are tender but not mushy. Drain, and reserve the liquid. Cut off any bits of meat on the ham bone. Discard the other seasonings. Cook the liquid down 5 minutes over brisk heat and thicken with beurre manié — butter and flour kneaded together. Add more salt if needed. Place the beans in a baking dish. Add the rum and Tabasco and pour in enough of the thickened liquid to just cover. Bake at 350 degrees until heated through and lightly browned — about 20 to 30 minutes. Serve with cold sour cream.

Caribbean Black Beans

2 pounds black beans
3 garlic cloves, finely chopped
½ cup finely diced salt pork
½ cup olive oil
Salt to taste
1 teaspoon freshly ground pepper
1 teaspoon oregano
½ cup finely chopped parsley
Fresh cilantro (coriander)

Prepare the beans as in the recipe above. Drain. Sauté the garlic and salt pork in the olive oil, add the seasonings, and combine with the beans and parsley. Garnish with cilantro leaves.

Pies and Pastry

Early English settlers of the Atlantic Coast brought their love of pies with them. These included meat, game, fish, fowl, fruit, and berry pies, and a variety of pastry. There were also cream, custard, and other open-face pies, but these were listed in old English cookbooks as puddings. As late as the mid-nineteenth century, some American cookbooks listed custard pies as puddings, although mainly by that time the custard was baked in a pie pan with a rim of pastry around the edge and no under crust.

In early America and well up into the nineteenth century, pie was a standard breakfast dish. Since the men of rural families rose early and had an hour or more of outside chores before breakfast, there was time to make such treats.

If winters were cold, pies were made in quantity and put out to freeze. The varieties were limited to the supplies at hand, but dried fruit was always available to the thrifty housekeeper. Sometimes the pies were layered. For instance, fresh or dried and simmered apple slices might be topped with custard or a cottage cheese custard; and mince might be topped with apple, cranberries, pumpkin, or sometimes apple and custard. Such recipes do not appear in cookbooks, but have come down to us in old diaries or literature of the time.

Apple Pie

5 cups peeled, cored, and thinly sliced apples
½ to ¾ cup sugar
½ to 1 teaspoon cinnamon
¼ teaspoon salt
2 tablespoons butter
Lemon juice (optional)
Pastry for two-crust 9-inch pie

So common has apple pie always been in this country — although it did not originate here — that many old American cookbooks did not bother to give a recipe. It was taken for granted that every housewife had her own favorite.

Whether to prepare the crust or the apples first is a matter of choice. If you are a quick pastry maker, then you'll probably want to start with the apples. Combine them with the sugar, cinnamon, and salt. Turn into a 9-inch pie pan lined with pastry. Dot the apples with butter and moisten the edge of the trimmed bottom crust. Put on the top pastry, trim, and crimp the edge. Bake in a 450-degree oven 15 minutes. Reduce the heat to 350 degrees and bake from 20 to 35 minutes longer. The length of time will depend upon the type of apples used. Summer apples, such as Transparents or Gravensteins, which should be used slightly green or underripe, will cook very quickly. It is best to leave a slit in the center of the pie crust so that the apples can be tested with a fork without disturbing the crust. If using very ripe apples or sweet apples, sprinkle with a tablespoon or two of lemon juice before adding the top crust. Serve apple pie warm or cold, plain or with aged Cheddar cheese, a cheese sauce, or ice cream, which makes it "à la mode."

Deep-Dish Apple Pie

6 cups cored, peeled, and thinly sliced apples
7/8 cup sugar (1 cup minus 2 tablespoons)
1 teaspoon cinnamon
2 or 3 tablespoons butter
Lemon juice (optional)
Pastry for one-crust 9-inch pie

This was often made along with a regular two-crust pie and left for future use, since it had no bottom crust to become soggy on standing. An inverted egg cup, or, for a large pie, an inverted teacup, was placed in the pie pan or casserole before the filling was put in. This gathered the juice and held up the crust. Here is a recipe for a small deep-dish pie, requiring a 9×9×2-inch pan.

Roll the pastry so it will extend about 1½ inches beyond the sides of the pan. Invert the pan on the pastry and cut around it, leaving a margin of about ½ inch. The amount of pastry used will depend upon whether you prefer a thick or thin crust. Roll the trimmings slightly wider, drape over the edge of the pan, and moisten the top. Mix the apples with the sugar and cinnamon. Sprinkle with a little lemon juice if they are of a sweet variety or seem a little old. Turn into the pan. Dot with butter. Adjust the top crust in place and press against the moistened bottom dough to seal. Cut slits or a design in the top to allow for the escape of steam, and crimp the edges. Bake in a 450-degree oven 15 minutes. Reduce the heat to 350 degrees, and bake 25 to 40 minutes longer, depending upon the variety of apples used. Serve hot or cold with cream, ice cream, or Cheddar cheese.

Deep Dish Peach, Apricot, Prune, or Berry Pie. Prepare as for deep-dish apple pie, adding 4 to 6 tablespoons flour to the sugar for fillings of berries or fruits that are quite juicy.

Cracker Pie (Mock Apple Pie)

3 egg whites
¼ teaspoon cream of tartar
1 cup sugar
½ teaspoon vanilla
½ to ¾ cup coarsely chopped, lightly toasted walnuts
1 cup soda crackers or rich round crackers crushed in hand (about 10 small soda crackers or about 16 round crackers)
½ to 1 cup whipping cream, whipped

More of a pudding than a pie, but old cookbooks considered it a pie because it was made in a pie pan.

Beat the egg whites until they begin to froth, add the cream of tartar, and beat until small bubbles begin to form. Gradually beat in the sugar and vanilla and continue to beat until the mixture is stiff and the granules of sugar have dissolved. Fold in the nuts and crumbled crackers. Pile roughly into a lightly oiled 9-inch pie pan. Bake in a 325-degree oven about 35 to 40 minutes. Cool on a rack. Chill in the refrigerator and top with whipped cream about 1 hour before serving.

Fresh Fruit Pie (Two-Crust)

4 to 5 cups prepared fruit
¾ to 1½ cups sugar
Flour
¼ teaspoon salt
Spice (optional)
1 to 2 tablespoons butter
Pastry for two-crust 9-inch pie

Prepare the pastry and roll out the bottom crust. Fit without stretching into the pan and trim the edge. Roll out the top crust. Prepare the fruit, and mix with the sugar, flour, salt, and spice. Turn the filling into the pie, and dot with butter. Moisten the edge of the bottom crust, place the top crust on it, and cut slits in it to allow the steam to escape. Trim the crust and crimp the edges to seal it. Bake in a 450-degree oven 15 minutes. Reduce the heat to 350 degrees, and bake about 25 to 30 minutes longer. Do not over-bake. The pie will continue to cook after it is out of the oven. Cool the pie on a rack, unless it is to be served warm.

Apricot Pie. Use 1¼ to 1½ cups sugar and 3 to 4 tablespoons flour. Add ½ teaspoon nutmeg or mace if you like.

Peach Pie. Peel, pit, and slice peaches about ½ inch thick. Very sweet peaches will be improved in flavor by the addition of 1 or 2 tablespoons lemon juice. Use 4 tablespoons flour combined with the sugar and salt. For very firm varieties of peaches, bake the pie slightly longer. For early peaches, generally of a very loose texture, bake the pie a total of about 40 minutes.

Pear Pie. Peel, core, and slice pears about ½ inch thick. Add 2 tablespoons lemon juice to the pears as soon as they are sliced, to intensify the flavor and to keep them from turning dark. Add 4 tablespoons flour for thickening, combined with 3/4 cup white sugar or slightly more of firmly packed brown sugar. Ginger (1/2 teaspoon ground, 1 tablespoon candied, or 1/2 teaspoon grated raw) is good in this pie. Or use 1/2 teaspoon mace or nutmeg.

Plum or Prune Pie. Plums should be peeled, for they usually have a thick skin that is rather acrid when cooked. Prunes (the type of plum that can be dried) do not need to be peeled. Cut the fruit in fourths as it is taken from the pits. Combine very juicy plums with 4 to 6 tablespoons flour and, for the very sweet varieties, 3/4 cup sugar. Add more for tarter fruit, according to taste. Prune pies like a sprinkling of cinnamon, allspice, and cloves. Plum pies are often made without spice. Generally white sugar is used to sweeten both.

Fruit Crisp or Crumb Pie

4 to 5 cups peeled and sliced apples, peaches, or pears, or cut-up apricots, prunes, or plums
1/2 cup butter
1 to 1 1/4 cups white or brown sugar
3/4 cup flour
1 teaspoon cinnamon or 1/2 teaspoon nutmeg or other spice
1/4 teaspoon salt
Unbaked 8 or 9 inch pastry shell

These are often made without a crust and served as a pudding topped with whipped cream or ice cream.

Place the fruit in an unbaked shell with fluted edges. Melt the butter in a 1 1/2 to 2 quart saucepan. Remove from the heat, stir in the sugar, flour, spices, and salt. The amount of sugar will depend upon the type of fruit used. Apricots and some tart plums may take more sugar. Apples, pears, peaches, and prunes may take slightly less than 1 cup. Brown sugar is generally preferred for apples, peaches, and pears. The amount of spice will depend upon taste. Cinnamon is generally used for apples; nutmeg, mace, or allspice is good with peaches or apricots. Add just a suggestion of clove along with cinnamon and nutmeg to prunes or plums. Pears are good with the addition of 1/2 teaspoon ginger. Scatter the mixture over the fruit, and bake the pie about 30 to 40 minutes in a 400-degree oven, or until the topping is crusty and the fruit is tender. Cool on a rack. Serve warm or cold, with whipped cream or ice cream, if you like.

Grape Crisp or Crumb Pie. Often grape pie (page 617) is made open face, with the above topping sprinkled over the filling.

Rhubarb Crisp or Crumb Pie. Use 4 cups fresh rhubarb stalks cut into pieces 1/2 to 1 inch long, and 1 1/2 to 1 3/4 cups sugar.

Apple Turnovers

Pastry
3 baking apples
1 cup sugar
1 inch of stick cinnamon
2 cups water

Preheat the oven to 400 degrees. Prepare, roll, and cut pastry into 6 squares as for apple dumplings (page 723). Peel and core the apples, cut them into moderately thin slices, and poach them just until they are tender but still firm in a syrup made by simmering together for 5 minutes the sugar, cinnamon, water, and vanilla. Drain the apples well and cool them. Arrange one-sixth of the slices in the center of

½ teaspoon vanilla
1 egg, beaten

each pastry square. Brush the edges with the beaten egg, fold the squares over to form triangles, and seal the edges to enclose the apples completely. Brush the triangles with the beaten egg and bake them on a baking sheet in the preheated oven for 20 minutes, or until they are lightly browned. Serve the turnovers warm, with vanilla sauce or chilled sweetened whipped cream.

Fried Pies

FILLING

1 pound dried apples, apricots, peaches, or prunes or 3½ to 4 cups thick cooked fruit (applesauce, pear butter, plum butter)
Sugar to taste
Spice (optional)

PASTRY

2 cups all-purpose flour
1 teaspoon salt
⅓ cup shortening or lard
4 to 5 tablespoons milk or water

Made most often with dried apples, peaches, apricots, or prunes, but other fresh or canned fruit sauces were used as well. Because they are fried, they require a less rich crust than normal.

Simmer the dried fruit in a covered saucepan with water to almost cover. When the fruit is tender, mash well. (Remove pits from prunes if using this fruit.) The amount of sugar for sweetening will depend upon the fruit. Apricots, for example, require more sugar than prunes or apples. Simmer the sweetened sauce, uncovered, until quite thick. Add spice to taste — cinnamon for apples, nutmeg for apricots, clove for prunes, nutmeg or allspice for peaches. Cool the sauce.

Turn the flour into a mixing bowl, add the salt, and stir well. Blend in the shortening with fingertips or a pastry blender. Add the milk or water (milk gives a nice brown to the crust). The dough should be slightly moist. Roll it out on a lightly floured board or pastry cloth, or between wax paper or plastic, to about ⅛ inch thick. Cut with a floured cutter into rounds 3 or 4 inches in diameter. (Old-time pies were cut with a paring knife, using a coffee saucer as a pattern.) Place about 2 tablespoons filling in the center of each round. Moisten edges with water or with beaten egg yolk or white thinned with 1 teaspoon of water. Fold the pastry over to form a half-round and press the edges together with a fork. Be sure they are sealed. Fry in 1 to 2 inches of fat heated to 375 degrees. Do only a few at a time, so the fat will not cool down and cause the pastry to become grease-soaked. Turn to brown on both sides. When nicely browned, take from fat with a slotted spoon and drain on paper towels. While still warm, sprinkle with granulated or powdered sugar. Serve hot or cold, but preferably while still warm. (Sometimes these pies were fried in about ¼ inch of shortening in a frying pan. Use medium heat to brown the crusts on both sides. However this method is not as successful as deep frying.)

Gooseberry Pie

3 to 4 cups gooseberries
¾ to 1 cup sugar

This greatly underrated pie is seldom found nowadays, but when you do, treasure it!

Line a deep 9-inch pie pan with pie crust. Add the gooseberries, the sugar and flour mixed together, and dot with butter. Cover with the top crust. Crimp the edges well, and make a vent for the steam to escape. Brush the crust with a little egg wash of egg yolk mixed with heavy cream. Bake the pie in a 450-degree oven 10 minutes, reduce the heat to 325 degrees, and continue baking until the pie is nicely browned and the fruit thoroughly cooked. This will take about 30 to 35 minutes. You may serve the gooseberry pie with a sweetened custard sauce or with heavy pouring cream or whipped cream.

¼ cup flour
1 egg yolk
2 tablespoons heavy cream
Crust for a two-crust pie
3 to 4 tablespoons butter

Grape Pie

1½ to 1¾ pounds Concord or other tart, slip-skin grapes (about 5 cups stemmed grapes)
1 cup sugar
4 to 6 tablespoons all-purpose flour
¼ teaspoon salt
½ teaspoon cinnamon (optional)
½ teaspoon allspice (optional)
1 to 2 tablespoons butter
Pastry for 9-inch covered pie

Seeded table grapes are used fresh in glazed tarts and are occasionally combined with tart fruits such as apricots in baked pies. But in earlier times slip-skin grapes were commonly baked in pies like any other fruit.

Slip the skins from the grapes and allow the pulp to fall into a 2-quart saucepan. Reserve the skins. Bring the pulp to a boil, remove from heat, and put through a sieve or colander or food mill to remove seeds. Cool. Combine the skins and pulp, sugar, flour, and salt. The amount of flour used will depend upon whether you prefer a rather firm filling. Add spices, if you like. Stir to combine the ingredients well. Roll out the bottom crust, fit without stretching into the pan, and trim the edge. Turn the filling into it, and dot with butter. Moisten the edge of the crust, put on the top pastry, cut steam vents, and crimp the edge. Bake the pie in a 450-degree oven 15 minutes. Reduce the heat to 350 degrees and continue to bake 25 minutes. Cool on a rack. Serve warm or cold. Many people like to serve this pie with cheese — aged Cheddar or a less flavorful cheese, such as cream cheese, Monterey jack, or one of the milder imported cheeses.

Rhubarb Pie

4 cups rhubarb stalks cut into ½ to ¾ inch pieces
1¼ to 1½ cups sugar
4 tablespoons flour or 2 tablespoons quick-cooking tapioca
¼ teaspoon salt
½ to 1 teaspoon grated orange or tangerine rind (optional)
1 to 2 tablespoons butter
Unbaked pastry for two-crust 9-inch pie

Since rhubarb was one of the first fresh garden products of the season in cold climates, it was looked upon as a tonic and was such a favorite for pie making that in many old cookbooks this was termed "pie plant pie."

Mix the rhubarb with the sugar, flour or tapioca, salt, and orange or tangerine rind. Turn into a pastry-lined pan. Dot with butter. Trim the edge of the pastry and moisten it. Top with pastry, trim the edge, and crimp the top and bottom edges together. Cut slits in the top for steam to escape. Bake at 450 degrees 15 minutes, reduce the heat to 350 degrees, and bake about 25 to 30 minutes longer. Cool on a rack. Serve warm or cold.

Rhubarb Custard Pie. Add 2 or 3 beaten eggs to the flour (2 tablespoons in this case), sugar, salt, and grated rind. Put the rhubarb in the pastry-lined pan, dot with butter, and pour the egg mixture over it. Add the top crust and bake as for plain rhubarb pie.

Lattice Rhubarb Pie. Either the plain or custard rhubarb pie is often baked with a lattice crust.

Rhubarb and Strawberry Pie. Use 1 to 2 cups sliced fresh or frozen strawberries instead of all rhubarb. This may take less sugar.

Berry Pies

4 cups prepared berries
3/4 to 1 1/2 cups sugar
4 to 6 tablespoons flour or 2 to 3 tablespoons quick-cooking tapioca
1/4 teaspoon salt
1 tablespoon lemon juice (for sweet berries)
1 to 2 tablespoons butter
Unbaked pastry for two-crust 9-inch pie

Wild or cultivated berries have long been top choice for pies. Here again, as for apples, there are few recipes for berry pies in old cookbooks, although they are mentioned in diaries and books from early American life. Apparently it was assumed that homemakers would know how to prepare them.

Pick over the berries. If they need washing, do not run water through them but put in a sieve or colander and dip up and down in a bowl of water, changing water if necessary. Drain well. Combine with the sugar, flour or tapioca, salt, and (if used) lemon juice. Turn into a pastry-lined pie pan. Dot with butter. Trim the pastry edge and moisten it. Cover with the top pastry, trim the edge, crimp the top and bottom edges together, and cut vents for steam. Bake at 450 degrees 15 minutes, reduce the heat to 350 degrees, and bake 25 to 30 minutes longer. Cool on a rack. Berry pies are usually served cold, although they can be served slightly warm. They are especially popular topped with ice cream.

Blueberry, Raspberry, or Strawberry Pie. These sweet berries usually require only about 3/4 cup sugar. However, if using lemon juice, add about 2 tablespoons more sugar for each tablespoon of lemon juice. Baked strawberry pie is not as popular as the others, but if you are making it, slice the berries. They are very juicy, so the maximum amount of flour (6 tablespoons) or quick-cooking tapioca (3 tablespoons) is preferred. Strawberries are considered best for pies when used fresh and then glazed. This is true also of raspberries and blueberries.

Wild Huckleberry Pie. Use 1 cup sugar and 1 to 2 tablespoons lemon juice. The amount of thickening depends on whether you like a rather runny or a firm pie.

Loganberry Pie. This tart, delicious berry used to be a favorite garden and commercial berry, but for some reason has lost its popularity in the past 30 years. Use 1 1/4 to 1 1/2 cups sugar and 5 to 6 tablespoons flour.

Blackberry Pie. There are many new commercial varieties of this fruit, as well as the tiny wild, flavorful blackberries found along the roadsides and fences. They can all be treated the same. For very ripe berries, wild or commercially grown, use 1 to 2 tablespoons lemon juice to enhance the flavor. The amount of thickening depends upon personal taste. Many of the new varieties of commercial blackberries are favored for use fresh in glazed pies.

Elderberry Pie. Generally elderberry bushes are not commercially grown for their fruit, and the berries must be gathered from the tall wild bushes or trees. Pick when fully ripe or the fruit will have an acrid taste. Blue elderberries are considered best. Strip the berries from the stem and proceed as in the basic recipe. Use 1 cup sugar and 1 to 2 tablespoons lemon juice in the filling.

Glazed Berry Pie

4 cups sliced strawberries or whole raspberries, sweet blackberries, or blueberries
Water
3/4 to 1 1/4 cups sugar
2 tablespoons cornstarch
1/4 teaspoon salt
2 tablespoons lemon juice
2 tablespoons butter
Baked pastry shell or crumb crust for 9-inch pie
1/2 to 1 cup whipping cream

Strawberries have been a favorite in this type of pie since the mid-nineteenth century. Now other berries, such as raspberries and many varieties of sweet blackberries and blueberries, are also used. Usually a crumb or sweet pastry crust is recommended.

Measure 1 cup berries. Add enough water to the cup to just cover the berries. Transfer to a saucepan, bring to a boil, and strain through a fine sieve or, for a clearer glaze, strain through cheesecloth. In a saucepan mix the sugar, cornstarch, and salt. Strawberries and blueberries will require the smaller amount of sugar, tart berries more. Measure the juice from the strained berries, and add enough water or fruit juice to make 1 cup. Stir into the sugar mixture and bring to a boil, stirring constantly, then reduce the heat. Allow the mixture to boil just until it looks clear — overboiling at this point will make the glaze thin. Remove from the heat, cool 5 minutes, and add the lemon juice and butter. Cool to room temperature. Meanwhile, chill the pie crust and remaining fruit. Spread a thin layer of cooled, not chilled, glaze in the crust. Add the berries and pour the remaining glaze over them. Chill. When ready to serve, top with whipped cream.

Glazed Berry Pie with Gelatine. Add 3/4 cup water to the cup of berries for the glaze, and after they come to a boil, simmer a few minutes to soften them. Put through a sieve or food mill, or strain through several layers of cheesecloth, Reheat, and add 1 tablespoon unflavored gelatine soaked in 1/4 cup cold water, stirring to dissolve thoroughly. Add the sugar, salt, and lemon juice (omit the butter), stir well, and chill until the consistency of egg white. Also chill the pie crust and berries. Spread a thin layer of gelatine glaze in the crust. Turn the berries into the crust and spoon (do not pour) the rest of the gelatine mixture over them to glaze the entire pie. Chill until firm, and top with whipped cream before serving.

Glazed Frozen Berry Pie. The gelatine version is probably easier to use if you are making the pie with frozen berries. Place two 10-ounce packages of frozen berries in a colander to thaw at room temperature. If possible, break the frozen mass of each package in half so that it will thaw faster. After about an hour the berries can be pulled apart readily. Pour off the juice and add water, if necessary, to make 3/4 cup. Continue as for glazed berry pie with gelatine (above), reducing the sugar as needed if the frozen berries are sweetened.

Glazed Berry Cream Pie. Make half the recipe for cream pie filling (page 624), using 1 or 2 eggs. Cool, and spread in the chilled crust. Continue as for glazed berry pie in either version (cornstarch or gelatine), using only half the recipe.

Glazed Berry Sour Cream Pie. Instead of cream pie filling, as in the version above, use 1 cup sour cream mixed with 2 tablespoons honey or 4 tablespoons berry jam. The jam will color the cream, so you may prefer to use the honey. Spread the sour cream mixture into the chilled crust, and continue as above. Serve plain.

Glazed Berry Cream Cheese Pie. Warm an 8-ounce package of cream cheese to room temperature. Whip until fluffy, adding 3 tablespoons milk to give a lighter texture. Stir in 2 tablespoons sugar or honey. Spread into the chilled crust and continue with either version of glazed berry pie, using only half the recipe. Serve plain.

Tart Cherry Pie

4 cups pitted pie cherries
1 to 1 1/2 cups sugar
4 to 6 tablespoons flour
4 or 5 drops almond flavoring
1 to 2 tablespoons butter
Unbaked pastry for two-crust 9-inch pie

Since "pie cherry" trees thrived in cold or moderately warm climates and developed fruit rather quickly, they were commonly grown in backyards. The pitted fruit was canned and was also used for a beautiful tart jam.

Combine the pitted fresh cherries with the sugar, flour, and flavoring. Turn into a pastry-lined pie pan. Trim the edge of the pastry, moisten it, and dot the filling with butter. Adjust the top crust in place, cut vents for steam, trim the edge, and crimp together the bottom and top crusts. Bake at 450 degrees 15 minutes, reduce the heat to 350 degrees, and bake 25 to 30 minutes longer. Cool on a rack. Cherry pie is usually served cool. Some people like to add a topping of cheese or ice cream.

Canned-Pie-Cherry Pie. Use one #2 1/2 can (3 cups) tart pie cherries. Drain the juice into a 2-quart saucepan. Combine with the sugar and flour. Bring to a boil, stirring constantly, and let cook a minute or two. Add the cherries and again bring to a boil. Cool, and add the flavoring. Continue as above, but bake only 15 minutes, or until the crust is browned.

Lemon Meringue Pie

1 cup sugar
3 tablespoons flour
3 tablespoons cornstarch
¼ teaspoon salt
1½ cups boiling or hot water
3 egg yolks
1 to 2 teaspoons grated lemon rind
⅓ cup lemon juice
1 to 2 tablespoons butter
Baked pastry shell or crumb crust for 8 or 9-inch pie
Meringue

Mix half the sugar with the flour, cornstarch, and salt in 1½ to 2 quart saucepan or top of a double boiler. Stir in the hot or boiling water. Cook and stir constantly over low heat until the mixture begins to boil. Immediately turn the heat very low and stir 3 or 4 minutes longer, or put the double boiler top over boiling water and cook slowly 5 or 6 minutes. Stir the remaining half cup of sugar into the egg yolks, then slowly stir in some of hot sugar mixture. When well combined, stir back into the sugar mixture. Continue to stir and cook about 2 minutes, or until the egg is cooked and set. Remove from the heat, and after 2 or 3 minutes stir in the grated lemon rind and juice. Stir in the butter (it will prevent a heavy scum from forming on the mixture). Cool, and turn into a baked pie shell or crumb crust. Make a meringue (see page 640), using 3 egg whites and 6 tablespoons sugar, flavoring if you like with a teaspoon of lemon juice. Spread roughly on the pie, and bake 20 minutes at 300 to 325 degrees. Serve slightly warm or cool.

Lemon Slice or Fresh Lemon Pie

1 cup thin slices of unpeeled lemon, or put whole unpeeled lemons through the coarse blade of a food chopper
1½ cups water
2 cups sugar or 1 cup sugar and 1¼ cups molasses
3 egg yolks
7 tablespoons flour
¼ teaspoon salt
2 tablespoons butter
Baked pastry shell or crumb crust for 9-inch pie

In some old Southern recipes for this pie, including this one, the filling was cooked separately and added to a baked crust; in others the filling was baked in the crust; and in still others raisins were added to the filling. Add a cup of raisins here if you like.

Place the prepared lemon slices or ground lemon in a 2-quart saucepan with the water and simmer about 10 minutes or until the rind is very tender. Add 1 cup sugar and let it simmer. Combine other cup of sugar or the molasses with the egg yolks, flour, and salt. Stir some of the lemon mixture into the egg and flour, then stir back into the lemon mixture and cook and stir over low heat until clear. Do not overcook or the acid of the lemons will begin to thin the filling. Add the butter and cool to room temperature. Pour into the pastry or crumb crust. Serve topped with whipped cream or meringue made with 3 egg whites (see page 640).

Grant's Lemon Pie

2 eggs
½ cup lemon juice
2 teaspoons grated lemon rind, or to taste
1¼ cups sugar
¼ teaspoon salt
1 cup raisins
¼ cup water
⅓ cup shredded coconut
Pastry for two-crust 9-inch pie

This recipe, which appears in different versions in old New York State sectional cookbooks, is from the third edition of a small collection by Lucy Bostwick, *Margery Daw in the Kitchen*, published by the author in 1883 in Auburn, New York.

Beat the eggs in a mixing bowl, and add the rest of the ingredients for the filling. Combine well, and turn into a pastry-lined pie pan. Trim the pastry, moisten the edge, and put on the top crust. Trim the edge of the top pastry, crimp the top and bottom edges together, and cut slits in the center for steam to escape. Bake at 450 degrees 15 minutes, reduce the heat to 300 degrees, and bake 25 minutes longer. Cool on a rack. This was often served with whipped cream.

Lemon Chiffon Pie

1 tablespoon unflavored gelatine
¼ cup cold water
4 eggs, separated
½ cup lemon juice
¼ teaspoon salt
1 cup sugar
1 teaspoon grated lemon rind
Baked pastry or crumb crust for 9-inch pie
½ to 1 cup heavy cream, whipped (optional)

Sprinkle the gelatine over the water and let stand to soften. Place the egg yolks, lemon juice, salt, and half the sugar in the top of a double boiler. Stir well to combine thoroughly. Cook and stir over boiling water (be sure the water does not touch the bottom) until the mixture thickens. Add the softened gelatine and stir until thoroughly dissolved. Add the grated lemon rind. Cool the mixture to room temperature or slightly cooler. Beat the egg whites until small bubbles begin to form. Gradually beat in the other ½ cup sugar and continue beating until the mixture holds stiff peaks and the sugar is dissolved. Fold into the lemon mixture until no streaks show. Heap into the pastry or crumb crust, and chill in the refrigerator until firm (4 to 5 hours). Or, if covered lightly, the pie can be stored in the refrigerator overnight. Before serving, top with whipped cream, if you like.

Served without whipped cream, this makes an especially nice dessert as the finale to a heavy dinner. Sprinkle an extra bit of lightly grated lemon rind over the top of the pie before serving.

Green Tomato Pie

4 cups peeled sliced tomatoes
1 tablespoon lemon juice or cider vinegar
1¼ cups sugar, white or brown
4 to 6 tablespoons flour
¼ teaspoon salt
Nutmeg or ginger to taste (optional)
2 tablespoons butter
Pastry for double-crust 9-inch pie

Tomatoes for this should be of mature size — those that would, in ordinary growing conditions, be about a week from turning very ripe. Very green small tomatoes will have an acrid taste.

Scald the tomatoes with boiling water, then peel them and remove the cores. Slice ¼ inch thick into a mixing bowl. Sprinkle with the lemon juice or vinegar. Combine the sugar, flour, salt, and spices, and fold into the tomato slices. Line a pie pan with pastry and trim the edge. Turn the tomatoes into the pastry and dot the top with butter. Moisten the edge of the bottom crust, top with pastry, trim the edge, and crimp. Cut steam vents in the top. Bake at 450 degrees 15 minutes, reduce the heat to 350 degrees, and bake 25 to 30 minutes longer. Cool on a rack.

Mock Mincemeat Pie

1 1/2 cups seedless or seeded raisins
1/3 cup dry sherry or brandy or rum
3 cups finely chopped apple
1/2 medium-size orange ground with peel
1/4 cup lemon juice
1 1/4 cups sugar
1/2 teaspoon salt
1 teaspoon cinnamon
1/2 teaspoon mace
1/4 teaspoon cloves
1/4 teaspoon ginger
Pastry for two double-crust 8-inch pies or one double-crust 10-inch pie
1/2 cup melted butter

There are many variations of this theme, imitating the pie that in former days began with the simmering of a piece of venison, neck of beef, or beef tongue. This is a rich pie, but does not require the long simmering of a true mincemeat filling.

Put the raisins in a mixing bowl and add the sherry or brandy, letting the fruit soak up the liquor while you prepare the crust and peel the apples. Add all the ingredients for the filling. If using two pie pans, line with pastry, trim, and moisten the edges. Divide the filling into the pans and pour half the butter in each. Top with pastry, trim, crimp the edges, and cut slits in the top of the crust to allow steam to escape. If using one large pie pan, it should be about 2 inches deep. Bake at 450 degrees 15 minutes. Reduce the heat to 350 degrees and bake 8-inch pies about 25 minutes longer and 10-inch pies about 35 minutes. Serve warm in small pieces with a sauce flavored with brandy, rum, sherry, or lemon.

Note. This pie may also be made with a lattice crust.

Raisin Pie

Pastry for two-crust 8 or 9 inch pie
1 1/2 cups raisins
1 1/2 cups water
3 tablespoons flour
1/8 teaspoon salt
1/2 to 3/4 cup white or brown sugar
1 to 2 tablespoons vinegar or lemon juice
1 teaspoon grated lemon rind (optional)
1/2 teaspoon mixed cinnamon, allspice and nutmeg
2 tablespoons butter

Called "funeral pie" in some parts of the United States. Why, I'm not sure. Almost invariably made with a cooked filling between two crusts, the recipe turns up occasionally as an open-face pie with a meringue topping.

Simmer the raisins in the water about 5 minutes, or until they begin to plump. Mix the flour, salt, and sugar, and slowly stir in some of the hot liquid in which the raisins have cooked. When well combined, turn into the raisins and liquid and cook and stir until thickened. Remove from the heat, let cool a few minutes, and add the remaining ingredients. Cool to room temperature. Turn into a pastry-lined pan, trim and moisten the pastry edge, and top with pastry. Trim and crimp the edges and cut slits in the top. Bake at 450 degrees 15 minutes, then reduce to 350 degrees and bake about 25 minutes more, or until the pastry is nicely browned.

Serve hot, warm, or cold. If served hot or warm the pie is sometimes topped with a slab of aged Cheddar cheese, or accompanied by a rum, sherry, or lemon sauce, or by ice cream. Serve cold with ice cream or with these.

Raisin Cream Pie. Use an 8 or 9 inch baked pastry shell or graham cracker, zweibach, or vanilla wafer crust. Combine only 1 tablespoon flour with the salt and sugar, and in addition stir in 2 or 3 egg yolks. Mix the filling as above, cool to room temperature, turn it into the shell, and top with meringue (see page 640). Bake at 300 to 325 degrees 20 minutes, or until the meringue is delicately brown.

Buttermilk Raisin Pie

6 tablespoons flour
¾ cup sugar
¼ teaspoon salt
2 cups buttermilk
½ to ¾ cup seedless raisins
2 eggs or 3 egg yolks
2 tablespoons lemon juice
2 tablespoons butter
⅓ teaspoon cinnamon
⅛ teaspoon cloves
¼ teaspoon nutmeg
Baked pastry shell or crumb crust for 8 or 9 inch pie

TOPPING

Meringue made with 3 egg whites (see page 640) or ½ cup whipping cream
¼ teaspoon cinnamon
⅛ teaspoon nutmeg
2 tablespoons sugar

This was a favorite summer pie, always made with homemade fresh churned buttermilk, which left little dots of butter atop the pie. Now, of course, we must be content with commercial buttermilk.

Combine the flour, sugar, and salt in a 1½ to 2 quart saucepan. Gradually stir in the buttermilk. Cook and stir over low heat until the mixture is thick. Add the raisins and turn to low heat. Stir the eggs or egg yolks in a bowl, and gradually stir in some of hot mixture. When well combined, slowly stir back into the hot mixture. Cook and continue to stir 1 or 2 minutes. Remove from the heat and cool several minutes. Stir in the lemon juice, butter, and spices. Cool to room temperature and turn into the baked pastry or crumb crust. Top with meringue to which the cinnamon and nutmeg have been added, and bake in a 350-degree oven until lightly brown. Or, just before serving, top with whipped cream to which the spices and sugar have been added.

Cream Pie

¾ cup sugar
7 tablespoons flour (½ cup minus 1 tablespoon)
¼ teaspoon salt
2 eggs
3 cups rich milk, scalded
1 teaspoon vanilla
Baked 8 or 9 inch pastry shell or crumb crust
½ cup heavy cream, whipped

Although there were "receipts" in old cookbooks for Boston cream pie, Martha Washington pie, and George Washington pie, these were really simple cakes, made in two or three layers with a cream or cream custard filling. Only in regional cookbooks of the late nineteenth century do cream pies, as we know them, begin to be listed.

Mix together the sugar, flour, salt, and eggs. Slowly stir in the scalded milk. You may use light cream in place of the milk or part cream and part milk; or, for a rich flavor, use part milk and part evaporated milk. Return the mixture to low heat, and stir constantly until it begins to boil. Reduce the heat to simmer and continue to stir and cook 2 to 3 minutes. Remove from the heat and add the vanilla. Cool to room temperature and spread into the baked shell. Serve topped with whipped cream that has been sweetened and flavored to your taste. For storage in refrigerator, top with gelatinized whipped cream (see page 743).

Meringue Cream Pie. Use 2 or 3 egg yolks instead of whole eggs in the pie filling and instead of whipped cream, top with meringue (see page 640). Brown lightly in a 375-degree oven.

Banana Cream Pie. Chill the cream pie filling slightly. Spread a thin layer over the bottom of the baked shell or crumb crust. Spread sliced bananas over this, add another layer of cream pie filling, then another layer of sliced bananas, and one more of filling. Just before serving, top with whipped cream and dot with sliced bananas. Or put sliced bananas on the filling and cover with gelatinized whipped cream (see page 743). Chill until ready to serve.

Chocolate Cream Pie. Add 1 to 2 ounces shaved unsweetened chocolate to the hot cream pie filling just after removing from the heat. Stir until the mixture is well blended and the chocolate has melted. This pie is generally topped with whipped cream, then sprinkled with shaved semisweet chocolate. To store in the refrigerator for any length of time before serving, chill the pie thoroughly, top with gelatinized whipped cream (see page 743), and decorate with chocolate shavings.

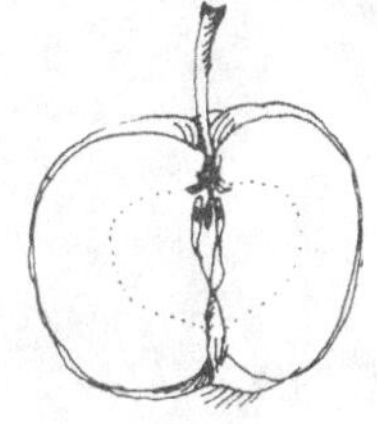

Coconut Cream Pie. Fold ½ to ¾ cup shredded or flaked coconut into the cooled cream pie filling, or add layers of coconut as you pour the filling into the shell. Top with whipped cream and sprinkle with coconut, or top with a meringue, sprinkle with coconut, and bake at 350 degrees 15 to 20 minutes.

Marlborough Pie (Apple Cream Pie)

3 cups finely chopped peeled cored apples
1 tablespoon lemon juice or cider vinegar
2 eggs
1 cup coffee cream, whipping cream, or evaporated milk
¾ cup sugar
2 to 3 tablespoons melted butter
½ teaspoon cinnamon
Unbaked pastry for single-crust or double-crust 9-inch pie or for tart shells

In cool climates, this pie was made with fresh, finely chopped apples; in warmer climates, where the storage of apples for long periods was not possible, applesauce was used.

Prepare the apples and sprinkle with the lemon juice or vinegar. Beat the eggs, stir in the cream or evaporated milk, sugar, butter, cinnamon (or reserve the cinnamon to sprinkle over the filling before baking), and apples. Turn the filling into a pastry-lined pie tin. Bake as a single-crust pie, or add a top crust (or lattice strips), crimp the edges, and make slits for steam to escape. Or use individual pastry-lined tart pans. Bake at 450 degrees 15 minutes (tarts 7 to 8 minutes). Reduce the heat to 325 degrees, and bake about 30 minutes longer (tarts about 12 minutes), or until the filling is firm. In some recipes the tarts are topped with meringue.

Butterscotch Pie

3 to 4 tablespoons butter
1¼ cups brown sugar (light brown preferred)
3 cups rich milk, light cream, or half milk and half evaporated milk
2 eggs
7 tablespoons flour
¼ teaspoon salt
1 teaspoon vanilla
Baked pastry or crumb crust for 9-inch pie

Melt the butter in 2-quart saucepan, add the brown sugar, and stir until the mixture bubbles up and looks slightly browner. Add 2 cups of the milk and stir to combine well. Stir the eggs with the flour and salt, then stir in the remaining milk. When the sugar mixture is hot but not boiling, slowly stir in the egg mixture. Stir and cook over medium low heat until the mixture boils up. Turn the heat very low and stir and cook 1 or 2 minutes more. Remove from the heat and stir in the vanilla. Cool to room temperature and turn into the baked pastry or crumb crust. Serve topped with whipped cream, if you like.

Butterscotch Meringue Pie. Use 3 egg yolks in the filling, top the pie with meringue made of the 3 egg whites (see page 640), and bake in a 350-degree oven until the meringue is lightly brown.

Butterscotch Nut Pie. Add ½ cup toasted pecans, walnuts, almonds, filberts, macadamia, or cashew nuts to the filling. Sprinkle a few over the top, or top with whipped cream or meringue sprinkled with nuts.

Date Butterscotch Pie. Use only ¾ cup brown sugar. Cool the filling and fold in 1 cup quartered dates. If you like, also fold in ½ cup toasted pecans or almonds with the dates.

Pumpkin or Squash Pie

3 eggs
2 cups cooked strained fresh or canned pumpkin or squash, or sieved frozen squash
1 cup brown sugar or ¾ cup white sugar
¼ teaspoon salt
¼ to ½ teaspoon ginger
½ to 1 teaspoon cinnamon
⅛ to ¼ teaspoon cloves
½ to 1 teaspoon nutmeg
1 to 1½ cups evaporated milk or coffee cream (10 percent cream)
Unbaked pastry shell for a deep 9 or 10 inch pie or for two 8-inch shells

In the eighteenth century this, like all one-crust pies, was called a pudding. Yankees preferred the recipe made with pumpkin, while Southerners preferred sweet potatoes. Spices were not included until clipper ships made them a more common commodity, and molasses or sorghum was used as part or all of the sweetening. Eventually white or brown sugar took over, but there are still cooks who use 3 to 4 tablespoons of molasses in this recipe.

Break the eggs into a mixing bowl and beat until the yolks and whites are combined. Add the pumpkin or squash, sugar, salt, and spices. Blend well. Add the milk or cream and stir to combine thoroughly. Have the pastry shell or shells ready. Stir the filling just before turning into the shell. This is rather a sloppy mixture to pour, and it is better to dip it from the bowl to the pastry. You might also position the pie pan on the oven rack, pulled forward, and ladle in the filling there, with the oven preheated to 450 degrees. Bake 9 or 10 inch pies 15 minutes at this temperature (8-inch pies 10 minutes), then reduce the heat to 300 to 325 degrees and bake about 30 minutes longer, or until the filling appears set when the pie is shaken gently, except for about 2 inches at the center. Or bake for the prescribed time at 450 degrees, then turn the oven off. Do not open the oven door. Leave the pie in the oven 40 to 45 minutes (8-inch pies about 35 minutes). It should be set when removed. This latter method of baking will only work with a well-insulated oven. Cool the pie on a rack.

Pumpkin or Squash Custard Pie. Reduce the sieved pumpkin or squash to 1 cup and increase the cream or evaporated milk to 2 to 2½ cups.

Sweet Potato or Yam Pie. Use sieved cooked sweet potatoes or yams, and add a dash of molasses. Seasoning and spicing depends upon sectional tastes. Some recipes claim that only nutmeg should be used, some prefer ginger, and others combine either spice with grated orange rind.

Sweet Potato or Yam Custard Pie. Use a larger proportion of milk and eggs to the sweet potato or yam, as in pumpkin or squash custard pie, above.

Sweet Potato and Apple Pie. This is also a Southern idea. It is usually a two-crust pie made with layers of sliced cooked sweet potatoes and apples arranged in an unbaked pie shell, with sugar, cinnamon, and nutmeg to taste. Or sometimes a one-crust version is made in which the slices are arranged in an unbaked crust and a custard mixture is poured over them. The top is given a "lump of butter the size of a small egg" (about 2 tablespoons) and sprinkled with cinnamon before baking.

Molasses Pie

4 tablespoons lemon juice or vinegar
3 tablespoons flour
4 egg yolks
½ teaspoon each of nutmeg, allspice, cinnamon, and salt
1 teaspoon ginger
2 cups molasses,
½ cup walnuts (black or English) or almonds
4 egg whites
½ cup sugar
2 tablespoons butter
Unbaked pastry shell for 9-inch pie

Combine the lemon juice or vinegar and flour in a bowl. Stir in the egg yolks, the spices and salt, the molasses and nuts. Spread the butter on the unbaked pastry shell and add the filling. Bake 10 to 12 minutes at 450 degrees, reduce the heat to 325 degrees, and continue baking about 35 minutes longer, or until almost firm. Remove and cool on a rack. When the pie is cool, make a meringue using 4 egg whites beaten until they hold soft peaks, then the sugar gradually added, a tablespoon at a time. Beat until the sugar is dissolved and the meringue stiff and glossy. Spread this over the pie, being certain to cover the edges. Place in a 350-degree oven to brown lightly. Serve cooled.

Cottage Cheese Pie

2 cups (1 pound) cottage cheese
2 tablespoons melted or softened butter
1 cup thin cream or milk
2 tablespoons lemon juice and 1 teaspoon grated lemon rind, or 1 teaspoon vanilla
1 cup sugar
1 tablespoon flour
¼ teaspoon salt
3 eggs, separated (egg whites for meringue)
Unbaked pie shell for 8 or 9 inch pie

This recipe, which found its way into many sectional cookbooks, probably came from the Pennsylvania Dutch. Both cottage cheese curd and creamed cottage cheese can be used. Many recipes call for sieving the curd first. In earlier days if vanilla or lemons were not available, lemon verbena leaves were used for flavoring.

Sieve the cottage cheese or whirl in a blender until the curds are broken up. Add the butter, cream or milk, flavoring, sugar, flour, salt, and egg yolks. Beat or stir well to blend. Turn into the pie shell. Bake 10 minutes at 450 degrees, then reduce the heat to 300 to 325 degrees. Continue baking 25 to 30 minutes, or until the filling is firm to within about 1 inch of the center. Cool on a rack. Just before serving top with a meringue (see page 640) made with the 3 egg whites, and brown lightly in a 350-degree oven. Some recipes recommend sprinkling nutmeg over the pie or over the meringue before baking.

Chess Pie or Tarts

½ cup butter
1 cup light brown sugar
2 eggs
¼ cup thin cream or evaporated milk
1 cup chopped walnuts
1 cup raisins, or raisins and currants, or chopped dates
¼ teaspoon vanilla
⅓ cup orange juice, grape juice, or sherry
Unbaked pastry for 8 to 12 patty pans or one 9-inch pie

Brought from England and prevalent mostly in New England and the Virginias, this was served more as a tea accompaniment than as a dessert pie. Traditionally it is made in patty pans as tarts. These were often carried on picnics when I was a child.

Cream the butter with the sugar and beat in the eggs. Stir in the remaining ingredients and spoon into pastry-lined patty pans, muffin pans, or a 9-inch pie pan. (Butter pastry, or half butter and half shortening, is generally used here.) Bake a pie 15 minutes at 450 degrees, reduce the heat to 325 degrees, and bake about 20 minutes longer. Bake individual tarts from 5 to 6 minutes at 450 degrees, reduce to 300 degrees, and bake 7 to 10 minutes longer, depending upon the thickness of the filling. Cool on a rack or serve slightly warm. Often a slice of maraschino cherry is put in the center of each tart or serving of pie.

Note. See the variations under Jefferson Davis pie.

Jeff Davis or Jefferson Davis Pie

1 cup coffee cream (10 percent cream) or evaporated milk
1 cup milk
1 whole egg
2 egg yolks
1 cup sugar
5 tablespoons flour
¼ teaspoon salt

Scald the cream and milk in the top of a double boiler or over low heat in a 1½ to 2 quart pan. In a bowl, stir together the egg and egg yolks, and add the sugar, flour, salt, and spices. (The amount of cloves varies among recipes, but even ½ teaspoon is very strong.) Slowly stir some of the hot cream or milk into the mixture. Pour this back into the hot milk and cream, and stir over low heat or boiling water until the mixture is thick. Remove from the heat and add the vanilla and butter. Cool to room temperature and turn into the baked pastry or crumb crust — a graham cracker or chocolate wafer crust is good for this. Top with the meringue and bake at 350 degrees until brown.

1 teaspoon cinnamon
¼ to 1 teaspoon cloves
1 teaspoon vanilla
2 tablespoons butter
Baked 9-inch pastry shell or crumb crust
Meringue made with 2 egg whites (see page 640)

Variations

In some old recipe books, ½ teaspoon allspice and 1 teaspoon nutmeg (freshly grated) were used instead of cloves and cinnamon; or brown sugar was used instead of white; or 1 cup chopped dates or ½ cup dates and ½ cup raisins were added to the cooled filling along with broken pecan meats.

Chess Pie (*Southern Version*). In the South, chess pie was sometimes made with the recipe for Jefferson Davis pie, omitting the spices, dates, raisins, and nuts. Most often this filling was served in tart shells and topped with whipped cream.

Sugar Pie, Maple Sugar Pie, or Tyler Pie

¾ cup white sugar and ¾ cup brown sugar, or 1½ cups maple sugar
3 eggs
1 tablespoon flour
¼ teaspoon salt
1 cup coffee cream, milk, or evaporated milk
1 teaspoon vanilla (optional)
¼ to ½ cup butter, melted
Unbaked pastry for 9-inch one-crust pie

This very sweet pie was called by different names from region to region. President Tyler gave his name to a number of the recipes. In parts of the Deep South it was called just sugar pie, and since in the Northern States it was made of maple sugar, it was usually called maple sugar pie.

Sprinkle the sugar into the pastry-lined pan. The edge of the pastry should be well crimped. Beat the eggs and add the flour, salt, cream, and vanilla if you are using it. Carefully pour the filling into the pie and top with the melted butter. Bake at 450 degrees 10 minutes. Reduce the heat to 300 degrees and bake until the filling is almost firm (about 25 minutes). Cool on a rack. Rich though this is, several recipes advised serving it with cream. I recommend serving it plain in small wedges.

Frangipani Pie

1 cup shelled almonds, unblanched
2 eggs
¼ to ½ cup powdered sugar
2 tablespoons melted butter
¼ teaspoon ground cinnamon
¼ teaspoon finely grated orange rind or 1 teaspoon orange flower water
¾ cup light rum
Unbaked pastry for 9-inch pie or 6 to 8 individual patty or pie pans

No doubt this pie was brought along by French immigrants during the time when most puddings were served in a pie crust. Today French frangipani is served as a pudding or a filling for cake or cream puffs. Recipes vary a good deal, particularly in the form of the almond flavoring. Here is an early New Orleans version.

Put half the almonds at a time in the blender and whirl until powdery. Or grate quite fine. Add 1 egg and the powdered sugar and melted butter, and combine very well. Add the cinnamon and orange rind or orange flower water (available these days at druggists, but not always). Beat in the second egg. Stir in the rum. Turn into a pastry-lined pie pan or pastry-lined individual patty or pie pans. Use sweet pastry or rich butter pastry (see pages 635 or 636). Bake a large pie 10 minutes at 450 degrees (small pies from 4 to 5 minutes); then reduce the temperature to 325 degrees and bake 10 to 25 minutes longer, or until the filling is set, as for custard.

Black Bottom Pie

1 tablespoon unflavored gelatine
1/4 cup cold water
2 cups milk or evaporated milk, or 1 cup coffee cream and 1 cup milk or evaporated milk
1/2 cup sugar
1/4 teaspoon salt
2 tablespoons flour
4 egg yolks
1 1/2 to 2 ounces unsweetened chocolate or 1/2 cup semisweet chocolate pieces, melted
1/2 teaspoon vanilla
2 tablespoons rum, light or dark
1/2 teaspoon rum flavoring (optional)
3 egg whites
1/4 teaspoon cream of tartar
1/3 cup sugar
Sweetened whipped cream (1/2 to 1 cup whipping cream and 2 to 3 tablespoons powdered sugar)
1/2 ounce shaved unsweetened or semisweet chocolate
Baked graham cracker, chocolate or vanilla cookie crumb crust, chilled

This recipe began appearing in cookbooks around the turn of the century. Obviously it was difficult to make without ice, so it was a real party dessert.

Soak the gelatine in the cold water. Scald the milk or milk and cream over very low heat. (Or prepare the entire filling in a double boiler over hot water.) Mix the 1/2 cup sugar and the salt, flour, and egg yolks. Slowly stir in some of milk until the mixture is blended. Pour back into the hot milk and stir over low heat until the mixture thickens enough to coat a spoon (about 15 to 20 minutes). Remove from the heat and take out 1 cup of custard. Add the melted chocolate and vanilla to this and stir until it is well combined. Set aside to cool to room temperature. Add the gelatine to the remaining custard and stir until dissolved. Then add the rum and rum flavoring. Chill until syrupy.

Spread the chocolate mixture into the chilled crumb crust and refrigerate. When the chilled gelatinized custard mixture is beginning to thicken, beat the egg whites until foamy, add the cream of tartar, and beat. Beat in the 1/3 cup of sugar gradually, and beat until it is dissolved and the mixture will hold stiff peaks when the beater is lifted. Fold into the gelatinized custard and spread over the chocolate layer. When ready to serve, top with sweetened whipped cream. Garnish with shaved chocolate. This is a rich pie and can be cut into 8 pieces for a luncheon dessert.

Crumb or Gravel Pie

1/2 cup hot water
1 cup brown sugar, honey, light molasses, or sorghum
1/2 teaspoon baking soda
2 eggs, beaten
1 1/4 cups all-purpose or cake flour
1/3 cup butter
1/4 teaspoon salt
1/2 to 1 teaspoon cinnamon
1/4 teaspoon nutmeg

The Pennsylvania Dutch spread the recipe for this pie to many other sections of the country. The difference in what it was called depended upon whether the crumbs were layered into the liquid or spread over the top of the filling. This is often served as a coffee cake in Pennsylvania Dutch homes.

In a mixing bowl combine the hot water and sugar or sweetening of your choice. Stir well and add the soda and beaten eggs. In another bowl mix the flour, butter, salt, and spices. Work until fine crumbs are formed. For crumb pie, turn the egg and sugar mixture into the pastry-lined pie pan; the edges should be well crimped. Spread the flour mixture over the top. For gravel pie, alternate the egg and sugar mixture with the crumbs, ending with a good thick

1/4 teaspoon ginger
Pastry for one-crust 9-inch pie

layer of crumbs. Either way, bake at 450 degrees 10 minutes, reduce heat to 350 degrees, and bake about 20 to 25 minutes longer, or until the top feels fairly firm.

Shoo Fly Pie. Make like either crumb or gravel pie, but first put 1/2 to 3/4 cup raisins into the pie shell. Some recipes use more flour (another 1/4 cup) in the crumbs, and some omit the eggs.

Pecan or Nut Pie

Pastry for one-crust 9-inch pie
1 cup pecan meats — halves or broken pieces — or walnuts or filberts
2 eggs
1 cup dark corn syrup or sorghum syrup
1/2 to 1 cup brown sugar
1 teaspoon vanilla or 2 tablespoons rum
1/4 teaspoon salt
2 to 4 tablespoons butter

This recipe varies throughout the Southern states, and although any of several nuts can be used, pecans are traditional. Formerly sorghum was used instead of dark corn syrup. However, there are still those who prefer light molasses. And in early nineteenth-century cookbooks recipes called for as much as 1 cup butter and 2 cups pecans.

Line the pie pan with pastry and crimp the edges. Sprinkle the nutmeats over the pastry. Beat the eggs in a mixing bowl, and stir in the syrup, sugar, flavoring, and salt. Pour over the nutmeats and dot with butter. Bake at 450 degrees 10 minutes, reduce the heat to 325 degrees, and bake until the filling is almost firm in the center, about 25 to 30 minutes. Cool on a rack. This very rich pie can be cut in 8 pieces.

Angel Pie

SHELL

4 egg whites
1/4 teaspoon cream of tartar
1 cup sugar

FILLING

4 egg yolks
1/2 cup sugar
1/4 teaspoon salt
1/4 cup lemon juice
2 tablespoons grated lemon rind
1 cup heavy cream, whipped

The most frequently printed of all the pie recipes in sectional cookbooks of the last sixty years.

For the shell, use a 9-inch pie pan or plate. Heat it slightly in a 300-degree oven, then grease very lightly with vegetable salad oil, using a piece of paper towel to spread the oil and blot the excess. Beat the egg whites until they form soft peaks with a rotary beater or in the small bowl of an electric mixer. Sprinkle in the cream of tartar and beat until uniform bubbles begin to form. Gradually add the 1 cup sugar and continue beating until the sugar is dissolved and the mixture stands in stiff peaks. Spread evenly in the prepared pan. Set in a 300-degree oven and bake about 1 hour. Do not open the oven for the first 30 minutes, or the shell will not be puffy. When the shell is a delicate yellow, turn off the oven and leave the door slightly ajar until cool. The shell will have sunk slightly in the center, but this is normal. Chill.

For the filling, beat the yolks slightly in the top of a double boiler. Add the sugar, salt, lemon juice, and rind. Place over slowly boiling water and cook and stir until thick. Remove from the heat and chill. Whip the cream until stiff. Spread half of it on the shell, leaving a margin of about an inch. Spread the filling on the cream, and top with the remaining cream. Some recipes recommend folding the cream into the filling. In either case, return the pie to the refrigerator and chill 24 hours or overnight.

Orange Angel Pie. In place of the lemon juice and rind, use 1/4 cup orange juice or 3 tablespoons undiluted thawed frozen orange juice concentrate, 1 tablespoon lemon juice, and 1 tablespoon grated orange rind.

Lime Angel Pie. In place of the lemon juice and rind, use 3 tablespoons lime juice, 1 tablespoon lemon juice, 1 teaspoon grated lime rind, and 1/2 teaspoon grated lemon rind. Key limes, if obtainable, are not as astringent as the limes generally available, and in this case the lemon juice can be omitted entirely, although you may still wish to use only 1 teaspoon grated lime rind.

Berry or Cranberry Angel Pie. In place of the lemon juice and rind, use 3/4 cup sieved fresh raspberries, strawberries, loganberries, or blackberries. Add 1 teaspoon lemon juice to the berry purée. If using cranberries — and this makes a pretty holiday pie — use 3/4 cup sieved cranberry sauce or jelly.

Pastry

Flaky, tender pie crust must have a delicate balance of fat and flour and not too much liquid. For this reason, measure the ingredients carefully. Too much flour can make a tough crust; too much fat, a greasy, crumbly crust; and too much liquid will in turn require more flour and result in a tough crust. This balance of ingredients applies also to the crumb crusts that are pressed or patted into a mold, or the cookie-type doughs that are pressed into a mold or rolled out and fitted in the usual way.

Pastry into the Pan

If you are not experienced, better keep the pie pan handy to measure the pastry dough. There should be enough pastry rolled out to go into the pan without stretching and to hang over the side about half an inch. If making a berry or other juicy fruit pie, you will want at least an inch overhang of crust, so the undercrust can overlap the upper crust to prevent the juice running over the edge. There are those who like to fold the dough over in half and pick it up to put into the pan. Others like to roll it up on the rolling pin, then unroll it on to the pan. In either case, lift the edge of the

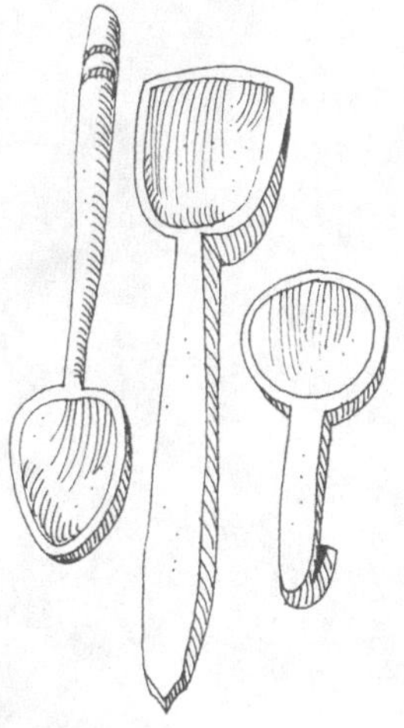

pastry and "full" it into the pan. Pastry shrinks in the baking, and if stretched into the pan will let some of the filling leak under the crust while baking. This, of course, leads to a soggy undercrust. Even off the overhang with a sharp knife held at a slant under the edge of the pan, or with scissors.

Do not heap the filling in a pie. Apples can, of course, be heaped slightly, for they will collapse. Large berries will cook down. But there'll be juice in the oven if the filling is excessive.

Moisten the edge of the bottom crust with a finger or pastry brush dipped in water before you put the top crust on. Trim the top crust overhang by cutting it from the underside of the pan with a sharp knife or scissors. Crimp the edges together with the fingers or the tines of a table fork.

There must always be a way for the steam to escape in a two-crust pie, so slit the crust near the center of the pie either before the top crust is placed on the filling or after. For very juicy pies, it was an old custom, no doubt brought from England, where it is still used, to put a china "bird" in the center before adding the filling. A hole was cut out of the top pastry dough and the dough fitted over the bird. The excess juice and steam seems to collect in this and does help to keep the oven clean.

Putting on a top crust only (as for meat pies, chicken pies, etc.). Usually the crust for these pies is a thickly rolled Rough Puff Paste (page 640) or Suet Pastry (page 640). Roll it out ¼ to ⅓ inch thick, then turn the pan or casserole over it and cut round the edge, leaving a margin of ½ to 1 inch. Roll the trimmings thinner, and cut in strips 1½ to 2 inches wide. Drape around the top of the container to make a pastry edge for the top crust to rest on. Spoon in the filling. Moisten the pastry strip and place the top crust on. Pinch the overhang from the top crust and the strip together and crimp up into a completely sealed edge. Cut steam vents in the top.

One-Crust Pies

One-crust pies are made by putting an uncooked filling into an uncooked shell and baking; or by baking the crust (prick the dough before baking), cooling it, and adding a cooked filling (or gelatine or glaze-type filling).

Baking filled one-crust pies. Start the pie in a hot oven at 450 degrees. It will take 10 to 12 minutes at this temperature to set the crust. Reduce the temperature to suit the filling. If it is a custard-type filling, thickened with eggs, reduce the temperature to 325 degrees.

Bake about 25 minutes longer or until, when the pie is lightly shaken on the oven rack, the center is still soft in an inch and a half to a two-inch circle. Remove to a rack to cool. If you have a well-insulated oven, try this method for custard-type pies. Bake 12 minutes at 450 degrees; then, without opening the oven, turn it completely off. Leave the pie in the oven about 35 to 40 minutes longer for the filling to cook at low heat. Remove to a rack to cool. If overcooked, custard fillings will separate and there will be a thin, syrupy layer on the bottom of the pie, just as in an overcooked custard pudding. This in turn will make a soggy crust.

Baked pie shells. To prevent a single crust from blistering and shrinking during baking, place a smaller pie pan inside the pastry-lined pan. Or put the unbaked pastry over an inverted pan, trim and crimp the edge, and prick the crust generously with a table fork. These holes, which usually close, prevent blisters from forming. Another highly popular method is to line the pastry with foil and then fill it with dry beans or rice. If a browned shell is required, remove the foil and filler and return the shell to the oven for 4 to 5 minutes. Watch carefully lest it brown too much on the edges.

Almost any temperature from moderate to very hot can be used for baking an unbaked crust. The length of time for baking will depend upon how thick it has been rolled and the oven temperature. Unless you are baking something else in the oven at the same time, you'll probably prefer 400 to 450 degrees. The average time for baking an unfilled crust set within two pans is about 8 minutes. The average time for baking a bean-filled or rimmed crust will be about 15 minutes at 400 degrees.

Cool pie shells on a rack and have at room temperature or chilled when prepared filling is added.

Pastry for Two-Crust Pie (9-inch)

2 cups sifted all-purpose flour
1 teaspoon salt
⅔ cup shortening or ⅓ cup butter and ½ cup vegetable shortening
¼ cup cold water, approximately

Sift the flour with the salt or stir together with a fork or pastry blender. Add the butter and shortening and cut it through the flour with a fork, pastry blender, wire potato masher, or two table knives; or rub between the fingers until the mixture is in pieces about the size of a pea. Add water a few drops at a time and toss the mixture with a fork to combine the water evenly. The dough should not be wet, but just moistened enough to hold together in a ball. The type of flour and the temperature of the mixture will make a difference in the amount of water used. Chill the dough in the refrigerator 15 to 30 minutes if it seems too soft.

Take out slightly more than half of the dough for the undercrust or, if you want a thinner top crust, take nearly two-thirds for the undercrust. Roll it out, fit it into the pie pan, and trim the edge. Roll out the upper crust. Fill the lower crust, moisten the edge, place the top crust on, cut steam vents, and trim and crimp the edges. Bake according to directions for the particular pie being made.

Flour Paste Method. After the flour and salt are combined, measure ⅓ cup of the mixture into a cup or bowl and add the cold water to it to form a smooth paste. Cut the butter or shortening into the remaining flour and salt until the size of small peas. Stir the water and flour mixture in very lightly. Chill if necessary before rolling out.

Pastry for One-Crust Pie (9-inch). Use 1½ cups sifted all-purpose flour, ¾ teaspoon salt, ½ cup shortening or butter and shortening, and about 3 tablespoons cold water.

Hot Water Pie Crust

2 cups sifted all-purpose flour
1 teaspoon salt
⅓ cup boiling water
⅔ cup lard, butter, or shortening (at room temperature)

Mix the flour and salt in bowl. Measure the boiling water into a measuring cup, and add lard, shortening, or butter until the cup is full. Stir the mixture until well combined, then stir lightly with a fork into the flour and salt. This will make a very soft dough that must be chilled 30 minutes or more before rolling out. When baked it will produce a crumbly crust rather than a flaky one.

Oil Pastry (Two-Crust)

2 cups sifted all-purpose flour
1 teaspoon salt
⅔ cup vegetable oil
3 tablespoons milk or water

Mix the salt with the flour in a mixing bowl. Stir the oil and milk or water together and then stir into the flour and salt. Turn out on wax paper or aluminum foil and chill before rolling.

One-Crust Oil Pastry. Use 1½ cups flour, ¾ teaspoon salt, ½ cup of oil and 2 tablespoons milk or water.

Butter Pastry for Two-Crust Pie (9-inch)

2 cups sifted all-purpose flour
½ teaspoon salt
⅓ cup shortening
½ cup butter
3 to 4 tablespoons cold water

This can be mixed in the same way as the standard pastry (see page 634), cutting the fats at one time into the flour and salt mixture. Or the fats can be added separately. In this event, blend the shortening into the flour and salt until about the consistency of cornmeal. Add the water a few drops at a time and toss with a fork. Chill the dough. Roll out the dough into a rectangle about ¼ inch thick. Spread the first two-thirds of the dough with butter. Fold the last third over the buttered dough, then fold the remaining buttered dough over this, to make a simple envelope. Chill the dough before dividing and rolling out for the pie. This will made a flaky pastry.

Sweet Egg Pastry (Murbeteig or Pâte Sucrée)

2 cups sifted all-purpose flour
½ teaspoon salt
¼ to ½ cup sugar
½ to 1 cup butter or margarine (at room temperature)
2 egg yolks or 1 whole egg
1 teaspoon vanilla (optional)
1 to 2 tablespoons lemon juice (optional)

This is a favorite with Europeans, who seldom make the English or American type of shortening pastry. It is generally used for tarts, tartlets, and pastry that is baked and then filled with fresh or cooked fruits. The recipe provides a variable amount of sugar, which should be added to taste — if you are using tart fruit, use a larger amount of sugar. The amount of butter is variable also and depends upon the richness desired. Often these crusts are made rather thick in small individual patty pans or crimped tartlet pans. They are baked, cooled, and served filled with ice cream topped with fresh fruit or chocolate or caramel sauce; or filled with sliced peaches, strawberries, or raspberries and topped with sweetened whipped cream.

If mixing by hand, put the flour on a pastry board or marble slab, make a hole in the center, and add the salt, sugar, and butter or margarine. Work in with the fingertips, then add the remaining ingredients and stir with the fingers until a smooth dough is formed. Or prepare at low speed in an electric mixer.) Break or pinch off pieces of the pastry and press into individual patty pans or tart pans and bake at 350 to 400 degrees until a very delicate brown.

Large Shells or Flan Rings. Roll the pastry and fit into two 7 or 8 inch pie pans or flan rings. When fitting pastry into the flan ring, be sure to trim the top so that it does not extend over the sides. Line the shell with foil and weight down with dried beans or rice to prevent the sides from falling while baking.

Cream Cheese or Viennese Pastry

2 cups all-purpose flour
½ teaspoon salt
1 cup butter or margarine
2 3-ounce packages cream cheese (at room temperature)

The slightly acid flavor of this rich pastry combines well with either sweet fillings or fillings for appetizers. It is often used for tarts, shells for fruit flans, tiny hors d'oeuvre shells, and bite-size turnovers that hold meat, fish, or fowl fillings.

Put the flour in a mixing bowl and stir in the salt. Cut in the butter or margarine and cream cheese to form a soft dough. Chill if it seems too soft to roll satisfactorily. Roll out very thin. Use only half the dough at a time when making small tarts or appetizer shells, for it is rich and becomes very soft in a warm kitchen. Fit the dough into tart pans or flan rings. Bake in a preheated 375 to 400 degree oven until a very light brown. The baking time will depend on the thickness of the dough.

Cottage Cheese or Pot Cheese Pastry. Use ¾ cup finely sieved cottage or pot cheese instead of cream cheese. The pastry will not be as rich, but it is very tender and especially good for appetizers filled with hot cheese, crab, shrimp, deviled ham, or chicken livers.

Crumb Crust for Pies

1½ cups fine crumbs
⅓ cup (about 6 tablespoons) butter
3 tablespoons white or brown sugar or 4 tablespoons powdered sugar
Spices, cocoa, or unsweetened or semisweet chocolate (optional)

Not a new idea — originally leftover cake, cookie crumbs, or breadcrumbs were combined with butter and syrup, molasses, sorghum, or a little sugar to make the foundation for cooked fillings, made in a basin and called pudding. Now all types of cracker and cookie crumbs (Graham crackers, zweibach, vanilla or chocolate wafers, gingersnaps, etc.) are used for the crusts.

Prepare the crumbs by rolling cookies or crackers between sheets of wax paper or plastic or tea towels. Or place a little at a time in a blender and turn to low until the fine crumbs form. Melt the butter over low heat in a 1½ to 2 quart saucepan. Remove from the heat, add the crumbs and sugar, and blend well. If using spices or cocoa in the crust, add with the sugar. If using chocolate, add 1 ounce unsweetened or 1 to 3 ounces semisweet chocolate to the butter after it is melted. Stir over very low heat until the chocolate is liquid, then add the crumbs and sugar and blend.

Turn the crumb mixture into an 8 or 9 inch pie pan, spread rather evenly and firmly, over the bottom and up the sides. Bake it at 325 degrees 7 to 10 minutes, depending upon the thickness of the crust. This will firm the crust. Some people like to chill the crust instead of baking, but if the filling is slightly moist, this will make the crust soggy.

Puff Pastry

4 cups flour
4 tablespoons softened butter
1 tablespoon lemon juice
1 teaspoon salt
¾ to 1 cup ice water
¾ pound (3 sticks) butter

Puff paste is thick, many layered, very delicate pastry. It was very often used in early cookbooks for meat pies, topping for tarts, patty shells, and various kinds of desserts and savory dishes. I think many people hesitate to try it because it is made out to be the most difficult thing in the world to do. It is not; neither is it the easiest. It needs care more than anything else.

First of all, you have a basic mixture, sometimes called the *détrempe*. Cut or work the butter into the flour with your fingers until the mixture is the size of small peas. Add the lemon juice, salt, and enough ice water to make a dough that is firm but not hard. Knead it slightly and press it out with your hand. You want the feeling of an easily workable dough, not one that you have to roll with some strength. Wrap the dough in wax paper and chill about 20 to 30 minutes in the refrigerator. Meanwhile, take 3 sticks of butter from the refrigerator (Danish or tub butter is best for this pastry as it has less water), beat them down with a rolling pin to soften slightly and form into a flat rectangular piece about 6 × 12 inches. Put it into the refrigerator on wax paper or foil. When the dough is chilled, roll out on a floured board or marble slab to a rectangle about 8 × 18 inches. Place the butter on the upper ⅔ of the dough, leaving enough room on the sides to seal the dough. Fold the bottom third of the dough, where there is no butter, over the butter about halfway, then fold the buttered part down over that, so that you have three layers of dough with butter between each layer. Seal the edges so that the butter does not ooze out during rolling. However, if it does, or the dough breaks, just pat a little flour into the wound to mend it. With the narrow part of the dough facing you, start rolling an inch away from the end and take a good full roll up to an inch away from the other end. Continue rolling until you have stretched the dough to about the same 8 × 18-inch rectangle you had in the beginning. Fold it in thirds again and roll again unless your butter has softened too much, in which case chill it in the refrigerator for 20 to 30 minutes. When you have made two turns (each rolling and folding process is a "turn"), mark the two turns with your fingertips at the corner of the dough. Wrap it in wax paper, put it in a plastic bag if you wish, and chill 30 to 40 minutes or longer. When it is chilled, place it again on the floured board or marble slab and roll it again to the 8 × 18 size. Fold it again in thirds, and if the butter is not too soft take the fourth turn and chill the dough again in the refrigerator.

After four turns you may use the pastry for meat pies, topping tarts, etc., but if you want a still flakier pastry give it two more turns after chilling it each time, so that in the end you will have given it six complete rollings and six turns. You will have many many layers of butter between flour. After your final turn let the pastry rest in the refrigerator an hour or overnight or two or three days if you like. Before you use it you will roll it again to a thickness of ¼ to ½ inch, and then it may be shaped as you want it for any kind of baking. Very often the trimmings are put together and rolled in sugar and made into little palm leaves or other kinds of small pastry.

Patty Shells or Bouchées. These can be made in many sizes, from the shells 3¼ or 3½ inches in diameter used for creamed chicken, seafood, ham, or other foods down to the bite-size shells used for appetizers or desserts. For large patty shells roll the dough about ½ inch thick. Cut into rounds with a 3 to 3½ inch cutter. Then use a second cutter about 2 to 2½ inches in diameter to cut about halfway down through each round. Place the rounds on a baking sheet about 1½ inches apart. Bake in a 450 to 500 degree oven 10 minutes without opening the oven door, then reduce the heat and bake at 350 degrees about 20 to 35 minutes longer. While the shells are still warm, but not hot, lift out the center portion with a knife.

Only about half of this will be puffy and crisp, the limp dough in the center is usually discarded. Before using patty shells for creamed mixtures, heat in a 350-degree oven 8 to 10 minutes.

Dessert patty shells are often sprinkled with or rolled in granulated sugar before baking and are made 2 to 3 inches in diameter. The dough is usually rolled about 1/4 inch thick to yield shells about 1 1/2 to 2 inches high. These are filled with fresh fruit and berries and topped with whipped cream or ice cream, or filled with ice cream and topped with sauce or fruit. You may prefer to remove the centers of the dough (see above) before baking, for they are not always used when the pastry is served. (These centers are then baked separately, split in half, filled with your favorite chocolate, brown butter or rum icing, reassembled, and glazed or frosted.) The patty shells are baked in a 450-degree oven about 4 to 5 minutes, then the temperature is reduced to 350 degrees for 20 to 35 minutes longer.

Petites bouchées, literally "small mouthfuls," are usually made with a cutter 1 1/2 inches in diameter and a center cutter 1 inch in diameter. These are baked a slightly shorter time than the dessert shells. Fill with sauced chunks of chicken, ham and chicken, veal and chicken, lobster, or crab.

Vol-au-vents are large patty shells. There are cutters in round or oval shapes especially for these, but in case you do not have them, you can make cutters out of cardboard. Be sure to plan the pattern to fit your baking pan. You will need enough dough to cut two circles or ovals. If making a vol-au-vent larger than 8 inches in diameter, the puff pastry recipe will require 3 or 4 cups of flour. Roll the dough slightly less than 1/2 inch thick. Place one round of puff paste in a shallow baking pan. Cut out the center of the second round, leaving a ring about 1 1/2 inches in width — for an 8-inch vol-au-vent, the hole would be 5 inches in diameter. Brush the first round very lightly around the top with 1 egg white or yolk mixed with 1 tablespoon cold water, being careful it does not drip over the sides, which would prevent the pastry from expanding. Or lightly moisten the edge with water. Place the ring of dough carefully on this. Bake in a 450 to 500 degree oven 10 minutes, then reduce the heat to 350 degrees and bake 35 to 45 minutes longer.

Palm Leaves. A favorite sweet pastry to serve with fresh sliced peaches or ice cream topped with fruit or berry sauce. Roll the puff paste slightly less than 1/4 inch thick and cut in strips about 6 inches wide. Sprinkle the dough with granulated sugar. Roll up the dough from each long side into the center, making a long double roll of pastry. Chill. Cut with a very sharp, thin-bladed knife in slices about 1/4 inch thick. Place cut side down on a lightly oiled or buttered baking sheet. Leave about 2 inches between pieces to allow for expansion, for these will expand horizontally, not vertically. Bake 5 minutes in a 450-degree oven, then reduce the heat to 350 degrees and bake 10 to 15 minutes longer.

Rough Puff Paste. Also called *Simple Puff Paste* or *Meat Puff Paste.* Although this can be used for any pie, it is more generally used as the topping for a meat, fish, or fowl pie. The recipe can easily be doubled or tripled if you are making, for example, Cornish pasties, or a large meat pie without undercrust. Rough puff paste is made like puff paste, but use half lard or shortening rather than all butter, and make only four turns before rolling it out to put on the pie. It should be thick — about 1/3 inch. To put it on the pie pan or casserole, see page 633.

Suet Pastry

2 cups sifted all-purpose flour
1 teaspoon salt
1 cup ground or very finely chopped beef suet (kidney suet preferred)
1/3 cup cold water, approximately

The use of suet for meat pies was an English custom, and in many sections of the country it is still preferred.

Mix the salt and suet into the flour with your fingertips or a pastry cutter. Add the water a few spoonfuls at a time and toss with a fork to distribute evenly. Add more water if the dough seems dry or crumbly. Chill the dough. Roll out on a lightly floured board to the thickness and shape desired. This amount of dough should be sufficient for a 2-quart casserole about 2½ inches deep with a top crust about 1/4 inch thick. If using a 10 × 14 × 2-inch pan, use one and a half to two times the recipe.

Suet and Egg Pastry. This is often used for richness and color. Mix an egg yolk or white with the water — use a scant 1/3 cup. Combine the remaining yolk or white with a teaspoon or two of water and use as the moistener for the pastry edge and as a glaze for the top crust.

Suet and Lemon Juice Pastry. Lemon juice (or sometimes vinegar) has long been a favorite addition to water in pie making, for it does make a more tender crust. Use 1 tablespoon of either as part of the liquid in suet pastries.

Meringue for Pies

3 egg whites
1 teaspoon cream of tartar

Beat the egg whites till they form soft peaks. Add the cream of tartar and salt and continue beating till the whites are stiff but not dry. Add sugar, a little at a time, beating it in well. Spread the meringue over the pie, being certain to cover the surface completely, including the edge of the crust. If you are deft with the pastry tube, you may pipe the meringue over the pie, using a #6 rosette tube. Bake the meringue at 350 degrees 15 to 18 minutes, or until it is lightly browned.

Pinch salt
6 tablespoons sugar

Cakes

I have never forgotten my early birthday cakes. Blessed with an insatiable taste for coconut, I always wanted a cake piled high with it. And since my birthday came in May, there were usually hawthorn blossoms available to decorate the plate. I felt that candles ruined the beauty of the cake and was firm about dispensing with the blowing out of candles ritual. These cakes, under their white icing and coconut, were usually a sunshine or moonshine cake or a white mountain cake.

The thought of a great round cake tin on our pantry shelf awakens memories of another type of cake that pleased me in my early years as it did most people in my generation — the pound cake, Madeira cake, or seed cake, which would keep for a fortnight or so and was sliced thin for tea or as an accompaniment to fruit or frozen desserts. These "good keepers" were standard fare for the well-stocked larder.

Cake baking in the home is a relatively recent accomplishment. During the seventeenth and eighteenth centuries, unless one mixed great Christmas cakes and toted them to the local baker to bake, little was done with delicate batters or lovely rich fruited cakes. The oven in the fireplace and the outdoor oven could produce breads of various kinds but were not particularly suited for fine baking. Often holiday cakes, made with fruits and nuts, were steamed or cooked in boiling water like a plum pudding. As a matter of fact, steamed fruit cakes were still in evidence when I was a child, and I am certain that many people continue to prepare them out of sheer nostalgia.

With the advent of kitchen stoves and ovens, baking became more common. Still, there were hazards. Accurate regulation of oven heat was impossible, there were no standards of measurement, and the quality of flours varied considerably. Furthermore, there were few artificial leaveners. Saleratus was not always available and pearl ash was used as a substitute, sometimes with disastrous results. Miss Leslie, in her cookbook, warns not to add too much pearl ash lest the cake have an unpleasant taste.

Many of the most reputable cookbooks of the day had recipes that were completely baffling, such as this one, gleaned from a book published in the early nineteenth century titled *Gentlewoman's Housewifery*. It called for "2 teacups sugar, butter the size of 2 eggs, 2 or 3 eggs, 1 coffee cup sour milk with 2 teaspoons soda added, salt, flavoring, and flour enough to make a good batter. Bake." With such directions and a primitive oven, it is miraculous that the housewife ever produced an edible bit of cake. Probably most of the time she didn't.

As the nineteenth century progressed and we imported fine cookbooks from England, such as Mrs. Acton's, there was a marked improvement in baking, aided by the introduction of standard measures and crude ideas of oven control. Housewives began to prepare luscious cream cakes and pound cakes, with many variations, and delicate cookies, and macaroons. Then the angel food cake was invented, really a form of soufflé in its way, and the layer cake came into its own after the introduction of baking powder. Chocolate layer cake became a standard item for baking days — it is more and more becoming only a dreamy memory — as well as such superlative creations as the devil's food and brownstone front, the white mountain and mahogany cakes — all new departures and all completely American.

As immigrants arrived from other countries and trekked across the continent to the West, the great European cakes became part of our heritage — fine sponge cakes, genoise, butter-laden pound cakes, fruited cakes, and torten. I well remember cake sales sponsored by churches, schools, or summer colonists to raise funds for some worthy cause. The display of cakes at these events was indicative of the scope of American baking. Naturally every woman put her best recipe forward and competed for eye appeal, too. There would be towering 1-2-3-4 cakes with marshmallow-chocolate icing, Schaumtorten, banana whipped cream cakes, delicate angel food cakes with almond icing, red devil's food, topped with a thick, fluffy boiled icing; sunshine cakes baked in a tube pan, uniced but wonderful, applesauce cakes, jam cakes, and other loaf cakes for those who preferred a moist texture and spicy flavor.

Today we are coming through another period of change in baking habits. The cake mix vogue, which began about twenty years ago, has had its day and is now on the wane. Cakes made from the box usually have good texture but are otherwise unpleasant, since they largely depend on a flavoring agent called vanillin — artificial vanilla. Nevertheless, the mix caught on because it put a homemade cake, if it can be called that, within the reach of every housewife. Some of the mixes, notably the angel food, can be highly successful. Now, I am told on very good authority, guilt (and perhaps improved taste) is driving people back to baking cakes from scratch, as is indicated by the increase in sales of certain cake ingredients.

Another development is the increased popularity of the refrigerated and the frozen cake. Usually these are of rather high quality, made from good ingredients, and are for the most part loaf cakes and sheet cakes, iced simply.

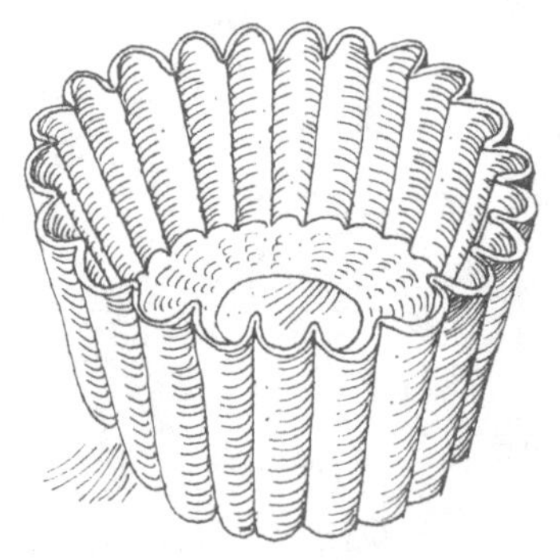

In this book I have reached into the past and attempted to present most of the famous cakes of the last century or so. Many of them were recipes enjoyed when I was a child, all rather distinctive in their way and baked by a variety of people.

Basic Facts About Cake Baking

Measuring ingredients accurately is the first step to a successful cake. For many "made" dishes such as stew, a bit more seasoning will not spoil the dish. However, too much leavening or not enough flour or liquid can ruin a cake.

Temperature of ingredients is important. Have all ingredients at room temperature (65 to 70 degrees) for an easily mixed, lighter, and better-textured cake.

Eggs separate easier right from the refrigerator. But both whites and yolks will whip to greater volume if warmed to room temperature.

Sizes of pans for baking cakes are fairly standard. Do not fill pans too full. Sometimes, as the result of overfilling, the cake crusts on the edge and the center appears fallen.

Clean, shining pans are important; burned or dark pans absorb heat and will usually burn the batter. If you must use dark pans, insulate them with several layers of well-greased letter paper. Even a streak of grease that has burned on will cause the cake to burn or overbake in the same area.

Preparation of pans depends upon the type of cake. Pans for sponge-type cakes, such as angel food and true sponge, should not be greased and should be washed well before using to eliminate any grease.

Pans for butter-type cakes should be greased or buttered, then sprinkled with flour. Tap the pan and turn it to distribute the flour evenly over the whole inside; then invert it and tap out excess flour. Or grease the pan, line the bottom with wax paper and grease the wax paper. To prepare paper of the proper size, place the pan bottom down on wax paper and trace around it with the tip of kitchen shears; then cut. If using more than one pan, fold the wax paper over in as many layers as you have pans, making layers slightly larger than the pan bottom; then trace and cut. If using letter paper or other heavy paper, simply trace around the pan with a pencil.

Oven heat. Oven heats are fairly standard in present-day ranges. However, thermostats in ovens can malfunction. Avoid smearing strong oven cleaners on the thermostat, which will often ruin it. Unless the manufacturer has planned the oven to accommodate aluminum foil placed on the bottom, do not use it. Foil will disturb the engineered distribution of heat and consequently make a difference in the baking.

Pan arrangement. Never bake with one pan directly over the other on the two oven racks. Stagger them, and be sure that the edges of the pans are at least 1½ inches — better 2 inches — away from the sides and back of the oven. Those edges can gather heat and prevent a good circulation of air. As a consequence, the cake will bake too much on one side and become lopsided.

Be sure your oven is level. If you do not own a carpenter's level, put a square pan on the bottom of the oven and pour in water until it comes to the top of the pan. If it is ready to overflow at one edge before the others, the oven is not level.

Cake Texture

A gummy texture in a cake or a soggy deposit on the bottom of the cake indicates that the heat was too low or the batter was beaten too much. All cakes have some sort of leavening — eggs, baking powder, soda, or a combination of these. Heat makes the leavening

expand. When it has expanded to the fullest, the oven must be hot enough to "set" the cake; otherwise it will collapse.

Overbeating can cause a very solid-looking fine grain with tunnels in it. A coarse grain — very large bubbles interspersed with bubbles of uniform size — indicates undermixing. To be mixed properly, ingredients should be stirred — especially after the flour is added — just long enough to be incorporated.

Flour. Varying types of flour will make a difference in cake textures. All-purpose flour, for example, will never make as light a cake as cake or pastry flour, inasmuch as it contains some hard wheat, hence more gluten. Gluten is the substance in flour that becomes elastic and holds the yeast gases when bread dough is kneaded. When using eggs, soda, or baking powder as the leavening with all-purpose flour, the more you beat or stir a cake the more likely it is to have a tough texture.

Using acid, such as sour milk, buttermilk, or citrus juice, helps to break down the gluten, which is why pioneer cake bakers, especially in the Midwest, preferred sour milk cakes. Some cake bakers used vinegar or cream of tartar to break down the gluten in flour for such cakes as angel food or sponge cakes.

Cornstarch blended with flour was also used in former days to achieve a fine-grained cake. More liquid had to be added, or 3/4 cup of cornstarch was substituted for 1 full cup of flour. Even then the cake was apt to have a raw starch or unbaked flavor.

Electric Mixers

Electric mixers have taken a good deal of tedium out of cake making. Before their advent, butter cakes were made by creaming the butter, creaming in the sugar, beating in the egg yolks, adding the flour and liquid alternately, and lastly, folding in the egg whites. To make butter cakes in a mixer, cream the butter, then cream in the sugar with the mixer at a low enough speed to keep the ingredients in the *bottom*, not up the sides, of the bowl. Have a rubber or plastic spatula handy to scrape down the sides. While the creaming is being done, measure out the other ingredients and prepare the pans. Increase the speed to add eggs — whole eggs are used, not separated. Use the lowest possible speed to fold in flour. Liquid should be added at medium speed.

Before using an electric mixer for cakes, read the instruction book. Some hand mixers are not powerful enough to mix cake batters or biscuit, muffin, and yeast doughs.

Freezing Cakes

Angel cakes do not freeze well and are apt to become tough.

Fluffy egg white frostings do not freeze well either, and usually turn to syrup when thawed. Any type of frosting that contains fat is fine for freezing. Cakes, like anything else, should be sealed in moistureproof and vaporproof material when put in the freezer. To freeze a fancy decorated cake, first freeze quickly, unwrapped, to firm the frosting. Put in a box and seal in a freezer bag.

Cupcakes

Cupcakes can be made from any cake batter, whether layer, fruit, angel food or sponge cake. One may use frilled paper cupcake containers set in muffin or cupcake pans, rather than grease and flour the pans themselves.

Rich fruit cakes, with fruits chopped fine, are often made in these frilled cups for holiday gift boxes, and more and more the cups are used to make bite-size morsels to be served along with holiday cookies. Oftentimes fruit cake (so-called groom's cake) for a wedding reception is baked in bonbon cups. This allows guests to eat the fruit cake at the reception, rather than carry off the too thin, usually dry packets of fruit cake that are to be slept on. Often tiny tea cakes or petits fours are made in small cupcake or muffin pans, frosted with fondant, or fluffy or butter frosting, and decorated with frosting, tiny candies, or chocolate.

Bake cupcakes at the same temperature called for in the full cake recipe but less time — usually 15 to 20 minutes is enough. In some instances, such as with a rather heavy batter, they should be baked at a temperature 25 degrees higher.

Saffron Nubbies

1/8 teaspoon powdered saffron
1/3 cup boiling water
1/3 cup cold water
1 cup raisins, golden preferred
1/2 cup butter
1 cup sugar
2 eggs
2 cups sifted all-purpose flour
1/2 teaspoon salt
2 teaspoons baking powder
1 cup quite finely chopped candied fruit (use greased knife for chopping)

Saffron cake was originally a much fruited yeast dough, but eventually developed into a quick cupcake with real flavor.

Steep the saffron in the boiling water about 30 minutes, then add the cold water. Wash the raisins and drain on a paper towel. In a mixing bowl cream the butter and cream in the sugar. Beat in the eggs. Sift the flour and sprinkle about a half cup of it over the drained raisins and chopped candied fruits. Sift the remaining flour with the salt and baking powder and add alternately with the saffron water to the creamed mixture. Do not overmix. Fold in the fruits. Spoon into greased and floured muffin or cupcake pans or into fluted cupcake papers set in muffin pans. Do not fill pans or papers more than half full. Bake in preheated 375-degree oven about 12 to 15 minutes or until the cake springs back when pressed lightly with a fingertip. Transfer to a rack to cool, loosen from the pans when still slightly warm, and continue cooling on the rack. These need no frosting.

Maids of Honor

PASTRY SHELLS

1 ½ cups unsifted all-purpose flour
½ cup butter (sweet — unsalted — butter preferred)
½ to 1 teaspoon salt, depending upon whether sweet butter is used
1 hard-boiled egg yolk, sieved
1 raw egg yolk
2 tablespoons sugar
1 teaspoon grated lemon rind

FILLING

¼ pound (½ cup) pot cheese (cottage cheese curd without cream added)
¼ cup sweet butter
3 tablespoons ground blanched almonds
½ teaspoon salt
1 teaspoon grated lemon rind
2 tablespoons lemon juice
4 egg yolks

It is difficult to decide whether these are cakes, cookies, or small pies. They are often mentioned in early Southern recipe collections.

For pastry shells, work the flour and butter together. Traditionally this is done on a bread board or marble slab. Make a well in the center of the flour, add the butter and remaining ingredients, and gradually incorporate the flour into the center mixture with the fingertips. Or put the ingredients into the bowl of the electric mixer and mix at low speed, scraping the sides and bottom of the bowl with a spatula. When mixed, turn onto wax paper or aluminum foil and fold the paper or foil around it. Or form into a ball and slip into a plastic bag. Put into the refrigerator to chill while making the filling.

For the filling, sieve the cheese. (If you are unable to purchase pot cheese, use large curd cottage cheese, put in a coarse sieve, and let as much of the cream run out as possible. This will probably take about half an hour or more.) Beat the softened butter until light, and stir in or beat in (use small bowl of electric mixer or hand mixer, if you like) the remaining ingredients. Roll the pastry into a log shape and divide into 12 pieces. Press each evenly with the thumbs into a tart pan, fluted or plain, about 3 inches in diameter. If you prefer to make these in smaller pans, divide the dough accordingly. Spoon the filling evenly into the crusts. Place the tart pans on a baking sheet and bake in preheated 350-degree oven until the tarts are brown and the filling is set, about 12 to 15 minutes. Transfer from the oven to a rack. Press from the pans while still slightly warm, but not hot.

Snickerdoodle (Snipdoodle)

1 cup sugar
1 cup flour
¼ teaspoon salt
1 teaspoon baking powder
1 teaspoon cinnamon
½ cup milk
1 egg
¼ cup melted butter
Additional sugar and cinnamon for topping

This version of snickerdoodle, which I have also heard called snipdoodle, is really a quick coffee cake and is delicious used as cake or bread for breakfast or luncheon.

Sift together the sugar, flour, baking powder, and cinnamon. Blend the eggs and milk and stir into the dry ingredients. Beat in the melted butter. Pour into a buttered 9 × 13-inch baking pan, sprinkle with granulated sugar and cinnamon. Bake at 400 degrees for about 25 minutes. Serve hot or cold.

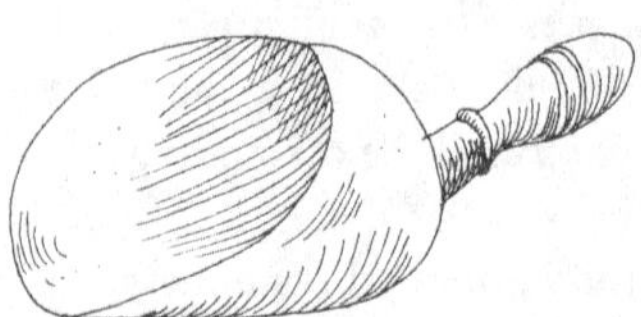

Snickerdoodle Cupcakes

½ cup butter
1 cup sugar
2 eggs
⅓ to ½ cup chopped, toasted nuts such as walnuts, pecans, almonds, filberts, hickory nuts, or peanuts
⅓ to ½ cup seedless raisins or finely cut dates
2½ cups sifted all-purpose flour
1 teaspoon baking soda
½ teaspoon salt
½ teaspoon cloves
½ teaspoon mace
1½ teaspoons cinnamon
¾ cup sour milk or buttermilk (or use sweet milk with 2 teaspoons vinegar stirred in, let stand 10 minutes)

This name seemed to appeal to homemakers at the turn of the century. It was applied in various forms to cupcakes, cookies, and to a form of breakfast or quick cake.

Cream the butter, cream in the sugar, then beat in the eggs, one at a time. Add the nuts and raisins, then stir in the sifted dry ingredients alternately with the sour milk or buttermilk. Stir just to mix. If using an electric mixer, add the flour and milk at lowest speed, and use a spatula to scrape the mixture down the sides of the bowl. Spoon into greased and floured cupcake pans or frilled paper cupcake containers set into muffin pans. Do not fill more than half full. Bake in preheated 375-degree oven about 15 minutes or until the cakes have shrunk slightly from the sides of the pans. Let stand a few minutes on a rack, then loosen and remove from the pans. These are usually left unfrosted but go well with orange butter frosting.

Loaf Cake

⅔ cup butter
1 cup sugar
3 eggs
2¼ cups sifted cake or 2 cups sifted all-purpose flour
3 teaspoons baking powder
½ teaspoon salt
½ cup milk
1 teaspoon vanilla or other flavoring

Loaf cakes were a favorite years ago, for the recipes were usually triple this size, and three loaf pans would fit in the coal or wood stove oven at one time.

Cream the butter and cream in the sugar until light and fluffy, easiest done with an electric mixer. If mixing by hand, beat in the eggs one at a time, then add the dry ingredients, sifted together, alternately with the milk and vanilla. If using a mixer, add the eggs at higher speed, then turn it off, add the sifted dry ingredients, turn to lowest speed, and add the milk and vanilla. Pour into a greased and floured loaf cake pan 9×5×2½ inches, or slightly deeper. Bake in a moderate 350-degree oven about 50 minutes, or until the cake springs back when touched lightly with a fingertip. Set the pan on a rack and let cool to lukewarm. Loosen the cake and turn it out onto the rack to continue cooling. Usually a butter icing, if any, is used on this cake.

Rum or Brandy Loaf Cake. Use 2 tablespoons rum or brandy instead of, or with, the vanilla. Or use only ¼ cup milk and add ¼ cup rum, brandy, bourbon, sherry, or port.

Orange Loaf Cake. Use ½ cup orange juice and 1 tablespoon grated orange rind instead of milk and vanilla. Use ½ teaspoon soda and 2 teaspoons baking powder instead of 3 teaspoons baking powder.

Lemon Loaf Cake. Use 2 teaspoons grated lemon rind instead of vanilla.

Spice Loaf Cake. Add to the flour when sifting: 1 teaspoon cinnamon, ½ teaspoon allspice, ½ teaspoon nutmeg or mace, ¼ teaspoon ground cloves, and 1 tablespoon cocoa. Also add at the end, if you like, ½ cup finely chopped toasted walnuts, pecans, almonds, or filberts. Vanilla may be omitted.

Nut Loaf Cake. Nut loaf cakes were a standard in the late nineteenth and early twentieth centuries, for they kept well for a week or 10 days when stored in the cooling cellar in a well-covered tin or crock. They were usually reserved for callers. In the Midwest, hickory nuts and black walnuts were much favored for these. Picking out the nutmeats was always the chore for the children. For a good nut loaf cake, use the above loaf cake recipe. Reduce the butter to ½ cup, and use 1 tablespoon rum or brandy instead of vanilla, if you like. Just before turning the batter into the pan, stir in 1 cup toasted chopped (medium coarse) walnuts, pecans, filberts, black walnuts, hickory nuts, Brazil nuts, almonds, or Macadamia nuts. (Toast the nutmeats lightly in a slow 325-degree oven to bring out the flavor, then chop and cool.) Usually this cake is not frosted, but some like a browned butter frosting.

1–2–3–4 Cake

1 cup butter
2 cups sugar
4 eggs
3 cups sifted cake flour
4 teaspoons baking powder
½ teaspoon salt
1 cup milk
1 to 1½ teaspoons vanilla

Several years ago I did an article for *Woman's Day* on birthday cakes, in which I gave my mother's recipe for this cake and pondered about the meaning of the name. Her recipe, you see, called for 2¾ cups of flour instead of 3 and thereby managed to obscure from me the very simple pattern of 1 cup of butter, 2 cups of sugar, 3 cups of flour, and 4 eggs. I received the greatest mail in the history of my association with that magazine, from both women and men whose mothers and grandmothers had handed down recipes for this famous cake. Some explained the all too obvious origin of the name, and others expressed indignation that I had dared to change the recipe. Now I, along with all the housewives of the past century, shall never forget the formula. Of all American cakes, probably this one has been the most popular through the years. Originally it was made as a loaf cake and contained no liquid, but it was increasingly preferred as a layer cake. Its fame no doubt has something to do with the ease of remembering the recipe. Also, before the days of standard measurements, the homemaker could use the same cup for measuring ingredients, thereby ensuring success.

Cream the butter and cream in the sugar until fluffy. If mixing by hand, separate the eggs, blend the beaten yolks into the butter mixture, sift the flour with the baking powder and salt, add alternately with the milk and vanilla, and fold in the beaten egg whites last. If using a mixer, beat the whole eggs in at medium to high speed, turn off the mixer and add the flour mixture, then turn to lowest speed and add the milk and vanilla. When smooth, pour into three 8 or 9 inch layer cake pans. Bake in a moderate 350-degree oven for about 25 minutes or until the cake springs back when touched lightly with a fingertip. Cool on a rack for a few minutes, then loosen from the pans and turn out on the rack to cool. This cake can be the base for many fillings and frostings.

Spice 1-2-3-4 Cake. Add 1½ teaspoons cinnamon, ½ teaspoon nutmeg, ½ teaspoon allspice, ½ teaspoon cloves, 1 tablespoon cocoa. Sift with the dry ingredients.

Sour Milk or Buttermilk 1-2-3-4 Cake. Use 1¼ cups buttermilk or sour milk instead of sweet milk; for leavening, instead of 4 teaspoons baking powder, use 3 teaspoons baking powder and ½ teaspoon soda sifted with the dry ingredients.

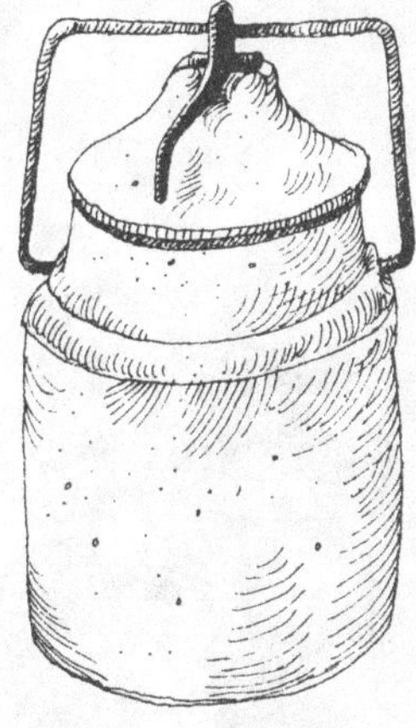

Orange Sundae 1-2-3-4 Cake. Use either the basic recipe or the buttermilk or sour cream version. Bake in a 10-inch tube pan or a 10×14×2-inch pan. When baked, let the cake cool 10 minutes or more, loosen from the pan, and turn out on a rack. For the frosting: Mix ¾ cup orange juice and 2 tablespoons lemon juice with ¾ cup sugar. Add 1 tablespoon grated orange rind also, if you like. Drizzle over the cake, being sure not to soak it all in one spot. Let the cake cool.

Lemon Sundae 1-2-3-4 Cake. Follow directions for orange sundae cake, above. For the frosting, mix ⅓ cup lemon juice, 1 teaspoon grated lemon rind, and ¾ cup sugar, and let stand for 10 minutes or more. Stir well to dissolve the sugar. Drizzle over the cake and cool.

Two-Egg Cake

½ cup butter
1 cup sugar
2 eggs
2 cups sifted cake flour
2 teaspoons baking powder
½ teaspoon salt
1 teaspoon vanilla
¾ cup milk

Cream the butter very well, add the sugar gradually and cream until the mixture is fluffy. If mixing by hand, beat in the eggs one at a time, sift the flour with the baking powder and salt, and add alternately with the milk, to which the vanilla has been added (or add the vanilla or other flavoring to the creamed butter and sugar mixture). Use a folding rather than stirring motion. If using a mixer, add both eggs at once, blend in the flour at low speed, then the milk and vanilla. When well blended, and be sure to scrape the sides and bottom of the bowl while mixing, turn into two greased and floured 8 or 9 inch layer cake pans or into a sheet pan about 10×13×2 inches. Bake in 350-degree oven about 25 minutes for layers or 35 minutes for sheet cake. Test for doneness with a fingertip — when the cake springs back in the center, it is done. Cool 3 or 4 minutes on the rack, loosen at the edges, and turn out onto rack to cool. Frost when cool.

Orange Cake. Use ½ teaspoon soda and 1 teaspoon baking powder, rather than all baking powder. Add 1 tablespoon grated orange rind to the butter. Use ¾ cup orange juice instead of milk, and omit the vanilla. Good with orange frosting or chocolate frosting.

Spice Cake. Sift with the flour 1 tablespoon cocoa, 1 teaspoon cinnamon, ½ teaspoon allspice, ½ teaspoon nutmeg, and ¼ teaspoon cloves.

Caramel Cake. Use 1¾ cups firmly packed brown sugar instead of white, and cream slightly with the butter instead of sifting with flour. For the liquid, if you like, use ½ cup evaporated milk, undiluted, with ⅔ cup milk.

Peppermint Candy Cake. Decrease the sugar by ¼ cup. Add ⅓ cup finely crushed peppermint stick candy with the eggs and milk at the end. This is good with a chocolate frosting or a fluffy white frosting with chocolate glaze.

Lemon Cake. Use ½ teaspoon soda and 1 teaspoon baking powder, rather than all baking powder. Add to the butter 1 to 1½ teaspoons grated lemon rind. Add 1 tablespoon lemon juice to the milk.

Sour Milk or Buttermilk Cake. Use ½ teaspoon soda and 1 teaspoon baking powder, rather than all baking powder. Use ¾ cup plus 2 tablespoons sour milk or buttermilk as liquid.

Marble Cake. Melt 2 ounces bitter (unsweetened) chocolate over very low heat or hot water with 3 tablespoons milk or water. Stir to combine well. Cool to room temperature. When the cake is mixed, transfer about half the mixture to a small bowl. Stir ¼ teaspoon soda into the cooled melted chocolate, and stir the mixture into half the cake batter. Spoon a little of the plain batter into the pan or pans, then add a little of the chocolate batter, and continue alternating. Use a separate spoon for each batter or the colors will not be as distinct. Smooth the batter with a spoon or by tapping the pan on the counter top several times. This is often frosted with a fluffy white frosting, then glazed with chocolate after the first frosting has set.

Spanish Bun Cake

½ cup butter
1 cup firmly packed brown sugar
2 egg yolks
2 cups sifted cake flour
2 teaspoons baking powder
¼ teaspoon salt
½ teaspoon cinnamon
½ teaspoon cloves
½ teaspoon allspice
½ cup milk
½ teaspoon vanilla

TOPPING

2 egg whites
½ teaspoon lemon juice or ¼ teaspoon cream of tartar
¾ cup firmly packed brown sugar
¾ cup chopped nutmeats

Cream the butter, then cream in the sugar until very light. Beat in the egg yolks thoroughly. Sift the flour with the dry ingredients and add alternately to the creamed mixture with the milk and vanilla. If using an electric mixer, turn it off and lift the beater before adding the flour mixture. Turn it on to the lowest speed, add the liquid, and mix only until the batter is smooth. Spread in a greased and floured pan (or pan lined with greased paper) 8 × 10 inches or 10 × 13 inches. Beat the egg whites until foamy, add the lemon juice or cream of tartar. Slowly beat in the brown sugar and beat until stiff and smooth and the sugar is dissolved. Fold in the nutmeats (or fold in half and sprinkle the remainder over the top after spreading). Add a few drops of vanilla, if you like. Spread evenly over the cake batter. Bake in a 350-degree oven about 50 minutes. Cool in the pan on a cake rack.

Blitz Küchen

½ cup butter
½ cup sugar
3 egg yolks
½ teaspoon vanilla
⅓ cup milk
1¼ cups sifted cake flour
1½ teaspoons baking powder
¼ teaspoon salt

MERINGUE TOPPING

3 egg whites
½ teaspoon lemon juice or ¼ teaspoon cream of tartar
½ cup sugar
½ cup chopped walnuts, almonds, pecans, or filberts

TOPPING

2 or 3 cups sliced fresh or frozen fruit, sliced strawberries, or whole raspberries
½ to 1 cup whipping cream

One of the best cakes for accommodating fresh or frozen fruits, such as peaches, apricots, strawberries, or raspberries.

Cream the butter, then cream in the sugar until very light. Beat in the egg yolks and vanilla. Add the milk alternately with the sifted dry ingredients. This will make a stiff batter. Spread in two greased and floured 8-inch cake pans. It will make a thin layer. Beat the egg whites until frothy. Add the lemon juice or cream of tartar. Slowly beat in the sugar and beat until well blended and stiff and the sugar is dissolved. Spread in swirls on the cake batter. Sprinkle with nuts and bake in a 350-degree oven 30 to 35 minutes, or until the cake shrinks from sides of pan. Remove to a rack. When cool, loosen the cake from one pan and turn meringue side down on a plate. Sprinkle with fruit and dot with whipped cream. Put on the other layer meringue side up. Decorate the top with spoonfuls of whipped cream and garnish the center with fruit.

Lady Baltimore Cake (Egg White Cake)

¾ cup butter
1½ cups sugar
3 cups sifted cake flour
3 teaspoons baking powder
¼ teaspoon salt
1 cup milk
1 teaspoon vanilla
½ teaspoon almond, rum or brandy extract
6 egg whites, beaten stiff

Said to have originated in Maryland, this was one of the first fine-textured cakes mentioned in old cookery books. It required a delicate touch in mixing and exact measurements — this, in the days of no standard measuring cups, teaspoons, or tablespoons. This makes a large three-layer cake, and you may prefer to make just two layers.

Cream the butter until very fluffy. Slowly cream in the sugar, and continue creaming until the mixture is like whipped cream. Sift the flour with the dry ingredients. Add a little to the creamed mixture, then add a little milk mixed with the flavorings, and continue alternating, ending with flour. Mix until a smooth batter is achieved. If using an electric mixer, cream the butter and sugar at medium speed, then turn off the mixer and add the dry ingredients. Set at lowest speed and pour the milk and flavorings down along the beaters. Keep the dough scraped down from the sides of the bowl. When the batter is well combined, fold in the beaten egg whites — best done by hand. Turn the batter into three 8 or 9 inch pans that have been greased and the bottom lined with greased letter paper. Bake in a 350-degree oven for about 25 minutes or until the center of the cake springs back when touched with a fingertip. Let cool for 5 minutes on a rack, then loosen around the edges with a spatula and turn out onto the rack. Allow to cool out of drafts. Spread two layers with Lady Baltimore filling. Frost the top and sides with seven-minute icing.

Lady Baltimore Filling

6 soft dried figs, finely cut
½ cup finely chopped seeded raisins
3 tablespoons Cognac
½ cup toasted, finely chopped pecans
1 recipe seven-minute frosting (see page 694)

Combine the fruits and Cognac and let stand 1 hour or more. Prepare the seven-minute frosting in the top of a double boiler, then transfer the top to a bowl of ice water and continue beating until the mixture is cooled. Fold in the fruit and nuts and spread between layers of cake.

Note. One may make a double recipe of frosting and divide into two parts — one for the filling and one for the frosting.

Lord Baltimore (Egg Yolk) Cake

¾ cup butter
1¼ cups sugar
8 egg yolks
3 cups sifted cake flour
3½ teaspoons baking powder

As a result of making Lady Baltimore Cake, there were egg yolks left. These often ended in a Lord Baltimore yellow cake, generally made in a tube pan.

Cream the butter well and cream in the sugar until fluffy. Beat the egg yolks until very light and lemon-colored and stir into the creamed ingredients. Sift the dry ingredients and stir in alternately with the milk and flavorings. If making with a mixer, add the egg yolks a few at a time to the creamed mixture and beat very well. Stop the mixer and add the sifted dry ingredients. Set the mixer at lowest speed, add the milk and flavorings gradually, and mix thoroughly. Turn into a well-greased 10-inch tube pan or into a sheet pan 11 × 14 × 2 inches. Bake in a 350-degree oven about 1 hour for the tube pan, about 45 minutes for the sheet pan. The cake is done when it springs back when touched lightly with a fingertip. Cool on a rack. The tube cake is usually removed from the pan after cooling about 15 minutes. When the cake is cool, frost with seafoam frosting.

½ teaspoon salt
¾ cup milk
1 teaspoon grated lemon rind and 1 teaspoon vanilla or 1 tablespoon dark rum

Egg Yolk Spice Cake. Use 2¾ cups sifted cake flour. Sift in with the dry ingredients ¼ cup cocoa, 1½ teaspoons cinnamon, ¾ teaspoon nutmeg, ½ teaspoon allspice, and ½ teaspoon ground cloves.

Fruit Upside Down Cake

⅓ cup melted butter
1 cup light brown or white sugar (depending upon fruit used)
Fruit
A butter cake (such as two-egg cake) or a sponge cake

Upside down cakes of many varieties have been known for generations, but most cooks think only of using pineapple.

This amount of butter and sugar is enough for a 10 × 14 × 2-inch sheet cake pan, two 9-inch square cake pans, or two 10-inch skillets. Melt the butter in the bottom of the pan. This is done easiest by putting the pan in the oven that is heating for the cake. Do not let the butter brown. Sprinkle the sugar evenly over the bottom of the pan. Lay well-drained slices of pineapple, halves of fresh or canned apricots, peeled fresh or canned sliced peaches, halved fresh or moist-dried prunes, pitted sweet cherries, or any fruit — or mixture of fruit — of your choice. Sometimes two kinds of fruit such as apricots and prunes are used alternately. If you like, put coarsely chopped nuts or maraschino cherries between the pieces of fruit for decoration and flavor.

Top the fruit with cake batter of your choosing; either a butter cake or a sponge cake is used most often. For the 10 × 14 inch pan, the standard two-egg cake, either one-bowl or conventional, provides the right amount. Or make a sponge cake using 4 to 6 eggs. Other types of cakes sometimes used include chocolate cake with apricots; spice cake with prunes, or with pears, which may be sprinkled with a little candied ginger; and orange cake with peaches.

Bake the cake as usual, allowing about 10 minutes more baking time. When the cake is pressed lightly in the center and springs back, it is done. Let it stand in the pan on a rack for 5 minutes; then loosen the edges, put a plate over the pan, and quickly invert the cake onto the plate. Serve hot or cold with or without whipped cream or ice cream.

Pineapple White Cake

½ cup butter
1 cup sugar
2 cups sifted cake flour
½ teaspoon baking soda
2 teaspoons baking powder
¼ teaspoon salt
1 cup crushed pineapple with most of juice drained
1 teaspoon lemon juice
4 egg whites

A moist cake, delicate in flavor.

Cream the butter well, and cream in the sugar until very light. Sift the flour with the soda, baking powder, and salt, and add alternately to the butter mixture with the pineapple and lemon juice. Combine thoroughly, but do not overbeat. Beat the egg whites stiff and fold into the cake batter. Turn into two 9-inch round cake pans and bake in a moderate 350-degree oven 25 to 30 minutes or until the cake springs back when pressed lightly in the center with a finger. Let cool 5 minutes on a cake rack, then loosen from the pan and turn onto the rack. Frost with pineapple fluffy frosting, using pineapple juice instead of water in standard recipe. Often coconut is put on the frosting. If you like, add ½ cup very well drained crushed pineapple to about three-quarters of the recipe for fluffy frosting, and spread between the layers.

Cream Cake

1 cup heavy cream
1 cup sugar
2 eggs
1 teaspoon vanilla
2 cups sifted cake flour
2 teaspoons baking powder
½ teaspoon salt

This was often made with the sour cream that collected on top of the milk pans or on top of the milk bottles, before the days of homogenization. This recipe uses heavy (whipping) cream instead.

Put the cream in a mixing bowl and beat with an electric mixer or rotary beater until fluffy. Add the sugar gradually, and after about half of it is added, add the eggs and vanilla and continue to add the sugar and beat until the mixture is very light and fluffy. Sift the flour with the baking powder and salt, fold into the cream mixture, and immediately turn into a greased and floured 9×12×2½-inch baking pan or into two 8-inch greased and floured pans. Bake in a preheated moderate 350-degree oven about 25 minutes for layers or 35 for a sheet cake. Test with a fingertip. When the cake springs back from light pressure, it is done. Cool a few minutes on a cake rack, then loosen from the pan and turn out on the rack. Good with many kinds of frosting.

Sour Cream Cake. This recipe does not work with commercial sour cream, which does not have enough butterfat content. To the cup of sweet whipping cream add 1 tablespoon vinegar and stir in well. Let stand 15 minutes. Use ½ teaspoon soda and 1 teaspoon baking powder as leavening.

Chocolate Cream Cake or Sour Cream Cake. Use only 1¾ cups flour and add 1 ounce bitter chocolate, melted, to either the sweet or sour cream cake recipe. Add the chocolate before the flour.

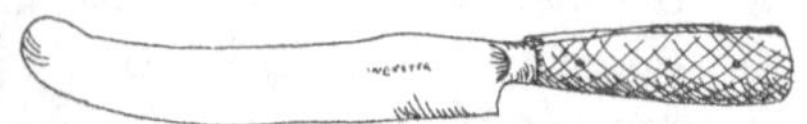

One-Egg Cake

¼ to ⅓ cup butter
1 cup sugar
1 egg
2 cups sifted cake flour
3 teaspoons baking powder
½ teaspoon salt
¾ cup milk
1 teaspoon vanilla

This cake is the foundation of Boston Cream Pie, Washington Pie, and Parker House Chocolate Pie. Then there is the Martha Washington or "Mrs. Washington's Pie" that is still another variation. Old recipes invariably called for sour milk or buttermilk and soda, but we'll give the sweet milk version.

Cream the butter, cream in the sugar, and beat in the egg until the mixture is very light. Sift the dry ingredients together and add alternately with the milk and vanilla. When using an electric mixer, add the flour at low speed. Turn the batter into two 8 or 9 inch cake pans. Bake in a preheated 350-degree oven about 25 minutes or until the cake tests done — it will spring back from a light pressure in the center. Put the pan on a rack to cool 5 minutes, then loosen the cake and turn out on the rack to cool.

Washington Pie. When the cake is cool, spread one layer generously with raspberry jam (sometimes jelly was used), top with the second layer, and sprinkle with sifted powdered sugar. Sometimes a lace paper doily was placed on top of the cake and the sugar sprinkled through it to form a pretty pattern.

Boston Cream Pie. Make a cream filling — beat 2 eggs slightly with a spoon or fork, then stir in ½ cup sugar, 5 tablespoons flour, ¼ teaspoon salt, and 2 cups scalded milk (scald over low heat or in a double boiler). Cook and stir over low heat until the mixture has boiled 1 minute. Let cool, and stir in ½ teaspoon vanilla and 1 tablespoon butter. Cool thoroughly. Spread between the cake layers. Sprinkle the top layer with powdered sugar. (*Note.* In recent years, sponge cake layers are sometimes used for this recipe.)

Parker House Chocolate Cream Pie. This is simply Boston Cream Pie with a thin layer of chocolate butter icing on top.

Martha Washington Pie. This is mentioned in a number of old cookbooks. Sometimes it is the same as Washington Pie, and at other times it uses a cream filling, made as above, on the bottom layer, raspberry jelly on a middle layer, and a sprinkling of powdered sugar on the top layer.

Lazy Daisy Cake

2 eggs
1 cup sugar
1 teaspoon vanilla
1 cup sifted all-purpose flour
¼ teaspoon salt

This cake has many names, but for the past forty years has generally been called by the "lazy" name. It does not have as fine texture as some other cakes but is meant to be served warm with a fruit sauce or topped with a broiled frosting. This was one of those cakes to be made when you suddenly discovered there was no dessert or unexpected guests arrived just before mealtime.

Beat the eggs until light and beat in the sugar gradually until the

1 teaspoon baking powder
½ cup milk
1 tablespoon butter

mixture is light and thick. Beat in the vanilla. Sift the flour with the salt and baking powder. In the meantime heat the milk just to scalding (when a slight scum begins to form) with the butter. Add the dry ingredients to the beaten eggs alternately with the hot milk. Stir just to mix. Turn into a greased 9-inch square baking pan and bake in a preheated 350-degree oven about 30 minutes or until the cake springs back when pressed lightly in the center. Serve iced or plain while still warm, or with fruit, chocolate or caramel sauce, or ice cream. The cake may also be eaten cold with whipped cream, icing, or fruit.

Bride's Cake or White Loaf Cake

2 cups butter
2 cups granulated or 3 cups powdered sugar
4½ cups sifted cake flour
5 teaspoons baking powder
1 teaspoon salt
1½ cups milk
1 teaspoon vanilla
½ teaspoon almond extract or 2 tablespoons light rum and ½ teaspoon nutmeg
8 to 10 egg whites

The cake was often baked by a good neighbor of the mother of the bride, especially during the era of smaller communities where there was no bakery. A variation of loaf cake, made white with the egg whites, it was baked in deep round or square pans. Graduating sizes of "tin milk pans" about 4 inches deep were the usual baking pan. The size and amount of cake it took to fill each pan depended upon the number of guests, but appetites were hearty and cakes large, despite the fact that other food was plentiful.

Cream the butter very well and cream in the sugar until fluffy and light. As in making any cake, the ingredients whip up lighter and better if all are at room temperature. Sift the dry ingredients together and add to the butter mixture alternately with the milk and flavorings. Beat the egg whites until stiff but not dry — the beater, when lifted, should form soft peaks that flop over — and fold into the first mixture with a rubber spatula or frilled whip. When well blended, turn into three or four 9-inch layer tins, two 11 × 14 × 2-inch sheet tins, a 12 or 14 inch round pan or a 10-inch tube pan, greased and floured and lined with greased paper. Fill not more than a little over half full. This will be a heavy batter, so it should be smoothed evenly over the top before baking. Baked in two regular loaf pans, it will take from 60 to 75 minutes. Test for doneness with the tip of the finger; when the cake springs back, it is done.

For a wedding, the cake was traditionally frosted with a boiled fluffy icing. After this was cool and a slight crust had formed, it was decorated with royal icing or decorating icing; or, lacking that, the platter was decorated with fresh flowers, and flowers were stuck into the center of the cake at the last minute.

Greenfield or Quick Tea Cake

2 cups sifted all-purpose flour
3 teaspoons baking powder
½ teaspoon salt
½ cup sugar
½ cup butter
1 cup milk
1 egg, unbeaten
½ cup seedless raisins

TOPPING

¾ cup sugar
1 to 3 teaspoons cinnamon

Good as a tea cake, a quick coffee cake for breakfast, or a quick dessert for lunch or dinner. This has many versions and many toppings.

Sift the flour, baking powder, salt, and sugar into a mixing bowl. Work in the butter with pastry blender or fingertips until the mixture resembles meal. Add the milk and egg, and stir in just until the dry ingredients are moistened. Stir in the raisins. Turn into a well-greased pan about 10 × 14 × 2 inches or into two 8-inch pans. Mix the sugar and cinnamon, sprinkle over the top, and bake in a preheated moderate to moderately hot oven, 375 to 400 degrees. This is good served cold but better when served warm. Some people prefer it with butter dotted over the cinnamon and sugar.

Quick Streusel Coffee Cake. Omit the raisins, if you like, and instead sprinkle the top with a streusel mixture, made as follows. In an electric mixer or with the fingertips, mix 4 tablespoons butter, 2 tablespoons flour, ⅓ to ½ cup white or firmly packed brown sugar, ½ to 1 teaspoon cinnamon, ¼ cup finely chopped almonds or other nuts. Sprinkle on the cake. The traditional streusel uses only almonds, but you don't have to be traditional.

Glenna McGinnis Lane Cake

1 cup butter
2 cups sugar
1 teaspoon vanilla
3¼ cups sifted all-purpose flour
3½ teaspoons double-acting baking powder
1 teaspoon salt
1 cup milk
8 egg whites

FILLING AND FROSTING

12 egg yolks
1¾ cups sugar
½ teaspoon salt
¾ cup butter
½ cup rye or bourbon whiskey
1½ cups coarsely chopped toasted pecans
1½ cups shredded fresh or flake coconut
1½ cups chopped seeded raisins

This Southern cake, considered a holiday cake, has a rich filling and is sometimes frosted with fluffy white icing. The McGinnis family have always used the filling as the frosting also, which makes the cake a long-keeping special — if you hide it.

Grease four round 9-inch layer cake pans with a little butter. Fit the bottoms with wax paper and butter the paper. If you have only two pans this size, bake only two layers at a time. Cream the butter until very fluffy; this is easiest done within the large bowl of the electric mixer. Cream in the sugar gradually. The mixture should be very light. Add the vanilla and beat a few seconds to mix. Sift the dry ingredients together several times. Add alternately with the milk to the creamed mixture. If using an electric mixer, turn it off, sprinkle in the flour mixture, then resume mixing at lowest speed, and slowly pour the milk in the center. Do not overmix, but mix just enough to incorporate flour evenly. Beat the egg whites until stiff but not at all dry. When the beater is lifted, they should have soft peaks that turn at the top. Fold into the cake batter carefully, using a rubber spatula or frilled whip. Spread evenly in the four cake pans. Bake in a preheated moderate 350-degree oven about 25 minutes or until the cake has shrunk from the sides of the pan and the center springs back when pressed lightly with the finger. Transfer to a rack and let stand 10 minutes to cool. Loosen from the pan and turn out on the rack to cool thoroughly. While it cools, make the filling-frosting.

Put the egg yolks in the top of a double boiler and beat slightly with rotary or electric beater. Add the sugar, salt, and butter. Cook over simmering water — the water should not touch the pan containing the yolks — stirring constantly until the sugar is dissolved, the butter melted, and the mixture slightly thickened. Do not overcook or the eggs will separate and harden like scrambled eggs. Remove from the heat, add the bourbon or rye whiskey, beat 1 minute with rotary or electric beater, and stir in nuts, coconut, and raisins. Cool and spread between layers and on the top and sides of the cake. After an hour, if any of the frosting has dripped from the cake, spread it back on. If you like, decorate the top, or top and sides, with halved pecans, preferably toasted. This cake is much better if left to age at least 3 to 5 days, covered, in a cool dry place. It will keep well as long as 3 or 4 weeks stored in this manner. It also freezes well. This is traditionally a handsome four-layer cake, but can be made as two two-layer cakes.

Old-Fashioned Six-Layer Cake

1/3 cup butter
1 1/2 cups sugar
3 eggs
2 1/4 cups sifted cake flour
2 1/2 teaspoons baking powder
1/4 teaspoon salt
3/4 cup milk
1 teaspoon vanilla

The sort of cake made for special occasions, since it is towering and impressive. Taken to church socials, it was generally made in double form — 12 layers — and the minister was given the first helping. Most often made with chocolate frosting, it was sometimes filled with sweetened whipped cream and thin-sliced bananas, which turned it into a real showpiece.

Cream the butter well, and cream in the sugar until a fluffy mixture is formed. Beat in the eggs one at a time. If mixing the cake by hand, it will be easier to cream about half the sugar into the butter, then beat in the eggs, and finally the remaining sugar. Sift the flour with the baking powder and salt, and add alternately with the milk and vanilla. Spread very thin in six 8 or 9 inch round layer cake pans that have been well greased. Or grease and flour three layer-cake pans to make layers to split later. Bake in a 375-degree preheated oven about 15 minutes for thin layers (six) and about 25 minutes for thicker layers. Test by pressing the center of the cake lightly with the finger. When done, the cake will spring back. Cool in the pans on racks for 5 to 10 minutes, then loosen and turn out on the racks to cool. If baking thick layers, place on the edge of the table or counter and with a sharp knife cut each in half horizontally to make two layers. Put together with old-fashioned chocolate frosting, or use sweetened whipped cream, plain or with fruits such as thin-sliced bananas.

Poppy Seed Cake

¾ cup poppy seeds
¾ cup milk, scalded
½ cup butter
1½ cups sugar
2 cups sifted all-purpose flour
3 teaspoons baking powder
½ teaspoon salt
1 teaspoon vanilla or 1 teaspoon grated lemon rind
4 egg whites

Thoroughly American, this is very different from the Mid-European poppy seed torte or mohntorte. It is a light cake, while the European version is firm in texture. Before starting this, smell the poppy seeds you have purchased, and if they smell rancid, do not use them.

Put the poppy seeds through the fine blade of a grinder or in a coffee mill, or whirl in a blender, or place between two layers of wax paper and roll until well broken up. Put in a bowl and pour in the scalding hot milk. Let stand until the milk has cooled to room temperature. Meantime cream the butter, cream in the sugar, and sift the flour with the baking powder and salt. Add the vanilla to the poppy seed mixture and add alternately with the flour mixture to the creamed butter and sugar. Beat the egg whites until stiff but not dry (they should come to peak and turn over slightly when the beater is lifted). Fold into the cake mixture very carefully. Turn into three greased and floured 8 or 9 inch cake pans. These will be rather thin layers, but the cake should be put together with a custard filling, made as for cream pie, and is better if assembled in three layers. Or bake in two 8-inch layer cake pans, then split the layers when cool, making a four-layer cake. Bake in a preheated 350-degree oven about 20 to 25 minutes. The cake is done when it shrinks from the sides of the pan and springs back when pressed lightly in the center. Cool a few minutes in the pan on a rack, then loosen in pan and turn out on the rack to cool. When cool, fill the layers with cream filling and top with a clear vanilla glaze or with a thin layer of butter frosting. Often the whole cake is covered with chocolate butter frosting.

Coconut Cake

1 cup firmly packed fresh grated coconut or commercial shredded or flaked coconut
1 cup scalded milk (coconut milk, if possible, supplemented by ordinary milk)
¾ cup butter
1½ cups sugar
1 teaspoon vanilla
3 cups sifted cake flour
4 teaspoons baking powder
¾ teaspoon salt
4 egg whites

The coconut flavor can come from using both coconut milk and shredded coconut in the cake or simply from sprinkling coconut over the frosting.

Put the coconut in a small mixing bowl and pour the scalded milk over it. Let stand until cool, then drain. If using the coconut in the cake, drain well by pressing in a strainer. If it is not fine enough to distribute well in the cake, chop it to make it finer. Cream the butter very well. Cream in the sugar until very light, adding the vanilla. Sift the flour with the baking powder and salt, and add alternately with the milk to the creamed mixture. Fold in the coconut, if using it in the cake. Beat the egg whites until stiff but not dry and fold into the cake mixture. Turn into two 10 or 11 inch greased and floured cake pans or two deep 9-inch cake pans. Bake in a preheated 350-degree oven 25 to 35 minutes. Test for doneness by touching lightly in the center. If it springs back, it is done. Remove to a rack and cool about 10 minutes. Loosen from the pan and turn out on the rack to cool. Frost with fluffy, seven-minute, or white boiled icing, and sprinkle with coconut before the frosting has begun to dry. Orange, lemon, or pineapple filling is superb in this cake.

This cake can be made in the electric mixer. Many people, however, still prefer to beat the egg whites separately and fold them in at the last. If you are not beating them separately, beat them into the creamed butter and sugar mixture at high speed. Reduce to lowest speed to add the flour and milk, and mix thoroughly, but do not overmix.

Scandinavian Gold Cake

1 cup soft butter
1 1/3 cups sifted all-purpose flour
5 eggs
1 1/3 cups sugar
1 1/2 teaspoons baking powder
1/2 teaspoon salt
1/2 teaspoon almond extract

Place the butter and flour in a mixing bowl. If using an electric mixer, mix 5 minutes on low speed or until the mixture is like meal and well blended. Or mix with the fingertips. Again on low speed, add the eggs one at a time. Or beat them in one at a time by hand with a whip or wooden or slotted spoon. Sift the sugar, baking powder, and salt together. Sift over the flour, butter and egg mixture, add the flavoring, and mix at low speed. Or, if mixing by hand, add gradually with the flavoring, and fold into first mixture. Turn into a greased and floured 10-inch tube pan. Bake in a preheated 325-degree oven about 1 hour or until the cake springs back when touched lightly in the center. Turn out on a rack to cool. This cake is so rich that it is usually served without frosting, but sometimes a lace paper doily is put on the top and powdered sugar is sifted through the doily to leave a pattern. It is frequently served as a coffee cake.

White Mountain Cake

1/2 cup butter
1 1/2 cups sugar
2 1/2 cups sifted cake flour
3 teaspoons baking powder
1/4 teaspoon salt
1 cup milk
1 teaspoon vanilla
4 egg whites, stiffly beaten

This was also called Colorado cake, and was sometimes baked in graduated cake pans to give a mountain effect. Later the cake was usually baked in a tube pan and heaped with white fluffy or white mountain icing.

Cream the butter and cream in the sugar until very light and fluffy. Sift the flour with other dry ingredients three times to incorporate as much air in the mixture as possible. Fold into the creamed mixture alternately with the milk and vanilla. For this particular cake, it is preferable to do the folding in of flour and milk by hand. Fold in the egg whites, which have been beaten until stiff but not dry. Turn into a greased and floured tube pan, or, fit a piece of paper into the bottom of the pan and grease this and the sides and tube. Bake in a preheated 350-degree oven 45 to 60 minutes or until the cake is pulling away from the sides of the pan and the cake springs back when touched lightly with the fingertip. Cool in the pan on a rack for 15 to 20 minutes before loosening from the sides and around the tube of the pan. Invert on the rack, and when cool heap with white mountain or white fluffy icing.

Blueberry Cake with Bourbon Cream

CAKE

1 cup butter
1 cup sugar
4 eggs
¼ teaspoon vanilla
¼ teaspoon salt
1 cup sifted cake flour

BOURBON CREAM FROSTING

1½ tablespoons cream
½ egg white (1 tablespoon)
1 tablespoon butter
1 pound confectioners' sugar
4 eggs
4 tablespoons bourbon
1 quart blueberries

Cream the butter, then cream in the sugar until light. Beat in the eggs one at a time with the vanilla, until well mixed. Sift the flour and salt over the mixture, and fold in gently. Have ready 6 or 7 rounds of baking parchment or greased paper, 7 or 8 inches across. Place on baking sheets and spread a very thin layer of batter on each round. Bake 3 minutes in a preheated moderate 375-degree oven. Let cool slightly before removing from paper. Cool.

For the frosting and filling, make a fondant by combining the cream, egg white, butter, and confectioners' sugar. Mix very well until light. Beat in the eggs and bourbon. Reserve 1 cup of this, and mix the blueberries into the rest. When the cake is cool, spread the blueberry filling between the layers. Chill the reserved cup of frosting until of spreading consistency, and spread it on top of the cake.

Pound Cake

2 cups butter
2 cups sugar
8 to 10 large eggs, separated
2 tablespoons rum, brandy, or orange juice
1 teaspoon vanilla
4½ cups sifted cake flour
¾ teaspoon salt

Every homemaker in the late nineteenth and early twentieth century kept a loaf or two of this cake in the pantry to serve to unexpected callers. As in 1-2-3-4 cake, the name is derived from the quantity of the ingredients — a pound each of butter, sugar, eggs, and flour.

Cream the butter until very fluffy, easiest done with an electric mixer. Cream in the sugar, or reserve ½ cup for the egg whites. The butter and sugar mixture should be like sweetened whipped cream in texture. If using a mixer, drop the egg yolks in one at a time with mixer on medium to high speed. If mixing by hand, beat the yolks with a rotary beater or whisk until very light and lemon-colored. Add to the butter and sugar mixture and beat vigorously. The mixture should be even lighter after the egg yolks are added. Stir or beat in the flavorings. It is customary to use several flavorings — that is, a combination of orange juice and vanilla or rum, or brandy with a little vanilla, or 1 tablespoon each of rum and brandy. (Some cooks insist that pound cake should also have 1 teaspoon of nutmeg or mace added, which was invariably true of New England pound cakes.) Sift the flour with salt, then sift several times more, holding the sifter high to incorporate as much air as possible. Stir into the creamed mixture until well blended. If using an electric mixer, do this at lowest speed. In any event, be sure to keep the batter wiped down from the sides and bottom of the bowl with a rubber or plastic spatula. Beat the egg whites until foamy, and if you like add 1 teaspoon lemon juice or cream of tartar at this point to stabilize the egg whites. If you have reserved ½ cup of sugar, add it gradually during beating of whites. Beat until stiff but not dry — the mixture should hold soft peaks. Fold into the cake batter with a rubber spatula. Turn immediately into two buttered and lightly floured loaf pans 9 × 5 × 3 inches. Or use smaller loaf pans, filling a little more than half full. (This cake works better in loaf than in sheet cake pans.) Bake in a moderately slow 325-degree oven for about an hour, depending upon size of the pans used — It may take 1¼ hours. Test by pressing the center of the cake lightly with the finger. When the cake springs back, and it has pulled away from the sides of the pan, it is done. Transfer to a rack and cool about 15 minutes before loosening from the pan and turning out on the rack to cool. Pound cake is generally considered best after a day or two of "resting." Store in a tightly covered container or place in plastic bags and seal. If kept for several weeks, it is better if stored in the refrigerator. It freezes well. Pound cake is not frosted.

Seed Cake. A variation of pound cake, which itself is made in a variety of ways in different sections of the country, true seed cake supposedly uses only 1 teaspoon to 1 tablespoon of caraway seed, stirred in with the flour. Other variations include adding, with the seeds, ½ cup finely shaved citron and 1 teaspoon grated lemon rind, and adding 4 teaspoons baking powder with the flour.

Fruit Cake with Pound Cake Base

- *1 recipe basic pound cake, using 3½ cups flour instead of 4½ (in this version all-purpose flour can be used)*
- *1½ cups seeded raisins*
- *1½ cups white raisins*
- *1½ cups currants*
- *1 tablespoon grated orange rind*
- *1 teaspoon grated lemon rind*
- *3 cups chopped mixed candied fruits*

This is an old standard, and the amount of nut meats, raisins, currants, and candied fruits used varies considerably. When using a total of more than 1 cup raisins, 1 cup currants, and 1 cup nuts, the temperature is lowered to 275 degrees and the cake is baked longer. Here is a mixture that gives a very fruity, rich cake. Whole eggs can be added to the creamed butter and sugar in the basic pound cake, if you like.

Rinse the raisins and currants with hot tap water and spread on a paper towel to dry. They will plump slightly. Or instead of plumping them, put all the fruits in a glass or porcelain bowl, add ½ cup sherry, brandy, or light rum, and let stand overnight, stirring a number of times until the fruit has absorbed the liquor. Add the nuts to the fruits and sprinkle with the flour.

1 cup candied cherries, whole or cut in half
1 cup moist-dried apricots, cut in small strips (optional)
2 cups halved or very coarsely chopped walnuts, pecans, almonds, Brazil nuts, or filberts
1 cup flour

Fold rather than stir the fruits and nuts into the pound cake batter — and you'll need a bowl larger than the electric mixer bowl for it, unless you have an institutional-size mixer. I like to mix this and any large fruit cake with the hands. First prepare the baking pans, then scatter the fruits and nuts on the pound cake batter, put your hands into the cake mixture, and bring the batter up and through the fruit and nuts to mix thoroughly. It is also often easiest to use hands to put the batter into the pans.

Baking pans should be filled not more than two-thirds full and should be well greased and lightly floured. If using tube pans, crown molds, or loaf pans that are old and blackened, better line the pans, both bottom and sides, with one or two layers of greased wrapping paper (I prefer this for fruit cakes rather than wax paper). Bake the cakes in a preheated slow oven, 275 degrees, for 1 to 3 hours, depending upon the sizes of the pans used. An ordinary loaf pan 9 × 5 × 3 inches will take about 1½ hours or slightly more, depending upon how full it is. If the cake springs back when pressed lightly in the center, it is done. It will also have begun to leave the sides of the pan.

When the cakes are done, glaze the tops by brushing on white corn syrup, preferably while they are still hot. This is also a good time to stick on any fruit and nut decoration you might like on the top. Cool in the pans. Remove, brush with brandy, bourbon, rum, or other liquor. Wrap well in aluminum foil — or easier, put into freezer bags — and seal. Brush with more liquor from time to time, if you like.

Simnel Cake

FILLING

6 to 7 ounces almond paste (this can be purchased in cans or sometimes in plastic bags)
⅓ cup softened butter
1 egg yolk

CAKE

¾ cup butter
1 cup unsifted all-purpose flour
3 eggs
½ cup sugar
¼ teaspoon salt
1 cup dried currants
⅓ cup chopped mixed candied fruit peel

Brought from England, this has been a classic for many years. Traditionally it was served in England on "Mithering Day," or as we would call it, Mother's Day.

For the filling, blend the ingredients until smooth. Set aside.

For the cake, cream the butter to a light fluffiness, and cream in the flour until well blended. This can be done with some electric mixers. Or rub in with the fingertips until evenly mixed with the butter. In another bowl beat the eggs until very light, and beat in the sugar and salt. Beat until very light and fluffy. Fold into the flour and butter mixture with the currants and candied fruit. Turn half the mixture into a buttered and floured 8-inch spring form pan. Put about half the filling on top of the cake batter in the pan. Add the remainder of the cake batter, and smooth it. Immediately put into a preheated moderately slow oven, 325 degrees, and bake about 1 hour. The cake should be set if it springs back when pressed lightly in the center. Remove from the oven, pipe the rest of the filling onto the top of the cake with a pastry tube, and return to the oven to lightly brown the topping (this will take 10 to 15 minutes). When the top is brown, transfer the cake to a rack. Loosen the edges and remove the rim from the pan. Allow the cake to cool on the rack.

Fabulous Nut Cake

2 pounds shelled pecans, walnuts or black walnuts
6 eggs
1 cup butter
1½ cups sugar
¾ cup milk
¼ cup Cognac
1 teaspoon almond extract
3⅓ cups sifted all-purpose flour
1 teaspoon cream of tartar

This cake keeps well for weeks when stored in a cool, dry place or in a cool place sealed in a freezer bag. It also freezes wonderfully.

Chop the nuts coarsely. Separate the eggs and beat the yolks slightly. Cream the butter, and then cream in the sugar until very fluffy. Add the yolks and beat until very light. Mix the milk, Cognac, and almond extract. Sift the flour, and add alternately with the milk to the first mixture. Add the nuts and mix well (sometimes easiest done with the hands). Beat the egg whites until foamy, add cream of tartar, and beat until they are stiff and hold a definite point when the beater is lifted. Fold into the cake mixture until well blended. Turn into a 10-inch tube pan that has been greased and floured or line the bottom with greased paper and grease the pan as well. Bake in a preheated slow oven, 275 degrees, about 2½ hours or more. When done, the cake will shrink from the sides of the pan and will spring back when touched lightly in the center with a fingertip. Cool on a rack 30 minutes before loosening from the pan and turning out on a rack to finish cooling. Do not ice the cake, but sprinkle with powdered sugar, if desired.

Whiskey, Moonshine, or Feuding Cake

1 pound walnuts, shelled (about 1¾ cups)
½ pound seeded raisins (1½ cups)
1½ cups sifted all-purpose flour
1 teaspoon double acting baking powder
½ teaspoon salt
½ cup butter
1⅛ cups sugar (1 cup plus 2 tablespoons)
3 eggs
2 teaspoons grated nutmeg
⅔ cup bourbon whiskey

This cake is moist and rich and will keep well. Makes a good gift from the kitchen when baked in short one-pound coffee cans. Or bake in small or large loaf pans.

Chop the nuts coarsely and cut the raisins in half. Use ½ cup of the flour to sprinkle over the nuts and raisins. Sift the remaining 1 cup of flour with the baking powder and salt. Cream the butter well, cream in the sugar, and beat or mix until fluffy. If using an electric mixer, add whole eggs. If mixing by hand, separate the eggs and beat in the yolks one at a time. Mix the nutmeg and whiskey together and add alternately with the flour to the creamed mixture. If using a mixer, turn it off, sprinkle the flour over the batter, and pour the whiskey-nutmeg in the center. Mix on lowest speed. Fold in the nuts and raisins. If mixing by hand, beat the whites until stiff but not dry and fold in at this point. Turn into a loaf cake pan (or pans) that has been greased and floured. Or line the bottom and sides with greased letter paper or brown wrapping paper. Bake in a preheated 325-degree oven 50 to 75 minutes, depending on the size of pan. Test by pressing the center with a fingertip; if the cake springs back, it is done. Transfer to a rack and let cool in pans for 1 hour before turning out onto the rack. Dribble more bourbon whiskey over the cake when cool, if you like, or brush it on the sides and bottom of the cake. Store in a cool, dry place, well covered, or slip into freezer bags, and store.

Burnt Leather, Brownstone Front, or Caramel Cake

CARAMEL SYRUP

1 cup sugar
1 cup hot water

CAKE

½ cup butter
1 cup minus 2 tablespoons sugar
2 eggs
4 tablespoons caramel syrup
2 cups sifted cake flour
3 teaspoons baking powder
½ teaspoon salt
¾ cup milk
1 teaspoon vanilla or 1 tablespoon rum

This has many more names, some of them very local. All evolved from the fact that the caramelized sugar makes the cake a rich brown.

Use a heavy skillet for the caramelizing. Put in the sugar and stir over moderate heat until it is a rich brown color and completely liquid. Remove from the heat and add the hot water. This will sputter, so stand back a bit. Return to the heat and cook and stir just until the sugar is again liquefied. Turn into a cup and cool.

For the cake, cream the butter, then cream in the sugar until very fluffy (easiest done with an electric mixer). Beat in the eggs and then the caramel syrup. Sift the flour with the baking powder and salt and add alternately with the milk and vanilla to the creamed mixture. If using an electric mixer, turn it off, pour in the flour, pour the milk in the center, set the mixer at lowest speed, and beat in the flour and milk. Turn into two 8 or 9 inch greased and floured layer cake pans, or greased and with the bottom fitted with greased paper. Bake in a preheated 350-degree oven about 25 minutes, or until the cake springs back when pressed lightly in the center. Cool in the pans on a rack for 10 minutes, then loosen and turn out onto the cake rack to cool. Frost with fluffy caramel icing, or add the remaining caramel syrup (there should be about 3 tablespoons left) to basic butter icing, and frost. Or use the syrup as the liquid in a 1-egg white or 2-egg white fluffy, double boiler, or seven-minute frosting.

Date Nut Torte

1 cup chopped pitted dates
¾ teaspoon baking soda
1 cup boiling water
3 tablespoons butter, melted
1 cup white sugar or 1¼ cups firmly packed brown sugar
1 egg
1 cup sifted all-purpose flour
½ cup coarsely chopped walnuts

Place the dates in a small bowl, sprinkle with the soda, and pour the boiling water over them. Put aside to cool. In a mixing bowl, cream the butter and sugar together until blended and beat in the egg until the mixture is light. Add the date mixture, then the flour and nuts that have been combined. Turn into a well-greased 8 or 9 inch square pan. Or bake in a thinner layer in a 10 × 12 × 2-inch pan, well greased. Bake in a 375-degree oven for 25 to 45 minutes, depending upon the size of pan used. When done, the cake will spring back when pressed lightly in the center. Serve hot or cold. This is often served rather more like a pudding, topped with whipped cream. Or, it is made in a thin layer, cut into thin strips and served as a tea cake.

Peanut Butter Cake or Cupcakes

1/3 cup butter
1 cup white or firmly packed brown sugar
1/2 cup peanut butter, crunch or creamy
2 eggs
2 cups sifted cake flour
3 teaspoons baking powder
1/2 teaspoon salt
3/4 cup milk
1 teaspoon vanilla

For peanut butter addicts *only*.

Cream the butter, and cream in the sugar and peanut butter. Beat in the eggs until fluffy (medium high speed on a mixer). Sift the dry ingredients together and add alternately with the milk and vanilla to the first mixture. Blend just until smooth. If using an electric mixer, set at lowest speed and add flour, then milk and vanilla. Mix until well blended, and use a rubber spatula to scrape down the sides and bottom of bowl. Turn into 12 to 18 well-greased cupcake pans or frilled paper cupcake holders set in muffin pans; or bake in two 8 or 9 inch layers or a 10 × 14 × 2-inch sheet pan. Grease and flour the cake pans. Bake in a moderate oven, 350 degrees, 15 to 25 minutes for layers or cupcakes or 35 minutes for sheet cake. Test by pressing lightly in the center of the cake. If it springs back, it is done. Cool the cake a few minutes, loosen it from the pan, and turn out on a wire rack to cool. Frost, if you like, with butter frosting, to which 1/2 cup chopped roasted peanuts have been added. Or use peanut butter instead of butter in the frosting.

Jam Cake

3/4 cup butter
1 cup sugar
3 eggs
1 cup thick jam
2 1/2 cups sifted all-purpose flour
1 teaspoon baking powder
1 teaspoon baking soda
1 teaspoon cinnamon
1/2 teaspoon each of allspice and nutmeg
1/4 teaspoon cloves
1/2 cup sour milk or buttermilk or 1/4 cup milk and 1/4 cup bourbon whiskey
1/2 cup nuts (optional)
1/2 cup seedless raisins (optional)

Moist and pretty in color when blackberry, currant, or some such jam was used, this was a favorite with pioneer women, for it kept well.

Cream the butter, then cream in the sugar until light. Beat in eggs one at a time (or if using electric mixer, add all at once and beat at high speed). Stir in the jam. Sift the flour with other dry ingredients, and if using raisins and nuts, toss them with a few tablespoons of the flour mixture. Add the flour mixture alternately with the liquid (or if using mixer, add the flour, then pour the liquid in the center). Mix on low speed until just combined. Fold in the nuts and raisins and turn into two greased and floured 9-inch layer cake pans or an 11 × 14 × 2 1/2-inch sheet cake pan. Bake in a preheated moderate 350-degree oven about 30 minutes for layers or 40 for sheet cake. Frost with jam, whipped cream, or fluffy frosting.

Southern Spicy Ginger Cake

2 eggs
3/4 cup firmly packed brown sugar
3/4 cup molasses (light preferred)

In a mixing bowl, beat the eggs and then beat in the sugar and molasses until very fluffy (easiest with electric mixer). Stir in the melted fat. (Many times, for family use, lard was used instead of butter, and often slightly less lard than the amount called for here was used.) Sift the dry ingredients together and stir into the first mixture. Add the boiling water and stir just to mix. Turn into a well-greased sheet pan about 10 × 14 × 2 inches. Bake in a preheated 350-degree oven about 35 minutes or until the cake springs back when pressed lightly in the center. Serve hot or cold, plain or topped with a fruit or chocolate sauce, whipped cream, or ice cream.

3/4 cup melted butter or lard
2 1/2 cups sifted all-purpose flour
1 teaspoon baking soda
1 teaspoon baking powder
1/2 teaspoon salt
1 1/2 to 2 teaspoons ginger
1/2 to 1 teaspoon cloves
1/2 teaspoon nutmeg
1 cup boiling water

Scripture or Bible Cake

This has many forms and is really just a variation of the old 1-2-3-4 Cake. It has been variously attributed to different states, so is sometimes called Missouri Scripture Cake or Vermont or New Hampshire Scripture Cake, etc.

1 cup butter	*Judges 5:25*
2 cups sugar	*Jeremiah 6:20*
6 eggs	*Isaiah 10:14*
1 tablespoon honey	*Exodus 16:31*
Spice to taste	*I Kings 10:2*
3 1/3 cups unsifted all-purpose flour	*I Kings 4:22*
4 teaspoons baking powder (not Biblical but it helps the cake)	
3/4 teaspoon salt (a little)	*Leviticus 2:13*
2 cups raisins	*I Samuel 30:12*
2 cups figs	*I Samuel 31:12*
1 cup almonds, chopped	*Genesis 30:12*
1 cup water (milk is better)	*Genesis 24:20*

To mix, follow Solomon's advice for making good boys—Proverbs 23:14.

I think you'll find it better, however, to mix this cake as you would any other, for overbeating will certainly not make a light cake. That is, cream the butter, cream in the sugar, beat in the eggs. Add the honey and either add the spices to it or sift them with the flour, baking powder, and salt. (Suggested spices are 1 1/2 teaspoons cinnamon, 1 teaspoon allspice, 1 teaspoon nutmeg, and 1/2 teaspoon cloves.) Sprinkle about 1/2 cup of the flour mixture over the raisins, figs, and nuts. The figs should be cut in small pieces, or use the same amount of cut-up dates. Add 1 cup chopped, candied fruit also, if you like, and other nuts can be used in place of the almonds. Lightly toasting them will give more flavor to the cake. Add the dry ingredients alternately with the water or milk. (Or use orange juice instead of water or milk. In this case use 1/2 teaspoon soda and

3 teaspoons baking powder for leavening. Adding 1 tablespoon grated orange rind will also make a tastier cake.) Add the fruits and nuts last, folding in thoroughly. Turn into two greased and floured loaf cake pans and bake in a preheated slow oven, 300 degrees, about 1½ hours, or until the cake has shrunk from the sides of the pan and the top springs back when pressed lightly in the center. Place on a rack to cool.

This was always considered a fruit cake and was aged at least 3 or 4 days before slicing. Often several were made a few months before using and rolled in a cloth — usually an old napkin that had been soaked in brandy or rum, depending upon the section of the country. Sometimes the "mountain dew" of Kentucky and Tennessee was used; or in some Southern states, sherry or port.

Mystery or Tomato Soup Cake

¼ cup butter (½ stick)
1 cup sugar
2 cups sifted all-purpose flour
1 teaspoon baking soda
¼ teaspoon salt
1 teaspoon cinnamon
1 teaspoon nutmeg
1 can (10¾ ounces) condensed tomato soup
1 teaspoon grated lemon rind
1 cup raisins
1 cup chopped toasted walnuts, pecans, filberts, or almonds

Originally this was made as a winter cake with canned tomatoes. Then condensed soup came into being, and the recipe was changed. Beating 1 or 2 eggs into the cake batter after the butter and sugar are creamed will make a richer cake. Also, this can be made into a layer or sheet cake with the addition of ¼ cup fruit juice, milk, or water.

Cream the butter and slowly cream in the sugar. Sift the dry ingredients together and sprinkle a few tablespoons of the mixture over the raisins and nuts. Add remainder to the creamed mixture alternately with the soup and lemon rind. Fold in the nuts and raisins. Turn into a greased and floured loaf pan, and bake in a preheated 350-degree oven about 1 hour, or until the center of the cake springs back when pressed lightly. Cool on a rack 10 minutes, then loosen from the pan and turn out onto the rack to cool. This is often frosted with a plain or chocolate cream cheese icing, or a plain, browned butter, or spiced butter icing.

Oatmeal Cake

1¼ cups boiling water
½ cup butter
1 cup rolled oats, quick-cooking or regular
1 cup white sugar
1 cup firmly packed brown sugar
2 eggs
1⅓ cups unsifted all-purpose flour
1 teaspoon baking soda

Though called oatmeal cake — and originally British immigrants, who brought the recipe, probably did use oatmeal — gradually recipes have changed to use more easily obtained rolled oats. There are many versions, some of which use nuts or raisins or cut-up prunes. There is a nice chewiness to these cakes.

In a mixing bowl put the boiling water, butter, and rolled oats. Stir and let stand 20 minutes. Add the sugars and eggs, and beat to blend. Add the remaining ingredients and stir just to mix. The mixture will be thin. Turn into a 9 × 13 × 2-inch pan, greased and floured. Bake in a preheated 350-degree oven 35 minutes or until the cake springs back when pressed gently with the finger. Cool

1 teaspoon baking powder
½ teaspoon salt
1 teaspoon cinnamon
½ teaspoon nutmeg
1 teaspoon vanilla (optional)

in the pan on a rack. Or immediately top with broiled nut frosting and put under the broiler for a few minutes, about 4 to 5 inches from heat, until the frosting bubbles. This burns easily, so watch carefully.

Pumpkin (or Squash) Spice Cake

½ cup butter
1 cup firmly packed brown sugar
2 eggs
¾ cup sieved cooked pumpkin (or winter squash)
2 cups sifted cake flour
½ teaspoon baking soda
1½ teaspoons baking powder
½ teaspoon salt
½ teaspoon cinnamon
½ teaspoon nutmeg
½ teaspoon allspice
½ teaspoon ginger
½ cup sour milk or buttermilk (or stir 1½ teaspoons vinegar into ½ cup sweet milk and allow to stand 10 minutes)
½ cup chopped toasted nuts (walnuts, pecans, filberts)

In a mixing bowl, cream the butter well, then cream in the sugar until fluffy. Beat in the eggs and the pumpkin. Sift the dry ingredients together and stir in alternately with the milk. If using an electric mixer, add the dry ingredients and milk and turn to lowest speed; push down the batter from the sides of the bowl with a rubber spatula, and mix just until the batter is smooth. Add the nuts and turn into a greased and floured sheet cake pan 11 × 14 × 2 inches or two 8 or 9 inch layer cake pans, greased and floured. Bake in a preheated 350-degree oven about 35 minutes for a sheet cake or 25 for layers, or until the cake springs back when pressed lightly in the center. Cool 5 minutes on a rack, loosen from the pan, and turn out onto the rack to cool. Frost with caramel fluffy, seven-minute, or sea foam frosting, or browned butter or chocolate frosting.

Dried Fruit Cake

½ cup dried prunes, apples, peaches, apricots, or a mixture
½ cup water
⅔ cup butter
1 cup sugar
1 egg
2 cups sifted all-purpose flour
1 teaspoon baking soda
½ teaspoon salt
½ teaspoon each of cinnamon and nutmeg
½ teaspoon grated orange rind

Obviously this, a museum piece, was the kind of fruit cake that used to be depended on during the winter and was often the holiday treat of the pioneer. Sometimes several types of fruit were combined for this cake, and old recipes generally called for four times this amount. We have livened the recipe with orange.

Combine the fruit and water in a small saucepan. Bring to boil, cover, and remove from heat. Let stand until cool. The fruit needs only to be softened. When cool, cut the fruit in pieces about the size of a seedless raisin. Pit the prunes. Cream the butter well and cream in the sugar until light. Beat in the egg and stir in fruit. Add the sifted dry ingredients alternately with the juice or wine and grated orange rind. Do not overstir. Add the nuts at the last. Turn into a greased and floured loaf pan or pans, and spread the

3/4 cup wine or juice from soaking dried fruit
1/2 cup toasted chopped walnuts, pecans, almonds, filberts, or hickory nuts

dough up the sides of the pan a bit to produce a more uniform top. Bake in a preheated 350-degree oven about 55 minutes. Test the center with a fingertip; when the cake springs back from light pressure and has shrunk from the sides of the pan, it is done. Let it stand in the pan on a rack about 10 minutes, then loosen from the pan and turn out on the rack to cool. This cake was generally not frosted but was stored in a crock or tightly covered tin until next day before being sliced.

Double Apple Cake or Cupcakes

1/2 cup butter
1 cup white or 1 1/4 cups firmly packed brown sugar
2 eggs
2 1/4 cups sifted cake or 2 cups sifted all-purpose flour
1/2 teaspoon baking soda
2 teaspoons baking powder
1/2 teaspoon salt
1 teaspoon cinnamon
1/4 teaspoon cloves
1/2 cup applesauce
3/4 cup finely chopped tart raw apple
1/2 cup raisins (optional)
1/2 cup chopped walnuts, pecans, or filberts (optional)

This cake uses both applesauce and chopped apples and is sometimes made without the spices or without the nuts and raisins.

Cream the butter and cream in the sugar very well (electric mixer is easiest). Beat in the eggs. Add the sifted dry ingredients alternately with the applesauce. Fold in the raw apple and, if you like, the raisins and nuts. Bake in a well-greased loaf pan or as a sheet cake in a preheated 350-degree oven about 55 minutes for a loaf cake or 35 minutes for a sheet cake. Cool in the pan on a rack.

This is the type of cake that is better eating the second or third day, for it becomes more moist. Usually it is not iced, but it can be, with a thin lemon, orange, or spice butter frosting. It freezes well.

Applesauce Cake

1/2 cup butter or lard
1 cup white sugar or firmly packed brown sugar (less if the fruit is sweetened)
1 egg
2 cups sifted all-purpose flour
1/2 teaspoon baking soda
1 teaspoon baking powder
1/2 teaspoon salt
1 teaspoon cinnamon

There are many old recipes for applesauce (or prune or peach or apricot) cake. Some of them use 2 or 3 eggs, some not any. This depended somewhat on the price of eggs, and in winter, when the hens were not laying, the cake was usually made without eggs.

Prunes, plums, peaches, or apricots may be used as well as apples. If using fresh or dried fruit, simmer it, covered, in a little water until it is quite soft. If canned, no cooking is needed. Drain, and sieve or chop well before adding to the cake.

Cream the butter or lard well and cream in the sugar very well (if using sweetened fruit, decrease the sugar by 1 or 2 tablespoons). Beat in the egg. Sift the flour with the other dry ingredients and add alternately with the fruit sauce. For a loaf cake use 1 cup sauce; for a sheet cake 1¼ cups. Turn into two 8 × 8 × 2-inch pans, an 11 × 14 × 2-inch sheet cake pan, or a 5 × 9 × 3-inch loaf pan. Grease the pan well or put greased paper in the bottom. Bake in a 350-degree oven about 35 minutes for layers, 45 minutes for a sheet cake, and 55 minutes for a loaf. The cake is done if it springs back when pressed lightly in the center. Cool in the pan on a rack.

Applesauce cake is not usually frosted, although some people like to frost it with browned butter frosting with nuts or serve it topped with ice cream or whipped cream. The cake is better after the first day, and keeps well.

½ teaspoon allspice
¼ teaspoon ground cloves
1 to 1¼ cups thick applesauce or other fruit (see below)
½ cup raisins or currants
½ cup finely chopped walnuts

Raw Apple Bread or Cake

½ cup butter
1 cup sugar
2 eggs
2 cups sifted all-purpose flour
¼ teaspoon salt
½ teaspoon baking soda
2 teaspoons baking powder
1½ tablespoons sweet or sour milk
1 cup coarsely ground or finely chopped unpeeled raw apples
1 teaspoon vanilla or 1 tablespoon rum
½ cup broken nut meats

Often served as a tea bread but really sweet enough to be a cake.

Cream the butter, then cream in the sugar. Beat in the eggs one at a time if mixing by hand; add both at once if using an electric mixer. Sift the dry ingredients together. If mixing by hand, add the egg mixture alternately with the combined milk, flavoring, apples, and nuts. With a mixer, put them all in together, turn the mixer to the lowest speed and scrape the sides of the bowl with a spatula while turning, just long enough to mix. Do not overmix. Turn into a well-greased loaf pan or into a 9 × 9 inch greased and floured square pan. Bake in a 350-degree oven about 35 minutes for the square pan, about 55 minutes for the loaf. Test for springiness with a fingertip. Let the cake cool in the pan on a rack for about 5 minutes, then loosen and turn out onto the rack to finish cooling.

This apple cake slices better the second or third day. It keeps well for several weeks in a covered tin or in a freezer bag in the refrigerator, or for months in the freezer. It can be frosted or left plain, as you like (if freezing, do not frost.)

Spiced Raw Apple Cake. Sift 1 teaspoon cinnamon, ½ teaspoon allspice, and ¼ teaspoon ground cloves with the dry ingredients.

Fresh Carrot Cake

1 cup butter
2 cups sugar
1 teaspoon ground cinnamon
½ teaspoon mace or nutmeg
½ to 1 teaspoon grated orange rind
4 eggs
1½ cups finely grated or shredded fresh carrots

Mid-European kitchens have known a carrot torte for generations. This is an evolvement that is lighter in texture than a torte and has a nutty flavor. It is sometimes made with currants and raisins in it, as well as nuts.

Cream the butter and then cream in the sugar until very light and fluffy. Add the spices and grated orange rind and beat. Add the eggs, one at a time, and beat well. Stir in the carrots and nuts. Sift the dry ingredients and add with the water. Do not beat when adding the flour, but rather fold in just until it is moistened well. If using an electric mixer, do this on the lowest speed. Turn into a

⅔ cup finely chopped, toasted walnuts, filberts, or black walnuts
2½ cups sifted all-purpose flour
3 teaspoons baking powder
½ teaspoon salt
⅓ cup warm water

greased and floured or greased paper-lined pan 11 × 15 × 2 inches, or into three 8 or 9 inch pans. Bake in a preheated 350-degree oven about 25 minutes for layers or 35 to 40 for a sheet cake; the cake is done if it springs back when pressed lightly in the center. Cool for a few minutes, then loosen from the sides of the pan, and turn out onto a cake rack to cool.

This cake is better when aged a day or two. It is served with or without frosting. Favorite frostings are browned butter, penoche nut, or caramel.

Pork Cake

¼ pound fat salt pork
½ cup boiling water
2 cups sifted all-purpose flour
½ teaspoon baking soda
1 teaspoon baking powder
¼ teaspoon salt
½ teaspoon each of cinnamon, cloves, allspice, nutmeg
½ cup raisins, chopped (or more)
1 egg
½ cup sugar
½ cup molasses

Distinctively flavored, this cake made imaginative use of salt pork when butter was scarce on the farm. The cake was revived during both world wars when butter was unobtainable. Originally this was made in huge quantities (usually using 4 pounds of flour) and the excess was stored.

Put the pork through a food chopper, using the finest blade. Put into a small, warm bowl and pour boiling water over it. Let stand 20 to 25 minutes. Sift the flour with the soda, baking powder, salt, and spices, then mix with the raisins. In mixing bowl, beat the egg, then beat in the sugar, followed by the molasses. Stir in the pork mixture, then the flour mixture. Continue to stir just enough to blend. Turn into a greased and floured loaf pan and bake in a preheated 325-degree oven about 60 minutes or until the cake is resilient when pressed lightly with a fingertip. Cool on a cake rack for a few minutes in the pan, then loosen the cake and turn it out on the rack. This cake was traditionally served plain. It freezes well.

Note. Additional raisins may be added to this cake, or moist dried prunes, cut up, or ½ cup coarsely chopped nuts.

Mayonnaise Cake

1 cup chopped raisins or dates
1 teaspoon baking soda
1 cup boiling water
¾ cup mayonnaise (not salad dressing)
1 cup sugar, white or firmly packed brown
2 cups sifted all-purpose flour
½ teaspoon salt
1 tablespoon cocoa
1 cup broken nut meats
1 teaspoon vanilla

This has had great popularity from time to time, mainly because it sounds daring.

Put the chopped raisins or dates in a small bowl. Sprinkle with the soda and pour the boiling water in. Set aside to cool. In a mixing bowl mix the mayonnaise and sugar very well. Sift the flour with the salt and cocoa and add alternately with the cooled fruit mixture to the mayonnaise and sugar. Stir in the nuts and vanilla. Turn into a greased and floured 9 inch loaf or 9 × 13 sheet pan and bake in a preheated moderate 350-degree oven about 35 minutes for sheet cake or 50 for a loaf. The cake is done when it springs back after the center is pressed lightly with the finger. Cool on a cake rack. This cake is not usually frosted, but is sometimes topped with a prune or pineapple butter frosting.

Chocolate or Chocolate Caramel Potato Cake

¾ cup butter
2 cups sugar
4 eggs, separated (or whole if you are using a mixer)
1 cup mashed or sieved potatoes, unseasoned
2 ounces unsweetened chocolate
2 cups sifted cake flour
½ teaspoon baking soda
2 teaspoons baking powder
½ teaspoon salt
1 teaspoon cinnamon
½ teaspoon nutmeg
¼ to ½ teaspoon cloves
½ cup milk
1 cup chopped walnuts, slightly toasted and coarsely chopped

Old recipes used more cloves for this rich, moist cake, easily made nowadays with instant mashed potatoes.

Cream the butter very well, then cream in the sugar until very light. Beat in the egg yolks until the mixture is fluffy and smooth. If using an electric mixer for this cake, the whole eggs can be beaten into the creamed butter and sugar. Have the potatoes ready and lukewarm — if using instant mashed potatoes, follow directions on the package but of course do not add butter, salt, or pepper. Melt the chocolate over warm (not hot) water, stir, and blend along with the potatoes into the butter mixture. Sift the flour with the soda, baking powder, salt, and spices, and add alternately with the milk. Add the nuts. Fold in the beaten egg whites last. Turn the batter into a greased and floured 10-inch tube pan or two loaf pans, filling not more than half full. Bake in a preheated moderate 350-degree oven about 60 minutes for a tube pan or 50 for loaves. To test, press the cake lightly in the center. If it springs back, it is done. Cool in the pan on a rack. Usually this cake is served plain.

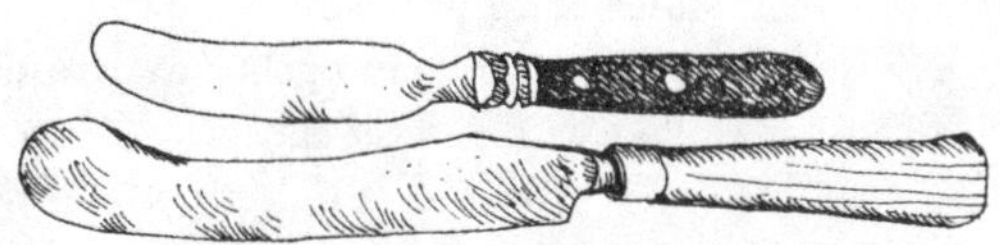

Fudge Cake

1 cup butter
1 cup sugar
4 eggs
4 ounces unsweetened chocolate, melted over warm (not hot) water
1 cup sifted all-purpose flour
2 teaspoons vanilla
1 cup broken walnuts

Made in a thin layer, this is cut in small squares and served as a tea cake or cookie. It is sometimes frosted, but this is perhaps too rich.

Cream the butter, and cream in the sugar very well. Beat in the eggs, one at a time. Stir in the melted chocolate, then stir in the flour, vanilla, and nutmeats just to combine. Turn into a well-greased and floured 8 or 9 inch square pan or 9 × 12 × 2-inch pan. Bake in a preheated 325-degree oven about 30 minutes for the square pan or about 40 minutes for the sheet pan. Do not overbake or it will be dry. Cool in the pan on a cake rack, and cut into pieces while still slightly warm.

This is often cut in squares and topped with ice cream. Sometimes it is frosted with double boiler frosting followed by a chocolate glaze; or it is frosted with chocolate butter frosting or mocha.

Mocha Fudge Cake. Add 2 tablespoons instant coffee after the eggs are added.

Chocolate Custard or Devil's Food Cake

3 eggs
1½ cups milk
1⅔ cups sugar
4 ounces sweet cooking chocolate or ¾ cup semisweet chocolate pieces
½ cup butter
1 teaspoon vanilla
2¼ cups sifted cake flour
1 teaspoon baking soda
½ teaspoon salt

This method of mixing chocolate cake is not a modern one. I'm sure some homemaker in the past figured that the chocolate combined better if melted with other ingredients. In many families this is considered tops in chocolate cake, for it is moist.

Beat 1 of the eggs slightly in a small saucepan, add ½ cup milk and ⅔ cup sugar. Cook and stir over low heat for several minutes or until the mixture begins to barely coat the spoon. Add the chocolate and continue stirring until it is melted and the mixture is thickened slightly. Cool to room temperature. Cream the butter until fluffy and cream in the rest of the sugar gradually. Continue creaming until very light. Add the vanilla and the remaining eggs, and beat well to combine. Sift the dry ingredients together and add alternately with the remaining cup of milk. If using a mixer, add at low speed. Stir in the chocolate mixture just to combine. Spread into three 8 or 9 inch pans that have been greased and floured or lined with greased paper. Or spread evenly into a greased and floured sheet pan 11 × 14 × 2 inches. Bake in a preheated 350-degree oven about 25 minutes for layers or 40 for a sheet cake. If the cake springs back when pressed lightly in the center, it is done. Cool in the pan on a rack 5 minutes, then loosen from pan, turn out on rack, and continue to cool. Frost with your favorite white or chocolate frosting. Frequently it is filled and frosted with a sweet chocolate filling.

Sweet Chocolate Cake

½ cup boiling water
1 4-ounce package sweet chocolate or ¾ cup semisweet chocolate pieces
1 cup butter
2 cups sugar
4 eggs, separated (or whole, if you use a mixer)
1 teaspoon vanilla
2½ cups sifted cake flour
½ teaspoon salt
1 teaspoon baking soda
1 cup buttermilk or sour milk (or add 1 tablespoon vinegar to 1 cup sweet milk, stir, and let stand 10 minutes)

Afterward called German sweet chocolate cake.

Pour the boiling water over the chocolate and stir to melt. Cool to room temperature. Cream the butter until fluffy. Beat in the sugar until the mixture is very fluffy. Beat in the unbeaten egg yolks. (If you are using an electric mixer, you can add the whole eggs, one at a time, which will make a fine-textured cake.) Add the vanilla, then the chocolate mixture, and stir to combine. Sift the dry ingredients together and add alternately with the milk. (If using the mixer, turn it off, add the flour, then set to lowest speed and pour the milk in the center. Scrape down the sides with a spatula from time to time. Mix only until smooth.) If mixing by hand, beat the egg whites until soft peaks form. Fold into the batter. Turn into three 8 or 9 inch greased and floured pans or cover bottoms of greased pans with well-greased paper. Or bake in a sheet pan 11 × 14 × 2 inches greased or lined with greased paper. Bake in a preheated 350-degree oven, about 25 minutes for layers or 40 for sheet cake. Test the center of the cake with light pressure of the finger. When it springs back, it is done. Cool the cake on a rack 5 minutes, then loosen from the pan and turn out on the rack to cool. Favored frostings for this cake are coconut or chocolate butter frosting.

Crazy Cake or Crazy Mixed-up Cake

1 1/2 cups unsifted all-purpose flour
1 cup sugar
3 tablespoons cocoa
1/2 teaspoon salt
1 teaspoon soda
6 tablespoons melted butter
1 tablespoon vinegar
1 teaspoon vanilla
1 cup cold water or milk

This is mixed in a bowl in conventional fashion and turned into a greased pan or sometimes mixed right in the baking pan.

Sift the dry ingredients together or not, as you prefer; or stir with a fork after putting them in a mixing bowl or ungreased 9 × 12 × 2-inch pan. Make three wells in the dry ingredients. Into these put, separately, the melted butter, vinegar, and vanilla. Pour the liquid over all. Mix with a fork just until the ingredients are well combined. If mixed in a bowl, turn into a greased pan. Bake in a preheated 350-degree oven about 30 minutes or until the cake springs back when pressed lightly in the center with the finger. Serve hot or cold with a chocolate or caramel sauce or with a boiled icing.

Red Devil's Food Cake

3/4 cup cocoa
1/3 cup sugar
1 1/4 cups scalded milk
2/3 cup butter
1 cup sugar
1 teaspoon vanilla
3 eggs
2 cups sifted cake flour
1 1/4 teaspoons baking soda
1/2 teaspoon salt

A cake that had great popularity at the beginning of this century and was made very red by the use of a good deal of soda, which achieved its purpose but had an objectionable flavor. This, I feel, does not have that problem.

Mix the cocoa and sugar in a small bowl and slowly stir in the scalded milk. Let cool to room temperature. Cream the butter, then cream in the sugar and vanilla. Beat in the eggs (if by hand, beat in one at a time). Stir in the cocoa mixture, then the sifted dry ingredients. Turn into greased and floured layer cake pans (this makes three 8 or 9 inch layers or two deeper 9 or 10 inch layers). Bake 25 to 30 minutes in a preheated oven at 350 degrees, or until the cake springs back when pressed gently in the center. Cool the cake a few minutes in the pan on a rack, then loosen from the pan and turn out on the rack. Red devil's food cake was usually filled and spread with boiled white frosting to intensify the red color.

Mahogany Cake. Sometimes red devil's food cake was called mahogany cake. However, in mahogany cake, occasionally only 1 cup milk was used, and 1/4 cup molasses was added after the milk had been stirred into the cocoa and sugar.

Red Velvet Cake

½ cup butter
1½ cups sugar
2 eggs
1 teaspoon cinnamon
1 teaspoon vanilla
½ teaspoon salt
3 tablespoons cocoa
1 teaspoon red coloring
2 tablespoons water
2½ cups sifted cake flour
1½ teaspoons baking powder
1 cup buttermilk or sour milk (or stir 1 tablespoon vinegar into sweet milk and let stand 10 minutes)
1 teaspoon baking soda
1 tablespoon vinegar

This has often been called the hundred-dollar cake, of which most versions have been chocolate. Although a very good-textured cake, the original lacked flavor. For that reason I've added vanilla and cinnamon. The color is definitely red.

Cream the butter, and cream in the sugar until very light. Beat in the eggs, one at a time, then the cinnamon, vanilla, and salt. Mix the cocoa, red coloring, and water, and add to the creamed mixture. Sift the flour with the baking powder and add alternately with the milk. Blend well. If using an electric mixer, turn to lowest speed when adding flour and buttermilk. Dissolve the soda in the vinegar and fold into the cake batter very carefully. Turn into two 9-inch greased and floured cake pans (or, if you like, grease the pans and then fit the bottoms with greased paper). Do not flour the pans heavily. Bake in a preheated 350-degree oven 25 to 30 minutes or until the cake springs back when pressed lightly in the center. Let cool in the pans on a rack for several minutes, then loosen and turn out onto the rack to cool. When cool, frost with white fluffy frosting, or use the white velvet icing, which is not excessively sweet.

Chocolate Upside Down Cake

CAKE
2 tablespoons butter, softened
¾ cup sugar
1 cup sifted all-purpose flour
1½ teaspoons baking powder
¼ teaspoon salt
1½ tablespoons cocoa
½ cup milk

TOPPING
½ cup broken walnut meats
½ cup sugar
½ cup firmly packed brown sugar
½ cup cocoa
1¼ cups boiling water

There has always been a discussion about whether this is a cake or pudding.

For the cake, mix the butter and sugar to cream slightly. Sift together the flour, baking powder, salt, and cocoa, and add with the milk to the creamed butter and sugar. Turn into a greased 9-inch square pan or its equivalent. For the topping, sprinkle with the nutmeats, then with the mixed white and brown sugar and cocoa. Pour the boiling water over the top of the batter in a thin stream. Bake in a preheated moderate 350-degree oven about 35 to 45 minutes, or until the cake leaves the sides of the pan and the center is springy to light pressure with the finger. Let it cool in the pan for a few minutes. Invert on a serving plate. Serve hot or cold, cut in squares, and top with cream, whipped cream, whipped cream cheese, or ice cream.

Roulage Léontine or Chocolate Roll

Made famous by Dione Lucas at her Cordon Bleu Cooking School, this flourless chocolate roll has always been associated with her. It is really a chocolate soufflé baked like a roll.

Prepare the pan first; it should be an 11 × 16 × ½-inch pan. Butter it well, then fit wax paper in the bottom and butter the wax paper (only wax paper will work with this). Preheat the oven to 350 degrees.

6 eggs
½ cup sugar
6 ounces semi-sweet chocolate pieces
1 teaspoon vanilla
¼ teaspoon salt
½ teaspoon cream of tartar
1 cup heavy cream, whipped, sweetened and flavored with vanilla, Cognac, or 1 or 2 tablespoons sherry or kirsch

Soften the chocolate over hot (not boiling) water and let cool to room temperature. Separate the eggs and beat the yolks until very light and lemon-colored. Add the sugar gradually, and continue beating until very light. Stir in the chocolate and beat again until the mixture is very light, adding the vanilla and salt while beating. Beat the egg whites until foamy, add the cream of tartar, and beat until the whites are light and hold a soft peak. Fold into the chocolate mixture with a rubber or plastic spatula. Turn the bowl as you do this to incorporate the two mixtures evenly and retain as much air as possible. Spread lightly into the prepared pan and bake in the preheated 350-degree oven approximately 15 minutes or until the roll pulls away from the sides of the pan. Transfer to a rack, put a damp towel over the pan, and leave 10 minutes. Take off the towel, loosen the sides of the roll, and turn onto wax paper sprinkled with cocoa or powdered sugar. Cool. Fill with the whipped cream, but do not spread it out to the edges. Lift the wax paper on one side, which will cause the cake to lift also and roll inward. Continue to roll, and roll off the paper onto a serving plate or onto a Roulage Léontine or special chocolate roll board. This roll will often crack, but it does not matter. Serve cut in diagonal slices.

This will freeze, but it is not as good. In fact I prefer it not even refrigerated. It will hold perfectly at room temperature for 4 or 5 hours.

Chocolate Soufflé. Instead of spreading in a pan, turn the mixture into a buttered and sugared 1-quart soufflé dish and bake about 45 minutes in a 375-degree oven. Serve with the whipped cream.

Nut Roll. Omit the chocolate. Fold 1 cup finely chopped almonds, pecans, walnuts, or filberts into the egg yolk mixture before folding in the egg whites. (Chop them in the blender, if you like.) The baking and rolling procedures are the same.

Sponge Roll or Sponge Layer

4 eggs
¼ cup sugar
½ teaspoon cream of tartar

Separate the eggs. Beat the whites until foamy, then slowly add sugar and cream of tartar, beating until the sugar is dissolved and the mixture stiff. Beat the yolks until foamy and light in color. Stir about 1 cup of the whites into the yolks, then pour back over the egg whites, Sprinkle with the flour, cornstarch, and salt sifted together. Add the vanilla and grated lemon rind. Fold the mixtures

¼ cup cake flour
¼ cup cornstarch
¼ teaspoon salt
½ teaspoon vanilla
½ teaspoon grated lemon rind

together just enough to combine. Spread into a buttered, wax-papered, and buttered 11 × 16-inch pan and bake at 400 degrees exactly 10 minutes. Let cool slightly before filling and rolling. This does not require rolling and unrolling and rerolling as do most other sponge or jelly rolls — I have kept it covered with foil for 24 hours before rolling it.

The sponge may be used filled with whipped cream and strawberries, for example, or with lemon curd mixed with an equal quantity of whipped cream, or with chocolate-flavored whipped cream and then rolled. Or it may be cut into small strips, spread with preserves, lemon curd, or flavored butter creams, and rolled tightly. It may also be cut into small squares, filled and iced with fondant or other icing used for small cakes. It is as versatile a cake as I know.

Genoise

⅓ cup to ½ cup sweet butter, melted and cooled to clarify
6 eggs (standard large size)
1 cup sugar (preferably fine granulated)
1 cup sifted cake flour
½ teaspoon salt
1 teaspoon vanilla

A light cake of Italian origin adopted by the French. It is used most often as the basis for a layer cake with butter cream frosting of various flavors. Often the layers are brushed lightly with liqueur before frosting. Usually, if to be made in thin layers with a rich frosting, a lesser amount of butter is used in the cake.

To clarify the butter, melt over low heat until the moisture and fat separate. Only the fat should be used in the cake. Chill the melted butter, lift the fat from the moisture underneath, and reheat it just slightly to soften.

Combine the eggs and sugar in a large mixing bowl. Beat for a minute or until they are combined. Set the bowl over a saucepan containing hot tap water. Do not let the bowl touch the water. Set the pan over very low heat (the water must not even simmer) and heat, beating occasionally until the eggs and sugar are lukewarm. Test with a knuckle or by putting a drop on your wrist. If the mixture feels neither warm nor cool, it is right. Begin to beat the eggs and sugar by hand with a whip or rotary beater or with an electric mixer. Beat at high speed 10 to 15 minutes, scraping the sides of the bowl with a rubber or plastic spatula when necessary. The batter is whipped enough when it has almost tripled in bulk. By hand this will take about 25 minutes.

Sprinkle the flour (that has been sifted several times with the salt) over the egg mixture, adding about a quarter at a time, and fold with a spatula. Add the butter and vanilla a little at a time along with the flour. Keep turning the bowl so that the flour, butter, and vanilla are well mixed without losing any more volume of the eggs and sugar than necessary. (If adding the flour, butter, and vanilla by electric mixer, use the lowest speed and put all into the mixer bowl at one time. Combine the ingredients just until mixed; do not overmix.) Turn the batter into greased and floured pans. This will fill two 8 or 9 inch round or square cake pans or one jelly roll pan 11 × 16 × ½-inch. Bake in a preheated 350-degree oven 20 to 35 minutes, depending upon the pan used. The jelly roll pan may take no more than 15 minutes. Test with a fingertip — when the cake springs back after light pressure, it is done. Cool in the pans on a wire rack for 15 minutes, then turn out on the rack to cool. Frost, if you like, with a butter or butter cream frosting. Often this is made in a jelly roll pan, and after rolling and cooling is filled with a Bavarian cream flavored with berries, peaches, or apricots. Or the cake is cut in squares and put together with fruit-flavored or berry-flavored creams.

Chocolate Genoise. Instead of 1 cup cake flour, use ¾ cup flour and ¼ cup cocoa (not sweetened). Sift together several times before adding with the butter and vanilla to the egg and sugar mixture.

Jelly Roll

¾ cup sifted cake flour
¾ teaspoon baking powder
¼ teaspoon salt
4 eggs
¾ cup sugar
1 teaspoon vanilla

Sift the flour with the baking powder and salt. Break the eggs into a mixing bowl, and beat with rotary beater, whip, or electric mixer until very fluffy. Gradually add the sugar and beat until very light and thick. Beat in the vanilla and fold in the flour mixture. Have ready a jelly roll pan about 11 × 16 × ½ inch that has been lined with wax paper. Spread the batter evenly in it and immediately put into a preheated 400-degree oven. Bake 8 to 9 minutes or until the cake springs back when pressed lightly in the center. Have ready a tea towel or foil lightly sprinkled with powdered sugar. Let the cake cool 2 to 3 minutes, then loosen at the edges, turn out onto the cloth, and remove the paper. If it is to be spread with jelly or jam, use a tart one. Spread while the cake is still slightly warm, and roll up in the cloth until cool. If the cake seems too dry and crisp around the edges after baking, trim the edges off before rolling. If the cake is to be filled with whipped cream, frosting, or filling that will melt, roll it up in the cloth and cool on a rack. When ready to fill, unroll but do not try to flatten the cake. Leave it rather cupped while you are spreading the filling. Reroll without the towel.

Chocolate Roll. Use ½ cup sifted cake flour sifted with ¼ cup cocoa instead of all flour. Proceed as above, rolling up the cake in the cloth to chill, unrolling just enough to spread the filling, and rolling up again. Usually chocolate roll is filled with sweetened whipped cream or a chocolate or vanilla Bavarian cream; or sometimes with chocolate or mocha cream frosting, which is used to frost the top as well.

Log Roll. Use chocolate or plain jelly roll. After turning out on sugared cloth, trim a ½-inch wide strip from one of the narrow sides and cut in half, roll up and fasten with a toothpick. Or cut these ½-inch wide slices from both of the narrow ends, if you like. (These will be frosted with chocolate butter, or chocolate or mocha cream frosting, and stuck on the cake with frosting to simulate the knots on the log.) Roll up the cake, chill, and fill with the chocolate or mocha butter or butter cream frosting. Frost the outside, then draw a fork down the length of the roll in slightly waving lines to simulate the bark of the tree. Place the little frosted knots here and there on the roll. This can, of course, be made a day in advance; or made, frosted, frozen, slipped into a freezer bag, and stored in the freezer for weeks. Remove from the freezer bag to thaw, allowing about 3 hours. This is the sort of whimsey often served on Lincoln's and Washington's birthday.

Bûche de Noel. This is a log roll traditional in France at Christmastime. It is made of either plain jelly roll or genoise, usually double the recipes given in this chapter, and baked in two 11 × 16 × ½-inch pans. Then each is rolled, and when the two cakes are filled and frosted they are put together to make one thick, long roll. The cake is itself white, and mocha cream frosting is used for the filling and the frosting. The outside is frosted and treated as for log roll, above.

Diplomas. Use plain jelly roll with your favorite filling. Use a thin vanilla butter cream icing on the outside, and either tie the roll with school colors to simulate a diploma, or pipe on the ribbon with colored icing.

Sponge Cake

1¼ cups sifted cake flour
1 cup sugar
½ teaspoon salt
½ teaspoon double-acting baking powder
½ cup egg yolks
¼ cup cold water or orange juice
1 teaspoon vanilla
½ teaspoon almond extract or 1 tablespoon grated orange rind

This is done by a quick-mix method, using the same ingredients as always.

Sift the flour with 1 cup sugar and the salt and baking powder (if using an electric mixer, sift into the small bowl). Add the egg yolks, liquid, and flavorings. Do not stir at this time. Put the egg whites in the large bowl of the mixer, or into a mixing bowl if working by hand. Beat until fluffy. Add the cream of tartar and continue to beat until small bubbles begin to form. Gradually beat in ½ cup sugar and continue beating until very stiff peaks are formed. With a rotary beater or the electric mixer on low speed, beat the flour, egg yolk, and flavoring mixture until well blended, about 1 minute.

Fold this mixture, about a quarter at a time, into the egg whites. *Fold; do not stir.* When the batter is smooth, turn into an ungreased 10-inch tube pan. Bake in a preheated 350-degree oven 40 to 50 minutes. If the cake springs back when pressed lightly in the center, it is done. It should also have begun to shrink from the sides of the pan. Immediately invert it and allow it to cool before removing from the pan (see angel food cake recipe).

¼ cup egg whites (about 6)
1 teaspoon cream of tartar
½ cup sugar (for egg whites)

Hot Water or Milk Sponge Cake

4 eggs
1½ cups sugar
½ cup boiling water or hot milk
1 teaspoon vanilla, 1 tablespoon grated orange rind, or 2 teaspoons grated lemon rind
1½ cups sifted cake flour
¼ teaspoon salt
1½ teaspoons baking powder

Popular in the '90's as a base for many combinations of fruit and whipped cream or ice cream.

Separate the eggs and beat the yolks until very thick, add ½ cup of the sugar, and beat until very light. Slowly add the water or milk and flavoring and beat in well. Sift the flour with the salt and baking powder and fold in. Beat the egg whites until foamy, and slowly beat in the remaining sugar (1 cup). Beat until soft peaks are formed. Fold into egg yolk mixture just until well combined. Turn into an ungreased 10-inch tube pan. Bake in a preheated 325-degree oven about 1 hour. When the cake springs back from light pressure with a fingertip, and has pulled from the sides of the pan, it is done. Invert the pan to cool the cake (see angel cake recipe). When cool, loosen from the pan with a fork and ice or leave plain.

Wind Cake

6 eggs
¾ cup cold water
1½ cups sugar
2 cups sifted cake flour
½ teaspoon salt
¾ teaspoon cream of tartar
1 teaspoon vanilla
Few drops almond extract

This used to require a strong arm, but now that we have electric mixers it is not so difficult. The idea appears in old cookbooks and was obviously contrived to produce a light cake before leavenings were general.

Separate the eggs. Put the yolks in a mixing bowl and the whites in a bowl large enough to beat them to high volume. Beat the yolks until beginning to be light. Add the water and beat until the mixture is quite fluffy — by hand this will take about 10 minutes, by mixer 4 or 5 minutes. Gradually beat in 1 cup of the sugar and continue beating with mixer until very fluffy. Fold in the sifted flour. Beat the egg whites with the salt and cream of tartar until foamy, gradually beat in the sugar, and continue beating until the mixture forms soft peaks that turn over as you lift the beater. Fold into the first mixture, and quickly turn into an ungreased 10-inch tube pan. Bake immediately in a preheated 350-degree oven about 50 minutes or until the cake springs back when touched lightly in the center. Invert the pan to cool (see angel cake recipe). Loosen the cake with a fork to remove, and "cut" for serving with two forks rather than a knife. This cake was often cut in three layers, filled with a whipped cream or custard filling, then frosted with slightly sweetened whipped cream.

Paula Peck's Melting Tea Cake

½ cup whole blanched almonds
1 cup butter (½ pound or 2 sticks), melted
1 teaspoon vanilla
1 teaspoon grated lemon rind
4 whole eggs
4 egg yolks
1 cup sugar
1½ cups sifted all-purpose flour
2 tablespoons sifted cornstarch
¼ teaspoon salt
⅛ teaspoon mace

One of my favorite cakes, delicate-textured and rich.

Preheat the oven to 350 degrees. Grease a 9-inch tube pan or a kugelhopf pan, or use a springform mold with the tube inset. Butter the pan well and dust with flour. Arrange the blanched almonds around the bottom of the pan.

Melt the butter over low heat and cool to lukewarm temperature (do not heat enough to clarify the butter, just enough to soften). Add the vanilla and grated lemon rind. In a mixing bowl combine the eggs, egg yolks, and sugar. Set the bowl over a saucepan of hot water and place the pan over low heat for about 10 minutes, stirring the mixture occasionally, until the eggs are slightly warmer than lukewarm. (The water should not touch the bowl and should never approach boiling.) When the eggs are warm, beat with a rotary beater, electric mixer, or whip until they are thick and tripled in bulk. Sprinkle the flour, cornstarch, salt, and mace on top. Fold in gently, adding the butter mixture at the same time. Continue to fold, turning the bowl so that the mixture will be well blended. Do not overmix. Turn into the prepared pan and bake in a preheated 350-degree oven about 45 minutes or until the cake is golden brown and pulls away from the sides of the pan. Cool on a rack 20 minutes, then loosen slightly and turn out onto the rack to cool.

Sunshine or Golden Glow Cake

11 egg yolks
2 cups powdered sugar
1 cup orange juice
1 teaspoon vanilla
2 cups sifted cake flour
2 teaspoons baking powder
½ teaspoon salt

This was always the cake made after the angel food had used the egg whites.

Put the egg yolks in a mixing bowl (this is preferably mixed and beaten with an electric mixer). Beat until very light and lemon-colored. Sift the sugar several times and beat into the yolks, adding the sugar gradually. Stir in the orange juice and vanilla. Sift the flour, baking powder, and salt four or five times to incorporate as much air as possible. Fold into the egg mixture, or if using a mixer, turn to lowest speed, keep scraping down the sides with a rubber spatula, and mix just until the flour is well incorporated. Turn into an ungreased 9 or 10 inch tube pan. Bake in a preheated 325-degree oven about 1 hour, or until the cake draws away from the pan and springs back when pressed lightly in the center with the finger. Invert the pan to cool (see angel cake recipe). When cool, pull the cake away from the pan with a fork. This cake usually has an orange icing.

Angel Food Cake

1 cup sifted cake flour
1½ cups fine granulated sugar

The angel cake is an achievement which came when ovens provided some sort of control and one no longer gauged oven heat by holding the hand in and saying, "One potato, two potatoes, three potatoes." As I said in the introduction to this chapter, this cake is very much like a soufflé, with more flour added. It is delicate and impressive and has developed many variations. Nowadays it is usually made in the electric mixer, but I can still remember people beating the egg whites on a large platter with a flat whisk — a process that took time and muscle. Angel cake is quite successful toasted, which few people seem to be aware of, and thus can be just as delightful in a different way the day after.

½ teaspoon salt
1½ cups egg whites (about 12 large)
1 teaspoon cream of tartar
1 tablespoon water or part water and part lemon juice
1½ teaspoons vanilla or 1 teaspoon vanilla and ½ teaspoon almond extract

This cake can be made in practically any shape of pan (loaf tins, sheet tins, or jelly roll tins), although the tube pan has become a stereotype.

Make sure the egg whites are allowed to warm to room temperature. Preheat the oven to 350 degrees.

Sift the flour, measure, and sift 5 or 6 more times with ½ cup sugar and the salt. Hold sifter high when sifting to incorporate as much air as possible. Beat the egg whites in a large, very clean bowl or on a large, very clean platter. If using the bowl, a frilled whip, rotary beater, or electric beater can be used. For the platter, a frilled whip is necessary. When the egg whites are foamy, add the cream of tartar and beat in the liquid. When the bubbles are uniform, start adding 1 cup sugar a few tablespoons at a time. Add the flavoring while adding the sugar. Beat until the egg whites will hold stiff peaks and the sugar is dissolved. Fold in the flour while sifting or spooning it over the egg whites. This can be done with a rubber spatula or frilled whip, using a down-the-side and up-through-the-batter motion. Turn the bowl to incorporate evenly. When the flour is thoroughly combined but not overmixed, turn the batter into a 10-inch tube pan (or use two bread pans). The pan must be absolutely free of grease, for the cake must cling to the sides as it rises. Bake the tube pan about 50 minutes, loaf pans about 45. Test by pressing lightly in the center — if the cake springs back it is done. Remove from oven and invert the pan until the cake cools — the edges of the pan must be lifted at least an inch or so while it cools. Many pans are equipped with legs for this purpose. Otherwise, rest the pan upside down on the edges of three or four teacups, or put the tube over a bottle neck to hang the cake. When the cake is cool it can be removed by pulling from the sides of the pan with a fork.

Frost or leave plain as you prefer. To serve the cake, pierce it with a fork at intervals to mark the portions, then pull apart with two forks. The cake will mash if cut in the usual fashion.

Uniced angel food cake is often used as the base for sweetened fresh or frozen fruit topped with whipped cream, or for ice cream and fruit, or ice cream with a chocolate, caramel, or butterscotch sauce. The cake is really elegant when sliced and toasted. If iced, use a fluffy white frosting or a thin vanilla, lemon, orange, or chocolate butter icing. Angel food cake does not freeze well, for it has no fat content and is apt to be a bit tough when thawed.

Chocolate or Cocoa Angel Food Cake. Reduce the flour to ¾ cup and sift with it (and the ½ cup sugar and salt) ¼ cup cocoa and, if you like, ½ teaspoon cinnamon. Often this is iced, when completely cool, with a mocha cream frosting.

Mocha Angel Food Cake. Make as chocolate or cocoa angel food cake above, with the addition of 2 teaspoons instant coffee to the sifted flour, cocoa, sugar, and salt. Sift 5 or 6 times as usual.

Praline Angel Food Cake. In a heavy frying pan, melt ½ cup sugar. When it is a light tan, add ¾ cup coarsely chopped pecans or slivered almonds, stir a few seconds to coat the nuts with the caramel, then turn immediately into a lightly oiled cake or pie pan and let cool completely. Pound into very small pieces, or better, break up and whirl in the electric blender to make a very fine, almost powdery, flavoring for the cake. Reduce the sugar in the angel food cake by ¼ cup — that is, sift only ¼ cup of sugar with the flour — and fold the praline into the beaten egg white mixture along with the flour. Use only 1 teaspoon vanilla or omit entirely, and use ½ to 1 teaspoon of almond flavoring. Frost or dust with powdered sugar.

Custard Angel Food Cake

8 eggs
1¼ cups sugar
½ cup water
1 cup sifted cake flour
½ teaspoon salt
1 teaspoon cream of tartar
1 tablespoon orange rind

A favorite cake at the turn of the nineteenth century. It was often cooled, sliced into three or four layers, and filled with a vanilla, lemon, or orange cream custard filling and then iced with lightly sweetened whipped cream.

Separate the eggs while cold. Use a large mixing bowl for the yolks, medium for the whites. Let whites and yolks warm to room temperature. In a 1½-quart pan, boil the water and 1 cup of the sugar until it spins a thread, 230 to 232 degrees on a candy thermometer. Meantime beat the egg yolks until very thick and lemon-colored. Slowly beat in the hot syrup (this can be done with an electric mixer using medium speed or with a rotary beater). When all the syrup is added, continue beating until the mixture is light, fluffy, and thick. Set aside to cool. Sift the flour 5 or 6 times with the salt to incorporate as much air as possible. Beat the egg whites until frothy, beat in the cream of tartar, sprinkle with ¼ cup sugar, and continue beating until stiff. Fold the flour into the cooled egg yolk mixture, along with the orange rind. Fold in the whites and turn immediately into an ungreased 10-inch tube pan. Bake in a preheated 350-degree oven about 1 hour or until the cake springs back when pressed lightly in the center and has pulled away from the sides of the pan. Invert the pan to cool the cake (see angel food recipe). When cool, remove by loosening with a fork.

Bread Torte or Brottorte

6 eggs
1 cup sugar
1¼ cups fine dry breadcrumbs
1 teaspoon baking powder
¼ teaspoon salt
½ teaspoon cinnamon
1 cup grated unblanched almonds
¼ cup lemon juice
1 teaspoon grated lemon rind

SAUCE

¾ cup sherry (dry preferred) or white wine
3 whole cloves
1 small stick of cinnamon
¼ cup sugar

This differs from other tortes in that it has a wine bath after baking.

Separate the eggs and beat the yolks until thick and lemon-colored. Gradually beat in half of the sugar. Combine the other ingredients (except egg whites) and fold into the yolks. Beat the whites until quite foamy, and start adding the rest of the sugar gradually. Beat well, until the whites hold a soft peak. Fold gently into the first mixture and turn into an 8 or 9 inch springform pan that has only the bottom buttered. Bake in a preheated 350-degree oven 1 to 1¼ hours. The cake will pull from the sides of the pan when done. Heat the ingredients for the sauce at just under simmer for a few minutes, strain into a pitcher, and pour very slowly over the hot cake. Be sure to distribute it evenly. Cool the cake and spread if you like, with crème patissière.

Linzer Torte

1 cup butter
½ cup sugar
2 egg yolks
½ teaspoon grated lemon rind
1 cup sifted all-purpose flour
¼ teaspoon salt
1 teaspoon cinnamon (optional)
¼ teaspoon powdered cloves (optional)
2 cups ground or very finely chopped unblanched almonds (or half almonds, half toasted filberts)
1 to 1½ cups redcurrant or raspberry jam

This well-known Austrian specialty is often made in a 10 × 14 × 2-inch pan, cut into squares, diamond shapes, or rectangles, and served as a cookie. It is crumbly and short (rich) compared to most of the other tortes, which are lighter. It is spectacular, made as a small cake or cookie, for the holiday season.

Cream the butter very well and cream in the sugar until very fluffy. Beat in the egg yolks and lemon rind. Sift the flour with the salt (and cinnamon and cloves if you like). Add to the creamed mixture, then add the almonds. (Almonds can be ground in a nut grater or whirled in the blender for a few minutes, about ½ to ¾ cup at a time.) For a real torte, roll out about two-thirds of the dough, ¼ inch thick. Line the bottom and spread the dough partway up the sides of an 8-inch springform pan. Spread the torte with the jam. Roll out the remaining dough very thin, cut into ½-inch strips, and arrange crisscross fashion on the torte. Or roll the remaining dough into 8 thin pencil shapes about 10 inches long, twist them slightly, and lay them across the torte to form pie-shaped markings. Crimp the edges. Bake in a preheated 350-degree oven about 55 to 60 minutes. When done, cool on a cake rack.

Mandel Torte or Almond Torte

6 eggs
1 cup fine granulated sugar
3 tablespoons lemon juice
1 teaspoon grated lemon rind
1 teaspoon cinnamon
1 cup ground unblanched almonds, finely chopped, grated, or whirled in an electric blender
½ cup dry white breadcrumbs, slightly toasted
½ teaspoon almond extract
½ teaspoon cream of tartar
¼ teaspoon salt

Separate the eggs and beat the yolks in a mixing bowl until light, gradually adding half of the sugar. Beat until very fluffy. Beat in the lemon juice, rind, and cinnamon. Fold in the almonds, then the breadcrumbs, and finally the almond extract. Beat the egg whites until foamy, beat in the cream of tartar and salt, and continue beating, adding the remaining sugar gradually, until the mixture holds stiff peaks. Fold into the yolk mixture just enough to combine well. Turn into an 8 or 9 inch springform mold that has only the bottom lightly greased. Bake in a preheated 350-degree oven about 50 to 60 minutes or until the cake pulls away from the pan. This cake is also often baked in two 8 or 9 inch layer pans with removable bottoms and made into a layer cake filled and frosted with crème patissière or chocolate, mocha, or lemon cream icing. Or the one large cake is split into layers and filled with sweetened flavored whipped cream.

Nut Torte or Nuss Torte

7 eggs
1 cup fine granulated sugar
1¼ cups grated or very finely chopped filberts or walnuts
½ cup fine dry breadcrumbs
½ teaspoon cream of tartar
¼ teaspoon salt

This typically Viennese dessert is of firmer consistency than our traditional cakes, although the texture is light.

Separate 6 of the eggs, putting the yolks in a mixing bowl, and add the seventh egg to the yolks. Beat until very light, then beat in half the sugar, and continue beating until very light. Fold in the nuts and breadcrumbs that have been put through a nut grater or whirled a few minutes in a blender. Beat the egg whites until foamy, add the cream of tartar and salt, and continue beating, gradually adding the sugar, until stiff peaks form. Fold into the yolk mixture carefully to retain as much air as possible. Turn into a buttered and floured 8-inch springform mold. Put immediately into a preheated 350-degree oven and bake about 1¼ hours or until the cake pulls from the sides of the pan. Cool in the pan on a rack. This cake is usually cut in half and filled with coffee, chocolate, or mocha cream, and is also often iced with the same mixture and sprinkled with chopped toasted nuts, either on top or just on the sides.

Chocolate Nut Torte. Melt over hot (not boiling) water 2 ounces semisweet chocolate (⅓ cup chocolate pieces), and let cool. Fold into the egg yolk and sugar mixture. After adding the crumbs, add 2 tablespoons rum, brandy, bourbon, or sherry.

Torta Lampo

2 ounces unsweetened chocolate
½ cup blanched almonds, finely chopped
¼ cup walnuts, finely chopped
5 eggs
¾ cup sugar
½ cup strong cold coffee
½ teaspoon cream of tartar

The Spanish adopted this torte generations ago, probably from the Viennese via France, and have used it with their own interpretation of flavor.

Melt the chocolate over hot (not boiling) water. Chop the nuts very fine or put through a grater or whirl for a few minutes in an electric blender. Separate the eggs and beat the yolks until thick. Beat the sugar until the mixture is very light, then fold in the nuts, chocolate, and finally coffee. (Coffee can be made by adding 2 teaspoons instant coffee to ½ cup hot water. Let cool.) Beat the egg whites until they are foamy, add the cream of tartar, and beat until soft peaks form. Fold into the chocolate mixture just enough to mix. Turn into a greased and floured 9×9×2½-inch baking pan. Bake about 1 hour in a preheated 350-degree oven. Transfer the pan to a rack to cool. Serve plain or with whipped cream slightly sweetened and flavored with sherry.

Schaum Torte or Meringue Shells

6 egg whites
½ teaspoon cream of tartar
¼ teaspoon salt
2 cups fine granulated sugar
2 teaspoons lemon juice or vinegar
1 to 1½ teaspoons vanilla (optional)

Made by all nationalities. During the nineteenth century in America, fancy individual meringues used to be served at tea. Meringues are still much in demand, made in large or in individual sizes to be served filled with fruit and sweetened whipped cream, or filled with ice cream and chocolate or caramel sauce.

Separate eggs while still cold. Put the whites into a large mixing bowl and let warm to room temperature. Beat until just foamy, add the cream of tartar and salt, and continue beating until the bubbles begin to be smaller. Start adding the sugar, beating in 3 or 4 tablespoons at a time. When part of it has been added, add the lemon juice or vinegar and continue beating until the sugar is completely dissolved and the meringue is stiff — it should hold peaks when the beater is lifted. If you like, flavor with vanilla. Spread as directed below on a baking sheet covered with white letter paper.

For a large schaum torte, intended to be cut as it is served, draw two circles on the sheets of paper, using a plate 6, 7, or 8 inches across as your guide. Either spread the meringue evenly into the circles or use a pastry bag and rosette tube to force it out in concentric ropes. For individual tortes or meringues, draw circles 3 to 4 inches in diameter (use a small saucer for a pattern), and spread as above. For a meringue with a built-up edge, first spread a flat layer of the meringue in a solid circle, then construct sides either with a spoon or a pastry bag fitted with a plain or preferably frilled tip. Meringues expand in the baking, so don't crowd the circles too close together.

Bake meringues 1 to 1½ hours — or perhaps more, if the mixture is thick — in a slow oven preheated to 275 degrees. They should be a delicate creamy white and quite dry on the outside when done.

Schaum tortes or meringues do not freeze well in most freezers, for they are apt to draw moisture and become syrupy. If you have a freezer that will keep a very low temperature, then you might try packaging meringues in a freezer bag; take out of the bag immediately when you remove them from the freezer. Well-baked tortes or meringues will keep several weeks if cooled well, then stored in tightly covered containers.

Meringue Eggs. Oil a tablespoon ever so lightly. Dip into the meringue mixture and turn it out on the letter paper in a large, half-egg shape. When baked, these are often put together with whipped cream or ice cream and fruit, and a berry or chocolate sauce is passed separately. They are often served at Eastertime with an apricot sauce, which can be made by sieving drained canned or fresh frozen apricots and adding sugar to your taste. A few drops of almond flavoring helps also.

Chiffon Cake

2½ cups sifted cake flour
1½ cups sugar
3 teaspoons baking powder
1 teaspoon salt
½ cup salad oil (not olive)
5 unbeaten egg yolks
¾ cup cold water
2 teaspoons vanilla
Grated rind of 1 lemon (about 2 teaspoons) (optional)
1 cup egg whites (8 to 9)
½ teaspoon cream of tartar

These cakes had a terrific popularity during the 30's. They come in many flavors, and sometimes instead of oil, clarified butter in the same quantity is used.

Sift together the flour, sugar, baking powder, and salt into a mixing bowl. Make a well in these dry ingredients, and add (in this order) the oil, egg yolks, water, vanilla, and lemon rind. Beat until smooth. In a separate bowl beat the egg whites (warmed to room temperature) with the cream of tartar until the whites form quite stiff peaks — stiffer than is usual for cakes. Do not underbeat the egg whites or the texture and volume of the cake will suffer. Pour the flour mixture gradually over the egg whites, folding in with a frilled whip or rubber spatula. Do not stir. When blended, turn into an ungreased 10-inch tube pan. Bake in a preheated moderately slow oven, 325 degrees, for 55 minutes, then at 350 degrees for 10 to 15 minutes, or until the top springs back when pressed lightly. Immediately invert the tube pan to stand on its legs, or hang the pan by putting the tube over a bottle neck, or rest the pan on the edges of three or four teacups. When cool, loosen from the pan and remove. Chiffon cakes are sometimes frosted, sometimes only dusted with powdered sugar.

Orange Chiffon Cake. Use orange juice instead of half the water, and instead of lemon rind and vanilla, use 1 to 1½ tablespoons grated orange rind.

Chocolate Chiffon Cake. Add 1 ounce unsweetened chocolate, melted, after the oil and egg yolks are added.

Mocha Chiffon Cake. In addition to the chocolate (see above), add 2 teaspoons powdered coffee.

Nut Chiffon Cake. Use the basic recipe or the chocolate or mocha variation. Just before turning the batter into the pan, fold in 1 cup very finely chopped toasted nuts (walnuts, filberts, almonds, black walnuts, or whatever you like). Omit the grated lemon rind if using the basic recipe.

Two-Egg Chiffon Cake

2 eggs
1½ cups sugar
2¼ cups sifted cake flour
3 teaspoons baking powder
¾ teaspoon salt
⅓ cup salad oil
1 cup milk
1½ teaspoons vanilla or other flavoring
¼ teaspoon cream of tartar

Separate the eggs and mix as in basic chiffon cake, except that the egg whites must be beaten stiff with the cream of tartar and folded into the flour mixture, instead of folding the flour mixture into the whites. Bake in a sheet pan or in layers in a preheated 350-degree oven, about 35 minutes for sheet cake and 25 for layers. This is not as flavorful as the basic chiffon cake, which has more eggs.

Election Cake, Raised Loaf Cake, Dough Cake, or March Meeting Cake

2 cups milk, scalded
½ cup brown sugar
1 teaspoon salt
2 cakes compressed or package active dry yeast
5 cups sifted all-purpose flour
¾ cup butter
1½ cups sugar
2 eggs
1½ cups raisins or raisins and currants
½ cup candied peel (optional)
1 teaspoon cinnamon
1 teaspoon nutmeg
½ teaspoon mace

A cake made originally in New England to be sold on election or town meeting days. The idea was taken by the New England pioneers into the Midwest and West, and this was often the cake taken to political rallies, revivals, or camp meetings, where everyone brought food for dinner (served in the middle of the day) and supper.

American Cookery, by Amelia Simmons, first published in the eighteenth century, later copied and added to, has in an 1812 edition this recipe for Election Cake. "Thirty quarts flour, ten pounds butter, fourteen pounds sugar, twelve pounds raisins, three dozen eggs, one pint wine, one quart brandy, four ounces cinnamon, four ounces fine coriander seed, three ounces ground allspice; wet the flour with the milk to the consistency of bread overnight, adding one quart yeast, the next morning work the butter and sugar together for half an hour, which will render the cake much lighter and whiter; when it has risen light, work in every other ingredient except the plumbs, which work in when going into the oven."

This recipe is more manageable.

Scald the milk and stir in the brown sugar and salt. Turn into mixing bowl, and when lukewarm stir in the yeast. Add about 4½ cups flour and beat well (either on low speed in electric mixer or by hand) until well blended and beginning to be elastic. Let stand in a warm place until very light and doubled in bulk. Cream the butter, then cream in the sugar until very light and fluffy. Beat in the eggs. Sprinkle the spices and remaining flour over the raisins (or raisins and currants) and the candied peel, if you are using it. Add to the creamed mixture. The two batters must be thoroughly combined. This will be a heavy dough. Turn into two or three well-greased loaf pans, filling the pans not more than half full, and again let rise until double in bulk. Bake in a preheated moderate oven, 350 to 375 degrees, until brown and pulled away from the sides of the pan, which will take from 35 to 50 minutes, depending upon the size. If you like, brush the top crusts with melted butter when the loaves are taken from the oven. Turn them out onto a rack to cool.

Election Cake was always considered better if left to ripen for a day or two in a covered crock. Nowadays we prefer to slip it into a plastic bag and let it age. These loaves freeze well, but will not age or mellow in the freezer. Remove from the freezer bags to thaw.

Saffron or Cornish Saffron Cake

¼ teaspoon powdered saffron or ½ teaspoon saffron threads
½ cup boiling water
5 cups sifted all-purpose flour
1 teaspoon salt
1 cup sugar
½ to ¾ cup butter or half butter and half lard
2 cakes compressed yeast or 2 packages active dry yeast
½ cup lukewarm water
1½ cups seeded raisins
1½ cups seedless raisins
1½ cups currants
¼ cup each of chopped candied orange peel, lemon peel, and citron
1 cup scalded and cooled milk or lukewarm water

Though made with yeast, this has always been classed as a true cake. It is known in every community where Cornishmen have settled and, of course, in all early mining communities.

Pour the boiling water over the saffron and let steep, covered, for a while. If using saffron threads, chop them after measuring, and steep. This is the amount of saffron that most cake makers like. Old-time Cornish homemakers liked more, but it is apt to overwhelm the flavor of all other ingredients. Measure the sifted flour into a large mixing bowl, add the salt, sugar, and shortening, and mix together well with the fingers. Be sure that the butter is well blended with the flour. In the meantime, soak the yeast in the ½ cup lukewarm water. Add 2 teaspoons of sugar to the yeast, if you like, to start the action sooner.

Mix the fruits into the flour mixture, then add the yeast and the scalded and cooled milk. (Sometimes 2 or 3 beaten eggs are added to this, but it is not traditional.) Beat until well blended and let stand in a warm place until doubled in bulk. Stir down and spoon into well-greased loaf pans or a 10-inch tube pan, filling not more than half full or a little less. Let stand again in a warm place until doubled in bulk. Bake in a preheated 350-degree oven about 50 to 60 minutes for a standard size loaf pan or about 1 hour and 15 minutes for the tube pan. The loaf or cake will shrink from the sides of the pan when done, and be lightly browned. This makes 2 large loaves. Cool in the pans on a rack. Sometimes this cake was dusted with powdered sugar or a thin marzipan frosting was used. Usually, however, the cake was cooled and stored for a week or perhaps more before using, and was eaten unfrosted.

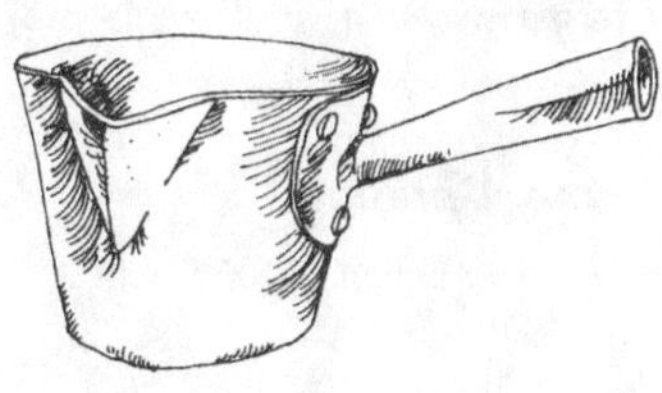

Frostings

Boiled Frosting

2 cups sugar
2/3 cup water
1/8 teaspoon cream of tartar
3 egg whites, stiffly beaten
1/8 teaspoon salt
1 teaspoon vanilla

In a saucepan combine the sugar, water, and cream of tartar. Bring the mixture slowly to a boil, stirring once or twice to dissolve the sugar before it bubbles. Cover, and boil 3 minutes, then uncover and boil to the soft ball stage (234 to 240 degrees). Remove the pan from the heat and pour the syrup in a thin stream over the stiffly beaten whites in a mixing bowl. Add the salt and vanilla and continue beating until the frosting cools and is firm enough to spread. If the frosting stiffens excessively, beat in about 1/4 teaspoon boiling hot water. This quantity is sufficient for a 9-inch two-layer cake or the equivalent.

Fluffy Frosting. Reduce the sugar to 1 1/2 cups and cook the syrup to 245 degrees.

Marshmallow Frosting. Cut 4 marshmallows into small bits and combine them with 2 tablespoons milk in the top pan of a double boiler. Cook over simmering water until the marshmallows melt. Stir this cream (there should be about 3 tablespoons) into the syrup before pouring over the egg whites.

Cinnamon Frosting. Cook the syrup with an inch of stick cinnamon. Discard it when the syrup has reached the soft ball stage. Omit the vanilla.

Ginger Frosting. Reduce the sugar to 1 3/4 cups, and instead of water use 1/4 cup syrup drained from preserved ginger. Omit the vanilla.

Seafoam Frosting. Use 2 2/3 cups firmly packed brown sugar instead of the granulated sugar.

Peppermint Frosting. Instead of vanilla, use 4 drops oil of peppermint and just a trace of red food coloring.

Seven-Minute Frosting

3 egg whites
¾ cup sugar
⅛ teaspoon salt
⅓ cup light corn syrup
1 teaspoon vanilla

In the top pan of a double boiler combine the egg whites, sugar, salt, and corn syrup. Set over simmering water and beat the mixture with a rotary beater or electric hand beater for about 7 minutes, or until soft peaks are formed when the beater is withdrawn. Remove the pan from over the water and stir in the vanilla. Continue beating until the frosting is stiff enough to spread. This quantity is sufficient for a 9-inch two-layer cake or the equivalent.

Caramel Frosting

2 cups dark brown sugar, firmly packed
1⅓ cups light cream
3 tablespoons butter
⅛ teaspoon salt
½ teaspoon vanilla

In a saucepan over low heat bring the sugar and cream to a boil. Cover the pan, and cook the mixture 3 minutes. Remove the cover and continue cooking until the mixture reaches 236 to 240 degrees. Remove the pan from the heat and stir in the butter, salt, and vanilla. Cool to lukewarm, then beat until the mixture is creamily smooth and of spreading consistency. This recipe provides sufficient frosting for a 9-inch two-layer cake or the equivalent.

Chocolate Fudge Frosting

3 ounces (3 squares) unsweetened chocolate
1¼ cups milk
3 cups sugar
¼ teaspoon salt
2 tablespoons light corn syrup
2 tablespoons butter
½ teaspoon vanilla

In a saucepan combine the chocolate and milk and heat them very gently, stirring constantly until the chocolate melts and is blended with the milk. Stir in the sugar, salt, and corn syrup. When they are incorporated, bring the mixture to a boil and cook it, covered, without further stirring for 3 minutes. Uncover the pan and continue cooking until the mixture reaches 236 to 240 degrees. Remove the pan from the heat, add the butter and vanilla, and let the mixture cool. When it is lukewarm, beat until it is very creamy and of spreading consistency. This quantity is sufficient for a 9-inch two-layer cake or the equivalent.

Chocolate Frosting, Helen Evans Brown

5 ounces semisweet chocolate (5 squares or the equivalent in morsels)
⅛ teaspoon salt
½ cup sour cream

Melt the chocolate in the top pan of a double boiler over hot water. Blend in the salt and sour cream and let the frosting cool. This recipe provides enough frosting to cover the top and sides of an 8-inch layer cake.

Butter Cream Frosting I

2 egg yolks
1/4 cup sugar
1/8 teaspoon salt
1/2 cup cream
1/2 teaspoon vanilla
1 cup unsalted butter

Prepare a boiled custard (page 728) with the sugar, salt, cream, and vanilla. Cream the butter until it is frothy and beat it vigorously, a little at a time, into the cooled custard. Chill the frosting slightly before using. If it separates, the emulsion may be restored by heating the frosting gently in the top of a double boiler over hot water, beating constantly.

Variations

Vary the flavor by omitting the vanilla and using one of the following in the custard instead:

(1) 1/4 teaspoon almond extract.
(2) 1/2 teaspoon lemon or orange extract.
(3) 1 teaspoon crème de cacao liqueur.
(4) 1 teaspoon concentrated coconut milk, made by steeping 1/4 cup packaged flaked or shredded coconut in 1/3 cup boiling water and reducing the strained liquid over moderate heat to the required amount.

Butter Cream Frosting II

1/3 cup softened butter
3 cups confectioners' sugar
3 to 4 tablespoons heavy cream
Flavoring

Cream together the butter and sugar and vigorously stir in the cream. Flavor with 1 teaspoon vanilla, or 1 tablespoon instant coffee dissolved in 1 teaspoon Cognac, or 1 tablespoon orange liqueur.

Maple Butter Cream. Use 1/4 cup maple syrup and omit the cream.

Chocolate Butter Cream with Orange. Sift 1/2 cup dark cocoa with the sugar. Omit the cream and use 1/3 cup strained orange juice instead. Add, if desired, 1/2 cup finely ground candied orange.

Butter Cream Frosting III

1 cup sugar
1/2 cup water
4 egg yolks, well beaten
1 cup butter, softened
Flavoring

In a saucepan cook together the sugar and water to the soft ball stage. Pour the syrup in a thin stream into the beaten yolks in a mixing bowl, beating constantly until the mixture is thick and cool. Flavor as desired; for suggestions see Butter Cream Frosting I and II. Whisk the butter to the consistency of whipped cream and beat the cooled yolk mixture into it, a little at a time.

Note. The quantity of each of the foregoing butter cream frostings is sufficient for a 9-inch two-layer cake or its equivalent. The frostings may be used also as fillings. So used, the indicated quantities are sufficient for two cakes.

Praline Butter Cream. Reduce the sugar by 2 tablespoons, and stir 2 tablespoons praline powder into the beaten yolks before adding the syrup. For praline powder see coffee jelly (page 735).

Vanilla Glaze

4 cups confectioners' sugar
1/4 cup cold water
1 teaspoon vanilla

In a saucepan combine 1 cup of the sugar with the water and cook them over moderately low heat until a syrup is formed of a consistency to spin a thread when a small quantity is dripped from a spoon (220 degrees). Skim the syrup several times during the cooking. Remove the pan from the heat and cool the syrup slightly. In a mixing bowl stir into the remaining sugar enough of the prepared syrup to reduce the sugar to the consistency of thick heavy cream. Stir the vanilla into it. Set the bowl over hot water, off the heat, and stir the icing until it is lukewarm and moderately runny. Use the icing as a glaze for puddings, cakes, or sweet breads or rolls. Simply pour it over the top of whatever is to be glazed and let it run down the sides. It will set in just a few minutes.

Any leftover sugar-water syrup may be kept in a tightly covered container. It may be used as bar syrup.

Cookies

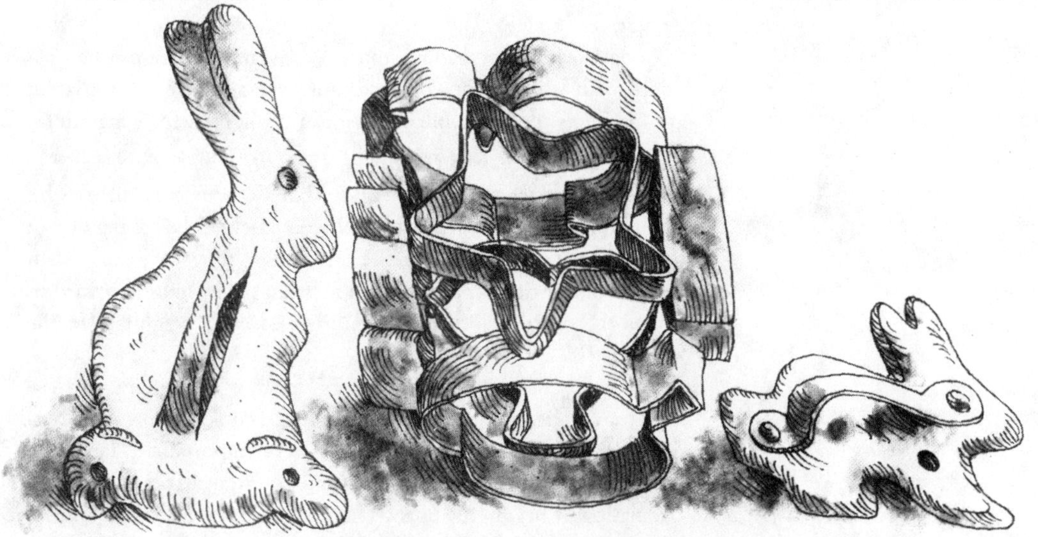

The New York Dutch were probably the first to popularize "koekjes," baked in outdoor ovens, in ovens built into the side of the fireplace, or on a griddle set over hot coals. But obviously cookies were difficult to bake until the wood-burning or coal-fired kitchen ranges were in general use. They became a standard item for lunch boxes and for snacks, and so constant was the demand that the cookie jar or tin was brought into fashion. Early twentieth-century housewives filled their cookie jars with not too sweet mixtures, rolled or dropped and spreading four to five inches in diameter. Tea or company cookies were made smaller and daintier.

How well I remember the cookies at Auntie Summers' when I was a child. Sadie, her extraordinary cook, made seven or eight different kinds that were stored in great tins nineteen inches high and twelve to fourteen inches in diameter. There were sugar cookies, fruit cookies, ginger cookies, and bar cookies; there were mock macaroons, an all-time favorite, which were nothing more than oatmeal drop cookies made with nuts and raisins; and there were true macaroons made with almonds or filberts or coconut. When Christmas rolled around there were galaxies of cookies — wonderful thin sugar cookies decorated with colored icings, anise-flavored springerle and anise bars, peppernuts and spice cookies. These never failed to delight me. They represented the art of cookie baking at its best.

Today, with temperature-controlled ovens, cookies can be produced with ease. I'm for a bulging cookie jar, and here in this chapter are the items that have filled American cookie jars for generations.

General Rules for Baking Cookies

Baking cookies requires attention, but with an oven timer, this is not difficult. Many cooks can tell by the smell of the baking dough just when the cookies are done. For this reason they leave the kitchen exhaust fan turned off during cookie baking. The natural hazard of this is the drawing of hungry family and even neighbors to the kitchen.

Properly shaped pans are important for any baking, and particularly for cookies. It is easier to remove baked cookies from a shallow-sided pan. The size of the pan, too, is very important. A large pan is better than a small one, but not one so large that it cuts off the circulation of heat in the oven. There should be at least 2 to 3 inches between the pan and the sides of the oven. Standard cookie baking pans are often called cookie "sheets" because they have no sides. These are fine, but a jelly roll pan about 11 × 15 × 1 inches is even better, because it can also be used for making a jelly roll and such cookies as brownies, cherubs, and matrimonials, that are baked in one piece and later sliced.

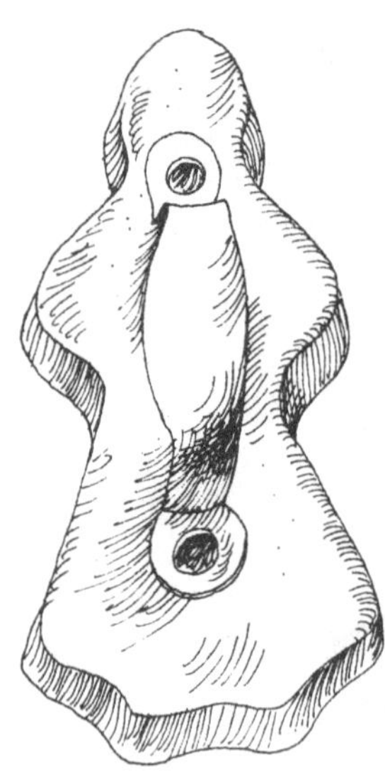

Production line baking usually can be accomplished by using two racks in the oven. Prepare one pan of cookies and place it on the lower rack of the oven. While it is baking, prepare another pan of cookies. Lift the first pan to the upper rack to finish baking before putting the second pan on the lower rack. Rotation in this way will allow the cookies to bake evenly. When baking a meringue type of cookie, it is best to bake one pan at a time to avoid opening the oven and exposing the cookies to cold air, which can cause them to fall.

Freezing Cookies and Cookie Dough

Refrigerators and freezers have made it possible to store both cookie dough and baked cookies. Cookie dough can be rolled in wax paper or aluminum foil, sealed in freezer bags to prevent drying, and stored in either the refrigerator or freezer. When ready to bake, cut with a sharp, thin-bladed knife into the thickness you prefer. If necessary, firm the rolls in the refrigerator before wrapping for freezing.

Remove baked cookies from the box or bag before thawing, so they will retain crispness. If they should lose it, place in a single layer on a cookie sheet or pan and heat in a 275 to 325 degree oven for a few minutes.

Many homemakers like to double or triple cookie recipes and keep the excess frozen for long periods or refrigerated for up to a month. Slicing off enough dough to produce a pan or two of baked cookies takes only few minutes.

To Use Chicken Fat or Bacon Fat in Cookies

Clarified chicken fat or bacon fat may be used instead of butter in many cookie recipes, such as rolled cookies. The fats are clarified by boiling with about half as much water for 5 to 6 minutes. Let cool, then chill. The fat can be skimmed or lifted from the water quite easily, leaving the "meat" flavor in the water. The Central Europeans also used goose fat for cookies. These fats were often used during the period when the cow had "dried up" and the butter supply had to be purchased. They were also used during World War I and II, when butter was in very short supply.

Nut Butter Balls

1 cup butter
4 to 6 tablespoons sugar
1 teaspoon vanilla or 1 tablespoon brandy, rum, or bourbon (optional)
2 cups sifted all-purpose flour
2 cups finely chopped or grated walnuts, pecans, filberts, or almonds
Powdered sugar for rolling

Nut butter balls, Russian tea cakes, and Mexican wedding cakes are a few of the names these cookies go by. Traditionally they are made with very little sugar and then heavily coated with powdered sugar, which is apt to leave a white moustache on the eater, or worse yet, a path of powdered sugar down the front of him. If you like, omit the powdered sugar and add 3/4 cup granulated sugar to the recipe. The Greeks like to put a whole clove in each cookie.

Cream the butter very well, then cream in the sugar until quite fluffy. Stir in the flavoring, the flour, and then the nuts. Mix together lightly until the flour is absorbed. Take small portions of the dough and roll into ropes on a lightly floured board. Cut into even sections. Roll in the palms to make very small, bite-size pieces. Place on ungreased cookie sheet and bake in a preheated 325-degree oven 8 to 12 minutes or more, until a delicate yellow. Remove from the pan and sift powdered sugar over them, or drop them while still warm into powdered sugar in a bag and shake lightly. This will give them a heavy coating of sugar. If less sugar is desired, cool the cookies before shaking them in the bag.

Peanut Butter Cookies

½ cup butter
½ cup peanut butter
1 cup firmly packed brown sugar
1 egg
2 cups sifted all-purpose flour
¼ teaspoon salt
1 teaspoon vanilla (optional)

This is a version dear to the set who favor peanut butter. Some people add from ½ to 1 cup of halved or chopped peanuts to make double peanut cookies.

Cream the butter and peanut butter, cream in the brown sugar, then beat in the egg. Sift the flour and salt and stir in. If desired, stir in the vanilla. This will make a very stiff dough. Form into long rolls about 1 inch in diameter. Cut into lengths of 1 inch or less, form into balls, and place an inch apart on greased cookie sheets. Press down the top of each cookie with a fork, first in one direction and then the other to make a crisscross design. Bake in a preheated 375-degree oven 9 to 12 minutes or until a delicate brown. Remove from pans while still slightly warm, and cool on a rack. Store in airtight containers. Yields about 4½ dozen small cookies.

Rich Peanut Butter Cookies. Use only 1¼ cups flour. Chill the rolls or freeze until firm. Slice about ¼ inch thick to bake. Place on greased or ungreased cookie pans or baking sheets, and bake until a delicate brown, about 8 minutes.

Pfeffernusse or Peppernuts

½ to 1 cup butter
2 cups sugar
2 eggs
1 teaspoon crushed baker's ammonia (ammonium carbonate, available at drug stores)
1 tablespoon lukewarm water
3 cups sifted all-purpose flour
½ teaspoon each of salt, nutmeg, and allspice
1 teaspoon cinnamon
¼ teaspoon fine ground pepper
¾ cup finely chopped candied fruit-cake fruits (optional)

One of the traditional Central European Christmas cookies. A great variance in recipes is to be found, depending upon the source. Some like their pfeffernusse rich, some like them made without fat, some like them slightly spiced, and some so spicy they bite back.

Cream the butter, then cream in the sugar and beat in the eggs until the mixture is light. Soak the baker's ammonia in the water about 5 minutes or until dissolved (the ammonia will give the cookies their characteristic crusty texture). Add the ammonia water to the creamed mixture. Sift dry ingredients together and stir into the creamed mixture. Add chopped fruits, if desired. Chill the dough about 30 minutes, then roll out into four long ropes about 1 inch in diameter. Cut off in ½-inch pieces. Roll each piece between the palms to create small balls. Place about 1 inch apart on greased or oiled cookie sheets. Bake in a preheated 375-degree oven about 8 minutes. Remove from the pan while slightly warm. Cool on a rack and store 5 or 6 days before using. Makes about 4½ dozen.

Refrigerator or Icebox Cookies

1 cup butter
1 to 1½ cups sugar

Cream the butter, then cream in the sugar until fluffy. Beat in the vanilla and eggs. Add the flour and salt, sifted together, and stir until well blended. Divide the dough into three or four parts and form rolls. Roll them up in wax paper or aluminum foil and store in the refrigerator or freezer until firm. With a sharp knife, slice

1 teaspoon vanilla
2 eggs
3 cups sifted all-purpose flour
½ teaspoon salt

⅛ to ⅜ inch thick. Place on greased or ungreased cookie sheets. Bake in a preheated 375-degree oven until a delicate beige — the time will depend upon the thickness of the cookies. Remove from the pan while warm and cool on a rack. Store in airtight containers. Yields 4½ dozen to 6½ dozen cookies.

Butterscotch Refrigerator Cookies. Instead of white sugar, use 1½ cups brown sugar.

Chocolate Refrigerator Cookies. Add 2 to 3 ounces bitter chocolate, melted, to the creamed butter and egg mixture. Use ¼ cup less flour.

Pinwheel Refrigerator Cookies. Divide the mixed dough approximately in half. Add 1 to 1½ ounces bitter chocolate, melted, to half the dough, mixing until no streaks remain. Roll half of the white dough between two sheets of heavy wax paper or foil until about ¼ inch thick and about 3 inches wide. Roll out half of the chocolate dough to the same size. Flip the chocolate dough over onto the plain dough and roll up like jelly roll, as tight as possible. Wrap in wax paper or foil and chill until very firm. Repeat with the remaining dough. Slice in ¼-inch slices and bake on a greased baking sheet until lightly yellow. Do not let these brown, or the contrasting stripes will not show up.

Orange or Lemon Refrigerator Cookies. Omit the vanilla and substitute 2 teaspoons finely grated lemon rind or 3 or 4 teaspoons finely grated orange rind.

Raisin, Date, Currant, or Prune Refrigerator Cookies. Put raisins, currants, or pitted dates or prunes through the medium blade of the food chopper (larger chunks of fruit are difficult to cut through and will break up the cookies) and beat into the creamed mixture before adding flour. From ½ to 1 cup ground fruit is sufficient. Use the spice recipe below, if you like.

Spice Refrigerator Cookies. Sift 1 tablespoon cocoa, 2 teaspoons cinnamon, 1 teaspoon nutmeg, and ½ teaspoon cloves with the flour and salt.

Filled Refrigerator Cookies. Shape spice, nut, chocolate, or butterscotch dough into a 2-inch roll. Chill until firm. Slice thin, place filling in the center, cover with another thin slice of dough, and press the edges down. For filling, use jelly or jam, or see filled cookies (page 715).

Rolled Oat Refrigerator Cookies. Use 1 to 1½ cups finely chopped rolled oats or oatmeal in place of 1 to 1½ cups of the flour. Rolled oats are too large to slice down successfully. Whirl them, about ½ cup at a time, in a blender for 30 to 40 seconds.

Nut Refrigerator Cookies. Mix ½ to ¾ cup finely chopped walnuts, pecans, Brazil nuts, filberts (hazelnuts), or peanuts into the sifted flour and salt. The nuts must be quite fine or the dough will crumble while being sliced.

Rocks

1 cup butter or ½ cup each of butter and lard
3 eggs
1½ cups firmly packed brown sugar
¾ cup raisins
2½ cups sifted all-purpose flour
½ teaspoon salt
1 teaspoon baking powder
1 teaspoon cinnamon

A recipe that appears in almost every cookbook of the late nineteenth and early twentieth century. Because these cookies kept well, the old recipes were made in huge quantities. Here the yield is about 3½ dozen instead of 12 dozen cookies.

Cream the shortening until very soft. Beat the eggs in a mixing bowl, and beat in the sugar until well blended. Add the creamed fat and the raisins. Stir in the flour sifted with the remaining ingredients. Dip up the dough with a greased teaspoon, and with the back of another greased teaspoon push it onto a buttered pan. Leave about 1½ inches between cookies for expansion. Bake in a preheated 350-degree oven 10 to 12 minutes or until a delicate brown. Remove from the pan while warm and cool on a rack. Store in airtight containers.

This dough freezes well if rolled 1½ to 2 inches in diameter, wrapped in wax paper or foil, and sealed in freezer bags. Cut or break off pieces and place on a buttered cookie sheet to bake. The baked cookies also freeze very well. Remove from the freezer bag when thawing so they will retain their crispness.

Rolled Cookies

½ to ¾ cup butter
1 cup sugar
2 eggs
1 teaspoon vanilla
2½ cups sifted all-purpose flour
2 teaspoons baking powder
½ teaspoon salt

A recipe that has many variations. Frequently the dough is rolled up and chilled, as with refrigerator cookies, and sliced thin to bake. The amount of butter used depends upon how rich you wish to make the cookies. For chewy cookies, use ½ cup butter and up to 1½ cups sugar.

Cream the butter and cream in the sugar until fluffy, then beat in the eggs and vanilla. Or use half vanilla and half another flavoring, such as almond. Add the flour sifted with the baking powder and salt. Blend well. Chill the dough for easier handling — if you are in a hurry, spread it out on aluminum foil in two portions, wrap, and place in the freezer for 10 to 30 minutes. Use only half the dough at a time for rolling and cutting. Roll with a floured pin on a lightly floured board, or roll between sheets of heavy wax paper. The thickness of the dough will depend upon your taste. For crisp cookies, roll very thin. If using wax paper, peel it off the top of the rolled dough, flop the dough over onto a lightly floured board, and peel off the other sheet. Cut the cookies with a floured cutter. Lift with a spatula onto a lightly oiled baking sheet or pan. Allow about 1 inch between them for expansion. Bake in a preheated 375-degree oven 8 to 10 minutes or until very lightly browned around the edges. Loosen from the pan while still quite warm. When they are cooled, on a rack, to room temperature, store in airtight containers. Makes about 4 dozen.

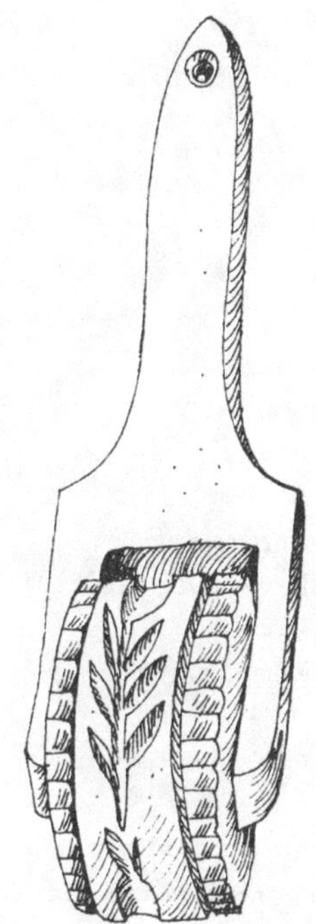

Caramel Rolled Cookies. Use ¾ cup butter and substitute 1½ cups firmly packed brown sugar for the white sugar.

Sugar Cookies. Use 2 teaspoons baking powder and only ½ cup butter. Roll ¼ to ⅓ inch thick. Before baking, sprinkle the cut-out cookies with sugar, preferably coarsely granulated white sugar. Sprinkle also with a little cinnamon, if you like.

Nut Rolled Cookies. Since it is difficult to cut through chunks of nutmeats with a cookie cutter, nuts are usually ground or whirled in a blender until quite fine. Mix in with the dry ingredients ½ to ¾ cup finely chopped or ground walnuts, pecans, peanuts, filberts, almonds, Brazil nuts, black walnuts, or butternuts. Or roll out the cookies, cut, brush with beaten whole egg, egg white, or egg yolk, and sprinkle the tops with finely chopped nutmeats.

Chocolate Rolled Cookies. Add ½ cup cocoa or 2 ounces melted unsweetened chocolate to the creamed butter and sugar mixture. Use only 2 cups flour.

Caraway, Sesame (Benne), or Anise Cookies. Mix 2 to 3 teaspoons caraway or sesame (benne) seed, or 1 teaspoon anise seed, into the sifted flour mixture. Or, in the old-fashioned way, brush the tops of the cut, unbaked cookies with beaten whole egg, egg white, or egg yolk, and sprinkle with the seeds.

Sandbakelse

1½ cups butter
⅞ cup sugar (1 cup minus 2 tablespoons)
1 egg yolk
¼ teaspoon almond extract
4 cups sifted all-purpose flour

Known by many different Scandinavian names, this can be made as a regular cookie or baked in patty pans or small muffin pans to provide a rather brittle shell for fresh berries or canned fruits — a great favorite when topped with whipped cream or ice cream.

Cream the butter, cream in the sugar, then mix in the egg yolk and flavoring. Add the flour a little at a time. Chill the dough, if not firm enough, before rolling out on a lightly floured board and cutting into thin cookies. Or press the dough into small or medium-size fluted patty pans or cake molds. Bake in a preheated 375 to 400 degree oven, for 8 to 10 minutes or until a very delicate brown. Remove cookies from the pans while warm and cool on a rack. If making patty shells, spring from pans when cool or almost cool by gently pressing the sides. Yields 6 to 7 dozen small tea cookies. The yield of fluted shells for fruit or ice cream depends upon the size of pans and thickness of dough.

Sand Tarts

½ cup butter
1 cup sugar
¼ teaspoon salt
1 egg
2 cups sifted cake flour
½ teaspoon vanilla (not traditional but often used)
1 egg white, lightly beaten with a fork
1 to 3 tablespoons coarse white sugar
¼ to ½ teaspoon cinnamon
Walnuts or almonds for decoration (optional)

So called because of the coarse sugar sprinkled on top of these very crisp cookies. We now use white decorating sugar to obtain that crunchy texture, for the present day granulated sugar will not give the proper "sand" effect.

Cream the butter until light, then cream in the sugar and salt, and beat in the egg, until the mixture is very light. Add the flour, and the vanilla if desired, or use almond flavoring and top with almond. When the dough is well blended, chill thoroughly. Roll out very thin and cut with floured cutter. Place the cookies on well-oiled baking sheets or pans and brush with beaten egg whites. Sprinkle with coarse white sugar to your taste, then with cinnamon. Do not overdo either sugar or cinnamon. Top with a walnut half or almond, if desired. Bake in a preheated 375-degree oven until a deep yellow around the edges. Allow to cool slightly before removing from the pans to a rack to cool. These will stay crisp 3 to 4 weeks when stored in airtight containers in a cool place, but are better if used within a week. The dough freezes very well or can be kept in the refrigerator (see page 698). When ready to use, slice very thin, sprinkle with sugar, and bake. Make about 5 dozen.

Scotch Shortbread

1½ cups butter
1 cup powdered or granulated sugar
4 cups sifted all-purpose flour

Never a holiday season goes by without shortbread in homes of the Scots or those of Scottish descent. Southerners are apt to call this "shortenin' bread" and often use brown instead of white sugar.

Cream the butter until almost like whipped cream. Gradually cream in the sugar and continue beating (easiest with electric mixer) until very light. Stir in the flour, then turn onto a lightly floured board or counter and knead the mixture until it is very smooth and will break slightly when the thumb is run from the center to the edge of the ball of dough. Traditionally this is pressed into shallow pie pans, the dough being about ½ inch thick. The edges are fluted as on a pie crust, and serving portions are stippled across the dough with a fork so that the shortbread can be broken easily into small pieces. I like to press the dough into tiny patty pans or into individual pie pans, crimping the edges. Prick the dough with a fork in even the smallest of pans, or it is apt to blister in the center. Bake in a preheated 275 to 300 degree oven until the palest brown around the edges. The length of time will depend upon the thickness of the dough and the size of the pan used. Remove from the pan, cool on a rack, and store in an airtight container, or place in freezer bags and seal. This is excellent eaten fresh, but traditionally it is aged a week or more in a cool place before being served. Makes 2 or 3 cakes and a number of small ones depending on the size.

Variation. Sometimes 1 to 2 tablespoons caraway seeds were added to the dough.

Snickerdoodles, Snipdoodles, or Schneckenoodles

1 cup soft butter
1½ cups sugar
1 teaspoon vanilla
2 eggs
¼ cup milk
3 cups sifted all-purpose flour
½ teaspoon salt
¾ teaspoon baking soda
1 teaspoon cream of tartar

TOPPING

3 tablespoons sugar
3 tablespoons cinnamon

In the middle to late nineteenth century regional cookbooks these appear under many names. The earliest church society cookbooks from the Hudson River region call them Schnecken Noodles, Schneckenoodles, or Snecke Noodles. Lower Midwest cookbooks, especially those of Kentucky and Missouri, list them as Snickerdoodles. Most recipes differ very little from crinkle cookies. Some recipes include ¾ cup raisins, mixed with the sifted flour mixture.

Cream the butter well, then cream in the sugar and vanilla. Beat in the eggs. Add the milk and the flour sifted with the salt, soda, and cream of tartar. Stir to combine well, easiest done with an electric mixer. Form into rolls about 1 inch in diameter and chill in the refrigerator. Cut off in 1-inch lengths and roll in the palms of the hand to form balls. Drop into the mixture of sugar and cinnamon, or dip only one side of the ball in the mixture and bake dipped side up. Place on a buttered cookie sheet or baking pan, leaving about 2 inches between each cookie. (These cookies can also be made without chilling the dough. When mixed, dip up with a greased teaspoon, scrape off with the back of another greased teaspoon onto buttered pans, then sprinkle the tops with cinnamon and sugar.) Bake in a preheated 375-degree oven until a delicate brown around the edges, about 10 minutes. Loosen from the pans while still warm. Makes about 40 to 45 cookies.

Spekulaas

2 cups (1 pound) butter
2 cups sugar
2 eggs
1½ teaspoons grated lemon rind
4½ cups sifted all-purpose flour
¾ teaspoon salt
2 teaspoons cinnamon
½ teaspoon ground cloves
½ teaspoon finely crushed or powdered cardamom seed

A rich and spicy cookie that can be rolled out and cut as any rolled cookie, but in Holland and Central Europe the dough is invariably pressed into a carved board to form interesting figures. The dough can be stored, chilled or frozen (see page 698) and then sliced before baking.

Cream the butter, then cream in the sugar until the mixture is very light. Beat in the eggs and lemon rind. Sift the flour with the remaining ingredients and blend well with the creamed mixture. If making molded cookies, sift flour over a spekulaas board, then brush lightly with a pastry brush to be sure flour goes into the carving. Press the dough into board and level it off by drawing a thin-bladed sharp knife across the board. Sometimes the dough is easier to handle if chilled. Unmold by holding the board over a cookie sheet and tapping lightly. If the cookies do not come out readily, turn the board over and with the tip of a paring knife lift an edge of the cookie, or tap the board on the kitchen counter.

A carved springerle rolling pin or board can also be used. Roll out the cookie dough about ⅓ inch thick, then roll with a well-floured springerle rolling pin or press into a floured springerle board. The springerle forms are never deep enough to use by pressing the dough into the design and cutting the dough away from the carving. Cut between the springerle designs to separate and transfer with a spatula to the cookie sheet.

Bake in a preheated 375-degree oven until a very delicate brown, 6 to 12 minutes, depending upon the thickness and circumference of the cookies. This recipe makes a large amount of cookies and can be easily halved.

Springerle

4 eggs
2 cups sugar
4 to 4½ cups sifted cake or pastry flour
1 tablespoon anise seed for pan or add 4 drops of anise oil to dough

The name of this cookie can be translated at a glance, for it does "spring up." Traditionally it is a Christmas cookie shaped with a springerle board or rolling pin, in which are carved charming little designs, so that the finished square or rectangle of cookie has a puffy top with a design embossed in it.

Beat the eggs until very light. Beat in the sugar gradually, and continue beating until the mixture is very light and creamy. Fold in the flour. If using anise oil, add it at this point. The Europeans never add salt to this cookie, but you may add ½ teaspoon, if you like. Also, they sometimes add 1 teaspoon baking powder with the flour. If standard-size eggs are used, 4 cups of flour should be ample, but a slight increase in size may call for the other cup. The dough should be soft enough to be rolled out on a lightly floured board or canvas. Lightly flour the top of the dough, and roll it out about ⅓ inch thick and approximately the size of the springerle board or the width of the springerle rolling pin. Dust the board or rolling pin with flour and blow away the excess. Press into the dough. Cut between the designs with a sharp, lightly greased knife or with a lightly greased pastry wheel. Transfer the pieces to a lightly oiled cookie sheet. If using anise seed, dust them onto the sheet before transferring the dough. Place the cookie sheets out of drafts and let stand 8 to 16 hours to set the design. Bake in a preheated 300-degree oven until a very delicate yellow. Do not overbake or these cookies will be hard, and even adding a cut apple or orange to the container in which they are stored will not soften them enough to make them edible. The length of time needed to bake them will depend upon the size of the cookies, but 10 to 14 minutes is usually enough. The cookies will puff up and have rather a crusty top. Makes about 60 cookies.

These cookies traditionally should be aged a week or two before eating, but many people like to eat them fresh. And there are those who claim that they should be very hard so they can be dunked in coffee. They freeze nicely if wrapped well in freezer bags. Better yet, pack between foil or wax paper, arrange in a box, and slip the box into a freezer bag and seal. Remove the bag and lid of the box to thaw.

Note: Some recipes add 2 tablespoons melted butter to the dough alternately with the flour.

Spritz or Cookie Press Cookies

1 cup butter
¾ cup sugar
1 egg or 3 egg yolks
1 teaspoon vanilla, almond, or brandy extract
2½ cups sifted all-purpose flour
¼ teaspoon salt

Scandinavian-Americans have made these fancily shaped cookies a specialty for many years. Commercial bakeries make them too, but not always with the quota of butter that gives them their distinctive flavor.

Cream the butter until very light and fluffy. Cream in the sugar gradually, and continue beating until very light. The degree of lightness determines the texture of the cookies. Beat in the egg or egg yolks and flavoring. Sift the flour with the salt and add to the mixture. In a warm temperature, this dough may have to be chilled about 30 minutes before putting through the cookie press. If the dough is too stiff it will be hard to press through the design plate; if too soft it may continue to ooze through the design plate and not break off when the press is lifted. To adjust a stiff dough, mix in a few drops of milk or white of egg. If despite chilling the dough is too soft, add a tablespoon or more of flour. Form a roll of dough slightly smaller than the tube of the cookie press and insert in the press after attaching the design plate you choose. Different makes of presses have their own directions for turning out the cookie dough, and you may wish to practice with a few turns. Press out the dough to be baked on a cold buttered cookie sheet or pan. Bake in a preheated 400-degree oven until a light yellow — baking time will depend upon the depth of the design used. Remove from the pans while still slightly warm, and let cool in one layer on a rack. When they are room temperature, store in airtight containers. They should be very crisp. To use the same baking pan for another batch of cookies, wipe the pan off very well with paper towels to remove grease and chill the pan slightly before pressing more cookie dough onto it. Makes 6 to 7 dozen.

These cookies, as do any rich cookies, freeze well. They are quite brittle, so it is best to line a box with wax paper or foil and layer the cookies in the box between foil or wax paper. Slip the box into a freezer bag and seal before freezing. To thaw, transfer cookies from box to a plate so they will not gather moisture. If they do not seem quite crisp when thawed, place on a cookie pan or sheet and freshen 4 or 5 minutes in a 300 to 325 oven.

Butterscotch Spritz. Substitute 7/8 cup (1 cup minus 2 tablespoons) firmly packed brown sugar for white sugar. If desired, use ½ teaspoon vanilla and 1 tablespoon rum as flavoring. If using rum, add 2 tablespoons more flour in recipe.

Chocolate Spritz. Add 2 ounces melted unsweetened chocolate to the creamed butter and sugar. Use 4 tablespoons less flour.

Spice Spritz. Sift with the flour and salt ½ to 1 teaspoon cinnamon, ½ teaspoon nutmeg, ½ teaspoon allspice, and ¼ teaspoon cloves.

Stick Candy Cookies

¾ cup butter
¾ cup sugar
2 eggs
2½ cups sifted all-purpose flour
½ teaspoon salt
⅓ to ½ cup crushed peppermint stick candy

Cream the butter, then cream in the sugar until light. Beat in the eggs. Stir in the flour mixed with salt. Fold in the crushed stick candy. This dough can be pushed from the tip of a teaspoon onto a greased baking sheet, or roll in aluminum foil or wax paper and chill or freeze until firm enough to slice about ¼ inch thick. Place on greased cookie sheets or pans and bake in a preheated 350-degree oven 8 to 12 minutes, depending upon the size of the cookies. Remove from the pan while still warm, cool on a rack, and store in airtight containers. Yields about 5 dozen cookies 2 inches in diameter.

Almond Pretzels

1 cup butter at room temperature
3 cups sifted cake flour
4 eggs
¼ cup heavy or whipping cream
1 teaspoon vanilla
1 cup sugar
¼ teaspoon salt

GLAZE

1 egg white
1 tablespoon milk
½ cup chopped blanched or unblanched almonds

Mid-Europe used these cookies as a party treat. The Pennsylvania Dutch probably made them popular in America, for the late nineteenth-century church society cookbooks of Pennsylvania and New York often mention them.

Mix the butter with the flour either with a pastry blender or by rubbing between the fingers until like fine meal. Beat the eggs, mix with the cream and vanilla, then with the sugar and salt. Turn into the flour mixture and stir well. Knead lightly in the bowl until thoroughly blended. Chill well. On a lightly floured surface, roll the dough quickly with the hands into thin rounds about 8 inches long and the diameter of a lead pencil. Form into bows or pretzel shapes. Brush lightly with the egg white beaten with the milk. Sprinkle with the almonds, or put the almonds in a pie pan and flop the pretzels into them. Place on a well-oiled cookie sheet or pan and bake in a preheated 325 to 350 degree oven until a very delicate yellow. This will take 10 to 15 minutes. Loosen from the baking sheet while still warm, and cool on a rack, and store in airtight containers. These freeze well but should be packed with wax paper in a box, then in a freezer bag, for they are brittle. Makes about 4½ dozen.

Chinese Almond Cookies

⅔ cup lard or half butter and half lard or all butter
½ to ⅔ cup sugar
½ to 1 teaspoon salt
1 teaspoon soda
1 teaspoon almond extract
2 eggs
3 cups sifted cake flour
1 egg yolk
1 teaspoon water or whiskey
Blanched almonds (about 36)

These and fortune cookies are a staple of Chinese restaurants. Almond cookies have been favorites in homes or bakeries on the West Coast for almost a hundred years and their fame has spread. Homemakers prefer to use all butter or half butter and half lard in their making. The former custom was to use lard and, instead of almond extract, 2 or 3 tablespoons of finely grated bitter almonds or peach or apricot pits.

Cream the shortening, cream in the sugar, and add the remaining ingredients except egg yolk, water and nuts. Or have all the ingredients at room temperature, place in a mixing bowl in the order given except the last three, and mix with the hands until well blended. If using all lard in the recipe, you will need 1 teaspoon of salt. The amount of sugar depends upon your taste. Roll the dough out on a floured board and form into four or five rolls about 1 inch in diameter. Cut off in about 1-inch pieces, and roll these into small balls. Press down on an oiled cookie sheet. Mix the egg yolk with the water or whiskey. Press an almond in the top of each cookie, and brush with the egg yolk mixture. Bake in a preheated 375-degree oven 8 to 12 minutes or until a delicate brown. Remove from the pans while warm, cool on a rack, and store in airtight containers. Makes about 4 dozen cookies.

Anise Caps

4 eggs
2 cups sugar
2 cups sifted all-purpose flour
¼ teaspoon salt
5 or 6 drops anise oil or anise seed for flavoring

Central Europeans make these as a Christmas cookie, and German Jews also make them for their holidays. Some Germans use caraway seeds instead of anise.

Combine the eggs and sugar in a double boiler top, and beat for several minutes with a whisk, rotary beater, or electric mixer at medium to medium high speed. Place over slowly boiling water and beat about 5 minutes or until the mixture is very fluffy and the bubbles are fine-textured. Remove from the heat. Fold in the flour sifted with the salt. Add the anise oil at this point, or sprinkle anise seed on the pan and on top of the cookies before baking. Push small dots of batter from tip of teaspoon with back of another teaspoon onto a greased and floured cookie sheet or pan. Bake immediately, or for the "cap" effect let the pans of cookies stand several hours in a draft-free spot. Bake in a preheated 350-degree oven just until a pale yellow. Overbaking will make these cookies hard. Cool before storing. They freeze only moderately well, but will keep several weeks in a tightly covered container in a cool place.

Apple, Prune, Apricot, or Pineapple Sauce Cookies

½ cup butter
1 cup white or firmly packed brown sugar
1 egg
2½ cups sifted all-purpose flour
½ teaspoon salt
1 teaspoon baking powder
¼ teaspoon baking soda
¾ cup thick apple, prune, apricot, or pineapple sauce
½ to ¾ cup coarsely chopped walnuts, pecans, or filberts
Spices (optional)

Cream the butter, cream in the sugar, and beat in the egg. Sift the flour with salt and leavenings. Add to the creamed mixture along with the sauce. The pineapple should be well-drained canned crushed pineapple. Apricot or prune sauce can be dried fruit steamed, well drained, and chopped; or use canned fruit drained very well, pitted, and crushed or chopped. If you want to flavor with spices, add 1 teaspoon cinnamon and ¼ teaspoon cloves. In pineapple cookies, use ¼ teaspoon ginger. Push the dough from the tip of teaspoon with the back of another onto a greased cookie or baking sheet. Bake in a preheated 375-degree oven 8 to 12 minutes until a delicate brown. Remove from the pans while still warm. Cool on a rack before storing in tightly covered containers. These keep well for several weeks, but are apt to become moist and stick together unless layers of wax paper are put between the cookies. Yields about 5 dozen small cookies.

Fresh Apple Cookies

½ cup butter
1⅓ cups firmly packed brown sugar
1 egg
2½ cups sifted all-purpose flour
½ teaspoon salt
½ teaspoon baking soda
1 teaspoon cinnamon
½ teaspoon nutmeg
½ teaspoon allspice
¼ teaspoon cloves
¼ cup apple juice, pineapple juice, orange juice, or milk
1 cup chopped, unpeeled raw apple
½ to 1 cup chopped walnuts, filberts, or pecans
1 cup raisins

Cream the butter, cream in the sugar, and beat in the egg. Sift the dry ingredients and add to the creamed mixture along with the juice or milk. Stir in the apple, nuts, and raisins. Push the dough from the tip of a teaspoon with the back of another onto a buttered cookie sheet, leaving about 1½ inches between each cookie. Bake in a preheated 375-degree oven 10 to 12 minutes or until a light brown. Yields about 4 dozen cookies.

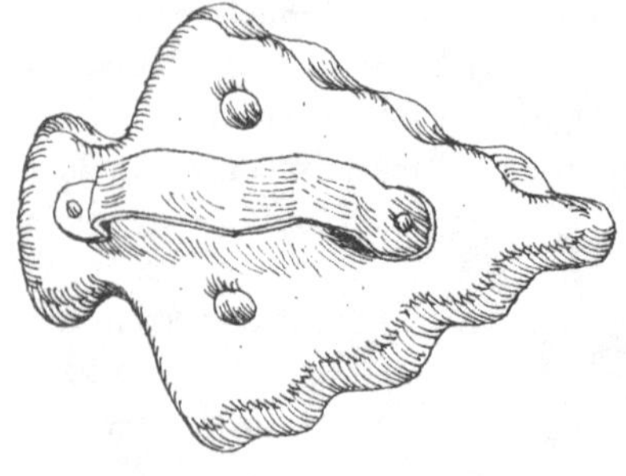

Bourbon, Sherry, Rum, or Brandy Balls or Walnut Spirit Balls

2½ cups finely crushed, rolled, or whirled-in-blender vanilla wafers or dried and crumbled yellow cake
1 cup confectioners' sugar
1 cup finely chopped walnuts, pecans, filberts, or almonds, lightly toasted
3 tablespoons corn syrup
¼ cup bourbon, sherry, light or dark rum, or brandy
Confectioners' sugar for rolling cookies

Since Prohibition was repealed, this cookie has been extremely popular. It is similar to the cookies made of dried cake crumbs that appear in several old regional cookbooks.

Mix the ingredients in the order given. Let stand a few minutes, then form into balls 1 inch in diameter and roll in confectioners' sugar. Store in a well-covered container packed between sheet of wax paper or foil for a day or two to ripen before serving. For keeping long periods, store in the refrigerator or freezer.

Cocoa or Mocha Spirit Balls. Add to the mixture 2 tablespoons cocoa, or heat the corn syrup and melt in it 1 to 2 ounces unsweetened chocolate. For mocha, use the cocoa and add 1 teaspoon instant coffee. These are especially good made with rum.

Brown Sugar or Tan or Pecan Kisses

1 egg white
¼ teaspoon cream of tartar
¼ teaspoon salt
1 cup firmly packed sugar (light brown preferred)
1 teaspoon vanilla
1 to 2 cups whole or very coarsely chopped pecans, walnuts, filberts, or almonds

In pecan-growing regions, these were considered a very special cookie confection at the turn of the century. Almost a candy, they are not really meant to fill the cookie jar, but are often made for Christmas boxes. Of course other nut meats can be used — including black walnuts and hickory nuts.

Beat the egg white with cream of tartar and salt until very foamy and beginning to hold shape. Beat in the brown sugar gradually, about ¼ cup at a time, while also adding the vanilla. Beat until the mixture is stiff and the sugar is dissolved — this is easiest done in the small bowl of an electric mixer. Fold in the nut meats. Push the dough from the tip of a greased teaspoon with the back of another onto a buttered and floured cookie sheet or pan. Bake at 300 to 325 degrees about 15 minutes or until the cookies are puffy and set. They will usually fall and crinkle on the top when removed from the oven. Take from the pans while still warm, and cool on a rack completely before storing between sheets of wax paper or aluminum foil.

Brownies

½ cup butter
2 to 4 ounces unsweetened chocolate
2 cups sugar

There are many variations of this theme, such as the recipe for butterscotch bars that follows. When this brownie recipe is made with creamed butter and sugar and 3 instead of 2 eggs, it is often called fudge cake and has a cake texture.

Melt the butter and chocolate in a saucepan (1½ to 2 quarts) over low heat. Remove from the heat, stir well, then stir in the sugar

2 eggs
1 teaspoon vanilla
1 cup sifted all-purpose flour
½ teaspoon salt
1 cup broken walnut meats

and beat in the eggs and vanilla. Quickly stir in the flour, salt, and nuts to just lightly mix. Spread into a well-greased 8 × 10-inch or 9 × 12-inch baking pan. Bake at 325 degrees, 35 minutes for the smaller pan, 30 for the larger. Do not overbake, or they will lose their nice chewy texture. Remove the pan to rack to cool. While still slightly warm, cut into squares with a greased knife. Yields 30 to 35 pieces about 1½ × 2 inches. These can be frozen packed into either freezer bags or a tightly covered box. Remove from the bag or box to thaw.

Frosted Brownies. Some people like to top baked brownies with cut up marshmallows or miniature marshmallows softened in the oven for about 4 minutes and then lightly spread. After cooling, the brownies are given a chocolate glaze.

Butterscotch Bars or Blond Brownies. This variation of the brownie is more like a confection than a cookie. Substitute 2½ cups (1 pound) light brown sugar for the chocolate and white sugar. After adding to the melted (not browned) butter, stir until just bubbly. Remove from heat and cool to room temperature before adding the other ingredients. Use pecans or filberts instead of walnuts, if you like. Use a well-greased 9 × 11 × 2-inch pan or one slightly larger. Bake at 325 degrees about 35 minutes for the 9 × 11-inch pan, slightly less for the larger one.

Polka Dot Brownies. Mix 6 ounces semisweet chocolate pieces into the dough for butterscotch bars (above).

Peanut Brownies. The first recipes called for 1 cup Spanish peanuts instead of walnuts.

Carrot Cookies

¾ cup butter
¾ cup sugar
1 cup grated or finely shredded raw carrot
1 egg
1 to 3 teaspoons grated orange rind
2¼ cups sifted all-purpose flour
½ teaspoon salt
2 teaspoons baking powder

The carrots give these cookies a rather crunchy texture. Sometimes chopped raw pumpkin or squash were used in place of carrots. Some old recipes call for spice or grated lemon rind, but most recipes seem to prefer the orange rind.

Cream the butter, cream in the sugar, beat in the carrot and egg, and blend well. Mix in the rind and the dry ingredients sifted together. Dip up about 1 teaspoonful of dough on a greased teaspoon and push off with the back of another onto a well-oiled or buttered baking pan or sheet. Bake in a preheated 375-degree oven 10 to 12 minutes or until the cookies are a delicate brown around the edges. Loosen from the pan while still warm, cool on a rack, and store in airtight containers. These freeze well, as does the unbaked dough.

Oatmeal Carrot Cookies. Use 1 cup rolled oats, the quick-cooking or regular variety, in place of 1 cup of the flour.

Cherubs, Honeymoon Bars, Dream Bars, or Lover's Morsels

1 1/3 cups unsifted all-purpose flour
1/2 teaspoon salt
1/2 cup butter
1/2 cup white or firmly packed brown sugar

TOPPING

2 eggs
1 cup white or firmly packed light brown sugar or 1/2 cup of each
1 1/2 cups flake coconut; or finely chopped walnuts, almonds, pecans, or filberts; or part coconut and part chopped nuts
1/8 teaspoon salt
1 teaspoon vanilla

This bar cookie has numerous names, and the topping has as many variations. Sometimes jam or a date filling is put between the pastry and the topping.

Put the flour, salt, butter, and sugar into a mixing bowl and blend with the hands or a pastry blender or in a mixer until the consistency of cornmeal. Press into the bottom of an 8 × 10-inch or 9 × 9-inch pan. This makes a pastry base for the cookies. Bake in a preheated 350-degree oven 8 to 10 minutes. In the meantime, prepare the topping. Beat the eggs until very fluffy and beat in the sugar until it is dissolved. Fold in the remaining ingredients. Spread on the partly baked pastry mixture and return to the oven for about 15 more minutes or until a delicate yellow. Put the pan on a rack to cool. While still warm, cut with a greased knife into small squares, diamonds, or strips.

Sweet Chocolate, Chocolate Chunk, Chocolate Chip, or Toll House Cookies

3/4 cup butter
3/4 cup white sugar
3/4 cup firmly packed brown sugar
1 egg
1 teaspoon vanilla (optional)
3 tablespoons milk
2 1/2 cups sifted all-purpose flour
1 teaspoon baking powder
1/4 teaspoon salt
1 12-ounce package semisweet chocolate pieces
1 cup chopped walnuts pecans,, almonds, or filberts

Long before semisweet or sweet chocolate was sold in small chips, bits, or morsels, homemakers cut up bars of chocolate to make these cookies. Ruth Wakefield, who ran the Toll House Restaurant in Massachusetts, made these cookies popular. She afterward sold the rights to the name to the Nestlé Company, who have perpetuated Toll House cookies. Some recipes use 1/4 cup more butter than is called for here, but this makes the dough so rich that the butter "fries out" during the baking.

Cream the butter, cream in the white and brown sugars, beat in the egg, vanilla, and milk. Sift the flour with the baking powder and salt, and stir into the batter, then stir in the chocolate pieces and nuts. Grease two teaspoons. Dip up about half a teaspoon of dough on a greased teaspoon, and with the back of another one scrape it off onto a buttered or oiled baking pan or sheet. Allow about 1 inch between cookies. Bake in a preheated 375-degree oven 8 to 12 minutes, depending upon the size of the cookies. Loosen from the pan with a spatula while still quite warm, cool on a cake rack, and store in airtight containers. These freeze well, and can also be stored in the refrigerator (see page 698). Yields about 5 dozen cookies 2 inches in diameter.

Crinkle Cookies

¾ cup butter
1⅔ cups granulated sugar
2 eggs
1 teaspoon vanilla
2½ cups sifted all-purpose flour
¼ teaspoon baking soda
1½ teaspoons baking powder
½ teaspoon salt
⅓ cup milk
½ cup finely chopped walnuts (optional)
Granulated or confectioner's sugar

Cream the butter very well, then cream in the sugar and beat in the eggs and vanilla. Stir in the flour sifted with the soda, baking powder, and salt. Add the milk, and finally the nuts. Chill the dough in the refrigerator several hours, or shape before chilling into long rolls about 1 inch in diameter. After chilling, cut into pieces of uniform size and roll into balls about 1 inch in diameter. Have granulated or sifted confectioner's sugar ready in a pie pan or similar shallow pan. Dip the cookies in the sugar to coat and place 2 or 3 inches apart on a greased cookie sheet or pan. Bake at 350 degrees about 12 minutes. The tops will be crinkly. Cool slightly and remove from the pan while still warm and cool on a rack. Yields about 4 dozen cookies.

Chocolate Crinkles. Use only ½ cup butter and 2 cups flour. Melt 2 squares unsweetened chocolate and add to the creamed mixture.

Spice Crinkles. Add 1 to 2 teaspoons powdered ginger or 3 tablespoons finely chopped candied or preserved ginger. Or add 1½ teaspoons cinnamon, ½ teaspoon nutmeg, and ¼ teaspoon cloves.

Eier Kringel or Egg Yolk Cookies

3 hard-boiled egg yolks
½ cup butter
½ cup sugar
1 raw egg or 2 raw egg yolks
2 cups sifted all-purpose flour or 2¼ cups sifted cake or pastry flour
¼ teaspoon salt
⅛ teaspoon mace (optional)
½ teaspoon finely grated lemon rind or 1 teaspoon vanilla

DECORATION

1 egg white
1 tablespoon water
Colored sugar, chopped candied fruits, etc.

Although these fine-textured cookies are excellent at any time of the year, they are usually made for holidays and are fashioned into wreaths, bows, and other suitable shapes. Central Europeans and Scandinavians invariably decorate these with colored sugar or paint them with frosting and dot with bits of candied cherry and other candied fruits.

Sieve the hard-boiled egg yolks by pushing through a medium to fine sieve (easiest done with the thumbs). Cream the sieved yolks and butter together until very light. Cream in the sugar until it is dissolved. Beat in the raw egg or yolks and stir in the flour sifted with the salt and mace. Add the flavoring. Blend well. Roll out on a very lightly floured board and cut with a floured cutter into whatever shape you choose. Or pull off small pieces of dough and roll to make long, very thin rolls. Cut in 3 to 4 inch lengths. Roll two or three of these together and join the ends to make a wreath. Or use a 6 to 7 inch length to make a bow or other design. Place on an ungreased cookie sheet and bake at 375 degrees until just a very delicate yellow. The length of time will depend upon the size of the cookie.

If colored sugar is to be used for decoration, beat the egg white and water until thin. Cool the baked cookies slightly, brush with the egg white mixture, and immediately sprinkle with colored sugar or invert the cookie in the sugar. Return to the oven for 2 or 3 minutes to set the egg white. Or cool the cookies (remove from pan while warm) and paint with colored royal frosting or egg yolk frosting. Finely chopped fruit cake fruits, if they are not too dry, will stick to the cookies as they are, if put on warm cookies. Otherwise, brush the cookies with the egg white mixture, apply the fruit in any design you like, and return to the oven for 1 or 2 minutes.

These cookies should not be kept for very long, although the dough can be made well ahead, wrapped in freezer bags, and refrigerated (see page 698). This is a crisp but not too brittle cookie that should not be shipped far, even with careful packing. If making these as Christmas cookies it would be wise to double the recipe or even triple it.

Fattigman's Bakelse or Poor Man's Cakes

6 egg yolks
3 tablespoons heavy cream or sour cream
3 tablespoons sugar
1⅓ cups sifted all-purpose flour or 1½ cups sifted cake or pastry flour
½ teaspoon salt
⅛ teaspoon ground cardamom seed, or flavor with 1 tablespoon brandy and reduce cream by 1 tablespoon

Scandinavians, Central Europeans, and Spanish and Italians consider these a holiday treat. Although fried in deep fat instead of being baked, they are served as one would a cookie, for they are thin, crisp, and dainty, not round and pudgy like a doughnut.

Beat the egg yolks slightly in a bowl, add the cream and sugar, and beat until very well blended. Add the flour sifted with the salt and cardamom seed. Stir well and knead slightly in the bowl to make a smooth mixture. Chill the dough well. Roll it very thin, about ⅛ inch thick — this can be done between two sheets of heavy wax paper. With a greased sharp knife or pastry wheel, cut in strips 4 inches long and 1 to 1½ inches wide, or cut in diamond shapes or squares. Each nationality seems to have its typical design. Cut a slit toward one end of the piece of dough and draw the opposite corner or side through. Drop into hot fat, 375 degrees on a deep-fat thermometer and 2 inches or more deep. When the cakes are a delicate brown on one side, turn and brown on the other. When done, remove to drain on paper towels or napkins. Sprinkle while still warm with powdered sugar or shake in a bag containing powdered sugar. Cool, and store in airtight containers until served. These can be freshened before serving by placing on a baking sheet and crisping in a slow oven, 275 to 300 degrees, for about 5 minutes.

Filled Cookies

½ to ¾ cup butter (¾ cup or more for a rich cookie)
½ to ¾ cup sugar (½ cup if filling is very sweet)
2 eggs
1 teaspoon vanilla
2½ cups sifted all-purpose flour

Apple, peach, pear, or prune butter was a favorite filling for cookies for the years when schoolchildren and many workingmen carried lunch pails. Fancier cookies were made with date, fig, or pineapple filling.

Cream the butter, and cream in the sugar until fluffy. Beat in the eggs and vanilla. Sift the flour with the salt and baking powder and stir into the creamed mixture just until blended. Chill. Remove half the dough at a time from the refrigerator. Roll out about ⅛ inch thick on a floured pastry cloth or lightly floured board. Cut into

½ teaspoon salt
1 teaspoon baking powder
1 cup filling or more

rounds with a floured cutter. Divide into two equal batches. One batch will receive the filling. Depending upon the size of the finished cookie, spoon from ¼ to 1 teaspoon filling into the center of each round. Cover with the remaining rounds and press the edges together with a fork. Sometimes the top rounds are cut out with a doughnut cutter so that the filling will show through the hole. Or cut the rounds 2½ to 4 inches in diameter, place the filling on one half of the round, fold the other half over it, and crimp the edges together. Whatever the shape, place the cut and filled cookies on greased cookie sheets. Bake in a preheated 375-degree oven 8 to 12 minutes, depending on the thickness and width of the cookies. Remove from the pan while warm and cool on a rack.

Date, Fig, Prune, or Apricot Cookie Filling

½ pound dried figs or pitted dates, prunes, or apricots
1¼ cups water
1 cup white or firmly packed sugar
1 tablespoon lemon juice
½ cup finely chopped walnuts, pecans, almonds, filberts or Brazil nuts (optional)

Bring the dried fruit and water to a boil in a saucepan. Cover, and simmer about 10 minutes or until the fruit is soft. Mash while warm, or cool and chop (prunes must be pitted). Sometimes the fruit can be broken sufficiently with a fork. Return the fruit to the pan, add the sugar, and simmer until thick. Remove from the heat, stir in the lemon juice, and add nuts, if desired. They will have more flavor if toasted lightly (spread in a shallow baking pan in a single layer and bake 5 to 8 minutes at 350 degrees). Cool the filling before using.

Pineapple Cookie Filling

2 cups crushed pineapple and juice (1-pound can)
½ cup sugar
4 tablespoons flour
1 tablespoon lemon juice

Bring the pineapple and juice to a boil in a saucepan. Mix the sugar and flour and stir in slowly. Bring again to a boil and boil 1 or 2 minutes until the mixture is quite thick. Remove from the heat and stir in the lemon juice. Cool before filling cookies.

Fruit Cake Cookies, or New Year's Cookies or "Cakes"

1 cup butter
2 cups sugar (all white or all firmly packed brown or 1 cup of each)
2 eggs

Fruit cake cookies have long been a holiday goody. From the evidence in old regional cookbooks, these rich cookies seem to have been made in large quantities, one recipe starting with 7 pounds (28 cups) of flour. Obviously this was during the mid-nineteenth century, when New Year's Day was the signal for the men of the family to spend the day calling on every household in town.

Cream the butter, cream in the sugar, and beat in the eggs. Stir in the flour sifted with the baking powder, salt, and spices. Add the liquid and then the raisins, nuts, and fruit cake fruits. With a greased teaspoon dip up 3/4 teaspoon of dough, push from the spoon with the back of another greased teaspoon onto a well-buttered or oiled cookie sheet or pan. Bake in a preheated 350-degree oven about 10 minutes or until the edges are a delicate brown. Do not overbake or the fruit will become hard. Remove from the pans while still warm. Cool on a rack to room temperature and store in airtight containers. These freeze well and are better if aged a week before eating.

3 cups sifted all-purpose flour
3 tablespoons baking powder
1/2 teaspoon each of salt, cloves, and nutmeg
2 teaspoons cinnamon
1/4 cup brandy, sherry, port, rum, wine, or fruit juice
1 cup raisins
1 cup coarsely chopped walnuts, pecans, filberts, or unblanched almonds
2 cups (1 pound) chopped fruit cake fruits

Gingerbread Men

3 cups sifted all-purpose flour
1/2 teaspoon baking soda
2 teaspoons baking powder
1/2 teaspoon salt
3/4 teaspoon ginger
1/3 cup butter or lard
1/3 cup firmly packed brown sugar
2/3 cup light or dark molasses
1 egg

There are so many versions of dough for gingerbread men. Some are very crisp, others puffy. In some countries the ginger, molasses, and flour are mixed and then stored in a crock in a cool cellar to age for a year. I've never found that it made that much difference in flavor, and few people these days have a cool basement — or a cellar.

Sift the flour with the soda, baking powder, salt, and ginger. Cream the fat, cream in the sugar, beat in the molasses and egg. Add the sifted dry ingredients and combine well. Chill slightly if the dough seems too soft. Roll out on a lightly floured board and cut into shapes with a floured cutter, cutters, or sharp knife. The thickness of the dough will depend upon the size of the cutters. If using a large cutter, have the dough at least 1/3 inch or, better, 1/2 inch thick. Large gingerbread men should be lifted from the board with a wide spatula. Bake cookies on greased baking sheets or pans. Allow room for expansion in baking. Bake in a preheated 375-degree oven, 8 to 15 minutes, depending upon the thickness. Remove from the pan while still warm and cool on a rack. The yield depends upon the sizes.

Gingersnaps

1 cup molasses or dark corn syrup
1 cup sugar
3/4 cup butter or lard
4 1/2 cups sifted all-purpose flour
3/4 teaspoon salt
1 teaspoon baking soda
1 tablespoon ginger

Long a cookie jar favorite, gingersnaps were considered a roll cookie in the nineteenth century. Homemakers nevertheless often dropped them on a greased cookie sheet to bake. Now they may be rolled or chilled and sliced.

Bring the molasses or corn syrup, sugar, and shortening just to the boil in a saucepan holding 2 or 3 quarts. Cool slightly. Add the flour sifted with the salt, soda, and spices. It is necessary, of course, to use the ginger, but the remaining spices may be omitted, if

2 teaspoons cinnamon
1 teaspoon nutmeg } *optional*
½ teaspoon cloves
⅓ cup water

desired. Add the water and stir until well blended. Chill the dough, then roll out on a lightly floured board. Cut with a floured cutter into rounds and place on a greased baking sheet or pan. Leave about 1 inch between the cookies. Or form the dough into rolls 1 to 1½ inches in diameter, wrap in wax paper or aluminum foil, and chill or freeze until firm. Slice with a thin sharp knife into cookies ⅛ to ¼ inch thick. Bake at 375 degrees 8 to 10 minutes, depending upon the size and thickness of the cookies. Remove from the pan while still slightly warm and cool on a rack.

Spice Snaps. Omit the ginger and use only the remaining spices.

Hermits

½ cup butter
1 cup firmly packed brown sugar
1 egg
½ cup sour cream
1½ cups unsifted all-purpose flour
½ teaspoon baking soda
½ teaspoon salt
1 teaspoon cinnamon
½ teaspoon each of cloves and allspice
1 cup chopped walnuts, pecans, hickory nuts, filberts, or almonds
½ to 1 cup raisins

Always a favorite of mine when young. Most old recipes use sour cream in these cookies, although in the Deep South molasses is often the liquid ingredient. All recipes, however, use some spice and always dried fruit — raisins or figs or dates, sometimes dried prunes cut in small pieces — and always nutmeats. Undoubtedly the choice of fruit in the old cookbooks depended upon availability.

Cream the butter, cream in the sugar well, beat in the egg, and stir in the sour cream. Add the sifted dry ingredients, then the nuts and raisins. Stir to lightly mix. Grease a teaspoon, dip up about a slightly rounded spoon of batter, and push with the back of another greased teaspoon onto a well-oiled cookie sheet or pan. Bake in a preheated 350-degree oven 8 to 12 minutes or until a delicate brown. Loosen from the pan while still hot. Cool on a rack to room temperature and store in airtight containers. These cookies freeze well and are better in flavor if they are aged several days before eating.

Jumbles

½ cup butter
1 cup sugar
2 eggs or 3 egg yolks
3 tablespoons sour cream
¼ teaspoon baking soda
½ teaspoon salt
2½ cups sifted all-purpose flour
1 teaspoon flavoring (optional)

Recipes for jumbles appear in many regional or sectional cookbooks from the 1870's through the first several decades of the twentieth century. *The Practical Cook Book*, compiled in 1882 by "A Committee of Ladies of the First Presbyterian Church of Meadville, Pennsylvania," out of twenty-one recipes for cookies and small cakes offers seven recipes for jumbles! Some use thick sour cream, some use buttermilk — which in those days was a home byproduct of churning and had many small dots of butter through it. We use commercially made sour cream to achieve the traditional flavor.

Cream the butter, and cream in the sugar until very light. Beat in the eggs or egg yolks. Stir in the sour cream mixed with the soda and salt. Stir in the flour. The traditional jumble had no flavor other than that of butter and sour cream, but you may add

1 teaspoon vanilla or ½ teaspoon vanilla and ½ teaspoon almond extract. Chill the dough, then roll out very thin on a lightly floured board. Cut with a floured cutter. Or form the dough into pencil-size rolls about 6 inches long and join the ends to make rings. Or cut the thin rolled-out dough with a doughnut cutter to form rings. Place on buttered baking sheets. Bake in a preheated 375-degree oven until a very delicate yellow around the edges. Or for a very crisp cookie that has a browned butter flavor, bake in a slow oven — 300 degrees.

Jumbles freeze nicely if well wrapped. They are fragile, so are better packed into a box with wax paper before being placed in a freezer bag and sealed. Remove from the box when thawing. The dough freezes very well and can also be rolled, wrapped, and chilled in the refrigerator to be sliced thin for baking (see page 700).

Lebkuchen

½ pound (⅔ cup) strained honey
1 cup firmly packed brown sugar
2 tablespoons water
2 tablespoons lard or butter
3½ cups sifted all-purpose flour
½ teaspoon baking soda
½ teaspoon salt
¼ teaspoon cloves
¼ teaspoon ginger
½ teaspoon cinnamon
¾ cup finely chopped candied citron or orange peel or some of each
1 cup blanched slivered almonds

GLAZE

1 tablespoon lemon juice or sherry
2 tablespoons hot water
1 cup sifted powdered sugar

This holiday cookie improves if aged 2 to 6 weeks. The recipe can vary greatly, depending upon the nationality of the baker or which Central European country she borrowed the recipe from.

Place the honey, sugar, water, and shortening in a large saucepan. Bring to a boil, remove from heat, stir to blend, and cool to room temperature. Sift the flour with the soda, salt, and spices. Stir into the honey mixture. Add the candied peel and slivered almonds. This dough can be rolled out immediately, although some recipes insist on packing into a bowl or loaf pan, covering well, and letting it ripen 2 or 3 days in a cool place. Roll about ⅓ inch thick on a lightly floured board. With a floured sharp knife, cut into strips about 1 × 3 inches. Place on a greased or oiled cookie sheet or pan and bake in a 300-degree oven about 10 minutes or until a very delicate brown. Do not overbake or the cookies will be very hard, although presumably they should be firm enough for dunking in coffee. Remove from the pan while still warm. Cool on a rack, then mix the transparent glaze icing and brush or spoon it on. When completely cool, store between sheets of wax paper in air-tight containers to age. These can also be decorated with bits of candied fruit cake fruits or candied cherries. Yields about 5 dozen strips.

Meringue Kisses

3 egg whites
½ teaspoon cream of tartar or 1 teaspoon lemon juice
1 cup fine granulated sugar
1 teaspoon vanilla, or rum or brandy flavoring

Considered "tea" specials in the days when ladies had certain days to receive callers. Invariably these were served in fancy shapes or decorated with colored sugars, nutmeats, or a powdering of cocoa or spice. They were often put through a pastry tube to make fluted fingers, and sometimes small rounds were baked and while still warm fastened to pastry "stems" to make "mushrooms." The mushroom caps were then sprinkled lightly with cinnamon.

This is easiest made in the small bowl of an electric mixer. Beat the egg whites until foamy. Add the cream of tartar or lemon juice and beat until fluffy but not at all dry. Be careful not to overbeat. Add the sugar gradually, about 3 or 4 tablespoons at a time. Add the flavoring when about half the sugar has been added. Continue beating until all the sugar is dissolved. Have ready cookie sheets or shallow pans lined with buttered letter paper or butcher paper or parchment. Push the meringue from the tip of a teaspoon with the back of another teaspoon onto the paper, or put in a pastry bag fitted with a plain or frilled tube and squeeze small amounts onto the paper, leaving at least an inch between meringues. These can also be baked in a greased and floured pan; they will stick if the pan is greased only. Bake at 275 to 300 degrees about 20 minutes or until the meringues are set and very lightly colored. Let cool slightly and remove from the paper. Set on a rack and cool completely before storing in airtight containers between sheets of foil or wax paper.

Forgotten Kisses. Make as above, but put in a well-insulated oven preheated to 350 degrees. Immediately turn off the heat and leave the oven door closed 2 hours or overnight.

Coconut Kisses or Macaroons. When the recipe is completely mixed, fold in 1 to 1½ cups flaked coconut. This mixture will not go through any but the plain tube (large) of a pastry bag. Or shape the cookies by pushing from the tip of a teaspoon.

Cornflake Kisses. When the recipe is completely mixed, fold in 1 to 1½ cups uncrushed cornflakes, or 1 cup cornflakes and ½ to 1 cup flaked coconut or ½ cup coarsely chopped nutmeats, such as walnuts, almonds, pecans, or filberts. Any of the ready-to-eat cereals can also be used in this.

Spicy Kisses. With the sugar, beat in 1 teaspoon cinnamon, ½ teaspoon mace or nutmeg, and ¼ teaspoon cloves.

Chocolate Kisses. Add 2 to 4 tablespoons of very dry cocoa after the sugar has been added. (Melted chocolate is not suitable, since even when cooled it is quite fat and is apt to liquefy the beaten egg white.) Fold in carefully, and drop or mold onto cookie sheets quickly and bake. Or better still, fold in 6 ounces semisweet chocolate pieces just before shaping with a spoon. Add ½ cup coarsely chopped nuts also, if you like.

Mincemeat Cookies

½ cup butter
1 cup sugar
2 eggs
1 cup mincemeat
2½ cups sifted all-purpose flour
2 teaspoons baking powder
½ teaspoon salt
½ to 1 cup chopped walnuts, pecans, or filberts (optional)

When huge jars or crocks of mincemeat were part of the stores prepared for winter, they provided the filling for many pies. But mincemeat was also used as a filling between two thinly rolled cookies, and when stirred into the batter made a very special party cookie.

Cream the butter, cream in the sugar, and beat in the eggs. Stir in the mincemeat, then the flour sifted with the baking powder and salt. If you are using nuts, stir them in. Push the dough from the tip of a teaspoon with the back of another onto a well-oiled baking sheet or pan. Bake in a preheated 375-degree oven just until the edges are light brown. Remove from the pan while still quite warm. Cool on a rack, and store in airtight containers between sheets of wax paper or foil. These cookies freeze well and so does the dough (see page 698). Slice off about ½ inch from a chilled dough roll for each cookie.

Molasses Cookies

½ cup butter or lard
½ cup sugar
1 cup molasses, dark or light
4 cups sifted all-purpose flour
1 teaspoon salt
1 teaspoon baking soda
1½ teaspoons cinnamon
¼ teaspoon cloves
1 teaspoon ginger

A standard item for cookie jars or crocks in young America. Recipes in old cookbooks vary in procedure and richness. Older recipes seldom mention sugar, for these cookies were made with whatever sweet was at hand, and molasses could mean sorghum syrup or cane sugar molasses. The former was often made from sorghum cane grown on the farm and crushed and boiled to make a sweetener that cost little and was readily available. For finer texture, the sugar and butter or lard were creamed, but for quicker mixing, the butter or lard was heated in the molasses before the remaining ingredients were added.

Melt the butter or lard in the molasses (stirring so it will not boil), let it cool to room temperature, and add the sugar. Sift the flour with the salt, soda, and spices, and add. Chill the dough if it is too soft to handle. Roll out about ¼ inch thick on a lightly floured board. Cut with a floured cutter (these cookies used to be made very large), place on a greased baking pan or sheet, and bake at 375 degrees 8 to 15 minutes, depending upon the size, until a light brown. Loosen from the pan while still warm, and cool in a single layer on a rack.

Puddings, Ice Creams, and Dessert Sauces

We have been one of the most dessert-minded of all countries except England. "What shall we have for dessert?" has been the cry of hostesses and family heads for generations, and the sweet tooth has been entertained in sundry ways. Shortage of the more refined ingredients led to experimentation with rougher meals and sweeteners — corn, whole meal, maple syrup, and molasses — and resulted in puddings and other sweets that still linger in our repertoire. Indian pudding, blueberry buckle, flummery, and steamed puddings are some of these holdovers, as well as custards and creams of various types. Perhaps the most extreme refinement of all appeared in the early part of this century when gelatine desserts became popular. "Dainty desserts for dainty people" became the catch phrase of one of the major manufacturers of gelatine. Certain rather doubtful inventions issued forth from kitchens during this period. Some of these gelatine concoctions have stayed with us on our daily round of menus, and others have become, shall we say, museum pieces.

Even with the surge of dieters in this country, when it comes to sweets the weakness of will shown by most people is striking, to say the least. The way of the transgressor is straight through the pastry tray.

Apple Brown Betty

3 cups coarse breadcrumbs
½ cup butter
3 large apples
1¼ cups sugar
½ teaspoon cinnamon
½ teaspoon nutmeg

Apple Brown Betty has many different guises. I don't think any two of the old recipes are alike. They all have unusual bits of personality attached to them. This one I like very much.

Toast the breadcrumbs. Cut the butter into small pieces. Peel and core the apples and cut them into thin slices. Combine the sugar and spices. Divide the crumbs into three parts, the butter into four, the apples into two, and the combined sugar and spices into three. Butter a 2-quart baking dish and arrange in it layers of, in order: 1 part each of crumbs, butter, apples, spices, butter, crumbs, butter, apples, spices, crumbs, butter, and spices. Bake 30 minutes at 375 degrees, or until the apples are tender and the crumb topping is well browned. Serve hot with heavy cream.

Apple Charlotte

12 tart apples
Sugar
¼ teaspoon vanilla
Thin slices of white bread
Melted butter

Wash the apples, cut them into quarters, and remove the cores but not the peel. Cook the apples in a little boiling water in a saucepan over moderate heat until they are soft. Drain them and force them through a sieve. Discard the residue. Measure the purée and combine it in the saucepan with an equal amount of sugar and the vanilla. Reduce the purée over moderate heat until it is very thick. Trim off the bread crusts, dip the slices in melted butter, and brown them on both sides in a skillet. Cut enough of the browned slices into triangles to fit tightly over the bottom of a 1½-quart mold, and set them in place. Cut enough additional slices into strips 2 inches wide to cover the sides completely and fit them around, overlapping them slightly. Fill the mold with the prepared purée and cover the top with more of the browned bread. Place the mold in a pan of hot water in a 350-degree oven and bake the charlotte 30 minutes, or until the bread lining is firm enough to support the filling. Unmold the charlotte and serve it, warm or cooled, with whipped cream or hard sauce.

Apple Dumplings

2 cups sifted flour
1 teaspoon salt
⅔ cup shortening
5 to 6 tablespoons ice water
6 small baking apples
⅓ cup sugar
½ cup butter
Nutmeg
1½ cups firmly packed brown sugar

Prepare pastry with the flour, salt, shortening, and as much of the ice water as may be needed (page 634). Roll the pastry ¼ inch thick and cut it into 6 squares, each large enough to enclose one of the baking apples. Peel and core the apples and fill the cavities with the sugar and butter combined. The cavities should be thoroughly filled. Use more butter and sugar if necessary. Sprinkle the fillings each with nutmeg. Enclose each apple in a square of the prepared pastry by molding the pastry around it. Chill the apples 30 minutes. Preheat the oven to 425 degrees. In a saucepan combine the brown sugar, water, and additional butter, and cook them at a gentle boil 5 minutes. Brush the pastry-enclosed apples each with

1 cup water
2 additional tablespoons butter

1 tablespoon of the syrup and arrange them in a baking pan. Bake them in the preheated oven 10 minutes. Reduce the heat to 350 degrees and continue baking 30 minutes longer, or until the apples are tender, basting them every ten minutes with the remaining syrup. Test for doneness by piercing the apples through the pastry with a cake tester. Serve the dumplings warm, with thick cream.

Apple Pan Dowdy

6 apples
1½ cups light molasses
1 teaspoon nutmeg
1 teaspoon cinnamon
½ teaspoon cloves
½ teaspoon ginger
Pastry for one-crust pie

Did you ever realize how many strange names there are for some early American desserts? Apple Pan Dowdy is related to Apple Grunt and also to Apple Charlotte, Apple Dumplings, and various other strange-named desserts. However, it's extremely good and great fun.

Peel, core, and dice the apples and put them into a buttered 8 × 10 or 9 × 9-inch baking dish and cover with the molasses and spices. Top with the pastry and bake 1 hour in a moderate oven (350 degrees). Allow it to cool, and serve warm with the crust down and the apple mixture on top, with pouring cream.

Charleston Pudding

3 eggs
1½ cups sugar
1 teaspoon vanilla
⅓ cup flour
2½ teaspoons baking powder
¼ teaspoon salt
2 tart apples, coarsely chopped, about 1½ cups
⅓ cup chopped pecans

In a mixing bowl beat the eggs with the sugar and vanilla until the mixture is thick and lemon-colored. Stir into it the flour sifted with the baking powder and salt. Gently fold in the chopped apples and pecans. Spread the batter evenly in a thickly buttered 8 × 12-inch baking pan and bake it at 325 degrees 35 minutes, or until the top is well browned and crisp. Heap the pudding in a serving bowl. Let it cool slightly, but serve it while it is still warm accompanied by lightly sweetened whipped cream flavored with Cognac.

Blueberry Grunt

3 cups blueberries
⅓ cup sugar
¼ teaspoon cinnamon
¼ teaspoon nutmeg
¼ teaspoon cloves
¼ cup molasses
2 tablespoons lemon juice

BISCUIT CRUST

1 cup flour
1½ teaspoons baking powder

Blueberry Grunt is — no one knows quite why, but it is — a grunt rather than a buckle.

Wash and pick over the berries and spread them in a deep 9-inch pie pan. Combine the sugar and spices and sift the mixture over the berries. Dribble the molasses over them and sprinkle them with the lemon juice. Bake the berries at 375 degrees 5 minutes, or just until they begin to render juice. Remove the pan from the oven. Increase the oven heat to 425 degrees.

Sift the flour with the baking powder and salt and blend in the butter and shortening. Stir in the egg and as much of the milk (or more) as is needed to produce a soft dough. Drop the dough by tablespoons over the berries and spread it evenly to cover them. Bake 20 minutes, or until the biscuit crust is well browned. Serve hot with hard sauce or heavy cream.

¼ teaspoon salt
3 tablespoons butter
1 tablespoon vegetable shortening
1 egg, lightly beaten
⅓ cup milk

Huckleberry Dumplings

2 cups sifted flour
4 teaspoons baking powder
1 tablespoon sugar
½ teaspoon salt
3 tablespoons butter
1 cup milk, more or less
4 cups huckleberries
½ cup boiling water
Thin peel of 1 lemon
½ cup sugar

Into a mixing bowl sift together the flour, baking powder, the tablespoon of sugar, and salt. With your fingers rub in the butter until the mixture resembles coarse cornmeal. Stir in the milk, adding as much of the cupful or a little more as may be needed to produce a stiff dough. Gently but thoroughly fold in 1 cup of the berries. Drop the dough by tablespoons into boiling lightly salted water, cover the pan, and cook the dumplings 12 minutes. Meanwhile, in a saucepan combine the remaining 3 cups of huckleberries with the boiling water and lemon peel. Simmer 12 minutes, then add the ½ cup sugar and continue cooking 3 minutes longer. Discard the lemon peel. Drop the finished dumplings into the hot stewed huckleberries. Leave them for 15 seconds, then drain, and serve them with the huckleberries passed separately.

Prune Whip

1⅓ cups pitted dried prunes
⅓ cup sugar
1 teaspoon vanilla
½ cup coarsely chopped walnuts
6 egg whites

A classic over a long period, this is related to a soufflé. It's good hot or cold and is nostalgic to a point.

Soak the prunes in water to cover until they are soft. Drain, chop them fine (or put them through the fine blade of a food chopper), and combine them with the sugar, vanilla, and nutmeats. Beat the egg whites until they are firm but not dry and fold them gently but thoroughly into the prune mixture. Pour into a buttered and lightly sugared 2-quart baking dish, and bake at 350 degrees 20 minutes, or until lightly browned and firm. Serve with whipped cream.

Vanilla Pudding

½ cup sugar
⅛ teaspoon salt
2 tablespoons cornstarch
3 cups milk
2 eggs
1 tablespoon butter
1½ teaspoons vanilla

In the top pan of a double boiler combine the sugar, salt, and cornstarch. Add gradually the milk, stirring to dissolve the dry ingredients. Cook over simmering water, stirring constantly, until the mixture is heated through. In a mixing bowl lightly beat the eggs and stir into them, a little at a time, enough of the hot mixture to heat the eggs to about the same temperature. Combine them with the remaining hot mixture. Continue cooking and stirring until the mixture thickens. Remove the pan from over the water and stir in the butter and vanilla. Cool the pudding slightly, apportion it equally among 6 individual serving dishes, and chill. Serve with cream, or fruit or berry purée.

Old-Fashioned Blancmange

¾ cup sugar
¼ cup cornstarch
¼ teaspoon salt
3 cups milk
1½ teaspoons vanilla

Old-fashioned blancmange, sometimes called "a cold shape," has often been made in fantastic molds and served for dinners and parties. It is a pleasant, innocuous dessert and a classic one.

In a saucepan combine the sugar, cornstarch, and salt, and blend in the milk. Bring the mixture to a boil over moderate heat, stirring constantly. Cook 1 minute. Remove the pan from the heat and add the vanilla. Pour the mixture into serving dishes. Cover the dishes and let the pudding cool. Serve with an accompaniment of berries or fruit.

Foamy Blancmange. Fold into the hot blancmange 1 egg white beaten into soft peaks.

Chocolate Blancmange. Increase the sugar to 1 cup and add 1 ounce (1 square) unsweetened chocolate, grated, to the dry ingredients.

Almond Blancmange. Omit the vanilla and flavor with ½ teaspoon almond extract.

Orange Blancmange. Omit the vanilla and flavor with 1 teaspoon pure orange extract.

Lemon Blancmange. Omit the vanilla and flavor with 1 teaspoon pure lemon extract.

Rose Blancmange. Omit the vanilla and flavor with 1 tablespoon rose blossom water.

The Coach House Bread and Butter Pudding

12 small thin slices French bread
Butter
5 whole eggs
4 egg yolks
1 cup sugar
⅛ teaspoon salt
4 cups (1 quart) milk
1 cup heavy cream
1 teaspoon vanilla extract
Confectioners' sugar

This is one of the best custards of all time as far as I am concerned.

Trim the crust from the bread, and butter each slice on one side. Beat together the eggs, yolks, sugar, and salt until thoroughly blended. In a saucepan combine the milk and cream. Scald them and blend the heated liquids very gradually into the yolk mixture. Stir in the vanilla extract. Arrange the slices of bread, buttered side up, in a 2-quart baking dish and strain the custard mixture over them. Set the dish in a roasting pan filled with hot water to a depth of about 1 inch and bake the pudding so in a preheated 375-degree oven 45 minutes, or until a knife inserted in the center of the pudding can be withdrawn clean. Sprinkle the pudding generously with confectioners' sugar and glaze it under a hot broiler. At The Coach House this elegant pudding is served with a purée of fresh raspberries.

Colonial Cheese Pudding

6 egg yolks
1 cup butter

One of those strange mixtures of pastry and pudding and tart that one finds in some of the early American dishes, this is rather good and unusual.

In a mixing bowl beat the yolks until they are thick and blend into them the butter and sugar creamed together, the nutmeg, and rum. Prepare pastry for a single crust, as indicated in the recipe, roll it 1/8 inch thick and with it linc 6 muffin tins. Partially bake the pastry at 400 degrees 12 minutes. Cool it. Coat the shells equally with the prepared batter and bake them 30 minutes or until the "cheese" is firm. Serve cooled.

1 1/2 cups brown sugar
1/4 teaspoon nutmeg
2 teaspoons rum
Pie pastry (page 634)

Cheese Pudding (with actual cheese)

Butter
6 thick slices white bread
4 large eggs
1 1/2 cups milk
1 teaspoon paprika
1/2 teaspoon salt
1/4 teaspoon prepared mustard
3/4 pound sharp Cheddar cheese, cubed

Butter the bread generously and cut the slices into cubes. Beat the eggs with the milk and seasonings and stir in the cubes of bread and cheese. Pour the mixture into a buttered 2-quart casserole and bake it at 325 degrees 40 minutes, or until the pudding is well browned and the custard is set. Serve warm as a savory or light entrée.

Cottage Pudding

1/3 cup butter
2/3 cup sugar
1 egg
2 1/4 cups flour
5 teaspoons baking powder
1/2 teaspoon salt
1 cup milk
1 teaspoon vanilla

In a mixing bowl thoroughly cream together the butter and sugar and beat in the egg. Sift the flour with the baking powder and salt and blend it, a little at a time, into the butter mixture, alternating with additions of the milk and vanilla combined. Spread the batter evenly in a buttered 8-inch square baking pan and bake it at 350 degrees 40 minutes, or until a cake tester, inserted in the center of the pudding, can be withdrawn clean. Serve with chocolate or butterscotch sauce, a fruit purée, or boiled custard.

Lemon Cake Pudding

3 well-beaten egg yolks
3 tablespoons flour
1 cup sugar
1/2 teaspoon salt
1 tablespoon melted butter
6 tablespoons lemon juice
1 tablespoon grated lemon rind
1 1/4 cups milk
3 egg whites, stiffly beaten

Combine the egg yolks with the dry ingredients which have been sifted together. Add the melted butter, lemon juice, lemon rind, and milk, and lastly fold in the stiffly beaten egg whites. Pour into a 2-quart baking dish and place in a 350-degree oven for 40 minutes until firm. The trick of this pudding is that it separates into a sponge-like cake on top and the custard rests on the bottom. Very good served with whipped cream.

Boiled Custard (Soft Custard)

6 egg yolks
½ cup sugar
¼ teaspoon salt
3 cups light cream
2 teaspoons vanilla

In the top pan of a double boiler combine the egg yolks, sugar, and salt. In another saucepan heat the cream just until it steams, and stir it very slowly into the yolk mixture. Cook over (but not touching) simmering water, stirring constantly until the mixture coats a metal spoon. Remove the pan from over the hot water and stir in the vanilla. Cool the custard and chill it. Pour it into 6 individual serving dishes or serve it as a sauce over cake or with pudding. Milk may be substituted for cream in the recipe. A thicker custard may be achieved by reducing the cream or milk content to 2 cups.

Floating Islands

Boiled custard (above)
3 egg whites
⅛ teaspoon salt
⅓ cup sugar

Pour the custard into a shallow serving bowl. Cool and chill it. Beat the egg whites with the salt to soft peak consistency. Add the sugar, 1 tablespoon at a time, continuing the beating until the whites are thick and glistening. Float rounded tablespoons of the meringue in hot milk to a depth of ½ inch in a baking pan. Set the pan under medium heat and broil the meringues until they are lightly browned, 1 to 2 minutes. Drain them in a slotted spoon and float them in the prepared custard. Chill the floating islands briefly before presenting them at the table. Lightly caramelized sugar may be drizzled over the meringues after chilling them.

Baked Custard

5 egg yolks
½ cup sugar
1 teaspoon vanilla
⅛ teaspoon salt
2½ cups milk
Nutmeg

Custards and Floating Islands were great Sunday desserts, and certainly nothing is more of an achievement than a perfect custard at any time. This is an extremely pleasant baked one, and the orange custard, which is a variation on the theme, is also an exciting dessert.

In a mixing bowl beat together the eggs, sugar, vanilla, and salt until the yolks are thick and the dry ingredients are incorporated. Scald the milk and add it very slowly. Pour the mixture equally into 6 custard cups arranged in a roasting pan and sprinkle the tops with nutmeg. Pour hot water to a depth of 1 inch around the cups and set the pan in a preheated 350-degree oven. Bake the custard 35 minutes, or until a knife inserted in the center can be withdrawn clean. If preferred, the custard may be baked in a single mold of 1½-quart capacity. So baked, the cooking time will be a few minutes longer.

Caramel Custard. Omit the nutmeg. In a heavy skillet melt ½ cup sugar over low heat until it caramelizes. Pour the caramel into the 6 custard cups or a 1½-quart baking dish, swirling the caramel around to coat the sides and bottom of the dishes evenly. Pour in the custard mixture and bake it as indicated in the recipe. To serve, run a knife around the sides to loosen the custard and unmold it onto a serving platter, or, if in custard cups, onto individual serving dishes.

Coconut Custard. Omit the nutmeg. Sprinkle the custard with ½ cup packaged flaked coconut before baking.

Baked Orange Custard

6 egg yolks
⅓ cup sugar
¼ teaspoon salt
½ teaspoon pure orange extract
2½ cups milk
2-inch strip orange peel, ½ inch wide

In a mixing bowl throughly beat together the egg yolks, sugar, salt, and orange extract. Scald the milk with the orange peel. Discard the peel. Pour the milk very slowly into the yolk mixture, beating constantly and vigorously. Pour the mixture into a buttered 1½-quart baking dish. Set the dish in a pan of hot water in a preheated 350-degree oven and bake 40 minutes, or until a knife inserted in the center can be withdrawn clean. Serve the custard warm or cooled with, if desired, slightly sweetened whipped cream.

Crème Brûlée

6 egg yolks
⅓ cup sugar
1 teaspoon cornstarch
3 tablespoons milk
3 cups heavy cream, scalded
¼ teaspoon vanilla
Light brown sugar

Crème brûlée wandered here from England, where it was originally a great recipe in King's College, Cambridge. The first recipe I know for it came from a seventeenth-century cookery book, and it was called Grilled Cream, I believe. Anyway, it has come a long way since then.

In the top pan of a double boiler beat the egg yolks with the sugar until the mixture is very thick. Blend into it the cornstarch dissolved in the milk. Stir in the heated cream, adding it very gradually. Set the pan over simmering water and cook the mixture, stirring it constantly until it thickens. Remove the pan from over the water and stir in the vanilla. Pour the custard into a shallow heat-proof serving dish, or into 6 such individual dishes, and cool and chill it until the surface is firm. Sift brown sugar over the top, covering the custard completely with an even layer about ⅛ inch thick. Set the dish or dishes on a baking sheet under a hot broiler and let the sugar caramelize. Turn frequently so that the sugar melts evenly and does not brown excessively. Let the glazed custard cool at room temperature. Chill it briefly in a freezer just before serving it.

Orange Crème Brûlée. Omit the vanilla and flavor the custard with, instead, 1 tablespoon orange liqueur (Cointreau, Grand Marnier, or such).

Spinach Dessert Pudding

2½ pounds spinach
½ cup milk
½ cup cream
3 egg yolks
¼ cup sugar
1 teaspoon orange liqueur
½ teaspoon finely grated lemon rind

Trim off the stems of the spinach. Wash the leaves, drain them, and cook them (in just the water that clings to the leaves) for 3 minutes, or just until they are completely wilted. Drain thoroughly, and force the spinach through a fine sieve or purée it in an electric blender. In the top pan of a double boiler combine the milk, cream, egg yolks, and sugar, and cook the mixture over simmering water until it coats a metal spoon. Stir constantly. Combine this custard with the puréed spinach, orange liqueur, and grated lemon rind, and transfer the mixture to a 1-quart buttered soufflé dish. Bake it at 350 degrees 30 minutes, or until a knife, inserted in the center of the pudding, can be withdrawn clean. Serve warm.

Tipsy Parson

1 8-inch layer of sponge cake, about 1½ inches thick
⅔ cup sweet sherry
3 whole eggs
2 egg yolks
½ cup sugar
¼ teaspoon salt
3 cups light cream, scalded
2 teaspoons vanilla
¾ cup slivered blanched almonds, toasted

When people still felt they should cover up the use of alcohol in their desserts they would serve Tipsy Parson, feeling that its sherry overtone was quite a daring variation on the usual non-alcoholic dessert theme.

Split the cake into two layers and douse them equally with the sherry. Chill well. Prepare a boiled custard (page 728), using the whole eggs, egg yolks, sugar, salt, scalded cream, and vanilla. Cool the custard and chill it. Thoroughly butter an 8-inch deep springform pan and place 1 layer of the chilled cake on the bottom. Stud the layer with ½ cup of the almonds and spread it with half the prepared custard. Cover with the second layer of cake and the remaining custard, and sprinkle with the remaining almonds, crushed. Chill 2 hours before unmolding onto a chilled platter.

Hindu Cream

1 medium pineapple, peeled and cored
1 cup sugar
⅓ cup water
½ teaspoon vanilla
Butter
3 egg whites
⅔ cup unblanched almonds, finely ground
⅔ cup heavy cream, whipped
1 teaspoon Cognac
2 tablespoons chopped toasted almonds

CUSTARD FILLING

3 egg yolks

Slice the pineapple thinly and cut the slices in half. In a saucepan dissolve ¼ cup of the sugar in the water and bring the liquid to a boil. Add the pineapple slices and simmer them 10 minutes, or until they are tender but still firm. Drain, and pat them dry. Butter a savarin mold, sprinkle it with 2 teaspoons of the sugar, and line it with the pineapple slices, overlapping them to cover the inside of the mold completely. Beat the egg whites into soft peaks. Add ½ cup of the sugar, a little at a time, beating constantly until the whites are very stiff. Fold the ground almonds into the beaten whites and spread the mixture over the pineapple in the mold. Set the mold in a pan of hot water in a 300-degree oven and bake 20 minutes, or until the meringue is firm. Remove the mold from the oven. Let the pudding cool, and chill it thoroughly.

Prepare the custard filling by combining the egg yolks, 3 tablespoons of the sugar, and the arrowroot powder in a saucepan. Very gradually stir in the scalded milk. Set the pan over low heat and cook the mixture, stirring constantly, until it thickens and is very smooth. Pour into a bowl, cool, and chill it. Sweeten the whipped cream with the remaining teaspoon of sugar and flavor it with the Cognac. Fold the cream into the chilled custard.

Unmold the pineapple and meringue pudding onto a chilled serving platter. Pour the creamed custard into the hollow of the mold and sprinkle the top with the toasted almonds.

1½ teaspoons arrowroot powder
1 cup milk, scalded

Steamed Ginger Pudding

2¼ cups flour
3½ teaspoons baking powder
¼ teaspoon salt
2 teaspoons ginger
½ teaspoon cinnamon
3 tablespoons butter
⅔ cup firmly packed brown sugar
2 eggs, beaten
⅔ cup milk
1 cup heavy cream, whipped
1 tablespoon syrup drained from a jar of preserved ginger

Sift the flour with the baking powder, salt, ginger, and cinnamon. Thoroughly cream together the butter and sugar and stir into them the beaten eggs. Blend in the dry ingredients, a half at a time, alternating with the milk. Pour the batter into a buttered 1-quart baking dish or pudding mold. Cover the container tightly and set it in a deep kettle. Pour around the mold boiling hot water to a depth of two-thirds its height. Cover the kettle and cook the pudding over low heat 1½ hours, replenishing the water as needed to maintain the level. Serve the pudding unmolded and hot, accompanied by whipped cream flavored with the ginger syrup.

Steamed Fig Pudding

1 cup beef suet
½ pound dried figs, chopped (about 1½ cups)
3 cups medium dry coarse breadcrumbs
½ cup milk
3 eggs
1 cup sugar

Fig pudding arrived in the nineteenth century, and was considered not quite as rich as a holiday pudding.

Put the suet and figs together through the fine blade of a food chopper and work them to a paste in a mortar with a pestle or in a bowl with a wooden spoon. Soften the crumbs in the milk and combine them with the paste. Blend in the eggs and sugar, beaten together. Pour the mixture into a pudding mold or a 1-pound coffee tin, cover tightly, and place on a rack over boiling water in a kettle. Cover the kettle and steam the pudding for 3 hours, replenishing the water as needed. Unmold the pudding and serve with Cognac sauce (page 742).

Steamed Date Pudding. Substitute pitted dates for figs.

Suet Pudding

3 cups flour
1 cup finely shredded suet
1 teaspoon baking powder
¼ teaspoon salt
Cold water
Additional flour as needed

In a mixing bowl combine the flour, suet, baking powder, and salt, and work them together with a wooden spoon, adding just enough cold water to produce a smooth firm paste. Shape the paste into a thick roll. Dampen a heavy cloth, such as a napkin, with boiling hot water, and coat one side with flour. Wrap the roll in the cloth (not too tightly; it swells during the cooking) and tie the ends. Set the wrapped roll in a deep pan, cover it with boiling water, and simmer it, covered, 2½ hours. Unwrap the pudding, cut it into slices, and serve it hot with jam, molasses, maple syrup, cooked fruit, or with rich beef gravy.

Plum Pudding

1 ½ cups sifted flour
1 teaspoon baking soda
1 teaspoon salt
1 teaspoon cinnamon
½ teaspoon nutmeg
½ teaspoon ground cloves
¼ teaspoon ginger
⅔ cup firmly packed brown sugar
1 ½ cups dry breadcrumbs
1 cup chopped nutmeats
1 cup shredded suet
1 cup chopped mixed candied fruit
2 cups seedless raisins
3 eggs, lightly beaten
⅓ cup molasses
¾ cup milk

Into a mixing bowl sift together the flour, soda, salt, cinnamon, nutmeg, cloves, and ginger. Combine with the mixture the brown sugar, crumbs, nutmeats, suet, candied fruit, and raisins. Blend in the eggs, molasses, and milk. Pour the mixture into a well-buttered 2-quart pudding mold and cover tightly. Place the mold on a rack over 2 inches of boiling water in a kettle. Cover the kettle and steam the pudding for 2 hours or until it is slightly resistant to the touch. Serve hot, in slices, with hard sauce.

Carrot Pudding

1 ½ cups finely grated raw carrots
1 ½ cups fine dry breadcrumbs
1 teaspoon nutmeg
1 teaspoon cinnamon
¼ teaspoon salt
6 eggs
¾ cup sugar
2 tablespoons butter, melted

An imitation of plum pudding, which was an imitation of English Christmas pudding, where all the family had a finger in mixing it. These recipes are not quite as elaborate as the English ones but they are extraordinarily good nevertheless.

In a mixing bowl combine the carrots, crumbs, and seasonings. Beat the eggs with the sugar until they are thick and blend into them the carrot mixture with the melted butter. Bake the pudding in a 2½-quart baking dish in a moderate oven (350 degrees) 45 minutes, or until it is set. Serve with lemon sauce or boiled custard blended with 1 teaspoon finely grated lemon rind. Serve hot or cooled, but not chilled.

Indian Pudding

¼ cup cornmeal
1 ⅔ cups cold milk
3 cups heated milk
¼ cup butter (½ stick)
1 cup molasses
½ teaspoon cinnamon

In the top pan of a double boiler moisten the cornmeal with 1 cup of the cold milk. Blend in the heated milk. Set the pan over gently boiling water and cook the mixture, stirring it frequently, until it is smooth. Cover the pan, reduce the heat to bring the water down to simmer, and continue cooking 25 minutes. Remove the pan from over the water and add the butter, molasses, spices, and salt. Vigorously stir in the beaten eggs. Transfer the mixture to a buttered 2-quart baking dish and pour the remaining ⅔ cup cold milk over the top. Bake the pudding at 350 degrees 1 hour. Serve it hot with well-chilled frothily beaten heavy cream or with vanilla ice cream.

½ teaspoon ginger
¼ teaspoon salt
2 eggs, well beaten

Pumpkin Pudding

2 cups cooked fresh or canned pumpkin
6 eggs
1¼ cups sugar
⅛ teaspoon salt
⅓ cup applejack
¼ teaspoon allspice
¼ teaspoon cinnamon
¼ teaspoon ground cloves
¼ teaspoon nutmeg
1 cup heavy cream, whipped

If fresh pumpkin is used, force the pulp through a fine sieve or purée it in an electric blender. Canned pumpkin is generally in purée form. In a mixing bowl beat the eggs, sugar, and salt together until the mixture is very thick. Stir into it the pumpkin, applejack, and spices, and lightly but thoroughly fold in the whipped cream. Transfer the mixture to a buttered 2-quart baking dish and bake it at 350 degrees 45 minutes, or until a knife inserted in the center can be withdrawn clean. Serve the pudding warm or cooled with slightly sweetened whipped cream flavored with applejack.

Tapioca Pudding

2 tablespoons quick-cooking tapioca
2⅔ cups milk, scalded
½ cup sugar
3 egg yolks
1 teaspoon vanilla
3 egg whites
¼ teaspoon salt

In the top pan of a double boiler stir the tapioca into the hot milk and cook it over simmering water 3 minutes, stirring frequently. In a heatproof mixing bowl stir ¼ cup of the sugar into the egg yolks and very slowly blend in the hot tapioca and milk. Return the mixture to the pan over the hot water and continue cooking until it has thickened. Remove the pan from over the water and stir in the vanilla. Cool the mixture slightly and fold in the egg whites, beaten until stiff with the salt and remaining sugar. Pour the pudding into 6 serving dishes and cool and chill it.

Fruit Tapioca. Fold ⅔ cup finely chopped fresh or dried fruit into the tapioca before folding in the beaten egg whites.

Old-Fashioned Tapioca Pudding

¼ cup pearl tapioca
⅓ cup cold water
2 cups milk
1 tablespoon butter
2 egg yolks
⅛ teaspoon salt
½ cup sugar
2 teaspoons orange flower water
2 egg whites

While this is delicious to the taste, it has sometimes been called "fish-eye" pudding and is the butt of many jokes. It is a most refreshing dessert.

In a mixing bowl soak the tapioca in water 1 hour. Drain it, and combine it with the milk in the top pan of a double boiler. Cook the mixture over gently boiling water until the tapioca is soft, stirring it occasionally. Remove the pan from over the water and stir in the butter. Beat the egg yolks with the salt and ⅓ cup of the sugar. Slowly blend the hot tapioca mixture into them and stir in the orange flower water. Pour the mixture into a buttered baking dish and bake it at 325 degrees 45 minutes, or until it is set. Beat the egg whites with the remaining sugar. Spread the meringue over the pudding and continue baking 15 minutes longer, or until the meringue is firm. Serve the pudding, slightly warm or cooled, with tart applesauce.

Basic Rice Pudding

1/3 cup rice
2 tablespoons butter
4 cups milk
3 tablespoons sugar
1/8 teaspoon salt
Nutmeg

Wash the rice in several changes of cold water. Drain the grains and dry them between sheets of paper toweling. In a heavy 1 1/2-quart casserole melt the butter over low heat. Add the rice and heat it, stirring constantly until the grains whiten. Do not let them brown. In a saucepan combine the milk with the sugar and salt, and scald it. Add it to the rice, stirring just long enough to blend. Let the milk bubble for a few seconds. Remove the casserole from the heat and sprinkle the top of the rice and milk with nutmeg. Cover the container securely and set it in an oven preheated to 250 degrees. Bake the pudding for 1 1/2 hours, or until it is firm and the grains of rice are very soft. Serve warm or cold.

Lemon Rice Pudding. Add to the milk mixture 1 teaspoon finely grated lemon rind and 1/4 teaspoon pure lemon extract. Omit the nutmeg.

Rice Custard Pudding

2 1/2 cups cooked rice
1 cup sugar
1 teaspoon vanilla
1/2 cup seedless raisins
1/4 cup Cognac
5 eggs
2 cups rich milk or light cream
1/8 teaspoon salt
Cinnamon

In a mixing bowl combine the rice with 1/2 cup of sugar, the vanilla, and the raisins, which have been soaked 1 hour in the Cognac. Add any remaining Cognac. In another bowl beat together the eggs, milk or cream, salt, and remaining sugar. Stir in the rice and raisin mixture, and pour the combined ingredients into a buttered 2-quart baking dish or into 6 individual baking dishes. Bake at 350 degrees 40 minutes (25 minutes for individual servings), or until the custard is firm and lightly browned. Remove from the oven and sprinkle lightly with cinnamon. Serve the pudding slightly chilled with heavy cream, liquid or whipped.

Maple Rice Pudding

4 cups milk
1/2 cup uncooked rice
1/3 cup pure maple syrup
1/8 teaspoon salt
1/4 teaspoon almond extract
3 tablespoons butter, melted

Combine all ingredients except the butter and pour into a 1 1/2-quart baking dish. Bake at 250 degrees 1 hour, stirring every 15 minutes. Blend in the melted butter and continue cooking, without further stirring, 2 hours longer. Serve warm or cooled, with cream.

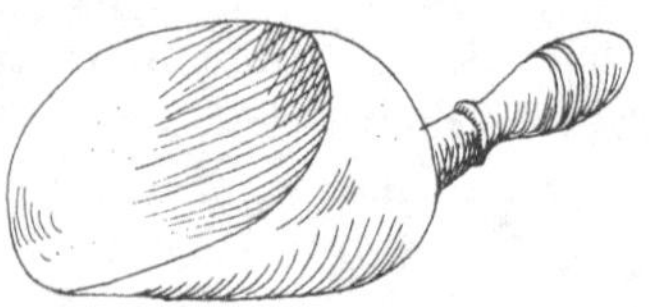

Coffee Jelly with Praline Cream

2 tablespoons (2 envelopes) unflavored gelatine
½ cup cold water
½ cup boiling hot water
3 cups strong brewed coffee
1½ tablespoons sugar
½ teaspoon vanilla

PRALINE CREAM

½ cup sugar
¼ cup unblanched almonds
¼ cup filberts
¾ cup heavy cream

Coffee jelly and wine jelly were considered quite elegant on the luncheon or dinner table as part of a collation. Both have an honesty and a delicacy that is very refreshing.

Soften the gelatine in the cold water, dissolve it in the hot water, and combine it with the coffee, sweetened with the sugar and flavored with the vanilla. Pour the mixture into six ¾-cup individual savarin molds. Chill in the refrigerator until the jelly is set. Unmold, and fill the centers with praline cream.

To make praline cream, first make praline powder. Slowly heat together in a skillet the sugar and nuts until the sugar melts and becomes dark amber in color. Pour the mixture onto a lightly greased baking sheet and let cool and harden completely. Roll this praline into a powder or pulverize it in an electric blender. Whip the cream stiffly and fold into it ⅓ cup of the praline powder. Reserve the remaining powder for future use, stored in a tightly covered container in a dry, fairly cool place (not in the refrigerator).

Wine Jelly

2 tablespoons (2 envelopes) unflavored gelatine
½ cup cold water
3 cups claret
½ cup sweet Madeira
½ cup strained orange juice
⅓ cup sugar

Soften the gelatine in the cold water. In a stainless steel or enamel-coated saucepan heat together, without boiling, the claret, Madeira, and orange juice. Dissolve the sugar in the heated liquids. Add the softened gelatine and stir to dissolve it also. Cool the mixture, pour into a mold, and chill until set. Unmold onto a chilled serving platter.

Spanish Cream

3 cups milk
1 tablespoon (1 envelope) unflavored gelatine
¼ cup cold water
½ cup sugar
3 egg yolks
¼ teaspoon salt
3 tablespoons sweet sherry
3 egg whites

Scald the milk in a saucepan. Soften the gelatine in the cold water and dissolve it and the sugar in the hot milk. Beat the egg yolks with the salt in the top pan of a double boiler, and beat the milk mixture into them, a very little at a time. Set the pan over simmering water and cook until the mixture thickens sufficiently to coat a metal spoon. Remove from over hot water and stir in the sherry. Let the custard cool, but do not let it set. Gently but thoroughly fold in the egg whites, beaten until stiff but not dry. Apportion the cream equally among 6 individual molds and chill until firm. Unmold onto serving plates, and decorate with rosettes of slightly sweetened whipped cream piped from a pastry tube.

Peppermint Candy Bavarian Cream

1 tablespoon (1 envelope) unflavored gelatine
¼ cup cold water
4 egg yolks
¼ cup sugar
⅓ cup pulverized peppermint candy
1 teaspoon cornstarch
⅛ teaspoon salt
1¼ cups milk
3 egg whites
1 tablespoon additional sugar
1¼ cups heavy cream, whipped
1 droplet red vegetable coloring
Additional whipped cream and crushed peppermint candy

Soften the gelatine in the cold water. In a saucepan combine the egg yolks, sugar, pulverized peppermint candy, cornstarch, and salt. Beat the mixture until the yolks are very thick and the dry ingredients are completely incorporated in them. Scald the milk and stir it in very gradually. Set the pan over low heat and cook the mixture, stirring constantly, until it coats a metal spoon. Add the softened gelatine and stir until dissolved. Transfer this custard to a bowl and cool it somewhat. Beat the egg whites into soft peaks. Add the additional sugar and continue beating until the whites are stiff. Fold them gently but thoroughly into the warm custard. Cool the custard completely and chill it. Fold in the whipped cream. Add the droplet of red coloring and whisk it through the Bavarian cream for a streaked effect to suggest striped peppermint candy. Chill 2 hours, or until very firm. Unmold onto a chilled serving platter and surround with a ruche of whipped cream piped through a pastry tube. Sprinkle the ruche with crushed peppermint candy.

Ice Creams and Sherbets

Ice cream dates back in our history to Revolutionary times and probably before. Jefferson was a great fancier of ice creams and brought many recipes from Italy and France which he put into use at Monticello and later the White House. In general, the story of ice creams or ices appears to go back into earliest history. There is a legend, which you may accept or not, that in Aztec times, Montezuma liked hot chocolate poured into snow and ice rushed from the mountaintops to Tenochtitlán. If this is true it certainly shows that ice cream has been a steady winner in the Americas from the very beginning.

Time was when Philadelphia was more famous for its ice cream than any other place in the country. This reputation had its beginnings about the last two decades of the eighteenth century, according to accounts of a cream machine dating from that period. The vogue continued into the nineteenth and twentieth centuries, when there were almost fifty ice cream factories in Philadelphia and at least that number of ice cream parlors, or saloons, as they sometimes called them. Sauter's was the most famous one of all, in existence until about the end of World War II.

There are various kinds of ice creams — among them one with a custard base of eggs and milk and flavorings, and another which uses just cream. Then there are such things as parfaits and bisques, but I think what we are most interested in here are the good simple ice cream recipes that have come up through the generations.

Miss Leslie gives quite a few recipes for ice cream; here is a very good one.

Miss Leslie's Strawberry Ice Cream

"Take two quarts of ripe strawberries, hull them and put them into a deep dish, strewing among them ½ pound of powdered loaf sugar [we can use granulated sugar – J.B.]. Cover them and let them stand an hour or two. Then mash them through a sieve until you have pressed out all the juice, and stir into it ½ pound more of powdered sugar or enough to make it sweet and like a thick syrup. Then mix it by degrees with two quarts of rich cream, beating it in very hard. Put it into a freezer and proceed as for directions."

You can use Miss Leslie's recipe for raspberry ice cream as well. Or use the one below.

Raspberry Ice Cream

1 quart raspberries
1 tablespoon lemon juice
1 quart heavy cream
Sugar

SIMPLE SYRUP

2 cups sugar
1½ cups water

Crush the raspberries and add the lemon juice. Make the simple syrup — boil the sugar with the water about 5 minutes, counting from the time it really boils. It must not be stirred while it is boiling. Add just enough of this syrup to the berries to sweeten to your taste (the rest you can keep refrigerated to use on fruits or other ice creams). Let the sweetened raspberries stand an hour or so, then mash and put them through a sieve. Scald the cream, add a tiny bit of sugar (if necessary), and stir until the sugar is dissolved. Cool. When it is quite cold, pour into the freezer, pack as directed above, and freeze until it is rather mushy (about half frozen). Then add the raspberries and continue freezing until it is thoroughly frozen. Remove the dasher, push down the ice cream, and cover the freezing can. Pack the freezer again, and let stand for about two hours before serving.

Basic Vanilla Ice Cream

4 cups light cream
¾ cup sugar
1½ teaspoons vanilla or the seeds scraped from 2 inches of vanilla bean
Pinch of salt

Stir the cream with the sugar constantly about 4 to 5 minutes. Add the vanilla or the seeds scraped from the vanilla bean and the pinch of salt, and stir again.

Note. If you like a richer ice cream you can add heavy cream to the mixture.

Pour the mixture into a freezing can fitted with a dasher. Cover it very tightly and lower it into the freezer. Pack with alternating layers of cracked ice and rock salt, using about 1 part salt to 6 to 8 parts ice. You can use either ice cream salt or kosher salt. Connect the dasher and the crank, if the machine is hand operated, and turn until the turning is very, very difficult. Then unpack the ice and remove the cover to see if the ice cream is thoroughly frozen. If not, return to the freezer, repack with the ice and salt, and continue turning another few minutes, or until frozen. Be very careful when you remove the lid not to spill salt into the ice cream. Remove the dasher, press the ice cream down, and cover the freezing can. Pack it with larger pieces of ice and more salt, and let it stand 2 to 3 hours before serving.

French Vanilla Ice Cream

6 egg yolks
2 cups milk
1 cup sugar
Pinch of salt
4 cups heavy cream
1½ tablespoons vanilla extract or the seeds scraped from 2½ inches of vanilla bean

This is a custard ice cream.

Make a rich custard in the upper part of a double boiler by combining the egg yolks, milk, sugar, and salt. Cook until the mixture is thick enough to coat a wooden spoon or spatula or a metal spoon, and let it cool. Stir in the heavy cream and the vanilla. Pour the mixture into the freezing can and freeze as in the recipe above.

Apricot Ice Cream. Add about 3 cups crushed ripe apricots and about 2 tablespoons Cognac to the ice cream when half frozen. Stir well, and continue freezing.

Peach Ice Cream. Add about 3 cups sliced sugared peaches and 1 tablespoon lemon juice to the ice cream when half frozen. Stir well, and continue freezing.

Strawberry Ice Cream. Add 2 cups crushed strawberries and 1 tablespoon lemon juice to the ice cream when half frozen. Stir well, and continue freezing.

Chocolate Ice Cream

3 ounces semisweet chocolate, melted
½ cup sugar

Melt the chocolate over hot water or in a 300 to 350 degree oven. Stir in the sugar, egg yolks, and salt. Add the hot milk and stir the mixture over medium heat about 3 minutes. Add the vanilla, strain through a fine sieve, and let the mixture chill. Whip the cream thoroughly until it is firm and fold in the chocolate mixture. Pour into the freezing can and freeze as above.

3 egg yolks, slightly beaten
1/4 teaspoon salt
2 cups hot milk
1 teaspoon vanilla extract
2 cups heavy cream, whipped

Orange-Chocolate Ice Cream. Add 1/4 cup Grand Marnier or Cointreau and 1 tablespoon grated orange rind to the chocolate custard.

Chocolate Ice Cream Made in the Refrigerator Freezer

4 egg yolks, well beaten
3/4 cup white corn syrup
4 ounces semisweet chocolate, melted
1/2 teaspoon cinnamon
2 teaspoons vanilla extract
1 cup heavy cream, whipped
Pinch of salt

Combine the egg yolks, corn syrup, and melted chocolate. Cook over medium heat until the mixture is smooth and thick. Remove from the heat, cool thoroughly, and flavor with the cinnamon and vanilla. Fold into the whipped cream. Pour the mixture into refrigerator ice trays and let stand in the refrigerator freezer about 2 1/2 to 3 hours, or until frozen.

Lime Ice (Sherbet)

3 cups water
1 1/2 cups sugar
1/2 cup lime juice
Pinch of salt
Tiny bit of green coloring (optional)
1 egg white

Sherbets have always been about as popular as ice cream with many people, and in these days of dieting sherbets are more popular than ever before. This lime ice is, I think, extraordinarily good.

Make a syrup with the water and sugar, boiling it for about 5 minutes and allowing it to cool. When it is quite cool add the lime juice and, if you wish, a little bit of coloring. You can freeze this in an old-fashioned freezer or an electric freezer, or you can put it into ice trays and freeze it in the refrigerator. If you do the former, freeze it until it becomes a mush and then add the white of egg, quite well beaten — not very stiff but in soft peaks. Return it to the freezer and freeze according to the directions for basic vanilla ice cream. If using trays in the refrigerator, let it freeze to a mush, remove it from the trays, beat it well with a fork or whisk, then beat in the beaten egg white and return it to the freezer. In either case, if you want an especially good sherbet, let it freeze to a mush a second time, beat it up again, and then return it to the trays or freezer to freeze until firm.

Lemon Sherbet. Substitute lemon juice for the lime juice.

Orange Sherbet. Substitute orange juice for the lime juice, and add 1 tablespoon grated orange rind and 2 tablespoons Grand Marnier or Cointreau.

Frozen Lemon Torte

3/4 cup vanilla wafer crumbs
3 eggs, separated
4 teaspoons grated lemon rind
1/4 cup lemon juice
1/8 teaspoon salt
1/2 cup sugar
1 cup heavy cream

Line a refrigerator tray or a 9 × 5 × 3-inch pan with half the vanilla wafer crumbs. Combine the egg yolks, lemon rind, lemon juice, salt, and sugar in the top of a double boiler, and mix thoroughly. Cook over boiling water, stirring constantly, until thick. Allow to cool. Beat the egg whites until stiff. Fold in the lemon mixture. Beat the cream until thick but not firm. Fold into the lemon mixture, spoon into the tray or pan, and top with the remaining crumbs. Freeze. This is very good unmolded and cut into sections.

Baked Alaska

1 cup sifted all-purpose flour
2/3 cup sugar
1 1/2 teaspoons baking powder
1/2 teaspoon salt
1/4 cup shortening
1/2 cup milk
1 egg
1 teaspoon vanilla extract
1 quart brick vanilla ice cream

MERINGUE

3 egg whites
1/2 cup granulated sugar

This has become a signature for elaborate dining in this country and is a dessert that causes ohs and ahs wherever it is presented. I think it is greatly overrated, but it is a part of American life.

You may use any other cake that you like, but this is a very quick, easy recipe. Butter and flour a 9-inch square pan. Sift the flour with the sugar, baking powder, and salt into a mixing bowl. Add the shortening and milk. Beat 1 1/2 minutes at low speed with a mixer or with a spoon until well blended and thick. Add the egg and the vanilla. Beat 1 1/2 minutes more. Pour into the pan and bake at 350 degrees 20 to 25 minutes, or until the cake springs back when lightly touched in the center. Cool. Place the cake on a cutting board or a cookie sheet and cut strips 2 inches wide from each side of the cake, and discard them. Make a meringue by beating the egg whites until they hold soft peaks, then beat in the sugar a tablespoon at a time until the whites are thick and glossy. Place the ice cream brick on top of the cake. Completely cover it and the cake with meringue. Bake at 450 degrees 5 minutes, or until delicately brown. Serve at once.

Orange Baked Alaska

3 very large oranges
1 medium-size banana, sliced
6 strawberries or maraschino cherries
1 pint vanilla ice cream
Meringue (as in previous recipe)

Cut the oranges in half. Cut a thin slice off the bottom of each half to prevent its tipping in the oven. Scoop out the pulp, reserving the orange segments. Fill the orange halves with the fruits. Top each half with a small scoop of ice cream and seal with meringue to the edges. Bake in a 400-degree oven 2 to 3 minutes, or until lightly browned. Serve immediately.

Dessert Sauces

Chocolate Sauce I

12 ounces semisweet chocolate
2 ounces unsweetened chocolate
1 cup heavy cream
2 tablespoons Cognac or Grand Marnier

Certainly few sweets are more loved in the American scene than chocolate sauce on ice cream, puddings, and many other desserts. This is a simple and good version, which I use consistently.

Melt the chocolate in the upper part of a double boiler over hot water. (If the chocolate should by any chance become lumpy, add a tablespoon of vegetable fat — not butter — and stir it in until smooth.) Add the cream, and stir until smooth. Add the Cognac and stir again until smooth. Serve hot. It may be reheated in a double boiler.

Chocolate Sauce II

¼ cup sugar
½ cup corn syrup
½ cup light cream
Salt
1 6-ounce package semisweet chocolate
1 teaspoon vanilla or 1 tablespoon Grand Marnier
1 tablespoon water

Combine the sugar, corn syrup, and cream in a saucepan, and bring to a boil. Add a dash of salt, remove from the heat, and stir in the chocolate till smooth. Add the vanilla or Grand Marnier and the water, and stir again until smooth. Serve hot, or cool for 10 minutes before serving.

Caramel Sauce

1 cup light brown sugar
¼ cup granulated sugar
½ cup corn syrup
1 cup heavy cream
Few grains salt

A delicious sauce which has always been fancied served warm with ice cream and toasted salted almonds or pecans.

Mix all ingredients together in a saucepan and bring to the boiling point. Cook until it reaches 238 degrees when tested with a candy thermometer or until it forms a soft ball when a small amount is dropped into cold water.

Butterscotch Sauce, Two Ways

1⅓ cups sugar
¾ cup corn syrup
3 tablespoons butter
2 tablespoons water
3 or 4 tablespoons heavy cream

Each of these sauces has merit and is a joy poured warm over ice cream and garnished with toasted nuts and a dab of whipped cream.

Mix all ingredients except the cream, and bring to a boil in a heavy saucepan. Boil 1 minute. Cool and stir in the cream until smooth and satiny.

Butterscotch Sauce II. Substitute dark brown sugar for the white.

Foamy Sauce

Whites of 2 eggs
1 cup powdered sugar
¼ cup hot milk
1 teaspoon vanilla

This sauce, for hot puddings, is easy to make with a hand mixer.

Beat the egg whites until they hold soft peaks, and gradually beat in the sugar until you have a stiff meringue. Continue beating while adding the hot milk and vanilla.

Hard Sauce

¾ cup soft butter
1½ cups sugar
Dash of salt

This may be made with a variety of flavorings — brandy, rum, fruit syrups, grated orange peel, or candied fruits.

Cream the butter and gradually beat in the sugar until creamy and quite light. Add flavoring to taste, and continue beating till thoroughly blended. Chill before serving with hot puddings. It is customary with plum pudding at Christmastime, and if you are a traditionalist you will serve a regular brandy sauce as well.

A Sauce for Plum and Other Puddings

¾ cup butter
3 cups light brown sugar
⅓ cup red Burgundy wine
¼ cup water
Thin peel of ½ orange

In a mixing bowl thoroughly cream the butter with the sugar. Bring the wine, water, and orange peel to a gentle boil in a saucepan over low heat and simmer 5 minutes. Discard the peel, and rapidly whisk the liquid into the combined butter and sugar. Reheat briefly in the saucepan and serve at once.

Cognac Sauce

6 tablespoons butter
⅔ cup confectioners' sugar
2 egg yolks
¾ cup heavy cream
3 tablespoons Cognac

In the top of a double boiler, cream the butter with the sugar. Stir in the egg yolks, one at a time, and ¼ cup of the cream. Set the pan over simmering water and cook, adding the remaining cream gradually and stirring constantly, until the mixture thickens just enough to coat a spoon. Remove from the heat and blend in the Cognac.

Brandy Sauce

4 tablespoons butter
1 cup powdered sugar
¼ cup Cognac
Yolks of 2 eggs, well beaten
½ cup cream
Whites of 2 eggs, beaten until stiff

Cream the butter well, and add the sugar gradually. When it is blended, add the Cognac slowly. Then add the egg yolks and the cream, and cook in the top of a double boiler over hot water, stirring constantly, till it thickens. Pour slowly over the beaten whites, continuing to beat with a whisk until well blended.

Whipped Cream

Although whipped cream has been an extraordinarily popular topping for everything from soups to fruit, time was, less than fifty years ago, when the cream delivered to our doors was so thick that one had to dilute it with a little milk before whipping to prevent it from turning to butter. Nowadays the cream sold as heavy or whipping cream is so lacking in butterfat that it is sometimes a struggle to get it to whip.

In view of the prevalence of electric mixers, there seems little need to explain how to whip cream. However, if you would like to revert to the simple hand method of earlier years, whip the cream with a whisk in a bowl placed on cracked ice. It is a much longer process than whipping in an electric mixer, and I am not sure that the result is better, but it might be more satisfying to do.

Cream should have a small amount of salt added to it before whipping, and if it is to be used for dessert, sugar should be added to taste. Also, you may add such seasonings as sherry, Madeira, Cognac, or a liqueur when the cream is all but ready to serve.

Cream for certain dishes, such as soufflés, hot puddings, and other warm desserts, should be beaten only to a runny thickness that is between the pouring and spooning stages.

In the days when ladies cared little about calories and cholesterol, hostesses at tea parties often served elaborately flavored cream as a rich little bonus with all the cakes and petits fours. Among the flavorings were crushed peanut brittle — and delicious it is if the brittle is a good one; finely cut bits of bittersweet and sweet chocolate; crushed dry macaroon crumbs; and praline powder.

Gelatinized Whipped Cream

Whipped cream to be used for decorating, piped through a tube, should be made firm. For each cup of cream to be whipped, dissolve 1 teaspoon unflavored gelatine in 1 tablespoon water and heat till it is thoroughly melted. Blend thoroughly with the cream just before it is whipped to your taste. This will give the piped cream a certain stability, although it changes the texture slightly.

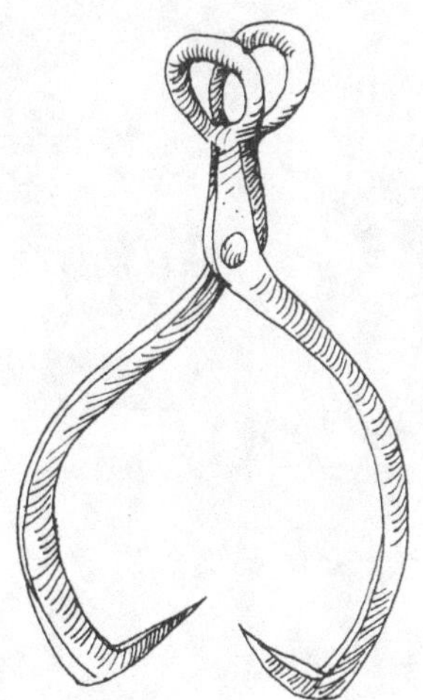

Fruit

Despite the wealth of fruit in this country, only in recent years has it become fashionable to serve it as a dessert or with a cheese course. Unfortunately, this custom comes at a time when the quality of fruit has sadly deteriorated compared to the fruit one used to eat in season. Modern refrigeration keeps fruit for long periods, though not always in its most flavorful state, and fast transportation carries it into all parts of the country. The benefits are found in bounty rather than quality, and we now take for granted such exotic items on our markets as fresh lichees, papaya, soursops, mangoes, fresh dates, and Chinese gooseberries, along with the more familiar fruits. The extended periods of availability have doubtlessly stimulated the appearance of fruit on our tables, aided by the national emphasis on slimming foods. Fruit is certainly among the kindest of desserts when it comes to caloric count, and fruit pies, which used to be a mainstay, are giving way to simpler dishes. Fruit is now often served plain, perhaps combined with other fruit, and sugared if needed; it is also served with cream or with liqueurs and brandies.

See the index for other recipes using fruits.

Almonds

Green almonds, extremely popular with the French, Italians, and Spanish, who frequently feast on them fresh from the tree, have just begun to have general distribution here.

Split the shells and pods with a sharp knife, remove the kernel, and peel it. Eat with a little salt.

Apples

Many of the apples we find on the market are refrigerated or temperature-controlled through the year to keep them more or less in harvest-fresh state, but a number of the old-fashioned varieties we used to know are in short supply or have disappeared from circulation entirely. We have come to depend on a few standards, such as the red Delicious, the yellow Delicious, and the McIntosh, all of which are extraordinarily good when picked fresh, but vary in flavor and texture when refrigerated for long periods. One also finds Northern Spies and occasionally Winesaps and Rome Beauties, which again are quite variable in quality. And in late spring we get shipments of Granny Smiths from Australia, which are excellent. Also, I find that the apples from Canada are often much better in New York than those shipped from the Northwest.

For cooking apples, in the East we get Greenings a good part of the year, which serve extremely well for most apple dishes, and we also get some Pippins, although they are far more plentiful on the West Coast. The great Gravensteins and Spitzenbergs seem to have vanished. The only way to get the best apple supply is to shop around at orchards when you drive into the countryside. The difference between apples from a local farmer and those refrigerated commercially can be astonishing. Recently in Pennsylvania I sampled apples that had been stored in a cold cellar for several months, and they were crisp, juicy, and thoroughly intriguing in flavor. One forgets how good an apple can be. Apples served with cheese are a most popular dessert.

Applesauce

6 to 8 cooking apples, 4 to 8 ounces each
½ to ¾ cup water
Sugar to taste

Our most common apple dish is applesauce, which has done duty as a dessert for generations and has also been used as an accompaniment to meats and poultry — notably pork, duck, and goose. In the days when people had apple trees in their backyards, the first fallen fruit was gathered, split, cored, and cooked with a little sugar. Then it was forced through a sieve and seasoned to taste. This made the initial applesauce of the season, much prized for its fresh flavor. However, sauce made from maturer apples is what most of us know.

Peel, core, and cut the apples into sixths. Place in a heavy saucepan and add a small amount of water — just enough to create the steam necessary to soften the apples. Cover, and cook over medium heat till the apples are done. Then stir with a wooden spoon or spatula and add sugar to taste, along with whatever spice you like, such as nutmeg, cinnamon, mace, or ginger. Apples vary so much in sugar content that it is folly to sweeten them before they are cooked.

Horseradish Applesauce. Add 2 or 3 tablespoons freshly grated or bottled horseradish to 1½ cups homemade applesauce, to serve with hot or cold meat. You may prefer to make it hotter (page 464).

Orange-Flavored or Lemon-Flavored Applesauce. Cook 1 or 2 slices of orange or lemon with the apples, and remove before you sweeten the fruit.

Apple Snow

3 egg whites
¼ cup granulated sugar
1 cup firm applesauce, puréed

A favorite dish in the early part of the century.

Beat the egg whites till they form peaks. Start adding the sugar in small amounts, and continue beating. When stiff and glossy, fold in the applesauce and serve heaped in glasses. Top with whipped cream or a soft custard.

Apple Compote

6 apples
1 cup sugar
1 cup water
Peel of a lemon, cut in fine strips

Peel, core, and cut the apples into sixths. Combine the sugar and water, bring to a boil, and add the lemon peel. Add the apples, and cook until just tender. Do not cook them down as you would for applesauce. Drain and transfer to a serving dish. Let the syrup boil down a little, and pour it over the apples. Chill, and serve with cream or whipped cream.

Baked Apples

The remarkable dining cars of the Northern Pacific Railroad used to feature two great products of the Northwest in the days when railroads catered to the public. One was an enormous baked potato, for which they became nationally famous. The second was a baked apple, also monumental in size and wonderful to eat.

Wash and core apples, and remove about 1 or 1½ inches of the skin around the tops. Arrange in a baking dish in about ½ inch water. Fill each apple with 1½ tablespoons sugar and 1 tablespoon butter. Sprinkle with 1 or 2 teaspoons sugar and add cinnamon or nutmeg if you like. Bake 30 to 60 minutes at 350 degrees. The cooking time varies considerably, depending on the texture of the apples. Baste once or twice with the juices in the pan. When done the apples should be firm and nicely shaped. Serve cold with cream or with a custard.

Variations

(1) Fill each center with a mixture of 2 tablespoons butter, 1 tablespoon sugar, and 1 to 2 tablespoons chopped raisins.

(2) Pour a mixture of sherry or white wine and water in the bottom of the baking dish instead of plain water, and baste with this.

(3) Use brown sugar or maple sugar instead of granulated sugar.

(4) Use maple syrup or simple syrup instead of sugar for filling the apples, and also substitute for the liquid in the pan.

(5) It was once thought delightful to fill the apples with red cinnamon candies, which colored the flesh pinky red and saturated it with the cinnamon flavor.

(6) Flavor each apple with 1 tablespoon Cognac or 1 tablespoon applejack before baking.

Fried Apple Rings

Often served with pork, ham, or chicken for a main course, and sometimes with bacon or sausages for breakfast. Fried apple rings are elegant to look upon and delicious to eat.

Choose cooking apples of uniform size. Peel and core, then cut into slices 3/8 to 1/2 inch thick. Sauté the rings in butter or bacon fat in a heavy skillet, turning once. Do not overcook.

Caramel Apple Rings. Fry as above, but sprinkle with sugar before turning. Turn a second time and allow the sugar to caramelize. Serve with a few drops of lemon juice.

Apricots

It is impossible nowadays to find perfect, ripe, fully mature apricots in the markets, which is a pity, since they can be so extraordinarily good. If you are close to a source of this fruit you are indeed lucky. California, Oregon, and Washington are all centers where apricots are available at their peak. Dried apricots are available all the year round, but one must shop for them carefully, for they vary a great deal in flavor and quality.

Few fruits are better than fresh apricots eaten as a dessert. They have a rich, smooth flavor and a lovely perfume. If they are really ripe, simply dip them in water and eat them as they are, savoring each bite. For another distinctive dessert, slice and serve them with sugar and heavy cream.

Poached Apricots

18 apricots, with pits
2 cups sugar
2 cups water
1-inch piece vanilla bean or 1½ teaspoons vanilla extract

Halve the apricots. Crack some of the pits and remove the kernels. Combine the sugar and water, bring to a boil, and cook 5 minutes. Add the vanilla, the fruit, and the kernels, and poach till the apricots are just tender. Serve cold.

Poached Whole Apricots

12 to 18 whole apricots, not too ripe
Boiling water to cover
2 cups sugar
2 cups water
1 teaspoon vanilla

Cover the apricots with boiling water in a deep saucepan. Simmer 5 minutes. Let them stand in the water 5 minutes more. Peel carefully. In a clean saucepan combine the sugar, water, and vanilla. Simmer 5 minutes and add the apricots. Poach until they are just cooked through — about 6 to 8 minutes. Do not overcook lest they become mushy. Cool, and serve with heavy cream or sour cream, or with a liqueur or brandy (kirsch or Cognac is probably best), or flame with brandy.

Poached Dried Apricots

1 pound dried apricots
1½ cups sugar
1½ cups water

Soak the apricots in water 2 hours or so, and then bring them to a boil. Drain well. Combine the sugar and water, bring to a boil, and simmer 5 minutes. Add the apricots, and when they begin to simmer cook them about 15 minutes over low heat. Chill. Serve with cream, or purée for sauces, fillings, or sherbet.

Tipsy Apricots

Bring dried apricots to a boil in water and drain. Place in a jar and add sherry, Madeira or port to cover; then seal and let stand several weeks. They may be used as they are, combined with other fruits, poached in a syrup, or poached and puréed for sauces or fillings.

Preserved Apricots

24 apricots
3 cups sugar
1 cup water
½ teaspoon vanilla
Pinch salt

These rich nuggets are absolutely without peer among summer fruit. In my youth, we often ate them with rich heavy cream or at times with homemade ice cream. They are also excellent with pound cake or sponge cake.

Halve the apricots. Crack some of the seeds and extract the kernels. Combine the water with 2 cups sugar and boil until the syrup reaches 238 degrees — the thread-spinning temperature. Add the apricots, vanilla, and remaining sugar, and boil rapidly approximately 12 to 15 minutes or until the fruit is cooked through. Add the kernels and cook 1 minute. From time to time while the apricots are boiling, scrape the sides of the pan with a rubber spatula or a wooden spatula covered with cheesecloth slightly dampened around the edges. This keeps the sugar from crystallizing and becoming gritty. Serve the apricots cold.

Apricot-Pineapple Preserve. Add ½ to 1 cup fresh, frozen, or canned pineapple cubes to the syrup with the apricots. It gives a delicious quality to the dish.

Bananas

Bananas, like apricots and mangoes, were not common in this country until late in the nineteenth century. Since then, they have become one of the most prevalent of fruits, with many different uses in ice creams, cakes, pies, and other dishes. A related fruit, the plantain, has also come into more general usage, introduced to our cookery by the Cubans and Puerto Ricans.

The ordinary banana is a development of several different varieties and is grown to last and to mature in transit. When the skin is a quite deep yellow and very speckled and the fruit inside is just soft, it achieves its finest flavor and is delicious raw or cooked. Red bananas, sometimes called claret bananas, also appear in our market. They are richer than the yellow variety and have a sweet, very unctuous quality, but may be used in the same way. Tiny finger bananas, too, are to be found in some markets. When ripe, they are exceptionally sweet and delightful to the palate. Dried bananas, found in many specialty markets, are really a sweetmeat, rich and extremely palatable, and should be eaten as they are.

Peel and slice bananas just before serving. Sprinkle with a little lime or lemon juice and with brown or white sugar. Serve heavy or sour cream separately. A good dish for breakfast or luncheon.

Baked Bananas in Their Jackets

Choose rather ripe bananas and arrange them, unpeeled, on a baking sheet. Usually one per person is ample. Bake in a 350-degree oven 20 to 30 minutes, or until the skins are quite black and soft to the touch. Transfer to warm plates and slit lengthwise with a sharp knife. Sprinkle with sugar and a bit of Cognac or rum. Or heat the liquor, ignite it, and serve the bananas flaming.

Baked Bananas

Butter
6 peeled ripe bananas
6 teaspoons butter
6 tablespoons brown sugar
Lime or lemon juice

Butter a baking dish and arrange the bananas on it. Spread each banana with a teaspoon of butter, sprinkle with brown sugar, and add a few drops of lime (preferably) or lemon juice. Bake at 350 degrees 15 to 20 minutes, or until the bananas are soft and the sugar and juice are blended. Serve warm with cream or sour cream, or flame with rum or Cognac.

Broiled Bananas. Increase the butter for each banana to 2 teaspoons instead of 1. Broil on a buttered broiling sheet about 5 inches from the source of heat till the fruit is soft and browned. Be careful they do not burn.

Sometimes hideous salads are fabricated with bananas. There is the banana and marshmallow combination, for example, and the one in which a banana is rolled in peanut butter, arranged on a lettuce leaf and dressed with mayonnaise. And probably most revolting of all is the "candlelight" or "candlestick" salad. This calls for lettuce and a slice of canned pineapple, surmounted by half a banana standing upright and decorated with a maraschino cherry and a dab of mayonnaise.

If you must combine bananas with anything, use other fruit. They are especially good with fresh pineapple, strawberries, or blueberries.

Blackberries

There are three varieties of blackberries. The low wild bramble blackberries which grow in such profusion in the Northwest over logged-off land are deliciously tart in flavor and lend themselves to jams and pies. Then there are the blackberries that sport magnificent blossoms in spring and come into fruit in the summer. Both the wild and the cultivated varieties of this type have a remarkably fresh flavor and are among the choicest of summer fruits. Unfortunately, they have large seeds, and thus, to my palate at least, are not particularly successful stewed, although they are just passable in a pie. They are ideal when served simply, with sugar and cream, or combined with other berries.

An unusually delightful way to enjoy blackberries is to extract the juice by putting them through a food mill or sieve. Pour it into a glass with ice, and add sugar if needed. This makes a superb and refreshing drink for summer.

A pie combining blackberries and apples is another unusual and delicious way to enjoy this berry.

Blueberries and Huckleberries

The blueberry and the huckleberry are interchangeable and equally wonderful to the taste. They come in many different varieties, wild and cultivated, and have a long season. The wild berries are available to those who live near heavily wooded, swampy, logged-off, or burnt-off land. Both blueberries and huckleberries make good pies and cakes and other typically American delights.

Blueberries make extraordinary eating. They need only sugar — granulated, powdered, brown, or maple — and heavy cream or sour cream. Or use maple syrup instead of sugar, and combine the berries with sliced peaches, if you like. Blueberries are very elegant sprinkled with either Cointreau or Grand Marnier, and they are delicious well sugared and spooned over vanilla ice cream or a fruit ice cream and topped with whipped cream.

Poached Blueberries

2 cups sugar
½ cup water
3 slices lemon
¼ teaspoon cinnamon
1½ pints blueberries or more

Prepare a syrup: Combine the sugar, water, lemon, and cinnamon and boil 5 to 8 minutes. Add the blueberries, and when they come to a boil reduce the heat and simmer 5 or 6 minutes. Let the berries cool in the syrup. Serve with heavy cream or whipped cream.

Blueberries in Whipped Cream

This is an old Pennsylvania way to serve blueberries or huckleberries.

For 6 persons, whip 1 pint cream, sweeten to taste with sugar or maple sugar, and fold in as many blueberries or huckleberries as possible — about a pint. Serve at once with crisp sugar cookies.

Blueberry Streusel

5 cups (2½ pints) ripe blueberries or huckleberries
Juice of a lemon or lime
¾ cup firmly packed brown or maple sugar
½ cup flour
⅓ cup butter

Combine the berries with the juice and let stand 25 minutes. Blend together the sugar and flour, and work in the butter. Add a touch of mace or nutmeg if you like. Continue to blend until the streusel mixture is crumbly but will adhere when squeezed together. Place the berries in a 6-cup baking dish and top with the streusel mixture. Bake in a 400-degree oven 20 to 25 minutes or until nicely browned. Serve hot with sour cream or whipped cream.

Apple Streusel. Apples, sliced and lightly sugared, may be prepared the same way (cooking time, about 30 minutes).

Dried and Frozen Blueberries

Blueberries and huckleberries, spread on trays or pans and dried in the sun, used to be stored in jars for winter use in sauces, pies, and cakes. Nowadays we can preserve them by freezing instead. They freeze exceedingly well, just as they come from the garden or the wilds. Simply wash and pack in plastic freezer bags.

Boysenberries

A hybrid berry which has made its debut in the last forty years. Boysenberries are excellent for jam or pies and tarts, and are quite good eaten as is with sugar and cream or sour cream. They are also good cooked lightly with sugar and served over ice cream.

Cherries

We grow some of the world's finest cherries, which include the Bing, developed in the Western hemisphere, perhaps the best cherry to be had anywhere; the Lambert, similar to the Bing and rarer than it used to be; the Royal Anne, a white cherry with red markings, which when matured and ripened is a great cherry for eating fresh or preserving; and the Kentish, Montmorency, or May Dukes — tart, brilliantly colored, and meaty when properly ripened — all excellent cooking cherries. California, Oregon, Washington, and parts of British Columbia appear to be the ideal part of the continent for cherries, and the Bings and Royal Annes grow to stupendous sizes in these regions.

Cherries are never better than when served fresh in a huge bowl with individual bowls of water for dipping. If ripe, juicy, and flavorful, they are a perfect dessert. Poached cherries are also excellent.

Poached Cherries

1½ to 2 pounds cherries
1 cup sugar
2 cups water
¼ cup kirsch or to taste

Stem the cherries and pit them if you like. Either use a cherry pitter — a gadget which has been part of American life for generations — or cut the cherries in half to pit them. Combine the sugar and water in a saucepan and bring to a boil. Add the cherries and cook until just heated through — be sure not to overcook. Add the kirsch and let the cherries cool in the syrup. Serve warm or chilled.

Cherries Jubilee

Prepare 2 pounds Bing cherries as above, but drain off most of their juices. Keep warm, or reheat. Heat 6 tablespoons kirsch, Cognac, or Armagnac, then ignite and pour it over the hot cherries. Serve at once either plain or over vanilla ice cream.

Red Cherry Compote

2 pounds red cooking cherries
2 cups sugar
1 cup water
½ teaspoon vanilla

Pick over the cherries, wash and stem. Pit them if you like. Combine the sugar, water, and vanilla, and simmer 5 minutes after it has come to a boil. Add the cherries and simmer 8 or 9 minutes, or until they are just cooked through. Cool. Serve at room temperature plain or with whipped cream.

Cherry Shrub

This was a tremendously popular summer drink in the nineteenth century. At that time it was made with Morello cherries, which still exist in some regions, but it can be made with other sweet cherries as well.

This is Mrs. Randolph's recipe: "Gather ripe Morello cherries, pick them from the stalk, put them in an earthen pot, which must be set into an iron pot of water; make the water boil but make sure that none of it gets into the cherries; when the juice is extracted pour it into a bag made of tolerably thick cloth, which will permit the juice to pass, but not the pulp of the cherries. Sweeten it to your taste and when it becomes perfectly clear — bottle it — put a gill of brandy into each bottle, before you pour in the juice — cover the corks with rosin. It will keep all summer, in a cool dry place, and is delicious mixed with water."

Currants

Ripe redcurrants are seldom used at table these days, but at one time they were a familiar sight, as in an old recipe for currants for tea: "Pick them from the stems and put them in a basin of water. shake them about; then take them up by the handful; shake off the water and put them in a deep dish; mix plenty of sugar with them and serve. These are better for standing an hour or so before serving."

Served alone, currants have great quality, and combined with fresh raspberries in summer pudding they are superb.

Summer Pudding

Thin slices of white bread with crusts removed
1½ pints raspberries
½ to ¾ pint currants
1 cup sugar

Line a 1 to 1½ quart pudding mold or bowl with the bread slices. Combine the fruit and sugar in a heavy saucepan, and simmer over low heat about 4 minutes to start juices flowing. Cool. Reserve some of the fruit juices. Pour the cooled fruit into the bread-lined mold and top with slices of bread. Cover with a plate or other flat object which will fit inside the mold, and weight it well. Let the pudding rest in the refrigerator overnight. To serve, unmold in a rather deep dish, and serve with the reserved juices, heavy cream, or whipped cream.

Figs

We are blessed with a great variety of figs and a long season. The first black figs appear as early as May, and we still have some slow-ripening figs in October, which are apt to be the most delicious of all, with a sweetness beyond belief. I remember traveling from Portland to San Francisco by car in my youth. We would plan a stop at Corning, California, in the center of fig and olive country. In season, large trays of ripe figs were available for the taking, and in the hotel dining room they would serve bowls of figs with cream.

To peel figs, cut a slice from the bottom of each; then with the tines of a fork or a small, sharp knife, carefully roll the skin away from the stem end. If you are deft, you can remove the skin without damaging the flesh.

Figs are delicious peeled, sliced, and served with sugar and heavy cream.

Figs with Prosciutto

The Italian custom of eating fresh figs with prosciutto has recently come into vogue in New York and California. To prepare, simply drape the ham over ripe figs, peeled or unpeeled, and serve as a first course. Two figs per person should be ample.

Roast Figs (Mrs. Crowen's)

A delightful old recipe seldom done any more.

"These are both palatable and nutritious for people in delicate health. Take fine large figs, put them on bird spits and roast them before the fire, or broil them over bright coals, on a gridiron; turn them when half done."

Gooseberries

Gooseberries were brought over by the English but have never become established here, mainly, I think, because most people are ignorant of how to use them. Gooseberries are usually sold in the markets green, in which state they are delicious in pies. When they ripen, they are a deep yellow, sometimes tinged with red, and may be eaten as they are.

They are also excellent poached and in gooseberry fool.

Gooseberry Fool

1½ pints gooseberries
1 to 1½ cups sugar, to taste
1 cup water
1½ cups heavy cream, or 1 cup heavy cream and 1 cup boiled custard

Fool is a fruit dish which the English brought with them and which has spread through the country. The South adopted it first, followed by New England and Pennsylvania. It is still a great delicacy and can be made with rhubarb, raspberries, strawberries, or greengage plums, as well as with gooseberries.

Pick the stems and tails from the gooseberries, wash them thoroughly, and drain. Combine the sugar and water and bring to a boil. Add the berries and simmer until they are just cooked through but not mushy. Stir them and shake the pan from time to time. Taste for sugar, and let cool in the syrup. When cool, drain well and put through a foodmill, sieve, or purée attachment on an electric mixer. Whip the cream (it should not be too stiff), or use 1 cup boiled custard combined with 1 cup heavy cream, whipped. Fold the gooseberry purée into the cream or the custard and cream, and chill thoroughly before serving. Serve with additional cream if you like.

Poached Gooseberries with Ice Cream. When the berries are poached, place 2 or 3 tablespoons of them in a glass, fill with vanilla ice cream, and top with whipped cream and chopped pistachio nuts.

Grapes

There are numerous varieties of grapes available in the fall and winter months. When ripe, few fruits are as refreshing. They are best, I feel, when chilled and served with small bowls of iced water for dipping. Provide grape shears — an inexpensive and versatile gadget — to avoid the nuisance of breaking off grapes.

Among the many varieties of grapes, probably the most popular is the Thompson seedless, a rather small white grape which comes early and late and is thoroughly refreshing but without particularly distinctive flavor. For flavor one must look for the spicy Muscat, also a white grape. The riper it grows and more discolored it becomes, the better the flavor. When almost shriveled and quite brown, on the verge of being raisins, Muscats are at their peak. Next in flavor, perhaps, are the Ribiers, the large black grapes, and the Tokays, which are a delightful reddish shade. The Malagas and the Ladyfingers, long and meaty, are also much sought after. In addition, we have a number of native grapes, such as the Concords and the Isabellas. These are spicy and of different texture entirely from the grapes described above.

Grapes with Brown Sugar and Sour Cream

The Thompson seedless are best for this dessert. Malagas and Muscats will do, but they must be split and seeded. Thompsons need only be split and arranged in a serving dish or in individual dishes. Sprinkle heavily with brown sugar, and top with sour cream. An excellent combination of flavors and textures.

Frosted Grapes

Dip bunches of grapes into slightly beaten egg white and then into granulated or crystallized sugar. Let them dry. Arrange on a plate and serve.

Grapefruit

Rather a recent addition to the citrus family, grapefruit has no significant tradition in our cookery. However, it is as popular as any fruit for breakfast, and the ever innovative American cook has thought of many other uses for it as well.

Broiled Grapefruit

Allow one half grapefruit per serving. Section the halves, sprinkle rather thickly with brown sugar or granulated sugar, and dot with butter. Place on a cookie sheet and broil about 5 inches from the heating unit till the sugar is caramelized and the fruit well heated. Serve plain or with a dash of rum or Cognac. If you must, decorate with a cherry.

Flavored Grapefruit Sections

Peel grapefruit well with a very sharp knife, being certain to remove all the outside membrane. With two strokes of a small pointed knife, cut through the membrane of each section and remove the meat. Place the sections in a bowl, sprinkle with sugar, and flavor with any of the following: sherry, port, or champagne. Serve in tall glasses or parfait glasses for breakfast or for a first course or dessert for luncheon or dinner.

Flavored Orange and Grapefruit Sections. Grapefruit is delicious combined with orange. Flavor the sections with Grand Marnier or Cointreau.

Ground-Cherries

Surprisingly little known nowadays, ground-cherries used to be one of the more common fruits and still are one of the more delicious. They grow wild throughout a great part of the country and are cultivated in Pennsylvania and the West. In Europe, where there are different types — they all belong to the genus *Physalis* — they are eaten raw and used for compotes. In Australia, where the larger ones are called Cape gooseberries, they are canned and shipped to the rest of the world. Ground-cherries make wonderful pocket fruit, for each one is securely packed in its own little husk. When eaten raw they are refreshingly sweet and rich. It is mystifying to me that they are not more prized.

Poached Ground-Cherries

2 cups sugar
1 cup water
4 slices lemon
1½ pints ground-cherries

Combine the sugar and water, bring to a boil, and boil 8 to 10 minutes. Add the lemon and ground-cherries and cook 5 minutes, at a rolling boil, removing any scum that forms. Reduce heat, and simmer until the ground-cherries are just cooked through, about 12 minutes in all. Cool in the syrup. Serve as a topping for ice cream, or serve warm over sponge cake or angel cake with whipped cream.

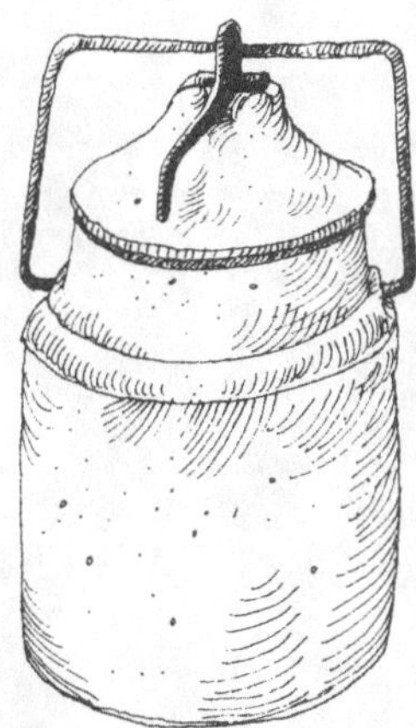

Huckleberries

See Blueberries.

Lichee Nuts

The Chinese fruit we have known so long dried and tinned is now available fresh in our markets throughout a large part of the year. I have seen lichee nuts in New York in the summer and in California, Oregon, and Washington in the spring. The pods are a rich coppery shade, and the fruit itself is a pearly white with an unbelievable flavor. One eats the fruit directly from the pod and removes the pit. I find lichee nuts delicious when chilled before serving.

The dried fruit has the same crisp pod and resembles a rather large raisin. Sold mainly in Chinese and Japanese shops, it is a delicious morsel, though not to be compared with the fresh fruit.

Mangoes

Mangoes have become increasingly common in this country during the last fifteen or twenty years. We now get the flat green-skinned Hawaiian and Caribbean mangoes and the rounder green- and red-skinned Haydens and Zills from Florida. Both types have luscious golden flesh and flavor unequaled by any other fruit. They also have large pits that cling tightly to the flesh and an abundance of juice, making them somewhat messy to handle. Actually, to most enjoy a mango one should probably eat it in a bathtub, or at the very least in private.

Mangoes can be peeled with a sharp knife and cut into sections by carving around the pit. In this way they can be served with sugar and with other fruit. A little kirsch may be added, but it is really not necessary, so highly delicious is the natural flavor of the ripe fruit.

Mangoes are also available canned, in which form they are excellent.

Melons

Probably the first melons spoken of in our cooking literature turn up in directions for pickling muskmelons or watermelons. One can assume that both these melons were eaten in the usual fashion as well. Also there were very popular pickles called "stuffed mangoes" which were really stuffed melons tied together. These I remember eating years ago, and they were delicious and unusual. Some recipes call for melons grown especially for pickling purposes, but this is not necessary.

Here is Mrs. Randolph's recipe for "mangoes": "Gather the melons a size larger than a goose egg — put them in a pot, pour boiling salt water made strong upon them, and cover them up; next day, cut a slit from the blossom end, and take out the seeds carefully — return them to the brine, and let them remain in it eight days; then put them in strong vinegar for a fortnight, wipe the insides with a soft cloth, stuff them and tie them, pack in a pot with the slit uppermost; strew some of the stuffing over each layer, and keep them covered with the best vinegar."

To make the stuffing for forty melons: "Wash a pound of white race ginger very clean; pour boiling water on it and let it stand twenty-four hours. Slice it thin and dry it; one pound of horse-radish scraped and dried, one pound of mustard seed washed and dried, one pound of chopped onion, one ounce of mace, one of nutmeg pounded fine, two ounces of turmeric and a handful of whole black pepper. Make these ingredients into a paste with a quarter of a pound of mustard, and a large cup full of sweet oil (olive). Put a clove of garlic into each mango."

Today we have melons all through the year from various parts of the globe, and they have become a standard part of our diet at breakfast, lunch, and dinner. The choice available to us is incredibly large and includes the muskmelon and cantaloupe, with orange flesh and roughish skins; the honeydew melon, with creamy green skin and brilliant green-white flesh, the least attractive of all the melons in flavor; the Persian melon, which looks like an enlarged cantaloupe, luscious, orange-fleshed, and with bouquet and flavor of great distinction; the Cranshaw melon, with somewhat dappled skin and flesh of pink-orange; the casaba melon, yellow-skinned, white-fleshed, and delicate in flavor, but which must be picked ripe to be at its best; the Hand melon, resembling the cantaloupe but more highly perfumed; the Spanish melon, with rough green skin and tawny whitish flesh, so delicate and delicious, available far into the winter months; the papaya, a tropical fruit with skin that runs from green to yellow, brilliant orange flesh, black seeds, and a delightful, distinctive flavor; and finally, the watermelon, crisp, red-meated, delicate in flavor, and good when eaten plain or plugged and soaked with liquor.

Melons, for the most part, are served in wedges with lemon or lime and are best when chilled. Below are a few of the better-known flavorings and accompaniments.

Melon with Port. Originally an English custom. Merely add 2 or 3 tablespoons port to a ripe melon wedge or half and make small gashes in the flesh with a spoon to permit the wine to penetrate.

Melon with Ginger. Many old-timers sprinkled a little powdered or ground ginger on melon to enhance the flavor.

Melon with Salt and Pepper. In the nineteenth century cantaloupe and muskmelon, especially, were often treated to salt or salt and pepper, a custom that carried over into the twentieth century. But I cannot see why, for the seasoning does not do a great deal for the melon.

Melon with Berries. A generous helping of sugared berries were often served in melon halves. Raspberries, particularly, seem to be very complementary, but so do blueberries and strawberries.

Melon with Ice Cream. Cantaloupe with ice cream, especially vanilla or strawberry, has always been a typically American favorite, sometimes embellished by raspberry syrup and whipped cream, or crushed raspberries or strawberries and whipped cream, just to make it a more stupendous dessert.

Melon Surprise or Melon Alaska

1 large melon — Persian, honeydew, Cranshaw, or Spanish
Lemon juice
Brandied fruits (peaches, apricots, cherries, plums, etc.) or ice creams (vanilla, strawberry, lemon, orange, pistachio, cherry, or peach)
4 or 5 egg whites
½ cup sugar

A dessert which used to be served frequently in the 1930's and occasionally before that. I seldom see it any more, which is a pity, since it is very impressive and delicious as well.

Peel the melon very carefully. Cut out a good-sized wedge, and through the opening remove all seeds. Add a touch of lemon juice. Replace the wedge. Cut a slice from the bottom of the melon opposite the wedge so that it will stand on a board securely. Chill the melon thoroughly. Preheat the oven to 425 degrees. Just before you are ready to serve the melon, beat the egg whites till they hold soft peaks and then beat in the sugar gradually till the meringue is stiff and glossy. Remove the chilled melon from the refrigerator and place on a board large enough to accommodate the melon and the meringue. Fill the melon with brandied fruits or with various flavors of ice cream, and cover the entire melon with meringue as you would for a baked Alaska. Place in the oven just long enough to brown the meringue. Remove and serve at once.

If you like, set several eggshell halves in the meringue before browning. After removing from the oven, fill with Cognac or kirsch, ignite, and take to the table flaming. Slice across the melon in thick slices and serve with a spoon and flat server.

Melon Surprise

This has long been a summer standard with party givers. Carve a large watermelon into a basket shape or scallop the edge of half a melon with a sharp knife. (Attach a paper pattern to the melon with Scotch tape to achieve an even design.) With a ball cutter — available at most kitchenware emporiums — scoop out balls of the melon and place in a large bowl. Also scoop balls from several other kinds of melon if you like. Combine the melon balls with other fruits — strawberries, blueberries, raspberries, sliced peaches — practically any combination you choose. Scrape out the watermelon well, and chill thoroughly. Sugar the fruit lightly and chill. When ready to serve, heap the mixed fruits in the watermelon shell and add kirsch, Cointreau, or Cognac to taste. Decorate with sprigs of mint dusted with powdered sugar. It is a good idea to keep some fruit in reserve for replenishment. Makes a spectacular dish for a party indoors or outdoors.

Melon with Ham

The Italians introduced us to melon and prosciutto years ago, and it has become a national favorite. A variation on this, done in New York and in other parts of the country, substitutes paper thin slices of Smithfield ham for the Parma ham or prosciutto. Both versions have distinction and are easy to prepare. Pass the pepper mill when you serve the melon and ham.

Tipsy Watermelon

This recipe is typical of several that were in circulation in the days before Prohibition and that have had a revival since. The liquor content varies from region to region. I have encountered recipes that call for champagne, bourbon, rum, applejack, or Cognac. All are commendable, and all make a pretty special watermelon for a picnic or garden party.

Cut a deep plug about 2 inches square in a ripe watermelon. Remove the plug and make several deep incisions in the flesh of the melon with an ice pick or similar tool. Slowly pour in light rum, Cognac or champagne — as much as the watermelon will take. Replace the plug, and seal with tape. Refrigerate the watermelon 24 hours, and turn four or five times to allow the liquor or wine to permeate the watermelon evenly.

Nectarines

Nectarines, which many years ago were called peach-plums, are one of our most delicious fruits and have a long season. Those imported from South America begin to come in February and March, and the locally grown ones appear in midsummer and last until late fall. Both the yellow-fleshed and pale green ones are available in most markets. Nectarines have a delicious peachy plum flavor and are at their best when eaten very ripe either sliced or in the hand. They may, however, be prepared as peaches, using any of the recipes given for that fruit.

Oranges

We have two schools of orange growing in the country now — the California citrus crop, which has served a great part of the country for years, and the Florida citrus crop, which has grown rapidly in popularity and in size over the last thirty years. Oranges are now in the market throughout the year, albeit they are not at their peak all that time, and care must be taken to get good ones. The difference in quality and flavor among oranges is obvious to anyone who really knows the fruit. Probably the finest eating oranges are the California navel oranges and the Florida Temples and Tangelos. These latter are in short season, but when ripe and in their prime they are among the most flavorful of fruits. The navels are in season a good part of the year and are dependable, easy to peel, and nicely flavored.

If ripe, oranges are delicious eaten just peeled and sectioned, and they combine with other fruits exceptionally well.

Orange Juice

Orange juice seems to be the universal breakfast tipple, but its quality has deteriorated in recent decades. Now one buys concentrated juice or pasteurized juice, and seldom does one bother to squeeze oranges for fresh juice any more. And much the pity, too. Nothing is quite as refreshing as a cool glass of fresh juice, whether plain or in combination with other juices. Also, orange juice makes a delicious dressing for fruits such as blueberries, strawberries, raspberries, or peaches.

Sliced Oranges

Peel the oranges or slice off the skin with a sharp knife so that the inner film of white is entirely removed. Slice quite thinly. Sprinkle with granulated sugar or powdered sugar, and with a little cinnamon.

Orange Sections

Peel oranges well, leaving none of the white film on them. With a sharp pointed knife cut between the sections and remove each section whole. Add sugar and/or a light splash of kirsch, Grand Marnier, Cointreau, or the Italian orange liqueur Aurum.

Orange Sections Dipped in Fondant

Orange sections used to be served this way for a Christmas treat. The sections were removed without having the film peeled from them and were then dipped into fondant, dried on a rack, and served with other Christmas sweetmeats.

Poached Oranges

4 oranges
Zest of 1½ oranges
2 cups sugar
1 cup water

These are not really poached, but heated in a syrup.

Remove the zest (thin outside peel) of 1½ oranges in even strips, and with a sharp knife cut into thin shreds. Peel the remaining oranges. Cut the oranges in halves and arrange in a serving dish. Bring the sugar and water to a boil, and boil 5 minutes. Add the finely cut orange zest, and boil again 3 or 4 minutes, or until the strips of zest are cooked through. Ladle the hot syrup over the oranges, and place the zest in small bunches atop them. Chill thoroughly. Garnish each orange half with candied violets or maraschino cherries.

Peaches

Peaches have been one of our staple fruits for well over a century. Early recipes for brandied peaches, pickled peaches, and peach mangoes can be found in many of the traditional old cookbooks, and peach preserves took on an almost legendary aura — everyone thought his grandmother or mother made the finest. (As a matter of fact, a famous play in the early part of the twentieth century, *Turn to the Right*, combined the Mother theme with a story of convicts rehabilitated by making peach preserves. It was a real tearjerker.)

Nowadays in many large cities it is difficult to get tree-ripened peaches, and we struggle with fruit which seems never to measure up to the flavor we expect of it. Quite often the first peaches to arrive in markets are the white ones, exceedingly delicate of meat, filled with remarkable flavor, and the best of the year until the very late-ripening peaches come along in the fall. Your success with peaches will depend in large part on your nearness to orchards and your persistence in shopping for mature fruit. Good peaches are exquisitely perfumed and wonderfully flavored; poor, they are dull indeed.

If peaches are very ripe, you can scrape the skin with the back of a knife and sometimes loosen it enough to remove it in one fell tug. Otherwise, blanch the peaches a few seconds in boiling water before removing the skin. Peaches discolor quickly, so be certain to peel and slice them at the last possible moment. A sprinkling of lemon juice will help to retard darkening.

It is sometimes pleasant to serve peaches whole and unpeeled, inviting family or guests to peel and slice their own. In this event, fingerbowls are required. Also, peaches prepared in almost any fashion are excellent when served with good ice cream, preferably homemade.

Sliced Peaches

Ripe and flavorful peaches are required for serving in this fashion. Peel and slice as above, sprinkle with sugar, and serve with cream, sour cream, or whipped cream.

Peaches with Red Wine. Sugar sliced peaches to taste, and pour in enough dry red wine to cover. Allow to stand a half hour or so before serving.

Peaches with Port or Madeira. Substitute either of these sweet wines for the dry red wine. Taste before adding sugar.

Peaches with Spirits. Sugar the peaches and flavor with Cognac, bourbon, one of the orange liqueurs — Grand Marnier or Cointreau — or kirsch or other white alcohol.

Peaches With Brown Sugar. Sprinkle with brown sugar to taste, and serve with sour cream or rum.

Peaches with Raspberries. Fresh sliced peaches and raspberries are particularly complementary to one another. Sugar the fruit and serve with cream or a liqueur. Or make a purée of the raspberries, sweeten to taste, and serve over the peaches — an attractive as well as a delicious dish.

Poached Peaches

6 fresh peaches
1 1/2 cups sugar
1 1/2 cups water
1 inch vanilla bean
Pinch salt

Peel and halve the peaches unless they are Clingstones, when peeling only is possible. Combine the sugar and water and add the vanilla bean. Bring to a boil and cook 5 minutes. Add the fruit and poach gently, basting them with hot liquid from time to time and turning them once during the cooking. When they are tender but not mushy, remove from the heat and allow to cool in the syrup. Serve with pouring cream or a custard sauce.

Variations

(1) Add 1/3 cup bourbon to the liquid 5 minutes before removing from heat.

(2) Omit the vanilla bean and add 1 or 2 slices of orange to the syrup. When they are cooled you may flavor with Grand Marnier.

Jellied Peaches

6 peaches
1 pound jar currant jelly
Cream or sour cream
Pistachio nuts

A rather old recipe I remember as a child. Beautiful to look upon and excellent to the palate.

Pour boiling water over the peaches and let them stand a few minutes to loosen the skins. Peel carefully and arrange in a serving dish. Melt the currant jelly and spoon over the peaches very carefully so that each peach receives a full coating. Chill, and serve with sour cream or whipped cream and a few chopped pistachio nuts for a garnish.

Broiled Peaches

6 ripe but firm peaches
Butter
Brown sugar
Maple sugar, currant jelly, or apricot preserves
Sliced toasted almonds

Broiled peaches may be served as a dessert or with certain meats, especially ham and duck, for a main course.

Pour boiling water over the peaches and let stand a few minutes, then peel. Halve the peaches, dot with butter, and sprinkle lightly with brown sugar. Place cut side up on a broiling rack and broil 4 to 5 inches from the heat until the sugar and butter are bubbling and the peaches heated through. Remove from the broiler, top with spoonfuls of maple sugar, currant jelly, or raspberry or apricot preserve. Run under the broiler 1 or 2 minutes to set, and serve on a hot plate. Or pour warmed bourbon or Cognac over the peaches and flame as you send them to table.

Note. Firm, well-drained canned peach halves can be treated the same way when fresh peaches are not available. Spoon a little of the syrup from the can into each peach half. No brown sugar is necessary. Merely add butter and the maple sugar, currant jelly, or raspberry preserve, and broil.

Baked Peaches

4 peaches
4 cloves
1 cup brown sugar
½ cup water
⅓ cup bourbon

In the early part of the century these were usually prepared without peeling, which makes not too pleasant a dish. Here is my version.

Choose large perfect peaches. Place in a deep bowl and pour boiling water over them. Let them stand 3 or 4 minutes. Peel very carefully and insert a clove into each. Transfer to a deep baking dish. Combine the brown sugar and water, and boil 5 minutes. Pour over the peaches. Bake at 350 degrees approximately 30 minutes or until the peaches are tender. Add the bourbon for the last few minutes of cooking. Serve warm or cold with bourbon-flavored custard sauce or bourbon-flavored soft whipped cream.

Brandied Peaches

From the late eighteenth century and throughout the nineteenth, no American cellar was complete without brandied peaches. This recipe of Mrs. Hale's is simple and good, and much resembles some of the old French family recipes.

"Take 4 pounds of ripe peaches, 2 pounds of powdered loaf [granulated] sugar. Put the fruit over the fire in cold water — simmer, but do not boil, till the skins will rub off easily. Stone them, if liked. Put the sugar and fruit in alternate layers in jars (quarts are best). Pour in brandy to cover. Cork tightly." Naturally these peaches stood for several months before using and developed a high degree of potency. They were served as a dessert taken from the bottle and they can be delicious when served warm or cold over ice cream.

Pears

Pears, like apples, when they are not superb seem to be exceedingly poor in quality. The latter condition, I am convinced, is because for the most part the fruit is too green when picked, and the ripening and storing processes are not as successful as they might be. There are months in the year when buying fresh pears is as much of a gamble as playing the tables at Las Vegas. If you buy pears that are still green, place them in a plastic or a paper bag to ripen. The Department of Agriculture claims that if you add a ripe apple and leave a small hole in the bag, the fruit will ripen rather quickly. I have found that this works with many different fruits, and it is indeed a help to those who are disconsolate over the state of fruit as it usually arrives from the fruiterers.

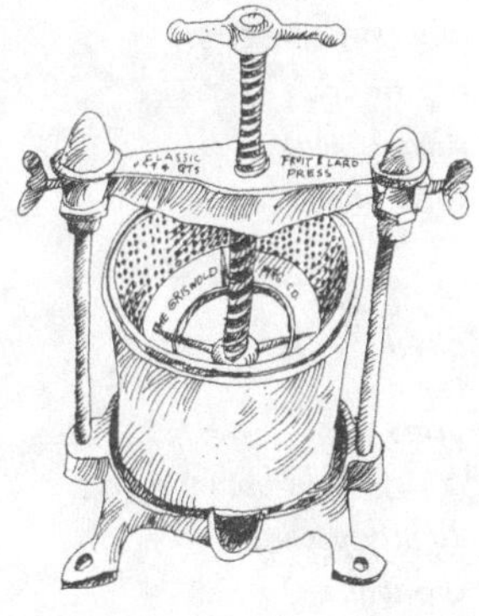

The finest pears for summer eating and for eating by hand are the Bartletts, known in Europe as the Williams. They have perfume that is intoxicating, and when perfectly ripened a flavor unmatched in any other pear. It is the pear from which is made the brandy called Williamine or eau de vie de poire. Bartletts flourish on the Pacific coast and in the East as well. They start coming into the market from California about July and continue through September. In the Northwest — Oregon, Washington, and British Columbia — they are later. To my mind, nothing in the world of fruit rivals this pear except fine strawberries, perfect peaches, and Tilton apricots.

Winter pears are different from Bartletts in texture, bouquet, and flavor. They ripen to a firmer meat, and they vary greatly in taste. The Bosc, a longish, rather russet pear, is probably the sweetest and most distinguished after the Bartlett. The Comice and the D'Anjou are later pears and usually suffer from refrigeration and long storage, but occasionally one finds them just at the peak when they prove to be delicious and thoroughly rewarding. The problem with winter pears as they are marketed now is that they take ages to mature, have a brief period of ripeness, and rot very quickly.

Ripe pears are really at their best as a dessert if served with a knife and fork and nothing else. If you are a cheese-and-pear person, then serve a cream cheese, or Roquefort, feta, or any one of a dozen other varieties. This, by the way, has become a distinctively American custom with pears. Ripe Bartlett, Comice, or Bosc pears are also excellent peeled, cut into thin slices, and served with sugar and heavy cream or sour cream.

Poached Pears

6 pears — Bosc, Bartlett, D'Anjou, or Comice
1½ cups sugar
2 cups water
1 teaspoon vanilla extract or 1 inch of vanilla bean

Peel, halve, and core the pears. (A small ball cutter used for melons and potatoes is ideal for removing the core of the pear. It makes a tidy indentation and gives a professional look.) Boil the sugar and water with the vanilla, add the pears, and reduce the heat. Simmer until the pears are just cooked through. Cool in their liquor, and serve plain, or with cream, or with a soft custard sauce.

Pears Hélène. Serve the pears over vanilla ice cream and top with hot chocolate sauce.

Pears in Red Wine

6 pears
1 pint port or sherry
1 cup sugar
3 slices lemon
3 slices orange

Peel the pears and core with a small ball cutter or paring knife, leaving them whole with the stem intact. Combine the wine and sugar, bring to a boil, and simmer 5 minutes. Add the pears and the lemon and orange slices, and reduce the heat to the barest ebullition. Poach until the fruit is just tender. It may take 1 to 1½ hours. Cool in the sauce, and serve very cold.

Baked Pears

6 pears
1½ cups light brown sugar, tightly packed
1 cup water
6 cloves

Leave the pears whole or split and core them. In either case, do not peel.

Wash the pears and arrange in a baking dish or casserole — about 2-quart capacity. Stand them upright if whole or overlap them if cut in half. Combine the sugar and water, bring to a boil, and simmer 5 minutes. Stick each pear with a clove. Pour the boiling syrup over the pears and bake in a 325-degree oven approximately 1 hour or until the pears are tender. Baste from time to time with the liquid in the dish. Cool the pears in the liquid. Serve with heavy cream.

Variations

(1) Add ¼ cup shaved preserved or candied ginger to the syrup.

(2) Sensationally good served with a little pear brandy (eau de vie de poire).

(3) Pour ½ cup brandy over the pears just as you remove them from the oven.

(4) Instead of using cream, serve warm with a hard sauce, or cold with a brandy-flavored custard.

Persimmons

This elegant, delicious, magnificently colored fruit was not very much appreciated in the early part of the country's history. One was warned not to eat them before frost, and then they were considered good only for fruit butter or marmalade. As Miss Leslie remarks in a somewhat haughty way, "they will be greatly appreciated in the backwoods." Nowadays the persimmon comes into the market in the late fall as a great delight after most of the peaches and pears have flown and one is bored with apples and other late fruits. Their brilliant orange hue and their glorious shapes make them showpieces for the table, and they are equally rewarding in flavor and texture.

The persimmon must be eaten fully ripe, when it is very soft. It is best split and served on a plate to be eaten with a spoon. A few drops of kirsch or pear brandy will give it additional zest.

Whole persimmons can be frozen and served slightly thawed for a sort of wonderful ready-made sherbet.

Pineapple

Pineapple is a thoroughly American fruit, although it has traveled around the world. Our principal sources are Hawaii and the Caribbean, which supply us with many varieties. Unfortunately, as is true of many other fruits, we seldom get pineapples in our markets that are dead ripe, when the flavor and smell are quite intoxicating. If the center pines can be pulled out easily and the smell is good and fruity, the pineapple is on the road to ripeness.

Small sugar pineapples from the Caribbean are often served cut in halves or quarters with the meat in the shell — see recipes below for small pineapples. Large pineapples must be peeled and have their pines removed. Sometimes the fruit is scored in diagonal stripes, following the pattern of the pines, which creates a handsome effect when it is sliced crosswise. If serving in slices, remove the coarse core. (Knives are available on the market that will cut into a whole pineapple, removing both the core and the pines at the same time.) Pineapple is also served cut in fingers, sections, or cubes, and in some countries thin slices are cut from the whole peeled fruit as needed. Whatever the form, sugar the fruit to taste and serve chilled with any of the liquors mentioned above.

Filled Pineapples

These can make rather spectacular desserts. Choose a large, decorative pineapple, remove the top very carefully, and set it aside. With a sharp knife or a ball cutter, remove the meat from the pineapple, discarding the core. Sprinkle with sugar and, if you like, with brandy, rum, or a liqueur. Combine the fruit with fresh strawberries or raspberries sugared to taste, and pack back into the pineapple shell. Set the top back in place, and chill the fruit well before serving.

Pineapple Filled with Ice Cream. Scoop out a pineapple as above. Sugar the meat, flavor with kirsch, and mix with vanilla ice cream; or combine the pineapple with raspberries and pineapple sherbet. Return to the pineapple shell and pack in ice and salt for an hour or two before serving.

Poached Pineapple

1 good-sized pineapple
1 cup water
1½ cups sugar
Pinch of salt

Peel and remove the pines from the pineapple. Cut the meat into fingers. In a saucepan large enough to accommodate the pineapple, boil together the water, sugar, and salt. When it has boiled 3 minutes, reduce the heat and add the pineapple. Simmer, turning from time to time, until the pineapple becomes more or less translucent and is tender. Allow it to cool in the syrup. Chill, and serve cold with kirsch or other liquors.

Small Pineapples with Rum

Cut 1 or 2 small pineapples into quarters, cutting through the plume as well. Run a sharp grapefruit or paring knife along under the core and around the shell of the pineapple, thus loosening the meat completely. Remove the meat and cut crosswise to make each quarter into four or five sections. Replace the sections in the shells, pulling alternate sections slightly to the left and the right to create a jagged effect. Sugar to taste and add rum, kirsch, or any other liqueur or flavoring you like. Serve very cold garnished with sprigs of mint.

Stuffed Small Pineapples. Cut the pineapple into halves rather than quarters, and combine the meat with other fruits — strawberries, raspberries, blueberries, peaches, or practically any fruit in season or a combination of several.

Plums and Prunes

Although we grow many different varieties of plums, few are in general circulation. There are four or five standards that one finds everywhere: the round red plum, the greengage plum (probably the first plum ever cultivated in this country), the tiny damson plum used so much for jam and butter, the egg plum (naturally, a yellow plum), and the Italian prune, which is purple, long in shape, comes late in the year, and is in the market longer than most of the others. Red and greengage plums are somewhat soft when ripe, while damsons are rather firm, as are Italian plums or prunes, which have a more solid meat than other varieties.

Ripe plums are delicious eaten in hand. They are also excellent poached.

Poached Plums

10 to 12 plums or prunes
2 cups sugar
1 cup water
Few grains salt
1 teaspoon vanilla or ¾ inch of vanilla bean

All varieties lend themselves to poaching and serving with a little brandy or mirabelle. They are also occasionally served with custard but seldom with cream.

To prepare the plums, split and remove the pits if possible. Some plums will not divide neatly. In this case, merely make an incision in the skin. Stir together the sugar, water, salt, and vanilla. Bring to a boil and remove any scum that forms. Add the fruit and poach gently until it is more or less translucent and tender. Cool in the syrup and serve either warm or chilled.

Baked Prunes

1 pound or more prunes
1 to 1½ cups brown sugar
½ cup water
¼ teaspoon cinnamon

Italian prunes, firmer than most of the plum family, lend themselves to baking exceedingly well.

Split and pit the prunes. Arrange them slightly overlapping in a shallow baking dish. Sprinkle with the brown sugar, add the water, and sprinkle with the cinnamon. Bake at 350 degrees 20 to 25 minutes or until they are tender. Serve warm or chilled with sour cream.

Note. These are equally good, if not better, simply sugared well and dotted with butter. Bake as above, and in this case, serve warm.

Quince

Few people know the delicacy and flavor of cooked quince, and they are brilliant in bouquet both cooked and raw. When peeled, cut into sections and baked, they make a nice change from other fruit dishes.

Baked Quince

3 large ripe quince
2 cups sugar
¾ cup water
Pinch of salt

Peel, cut into eighths, and arrange in a 1½-quart casserole equipped with a cover. Combine the sugar and water and bring to a boil. Add the salt. Pour over the quince, cover the casserole, and bake at 325 degrees 45 minutes, or until the fruit is tender but not mushy. Cool, and serve with heavy cream or sour cream.

Raspberries

This most elegant of fruits has been cherished for centuries. No other berry is as delicate in flavor, as meaty, and as satisfying to the palate. Raspberry flavor is unsurpassed in mousses, ices, creams, and tarts. The West — the Northwest in particular — produces some of the greatest of raspberries, as does the country around Baltimore.

Raspberries are best when eaten simply with sugar and, if you like, heavy cream or sour cream. If they are really ripe and freshly picked, they need nothing at all. Raspberries are good chilled, but those picked from the vines and rushed to the table with the warmth of the sun still on them should be eaten in their natural state. Kirsch and raspberry brandy (eau de vie de framboise) are both highly complementary to raspberries if used in small quantities — they should enhance, not drown, the flavor of the fruit. Raspberries themselves are especially complementary to currants, melon, and peaches.

Raspberry Purée

1 quart raspberries
Granulated sugar or powdered sugar
3 tablespoons crème de cassis (optional)

Put the raspberries through a sieve or food mill and blend in enough sugar to thicken. Add a little crème de cassis for flavoring if you like. Serve over fresh raspberries or strawberries, poached peaches, or half a melon filled with vanilla ice cream.

Raspberry Vinegar

A very old recipe from Mrs. Randolph for one of the most excellent of summer drinks. To serve, pour some of the vinegar into a glass, add ice and sugar, if desired, and water or soda.

"Put a quart of ripe red raspberries in a bowl; pour on them a quart of strong well-flavored vinegar — let them stand 24 hours, strain them through a bag, put this liquid on another quart of raspberries, which strain in the same manner — and then on a third quart; when this last is prepared, make it sweet with pounded loaf [granulated] sugar; refine and bottle it. It is a delicious beverage mixed with iced water."

Raspberry Cordial

Also from Mrs. Randolph, this is really better when made with vodka, which seems to intensify the raspberry flavor. Mrs. Randolph, of course, did not know vodka.

"To each quart of ripened raspberries, put one quart of best French brandy, let it remain about a week. Then strain through a sieve or a bag, pressing out all the liquid; when you have got as much as you want, reduce the strength with water and put a pound of powdered loaf [granulated] sugar to each gallon — let it stand till refined. Strawberry cordial is made the same way. It destroys the flavor of these fruits to put them on the fire."

Rhubarb

Rhubarb is held in poor esteem by some of the early cooking authorities. Miss Leslie says: "This is sometimes called spring fruit or pie plant. It comes earlier but is by no means as good as gooseberries. We do not think it worth preserving or making it into a sweet."

Despite Miss Leslie, rhubarb has come into general use, although I would not describe it as a champion among spring fruit. It does come into the market fresh early in the year and is delicious to eat occasionally. It can be stewed successfully, but it is much better baked, either by itself or as a rhubarb pie.

Baked Rhubarb

1½ pounds rhubarb, peeled if necessary, and cut in 3 or 4 inch stalks
¼ cup water
1 to 1½ cups sugar
Dash of salt

Arrange the rhubarb in a 1½-quart casserole with a cover. Add the water, sugar to taste, and salt. Cover tightly and bake at 350 degrees 20 to 25 minutes or until tender. Chill and serve. Cooked rhubarb is good served with heavy cream or sour cream, with fresh strawberries if you like.

Rhubarb Fool

1½ pounds rhubarb
1 to 1½ cups sugar
¼ cup water
Whipped cream, sour cream, or rich custard

Cut the rhubarb into 2-inch lengths and combine with sugar and water in a heavy 2-quart saucepan. Cover, and simmer until the rhubarb is quite tender — about 25 to 30 minutes. When cool, chill in the refrigerator. Then force the rhubarb through a food mill or sieve and fold into whipped cream, sour cream, or a rich boiled custard. Serve very cold.

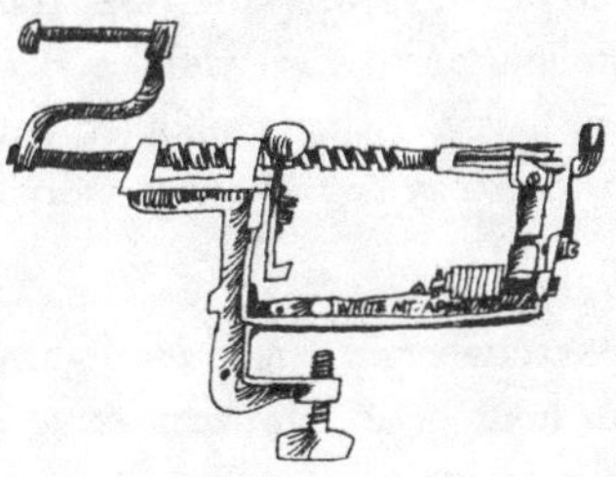

Harriet Coe's Rhubarb Ring with Strawberries

3 cups rhubarb cut in small dice
2 cups sugar
1 cup boiling water
2 envelopes gelatine
½ cup cold water
Strawberries
Powdered sugar
1 cup heavy cream, whipped
1 tablespoon sugar
2 tablespoons kirsch

Cook the rhubarb with the sugar and boiling water in a 2-quart saucepan until tender. Dissolve the gelatine in cold water, add to the rhubarb, and stir until dissolved. Pour into an 8-cup ring mold which has been oiled. Chill till firm. To serve, unmold the ring on a serving plate, fill the center with strawberries, and dust with powdered sugar. Serve with the whipped cream, into which the sugar and kirsch have been folded.

Strawberries

We have been lucky with strawberries in our country. We have always had quantities of delicious wild ones, and cultivated berries go back far into the past. The first strawberries of the season used to be marked by strawberry socials, a standard fund-raising event for churches and other groups up until recent years, when berries became an all-year crop. I still remember the socials in New York at the First Presbyterian Church on Fifth Avenue, where they emulated the small-town affairs — Japanese lanterns, lawn tables, loads of strawberries, thick cream, cakes, sometimes ice cream as well. What lovely days they were.

There are those who tell you that strawberries must never be washed except by a little wine, and that to be discarded.

Strawberries, if quite ripe, are best served with their hulls. Simply provide bowls for dipping — a bowl of water, of sugar, and of heavy cream, whipped cream, or sour cream. A recent innovation is to provide a bowl of kirsch into which the berries are dipped before going into the sugar.

Strawberries and Cream

This has always been a favorite. Hull ripe strawberries, sugar them, and let stand an hour or so. Serve with heavy cream, whipped cream, or sour cream, passed separately. Sometimes the berries are served unsugared, so they may be sugared to individual taste.

Strawberries with Ice Cream

Hull and sugar ripe strawberries, and crush lightly with a potato masher. Let stand an hour or so, and then serve over ice cream with a dab of whipped cream.

Strawberries with Raspberry Purée

Pile large ripe strawberries in a pyramid in a very beautiful serving dish. Carefully spoon raspberry purée over the berries, and serve with whipped cream.

Strawberries with Orange Juice

Hull strawberries and arrange in a serving dish. Add freshly squeezed orange juice to taste, and add sugar if needed.

American Strawberry Bowl

Add half orange juice and half port wine to the berries, and serve with whipped cream. This is an old recipe.

Bread

In 1857 Mrs. Sara Hale wrote in her huge cookbook, *Receipts for the Millions:* "To make good bread or to understand the process of making it is the duty of every woman; indeed an art that should never be neglected in the education of a lady. The lady derives her title from 'dividing or distributing bread'; the more perfect the bread the more perfect the lady."

Perfection in this art, however, was not easily achieved in the middle of the nineteenth century. Flour was variable, and so was yeast, which was made with hops, potatoes, and sour dough starter, or with salt rising, a form of fermented cornmeal which creates a rather smelly leavening. There were no standard measurements for the cook in those days, and to top it off, it was difficult to control oven temperatures. Ovens, if they were not made of brick, were of the reflector type used in front of an open fire, or they were Dutch ovens buried in coals. (As recently as 1969 I ate bread cooked in a huge Dutch oven by a Basque shepherd in the mountains of Colorado. It was as good a loaf of bread as I have ever eaten, excellent in texture and flavor and overpowering in aroma.) In later years the ovens of coal or wood stoves were tested by tossing in a little flour. If it browned as you counted twenty the oven was ready for bread. If it blackened, the oven door was left open until the temperature was sufficiently cooled. Kneading depended upon the baker's intelligence and muscle. Miss Leslie gave these directions: "To knead, double up your hands, put them deep into the bread, and work it with your knuckles, exerting all your strength. When the dough sticks to them no longer, but leaves your bent fingers clean and clear, it is time to cease kneading, for you have done enough for that time." Considering the fact that the average recipe called for a peck of flour, a ruined batch of bread meant a dreadful loss of effort and ingredients.

Fortunately, the hazards of bread baking are not as great as they once were. We have standard recipes, oven thermostats, reliable yeast in cake or granulated form, and electric mixers equipped with dough hooks to do most of the work of kneading.

Flours

One problem that still remains is the uncertain characteristics of flours, which deviate in their ability to absorb liquid. Most all-purpose flours are blended and bleached and vary a great deal from region to region. They are the most readily available. I prefer the unbleached and rather "strong" flours found in some sections of the country, which are ideal for bread making but not for cakes and pastries. Whole-meal flours are not as easy to come by as they are in Europe, but they can be tracked down, too. There are increasing numbers of shops and markets specializing in organic and natural foods. Whole-wheat, graham, rye, barley, and oatmeal are all excellent in breads. Cornmeal, which is so good in many different quick breads made with baking powder or without leavening, is not particularly suited to risen breads except as an additive. Since it has no gluten, it does not combine with yeast, as the Massachusetts Bay colonies discovered early in our history. However, cornmeal is an ingredient in the famous Boston brown bread, along with rye and wheat flour.

Once you find a flour that produces a fine loaf of bread for you, use it consistently. Then you'll learn how much is required, how much water it will take, and how it reacts to mixing and kneading. Bread making will become an automatic process.

Yeast

Next to flour, certainly yeast is the most important factor in making good bread. I have become used to granular yeast at this point and find that it produces good results, although it lacks the wondrous smell of fresh yeast proofing. Since it is the only yeast one can find, generally, we must adjust to it. If you do a great deal of baking, occasionally you can persuade your local baker to sell you a pound of fresh yeast, which will keep under refrigeration or can be frozen for some time.

Though it is not considered necessary these days, I like to proof the yeast — that is, allow it to begin its fermentation — before adding it to the other ingredients. Many modern recipes call for adding dry yeast to the liquids without proofing and it appears to work quite well. Nevertheless, I continue to proof. Perhaps it is merely habit. While warm water — about 110 degrees — is usually recommended for dissolving and proofing yeast, it will proof just as well, though it will take longer, in cold water. Water that is too hot will kill the yeast, and it will fail to proof. Sugar and warm milk will accelerate proofing. If you are using fresh yeast, cream it with the sugar, which will greatly speed up the action of the dough.

Salt and Sugar

On the other hand, salt slows down fermentation. Therefore it is best to add it after you have mixed the yeast with the flour and liquids. I like bread with a high salt content. A tablespoon of kosher or coarse salt to a pound (3 ½ cups) of flour is about right, although some of my friends find it excessive. One of the reasons I dislike most commercial breads is that they contain too little salt — and too much sugar. Sugar, except for a very small amount, is not a pleasing additive to bread. I seldom use it myself, but I usually include it in recipes for other people. Nor do I like butter and milk in my bread as most people do, which produce too soft and cake-like a loaf. I prefer the rough, simple quality of bread made with flour, water, salt, and yeast. These are the ingredients of the finest of French bread, which is prized above all other breads.

The time prescribed for the rising of the dough is another variable. Overheating tends to be damaging to rising, although such a place as an oven faintly heated by a pilot light will be ideal. One may also set bread to rise in a cold room, without drafts, or even in the refrigerator. In either case rising will take double the usual time.

Pans

Bread pans should be well greased with butter, oil, or vegetable shortening. If you are baking French or Italian style loaves, sprinkle the baking sheets with cornmeal.

Mixers

Most of the breads in this chapter may be made in a heavy-duty electric mixer equipped with a dough hook, but it takes careful watching for the point when the dough becomes glossy and elastic and loses any stickiness. Perhaps the safest method to follow is to remove the dough before it is ready and finish it off with a bit of kneading.

A Simple Recipe for Bread

Butter
1 yeast cake or 1 package active dry yeast
1 tablespoon sugar (optional)
1 cup (approximately) warm water
1 tablespoon salt, preferably kosher or coarse
3½ to 4½ cups all-purpose or unbleached hard wheat flour, or mixed flour (see text above).

I discover more and more men and women who are baking their own bread — and good bread. It can be a delightful occupation, and once you get hooked on working with yeast, it is hard to find any pursuit in cookery more satisfying. For a beginning you might try this recipe, the simplest recipe for bread I know. It will please those who appreciate a good solid, flavorful loaf, and may be made with equal parts of whole-wheat and white flour, or with ¼ white flour and ¾ whole-wheat, barley meal, rye meal, or graham flour. A little more water may be required. Sprinkle a bit of the meal on the loaves before baking.

Butter an 8 × 5 × 3-inch loaf tin. Place the yeast in a cup. If it is in cake form, crumble it. Add ¼ cup warm (110 degrees) water and allow the yeast to dissolve. Add the sugar (if you are using it) and let the yeast proof slightly. Put the flour and salt into a mixing bowl or the bowl of a heavy-duty electric mixer fitted with a dough hook. Add the yeast mixture and about ¾ cup more water.

To prepare by hand: Mix well with a wooden spoon. When the mixture has formed a ball or breaks away from the sides of the bowl, roll it out on a floured board and dust lightly with flour. Begin kneading by pushing into the dough firmly and away from you with the heel of the hand. Fold it back after each push and rotate the dough a little each time. Keep up a steady rhythm. Continue until the dough is elastic and forms blisters on its surface when squeezed. If the dough still seems sticky, sprinkle with a little additional flour and continue to knead. On the other hand, if the dough is too stiff before kneading, add a little more water. Only practice will teach you when you have the right balance of ingredients and the right amount of kneading.

To prepare in an electric mixer: Mix at low speed. When the mixture has formed a ball or breaks away from the sides of the bowl, increase the speed. Continue to knead until the dough is glossy and elastic. You will have to watch carefully and test it. I prefer to take the dough from the mixer just before it is ready and give it a few kneadings by hand till I am sure of the feel of the dough.

In either case, when you have a ball of well-kneaded dough place it in a thoroughly buttered bowl and turn it several times to coat the surface with butter. Cover the bowl lightly and set it in a

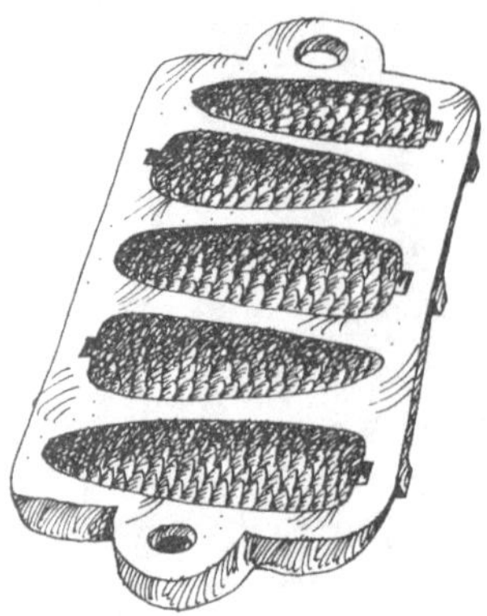

draft-free spot to rise till the dough has doubled in bulk. This will take anywhere from 45 minutes to 2 hours. Punch it down with the fist, knead gently about 3 minutes, and then slap it vigorously on the kneading board a few times. Shape it and place in the buttered loaf tin. Cover, and set again in a warm draft-free place to rise to the top of the pan.

Meanwhile, heat the oven to 425 degrees. Some people like to brush the dough with a wash just before baking. A yolk of egg beaten lightly with 2 tablespoons cream or milk gives color and glazes the bread. Very lightly beaten egg white achieves somewhat the same result. A salt and water solution yields a crisper crust. Try each of these to see which pleases you the most. And, if you like, slash the dough diagonally across the top three times with a very sharp knife or cutter dipped in hot water. This will give the bread a more professional look and decrease the baking time a bit. Place the loaf in the center of the rack and bake 20 minutes. Reduce the heat to 400 degrees and bake another 20 minutes. Test to see if it is done by tapping it. If it produces a hollow sound, the loaf is baked. If not baked, reduce the heat to 375 degrees and return the bread to the oven without the tin to get a crisper bottom crust. Allow 5 to 8 minutes.

Transfer the loaf to a rack to cool. It is sometimes the custom to brush the hot loaf with melted butter, but since this has the effect of softening the crust, I do not particularly recommend it. When thoroughly cool, store wrapped in foil, plastic, or cloth. I frequently keep it in the refrigerator.

Basic White Bread I

1 yeast cake or 1 package active dry yeast
1/4 cup warm water
1 tablespoon sugar
1 cup milk
1 teaspoon salt
3 tablespoons butter
3 1/2 to 4 1/2 cups all-purpose flour
1 egg white
1 tablespoon water

This is what I call tea bread — because it is enriched with butter and milk and somewhat lacks the guts of the breads made with water and without shortening. However, I know it has a real public and is many people's idea of perfect bread.

Proof the yeast in the warm (110 degrees) water with the sugar. Heat the milk with the salt. Stir in the butter until melted. In a large mixing bowl, combine the yeast and milk mixtures. Beat until smooth. Stir in flour to form a stiff dough, kneading in more flour if necessary. Knead on a floured surface until the dough is no longer sticky, about 10 minutes. Place the ball of dough in a buttered bowl, turning it to coat with butter. Cover, and let rise in a warm place until it is light and doubled in size, about 1 to 1 1/2 hours. Punch down the dough. Shape into one large or two smaller loaves, and place in buttered loaf pans. Cover, and let rise again in a warm place until light and doubled in size, about 45 minutes. Combine the egg white and water, and brush the top of the loaves. Bake at 400 degrees 20 minutes, reduce the heat to 350 degrees, and continue baking another 20 to 30 minutes until well browned and hollow-sounding when tapped.

Basic White Bread with Cheese. A traditional bread in the West, where it is frequently used for toast and sandwiches or toasted sandwiches. The cheese and seasoning give a delicious flavor to the bread that is especially good with sandwiches made with ham, sausage, corned beef, chicken, or tongue. Use unbleached flour. After you have punched down the dough, knead in ¾ cup grated sharp Cheddar cheese and sprinkle in ¼ teaspoon Tabasco. Shape into one round loaf and place in a buttered 8-inch round cake pan to rise. When the dough is light and doubled in size (about 45 minutes) brush it with the egg wash, using ¼ cup evaporated milk instead of water. Bake as above.

Basic White Bread II

⅓ cup nonfat dry milk powder
3 tablespoons sugar
1 tablespoon salt
3 tablespoons butter or vegetable shortening
2 cups warm water (120 degrees)
1 package active dry yeast
5 to 6 cups all-purpose flour

This is typical of the breads of today using nonfat milk solids, which give a delicate texture and tighter grain, especially good for toasting. You may want to cut the sugar content after one or two trials.

This bread may also be made by hand, following the method for Basic White Bread I.

In the large bowl of an electric mixer, combine the dry milk, sugar, salt, shortening, and water. Add the yeast and 3 cups flour. Blend 30 seconds at low speed, then beat 2 minutes at medium speed. Gradually stir in enough of the remaining flour to form a stiff dough. Knead on a floured surface until smooth and satiny (about 10 minutes). Place in a buttered bowl, turning the dough to coat all sides. Cover, and let rise in a warm place until light and doubled in size, about 1½ hours. Punch down the dough. Fold the edges toward the center and turn upside down in the bowl. Cover, and let rise another 30 minutes. Divide the dough into two parts. Mold into balls. Allow to rest on the counter, covered with inverted bowls, for 10 minutes. Shape into loaves. Place in well-buttered 8½ × 4½-inch pans. Cover, and let rise in a warm place until the tops of the loaves are well above the pan edges, about 1 hour. Bake at 375 degrees 40 to 50 minutes. Remove from the pans immediately. Cool thoroughly on a rack.

Refrigerator Rolls

One of the favorite recipes for rolls in the American kitchen. To make these rolls, use either basic white bread recipe. Punch the dough down as usual after the first rising, then refrigerate it not less than 2 hours and not more than 72. The dough may then be worked into any of various shapes, such as those listed below.

Cloverleaf Rolls. Shape into small balls about 1 inch in diameter. Place 3 balls in each cup of well-buttered muffin tins.

Bowknots. Roll about ½ inch thick, and cut into 9-inch strips. Tie in loose knots and place on a well-buttered cookie sheet.

Braids. Roll ¼ inch thick and cut into strips 5 to 6 inches long. Put three together and pinch one end. Braid, and pinch the other end. Place on a well-buttered cookie sheet.

Crescents. Roll into 12-inch circles about ¼ inch thick. Brush each round well with melted butter. Cut in 8 to 12 wedges, and starting with the wider edge, roll each into the point. Shape into crescents and place on a well-buttered cookie sheet.

Parker House Rolls. Roll about ½ inch thick. Brush well with melted butter. Cut into rounds with a cutter 3 to 4 inches in diameter. Fold over each round to make a half circle. Press the edges to seal and arrange on a well-buttered cookie sheet.

Any of these rolls may be brushed with beaten egg yolk, cream, or with melted butter, and then if you like sprinkled with poppy seeds or sesame seeds. Allow them to rise until almost double in bulk. From the refrigerator to the oven will take a minimum of 2 hours. Bake at 400 degrees 12 to 15 minutes. Eat hot, or cool and reheat.

Sally Lunn

1 package active dry yeast or 1 yeast cake
¼ cup warm water
1¾ cups milk
2 tablespoons sugar
4 tablespoons butter
1 teaspoon salt
2 eggs, well beaten
5 cups flour, approximately

There are so many recipes for Sally Lunn that one would be hard pressed to find the original or the "correct" one. Though they vary greatly in content and method, the recipes tested produced more or less similar results. This one seemed the best of the lot.

Dissolve the yeast in the warm water. Heat the milk to almost boiling, and pour over the sugar, butter, and salt in a mixing bowl. Cool. Sift the flour and beat the eggs slightly. When the mixture has cooled, stir in the yeast, eggs, and 3 cups flour. Add enough additional flour to make a soft dough. Place the dough in a buttered bundt mold, or divide in half and place in buttered 9×5×3-inch loaf pans. Let rise till double in bulk. Bake at 400 degrees 15 minutes, then reduce to 350 for another 15 to 18 minutes. Delicious served with butter and jam when fresh, and excellent for toasting and buttering.

Raisin Bread

1 package active dry yeast or 1 yeast cake
2 cups warm milk
⅓ cup sugar
1 tablespoon salt
3 tablespoons butter
5 to 6 cups all-purpose flour
Melted butter
1½ cups sultana raisins plumped overnight in sherry or Cognac and mixed with ½ teaspoon mace and 2 teaspoons grated fresh orange rind
1 egg yolk beaten with 2 tablespoons cream

Raisin bread always has been a favorite in this country and still is the great specialty for toast at the Palace Hotel in San Francisco. Years ago my mother asked for their recipe and, failing to get it, made up her own. This is it. It is good, and it toasts well.

This can also be made in an electric mixer fitted with a dough hook.

Dissolve the yeast in ¼ cup of the milk. Combine the rest of the warm milk, sugar, salt, and butter in a large bowl. Add the yeast and gradually beat in 3 cups flour. Beat well. Gradually stir in with the hands or a heavy wooden spoon enough additional flour to make a stiff dough. Turn out on a floured surface and knead until smooth, elastic, and glossy. This will take about 10 minutes. Place in a buttered bowl and turn well so the entire surface is lightly coated with butter. Cover, and allow to rise until doubled in bulk, about 2½ hours.

Punch the dough down. Knead again 3 minutes. Return to the bowl and let rise again 30 minutes. Divide the dough into two parts and roll each into a rectangle about 20 × 7 inches. Brush each with melted butter and sprinkle with the raisin-orange mixture. Roll the dough tightly into two loaves, turning in the ends slightly as you roll. Place in well-buttered 8½ × 4½-inch pans. Cover, and let rise in a warm place till the loaves fill the pans and extend above the top. Brush with the egg yolk and cream. Bake at 400 degrees 20 minutes, then reduce the heat to 350. Continue baking an additional 20 to 30 minutes, or until the loaves give off a hollow sound when tapped with the knuckles. If you like, return them briefly to the oven without pans to brown the bottom crust.

Cinnamon Bread. When you roll out the rectangles of dough, spread well with 3 tablespoons softened butter. Sprinkle with ¼ cup sugar and 2 teaspoons cinnamon.

Nut Bread. Sprinkle the buttered dough fairly heavily with 1½ cups lightly salted and broken walnut or pecan meats, instead of raisins.

Pizza Loaf

1 yeast cake or 1 package active dry yeast
1 tablespoon sugar
¼ cup warm water (about 110 degrees)
1 tablespoon coarse salt
1 cup hot water
3 tablespoons olive oil

This unusual loaf of seasoned bread is an outgrowth of the enormously popular pizza.

Proof the yeast and sugar in the warm water. Dissolve the coarse salt in the hot water. Stir in the flour, yeast mixture, and oil to make a fairly stiff dough. Turn out on a floured board and knead until the dough is no longer sticky, about 10 minutes. Place in an oiled bowl, and turn to coat with a film of oil. Cover, and allow to rise until doubled in bulk. Punch down the dough and knead 3 minutes. Roll into a 15 × 7-inch rectangle. Spread with the tomato

3½ cups hard wheat flour or all-purpose unbleached flour
3 to 4 tablespoons tomato paste
2 finely chopped garlic cloves
½ teaspoon dried basil or 1 tablespoon chopped fresh basil
4 tablespoons freshly grated Parmesan cheese
1 egg white lightly beaten with 1 tablespoon water

paste, garlic, basil, and cheese. Roll up, turning in the ends slightly as you roll. Place in an 8½ × 4½-inch well-buttered pan. Cover, and let rise in a warm place 30 minutes. Brush with the beaten egg white and water. Bake at 400 degrees 20 minutes, then reduce the heat to 350. Bake 30 minutes more, or until the loaf is well browned and sounds hollow when tapped with the knuckles. This bread is best when eaten warm, and should be cut with a good serrated knife.

Potato Bread

1 yeast cake or 1 package active dry yeast
1 tablespoon sugar
¼ cup warm potato water
¼ cup butter (½ stick)
1 tablespoon salt
¾ cup warm potato water and ¾ cup warm milk, or 1½ cups warm potato water
¾ cup mashed potatoes
5½ to 6 cups unbleached or all-purpose flour

Potatoes have always been a part of bread baking in this country. In former days people made yeast and starters with potato water—water in which potatoes had cooked. And often potato water and mashed potatoes were used together in bread to make this rather soft, nicely textured loaf, which has great appeal.

Proof the yeast and sugar in the ¼ cup warm potato water. In a large mixing bowl combine the butter, salt, and liquids. Stir to melt the shortening. Add the potatoes, stir in the yeast mixture, and add enough flour to make a stiff dough. Turn out on a floured board and knead until the dough is no longer sticky, 5 to 10 minutes. Place in a buttered bowl, and roll the dough around so that it becomes coated with butter. Cover, and allow to rise until doubled in bulk, 1½ to 2 hours. Punch down the dough and knead briefly. Cover, and allow to rise again about 30 minutes. Place on a floured board and divide into two parts. Mold into balls. Cover the dough and let it rest 15 minutes. Shape into loaves and place in well-buttered 8½ × 4½-inch bread pans. Cover, and allow to rise in a warm place till the dough appears above the top of the pans. Dust the loaves with flour. Bake at 400 degrees 20 minutes, then reduce the heat to 350. Bake another 20 to 30 minutes, or until brown and hollow-sounding when tapped with the knuckles. Immediately transfer to a rack to cool.

Orange Bread

1 package active dry yeast or 1 yeast cake
¼ cup warm water
1 tablespoon sugar
1 cup orange juice
1 tablespoon salt
3 tablespoons melted butter

This is a whimsy which was introduced about fifty years ago when people were experimenting with fruits in breads. I think it is rather appealing when it is made with freshly squeezed juice from exceptionally fine oranges.

Proof the yeast and sugar in the warm water. Combine the orange juice, salt, melted butter, and orange peel, and mix with the flour and the yeast mixture to form a rather stiff dough. Turn out on a floured surface and knead until the dough is no longer sticky, about

8 to 10 minutes. Place in a buttered bowl and turn to coat all sides with a film of butter. Cover, and allow to rise in a warm draft-free place about 1½ hours, or until doubled in bulk. Punch down and knead again about 3 minutes. Shape into one large or two small loaves, and place in an 8½ × 4½-inch bread pan or two small loaf pans, well buttered. Cover, and allow to rise again until the dough appears above the edge of the pan. Combine the water and egg white, and brush the top of the bread. Bake at 400 degrees 20 minutes, then reduce the heat to 350 degrees and bake 25 to 30 minutes longer, or until the loaf is brown and sounds hollow when tapped. Turn out on a rack at once to cool.

3 tablespoons grated orange peel
3 to 3½ cups all-purpose flour
1 tablespoon water
1 egg white

A Good Whole-Wheat Bread

2 packages active dry yeast or 2 yeast cakes
2 cups warm water
½ cup honey
1 tablespoon salt
2 tablespoons oil
3 cups whole-wheat flour
3 to 3½ cups all-purpose flour

Although whole-meal breads have been with us for centuries, within the last fifty years they have increased enormously in popularity.

This typical recipe is oversweet to my taste. If it promises to be too sweet for you, reduce or omit the honey. This can be made in an electric mixer with a dough hook.

Proof the yeast in ½ cup warm water. Combine the honey, remaining water, salt, oil, and whole-wheat flour. Add the yeast and stir well. Gradually add enough white flour to make a stiff dough. Remove the dough to a floured surface and knead until it is smooth and satiny. Place in an oiled bowl and toss to coat all surfaces. Cover, and allow to rise until doubled in bulk, about 1 to 1½ hours. Punch down the dough. Knead again 3 minutes and divide in half. Roll each half to a 14 × 7-inch rectangle and, starting with the narrower side, roll tightly and seal the edges. Place each roll in a well-buttered 8½ × 4½-inch bread pan. Cover, and allow to rise until doubled in bulk — about an hour. Sprinkle the loaves with a little whole-wheat flour. Bake at 375 degrees about 40 to 50 minutes. Remove the loaves from the pans and return to oven for 10 minutes to crisp the bottoms.

Whole-Grain Bread

1 package active dry yeast or 1 yeast cake
1½ cups warm water
2 tablespoons butter
2 tablespoons molasses or 1 tablespoon sugar
1 tablespoon salt
1 egg, slightly beaten

This rather simple whole-grain bread is moist, pleasant when eaten fresh, and also a fairly interesting bread for toast. If it is baked in a 2-pound coffee can or a 2-quart soufflé mold it makes rather nice slices. It can be prepared in a heavy-duty mixer very easily.

Proof the yeast in ½ cup warm water. Combine the remaining water, butter, molasses or sugar, salt, beaten egg, and whole-grain cereal. Add the yeast and beat very well in the mixer with a dough hook or by hand with a wooden spoon. Beat in 2½ cups all-purpose flour, then beat in the final cup of flour and continue to beat

1 cup whole-grain cereal (cereal for cooking — not flakes)
3½ cups all-purpose flour or unbleached flour

thoroughly till the dough is elastic. Turn into a well-buttered 2-pound coffee tin or a 2-quart soufflé dish. Cover — with the coffee can, you may use the top — and set to rise in a warm place until doubled in bulk. The dough should reach the top of the can or mold. Bake at 350 degrees 1 hour and 10 to 15 minutes, or until deliciously brown. Allow it to rest in the tin or mold 10 minutes, then remove and cool on a rack.

Health Bread

¼ cup warm water
1 package active dry yeast
2 cups milk, heated to 100 degrees
2 tablespoons melted butter
2 teaspoons salt
2 tablespoons molasses
About 4 cups whole-wheat flour, or you may use ½ cup wheat germ, ½ cup barley flour or buckwheat flour, 1 cup rye flour, and 2 cups whole-wheat

Dissolve the yeast in the warm water. Then stir in the milk, melted butter, salt, and molasses, and stir until well blended. Mix the flours together and stir 3 cups flour into the mixture a cup at a time. Beat until the dough is quite smooth. Then add about a cup, enough to make a very stiff dough. Sprinkle some of the flour onto a board, turn out the dough, and knead it so that it will absorb the extra flour. Knead until the bread seems quite smooth. With all this mixture of whole-grain flours it will never be quite as non-sticky as white dough but will have a slightly gummy quality. When it is kneaded thoroughly, put the dough into a well-buttered bowl and turn it over so that it gets a covering of fat. Cover it lightly and put in a warm place to rise until about double in bulk. This will take 1½ to 2 hours. Don't worry, let it rise slowly. Punch the dough down, knead it 2 to 3 minutes, and shape into a ball. Cut it in half for two loaves, and form each loaf by pressing the dough down and making a rather thick oval. Now pull the ends together and pinch the seam to seal it. Turn the ends in and pinch those, and you have a nicely shaped loaf. Put these loaves in two buttered 9 × 5 × 3-inch pans with the seams down. Set in a warm spot and let rise until nearly doubled in bulk. Then place in a 375-degree oven and bake from 45 to 50 minutes, or until the loaf sounds hollow when tapped with the knuckles. Remove from the pans and return to the rack of the oven for a few minutes to give a crisp finish to the bottom crust. This is a moist, not very light bread, but a good one.

Anadama Bread

2½ to 3 cups all-purpose flour
1 cup cornmeal
2 packages dry active yeast
1 tablespoon salt
2 cups hot water
5 tablespoons butter
½ cup molasses

Many tales surround Anadama bread. The most popular is that Anna was a damn good baker, and her husband, when praising her bread, referred to her as Anna, damn her. You can accept that story or not, as you like.

This is a much simplified version of the bread, exceedingly good and excellent for toast.

Combine the flour, cornmeal, dry yeast, and salt. Combine the hot water, butter, and molasses, and add to the flour mixture. Beat either by hand or in the electric mixer — 3 minutes in the mixer or about 150 strokes if by hand. Add flour to make a rather stiff dough. Turn out on a floured board and knead until no longer sticky, about 10 minutes. Place in a buttered bowl, turning to coat the surface. Let rise in a warm, draft-free place until doubled in size — 1 to 1½ hours. Punch down the dough, shape into two balls, and place each in a well-buttered 8-inch round cake tin. Allow to rise again until doubled in bulk, about 1 hour. Bake at 375 degrees about 55 minutes, or until deep brown and hollow-sounding when rapped with the knuckles.

Rye Bread

2 cups rye flour
2 cups boiling water
¾ cup molasses
⅓ cup butter or other shortening
1 tablespoon salt
1 package dry active yeast or 1 yeast cake
½ cup warm water
6¼ cups unbleached flour, approximately

Rye meal and rye flour have been used in sundry combinations for bread since the early days of the Massachusetts Bay Colony. Today, rye bread is made in many parts of the country, but it is especially common in the Middle West, where the greatest number of Scandinavians are congregated. These two Scandinavian-inspired recipes have long been standard throughout the States.

Combine, in a large mixing bowl, the rye flour, boiling water, molasses, shortening, and salt. Cool. Proof the yeast in the warm water, and add to the rye flour mixture. Gradually add enough unbleached flour to make a stiff dough. Turn out on a floured board and knead till no longer sticky, about 10 to 12 minutes. Place in a buttered bowl, turning the dough to coat the surface. Cover, and let rise till doubled in bulk, about 2 to 2½ hours. Punch down the dough and let rise again, covered, 30 minutes. Turn out on a floured board and knead 3 to 4 minutes. Divide the dough into thirds and shape into round loaves. Place on cookie sheets sprinkled with cornmeal or on buttered cookie sheets. Cover, and let rise in warm place until doubled in bulk. Bake at 350 degrees 40 to 50 minutes, or until dark brown and hollow-sounding when rapped with the knuckles. Cool on racks.

Hot-Water Bread

1½ packages active dry yeast or 1½ yeast cakes
2 cups hot water
1 tablespoon sugar
5 to 6 cups unbleached flour or hard wheat flour
1 tablespoon salt
Yellow cornmeal for cookie sheets
1 egg white
1 tablespoon cold water

This loaf, which originated in the West Indies is a quick bread with a good crust, and is easily prepared. It lasts only a day unless frozen.

Proof the yeast in hot water with the sugar. Combine with 3 cups flour and the salt and work well. Stir in additional flour to make a stiff dough. Turn out on a floured board and knead till no longer sticky, about 10 minutes. Then beat the dough a few times against the kneading board. Place in a buttered bowl and turn to coat the surface. Cover, and let rise about 1 to 1½ hours, or until doubled in bulk. Remove, punch down, and knead 3 to 4 minutes. Form into two long French-style loaves and make three diagonal slashes in the top of each loaf with a sharp knife. Place on a cookie sheet well sprinkled with cornmeal. Allow to rise 5 minutes. Mix egg white and water and use to brush loaves well. Place in a cold oven set for 400 degrees and turn on heat. Bake about 40 minutes, or until the bread is browned lightly and sounds hollow when rapped with the knuckles. Cool on a rack.

Notes. (1) If you place a pan of boiling water in the oven with the bread, it will produce a little better finish and crust. (2) You may substitute whole-wheat or other coarse flour for half the flour. (3) The dough may be molded into rolls, in which case baking time will be about 25 minutes.

Swedish Limpa

2 packages active dry yeast or 2 yeast cakes
1½ cups warm water (or use water and orange juice)
⅓ cup sugar
¼ cup molasses
2 tablespoons butter, melted
1 tablespoon salt
2 tablespoons finely chopped candied orange peel
1 teaspoon ground cardamom
2½ cups rye flour
2½ cups all purpose or unbleached flour

This has a slight orange overtone that is extremely pleasant to many people. I have seen this bread made with orange juice instead of water with rather good results. In either version it makes an unusual, appetizing loaf.

Proof the yeast in the warm water with the sugar. Combine in an electric mixer bowl or, if mixing by hand, a large mixing bowl, the molasses, melted butter, salt, orange peel, cardamom, and 1 cup each of rye and white flour. Blend to a smooth paste by hand, or with a dough hook in the mixer, adding yeast mixture. Gradually beat in the remaining flour to form a stiff dough. Knead until smooth, about 3 minutes. Place in a buttered bowl and turn to coat all sides. Cover, and let rise until doubled in bulk. Punch down the dough and knead 3 minutes. Divide into two parts and shape into oval loaves. Place on a greased cookie sheet. Let rise again 45 to 60 minutes or until about doubled in bulk. Bake at 375 degrees approximately 1 hour. Brush with melted butter while warm.

Middle Eastern Bread

2½ cups warm water (110 degrees)
2 packages active dry yeast or 2 yeast cakes
½ teaspoon sugar
5½ to 6 cups unbleached all-purpose flour
1 tablespoon salt
3 tablespoons olive oil

In their native land these flat loaves are used to wrap around pieces of meat from a skewer or to dip into sauces or other dishes, thus serving as knife, fork, and plate. It is as versatile as any bread I know — it splits easily for sandwiches — and is becoming more and more in demand throughout the country. It can be bought packed in plastic bags, refrigerated or frozen. But it is also easy to make.

Proof the yeast in ½ cup of the warm water with the sugar. Combine the flour, salt, and oil in a large bowl and add the yeast and remaining liquid. Mix thoroughly. Turn out on a floured board and knead well until smooth and no longer sticky. Place in a buttered bowl and turn to coat the surface. Cover, and allow to rise until doubled in bulk — about 2 hours. Turn out the dough, and knead again about 4 minutes. Tear off pieces of dough to make

16 balls of the same size. Roll each ball into a round about 6 inches in diameter and about 3/16 inch thick. Be as accurate as possible about the thickness — this is very important. Place each piece of dough on a 6½-inch square of buttered aluminum foil. Let stand at room temperature 1 hour to rise. Set a rack in the lowest oven position, and preheat the oven to 500 degrees. Place about 4 breads (on foil) at a time on the rack and bake about 5 minutes, or until they puff and become delicately brown. Use at once or cool and store in plastic bags.

Egg Breads

Egg breads, which have been enormously popular for generations, were probably introduced to America with the Jewish traditional bread challah and the French brioche. One finds them, after a hundred years or so, practically anywhere in the country. A highly simplified brioche bread is available in bakeshops and by special order. Formerly it was found in that rare thing which America boasted during the nineteenth and twentieth centuries — the Woman's Exchange. (An exchange still exists in New York and in a few other cities but they do not flourish as they once did.) Here is a recipe for it.

Brioche Bread

1½ packages active dry yeast or 1½ yeast cakes
½ cup warm water (110 degrees)
2 tablespoons sugar
1 cup butter, melted
1½ teaspoons salt
4 to 5 cups all purpose flour
4 eggs
1 egg yolk, mixed with 2 tablespoons cream

Proof the yeast in the warm water with the sugar. Melt the butter and add the salt. In a large mixing bowl or in the bowl of a heavy-duty electric mixer, combine 4 cups flour and the eggs, melted butter, and yeast mixture. Using a wooden spoon if preparing by hand, or a dough hook if with the electric mixer, beat the dough until it is smooth, glossy, and without stickiness. Add more flour as needed. The dough may not be very firm. Transfer to a buttered bowl. Cover, and allow to rise until doubled in bulk — about 1 to 1½ hours. Punch down the dough. Separate into two equal parts and transfer to well-buttered 8½ × 4½-inch loaf pans. Let rise in a warm place until doubled in size. Brush with the egg yolk and cream, and bake at 400 degrees 30 to 40 minutes. Cool on wire racks.

Country Fair Bread

5 to 5½ cups all-purpose flour
¼ cup sugar
2 teaspoons salt
1 package active dry yeast

In a large mixer bowl, combine 1 cup flour with the sugar, salt, and dry yeast. In a saucepan, heat the milk with the butter until warm (the butter does not need to melt). Add the eggs and liquid to the flour mixture. Blend at the lowest speed until moistened; then beat 3 minutes at medium speed. By hand, stir in the remaining flour

1½ cups milk
¼ cup butter
2 eggs
1 egg white, slightly beaten
1 tablespoon water
Sesame or poppy seeds

to form a stiff dough. Knead on a floured surface until smooth and elastic, about 3 minutes. Place in a greased bowl, turning to grease the top. Cover, and let rise in a warm place until light and doubled in size, 1 to 1½ hours. Punch down the dough and divide it into 6 portions. Shape each portion into a strip 8 inches long by rolling between the hands. Braid three strips together and place on a greased cookie sheet. Do the same with the remaining three strips. Cover, let rise in a warm place until light and doubled in size, about 45 minutes. Brush with the egg white and water mixed. Sprinkle with the seeds. Bake at 375 degrees 35 to 40 minutes, until golden brown. Cool on wire racks.

Sweet Potato Batter Bread

2 packages active dry yeast or 2 yeast cakes
½ cup warm water
½ cup mashed sweet potato or yam
¼ cup sugar
3 tablespoons butter, melted
1 tablespoon salt
2 eggs
3 to 3½ cups all-purpose flour

This batter bread, made with sweet potatoes, might be called a quick bread and is extremely pleasant to eat.

Proof the yeast in the warm water. Add the mashed sweet potato, sugar, butter, salt, eggs, and 1½ cups flour. Beat several minutes in an electric mixer or by hand to blend well. Beat in the remaining flour to form a rather stiff dough. Cover, and allow to rise in a warm draft-free spot until doubled in bulk, about 1½ hours. Stir vigorously with a wooden spoon or spatula. Transfer to a well-buttered 2-pound coffee tin or two well-buttered 8½ × 4½-inch loaf tins. Allow to rise again until doubled in bulk. Bake at 375 degrees 35 to 45 minutes, or until nicely browned. After 5 minutes, turn out on a rack to cool.

Quick Batter Bread

2½ to 3 cups all-purpose flour
1 tablespoon sugar
1 tablespoon chopped chives or finely chopped onion
2 teaspoons dillweed or chopped fresh dill
1 tablespoon salt
¼ teaspoon baking soda
1 package active dry yeast
1 cup creamed cottage cheese
¼ cup water
1 tablespoon butter
1 egg
1 egg, slightly beaten

This particular recipe has appeared in various versions for the last twenty-five years. It can be baked in a 2-pound coffee can, a 2-quart soufflé mold, or a charlotte mold. It is best when eaten fresh.

Combine 1 cup of flour with the sugar, chives or onion, dill, salt, soda, and dry yeast in a large mixing bowl or the bowl of an electric mixer. Heat the cottage cheese, water, and butter in a small saucepan. Add to the flour mixture along with the egg, and blend 3 minutes. Beat in the remaining flour to make a stiff dough. Cover, and allow to rise in a warm draft-free place until doubled in bulk — about an hour. Stir the dough down. Turn into a well-buttered 2-pound coffee can or a 2-quart soufflé or charlotte mold. Allow to rise again 35 to 40 minutes. Brush lightly with beaten egg. Bake at 350 degrees 35 to 40 minutes, or until nicely browned and hollow-sounding when rapped. Cool in the container 10 minutes, then slip out onto a rack to finish cooling.

Sourdough

Sourdough Starter

2 cups lukewarm water
1 package active dry yeast or 1 yeast cake
2 cups all-purpose flour
½ teaspoon salt

Mix the ingredients in a medium-size crock. Cover loosely with cheesecloth and place in a warm spot in the kitchen. Every day, for 4 days, add ½ cup lukewarm water and ½ cup flour to feed the starter. At the end of 4 to 6 days, it should begin to give off a sour smell. If you do not plan to use the starter or part of it immediately, add a little more flour and lukewarm water and store in the refrigerator. It should be fed every week by adding additional water and flour. When using the starter take out 1 or 2 cups and be certain to replace them with equal amounts of lukewarm water and flour. Be careful not to let fat or egg get into the starter.

Sourdough Bread

1 cup lukewarm water or potato water
1 tablespoon sugar
1 to 2 tablespoons melted butter, bacon fat, or lard
1 tablespoon or more salt
1 cup sourdough starter
¼ teaspoon baking soda
4½ cups (about) all-purpose flour
Melted butter or margarine

In a mixing bowl, stir together the lukewarm water or potato water, sugar, fat and salt. Measure the starter, mix in the soda, and stir into the water mixture. Gradually beat in the flour to make a very stiff dough. Turn out onto a floured surface and knead in about ½ cup more flour to make a smooth, satiny dough. Put back into the bowl, brush the top of the dough with melted butter or margarine. Cover with a cloth, wax paper, or foil, and let stand in a warm place until double in bulk. Again turn out on a lightly floured surface. Cut the dough in half and shape into two loaves. Let stand in a warm place until the loaves are double in bulk. Carefully place in a preheated 375-degree oven and bake about 40 minutes, or until the loaves shrink from the sides of the pan. Turn on a rack to cool.

Sourdough Biscuits or Buns

1½ cups all-purpose flour
1 teaspoon salt
¼ cup butter
1 cup sourdough starter
½ teaspoon baking soda

These were standard breakfast bread on farms and ranches, where chores were done before the morning meal. On cattle drives, where nights were apt to be chilly, the cook-wagon "chef" usually mixed the dough the night before and set the biscuits in a reflector oven or frying pan to be cooked the next morning.

Measure the flour, salt, and fat into a mixing bowl. With a pastry blender or tips of the fingers, rub in the fat until the mixture is the texture of cornmeal. Measure the sour dough starter, stir in the soda, and add to the flour. Stir to combine. Turn out on a lightly floured surface and knead until smooth. If the starter is quite thick, add a little water, about a teaspoon at a time, to the mixture. When the dough is smooth, roll or pat out, and cut with a floured cutter into rolls. Or pinch off pieces of dough and roll or pat out into rounds about 1½ to 2 inches in diameter. The dough may also be

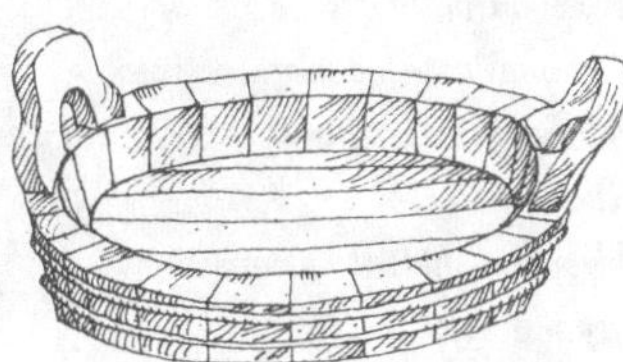

patted or rolled into a rectangle and cut into squares with a greased knife. Melt 2 or 3 tablespoons of butter or margarine in a 9×9×2-inch or larger pan. Put the biscuits or rolls in the pan and turn so that the top of the dough will be buttered. Let rise about 1 hour, or until doubled in bulk. Bake in a 425-degree oven until light brown, about 12 to 20 minutes, depending upon the size of the pan and the thickness and size of the biscuits. Serve hot. These can also be given a light bake and then frozen.

Salt Rising Bread

The distinct flavor of this bread comes from the "wild yeast" that is developed in the starter. Cooking authorities give several methods for preparing the starter, using potato slices or cornmeal or sometimes a combination of them. The starter must be kept warm for 12 to 24 hours. Originally the baker enveloped the starter in blankets. Those who could boast of making salt rising bread were apt to be a bit smug. The flavor is distinctive and the smell rather startling.

Salt Rising Starter

1½ cups scalded milk or hot water
1 medium-size potato, peeled and sliced thin
2 tablespoons white or yellow cornmeal
1 teaspoon sugar
½ teaspoon salt

Mix the ingredients and pour into a 2-quart jar or deep bowl which has been rinsed well with hot tap water. Cover with a lid or plate. Put the jar into a larger bowl or pan and surround with boiling water. Cover the large bowl with plastic or a towel, and cover this with three or four bath towels or a blanket. It should stand at a temperature of 100 degrees when the mixture is finally foaming. The electric oven turned to warm will provide the right temperature, and so will a gas range with a pilot light on. In either case let the starter stand about 12 hours, or until the top is covered with ½ to 1 inch of foam. Sometimes it will take longer to foam, even 24 hours, but continue to keep it warm.

Salt Rising Bread

Liquid from starter
½ cup warm water (about 100 degrees)
¼ teaspoon baking soda
½ cup undiluted evaporated milk or ½ cup scalded and cooled milk
1 tablespoon melted butter
1 teaspoon salt
4½ to 5½ cups all-purpose flour or hard wheat flour

Drain the starter from the potato into a mixing bowl and pour warm water through the potatoes. Discard the potatoes, but save the rinse water, and add to the starter. Add the soda, milk, melted butter, and salt, and stir well. Stir in 2 cups flour and beat until very smooth. Stir in the remaining flour, a cup at a time, until a soft dough is formed. Put a cup of flour on the bread board and turn the dough onto it. Sprinkle a little of the flour on top of the dough and knead lightly until the dough is smooth but still soft. Divide the dough and shape into two loaves (this bread does not have a rising between the kneading and the shaping). Place in well-buttered bread pans, brush the top of each loaf with melted butter, and place them out of drafts in a warm place to rise. Let rise to double in bulk. This will take longer than regular bread — as long as 4 to

5 hours. Bake at 375 degrees 35 to 45 minutes, or until the loaf shrinks from the sides of the pan. Remove from pan to cool. If only using one loaf, freeze the second loaf in an airtight wrap.

Baking Powder Breads

Baking powder breads have been in favor ever since the tea room craze of forty years ago, when gooey sweetened breads such as these were served in place of rolls with lunch or dinner. No other country, to my knowledge, has followed this practice.

Orange Bread

2 cups sifted flour
1 teaspoon baking powder
½ teaspoon baking soda
½ teaspoon salt
2 tablespoons butter
1 cup sugar
1 egg
¼ cup orange juice
¾ cup hot water
2 to 3 tablespoons grated orange rind

This has been one of the more delicious and prevalent of all the sweetened breads.

Sift together the flour, baking powder, baking soda, and salt onto a piece of waxed paper or foil. Cream the butter and sugar together in a large mixing bowl. Add the egg and beat well. Combine the orange juice and hot water. Alternately, add the liquids and the dry ingredients to the creamed mixture, blending well after each addition. One should begin and end with dry ingredients. Stir in the grated orange rind. Pour the batter into a well-buttered 9×5×3-inch loaf pan. Bake at 350 degrees 50 to 60 minutes. Remove from the pan and cool on a wire rack. This bread is often cut very thin and buttered for tea. It is also used for certain sandwiches, naturally those that will stand a sweet bread as the base. Such things as cream cheese and nuts, chopped fruits and nuts, or marmalade go with it exceedingly well.

Date Nut Bread

1 cup boiling water
1¼ cups dates (the equivalent of an 8-ounce package) cut into large pieces
2 teaspoons baking soda
2 cups sifted all-purpose flour
1 teaspoon salt
½ cup chopped nuts — filberts or pecans
2 tablespoons shortening
1 cup firmly packed brown sugar
2 eggs, beaten

Another quite popular bread in this category. It is very sweet and slightly gooey, but quite good with cheese or fruit fillings. It is also a pleasant tea bread when thickly spread with good sweet butter.

Pour the boiling water over dates and soda. Cool until lukewarm. Sift the flour with the salt and add the nuts. Cream the shortening and brown sugar in a mixing bowl. Add the beaten eggs. Beginning with the dry ingredients, alternately add the dry ingredients and the date mixture to the creamed mixture. Blend well after each addition, and end with the dry ingredients. Pour into a well-buttered 9×5×3-inch loaf pan. Bake at 350 degrees 60 to 70 minutes. Cool on a wire rack.

Brown Bread

1 cup sifted all-purpose flour
1 cup whole-wheat or rye flour
2 teaspoons baking soda
1 teaspoon salt
1 cup cornmeal
1 cup raisins
2 cups sour milk or buttermilk
¾ cup dark molasses
2 tablespoons melted butter or other shortening

Brown bread is as old as our country. Everyone seems to treasure an "original" recipe, handed down from the founding families. Although we do not know which recipes are genuine, we do know that the original was a mixture of three flours or meals. The white flour, which was a luxury item, was used only for binding, because of its gluten content. Nowadays most people use whole-wheat flour instead of rye flour, which was used to a great extent in former times and which I still prefer.

Naturally, brown bread is wedded to baked beans. This gastronomic marriage was a staple of Massachusetts and the other colonies and has continued to be a great American specialty.

Sift the flour with the soda and salt into a mixing bowl and stir in the cornmeal. Add the raisins and toss well. Add the buttermilk (or sour milk), molasses, and shortening, and blend thoroughly. Pour into three well-buttered 1-pound coffee, fruit, or vegetable tins, filling about two-thirds full. Cover tightly with foil and set in a steamer in boiling water to a depth of one-third of the tins. Cover, and steam 3 hours. Remove from the water bath and discard the foil. Cool 15 minutes, then remove to a rack. Best when eaten warm.

Jeanne Owen's Corn Bread

½ cup sifted flour
1½ cups yellow corn meal
1 teaspoon salt
1 teaspoon sugar
3 teaspoons baking powder
3 eggs, well beaten
1 cup milk
¼ cup cream
⅓ cup melted butter

The finest corn bread I have ever eaten came from the recipe of the late Jeanne Owen, who was a brilliant cook and a stalwart disciple of the art of good living. Mrs. Owen often served it for cocktails in the form of small square sandwiches filled with bits of ham.

Sift all the dry ingredients together in a mixing bowl. Add the eggs and milk and beat with a wooden spoon. Beat in the cream, and lastly the melted butter. Pour into an 8½ × 11-inch well-buttered pan, and bake at 400 degrees approximately 15 to 18 minutes. Cut in squares while still hot and fold into a napkin before serving.

Gingerbread

1 cup light or dark molasses
½ cup boiling water
5 tablespoons butter
½ teaspoon salt
1½ to 2 teaspoons ginger
1 teaspoon baking soda
2 cups all-purpose flour

To the present generation gingerbread is usually thought of as a dessert that is perhaps served topped with applesauce or apple butter and whipped cream or ice cream. But in earlier years it was considered a bread to be served with a meal.

Put the molasses in a mixing bowl and add the boiling water and butter. Stir until well mixed. Add the salt, ginger, and soda, and stir lightly. Stir in the flour just enough to moisten and mix. Turn into a 9 × 9 × 2-inch or 9 × 13 × 2-inch baking pan. Bake at 375 degrees

25 to 35 minutes, or until the top springs back when pressed lightly and the mixture is pulling away from the sides of the pan.

Baking Powder Biscuits

2 cups sifted all-purpose flour
1 tablespoon baking powder
½ teaspoon salt
¼ cup shortening
¾ cup milk
1 tablespoon sugar (optional)

In former times, biscuits were the bread of many people. Breakfast, lunch, and dinner brought them to the table hot, light, and fresh. Made with butter, lard, bacon fat, chicken fat, or vegetable shortening, they were also commonly used as toppings for savory pies — fried, of course — and for shortcakes. They are still standard countrywide, but homemade varieties have been supplanted by the advent of refrigerated biscuits, which may be bought and with very little preparation (brushing or dipping in melted butter does make a great difference) placed on a cookie sheet and baked. They are so good that I sometimes feel it is foolish to put these biscuits together from scratch. (Cream biscuits and shortcake are another matter.)

Sift the flour, baking powder, and salt (and sugar if used) into a bowl. Cut in the shortening (butter, lard, vegetable shortening, chicken fat — what you will). The pieces of fat should be quite fine. Add the milk and stir quickly until the dough clings together. Turn out on a floured board, knead a few times, and pat or roll out to ¼ to ½ inch thickness. Cut into rounds with a floured cutter 1 to 2 inches in diameter. Place on a buttered cookie sheet, or, if you like biscuits crisp on top and bottom and soft in the center, place in a buttered 9×9 inch pan. Bake at 450 degrees 12 to 15 minutes, or until light and brown.

Note. For richer biscuits, turn each one in a bowl or pan of melted butter before placing on the baking sheet.

Parsley Biscuits. Add 2 tablespoons finely chopped parsley to the dough.

Cream Biscuits. These were a specialty of my mother's. I find them very light and thoroughly different from other biscuits. Use no shortening, but add ¾ to 1 cup heavy cream to make a light dough. Pat or roll ½ inch thick. Melt 4 tablespoons butter in a 9×9-inch baking pan or a small skillet. Dip each biscuit in the melted butter and place either in the pan or on a cookie sheet. Bake as above.

Shortcake. Use either biscuit recipe above. If you use the basic one, add 2 to 3 tablespoons sugar and substitute evaporated milk or heavy cream for the milk. Divide the dough in half or into two unequal portions, one twice as large as the other. Roll the larger portion into a circle about 8 inches in diameter and the smaller one into a circle 6 to 7 inches in diameter. Place the larger one on a

well-buttered cookie sheet and brush thoroughly with melted butter. Top with the smaller one, and also brush with melted butter. Bake at 450 degrees 15 to 18 minutes. Transfer to a serving plate and remove the top (smaller) layer very carefully. Cover the bottom layer with sugared berries and then replace the top layer. Add more berries, and top with whipped cream or serve with a pitcher of heavy pouring cream. This base will serve for strawberry, raspberry, blackberry, peach, or plum shortcake.

Buttermilk Biscuits

2 cups unsifted all-purpose flour (may be unbleached)
2½ teaspoons baking powder
½ teaspoon salt
½ teaspoon baking soda
⅓ cup butter
¾ cup buttermilk or sour milk

Years ago biscuits were usually made with sour milk, sour cream, or buttermilk. Sometimes baking powder and soda were used for the leavening, and sometimes a combination of cream of tartar and baking powder. Prior to that, a leaven of pearl ash was used. Buttermilk biscuits, which resemble these earlier biscuits, have a distinctive flavor. They were made with real buttermilk, which had bits of butter floating in it.

Combine all the dry ingredients and sift into a mixing bowl. Add the butter and blend in well. Stir in the buttermilk and blend till the dough holds together, Turn out on a floured board and flour the top of the dough lightly. Knead about 3 minutes and pat or roll out in a circle about ½ inch thick. Cut the biscuits any size you like, dip them into melted butter, and arrange on a baking sheet or in a 9 × 9-inch buttered pan. Bake at 450 degrees 12 to 15 minutes.

Note. To sour milk nowadays, combine ⅞ cup milk with 1½ tablespoons vinegar and let stand a half hour.

Muffins

Muffins have been inordinately popular for years. I, for one, have never been able to understand why. They must be eaten piping hot and are not very good when warmed over. An exception might be made for bran muffins, but then we could get along just as well without them, too.

Simple Muffins

2 cups sifted flour—all-purpose or unbleached all-purpose
¼ cup sugar
1 tablespoon baking powder
½ teaspoon salt
1 egg, beaten
1 cup milk
¼ cup melted butter

This recipe makes 10 to 12 normal-size muffins, or double the number of tiny muffins.

Butter the muffin tins. Sift all the dry ingredients — flour, sugar, baking powder, and salt — into a mixing bowl. Combine the egg, milk, and melted butter. Make a well in the center of the dry ingredients and add the liquid at one time. Mix very lightly, just until the dry ingredients are moistened. Fill the buttered tins about two-thirds full. Bake at 425 degrees 20 to 25 minutes, or until nicely browned and puffy.

Rich Muffins. Increase the sugar to ½ cup, use 2 beaten eggs instead of 1, increase the melted butter to ½ cup, and decrease the milk to ½ cup.

Cheese Muffins. Add ½ to 1 cup shredded sharp Cheddar or Switzerland Swiss cheese, and a few drops of Tabasco. Omit the sugar.

Fruit Muffins. Add ½ cup lightly floured fruit (raisins, blueberries, or chopped dates, prunes, figs, or apricots) to the dry ingredients.

Nut Muffins. Add ½ cup chopped walnuts, peanuts, hazelnuts, or pecans to the dry ingredients.

Cornmeal Muffins

1 cup sifted all-purpose flour
1 cup cornmeal
1 to 2 tablespoons sugar, to your taste
4 teaspoons baking powder
1½ teaspoons salt
2 eggs, slightly beaten
1 cup milk
¼ cup melted butter

Sift all the dry ingredients together into a mixing bowl. Make a well in the center and add the eggs, milk, and butter. Stir to a smooth batter. Fill well-buttered muffin tins or corn stick pans two-thirds full. Bake at 425 degrees 15 to 20 minutes, or until nicely browned and baked through.

Bran Muffins

1½ cups bran
1¼ cups milk
1½ cups sifted all-purpose flour
2½ teaspoons baking powder
1 teaspoon salt
¼ cup butter or margarine
⅓ cup sugar
¼ cup light molasses
1 egg

Combine the bran and milk and let stand 10 minutes. Sift the flour, baking powder, and salt. Cream the butter or margarine and sugar and blend in the molasses, egg, and bran mixture. Mix in the dry ingredients until all particles are moist. Butter well 12 large or 24 small muffin tins, and fill two-thirds full. Bake at 400 degrees 20 to 30 minutes.

Note. You may add ½ cup raisins or ½ cup coarsely chopped walnuts with the molasses, egg, and bran mixture.

Popovers

2 eggs
1 cup flour, sifted
1 teaspoon salt
1 cup milk
2 tablespoons melted butter

Popovers — once known as Laplanders — are made without leavening, and are a delight to the eye, the tooth, and the palate. They are purely American. Although the batter is almost that of Yorkshire pudding, I do not believe that this was the inspiration, inasmuch as the popover went through a number of transitions over the years till it became the standard recipe we know.

The latest development in popovers — after we were advised for years to pour the batter into sizzling tins, put the tins into a very hot

oven, and reduce the heat after 20 to 30 minutes — comes from the discovery that they can be started in a cold oven set for 425 degrees. They pop and rise magnificently this way. Also, it is certain that the less they are beaten the better they are.

Beat the eggs lightly and beat in the flour and salt. Stir in the milk. Blend to make a fairly smooth batter. Add the melted butter. Pour into 10 to 12 buttered muffin tins or custard cups, filling about two-thirds full. Place in a cold oven set for 425 degrees and bake 30 to 35 minutes. Reduce the temperature if the popovers seem to brown too much. When they are baked, pierce each one with a skewer or knife to dry them out, if you like.

Pancakes, Waffles, Doughnuts

Pancakes, Griddlecakes, Flapjacks, Stack o' Wheats

Griddlecakes and pancakes have been as much of a mainstay for our ancestors as any other article of food. They can be cooked over a fire in the wilds as well as in a kitchen — practically any place where there is heat and a griddle or pan. I can remember cooking pancakes on the beach when I was a child and savoring the wonderful sweet-sour taste of the sour milk cake combined with the syrup and butter and served with ham or bacon and eggs and coffee (made in an old-fashioned pot with eggshells and whites in it). It seemed there was no satiation for our appetites. I also remember a sign in a diner in the Siskiyou mountains — this, at breakfast time — "Short stack for light appetites." Well, the short stack turned out to be four rather thickish light griddlecakes about 8 inches in diameter! What a long stack would have been I hesitate to think.

Practically no one makes pancakes from scratch these days. With the mixes, refrigerated batters, and frozen pancakes available on the market, there seems little need. However, I feel that homemade cakes are better and worth the trouble.

Basic Griddlecakes

2 cups sifted all-purpose flour
1 tablespoon sugar
4 teaspoons baking powder

Combine all the dry ingredients and sift into a mixing bowl. Combine the eggs, milk, and butter and stir into the dry ingredients until the large lumps disappear. It is wise to remember that as this batter stands, it thickens. If this should happen while you are baking the cakes, add a little more milk, stirring it in with a wooden spoon

1 teaspoon salt
2 eggs, lightly beaten
1½ cups milk
¼ cup melted butter or oil

or spatula. To bake, pour the batter on a hot, lightly greased griddle. The cakes should be about 4 to 6 inches in diameter. They are ready to turn when bubbles form and break and the edges seem cooked. Turn, and brown lightly on the reverse side. These are best served with melted butter and hot syrup or honey.

Buttermilk Pancakes

2 cups all-purpose flour
1 teaspoon baking soda
1 teaspoon salt
2 cups buttermilk
3 eggs, separated
¼ cup butter, melted

Pancakes made with buttermilk, sour milk, or sour cream used to have a dedicated public. Alas, most of us never see real buttermilk or sour milk any more, but one can make pretty good cakes with cultured buttermilk. Sometimes it needs a little thinning with regular milk to give the batter the right texture.

Sift all the dry ingredients into a mixing bowl. Stir in the buttermilk and well-beaten egg yolks. Add the butter and beat until smooth. Beat the egg whites until they are stiff but not dry. Fold into the batter very gently. Drop the batter by spoonfuls on a lightly greased hot griddle and bake until brown. Turn and brown the other side. Serve at once. Good with butter and hot syrup or honey or the berry jams.

Henri Thiele's German Pancakes

1 cup sifted all-purpose flour
2 teaspoons salt
3 tablespoons sugar
1 cup cream
9 eggs
4 tablespoons butter for the pan
Melted butter
Additional sugar
Lemon juice

When I was young in Portland, Henry Thiele's restaurant and the Pine Street Coffee House made a great specialty of these pancakes, and I find them in German restaurants throughout the country. This recipe will make three delicious 12-inch pancakes.

Mix the flour, salt, sugar, and cream to form a rather smooth paste. Beat in the eggs, one at a time. Heat a 12-inch iron or metal skillet and melt the butter for the pan until it is foamy and bubbly. Add approximately a third of the batter and cook over medium heat until it browns lightly on the bottom and seems to be cooked at the sides. Place in a 400-degree oven until it puffs and browns on the top. Remove from the oven and slip the pancake onto a heated plate. Brush lavishly with melted butter, sprinkle with sugar and a few drops of lemon juice. Roll and serve at once.

Variations

(1) Serve with warm syrup or apricot jam instead of the sugar and lemon juice.

(2) Roll the pancakes and flambé with rum or Cognac. In that case, sprinkle with additional granulated sugar before you pour the warmed liquor over it.

(3) Make smaller pancakes in an 8-inch or 10-inch skillet, using less of the batter in each.

Waffles

Waffles date from the beginning of the nineteenth century in this country. Miss Leslie gives recipes for yeast waffles and directions for using the early waffle irons, which were put over an open flame or on top of the stove and had to be turned at least once during the cooking process. With the advent of the electric waffle iron, waffles became almost too popular. People served them with syrup, with butter, with honey and butter, with creamed chicken, with tuna fish, with ham and bacon. Waffles were served as breakfast food, luncheon food, and supper food. It was an easy way to entertain. Many people felt if they mastered waffle batter and had a waffle iron, no extension of their gastronomic repertoire was needed. Waffles are delicious when properly served and are a bore when served too often.

Waffles

1¾ cups sifted all-purpose flour
2 teaspoons baking powder
½ teaspoon salt
2 tablespoons sugar
3 eggs, separated
1¾ cups milk
6 tablespoons melted butter or bacon, sausage, or ham fat

Waffles are best served with melted butter and heated syrup or honey on heated plates, although some people enjoy them with apple butter or various preserves. The following recipe will make about four servings.

Sift the flour with the baking powder, salt, and sugar. In a mixing bowl, beat the egg yolks. Add the milk and melted fat. Stir in the flour mixture just until moistened. Do not beat. Beat the egg whites until they hold firm peaks, then fold into the batter. Use immediately by spooning into a preheated waffle iron. The batter will spread considerably in the waffle iron, so test the first waffle by putting in a rounded tablespoon of batter. A running-over waffle iron is bound to create a good deal of smoke and is hard to clean. Bake until the steam has stopped coming from around the edge of the iron, usually about 5 minutes, then lift the lid of the iron and see if the waffle is nicely browned.

Belgian Waffles. Serve with strawberries or other fresh fruits and whipped cream, like a shortcake. They should be buttered, topped with sugared fruit and sweetened whipped cream, and served piping hot.

Rich Cream Waffles. Use 1 cup heavy cream and ¾ cup milk Reduce the melted butter to 3 tablespoons.

Buttermilk Waffles. Use 1 teaspoon baking soda and 2 to 2½ cups buttermilk in place of the baking powder and milk.

Sour Cream Waffles. Use 1 teaspoon baking powder and ½ teaspoon baking soda with 2 cups sour cream.

Cornmeal Waffles. Use ½ cup white or yellow cornmeal instead of ½ cup flour.

Doughnuts

Doughnuts, crullers, and other fried cakes have been standard fare in this country for centuries. The New Englanders, the Pennsylvania Dutch, and practically everyone who settled this country soon adopted the habit of eating doughnuts for breakfast or lunch or a between-meal snack. Sometimes they are pretty fat-sodden, sometimes they are light and fluffy, sometimes they are tough, but none of this seems to make too much difference.

Cake doughnuts, or doughnuts without yeast, are the most common ones today. They are usually served coated with granulated or powdered sugar, and in the last few years have been insulted by having various colors of icing poured over them. Raised doughnuts came with the Dutch and Germans. They were made with risen dough cut and fried, then shaken with granulated sugar and sometimes cinnamon. They were often filled as well (originally called Berliner Pfannkuchen), sometimes with jelly or jam and sometimes a pastry cream. These have been referred to as cannonballs, jelly doughnuts, cream doughnuts, etc. They are heavy, but if well made, absolutely delicious. With the development of raised doughnuts, which seem to be Western more than anything else, came rectangular pieces of fried cake made from risen dough which are topped with maple-flavored frosting and called maple bars. I must confess a great weakness for them.

Cake Doughnuts

2 eggs
1 cup sugar
3½ cups sifted all-purpose flour
4 teaspoons baking powder
1 teaspoon salt
½ teaspoon nutmeg
2 tablespoons melted butter
1 cup milk
1 teaspoon vanilla (optional)
3 pounds lard or shortening or 2 quarts oil, for frying

Break the eggs into a mixing bowl and beat until light and lemon-colored. Gradually beat in the sugar until the mixture is thick and ribbony. Sift together the flour, baking powder, salt, and nutmeg. Add this to the beaten eggs and sugar alternately with the milk and melted butter, and stir lightly until the flour is moistened. Allow the mixture to stand about 15 minutes. If the dough should seem very thin, chill it a half hour before rolling. Take half the dough and roll about ¾ inch thick. Cut with a floured doughnut cutter, and be sure to save the holes. They are most delicious when fried. With the aid of a spatula, lift the cut doughnuts to wax paper or a lightly floured board. Allow them to stand in a cool place 15 minutes before frying. The fat for frying the doughnuts should be 2 to 3 inches deep and should be heated to 365 degrees. Lower the doughnuts, one or two at a time, into the hot fat. When they are brown on one side, turn with the aid of a spatula or tongs and brown the other side. When nicely browned, remove to absorbent paper. Be sure to reheat the fat to 365 degrees before adding additional doughnuts. When all are fried, sprinkle with granulated or confectioner's sugar. Fry the holes separately and roll them in sugar as well.

Potato Doughnuts. Use only ¾ cup milk and add ½ cup mashed potatoes.

Raised Doughnuts

½ yeast cake or 1 package active dry yeast
2 tablespoons warm water
½ cup sugar
1 egg
1 cup scalded milk cooled to lukewarm or ½ cup evaporated milk and ½ cup warm tap water
2 tablespoons melted butter or margarine
3¾ cups sifted all-purpose flour

These are eternally popular and best eaten when freshly fried rather than cold.

In a mixing bowl place the yeast, add the warm water, and stir. Add the sugar and mix well. Let stand 10 to 15 minutes. Stir in the egg, then the milk, melted butter, and flour. Stir until the dough seems springy. Brush the top of the dough lightly with melted butter or margarine and cover with wax paper or foil. Place in a warm part of the kitchen to rise until double in bulk, about 1½ hours. (*Note.* This is easier to roll out if put in the refrigerator to rise overnight, or at least 4 hours.) Roll out half the dough at a time about ½ inch thick. Cut with a floured cutter and place on a bread board or wax paper–covered cookie sheet to rise until double in bulk. Fry in 2 or more inches of hot lard, shortening, or cooking oil heated to 370 degrees in a large, deep kettle. Put the doughnuts in with the top-risen side down. Fry until brown on one side and turn to brown on the other side. When nicely browned, remove from the hot fat and drain on absorbent paper. Sprinkle with confectioner's or granulated sugar while still warm. The easiest way to attain an even sugaring of the doughnuts is to put the sugar in a large plastic or paper bag and add a few doughnuts at a time.

Filled Doughnuts, Jellied Doughnuts, or Cannonballs. These are famous throughout Central Europe and the custom spread to America. Sometimes 3 egg yolks are used instead of the whole egg, and often a plain bread dough is used. After the dough has been mixed and allowed to rise once, roll out about ¼ inch thick. Cut into rounds 3 to 4 inches in diameter — no holes in these — and place ½ teaspoon jam, jelly, or pastry cream into the centers of half of the rounds. Brush the edges with slightly beaten egg mixed with 2 tablespoons water. Place the plain rounds over the filled rounds and press the edges together gently. Allow to rise until almost double in bulk, and fry as for any other doughnut, in hot fat heated to 370 degrees. Do not try to fry too many doughnuts at one time.

Maple Bars. Prepare a yeast bread dough or a richer dough such as described above for filled doughnuts. Roll out the risen dough on a lightly floured board or surface to a square or rectangle about ½ inch thick. Cut into pieces about 1½ to 2 inches wide and 4 inches long. Transfer to another board or cookie sheet to rise until almost double in bulk. Fry in deep fat heated to 370 degrees until nicely brown on each side. Drain on absorbent paper, and spoon a maple glaze on one side. (*Maple Glaze I:* Mix maple syrup with confectioners' sugar, using about ¼ cup to 1 cup of sugar. *Maple Glaze II:* Add 2 to 3 tablespoons hot water to 1 cup sugar and about ⅓ teaspoon imitation maple flavoring.)

Crullers

4 eggs
⅔ cup sugar
1 teaspoon grated lemon rind
⅓ cup melted butter or margarine
3½ cups sifted all-purpose flour
½ teaspoon salt
2 teaspoons baking powder
⅓ cup milk

Richer than doughnuts, these are a delicate accompaniment to coffee.

Beat the eggs until very light, and beat in the sugar a little at a time. Stir in the lemon rind and melted butter or margarine. Sift the flour with the salt and baking powder, and add to the egg mixture alternately with the milk. Stir just to combine. Chill the dough about 30 minutes, then roll out about ¼ inch thick (roll half at a time on a lightly floured board). Cut, preferably with a pastry wheel to give a decorative edge, into strips ½ inch by 2 to 2½ inches. Twist the strips as you drop them into deep hot fat, heated to 370 degrees. When lightly browned on one side, turn and brown on the other side. Do not overcrowd the fat or the crullers will be grease-soaked. When browned, drain on absorbent paper. Sprinkle with powdered sugar and serve hot or cold. These can be reheated, if you prefer them warm. Place one layer of crullers in a shallow pan and heat at 350 degrees for a few minutes. Store in airtight containers to keep them crisp.

Fried Rice Cakes

2 cups cooked rice
1½ cups flour
1½ teaspoons baking powder
1 teaspoon cinnamon
1 teaspoon nutmeg
2 tablespoons sugar
¼ teaspoon salt
2 eggs, well beaten

These are a version of the great New Orleans dish called Calas. The Creole cooks were known to wander into the streets of New Orleans calling out, "*Calas tout chaud.*" Some of them were made with yeast dough, which I think are extremely good, and some with baking powder.

Combine the rice with the sifted flour, baking powder, cinnamon, nutmeg, sugar, and salt. Stir in the beaten eggs and form the mixture into small rolls about 2½ inches long. Carefully lower them into very hot fat heated to 350 degrees and cook until well browned, about 8 minutes. Drain on absorbent paper. Sprinkle with granulated sugar and serve hot.

Sandwiches

When Lord Sandwich sent out for some meat to be placed between two pieces of bread so he could continue with his game of cards, he had no idea what a revolution in food he was causing. He influenced the food habits of the Danes, the English, and the French. But for Americans, he started a way of life.

The sandwich has been put into service at every meal and can turn up as a luncheon dish, as a snack, as a dinner entrée, as a supper dish, and as an all-night resuscitator, to say nothing of its dainty and refined versions for tea and for cocktail parties. Apart from the traditional two slices of bread with a filling, sandwiches are prepared as two-deckers, three-deckers, on buns, on rolls, and even on whole loaves of bread.

Some Advice About Sandwiches

Bread for sandwiches. The soft, rather flabby substance which we are fools enough to accept as daily bread in this country makes dreadful sandwiches, even if toasted. There are numerous other choices that lend themselves perfectly to sandwiches: homemade breads, rye breads, pumpernickel, various meal breads — (oatmeal, barley, whole meal, corn), onion breads, herb breads, breads such as the Italian variety studded with tiny nuggets of crisp pork and coarse pepper, nut breads, and cheese breads. Armenian and Syrian breads are also novel for producing the sandwich. Some of the quick breads made with baking powder, such as orange bread, fruit breads, and fruit and nut loaves, are particularly good for tea sandwiches or other sandwiches requiring a rather sweet overtone. French rolls — the very crisp long ones and the round and oblong rolls — are ideal sandwich rolls. Also the soft finger roll and what we are wont to accept as the hot dog roll make extremely good sandwich rolls.

Crusts are a matter of personal taste. I prefer to remove the crusts for a delicate sandwich, such as one filled with chicken white meat or pâté. With a hearty sandwich, however — meat loaf or roast beef, for example — the crust, if good and crisp, adds to the flavor.

Spreading sandwiches. Butter for sandwiches should be sweet — unsalted — and soft enough to spread evenly. If hard it can tear the bread and remain in small chunks. Flavored butters, creamed with contrasting flavors, are excellent with certain sandwiches — see the index.

Many people have become devoted to mayonnaise in place of or in addition to — butter. It can offer a pleasantly moist flavor to the finished sandwich, but it can also ruin many delicate fillings. Generally it should be used judiciously as an additive, like mustard, catsup, pickle relish, or chowchow.

Wrapping and storing sandwiches. Sandwiches are best when served fresh. If they must be stored, wrap securely in foil or in plastic wrap or bags, and chill in the refrigerator till ready to use. If they are being prepared for a picnic, wrap first in plastic or foil, then wrap in damp towels. Or store them in a portable icebox.

Toasted sandwiches. Toasted sandwiches — those served on *hot, crisp* toast — are extremely good and popular. There is nothing more unappetizing than a flabby, lukewarm toasted sandwich.

French-toasting has become one of the more popular approaches to sandwich making. The sandwich is dipped into a batter of beaten egg and milk (1 egg to each ½ cup milk) and then fried in butter or deep fat for a few moments at 350 degrees. Naturally such sandwiches are not suitable for feeding a crowd — they must be eaten promptly after they are made.

Broiled, grilled, or sautéed sandwiches. These, like toasted sandwiches, must be made and served practically at the last minute, lest they become soggy and tired.

Club Sandwich

For this, the supreme example of the sandwich art, see page 219 in the poultry chapter.

Hamburger Sandwich

For hamburgers and cheeseburgers, see pages 311–316. Here are a few variations for their use as sandwiches.

(1) Cheeseburger, topped with a slice of real Cheddar or Swiss cheese, and broiled for the last few minutes to melt the cheese.

(2) Cheeseburger, with grated cheese incorporated into the meat with seasonings.

(3) Chiliburger, with a generous helping of chili over the hamburger.

(4) Hamburger rarebit, with Welsh rarebit spooned over the hamburger.

(5) Hamburger covered with smothered onions.

(6) Hamburger pan-fried, with red wine and onions or mushrooms added.

Frankfurter Sandwich

This has had a long and successful career in the country, and at one point, in fact, was thought to be the most popular food item in the world. I can remember birthday parties where frankfurters and rolls were the pièce de résistance among the refreshments. And of course they were sold more or less by the millions to hungry mobs of children assembled at local amusement parks. Mustard, relish and/or catsup were the standard accompaniments then and still are, although there are a few very fancy changes in the field. Some of these are:

(1) Split the frankfurter, stuff with a finger of Cheddar cheese, wrap with bacon, and broil. Serve in a roll with mustard.

(2) Dip the frankfurter into a corn batter, deep-fry, and serve on a stick.

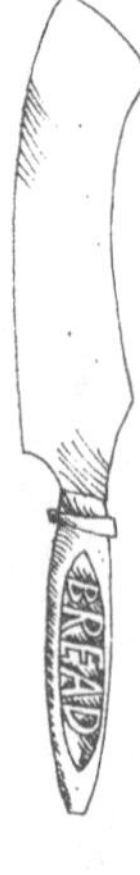

(3) A real Coney Island is a good frankfurter on a roll with a swab of mustard, some chili — without beans — and a hearty sprinkling of chopped raw onions. These thoroughly delicious morsels are available throughout the country, albeit occasionally in the tougher neighborhoods for some unexplainable reason. You can make them yourself, using the chili recipe on page 18 and adding the ingredients mentioned above. They are wonderful for a cocktail party.

(4) The barbecued frankfurter is cooked in a smoky barbecue sauce, then placed in a frankfurter bun and often doused with additional sauce.

Frankfurters have been made of tuna fish, chicken, and who knows what else. Lately they have become skinless and have lost much of the snap and juiciness they used to have. There are, however, still markets where one can find kosher (all beef) frankfurters and German-style ones. These have good flavor and texture and are less apt to be filled with artificial ingredients.

Bacon Rolls

These had many years of service. They were originally served at Schrafft's, I believe, but were copied and sometimes not successfully.

They are composed of soft finger rolls, similar to hot dog rolls, filled with rashers of bacon and served crisp and hot. Perfect for breakfast, though delicious at any time of day.

Bacon and Tomato Sandwich

2 pieces of toast, buttered
3 or 4 (or to taste) slices tomato
Mayonnaise
Crisp bacon

This can be delicious if well made and served hot. Lettuce is sometimes included in either version. But why?

With Cheese. Lay a piece of Cheddar cheese atop the tomatoes and grill this portion of the sandwich till the cheese melts. Add the bacon and top with the second piece of toast.

Corned Beef Sandwich

Corned beef is best served warm and cut paper-thin. Pile thin slices on well-buttered rye or pumpernickel bread — any of the many varieties of rye bread is ideal for the sandwich — and serve with good mustard and fresh pickles.

With Cheese. Add a thin slice or two of Swiss cheese to the sandwich, on rye or pumpernickel bread.

With Chutney. A julienne of corned beef tossed with India relish and served on white bread used to be one of the more successful sandwiches at Schrafft's. It is a piquant combination good for lunch boxes because the pickle keeps the corned beef moist.

Reuben Sandwich. There are many different versions of this sandwich. Basically, it is made with corned beef, Swiss cheese, and sauerkraut, after which it is toasted. The old Reuben sandwiches I remember were made of thickish slices of pumpernickel, corned beef, sauerkraut, chicken breast or turkey breast, Swiss cheese, and Russian dressing. They were rather stupendous, but made a perfect summer meal and were also well fitted for a picnic. For cocktail-size Reuben sandwiches, see page 23.

Cold Boiled or Pressed Beef Sandwich

Cold beef from a boiled dinner or pressed beef on white bread makes a delicious sandwich for summer, served with horseradish cream or horseradish mayonnaise, and combined with coleslaw or a potato salad.

Hot Pastrami Sandwich

One of the more delicious of the cured meats, but one which can be so badly treated as to be almost inedible. It resembles very much the famous spiced beef of England and early America, and is easy to make (page 306). It takes a good deal of marinating to make it perfect, but it is worth it.

Pastrami should be carved hot and rather thinnish — not as thin as corned beef — and piled on well-buttered rye or pumpernickel bread, or on truly good white bread. Serve with good mustard. One delicious specialty of the now departed Lindy's in New York was a pastrami sandwich with one slice of bread spread with chopped chicken livers.

London Broil

Many different cuts — flank, hanging tenderloin, skirt, rump — but none of the prime ones are used for London broil. This started not in London but in Philadelphia and has swept the country as a luncheon dish. The steaks are broiled, cut in thin diagonal slices, and served often on toast or toasted French bread. Sometimes a Béarnaise sauce, a Bordelaise sauce, or rosemary butter is served with it. Various mustards, also, are excellent with London broil. For accompaniments, one wants crisp potatoes and a salad. This is an ideal sandwich for outdoor entertaining.

Roast Beef Sandwich

One of the perfect sandwiches, whether made with good white bread, rye, or pumpernickel. Use either cold prime rib with some of its fat (if you can take fat) or the wonderful top sirloin or sirloin tip roast one finds in good delicatessens. Slice paper-thin and pack generously into a sandwich spread with butter and mustard or horseradish. For picnics, roast beef on homemade white bread with thin slices of onion is extraordinarily good. Roast beef on rye toast or white toast is also excellent. Mustard pickles go well with all roast beef sandwiches.

Steak Sandwich

Cold sliced steak on toast or rye bread makes a superb sandwich. Carve the meat in thin diagonal slices. Serve with a good mustard or a barbecue sauce that can be eaten cold. For a picnic, broil steaks and allow them to cool. Prepare sandwiches in advance at home, or carve the steak at the picnic and arrange on rolls or bread. (See grilled flank steak sandwiches, page 22.)

Cold Lamb Sandwich

A much neglected treat, cold lamb from the leg or shoulder affords a pleasant sandwich, thinly sliced and placed on buttered white or rye bread. The lamb is best when it is cooked pink rare. Salt and pepper, and chutney or a bit of mint sauce, will enhance the flavor. Ideal for packing and carrying on a trip or to a picnic.

Cold Pork Sandwich

Pork is another much neglected meat for sandwiches. Use loin meat or fresh ham sliced very thin, and combine with white or nut bread and butter. Try adding a little pickled walnut, finely cut, or some mango chutney. Otherwise, plain mustard mayonnaise makes a delicious sandwich.

Finely chopped pork blended with Russian dressing and a bit of dill or tarragon makes a very satisfactory spread for sandwiches as well.

Ham Sandwich

A good ham sandwich is an achievement. All too often the filling for a ham sandwich is a thin slice of some vaguely familiar pink meat that is almost totally without flavor. There are still good hams to be found which roast or boil to perfection and whose flavor lingers in the slices put between two pieces of well-buttered bread. Rye bread, good white bread, and crisp French rolls are excellent with ham. Soft rolls are also used frequently, and nut bread and fruit breads are successful with certain types of ham sandwiches.

Baked Ham Sandwich. Use country ham or regular cured ham if it has good flavor. Carve the ham rather thin, but give the sandwiches ample fillings. Hot English mustard or French mustard is a standard accompaniment, and white or rye bread is recommended. A sandwich of baked ham on buttered nut bread spread with Russian or Thousand Island dressing can have interesting flavor. Baked ham may also be served on toast.

Smithfield Ham Sandwich. The flavor of Smithfield, which is different from all other hams, seems to be best enhanced when served on homemade bread, preferably white, with whole wheat or Graham being next in preference. The bread should be cut thin and the ham not too thick. No other additive is required except a bit of mustard. Pickles accompany it extremely well. For snacks, it is delicious served between thin squares of very hot corn bread, well buttered. Also excellent with hot biscuit and beaten biscuit.

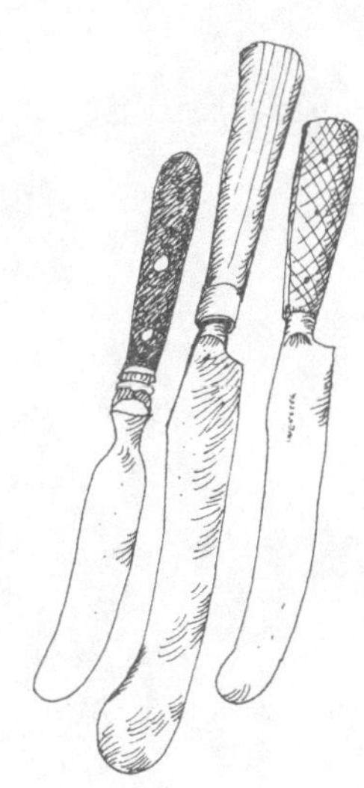

Frizzled or Fried Ham Sandwich. Serve ham cut thin and frizzled in butter, or thickish slices of fried ham, on well-buttered hot toasted English muffins or corn bread. Or top the ham with a fried egg and served on hot toast or a toasted bun. Naturally the fried egg should be rather well done, the yolk broken and just cooked through. This used to be a favorite picnic sandwich, for what reason I cannot imagine.

Prosciutto Sandwich. Italian ham grows in popularity more each year. For a regular sandwich, it is best cut into shreds with a sharp knife or scissors and arranged on French or Italian bread with plenty of butter. For a more interesting sandwich, combine it with beaten eggs, scramble, and use as a filling for hot toasted buns.

Westphalian Ham Sandwich. Treat as you would prosciutto, above. For sandwiches, it is best cut into thin strips. It is especially good combined with mild cream cheese or shredded Cheddar cheese.

Deviled Ham Sandwich. Long an American favorite, deviled ham (see page 449) was usually made of the last bits of a baked ham and kept in jars just for sandwiches. Naturally, the better the ham, the better the flavor of the deviled ham, and the Smithfield probably makes the best of all. My preference is to combine it with mustard and mayonnaise for a spread, without chopped pickles or such additions — one can serve sweet gherkins or mustard pickles separately. Canned deviled ham has no relation to the homemade variety. It is merely a salty spread of pork, with none of the finesse of carefully ground or chopped ham.

Ham Salad Sandwich. Ham salad (page 70) has come into being in the last twenty-five years and is used primarily for sandwiches, particularly for ham salad rolls — tiny finger rolls or hot dog rolls filled with the ham mixture. To vary, combine the ham salad with chopped hard-boiled egg, which makes a rather pleasant spread.

Ham and Cheese Sandwich

Usually this common sandwich is made with a slice of ham — baked or boiled — and Swiss cheese, combined with mustard and served on rye or white bread. Occasionally it is toasted after being assembled. Frizzled or fried ham, and Cheddar rather than Swiss cheese, are especially good in the sautéed and French-toasted varieties.

Sautéed Ham and Cheese Sandwich. Butter the outside of the bread and sauté the sandwich gently in a skillet till the bread is crisp and buttery and the cheese melted.

French-Toasted Ham and Cheese Sandwich. Dip the sandwich into a mixture of beaten eggs and milk such as one prepares for French toast, then sauté in butter until both sides are brown and the cheese is melted. The bread should be fairly well soaked in the egg-milk mixture to achieve a soft quality beneath the crisp exterior.

Ham, Cheese, and Chicken or Turkey Sandwich. Add a slice of chicken or turkey to the sandwich and sauté or French-toast it as above.

Tongue Sandwich

Boiled smoked tongue, while not a favorite table meat in the United States, has always been a choice and very expensive sandwich specialty. It is best, certainly, on well-buttered rye or good white bread. Carve very thin, fill the sandwich generously, and serve with butter and horseradish.

Variations

(1) Combine sliced tongue and turkey on white bread with mayonnaise and horseradish.

(2) Combine ½ cup cream cheese, ¼ cup sour cream and 2 or 3 tablespoons horseradish, and spread on thin rye or white bread. Add sliced tongue.

(3) Use freshly shredded horseradish with thin slices of tongue on rye bread. For a very spicy sandwich, add a touch of English mustard.

(4) Combine shredded tongue with chutney in a sandwich.

(5) Combine sliced tongue, sliced chicken or turkey white meat, and Swiss cheese on white or rye bread, and add a touch of mustard. Toast, sauté, or French-toast the sandwich.

Bologna Sandwich

Bologna and its parent mortadella combine with cheese, peppers, and tomato for a version of a hero, and also with cream cheese and black olives.

Liverwurst Sandwich

Liverwurst, mashed and blended with mustard, mayonnaise, or chopped pickle, is extremely popular on whole-grain bread or pumpernickel. Thinly sliced with slices of raw onion on rye or pumpernickel, it is a delight in the picnic hamper.

Chicken Salad Sandwich

This sandwich is quite different in quality from one made with sliced chicken, but it can be equally good. Combine 1½ cups diced chicken (white meat or white and dark mixed), 3 tablespoons finely cut celery, a few capers, 2 tablespoons chopped ripe olives, and mayonnaise to bind. The mixture should be on the firm side; thus the mayonnaise should be heavy and thick, not wet.

Chopped Chicken Sandwich. Finely chopped chicken makes another good sandwich filling. Combine 1½ cups cold chopped chicken with salt and pepper to taste, a teaspoon of crushed tarragon, and mayonnaise to bind to a tight paste. Chopped green peppers may also be added. Spread on toasted white or dark bread, adding more mayonnaise, if you like.

Chicken Sandwich

Next to ham, probably the most staple filling for sandwiches the world over is chicken. Nowadays a chicken sandwich is far more difficult to get in restaurants than the eternal turkey sandwich. Naturally at home it is always within one's grasp.

Chicken sandwiches are best made on thin, well-buttered slices of bread trimmed of crusts, preferably white (homemade bread or what is referred to as Pullman bread), or try a well flavored rye bread, preferably one without seeds and not too overpowering, or Swedish limpa bread. Use thinnish slices of white meat. Salt to taste. Mayonnaise is optional and should be served separately in a small sauceboat or bowl. No lettuce is necessary.

Variations

(1) Sliced chicken and ham on white or whole wheat, or — especially for those interested in lowering the calorie count — on protein toast.

(2) Sliced chicken, ham, and Swiss cheese on white bread, dipped in batter (as for French toast) and sautéed in butter or fried in deep fat for a few moments at 350 degrees.

(3) Sliced chicken on well-buttered whole wheat bread with a few slices of peeled and seeded cucumber, a dash of salt, and mayonnaise.

Chicken Giblet Sandwich

½ pound chicken gizzards
¼ pound chicken hearts
2 cups (approximately) well-flavored chicken broth
½ pound chicken livers
Salt and freshly ground pepper
1 tablespoon grated onion
Mayonnaise
Bread or Toast

I first remember this sandwich in a delightful small restaurant in the Northwest where it was a luncheon feature. Soon it was copied by other restaurants, but as usual, without the same success. The original had one or two secrets undiscovered by the imitators.

Cook the gizzards and hearts in broth to cover. When they are just tender, in about 30 minutes, add the livers and correct the seasoning. The livers will take no longer than about 4 or 5 minutes to cook. Drain well and chop while the ingredients are still warm, discarding fat and gristle around the gizzards. Season with the grated onion and enough well-seasoned mayonnaise to bind. Keep warm. Spread generously on hot toast and serve warm; or use untoasted bread, spread the outer sides of the sandwich with butter, and sauté slowly until the bread is crisp and brown on both sides.

Turkey Sandwich

Turkey can be used in any of the fashions suggested for chicken. It lacks the delicacy of chicken but is very agreeable if it has not been overcooked to the dry stage.

Tuna Fish Sandwich

Canned flaked tuna is without doubt one of the all-time favorites as a sandwich spread. It is almost always combined with mayonnaise. The most common formula uses 4 parts tuna to 1 part finely chopped celery — the celery content increases in more modest restaurants — bound with mayonnaise and sometimes including a bit of onion and a little chopped egg. It should make a quite thick, flavorful paste. Spread generously on white or rye bread or on toast.

Here are other combinations:

(1) Tuna, hard-boiled egg, and chopped chives, mixed with mayonnaise (a favorite Southern version).

(2) Tuna, chopped celery, a little pickle relish, and mayonnaise.

(3) Tuna, a tiny bit of grated apple, chopped celery, and mayonnaise.

(4) Tuna, finely chopped green pepper, finely chopped celery, and mayonnaise.

Salmon Sandwich

Salmon, fresh or canned, can be used in much the same way as tuna, although for some reason it has never achieved the same status as a sandwich spread.

Smoked Salmon (Lox) and Cream Cheese. This combination, served on rye bread or on bagels, is one of the highly popular delicatessen sandwiches. It can be excellent, depending on the quality of the salmon. A little chopped fresh dill makes an agreeable additive.

Sardine Sandwich

Canned sardines have long been imported from Portugal, Norway, and France, but in the last twenty years American sardines have become a contender for the market. Whatever its source, the sardine is a perennial favorite for filling sandwiches, in any of the following ways:

(1) Arrange whole sardines on a slice of buttered rye bread, and serve open-faced with a second buttered slice beside it. This is often accompanied by a slice of hard-boiled egg and a half lemon.

(2) Serve the sardines in their tin, along with buttered rye slices, so that one can make his own sandwiches. This is frequently done in restaurants.

(3) Mash sardines, blend with lemon juice and some of the oil from the tin, and serve on thin, buttered white bread with a thin slice of onion.

(4) Top sardines with sliced eggs, and add mayonnaise.

Anchovy Sandwich

An old favorite consists of anchovy fillets and sliced eggs on white toast, sprinkled with a touch of lemon juice. For a more interesting sandwich, combine anchovy fillets with scrambled eggs, chopped parsley, a touch of lemon juice, and, if you like, a thin slice of onion. Serve hot on well-buttered toast or toasted English muffins or buns.

Lobster, Shrimp, or Crabmeat Sandwiches

For sandwiches, lobster, shrimp, or crabmeat is best chopped. To every cup of the chopped meat, add 3 to 4 tablespoons well-flavored mayonnaise and, if you like, ¼ cup finely chopped celery. A little mustard added to the mayonnaise gives the flavoring an extra lift. Serve on buttered white bread or soft rolls. These sandwiches are excellent for luncheon, a supper snack, or summer eating, but are not recommended for carrying to picnics, since seafood and mayonnaise both spoil easily in hot weather.

Egg Sandwich

Fried Egg Sandwich. A fried egg sandwich has been a steady diner item over the years. It is just what it says it is — a fried egg, usually served on white bread or a toasted bun. It is filling and good, and safe to order in strange or doubtful little restaurants.

Egg Salad Sandwich. Egg salad is a sandwich filler that vies with tuna for popularity. Combine chopped hard-boiled eggs with chopped green pepper or chopped pimiento or both, chopped celery, and mayonnaise. Serve on white, whole wheat, or rye bread, or on toast. A little crumbled crisp bacon may also be added.

Sliced Egg Sandwich. Sliced hard-boiled egg served on rye or whole-wheat bread or protein bread toast is excellent. Mayonnaise is a necessity. Other delicious additions are sliced tomato, thinly sliced onion, sardines, or anchovies.

Cucumber Sandwich

These are usually enjoyed by everyone except the very young. They should be made on thin buttered white or whole wheat bread or on paper-thin rye, first removing the seeds from the cucumbers. Or marinate the cucumbers in sour cream and dill or in equal parts mayonnaise and sour cream, with dill added, if you like. The sandwiches should be nicely firm and easily handled. They do not keep, because of the high moisture content, and should be eaten before they become soggy.

Tomato Sandwich

Tomato sandwiches should be made on thin, lightly buttered white or whole wheat bread. Slice the tomatoes thin, drain briefly on absorbent paper, and salt and pepper to taste. Or peel, seed, and chop the tomatoes and spread on buttered bread, adding salt and pepper or just a hint of mayonnaise. Trim the crusts. Do not allow the sandwiches to stand too long, for they quickly become soggy.

Onion Sandwich

Few sandwiches are better than thinly sliced onions on good buttered homemade bread as a snack or as an accompaniment to other food. Or chop the onion, and blend with mayonnaise and a little chopped parsley. As an accompaniment for cold meats or chicken — especially for picnics — make sandwiches of very thin bread, well buttered, and salted slices of onion.

Cheese Sandwich

A slab of Cheddar or Swiss cheese on buttered bread makes a dry, uninteresting sandwich, it seems to me. However, when the sandwich is toasted or sautéed in butter long enough to melt the cheese, it becomes quite another dish.

(1) Butter slices of white or light rye bread, add slices of Cheddar or Swiss cheese, and spread with good mustard. Close the sandwich and butter the outside. Sauté gently on both sides till the bread is crisp and brown and the cheese melted.

(2) Spread one slice of lightly toasted bread with butter and top with cheese. Place under the broiler just long enough to melt the cheese. Top with another slice of toast.

(3) Shred 1½ cups Cheddar, jack, or Swiss cheese. Combine with 1 teaspoon mustard, 1 teaspoon pickle relish or 1 tablespoon chutney, and ½ cup mayonnaise. Mix well, spread on slices of toast, and melt cheese under the broiler. Top with toast.

Cottage Cheese Sandwich

Cottage cheese make good sandwich fillings when mixed with savory additives, such as any of the following, to be added to 1 cup cottage cheese:

(1) Three tablespoons chopped chives, 1 tablespoon chopped parsley, and salt and pepper to taste.

(2) Three tablespoons chopped gherkin, 2 tablespoons chopped onion, and 1 tablespoon chopped parsley.

(3) A quarter-cup each of chopped ripe olives, chopped stuffed olives, and chopped pecans.

(4) Three tablespoons each of chopped onion and chopped red or green pepper, with salt and freshly ground pepper to taste.

Hero Sandwich (Grinder, Submarine Sandwich, Sub)

Hero sandwiches have become a national dish in the last ten years. Basically Italian, the sandwiches are made with loaves of Italian bread of varying sizes. One shop in New York makes them

6 feet long. For the most part, though, the loaves are 10 to 14 inches long, split, and sometimes buttered.

Naturally the contents draw on Italian delicatessen to a great extent — salami, capocollo, prosciutto, mortadella, provolone, Italian peppers, baked peppers, crushed olives, and sliced meatballs, among other items. They are constructed in quite fantastic proportions, and there are no fixed combinations. Imitation heroes are made with boiled ham, chopped cabbage, shredded lettuce, and processed cheese, generally pretty dreadful, and one now sees veal cutlet heroes and filet of sole heroes advertised. Apparently anything goes. The only unvarying element in a hero, then, is the loaf of Italian bread. Taking the cue from the trend, you can proceed to make up any wild combination of your own.

Do not prepare heroes in advance for a picnic or similar outing. They do not keep well but become soggy. Instead, carry the bread and delicatessen items separately, and make the sandwiches on the spot.

Po' Boy Sandwich

These sandwiches were typical of New Orleans in the late nineteenth and early twentieth century and were probably sandwiches made up when hungry people begged for food. They were made with a New Orleans French loaf (which resembles the bread of the West Indies more than anything else), split and filled with meats, cheeses, and sometimes fish and relishes. They were as elastic in content as the hero is today.

Picnic, Lunch Box, or Tea Sandwiches

The following are some of the established sandwiches packed daily in lunch boxes or produced for more special occasions:

(1) Chopped stuffed olives and walnuts (about ¾ cup of each) well mixed.

(2) Chopped stuffed olives blended with ½ cup cream cheese — about 1½ cups olives to ½ cup cheese.

(3) A half-cup each of chopped raisins and walnuts blended with 1 cup cream cheese and a little heavy cream.

(4) A half-cup each of chopped preserved ginger and walnuts, on nut bread or Boston brown bread.

(5) Chopped chutney, chopped almonds, and cream cheese.

(6) Jelly or jam on lightly buttered white bread — long a standby for tea, luncheon, and snacks for children.

(7) Cream cheese and jelly or jam or marmalade has a never-wavering public. The bread — white, rye, or whole-wheat — is heavily encrusted with cream cheese and sometimes butter, as well

as the jelly or jam of one's choice. Sometimes nuts are sprinkled on to make a very super combination sandwich.

(8) Peanut butter. There are other nut butters, but the most popular sandwich of all without any doubt is peanut butter and jelly. It is the ideal luncheon of the younger younger set and lasts far into teens and youth for many people. The bread can be buttered or not. Other combinations with peanut butter are crumbled bacon, bananas, mayonnaise — but it is peanut butter and jelly that wins all the way.

Dainty Sandwiches

At the other end of the spectrum from the heroes and po' boys are the little sandwiches sometimes called "reception sandwiches," so popular from the turn of the century up to the end of the First World War, lingering to some degree until the present time. The idea was to combine color, charm, and daintiness, and I must confess that some of the rolled sandwiches, notably those made with asparagus or watercress, are utterly delicious.

Rolled sandwiches were the favorites. To make them requires unsliced soft bread with crusts removed, cut in slices lengthwise. They may be made from 1½ to 2½ inches wide. Spread the slices with a filling, and roll. Wrap in wax paper or secure with toothpicks (in the Edwardian era they were tied with dainty silk ribbons). Then chill in the refrigerator to firm the roll for slicing. One secret for keeping the rolled sandwich intact is to use softened butter (not melted), which will penetrate the bread and harden nicely during refrigeration. Below are a few suggestions for fillings:

(1) Thin slices of smoked salmon sprinkled with lemon. The pink of the salmon contrasts nicely with the bread.

(2) Chopped watercress and mayonnaise, with sprigs of watercress stuck in either end of the roll just before serving.

(3) Cooked asparagus tips with mayonnaise, rolled into the sandwiched with the tips protruding.

(4) Chopped nuts, chopped olives, and cream cheese.

(5) Chopped pimientos and chopped almonds with a little binding of mayonnaise.

(6) Deviled ham, tongue, or chicken.

(7) Chopped dates, chopped toasted filberts, and chopped raisins.

Sandwich Loaves

The sandwich loaf is an innovation of the twentieth century. It is used primarily for feeding a large number of people, and it can be quite good or quite horrid. Its principle is simply one of cutting long loaves of bread lengthwise into slices, adding a filling between the slices, then cutting the loaf crosswise into serving portions. One can use either a square loaf of bread, known as Pullman bread, 12 to 14 inches long, with crusts removed, which will yield perhaps six slices lengthwise; or a round loaf, which will yield 4 to 6 slices 9 to 10 inches in diameter. White bread and rye or whole wheat can be alternated if the slices are of identical size.

Each layer may be spread with a different filling, or two fillings may be alternated throughout. The fillings should be reasonably firm to prevent the slices from slipping when the loaf is cut for serving. Once the entire loaf is assembled it is iced with a cream cheese mixture, sometimes piped through a rosette pastry tube to make an elaborate pattern or decorated with carved vegetables. If done in a tailored fashion, the loaf can be very handsome; otherwise it can resemble nothing so much as a creation for the Thursday afternoon Chew and Chat Society.

Suggested fillings for sandwich loaves — choose two or three, and alternate them.

(1) Deviled ham.

(2) Chopped chicken paste.

(3) Shrimp salad (the shrimps should be finely chopped).

(4) Crab salad (the crab should be in smallish pieces).

(5) Deviled tongue or chopped tongue with mayonnaise and horseradish.

(6) Olives and nuts with mayonnaise.

(7) Cottage cheese or cream cheese with chives.

(8) Liverwurst with mustard.

(9) Chopped cold pork with mayonnaise and mustard.

(10) Chopped green pepper and cream cheese or mayonnaise.

(11) Thinly sliced onion, mayonnaise, and chopped parsley.

(12) Chopped pimientos, chopped green chilies, and cream cheese.

Butter the bread, fill with the mixtures, and press the layers together well. Ice with cream cheese mixed with enough heavy cream or sour cream to make a good spreading consistency. Decorate with cheese forced through a pastry bag fitted with a large rosette tube. Garnish with olives, pickles, or nuts in any pattern you like. Chill well before serving. Cut a square loaf into slices and a round loaf into thin wedges, and serve along with a salad or with various finger vegetables and pickles.

A Rye and White Bread Sandwich Loaf. This makes a little hardier fare than the preceding loaf, but is prepared, iced, and cut in the same way. Again, it is wise to avoid fillings that will cause the layers to slip. Any of the following will work extremely well.

(1) Chopped corned beef, chopped onion, and chopped pickles, moistened with a small amount of mayonnaise.

(2) Crumbled crisp bacon, chopped hard-boiled eggs, and mayonnaise.

(3) Thinly sliced salami.

(4) Thinly sliced summer sausage.

(5) Chopped peppers, chopped celery, chopped olives, and mayonnaise.

(6) Tuna fish, chopped anchovies, chopped onion, and a tiny bit of chopped celery.

(7) Thinly sliced bologna or mortadella.

(8) Thinly sliced smoked salmon, chopped onion, dill, and mayonnaise.

(9) Mashed sardines, mashed hard-boiled eggs, lemon juice, and capers.

(10) Chopped anchovies, chopped eggs, and mayonnaise.

Pickles and Preserves

Salting and drying food, and the use of "root" cellars for storing such garden produce as cabbage, squash, winter apples, potatoes, and other root vegetables, were necessary for survival in early America, particularly in the colder climates. Only in old diaries and letters are there references to these methods of food preservation. Since every household knew how to stock its own larder, apparently it was not deemed necessary to publish directions for this in cookbooks. It was not until sugar became generally available that jams, jellies, conserves, and marmalades were introduced to cookbooks on any scale. The same is true of pickles and relishes, although in many early cookbooks one finds directions for these handwritten on flyleaves and on notes tucked between the pages.

The advent of glass canning jars that could be easily sealed added new chapters to late nineteenth-century cookbooks. This was during an era when most families, climate permitting, grew a few fruit trees and a home garden. By the beginning of the twentieth century, commercial canners had taken over much of the food preservation for urban dwellers, and glass canning jar companies began supplying homemakers with more advanced and more precise instructions than could be found in cookbooks.

Fewer and fewer chapters on food preservation appear now in

books, although since World War II we have added freezing to home techniques for food preservation.

We give here some of the specialties of pickle, relish, and jam making that are still favored in many parts of the United States. Some of these recipes are very old, but also included are new methods of making jams, considered by many to be excellent in flavor, as well as easy to prepare.

To Sterilize Jars

Place the jars on an oven rack 1 inch apart, turn the oven to 250 degrees, and let the jars remain 20 to 25 minutes. Or place the jars upside down in about 4 inches of boiling water and let boil gently 6 to 8 minutes.

To Pack and Seal Jars

Unless the recipe indicates otherwise, use jars with vacuum-seal metal disk tops and screw bands. Place the hot sterilized jars on a rack over a surface that will not be harmed by heat or spills. Fill to within 1/4 inch of the top, or, if the recipe has pickling liquid, pack the jar first with the pickles, then pour the hot pickling liquid up to 1/4 inch of the top. Wipe the sealing edge of each jar clean. Dip the metal disk lid in boiling water and place on the jar. Screw the sealing band on tight. Allow the jars to cool overnight away from drafts. If they must be moved from the rack, put them on a wooden surface or a surface heavily padded with paper towels. When thoroughly cool, test the seal by turning the jar upside down and checking for leakage. Wash the jars clean, and store.

It is imperative that the jars and lids be as hot as possible when you are filling jars, since without heat there will be no vacuum.

Six-Minute Strawberry Preserves

6 cups whole strawberries
6 cups sugar
2 to 4 tablespoons lemon juice

Easily made, this, along with sunshine strawberry preserves, has been popular for years.

Hull firm-ripe, medium to large strawberries. Measure into a colander and wash by rinsing up and down in cool water. Never let water run over the berries. Drain, place the colander with the berries in a large bowl or pan and cover with boiling water. Let stand 1 minute and drain very well. (This will allow the berries to absorb the sugar more readily.) Turn the berries into a 6 to 8 quart kettle. Add half the sugar and the lemon juice. Bring to a full rolling boil (a rolling boil cannot be stirred down). Boil 3 minutes. Remove from the heat and skim. Add the remaining sugar and again boil 3 minutes. Remove from the heat, skim, and allow the preserves to stand overnight. Push the berries down into the syrup occasionally. Standing overnight allows the berries to absorb more sugar and plumps them. Strawberries grown during a normal season will produce a plump preserve surrounded with a thick, rich red syrup. If the season has been abnormally rainy, the berries might have to be cooked again for a minute or two. When the preserve is completely cold, seal in hot sterilized jars, or use jelly glasses and cover the tops with paraffin. Yields 5 to 6 cups of preserves.

Sunshine Strawberry Preserves

1 to 3 quarts washed, hulled, firm-ripe strawberries
1 to 3 quarts sugar
2 to 6 tablespoons lemon juice (optional)

Strawberries for this should be without blemishes to make a perfect finished product. Use as much sugar as strawberries, and since this makes a very sweet preserve it is advisable to add lemon juice. Layer the measured berries with an equal amount of sugar in a large kettle. Let stand 30 to 60 minutes so the sugar will draw a little juice from the berries. Bring to very slow boil, stirring carefully to be sure that no undissolved sugar is on the bottom of the kettle. Simmer about 5 minutes. Remove to flat sheet cake pans or similar pans or glass baking dishes. Skim if necessary. Cover the pans with panes of glass, nylon net, or mosquito netting. Place in a sunny spot during the daytime. Some people like to keep changing the pans from window to window. In former days the pans were placed on top of the woodpile! The berries should be stirred several times a day. The pans should be returned to the warmth of the kitchen when the sun goes down, for usually dew will collect on the pans, and the idea is to evaporate the liquid until a thick, rich syrup surrounds the plump berries. If there is no sun, place the pans in a very slow oven, 150 to 200 degrees, stirring occasionally until the syrup is as thick as desired. Seal, without heating, in hot sterilized jars.

Apricot Pineapple Conserve

3 cups finely diced apricots
¼ cup orange juice
2 tablespoons lemon juice
1 cup drained crushed or finely diced canned, fresh, or frozen pineapple
½ teaspoon grated orange rind (optional)
3½ cups sugar

Combine all ingredients in a 3 or 4 quart kettle. Stir several times while bringing to slow boil. Boil gently until a few drops poured on a cold plate are thick enough to spread on toast or other bread. Seal immediately in hot sterilized jars. This conserve will not keep when sealed with paraffin.

Note. Firm ripe apricots should be used for this conserve. Some varieties of apricot have a thick skin; if so, the fruit should be dropped into boiling water and left a few seconds until the skins can be loosened easily. The fruit should be put immediately into cold water before the skin is removed.

Fruit Butters

Apples or other fruit (peaches, plums, prunes, pears) — enough to supply 1 quart sieved cooked fruit
1 cup sugar or honey
1 teaspoon powdered cinnamon (optional)
¼ teaspoon powdered cloves (optional)

Back in Colonial America it was a practice to make "butter" from very ripe fruits such as apples, prunes, plums, peaches, pears, grapes and at times even cherries. If no sugar or honey was available, the fruit alone furnished the sweetness of this favorite spread.

Butters often were made in large copper kettles over open fires in the backyard, constantly stirred with a long wooden paddle. If made on top of the stove, even constant stirring will sometimes not prevent a slight scorch. For that reason the oven method of cooking down is recommended. Often it was still further cooked down and dried into a popular early candy (see fruit leather, page 832).

The basic recipe below is for apple butter, and directions for other fruits follow.

Place the prepared raw apples (see below) in a kettle, and add about 1 inch of water, cider, or apple juice for every 4 to 6 inches of apples. Cover the kettle and simmer the fruit until it is tender. Put it through a food mill or colander, then measure, and turn into a large baking pan or pans. Add the sugar or honey and, if desired, spice. Stir well to combine. Place in a 300-degree oven. Stir every 20 to 30 minutes until thick. Spoon boiling hot into hot sterilized jars, and seal.

To Prepare the Fruit

Apples can be peeled, if you like, but usually they are simply washed and quartered, and the core, stem, and blossom end removed.

Peaches must be peeled and pitted before cooking.

Plums of some kinds have a very acrid skin that will give rather a bitter flavor to the plum butter. Therefore, it is better, before cooking, to drop the plums into boiling water a few seconds, then into cold water, so that the skins can be removed easily. They must be pitted, too.

Prunes do not need to be skinned. Cook with a small amount of water before sieving.

Pears are sometimes put through a food mill without being peeled; however, they should first be quartered and the stem, blossom end, and core removed.

Pear Butter. If you like, flavor with ½ teaspoon powdered ginger instead of cinnamon and cloves. Brown sugar can be used instead of white (about 1¼ cups of firmly packed brown sugar per quart of pulp).

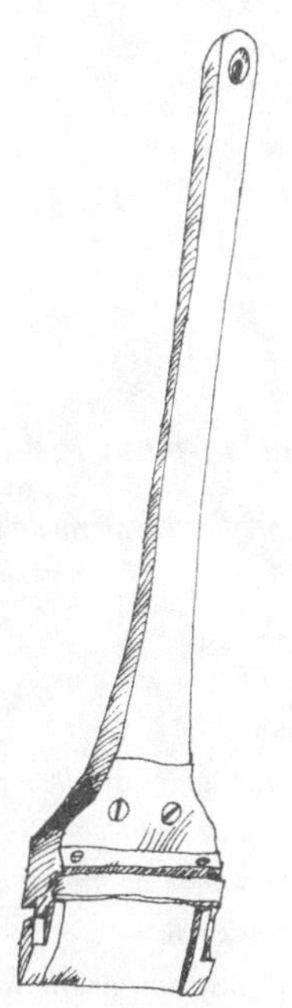

Uncooked Frozen Jams

These jams, made with powdered pectin, are easily prepared and require no cooking. They are preserved by freezing, and are

notable for their fresh fruit flavor. Fresh or frozen berries are especially favored for this type of jam, as well as peaches, sour cherries, plums, prunes, and grapes. Since pectin brands vary in their methods for making uncooked jams, it is best to follow the directions found in each package. Here are a few additional suggestions.

Blenders are excellent for mashing fruits. Or mash fruit into a pint or quart measure and cut across several times with a paring knife. Turn into the large bowl of the electric mixer, break up with the blades of the mixer, then stir in the pectin, sugar, and other ingredients.

Ingredients should be warmed to room temperature or slightly warmer, and many pectins call for the jam to be heated to about 98 degrees. Placing the bowl of ingredients in a 120-degree oven (the temperature for warming plates) and stirring occasionally works very well, especially when you are making more than one recipe at a time.

When filling jars for freezing, be sure to leave room for expansion. Any sturdy jar can be used for the freezing, but baby and junior food jars, which hold 1 cup, are convenient, especially for gifts.

Frozen jams do not have to be stored in the freezer. The freezing will make them more firm, but if storage is a problem, after being left to freeze for several days they can be stored in the back of the refrigerator.

Watermelon Rind Pickles

4 quarts prepared watermelon rind cubes
½ cup salt
1 teaspoon powdered alum
Cold water
3 cups white wine vinegar or white distilled vinegar
2 sticks cinnamon or 3 or 4 drops oil of cinnamon
1 rounded teaspoon whole cloves (about 16 cloves) or 1 or 2 drops oil of cloves
3 cups white sugar

In these days of thinner watermelon rinds, it will take one very large or two small melons to yield the amount of rind called for in the recipe.

To prepare the rind, cut away all of the outside green, leaving a bare rim of red inside, and cut into ½-inch (or up to ¾-inch) cubes. Measure, and place in a large glass, plastic, or crockery mixing bowl. Mix the salt and alum together very well. Add about 1 quart cold water and stir well to dissolve the salt. Pour over the rind, then add enough more water to cover it. The cubes will float, so it is best to weight them down with a plate. Let stand at least 8 hours or up to 24 hours. Drain well and rinse for several minutes under cold running water. Drain well again. Bring the vinegar to boil in 8-quart kettle. If using whole spices, tie them in cheesecloth or other thin cloth bag and simmer in the vinegar 10 minutes. The amount of oil of spice used will depend upon its strength, which often varies, and upon your taste. Therefore it is best to use very little at first.

Add 1 cup sugar to the vinegar, stir well, and add the watermelon rind. Bring just to simmer. Remove from the heat and let stand off the range until cool. Add another cup of sugar and again bring just to the boil. Again remove from the heat and let cool. Now taste for sweetness. This amount of sugar will give a sour-sweet flavor. If more sugar is desired, after the melon has cooled, add the last cup of sugar and again bring to the boil. Remove the spice bag and simmer the rind just until it looks translucent. Stir occasionally to make sure all the watermelon cubes are cooking. Seal in hot sterilized jars. Yields 4 pints.

Oil or Olive Oil Pickles

10 fresh cucumbers about 4 inches long
2 to 4 medium-size onions
½ cup salt
1 teaspoon alum
Vinegar
Olive or salad oil
2 tablespoons celery seed
2 tablespoons mustard seed

These appear in almost every cookbook of the late nineteenth century and the early twentieth. They were especially savored as a treat for company.

Wash the cucumbers well and remove any wax with hot water and vigorous rubbing. Cut into thin slices — they do not have to be paper-thin, but should not be over ¼ inch thick. Peel and slice the onions, mix with the cucumbers in a large bowl, and sprinkle with the salt and alum that have been well mixed together. Let stand in a cool place overnight. In the morning drain well and rinse well, put back in the bowl, and pour over enough vinegar to just cover the vegetables. Let stand 1 to 4 hours. Again drain, saving the vinegar. Measure the vinegar into a kettle, and for each cup add 2 tablespoons olive oil or salad oil. Mix in the celery seed and mustard seed. Bring to a boil. Pack and seal in hot sterilized jars. These should stand a week before using. Yields about 5 pints.

Dill Pickles

2 quarts fresh cucumbers, 3 to 4 inches long
4 to 8 heads and stems of dill
1 to 2 tablespoons mixed pickling spices
1 clove garlic or more, split
Peeled pickling onions or slices of dry onion
2 to 3 tablespoons salt
Cold water
1 cup vinegar

Although our forebears didn't realize it, this all-time favorite pickle was a good source of vitamin C during long cold northern winters. Dill pickles, like sauerkraut, were fermented and stored in crocks or barrels. While damp climates and the lack of a "cool cellar" makes natural fermentation and large-scale storage of any pickle impractical, many people still like to make dill pickles in fruit jars with a vinegar brine (note pack method below). In the first (cold-pack) recipe, the pickles ferment.

Wash the cucumbers, prick several times with a fork, and pack into jars — 2-quart, 1-quart, or pint. The cucumbers should not reach past the shoulder of the jar. Add the dill, pickling spices, garlic, and onion. Sprinkle with salt. (If making pickles in a damp climate, it is best to use 3 tablespoons.) Fill each jar to the halfway mark with cold water, add vinegar, then fill to within a half-inch of the top with more cold water. Place a metal disk lid on and screw the band down until almost tight. Leave in the kitchen or other warm place until the pickles start to ferment — shown by bubbling activity. When they are through fermenting, you will notice a cessation of activity. Tighten the screw bands and store.

Hot-Pack Dill Pickles. Pack the washed and pricked cucumbers and seasonings in a sterilized jar (or jars). Place on a rack in a hot sterilizing container. Bring to a boil 1 cup vinegar, 3 cups water, and 1/4 cup pickling salt (without filler) or 1/4 cup plus 1 tablespoon table salt. Pour slowly over the cucumbers to within a half-inch of the top, and seal. These pickles will not "work" or ferment like the cold-pack, so they can be stored immediately. They will not be good to eat until the flavors have blended, in about 6 weeks.

Sweet Dill Pickles. Allow dill pickles to stand at least 6 weeks — longer if possible. Cut into long strips or slice in 1/2-inch to 1-inch pieces. Pack not too tightly into hot sterilized jars. Add sliced sweet onion, if you wish. Mix 1 cup vinegar and 1 3/4 cups white sugar until the sugar is dissolved. Pour over the pickles and seal. These should stand a week before using.

Bread and Butter (Old-Fashioned Sliced) Pickles

6 quarts cucumbers 3 to 4 inches long, measured after slicing about 1/4 inch thick
6 medium-size onions, sliced
1 cup salt
6 cups vinegar
6 cups sugar
1 teaspoon turmeric
1/2 cup mustard seed
1 tablespoon celery seed
1/4 to 1/3 teaspoon cayenne pepper

Recipes for these vary from one section of the United States to another, but commercial producers have made this easy-to-prepare version so popular that many homemakers use the same formula. Those with an abundance of very small zucchini in their gardens can substitute this vegetable for the cucumbers.

Pickling cucumbers are best for this, but the usual table cucumbers can be used if they are quite firm. The long ribbed cucumbers variously called Armenian, Belgian, Syrian, and, so on, are also good. Wash the cucumbers well, remove the blossom and stem ends, and slice on a cutting board with a chef's knife, or preferably with a "kraut" or slicing board. Place with the sliced onions in a large bowl or roasting pan, sprinkle with the salt, and mix thoroughly. Allow to stand 3 to 6 hours. Drain well, and rinse well under cold water. Taste for salt. If excessively salty, rinse some more, or cover with cold water, let stand a few minutes, then drain. Prepare 9 or 10 sterilized pint jars. (To sterilize, place on an oven rack 1 inch apart, turn the oven to 250 degrees, and let the jars remain 20 to 25 minutes. Or place upside down in about 4 inches of boiling water and let boil gently 6 to 8 minutes.) Bring the remaining ingredients to a boil in a large kettle, about 8-quart capacity. Add the cucumbers and onions and bring just to the simmering point. Do not let the mixture boil, or it will make the finished pickles limp. Immediately fill the hot sterilized jars to within 1/4 inch of the top. Wipe the sealing edges with a clean, damp cloth, dip the metal disk lids in boiling water and place on top. Seal with the screw bands. Allow to cool overnight, remove the bands, test the seal, wash jars and store. Yields 8 to 10 pints.

Zucchini Sliced Pickles. Use small zucchini, not more than 6 to 7 inches long and very firm. Slice and proceed as above. For firmer slices, combine 1 teaspoon powdered alum (available at drugstores) with the salt before mixing it in.

Lazy Housewife (Sour) Pickles

8 quarts fresh pickling cucumbers about 3 inches long
2 cups pickling salt (salt without filler)
Water to cover
4 quarts cider vinegar
1 to 4 cups sugar
1 cup salt
1/4 to 1 cup powdered mustard

These are very sour and often very, very hot, depending upon the amount of mustard used. Like many pickles, these were stored in crocks in the "cool cellar" in the old days. With today's accommodations, these are best put in jars.

Wash the cucumbers well. Do not peel or slice. Place in a large bowl or utensil such as a plastic dishpan. Sprinkle with the pickling salt and cover with cold water. Stir carefully to distribute the salt. Let stand 24 hours. Drain, rinse, and pack the cucumbers into hot sterilized jars. Bring the remaining ingredients to a boil, pour over the cucumbers to within 1/4 inch of the jar tops, and seal. Yields 7 to 8 quarts.

Pickled Onions

4 quarts small white pickling onions
1 cup salt
Cold water
6 cups white wine vinegar or 4 cups white wine vinegar and 2 cups dry white wine
2 cups sugar
1/4 cup mixed pickling spices (optional)

Even before the advent of the Gibson cocktail, pickled onions were considered quite a delicacy. Now we often make them with white wine vinegar, and they are even better eating.

Bring about a gallon of water to boil in a large kettle. Add the onions and let stand 5 to 10 minutes. Test occasionally to see if the outer husk will slip from an onion. When it does, immediately drain the onions, pour on cold water, slip them out of the outer skins, and cut away the root ends, but be sure to leave enough root so the onion will not go to pieces. Place the onions in a bowl, sprinkle with the salt and cover with cold water. Let stand overnight. Drain, and rinse very well with cold water. Bring the vinegar (and wine if used) and sugar to a boil. If spices are to be used, tie in cheesecloth and simmer in the mixture about 10 minutes. Have ready 5 or 6 sterilized pint jars, or preferably half-pint jars. Bring the onions just to a simmer. Do not boil. Pack the onions in the jars, fill to within 1/4 inch of the top with the hot vinegar solution, and seal.

Piccalilli

5 pounds of green tomatoes sliced

Slice the tomatoes rather thin and let them stand overnight with the salt. In the morning, wash off the salt and add the pickling spices, sliced onions, brown sugar, and vinegar. Cook very slowly

1 cup salt
3 ounces mixed pickling spices tied in a bag
6 large onions, sliced
1 pound brown sugar
8 cups mild cider vinegar

until tender. Ladle into sterilized jars and seal. If you find you have a great deal of liquid, let it simmer a little longer to reduce the quantity. This makes about 12 pints.

Mustard Pickles

4 cups green tomatoes cut in wedges (about 3 to 4 pounds)
About 50 small white onions
3 red peppers
1½ pounds whole green beans
1 large cauliflower broken into small flowerets
6 carrots cut into long thin strips
1 cup salt
8 cups mild cider vinegar
6 cups sugar
7 tablespoons dry mustard
1 cup flour
1½ tablespoons turmeric
1½ ounces pickling spices

Cut all the vegetables into pieces (the green beans may be just cut at either end), place them in enough water to cover, and add the salt. Let stand overnight. In the morning, boil 10 minutes and strain. Combine the vinegar, sugar, mustard, flour, turmeric, and spices, and heat with enough water to make a smooth paste. Pour this over the vegetables and pour into jars and seal. Makes 8 pints. If you wish to keep the vegetables very crisp, add a small amount of alum to each jar. Do not overcook.

Chow Chow

6 large cucumbers
6 large onions
1 small head firm cabbage
1 head cauliflower
About 50 smallish green tomatoes
1 red pepper
1 cup salt
3 tablespoons pickling spices tied in a cheesecloth bag
1 tablespoon mustard seed
1 tablespoon celery seed
2 cups white sugar
About 1½ quarts cider vinegar

Chop the vegetables very fine, mix together, and cover with the salt. Let stand overnight. Drain. Place in a large kettle and add the pickling spices. Combine the rest of the ingredients, pour over the chopped vegetables, bring to a boil, and simmer ½ hour. Fill sterilized jars and seal.

Chutney

1½ cups cider vinegar
2 to 2½ cups firmly packed light brown sugar
5 cups peeled, pitted, and chopped firm ripe fruit
1 medium-size lemon cut in thin slices or seeded and chopped
1 large or 2 small cloves garlic, peeled and chopped
⅓ cup peeled chopped green gingerroot or ½ cup chopped candied or preserved crystallized ginger
1½ cups seeded raisins
1 teaspoon salt
¼ teaspoon ground cayenne pepper
1 cup chopped onion (optional)
¾ cup red sweet bell pepper, seeded and chopped (optional)

The "India trade" brought curried dishes to seaports in America, with a consequent taste also for the condiments to accompany the curries. Ginger, the essential flavoring of chutney, was originally used as a powder, or the dried root was soaked and simmered. More and more supermarkets now carry the green gingerroot, and it is, of course, available in Oriental markets. For this recipe, preserved or candied ginger can also be used.

Bring the vinegar and brown sugar to a boil. Add the fruit and bring to simmer. Add the remaining ingredients. Again, bring just to simmer, turn off the heat, and allow to cool. This will plump the fruit and give it a chance to absorb the flavors and the sugar. Simmer until as thick as desired, fill hot sterilized jars to within about ¼ inch from the top, and seal.

Peach Chutney. Resembles the mango chutney generally used in India.

Apple, Pear, or Green Tomato Chutney. Use very firm apples such as Newtown Pippins or other winter apples, or use apples slightly on the green side. Peel, quarter, core, slice, and measure. The slices should be about ¼ inch thick and 1 inch long. Also use pears on the green side so the slices will remain firm. Scald green tomatoes with boiling water or immerse in boiling water until the skin will peel off readily. Place in cold water, peel, cut in half, squeeze out the seeds, cut in small pieces, and measure. For the apple or green tomato chutney, you may add more ginger and more garlic.

Chili Sauce

About 24 large ripe tomatoes
3 large or 5 small red peppers
4 green peppers
1 or 2 tiny hot red peppers
1 cup sugar
3 cups vinegar (a good cider vinegar is best)
2 tablespoons salt, or to taste
3 or 4 large onions, finely chopped
2 garlic cloves, fiinely chopped
1 teaspoon ground cloves
2 teaspoons ground ginger
1½ teaspoons ground cinnamon
1½ teaspoons freshly ground pepper

This old favorite is decidedly easy to made if you use good ripe tomatoes. It is an all-round sauce for meats, barbecues, salad dressings, and an endless variety of dishes.

Scald and peel the tomatoes, and chop coarsely. Seed the peppers and chop. Combine everything but the spices in a heavy kettle, bring to a boil, and simmer for 2 hours. Stir occasionally. Fifteen minutes or so before the sauce is ready, add the spices. Stir well and taste for seasoning and texture. If the sauce seems too thin you may want to cook it down a bit longer.

Pour into hot sterilized jars or bottles and seal. It is best if allowed to ripen for a couple of weeks.

Candy

It is very evident these days that candy making is not the delightful pastime it was when I was young. Taffy pulls and parties where guests made fudge, divinities, and other luscious bits were very common. A dark day was always the signal to make candy, and on such occasions one went to a friend's house after school and messed up the kitchen magnificently making penoche.

At Christmastime people made varieties of candy to pack in "treat boxes" for stockings and to include in gift boxes for friends. I remember a friend of my mother's who made extraordinary chocolates, marshmallows — very fashionable then — and wonderful nougat, redolent with the flavor of nuts and sometimes fruits.

Candies had very modest beginnings in this country. The sugaring-off periods in New England provided one of the principal sweets, maple sugar, and sorghums and molasses were combined with various ingredients for taffies and other simple candies. There was no efficient way to gauge cooking temperatures, essential in candy making, so the techniques for preparing more elaborate candies did not become common until the 1880's, when cookbooks introduced candy or "confectionery" chapters.

Today people settle for fudge mixes and melt chocolate for a form of Rocky Road, and occasionally someone will make a popcorn ball batch. But the tradition of candy making is not what it was —

and more's the pity, too. Just the smell of good candy cooking in the house is enough to warrant the renascence of homemade candy.

Testing Temperature

Not until after World War I were candy thermometers generally available except to the professional candy maker. Before that, the stages — soft ball, hard ball, hard crack, thread, and such — were mentioned in cookbooks in terms vague enough to tax the skill of experienced cooks. Many a batch of candy must have been cooked and recooked if most of the early recipes were faithfully followed, Candy thermometers take the guesswork out of candy making and make it a simple matter to achieve these prescribed conditions for the syrup.

Soft ball stage (234 to 240 degrees). A half-teaspoon of the boiling syrup dropped into a cup of cold water and worked with the fingers will form a soft ball that can be picked up.

Firm ball stage (242 to 248 degrees). A half-teaspoon of syrup dropped into a cup of cold water will form a definitely firm ball.

Hard ball stage (250 to 268 degrees). A half-teaspoon of syrup dropped into a cup of cold water will form a hard ball.

Crack stage (270 to 290 degrees). A half-teaspoon of syrup dropped into a cup of cold water will form a string that will crack when hit on the side of the cup.

Hard crack stage (300 to 310 degrees). A half-teaspoon of syrup poured from a height of about 6 inches into a cup of cold water will form thin, very brittle strings. Some will float off in the air; those that fall in the cup will crack when taken up in the fingers.

Butterscotch

1 cup granulated sugar
1 cup firmly packed light brown sugar
½ cup water
½ cup dark corn syrup
1 tablespoon vinegar
½ cup butter (1 stick)

Old recipes for butterscotch often used brown sugar or part white and part brown sugar. Some contained molasses, some vinegar. This recipe is something of a synthesis, but if you wish, molasses can be substituted for the corn syrup.

Combine the sugars, water, corn syrup, and vinegar in a 3-quart saucepan. Bring to a boil, and wash down the sides of the pan with a pastry brush dipped in water to remove sugar granules. Boil until the hard ball stage (about 260 degrees), then add the butter a quarter at a time, stirring constantly. Continue to stir until the mixture is at a definite crack stage (280 to 290 degrees). Pour out into a buttered pan about 9×9×2 inches or, for thinner pieces of candy, into a slightly larger pan. Mark into squares with a well-buttered knife while the candy is still warm (not hot). Cool, and break into pieces. Work quickly, for the candy is very brittle when cold.

Caramel Corn and Caramel Nuts

3 quarts lightly salted popped corn or 2 quarts popped corn and 3 cups toasted nutmeats
2½ cups firmly packed brown sugar
½ cup light or dark corn syrup
½ cup water
¼ to ½ cup butter
2 teaspoons vanilla

How I used to love various forms of caramel corn, and sometimes I still dip into a can just for nostalgia's sake. This came into national popularity during the 1920's, when seldom anything but the caramel syrup coated the corn. Now there are many fancy names for a mixture of caramelized popcorn and nut meats. The nut meats should be toasted lightly before being covered with the syrup. Place them in a baking pan in a single layer and heat in the oven at 300 degrees 8 to 15 minutes, depending upon the type and size of the nut meat.

Put the popped corn or the corn and nuts in an oiled or buttered mixing bowl and place in an oven heated to about 120 degrees. Oil a large piece of aluminum foil. Measure the sugar, corn syrup, and water into a 3-quart saucepan. Bring to a rolling boil, and wash down the sides of the pan with a pastry brush dipped in water to remove sugar granules. Add the butter and cook to the very hard ball stage (264 to 270 degrees). Stir in the vanilla. Immediately pour into the popped corn and stir well to coat evenly. While the mixture is still very hot, turn out onto the oiled foil, and with two forks pull it apart to make bite-size or slightly larger pieces. Let cool thoroughly, and store in airtight containers or freezer bags.

Cooked Fondant

2 cups sugar
¾ cup water
¼ teaspoon cream of tartar or 1 tablespoon light corn syrup
Flavoring to taste
Coloring (optional)

Used for little flat mints, as the base for chocolate-covered creams, or for frosting the tiny tea cakes or petit fours that were always at hand when "at homes" were considered necessary.

Place the sugar, water, and cream of tartar or corn syrup in a 3-quart saucepan. Bring to a full boil and wash down the sides of the pan with a pastry brush dipped in water to remove all sugar granules. Boil without stirring to the soft ball stage (236 to 238 degrees). Pour out on a marble slab or lightly oiled pan or platter. Let cool to lukewarm. With a broad spatula start turning the mixture from the outside toward the center until it begins to thicken and lose its gloss. Now knead the mixture until it is smooth. Place in a bowl and cover tightly. Let stand overnight or for 5 to 6 hours to allow the fondant to ripen and become very creamy.

When ready to use, put in the top of a double boiler over hot water and stir occasionally until of a consistency to mold into mints or other candy. Add the flavoring of your choice. Also, if you like, add food colors at this point.

For flavoring, use mint (see below) or any of the following: 1 teaspoon vanilla; 1 to 2 tablespoons water or orange juice and 1 to 2 teaspoons finely grated orange rind; 1 teaspoon lemon juice and 1 teaspoon grated lemon rind; 1 teaspoon lemon juice and

¼ cup very well drained and very finely chopped crushed pineapple.

Fruit Fondant. Flavor the fondant with orange or lemon (above). Add chopped candied fruits, and use to fill pitted prunes or dates. Half a walnut or pecan meat is sometimes set on the fondant filling to decorate the fruit.

Mints. Flavor the fondant with a few drops of oil of mint or peppermint, or ¾ teaspoon mint flavoring. Add food coloring, if you like. Pour the fondant onto foil into circles about the size of a quarter, and allow to dry several hours. Then pack between wax paper or foil in an airtight container.

Butter Fondant. This is used mainly for frosting petits fours or filling the centers of chocolate creams. It is made by working 4 tablespoons butter into the fondant after cooking and cooling. Usually this can be incorporated into the creams without first melting, after the ripening period

Petits Fours. Heat the fondant in the double boiler until quite liquid. Flavor (see above), and add coloring if you like. Cut a sponge cake, angel food, or génoise (other cakes are apt to crumble on the edges) into small pieces. Place the pieces of cake so they do not touch each other on cake racks set on cookie sheets, jelly roll pans, or aluminum foil. Pour the fairly liquid fondant over the cakes. You can use a tin can for this operation, with one side bent to make a flat pouring edge, unless you have a flat-spouted pitcher or a mixing bowl with a flat pouring edge. Cover the tops and sides of the cakes completely. The fondant that flows off the cakes can be gathered up, remelted, and used again.

Fruit Paste

2 cups pitted dried prunes
2 cups pitted dates
2 cups pitted dried apricot or peaches
3 tablespoons honey
Coarse granulated sugar, or flaked or shredded coconut, or both

Considered a healthful addition to holidy candy trays, these could also have a cathartic effect, depending upon the fruit used.

Grind the fruit through the medium to coarse blade of a food chopper. Mix well with the honey, and if the mixture seems very dry, add a bit more. Form into long thin rolls. This is easiest done by rolling by hand on wax paper or aluminum foil, first lightly greasing the hands with vegetable oil. Cut off even sections of the roll, and work in the palms of the hands to form balls about ¾ to 1 inch in diameter. Drop into granulated sugar or into flaked or shredded coconut; or drop into sugar, then roll in coconut. Let stand on wax paper, foil, or cake racks to dry before storing between wax paper or foil in airtight containers.

Fruit Leather (Peach, Apple, Prune, Plum, Apricot)

This old-fashioned sweet, made with sweetened fruit sauce cooked down and dried, can still sometimes be purchased in specialty shops. Babies used to teeth on long strips of chewy fruit leather, and it was a favorite sweet for school lunches.

Directions for making fruit leather in old manuscript cookbooks — it is seldom mentioned in printed cookbooks — generally called for cooking down a fruit butter (see the recipe for fruit butters, page 821) until very thick. It was then spread about a half-inch deep on lightly greased hardwood boards or on graniteware or pottery pie plates. These were covered with netting and placed in a sunny spot (usually the woodshed roof) to evaporate further and turn a rich brown. When quite leathery, the mixture was cut in strips and strung on heavy thread to be hung from the kitchen ceiling or in a dry attic. This pioneer candy was welcome during the winter, especially when sugar, sorghum, and honey were difficult to make or purchase.

Divinity Fudge

2 egg whites
2 cups sugar
½ cup light corn syrup
½ cup water
1 teaspoon flavoring — vanilla, orange, lemon, or mint extract
¾ cup candied (not maraschino) cherries cut in rings (optional)
¾ cup coarsely chopped, lightly toasted almonds, walnuts, filberts, or pecans

I loathed divinity fudge when I was young, and I still have no taste for it. But it is certainly one of our most important sweets and therefore belongs in this volume. It used to be considered a holiday candy because sliced candied cherries were folded in the mixture, and earlier in our history it was flavored with vanilla or mint and served as a dainty at fancy teas.

The egg whites should be at room temperature. Pour into a medium-size mixing bowl or the large bowl of an electric mixer. Place the sugar, corn syrup, and water in a 2 or 3 quart saucepan. Bring to a full boil and wash sugar crystals from the sides of the pan with a pastry brush dipped in water. Continue boiling until the syrup is at 254 degrees. In the meantime, beat the egg whites until they will hold peaks that droop very slightly when the beater is lifted out of the mixture.

Slowly beat one-third of the hot syrup into the egg whites. (Use a frilled whip, a French whip, or similar whip if doing this by hand. A rotary beater is not suitable, since the syrup must be poured and beaten into the whites simultaneously. If using an electric mixer, add the syrup at medium speed.) Put the pan of syrup back on the heat, and cook to a firmer stage, 262 degrees. This will take only a few minutes. Continue beating the egg white mixture in the meantime. Slowly beat in the hotter syrup, adding again in a very thin stream at first and gradually increasing the flow. If using an electric mixer, add this second batch of syrup at a higher speed. Continue beating with the mixer or by hand until the mixture begins to be quite creamy and stiff. Add the flavoring of your choice. Fold in cherries, if you like, and nuts. Quickly drop on wax paper or aluminum foil by spoonfuls, or turn out onto foil and cut into serving-size pieces. Store in airtight containers, for this dries rapidly.

Fudge

2 cups sugar
2 tablespoons corn syrup, light or dark
⅔ cup rich milk or evaporated milk
2 to 4 tablespoons butter
¼ teaspoon salt
1 teaspoon vanilla
½ cup coarsely broken or chopped, lightly toasted nutmeats (walnuts, pecans, filberts, almonds, Brazil nuts, etc.)

With the help of a candy thermometer, this, like many other candies, is easily made. Although numbers of people think that fudge comes only in one flavor — chocolate — it is also commonly flavored with vanilla, coconut, or orange, among several variations.

Combine the sugar, corn syrup, milk, butter, and salt in a 3 or 4 quart saucepan. Stir and bring to boil. Wash down the sides of the pan with a pastry brush dipped in water to be sure that all sugar crystals are dissolved. Cook to 234 to 236 degrees. If it is a rainy day and there is much moisture in the air, cook to 238 degrees. It may be necessary to stir the mixture while cooking, but do not splash the candy on the sides of the saucepan for it might granulate later. Pour the mixture out on a marble slab, or place the saucepan on a cake rack to cool.

When the bottom of the pan is cool enough so that the hand can be held on it, start stirring (it is not necessary to beat) the fudge. If using a marble slab, the candy is ready to be worked when you can tolerate putting a greased finger into the center. Using a spatula, keep turning the mixture from the outer edges in toward the center. When it begins to lose its gloss, add the vanilla and nuts, continue to mix. Turn out onto foil, wax paper, or a buttered pan or plate, and while still slightly warm mark into serving-size pieces.

Chocolate Fudge. Add 1 to 2 ounces (squares) of unsweetened chocolate.

Peanut Butter Fudge. Omit the nut meats and butter and substitute ½ cup peanut butter, either the smooth or crunchy type. Add also, if you like, ½ cup roasted peanuts after the fudge has been stirred.

Brown Sugar Fudge. Use either 2½ cups firmly packed brown sugar or 1¼ cups brown and 1 cup white. This will look curdled as it is cooking, but the mixture will become smooth during stirring after it is cooked and slightly cooled.

Sour Cream Fudge. Use 1 cup sour cream instead of the milk in either the vanilla or chocolate fudge recipe.

Orange Fudge. Omit the vanilla. Add 1 to 2 tablespoons grated orange rind, or use orange juice instead of milk.

Candied, Fudged, or Spiced Walnuts, Pecans, or Filberts. Use the brown sugar fudge recipe. For a spicy flavor, add 2 teaspoons ground cinnamon and ½ teaspoon ground cloves while cooking. When the mixture reaches the soft ball stage, remove from the stove and add 2½ to 3 cups lightly toasted walnut or pecan halves or whole filberts. Stir just to coat the nuts. Turn out onto wax paper or foil, and pull the nuts apart with forks to cool.

Fudge Roll. Make any of the fudges above. While still slightly warm, work with the hands and form into rolls about 1 to 1½ inches in diameter. Allow to cool, dip in melted caramels, and roll in coarsely chopped and slightly toasted nutmeats.

Never-Fail Fudge

4 cups sugar
1⅔ cups evaporated milk (14½ ounce-can)
¼ to ½ cup butter
¼ teaspoon salt
12-ounce package semisweet chocolate pieces
4 ounces unsweetened chocolate (optional), cut into small bits
½ pound marshmallows
1 to 2 cups slightly toasted walnuts, pecans, or filberts

For some, the making of fudge without a graininess or "sugar" texture is difficult. This, in a modernized version, is one of the recipes that has been popular for sixty years.

Combine the sugar, evaporated milk, butter, and salt in a 4-quart saucepan. Stir well. Bring to a full rolling boil (that cannot be stirred down) and boil 4 minutes. Have the chocolate and marshmallows ready in a mixing bowl. If you prefer, cut the marshmallows in half with greased scissors, or use tiny ones. Pour the sugar mixture over the marshmallows and chocolate, and stir until they are melted and well blended. Stir in the nuts, and turn into a well-buttered pan about 10 × 14 × 2 inches. Cool at room temperature. This will take about 8 hours to set firmly. Cut into serving-size pieces after cooling. Yields about 4½ pounds candy.

Peanut Brittle

3 cups sugar
1¼ cups white corn syrup
1 cup water
2 tablespoons butter
3 to 4 cups (1 to 1⅓ pounds) unroasted (raw) shelled peanuts
½ teaspoon salt
1 teaspoon baking soda
1 teaspoon vanilla

After sixty years I can still enjoy good peanut brittle and get great satisfaction in making it from scratch. Raw peanuts are always best for this, but roasted nuts can be used as well.

This should be prepared on a marble slab, stainless steel counter top, or 3 or 4 cookie sheets, or in 11 × 15 × ½-inch jelly roll pans. If using a marble slab, have at room temperature, or allow warm tap water to run over it for a few minutes, then dry thoroughly and brush with vegetable oil. If using pans or counter top, rub with oil.

Place the sugar, corn syrup, water, and butter in a 4 to 5 quart kettle. Stir well. Bring to a full rolling boil and wash down the sides of the pan with a pastry brush dipped in water to dissolve all the sugar crystals. Boil until the candy thermometer registers 140 to 145 degrees, then add the peanuts. (If using roasted peanuts, do not add yet.) Continue cooking, stirring occasionally very carefully, until the mixture reaches about 300 degrees. In the meantime, mix the salt, soda, and vanilla. Continue to cook to 315 degrees, stirring occasionally, watching carefully to prevent burning. Remove from the heat. (If using roasted peanuts, add them now, bring to a boil again, and remove from the heat.) At once thoroughly stir in the salt, soda, and vanilla, which will cause the candy to foam up. Quickly turn out the peanut brittle, moving the kettle along the marble slab or counter. If using pans, put only a small amount on each pan. Have a greased spatula handy and spread the peanuts to the edge of each batch of candy. The candy will tend to melt away from the peanuts. Be careful to spread it well. The next steps, turning and stretching the peanut brittle, are important. Many people turn the candy wearing garden gloves that have the fingers and palms oiled. Since this is a very hot candy, don't attempt this step with the bare hands, even if they are oiled. When the edge of the brittle is cool enough to turn up slightly, grasp it and turn it over. Allow it to cool a bit more. Now, with greased hands, stretch the mixture, beginning at the edges, to make it wafer-thin between the peanuts. This is the secret of good brittle. Peanut brittle draws moisture, so when cool it should be stored in an airtight container or in sealed plastic bags. Break it into pieces of a convenient size.

Penoche

3 cups sugar
2 tablespoons corn syrup, light or dark
1½ cups rich milk or evaporated milk
¼ teaspoon salt
3 or 4 tablespoons butter
1 teaspoon vanilla or 1 or 2 tablespoons grated orange rind
½ to 1 cup coarsely chopped or broken lightly toasted walnuts or pecans

Although brown sugar fudge is often called by this name, generally old Southern cooks insist that the flavor and color of penoche must come from caramelized sugar.

Put 1 cup of the sugar into a heavy frying pan over medium high heat. Watch carefully. Have a long-handled spoon or wooden spoon handy to stir the mixture. Place the remaining sugar, half the milk (¾ cup), and the corn syrup, salt, and butter in a 3 to 4 quart saucepan over medium heat. Stir the sugar in the frying pan and have the remaining ¾ cup milk at hand. When the sugar is caramelized to a rich brown, take the pan from the heat quickly. Stir the remaining milk into the hot sugar at arm's length, for it will spatter. Return to the heat and cook and stir until it forms a syrup. Pour into the other sugar mixture that by now should be boiling. Continue boiling until a good soft ball forms in cold water (236 to 238 degrees). Turn out onto a marble slab, or cool in the pan, until about 110 degrees (cool enough on the bottom of the pan to place the hand on it). Stir in the pan with a spoon, or work with a spatula on the slab, folding it inward, until the mixture begins to lose its gloss. Quickly add the flavoring and the nuts. Turn out onto a buttered platter or foil. Mark into serving-size pieces while still warm.

Pralines. Pralines are a Southern specialty that are made in many forms. Sometimes a base of brown sugar fudge is used, but for the most flavorful version usually it is penoche, often made with water instead of milk. To the basic penoche recipe, add 2 cups lightly toasted pecan halves when the syrup is taken from the heat, first allowing the candy to cool about 5 minutes, which will give a smoother and not so sugary product. Stir for only a few minutes, and drop by large spoonfuls onto buttered foil.

Popcorn Balls

3 to 4 quarts lightly salted popped corn
2 cups sugar
½ cup light corn syrup
½ cup water
2 teaspoons vanilla

Middle West pioneers knew the pleasures of eating buttered popcorn, usually popped in the open fireplace. Popcorn balls are favored for trick or treat bags on Halloween, and are now often wrapped in plastic and hung on Christmas trees.

Place the popped corn in a large buttered mixing bowl and put in a warm oven (110 to 120 degrees). Put wax paper or aluminum foil on a counter top. Measure the sugar, corn syrup, and water into a 3-quart saucepan. Bring to a boil and wash down the sides of the pan with a pastry brush dipped in water, to avoid sugar granules. Cook to the hard ball stage (264 to 270 degrees). Remove from the heat and immediately stir in the vanilla. Take the popcorn from oven, and slowly pour the syrup over it while stirring thoroughly with a large long-handled spoon. Butter or oil the hands very well, and as soon as the mixture can be handled without burning, take up enough popcorn into the hands to be pressed into a ball. Space the balls on the wax paper or aluminum foil until cool. Work rapidly so that the syrup will not harden before the balls can be formed. Store in freezer bags or in tightly covered airtight containers, for the syrup will draw moisture and make the popcorn soggy. If to be used for decoration, wrap the popcorn balls in small plastic bags or plastic wrap. This recipe yields about 12 rather good size popcorn balls.

Rocky Road

1 pound milk chocolate
1 tablespoon vegetable oil or 1 ounce cocoa butter
½ pound large marshmallows
1 cup broken, lightly toasted walnuts

Break up the chocolate in the top of a double boiler. Add the vegetable oil or cocoa butter (purchased at drugstores). Place over a small amount of hot water in the bottom of the double boiler; the water should not touch the pan containing the chocolate. Without covering, allow the chocolate to melt, stirring occasionally. Cut the marshmallows in halves or quarters and have at room temperature. The nuts should be at room temperature also. Spread half of the chocolate in a thin layer in the bottom of a well-buttered 9×9×2-inch pan. Sprinkle with the marshmallows and nuts. Spread the remaining chocolate over the top. If you like, save a few nuts and marshmallows to stick into the top layer. Cool overnight or at least 8 hours to firm the chocolate. Cut with an oiled knife into serving-size pieces.

Candied or Crystallized Rose Petals

Candied rose petals or violets were the ultimate in daintiness in the late nineteenth century. They are still used for decorating many desserts, and fragrant rose petals are rather a novelty for floating on a cup of tea.

Select firm petals of deep pink or red roses. Some red petals will crystallize into a faded purple, so you may prefer the pink. It is best to gather the petals early in the morning. Wash and drain very well between towels. Cut the white end of the petal away with a scissors, for this is quite bitter. Dip the petals in white of egg that has been beaten to a light foam with 1 tablespoon water. The petal should be coated on both sides. Drop into granulated sugar and sprinkle with sugar to coat the petal evenly. Lay on cake racks or on aluminum screening, if candying many petals, and allow to dry until rather brittle. Store in airtight containers so that moisture will not get to the sugar. These are sometimes used to decorate the top of small tea cakes or ice cream or are placed in a wreath around a cake.

Candied Violets. These are made the same way, but it is often difficult to get the egg white into the violet. Cut the stems off firm violet blossoms, stick with a pin or sharp end of a round wooden toothpick. Dip the violet in the egg white beaten with water in a cup deep enough to cover the flower. After dipping, be sure to sprinkle sugar into the center of the violet. Dry as for rose petals, and store in airtight containers.

Taffy

3 cups sugar
1 cup water
1 cup light corn syrup
¼ teaspoon salt
4 tablespoons (½ stick) butter
1½ teaspoons vanilla or mint flavoring, or a few drops oil of mint or rum or brandy extract

Except for variations of molasses taffy, taffy recipes were seldom spelled out in old cookbooks. As with many other common "receipts," it was undoubtedly taken for granted that every homemaker would have the formula in her head. "Taffy pulls" were one of the favorite forms of party entertainment for young people from the late eighteenth century up into the twentieth.

Combine the sugar, water, corn syrup, and salt in a 4-quart saucepan. Stir until boiling, and wash down any undissolved sugar from the sides of the pan with a pastry brush dipped in water. Add the butter and continue boiling without stirring until the candy thermometer registers 256 to 264 degrees. The lower temperature will give a chewier taffy, and the higher heat a more brittle product. Turn out on a marble slab or large platter or pan that has been oiled well with vegetable oil. If using a large marble slab, turn out the hot batch into two pools. After a few minutes sprinkle with the flavoring. A few drops of food coloring can also be added to the top of the candy now. Or you may wait until it is being pulled and add several colors.

The edge of the taffy will cool fairly quickly, and when it can be comfortably touched with well-buttered or oiled fingers, turn it inward to form a mass. Taffy is ready to pull as soon as it can be handled, which is usually sooner than expected. It is easier (and more fun) if two pull this large amount together. Have the palms and fingers well greased. You'll probably like the flavor of butter for this, although margarine or vegetable oil can be used. Take the warm, flowing candy up with the fingertips and pull out about 12 inches at first. Quickly turn the candy back from the fingertips of one hand to the other hand, then catch the center and again pull, always with the fingertips. This incorporates air in the mixture and gives its typical texture.

If adding food coloring at this point, pause briefly and put a drop or two of color along the taffy and then flop the mixture over on the color and continue pulling until the color is mixed evenly.

When the taffy is very hard to pull and will hold its shape if laid out on the marble slab or pan, it is ready to break off into pieces, but preferably it should be cut with greased scissors. If making several colors of taffy, you may pull each out until thin and then twist them together. For a completely round candy, like a peppermint candy stick or cane, roll this twisted mixture on the marble slab to make it even. Store taffy in airtight containers, such as cookie tins, between sheets of wax paper or foil, for any moisture in the air will make it quite sticky. It is for this reason that taffy is generally sold with the pieces individually wrapped.

Salt Water Taffy. A feature of shops near the seashore, this is made by merely adding salt to the taffy recipe while cooking it. For this recipe use 1 to 1½ teaspoons.

Vinegar Taffy. Vinegar was the flavoring formerly used when mint or vanilla were unavailable. Add 2 to 4 tablespoons of vinegar to the standard taffy recipe.

Molasses Taffy

1½ cups sugar
1½ cups light molasses
½ cup water
1 tablespoon vinegar
¼ teaspoon salt
3 tablespoons butter
1 teaspoon vanilla or a few drops of oil of peppermint (optional)

This is still in favor, but was especially popular before granulated sugar was readily available.

Combine the sugar, molasses, water, vinegar, and salt in a 4-quart saucepan. Stir until the sugar is dissolved. Cook until boiling and wash down sugar granules from the sides of the pan, using a pastry brush dipped in water. Add the butter and cook without stirring until a candy thermometer registers 268 degrees. Pour out on oiled marble slab or large oiled platter and proceed as for taffy. Often the molasses is the only flavoring used.

Toffee or English Toffee

4 cups sugar
1 cup water
⅓ cup light corn syrup
1 pound (2 cups) butter, cut in 12 to 16 pieces
1 teaspoon salt
½ cup very finely chopped, grated or ground almonds (not roasted)
1 teaspoon vanilla
3 to 6 ounces semisweet chocolate pieces
¼ to ½ cup finely chopped lightly toasted almonds

English toffee seems to have been a glorified import from England, and has been an outstanding candy for generations. I still order pounds of it from Rogers in Victoria, British Columbia, where the tradition is at least seventy years old. Originally, Mr. Rogers made just so much candy each day, and when he sold it he shut the shop in the most independent manner. His heirs maintain the same quality (the Victoria Chocolates from there are unbelievable) but provide quantities usually sufficient for the trade. At any rate, it's one of the better candies in the American tradition.

Place the sugar, water, and corn syrup in a 4-quart kettle. Stir until blended, bring to a full boil, and wash down the sides of the pan with a pastry brush dipped in water. Boil to 280 degrees. Stir in the butter a few pieces at a time, and continue to stir until the butter is blended in. Add the salt, and stir until the temperature reaches 315 degrees. Add the ½ cup of unroasted almonds and continue stirring until the candy registers 320 degrees or slightly below. Immediately remove from the heat, stir in the vanilla, and turn onto an oiled marble slab or two oiled 11 × 15 × ½-inch jelly roll pans. While the candy is still quite hot, mark into squares with an oiled spatula.

It is easiest to spread a thin layer of chocolate on the candy while it is still warm. Melt the chocolate in the top of a double boiler set over warm water. Do not have the water touching the top part of the boiler. Spread the melted chocolate on the candy and sprinkle with the chopped toasted almonds. This candy can also be broken apart into individual pieces, dipped in coating chocolate or in melted semisweet or milk chocolate, and rolled in finely chopped toasted almonds.

Toffee has a better texture if left to mature overnight in a cool dry place. Store in an airtight container.

Reading List and Sources

Abell, Mrs. L. G. *The Skillful Housewife's Book*. New York 1853. 216 pp.

Alcott, William A. *The Young Housekeeper*. Boston 1838. 424 pp.

Allen, Ida Bailey. *Step-by-Step Picture Cook Book*. New York 1952. 247 pp.

American Daughters of Sweden. *Swedish Recipes Old and New*. Chicago 1955. 180 pp.

[Andrews, Julia C.]. *Breakfast, Dinner and Tea: Viewed Classically, Poetically, and Practically*. New York 1859. 351 pp.

Barber, Edith M. *Edith Barber's Cook Book*. New York 1940. 524 pp.

[Beecher, Catharine]. *Miss Beecher's Domestic Receipt Book*. New York 1846. 293 pp.

Bitting, Katherine Golden. *Gastronomic Bibliography*. San Francisco 1939. 718 pp.

Blot, Pierre. *What to Eat, and How to Cook It*. New York 1886. 259 pp.

Blot, Pierre. *Hand-Book of Practical Cookery, for Ladies and Professional Cooks*. New York 1868. 478 pp.

Bostwick, Lucy. *Margery Daw in the Kitchen*. Auburn, New York 1883.

Bradley, Alice. *The Alice Bradley Menu-Cook-Book*. New York 1937. 253 pp.

Brown, Helen. *West Coast Cook Book*. Boston 1956. 443 pp.

Brown, Margaret. *Margaret Brown's French Cookery Book*. Washington, D.C. 1886. 120 pp.

Brown, Susan Anna. *The Book of Forty Puddings*. New York 1882. 52 pp., unnumbered.

Buckeye Cookery and Practical Housekeeping. Marysville, Ohio 1877. 464 pp.

Caron, Pierre. *French Dishes for American Tables*. Translated and edited by Mrs. Frederic Sherman. New York 1886. 231 pp.

Carson, Rachel L. *Fish and Shellfish of the South Atlantic and Gulf Coasts*. Conservation Bulletin #37. Washington, D.C. 1944. 45 pp.

———. *Fishes of the Middle West*. Conservation Bulletin #34. Washington, D.C. 1943. 44 pp.

Castelar Creche Cook Book. Los Angeles 1922. 296 pp.

Chadwick, Mrs. J. *Home Cookery*. Boston 1853, 161 pp.

Charleston Receipts. Collected by the Junior League of Charleston [S.C.]. 1950. 308 pp.

Chase, A. W. *Dr. Chase's Recipes.* Ann Arbor 1866. 384 pp.

Child, Mrs. [Lydia Maria]. *The American Frugal Housewife, Dedicated to Those Who Are Not Ashamed of Economy.* Boston 1836. 130 pp.

Child, Theodore. *Delicate Feasting.* New York 1890. 214 pp.

Circle 3 of the Women's Fellowship. *Moravian Church Cook Book.* Republished with Additions by Circle 5. Wisconsin Rapids, Wisconsin 1964. 206 pp.

Circles 6 and 8, First Presbyterian Church. *The Betty Cowan Cook Book.* Revised edition. St. Joseph, Missouri 1933. 192 pp.

Cooked to Taste: The Junior League of Portland Cookery Book. Oregon 1951.

Cooper, Lenna Frances. *The New Cookery.* Battle Creek, Michigan 1913. 298 pp.

Cornelius, Mrs. [Mary]. *The Young Housekeeper's Friend.* Boston 1846. 190 pp.

Council of Jewish Women. *The Neighborhood Cook Book.* Portland, Oregon 1914. 329 pp.

[Crowen, Mrs. Thomas J.]. *The American System of Cookery.* By a Lady of New York. New York 1847. 431 pp.

Dauzvardis, Josephine J., ed. *Popular Lithuanian Recipes.* Chicago 1967. 128 pp.

Detroit Women's Chapter of the Armenian General Benevolent Union. *Treasured Armenian Recipes.* Detroit 1965. 126 pp.

de Wolfe, Elsie. *Elsie de Wolfe's Recipes for Successful Dining.* New York 1934. 102 pp.

Ellwanger, George H. *The Pleasures of the Table.* New York 1902. 477 pp.

Farmer, Fannie Merritt. *The Boston Cooking-School Cook Book.* Boston 1896. 682 pp.

Florence Crittenton League, The. *Specialty of the House.* New York 1955. 113 pp.

Giger, Mrs. Frederick Sidney, ed. *Colonial Receipt Book.* Philadelphia 1907. 275 pp.

Gilbert, Fabiola C. *Historic Cookery.* New Mexico State College, New Mexico 1914.

Goodfellow, Mrs. *Mrs. Goodfellow's Cookery As It Should Be.* Philadelphia 1865. 362 pp.

Green, Olive. *What to Have for Breakfast.* New York 1905. 283 pp.

Hale, Mrs. S[arah] J[osepha]. *The Good Housekeeper, or The Way to Live Well and to Be Well While We Live.* Boston 1839. 132 pp.

———. *Mrs. Hale's New Cook Book.* Philadelphia 1857. 526 pp.

———. *Receipts for the Millions.* Philadelphia 1857.

Harland, Marion. *Common Sense in the Household.* New York 1881. 546 pp.

———. *The Dinner Year-Book.* New York 1878. 713 pp.

Harvey, Peggy. *Season to Taste.* New York 1957. 288 pp.

Henderson, Mrs. Mary F. *Practical Cooking and Dinner Giving.* New York 1876. 376 pp.

Herter, George and Bertha. *Bull Cook and Authentic Historical Recipes and Practices.* Waseca, Minnesota 1969. 384 pp.

Hibben, Sheila. *The National Cookbook: A Kitchen Americana.* New York 1932. 452 pp.

Hill, Janet McKenzie. *Salads, Sandwiches, and Chafing-Dish Dainties.* Boston 1903. 230 pp.

[Hodgson, Mary]. *The Philadelphia Housewife.* By Aunt Mary. Philadelphia 1855. 64 pp.

Home Institute of the New York Herald Tribune. *America's Cook Book.* New York 1943. 1032 pp.

Howard, Maria Willett. *Lowney's Cook Book.* Boston 1907. 367 pp.

Howland, Mrs. E. A. *The American Economical Housekeeper and Family Receipt Book.* Worcester, Massachusetts 1852. 108 pp.

Ladies Aid Society of the Congregational Church. *Tried and Tested Recipes of Webster City's Best Cooks.* Webster City, Iowa 1916. 121 pp.

Ladies Auxiliary of the Homestead Welfare Club. *A Collection of Traditional Amana Recipes.* Homestead, Iowa 1948. 120 pp.

Ladies of Leavenworth. *The Kansas Home Cook-Book.* Published for the Benefit of the Home for the Friendless. Leavenworth 1874. 264 pp.

Ladies of the Presbyterian Church. *The Logan Cook Book.* Logan, Ohio ca. 1910. 70 pp., unnumbered.

Ladies of Trinity Methodist Episcopal Church. *Pittsburgh Tested Recipes.* Pittsburgh 1885. 178 pp.

Larned, Linda Hull. *One Hundred Picnic Suggestions.* New York 1915. 123 pp.

Lea, Elizabeth E. *Domestic Cookery, Useful Receipts, and Hints to Young Housekeepers.* Baltimore 1856. 310 pp.

Leslie, Miss [Eliza]. *Directions for Cookery, in Its Various Branches.* Philadelphia 1837. 450 pp.

———. *Domestic French Cookery.* Philadelphia 1832. 120 pp.

———. *Miss Leslie's New Cookery Book.* Philadelphia 1857. 662 pp.

———. *New Receipts for Cooking.* Philadelphia 1854. 520 pp.

———. *Miss Leslie's Seventy-five Receipts for Pastry, Cakes, and Sweetmeats.* Boston 1851. 120 pp.

Lincoln, Mrs. D. A. *Mrs. Lincoln's Boston Cook Book.* Boston 1896. 536 pp.

Lowenstein, Eleanor. *Bibliography of American Cookery Books 1742–1860.* In press.

Lutes, Della. *The Country Kitchen.* Boston 1936. 264 pp.

MacDougall, Allan Ross. *The Gourmets' Almanac.* New York 1930. 308 pp.

Mann [Mary T. Peabody], Mrs. Horace. *Christianity in the Kitchen.* Boston 1858. 189 pp.

Mazza, Irma. *Herbs for the Kitchen.* Boston 1947.

Moody, Mrs. William Vaughn. *Mrs. William Vaughn Moody's Cook-Book.* New York 1931. 475 pp.

Morristown Cook Book. Morristown, New Jersey 1900. 110 pp.

Mosser, Marjorie. *Good Maine Food.* Introduction by Kenneth Roberts. New York 1939. 381 pp.

Neil, Marian Harris. *A "Calendar of Dinners" with 615 Recipes.* Cincinnati 1920. 231 pp.

Owen, Jeanne. *Lunching and Dining at Home.* New York 1942. 284 pp.

Paddleford, Clementine. *How America Eats.* New York 1960. 495 pp.

Parloa, Maria. *Miss Parloa's New Cook Book and Marketing Guide.* Boston 1880. 430 pp.

[Peterson, Hannah Mary Bouvier]. *The National Cook Book.* By a Lady of Philadelphia, a Practical Housewife. Philadelphia 1856. 301 pp.

Picayune's Creole Cook Book, The. 4th edition. New Orleans 1910. 418 pp.

Pixley, Aristene. *The Green Mountain Cook Book.* Brattleboro, Vermont 1934. 90 pp.

[Platt, June]. *June Platt's Plain and Fancy Cook Book.* Boston 1941. 356 pp.

Porter, Mrs. M. E. *Mrs. Porter's New Southern Cookery Book.* Philadelphia 1871. 416 pp.

Portland Woman's Exchange. *The Portland Women's Exchange Cook Book.* Portland, Oregon 1913.

Putnam, Mrs. [Elizabeth H.]. *Mrs. Putnam's Receipt Book.* New York 1860. 228 pp.

Randolph, Mrs. Mary. *The Virginia Housewife.* Baltimore 1836. 180 pp.

Rawlings, Marjorie Kinnan. *Cross Creek Cookery.* New York 1942. 230 pp.

Rombauer, Irma. *The Joy of Cooking.* Indianapolis 1943. 884 pp.

Rorer, Mrs. S[arah] T[yson]. *Mrs. Rorer's New Cook Book.* Philadelphia 1902. 731 pp.

———. *Mrs. Rorer's Philadelphia Cook Book.* Philadelphia 1886. 581 pp.

Rosický, Marie. *Bohemian-American Cook Book.* 5th edition. Omaha 1949. 290 pp.

San Grael Society of the First Presbyterian Church. *The Web-Foot Cook Book.* Portland, Oregon 1885. 218 pp.

Shute, Miss T. S. *The American Housewife Cook Book.* Philadelphia 1877. 212 pp.

Simmons, Amelia. *American Cookery.* A facsimile of the first edition, 1796. New York 1958. 47 pp and an introductory essay by Mary T. Wilson.

Sisters of Ravanica Serbian Eastern Orthodox Church. *Serbian Cookery.* Detroit 1955. 143 pp.

Somerset Club Cook Book, The. Boston 1963. 113 pp.

Spencer, Evelene, and John Cobb. *Fish Cookery.* Boston 1921. 364 pp.

Sunset Adventures in Food. Menlo Park, California 1964. 192 pp.

Thomas, Gertrude. *Foods of Our Forefathers.* Philadelphia 1941. 227 pp.

Twentieth Century Cook Book. Chicago 1921. 182 pp.

Vehling, Joseph. *America's Table.* Chicago 1950. 882 pp.

Webster, Mrs. A. L. *The Improved Housewife.* Hartford, Connecticut 1852. 236 pp.

Widdifield, Hannah. *Widdifield's New Cook Book.* Philadelphia 1856. 410 pp.

Winslow, Mrs. *Mrs. Winslow's Domestic Receipt Book for 1866* [etc.; an almanac issued annually]. New York. 31 pp.

Yankee Cook Book The. Imogene B. Wolcott, ed. New York 1939.

Young Ladies of the First Baptist Society. *Young-Mother-Hubbard's Cupboard.* Brattleboro, Vermont 1889. 52 pp.

Ziemann, Hugo, and Mrs. F. L. Gillette. *The White House Cook Book.* New York 1908. 590 pp.

Acknowledgments

Many people have helped with the preparation of this script. John Ferrone has given of his time and advice and been a constant source of comfort when discussions and problems put themselves forward. Catherine Laughton Hindley did testing and research for the baking chapters and has been a most satisfactory consultant on the book. Philip Brown was generous in loaning books from his vast collection on gastronomy. Eleanor Lowenstein of the Corner Book Shop has been tireless in organizing and arranging reference material. A large word of thanks to Suzette Hennion for her typing and the same to Betty Ward for hers. Between the two of them they used up a great deal of energy, to say nothing of typing paper.

J.B.

Index

About the Author

James Beard was the most acclaimed American chef and food writer of his time, and a true pioneer in cooking. His life's work helped to lay the groundwork for American culinary practice as we know it today. Born in 1903 in Portland, Oregon, Beard played a major role in New York City's food community. In 1955, he established the legendary James Beard Cooking School, where he taught his signature principles of wholesome American food for thirty years. After his death in 1985, at the behest of Julia Child, the James Beard Foundation opened the James Beard House at his former home. Today, the foundation continues to honor Beard's legacy through a series of culinary events at the James Beard House and the annual James Beard Foundation Awards.